THE ROUGH GUIDE TO

New Zealand

This ninth edition updated by

Jo James, Alison Mudd, Helen Ochyra and Paul
Whitfield

In memory of Tony Mudd

ROUGH
GUIDES

roughguides.com

D0062049

Contents

OPPOSITE CASTLEPOINT, WAIRARAPA **PREVIOUS PAGE** TE WHARE RUNANGA MEETINGHOUSE, WAITANGI

Introduction to
New Zealand

Kiwis – the people, not the emblematic flightless bird – can't believe their luck at being born in what they call "Godzone" (God's own country). Year after year, travellers list New Zealand in the top ten of places they'd like to visit – and you rarely meet anyone who has been and didn't love the place. And what's not to like? With craggy coastlines, sweeping beaches, primeval forests, snowcapped mountains and explosive geysers, the scenery is truly majestic. The forests come inhabited by strange birds that have evolved to fill evolutionary niches normally occupied by mammals, while penguins, whales and seals ring the coast. And in a land that's larger than the UK and two-thirds the size of California there are just 4.5 million people. Maori have only been here for around eight hundred years but retain distinct and fascinating customs overlaid by colonial European – and increasingly Asian – cultures that together create a vibrant, if understated, urban life.

Given this stunning backdrop it's not surprising that there are boundless diversions, ranging from strolls along moody windswept beaches and multi-day tramps over alpine passes to adrenaline-charged adventure activities such as bungy jumping, skiing, sea-kayaking and whitewater rafting. Some visitors treat the country as a large-scale adventure playground, aiming to tackle as many challenges as possible in the time available.

Much of the scenic drama comes from tectonic or volcanic forces, as the people of Canterbury know only too well following the **Christchurch earthquakes** of September 4, 2010, and February 22, 2011. The quakes, along with several thousand aftershocks, collectively devastated the city but the rebuild is now in full swing.

So many residents have left Christchurch that by most measures **Wellington** now outranks it as the country's second largest city, both well behind **Auckland**. Elsewhere, you can travel through stunning countryside without seeing a soul: there are spots so remote that, it's reliably contended, no human has yet visited them.

ABOVE SHEEP GRAZING IN THE CATLINS **OPPOSITE** HIKING IN THE FOX GLACIER AREA

Geologically, New Zealand split away from the super-continent of Gondwana early, developing a unique **ecosystem** in which birds adapted to fill the role of mammals, many becoming flightless because they had no predators. That all changed about eight hundred years ago, with the arrival of Polynesian navigators, when the land they called **Aotearoa** – "the land of the long white cloud" – became the last major landmass to be settled by humans. On disembarking from their canoes, these **Maori** proceeded to unbalance the fragile ecosystem, dispatching forever the giant ostrich-sized moa, which formed a major part of their diet. The country once again settled into a fragile balance before the arrival of **Pakeha** – white Europeans, predominantly of British origin – who swarmed off their square-rigged ships full of colonial zeal in the mid-nineteenth century and altered the land forever.

An uneasy coexistence between **Maori** and **European** societies informs the current wrangles over cultural identity, land and resource rights. The British didn't invade as such, and were to some degree reluctant to enter into the 1840 **Treaty of Waitangi**, New Zealand's founding document, which effectively ceded New Zealand to the British Crown while guaranteeing Maori hegemony over their land and traditional gathering and fishing rights. As time wore on and increasing numbers of settlers demanded ever larger parcels of land from Maori, antipathy surfaced and escalated into hostility. Once Maori were subdued, a policy of partial integration all but destroyed **Maoritanga** – the Maori way of doing things. Maori, however, were left well outside the new European order, where difference was perceived as tantamount to a betrayal of the emergent sense of nationhood. Although elements of this still exist and Presbyterian and Anglican values

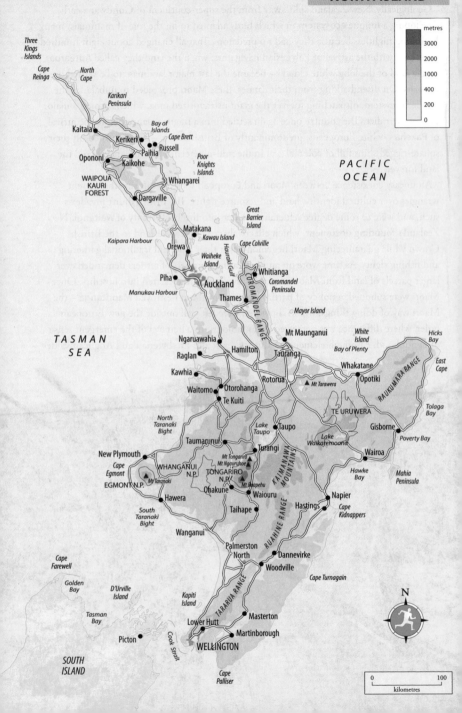

NORTH ISLAND

metres
3000
2000
1000
400
200
0

Three Kings Islands

Cape Reinga
North Cape

Karikari Peninsula

Kaitaia

Kerikeri
Paihia
Russell
Cape Brett

Bay of Islands

Opononi
Kaikohe

Poor Knights Islands

WAIPOUA KAURI FOREST

Whangarei

Dargaville

Kaipara Harbour

Matakana

Great Barrier Island

Orewa

Kawau Island

Cape Colville

Waiheke Island

Hauraki Gulf

Piha

Auckland

Manukau Harbour

Thames

Whitianga

Coromandel Peninsula

COROMANDEL RANGE

Mayor Island

PACIFIC OCEAN

TASMAN SEA

Ngaruawahia

Mt Maunganui

White Island

Bay of Plenty

Hicks Bay

Raglan

Hamilton

Tauranga

Whakatane

Opotiki

East Cape

Kawhia

Rotorua

RAUKUMARA RANGE

Waitomo

Otorohanga

▲ Mt Tarawera

Tolaga Bay

Te Kuiti

TE URUWERA

Gisborne

Poverty Bay

North Taranaki Bight

Taumarunui

Lake Taupo

Taupo

Lake Waikaremoana

Wairoa

New Plymouth

Cape Egmont

WHANGANUI N.P.

Turangi

Mt Tongariro
Mt Ngauruhoe ▲
TONGARIRO N.P.

KAIMANAWA MOUNTAINS

Mahia Peninsula

Mt Taranaki ▲

EGMONT N.P.

Ohakune
Mt Ruapehu ▲
Waiouru

Hawke Bay

Hawera

Napier

Hastings

Cape Kidnappers

South Taranaki Bight

Taihape

RUAHINE RANGE

Wanganui

Palmerston North

Dannevirke

Woodville

Cape Turnagain

Cape Farewell

Golden Bay

D'Urville Island

Kapiti Island

TARARUA RANGE

Masterton

Martinborough

Tasman Bay

Picton

Cook Strait

Lower Hutt

WELLINGTON

SOUTH ISLAND

Cape Palliser

N

0   kilometres   100

SOUTH ISLAND

NORTH
ISLAND

metres
3000
2000
1000
400
200
0

Kapiti
Island

Cape
Farewell
Farewell
Spit
D'Urville
Island
Marlborough
Sounds
WELLINGTON
Collingwood
Golden
Bay
ABEL
TASMAN
N.P.
Takaka
Tasman
Bay
Picton
KAHURANGI
N.P.
Nelson
Blenheim
Cook Strait
Cape
Palliser

Karamea
Bight
St Arnaud
Karamea

Westport
Murchison
NELSON
LAKES N.P.
Kaikoura
Cape Foulwind
PAPAROA
N.P.
Reefton
Hanmer
Springs
TASMAN SEA
Punakaiki
Lewis Pass
Greymouth
Lake Brunner
Hokitika
Arthur's Pass
Ross
ARTHUR'S
PASS N.P.
Arthur's
Pass Village
Pegasus
Bay
Christchurch
Whataroa
Banks
Peninsula
Franz Josef Glacier
Methven
Lyttelton
Fox Glacier
WESTLAND N.P.
Akaroa
Aoraki/Mount Cook
AORAKI/MOUNT COOK N.P.
Ashburton
Aoraki/Mount Cook Village
LakeTekapo
Canterbury Bight
Haast
Lake Pukaki
Twizel
Timaru
PACIFIC OCEAN
Jackson Bay
Haast
Pass
Lake
Ohau
MOUNT ASPIRING N.P.
Mount
Aspiring
Lake Hawea
Lindis Pass
Mount
Tutoko
Lake Wanaka
Oamaru
Milford Sound
Wanaka
Milford Sound
Arrowtown
Cromwell
Moeraki
Glenorchy
Ranfurly
George Sound
Queenstown
Alexandra
Palmerston
Otago
Peninsula
Secretary Island
Lake
Te Anau
FIORDLAND
N.P.
Lake
Wakatipu
Dunedin
Doubtful Sound
Te Anau
Lumsden
Manapouri
Lake
Manapouri
Ohai
Resolution
Island
Lake Hauroko
Gore
Balclutha
Dusky Sound
Tuatapere
Invercargill
Puyseger Point
Riverton
Bluff
Foveaux Strait
Oban (Halfmoon Bay)
RAKIURA
N.P.
Stewart Island

N

0   100
kilometres

FACT FILE

• At latitude 41° south, Wellington is the world's southernmost capital city and shares the honour of being the most remote with Canberra, over 2000km away.

• Possums are the national pest. When seen on the road, these introduced marsupials turn normally mild-mannered folk into killers. Flattened examples are everywhere.

• Kiwis love foreign affirmation: *Flight of the Conchords* was turned down by domestic television and only became a local success after their HBO hit series.

• Maori ex-prostitute Georgina Beyer became the world's first transsexual MP in 1999.

• There are no snakes in New Zealand, and only a few venomous spiders, rarely seen.

• The numerous Maori words that have crept into everyday conversation easily confound visitors: *aroha* is love; *kia kaha* means be strong; *kia ora* can be hi or might signify agreement; and *koha* is a donation or offering.

• New Zealand's eels live to 80 years and only breed once, at the end of their lives – and they swim all the way to Tonga to do it.

have proved hard to shake off, the Kiwi psyche has become infused with Maori generosity and hospitality, coupled with a colonial mateyness and the unerring belief that whatever happens, "she'll be right".

Only in the last forty years has New Zealand come of age and developed a true national self-confidence, something partly forced on it by Britain severing the colonial apron strings, and by the resurgence of Maori identity. Maori demands have been nurtured by a willingness on the part of most Pakeha to redress the wrongs perpetrated over the last 175 years, as long as it doesn't impinge on their high standard of living or overall feeling of control. More recently, integration has been replaced with a policy of **biculturalism** – the somewhat fraught notion of promoting two cultures alongside each other, but with maximum interaction. This policy has been somewhat weakened by relatively recent and extensive **immigration** from China, Korea and South Asia.

Despite having and achieving much to give them confidence, Kiwis (unlike their Australian neighbours) retain an underlying shyness that borders on an inferiority complex: you may well find yourself interrogated about your opinions

Author picks

Our authors have bussed, walked, rafted and ridden the length and breadth of New Zealand. These are some of their own favourite travel experiences.

Superb natural hot pool Kerosene Creek has no changing rooms, no café, no gift store – just a naturally heated stream which tumbles over a short waterfall into a bath-like pool. Bliss. See p.281.

The kleptomaniac kea It's hard not to love these trickster alpine parrots, even if one has just shredded your windscreen wipers. See p.565.

DIY caving There's something raw and thrilling about an unaided exploration of Cave Stream, a 600m-long tunnel carved by an alpine stream. See p.562.

Most entertaining stroll For a diverse slice of Kiwi life, take a late evening wander along Auckland's Karangahape Road, a grungy yet vibrant strip of cafés and shops where boozy suits, gay couples, dining suburbanites and preening transvestites all mix to kaleidoscopic effect. See p.79.

Seafood restaurant heaven At *Fleur's Place*, a quirky shed restaurant, you know the fish is fresh as you can see Fleur's fishing boat bobbing in the bay outside. See p.551.

Best coastal drive Savour the Picton–Kaikoura route, with Sauvignon Blanc vineyards heralding a craggy coastal ribbon of crashing azure waves backed by the magnificent Kaikoura Ranges. See p.498.

Southern sky stargazing Join the excellent Earth & Sky stargazing trips to the summit of Mt John near Lake Tekapo or simply gaze overhead from your tent. See p.577.

Hiking the Hump Ridge Track A dream combination of thick bush, subalpine tops and coastal scenery with a smattering of pioneer logging heritage make this a wonderful hike. Pay a little extra for nightly hot showers and helicopter bag transfer up the stiffest climb. See p.782.

> Our author recommendations don't end here. We've flagged up our favourite places – a perfectly sited hotel, an atmospheric café, a special restaurant – throughout the Guide, highlighted with the ★ symbol.

LEFT QUEENSTOWN **FROM TOP** A KEA GETS CURIOUS; VINE ROWS AT SUNSET; A PLATTER OF SEAFOOD

THE MAORI

Tribal costume is only worn on special occasions, facial tattoos are fairly rare and you'll probably only see a *haka* performed at a rugby match or cultural show. In fact, Maori live very much in the modern world. But peel back the veneer of the song-dance-and-*hangi* performance and you'll discover a parallel world that non-Maori are only dimly aware of.

Knowledge of **whakapapa** (tribal lineage) is central to Maori identity. **Spirituality** connects Maori to their traditional local mountain or river, while **oratory**, and the ability to produce a song at a moment's notice, are both highly valued. All New Zealanders understand **mana**, a synthesis of prestige, charisma and influence, which is enhanced through brave or compassionate actions.

Sadly, the Maori community is riven by social problems: average incomes are lower than those of Pakeha; almost half of all prison inmates are Maori; and health statistics make appalling reading.

Hope for redress comes through a **bicultural** approach stressing equality and integration while allowing for parallel identities.

For more on what it means to be Maori, and how visitors are likely to tap into it, see p.801.

on the country almost before you've even left the airport. Balancing this is an extraordinary enthusiasm for **sports** and **culture**, which generate a swelling pride in New Zealanders when they witness plucky Kiwis taking on and sometimes beating the world.

Where to go

New Zealand packs a lot into a limited space, meaning you can visit many of the main sights in a couple of weeks, but allow at least a month (or preferably two) for a proper look around. The scenery is the big draw, and most people only pop into the big cities on arrival and departure (easily done with open-jaw air tickets, allowing you to fly into Auckland and out of Christchurch) or when travelling to Wellington from the South Island across the **Cook Strait**.

Sprawled around the sparkling Waitemata Harbour, go-ahead **Auckland** looks out over the island-studded Hauraki Gulf. Most people head south from here, missing out on **Northland**, the cradle of both Maori and Pakeha colonization, cloaked in wonderful subtropical forest that harbours New Zealand's largest kauri trees. East of Auckland the coast follows the isolated greenery and long, golden beaches of the **Coromandel Peninsula**, before running down to the beach towns of the **Bay of Plenty**. Immediately south your senses are assailed by the ever-present sulphurous whiff of **Rotorua**, with its spurting geysers and bubbling pools of mud, and the volcanic plateau centred on the trout-filled waters of **Lake Taupo**, overshadowed by three snowcapped volcanoes. Cave fans will want to head west of Taupo for the eerie limestone caverns of **Waitomo**; alternatively it's just a short hop from Taupo to the delights of canoeing the

LEFT MAORI WOODCARVING

HOT POOLS, GEYSERS AND BOILING MUD

One of New Zealand's most sensual pleasures is lying back in a **natural hot pool** surrounded by bush and gazing up at the stars. The country lies on the Pacific Ring of Fire, and earthquakes and volcanic activity are common. Superheated steam escapes as **geysers** (around Rotorua), **boiling mud pools** (Rotorua and Taupo) and **hot springs** – around eighty of them across the northern two-thirds of the North Island and another fifteen along a thin thread down the western side of the Southern Alps.

Over thirty are commercial **resorts** offering tepid swimming pools, near-scalding baths, mineral mud and hydrothermal pampering. The remainder are **natural pools** – in the bush, beside a stream or welling up from below a sandy beach – which require a little sleuthing; locals like to keep the best spots to themselves. Check out ⓦ **nzhotpools.co.nz**, read the notes on **amoebic meningitis** (see p.63) and sample the following (listed north to south).

Polynesian Spa Commercial resort in Rotorua with something for everyone: mineral pools, family spa, adult-only open-air complex and all manner of body treatments. See p.268

Hot Water Beach Come at low tide, rent a spade and dig a hot pool beside the cool surf. See p.336

Maruia Springs Small resort in the hills 200km north of Christchurch. Particularly magical in winter. See p.560

Welcome Flat Hot Springs Four natural pools sited amid mountain scenery just south of Fox Glacier. It is a six- to seven-hour walk in and you can stay at the adjacent DOC hut. See p.681

Whanganui River, a broad, emerald-green waterway banked by virtually impenetrable bush thrown into relief by the cone of **Mount Taranaki**, whose summit is accessible in a day. East of Taupo lie ranges that form the North Island's backbone, and beyond them the **Hawke's Bay wine country**, centred on the Art Deco city of Napier. Further south, the wine region of Martinborough is just an hour or so from the capital, **Wellington**, its centre squeezed onto reclaimed harbourside, the suburbs slung across steep hills

ABOVE HOT WATER BEACH

overlooking glistening bays. Politicians and bureaucrats give it a well-scrubbed and urbane sophistication, enlivened by an established café society and after-dark scene.

The **South Island** kicks off with the world-renowned wineries of **Marlborough** and appealing **Nelson**, a pretty and compact spot surrounded by lovely beaches and within easy reach of the hill country around the **Nelson Lakes National Park** and the fabulous sea-kayaking of the **Abel Tasman National Park**. From the top of the South Island you've a choice of nipping behind the 3000m summits of the Southern Alps and following the West Coast to the fabulous, if rapidly shrinking, **glaciers** at Fox and Franz Josef, or sticking to the east, passing the whale-watching territory of **Kaikoura** en route to the South Island's largest centre, **Christchurch**. Its English architectural heritage may have been ravaged by earthquakes – and its people still reeling from the upheaval – but as the rebuild process kicks into top gear the city has become one of the country's most exciting.

From here you can head across country to the West Coast via Arthur's Pass on the scenic TranzAlpine train trip, or shoot southwest across the patchwork Canterbury Plains to the foothills of the **Southern Alps** and **Aoraki/Mount Cook** with its distinctive drooping-tent summit.

The patchwork-quilt fields of Canterbury run, via the grand architecture of **Oamaru**, to the unmistakably Scottish-influenced city of **Dunedin**, a base for exploring the wildlife of the **Otago Peninsula**, with its albatross, seal, sea lion and penguin colonies. In the middle of the nineteenth century, prospectors arrived here and rushed inland to gold strikes throughout central Otago and around stunningly set **Queenstown**, now a

LOCATION, LOCATION, LOCATION...

When Peter Jackson filmed his *Lord of the Rings* trilogy in New Zealand the nation rejoiced, even appointing a special minister for the project. However, few could have anticipated how completely it would take over the country, nor for how long. The final of *The Hobbit* trilogy screened late in 2014, thirteen years after the first J.R.R. Tolkien adaptation. For thousands of visitors, no stay in Aotearoa is complete without a hobbit hole visit to Hobbiton, a pilgrimage to Wellington's Weta Workshop, where the prosthetics and miniatures were done, and a tour of film locations around Queenstown.

Scene-seeking tourists also follow Disney's two *Chronicles of Narnia* movies, and tour guides will often reference *X-Men Origins: Wolverine* or Jane Campion's 2013 TV miniseries *Top of the Lake*. Trips to location sites undoubtedly visit some magnificent scenery, but don't expect things to look as they did in the films. Digital enhancement works wonders, but the landscape stands up just fine without CGI trickery.

commercialized activity centre where bungy jumping, rafting, jetboating and skiing hold sway. Just up the road is Glenorchy, a tramping heartland, from which the **Routeburn Track** sets out to rain-sodden **Fiordland**; its neighbour, Te Anau, is the launch pad for many of New Zealand's most famous treks, including the **Milford Track**. Further south you'll feel the bite of the Antarctic winds, which reach their peak on New Zealand's third landmass, isolated **Stewart Island**, covered mostly by dense coastal rainforest that offers a great chance of spotting a kiwi in the wild.

When to go

With ocean in every direction it is no surprise that New Zealand has a maritime climate, warm in the summer months, December to March, and never truly cold, even in winter. **Weather** patterns are strongly affected by prevailing westerlies, which suck up moisture from the Tasman Sea and dump it on the western side of both islands. The South Island gets the lion's share, with the West Coast and Fiordland ranking among the world's wettest places. Mountain ranges running the length of both islands cast long rain shadows eastward, making those locations considerably drier. The south is a few degrees cooler than elsewhere, and subtropical Auckland and Northland are appreciably more humid. In the North Island, warm, damp summers fade imperceptibly into cool, wet winters, while the further south you travel the more the weather divides the year into four distinct seasons.

Most people visit New Zealand in the summer, but it is a viable destination at any time provided you pick your target. From December to March you'll find everything open, though often busy with holidaying Kiwis from Christmas to mid-January. In general, you're better off joining the bulk of foreign visitors during the **shoulder seasons** – October, November and April – when sights and attractions are quieter, and accommodation easier to come by. **Winter** (May–Sept) is the wettest, coldest and consequently least popular time, unless you are enamoured of winter sports, in which case it's fabulous. The switch to prevailing southerly winds tends to bring periods of crisp, dry and cloudless weather to the West Coast and heavy snowfalls to the Southern Alps and Central North Island, allowing for some of the most varied and least-populated **skiing and snowboarding** in the world.

29

things not to miss

It's not possible to see everything that New Zealand has to offer in one trip – so don't try. What follows, in no particular order, is a selective taste of the islands' highlights, including outstanding national parks, natural wonders, adventure activities and exotic wildlife. All highlights have a page reference to take you straight into the Guide, where you can find out more. Coloured numbers refer to chapters in the Guide.

1

1 MILFORD SOUND
Page 765

Experience the grandeur and beauty of Fiordland on the area's most accessible fiord, great in bright sunshine and wonderfully atmospheric in the mist with the waterfalls at their most impressive.

2 FAREWELL SPIT
Page 486

This slender 25km arc of sand dunes and beaches is a nature reserve protecting a host of birds including black swans, wrybills, curlews and dotterels.

3 JETBOATING
Page 52

Charging up rapids perilously close to rocks is a countrywide obsession, with some superb trips around Queenstown, in Fiordland and just north of Taupo.

4 TAIERI GORGE RAILWAY
Page 606

Ride the stately old train through otherwise inaccessible mountain landscapes on this dramatic journey along a line established back in 1859.

5 WHALE WATCHING
Page 502

An impressive range of cetaceans populates the deep canyons off the Kaikoura Peninsula, visited on a cruise or spied from a plane or helicopter.

6 OTAGO CENTRAL RAIL TRAIL
Page 743

Taking three leisurely days on a bike is the best way to tackle this 150km trail, which follows the route of a former rail line through some ruggedly barren country.

7 WHITE ISLAND
Page 356

Take an appealing boat trip out to New Zealand's most active volcano, and stroll through the sulphurous lunar landscape to peer into the steaming crater.

8 NINETY MILE BEACH
Page 185

This seemingly endless wave-lashed golden strand is a designated highway, plied by tour buses that regularly stop to let passengers toboggan down the steep dunes.

9 EAST CAPE
Page 360

A varied coastline, tiny, predominantly Maori communities and the slow pace of life make this isolated region a place to linger.

8

9

14

10 THE GLACIERS
Page 668

The steep and dramatic Fox and Franz Josef glaciers can be explored by valley walk, ice climbing or heli-hiking on the glacier.

11 TREE FERNS
Page 812

Sometimes reaching up to 10m, these outsize specimens provide shade for some of the more delicate species in New Zealand's unique ecosystem.

12 DIVING AT THE POOR KNIGHTS ISLANDS
Page 157

Two-dive day-trips visit any of several dozen sites at one of the world's best diving destinations. A couple of scuttled navy boats nearby add to the possibilities.

13 THE CATLINS
Page 613

Seals and dolphins and a laidback approach to life make this rugged coast a great place to unwind for a few days.

14 MUSEUM OF NEW ZEALAND (TE PAPA)
Page 418

A celebration of the people, culture and art of New Zealand that's as appealing to kids as it is to adults, with an impressive use of state-of-the-art technology.

15 HOKIANGA HARBOUR
Page 190

As a low-key antidote to the commercialization of the Bay of Islands, the sand dunes, quiet retreats and crafts culture of this vast inlet are hard to beat.

15

16

17

18

23 THE ROUTEBURN TRACK
Page 715

One of the country's finest walks, showcasing forested valleys, rich birdlife, thundering waterfalls, river flats, lakes and wonderful mountain scenery.

24 MOERAKI BOULDERS
Page 550

Stroll along the beach to visit these large, perfectly round, natural spheres with a honeycomb centre, just sitting in the surf.

25 BUNGY JUMPING
Page 53

New Zealand's trademark adventure sport can be tried at Kawarau Bridge, the original commercial jump site, and other spots around the country.

26 HANGI
Page 41

Sample fall-off-the-bone pork and chicken along with sweet potatoes and pumpkin, disinterred after several hours' steaming in a Maori earth oven.

27 TONGARIRO ALPINE CROSSING
Page 300

A superb one-day hike through the volcanic badlands of the Tongariro National Park, passing the cinder cone of Mount Ngauruhoe.

28 ART DECO, NAPIER
Page 387

The world's most homogeneous collection of Art Deco architecture owes its genesis to the 1931 earthquake that flattened this lovely provincial city.

29 THE PENGUIN PLACE
Page 611

Watch yellow-eyed penguins waddle up the beach to their nests each night from hides and viewing platforms all along the South Island's southwestern coast.

23

24

Itineraries

The following itineraries pick out New Zealand's best, from a quick overview combining beaches, Maori culture, cool cities and majestic scenery, to something more specific – either the strange birdlife, soaking in hot pools and stargazing, or going for the giant adventure playground experience. Complete one list or mix and match to gain a wonderful insight into Aotearoa's stunning diversity.

THE GRAND TOUR

New Zealand may be small but it really packs in the sights, so allow at least 3 weeks to see it all.

❶ Northland Drive sweeping beaches, slide down vast sand dunes and visit the quaint harbours of the winterless north. **See p.140**

❷ Rotorua Don't let the bad-egg smell put you off this geothermal wonderland of geysers and boiling mud pools where *haka*, dance and an earth-steamed *hangi* dinner showcase Maori culture. **See p.265**

❸ Napier The small-scale Art Deco architecture provides the backdrop to Hawke's Bay's fine food and some of New Zealand's best Bordeaux-style red wines. **See p.385**

❹ Wellington The capital is New Zealand's most beguiling city, with a walkable heart of museums, cafés and lively bars elegantly strung around a picturesque harbour. **See p.412**

❺ Nelson and Golden Bay Golden beaches, hippy markets and the coastal pleasures of the Abel Tasman National Park make this the most blissed-out corner of the country. **See p.459**

❻ The West Coast Native bush and precipitous glaciers plunge steeply to the crashing surf along this wild and fabulously scenic coast. **See p.638**

❼ Aoraki/Mount Cook New Zealand's highest peak stands as snowy sentinel over the impossibly blue lakes and golden grasses of the Mackenzie Country. **See p.578**

❽ Queenstown Don't miss the fabulous mountain scenery, incredible concentration of adventure activities, great hikes, and some of the South Island's best restaurants and bars. **See p.688**

❾ Fiordland Cruise, kayak or even dive the waters of Milford and Doubtful sounds in between multi-day tramps along the Kepler Track or the exalted Milford Track. **See p.750**

NATURAL NEW ZEALAND

Geysers, fiords, alpine parrots, cute penguins, whales and several species of dolphin supplement New Zealand's clear skies and stunning scenery.

❶ Kiwi spotting in the kauri forest Move quietly among the kauri forest night as kiwi call plaintively and maybe – just maybe – show themselves. **See p.195**

❷ Hot Water Beach Dig a hole in the beach and ease into a shallow pool of hot water occasionally cooled by the surf. **See p.336**

❸ Birds on Kapiti Island Explore this island sanctuary full of intriguing birds – bush parrots, parakeets, fantails, little spotted kiwis and even a few of the 250 takahe left in the world. **See p.256**

ABOVE VIEW OF AORAKI/MOUNT COOK

❹ Swimming with seals Give the dolphins a break: seals are often more playful, particularly in the waters off Kaikoura. **See p.503**

❺ Night sky viewing The wonderful stargazing is helping Tekapo get itself declared the country's first Starlight Reserve. **See p.576**

❻ Otago Peninsula wildlife Dunedin's doorstep harbours a fabulous concentration of wildlife with two species of penguin, seals and an accessible colony of albatross. **See p.608**

❼ Stewart Island After being welcomed by flocks of parrots, visit saddlebacks, red-crowned parakeets and bellbirds on Ulva Island then spot kiwi at Mason Bay. **See p.630**

ADVENTURE NEW ZEALAND

Nowhere in the world has as many adrenaline-fuelled and low-key adventures as New Zealand.

❶ Raft the Kaituna Short and sweet, the Kaituna packs in a gorgeous verdant gorge, plunging rapids and a massive 7m waterfall. **See p.272**

❷ Lost World caving The ground below Waitomo is riddled with limestone caverns, best explored by a massive abseil followed by several hours of squeezes, scrambles and floating. **See p.221**

❸ Hiking the Tongariro Alpine Crossing Take on New Zealand's finest one-day tramp across the barren volcanic wastes of the Tongariro National Park. **See p.300**

❹ Kayaking Abel Tasman National Park Opt for an overnight paddle on the sheltered, warm waters then camp beside a golden beach. **See p.476**

❺ Glacier hike Franz Josef Get choppered up onto the glacier and left for a couple of hours of guided hiking across snowfields and through ice caves. **See p.676**

❻ Canyon the Niger Stream Jump into deep pools and abseil down waterfalls in Wanaka's beautiful canyons. **See p.734**

❼ Bungy the Nevis Go for the big one, a 134m monster from a gondola eight freefall seconds above a tiny stream. **See p.699**

❽ Bike the Wakatipu Basin Easy lakeside jaunts, great cross-country rides, and the country's only cable-car-assisted downhill mountain-bike tracks make Queenstown the perfect biking destination. **See p.701**

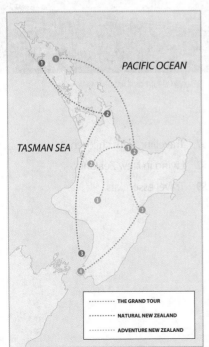

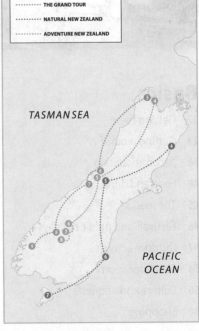

AORAKI/MOUNT COOK NATIONAL PARK

Basics

Getting there

The quickest, easiest and cheapest way to get to New Zealand is to fly. It is possible to arrive by sea, but there are no international passenger ferries, so unless you own a boat this means joining a cruise, crewing on a private yacht, or paying for your passage on a cargo ship (a rewarding experience for those who like sea journeys – find out more at ⓦfreightertravel.co.nz).

Air fares depend on the season, with the highest during the New Zealand summer (Dec–Feb); prices drop during the shoulder seasons (Sept–Nov & March–May) and you'll get the cheapest rates during the low (ski) season (June–Aug).

Arriving in New Zealand, your only real choice, unless you're coming from Australia, is between the **international airports at Auckland and Christchurch**. Christchurch receives fewer direct flights but many scheduled airlines have a codeshare shuttle from Auckland at no extra cost. The most desirable option, an **open-jaw ticket** (flying into one and out of the other), usually costs no more than an ordinary return. For **internal flights** within NZ, see box, p.29.

Tourists and those on short-term working visas (see p.58) are generally required by New Zealand immigration to arrive with an **outward bound ticket**, so one-way tickets are really only viable for Australian and NZ residents.

If you've purchased a return ticket and find you want to stay longer or head off on a totally different route, it's possible to **change** the dates and, more rarely, the route, with the airline or travel agent, depending on the conditions of your ticket, though there is often a fee.

Flights from the UK and Ireland

Over a dozen airlines compete to fly you **from Britain** to New Zealand for as little as £745, but prices depend upon the time of year, and can be double that amount at Christmas. Going for the **cheapest flight** typically means sacrificing some comfort (multiple stops, longer layovers), which you may regret, given that even the shortest journey will last at least 24 hours including an obligatory refuelling stop. There are no direct flights to New Zealand **from Ireland**, so you'll need to factor in the short hop to London (£100 return, cheaper with internet deals) or the additional stop in Australia.

Most **scheduled flights** allow multiple **stopovers** either in North America and the Pacific, or Asia and Australia. Most direct scheduled flights depart from London Heathrow, though some services operate from London Gatwick, and regional airports including Manchester and Newcastle.

Flights from the US and Canada

Direct trans-Pacific flights to Auckland operate from Los Angeles, San Francisco (12 hours) and Vancouver (13 hours). Assorted codeshare partners sell tickets to New Zealand, usually offering several connections a day to Wellington and Christchurch.

From the US a direct LA–Auckland or San Francisco–Auckland round-trip **fare** goes for around US$1200 during the southern winter, rising to around US$1600 or more in peak southern summer season. Flights from all other US cities are routed via California. Off-peak you might expect to pay US$1500–1700 from New York or Chicago, but shopping around should save you money.

From Canada, you can fly direct to Auckland. Depending on the season, fares from Vancouver are around CA$1700; from Toronto, around CA$1900; and from Montréal, around CA$2000. Substantial savings can often be made through discount travel companies and websites.

Apart from an **RTW** ticket (see p.28), an alternative approach from North America is to fly **via Asia**, which may work out cheaper. Another option is to stop off at a **Pacific island** or two along the way, which often costs less than US$200 per stopover.

Flights from Australia and South Africa

Prices for flights between **Australia** and New Zealand vary enormously depending on demand

---

A BETTER KIND OF TRAVEL

At Rough Guides we are passionately committed to travel. We believe it helps us understand the world we live in and the people we share it with – and of course tourism is vital to many developing economies. But the scale of modern tourism has also damaged some places irreparably, and climate change is accelerated by most forms of transport, especially flying. All Rough Guides' flights are carbon-offset, and every year we donate money to a variety of environmental charities.

(book well in advance in summer), but the level of competition generally keeps them reasonable – as low as AU$250 return from Australia's east coast (including a basic baggage allowance) if you're prepared to go for nonrefundable tickets. Return flights from Perth start at around AU$480.

Flying time from Sydney or Melbourne to New Zealand is around three and a half hours. Auckland, Christchurch, Dunedin, Rotorua, Queenstown and Wellington international airports all have direct flights to/from Australia.

From Australia, there's a huge variety of **package holidays** to New Zealand, including short **city-breaks** (flight and accommodation), winter skiing packages and **fly-drive** deals for little more than the cost of the regular air fare.

Travelling to New Zealand **from South Africa** invariably involves flying via Australia. Expect to pay around ZAR14,000–30,000, depending on the season and airline.

Round-the-world flights

If New Zealand is only one stop on a longer journey, you might consider buying a **Round-the-World (RTW)** ticket. An "off-the-shelf" RTW ticket will have you touching down in about half a dozen cities (Auckland is on many itineraries), or you can assemble one tailored to your needs, though this is liable to be more expensive.

INTERNATIONAL AIRLINES

Air Canada (W aircanada.com)
Air New Zealand (W airnewzealand.com)
American Airlines (W aa.com)
British Airways (W ba.com)
Cathay Pacific (W cathaypacific.com)
China Southern (W csair.com/en)
Emirates (W emirates.com)
Etihad (W etihad.com)
Fiji Airways (W fijiairways.com)
LAN (W lan.com)
Malaysia (W malaysiaairlines.com)
Qantas (W qantas.com.au)
South African Airways (W saa.co.za)
Thai (W thaiairways.com)
Virgin Australia (W virginaustralia.com)

Agents and operators

If time is limited and you have a clear idea of what you want to do, numerous companies offer **organized tours**, from backpacker excursions to no-expense-spared extravaganzas. Full "see-it-all" packages, with most meals and transport included, can be good value, considering what you'd be spending anyway. Some companies offer tours specifically for those aged 18–35, seniors, or the adventurous. You can also find tours to suit your interest (such as hiking or kayaking). For details of **NZ-based tour operators**, see box, p.50.

A number of companies operate **flexible bus tours**, which you can hop off whenever you like and rejoin a day or two later when the next bus comes through (see box, p.30).

Pretty much all the major tour operators can also book you onto **tramping trips**, including some of the guided Great Walks (see p.49); you'll still need to book way in advance, though. For **skiing trips**, the cheapest option is usually to contact ski clubs at the fields directly (contact details at W snow .co.nz).

Even if an all-in package doesn't appeal, it still may be worth investigating potential savings by pre-booking some accommodation, tours or a rental vehicle.

AGENTS AND OPERATORS

Adventures Abroad W adventures-abroad.com. US-based agent with a broad range of New Zealand options.

Backpackers World Travel Australia T 1800 997 325, W backpackersworld.com.

Contiki W contiki.com. 18–35 package tour bracket.

Intrepid W intrepidtravel.com. Adventurous, excellently led small-group tours, aimed mainly at the younger end of the market.

North South Travel UK T 01245 608 291, W northsouthtravel .co.uk. Competitive travel agency, offering discounted fares worldwide. Profits are used to support projects in the developing world, especially the promotion of sustainable tourism.

Road Scholar W roadscholar.org. Not-for-profit educational and adventure tours, mostly small-group, with strong package of New Zealand options.

STA Travel UK T 0333 321 0099, US T 1 800 781 4040, Australia T 134 782, NZ T 0800 474 400, South Africa T 0861 781 781; W statravel.co.uk. Worldwide specialists in independent travel; also student IDs, travel insurance, car rental, rail passes and more. Good discounts for students and under-26s. Experts on NZ travel with branches in major Kiwi cities.

Trailfinders UK T 0207 368 1200, Ireland T 01 677 7888; W trailfinders.com. One of the best-informed and most efficient agents for independent travellers.

Travel Cuts Canada T 1 800 667-2887, W travelcuts.com. Canadian student-travel organization.

USIT Ireland T 01 602 1906, Australia T 1800 092 499; W usit.ie. Ireland's main student and youth travel specialists.

Getting around

New Zealand is a relatively small country and getting around is easy, with some form of public transport going to many destinations, though sometimes limited to one service per day. There are still a few places that are hard to access, yet all of these can be reached with will, flexibility and a little ingenuity.

Internal **flights** are reasonably priced if booked well in advance, but you'll appreciate the scenery better by travelling at ground level. The cheapest and easiest, though slowest, way to get around is by **bus** (coaches or shuttle buses). The **rail service**, by contrast, is limited and expensive.

Rental **cars** and campervans, particularly the little ones (see p.32), can be remarkably good value for two or more people, but if you are staying in the country for more than a couple of months, it's more economical to buy a vehicle. New Zealand's green countryside encourages **cyclists**, but even the keenest vary their transport options.

Competition on the **ferries** connecting the North and South islands means passenger fares are good value, though transporting vehicles is pricey. Planes and boats give limited access to offshore islands and the parts of the mainland that remain stubbornly impenetrable by road, though more specialist **tours** make getting into the wilds easier.

The frequency of long-distance bus, train and plane services is listed, where relevant, in each chapter in "Arrival and departure", while local buses and trains, again where relevant, appear in "Getting around".

By plane

Many visitors fly into Auckland at the beginning of their trip and out from Christchurch at the end, so don't touch **domestic flights**, but those with a tight timetable wanting to hit a few key sights in a short time might be tempted by reasonable-value internal fares.

The biggest domestic operator is **Air New Zealand**, serving all the main centres and numerous minor ones (20 destinations). The main competition is from **Jetstar**, which serves Auckland, Wellington, Christchurch, Queenstown and Dunedin. Air New Zealand runs single-class planes with **fares** that come in four levels, offering lower fares for decreased flexibility: there are fewer low-cost fares at popular times. Jetstar has a similar system. For example, a one-way standard flight between Auckland and Christchurch is about $200, a seat+bag $139, seat only (no hold baggage) as little as $59 – or only $45 on Ⓦgrabaseat.co.nz. Other flights you might take are scenic jaunts from Auckland to Great Barrier Island, the hop over Cook Strait, or the short trip from Invercargill to Stewart Island.

AIRLINES

Air New Zealand ☎ 0800 737 000, Ⓦ airnewzealand.co.nz.

Fly My Sky ☎ 0800 222 123, Ⓦ flymysky.co.nz. Flights between Auckland and Great Barrier Island.

Great Barrier Airlines ☎ 0800 900 600, Ⓦ greatbarrierairlines .co.nz. Flights to Great Barrier Island from Northland, Auckland, the Coromandel or Tauranga.

Jetstar ☎ 0800 800 995, Ⓦ jetstar.com.

Soundsair ☎ 0800 505 005, Ⓦ soundsair.com. Small planes across Cook Strait.

Stewart Island Flights ☎ 03 218 9129, Ⓦ stewartislandflights .com. Scheduled services between Invercargill and Stewart Island.

By bus

You can get most places on long-distance **buses** ("coaches") and smaller **shuttle buses**, which essentially offer the same service but are more likely to drop you off and pick up at hotels, hostels and the like. Services are generally reliable and reasonably comfortable, and competition keeps prices competitive. The larger buses are usually air-conditioned and may have wi-fi. Some have toilets, though all services stop every couple of hours, at wayside tearooms and points of interest along the way. Most of your fellow passengers are likely to be visitors to New Zealand so drivers often give a commentary, the quality of which varies.

INTERNAL FLIGHTS

If you decide to use **internal flights**, booking tickets online can save you up to fifty percent. Check out Air New Zealand's (Ⓦairnewzealand.com) **air passes** if you've used the airline to get to New Zealand. You can buy one-way tickets to create your own multi-stop itinerary. Jetstar (Ⓦjetstar.com) offers similar multi-destination tickets at less favourable rates. Air New Zealand also offer last minute (or 90 minutes before departure, to be precise) Regional Gotta Go fares. Their discount website Ⓦgrabaseat.co.nz has cheap seats as well as a weekly reverse seat auction.

InterCity and Newmans

The biggest operator, **InterCity**, runs high-quality full-size buses all over the country. **Newmans** are part of the same company, and pitch themselves as slightly more luxurious and target sightseeing excursions. In practice, the two companies share a timetable and InterCity passes can often be used on Newmans buses: when we refer to InterCity we are generally referring to services run collectively by InterCity and Newmans. Some services have luxury leather seats with USB charging and wi-fi.

As an example, a standard one-way fare on the North Island, Auckland to Rotorua, is $55 (nonrefundable tickets start at $21), while on the South Island, Christchurch to Queenstown, it's $75 (nonrefundable $55). Prices drop during off-peak periods.

Book early for the best prices. There's one $1 seat sold on each service, but as they're available a year in advance, you may feel you've better odds of spotting a hobbit. YHA, VIP, ISIC and BBH cardholders get small discounts off Flexible Fares but you'll find cheaper deals by chasing down the various nonrefundable fares.

InterCity also offers numerous **passes**. Fixed-route TravelPasses include Auckland to Paihia (Bay

---

BACKPACKER BUSES

One of the cheapest ways to cover a lot of ground is on a **backpacker bus**, which combines some of the flexibility of independent travel with the convenience of a tour. You typically purchase a ticket for a fixed route (usually valid for 12 months), and then take it at your own pace. You can either stick with the one bus for the entire journey with nights spent at various towns along the route, or stop off longer in places and hop on a later bus. During peak times some buses may be full, so you'll need to plan onward travel several days in advance. Most companies operate year-round, though services are reduced in winter.

The emphasis is on **experiencing the country** rather than travelling from one town to the next, so you'll be stopping off to bungy jump, hike or some such. Being part of a group of forty rowdy backpackers arriving at some idyllic spot isn't everyone's idea of a good time and, by using assorted public transport, it is often just as cheap to make your own way around New Zealand. But if you want almost everything organized for you, and a ready-made bunch of like-minded fellow travellers, this sort of travel might appeal.

It can be slightly **cheaper** to book before you arrive, as some deals are not available once you step off the plane: check the websites. You might also save a few dollars by being a YHA, VIP, BBH or ISIC cardholder. Tickets don't generally cover accommodation, activities (although these are often discounted), side trips, food or travel between the North and South islands.

Operators are listed below. Those interested in multi-day tours and adventure activities should check out "Outdoor activities" (see box, p.50), where more intimate and specialized excursions are listed.

Flying Kiwi Wilderness Expeditions

(w flyingkiwi.com). Operator specializing in tours that get off the beaten track and eschew city hostels in favour of camping. Converted buses are equipped with bikes, canoes, kitchen, awning, fridge, mattresses, tents and hot shower, and everyone mucks in with domestic chores. Trips operate all year and once on board you stick with the same group. Options range from the Northern Express from Wellington to Auckland via Taupo (2 days; $296) to a full NZ tour (27 days; $3950 including food and camping fees).

Haka Tours (w hakatours.com). Fully guided, small-group tours. You'll travel together, sleep together (all tours include accommodation), and breakfast together. Save money by booking activity packages in advance – useful if you're worried you might squander that money you saved for a dolphin-swim on beer. Tours include the Epic (24 days; $3600 including handful of activities) and the South Island LICK (7 days; $1299 with a trip on the TranzAlpine).

Kiwi Experience (w kiwiexperience.com). With a deserved reputation for attracting high-spirited party animals, Kiwi Experience offers a huge array of passes, from a trip to Cape Reinga starting in Auckland (min 3 days; $225) to the Whole Kit and Caboodle (minimum 30 days; $1935).

Stray (w straytravel.com). Stray see themselves as a bit more intrepid than Kiwi Experience; you're as likely to be necking beers around a campfire as a city bar. Trips include a Round South Island (RON) circuit (minimum 16 days; $1035) and a North Island circuit (minimum 13 days; $985).

TRAVEL PASSES

If you're doing a lot of travelling by bus and train, there are savings to be made with travel passes. **KiwiRail Scenic Rail Pass** (ⓦ kiwirailscenic.co.nz/scenic-rail-pass) gives unlimited travel on Tranz Scenic trains for 1–3 weeks (from $599).

InterCity/Newmans (ⓦ intercity.co.nz) offer their own **FlexiPass**, allowing you to buy bus travel by the hour – the more hours you buy the better the savings. You would typically need 45 hours ($349) to cover one of the main islands, and 60 hours upwards ($449) for a full tour. If that's not enough, you can top-up your pass with, say, 15 hours ($119). The Flexi-Pass is valid for 12 months and journeys can be booked online.

Travellers wanting to move around pretty quickly might be better off with one of the **New Zealand Travel Passes** (ⓦ travelpass.co.nz) which make extensive use of InterCity and throw in a ferry journey and a few extras (the cheapest option is $738); other options and more money get you a train journey.

The backpacker tour buses (see box, p.30) offer lower prices in return for older buses and – often – a more boisterous time.

Escape $119); Auckland to Wellington via Matamata (includes Hobbiton tour), Rotorua and Taupo (Big Fish: $209); or Nelson to Queenstown via the west coast ($189). For complete freedom choose a Flexipass (see box above) or Flexitrips (ⓦ flexitrips .co.nz), which is like a carnet: 5 tickets start from $156, but the more you buy the bigger the saving (you can use trips to pay for Interislander crossings and some sightseeing tours).

Other buses

Other companies compete directly with InterCity/Newmans on the main routes and fill in the gaps around the country, often linking with the major operators, to take you off the beaten track. Generally they cost less (sometimes appreciably) and can be more obliging when it comes to drop-offs and pick-ups, though seldom as comfortable over distance.

Newcomer **Manabus** is competing on a few North Island routes, offering leather seats, free wi-fi and onboard toilets, with a one-way fare from Auckland to Rotorua of $1 to $3. We've listed a number of other operators below, but there are many more mentioned in the appropriate sections of this guide.

Official (i-SITE) visitor centres carry **timetables** of bus and shuttle companies operating in their area, so you can compare frequencies and prices. **Fare structures** are generally straightforward, with fixed prices and no complicated discounts. Auckland to Rotorua, on the North Island, costs about $20, while on the South Island, Christchurch to Queenstown will be roughly $50.

BUS COMPANIES

Atomic Shuttles ☎ 03 349 0697, ⓦ atomictravel.co.nz. Major long-distance bus operator in the South Island.

InterCity & Newmans Auckland call centre ☎ 09 583 5780, ⓦ intercitycoach.co.nz. Long-distance buses nationwide.

Manabus ⓦ manabus.com.

NakedBus ☎ 0900 62533 (premium rate), ⓦ nakedbus.com. Cheap trips on both islands, including free wi-fi – and beds.

Northliner Express ☎ 09 583 5780, ⓦ northliner.co.nz. Bus travel around Northland, owned by InterCity.

By train

Not much is left of New Zealand's passenger train service besides **commuter** services in Wellington and Auckland and a few inter-city trains. The **long-distance services** that exist are scenic runs, primarily used by tourists; trains are so slow that they have ceased to be practical transport for New Zealanders. Minimal investment in infrastructure and rolling stock is beginning to have an effect on standards, but railway travel remains a pleasant experience.

Long-distance trains are all run by **KiwiRail Scenic Journeys** (☎ 04 495 0775 & ☎ 0800 872 467, ⓦ kiwirailscenic.co.nz), which operates three passenger routes. Trains have reclining seats, buffet cars with reasonable food, beer, panoramic windows, glass-backed observation cars or open-air viewing decks. Tickets guarantee a seat: passengers check in on the platform before boarding and bags are carried in a luggage van.

The longest is the **Northern Explorer** between Auckland and Wellington, past the volcanic peaks of the Tongariro National Park. Interesting **stops along the way** include Otorohanga (where the train is met by a shuttle bus to Waitomo Caves) and National Park (with access to Mount Ruapehu and the Tongariro Alpine Crossing). The service leaves both Auckland and Wellington daily around 7.50am and reaches its destination around 6.40pm.

In the South Island, the **Coastal Pacific** makes a pretty run **between Christchurch and Picton**, sometimes hugging the coast. Every day in the summer (October through April), it leaves Christchurch at 7am for the run up through Kaikoura (9.54am) and Blenheim (11.46am) to Picton (12.13pm). It then returns from Picton (1pm) through Blenheim (1.33pm) and Kaikoura (3.28pm) to Christchurch (6.21pm).

The finest rail journey in New Zealand is the **TranzAlpine between Christchurch and Greymouth** on the West Coast, covered in detail on p.524.

Fares are higher than the comparable bus tickets, but with discounts and the use of a **travel pass** (see box, p.31), travelling is still reasonably good value. Most people get the standard or **Flexi Fare**, which gives a discount in return for advance booking and a full refund if you cancel or change more than 48 hours before the departure time. As an example, a standard, one-way ticket from Auckland to Wellington or from Christchurch to Greymouth is around $199. Seniors (60-plus) can get discounts on standard fares, though most folk do better by going for a Scenic Rail Pass (see box, p.31).

Apart from a couple of short-run steam trains, the only other passenger trains are along the **Taieri Gorge Railway** (see box, p.606) between Dunedin and Middlemarch, an extremely beautiful route again run almost entirely for the benefit of tourists.

By car

For maximum flexibility, it's hard to beat **driving** around New Zealand: you'll be able to get to places beyond the reach of public transport and to set your own timetable. With the freedom to camp or stay in cheaper places away from town centres this can be a very economical option for two or more people.

Plan routes carefully to allow sufficient time to enjoy your journey: even the highways may be narrower, steeper and more winding than you are used to.

In order to drive in New Zealand you need a valid **licence** from your home country, or an International Driver's Licence (valid for up to a year in New Zealand). You must always carry the licence when driving.

In New Zealand you **drive on the left** and will find **road rules** similar to those in the UK, Australia and the US. All occupants must wear **seatbelts** and drivers must park in the same direction as the traffic

flow. The Transport Agency (**@** nzta.govt.nz) publish guides in several languages on *What's different about driving in New Zealand.*

The **speed limit** for the open road is 100kmph, reduced to 70kmph or 50kmph in built-up areas. Speeding fines start at $30 and rapidly increase as the degree of transgression increases. Some drivers flash their headlights at oncoming cars to warn of lurking police patrols, but there are also hidden cameras on the roads. **Drink driving** has traditionally been a problem in New Zealand: as part of a campaign to cut the death toll the alcohol limit is low, random breath tests exist and offenders are dealt with severely.

Road conditions are generally good and traffic is relatively light except around Auckland and Wellington in the rush hour. Most roads are sealed (paved), although a few have a metalled surface, composed of an aggregate of loose chippings. Clearly marked on most maps, these are slower to drive along, prone to washouts and landslides after heavy rain, and demand considerably more care and attention from the driver. Always check conditions locally before setting off on these routes. All rental companies should insure you on gravel (unsealed) roads, though some prohibit the use of their cars on the worst – typically those at Skippers Canyon and around the northern tip of Coromandel Peninsula.

Other **hazards** include one-lane bridges: a sign before the bridge will indicate who has right of way, and on longer examples there'll be a passing place halfway across.

Unleaded and super unleaded **petrol** and diesel are available in New Zealand, and in larger towns petrol stations are open 24hr. In smaller towns, they may close after 8pm, so be sure to fill up for long evening or night journeys.

If you're driving your own vehicle, check if the **New Zealand Automobile Association** (**@** aa.co.nz) has reciprocal rights with motoring organizations from your own country. Apart from a free 24hr **emergency breakdown** service (**☎** 0800 500 222) – excluding vehicles bogged on beaches – membership entitles you to free maps, accommodation guides and legal assistance, discounts on some rental cars and accommodation, plus access to insurance and pre-purchase vehicle inspection services.

Car rental

Visitors driving in New Zealand typically pick up a car in Auckland, tour the North Island to Wellington where they leave the first vehicle, cross Cook Strait, pick up a second car in Picton, then drive around the South Island dropping off the car in Christchurch. The whole thing can be done in reverse, and may work out cheaper, or you can stick with the same car across Cook Strait, which doesn't entail a big price hike from domestic companies (though some international agencies forbid it).

You'll see rental deals for under $19 a day, though only for older, small cars rented for over a month in winter (June–Aug). Demand is high over the main summer season and prices rise accordingly.

Most of the major **international companies** are represented and offer good deals for virtually new cars. **Domestic** firms offer cheaper rates partly by minimizing overheads and offering older (but perfectly serviceable) vehicles. You may find even cheaper deals with cut-rate local companies, which are fine for short stints, though for general touring domestic nationwide companies are the best bet. Their infrastructure helps when it comes to crossing between the North and South islands (see p.431) and they typically offer free breakdown assistance.

In peak season it usually pays to have a car **booked in advance**. At quieter times you can often pick up something cheaper once you arrive; and in winter (except in ski areas) you can almost name your price. Provided your rental period is four days or more the deal will be for **unlimited kilometres**. The rates quoted below are for summer season assuming a two-week rental period, but don't be afraid to haggle at any time.

As a general rule, Ace, Apex, Omega and Pegasus offer reasonably new cars at moderate prices, while the rest of the companies listed below try desperately to undercut each other and offer **low prices**.

Based on a two-week rental in summer, for two people, a **small car** (1.3–1.8 litre) might cost $45–80 a day from the majors and $40–60 from domestic national firms. A **medium-sized car** (2–3 litre) might cost $90–120 from the majors and $60–70 from domestic national companies. Unless you're here in winter and want to get up to the ski-fields without tyre chains you don't really need a **4WD**, which generally cost $70–140 a day; you'll be better off renting one for short trips in specific areas.

If you are renting for several weeks, there is often no **drop-off fee** for leaving the vehicle somewhere other than where you picked it up. For shorter rental periods you may be charged around $200, though if you're travelling south to north, you may be able to sweet-talk your way out of drop-off charges. At different times in the season Wellington, Picton, Christchurch and Queenstown have a glut of cars that are needed elsewhere, and companies will offer **relocation deals**. Look at hostel notice

boards or call the firms listed below. Some companies want quick delivery, while others will allow you to spend a few more days en route for a reduced rental rate.

You must have a full, clean **driver's licence** and be over 21; drivers under 25 often pay more for insurance. In most cases insurance is included in the quoted cost but you are liable for any windscreen damage and the first $2000 of any damage. With some of the major international companies, and also cheaper companies, this excess can be as much as $3500 if the accident is your fault. This can usually be reduced to $350 or zero by paying an additional $10–25 a day Collision Damage Waiver. Usually before giving you a car rental companies take a credit-card imprint or a cash bond from you for $2000. If you have an accident, the bond is used to pay for any damage: in some cases you can pay anything up to the value of the bond; in others you pay the entire bond no matter how slight the damage. Read the small print, look around the car for any visible **defects**, so you won't end up being charged for someone else's mistakes, and check whether there are any restrictions on driving along certain roads.

DOMESTIC CAR-RENTAL AGENCIES

A2B Rentals ☎ 0800 545 000, ⓦ a2b-car-rental.co.nz.
Ace Rental Cars ☎ 0800 502 277, ⓦ acerentalcars.co.nz.
Apex ☎ 0800 500 660, ⓦ apexrentals.co.nz.
Bargain Rental Cars ☎ 0800 001 122, ⓦ bargainrentals.co.nz.
Jucy ☎ 0800 399 736, ⓦ jucy.co.nz.
Omega ☎ 0800 525 210, ⓦ omegarentalcars.com.
Pegasus ☎ 0800 803 580, ⓦ rentalcars.co.nz.

Campervan rental

Throughout the summer, roads are clogged with **campervans**, almost all driven by foreign visitors who rent them for a few weeks and drive around the country staying in campsites and freedom camping (see p.40). A medium campervan is generally suitable for two adults and a couple of kids and comes with a fold-down bed and compact kitchen. Larger models sleep four or more and often have a shower and toilet.

Medium **campervan rentals** (based on a 3-week rental) can be anywhere between $150 and $400 a day during the high season (Dec–Feb), dropping to $70–240 for a couple of months either side and plummeting to $40–150 in winter. The most well known brands (Kea, Britz, Mighty and Maui) are effectively one company. The smaller firms (listed below) offer cheaper rates, often saving 30 percent or more.

Small vans are often cramped and aimed at backpackers prepared to sacrifice comfort to save money. These typically cost $60–140 a day during summer, $30–90 in the shoulder season and $25–35 in the depths of winter. The trend is for wildly painted bodywork, often with arcane, quirky or downright offensive comments graffitied on them: witness Escape Rentals and Wicked Campers. Other good bets are the distinctive orange Spaceships that have been imaginatively converted to suit two adults. For an affordable and slightly offbeat experience go for a restored, classic VW campervan (possibly with a pop-top), from Auckland-based Kiwi Kombis, who charge $130–190 a day, depending on dates and van.

For all vans you get unlimited kilometres, a kitchen kit and perhaps airport transfer. If you're renting for less than a week, there may be an additional charge, especially in high summer. Insurance is included but you'll be liable for the first $3000–4000 and you should seriously consider paying extra fees to get this liability reduced. Most companies have a supply of tents, camping kits, outdoor chairs and tables that can be rented for a few dollars.

No special **licence** is required to drive a campervan, but some caution is needed, especially in high winds and when climbing hills and going around tight corners.

CAMPERVAN RENTALS: MEDIUM TO LARGE

Adventure ☎ 0800 123 555, ⓦ nzmotorhomes.co.nz.
Britz ☎ 0800 831 900, ⓦ britz.com.
Eurocampers ☎ 03 347 3285, ⓦ eurocamper.co.nz.
Freedom Campers ☎ 0800 325 939, ⓦ freedomcampers.co.nz.
Jucy ☎ 0800 399 736, ⓦ jucy.co.nz.
Kea Campers ☎ 0800 520 052, ⓦ keacampers.com.
Maui ☎ 0800 651 080, ⓦ maui.co.nz.
Mighty Cars and Campers ☎ 800 422 267, ⓦ mightycampers .com.

SMALL VANS AND CONVERSIONS

Escape ☎ 0800 216 171, ⓦ escaperentals.co.nz.
Jucy ☎ 0800 399 736, ⓦ jucy.co.nz.
Kiwi Kombis ☎ 09 533 9335, ⓦ kiwikombis.com.
Spaceships ☎ 0800 772 237, ⓦ spaceshipsrentals.co.nz.
Wicked Campers ☎ 0800 246 870, ⓦ wickedcampers.co.nz.

Buying a used vehicle

Buying a **used vehicle** can be cost-effective if you are staying in the country for more than a couple of months. Reselling can recoup enough of the price to make it cheaper than using public transport or renting. However, if you buy cheap there's a greater risk of breakdowns and expensive repairs. The majority of people buy cars in Auckland and then try to sell them in Christchurch, so there's something to be said for buying in Christchurch where you'll often have more choice and a better bargaining position.

Some of the best deals are found on backpacker **hostel notice boards** where older cars and vans are typically offered for $500–5000. Realistically you can expect to pay upwards of $3000 for something half-decent. It may not look pretty and with a **private sale** there's no guarantee the vehicle will make yet another trip around the country, but you might get an added bonus like camping gear thrown in with the car (or offered at a snip).

For a little more peace of mind, buy from a **dealership**. There are plenty all over the country, especially in Auckland, Christchurch and Wellington. Prices begin at around $5000 and some yards offer a **buy-back service**, usually paying about fifty percent of the purchase price. If you're confident of your ability to spot a lemon, you can try to pick up a cheap car at an **auction**; they're held weekly in Auckland and Christchurch and are advertised in the local press. Be aware that you'll usually be liable for a **buyer's premium** of around ten percent over your bid.

Before you commit yourself, consult the My Vehicle section of the NZ Transport Agency website (ⓦ nzta.govt.nz), which has good advice on buying and the pitfalls. Their **tips for buying a used car** are particularly helpful.

Unless you really know your big end from your steering column you'll want to arrange a **mobile vehicle inspection**, either from the AA (☎ 0800 907 788, ⓦ aa.co.nz; members $149, nonmembers $169) or the Car Inspection Services (☎ 0800 500 800 in Auckland and Wellington, ⓦ carinspections .co.nz). The inspection may give you enough ammunition to negotiate a price reduction. Finally, before you close a private sale, call LemonCheck (☎ 0800 536 662, ⓦ lemoncheck.co.nz) – its staff will fill you in on the vehicle history, including possible odometer tampering ($20) and let you know about any debts on the vehicle ($7.50).

All vehicles over three years old must have a **Warrant of Fitness** (WOF), which is a test of its mechanical worthiness and safety. WOFs are carried out and issued by specified garages and testing stations and last for a year if the vehicle was registered this century, or six months if older. Check the expiry date, as any vehicle for sale must have had a WOF carried out no more than one month before sale. The vehicle should also have a current **vehicle licence** ("rego"), which must be renewed before it expires (6 months, starting at $291.08; 12 months $431.25 for petrol-driven, private vehicles of 1301–2600cc): post offices and AA offices are the most convenient for this, though you can also do it online at ⓦ nzta.govt.nz.

You **transfer ownership** by completing buyer and seller forms online (buyers can also complete forms at a post office or AA office): the licence plates stay with the vehicle. Next, even though it's not compulsory, you'll want **insurance**: Comprehensive (which covers your vehicle and any other damaged vehicles), or Third Party, Fire & Theft (which covers your own vehicle against fire and theft, but only pays out on damage to other vehicles in case of an accident). Shop around as prices vary widely, but expect to pay a minimum of $150 for six months' Third Party, Fire & Theft cover (depending on age, experience, car value and so on).

By motorcycle

Visitors from most countries can ride in New Zealand with their normal or international licence, though it must specify motorbikes. **Helmets** are compulsory, and you'll need to be prepared to ride on gravel roads from time to time.

Few people bring their own bike but **bike rental** is available from the companies running guided bike tours (see below). It isn't cheap: expect to pay $110–190 a day for a 650cc machine in summer, and up to $350 for a Harley tourer. Bike Adventure New Zealand (ⓣ0800 498 600, ⓦbikeadventure .co.nz) offers 600cc enduro machines for $95 per day for short periods, dropping to $50 per day for ten weeks. Alternatively, try the same channels as for "Buying a used vehicle", p.34.

MOTORBIKE TOURS

Organized tours come in self-guided or guided varieties, usually incorporating top-of-the-range accommodation, restaurants and bikes.

Adventure New Zealand Motorcycle Tours & Rentals
ⓦ gotournz.com. Nelson-based company providing upmarket, small-group guided or self-guided tours around the South Island, with itineraries tweaked to suit and a luxury coach in your wake. Rates start at $9190 for a guided 10-day trip on a relatively modest bike.

New Zealand Motorcycle Rentals & Tours ⓦ nzbike.com. Another specialist top-end company, offering guided all-inclusive tours staying in quality accommodation, semi-guided tours and bike rental. A fully guided 19-day tour round both islands will set you back about $8800, staying in hotels and riding a modest bike.

Te Waipounamu Motorcycle Hire & Tours ⓦ motorcycle-hire .co.nz. These folk do upscale tours across New Zealand and bike rentals including Beamers at $235/day in the high season.

By bike

If you have time, **cycling** is an excellent way of getting around. Distances aren't enormous, the weather is generally pretty benign, traffic is light, and the countryside is gorgeous. Most everywhere you go you'll find hostels and campsites well set up for campers, but also equipped with rooms and cabins for when the weather really fails.

But there are downsides. New Zealand's road network is skeletal, so in many places you'll find yourself riding on main roads or unsealed minor roads. You'll also experience a fair bit of wind and rain and have to climb quite a lot of hills.

Cycling the **South Island** is an easier proposition than the **North Island**. The South Island's alpine backbone presents virtually the only geographical barrier, while the eastern two-thirds of the island comprise a flat plain. In the North Island you can barely go 10km without encountering significant hills – and you have to contend with a great deal more traffic, including intimidating logging trucks.

New Zealand law requires all cyclists to wear a **helmet**. Some **fitness** is important, but distances don't have to be great and you can take things at your own pace. If you'd rather go with a **guided group**, see box, p.50.

NGA HAERENGA – THE NEW ZEALAND CYCLE TRAIL

With quiet roads, brilliant scenery and superb camping, New Zealand has long been on the cycle touring map and is set to become a major off-road cycle touring destination.

The government has funded a series of **23 Great Rides**, stand-alone, mostly off-road routes that comprise **Nga Haerenga** (ⓦnzcycletrail.com). Most of the rides (from a few hours to several days) are now complete and it's hoped that they will emulate the successful Otago Central Rail Trail (see box, p.743), providing superb riding while boosting the local economy. Eventually these may be linked together in an end-to-end network along the lines of Te Araroa (see box, p.48).

Rent a bike locally and just tackle rides such as "From the Mountains to the Sea" in the north and "The Old Ghost Road" in the south, or come for a month or so and collect the set.

For more **information**, and to plan your trip, use the *Pedallers' Paradise* guides (⒲paradise-press .co.nz), Bruce Ringer's *New Zealand by Bike* or the Kennett brothers' *Classic New Zealand Cycle Trails* (which has a two-month route from Cape Reinga to Bluff).

The bike

Since the vast majority of riding will be on sealed roads with only relatively short sections of gravel, it is perfectly reasonable (and more efficient) to get around New Zealand on a touring bike. But fashion dictates most people use a **mountain bike** fitted with fat but relatively smooth tyres.

On long trips it's cheaper to **bring your own bike**, already set up to your liking. Most international airlines simply count bikes as a piece of luggage and don't incur any extra cost as long as you don't exceed your baggage limit. However, they do require you to use a **bike bag** or box, or at the very least remove pedals and handle-bars and wrap the chain. Some airlines will sell you a cardboard bike box at the airport. Soft bags are probably the most convenient (they're easy to carry on the bike once you arrive), but if you are flying out from the same city you arrive in you can often store hardshell containers (free or for a small fee) at the backpacker hostel where you spend your first and last nights: call around.

Renting bikes for more than the odd day can be an expensive option, costing anything from $30–60 a day, depending on whether you want a bike with little more than pedals and brakes, a tourer or state-of-the-art mountain bike. Specialist cycle shops do more economical monthly rentals for around $200–250 for a tourer and $300 or more for a full-suspension superbike.

For long-distance cycle touring, it's generally cheaper to **buy a bike**. It will cost at least $1500 to get fully kitted out with new equipment, but it's worth checking hostel notice boards for **secondhand bikes** (under $500 is a reasonable deal), often accompanied by essential extras such as wet-weather gear, lights, a helmet and a pump. Some cycle shops offer **buy-back deals**, guaranteeing to refund about fifty percent of the purchase price at the end of your trip – contact Adventure Cycles, 9 Premier Ave, Western Springs, in Auckland (☎09 940 2453, ⒲adventure-auckland .co.nz/adventurecycles). If you're bringing your own bike, the same folk will let you store the bike box you transported your machine in ($20 a month, free if you buy stuff from their shop), help organize an emergency package of spare parts and extra

clothing to be forwarded at your request, and give your bike a once-over before you set off.

Transporting bikes

Lethargy, boredom, breakdowns or simply a need to shift your bike between islands mean you'll use **public transport** at some point. You can usually get your bike onto a bus (generally $10–15) or train ($10/journey), though space is often limited so book well in advance. Crossing Cook Strait, the Interislander and Blue Bridge ferries charge $10–15.

Air New Zealand and Jetstar will fly your bike free, if it is packed in a bike bag and is within your baggage allowance.

By ferry

The **ferries** you're most likely to use are vehicle-carrying services plying Cook Strait between Wellington on the North Island and Picton on the South Island. Details are given on p.431.

Passenger ferries link Bluff, in the south of the South Island, to Stewart Island, and vehicle ferries connect Auckland with the Hauraki Gulf islands, principally Waiheke and Great Barrier. Information about these short trips is included in the sections on Invercargill and Auckland. Most visitors spend more boat time on cruises – whale watching, dolphin swimming, sightseeing – or **water taxis**.

Accommodation

Accommodation will take up a fair chunk of your money while in New Zealand, but the good news is that standards are uniformly excellent. Almost every town has a motel or hostel of some description, so finding accommodation is seldom a problem – though it's essential to book ahead during the peak summer season from Christmas to the end of March.

Kiwis travel widely at home, most choosing to self-cater at the country's huge number of well-equipped **campsites** (a.k.a. holiday parks) and **motels**, shunning **hotels**, which cater mainly to package holiday-makers and the business community. The range of **backpacker hostels**, **B&Bs**, **homestays**, **farmstays** and **lodges** forms an appealing alternative, covering the whole spectrum from a room in someone's suburban home to pampered luxury in a country mansion.

Wherever you stay, you can expect unstinting hospitality and a truckload of valuable advice on

BOOKING ACCOMMODATION

You should **book accommodation** at major towns and popular tourist locales at least a few days in advance from December to March. Reserving several weeks ahead is a good idea if you're particular about where you stay. Most Kiwis take two to three weeks off from Christmas onwards, so from **December 26 to mid-January** anywhere near a nice beach or lake is likely to be packed, particularly holiday parks (campsites) and motels, which usually rack up their prices considerably during this period. Places that don't attract Kiwi holiday-makers can be relatively peaceful at this time. Towns near **ski resorts** are typically busiest between July and September, particularly on weekends and during school holidays.

local activities and onward travel. Many places are now accredited using the nationwide **Qualmark** system (W qualmark.co.nz), which grades different types of accommodation from one to five stars. Most fall between three stars (very good) and four plus (at the top end of excellent), but there is no way of knowing whether, for example, a four-star backpacker is superior to rooms at a five-star holiday park. Many places choose not to join the system, but may be just as good or better.

ACCOMMODATION GUIDES AND WEBSITES

AA Accommodation Guide W aatravel.co.nz. Accommodation providers pay to be in this annual guide for the whole country that concentrates mostly on motels and holiday parks. Also a B&B guide and various regional variants. Available free from most motels and i-SITE offices.

BookABach W bookabach.co.nz. Many Kiwis own a holiday home (a.k.a. *bach* or *crib*), which they may rent out when they're not using them. Some are in superb locations next to beaches or lakes. Some have a two- or three-night minimum stay, rising to a week from Christmas to late February when rates rise dramatically and availability is reduced. There are real bargains in winter. Holiday houses (W holidayhouses.co.nz) has a similar range of places.

Charming places to stay W charmingaccommodation.co.nz. Glossy B&B guide concentrating on mid-range places but also country and farmstays. View online, download as one massive PDF, get the book for the price of postage, or pick up (often free) at B&Bs.

Hotels, motels and pubs

In New Zealand, **hotel** is a term frequently used to describe old-style **pubs**, once legally obliged to provide rooms for drinkers to recuperate. Many no longer provide accommodation, but some have transformed themselves into backpacker hostels, while others are dedicated to preserving the tradition. At their best, such hotels offer comfortable rooms in historic buildings (for $100–140/night), though just as often lodgings are rudimentary. Hotel bars are frequently at the centre of small-town life and at weekends in particular can

be pretty raucous, so you may find a budget room at a hostel a better bet.

In the cities and major resorts, you'll also come across **hotels** in the conventional sense ($150–400), predominantly business- or tour-bus-oriented places. Rack rates are generally high but bargains can definitely be had, particularly at weekends, by checking their websites.

Most Kiwi families on the move prefer the astonishingly well-equipped **motels** ($100–250) which congregate along the roads running into town, making them more convenient for drivers than for those using trains or buses. They usually come with Sky TV, bathroom, some sort of kitchen and tea and coffee, but are often fairly functional concrete-block places with little to distinguish one from another. Rooms range from all-in-one **studios**, with beds, kettle, toaster and a microwave, through **one-bedroom units**, usually with a full and separate kitchen, to two- and **three-bedroom suites**, sleeping six or eight. Suites generally go for the same basic price as a one-bedroom unit, with

ACCOMMODATION PRICES

Accommodation rates quoted represent the cheapest available double or twin room in high season, though we have generally ignored the short spike in prices around Christmas and New Year. Single rooms usually cost only ten to twenty percent less than doubles or twins. In hostels and campsites where individual dorm beds are available, we have given the full price assuming no discount cards. YHA members get 10 percent discount at YHAs and associate YHAs, while BBH members typically save $3 at BBH-affiliated establishments. DOC hut and camping fees are also per person, unless otherwise stated.

Our prices always include the 15 percent Goods and Services Tax (GST).

each additional adult paying $20–30, making them an economical choice for groups travelling together. Anything calling itself a **motor inn** ($140–240) or similar will be quite luxurious, with a bar, restaurant, swimming pool and sauna but no cooking facilities.

B&Bs, lodges and boutique hotels

While families might prefer the freedom and adaptability of a motel, couples are often better served by a **bed and breakfast** (B&B; $120–250). This might be a simple room with a bathroom down the hall and some toast and cereal included in the price. But the term also encompasses luxurious colonial homes with well-furnished en-suite rooms and sumptuous home-cooked breakfasts. Those at the top end – and sometimes more basic places – fashion themselves as **lodges**, **boutique hotels** and "exclusive retreats" ($300–2000), where standards of service, comfort and prices can reach extraordinary levels.

Rates drop in the low season, when these places can often be good value. If you're travelling alone, want to be chatting to people and don't fancy hostels, B&Bs are a good alternative, usually charging **lone travellers** 60–80 percent of the double room rate, though some only ask fifty percent.

Homestays and farmstays

Homestays ($100–200) usually offer a guest room or two in an ordinary house where you muck in with the owners and join them for breakfast the following morning. Staying in such places can be an excellent way to meet ordinary New Zealanders; you'll be well looked after, sometimes to the point of being overwhelmed by your hosts' generosity. It is courteous to **call in advance**, and bear in mind you'll usually have to **pay in cash**. Rural versions often operate as **farmstays** ($120–200), where you're encouraged to stay a couple of nights and might be able to spend the intervening day trying your hand at farm tasks: rounding up sheep, milking cows, fencing, whatever might need doing. Both homestays and farmstays charge for a double room, including breakfast; some cook dinner on request for $25–75 per person, and you may pay a small fee for lunch if you spend the day at the farm or for a packed lunch.

Hostels, backpackers and YHAs

New Zealand has over 350 budget and self-catering places, pretty much interchangeably known as **hostels** or **backpackers** and offering a

For advice on **backcountry camping** and **trampers' huts**, see the "Outdoor activities" section (see p.49).

dorm bed or bunk for around $20–32. They're often in superb locations – bang in the centre of town, beside the beach, close to a ski-field or amid magnificent scenery in a national or forest park – and are great places to meet other travellers and pick up local information. Backpacker hostels range in size from as few as four beds up to huge premises accommodating several hundred. Beds are generally fully made up (sleeping bags were banned years ago to prevent the spread of bed bugs); you should bring your own towel, though you can rent one for a few dollars. **Internet access** (and increasingly wi-fi) is pretty standard, though a few rural places intentionally eschew such mod cons. Depending on the area, there may be a pool, barbecue, bike and/or canoe rental and information on local work opportunities. Many offer cupboards for your gear, though you'll usually need your own padlock. Almost all hostels are affiliated with local and international organizations that offer **accommodation discounts** to members, along with an array of other travel- and activity-related savings.

Some hostels allow you to pitch a tent in the grounds and use the facilities for around $20 per person, but generally the most basic and cheapest accommodation is in a six- to twelve-bunk **dorm** ($20–28), with three- and four-bed rooms (also known as three-shares and four-shares) usually priced a couple of dollars higher. Most hostels also have **double**, **twin** and **family rooms** ($55–100 for two), the more expensive ones with en-suite bathrooms. Lone travellers who don't fancy a dorm can sometimes get a **single room** ($40–70), and many larger places (especially YHAs and Base backpackers) also offer **women-only dorms**.

YHA

YHA New Zealand (Ⓦ yha.co.nz) has around 17 hostels across the country, and another 27 hostels are affiliated **associate YHA hostels**. It's run as a charity, and has a couple of hundred employees, so staff are well-trained, knowledgeable and keen to help.

Newer purpose-built hostels have won awards for embodying the charity's commitment to sustainability, while all promote recycling and energy conservation. Most have double and family rooms as well as single-sex dorms. None have bars.

Nonmembers pay the price we've quoted but you can save 10 percent if you've got a **Hostelling International Card**. You may be better off getting $25 annual YHA membership in New Zealand, which aside from accommodation discounts nets you free wi-fi at YHA hostels and further discounts with travel and activity companies.

You can **book ahead** online, from another hostel or through the YHA National Reservations Centre and through Hostelling International offices in your home country.

YHA and associate YHA hostels are listed on the annual *YHA Backpacker Map*.

BBH

YHAs are vastly outnumbered by other **backpacker hostels**, where the atmosphere is more variable; some are friendly and relaxed, others more party-oriented. Many are aligned with the NZ-based **Budget Backpacker Hostels** (@bbh.co.nz), and are listed (along with current prices) in the *BBH Accommodation Guide*, widely available from hostels and visitor centres. The entries are written by the hostels and don't pretend to be impartial, but each is also given a customer **rating** which is determined by an annual survey and by online voting. These are a fairly reliable quality indicator, though city hostels tend not to rate as well as similarly appointed places next to nice beaches. Anything above 80 percent will be excellent: those rating below 60 percent should be treated with suspicion.

Savings can be made by buying a **BBH Club Card** ($45), which nets a $3–4 discount on each night's stay. Cards are available from BBH and all participating hostels, and each card doubles as a rechargeable phonecard loaded with $20 worth of calling time.

Base and Nomads

Two Australasian hostel chains, **Base** (@stayatbase .com) and **Nomads** (@nomadsworld.com), each run around ten hostels across the country, in major tourist hangouts. Both offer discounts if you sign up to a card or accommodation package.

Holiday parks, cabins and camping

New Zealand has some of the world's best **camping** facilities, and even if you've never camped before, you may well find yourself using **holiday parks** (also known as **motor camps**), which come with space to pitch tents, numerous powered sites (or hook-ups) for campervans and usually a broad range of dorms, cabins and motel units. You'll find more down-to-earth camping at wonderfully located **DOC sites**.

Camping is largely a summer activity (Nov–May), especially in the South Island. At worst, New Zealand can be very wet, windy and plagued by voracious winged **insects**, so the first priority for tent campers is good-quality gear with a fly sheet which will repel the worst that the elements can dish out, and an inner tent with bug-proof ventilation for hot mornings.

Busy times at motor camps fall into line with the school holidays, making Easter and the summer period from Christmas to the end of January the most hectic. Make **reservations** as far in advance as possible at this time, and a day or two before you arrive through February and March. DOC sites are not generally bookable, and while this is no problem through most of the year, Christmas can be a mad free-for-all.

See p.40 for information about responsible overnight stops outside official areas.

Holiday parks

Holiday parks are typically located on the outskirts of towns and are invariably well equipped, with a communal kitchen, TV lounge, games area, laundry and sometimes a swimming pool. You should bring your own pans, plates and cutlery, though some places have limited supplies and full sets can be rented for a few dollars a night. Nonresidents can often get **showers** for around $2–5. **Campers** usually get the quietest and most sylvan corner of the site and are charged around $15–25 per person; camping prices throughout the Guide are per person unless followed or preceded by "per site". There is often no distinction between tent pitches and the **powered sites** set aside for campervans, but the latter usually cost an extra $2–5 per person for the use of power hook-ups and dump stations.

Most holiday parks also have some form of on-site accommodation (see p.40). **Sheets and towels** may not be included at the cheaper end, so bring a sleeping bag or be prepared to pay to rent bed linen (typically $5–15/stay).

Holiday parks are independently run but often align themselves with nationwide organizations that set minimum standards. Look out for **Top 10** sites (@top10.co.nz), which maintain a reliably high standard in return for slightly higher prices and a degree of identikit sameness. By purchasing a **membership card** ($49) you save ten percent on each night's stay and get local discounts; the card (valid 2 years) can also be used at some sites in Australia.

HOLIDAY PARK ACCOMMODATION OPTIONS

Tent site ($15–25/person). Usually a patch of grass with a tap nearby.

Powered site ($18–28/person). Patch of grass or concrete with electrical hook-up and a dump station nearby. Fancier places charge a minimum of two people per site.

Lodge or backpackers ($20–30/person). Dorm accommodation, often 8–12 bunks.

Standard cabin ($50–90 for two, plus $10–15 for each extra person). Often little more than a shed with bunks and perhaps a table. They sleep 2–4 and bedding is usually extra.

Kitchen cabin ($70–120 for two, plus $10–20 for each extra person). Like a standard cabin but with some cooking facilities, table and chairs, and pans and plates provided. Often sleeps four and bedding is extra.

Tourist cabin/flat ($80–140 for two, plus $15–25 for each extra person). A kitchen cabin but with your own shower, toilet and maybe TV. Sometimes known as a self-contained unit, it typically sleeps four, and bedding is sometimes included.

Motel unit ($100–200 for two, plus $15–30 for each extra person). Larger than cabins and probably with one or more separate bedrooms and TV/DVD. Bedding and towels included.

DOC campsites

Few holiday parks can match the idyllic locations of the 250 or so **campsites** operated by the **Department of Conservation** (DOC; Ⓦ doc.govt.nz) in national parks, reserves, maritime and forest parks, the majority beautifully set by sweeping beaches or deep in the bush. This is back-to-nature camping, low-cost and with simple **facilities**, though sites almost always have running water and toilets of some sort. Listed in DOC's free North Island and South Island *Conservation Campsites* booklets (available from DOC offices), the sites fall into one of five categories: **Basic** (free), usually with nothing but a long-drop toilet and water nearby; **Backcountry** ($6), with perhaps a cooking shelter and/or fireplace; the more common **Standard** ($6), all with vehicular access and many with barbecues, fireplaces, picnic tables and refuse collection; **Scenic** ($10), popular coastal sites with toilets, tap water and possibly cold showers, barbecues and bins; and the rare **Serviced** ($15), which are similar in scope to the regular holiday parks. Children aged 5–17 are usually charged half the adult price. Serviced sites and some Scenic and Standard sites must be **booked in advance** from October to April.

Freedom camping

One of the pleasures of driving a campervan around New Zealand is the ability to sneak the odd free night in wayside rest areas or in car parks beside beaches. This **freedom camping** has never been strictly legal, but when numbers were small nobody worried too much. However, the popularity of the privilege and indiscriminate littering took its toll and a new law now gives councils the power to hand out **instant fines** (minimum $200) to people found camping where they are instructed not to. "No Camping" signs have sprung up in likely spots all over the country, forcing freedom campers to quieter places between towns.

Freedom camping is definitely getting tougher but the approach varies throughout the country. Almost everyone takes a dim view of freedom camping in vehicles without a plumbed-in toilet. **Full self-contained campers** (with a blue warrant, and rear vehicle sticker) have more options. Some councils impose a blanket ban on freedom camping within 10km of town, other places designate specific spots for freedom campers. DOC have responded to the changes by opening up more **campsites**; there's also **Native Parks** (Ⓦ nativeparks.co.nz), a scheme where travellers in fully self-contained campervans can stay free on hosts' property. When you join ($75) you get a guidebook outlining around 90 member properties spread all over the country.

We've listed many of the best and most convenient camping areas throughout the Guide, but there's lots more information out there. Consult Ⓦ **camping.org.nz** for guidelines on freedom camping and useful links including the AA maps of dump stations and public toilets. There are also useful **apps**; try the free one from Ⓦ campermate .co.nz showing camping spots, toilets, budget accommodation and wi-fi hotspots all over the country, and **Respect NZ**, a free website (Ⓦ rankers .co.nz/respect) or charged-for app (Official Camping NZ; $15), which focuses on the camping but has deeper coverage.

Food and drink

New Zealand's food scene is brilliant all round, from the quality of the ingredients and cooking, to its presentation and the places where it's served.

Kiwi **gastronomy** has its roots in the British culinary tradition – an unfortunate heritage that still informs cooking patterns for older New Zealanders – and it is only comparatively recently that the country's chefs have woken up to the possibilities presented by the fabulous larder of super-fresh, top-quality ingredients available locally. Along with tender lamb, succulent beef and venison, and

THE HANGI

To sample traditional cooking methods go to a **hangi** (pronounced nasally as "hungi"), where meat and vegetables are steamed for hours in an earth oven then served to the assembled masses. The ideal way to experience a *hangi* is as a guest at a private gathering, but most people have to settle for one of the commercial affairs in Rotorua or Christchurch. There you'll be a paying customer rather than a guest but the *hangi* flavours will be authentic, though sometimes the operators may have been creative in the more modern methods they've used to achieve them.

At a traditional *hangi*, the men first light a fire and place river stones in its embers. While these are heating, they dig a suitably large pit and place the hot stones in the bottom, covering them with wet sacking. Meanwhile the women prepare lamb, pork, chicken, fish, shellfish and vegetables (particularly *kumara*), wrapping the morsels in leaves then arranging them in baskets (originally of flax, but now more commonly of steel mesh). The baskets are lowered into the cooking pit and the *hangi* is covered over, sealing in the steam and flavours. A couple of hours later, the baskets are disinterred, revealing fabulously tender steam-smoked meat and vegetables with a faintly earthy flavour. A reverential silence, broken only by munching and appreciative murmurs, usually descends.

superb seafood you'll find some of the world's best dairy products and stone and pip fruit which, at harvest time, can be bought for next to nothing from roadside stalls.

All this has been combined into what might be termed **Modern Kiwi cuisine**, drawing on Californian and contemporary Australian cooking, and combining it with flavours drawn from the **Mediterranean**, **Asia** and the **Pacific Rim**: sun-dried tomatoes, lemongrass, basil, ginger, coconut, and many more. Restaurants and cafés throughout the country feel duty-bound to fill their menus with as broad a spectrum as possible, lining up seafood linguini, couscous, sushi, Thai food, venison meatballs and chicken korma alongside the rack of lamb and gourmet pizza. Sometimes this causes gastronomic overload, but often it is simply mouthwatering.

Meat and fish

New Zealanders have a taste for **meat**, the quality of which is superb, with New Zealand lamb often at the head of the menu but matched in flavour by venison and beef.

With the country's extensive coastline, it's no surprise that **fish and seafood** also loom large. The white, flaky flesh of the **snapper** is the most common saltwater fish, but you'll also come across blue cod, tuna, John Dory, groper (often known by its Maori name of **hapuku**), flounder, gurnard, and the firm, delicately flavoured **tarakihi**. Salmon is common, but not trout, which cannot be bought or sold, though most hotels and restaurants will cook one if you've caught it. This archaic law was originally intended to protect sportfishing when trout were introduced to New Zealand in the nineteenth century. All these fish are very tasty smoked, but smoked tarakihi, hapuku, blue cod, marlin and eel are particularly good.

One much-loved delicacy is **whitebait**, a collective name for five species of tiny, silvery, native fish mostly caught on the West Coast and eaten whole in fritters during the August to November season.

Shellfish are a real New Zealand speciality. You'll occasionally come across **tuatua**, dug from Northland beaches, on menus, but you're more likely to find fabulous **Bluff oysters** (see box, p.630), scallops and sensational **green-lipped mussels**, which have a flavour and texture that's hard to beat and are farmed in the cool, clear waters of the Marlborough Sounds, especially around Havelock. Live green-lipped mussels can be bought from any decent supermarket.

Wonderfully rich and delicate **crayfish** is also available round the coast and should be sought out, particularly when touring Kaikoura and the East Cape.

Maori and ethnic food

In New Zealand restaurants you'll find few examples of Polynesian or **Maori cuisine**, though the cooking style does now have a foothold in forward-looking establishments where you might find a fern frond salad, or steak rubbed with peppery *horopito* leaves. To sample Maori food you'll really need to get along to a *hangi* (see box above), most likely in Rotorua. One Pacific staple you'll certainly come across is **kumara** (sweet potato), which features in *hangi* and is often deep-fried as *kumara* chips.

THE EDMONDS COOKERY BOOK AND KIWI DESSERTS

Almost every Kiwi household has a battered copy of the **Edmonds Cookery Book**, first published in 1908 and still selling over 20,000 copies a year, parents often giving their kids a copy when they first leave home. The recipes are wide-ranging but the focus is on baking, usually using Edmond's baking powder, which is still prominent on supermarket shelves. The book is the first place people turn for making the sort of cakes and desserts that fill the shelves of rural tearooms. Fancier modern cafés are now reinventing these retro Kiwi classics.

Afghans The origin of the name is lost, but these chocolate-and-cornflake-dough biscuits topped with cocoa icing are a perennial favourite.

Anzac biscuit Textured cookie made with oats and coconut.

Carrot cake A Kiwi favourite found in cafés and tearooms all over.

Lamington A light sponge slice slathered in pink icing and desiccated coconut.

Pavlova No more than a giant, soft meringue covered in cream and fruit, the "pav" is the apotheosis of Kiwi desserts.

A major influx of immigrants from south and east Asia has really changed the Kiwi restaurant scene over the last couple of decades; there's barely a town in the land without an **Indian** or **Chinese** restaurant. **Thai** is also common though you'll need to go to larger towns to find **Malaysian**, **Singaporean**, **Japanese** and **Korean** places. In the bigger cities there has recently been a resurgence of **Mexican** restaurants after years out of favour.

Vegetarian food

Self-catering **vegetarians** can eat well, though they are less well served in restaurants. Outside the major centres dedicated vegetarian restaurants are rare and you will have to rely on the token meat-free dishes served in most cafés. **Vegans** may develop an unhealthy reliance on the ubiquitous veggieburger, though these days many new organic outlets offer a decent selection of plant-based meals.

If you are taking a multi-day expedition on which food is provided, give the operator plenty of notice of your dietary needs.

Eating out

The quality of **cafés** and **restaurants** in New Zealand is typically superb, portions are respectable, and many are good value for money. In most restaurants you can expect to pay upwards of $25 for a main course, perhaps $55 for three courses without wine. There is no expectation of a tip, though a reward for exceptional service (usually around 10 percent) is welcomed. On **public holidays** you may be expected to pay a surcharge (typically 15 percent) to ensure staff get financially compensated for giving up a statutory holiday.

The traditional staple of the Kiwi dining scene is the **tearoom**, a self-service cafeteria-style establishment with old school atmosphere, cheap sandwiches, unsavoury savouries, sticky cakes and very average coffee. You'll still find such places in rural towns: long-distance buses sometimes make their comfort stops at them.

In more urbane areas, tearooms are replaced by **cafés** selling everything from often excellent espresso and muffins to full breakfasts and lunch with a range of wines. Many close around 4pm, but others stay open late, transforming into **restaurants**. There is minimal distinction between the two so you may find yourself eating a full meal alongside folk just out for a beer or coffee. At a café you normally order and pay at the front counter and then are brought your food. In restaurants full table service is the norm, although you may be expected to settle the bill at the counter after your meal.

Restaurants, and many cafés, have alcohol licences, but some still maintain the old **BYO** tradition. Corkage fees are typically $5–20 per bottle, though some places charge per person.

Most **bars** serve **pub meals**, often the best-value budget eating around, with straightforward steak and chips, lasagne, pizza or burgers for under $20. The country's ever-burgeoning wine industry has also spawned a number of moderate-to-expensive **vineyard restaurants**, particularly in the growing areas of Hawke's Bay and Marlborough. The food is almost invariably excellent, with many of the dishes matched to that vineyard's wines.

Snacks and takeaways

In the cities you'll come across **food courts**, usually in shopping malls with a dozen or so stalls selling

TOP 5 FOR FISH & CHIPS
Kai Kart Stewart Island. See p.637
Kaiaua Fisheries Kaiaua. See p.118
The Smokehouse Mapua. See p.472
Tiki's Takeaway Kaikoura. See p.505
Wellington Seamarket Wellington.
See p.438

bargain plates of all manner of ethnic dishes. Traditional **burger bars** continue to serve constructions far removed from the limp international-franchise offerings: weighty buns with juicy patties, thick ketchup, a stack of lettuce and tomato and the ever-present Kiwi favourite, slices of beetroot. **Meat pies** are another snack-time stalwart; sold in bakeries and from warming cabinets in pubs everywhere, the traditional steak and mince varieties now augmented by bacon and egg, venison, steak and cheese, steak and oyster, smoked fish and *kumara* and, increasingly, vegetarian versions.

Fish and chips are also rightly popular – the fish is often shark (euphemistically called lemon fish or flake), though tastier species are always available for a small premium. Look out too for **paua fritters** – battered slabs of minced abalone that are something of an acquired taste.

Self-catering and farmers' markets

If you're **self-catering**, your best bet for cheap supplies is the local supermarket: Pak 'n Save is usually the cheapest; New World usually has the widest variety of quality foods. In emergencies you can top up with supplies from the plethora of convenience corner shops (known as "dairies") stocking bog-standard essentials. These, along with shops at campsites and those in isolated areas with a captive market, tend to have inflated prices.

Gourmet foodstuffs are best sought at small independent outlets, offering predominantly local and/or organic supplies. **Farmers' markets** are another good source of local produce; every town of any size now seems to have one, usually on Saturday or Sunday morning – we've mentioned several throughout the Guide.

Drinking

Licensed cafés and restaurants across the land make a point of stocking a wide range of New Zealand wines and beers, but for the lowest prices and a genuine Kiwi atmosphere you can't beat the **pub**. It's a place where folk stop off on their way home from work, its emphasis on consumption and back-slapping camaraderie rather than ambience and decor. In the cities, where competition from cafés is strong, pubs tend to be more comfortable and relaxing, but in the sticks little has changed. Rural pubs can initially be daunting for strangers, but once you get chatting, barriers soon drop. Drinking hours are barely limited; theoretically you can drink in most bars until at least midnight on weeknights and until 4am or later at weekends though places often close much earlier if there are few customers. The **drinking age** is 18. Smokers are banished to the open air, often in small, purpose-built shelters.

Beer

Beer is drunk widely and often. Nearly all of it is produced by two huge conglomerates – Lion Nathan and DB – who market countless variations on the lager and Pilsener theme, as well as insipid, deep-brown fizzy liquid dispensed from taps and in bottles as "draught" – a distant relation of British-style bitter. One eternal favourite is Steinlager, now also marketed in a "no-additive" version Pure. There

QUALITY FOOD AND DRINK TO LOOK OUT FOR
Ice cream Firm scooped ice cream in a cone is a Kiwi institution and is sold all over. To taste some of the best head for a good supermarket and look for Kapiti or Kohu Road, both available in numerous delicious flavours.
Jams and preserves Artisans sell preserves at various farmers' markets but supermarket brands Anathoth Farm and Te Horo are amazingly flavoursome at modest prices.
Cheese Bland cheddar is the de facto national standard, but New Zealand now makes a wide range of delicious cheeses, with the Kapiti brand widely available. Their super-rich Kikorangi blue is particularly good. Look out, too, for smaller producers such as Whitestone, Meyer and Puhoi Valley.
Beer Shun the mainstream stuff and zero in on small-batch craft brews such as Auckland's Epic; Croucher from Rotorua; McCashin's, from Stoke outside Nelson; Emerson's from Dunedin; and the deep south's Invercargill Brewery. Most are available in bottle stores and good supermarkets.

really isn't a lot to choose between the beers except for alcohol content, normally around four percent, though five percent is common for premium beers usually described as "export".

Beer consumption generally is declining, but there has been a boom in microbreweries making **craft beers**. Tap into the craft beer scene at ⓦrealbeer.co.nz and ⓦbeertourist.co.nz.

Draught beer is usually sold in **pints** (just over half a litre). Keep in mind that a half-pint will always be served as a ten fluid ounce glass and therefore will be a little over half the price of a pint. In rural areas, traditions die hard and you can buy a one-litre **jug**, which is then decanted into the required number of glasses, usually a **seven** (originally seven fluid ounces, or 200ml), a **ten**, or even an elegantly fluted **twelve**.

Prices vary enormously, but you can expect to pay $6–9 for a pint. It is much cheaper to buy in bulk from a **bottle shop** (off-licence or liquor store) which will stock a fair range of mainstream and boutique beers, usually in a six-pack of 330ml bottles (around $12–15) or multiple thereof.

Wine

Kiwis are justifiably loyal to New Zealand winemakers, who now produce **wines** that are among the best in the world, especially **white wines**. New Zealand is rapidly encroaching on the Loire's standing as the world benchmark for Sauvignon Blanc, while the bold fruitiness of its Chardonnay and apricot and citrus palate of its Rieslings attract many fans. **Red wines** were once of the broad-shouldered Aussie variety, but this has changed as improved canopy management and better site selection have brought Kiwi reds up alongside their Australian cousins. Today

there are some superb wines based on Cabernet Sauvignon and Merlot (particularly from Waiheke Island and Hawke's Bay), but the reds garnering the most praise are Pinot Noirs from Central Otago, Marlborough and Martinborough, and Hawke's Bay Syrah – essentially a Shiraz but made in a subtler fashion than the Aussie style.

A liking for **champagne** no longer implies "champagne tastes" in New Zealand: you can still buy the wildly overpriced French stuff, but good Kiwi Méthode Traditionelle (fermented in the bottle in the time-honoured way) starts at around $13 a bottle. Montana's Lindauer Brut is widely available, and justly popular. Many people round out their restaurant meal with **dessert wines** (or "stickies"), with the sweetest made from grapes withered on the vine by the **botrytis** fungus, the so-called "noble rot".

Most bars and licensed restaurants have a tempting range of wines, many sold by the glass ($7–12; $8 and up for dessert wine), while in shops the racks groan under bottles starting from $11 ($15–25 for good quality).

If you want to try before you buy, visit a few wineries, where you can sample half a dozen different wines; occasionally these are free of charge, but more often you will pay a small fee ($10–15), especially to try the reserve wines. A good starting point for information on the Kiwi wine scene is ⓦnzwine.com.

Spirits

The big success story for New Zealand spirits is **42 Below vodka** (ⓦ42below.com). It has won awards and comes infused with fruity flavourings including kiwifruit, passionfruit, and local favourites feijoa and manuka honey. With 42 Below purchased by Bacardi in 2006, the vodka's Kiwi creators have

---

MAJOR WINE AREAS

The following wine areas are listed from north to south:

Henderson and Kumeu Most of these wineries, 15km west of Auckland, source their grapes elsewhere, making this a good place to sample wines from around the country, though Chardonnay and Merlot are particular highlights.

Hawke's Bay Premium wine area around Napier and Hastings with over seventy wineries open to the public, some with tours and restaurants. Produces some of the country's best Chardonnay, Cabernet Sauvignon blends and Syrahs.

Martinborough The most accessible cluster of vineyards, many within walking distance of the town, with fine Pinot Noir and Sauvignon Blanc, as well as dessert wines.

Marlborough Seventy percent of New Zealand's grapes are grown around Blenheim and Renwick, with a huge range of fantastic vineyards, several with restaurants. Famous for its Sauvignon Blanc, the region also produces excellent Pinot Noir and other aromatic white wines.

Central Otago Cool-climate wine growing at the limit of practicability, mostly around Bannockburn near Queenstown. Excellent Pinot Noir in particular.

turned their hand to producing delicious South Gin (Ⓦsouthgin.com).

The commercial success of these tipples has spawned domestic pretenders such as Stolen Rum (Ⓦstolenrum.com), Smoke & Oakum's rum (Ⓦgunpowderrum.com), Broken Shed vodka (Ⓦbrokenshed.com) and others.

A few places, mostly in the south of the South Island, produce single malt **whisky**, the best being Oamaru's New Zealand Malt Whisky Co. (Ⓦthenz whisky.com). Minor players dabble in fruit **liqueurs**; some are delicious, though few visitors develop an enduring taste for the sickly sweet kiwifruit or feijoa varieties, which are mostly sold through souvenir shops.

Tea and coffee

Tea is usually a down-to-earth Indian blend (sometimes jocularly known as "gumboot"), though you may also have a choice of a dozen or so flavoured, scented and herbal varieties. **Coffee** drinking has been elevated to an art form with a specialized terminology: an Italian-style espresso is known as a **short black**; an espresso diluted with hot water is a **long black** (with the hot water occasionally served on the side); an espresso topped with velvety smooth hot milk becomes a **flat white**. Better places will serve all these decaffeinated, skinny or made with soya milk. Flavoured syrups are widely available.

The media

For a country of only 4.5 million inhabitants, New Zealand has a vibrant media scene. Auckland claims to have more radio stations per capita than any other city in the world, and magazine racks are crammed with Kiwi-produced weeklies and monthlies. The standard of media coverage sometimes leaves a little to be desired, but for the most part this is a well-informed country with sophisticated tastes. Online, a good starting point is Ⓦpublicaddress.net, the leading Kiwi blog site.

TV

New Zealanders receive five main free-to-air **broadcast channels**, a handful of local channels and Sky TV (which you'll find in most motels).

The biggest broadcaster is the state-owned **TVNZ**, which operates two advertising-heavy channels. TV ONE has slightly older and more information-based programming while TV2 is younger and more entertainment-oriented. Both channels present a diet of local news, current affairs, sport, drama and entertainment, plus a slew of US, British and Australian programmes: you'll find most of your favourites, often three to six months behind. Visitors may already be acquainted with long-running, home-grown Kiwi soap opera, *Shortland Street*, set in the fictional suburb of Ferndale in Auckland.

The main opposition comes from **TV3**, which pitches itself roughly between TV ONE and TV2, and **Prime**, backed by Sky TV, which often has quirkier programming.

Maori TV launched in 2004 with substantial government support (though it also has ads). Broadcasting in Maori and English, it promotes the language and culture but is far from a stuffy educational channel. Along with good movies and engaging Maori language lessons, you might catch Maori cooking shows, lifestyle makeovers, sitcoms and Maori angles on news, current affairs and sport.

Radio

New Zealand has few countrywide radio stations, but syndication means that some commercial stations can be heard in many parts of the country, with local commercials. All websites listed stream the channel over the **internet**.

For news, current affairs and a thoughtful look at the arts and music, tune into the government-funded **Radio New Zealand National** (101.0–101.7 FM; Ⓦradionz.co.nz), which is the nearest New Zealand gets to, say, NPR or BBC Radio 4. You'll pick it up most places, though there are blank spots. Its sister station, **Radio New Zealand Concert** (89–100 FM), concentrates on classical music.

Though often amateurish, **student radio stations** provide excellent and varied "alternative" listening in their home cities. In Auckland tune to bFM (95.0; Ⓦ95bfm.co.nz); in Wellington to Active (88.6; Ⓦradioactive.co.nz); in Christchurch to RDU (98.5; Ⓦrdu.org.nz); and in Dunedin to Radio One (91.0; Ⓦr1.co.nz).

The rest of the airwaves are clogged by **commercial stations**: keep an ear out for **KiwiFM** (102.1–102.5; Ⓦkiwifm.co.nz), predominantly Kiwi music to Auckland, Wellington and Canterbury.

Newspapers and magazines

New Zealand has no national **daily newspaper**, but rather four major regional papers (all published

Mon–Sat mornings) as well as a plethora of minor rags of mostly local interest. All are politically fairly neutral. The North Island is shared between the Auckland-based *New Zealand Herald* (W nzherald .co.nz) and Wellington's *Dominion Post*, while *The Press* covers Christchurch and its environs (the *Dominion Post* and *The Press* are both available online at W stuff.co.nz), and the *Otago Daily Times* (W odt.co.nz) serves the far south of the country. All offer a pretty decent selection of national and international news, sport and reviews, often relying heavily on wire services and syndication deals with major British and American newspapers. On **Sunday**, check out the tabloid-style *Sunday News*; the superior broadsheet *Sunday Star-Times*; or Auckland's *Herald on Sunday*.

Kiwi newspaper journalists get little scope for imaginative or investigative journalism, though the broad-ranging and slightly left-leaning **weekly magazine** the *Listener* (W listener.co.nz) does its best. With coverage of politics, art, music, TV, radio, books, science, travel, architecture and much more, it's perhaps the best overall insight into what makes New Zealand tick.

Topics are covered in greater depth in the nationwide **monthly** *North and South*, though for an insight into the aspirations of Aucklanders you might be better off with the snappier glossy, *Metro* (W metromag.co.nz).

Specialist magazines cover the range: *Wilderness* (W wildernessmag.co.nz) has a good spread of tramping, kayaking, climbing and mountain biking, and *Rip It Up* (W ripitup.co.nz) is the best of the music mags.

The bi-monthly *Mana* (W mana.co.nz) pitches itself as presenting "the Maori perspective", and gives an insight into what sometimes seems like a parallel world barely acknowledged by the mainstream media. It is in English, but comes peppered with Maori words and concepts, with a convenient glossary.

Festivals and public holidays

In the southern hemisphere, Christmas falls near the start of the school summer holidays, which run from mid-December until early February. From Boxing Day through to the middle of January Kiwis hit the beaches en masse and during this time you'll find a lot more people about.

Motels and campsites can be difficult to book and often raise their prices, though B&Bs and hostels rarely up their rates.

To help you chart a path through the chaos, i-SITE visitor centres are open longer hours, as are many other tourist attractions. **Other school holidays** last for two weeks in mid- to late April, a fortnight in early to mid-July and the first two weeks of October, though these have a less pronounced effect.

Public holidays are big news in New Zealand and it can feel like the entire country has taken to the roads, so it's worth staying put rather than trying to travel on these days. Each region also takes one day a year to celebrate its **Anniversary Day**, remembering the founding of the original provinces that made up New Zealand, and generally celebrated with an agricultural show, horse-jumping, sheepshearing, cake-baking and best-vegetable contests and novelty events (such as gumboot throwing). We've listed official dates below, but days are usually observed on the nearest Monday (or occasionally Friday) to make a long weekend.

PUBLIC HOLIDAYS AND FESTIVAL CALENDAR

Many of the festivals listed below are covered in more detail in the relevant section of the Guide. **PH** indicates a public holiday.

January 1 New Year's Day (PH) Whaleboat Racing Regatta, Kawhia (W kawhiaharbour.co.nz); Highland Games, Waipu (W highlandgames.co.nz).

January 2 (PH)

First Saturday in January Glenorchy Races (W glenorchy-nz .co.nz).

January 17 Anniversary Day (PH in Southland).

Mid-January in odd-numbered years Wings over Wairarapa (W wings.org.nz).

January 22 Anniversary Day (PH in Wellington).

January 29 Anniversary Day (PH in Auckland, Northland, Waikato, Coromandel, Taupo and the Bay of Plenty), celebrated with a massive regatta on Auckland's Waitemata Harbour.

February 1 Anniversary Day (PH in Nelson).

February 6 Waitangi Day (PH); formal events at Waitangi.

First Saturday in February (in even-numbered years) Rippon Open Air Festival, Wanaka (see box, p.737).

First Saturday in February Martinborough Fair, Martinborough W martinboroughfair.org.nz.

Second Saturday in February Wine Marlborough Festival, Blenheim (W wine-marlborough-festival.co.nz).

Second weekend in February Coast-to-Coast multisport race, South Island (W coasttocoast.co.nz).

Mid-February Out in the Park, Wellington (W outinthepark.co.nz).

Third weekend in February Art Deco Weekend, Napier (W artdeconapier.com).

Mid-February to early March Wellington Fringe Festival (Ⓦ fringe.org.nz).

Mid-February to mid-March Burst: The Festival of Flowers, Christchurch (Ⓦ festivalofflowers.co.nz).

Late February to late March NZ International Arts Festival, Wellington (even-numbered years only; Ⓦ nzfestival.co.nz).

Last weekend in February or first weekend in March Golden Shears sheepshearing competition in Masterton (Ⓦ goldenshears .co.nz).

First Saturday in March Martinborough Fair, Martinborough (Ⓦ martinboroughfair.org.nz).

Second Saturday in March Pasifika Festival, Auckland (Ⓦ aucklandnz.com/pasifika); Wildfoods Festival, Hokitika (Ⓦ wildfoods.co.nz).

Mid-March WOMAD world music festival, New Plymouth (see box, p.230).

Mid-March Round-the-Bays Sunday fun run, Auckland (Ⓦ roundthebays.co.nz).

Third weekend in March Te Houtaewa Challenge and Te Houtaewa Surf Challenge, Ahipara (see box, p.183).

Closest Saturday to March 17 Ngaruawahia Maori Regatta, near Hamilton (see p.209).

March 23 Anniversary Day (PH in Otago).

March 31 Anniversary Day (PH in Taranaki).

Late March to late April Good Friday (PH) and Easter Sunday (PH).

Easter week Royal Easter Show, Auckland (Ⓦ royaleastershow .co.nz); Warbirds Over Wanaka airshow (even-numbered years only; see box, p.737); National Jazz Festival, Tauranga (Ⓦ jazz.org.nz).

April 25 ANZAC Day (PH). Dawn services at cenotaphs around the country.

Late April Festival of Colour, Wanaka (odd-numbered years only; five-days; see box, p.737).

Mid-April to late April Arrowtown Autumn Festival (Ⓦ arrowtownautumnfestival.org.nz).

First Monday in June Queen's Birthday (PH).

Middle weekend in June Fieldays, the southern hemisphere's largest agricultural show, Hamilton (Ⓦ fieldays.co.nz).

Mid- to late June Matariki, Maori New Year festivities (Ⓦ matarikievents.co.nz).

Late June to early July Queenstown Winter Festival (Ⓦ winterfestival.co.nz).

Early July to late November New Zealand International Film Festival, held for two weeks each in 14 sites around the country (Ⓦ nzff.co.nz).

Third weekend in June Deco Winter Weekend, Napier (Ⓦ artdeconapier.com).

Early August Taranaki International Festival of the Arts (odd-numbered years only; see box, p.230).

Late September to early October Alexandra Blossom Festival (Ⓦ blossom.co.nz).

Late September to early October World of Wearable Art Awards (WOW), Wellington (Ⓦ worldofwearableart.com).

Fourth Monday in October Labour Day (PH).

October 31 Halloween.

Late October to early November Taranaki Garden Spectacular, New Plymouth (see box, p.230).

Early November Food and Wine Classic, Hawke's Bay (Ⓦ fawc.co.nz).

November 1 Anniversary Day (PH in Hawke's Bay and Marlborough).

November 5 Guy Fawkes' Night fireworks.

Second week in November New Zealand Cup & Show Week, Canterbury (Ⓦ nzcupandshow.co.nz).

Third Friday in November Anniversary Day (PH in Canterbury).

Third Sunday in November Toast Martinborough Wine, Food & Music Festival (Ⓦ toastmartinborough.co.nz).

December 1 Anniversary Day (PH in Westland).

Mid-December to January Festival of Lights, New Plymouth. See box, p.230.

December 25 Christmas Day (PH).

December 26 Boxing Day (PH).

Late Dec Rhythm and Vines three-day music festival, culminating on New Year's Eve, Gisborne (Ⓦ rhythmandvines.co.nz).

Outdoor activities

Life in New Zealand is tied to the Great Outdoors, and no visit to the country would be complete without spending a fair chunk of your time in intimate contact with nature.

Kiwis have long taken it for granted that within a few minutes' drive of their home they can find a deserted beach or piece of "bush" and wander freely through it, an attitude enshrined in a fabulous collection of national, forest and maritime parks. They are all administered by the **Department of Conservation** (DOC; Ⓦ doc.govt.nz), which seeks to balance the maintenance of a fragile environment with the demands of tourism. For the most part it manages remarkably well, providing a superb network of signposted paths studded with trampers' huts, and operating visitor centres that present highly informative material about the local history, flora and fauna.

The lofty peaks of the Southern Alps offer challenging **mountaineering** and great **skiing**, while the lower slopes are ideal for multi-day **tramps** which cross low passes between valleys choked with subtropical and temperate rainforests. Along the coasts there are sheltered lagoons and calm harbours for gentle **swimming** and **boating**, but also sweeping strands battered by some top-class **surf**.

The country also promotes itself as the **adventure tourism** capital of the world. All over

TE ARAROA – THE LONG PATHWAY

Since the mid-1970s it has been a Kiwi dream to have a continuous path from one end of the country to the other. **Te Araroa** (🌐 teararoa.org.nz) opened in 2011 under the auspices of the private Te Araroa Trust, which has linked a fragmented network of existing tracks into a continuous 3000km route from Cape Reinga to Bluff. Improvements are made as new access is negotiated, but the impressively varied route is essentially complete. Much of it runs through fairly remote country, although it intentionally visits small communities so that trampers can resupply.

Some hardy souls have tramped the whole route but it's envisaged that most people will tackle short sections.

New Zealand you'll find places to bungy jump, whitewater or cave raft, jetboat, tandem skydive, mountain bike, scuba dive and much more – you name it, someone somewhere organizes it. While thousands of people participate in these activities every day without incident, standards of instructor training vary. It seems to be a point of honour for operators, instructors and guides to put the wind up you as much as possible. Such bravado shouldn't be interpreted as a genuine disregard for safety, but the fact remains that there have been a few well-publicized injuries and deaths – a tragic situation that's addressed by industry-regulated codes of practice, an independent system of accreditation and home-grown organizations that insist upon high levels of professionalism and safety instruction.

Before engaging in any adventure activities, check your insurance cover (see p.63).

Tramping

Tramping, trekking, bushwalking, hiking – call it what you will, it is one of the most compelling reasons to visit New Zealand, and for many the sole objective.

Hikes typically last three to five days, following well-worn trails through relatively untouched wilderness, often in one of the country's national parks. Along the way you'll be either camping out or staying in trampers' huts, and will consequently be lugging a pack over some rugged terrain, so a moderate level of fitness is required. If this sounds daunting, you can sign up with one of the guided tramping companies that maintain more salubrious huts or luxury lodges, provide meals and carry much of your gear. Details are given throughout the Guide.

The main tramping season is in summer, from October to May, although the most popular tramps – the Milford, Routeburn and Kepler – are in the cooler southern half of the South Island, where the season is shorter by a few weeks at either end.

The tramps

Rugged terrain and a history of track-bashing by explorers and deer hunters has left New Zealand with a web of tramps following river valleys and linking up over passes, high above the bushline. As far as possible, we've indicated the degree of difficulty of all tramps covered in the Guide, broadly following DOC's classification system: a **path** is level, well graded and often wheelchair-accessible; **walking tracks** and **tramping tracks** (usually way-marked with red and white or orange flashes on trees) are respectively more arduous affairs requiring some fitness and proper walking equipment; and a **route** requires considerable tramping experience to cope with an ill-defined trail, frequently above the bushline. DOC's estimated **walking times** can trip you up: along paths likely to be used by families, for example, you can easily find yourself finishing in under half the time specified, but on serious routes aimed at trampers you might struggle to keep pace. We've given estimates for moderately fit individuals and, where possible, included the distance and amount of climbing involved, aiding route planning.

Invaluable information on walking directions, details of access, huts and an adequate map are contained in the excellent DOC tramp **leaflets** (usually $1–2 but downloadable free at 🌐 doc.govt .nz) for major walking tracks).

The maps in each DOC leaflet should be sufficient for trampers sticking to the designated route, but experienced walkers planning independent routes and folk after a more detailed vision of the terrain should fork out for specialized **maps** that identify all the features along the way. Most trampers' huts have a copy of the local area map pinned to the wall or laminated into the table. In describing tramps we have used "**true directions**" in relation to rivers and streams, whereby the left bank (the "true left") is the left-hand side of the river looking downstream.

Eight of New Zealand's finest, most popular tramps, plus one river journey, have been classified

TREMENDOUS TRAMPS

Eight of New Zealand's finest tramps, and one river journey, have been classified as Great Walks; even the most well-trodden of these reveal magnificent natural wonders in the raw. To get more information about the Great Walks and other tramps, check ⓦtramper.co.nz.

NORTH ISLAND

The Tongariro Northern Circuit (3–4 days; see p.301) Takes in magnificent volcanic and semi-desert scenery.
Waikaremoana Track (3–4 days; see p.381) A gentle circumnavigation of one of the country's most beautiful lakes.
The Whanganui River Journey (2–4 days; see p.242) Best explored by canoe and a series of highly atmospheric short walks.

SOUTH ISLAND

The Abel Tasman Coast Track (2–4 days; see p.475) Skirts beaches and crystal-clear bays, ideally explored by sea kayak.
The Heaphy Track (4–5 days; see p.488) Passes through the Kahurangi National Park, balancing subalpine tops and surf-pounded beaches.
The Kepler Track (4 days; see p.761) Renowned for ridge walks and virgin beech forest.
Milford Track (4 days; see p.773) The world-famous track accesses stunning glaciated alpine scenery and stupendous waterfalls.
The Rakiura Track (3 days; see p.635) Follows the rainforest-bordered coast of Stewart Island and provides opportunities to see kiwi in the wild.
The Routeburn Track (3 days; see p.715) One of the country's finest walks, with quality time spent above the bushline.

by DOC as **Great Walks** and are covered in detail in the Guide. Great Walks get the lion's share of DOC track spending, resulting in relatively smooth, broad walkways, with boardwalks over muddy sections and bridges over almost every stream – a sanitized side of New Zealand tramping.

Access to tracks is seldom a problem in the most popular tramping regions, though it does require planning. Most finish some distance from their start, so taking your own vehicle is not much use; besides, cars parked at trailheads are an open invitation to thieves. Great Walks always have transport from the nearest town, but there are often equally stunning and barely used tramps close by which require a little more patience and tenacity to get to – we've included some of the best of the rest in the Guide, listed under "Tramps" in the index.

Backcountry accommodation: huts and camping

New Zealand's backcountry is strung with a network of over 950 **trampers' huts**, sited less than a day's walk apart, frequently in beautiful surroundings. All are simple, communal affairs that fall into four distinct categories as defined by DOC.

Basic Huts (free) are often crude and rarely encountered on the major tramps. Next up is the **Standard Hut** ($5/person/night): basic,

weatherproof, usually equipped with individual bunks or sleeping platforms accommodating a dozen or so, an external long-drop toilet and a water supply. There is often a wood-burning stove but there are no cooking facilities. **Serviced Huts** ($15) tend to be larger, sleeping twenty or more on bunks with mattresses. Water is piped indoors to a sink, and flush toilets are occasionally encountered. Again, you'll need to bring your own stove and cooking gear, but heating is provided; if the fire is a wood-burning one, you should replace any firewood you use. More sophisticated still are the **Great Walk Huts** ($22–54 per adult per night), found along the Great Walks. They tend to have separate bunkrooms, gas rings for cooking (but no utensils), stoves for heating, a drying room and occasionally solar-powered lighting and flush toilets. Under-18s pay half the adult fee at Serviced and Standard huts and stay free on Great Walks – though you must still book in advance.

Hut fees are best paid in advance online, at the local DOC office, visitor centre or other outlet close to the start of the track. For Great Walks you need to book (and pay for) specific nights at each hut where you want to stay, then carry the confirmation with you, otherwise the wardens will charge you for each hut again. The booking guarantees you a bed and can be altered online subsequently if there is space left in the hut you want.

Should you wish to do a lot of tramping outside the Great Walks system, or on the Great Walks out of season, it's worth buying a **Backcountry Hut Pass** ($122 for 12 months; $92 for 6 months), which allows you to stay in all Standard and Serviced huts.

In winter (May–Sept) the huts on Great Walks are often stripped of heating and cooking facilities and downgraded to Standard status, so if you have a Backcountry Hut Pass you can use them, though possessing the pass or a ticket doesn't guarantee you a bunk; beds go on a first-come-first-served basis.

Camping is allowed on all tracks except the Milford. Rules vary, but in most cases you're required to minimize environmental impact by camping close to the huts, whose facilities (toilets, water and gas rings where available) you can use.

Equipment

Tramping in New Zealand can be a dangerous and/or dispiriting experience if you're not equipped for both hot, sunny days and wet, cold and windy weather. Conditions can change rapidly. The best tramps pass through some of the world's wettest regions, with parts of the Milford Track receiving over 6m of rain a year. It's essential to carry a good waterproof jacket. Keeping your lower half dry is less crucial and many Kiwis tramp in shorts. Early starts can involve wading through long, sodden grass, so a pair of knee-length gaiters can be useful. Comfortable boots with good ankle support are a must; take suitably broken-in leather boots or light-weight walking boots, and some comfortable footwear for the day's end. You'll also need a warm jacket or jumper, plus a good sleeping bag; even the heated huts are cold at night and a warm hat never goes amiss. All this, along with lighter clothing for sunny days, should be kept inside a robust backpack, preferably lined with a strong waterproof liner such as those sold at DOC offices.

Once on the tramp, you need to be totally self-sufficient. On Great Walks, you should carry **cooking** gear; on other tramps you also need a cooking stove and fuel. **Food** can be your heaviest burden; freeze-dried meals are light and reasonably tasty but expensive; many cost-conscious trampers prefer pasta or rice, dried soups for sauces, a handful of fresh vegetables, muesli, milk powder and bread or crackers for lunch. Consider taking biscuits, trail mix (known as "scroggin"), tea, coffee and powdered fruit drinks (the Raro brand is good), and energy-boosting spreads. All huts have drinking **water** but DOC advise treating water taken from lakes and rivers to protect yourself from giardia; see p.63 for more on this and water-purification methods.

You should also carry basic supplies: a first aid kit, blister kit, sunscreen, insect repellent; a torch (flashlight),

---

MULTI-DAY TOURS

Tours included in this box involve taking part in one or other several of the activities featured in this section. Although New Zealand is an easy place to explore independently, tours offer specialist insight, logistical help and company along the way.

HIKING AND WILDLIFE

Active Earth Adventures ⓦ activeearthadventures.com. Suitable for anyone who is reasonably fit and wants to see things few other tourists will. Good-humoured and informative guides take small groups tramping, climbing, cycling, Nordic skiing and wilderness camping in virtually untouched country from $1095 for four nights.

Hiking New Zealand ⓦ hikingnewzealand.com. Conservation-minded company offering everything from hiking trips around the far north of Northland (6 days; NZ$1280) to boat trips to NZ's subantarctic islands (8 days; US$4100, plus US$375 landing fees).

Kiwi Wildlife Walks ⓦ nzwalk.com. Expertly run guided walks including Stewart Island, where they go kiwi spotting (4 days; $2295).

Ruggedy Range ⓦ ruggedyrange.com. Stewart Island-based company offering enthusiastic and entertaining trips visiting the unique wildlife (overnight from $650).

CRUISES

Heritage Expeditions ☎ 0800 262 8873, ⓦ heritage-expeditions.com. Several pricey but spectacular cruises each southern summer to New Zealand's subantarctic islands – Antipodes, Auckland, Campbell etc – plus the Australian Macquarie Island and even the coast of Antarctica. Prices from US$6000 for 10 days.

Real Journeys ⓦ realjourneys.co.nz. As well as their Milford Sound and Doubtful Sound trips, Real Journeys run remoter multi-day trips to Dusky Sound (5 days from $2150).

candles, matches or a lighter; and a compass (though few bother on the better-marked tracks).

In the most popular tramping areas you will be able to **rent equipment**. Most important of all, remember that you'll have to carry all this stuff for hours each day. Hotels and hostels in nearby towns will generally let you leave your surplus gear either free or for a small fee.

Safety

Most people spend days or weeks tramping in New Zealand with nothing worse than stiff legs and a few sandfly bites, but **safety** is nonetheless a serious issue and deaths occur every year. The culprit is usually New Zealand's fickle **weather**. It cannot be stressed too strongly that within an hour (even in high summer) a warm, cloudless day can turn bitterly cold, with high winds driving in thick banks of track-obscuring cloud. Heeding the mountain weather forecast (posted in DOC offices) is crucial, as is carrying warm, windproof and waterproof clothing.

Failed **river crossings** are also a common cause of tramping fatalities. On Great Walks, rivers are always bridged, but elsewhere if you are confronted with something that looks too dangerous to cross, then it is, and you should wait until the level falls or backtrack. If the worst happens and you get swept away while crossing, don't try to stand up; you may trap your leg between rocks and drown. Instead, lie on your back and float feet first until you reach a place where swimming to the bank is feasible.

If you do get lost or injured, your chances of being found are better if you've left word of your intentions with a **friend** or with a **trusted person** at your next port of call, who will realize you are overdue. DOC make no attempt to track hikers so make your intentions clear to friends by using Ⓦadventuresmart.org.nz. While on the tramp, fill in the hut logs as you go, so that your movements can be traced, and check in with the folk you told about the trip on your return.

Animals are not a problem in the bush, the biggest irritants being sandflies whose bites itch (often insufferably), or kea, alpine parrots that delight in pinching anything they can get their beaks into and tearing it apart to fulfil their curiosity.

Swimming, surfing and windsurfing

Kiwi life is inextricably linked with the beach, and from Christmas to the end of March (longer in warmer northern climes), a weekend isn't complete without a dip or a waterside barbecue – though you should never underestimate the ferocity of the southern **sun** (see p.62 for precautions). Some of

---

CYCLING, HORSERIDING AND KAYAKING

Adventure South Ⓦadvsouth.co.nz. This environmentally conscious company runs guided cycling and multi-activity tours around the South Island, with accommodation in characterful lodges or track huts. Their 6-day West Coast trip ($2340) can be combined with their Marlborough trip to form a South Island grand tour. All tours carry a single supplement.

Alpine Horse Safaris Ⓦalpinehorse.co.nz. Multi-day rides in North Canterbury and the central South Island that follow old mining and farm tracks well away from civilization and most roads. They're intended for serious riders and start at $1090 for 3 days including food and simple accommodation.

Natural High Ⓦnaturalhigh.co.nz. A vast range of guided road and MTB trips from half a day to over two weeks, plus self-guided trips, bike rentals and even hire of cycle-friendly campervans.

New Zealand Sea Kayak Adventures Ⓦnzkayaktours.com. Fully catered, guided sea-kayak camping tours around Northland catering to a wide range of abilities. Go for the Bay of Islands (3 days; $750) or the Northeast Coast around the Cavalli Islands and Whangaroa Harbour (7 days; $1400).

Pacific Cycle Tours Ⓦbike-nz.com. Mountain-bike, road-bike and hiking tours round both islands with varying degrees of adventurousness, including a five-day cycling and wine-tasting trip (from $2065).

Pakiri Beach Horseriding Ⓦhorseride-nz.co.nz. Multi-day tours through Northland's native bush and along clifftops including an epic coast-to-coast trip (7 days; $3999).

Pedaltours Ⓦpedaltours.co.nz. Guided road- and mountain-biking tours of both islands, including a week-long ride around the southern South Island ($2785).

the most picturesque beaches stretch away into salt spray from the pounding Tasman surf or Pacific rollers. **Swimming** here can be very hazardous, so only venture into the water at beaches patrolled by surf lifesaving clubs and always swim between the flags; see box, p.63. Sharks are occasionally seen at swimming beaches, so if you notice everyone heading for safety, get out of the water.

New Zealand's coastline offers great conditions for **surfing**, windsurfing and kite-boarding. At major beach resorts there is often an outlet renting dinghies, catamarans, canoes and stand-up paddle-boards; in regions where there is reliably good surf you might also come across boogie boards and surfboards, and seaside hostels often have a couple for guests' use. For more information, see Ⓦsurf .co.nz and Ⓦsurf2surf.co.nz.

Sailing

New Zealand's numerous harbours, studded with small islands and ringed with deserted bays, make **sailing** a favourite pursuit, which explains why New Zealand and Kiwi sailors have been so influential in the fate of the America's Cup. People sail year-round, but the summer months from December to March are busiest. Unless you befriend a yachtie you'll probably be limited to commercial yacht **charters** (expensive and with a skipper), more reasonably priced and often excellent **day-sailing trips**, or renting a dinghy for some inshore antics.

Scuba diving and snorkelling

The waters around New Zealand offer wonderful opportunities to **scuba dive** and **snorkel**. What they lack in long-distance visibility, tropical warmth and colourful fish they make up for with the range of diving environments. Pretty much anywhere along the more sheltered eastern side of both islands you'll find somewhere with rewarding snorkelling, but much the best and most accessible spot is the **Goat Island Marine Reserve**, in Northland, where there's a superb range of habitats close to the shore. Northland also has world-class scuba diving at the **Poor Knights Islands Marine Reserve**, reached by boat from Tutukaka, and wreck diving on the *Rainbow Warrior*, from Matauri Bay, plus a stack of good sites around Great Barrier Island and White Island. On the South Island, there are wrecks worth exploring off **Picton** and fabulous growths of **black and red corals** relatively close to the surface, in the southwestern fiords near Milford.

For the inexperienced, the easiest way to get a taste of what's under the surface is to take a **resort dive** with an instructor. If you want to dive independently, you need to be PADI-qualified. For more information consult Ⓦdivenewzealand.com.

Rafting

The combination of challenging rapids and gorgeous scenery makes **whitewater rafting** one of New Zealand's most thrilling adventure activities. Visitor numbers and weather restrict the main **rafting season** to October to May, and most companies set an **age limit** at 13. Take a swimming costume and an old pair of trainers, and after safety instruction you'll generally spend a couple of hours on the water.

Thrilling though it is, rafting is also one of the most **dangerous** of the adventure activities, claiming a number of lives over the years. Operators have a self-imposed code of practice, but there are still cowboys out there. It might be stating the obvious but fatalities happen when people fall out of rafts: heed the guide's instructions about how best to stay on board and how to protect yourself if you do get a dunking.

Canoeing and kayaking

New Zealand is a paddler's paradise, and pretty much anywhere with water nearby has somewhere you can rent either canoes or kayaks. Sometimes this is simply an opportunity to muck around in boats but often there are guided trips available, with the emphasis being on soaking up the scenery. The scenic **Whanganui River** is a perennial favourite.

Jetboating

The shallow, braided rivers of the high Canterbury sheep country posed access difficulties for run-owner Bill Hamilton, who got around the problem by inventing the **Hamilton Jetboat** in the early 1960s. His inspired invention could plane in as little as 100mm of water, reach prodigious speeds (up to 80km/hr) and negotiate rapids while maintaining astonishing, turn-on-a-sixpence manoeuvrability.

The jetboat carried its first fare-paying passengers on a deep and glassy section of the Shotover River, which is still used by the pioneering Shotover Jet. **Rides** last around thirty eye-streaming minutes, time enough for hot-dogging and as many 360-degree spins as anyone needs. **Wilderness trips** can last two hours or longer.

Bungy jumping and bridge swinging

For maximum adrenalin, minimum risk and greatest expense, bungy jumping is difficult to beat. Commercial bungy jumping was pioneered by Kiwi speed skiers A.J. Hackett and Henry Van Asch. They began pushing the bungy boundaries, culminating in Hackett's jump from the Eiffel Tower in 1987. He was promptly arrested, but the publicity sparked worldwide interest that continues to draw bungy aspirants to New Zealand's sites – some of the world's best, with bridges over deep canyons and platforms cantilevered out over rivers. The first commercial operation was set up just outside Queenstown on the 43m Kawerau Suspension Bridge. Its accessible location and the chance to be dunked in the river make this the most popular jump of many on both islands. For a bit of variety you could try a close relative of the bungy, **swinging**, which provides a similar gut-wrenching fall accompanied by a super-fast swing along a gorge while harnessed to a cable.

Ziplines

New Zealand was slow off the mark installing **zipwires** or flying foxes through the trees, but is quickly catching up with sites – Waiheke Island, Taihape, Rotorua, Nelson and Queenstown. Some are just single lines across ravines, but most modern installations feature a sequence of lines with changeovers on platforms high in the trees.

Canyoning

The easiest way to get your hands on New Zealand rock is to go **canyoning**, which involves following steep and confined river gorges or streambeds down chutes and over waterfalls for a few hours, sliding, jumping and abseiling all the way. Guided trips are available in a handful of places, the most accessible being in Auckland, Thames, Queenstown and Wanaka.

Mountaineering

New Zealand is better suited to **mountaineering** than rock climbing, though most of what is available is fairly serious stuff, suitable only for well-equipped parties with a good deal of experience. For most people the only way to get above the snowline is to tackle the easy summit of Mount Ruapehu, the North Island's highest point, the summit of Mount Taranaki, near New Plymouth, or pay for a guided ascent of one of the country's classic peaks. Prime candidates are New Zealand's highest mountain, Aoraki/Mount Cook (3754m), accessed from the climbers' heartland of Aoraki/Mount Cook Village, and the nation's most beautiful peak, the pyramidal Mount Aspiring (3030m), approached from Wanaka. In both cases networks of climbers' huts are used as bases for what are typically twenty-hour attempts on the summit.

Flying, skydiving and paragliding

Almost every town in New Zealand seems to harbour an airstrip or a helipad, and there's inevitably someone happy to get you airborne for half an hour's **flightseeing**. Helicopters cost around fifty percent more than planes and can't cover the same distances but score on manoeuvrability and the chance to land. If money is tight take a regular flight somewhere you want to go anyway. First choice here would have to be the journey from either Wanaka or Queenstown to Milford Sound, which overflies the very best of Fiordland.

In **tandem skydiving**, a double harness links you to an instructor, who has control of the parachute. The plane circles up to 12,000ft (around 2500m) and after you leap out together, you experience around 45 seconds of eerie freefall before the instructor pulls the ripcord. Higher jumps are also available.

Tandem paragliding involves you and an instructor jointly launching off a hilltop, slung below a manoeuvrable parachute, for perhaps ten to twenty minutes of graceful gliding and stomach-churning banked turns. **Tandem hang-gliding** and **parasailing** are also offered in a few places.

Skiing and snowboarding

New Zealand's **ski season** (roughly June–Oct) starts as snows on northern hemisphere slopes melt away, which, combined with the South Island's backbone of 3000m peaks makes New Zealand an increasingly popular international ski destination. Most fields are geared to the domestic downhill market, and the eastern side of the Southern Alps is littered with **club fields** sporting a handful of rope tows, simple lifts and a motley collection of private ski lodges. They're open to all-comers, but some are only accessible by 4WD vehicles, others have a long walk in, and ski schools are almost unheard of. A dozen exceptions are scattered throughout the country – **commercial resorts**, with high-speed chairs, ski schools, gear rental and groomed wide-open slopes. What you won't find are massive on-site resorts of the scale found in North America and Europe; skiers commute daily to the slopes from nearby après-ski towns and **gear rental** is either from shops in these or on the field.

The main **North Island ski-fields** are Turoa and Whakapapa, both on the volcanic Mount Ruapehu. The best combination of uncrowded runs, a party atmosphere and some of the most spectacular snow-dusted scenery you'll ever see is on the **South Island. The main commercial fields are:** Porters and Mount Hutt, both within two hours' drive of Christchurch; Coronet Peak and The Remarkables near Queenstown; and Treble Cone, Cardrona and the Snow Farm, all accessed from Wanaka.

For up-to-date skiing information, consult Ⓦ snow.co.nz which lists snow, lift and terrain details of all the major fields and most of the smaller ones, plus has links to local accommodation and gear rental places.

Fishing

All around the coast there are low-key canoe, yacht and launch trips on which there is always time for a little **casual fishing**, but you'll also find plenty of trips aimed at more dedicated anglers. From December to May these scout the seas off the northern half of the North Island for marlin, shark, tuna and lots of smaller quarry. Regulations and bag limits are covered on the Ministry for Primary Industries website, Ⓦ fish.govt.nz.

Inland, the **rivers** and **lakes** are choked with rainbow and brown trout, quinnat and Atlantic salmon, all introduced for sport at the end of the nineteenth century. Certain areas have gained enviable reputations: Lake Taupo is world-renowned for its rainbow trout; South Island rivers, particularly around Gore, boast the finest brown trout; and the braided gravel-bed rivers draining the eastern slopes of the Southern Alps bear superb salmon.

A national **fishing licence** ($123 for the year from Oct 1–Sept 30, $25/24hr) covers all New Zealand's lakes and rivers except for those in the Taupo catchment area, where a local licensing arrangement applies. They're available from sports shops everywhere and directly from Fish and Game New Zealand (Ⓦ fishandgame.org.nz), the agency responsible for managing freshwater sports fisheries. The website also lists bag limits and local regulations.

Wherever you fish, **regulations** are taken seriously and are rigidly enforced. If you're found with an undersize catch or an over-full bag, heavy fines may be imposed and equipment confiscated. The NZ Fishing Rules app is a handy reference. Other fishy websites include Ⓦ fishingin newzealand.com and Ⓦ fishing.net.nz.

Horse trekking

New Zealand's highly urbanized population leaves a huge amount of countryside available for **horse trekking**, occasionally along beaches, often through patches of native bush and tracts of farmland. There are schools everywhere and all levels of experience are catered for, but more experienced riders might prefer the greater scope of full-day or even week-long wilderness treks (see box, p.51). We've highlighted some noteworthy places and operators throughout the guide, and there's a smattering of others listed at Ⓦ truenz .co.nz/horsetrekking.

Mountain biking

With the explosion of the New Zealand Cycle Trail network of bike routes (Ⓦ nzcycletrail.com), getting around the country by bike has never been easier or more pleasurable (see p.35). But several of the routes are more appropriate for mountain-bikers, supplementing an already generous selection of off-road rides. The two big centres are **Rotorua**, principally for the tortuous pleasures of Whakarewarewa Forest (aka "The Redwoods"; see p.279), and **Queenstown**, where there's everything from relatively easy cross-country trails to extreme downhill and heli-biking. In between there are a couple of excellent rides at the top of the South Island. You can ride the whole 71km of the Queen Charlotte Track for most of the year, though the northernmost 26km is off limits in Dec, Jan and Feb. Riding the Heaphy Track is even more time constrained, but if you're considering being in New Zealand between May and September, inclusive, this is one you shouldn't miss.

Spectator sports

If God were a rugby coach almost every New Zealander would be a religious fundamentalist. News coverage often gives headline prominence to sport, particularly the All Blacks, and entire

radio stations are devoted to sports talkback, usually dwelling on occasions when Kiwi underdogs overcome better-funded teams from more populous nations.

Most major sports events are televised. Increasingly these are on subscription-only Sky TV, which encourages a devoted following in pubs.

Anyone with a keen interest in sport or just Kiwi culture should attend a rugby game. Local papers advertise games along with ticket booking details. **Bookings** for many of the bigger events can be made through Ticketek (Ⓦ ticketek.co.nz), although, except for the oversubscribed internationals and season finals, you can usually just buy a ticket at the gate.

Rugby

Opponents quake in their boots at the sight of fifteen strapping **All Blacks**, the national **rugby** team, performing their pre-match *haka*, and few spectators remain unmoved. Kiwi hearts swell at the sight, secure in the knowledge that their national team is always among the world's best, and anything less than a resounding victory is considered a case for national mourning in the leader columns of the newspapers – although, thanks to the All Blacks' dominance, this is relatively rare. The team won the **2011 Rugby World Cup** by defeating France at home in Auckland.

Rugby is played through the winter, the season kicking off with the **Super 15 series** (mid-Feb to May) in which regional southern hemisphere teams (five apiece from New Zealand, South Africa and Australia) play each other with the top four teams going on to contest the finals series. Super 15 players make up the All Blacks team which, through the middle of winter, hosts an international test series or two, including the annual **Rugby Championship** (mid-July to Aug) against South Africa, Australia and Argentina. Games between the All Blacks and Australia also contest the **Bledisloe Cup**, which creates much desired bragging rights for one or other nation for a year.

The international season often runs over into the **ITM Cup**, a national provincial competition, played from the middle of August until the end of October. Throughout the ITM Cup season, teams also do battle for the right to hold the **Ranfurly Shield**, affectionately known as the "log of wood". The holders accept challenges at their home ground, and the winner takes all. Occasionally minor teams will wrest the shield, and in the smaller provinces this is a huge source of pride, subsequent defences of the shield prompting a surge of community spirit.

Domestic rugby ticket prices vary, depending on where you are in the ground, but start at around $15, while a similar seat for an international will start at $45. To find out more, visit the New Zealand Rugby Union's official **website** (Ⓦ nzrugby.co.nz).

Rugby league (Ⓦ rugbyleague.co.nz and Ⓦ nzrl .co.nz) has always been regarded as rugby union's poor cousin, though success at international level has raised its profile. New Zealand's only significant provincial team are the Auckland-based **Warriors**, who play in Australia's NRL during the March to early September season, with home games played at Mount Smart Stadium, where you can buy tickets at the gate. The top eight teams in the league go through to the finals series in September.

Cricket

Most visitors spend their time in New Zealand from October to March, when the stadiums are turned over to the country's traditional summer sport, **cricket** (Ⓦ nzcricket.co.nz). The national team – the **Black Caps** – hover mid-table in international test and one-day rankings but periodic flashes of brilliance, the odd unexpected victory over Australia, and the co-hosting of the 2015 **Cricket World Cup** keep fans interested. You can usually just turn up at a ground and buy a ticket, though games held around Christmas and New Year fill up fast and internationals sell out in advance. **Tickets** start at around $25–30 for an international, less for a domestic match.

Other sports

Other team sports lag far behind rugby and cricket, though women's **netball** (Ⓦ netballnz.co.nz) has an enthusiastic following and live TV coverage of the Silver Ferns' international fixtures gets good audiences.

Although more youngsters play **soccer** than rugby, it was the New Zealand All Whites' participation in the 2010 World Cup that boosted the game's profile nationally. For domestic fixtures, see Ⓦ nzfootball.co.nz. New Zealand's only representative in the Australian A-League is the Wellington Phoenix (Ⓦ wellingtonphoenix.com). The season runs from October to early April and home games are played at Westpac Stadium in Wellington; **tickets** (from around $40 for a domestic match) can be bought at the gate or on the team's website.

Auckland is a frequent midway point for round-the-world **yacht** races and has twice hosted the

America's Cup. New Zealand's **Olympic** heritage is patchy, with occasional clutches of medals from rowing and yachting and a long pedigree of **middle-distance runners**. These days, however, multi-event championships and endurance events like triathlons and Iron Man races seem to dominate.

Culture and etiquette

Ever since Maori arrived in the land they named Aotearoa, New Zealand has been a nation of immigrants. The majority of residents trace their roots back to Britain and Ireland, and northern European culture prevails with a strong Maori and Polynesian influence. New Zealand's policy of bi-culturalism gives Maori and Pakeha (white European) values equal status, at least nominally. In practice, the operation of Parliament and the legal system is rooted in the old country, the Queen continues as head of state and beams out from all coins and the $20 note, and, along with "God Defend New Zealand", "God Save the Queen" remains one of the country's two official national anthems.

That said, **Maori** are very much part of mainstream contemporary NZ society (see p.801). The racial tension that does exist mostly stays below the surface (aside from some issue-specific protests), and as a visitor you'll probably come away from New Zealand with the impression of a relatively tolerant society.

In the last couple of decades **Asian immigration** (principally from China and Korea, as well as the Indian subcontinent) has seen Asians make up around 12 percent of the population (with Maori comprising just under 15 percent) nationwide. In the Auckland region, though, this figure rises to over eighteen percent, making some form of tri-culturalism a possibility in the future.

Notwithstanding this mix, the archetypal **Kiwi personality** is rooted in the desire to make a better life in a unique and sometimes unaccom-modating land. New Zealanders are inordinately fond of stories of plucky little Kiwis overcoming great odds and succeeding, perceiving the NZ persona to be rooted in self-reliance, inventiveness and bravery, tempered by a certain self-deprecating humour. Overachieving "tall poppies" are routinely cut down.

Sport is a huge passion; the country has consistently punched above its weight in international competition, especially on the rugby field. Despite a reputation for a rugby-playing, beer-swilling, male-dominated culture, Kiwis like to point out that they run an open-minded and egalitarian society, in everything from same-sex marriage to nuclear-free waters (see p.798), and broadly liberal social attitudes prevail, with Japanese whaling and genetic modification hot topics.

New Zealand's relationship with its larger neighbour, Australia, is a cause for endless enter-tainment on both sides of "the ditch" (the Tasman Sea). Kiwis and **Aussies** are like siblings: there are lots of scraps (mostly just good-natured ribbing), especially when it comes to sport, but they're the first to jump to each other's defence in everything from military conflict to pub brawls.

Etiquette

New Zealanders are refreshingly relaxed, low-key and free of pretension, and you're likely to be greeted with an informal "gidday!", "Kia ora!" (Hi) or "Kia ora, bro!" (Hi, mate). **Dress standards** are as informal as the greetings, and unless you're on business or have a diplomatic function to attend you can leave your suit and tie at home; even the finest restaurants only require smart-casual attire.

The legal **drinking age** is 18, but by law you may be asked to prove your age by showing ID, which must be either a New Zealand driver's licence or a passport (foreign driver's licences aren't accepted).

Smoking is increasingly outlawed. It's banned on all public transport and in public buildings and some outdoor areas – see ⓦsmokefree.org.nz.

The Kiwi attitude to **tipping** is pleasingly uncom-plicated. No tip is expected, though reward for excellent service in restaurants and cafés is appreciated.

Shopping

One of the most popular souvenirs from NZ is a curvaceous greenstone (jade) pendant, probably based on a Maori design. They're available all over the country, though it makes sense to buy close to the main source of raw material around Greymouth and Hokitika on the West Coast of the South Island. Cheaper

items are manufactured from Chinese jade or inferior stones such as soapstone: for the genuine article, insist on NZ pounamu carved locally (see box, p.668).

A variation on this theme is the **bone pendant**. Several places around the country give you a chance to work a piece of cattle bone into your own design or something based on classic Maori iconography. With a little talent and application you should be able to whip up something to be proud of in a few hours. Something similar can be made of iridescent paua shell, or you can simply buy ready-made pieces fashioned into anything from buttons to detailed picture frames.

Sheepskin and **wool** products are also big, as are garments – socks, sweaters etc – at least partly made from **possum fur**. New Zealanders hate these pests and will thank you for supporting any industry which hastens their demise. A quality possum-fur throw will set you back over $1000 but cushion covers come much cheaper. Sheepskins go for around $100.

There's plenty of outdoor clothing around, but look out for the Icebreaker (Ⓦnz.icebreaker.com), Untouched World (Ⓦuntouchedworld.co.nz) and Glowing Sky (Ⓦglowingsky.co.nz) brands of stylish merino-wool garments, which are fairly pricey but feel great, keep you warm and don't harbour nasty odours.

Some of New Zealand's top fashion designers are world-class. Garments by Karen Walker, Kate Sylvester, Trelise Cooper, Alexandra Owen, Zambesi and World are expensive but coveted and unique.

Travelling with children

New Zealand is a child-friendly place, and while other people's kids aren't revered in the way they are in Mediterranean Europe, if you're travelling with children you'll find broad acceptance.

Accommodation is well geared for families: family rooms are almost always available at motels and hostels, and holiday parks (campsites) typically offer self-contained units where the whole family can be together. The better holiday parks also have kids' play areas and often a swimming pool. To be more self-sufficient, consider renting a medium-sized **campervan** with its own shower and toilet, though the downside is that you'll have no escape.

Travelling around you'll find **public toilets** in most towns and anywhere tourists congregate – cleanliness standards are usually good.

Older kids can often join in adult **adventure activities**, though restrictions may apply. Bungy operators usually require a **minimum age** of 10, though this might rise to 12 or 13 for the bigger jumps. Whitewater rafting is typically limited to those 13 and over, though there are a few easier family-oriented trips. Similar restrictions apply to other activities – ask when you book. **Family tickets** are often available and usually cost about the same as two adults and one child.

Children are welcomed in most cafés and **restaurants**, and most will make a reasonable effort to accommodate you.

Living in New Zealand

New Zealand is the sort of place people come for a short visit and end up wanting to stay (at least for a few months). Unless you have substantial financial backing, this will probably mean finding some work. And while your earning potential in New Zealand isn't necessarily going to be great, you can at least supplement your budget for multiple bungy jumps, skydiving lessons and the like. Paid casual work is typically in tourism-linked service industries, or in orchard work.

For the last few years unemployment has remained relatively low and, providing you have the necessary paperwork, finding casual work shouldn't be too difficult, while better-paid, short-term **professional jobs** are quite possible if you have the skills. Employment agencies are a good bet for this sort of work, or simply look at general job-search websites such as Ⓦseek.co.nz or the jobs section of Ⓦtrademe.co.nz. The **minimum wage** for all legally employed folk over the age of 16 (other than 16- and 17-year-old new entrants or trainees) is $14.25 an hour. If you'd rather not tackle the red tape you can simply reduce your travelling costs by **working for your board** (though technically the Immigration Department still considers this to be work).

Working for board and lodging

A popular way of getting around the country cheaply is to **work for your board and lodging**, typically toiling for 4–6 hours a day. **FHiNZ** (Farm Helpers in New Zealand; ☻fhinz.co.nz) organizes stays on farms, orchards and horticultural holdings for singles, couples and families; no experience is needed. Almost 350 places are listed in its booklet ($25; sold online) and accommodation ranges from basic to quite luxurious. The international **WWOOF** (originally Willing Workers on Organic Farms; ☻wwoof.co.nz) coordinates over a thousand properties (membership, for one or a couple, with online access $40 or printed booklet $52), mostly farms but also orchards, market gardens and self-sufficiency-orientated smallholdings, all using organic methods to a greater or lesser degree. Many backpacker hostels also take WWOOFers. They'll expect a minimum stay of around five nights, though much longer periods are common; you **book direct** (preferably a week or more in advance). There have been occasional reports of taskmasters; make sure you discuss what's expected before you commit yourself. Property managers are vetted but **solo women** may prefer placements with couples or families. Other organizations have fewer guarantees, though many are perfectly reputable.

A similar organization is the online **Help Exchange** (☻helpx.net), which supplies a regularly updated list of hosts on farms as well as at homestays, B&Bs, hostels and lodges, who need extra help in return for meals and accommodation; you register online and book direct.

Visas, permits and red tape

Australians can work legally in New Zealand without any paperwork. Otherwise, if you're aged 18–30 (up to 35 for Canadians), the easiest way to work legally is through the **Working Holiday Scheme** (WHS), which gives you a temporary work permit valid for twelve months. An unlimited number of Brits, Irish, Americans, Canadians, Japanese, Belgian, Danish, Finnish, French, German, Italian, Dutch, Norwegian and Swedish people in this age bracket are eligible each year, plus various annual quotas for two dozen other nationalities on a first-come-first-served basis; apply as far in advance as you can. You'll need a passport, NZ$165 for the application, evidence of an onward ticket out of New Zealand (or the funds to pay for it), and a minimum of NZ$350 per month of your intended stay (or, depending on your country of origin, NZ$4200 in total) to show you can support yourself – work is not meant to be the main reason for your visit. Brits can apply for a 23-month stay, the last 11 months of which can be applied for in New Zealand

as an extension. Working holiday-makers who can show they've worked in the horticulture or viticulture industries for at least three months may be eligible to obtain an extra three-month stay in New Zealand with a **Working Holidaymaker Extension** (WHE) permit. Applications are made through **Immigration New Zealand** (☎0508 558 855, ☻immigration.govt.nz), which has details and downloadable forms on its website.

Some visitors are tempted to **work illegally**, something for which you could be fined or deported. However, there is a variety of other visa options, including the Silver Fern visa for 20–35-year-olds, and visas for seasonal horticulture and viticulture work – contact the **Immigration Service** for details. The only other legal option is trying to gain resident status – not something to be tackled lightly.

Anyone working legally in New Zealand needs to obtain a **tax number** from the local Inland Revenue Department office (☻ird.govt.nz); without this your employer will have trouble paying you. The process can take up to ten working days, though you can still work while the wheels of bureaucracy turn. Inland Revenue will take 10.5 percent of your first $14,000 of earnings, 17.5 percent of the next $34,000, and higher rates above that. Many companies will also only pay wages into a New Zealand **bank account** – opening one is easy (see p.65).

Casual work

One of the main sources of casual work is **fruit-picking** or related **orchard work** such as packing or pruning and thinning. The main areas are Kerikeri in the Bay of Islands for citrus and kiwifruit, Hastings in Hawke's Bay for apples, pears and peaches, Tauranga and Te Puke for kiwifruit, Blenheim for grapes and Alexandra and Cromwell in Central Otago for stone fruit. Most work is available during the autumn **picking season**, which runs roughly from January to May, but you can often find something just as easily in the off season. In popular working areas, some hostels cater to short-term workers, and these are usually the best places to find out what's going.

Picking can be hard, physical work and **payment** is usually by the quantity gathered, rather than by the hour. When you're starting off, the poor returns can be frustrating, but with persistence and application you can soon find yourself grossing $130 or more in an eight-hour day. Rates vary considerably so it's worth asking around, factoring in any transport, meals and accommodation, which are sometimes included. Indoor packing work tends to be paid hourly.

Particularly in popular tourist areas – Rotorua, Nelson, Queenstown – **cafés**, **bars** and **hostels** often need extra staff during peak periods. If you have no luck, try more out-of-the-way locales, where there'll be fewer travellers clamouring for work. Unless you have good experience, bar and restaurant work only pays minimum wage and tips are negligible. Generally you'll need to commit to at least three months. **Ski resorts** occasionally employ people during the June to October season, usually in catering roles. Hourly wages may be supplemented by a lift pass and subsidized food and drink, though finding affordable accommodation can be difficult and may offset a lot of what you gain. Hiring clinics for ski and snowboard instructors are usually held at the beginning of the season at a small cost, though if you're experienced it's better to apply directly to the resort beforehand.

In addition to local hostels and backpackers, handy **resources** include ⓦbackpackerboard.co.nz and ⓦjob.co.nz; for fruit picking and the like, check out ⓦseasonalwork.co.nz and ⓦpicknz.co.nz.

Volunteering

A useful starting point is the online service from the UK-based **The Gapyear Company** (ⓦgapyear.com), which offers free membership plus heaps of information on volunteering, travel, contacts and living abroad. The Department of Conservation's **Conservation Volunteer Programme** (search at ⓦdoc.govt.nz) provides an excellent way to spend time out in the New Zealand bush while putting something back into the environment. Often you'll get into areas most visitors never see, and learn some skills while you're at it. Projects include bat surveys, kiwi monitoring and nest protection, as well as more rugged tasks like track maintenance, tree planting and hut repair. You can muck in for just a day or up to a couple of weeks, and sometimes there is a fee (of around $50–200) to cover food and transport. Application forms are often available on the website. Programmes are in high demand and often book up well in advance, so it's worth applying before you reach New Zealand.

Travel essentials

Climate

The sunny summer months (October to April) are the most popular time for travellers visiting New Zealand, but winter offers great skiing and snowboarding and the days are often clear and bright, if chilly. The far north of the country is often

AVERAGE MONTHLY TEMPERATURES AND RAINFALL

	Jan	Feb	Mar	Apr	May	Jun	July	Aug	Sep	Oct	Nov	Dec
AUCKLAND												
max/min (°C)	23/16	23/16	22/15	19/13	17/11	14/9	13/8	14/8	16/9	17/11	19/12	21/14
max/min (°F)	73/61	73/61	72/59	66/55	63/52	57/48	55/46	57/46	61/48	63/52	66/54	70/57
rainfall (mm)	79	94	81	97	112	137	145	117	102	102	89	79
WELLINGTON												
max/min (°C)	21/13	21/13	19/12	17/11	14/8	13/7	12/6	12/6	14/8	16/9	17/10	19/12
max/min (°F)	70/55	70/55	66/54	63/52	57/46	55/45	54/43	54/43	57/46	61/48	63/50	66/54
rainfall (mm)	81	81	81	97	117	117	137	117	97	102	89	89
CHRISTCHURCH												
max/min (°C)	21/12	21/12	19/10	17/7	13/4	11/2	10/2	11/2	14/4	17/7	19/8	21/11
max/min (°F)	70/54	70/54	66/50	63/45	55/39	52/36	50/36	52/36	57/39	63/45	66/46	70/52
rainfall (mm)	56	43	48	48	66	66	69	48	46	43	48	56
HOKITIKA												
max/min (°C)	19/12	19/12	18/11	16/8	14/6	12/3	12/3	12/3	13/6	15/8	16/9	18/11
max/min (°F)	66/54	66/54	64/52	61/46	57/43	54/37	54/37	54/37	55/43	59/46	61/48	64/52
rainfall (mm)	262	191	239	236	244	231	218	239	226	292	267	262
QUEENSTOWN												
max/min (°C)	21/10	21/10	20/9	15/7	11/3	9/1	9/0	11/1	14/3	18/5	19/7	20/10
max/min (°F)	70/50	70/50	68/48	59/45	52/37	48/34	48/32	52/34	57/37	64/41	66/45	68/50
rainfall (mm)	79	72	74	72	64	58	59	63	66	77	64	62

dubbed the "winterless north", although even in this subtropical area, winters can be nippy. The far south is the coldest part of the country – if you're surfing you'll need a wetsuit year-round.

Costs

The strong Kiwi dollar and lingering effects of the global financial crisis means that New Zealand is no bargain, but with high standards of quality and service the country is still decent value for money.

Daily costs vary enormously, and the following estimates (in NZ dollars) are per person for two people travelling together. (With the prevalence of good hostels, **single travellers** can live almost as cheaply as couples, though you'll pay around thirty percent more if you want a room to yourself.)

If you're on a tight budget, using public transport, camping or staying in hostels, and cooking most of your own meals, you could scrape by on $60 a day. Renting a car, staying in budget motels, and eating out a fair bit, you're looking at more like $160 a day. Step up to comfortable B&Bs and nicer restaurants, throw in a few trips, and you can easily find yourself spending over $350 a day. Also, you can completely blow your budget on **adventure trips** such as a bungy jump or tandem parachuting, so it pays to think carefully about how to get the maximum bang for your buck.

The price quoted is what you pay. With the exception of some business hotels, the 15-percent Goods and Service Tax (**GST**) is always included in the listed price. GST refunds are available on more expensive items bought then taken out of the country – keep your receipts and carry the items as hand luggage.

Student **discounts** are few and far between, but you can make substantial savings on accommodation and travel by buying one of the backpacker or YHA cards (see p.38). **Kids** (see p.57) enjoy reductions of around fifty percent on most trains, buses and entry to many sights.

Crime and personal safety

New Zealand's rates of violent crime are in line with those in other developed countries and you'll

EMERGENCY PHONE CALLS

☎ **111** is the free emergency telephone number to summon the police, ambulance or fire service.

almost certainly come across some grisly stories in the media. Still, as long as you use your common sense, you're unlikely to run into any trouble. Some caution is needed in the **seedier quarters** of the larger cities where it's unwise to walk alone late at night. One major safety issue is "**boy racers**" using city and town streets as racetracks for customized cars, leading to bystander fatalities. Although the police do take action, their presence is relatively thin on the ground so be careful when out late in city suburbs.

Always take precautions against **petty theft**, particularly from cars and campervans. When staying in cities you should move valuables into your lodging. Thieves also prey on visitors' vehicles left at trailheads and car parks. Campervans containing all your possessions make obvious and easy pickings. Take your valuables with you, put packs and bags out of sight and get good insurance. When setting out on long walks use a secure car park if possible, where your vehicle will be kept safe for a small sum.

Police and the law

If you get **arrested**, you are entitled to talk to a lawyer. One will be appointed if you can't afford one and you may be able to claim legal aid. It's unlikely that your consulate will take more than a passing interest unless there is something strange or unusual about the case against you.

The laws regarding **alcohol consumption** have traditionally been pretty lenient, though persistent rowdy behaviour has encouraged some towns to ban drinking in public spaces. Still, most of the time nobody's going to bother you if you fancy a beer on the beach or glass of wine at some wayside picnic area. The same does not apply to drink driving (see p.32), which is taken very seriously.

Marijuana has a reputation for being very potent and relatively easily available. It is, however, illegal, and although a certain amount of tolerance is sometimes shown towards personal use, the police and courts take a dim view of larger quantities and hard drugs, handing out long custodial sentences.

Prejudice

New Zealanders like to think of themselves as a tolerant and open-minded people, and foreign visitors are generally welcomed with open arms. Racism is far from unknown, but you're unlikely to experience overt **discrimination** or be refused service because of your race, colour or gender. In out-of-the-way rural pubs, women, foreigners – and just about anyone who doesn't live within a 10km radius – may get a frosty reception, though this soon breaks down once you get talking.

Despite constant efforts to maintain good relations between Maori and Pakeha, tensions do exist. Ever since colonization, **Maori** have achieved lower educational standards, earned less and maintained disproportionately high rates of unemployment and imprisonment. Slowly Maori are getting some restitution for the wrongs perpetrated on their race, which of course plays into the hands of those who feel that such positive discrimination is unfair.

Recent high levels of immigration from east Asia – Hong Kong, China and Taiwan in particular – have rapidly changed the demographics in Auckland, where most have settled. Central Auckland also has several English-language schools that are mostly full of Asian students. The combined effect means that in parts of Auckland, especially downtown, longer-established New Zealanders are in the minority. It is a sensation that some Maori and Pakeha find faintly disturbing. There's little overt racism, but neither is there much mixing.

Electricity

New Zealand operates a 230/240-volt, 50Hz **AC power supply**, and sockets take a three-prong, flat-pin type of plug. Suitable socket adaptors are widely available in New Zealand and at most international airports; and for phone chargers and laptops that's all you'll need. In most other cases, North American appliances require both a transformer and an adaptor, British and Irish equipment needs only an adaptor and Australian appliances need no alteration.

Entry requirements

All visitors to New Zealand need a passport, which must be valid for at least three months beyond the time you intend to stay. When flying to New Zealand you'll probably need to show you have an **onward or return booking** before they'll let you board the plane.

On arrival, British citizens are automatically issued with a permit to stay for up to six months, and a three-month permit is granted to citizens of most other European countries, Southeast Asian nations, Japan, South Africa, the US and Canada, and several other countries. Australian citizens can stay indefinitely.

Other nationalities need to obtain a visitor visa in advance from a New Zealand embassy, costing the local equivalent of NZ$160 and usually valid for three months. Visas are issued by Immigration New Zealand (Ⓦ immigration.govt.nz). See p.58 for advice on working visas.

Websites and contact details for all NZ embassies and consulates **abroad** can be found at Ⓦ nzembassy.com.

Quarantine and customs

In a country all too familiar with the damage that can be caused by introduced plants and animals, **biosecurity** is taken seriously (Ⓦ biosecurity.govt .nz). On arrival you'll be asked to **declare any food**, plants or parts of plants, animals (dead or alive), equipment used with animals, wooden products (including musical instruments), camping gear, golf clubs, bicycles, biological specimens and hiking boots. Outdoor equipment and walking boots will be inspected and perhaps cleaned then returned shortly thereafter. After a long flight it can seem a bit of a pain, but such precautions are important and there are huge fines for non-compliance. Be sure to dispose of any fresh fruit, vegetables and meat in the bins provided or you're liable for an instant $400 fine (even for that orange you forgot about in the bottom of your bag). Processed foods are usually allowed through, but must be declared.

Visitors aged 18 and over are entitled to a **duty-free allowance** (Ⓦ customs.govt.nz) of 200 cigarettes (or 250 grams of tobacco, or 50 cigars), 4.5 litres of wine or beer, three 1125ml bottles of spirits, and up to $700 worth of goods. There are **export restrictions** on wildlife, plants, antiquities and works of art.

Gay and lesbian travellers

Homosexuality was decriminalized in New Zealand in 1986 and the **age of consent** was set at 16 (the same as for heterosexuals). It is illegal to discriminate against gays and people with HIV or AIDS, and New Zealand makes no limitation on people with HIV or AIDS entering the country. Civil unions were legalized in 2005 and full marriage made it into the statute books in 2013.

Though there remains an undercurrent of redneck intolerance, particularly in rural areas, it generally stays well below the surface, and New Zealand is a broadly gay-friendly place. The mainstream acceptance is such that the New Zealand Symphony Orchestra and Auckland Philharmonia composer, Gareth Farr, also performs as drag queen Lilith LaCroix. This tolerant attitude has conspired to de-ghettoize the gay community;

even in **Auckland** and **Wellington**, the only cities with genuinely vibrant gay scenes, there aren't any predominantly gay areas and most venues have a mixed clientele. Auckland's scene is generally the largest and most lively, but the intimate nature of Wellington makes it more accessible and welcoming. Christchurch, Nelson and Queenstown also have small gay scenes.

The best source of on-the-ground information is the fortnightly gay newspaper *Express* (W gay express.co.nz), available free in gay-friendly cafés and venues and almost any decent bookshop.

GAY EVENTS

Asia Pacific Outgames W asiapacificoutgames.org. Auckland is host city for the 2016 edition of this gay sporting jamboree with competitors from 20 countries expected. To be held at the same time as the Auckland Pride Festival.

Auckland Pride Festival W aucklandpridefestival.org.nz. See box, p.107.

Gay Ski Week W gayskiweekqt.com. Late Aug to early Sept. Aussie and Kiwi gay men and women fly in to party up large at cabaret nights, a trannie-hosted bingo night, live music gigs and yet more partying in venues around Queenstown. There's even time for skiing.

Vinegar Hill Summer Camp search for Vinegar Hill Gay Camping at W facebook.com. Very laidback affair, with a couple of hundred gay men and women camping out, mixing and partying 5km north of the small town of Hunterville, in the middle of the North Island. Runs from Boxing Day to just after New Year. There's no charge (except around $5 for camping) and no hot water, but a large river runs through the grounds and everyone has a great time.

GAY TRAVEL WEBSITES

W **gaynewzealand.com** A virtual tour of the country with a gay and lesbian slant.

W **gaynz.com** Useful site with direct access to gay, lesbian, bisexual and transgender information including a guide to what's on in the gay community and a calendar of events all over the country.

W **gaytravel.co.nz** A gay online accommodation and travel reservation service.

W **rainbowtourism.com** An excellent resource for gay and lesbian travellers in NZ and wider afield, listing accommodation, events, clubs and tours.

W **samesextravel.com** Lists gay- and lesbian-owned and -operated accommodation throughout NZ and Oz.

W **purpleroofs.com** Comprehensive listing for gay-owned and gay-friendly accommodation in NZ and beyond.

Health

New Zealand is relatively free of serious health hazards and the most common pitfall is simply underestimating the power of nature. **No** **vaccinations** are required to enter the country, but you should make sure you have adequate health cover in your travel insurance, especially if you plan to take on the great outdoors (see p.51 for advice on tramping health and safety).

New Zealand has a good **health service** that's reasonably cheap by world standards. All visitors are covered by the accident compensation scheme, under which you can claim some medical and hospital expenses in the event of an accident, but without full cover in your travel insurance you could still face a hefty bill. For more minor ailments, you can visit a doctor for a consultation (from around $65) and, armed with a prescription, buy any required medication at a pharmacy at a reasonable price.

Sun, surf and earthquakes

Visitors to New Zealand frequently get caught out by the intensity of the **sun**, its damaging ultraviolet rays easily penetrating the thin ozone layer and reducing burn times to as little as ten minutes in spring and summer. Stay out of the sun (or keep covered up) as much as possible between 11am and 3pm, and always slap on plenty of sunblock. Reapply every few hours as well as after swimming, and keep a check on any moles on your body: if you notice any changes, during or after your trip, see a doctor right away.

The sea is a more immediate killer and even strong swimmers should read our **surf** warning (see box opposite).

New Zealand is regularly shaken by **earthquakes** (see p.808), but, although Christchurch experienced major quakes in 2010 and 2011, most are minor and it is generally not something to worry about. If the worst happens, the best advice is to stand in a doorway or crouch under a table. If caught in the open, try to get inside; failing that, keep your distance from trees and rocky outcrops to reduce the chances of being injured by falling branches or debris.

Wildlife hazards

New Zealand's wildlife is amazingly benign. There are no snakes, scorpions or other nasties, and only a few poisonous **spiders**, all rarely seen. No one has died from spider venom for many years, but if you get a serious reaction from a bite be sure to see a doctor or head to the nearest hospital, where antivenin will be available.

Shark attacks are also rare; you're more likely to be carried away by a strong tide than a great white, though it still pays to be sensible and obey any local warnings when swimming.

SWIM BETWEEN THE FLAGS

The New Zealand coast is frequently pounded by ferocious surf and even strong swimmers can find themselves in difficulty in what may seem benign conditions. Every day throughout the peak holiday weeks (Christmas–Jan), and at weekends through the rest of the summer (Nov–Easter), the most popular surf beaches are monitored daily from around 10am to 5pm. Lifeguards stake out a section of beach between two red and yellow flags and continually monitor that area: **always swim between the flags**.

Before entering the water, watch other swimmers to see if they are being dragged along the beach by a strong along-shore **current** or **rip**. Often the rip will turn out to sea, leaving a "river" of disturbed but relatively calm water through the pattern of curling breakers. On entering the water, feel the strength of the waves and current before committing yourself too deeply, then keep glancing back to where you left your towel to judge your drift along the shore. Look out too for **sandbars**, a common feature of surf beaches at certain tides: wading out to sea, you may well be neck deep and then suddenly be only up to your knees. The corollary is moments after being comfortably within your depth you'll be floundering around in a **hole**, reaching for the bottom. Note that **boogie boards**, while providing flotation, can make you vulnerable to rips, and riders should always wear fins (flippers).

If you do find yourself in **trouble**, try not to panic, raise one hand in the air and yell to attract the attention of other swimmers and surf rescue folk. Most of all, don't struggle against the current; either swim across the rip or let it drag you out. Around 100–200m offshore the current will often subside and you can swim away from the rip and bodysurf the breakers back to shore. If you have to be rescued (or are just feeling generous), a large donation is in order. Surf lifeguards are dedicated volunteers, always strapped for cash and in need of new rescue equipment.

A far bigger problem is the country's **mosquitoes** and **sandflies**, although they're generally free of life-threatening diseases. The West Coast of the South Island in the summer is the worst place for these irritating insects, though they appear to a lesser degree in many other places across the country. A liberal application of repellent helps keep them at bay; for a natural deterrent, try lavender oil.

At the microscopic level, **giardia** inhabits many rivers and lakes, and infection results from drinking contaminated water, with symptoms appearing several weeks later: a bloated stomach, cramps, explosive diarrhoea and wind. The Department of Conservation advises you to purify drinking water by using iodine-based solutions or tablets (regular chlorine-based tablets aren't effective against giardia), by fast-boiling water for at least three minutes or by using a giardia-rated filter (obtainable from any outdoors or camping shop).

The relatively rare **amoebic meningitis** is another waterborne hazard, this time contracted from hot pools. Commercial pools are always safe, but in natural pools surrounded by earth you should avoid contamination by keeping your head above water. The amoeba enters the body via the nose or ears, lodges in the brain, and weeks later causes severe headaches, stiffness of the neck, hypersensitivity to light, and eventually coma. If you

experience any of these symptoms, seek medical attention immediately.

Insurance

New Zealand's Accident Compensation Commission (W acc.co.nz) provides limited medical treatment for visitors injured while in New Zealand, but is no substitute for having comprehensive **travel insurance** to cover against theft, loss and illness or injury.

Before paying for a new policy, it's worth checking whether you are already covered: some home insurance policies may cover your possessions when overseas, and many private medical schemes include cover when abroad. Students will often find that their student health coverage extends during the vacations and for one term beyond the date of last enrolment.

After exhausting the possibilities above, you might want to contact a specialist travel insurance company. Most policies exclude so-called **dangerous activities** unless an extra premium is paid. In New Zealand this can mean scuba diving, bungy jumping, whitewater rafting, windsurfing, surfing, skiing and snowboarding, and even tramping under some policies.

Many policies can exclude coverage you don't need. If you do take medical coverage, ascertain

ROUGH GUIDES TRAVEL INSURANCE

Rough Guides has teamed up with WorldNomads.com to offer great **travel insurance** deals. Policies are available to residents of over 150 countries, with cover for a wide range of **adventure sports**, 24hr emergency assistance, high levels of medical and evacuation cover and a stream of **travel safety information**. Roughguides.com users can take advantage of their policies online 24/7, from anywhere in the world – even if you're already travelling. And since plans often change when you're on the road, you can extend your policy and even claim online. Roughguides.com users who buy travel insurance with WorldNomads.com can also leave a positive footprint and donate to a community development project. For more information, go to ⓦroughguides.com/travel-insurance.

whether benefits will be paid as treatment proceeds or only after return home, and if there's a 24-hour medical emergency number. When securing **baggage cover**, make sure that the per-article limit will cover your most valuable possession. If you need to make a claim, you'll need to keep receipts for medicines and medical treatment, and in the event you have anything stolen, you must obtain an official statement from the police.

Internet

Internet access is abundant and fairly cheap though seldom blindingly fast. You'll find coin-operated machines at most **visitor centres**, backpacker hostels, motels and campsites, generally charging around $6 an hour. Most are set up with card readers, headsets and webcams, and often loaded with Skype and iTunes. At more expensive accommodation there'll often be a free-use computer, and laptop connections may be available.

There's often better functionality and lower prices at the abundant **internet cafés** lining city streets, which charge $3–6 per hour. **Libraries** typically have internet access – some offer this service free, while others charge.

Wi-fi access is increasingly widespread. In addition to internet **cafés**, many holiday parks, hostels, motels and hotels have hotspots accessible using your credit card or by buying access from reception. Some Spark phonebooths also double as wi-fi hotspots, although you'll need a Kiwi or Australian mobile phone number to use the service. Rates vary considerably: an hour might cost $10 but you can often get a full 24-hour day for under $25. Swankier B&Bs and lodges will usually have free wi-fi in all rooms. Organizations such as Zenbu (ⓦzenbu.net.nz) allow you to store your purchased time for future use. Note that in New Zealand, there's often a

kilobyte cap, so make sure your device isn't using up your kilobytes in automatic updates.

Mail

Stamps, postcards, envelopes, packing materials and a lot more can be bought at **post offices** (a.k.a. **PostShops**), which are open Monday to Friday 8.30am to 5pm, plus Saturday 9 or 10am to noon or 1pm in some large towns and cities. Red and silver **post boxes** are found outside post offices and on street corners, with mail collected daily.

Parcels are quite expensive to send overseas as everything goes by air; regular airmail takes up to ten days, while the more expensive courier services will deliver your package in less than six days.

One post office in each major town operates a **Poste Restante** (or **General Delivery**) service where you can receive mail; we've listed the major ones in town accounts. Most hostels and hotels will keep mail for you, preferably marked with your expected date of arrival.

Maps and GPS

Specialist outlets should have a reasonable stock of **maps** of New Zealand. **Road atlases** are widely available in bookshops and service stations; the most detailed are those produced by Kiwi Pathfinder, which indicate numerous points of interest and the type of road surface. Also look out for *A Driving Guide to Scenic New Zealand* ($40) with handy angled projections giving a real sense of the lay of the land. Many car- and van-rental places have **GPS navigation systems**, usually for an additional $5–15 a day.

With a road atlas and our city plans you can't go far wrong on the roads, but more detailed maps may be required for tramping. All the major walks are covered by the **Park Map** series, complete with photos (around $19 from DOC offices and bookshops in NZ), while the larger-scale 1:50,000 Topo50 and 1:250,000 Topo250 (downloadable at ⓦ linz.govt.nz and sold in i-SITEs, book and outdoors shops and DOC offices) cover the whole country.

Money

The **Kiwi dollar** is divided into 100 cents. There are $100, $50, $20, $10 and $5 notes made of a sturdy plastic material, and coins in denominations of $2, $1 (both gold in colour), 50¢, 20¢ and 10¢. Grocery prices are given to the nearest cent, but the final bill is rounded up or down to the nearest ten cents. All prices quoted in the Guide are in New Zealand dollars.

Cards, cheques and ATMs

For purchases, visitors generally rely on **credit cards**, particularly Visa and MasterCard, which are widely accepted, though many hostels, campsites and homestays will only accept cash. American Express and Diners Club are far less useful. You'll also find credit cards handy for advance booking of accommodation and trips, and with the appropriate PIN you can obtain **cash advances** through 24-hour ATMs found almost everywhere. **Debit cards** are also useful for purchases and ATM cash withdrawals.

Banks

The major **banks** – ASB, ANZ, BNZ, Kiwibank (found in post offices), National Bank and Westpac – have branches in towns of any size and are open Monday to Friday from 9.30am to 4.30pm, with some city branches opening on Saturday mornings (until around 12.30pm). The big cities and tourist centres also have **bureaux de change**, which are typically open from 8am to 8pm daily.

Especially if you are working in New Zealand you may want to open a **bank account**. A New Zealand EFTPOS (debit) card can be used just about anywhere for purchases or obtaining cash. An account can usually be set up within a day; remember to take your passport.

Opening hours

New Zealand's larger cities and tourist centres are increasingly open all hours, with cafés, bars and supermarkets open till very late, and shops open long hours every day. Once you get into rural areas, things change rapidly, and core **shopping**

hours (Mon–Fri 9am–5.30pm, Sat 9am–noon) apply, though tourist-oriented shops stay open daily until 8pm.

An ever-increasing number of **supermarkets** open 24/7 and small "dairies" (corner shops or convenience stores) also keep long hours and open on Sundays. **Museums** and sights usually open around 9am, although small-town museums often open only in the afternoons and/or only on specific days.

Public holidays and festivals are listed on p.46.

Phones

Given the near-ubiquity of mobile phones, and the prominence of Skype (or similar services) for international calling, most people don't have much need of **public payphones**, though they are still fairly widespread across New Zealand. Coin-operated phones are now rare, but all payphones accept major credit cards, account-based phone-cards and slot-in disposable PhoneCards sold at post offices, newsagents, dairies, petrol stations, i-SITEs and supermarkets.

Phone numbers

New Zealand **landline numbers** have only five area codes. The North Island is divided into four codes, while the South Island makes do with just one (❶03); all numbers in the Guide are given with their code. Even within the same area, you may have to dial the code if you're calling another town some distance away. **Mobile numbers** start with ❶021, ❶022, ❶027 or ❶029, and you'll come across **freephone** numbers which are all ❶0800 or ❶0508. Numbers prefixed ❶0900 are **premium-rated** and cannot be called from payphones.

IMPORTANT PHONE NUMBERS

National directory assistance ❶018
International directory assistance ❶0172
Emergency services Police, ambulance and fire brigade (no charge) ❶111

International dialling codes

To call New Zealand from overseas, dial the international access code (❶00 from the UK, ❶011 from the US and Canada, ❶0011 from Australia, ❶09 from South Africa), followed by ❶64, the area code minus its initial zero, and then the number.

To dial out of New Zealand, it's ❶00, followed by the country code (see box p.66), then the area code (without the initial zero if there is one) and the number.

CALLING HOME

Australia 00 + 61 + area code.
Republic of Ireland 00 + 353 + area code.
South Africa 00 + 27 + area code.
UK 00 + 44 + area code.
US and Canada 00 + 1 + area code.

Phonecards and calling cards

For **long-distance and international calling** you are best off with pre-paid account-based **phonecards** that can be used on any phone. There are numerous such cards around offering highly competitive rates, but be wary of the very cheap ones: they are often internet-based and the voice quality can be poor and delayed. Be warned, though, that public payphones have an additional per-minute charge for account-based phonecards, so try to use them from private phones whenever possible.

Mobile phones

New Zealand has three **mobile** providers: Spark (Ⓦspark.co.nz), Vodafone (Ⓦvodafone.co.nz) and 2degrees (Ⓦ2degreesmobile.co.nz). All have excellent reception in populated areas but sporadic coverage in remoter spots.

If you're thinking of bringing your phone from home, check with your service to see if your phone will roam in New Zealand and check roaming costs, which can be excessive. Providing your phone is unlocked, you can also buy a New Zealand SIM card and pre-pay.

Time and seasons

New Zealand Standard Time (NZST) is twelve hours ahead of Greenwich Mean Time, but, from the last Sunday in September to the first Sunday in April, Daylight Saving puts the clocks one hour further forward (GMT+13). Throughout the summer, when it is 8pm in New Zealand, it's 6pm in Sydney, 7am in London, 2am in New York, and 11pm the day before in Los Angeles.

New Zealand follows Britain's lead with **dates**, and 1/4/2016 means April 1 not January 4.

Don't forget that the southern hemisphere **seasons** are reversed: summer is officially December 1 to February 28 (or 29), and winter is June 1 to August 31.

Tourist information

New Zealand promotes itself enthusiastically abroad through **Tourism New Zealand** (Ⓦnewzealand.com).

Many information centres, as well as some cafés, bars and hostels, keep a supply of **free newspapers** and **magazines** oriented towards backpackers – they're usually filled with promotional copy, but are informative nonetheless. *TNT* (Ⓦtntdownunder .com) is about the best.

Visitor centres

Every town of any size has an official **i-SITE visitor centre**, staffed by helpful and knowledgeable personnel and sometimes offering some form of video presentation on the area. Apart from dishing out local maps and leaflets, they offer a **free booking service** for accommodation, trips and activities, and onward travel, but only for businesses registered with them. Some (usually small) businesses choose not to register and may still be worth seeking out; we've mentioned them where relevant. In the more popular tourist areas, you'll also come across places representing themselves as **independent information centres** that usually follow a hidden agenda (ie commission), typically promoting a number of allied adventure companies. While these can be excellent, it's worth remembering that their advice may not be impartial.

Other useful resources are **Department of Conservation** (DOC; Ⓦdoc.govt.nz) offices and field centres, usually sited close to wilderness areas and popular tramping tracks, and sometimes serving as the local visitor centre as well. These are highly informative and well geared to trampers' needs, with local weather forecasts, intentions forms and maps as well as historic and environmental displays and audiovisual exhibitions. The website contains loads of detail on the environment and the latest conservation issues plus details of national parks and Great Walks.

Travellers with disabilities

Overall, New Zealand is disabled traveller-friendly. Many public buildings, galleries and museums are **accessible**, and many tour operators will make a special effort to help you participate in all manner of activities, such as swimming with dolphins or seals. However, restaurants and local public transport generally make few concessions.

Planning a trip

Independent travellers should advise travel agencies, insurance companies and travel companions of limitations. Reading your travel **insurance** small print carefully to make sure that people with a pre-existing medical condition aren't excluded could save you a fortune. Your travel agent can help make your journey simpler: airline or bus companies can better cater to your needs if they are expecting you. A **medical certificate** of your fitness to travel, provided by your doctor, is also extremely useful; some airlines or insurance companies may insist on it.

Accommodation

New accommodation must have at least one room designed for disabled access, and many pre-existing places have converted rooms, including most YHA hostels, some motels, campsites and larger hotels. Older buildings, homestays and B&Bs are the least likely to lend themselves to such conversions.

For listings, visit ⓦ tourism.net.nz/accommodation /accessible-accommodation, which has a searchable database of places that offer disability-friendly facilities.

Travelling

Few airlines, trains, ferries and buses allow complete independence. Air New Zealand provides aisle wheelchairs on international (but not domestic) flights, and the rear toilet cubicles are wider than the others to facilitate access; for more details search for "Special Assistance" on its website. Other **domestic airlines** have poorer facilities. Inter-islander Cook Strait **ferries** have reasonable access for disabled travellers, including help while boarding, if needed, and adapted toilets. If given advance warning, trains will provide attendants to get passengers in wheelchairs or sight-impaired travellers on board, but moving around the train in

a standard wheelchair is impossible and there are no specially adapted toilets; the problems with **long-distance buses** are much the same.

In cities there are some **taxis** specifically adapted for wheelchairs, but these must be pre-booked; otherwise taxi drivers obligingly hoist wheelchairs into the boot and their occupant onto a seat.

CONTACTS IN NEW ZEALAND

Access Tourism NZ ⓦ accesstourismnz.org.nz. Informative advocacy blog.
Disability Resource Centre 14 Erson Ave, Royal Oak, Auckland ☎ 09 625 8069, ⓦ disabilityresource.org.nz. General resource centre.
DPA Level 4/173–175 Victoria St, Wellington, NZ ☎ 04 801 9100, ⓦ dpa.org.nz. Disability advocacy organization with useful links.
Enable New Zealand ☎ 0800 362 253, ⓦ enable.co.nz. Organization assisting people with disabilities, though not specifically focused on travellers.

Women travellers

Kiwi men have fairly progressive attitudes towards women, and travelling in New Zealand doesn't present any particular problems.

In the unlikely event of trouble, contact RPE (Rape Prevention Education), ⓦ www.rpe.org.nz, which coordinates a series of sexual assault support centres across the country. You might also consider partly organizing your holiday through **Women Travel New Zealand** (ⓦ womentravel.co.nz), which offers information, links to retreats, women-oriented tour operators and accommodation. Auckland's Women's Bookshop (p.109; ⓦ womens bookshop.co.nz) is a handy resource and hosts literary events.

Auckland
and around

AUCKLAND'S SKYLINE AS SEEN FROM MOUNT EDEN

1

Auckland and around

Auckland is New Zealand's largest city and, as the site of the major international airport, most visitors' first view of the country. Planes bank over the island-studded Hauraki Gulf and yachts with bright spinnakers tack through the glistening waters of the Waitemata Harbour towards the "City of Sails". The skyscrapered downtown is surrounded by the grassy humps of some fifty-odd extinct volcanoes, and a low-rise suburban sprawl of prim wooden villas surrounded by substantial gardens. Look beyond the glitzy shopfronts and Auckland has a modest small-town feel and measured pace, though this can seem frenetic in comparison with the rest of the country. In fact, Auckland is one of the least densely populated cities in the world, the size of London and yet home to only 1.5 million inhabitants. It is also the world's largest Polynesian city. Around eleven percent of the population claim Maori descent while fourteen percent are families of migrants who arrived from other South Pacific islands during the 1960s and 1970s.

Nevertheless, the Polynesian profile has traditionally been confined to small pockets, and it is only in the last decade or so, as the second generation matures, that Polynesia is making its presence felt in mainstream Auckland life, especially in the arts.

Many visitors only stay in the city long enough for a quick zip around the smattering of key sights, principally the **Auckland Museum**, with its matchless collection of Maori and Pacific Island carving and artefacts. A better taste of the city is gleaned by ambling around the fashionable **inner-city suburbs** of Ponsonby, Parnell, Newmarket and Devonport, and using the city as a base for exploring the wild and desolate West Coast **surf beaches** and the **wineries**, all less than an hour from the city centre. With more time, head out to the **Hauraki Gulf islands**: craggy, volcanic Rangitoto, sophisticated Waiheke, bird-rich Tiritiri Matangi and chilled-out Great Barrier.

Auckland's **climate** is temperate and muggy, though never scorching hot, and the humidity is always tempered by a sea breeze. Winters are generally mild but rainy. The average daytime high is 23°C in January and February, and drops down to 14°C in July and August.

MAUNGAUIKA (NORTH HEAD), DEVONPORT

Highlights

❶ Auckland Art Gallery With an impressive $90 million refit, Auckland's Art Gallery now ranks as the best showcase for Kiwi art in the country. **See p.78**

❷ Auckland Museum The exemplary Maori and Pacific Island collection is the highlight of this landmark museum. **See p.80**

❸ Devonport Stroll the streets of this refined waterside suburb where Maungauika (North Head) provides wonderful harbour views. **See p.87**

❹ Otara Market Island print fabrics, veg stalls and a lot of life make this New Zealand's finest multicultural market. **See p.90**

❺ Karekare and Piha Swim, surf, go canyoning or simply laze on the black-and-gold sands of these wild, bush-backed beaches less than an hour from the city. **See p.113**

❻ Rangitoto Island Make a day-trip to this gnarled lava landscape draped in pohutukawa forest with great views back to the city. **See p.119**

❼ Great Barrier Island Step back in time to this compact, laidback land of golden beaches, mountain bushwalks, indented harbours and hot springs. **See p.129**

❽ Tiritiri Matangi Enjoy close encounters with some of New Zealand's rarest birds amid regenerating bush on one of the Hauraki Gulf's prettiest islands. **See p.136**

HIGHLIGHTS ARE MARKED ON THE MAP ON P.72

1 Auckland

AUCKLAND's urban sprawl smothers the North Island's wasp waist, a narrow isthmus where the island is all but severed by river estuaries probing inland from the city's two harbours. To the west, the shallow and silted **Manukau Harbour** opens out onto the Tasman Sea at a rare break in the long string of black-sand beaches continually pounded by heavy surf. Maori named the eastern anchorage the **Waitemata Harbour** for its "sparkling waters", which constitute Auckland's deep-water port and a focus for the heart of the city. Every summer weekend the harbour and adjoining Hauraki Gulf explode into a riot of brightly coloured sails.

Auckland is increasingly focusing on its **waterfront**, with former docks and fishing wharves now dotted with bobbing yachts and the rejuvenated surrounds converted to flashy restaurants and swanky apartments. This is very much the place to hang out, sucking life from **downtown Auckland**, which is fighting back with the superbly renovated Auckland Art Gallery.

At the top of Queen Street lies **Karangahape Road**, an altogether groovier strip of cheaper shops, ethnic restaurants and more down-and-dirty clubs. To the east lies

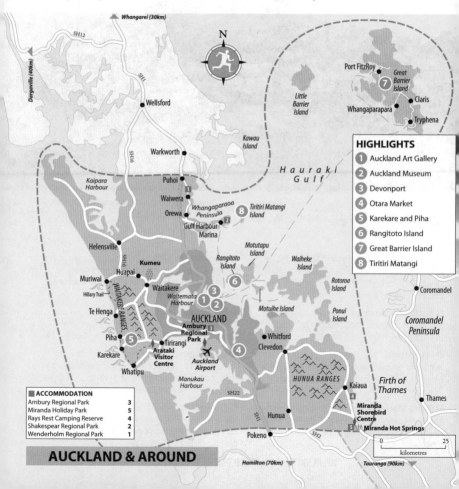

HIGHLIGHTS

1. Auckland Art Gallery
2. Auckland Museum
3. Devonport
4. Otara Market
5. Karekare and Piha
6. Rangitoto Island
7. Great Barrier Island
8. Tiritiri Matangi

■ ACCOMMODATION

Ambury Regional Park	3
Miranda Holiday Park	5
Rays Rest Camping Reserve	4
Shakespear Regional Park	2
Wenderholm Regional Park	1

AUCKLAND & AROUND

1

The Domain, an extensive swathe of semiformal parkland centred on the city's most-visited attraction, the **Auckland Museum**, exhibiting stunning Maori and Pacific Island artefacts.

Neighbouring **Parnell** forms the ecclesiastical heart of the city, with one of Auckland's oldest churches and a couple of historical houses. At the foot of the hill, **Tamaki Drive** follows the eastern waterfront past the watery attractions of Kelly Tarlton's aquarium to the city beaches of Mission Bay and St Heliers. West of the centre, the cafés, shops and bars of **Ponsonby Road** give way to Western Springs, home of the MOTAT transport museum and the excellent **zoo**.

Across the Waitemata Harbour the seemingly endless suburbs of the **North Shore** stretch into the distance, though you're only likely to want to spend much time in the old waterside suburb of Devonport and perhaps the long golden beach at **Takapuna**.

Immediately south of the centre, two of Auckland's highest points, **Maungawhau** (Mt Eden) and **Maungakiekie** (One Tree Hill) with its encircling **Cornwall Park**, provide wonderful vantage points for views of the city. **Pah Homestead** presents more great art, but the main reason for heading further south is to visit Saturday's **Otara Market**.

Brief history

The earth's crust between the Waitemata and Manukau harbours is so thin that, every few thousand years, magma finds a fissure and bursts onto the surface, producing yet another volcano. The most recent eruption, some six hundred years ago, formed Rangitoto Island. The Rangitoto eruption was witnessed by some of the region's earliest **Maori inhabitants**, settled on adjacent Motutapu Island. Legend records their ancestors' arrival on the Tamaki isthmus, the narrowest neck of land. With plentiful catches from two harbours and rich volcanic soils on a wealth of highly defensible volcano-top sites, the land, which they came to know as **Tamaki Makaurau** ("the maiden sought by a hundred lovers"), became the prize of numerous battles over the years. By the middle of the eighteenth century it had fallen to **Kiwi Tamaki**, who established a three-thousand-strong *pa* (fortified village) on Maungakiekie ("One Tree Hill"), and a satellite *pa* on just about every volcano in the district, but who were eventually overwhelmed by rival *hapu* (subtribes) from Kaipara Harbour to the north.

The Europeans arrive

With the arrival of musket-trading **Europeans** in the Bay of Islands around the beginning of the nineteenth century, Northland Ngapuhi were able to launch successful raids on the Tamaki Maori, which, combined with smallpox epidemics, left the region almost uninhabited, a significant factor in its choice as the new capital after the signing of the Treaty of Waitangi in 1840. Scottish medic **John Logan Campbell** was one of the few European residents when this fertile land, with easy access to major river and seaborne trading routes, was purchased for £55 and some blankets. The capital was roughly laid out and Campbell took advantage of his early start, wheeling and dealing to achieve control of half the city, eventually becoming mayor and "the father of Auckland". After 1840, immigrants boosted the population to the extent that more land was needed, a demand which partly precipitated the **New Zealand Wars** of the 1860s (see p.792).

Loss of capital status

During the depression that followed, many sought their fortunes in the Otago goldfields, and, as the balance of European population shifted south, the capital moved to Wellington in 1865 and the city slumped further. Since then, Auckland has never looked back, almost continuously growing faster than the country as a whole and absorbing waves of migrants, initially from Britain, then, in the 1960s and 1970s, from the Polynesian Islands of the South Pacific. A steady stream of rural Maori has been arriving on Auckland's doorstep for over half a century, now joined by an influx of East

GREATER AUCKLAND

▲ Waiheke

■ ACCOMMODATION	
Aarangi Motel	3
Auckland North Shore Motels and Holiday Park	2
Kohi Beach B&B	4
Takapuna Beach Holiday Park	1

● RESTAURANTS	
The Attic	4
Café on Kohi	5
Little & Friday	3
Madam Woo	1
Takapuna Beach Café	2

N

Rangitoto

Motukorea Channel

Browns Island

HOWICK

PAKURANGA

Half Moon Bay Marina

PANMURE

▶ Otara Market (2km) & Auckland Botanical Gardens (12km)

Rangitoto Channel

Cheltenham & Narrow Neck Beaches

DEVONPORT

SEE 'DEVONPORT' MAP FOR DETAIL

Northcote Point

Kelly Tarlton's Sea Life Aquarium

Ferg's Kayaks

Achilles Point

ST HELIERS

GLEN INNES

TAMAKI

KOHIMARAMA

M. J. Savage Memorial Park

Bastion Point

MISSION BAY

TAMAKI DRIVE

Tamaki River

ELLERSLIE

▶ Auckland Airport (7km)

Long Bay (12km) ▲

TAKAPUNA

Rangitoto Channel

Waitemata Harbour

Harbour Bridge

BIRKENHEAD

Judges Bay

Parnell Baths

PARNELL

NEWMARKET

SEE 'PARNELL & NEWMARKET' MAP FOR DETAIL

REMUERA

GREENLANE

Huia Lodge and Acacia Cottage

Cornwall Park

Maungakiekie (One Tree Hill)

One Tree Hill Domain

Pah Homestead and the Wallace Arts Centre

Manukau Harbour

SEE 'CENTRAL AUCKLAND' MAP FOR DETAIL

ST MARY'S BAY

FREEMANS BAY

PONSONBY

HERNE BAY

GREY LYNN

SEE 'PONSONBY AND HERNE BAY' MAP FOR DETAIL

Eden Garden

Maungawhau (Mt Eden)

MOUNT EDEN

BALMORAL

SEE 'MT EDEN AND EPSOM' MAP FOR DETAILS

Highwic

Eden Park

KINGSLAND

SANDRINGHAM

WESTERN SPRINGS

MOTAT

MOTAT MEDIA ROAD

Coyle Park

MOTAT Aviation Hall

Auckland Zoo

PT CHEVALIER RD

▶ Titirangi (8km)

▲ Henderson (10km)

0 ————— 2

kilometres

AUCKLAND'S VOLCANIC CONES

Within 20km of the centre of Auckland there are **fifty small volcanoes**, but on the whole the city hasn't been very respectful of its geological heritage. Even the exact number is hard to pin down, not least because several cones have disappeared over the last 150 years, mostly chewed away by scoria and basalt quarrying.

That might sound a Herculean feat, but almost all are under 200m high and many are pimples that only just poke above the surrounding housing. Early on, **Maori** recognized the fertility of the volcanic soils, and set up *kumara* gardens on the lower slopes, usually protected by fortified *pa* sites around the summit. Europeans valued the elevated positions for water storage – most of the main volcanoes have **reservoirs** in the craters.

It is only in the last few decades that volcanic features have been protected from development, often by turning their environs into parks – all or part of 37 of them have some form of protection. The council's "volcanic viewshafts" dictate that some summits can't be obscured from certain angles, and yet a few years ago the edge of one volcano was only just saved from removal for a motorway extension. Some seek UNESCO World Heritage Site status for the cones, but protection looks more likely to come from a 2014 transfer of ownership to a collective of Maori tribes with historic claims to the Auckland (Tamaki Makaurau) isthmus. Fourteen of the major cones are now under Maori ownership though Auckland Council will still maintain them.

Crucially, public access will be maintained. The volcanoes make wonderful **viewpoints** dotted all over the city, notably from central Auckland's Maungawhau and Maungakiekie, Devonport's Maungauika and the top of Rangitoto Island where you can also explore lava caves.

The oldest volcanoes erupted 250,000 years ago, though it is only 600 years since the last eruption, and the volcanic field remains active. No one knows when the next eruption will be, but it is unlikely to be through one of the existing volcanoes – meaning one day a new peak will emerge.

Asians whose tastes have radically altered the city centre. Asians now comprise almost twenty percent of Greater Auckland's population, many of them inhabiting the high-rise apartments that pepper the city centre, and Korean, Thai, Malaysian, Chinese and Japanese restaurants are everywhere. Almost forty percent of Aucklanders were born overseas compared to an average of eighteen percent throughout the rest of the country.

The waterfront

 waterfrontauckland.co.nz

Through much of the twentieth century, Auckland's city centre was cut off from its harbour frontage by working docks. As business gradually moved to the container port, the **waterfront** is finally getting a chance to shine.

The 1912 **Ferry Building** remains the nexus of the harbour ferries, whose history and social importance are covered at the nearby **Voyager** maritime museum. **Viaduct Harbour** and **Princes Wharf** were smartened up around the Millennium, though the torch has now moved a little west to the revitalized **Wynyard Quarter**.

Voyager: New Zealand Maritime Museum

Corner of Quay and Hobson sts • Daily 9am–5pm; guided tours Mon–Fri 10.30am & 1pm; cruises $12–35 • 09 373 0800, maritimemuseum.co.nz

Voyager: New Zealand Maritime Museum pays homage to the maritime history of an island nation reliant on the sea for colonization, trade and sport. A short movie on an imagined Maori migration voyage sets the scene for a display of South Pacific outrigger and double-hulled canoes. Designs for fishing, lagoon sailing and ocean voyaging include the massive 21m-long *Taratai*, which carried New Zealand film-maker and writer James Siers over 2400km from Kiribati to Fiji in 1976. The creaking and rolling innards of a migrant ship and displays on New Zealand's coastal traders and whalers lead on to *Blue Water Black Magic*, a tribute to New Zealand's most celebrated sailor,

1

Peter Blake. Wins in the 1990 Whitbread Round the World Race and two America's Cups (1995 and 2000) are celebrated along with high-tech boat construction and an opportunity to work as a team at the helm and grinders of an interactive America's Cup yacht. Other highlights include an early example of the Hamilton Jetboat, which was designed for shallow, braided Canterbury rivers, and a fine collection of boat figureheads and maritime art.

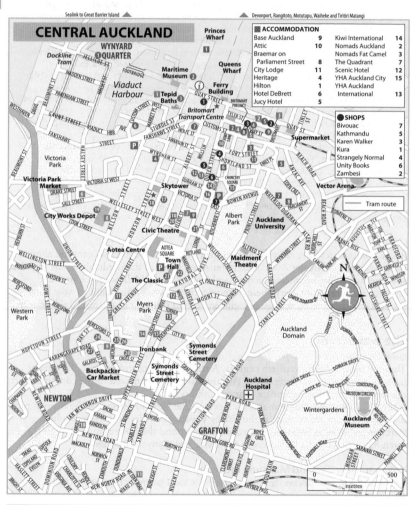

CENTRAL AUCKLAND

Sealink to Great Barrier Island — Devonport, Rangitoto, Motutapu, Waiheke and Tiritiri Matangi

■ ACCOMMODATION

Base Auckland	9	Kiwi International	14
Attic	10	Nomads Auckland	2
Braemar on		Nomads Fat Camel	3
Parliament Street	8	The Quadrant	7
City Lodge	11	Scenic Hotel	12
Heritage	4	YHA Auckland City	15
Hilton	1	YHA Auckland	
Hotel DeBrett	6	International	13
Jucy Hotel	5		

● SHOPS

Bivouac	7
Kathmandu	5
Karen Walker	3
Kura	1
Strangely Normal	4
Unity Books	6
Zambesi	2

Tram route

● CAFÉS & RESTAURANTS

Alleluya	26	Ebisu	5	Misters	13
Bellota	18	Federal Delicatessen	17	Ortolana	4
Better Burger	8	Food Alley	7	Ostro	5
Black Hoof	12	Grand Harbour	6	No. 1 Pancake	21
Bombay Chinese	22	Jack Tar	1	Pok Pok	24
The Botanist	19	Ima	11	Rasoi	25
Cassia	10	Imperial Lane	10	Soul	3
Chuffed	14	Mamak Malaysian	15	Sri Pinang	28
Coco's Cantina	27	Mexico	9	Tanuki's Cave	23
The Depot	17	Mezze Bar	16	Wildfire	2
		Middle East Café	20		

■ PUBS, BARS & CLUBS

1885 Britomart	5	Sweat Shop
Brew on Quay	3	Brew Kitchen	6
Brothers Beer	8	Tyler St Garage	2
Britomart Country Club	5	Xuxu	4
Cowboys	1		
Galbraith's Alehouse	11		
Family Bar	9		
Globe	7		
Kings Arms	10		
O'Hagan's	1		

Book ahead for **cruises** on the *Ted Ashby*, a 1990s replica of one of the traditional flat-bottomed, ketch-rigged scows that once worked the North Island tidal waterways, or *Breeze*, a replica of a nineteenth-century coastal trader.

Viaduct Harbour and Princes Wharf

Viaduct Harbour was a scruffy fishing port until it was smartened up for New Zealand's successful defence of the **America's Cup** in 2000. Bobbing yachts still dominate a waterfront lined with exclusive apartments, a lively cluster of restaurants and bars. More restaurants and bars flank **Princes Wharf**, which spears out into the harbour to the dramatically sited *Hilton* hotel.

Wynyard Quarter

Cross Wynyard Crossing pedestrian bridge from Viaduct Harbour or get the City Link bus from Queen St • Dockline Tram 20 Dec–Jan daily 10am–4pm; Nov–19 Dec, Feb & March Sat & Sun 10am–4pm; every 10min • Adults $2 all day, under-16s $1 • ⓦ aucklandtram.co.nz

Further west, **Wynyard Quarter** successfully blends the still-operational fish market and Great Barrier Island ferry terminal with parks and a dozen or so nicely-sited restaurants. A "six pack" of old industrial silos has been retained and provides a backdrop for the Friday-evening movies, and kids splash in the fountain. Catch it on a fine day and the whole area can be a delight.

The quarter is prettified by the **Dockline Tram**, on which restored 1920s trams make a pleasant enough 1.5km loop which doesn't take you anywhere you couldn't easily walk.

Downtown

Downtown Auckland spreads south from the waterfront along downbeat **Queen Street**, the main drag, largely sustained by banks and fairly dull shops. That said, there are still a couple of lovely Victorian shopping arcades along Queen Street – Queens Arcade at no. 34 and Stand Arcade at no. 233.

Either side is a grid of streets commemorating prime movers in New Zealand's early European history: the country's first governor-general, William Hobson; Willoughby Shortland, New Zealand's first colonial secretary; and William Symonds, who chivvied along local Maori chiefs reluctant to sign the Treaty of Waitangi.

Immediately east of Queen Street, restored old warehouses and a couple of new office blocks from the lively **Britomart Precinct**, home of many of the city's **top fashion shops**, but at its best in the evening when the restaurants and bars are packed.

Further south, spurn Queen Street in favour of the shops and cafés along O'Connell Street and High Street, heading for the kitsch beauty of the **Civic Theatre**, the **casino** and **Skytower**, and the superbly revamped and expanded **Auckland Art Gallery**. Wedged between the Art Gallery and the University, Albert Park makes a nice break from the concrete jungle.

Britomart Precinct

At the foot of Queen Street the neoclassical 1910 former post office has been transformed into the striking **Britomart Transport Centre** which goes some way to recapturing the majesty of train travel, though useful services are limited.

The transport centre opens out into the **Britomart Precinct**, a cluster of heritage buildings centred on **Takutai Square** with its fountain, lawns and scattered beanbags. Some hip new café, stylish bar or chic clothes shop seems to open every week; check out top Kiwi fashion at Karen Walker, World and Kate Sylvester.

Fort Street, High Street and Vulcan Lane

The waterfront once lapped at **Fort Street** (originally Fore Street), but progressive reclamation shifted the shoreline 300m to the north. Something of a backpacker ghetto (with three hostels and several bars catering to them), it is also Auckland's (admittedly

1

tame) red-light district, with a few raunchy clubs. But Britomart's rejuvenation has spread south. Fort Lane, in particular, is packed with fun places and **High Street** and **O'Connell Street** are regaining some of the buzz they lost when everyone decamped to Britomart. Around the corner, **Vulcan Lane** was originally a street of blacksmiths, now replaced by bars and restaurants.

Civic Theatre

One of Queen Street's few buildings of distinction is the Art Nouveau **Civic Theatre**, on the corner of Wellesley Street. The talk of the town when it opened in 1929, the management went so far as to import a small Indian boy from Fiji to complement the ornate Moghul-style decor, all elephants, Hindu gods, a proscenium arch with flanking red-eyed panthers and star-strewn artificial sky. You may be able to stick your head in for a glimpse, but, sadly, the only way to see inside properly is to attend a performance (see p.108).

Skytower

Corner of Victoria and Federal sts • Mon–Thurs & Sun 8.30am–10.30pm, Fri & Sat 8.30am–11.30pm • $28 • ☎ 0800 759 2489, ⓦ skycityauckland.co.nz/attractions

At 328m, the **Skytower**, which sprouts from the **Skycity Casino**, is New Zealand's tallest structure and just pips the Eiffel Tower and Sydney's Centrepoint. You can admire the stupendous views over the city and Hauraki Gulf either from one of two observation decks (186m and 220m) or from the classy *Sugar Club* revolving restaurant.

SkyWalk

Daily 10am–6pm • $145; students and BBH $125 • ☎ 0800 759 925, ⓦ skywalk.co.nz

The views from inside the Skytower are surpassed by those from the **SkyWalk** – if you dare to look around. At the 192m level you tentatively make a twenty-minute circumnavigation of the Skytower exterior on a metre-wide, handrail-free walkway with just a rope tether to steady the nerves. At first it is petrifying, but the guide will soon have you hanging over the edge trusting that tether with your life.

SkyJump

Daily 10am–6pm • $225; students $195, BBH $205 • ☎ 0800 759 586, ⓦ skyjump.co.nz

The **SkyJump** is a close relation of bungy jumping. You plummet 192m in a kind of ten-second arrested freefall at 80km/hr, with a cable attached to your back. You approach the ground frighteningly fast, but miraculously touch gently down onto the target platform.

Auckland Art Gallery

Corner of Kitchener and Wellesley sts • Daily 10am–5pm; free tours 11.30am & 1.30pm • Free • ☎ 09 379 1349, ⓦ aucklandartgallery.com

A recent major expansion of the **Auckland Art Gallery** has garnered a slew of international architectural awards and made the country's best art gallery a whole lot better. The elaborate old mock-chateau galleries have been elegantly integrated with the superb new glass-cube atrium supported by kauri-wood columns that fan out to form an organic, forest-like canopy. The gallery feels open to the street and integrated with Albert Park behind, allowing everyone to see the atrium's keynote sculpture, which changes annually. Park and atrium can both be seen from the excellent, smart but relaxed **café**.

There is a significant international collection, but the emphasis is on the world's **finest collection of New Zealand art**.

Europeans depicting Maori

Maori life romanticized through European explorers' eyes is best seen in a couple of contrasting but equally misleading views: Kennett Watkins' 1912 *The Legend of the*

Voyage to New Zealand, with its plump, happy natives on a still lagoon; and Charles Goldie's 1898 *The Arrival of the Maoris in New Zealand*, modelled on Géricault's *Raft of the Medusa* and showing starving, frightened voyagers battling tempestuous seas.

Much of the early collection is devoted to works by artists who remain highly respected by Maori for their accurate portrayal of their ancestors. **Gottfried Lindauer** emigrated to New Zealand in 1873 and spent his later years painting lifelike, almost documentary, portraits of *rangatira* (chiefs) and high-born Maori men and women, in the mistaken belief that the Maori people were about to become extinct. In the early part of the twentieth century, **Charles F. Goldie** became New Zealand's resident "old master" and earned international recognition for his more emotional portraits of elderly Maori regally showing off their traditional tattoos, or *moko*, though they were in fact often painted from photographs (sometimes after the subject's death).

New Zealand art comes of age

It took half a century for European artists to grasp how to paint the harsh Kiwi light, an evolutionary process that continued into the 1960s and 1970s, when many works betrayed an almost cartoon-like quality, with heavily delineated spaces daubed in shocking colours.

Look out for oils by **Rita Angus**, renowned for her landscapes of Canterbury and Otago in the 1940s; **Colin McCahon**, whose fascination with the power and beauty of New Zealand landscape informs much late twentieth-century Kiwi art; and **Gordon Walters**, who drew inspiration from Maori iconography, controversially appropriating vibrant, graphic representations of traditional Maori symbols.

More recent acquisitions are strong on art by Maori artists. You'll usually find some of the excellent contemporary work by painter **Shane Cotton**, dark pieces by **Ralph Hotere**, and sculptures by **Michael Parekowhai**, whose bull-on-a-grand-piano entry for the 2011 Venice Biennale turned more than a few heads.

Albert Park

East of Queen Street, the formal Victorian-style gardens of **Albert Park** were originally the site of a Maori *pa* before becoming Albert Barracks in the 1840s and 50s. Its oaks and Morton Bay figs are now thronged with sunbathing students and office workers, mostly unaware they're sitting atop a labyrinth of World War II air-raid shelters.

Karangahape Road

The southern end of Queen Street climbs to vibrant and grungy **Karangahape Road**, universally known as **K' Road**. Originally home to prosperous nineteenth-century merchants, it became the heart of Auckland's Polynesian community in the 1970s, and was subsequently notorious for its massage parlours, strip joints and gay cruising clubs. For thirty years K' Road has been slated for a mainstream shopping renaissance, and while most of the strip joints and sex shops are gone, the atmosphere remains determinedly niche. In the evening, particularly at weekends, K' Road becomes an entertaining kaleidoscope of preening transvestites, boozed-up office workers, gay couples, spaced-out street people and the upwardly mobile in from the suburbs. Fun, if a little edgy.

Along K' Road

There are few specific sights, but groovy cafés, bars and vinyl music shops rub shoulders with colourful Indian- and Chinese-run stores along the road, and a handful of intriguing boutiques, particularly The Keep, at no. 504, and Hailwood, at no. 516. While you're in the area, take a look in the contemporary Starkwhite gallery at no. 510.

Architecture buffs won't miss the stunning **Ironbank** at no. 150, an eight-storey office block that looks like five stacks of rusty steel boxes. Opposite, the 1920s

1

GUIDED AND SELF-GUIDED WALKS IN AUCKLAND

The most ambitious **walking** normally attempted by visitors to Auckland is a stroll through The Domain or a short hike up to one of the volcano-top viewpoints. More ambitious hikers can head to Rangitoto Island (see p.119) or pick off sections of the **Hillary Trail** (see p.111) out west in the hills of the Waitakere Ranges. Most of the West Coast tours (see p.110) also include some gentle walking.

SELF-GUIDED WALKS

Coast to Coast Walkway (16km one way; 4hr) The best of the city's sights are threaded together on this fine walk which straddles the isthmus. A route map can be downloaded free from ⓦ aucklandcouncil.govt.nz and the route is marked on the council's free and widely available *Explore Central Auckland* map. Either stop after Maungakiekie (12km; 3hr) and get the #304, #305 or #312 bus back to the city from Manukau Road or do the full walk and catch the train back from Onehunga.

North Shore Coastal Walk (23km one way) Free leaflet from visitor centres. The Devonport ferry wharf marks the southern end of the North Shore Coastal Walk (part of the tip-to-toe Te Araroa; see box, p.48) which follows the waterfront past the Navy Museum, close to Maungauika then up the coast past several pretty beaches with views of Rangitoto. If you've come over by ferry, consider following the walk as far as Takapuna (10km; 2–3hr) then getting the bus back to the city from there. Best either side of low tide when you can stick to the water's edge.

GUIDED WALKS

Auckland Walks ☎ 0800 300 100, ⓦ aucklandwalks.co.nz. Learn more about the city centre on these informative guided walks (daily 10am; 2hr; $35; booking essential) leaving the Harbour Information Centre at the Ferry Building, 99 Quay St. **Tamaki Hikoi** ☎ 0800 282 552, ⓦ tamakihikoi .co.nz. Maori-led walks giving a Ngati Whatua perspective on Tamaki Makaurau. Choose from a tour of Pukekawa (Auckland Domain; 1hr 30min; $40), an interpretation of the Maori galleries at the Auckland

Museum complete with the cultural performance (3hr; $95), or a visit to Takaparawhau (Bastion Point; 1hr; $40). All come with lots of stories and give a completely different perspective on Auckland and colonization. **TIME Unlimited** ☎ 0800 868 463, ⓦ newzealand tours.travel. Maori-led city full-day tour ($265) explaining the significance to Maori of locations around the city. Their "Extra" package ($295) includes a guided tour through the Maori galleries at the Auckland Museum plus entry to the Maori Cultural Performance.

St Kevin's Arcade is packed with vintage clothing stores, chic brac-a-brac and breakthrough clothing designers. To the east, the **Symonds Street Cemetery** houses the somewhat neglected grave of New Zealand's first governor, William Hobson, tucked away almost under the vast concrete span of Grafton Bridge.

The Domain

The Domain is the city's finest park, draped over the low profile of an extinct volcano known as Pukekawa or "hill of bitter memories" (a reference to the bloodshed of ancient inter-tribal fighting) and furnished with mid-nineteenth-century accoutrements: a band rotunda, phoenix palms, formal flowerbeds and spacious lawns. In summer, the rugby pitches metamorphose into cricket ovals, and stages are erected in the crater's shallow amphitheatre for outdoor musical extravaganzas.

Auckland Museum

Auckland Domain • Daily 10am–5pm • $25, free to Auckland residents; Maori cultural performance daily 11am, noon & 1.30pm plus Nov–March 2.30pm, additional $20 • ☎ 09 309 0443, ⓦ aucklandmuseum.com • The museum is on the route of the Coast to Coast Walkway and city tour buses; the Inner Link bus stops on Parnell Rd, five minutes' walk away

The imposing Greco-Roman-style **Auckland Museum** sits at the highest point of the Auckland Domain, and contains the world's finest collections of Maori and Pacific art and craft. Traditional in its approach yet contemporary in its execution, the museum was built as a World War I memorial in 1929 and has been progressively expanded, most recently with the **Auckland Atrium** entrance, a former courtyard capped with a copper dome and slung with a kind of upturned beehive of slatted Fijian kauri.

Several times a day a conch-blast that echoes through the building heralds the thirty-minute **Maori Cultural Performance** of frightening eye-rolling challenges, gentle songs and a downright scary *haka*.

Maori Court

As traditional Maori villages started to disappear towards the end of the nineteenth century, some of the best examples of carved panels, meeting houses and food stores were rescued and relocated here. The large and wonderfully carved **Hotunui** meeting house was built in 1878, late enough to have a corrugated-iron rather than rush roof. The craftsmanship is superb; the house's exterior bristles with grotesque faces, lolling tongues and glistening paua-shell eyes, while the interior is lined with wonderful geometric *tukutuku* panels. Outside is the intricately carved prow and stern-piece of **Te Toki a Tapiri**, a 25m-long *waka taua* (war canoe) designed to seat a hundred warriors, the only surviving specimen from the pre-European era.

The transition from purely Polynesian motifs to an identifiably Maori style is exemplified by the fourteenth- or fifteenth-century **Kaitaia Carving**, a 2.5m-wide totara carving thought to have been designed for a ceremonial gateway, guarded by the central goblin-like figure with sweeping arms that stretch out to become lizard forms: Polynesian in style but Maori in concept.

Pacific Masterpieces

Exquisite Polynesian, Melanesian and Micronesian works to look out for include the shell-inlaid ceremonial food bowl from the Solomon Islands, ritual clubs and a wonderfully resonant slit-drum from Vanuatu. The textiles are fabulous too, with designs far more varied than you'd expect considering the limited raw materials: the Hawaiian red feather cloak is especially fine.

Pacific Lifeways

Daily life of Maori and the wider Pacific peoples is covered in the Pacific Lifeways room, which is dominated by a simple yet majestic breadfruit-wood statue from the Caroline Islands depicting **Kave**, Polynesia's malevolent and highest-ranked female deity, whose menace is barely hinted at in this serene form.

Middle floor

The middle floor of the museum comprises the **natural history galleries**, an unusual combination of modern thematic displays and stuffed birds in cases. Displays such as the 3m-high giant moa and an 800kg ammonite shouldn't be missed, but there's also material on dinosaurs, volcanoes and a **Maori Natural History** display, which attempts to explain the unique Maori perspective unencumbered by Western scientific thinking. The middle floor is also where you'll find hands-on and "discovery" areas for kids.

Upper floor

Scars on the Heart occupies the entire upper floor and explores how New Zealanders' involvement in war has helped shape national identity. The New Zealand Wars of the 1860s are interpreted from both Maori and Pakeha perspectives and World War I gets extensive coverage, particularly the Gallipoli campaign in Turkey, when botched leadership led to a massacre of ANZAC – Australian and New Zealand Army Corps – troops in the trenches. Powerful visuals and rousing martial music accompany newsreel footage of the Pacific campaigns of World War II and Vietnam, with personal accounts of the troops' experiences and the responses of those back home.

1

The Wintergardens and the Fernz Fernery
Auckland Domain • Nov–March Mon–Sat 9am–5.30pm, Sun 9am–7.30pm; April–Oct daily 9am–4.30pm • Free

The Domain's volcanic spring was one of Auckland's original water sources and was used by the Auckland Acclimatization Society to grow European plants, thereby promoting the rapid Europeanization of the New Zealand countryside. The spirit of this enterprise lingers on in the lovely **Wintergardens**, a formal fishpond flanked by two barrel-roofed glasshouses – one temperate, the other heated to mimic tropical climes. Next door, a former scoria quarry has been transformed into the **Fernz Fernery**, a green dell with over a hundred types of fern in dry, intermediate and wet habitats.

The inner east: Parnell and Newmarket

The Auckland Domain separates the city from established, moneyed **Parnell**. Once the city's ecclesiastical heart, it was revived in the 1960s when eccentric dreamer **Les Harvey** saved the dilapidated villas from the developers' wrecking ball. Through to the 1980s Parnell was the only place in Auckland where you could shop on a Saturday (let alone a Sunday) and while its long-standing reputation for chic clothes shops and swanky restaurants has waned of late, the dealer art galleries remain.

Parnell Road leads south past the cathedral becoming Broadway, the main drag of **Newmarket**, lined with middle-of-the-road clothes shops. A few classier boutiques hide among the backstreets – Teed, Kent, Osborne and Nuffield.

St Mary's and the Holy Trinity Cathedral
Corner of Parnell Rd and St Stephens Ave • **St Mary's** Mon–Sat 10am–4pm, Sun 11am–4pm; **Holy Trinity Cathedral** Mon–Sat 10am–4pm, Sun 12.30pm–4pm • Free • ☏ 09 303 9500, ⓦ holy-trinity.org.nz

At the southern end of Parnell Road stands one of the world's largest wooden churches, **St Mary's**, built from native timbers in 1886 and almost 50m long. Inside, check out the series of photos taken on the dramatic day in 1982 when the church was rolled in one piece from its original site across Parnell Road to join its more modern kin.

The original Gothic chancel of the **Holy Trinity Cathedral** was started in 1959 then left half-finished until the early 1990s, when an incongruous, airy nave with a Swiss chalet-style roof was grafted on, supposedly in imitation of the older church alongside. Pop in to admire the stained-glass windows at the back symbolizing Maori and Pakeha contributions to society, and Maori artist Shane Cotton's panels along the side in unifying muted tones of red, brown and green. The massive cast-glass font is by internationally-renowned Kiwi artist Ann Robinson.

Kinder House
2 Ayr St, Parnell • Wed–Sun noon–3pm • Free • ☏ 09 379 4008, ⓦ kinder.org.nz

The Gothic flourishes of nearby St Mary's church show the influence of New Zealand's prominent ecclesiastical architect, Frederick Thatcher, who designed **Kinder House** for the headmaster of the new grammar school – a post filled by John Kinder, an accomplished watercolourist and documentary photographer. Built of rough-hewn volcanic rock from nearby Maungawhau, the house contains some interesting photos and reproductions of Kinder's paintings of nineteenth-century New Zealand.

Ewelme Cottage
14 Ayr St, Parnell • Sun 10.30am–4.30pm • $8.50 • ☏ 09 524 5729, ⓦ historicplaces.org.nz

For a glimpse of pioneer life in New Zealand, visit **Ewelme Cottage**, built in 1864 for the wonderfully named clergyman Vicesimus Lush, who lived further afield but built in town so that he could get his kids into a good school – some things never change. The appeal of the place lies not so much in the large kauri cottage itself but in its furniture and possessions, left just as they were when Lush's descendants finally moved out in

1968, the family heirlooms betraying a desire to replicate the home comforts of their native Oxfordshire.

Highwic

40 Gillies Ave, Newmarket • Wed–Sun 10.30am–4.30pm • $10 • ☎ 09 524 5729, ⊛ historicplaces.org.nz

The Gothic timber mansion of **Highwic** was built as a "city" property by a wealthy rural auctioneer and landowner in 1862. Its vertical battening and gingerbread barge-boards make it quite unlike most New Zealand architecture of the time. Though hardly *Downton Abbey*, the estate, complete with outbuildings and servants' quarters, gives a fair indication of the contrasting lives of the time.

Eden Garden

24 Omana Ave, Newmarket • Daily: Sept–April 9am–4.30pm; May–Aug 9am–4pm • $8 • ☎ 09 638 8395, ⊛ edengarden.co.nz

Occupying a small former quarry hewn into the eastern flank of Maungawhau, **Eden Garden** is a remarkably manageable place with year-round interest in the form of ferns, tulips, roses, proteas, a small waterfall and Australasia's largest and widest collection of camellias, in bloom from April to October. Everywhere you look there are peaceful dells where you can sit awhile and listen to the birdlife, sustained by visits to their very good *Bloom Café*.

The waterfront: along Tamaki Drive

Tamaki Drive twists past 8km of waterfront immediately east of the city centre past Auckland's most popular city beaches – **Mission Bay**, **Kohimarama** and **St Heliers** – the undersea world of **Kelly Tarlton's** and a couple of headland viewpoints. During the summer, the waterfront is the favoured hangout of joggers and cyclists.

Kelly Tarlton's Sea Life Aquarium

23 Tamaki Drive, Okahu Bay, 6km east of the city • Daily 9.30am–5pm • $36 valid all day; get discounts on all tickets by booking online • Shark dive $165 including Kelly Tarlton's entry for certified diver, $230 for non-certified; Shark Cage snorkel $95 including entry • ☎ 0800 805 050, ⊛ kellytarltons .co.nz • Explorer Bus and city buses #710, #750 and #769 from Tyler St in Britomart stop outside; Tarlton's free shuttle runs on the hour (9.30am–3.30pm) from opposite the Ferry Building, 172 Quay St

Kelly Tarlton's Sea Life Aquarium was opened in 1985 by Kiwi diver, treasure hunter and salvage expert

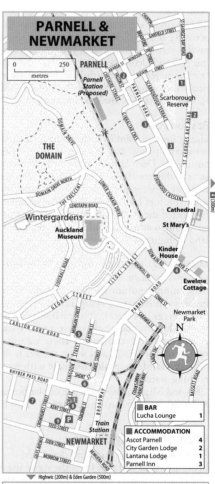

PARNELL & NEWMARKET

● RESTAURANTS, CAFÉS & BARS			
Asian Food Hall	9	Little & Friday	7
Basque Kitchen Bar	6	Mojo	5
Best Ugly Bagels	8	Non Solo Pizza	3
Domain & Ayr	4	Oh Calcutta!	2
La Cigale French Market	1		

■ BAR	
Lucha Lounge	1

■ ACCOMMODATION	
Ascot Parnell	4
City Garden Lodge	2
Lantana Lodge	1
Parnell Inn	3

1

Kelly Tarlton in some huge converted sewage tanks which, from 1910 until 1961, flushed the city's effluent into the Waitemata Harbour on the outgoing tides. Its pioneering walk-through acrylic tunnels have since become commonplace, but it is still a pleasure to stand on the moving walkway and glide through two tanks: one dominated by flowing kelp beds, colourful reef fish and twisting eels; the other with smallish sharks, all appearing alarmingly close in the crystal-clear water. If you want to get in among them, join one of the dives. Tanks in the **Stingray Bay** section feature specimens with a 2m wingspan. New Zealand is also home to six penguin species, but the gentoo and king penguins seen here reside much further south. You get great close-up views of their icy home (inside one of the old sewage tanks) both topside and underwater.

Scott Base

The Antarctic connection is further explored in the **Scott Base section**, which covers activities at New Zealand's Antarctic foothold and the Antarctic Heritage Trust which preserves historic huts. Here you walk through a convincing replica of the capacious hut Robert Falcon Scott and his team used on their ill-starred 1911–12 attempt to be the first to reach the South Pole. It contains expedition artefacts, including a printing press from which the *South Polar Times* rolled every few months, and contemporary footage and tales of their exploits add to the haunting atmosphere.

Bastion Point

Grassy **Bastion Point** (Takaparawhau) has great views of the Hauraki Gulf and makes a wonderful picnic spot. It's topped by the **M.J. Savage Memorial Park**, the nation's austere Art Deco homage to its first Labour prime minister, who ushered in the welfare state in the late 1930s. More recently, Bastion Point was the site of a seventeen-month standoff between police and its traditional owners, the Ngati Whatua, over the subdivision of land for housing. The occupiers were removed in 1977, but the stand galvanized the land-rights movement, and paved the way for a significant change in government attitude. Within a decade, the Waitangi Tribunal recommended that the land be returned.

Mission Bay, Kohimarama and St Heliers

Tamaki Drive, 7km east of the city

Swimming conditions are best at half-tide and above at three pohutukawa-backed beach suburbs strung along Tamaki Drive. Just past the kayak and bike rental place, Fergs (see p.92), you reach **Mission Bay**, the closest of the truly worthwhile city **beaches**, where a grassy waterside reserve is backed by a lively row of cafés and restaurants. There are usually kayak and stand-up paddleboard rentals on the beach, and when the sea is shallow, kids make good use of the Sicilian marble **fountain** complete with its three bronze ornamental sea monsters gushing water.

Beyond Mission Bay there are similar but usually quieter café-backed beaches at **Kohimarama** (1km on) and **St Heliers** (1km beyond that).

West of the city centre

The suburbs of west Auckland developed later than their eastern counterparts, mainly because of their distance from the sea in the days when almost all travel was by ferry. The exceptions were the inner suburbs of **Ponsonby** and **Herne Bay**.

Sights are scarce until you get out to **Western Springs**, which, in the late nineteenth century, was the major water source for the burgeoning city of Auckland. The area is now home to a pleasant park flanked by the classy **Auckland Zoo** and the transport and technology museum known as **MOTAT**.

Ponsonby

Ponsonby Road has long been a byword for designer clothing, cafés and see-and-be-seen lunching for long-term residents and the overspill from the adjacent suburbs – the media luvvies stronghold of **Grey Lynn**, and **Herne Bay**, which with average property prices approaching $2 million is the priciest in the country. It's all a far cry from the 1960s when large numbers of immigrant Pacific Islanders made the area their home, followed a decade later by an influx of bohemians and artists.

Ponsonby Road itself is not especially beautiful, but the people sure are: musicians, media folk and the well-scrubbed Audi set congregate to lunch, schmooze and be seen in the latest fashionable haunt here. If it all sounds a bit too swanky, don't be deterred. Ponsonby retains a lively vibe with loads of places to eat that are no more expensive than many other areas of the city. The best names in Kiwi fashion are also here (see p.108).

MOTAT

805 Great North Rd, Western Springs, 5km southwest of the city centre • Daily 10am–5pm • $16 • ☎ 0800 668 286, Ⓦ motat.org.nz • Numerous buses including #030 from Britomart

While slightly run-down, the **Museum of Transport and Technology** (MOTAT) still

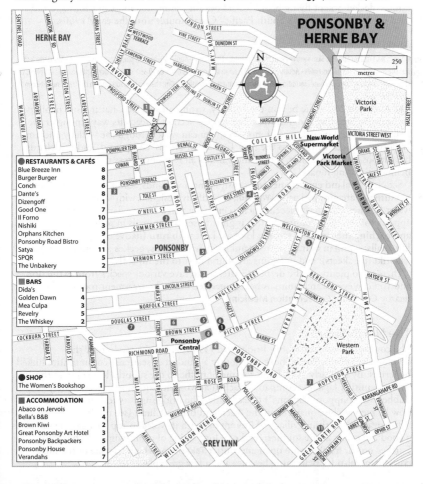

1

manages to showcase New Zealand's vehicular and industrial past while keeping the kids entertained. The jumble of sheds and halls is centred on the restored Western Springs' **pumphouse** where the massive 1877 beam engine mostly sits grandly immobile, unless they find someone to fire up the boiler.

Appropriately for an agricultural nation there's an impressive array of tractors, including one Edmund Hillary took to the South Pole in 1958, the first overland party there since Scott and Amundsen 46 years earlier. Elsewhere there's a science-oriented, hands-on section, a Victorian village built around the original pumphouse engineer's cottage, and a shed full of trams that plied the city's streets from 1902–56.

Aviation Display Hall

One **tram** (every 15–30min; included in admission price) takes you 1km to MOTAT's impressive **Aviation Display Hall**, a hangar eco-designed with vast laminated wood beams. Star attractions are one of the few surviving World War II Lancaster bombers, early crop-dusting planes and fragile-looking things that took early tourists to the Fox and Franz Josef glaciers in the days before decent roads. Restoration continues on a double-decker Solent flying boat, decked out for dining in a more gracious age and used on Air New Zealand's South Pacific "Coral Route" until the early 1960s.

Auckland Zoo

Motions Rd, Western Springs, 5km southwest of the city centre • Daily: Sept–April 9.30am–5.30pm; May–Aug 9.30am–5pm; check the website for Animal Encounters times • Adults $28, kids $12; Animal Encounters free • ☎ 09 360 3805, Ⓦ aucklandzoo.co.nz • Explorer bus stops here and numerous city buses including #030 from Britomart pass within 200m; there's also a zoo stop on the tramline between the two MOTAT sites

The **Auckland Zoo** is the best in the country, strong on spacious, naturalistic habitats and captive breeding programmes. The Tropics section threads its way among artificial islands inhabited by colonies of monkeys, you can walk through the wallaby and emu enclosure straight through to the new Tasmanian Devils' compound, and Pridelands has hippos, rhinos, giraffes, zebras and gazelles all roaming across mock savannah behind enclosing moats.

Six New Zealand environments – coast, islands, wetlands, forest, high country and nocturnal – are grouped as **Te Wao Nui**, beautifully designed with loads of sculptures, water features and clever deceits such as entering a free-flight aviary through what appears to be a high-country hut. It is great to see the animals in something approaching their natural setting: kiwi are kept with ruru (native owls) and nocturnal flax snails; reptilian tuatara share island space with skinks, geckos and luminous green kakariki (parakeets); and penguins are found next to the fur seals.

There's also plenty on the desperate attempt to save various species from extinction, and you can even watch animals being operated on in the treatment room at the nearby **Centre for Conservation Medicine**.

The North Shore

The completion of the harbour bridge in 1959 provided the catalyst for the development of the **North Shore**, previously a handful of scattered communities linked by ferries. By the early 1970s, the volume of traffic to the suburbs log-jammed the bridge – until a Japanese company attached a two-lane extension (affectionately dubbed "the Nippon Clip-ons") to each side. The bridge and its additional lanes can now be seen at close quarters on the Auckland Bridge Climb (see p.92).

The peaceful maritime village of **Devonport** with its volcano-top harbour views makes a good target, set at the southern end of a long string of calm swimming **beaches**. Further north, try the more open and busier **Takapuna**, which has one of the most convenient all-tides swimming beaches and a few great places to eat.

Devonport

Devonport is one of Auckland's oldest suburbs, founded in 1840 and still linked to the city by a ten-minute ferry journey. The naval station was an early tenant, soon followed by wealthy merchants, who built fine kauri villas. The essence of Devonport's appeal is wandering the tree-fringed waterfront, up the volcanoes or along the **North Shore Coastal Walk** (see box, p.81) before grabbing fish and chips on Cheltenham Beach, then attending an aged cinema (see p.108).

Navy Museum

64 King Edward Parade, Torpedo Bay • Daily 10am–5pm; free guided tours Sat & Sun 10.30am & 1.30pm • Free • ☎ 09 445 5186, ⓦ navymuseum.mil.nz

A pleasant 1km waterfront stroll from central Devonport, this former submarine mining station has the expected guns, medals and naval uniforms, supplemented with coverage of New Zealand's military involvement in the Battle of the River Plate in World War II to the HMNZS *Otago*'s visit to Mururoa Atoll in 1973 to protest against French nuclear testing. Try your hand at sending Morse code and don't miss the World War II Japanese map of New Zealand with a detail of Auckland; kids can try on uniforms. The on-site *Torpedo Bay Café* has great views across the harbour to the city.

North Head Historic Reserve

Daily 6am–10pm; vehicles 6am–8pm • Free

The grassy volcanic plug of **Maungauika** (North Head) guards the harbour entrance and makes a wonderful vantage point during yachting events or on any sunny afternoon. A strategic site for pre-colonial Maori, it was later co-opted to form part of the young nation's coastal defences. In the wake of the "Russian Scares" of 1884–86, which were precipitated by the opening of the port of Vladivostok, North Head became Fort Cautley. It is now operated by DOC and comes riddled with pillboxes, concrete tunnels linking gun emplacements and even a restored eight-inch "disappearing gun", which recoiled underground for easy reloading. Learn their significance from two short movies screening in hilltop buildings then explore along three intriguing walking loops (15–30min each).

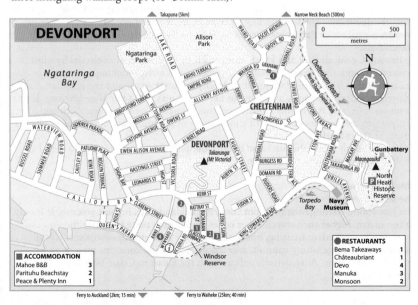

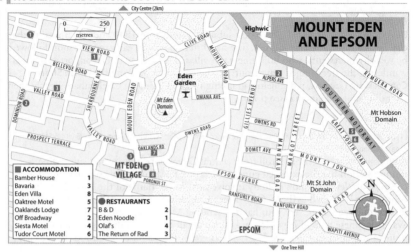

Takapuna
From Devonport catch bus #813

The best thing about **Takapuna**, 5km north of Devonport, is its broad sweep of golden sand with that rarity for Auckland beaches, good swimming even at low tide. There are views across to Rangitoto, waterside camping (see p.99) and some great places to eat (see p.105). The North Shore Coastal Walk (see p.81) runs here from Devonport.

South of the city centre

Immediately south of downtown Auckland, the city's most lofty volcano, **Maungawhau** (Mount Eden), offers superb views, and its near-identical twin, **Maungakiekie** (One Tree Hill), has some of the best surviving examples of the terracing undertaken by early Maori inhabitants. The surrounding Cornwall Park is one of the city's best, while the nearby art gallery at **Pah Homestead** complements the Auckland Art Gallery beautifully.

Beyond Cornwall Park and Pah Homestead is **South Auckland**, neglected by most visitors, though the airport at Mangere is where most arrive. Arching around the eastern end of Manukau Harbour, it is the city's poorest sector and the less-than-flatteringly-depicted gangland setting of Lee Tamahori's film *Once Were Warriors*. It isn't a no-go zone, and is certainly worth a look on Saturday morning when Auckland's Polynesian community (along with almost every other immigrant community) plies its wares at **Otara Market**.

Further south again, the **Auckland Botanic Gardens** are a relaxing place to spend an hour before continuing out of town.

Maungawhau
2km south of the city centre

At just 196m, Maungawhau (**Mount Eden**) is Auckland city's highest volcano. It is only a few metres higher then several other cones, and doesn't poke far above the surrounding suburban housing, but the summit car park affords extensive views all around. At the often-busy summit, take a walk around the cone rim for a more peaceful viewpoint. Alternatively, walk here on the Coast to Coast Walkway (see p.80).

ONE TREE HILL

Sir **John Logan Campbell** is buried at the summit where a single totara tree originally gave **One Tree Hill** its English name. Settlers cut it down in 1852, and Campbell planted several pines as a windbreak, a single specimen surviving until the millennium. Already ailing from a 1994 chainsaw attack by a Maori activist avenging the loss of the totara, the pine's fate was sealed by a similar attack in 1999 and the tree was removed the next year. Immediate demands for a replacement have been replaced by resignation that it will continue as "None Tree Hill" until Treaty of Waitangi grievances are settled with the local Ngati Whatua people.

One Tree Hill Domain

7km south of the city centre • Daily 7am–11pm • Free • Accessible off Manukau Rd, which can be reached on bus #305 from Stop 7055 outside the Civic Theatre

Auckland's most distinctive peak is **Maungakiekie** (One Tree Hill; 183m), topped by a 33m-tall granite obelisk – but no tree. The hilltop views are as good as those from Mount Eden and the surrounding **One Tree Hill Domain** makes this a more rewarding destination overall.

For a century, until just before the arrival of Europeans, the "mountain of the kiekie plant" was one of the largest *pa* sites in the country; an estimated 4000 people were drawn here by the proximity to abundant seafood from both harbours and the rich soils of the volcanic cone, which still bears the scars of extensive earthworks including the remains of dwellings and *kumara* pits. The site was abandoned and then bought by the Scottish medic and "father of Auckland", Sir John Logan Campbell, one of only two European residents when the city was granted capital status in 1840.

Cornwall Park

Off Green Lane West, 7km south of the city centre • Daily 7am–dusk • Free • ⊕ cornwallpark.co.nz

One Tree Hill Domain is almost entirely encircled by **Cornwall Park**, which Sir John Logan Campbell created from his One Tree Hill Estate and gifted to the people of New Zealand to commemorate the 1901 visit of Britain's Duke and Duchess of Cornwall. There are attractive formal areas, but large sections of the park are farmed, the grazing sheep and cattle making for an odd sight in the midst of a large modern city. Cornwall Park puts on its best display around Christmas, when avenues of pohutukawa trees erupt in a riot of red blossom.

Huia Lodge and Acacia Cottage

Green Lane Rd entrance • Huia Lodge daily 10am–4pm; Acacia Cottage daily 7am–dusk • Free • Huia Lodge ☎ 09 630 8485

Cornwall Park's amenities are clustered around **Huia Lodge**, built by Campbell as the park caretaker's cottage and now containing displays on the park and the man. It also contains a **visitor centre**, which has free leaflets outlining the archeological and volcanic sites of the hill.

Immediately opposite Huia Lodge is the pit-sawn kauri **Acacia Cottage**, Campbell's original home and the city's oldest surviving building, built in 1841 and re-sited from central Auckland in 1920. Inside, the four simple rooms are furnished as they might have been in the 1840s.

Pah Homestead and the Wallace Arts Centre

72 Hillsborough Rd, 9km south of the city centre • Tues–Fri 10am–3pm, Sat & Sun 10am–5pm • Free • ☎ 09 639 2010 • Bus #299 takes 30min from Queen St beside the Civic Theatre

One of the best reasons to stray south from the city centre is to visit **Pah Homestead**, an Italianate residence perched on a low hill overlooking the graceful, mature cedars and Moreton Bay fig trees of the surrounding **Monte Cecilia Park**. When completed in

1

1879, the house was the largest in Auckland and home to lavish parties. Despite spending time as a novitiate home and a boarding house, the wood panelling and elaborate ceiling bosses are original.

The Wallace Arts Centre

ⓦ tsbbankwallaceartscentre.org.nz

While fairly impressive, Pah Homestead wouldn't warrant a special trip if it wasn't for the contents: an array of pieces from the seven thousand-work art collection housed in the **Wallace Arts Centre**. In the mid-1960s, Kiwi agribusiness magnate James Wallace began collecting works by emerging New Zealand artists and has continued to buy their best stuff (and commission more) as they've risen to become some of the country's most eminent. The result is a wide-ranging collection particularly strong on artists such as Toss Woollaston, Philip Trusttum and Michael Parekowhai. What's on show is constantly changing and typically superb, especially in September and October when the winners of the annual Wallace Arts Awards are on show. The *Pah Café* spills out onto the veranda, overlooking the sculpture garden.

Otara Market

Otara Town Centre, 18km southeast of the city centre • Sat 6am–noon, but liveliest 8–11am • ⓦ otarafleamarket.co.nz • Take East Tamaki Rd (Exit 444) off the southern motorway or catch the Waka Pacific bus (#487 or #497) for the 50min journey from 55 Customs St East downtown

On Saturday morning, **Otara Market** sprawls across the car park of the Otara Town Centre. Billed as the largest Maori and Polynesian market in the world, it certainly sells Maori greenstone carvings and Maori sovereignty shirts (look for tees emblazoned with the words "*Tino Rangatiratanga*"), and Pasifika rhythms and reggae beats ringing out to the adjacent Community Hall, typically full of *kete* (woven baskets), tapa cloth and island-style floral print fabrics. But these days the diversity reflects the racial make-up of modern south Auckland with Sikhs flogging gold bracelets next to Korean-language DVD vendors and lots of Chinese selling truckloads of cheap fruit and veg. There's plenty of low-cost **eating** here too, from coffee and pastries to wieners, goat curry, pork buns, whitebait fritters and even a classic Maori boil-up of pork bones, watercress, pumpkin and "fry bread".

Auckland Botanic Gardens

102 Hill Rd, Manurewa, 24km southeast of the city centre • Daily: Oct–March 6am–8pm; April–Sept 7am–6pm • Café daily 8am–4pm • Free • ☎ 09 267 1457, ⓦ aucklandbotanicgardens.co.nz

Southbound drivers might want to spend an hour or two just off the motorway at the extensive **Auckland Botanic Gardens**, which only opened in 1982. What was once farmland has a long way to grow, but already there's a beautiful rock garden, a children's garden, a great section of African plants, instructive sections on threatened New Zealand native species and, at the far northern end, bushwalks through native bush that form part of the Te Araroa pathway. There are great picnic spots, or visit *Café Miko*.

ARRIVAL AND DEPARTURE   AUCKLAND

As New Zealand's major gateway city, Auckland receives the bulk of **international arrivals**, a few disembarking from cruise ships at the dock by the Ferry Building downtown, but the vast majority arriving by air.

BY PLANE

Auckland International Airport The airport (ⓦ aucklandairport.co.nz) is 20km south of the city centre in the suburb of Mangere. There is no train service, but buses, collective minibuses and taxis run into the city.

Destinations Bay of Islands (4–5 daily; 45min); Blenheim (4 daily; 1hr 25min); Christchurch (20 daily; 1hr 20min); Dunedin (3 daily; 1hr 50min); Gisborne (4 daily; 1hr); Great Barrier Island (6–8 daily; 40min); Napier/Hastings (6–8 daily; 1hr); Nelson (9 daily; 1hr 25min); New Plymouth (5 daily;

FROM TOP PIHA BEACH AND LION ROCK (P.113); CORNWALL PARK, ONE TREE HILL, AUCKLAND (P.89) >

1

AUCKLAND HARBOUR ACTIVITIES

Auckland is so water-focused that it would be a shame not to get out on the harbour at some point, either on a ferry to one of the outlying islands (see p.119), a **cruise**, a **dolphin and whale safari** or a **sea-kayaking** trip. You can also do a bridge climb and a bungy jump off the Harbour Bridge. For more activities nearby, check out the boxes on p.110 and p.113.

CRUISES AND SAILING

America's Cup Sailing ☎0800 397 567, ⊛exploregroup.co.nz. Crew on old-style monohull America's Cup racing yachts *NZL41* (raced by Japan in the 1995 cup) and *NZL68* (used as a trial boat by New Zealand in 2007) from Viaduct Harbour. There's a chance to grind the winches or take the helm as you get a real sense of power and speed. $160 for a two-hour sail or $195 as part of a team in a three-hour match race between the two boats.

Auckland Harbour Cruise ☎09 367 9111, ⊛fullers.co.nz. Fullers offer a two-hour cruise (daily 10.30am & 1.30pm; $40) that leaves the Ferry Building, briefly visiting the Harbour Bridge and Rangitoto Island. You can stay on Rangitoto and return on a later cruise, and the ticket gives you a free return ferry ride to Devonport.

Explore Sailing ☎0800 397 567, ⊛exploregroup.co.nz. Leisurely sailing trips (year-round at 3.15pm plus Nov–March 1pm; 1hr 30min; $75), plus a dinner cruise (6pm; 2hr 30min; $120). Also offers a great Waiheke Island deal with a return ferry trip and 3hr sailing while there (Dec–March daily 9am; 3hr; $85).

DOLPHIN AND WHALE WATCHING

Whale & Dolphin Safari Viaduct Harbour ☎0508 DOLPHINS, ⊛awads.co.nz. There are stacks of common and bottlenose dolphins out in the Hauraki Gulf year-round, often forming huge pods in winter and spring when Bryde's whale and orca sightings increase. Daily educational and entertaining trips (4hr30min; $160) head out on a fast, 20m catamaran which also undertakes marine mammal research. Dolphins (which are seen on ninety percent of trips) are often located by the cluster of gannets spectacularly dive-bombing schools of fish. If you don't see any marine mammals you can go again, free.

KAYAKING AND KAYAK FISHING

Auckland Sea Kayaks ☎0800 999 089, ⊛aucklandseakayaks.co.nz. Great guided kayak tours including an easy paddle over to Motukorea (Browns) Island (4hr; $135), a longer trip to Rangitoto with a summit hike (7hr; $175), a Rangitoto evening/night trip with sunset from the summit and excellent food along the way (7hr; $185), and a range of overnight trips including camping on Motuihe Island, where there are little spotted kiwi ($365).

Fergs Kayaks 12 Tamaki Drive, Okahu Bay ☎09 529 2230, ⊛fergskayaks.co.nz. Offers guided trips 7km across the Waitemata Harbour to Rangitoto Island, hiking to the summit, then paddling back (departures 9.30am plus Mon–Fri 5.30pm, Sat & Sun 4pm; 6hr; $140). The later departure gives you a chance to paddle by moon or torchlight. Alternatively, opt for their 3km paddle to Devonport (9.30am; 3hr; $100), usually with a hike up North Head. Single sea kayaks ($25/hr, $60/half-day), doubles ($50/hr, $120/half-day), or slightly cheaper sit-on-tops are also available to rent; trips to Rangitoto and Devonport are not generally allowed for rentals.

AUCKLAND BRIDGE CLIMB AND BUNGY

Auckland Bridge Climb ☎0800 286 4958, ⊛aucklandbridgeclimb.co.nz. Spend 90min (3 climbs daily; $125) strolling along steel walkways while harnessed to a cable as guides relate detail on the bridge's fulcrums, pivots and cantilevers, and guide you to the city views some 65m above the Waitemata Harbour. Free transport from Voyager maritime museum. Bridge Climb and Bungy combo $230.

Auckland Bridge Bungy ☎0800 286 4958, ⊛bungy.co.nz. The place to go for an adrenalin rush, a 40m leap and a water touch (5 times daily; $160). There's free transport from the Voyager maritime museum on the waterfront and you get the free bragging T-shirt.

50min); Palmerston North (6 daily; 1hr 10min); Queenstown (6 daily; 1hr 50min); Rotorua (3–4 daily; 40min); Taupo (2–3 daily; 45min); Tauranga (4–5 daily; 35min); Wanganui (3–4 daily; 1hr); Wellington (5+ daily; 1hr); Whakatane (2–3 daily; 45min); Whangarei (3–4 daily; 35min).

AIRPORT INFORMATION
i-SITE There's a well-stocked international terminal office (daily 5.30am–1.30am; ☎09 275 6467) with a free accommodation booking service, courtesy hotel-booking phones and free showers.

Services There are several ATMs at both terminals, as well as foreign exchange offices at the international terminal that are open whenever flights arrive.

AIRPORT TRANSPORT

Between terminals The international terminal is connected to the domestic terminal by a free shuttle bus (5am–10.30pm; every 15min), or you can walk in around ten minutes – follow the blue and white lines.

Taxis Expensive taxis wait outside both terminals. Expect to pay $80 into the central city, Ponsonby or Parnell; over $100 to Northcote or Devonport.

Bus The Airbus Express (24/7 every 10–30min; $16 one way, $28 return; ⓦ airbus.co.nz) is good value for solo travellers. It calls at both airport terminals then alternates between two fixed routes (along Mt Eden Rd or Dominion Rd) into the city (roughly 45min). The cheapest way into town is to take the #380 Airporter bus to Papatoetoe train station (every 30–40min; 30min; $4 from driver) then catch the train to central Auckland (frequent; 40min; $6).

Collective minibus Most travellers catch one of the shared, door-to-door minibuses that wait outside the terminals. Ask at the first in line and if they're not going to the part of town where you're staying they'll point you to one that is: you'll seldom have to wait more than 15min. Fares are $35 to downtown and $60 to Devonport; groups travelling to the same location get a significant reduction, adding only $8–11 per additional person.

To the airport For pick-up on departure call Super Shuttle (ⓣ 0800 748 885) or phone a taxi (see p.95).

BY TRAIN

Northern Explorer ⓣ 0800 872 467, ⓦ kiwirailscenic .co.nz. The train from Wellington, National Park and Hamilton arrives at the Britomart Transport Centre, at the harbour end of Queen St on Tues, Fri and Sun evenings. Southbound services run on Mon, Thurs and Sat.

Destinations Hamilton (3 weekly; 2hr 30min); National Park (3 weekly; 5hr 30min); Ohakune (3 weekly; 6hr); Otorohanga (3 weekly; 3hr); Palmerston North (3 weekly; 8hr 30min); Wellington (3 weekly; 11hr 30min).

BY BUS

InterCity/Newmans, Great Sights and Northliner long-distance bus services arrive at the Sky City Coach Terminal. Other operators stop outside 172 Quay St, opposite the Downtown Ferry Terminal.

Bus companies Go Kiwi (ⓣ 07 866 0336, ⓦ go-kiwi.co.nz), daily to the Coromandel Peninsula with en route pick-ups at Auckland Airport, ideal if you want to head straight to Whitianga; InterCity/Newmans, Northliner, Great Sights (ⓣ 09 583 5780, ⓦ intercity.co.nz) and NakedBus (ⓣ 0900 62 533, ⓦ nakedbus.com) all offer national coverage.

Destinations Gisborne (1 daily; 9hr 15min); Hamilton (25 daily; 2hr); Hastings (1 daily; 7hr 30min); Kerikeri (5–6 daily; 4hr 30min); Napier (1 daily; 7hr); National Park (1 daily; 6hr); New Plymouth (3 daily; 6hr–6hr 30min); Ohakune (1 daily; 6hr 30min); Paihia (7–8 daily; 4hr); Palmerston North (8 daily; 9–10hr); Rotorua (11 daily; 4hr); Taihape (6 daily; 7hr); Taupo (7 daily; 5hr); Tauranga (7 daily; 3hr 20min–5hr); Thames (4 daily; 1hr 45min); Waipu (5–6 daily; 2hr 15min); Waitomo Caves (1 daily; 3hr 30min); Warkworth (5–6 daily; 1hr); Wellington (7 daily; 11–12hr); Whangarei (6–7 daily; 2hr 50min); Whitianga (1 daily; 3hr).

BY CAR

Car rental For information on car rental, see p.94.

Departing Northbound drivers can take either SH1 directly over the Harbour Bridge, or go west around the head of the Waitemata Harbour past the wineries and West Coast beaches to meet SH1 at Wellsford. Southbound, either head straight down SH1 to Hamilton, branch east to the Coromandel Peninsula, or take the slow road down the Seabird Coast.

BY BIKE

Northbound The Harbour Bridge is off limits so catch the Devonport Ferry or take the western route, possibly riding a suburban train as far as Waitakere (bike goes free; travel outside peak hours).

Southbound Cyclists heading south are better off following the Seabird Coast, avoiding the Southern Motorway, the main route south out of the city.

AUCKLAND TRANSPORT INFORMATION AND TICKETS

For integrated information on Auckland's buses, trains and ferries consult **AT** (ⓣ 09 355 3553, ⓦ at.govt.nz), which includes timetables and a journey planner. Alternatively, pick up the five free AT **public transport maps** from Britomart: the *Central Suburbs* region is the most useful.

You can pay cash for bus, train and ferry journeys, but it is much more convenient (and may end up cheaper) obtaining a stored-value tag-on-tag-off **AT Hop card** ($5 nonrefundable) from Britomart, train stations and Fullers ferry offices. Use it for individual journeys (at 10–15percent off the cash fare), or use a top-up machine to buy an **AT Hop day-pass** ($16 for 24hr from your first tag-on) which covers all trains and buses (including Waiheke Island buses) plus Devonport ferries, but not ferries to Rangitoto or Waiheke.

1

GETTING AROUND

You can get to many of the most interesting parts of Auckland on foot, notably along the Coast to Coast Walkway. Auckland's poor but improving public transport system is centred on the Britomart Transport Centre at the harbour end of Queen St – suburban trains pull in here while buses have various stops nearby. Out on the harbour, ferries connect the city to the inner suburb of Devonport and the islands. Taxis are best contacted by phone (see opposite). Parking isn't a major headache, but drivers aren't courteous and you may be better off renting a car just before you leave the city.

BY TRAIN

Suburban trains The recent introduction of modern electric trains has drastically improved Auckland's rail service but sadly they mostly call at places of little interest to tourists. The main exception is the route from the downtown Britomart Transport Centre to Newmarket (every 10–20min; 10min). The planned new Parnell station probably won't be built until 2017 or later. Tickets ($2) can be bought at Britomart or on platforms.

BY BUS

Departures Most buses don't depart from the Britomart Transport Centre (see above) but from any of a couple of dozen stops along city streets within a 10min walk of there. It is confusing, so ask at Britomart or get the exact stop location from ⓦ at.govt.nz. The Link buses listed below are the most useful services.

Fares For buses other than the Link, fares are roughly: $2 to Parnell, Newmarket, Mount Eden, Ponsonby and Kingsland; $4 to MOTAT, the Zoo and Mission Bay; and $5 to St Heliers.

LINK SERVICES

City Link (Mon–Sat 6.30am–11.30pm every 7–8min; Sun 7am–11pm every 20min; 50¢; free to AT Hop card users). The red buses of this central city service travel the length of Queen St from K'Rd to Britomart Transport Centre then west to Wynyard Quarter.

Inner Link (Mon–Fri 6.30am–11pm, Sat & Sun 7am–11pm; every 10–15min; $1.90). The single most useful route, with green buses continuously looping through the city, Parnell, Auckland Museum, Newmarket, K'Rd and Ponsonby; buy tickets on the bus.

Outer Link (Mon–Sat 6.30am–11pm, Sun 7am–11pm; every 15min; $1.90–3.40). Orange buses making a larger loop than the Inner Link and visiting Mt Eden, MOTAT and Herne Bay. Connects with the Inner Link in Parnell, the Auckland Museum, Newmarket and in Ponsonby.

OTHER BUS SERVICES

NiteRider Journey planner at ⓦ at.govt.nz. A series of secure night buses designed to get you home after a night out (Sat & Sun 1–3.30am; $4.50).

Explorer Bus ☎ 0800 439 756, ⓦ explorerbus.co.nz. Get around the main sights on this commentated hop-on-hop-off bus with two intersecting circuits (Oct–March

every 30min 9am–4pm; April–Sept hourly 10am–4pm; 1-day pass $45, 2-day pass $75, pay cash to the driver).

BY FERRY

The Waitemata Harbour was once a seething mass of ferries bringing commuters in from the suburbs, and ferries remain a fast, pleasurable and scenic way to get around. The main destinations are the Hauraki Gulf islands and Devonport; Rangitoto-bound and several Waiheke-bound ferries also stop at Devonport.

FERRY OPERATORS

Fullers ☎ 09 367 9111, ⓦ fullers.co.nz. Auckland's principal ferry company runs ferries to Devonport (Mon–Thurs 6am–11.15pm, Fri & Sat 6am–1am, Sun 7.30am–10pm; $6 each way, bikes free), the cheapest cruise in town. It also operates ferries to Rangitoto and Waiheke islands.

360 Discovery ☎ 09 307 8005, ⓦ 360discovery.co.nz. Passenger ferry services to Tiritiri Matangi, Rotoroa Island and a regular service across the Hauraki Gulf to Coromandel Town ($57 one way): for nondrivers it's a pleasant alternative to taking the bus via Thames.

Explore ☎ 0800 397 567, ⓦ exploregroup.co.nz. Ferries to Waiheke and Motutapu islands.

Sealink ☎ 0800 732 546, ⓦ sealink.co.nz. Car and passenger ferries to Waiheke and Great Barrier islands. Destinations Coromandel (Oct–March 5–7 weekly; 2hr); Devonport (every 15–30min; 10min); Great Barrier (4–7 weekly; 2–5hr); Motutapu (1 daily in peak summer; 30min); Rangitoto (4–5 daily; 40min); Rotoroa Island (Oct–March 5–7 weekly; 1hr 15min); Tiritiri Matangi Island (5 weekly; 1hr 30min); Waiheke (every 30min; 35–45min).

BY CAR

With many sights accessible on foot or by public transport, a car isn't a huge advantage in the city centre, though you'll need one to explore the Kumeu wineries and surf beaches of the West Coast. If you've just flown in you may want to wait and rent a car when you're ready to leave the city.

Car rental The international and major national companies all have depots close to the airport and free shuttle buses to pick you up; smaller companies are mostly based in the city or inner suburbs. In the central city, you'll find several close together on Beach Rd. The main international and local operators are listed in Basics (see p.33).

Buying a car For general advice, consult Basics (see p.34), then peruse the notice boards in hostels, or visit ⓦ trademe. co.nz and ⓦ autotrader.co.nz. At Backpacker Car World, 19 East St (Mon–Fri 9.30am–5pm; ☎ 09 377 7761, ⓦ backpackercarworld.com), just off K' Rd, where backpackers buy and sell directly to each other, there are also insurance and roadside deals. Alternatively, head to the Auckland Carfair, Ellerslie Racecourse, Greenlane (every Sun 9am–noon; ☎ 09 529 2233, ⓦ carfair.co.nz), which is well organized, with qualified folk on hand to check roadworthiness.

Driving On first acquaintance, Auckland's urban freeways are unnerving, but driving around Auckland by car isn't especially taxing if you avoid the rush hours (7–9am & 4–6.30pm). Inner-city streets are metered, which means that parking is best done in the multistorey car parks dotted round the city; we've marked the cheapest for short-term stays on our map (see p.76). Some are not open 24hr, so check the latest exit time.

BY TAXI

Taxi ranks are scattered around the city including along Queen St, at Viaduct Harbour and along K' Rd. Alternatively, call Discount (☎ 09 529 1000) which is cheap, or sustainability-oriented Green Cabs (☎ 0508 447 336, ⓦ greencabs.co.nz) whose hybrids are only a little pricier. From the city centre to Ponsonby should be $12–14.

BY BIKE

Routes Auckland's hills can make cycling a tiring and dispiriting exercise, compounded by motorists' lack of bike-awareness. However, a few areas lend themselves to exploration, most notably the delightful harbourside Tamaki Drive which follows the waterfront for 10km to the east of the city centre.

BIKE RENTAL

Adventure Capital 23 Commerce St ☎ 09 337 0633, ⓦ adventurecapital.co.nz. Handy downtown location for low-grade mountain bikes ($15 4hr; $20/day; $60/5 days) that are ideal for knocking about town, through parks and along the waterfront.

Adventure Cycles 9 Premier Ave, Western Springs ☎ 0800 245 3868, ⓦ adventure-auckland.co.nz. Somewhat inconveniently sited west of the zoo, but a great resource for short-term bike rental (city bikes $20/day; mountain bikes $25/day) and touring bikes ($90/week; $200/month). Call ahead to make sure they have what you want and for transport details. Thurs–Mon 7.30am–7pm.

Cycle Auckland Devonport Wharf ☎ 09 445 1189, ⓦ cycleauckland.co.nz. A great selection (from $28/day; $115/week), including road, touring, tandem, hybrid and kids' bikes, plus self-guided and guided tours. The people to talk to if you fancy more than just a meander around town.

Fergs Kayaks 12 Tamaki Drive, Okahu Bay ☎ 09 529 2230, ⓦ fergskayaks.co.nz. Rents cruisers ($25/2hr; $60/day) perfect for a spin along the waterfront. Daily 10am–5pm.

Natural High 10 Uenuku Way ☎ 0800 444 144, ⓦ naturalhigh.co.nz. Cycle tourists should consider these guided and self-guided tours or go for their bike rental or buy-back schemes.

INFORMATION AND TOURS

Tourist information i-SITE Auckland has two central visitor centres: 137 Quay St (daily 9am–5pm and sometimes later in summer; ☎ 0800 282 552, ⓦ aucklandnz.com); and the more cramped branch inside the Sky City Casino (daily 9am–5pm; same contact details), on the corner of Victoria and Federal streets. Both stock leaflets from around the country including a number of advertisement-heavy free publications. The Devonport branch at Devonport Wharf (daily 9am–5pm; ☎ 09 365 9906, ⓦ devonport.co.nz) stocks maps and the free *Old Devonport Walk* leaflet outlining points of historic and architectural interest.

DOC office Inside the Quay St i-SITE (Mid-Oct–April Mon–Fri 9am–5pm, Sat & Sun 10am–4pm; May to mid-Oct Mon–Fri 9am–5pm; ☎ 09 379 6476, ⓔ aucklandvc@doc .govt.nz). Great for hiking information, stocks DOC leaflets and does track bookings for the whole country although it specializes in the Auckland and Hauraki Gulf region.

Maps For most purposes you can get by with the maps in this guide and Auckland Tourism's *Explore* series of free maps available from i-SITEs, hotels and hostels.

Backpacker information Check the notice boards in hostels, where the adverts cover rides, vehicle sales and job opportunities.

ACCOMMODATION

With efficient door-to-door shuttle services into central Auckland there's little reason to stay at the **airport**, though Auckland is a place where you might choose to stay **outside the city centre**, particularly: Ponsonby, 2km west; Mount Eden, 2km south; Parnell, 2km east; and Devonport, a short ferry journey across the harbour. All are more peaceful than the city centre but still well supplied with places to eat and drink, and access is good on the Inner Link and Outer Link buses (see opposite). **Camping** involves staying further out and it's not really worth the hassle unless you've rented a campervan.

1

FIRST-NIGHT CAMPING

If you're picking up a car or campervan near the airport after a long flight you may not fancy tangling with central city traffic. The closest appealing **campsite** is *Ambury Regional Park* (see p.99). There are also numerous tempting beachside spots only an hour or two from the airport, including: *Miranda Holiday Park* (p.119); *Rays Rest Camping Reserve* (p.119); *Muriwai Motorcamp* (p.115); *Orewa Beach Top 10 Holiday Park* (p.116); *Wenderholm Regional Park* (p.117); *Piha Domain Motor Camp* (p.114); and *Shakespear Regional Park* (p.116). If you just need a place to park up your toilet-equipped campervan, see our box on p.99.

ESSENTIALS

Seasons From December to March you should book ahead. At other times it's less critical, and through the quiet winter months (June–Sept) you'll be spoiled for choice and significant discounts on room rates can be had; it's worth asking.

Costs Room rates in Auckland are across the board a touch higher than in the rest of the country, though not unreasonably so.

CENTRAL AUCKLAND

International hotels (with high walk-up rates but good weekend and internet deals) brush shoulders with backpacker hostels, many with on-site travel services. Most downtown hostels cram in the beds and, with bars and clubs only a short stagger away, cater to a party crowd. Wherever you stay, you'll probably have to pay for parking.

Attic 15–31 Wellesley St W ☎09 973 5887, ⓦatticbackpackers.co.nz; map p.76. An ancient lift takes you up to this friendly and well-managed, 94-bed backpackers atop a five-storey city hotel. Even the 12- and 10-bed dorms feel spacious, and the mixed and female-only smaller dorms ($34–36) often have beds rather than bunks. Common areas include a quiet lounge and BBQ deck. Big dorms $29, twins $84

Base Auckland 229 Queen St ☎0800 227 369, ⓦstayatbase.com; map p.76. Well-run 500-bed hostel in a ten-storey office building with bar, massive internet centre, travel office, jobs centre, laundry, gear storage and swipe card access. Pay a little extra for the smaller dorms ($33) or en suites with TV ($110). Dorms $30, double $90

Braemar on Parliament Street 7 Parliament St ☎09 377 5463, ⓦparliamentstreet.co.nz; map p.76. This very welcoming 1901 townhouse B&B in the heart of the city has retained its late Victorian feel. There's a large suite ($350), a smaller en-suite room and two rooms that share a bathroom (all baths are clawfoot), and breakfast is a major affair with dishes cooked to order. There's free wi-fi, guest parking and a strong sustainability ethic. Shared bath $225, doubles $250

City Lodge 150 Vincent St ☎0800 766 686, ⓦcitylodge .co.nz; map p.76. YMCA-run tower block packed with en-suite rooms each with TV, fridge, tea & coffee. While there are no dorms or shared rooms, there are quads ($165; they don't put strangers together in the same room) and there's a decent communal kitchen/lounge. Weekly rates make it good for long stays. $115

Heritage 35 Hobson St ☎0800 368 888, ⓦheritagehotels.co.nz; map p.76. Top-class hotel partly fashioned from the original Farmers department store. Occasional bits of aged planking and wooden pillars in public areas augment the high standard fit-out and many rooms have views across the harbour or into the glassed-in atrium restaurant. The outside pool has great views over the city. $200

Hilton Princes Wharf, 147 Quay St ☎09 978 2000, ⓦhilton.com; map p.76. Fabulously sited on a wharf jutting into the harbour, this majestic hotel comes with a classy restaurant and the *Bellini* cocktail bar. The beautifully decorated rooms all have a terrace or balcony but it is worth paying the extra $80 for a good view. Valet parking $35 a day. $350

★**Hotel DeBrett** 2 High St ☎09 925 9000, ⓦhoteldebrett.com; map p.76. The height of Auckland chic, this classy 25-room boutique hotel references its Art Deco origins while adding bold colours and mismatched but complementary furniture. Bathrooms are gorgeous, continental breakfast and wi-fi are included and guests have access to a lovely drawing room with honesty bar. Rooms $330, suites $440

Jucy Hotel 62 Emily Place ☎09 379 6633, ⓦjucyhotel .com; map p.76. Budget hotel (by the cars and camper rental people) with decent value and surprisingly quiet (though garishly painted) rooms. Some are small and lack much natural light – the en suites with TV ($99) are considerably nicer. There's a small communal kitchen and lounge, and parking is available for $15/day. $69

Kiwi International 411 Queen St ☎0800 100 411, ⓦkiwihotel.co.nz; map p.76. Rambling 120-room budget hotel, where basic rooms have just a bed, hand basin, small desk and tea-making facilities: ensuites add a TV ($99), or go for an apartment with full cooking kit ($169). Limited off-street parking and a few rooms overlook Myers Park. Rates increase $5–10 on Friday and Saturday nights. $79

1

TOP 5 ROOMS WITH A VIEW
Hilton p.76
The Quadrant p.76
Ascot Parnell p.83
Peace and Plenty Inn p.87
Takapuna Beach Holiday Park p.74

Nomads Auckland 16–20 Fort St ☎0508 666 237, ⓦnomadshostels.com; map p.76. Classy conversion of a city office building into an upscale hostel with women-only dorms, rooftop kitchen and outdoor barbecue area. There's also a spa pool, sauna, good travel desk and the lively *Fort Street Union* bar, which offers very cheap meals to guests. Dorms have 6–12 beds and there are en-suite 4-shares ($37). Dorms $25, en-suite doubles $96

Nomads Fat Camel 38 Fort St ☎09 307 0181, ⓦnomadshostels.com; map p.76. Solid downtown hostel with six- and eight-bed mixed and female dorms (windowless ones are some of the cheapest in town at $21), twins and doubles all arranged in small apartments, each group having its own kitchen, lounge and showers. There's a bar with very cheap meals for guests, and a travel desk. Dorms $24, doubles $72

★**The Quadrant** 10 Waterloo Quadrant ☎09 984 6000, ⓦthequadrant.com; map p.76. Designer hotel chic without the high prices, this four-star place has a fresh appearance and great city and harbour views from the balcony of most of its 270 rooms. Most come with kitchenette and some have a washing machine and dishwasher. There's also a compact and intimate bar, a breakfast and lunch café, spa, sauna, a small gym and unlimited free wi-fi. Studio $165, one-bed apartment $180

Scenic Hotel 380 Queen St ☎09 374 1741, ⓦscenichotels.co.nz; map p.76. Good mid-range hotel with lobby areas restored to their Art Deco glory. Many of the hundred rooms have city views and/or full kitchens and there's a small fitness room. $160

YHA Auckland City 18 Liverpool St ☎09 309 2802, ⓦyha.co.nz; map p.76. Large and central YHA with seven floors of mostly twin and double rooms – the upper ones with fine city views – plus four-shares ($30) and well-equipped common areas. No dedicated parking but 1Gb free wi-fi a day for YHA members. Single-sex and mixed dorms $27, doubles $85

★**YHA Auckland International** 5 Turner St ☎09 302 8200, ⓦyha.co.nz; map p.76. The pick of the two YHAs, this purpose-built 168-bed establishment comes with spacious single-sex dorms and four-shares ($35), en suites ($108), excellent cooking facilities, separate TV and quiet lounges, a travel centre and wi-fi (free 1Gb a day to YHA members). There are even a few free parking spaces; book early. Dorms $28, doubles $94

PARNELL
Parnell is strong on B&Bs and hostels, is close to the Auckland Museum, has plenty of places to eat and drink and has good Inner and Outer Link bus connections.

Ascot Parnell 32 St Stephens Ave ☎09 309 9012, ⓦascotparnell.com; map p.83. Tranquil, comfortable Belgian-run B&B in a small, modern apartment block, with two mini-suites and a huge harbour suite. An enormous guest lounge with balcony overlooks the city and harbour, and there's a 12m pool, lift access from the secure parking, free wi-fi and computer, and airport pick-up (for a small fee). Try the signature savoury Flemish toast for breakfast. $225, harbour suite $265

City Garden Lodge 25 St George's Bay Rd ☎09 302 0880, ⓦcitygardenlodge.co.nz; map p.83. Friendly backpackers in a large, well-organized villa originally built for the Queen of Tonga, and surrounded by lawns. Along with spacious dorms and some lovely doubles/twins there are little touches such as hot water bottles in winter and even a yoga/meditation room (classes available). Dorms $28, doubles $72

Lantana Lodge 60 St George's Bay Rd ☎09 373 4546, ⓦlantanalodge.co.nz; map p.83. Clean and friendly hostel with a maximum of 25 guests, free wi-fi, free local calls and a homely feel. Four-shares are $31. Dorms $27, doubles $72

Parnell Inn 320 Parnell Rd ☎0800 472 763, ⓦparnellinn.co.nz; map p.83. Compact and simple hotel right in the heart of Parnell. Rooms are fairly small but there are some good views and kitchenettes are available. Off-street parking. $105

PONSONBY AND HERNE BAY
Ponsonby isn't especially close to the main sights, but its B&Bs and hostels are well-sited for the Ponsonby Rd café, bar and shopping strip. The Inner Link bus runs right along Ponsonby Rd.

Abaco on Jervois 59 Jervois Rd ☎0800 220 066, ⓦabaco.co.nz; map p.85. Stylish motel with plenty of off-street parking, unlimited free wi-fi, Sky TV and a/c in all rooms. Choose from compact studios, spacious rooms come with cooking facilities and deluxe suites ($195) with spa baths. $135

★**Bella's B&B** 33 England St, Freeman's Bay ☎09 378 8819, ⓦbellasbedandbreakfast.co.nz; map p.85. Glamorously decorated B&B well-sited for Ponsonby and the city centre. Immaculate rooms, including the spacious City Lights Suite ($295) with its city skyline views, lead off from a grand guest lounge where an elaborate breakfast is served. There's even a guest library, unlimited free wi-fi and off-street parking. $225

Brown Kiwi 7 Prosford St ☎09 378 0191, ⓦbrownkiwi .co.nz; map p.85. Compact, home-away-from-home hostel in a restored Victorian villa on a quiet street close to

1

the Ponsonby cafés. A patio and tiny garden is a relaxing oasis, and though daytime parking isn't great, there are good bus connections. Shares cost $32. Dorms $\overline{\$29}$, doubles $\overline{\$76}$

Great Ponsonby Art Hotel 30 Ponsonby Terrace ☏080 766 792, ⓦgreatpons.co.nz; map p.85. Welcoming boutique hotel based around a restored 1898 villa and boldly decorated in ocean tones and Pacific artworks. You can even choose your own breakfast from a short menu. Luxurious en-suite rooms, and self-catering studio units ($265) come with Sky TV and unlimited free wi-fi. $\overline{\$245}$

★**Ponsonby Backpackers** 2 Franklin Rd ☏09 360 1311, ⓦponsonby-backpackers.co.nz; map p.85. Well-managed hostel in a large villa perfectly sited just off Ponsonby Road. Does all the usual stuff, just better than most. Four-shares and the female-only dorm go for $32. Dorms $\overline{\$29}$, doubles $\overline{\$74}$

★**Ponsonby House** 8 Douglas St ☏09 361 1368, ⓦponsonbyhouse.co.nz; map p.85. Understated yet elegant B&B in a nice old villa. The three airy guest rooms (named Darjeeling, Jasmine and Earl Grey) are spacious and breakfast (fresh croissants, organic yoghurt etc) is taken in the privacy of your room, but the amiable hosts are always happy to chat if you need them. Great beds, free wi-fi and everything is cleaned with hypoallergenic, nontoxic products. $\overline{\$210}$

★**Verandahs** 6 Hopetoun St ☏09 360 4180, ⓦverandahs.co.nz; map p.85. Welcoming and beautifully appointed backpackers in a pair of grand 1905 villas overlooking a leafy park close to the Ponsonby Rd and K'Rd nightlife. The hostel has a selection of spacious dorms with no bunks, shares ($31), en suites ($96), limited off-street parking and the main lounge favours piano and guitar over TV. Dorms $\overline{\$29}$, doubles $\overline{\$76}$

NEWMARKET

The widest selection of motels is in Newmarket where nine nestle in one kilometre. They're close to Newmarket's shopping but relatively far from most sights and beaches.

Oaktree Motel 104 Great South Rd ☏0800 625 8733, ⓦoaktree.co.nz; map p.88. Fairly upscale motel comprising nicely modernized studios with a basic kitchen, and one-bedroom apartments. Some of both have a/c. Studios $\overline{\$120}$, apartments $\overline{\$195}$

Off Broadway 11 Alpers Ave ☏0800 427 623, ⓦoffbroadway.co.nz; map p.88. Business-oriented hotel with a/c, soundproofed en-suite studios and several one-bedroom suites with spa bath. There's undercover parking, a small gym, and breakfast can be served in your room. Studios $\overline{\$127}$, suites $\overline{\$198}$

Siesta Motel 70 Great South Rd ☏0800 743 782, ⓦsiestamotel.co.nz; map p.88. Ageing but decent motel with studios and self-catering units ($115), some recently remodelled. There's limited free wi-fi and Sky TV comes with sport and movie channels. Studios $\overline{\$105}$, apartment $\overline{\$125}$

Tudor Court Motel 108 Great South Rd ☏0800 826 878, ⓦtudor.co.nz; map p.88. Compact motel with small hotel-style rooms and slightly larger ones with kitchenettes ($129). Free wi-fi and Sky TV including sport and movies. $\overline{\$119}$

MOUNT EDEN

Suburban Mount Eden is strong on hostels and B&Bs. The Outer Link bus runs close to all the places listed below.

★**Bamber House** 22 View Rd ☏09 623 4267, ⓦbamberhouse.co.nz; map p.88. Spacious, well-managed hostel spread across a lovely old two-storey villa and a swish modern house in expansive grounds, plus several en-suite cabins ($90) that come with a kettle and fridge. There's a large lawn out front and free wi-fi as well as movie, games, pizza and poker nights. Dorms $\overline{\$26}$, doubles $\overline{\$72}$

Bavaria 83 Valley Rd ☏09 638 9641, ⓦbavariabandbhotel.co.nz; map p.88. The exuberant new host has rejuvenated this eleven-room B&B in a quiet suburban villa. Rooms are airy and spacious and the king rooms ($185) have balcony views. With no TV in rooms guests are encouraged to use the big lounge (which does have TV), and there's unlimited free wi-fi throughout. Generous breakfasts are served. $\overline{\$145}$

Eden Villa 16 Poronui St ☏09 630 1165, ⓦedenvilla.co.nz; map p.88. You're always well looked after at this delightful, art- and antique-filled three-room villa in a quiet street just steps from the Mt Eden shops. One room opens out onto the sunny back garden where superb breakfasts are served on fine mornings. TV with Sky is in the guest lounge and there's free wi-fi throughout. $\overline{\$250}$

Oaklands Lodge 5a Oaklands Rd ☏09 638 6545, ⓦoaklands.co.nz; map p.88. This large Victorian house right by Mount Eden shops is well-managed and mostly comprises dorms with beds rather than bunks (four-shares $27). Good kitchen and lounge areas plus a packed schedule of film, pizza and curry nights through the busier months. Dorms $\overline{\$25}$, doubles $\overline{\$68}$

KOHIMARAMA

Aarangi Motel 1 Melanesia Rd ☏09 521 2649, ⓦaarangimotel.co.nz; map p.74. Proximity to a good beach and café, both a block away, is the main selling point for this ageing but neat and tidy hacienda-style motel in a quiet neighbourhood. Several units have separate bedroom and kitchenette, and some have a balcony overlooking the little, manicured garden. $\overline{\$190}$

Kohi Beach B&B 72 Kohimarama Rd ☏09 521 1715, ⓦkohibedandbreakfast.com; map p.74. Lovely little German-Kiwi-run B&B a short walk from the beach, with a

CAMPERVAN PARK-UPS

Auckland Council aids those who want to maximise your nights spent outside official campsites by allowing **self-contained campervans** to stay overnight at designated SCC parking areas for $6 per person. No facilities are provided. In summer (Oct–early April), there's a one-night limit though some places allow 2 or 3 nights in winter. Book (and pay) through ⓦ aucklandcouncil.govt.nz (search for SCC) where there's a full list of sites including most regional parks and a few appealing car parks in the Waitakere Ranges. We've also mentioned campervan parking in a few places in the text.

couple of clean, well-appointed rooms (one with sea views; $165), off-street parking and continental breakfast. $150

DEVONPORT

Devonport has a cluster of fine B&Bs, all close to the Devonport ferry and some reasonable cafés (though none of the city's really good restaurants).

Mahoe B&B 15b King Edward Parade ☎ 09 445 1515, ⓦ mahoe.co.nz; map p.87. Lovely property in the heart of Devonport, set back from the waterfront, tastefully furnished and offering either B&B accommodation in the house or a separate, self-contained apartment. Breakfast is $15/person extra. Rooms $170, apartment $200

★**Parituhu Beachstay** 3 King Edward Parade ☎ 09 445 6559, ⓦ parituhu.co.nz; map. p.87. Helen and Lindsay will look after you at this gay-friendly budget B&B homestay in the heart of Devonport that overlooks the harbour. There's just the one room, a private bath, access to a secluded garden and continental breakfast. $155

Peace & Plenty Inn 6 Flagstaff Terrace ☎ 09 445 2925, ⓦ peaceandplenty.co.nz; map p.87. There's a strong ethical bias to this beautifully presented, Victorian-styled B&B in a grand villa. Kauri floorboards lead through to a lovely veranda, past rooms filled with fresh flowers and stocked with sherry and port. They even put on afternoon teas at weekends ($45). $310

CAMPSITES AND HOLIDAY PARKS

There are several well-equipped motor camps within the city limits that are fine for campervans and offer bargain cabins, though without your own vehicle you'll end up spending a lot of money on buses. Ambury is the nicest spot to pitch a tent.

Ambury Regional Park Mangere, 6km north of the airport ☎ 09 366 2000; map p.72. Basic, flat sites (no power) in a field overlooking the Manukau Harbour – a great location for those wanting to rest up after flying in to NZ. The adjacent farm park (with pigs, sheep, rabbits etc) has toilets and coin-op showers. Call ahead in winter. Camping per person $13, campervan parking per night $6

Auckland North Shore Motels and Holiday Park 52 Northcote Rd, Northcote ☎ 0508 909 090, ⓦ top1.co.nz; map p.74. Well-appointed site with an indoor swimming pool, extensive BBQ areas and a range of tourist flats ($110) and motel units ($140). Located just off the northern motorway and only a 15min drive from the city centre – bus #922 from lower Albert St, City (and others) stop nearby. Tent and van sites $40, cabins $70

★**Takapuna Beach Holiday Park** 22 The Promenade, Takapuna ☎ 09 489 7909, ⓦ takapunabeachholiday park.co.nz; map p.74. Small, perfectly-located caravan park that's neither very well equipped nor particularly spacious but you can't beat the views from the waterfront sites ($47). Frequent buses (#822, #839, #858, #879 etc) from lower Albert St in central Auckland. Book ahead as it is popular, and it may be forced to close. Camping $42, kitchen cabins $72

EATING

Auckland has a huge range of places to eat, and standards are generally very high. Daytime cafés often morph into full-blown restaurants, with alcohol consumption becoming an increasingly significant activity, as the night wears on. Britomart and Ponsonby are the big eating destinations but there are plenty of good spots elsewhere. Many new and fashionable haunts don't take bookings, though they're happy to sell you a drink or call you as soon as a table is ready.

THE WATERFRONT

Fine summer days are a perfect time to venture down to the cafés, restaurants and bars of Princes Wharf, Viaduct Harbour and Wynyard Quarter. Some places are ostentatious and soulless, though the best (listed below) have great food and luscious vistas of super-yachts.

Grand Harbour 18 Customs St West ☎ 09 357 6889, ⓦ grandharbour.co.nz; map p.76. More opulent than

TOP 5 PLACES TO DINE IN STYLE

Bellota p.76
The Depot p.76
Orphan's Kitchen p.85
Ortolana p.76
Ostro p.76

1

most of the city's Chinese places and heavily patronized by the Chinese community, this bustling modern restaurant is popular for business lunches and serves great *yum cha* (daily 11am–3pm). Daily 11am–3pm & 5.30–10pm.

Jack Tar North Wharf, Wynyard Quarter ☎09 303 1002, ⓦjacktar.co.nz; map p.76. A great spot to soak up the afternoon sun overlooking the fishing boats. A beer and squid rings ($18) is perfect appetizer for pizzas ($24), burgers ($18–24) and hoisin pork belly ($29). Mon–Thurs 11.30am–10pm, Fri–Sun 8am–11pm or later.

Soul Viaduct Harbour ☎09 356 7249, ⓦsoulbar .co.nz; map p.76. An icon of Auckland's waterfront dining scene, *Soul* is perfect for slick, modern bistro meals or a glass of wine on the terrace overlooking the yachts. Go for their classic salt-and-pepper squid ($20) followed perhaps by pan-fried hapuku with white bean cassoulet and salsa verde ($35). Daily 11am–10pm or much later.

Wildfire Princes Wharf ☎09 353 7595, ⓦwildfire restaurant.co.nz; map p.76. Flashy Brazilian barbecue restaurant with waterside tables that are perfect for a *caipirinha* cocktail. Their *churrasco* experience ($56) involves assorted tapas-style appetizers followed by a vast selection of meats and seafood marinated in herbs, roasted over manuka coals then carved off skewers at the table. Come early and you can drop the tapas for their *churrasco* special (noon–3pm, $40; 5–7pm, $46). Daily noon–11pm or later.

BRITOMART PRECINCT

Waterside seating is traded for urban chic around the Britomart Precinct, home to some of the city's best dining and chic-est bars, lively day and night.

Better Burger 31 Galway St ☎09 303 2541, ⓦbetterburger.co.nz; map p.76. Nothing fancy, just a limited range of straightforward but delicious burgers such as the double cheeseburger, fries and shake combo ($14.50). Bring a beer from the *Britomart Country Club* next door. Daily noon–10pm or later.

Cassia 5 Fort Lane ☎09 379 9702, ⓦcassiarestaurant .co.nz; map p.76. Not a gloopy curry in sight as top chef Sid Sahrawat draws on his heritage to create magic with the freshest local ingredients and traditional Indian spices. Slink into this stylish basement for starters such as fennel brioche with chicken tikka and kachumber ($8 each), followed by Kerala-style lamb rump with radish, turnip and saffron. Lunch Wed–Fri noon–3pm, dinner Tues–Sat 5.30–11pm.

Ebisu 116 Quay St ☎09 300 5271, ⓦebisu.co.nz; map p.76. Classy take on traditional Japanese *izakaya* dining effused with a few European ideas to produce a wonderfully modern combination. Try the Hokkaido scallops with *kumara* ginger purée and shiitake mushrooms ($25), or the

snapper sashimi with jalapeño salsa and lemon wafu sauce ($23) and enjoy the bare brick decor of the old Union Fish Company premises. Reservation taken for lunch only. Mon–Fri noon–10pm or later, Sat & Sun 5–10pm or later.

Ima 57 Fort St ☎09 300 7252, ⓦimacuisine.co.nz; map p.76. A relaxed Israeli and Middle Eastern café, where everything they make is super-fresh, including the best falafel in town ($16). The Arab chicken *meschuan* ($30) is also excellent. Tues–Sat 6–10pm.

★**Imperial Lane** 7 Fort Lane ☎09 929 2703, ⓦtheimperiallane.co.nz; map p.76. Industrial-chic café and bar with metal tables flanking a broad service ramp that links through to Queen St. Come for coffee and superb sandwiches and pastries during the day, and return later for drinks and hot dogs such as their Tijuana, stuffed with guacamole, chipotle and jalapeños ($11). Mon–Thurs 7.30am–7pm, Fri 7.30am–9pm, Sat & Sun 9am–3pm.

Mexico 23 Britomart Place ☎09 366 1759, ⓦmexico .net.nz; map p.76. Kitsch Mexicana decor (all skulls, bullfighting and Frida Kahlo portraits) sets the tone for this fun joint where south-of-the-border staples are replaced by the likes of tacos with Pipian chicken, candied *pepitas*, and lemon confit ($6); *ceviche* with pork crackling and watermelon ($16); and chicken *mole quesedillas* ($15). Kick off with a coriander and lime *agua frescas* ($4) or one of their sixty-odd tequilas then ease into the Bohemias. No bookings. Daily noon–10pm or later.

★**Ortolana** The Pavilions, 31 Tyler St ☎09 368 9487, ⓦhipgroup.co.nz/ortolana.html; map p.76. If you desire quality food, expertly presented and served but without fuss or pretension then *Ortolana* is the place for you. Fresh produce from their own farm and trusted suppliers is imaginatively combined into loosely Italian small and large plates like pork, *stracciatella* and mustard leaves *piadina* ($16) and lamb, lentils and grapes with *labneh* ($25). The wine list is equally well thought out. Not exactly cheap, but great value for food of this quality. No bookings. Daily 7am–11pm.

Ostro 52 Tyler St ☎09 280 3789, ⓦseafarers.co.nz; map p.76. Sexy brasserie and bar where the unfussy yet superb food is almost upstaged by the spectacular setting, with one entirely-glass wall overlooking the docks and harbour. Come for a meal here – perhaps slow-roasted pork belly with caramelized pear, celeriac remoulade, salsa verde and crackling ($38) – or just sip a killer cocktail ($16–18) on the more casual city side overlooking Britomart. Daily noon–11pm.

CITY CENTRE

Away from the water, office workers dine at low-cost Asian restaurants and food halls while a couple of hubs meet the needs of more sophisticated tastes and deeper pockets. A short section of Federal Street at the foot of the Skytower comes packed with top-class places while some former council workshops have been transformed into the City Works Depot (ⓦ cityworksdepot.co.nz) on the corner of Wellesley and Nelson streets, where cafés, a bakery, a coffee roaster and a bagelry surround a knot of architecture, design and media businesses.

★**Bellota** 91 Federal St ☎09 363 6301, ⓦbellota .co.nz; map p.76. Fans of celebrated Kiwi chef Peter Gordon flock to the booths in this retro 1970s cave for his fusion take on Spanish tapas (around $12), such as lamb chilli and feta spring rolls with tamarind aioli. The name means "acorn", a reference to the acorn-fed pigs that feature on the menu (though there are plenty of veggie options). Daily 4.30–10.30pm or later.

Black Hoof 12 Wyndham St ☎09 366 1271, ⓦtheblackhoof.co.nz; map p.76. Dried hams hang over the bar in this Spanish taverna that's perfect for a few tapas and the best cured meats ($14–36 for 40g portions) over a sherry or two. Squid-ink rice with crispy calamari or grilled beef skirt with roast cauliflower and olives (both $26) are helped down with mostly Kiwi and Spanish wines, and the $20 plate-and-a-glass weekday lunches are great value. Mon–Thurs 11am–10pm, Fri 11am–11pm, Sat–11pm.

Bombay Chinese 370 Queen St ⓦbombaychinese .co.nz; map p.76. The food court ambience only detracts a little from this excellent take on Indian-Chinese street food where $15 gets you a huge portion. Sample the *momos* and the legendary "chicken 65" with ginger, garlic, chillies and mustard seeds, and try the super-hot Death Valley chicken ($16) if you dare. Mon–Fri 10am–9pm, Sat & Sun 5–9pm.

★**The Botanist** City Works Depot, 90 Wellesley St ☎09 308 9494, ⓦbotanist.co.nz; map p.76. Creatives from surrounding media and design studios meet at this stylish concrete bunker, softened by bent-ply stools and plants from the adjacent florist. Gather around the communal table or perch at the counter and tuck into their potato and cheddar waffle topped with mushrooms, haloumi and wilted greens ($19) or pea-pesto-topped lamb shoulder with roasted cauliflower ($14). Quality wine and beers accompany light snacks some evenings. Mon & Tues 7am–4pm, Wed–Fri 7am–9pm or later, Sat & Sun 8am–3pm.

Chuffed 43 High St ☎09 367 6801, ⓦchuffedcoffee .co.nz; map p.76. An oasis of good coffee (cold-drip, batch brewed if you wish) tucked down an unlikely looking alley and even boasting a shaded terrace with outdoor fireplace. Delectable cabinet food is supplemented by house-made crumpets with strawberry jam and ricotta ($11) or a braised duck leg salad ($21). Licensed. Mon–Fri 7am–5pm, Sat 9am–5pm.

★**The Depot** 86 Federal St ☎09 363 7048, ⓦeatatdepot.co.nz; map p.76. Waiters carrying plates of fresh oysters weave around stools clustered at high tables at this bustling, hip, industrially-styled bar and restaurant run by celebrity chef Al Brown. Quality wine comes by the carafe and the menu offers small plates of cumin-battered warehou tortillas ($18) and large dishes of wood-roasted lemon chicken with white bean ragout ($30). They don't take bookings, so add your name to the list and pop across to *Bellota* for a sherry while you wait. Daily 7am–around 11pm.

★**Federal Delicatessen** 86 Federal St ☎09 363 7184, ⓦthefed.co.nz; map p.76. Brash and confident, this upscale licensed diner is celebrity chef Al Brown's take on a 1950s New York Jewish deli. Slip into olive green booths or perch at the counter for crispy salmon latkes ($18), a delectable toasted Reuben ($22) and pumpkin pie with pecans ($10). Aucklanders find the lack of espresso a little too authentic, but the bottomless filter coffee ($3.50) is fine. No bookings. Daily 7am–11pm or later.

Food Alley 9 Albert St ☎09 373 4917; map p.76. Auckland's best food hall is spartan and inexpensive, with over a dozen kitchens exhibiting a strong East Asian bias – *Marigold Thai* is particularly good for its light-as-a-feather curry puffs ($6) and tasty Isaan dishes. Daily 10am–10pm.

★**Mamak Malaysian** Chancery Square, 50 Kitchener St ☎09 948 6479; map p.76. The fabulously flaky *roti* are made on site at this quick-serve little restaurant known for its *roti* chicken curry ($14.50) but also good for Chinese-style salt and pepper squid ($10) and seafood *laksa* ($14). Add a *teh tarik* (tea made with condensed milk) for that true Malaysian experience. Licensed and also does takeaways. Tues to Sun 11.30am–3pm & 5–9.30pm.

★**Mezze Bar** 9 Durham Lane East ☎09 307 2029, ⓦmezzebar.co.nz; map p.76. Relaxed, sepia-toned café and bar serving up predominantly Spanish, Moroccan and Middle Eastern dishes. Great for coffee and a slice of orange almond cake, tapas and meze (mostly $12–17) with sherry or Spanish wine, or dishes such as lamb tajine ($28) or chargrilled salmon Niçoise ($27). Mon–Thurs & Sun 7am–10.30pm, Fri & Sat 7am–11.30pm.

Middle East Café 23a Wellesley St West ☎09 379 4843, ⓦmiddleeastcafe.co.nz; map p.76. Tiny, simple, camel-themed eat-in or takeaway unlicensed café that's an Auckland institution, deservedly celebrated for its shawarma and falafel ($10), both cloaked in creamy garlic, spicy tomato sauce or hot chilli sauce. Mon 11am–3pm, Tues–Fri 11am–3pm & 5–10pm, Sat 5–10pm, Sun 5–9pm.

Misters 12 Wyndham St ☎09 379 9939, ⓦmisters .co; map p.76. Great little, mostly dairy- and

1

gluten-free breakfast and lunch joint with a frequently changing menu which might include buckwheat griddle cakes with blueberries and coconut yoghurt ($10) or beef and pork-ball tabouleh ($14). Mon–Fri 7am–3pm, Sat 8am–3pm.

No. 1 Pancake 10 Wellesley St, at Lorne St; map p.76. Bargain hole-in-the-wall serving Korean pancakes with delectable fillings such as pork, red bean, chicken and cheese, or sugar and cinnamon for $3–4.50 each. Mon–Fri 10am–7pm, Sat 11am–6pm.

Tanuki's Cave 319b Queen St ☎09 379 5151, ⓦsakebars.co.nz; map p.76. Excellent *yakitori* and sake bar in a cave-like basement setting, with a more formal restaurant above. Tuck into meaty skewers (around $5 each), octopus balls ($8) or order a *yakitori* set ($17) and wash it all down with sake or Japanese beer. Often busy; no bookings. Daily 5–11.30pm or later.

KARANGAHAPE ROAD AND AROUND

There's a relaxed vibe along Karangahape Road with laidback cafés, an abundance of low-cost ethnic restaurants and a couple of smarter places moving in.

★**Alleluya** St Kevin's Arcade, 179 K' Rd ☎09 377 8482; map p.76. K' Road life comes together at this shabby-chic café among the potted kentia palms in a pretty 1920s arcade. Grab a city-view window seat and tuck into a fiery breakfast burrito ($15), kedgeree ($15), or excellent coffee and cake. Licensed. Mon–Sat 8am–5pm, Sun 9am–3pm.

★**Coco's Cantina** 376 K' Rd ☎09 300 7582, ⓦcocoscantina.co.nz; map p.76. A funky and very popular restaurant with a strong gay following. Its short, rustic-Italian menu might include *arancini* risotto balls ($12) followed by steak with anchovy butter and home fries ($30) or its signature spaghetti and meatballs ($33). The outside tables are great for watching the characters along K' Rd, especially on Friday and Saturday nights. No bookings, so grab a glass of wine at the bar and wait your turn. Tues–Sat 5pm–midnight.

★**Pok Pok** 261 K' Rd ☎09 963 9987, ⓦpokpokthai .co.nz; map p.76. The place is nothing to look at, but the flavours at this modestly priced restaurant leave most Thai places for dead. The duck spring rolls ($8) are crispy and delicious, the *tom yum* prawn ($20) zings with galangal and lemongrass and you must leave room for the dark chocolate chilli mousse ($14) and the black sticky rice with coconut ice cream ($10). Licensed and BYO. Mon–Fri 11am–2.30pm & 5–10pm, Sat & Sun 5–10pm or later.

Rasoi 211 K' Rd ☎09 377 7780; map p.76. It feels almost like you're in South India at this budget vegetarian café that dishes up *dosas*, *uttappams* and *thalis* for $13–20; there's also an all-you-can-eat maharajah *thali* for $27. Great Indian sweets, too. Mon–Sat 11am–9pm.

Sri Pinang 356 K' Rd ☎09 358 3886; map p.76. A simple but ever-popular Malaysian restaurant where you can start with half a dozen satay chicken skewers and follow with dishes such as *sambal* okra, beef *rendang* or clay-pot chicken rice scooped up with excellent *roti*. Most dishes $15–24. BYO wine or beer from the shop across the road. Mon 5.30–10pm, Tues–Fri 11am–2.30pm & 5.30–10pm, Sat 5.30–11pm.

PARNELL AND NEWMARKET

Neither Parnell nor Newmarket are culinary hotbeds, but both have a respectable range of great places to eat, and lots of middling contenders.

Asian Food Hall Newmarket Plaza, 11 Kent St ☎09 529 1868; map p.83. A little slice of East Asia with Malaysian, Thai, Japanese and Chinese places all serving national staples for $10–17. *Laksa House* is particularly good for its *wat tan hor* (fried flat noodles; $12). Daily 10.30am–9pm.

Basque Kitchen Bar 61 Davis Crescent ☎09 523 1057 ⓦbasquekitchenbar.co.nz; map p.83. All the wines are Spanish (ask for recommendations) at this fun concrete-floored tapas bar where you might tuck into serrano ham and manchego cheese croquettes ($5) and smoked paprika grilled octopus ($14.50), perhaps washed down with one of their delectable sherries ($10–20). Mon–Sat 4.30–10pm or later.

Best Ugly Bagels 3a Yorke St, Newmarket ☎09 529 5993, ⓦbestugly.co.nz; map p.83. The coolest corner of Newmarket centres on this joint where wood-fired Montreal-style bagels are served up inside or out in their courtyard with its outdoor fire. Come early for their breakfast bagel or opt for classics like pastrami, swiss and habanero mustard ($10) or lox and cream cheese ($14). Mon–Fri 7am–3pm, Sat & Sun 7am–4pm.

★**Domain & Ayr** 492 Parnell Rd ☎09 366 4464; map p.83. Join the communal table or tuck yourself away with a magazine at this modern organic and free-range café serving Fairtrade organic coffee, all made with organic milk. The growers are namechecked on the recycled-paper menus, which include the likes of *huevos rancheros* ($16.50), bubble and squeak ($18.50) and great salads. Mon–Fri 7am–3pm, Sat & Sun 8am–3pm.

La Cigale French Market 69 St George's Bay Rd, ⓦlacigale.co.nz; map p.83. Beautiful people flock here for delicious morsels and perhaps to pick up some picnic ingredients. It's always alive with folk sampling savouries such as raclette, delicious dips, paella, Cornish pasties and whitebait fritters, or just sitting around over a coffee and Auckland's best French pastries. Sat 8am–1.30pm, Sun 9am–1.30pm.

★**Little & Friday** 12 Melrose St, Newmarket ☎09 524 8742 ⓦlittleandfriday.com; map p.83. Less cool but handier than their Takapuna mothership, this café/bakery in the corner of a fabric warehouse serves up pies, sandwiches and cakes on delicate old-fashioned plates. Try a beetroot quiche ($11) or a pear and almond tart ($8). Mon–Fri 8am–3.30pm, Sat & Sun 9am–4pm.

Mojo 110 Carlton Gore Rd ☎09 524 9619, ⓦmojocoffee.co.nz; map p.83. A former car workshop has been transformed into this slick but welcoming café where great coffee and toothsome muffins supplement the likes of egg and minced beef cheek on rosemary sourdough, and Basque-style baked eggs with capsicum and smoked paprika piperade (both $17). Mon–Fri 7am–4.30pm, Sat & Sun 8am–4.30pm.

Non Solo Pizza 259 Parnell Rd ☎09 379 5358, ⓦnonsolopizza.co.nz; map p.83. As the name says, not just pizza, but they do create wonderfully thin-crust concoctions with classic Italian toppings. Pasta and assorted *secondi piatti*, such as confit of duck with beans and chorizo ($37), is served inside or on the intimate patio. Daily noon–10pm or later.

★**Oh Calcutta!** 151 Parnell Rd ☎09 377 9090, ⓦohcalcutta.co.nz; map p.83. Bronzed statues of Shiva and Ganesh look down on diners from Moghul alcoves in this classy curry restaurant that picks the best dishes from across the subcontinent – Malabar prawn cutlets with coriander and coconut cream ($25) – and imbues them with wonderfully distinct flavours. A range of lunchtime tiffin menus lets you sample three curries, rice, naan and poppadoms for $25. Lunch Wed–Fri noon–2pm, dinner nightly 5.30–10pm.

MOUNT EDEN AND DOMINION ROAD

Dining options in Mt Eden Village are getting better all the time while the strip along Dominion Road is home to one of the city's densest concentrations of cheap East Asian restaurants.

B & D 296c Dominion Rd ☎09 623 2123; map p.88. Take a friend to share the enormous portions at this cheap and cheerful Chinese where noodle soups, dumplings and the likes of garlicky and spicy green beans with pork mince ($14) and hot and spicy fish fillet ($18) come with free jasmine tea. $10 lunches too. Mon–Sat 9am–10pm, Sun 9am–9pm.

Eden Noodles 105 Dominion Rd ☎09 630 1899; map p.88. Go for the hand-pulled Dan Dan noodles with Sichuan sauce and crunchy pork at this ever-popular but atmosphere-free joint. Mon–Sat 11am–9.30pm.

★**Olaf's** 1 Stokes Road, Mt Eden ☎09 638 7593, ⓦolafs.co.nz; map p.88. Casual café that's best for superb baked goods like the rhubarb galette, ginger torte or a couple of Portuguese specialities – *pastel de nata* and *barquinhos de coco* (all under $5). Their breads (available by the loaf) work perfectly in their roast chicken ficelle ($13.50) and Reuben on rye ($14.50). Mon & Tues 6.30am–6pm, Wed–Fri 6.30am–11pm, Sat 7am–11pm, Sun 7am–5pm.

The Return of Rad 397 Mt Eden Rd, Mt Eden ☎09 631 5218, ⓦthereturnofrad.co.nz; map p.88. Hipster cool breaks out in Mt Eden at this great little café which, naturally, serves cold-drip single-origin coffee along with excellent espresso. Smart (often bearded) staff navigate the rough-brick and bare-bulb interior serving the likes of mushrooms with goat curd cheese and truffle oil ($17), pork *bánh mì* ($13) and fresh-squeezed juices and smoothies ($7). Mon–Fri 6.30am–4pm, Sat 7am–4pm, Sun 8am–4pm.

TAMAKI DRIVE: OKAHU BAY AND MISSION BAY

Dining along Auckland's beach strip can be a hit-and-miss affair, but these spots are reliably good.

The Attic upstairs at 55 Tamaki Drive ☎09 521 0000, ⓦtheatticbar.co.nz; map p.74. Reliable spot for a beer or a cocktail, especially if you score a seat on the terrace overlooking the park and beach. The tap beer is boring but there are plenty of good wines by the glass and meals like pork ribs in Jack Daniels BBQ sauce ($29). Mon–Thurs 4–11pm, Fri–Sun noon–11pm or later.

Café on Kohi 237 Tamaki Drive, Kohimarama ☎09 528 8335; map p.74. A touch more formal than other Tamaki Drive cafés, and a dollar or two more expensive, but worth it for the best café food in these parts and great views across the beach to Rangitoto. The associated *The Store on Kohi*, around the corner in the same building, does superb pastries, savouries, gelati and coffee all to take away and eat on the beach. Daily 7am–4pm.

PONSONBY

Fashion-conscious foodies should make for Ponsonby, where devotion to style is as important as culinary prowess. But don't be intimidated; the food is excellent and competition keeps prices reasonable. There are stacks of excellent cafés (nowhere below par lasts long) so we've selected a few of the more unusual or tucked-away places. First stop should be Ponsonby Central, 136 Ponsonby Rd (ⓦponsonbycentral.co.nz), a dense knot of mostly excellent cafés, restaurants and food stores – including a crêperie, fish and chips, coffee roastery – that's always buzzing.

Blue Breeze Inn 136 Ponsonby Rd ☎09 360 0303, ⓦthebluebreezeinn.co.nz; map p.85. Hawaiian bar meets modern Chinese cuisine at this bustling Ponsonby Central darling where a rum cocktail is the perfect aperitif for the likes of tiger prawn and sesame dumplings ($12) , Szechuan wagyu tartare ($20) and roasted duck with hoisin sauce ($30). Daily noon–10pm or later.

Burger Burger Ponsonby Central, 136 Ponsonby Rd ☎09 360 8030, ⓦburgerburger.co.nz; map p.85. Very Ponsonby eat-in and takeaway where the chicken burger (thigh meat with red pepper salsa) can come with potato skins and aioli and either a super-rich milkshake (organic milk, naturally) or even champagne. Delicious. Daily noon–9pm or later.

Conch 115a Ponsonby Rd ☎09 360 1999, ⓦconch .co.nz; map p.85. Cult vinyl-heavy record store which is increasingly becoming a cool café and bar. It's perfect for a sidewalk coffee, or slip into a booth out back for Venezuelan flatbreads stuffed with pork *carnitas* and pickles or one of their wood-fired pizzas ($24) with a *caipirinha* or two. Wed–Sun 10am–10pm.

Dante's 136 Ponsonby Rd ☎09 378 4443, ⓦdantespizza.co.nz; map p.85. They keep it simple with just six choices of topping on their wonderful wood-fired pizza ($24) done the Neapolitan way – they've even got special certification from Naples – using only the freshest ingredients. No other food and just three wines, all Italian, and Peroni on tap. Daily 11am–10pm.

Dizengoff 256 Ponsonby Rd ☎09 360 0108; map p.85. Buzzy breakfast and lunch café specializing in wonderful bagels, eggs with fried pastrami and other Jewish deli favourites, plus luscious chargrilled vegetables, all at reasonable prices. No alcohol. Mon–Fri 6.30am–5pm, Sat & Sun 7am–5pm.

Good One 42 Douglas St ☎09 376 2784, ⓦcoffeesupreme.com; map p.85. Hip backstreet café in an old manufacturing building. There are gourmet pies and delicious *Little & Friday* cakes but it's mainly about the coffee, espresso or batch filtered. Mon–Fri 7am–3pm, Sat 8am–3pm, Sun 9am–3pm.

★**Il Forno** 55 Mackelvie St; map p.85. Simple daytime bakery and café, especially notable for its delectable made-on-the-premises cakes, pastries and coffee, but also doing fine sandwiches, rolls and cannelloni, lasagne and chicken schnitzel lunches (10.30am–1.30pm; $12). Daily 7am–4pm.

Nishiki 100 Wellington St ☎09 376 7104, ⓦnishiki .co.nz; map p.85. Authentic, loud and busy *izakaya* with a vast menu of freshly cooked goodies. Try the pork belly skewers ($5), crispy *gyoza* ($7), okra tempura ($7) and made-to-order sushi. Licensed and BYO. Tues–Sun 6–10.30pm.

Orphans Kitchen 118 Ponsonby Rd ☎09 378 7979, ⓦorphanskitchen.co.nz; map p.85. Bright, fresh and imaginative restaurant where bookings are absent and tables often communal. By the time you read this the shared plates (around $25) almost certainly won't include smoked salmon with celeriac, black rice, apple and horseradish or braised venison shin with swede, feijoa and rainbow chard, but you get the idea. A well-thought-out wine list helps things along and they even open for only slightly less adventurous brunches. Tues 5–11pm, Wed–Sat 7am–2pm & 5–11pm, Sun 7am–2pm.

★**Ponsonby Road Bistro** 165 Ponsonby Rd ☎09 360 1611, ⓦponsonbyroadbistro.co.nz; map p.85. Blackboard specials lend a relaxed ambience to this consistently good, casually sophisticated restaurant where pork, venison and prune terrine with pickled vegetables ($20) might be followed by chargrilled steak and chips ($33) or pizza ($25). Mon–Fri noon–midnight, Sat 5.30pm–midnight.

★**Satya** 17 Great North Rd ☎09 361 3612, ⓦsatya .co.nz; map p.85. This excellent South Indian place steps outside the usual range of curries with the likes of *bhel puri* ($8) followed by *murg badami* with almonds and marinated chicken ($22). Lunches from $10. Licensed & BYO. Mon–Sat 11.30am–2.30pm & 5.30–10pm, Sun 5.30–10pm.

★**SPQR** 150 Ponsonby Rd ☎09 360 1710, ⓦspqrnz .co.nz; map p.85. Dimly lit and eternally groovy restaurant/bar with a strong gay following that's always popular for its quality Italian-influenced food. The crispy pizzas ($26) are superb and there's nothing the slightest bit shabby about the likes of roast snapper on saffron lime risotto ($36) or veal *scallopine* ($33). Many treat it more as a bar and venue for spotting actors and rock stars. Excellent cocktails and a wide range of wines (sold by the glass). Daily noon–11pm or much later.

The Unbakery 1a Summer St ☎09 555 3278 ⓦlittlebirdorganics.co.nz; map p.85. Not just an unbakery, this oh-so-fashionable café also uncooks breakfast and lunch using (mostly) raw organic ingredients. Expect the likes of raw corn taco with spiced Mexican mushrooms and cooked black beans ($18.50), a changing roster of flavoured kombucha, cold brewed filter coffee served on ice (with hazelnut milk if you wish) and delicious cakes from the counter. Daily 7am–4pm.

DEVONPORT

Bema Takeaways 87 Vauxhall Rd ☎09 445 4441; map p.87. On a nice evening it's hard to beat fish and chips or a straightforward burger on the adjacent Cheltenham Beach. Daily noon–9pm.

Châteaubriant 87a Vauxhall Rd ☎09 445 002, ⓦchateaubriant.co.nz; map p.87. This little piece of France blends a *boulangerie*, *charcuterie* and *fromagerie* in a tiled former butchers shop. Gather around the communal table for filled baguettes ($8), quiche Lorraine ($6.50) and éclairs or grab a baguette, free-range rotisserie chicken, cheese and pâté for a picnic at the beach. Tues–Sun 8am–3.30pm or later.

Devo 23 Wynyard St; map p.87. Tiny, unassuming place squeezed in next to a hardware store, dishing up top espresso and gluten-free muffins to go – or sit perched in the morning sun. Mon–Fri 5.45am–1pm, Sat & Sun 7am–2pm.

Manuka 49 Victoria Rd ☎09 445 7732,

ⓦmanukarestaurant.co.nz; map p.87. Reliable restaurant specializing in pasta, wood-fired pizza (around $26) and the likes of chicken Caesar salad ($20) or pumpkin and feta ravioli ($22), but good at any time of the day for light snacks and salads or just for coffee and cake. Daily 7am–9pm or later.

Monsoon 71 Victoria Rd ☎09 445 4263, ⓦmonsoonthai.co.nz; map p.87. Value-for-money Thai/Malaysian place with tasty dishes such as fish and prawns in a red curry sauce ($21). Licensed & BYO. Daily 5–10pm or 11pm.

TAKAPUNA

★ **Little & Friday** 43 Eversleigh Rd, Belmont ☎09 489 8527, ⓦlittleandfriday.com; map p.74. Make the effort to visit this fabulous café and bakery that has gradually taken over a nondescript suburban strip-mall. Pies, tarts, pastries and cakes are all magic and they operate in the evenings as *Afterhours*, serving a choice of a pizza or a bistro-style dish (both change daily and cost $18–22: check the website for the week's line-up). Café daily 8am–4pm, Afterhours Tues–Sat 5–8pm.

Madam Woo 486 Lake Rd ⓦmadamwoo.co.nz; map p.74. The new Auckland branch of this Queenstown darling had yet to open but aims to replicate the original with its lively atmosphere and wide range of Southeast-Asian influenced dishes to die for. Half of foodie Auckland was hanging out for their famed hawker rolls.

Takapuna Beach Café 22 The Promenade ☎09 484 0002, ⓦtakapunabeachcafe.co.nz; map p.74. High prices are justified by the superb location and great food at this highly formal café overlooking Rangitoto. Come for freekah fritter with smoked trevally, poached egg and citrus vinaigrette ($22) or lamb burger with *labneh* and chips ($26), or just grab a coffee. The adjacent *Store* serves excellent takeaway coffee, pastries, gelato and some of the city's best fish and chips – perfect for a seawall sunset. Daily 7am–6pm or later.

DRINKING, NIGHTLIFE AND ENTERTAINMENT

With 1.5 million people to entertain, there's always something going on in Auckland. One of the best ways to see local acts is to attend one of the free summer concerts held in The Domain and elsewhere under the Music in Parks banner (Jan–March; ⓦmusicinparks.co.nz), mostly on Friday, Saturday and Sunday afternoons.

ESSENTIALS

Listings and tickets Find out what's on at the Entertainment Guide section of the bFM radio station website ⓦ95bfm.co.nz or ⓦundertheradar.co.nz, which has links for ticket purchases.

Gay and lesbian Auckland Auckland has a fairly small but progressive and proactive gay scene largely woven into the café/bar mainstream of Ponsonby and K' Road, where strip clubs mingle freely with gay bars and cruise clubs. The best way to link into the scene is to pick up the free, monthly *exPress* magazine (ⓦgayexpress.co.nz), found in gay-friendly shops, cafés and bars. Alternatively, pick up a copy of the free *Gaynz.com* guide, which covers gay hotspots around the country.

PUBS, BARS, CLUBS AND LIVE MUSIC

As elsewhere in the country, the distinction between eating and drinking places is frequently blurred. The places listed below concentrate on the drinking, though even basic pubs serve simple meals. Closing times are relaxed, with rowdier places staying open until 3am at weekends.

The clubbing torch currently burns brightest around Britomart and Viaduct Harbour, where you can join the nightly flow of young things meandering between venues. Unless someone special is on the decks or a band is playing, most clubs are free early in the week, charge $5–10 on Thursday and over $10 on Friday and Saturday. Lots of pubs and bars double as venues for live acts, employ DJs or put on some form of entertainment.

Many of the clubs have one area set up as a stage, and on any night of the week you might find top Kiwi acts and even overseas bands blazing away in the corner; a few pubs may also put on a band from time to time. Big acts from North America and Europe visit sporadically and tend to play only in Auckland, usually in the larger venues.

THE WATERFRONT

Cowboys 95 Customs St West ☎09 377 7778; map p.76. Faux-Western bar where the trick is to knock back a few bourbons, tequilas or whatever, help yourself to a cowboy hat and dance around to 1980s music. It might sound cheesy but everyone has a great time. Daily noon–midnight or later.

O'Hagan's 103 Customs St West ☎09 363 2106, ⓦohagans.co.nz; map p.76. Classy Irish-themed pub spilling out onto the Market Square. Guinness, Kilkenny and English ales on tap, a good range of meals (chicken and mushroom pie and a pint $23), big-screen sports and live music on weekends from 11pm. Daily 8am–10pm or later.

BRITOMART

1885 Britomart 27 Galway St ☎09 551 3100, ⓦ1885 .co.nz; map p.76. Ever-popular martini bar and club where there's almost always a DJ or two on the platters and cocktails are raised to a fine art. Befriend a member to get

1

into the plush New York-clubby *Basement* bar. Wed–Sat 5pm–3am.

Brew on Quay 102 Quay St ☎09 302 2085, ⓦbrewonquay.co.nz; map p.76. Seek out one of the semi-private rooms or the rooftop deck in this historic former Wharf Police building where craft beer is king. Try the frequently changing roaster of guest tap beers with a 5-beer sample paddle ($22) or trawl the strong selection of wines, whiskies (including Japanese, Indian and NZ variants). There are quality pub meals (lunch specials $10, otherwise mostly $20) and live music at weekends. Daily 11am–11pm or later.

Britomart Country Club 31 Galway St ☎09 303 2541, ⓦbritomartcountryclub.co.nz; map p.76. Buzzing garden bar linked to *1885 Britomart*, and when it rains there's weather protection and cheaper beer. Early day coffee and fresh juices give way to shared jugs of Thai punch ($35) poured into jars and a menu of *kumara* fries, squid rings, burgers and sandwiches ($8–16). DJs most nights. Daily noon–midnight.

Tyler St Garage 120 Quay St ☎09 300 5279, ⓦtylerstreetgarage.co.nz; map p.76. Stylish and bustling semi-industrial bar topped by a great roof terrace for sipping cocktails $12–16) with views across the docks. There's half-price pizza on Tues and live music and DJs at weekends. Daily 11.30am–11pm or much later.

Xuxu Cnr Galway St & Commerce St ☎09 309 5529, ⓦxuxu.co.nz; map p.76. Though it calls itself a dumpling bar (the prawn *har gao* and chicken potstickers are delicious) this is really an exotic little cocktail bar, perfect for that pre-dinner drink or late-night tipple. Mon–Sat 3pm–late.

CITY CENTRE

Brothers Beer 90 Wellesley St, ☎09 366 6100, ⓦbrothersbeer.co.nz; map p.76. There's nothing but top-class beer and cider at this casual City Works Depot brewpub with 18 beers on tap, including their own contributions. A 5-beer tasting paddle ($20 for Brothers, $25 for others) is a great starting point and the tables outside are a fine spot for one of their thin-crust pizzas. Tues & Sun noon–8pm, Weds–Sat noon–10pm.

Globe 229 Queen St, under Base Auckland hostel ☎09 357 3980, ⓦglobeauckland.wordpress.com; map p.76. Long, thin, noisy backpackers-get-drunk bar that's full most nights of the week. Nightly 6pm–late.

Sweat Shop Brew Kitchen 7 Sale St, Freeman's Bay ☎09 307 8148, ⓦsweatshopbrew.co.nz; map p.76. Big, open semi-industrial space (a former garment factory, hence the name) and a massive deck that's ideal for sampling their house-brewed beers and a slab of pork or

beef from their smokehouse grill. Daily 11.30am–10pm or much later.

KARANGAHAPE ROAD AND NEWTON

Family Bar 270 K' Rd ☎09 309 0213, ⓦfacebook.com /FamilyBar; map p.76. Lively, predominantly gay and lesbian bar that welcomes all comers for drinks during the day and plenty of action at night – karaoke on Wed, DJs Thurs–Sat and drag shows from 1am on Fri and Sat nights. Daily 9.30am–4am.

★**Galbraith's Alehouse** 2 Mount Eden Rd, Newton ☎09 379 3557, ⓦalehouse.co.nz; map p.76. The closest Auckland gets to an English pub, with some of NZ's finest English-style ales brewed on site plus guest beers by other craft brewers and fifty-odd bottled varieties. Very good bar meals kick off with stuffed jalapeños ($12) and include burger and fries ($18), Thai red chicken curry ($20) and chargrilled Scotch fillet ($25). Tues–Sat noon–11pm, Sun & Mon noon–10pm.

Kings Arms 59 France St, Newton ☎09 373 3240, ⓦkingsarms.co.nz; map p.76. Popular pub and second-string venue hosting local and touring acts who can't quite fill the bigger venues. There's something on most nights (typically $10–20) and blues on Sunday afternoons. Daily noon–11pm or later.

PONSONBY

★**Dida's** 54 Jervois Rd ☎09 376 2813, ⓦdidas.co.nz; map p.85. The smart set flocks to this classy tapas bar and wine lounge, sinking into the leather sofas to choose from a fantastic wine selection and an array of delectable small plates such as fino-braised pork belly ($14) or prawn and coriander *buñuelo* ($9). Daily noon–midnight.

Golden Dawn 134 Ponsonby Rd ☎09 376 9929, ⓦwww.goldendawn.co.nz; map p.85. Listen for the clamour or follow the cool folk to this quirky and unconventional, signage-free corner bar. The music (sometimes live) is always a treat, so grab a pre-dinner craft beer or wine and make yourself at home in the grungy courtyard. Stay for something from their small but considered menu or dine elsewhere and return when things hot up. Tues–Thurs 4pm–late, Fri–Sun 3pm–late.

Mea Culpa 175 Ponsonby Rd ☎09 376 4460; map p.85. There's a cosy feel to this tiny bar where you can sit outside on wrought-iron chairs on the Turkish rug. Mon–Thurs 5pm–1am, Fri 5pm–3am, Sat 6pm–3am.

Revelry 106 Ponsonby Rd ☎09 376 8663, ⓦrevelry .co.nz; map p.85. It is usually pretty boisterous both out on the deck or in the colonial Shanghai interior that is at once unpretentious yet sexy. The beer, wine and food menus are fine but it is really about the cocktails – try the tequila-based Smokin' Tommy. Mon–Thurs 4pm–11pm, Fri & Sat noon–3am, Sun noon–10pm or later.

FESTIVALS

As befits a city of its size, Auckland has numerous festivals and annual events. These are some of the best.

JANUARY

Anniversary Day Massive sailing regatta on Auckland's Waitemata Harbour. Last Monday.

International Buskers Festival ⓦaucklandbuskersfestival.co.nz. Buskers from around the world take over the city streets. Free. Late January.

Laneway Festival ⓦauckland .lanewayfestival.com. One-day alt music festival held at Silo Park in Wynyard Quarter with class acts for NZ and abroad – Belle & Sebastian, Flying Lotus and Rackets in recent years. Last Monday.

FEBRUARY

Auckland Pride Festival ⓦaucklandpride festival.org.nz. Highlight of the gay year with lavish gala-night opener, the Big Gay Out one-day festival (ⓦbiggayout.co.nz; second Sun) in Coyle Park, Point Chevalier, just west of the zoo, gay garden visits, the Pride Parade along Ponsonby Road (third Sat) and a big party to finish. In 2016 the Pride Festival will coincide with Auckland hosting the Asia Pacific Outgames. Last 3 weeks.

MARCH

Auckland Arts Festival ⓦauckland festival.co.nz. Major international arts and culture festival at venues all over the city with everything from street performances to ballet. Held during two middle weeks every odd-numbered year.

Pasifika ⓦaucklandnz.com/pasifika. Twenty thousand people enjoy this free, two-day celebration of Polynesian and Pacific Island culture – music, culture, food and crafts – at Western Springs Park. Free. Second weekend.

Round the Bays Fun Run ⓦroundthebays .co.nz. Up to 70,000 people jog 9km along the Tamaki Drive waterfront. Second or third Sunday.

Easter Show ⓦeastershow.co.nz. Family entertainment, Kiwi-style, with equestrian events, lumberjack show, wine tasting and arts and crafts, all held at the ASB showgrounds along Greenlane. Easter weekend.

MAY

International Comedy Festival ⓦcomedyfestival.co.nz. Three weeks of performances by the best from New Zealand and around the world; recent acts have included Sara Pascoe and Rhys Darby. Early May.

JUNE

Matariki ⓦmatarikifestival.org.nz. The Maori New Year, marking the rising of Matariki (the Pleiades) in the winter sky, is marked by music, theatre and exhibitions throughout the month across the city.

JULY

Auckland International Film Festival ⓦnzff.co.nz. The nationwide film tour usually kicks off in the city where it all started back in 1969. Tickets $17. Late July.

NOVEMBER

Art in the Dark ⓦartinthedark.co.nz. Western Park, 13–16 Nov, 2014. Ponsonby's Western Park is transformed by light-art installations for 4 nights mid-month.

DECEMBER

Christmas in the Park ⓦchristmasinthe park.co.nz. Free family music extravaganza in the Domain. Saturday night in mid-Dec.

Franklin Road Christmas Lights Residents decorate their houses with elaborate lights. 1–24 December. Free.

The Whiskey 210 Ponsonby Rd ☎09 361 2666; map p.85. Stylish bar with something of the feel of a groovy gentleman's club, all chocolate leather sofas and white brick walls hung with superb photos of Little Richard, the New York Dolls, Jimi Hendrix and more. Great cocktails ($17–20). Daily 5pm–3am.

1

NEWMARKET

Lucha Lounge 1 York St ☎ 09 524 6370, ⓦ luchalounge .co.nz; map p.83. Tiny, dark bar mashing the look of a 1960s lounge with a Mexican *lucha libre* wrestling theme. Odd but it works. Tecate and Bohemia beers and passionfruit chilli margarita ($15) work perfectly and rowdy bands play at weekends. Arrive late and stay later. Tues–Fri 5pm–late, Sat 6pm–late.

CLASSICAL MUSIC, THEATRE AND COMEDY

Auckland's theatre, classical music and comedy scene seldom sets the world alight, though it is reasonably lively, and you'll usually have a choice of a couple of plays, comedy and dance or opera.

Aotea Centre Aotea Square, Queen St ☎ 09 309 2677, ⓦ aucklandlive.co.nz. New Zealand's first purpose-built opera house (Kiri Te Kanawa performed on the opening night in 1990) and the Auckland home of the Royal New Zealand Ballet.

Civic Theatre Corner of Queen & Wellesley sts ☎ 09 309 2677, ⓦ aucklandlive.co.nz. A lovely theatre that's worth visiting if there's anything at all on; it hosts July's International Film Festival along with musicals and visiting extravaganzas.

The Classic 321 Queen St ☎ 09 373 4321, ⓦ comedy .co.nz. Bar and comedy venue hosting top local names and touring acts. Shows are Mon–Sat with the best line-ups at weekends. $25 for the main acts, $15 for the regular late show (Fri & Sat at 10.30pm).

Maidment Theatre 8 Alfred St ☎ 09 308 2383, ⓦ maidment.auckland.ac.nz. Two university theatres, with mainstream works in the larger venue and more daring stuff in the studio. The Auckland Theatre Company (ⓦ atc.co.nz) mainly performs here.

Q 305 Queen St ☎ 09 309 9771, ⓦ qtheatre.co.nz. Auckland's newest theatre space, flexible enough to handle everything from Maori contemporary dance to cutting-edge plays and burlesque.

CINEMAS

Academy 44 Lorne St ☎ 09 373 2761, ⓦ academycinemas.co.nz. Dedicated art-house cinema with two screens tucked underneath the main library. Cheaper weekdays before 5pm, and $5 all day Wed.

Rialto 167 Broadway, Newmarket ☎ 09 369 2417, ⓦ rialto.co.nz. Handy 7-screener offering mainstream and slightly left-field fare. Cheap tickets before 5pm on Tues.

Silo Cinema ⓦ silopark.co.nz/silo-park/cinema. Free open-air movies in the main plaza in Wynyard Quarter. Dec–March Fri at 9pm. Market stalls and bar open from 5pm.

The Vic 48 Victoria Rd, Devonport ☎ 09 446 0100, ⓦ thevic.co.nz. New Zealand's oldest cinema (built in 1912) has been revived with a programme of mainstream and more arty new releases. Tickets are $14 (Tues $11) and Fullers do a $17 deal including return ferry trip from the city. Great for an evening out in Devonport.

SHOPPING

As New Zealand's biggest city, Auckland has its best range of shopping. For high-end fashion, the richest veins run through the Britomart Precinct and along Ponsonby Road with many of the top labels having shops in both locations. Newmarket also has a few notable names, plus a number of more mass-market outlets. Other names to look out for include: Deadly Ponies, Juliette Hogan, Kate Sylvester, Trelise Cooper, Twenty-seven Names and World.

ARTS, CRAFTS AND SOUVENIRS

Auckland Museum Store ☎ 09 309 2580, ⓦ aucklandmuseum.com. Excellent selection of everything from quality crafts through Kiwiana and classy homeware to books, prints and kids' toys. And every purchase goes to support the museum. Daily 10am–5pm.

Kura 188 Quay St, downtown ☎ 09 302 1151, ⓦ kuragallery.co.nz. Classy gallery focused on contemporary Maori art and design. Everything from paua inlaid bookmarks and greenstone pendants to $2000 korowai feather cloaks and some wonderfully patterned carvings. Mon–Fri 10am–6pm, Sat & Sun 11am–4pm.

FASHION

Karen Walker 18 Te Ara Tahuhu Walking Street, Britomart ☎ 09 309 6299, ⓦ karenwalker.com. New Zealand's biggest international brand as worn by Björk, Lady Gaga and many more. The clothes are cute

conservative and she also excels in eyewear and jewellery. Also in Newmarket and Ponsonby. Mon–Fri 10am–6pm, Sat 10am–5pm, Sun 11am–4pm.

Strangely Normal 19 O'Connell St, downtown ☎ 09 309 0600, ⓦ strangelynormal.com. Witty, modern take on Fifties men's style with some wonderfully bold patterned shirts. Mon–Fri 10am–6pm, Sat 10am–5pm, Sun 11am–4pm.

Zambezi 56 Tyler St, downtown ☎ 09 303 1701, ⓦ zambesi.co.nz. Long-standing and quirky fashion label featuring a lot of black. There's also menswear at this store but not at their Britomart and Newmarket branches. Mon–Fri 9.30am–5.30pm, Sat 10am–5pm, Sun 11am–4pm.

BOOKSHOPS

Unity Books 19 High Street, downtown ☎ 09 307 0731, ⓦ unitybooks.co.nz. Probably the city's best

independent bookshop. Mon–Thurs 9am–6pm, Fri 9am–7pm, Sat 10am–6pm, Sun 11am–5pm.
The Women's Bookshop 105 Ponsonby Rd, Ponsonby ☎09 376 4399, ⓦwomensbookshop.co.nz. Excellent small shop with knowledgeable staff and plenty for men too. Mon–Fri 10am–6pm, Sat & Sun 10am–5pm.

OUTDOOR CLOTHING AND CAMPING
Bivouac 210 Queen St, downtown ☎09 366 1966,

ⓦbivouac.co.nz. Stocks the best range of quality outdoors gear. Also open similar hours at 312 Broadway, Newmarket. Mon–Thurs 10am–6pm, Fri 9am–7pm, Sat 10am–6pm, Sun 10am–4pm.
Kathmandu 151 Queen St, downtown ☎09 309 4615, ⓦkathmandu.co.nz. Budget outdoor-clothing chain where there always seems to be a major sale on. Don't pay full price. Stores across Auckland and nationwide. Mon–Fri 9am–6pm, Sat & Sun 10am–5pm.

DIRECTORY

Automobile Association 99 Albert St ☎09 966 8800, ⓦaa.co.nz.
Consulates Australia Level 7, PWC Tower, 186–194 Quay St ☎09 921 8800, ⓦnewzealand.embassy.gov.au; Canada 9th floor, 48 Emily Place ☎09 309 3690, ⓦcanadainternational.gc.ca; Ireland Level 3, 205 Queen St ☎09 977 2252, ⓦireland.co.nz; UK Level 17, 151 Queen St ☎09 303 2973, ⓦukinnewzealand.fco.gov.uk; US Level 3, Citibank Centre, 23 Customs St East ☎09 303 2724, ⓦnewzealand.usembassy.gov.
Emergencies Police, fire and ambulance ☎111; Auckland Central police station ☎09 302 6400.
Gay and lesbian Helpline ☎0800 688 5463, ⓦoutline .org.nz. Operates Mon–Fri 9am–9pm, Sat & Sun 6–9pm.
Internet Libraries have free-use computers and wi-fi (max 200Mb/day). There's also free wi-fi (1Gb/day) in Britomart's outdoor spaces.
Laundry Travellers Laundromat, 458 K' Rd ☎09 376 6062; daily 5am–9.30pm. Parnell Laundry, 409 Parnell Rd, ☎09 373 2680; Mon–Fri 8am–6pm, Sat 8am–5pm, Sun 9am–3pm.
Left luggage Sky City Bus Terminal, 102 Hobson St, has lockers (daily 7am–8pm; small $5 all day, large $8; ☎09 300 6130), and most of the larger hostels also have long-term storage for one-time guests at minimal or no charge.
Library Central City Library, 44 Lorne St ☎09 377 0209, ⓦaucklandlibraries.govt.nz; Mon–Fri 9am–8pm, Sat & Sun 10am–4pm.

Medical treatment For emergencies go to Auckland City Hospital, Park Rd, Grafton ☎09 367 0000. The Travel Doctor, Level 1, 170 Queen St (Mon–Fri 9am–5pm; ☎09 373 3531, ⓦwww.traveldoctor.co.nz), offers vaccinations and travel health advice. CityMed, 8 Albert St (Mon–Fri 8am–6pm; ☎09 377 5525, ⓦcitymed.co.nz), has doctors and a pharmacy.
Pharmacy Medicines to Midnight, 160 Broadway, Newmarket (Mon–Sat 9.30am–midnight, Sun 10am–midnight; ☎09 520 6634, ⓦmedicinestomidnight.co.nz), is the most convenient late-closing pharmacy. Emergency departments of hospitals (see above) have 24hr pharmacies.
Post office The central city branch at 24 Wellesley St (Mon–Fri 8.30am–5.30pm; ☎0800 501 501) has poste restante facilities.
Swimming Central pools include the stylishly revamped, indoor Edwardian Tepid Baths at 100 Customs St West (☎09 379 4745), and the lovely open-air saltwater Parnell Baths on Judges Bay Rd (late Nov–Easter Mon–Fri 6am–8pm, Sat & Sun 8am–8pm; ☎09 373 3561). Check ⓦaucklandleisure.co.nz for these and others, or simply head for one of the beaches (see p.84 & p.88).
Women's centre Auckland Women's Centre, 4 Warnock St, Grey Lynn (Mon–Fri 9am–4pm; ☎09 376 3227, ⓦawc .org.nz), offers counselling and health advice and has a library.

West of Auckland

Real New Zealand begins, for many, in **West Auckland**, where verdant hills and magnificent beaches replace tower blocks, suburbs and sanitized wharves. The suburban sprawl peters out 20km west of the centre among the enveloping folds of the **Waitakere Ranges**. Here, some of Auckland's finest scenery and best adventures can be had little more than thirty minutes' drive from downtown. Despite being the most accessible expanse of greenery for 1.5 million people, the hills remain largely unspoilt, with plenty of trails through native bush. The soils around the eastern fringes of the Waitakeres nurture long-established **vineyards**, mainly around Kumeu.
    On hot summer days, thousands head over the hills to one of half a dozen thundering **West Coast surf beaches**, largely undeveloped but for a few holiday homes (known as *baches*), the odd shop and New Zealand's densest concentration of surf-lifesaving patrols.

1

WEST COAST TOURS

You'll need your own transport to do justice to the beaches and most of the ranges, unless you join one of the West Coast tours, or perhaps join a canyoning trip (see p.113). All trips pick up around central Auckland.

Bush & Beach ☎ 0800 423 224, � bushandbeach .co.nz. Afternoon trips ($145) include a short bushwalk to waterfalls and kauri trees, and a visit to Piha beach. The more satisfying full-day tour ($230) has longer guided walks and more bushcraft.

Fine Wine Tours ☎ 0800 023 111, � insidertouring .co.nz. Phil Parker personally leads small-group, half-day tours ($199; $30 for optional beer tasting) including three Kumeu wineries, lunch and a visit to Muriwai. Also full-day wine tours to Kumeu ($245)

with five wineries and optional beer tasting, plus tours to Waiheke Island ($339 including classy lunch and premium tasting but not the ferry).

TIME Unlimited ☎ 09 846 3469, � newzealandtours.travel. Personal service and a willingness to go the extra mile characterize these full-day small-group tours which include excellent bushwalking (matched to the group) along with the pounding surf of either Whatipu, Karekare or Piha beaches ($295).

GETTING AROUND

By train Auckland's suburban trains make it to the outlying communities of Henderson and Waitakere but don't get you to the wineries or beaches.

By car The easiest access to the majority of the walks and

beaches is via the Waitakere Scenic Drive (Route 24), which winds through the ranges from the dormitory suburb of Titirangi, in the foothills past the informative Arataki Visitor Centre.

Kumeu and Huapai

Once a viticultural powerhouse, West Auckland has been eclipsed by bigger enterprises elsewhere. There is still some production, centred on the contiguous and characterless communities of **KUMEU** and **HUAPAI**, though much of the grape juice comes from Marlborough, Gisborne and Hawke's Bay.

As early as 1819 the Reverend Samuel Marsden planted grapes in Kerikeri in the Bay of Islands, ostensibly to produce sacramental wine. But commercial winemaking didn't get under way until Dalmatians turned their hand to growing grapes, after the kauri gum they came to dig ceased to be profitable. Many of today's businesses owe their existence to immigrant families, a legacy evident in winery names such as Babich, Nobilo, Selak and Soljan. The region's vines still produce Pinot Noir, Pinot Gris and superb Chardonnay. If you plan some serious tasting, designate a non-drinking driver or join Fine Wine Tours (see box above).

ARRIVAL AND INFORMATION   KUMEU AND HUAPAI

By bus Richies bus #060 runs to Kumeu and Huapai (check � at.govt.nz for schedules) but you're lost without transport once you get there. Drive or take a wine tour.

Information The free *Kumeu Wine Country* booklet details almost a dozen wineries that can be visited.

EATING AND DRINKING

★**Hallertau Brewbar & Restaurant** 1171 Coatsville Riverhead Hwy, off SH16 ☎ 09 412 5555, ☻ hallertau .co.nz. Airy restaurant/bar and refreshing alternative to the wineries hereabouts. Sink a pint or two of their superb brewed-on-the-premises kolsch, pale ale, red ale, schwartzbier and cider, or try a tasting "paddle" of five ($14). Afterwards, tuck into light snacks ($14–16) or full meals such as pumpkin risotto, duck confit pasta or steak ($25–34). Daily 11am–midnight.

★**The Riverhead** 68 Queen St, Riverhead ☎ 09 412

8902, ☻ theriverhead.co.nz. Mangrovy tentacles of the Waitemata Harbour reach up to one of New Zealand's oldest taverns. Grab a beer and play pool in the public bar or head for the lounge bar for salt-and-pepper squid ($18), barbecue ribs and fries ($27) or pizza ($20) under the oaks at high water. Daily 11am–10pm or later.

THE WINERIES

Kumeu River 550 SH16, Kumeu ☎ 09 412 8415, ☻ kumeuriver.co.nz. The Brajkovich family produces

several of New Zealand's finest Chardonnays, all grown hereabouts. Generous tastings, including three single-vineyard varieties, make this an essential stop. Mon–Fri 9am–5pm, Sat 11am–5pm.
Soljans 366 SH16, Kumeu ☎09 412 2680,

ⓦsoljans.co.nz. Quality winery making locally grown Pinot Gris and a fun sparkling Muscat. There are free tastings and a smart but casual café serving the likes of beer-battered fish ($22) or a Mediterranean platter for two ($55). Daily 9am–4pm.

Waitakere Ranges and the West Coast beaches

Auckland's western limit is defined by the bush-clad, 500m-high **Waitakere Ranges**, perennially popular with weekending Aucklanders intent on a picnic or a stroll. The western slopes roll down to the wild, gold-and-black-sand **West Coast beaches** of Whatipu, Karekare, Piha and Muriwai. A counterpoint to the calm, gently shelved beaches of the Hauraki Gulf, these tempestuous shores are pounded by heavy surf and punctuated by precipitous headlands threaded by moderate walks.

WAITAKERE WALKS AND THE HILLARY TRAIL

The Waitakeres have some beautiful walks to waterfalls, kauri trees and lookouts over the wild ocean. Arataki Visitor Centre is the place to go for information, though few walks actually start there. The maps in several free leaflets – *Scenic Drive*, *Piha*, *Karekare and Anawhata* etc – are fine for most walks, though for the Hillary Trail you'll need the comprehensive *Waitakere Ranges Regional Park Recreation map* ($5).

WAITAKERE WALKS

The following walks are listed roughly from south to north.

Omanawanui Track Whatipu (3km; 2hr 15min; 220m descent). Superb views of the Manukau Harbour and its churning bar are the main reason to tackle this ridgeline descent which has some steep sections. Works best if you have someone to drop you off at the start, or turn it into a 5hr loop from Whatipu Kura Track.
Zion Hill–Pararaha Valley–Tunnel Point circuit Karekare (8km; 4hr; 200m ascent). This lovely loop at the south end of Karekare beach follows part of the old Pararaha Tramway to Whatipu visiting an old tunnel that proved too tight a squeeze for a large steam engine whose boiler still litters the shore.
Kitekite Falls Piha (3.5km; 1hr 30min loop; 220m ascent). Starting 1km up Glen Esk Rd, which runs inland opposite Piha's central

Domain, this fairly easy track passes the three-stage plunge of Kitekite Falls (totalling 40m), below which is a cool pool.
Lion Rock Piha (500m return; 20–30min; 60m ascent). An energetic climb to a shoulder two-thirds of the way up Lion Rock, best done as the day cools. The summit is out of bounds.
Tasman Lookout Track Piha (600m return; 30–40min; 40m ascent). From the south end of the beach this track climbs up to a lookout over the tiny cove of The Gap, where a spectacular blowhole performs in heavy surf.
Auckland City Walk (1hr loop; 1.5km; 50m ascent). Not a city walk at all but a delightful amble which threads its way through native bush, alongside a peaceful stream and offers an adventurous side scramble up to a hidden waterfall.

THE HILLARY TRAIL

In honour of the 2008 passing of New Zealand's mountaineering hero, Sir Edmund Hillary, Auckland has linked a series of existing walking tracks through the Waitakere Ranges into the **Hillary Trail** (77km; 3–4 days; download map at ⓦaucklandcouncil.govt.nz). Running from the Arataki Visitor Centre via Whatipu, Karekare, Piha and Te Henga to Muriwai, it gives a great sense of the region – regenerating rainforest, stands of kauri, rocky shores, black-sand beaches and historic remains. The highest point is only 390m but it is an undulating track and tougher than you might expect. Occasionally slippery, steep paths and unbridged streams can make it a good deal harder in winter, and in any season the last 27km day takes most people at least 10hr.

Nights are generally spent in primitive campsites ($5; book on ☎09 366 2000), though you can stay under a roof in Whatipu, Piha and Te Henga. The best source of on-the-ground information is the Arataki Visitor Centre (see p.112).

1

Some history

The Kawerau a Maki people knew the region as Te Wao Nui a Tiriwa or "the Great Forest of Tiriwa", aptly describing the kauri groves that swathed the hills before the arrival of Europeans. By the turn of the twentieth century, diggers had pretty much cleaned out the kauri gum, but logging continued until the 1920s, leaving the land spent. The Auckland Council bought the land, built reservoirs and designated a vast tract as the Centennial Memorial Park, with 200km of walking tracks leading to fine vistas and numerous waterfalls that cascade off the escarpment.

Arataki Visitor Centre

300 Scenic Drive • Sept–April daily 9am–5pm; May–Aug Mon–Fri 10am–4pm, Sat & Sun 9am–5pm • ☎ 09 817 0077

The best introduction to the area is the **Arataki Visitor Centre**, entered past a striking *pou*, or guardian post created from a fallen kauri by Te Kawerau a Maki carvers. Duck into the ground-floor auditorium for the inspiring **movie** about the Waitakeres (12min; on demand; free) then head upstairs for more carvings and displays on the area. Outside, walkways forge into the second-growth forest: the ten-minute plant identification loop trail identifies a dozen or so significant forest trees and ferns; a longer trail (45min) visits one of the few mature kauri stands to survive the loggers. Arataki is also the place to pick up leaflets and maps for the numerous **short walks** in the ranges (see box, p.111). Up to five self-contained campervans can park here for one night, or two in winter (see box, p.99).

Whatipu

45km southwest of the city centre, at the north head of Manukau Harbour

Whatipu is the southernmost of Auckland's West Coast surf beaches and is located by the sandbar entrance to Manukau Harbour, the watery grave of many a ship. The wharf at Whatipu was briefly the terminus of the precarious coastal **Parahara Railway**, which hauled kauri from the mill at Karekare across the beach and headlands during the 1870s. The tracks were continually pounded by surf, but a second tramway from Piha covered the same treacherous expanse in the early twentieth century.

Over the last few decades, the sea has receded more than a kilometre, leaving a broad beach backed by wetlands colonized by cabbage trees, tall toetoe grasses and waterfowl. It's a great, wild place to explore, particularly along the base of the cliffs to the north where, in half an hour, you can walk to the **Ballroom Cave**, fitted with a sprung kauri-wood dancefloor around 1900 that apparently still survives, buried by 5m of sand that drifted into the cave in the intervening years. For a longer walk try the Omanawanui Track (see box, p.111).

ACCOMMODATION AND EATING   WHATIPU

Huia Foodstore 1194 Huia Rd, Huia, 10km east of Whatipu ☎ 09 811 8113, ⓦ huiafoodstore.co.nz. On the way to Whatipu the last supplies are from this revamped take on a traditional Kiwi takeaway and café. There's fresh baking, superb espresso, jars of sweets along the walls, scoop ice cream. The take aways are top notch (fish is freshest on Fri, Sat & Sun) and the waterside park across the road is a perfect spot to take them. Mon–Thurs 8am–4pm, Fri–Sun 8am–7pm; check website for reduced winter hours.

Whatipu Lodge ☎ 09 811 8860, ⓦ whatipulodge .co.nz. This 1870 former mill manager's house is the only habitation at Whatipu and a great base to experience a wild area of New Zealand, just an hour's drive from Auckland. Twin and single rooms are simple, there's no mains electricity (it generates its own for limited hours) and no mobile phone coverage but there are communal cooking facilities, good hot showers, a tennis court and full-sized billiard table. Bring a sleeping bag or sheets and duvets. Booking is essential. Rooms are charged at $35 per person, but $45 for one-night stays. Camping $7.50, double $90

Karekare

Perhaps the most intimate and immediately appealing of the West Coast settlements is **KAREKARE**, 17km west of the Arataki Visitor Centre and accessed along Piha Road,

1

WEST COAST BEACHES: WALKS, TOURS AND ACTIVITIES

The West Coast's bush-clad hills, steep gullies and wild, open beaches are the setting for a bunch of activities including horseriding in the dunes, sand yachting and a couple of the best canyoning trips around.

HORSERIDING

Muriwai Beach Horse Treks Horse Park, Coast Rd ☎ 09 411 8948, ⓦ muriwaibeachhorsetreks.co.nz. Offers the chance to explore the beach, dunes and pine forests to the north ($95/2hr). Treks leave daily at 10am, 2pm and in summer 4pm, but call ahead.

SURFING

Muriwai Surf School By the beach ☎ 021 478 734, ⓦ muriwaisurfschool.co.nz. Rents surf gear (board and wetsuit $40/3hr), bodyboards ($10/hr) and mountain bikes ($10/hr), and conducts surf lessons (introductory $60, advanced $100).

Piha Surf Shop 122 Seaview Rd ☎ 09 812 8723, ⓦ pihasurf.co.nz. Mike Jolly sells his own handcrafted longboards and a good range of secondhand boards from what is essentially Piha's surf central. There are rentals too (from $25 for 3hr) and if you need to brush up your skills Mike can hook you up with a local guide/ instructor.

CANYONING

AWOL Adventures ☎ 0800 462 965, ⓦ awoladventures.co.nz. About the most fun you can have in a wetsuit around Auckland is canyoning, a combination of swimming, abseiling, jumping into deep pools and sliding down rock chutes. AWOL run excellent trips in two canyons near Piha, with pick-ups at SkyCity in Auckland. In Piha Canyon the emphasis is on abseiling, particularly on their full-day trip ($195).

The lower canyon is host to the half-day trip ($165) and night canyoning ($185; mostly in winter) with just a headtorch and glowworms for illumination. If you're feeling fit and robust, opt for the full day in the Blue Canyon ($195) which involves slightly fewer abseils but more slides, bigger jumps and considerably more bushwalking. Bring your swimsuit, a towel and a pair of old trainers.

---

with manuka, pohutukawa and cabbage trees running down to a broad beach and only a smattering of houses. In one hectic year, this dramatic spot provided the setting for beach scenes in Jane Campion's 1993 film *The Piano* and the inspiration for Crowded House's *Together Alone* album. The Karekare Surf Club patrols the beach on summer weekends, or there is a pool below **Karekare Falls**, a five-minute walk on a track just inland from the road. There is nowhere to stay here, and no facilities.

Piha

For decades **PIHA**, 20km west of the Arataki Visitor Centre and accessed along Piha Road, has been an icon for Aucklanders. A quintessential West Coast beach with a string of low-key weekend cottages and crashing surf, it lures a wide spectrum of day-trippers and the party set, whose New Year's Eve antics hastened in a dusk-till-dawn alcohol ban on holiday weekends. Despite the gradual gentrification of the old *baches* and the opening of the modern *Piha Café*, it is hanging onto its rustic charm.

The 3km beach is hemmed in by bush-clad hills and split by Piha's defining feature, 101m-high **Lion Rock**. With some imagination, this former *pa* site resembles a seated lion staring out to sea. The rock was traditionally known as Te Piha, referring to the wave patterns around it that resemble the bow wave of a canoe.

Most **swimmers** head for South Piha, where the more prestigious of two surf-lifesaving clubs hogs the best **surf**. *Piha Surf Shop* (see box above) sells and rents gear. If battling raging surf isn't your thing, head for **Kitikite Falls** (see box, p.111).

ARRIVAL AND DEPARTURE   PIHA

By shuttle The Piha Surf Shuttle (Dec–Feb daily; March– Nov on demand; $45 each way, $70 same-day return; ☎ 0800 952 526, ⓦ surfshuttle.co.nz) picks up at lodgings around Auckland around 9am and leaves Piha for the city at 4pm. Also runs here straight from Auckland International Airport for $70.

1

ACCOMMODATION

Black Sands Lodge 54 Beach Rd ☎021 969 924, ⓦpihabeach.co.nz. A beach-chic style runs through these three tasteful *baches*: a beach cabin and two suites with big decks, French doors and quality furnishings and bedding. The genial lesbian hosts will also prepare romantic four-course dinners, served in your suite (around $140 a head, excluding wine). Cabin $\overline{\$140}$, suites $\overline{\$210}$

Campervan parking Up to five self-contained campervans can park at the end of Glen Esk Road for one night, or two in winter. Five more can stay at the end of Log Race Road (see box, p.99). Per person $\overline{\$6}$

★**Piha Beachstay** (aka Jandal Palace) 38 Glenesk Rd ☎09 812 8381, ⓦpihabeachstay.co.nz. Excellent and very peaceful modern backpackers sleeping just ten, tucked away from the beach in a verdant valley. There's free wi-fi, late checkout and rooms (including one with en suite and bath at $120) that open onto sunny decks. Dorm $\overline{\$33}$, doubles $\overline{\$86}$

Piha Domain Motor Camp 21 Seaview Rd ☎09 812 8815. Classic Kiwi campsite, close to the beach with flat camping, fairly simple facilities (though there's a flash new bathroom block) and some tiny but well-maintained cabins. Camping $\overline{\$15}$, powered sites $\overline{\$18}$, cabins $\overline{\$60}$

Piha Ocean Lookout 14 Log Race Rd ☎09 812 8207, ⓦpihaoceanlookoutbandb.co.nz. Set high on a headland about 4km from Piha beach, this B&B has two rooms but they're only let to one party as they share a bathroom and mini-kitchen. There are great views from the lounge or deck where a lovely continental breakfast is served, and clifftop walks (including the Hillary Trail) run right by. $\overline{\$140}$

Piha Surf Shop 122 Seaview Rd ☎09 812 8723, ⓦpihasurf.co.nz. The principal surfers hangout, located a kilometre or so before the beach on the road in to Piha. This chilled place has a range of rustic self-contained caravans, plus cabins with long-drop toilets and a shared single shower. There are great distant views over the beach and everything you need for surfing (see box, p.113). Per person $\overline{\$30}$

EATING AND DRINKING

Blairs on the Beach 23 Marine Parade South ☎09 812 8309. Salty hair and black sand on your feet is the correct dress code for this classic Kiwi beach takeaway that does excellent fresh fish and chips, hearty burgers and toasted sandwiches. A chocolate milkshake with a shot of espresso makes a great ersatz iced mocha. Daily 11am–6.30pm or later.

★**The Piha Café** 20 Seaview Rd ☎09 812 8808, ⓦpihacafe.com. Piha's only real café, a casual but stylish rough-hewn timber place with plenty of seating inside and out. Plenty of good baking, fresh salads, counter food and a blackboard menu of seasonal dishes (mostly $15–25). The coffee's great and they even do takeaway pizzas ($19–25). Hours flexible and much reduced in winter. Licensed. Mon–Thurs 8.30am–4pm or later, Sat & Sun 8.30am–9pm or 10pm.

Piha Surf Lifesaving Club 23 Marine Parade South, overlooking South Piha beach ☎09 812 8896, ⓦpihaslsc.com. You can eat here, but it's really more of a spot to watch the sunset over the sea with a beer in hand. Sign yourself in. Oct–April Mon–Fri 5–10pm, Sat & Sun noon–10pm.

Cascade Kauri

3km along Falls Rd, accessed 1.5km along Te Henga Road off Scenic Drive • Daily: Oct–March 6am–9pm; April–Sept 8am–7pm • Free

The drive through the Waitakere Golf Club is an odd introduction to **Cascade Kauri**, a delightful patch of forest that's also known as the **Ark in the Park**. Forest & Bird partly maintain this open sanctuary, its volunteers undertaking pest and weed control with superb results. The bush is looking great and North Island robins, kokako and whiteheads have all been reintroduced to the area. There are longer tracks, but the best introduction is the delightful **Auckland City Walk** (see box, p.111).

Te Henga

TE HENGA (also known as Bethell's Beach), 27km northwest of the Arataki Visitor Centre, is similar to, but less dramatic than Karekare, Piha or Muriwai, and is correspondingly less visited, making it good for escaping the crowds in the summer. There are no shops, but there is a surf club and occasional café. If you fancy some freshwater swimming or just sliding down sand dunes, head to **Lake Wainamu**, reached on foot along a sandy streambed path (30min each way) from a car park 1km back from the beach.

ACCOMMODATION AND EATING
TE HENGA

Bethells Beach Cottages 267 Bethells Road ☎ 09 810 9581, ⓦ bethellsbeach.com. Located on a hill just behind the dunes, these three casually bohemian self-contained cottages have great sea views and a wonderfully relaxing tenor. Hot tub and holistic health treatments available. Bring everything you need to cook. **$260**

The Bethells Café Main beach car park off Bethells Road ☎ 09 810 9387, ⓦ facebook.com/TheBethellsCafe. Good food and coffee are reason enough to stop by this caravan café, but it is more about the chilled vibe and occasional live music. Nov Sat & Sun 10am–6pm; Dec–Feb, Fri 5.30–9pm, Sat & Sun 10am–6pm.

Campervan parking Up to five self-contained campervans can park at Cascade Kauri for one night, three in winter (see box, p.99). Per person **$6**

Muriwai

MURIWAI, 15km north of Piha and 15km southwest of Huapai, is the most populous of the West Coast beach settlements and has wonderful surf, and a long beach stretching 45km north to the heads of Kaipara Harbour.

Muriwai Gannet Colony

Muriwai's main attraction is at the southern end of the beach where a **gannet colony** (best seen late Oct to mid-Feb) occupies Motutara Island and Otakamiro Point, the headland between the main beach and the surfers' cove of Maori Bay. The gannets breed here before migrating to sunnier climes, a few staying behind with the fur seals that inhabit the rocks below. Gannets normally prefer the protection of islands, but this is one of the few places where they nest on the mainland, just below viewing platforms from where you get a bird's-eye view. Short paths lead up here from near the surf club and off the road to Maori Bay.

ACCOMMODATION AND EATING
MURIWAI

Muriwai Motorcamp 451 Motutara Rd ☎ 09 411 9262, ⓦ muriwaimotorcamp.co.nz. Pines shade this spacious campsite behind the dunes. There are power sites, hot showers (50¢ coins), kitchen, laundry and a small lounge. Camping **$14**

Sand Dunz Café 455 Motutara Rd ☎ 09 411 8558. Good café with sandwiches and salads from the counter food, a standard range of breakfasts and lunches (mostly $16–20; served until 4pm or 5pm) and takeaway burgers and chips. Daily: April–Sept 7.30am–4pm (takeaways to 5pm); Oct–March 7.30am–7.30pm.

North of Auckland

Some 40km north of the city, Auckland's straggling suburbs merge into the **Hibiscus Coast**, centred on the suburban **Whangaparaoa Peninsula** and the anodyne beachside community of **Orewa**, now bypassed by the Northern Motorway. Immediately to the north, the hot springs at **Waiwera** herald the beach-and-barbecue scene of **Wenderholm Regional Park** and the classic old village of **Puhoi**.

Passing beyond Puhoi puts you into **Northland**; coverage of that region begins with Warkworth (see p.144).

Orewa and the Whangaparaoa Peninsula

The most striking of the Hibiscus Coast beaches is the 3km strand backed by **OREWA**, predominantly a retirement and dormitory town dominated by the twelve-storey Nautilus apartment block. It's a relaxing spot with accommodation, restaurants and plenty of good spots for swimming, kitesurfing and paddleboarding.

South of Orewa, the **Whangaparaoa Peninsula** juts out 12km into the Hauraki Gulf to Gulf Harbour Marina, launching point for trips to the delightful bird sanctuary of **Tiritiri Matangi** (see p.136).

1

NORTHERN GATEWAY TOLL ROAD

To avoid paying the $2.20 **toll** for the final 5km of Auckland's Northern Motorway, come off at Silverdale and follow the coast road through Orewa – it'll only add ten minutes to your journey. Otherwise, pay online (@tollroad.govt.nz) either before or up to five days after your journey, or use the roadside pay kiosks.

Shakespear Regional Park

20km southeast of Orewa • Daily: Oct–March 6am–9pm; April–Sept 6am–7pm

You can spend a few pleasant hours swimming, camping and birdwatching at **Shakespear Regional Park**, which envelops the tip of the Whangaparaoa Peninsula. This open sanctuary is protected by a predator-proof fence and, after extensive pest poisoning and trapping in 2011, bird numbers are on the up. Easy walks wander through regenerating bush where you might see red-crowned parakeets, bellbirds and tui.

ARRIVAL AND ACTIVITIES

OREWA

By bus Catch North Star-branded Auckland bus routes #893–896 from 13 Albert St in central Auckland. Destinations Auckland (11 daily; 1hr).

SUP Shed 12 Bakehouse Lane @09 426 7873, @supshed.com. Stand-up paddleboard rentals ($20/hr) either from the shop or in summer from a tent on the beach. One-hour lessons for $70 including board rental. Daily 10am–5.30pm; closed Mon in winter.

ACCOMMODATION

Orewa Beach Top 10 Holiday Park 265 Hibiscus Coast Hwy @09 426 5832, @orewabeachtop10.co.nz. Large, high-standard and very popular campsite with kitchen cabins ($80) and tourist cabins ($120) shaded by pohutukawas backing Orewa Beach. Camping $20, cabins $64

Pillows Lodge 412 Hibiscus Coast Hwy @09 426 6338, @pillows.co.nz. Central hostel that's ranged around a central courtyard with a piano in the lounge. Two kayaks to rent, and en-suite rooms ($95) and a family room ($115) come with TV and fridge. Dorms $31, doubles $85

Shakespear Regional Park Whangaparaoa Rd @09 301 0100, @aucklandcouncil.govt.nz. Large camping area close to a great swimming beach. There's tap water, flush toilets, and provision for self-contained campervan parking. Booking essential. Per person: camping $13, campervan parking $6

Villa Orewa 264 Hibiscus Coast Hwy @09 426 3073, @villaorewa.co.nz. Classy, whitewashed Greek-island-style B&B offering airy rooms with bold-coloured furnishings, beach-view balconies and delicious breakfasts. Dinner is available on request. $210

Waves 1 Kohu Rd, off Hibiscus Coast Hwy @0800 426 6889, @waves.co.nz. The town's fanciest motel is just steps from the beach, has underfloor heating and stylish decor. The premium rooms have the best views. $180, premium $230

EATING

Alley Katz 358 Hibiscus Coast Hwy @09 426 0548. Catch the morning sun roadside at this relaxed café with a tempting array of counter food, a yummy breakfast wrap ($10) and calamari salad ($18). Daily 7am–4pm.

Coast Bites and Brews 342 Hibiscus Coast Hwy @09 421 1016, @dcbrewing.co.nz. Fun bar showcasing Deep Creek Brewing's excellent range of small-batch craft beers and serving up the likes of skirt steak wraps ($21) and surf-and turf platters ($35). Daily 11am–11pm.

Waiwera Thermal Spa Resort

21 Waiwera Rd • Mon–Thurs & Sun 9am–8pm, Fri & Sat 9am–9pm; movies daily noon, 3pm & 7pm • $26; children $15; adult residents $14; child residents $8 • @0800 WAIWERA, @waiwera.co.nz

The coastal highway runs 6km north of Orewa to **WAIWERA** where naturally hot waters are channelled into the family-oriented **Waiwera Thermal Resort**, a cluster of indoor and outdoor pools naturally heated to between 24°C and 40°C. Hurtle down suicidal waterslides, drift along the fairly functional Lazy River or soak your bones while watching a PG-rated movie. Spa treatments, massages and wood-fired pizza are all available and if you're staying in the area ask your accommodation about the temporary resident discount.

Wenderholm Regional Park

SH1, 1km north of Waiwera • Daily 6am–dusk • Kayak rental $25/hr: Christmas to mid-Jan daily; mid-Jan–Feb Sat & Sun only • Free

Wenderholm Regional Park is bordered by the Puhoi River estuary and a sweeping golden beach backed by pohutukawa-shaded swathes of grass that's often packed with picnicking families on summer weekends. There are coin-op barbecues, cold showers and, three hours either side of high tide, the chance to rent sit-on-top **kayaks** and muck about on the estuary. Walking tracks (20min–2hr) wind up to a headland viewpoint through nikau palm groves alive with birds that have repopulated the area from Tiritiri Matangi (see p.136).

Couldrey House

Christmas–Easter daily 1–4pm; Easter–Christmas Sat & Sun 1–4pm • $5 • ☎ 09 528 3713, ⓦ historiccouldreyhouse.co.nz

This 1860s beach house was built as a winter home (hence the name of the surrounding park) and has been restored and decorated in period fashion (except for the classic pink and Formica 1950s bathroom). Check out the beautiful 1884 map of Greenwood Estate, a proposed resort and housing development that would have seen all of Wenderholm covered by a housing subdivision.

ACCOMMODATION   WENDERHOLM

Wenderholm Camping SH1, 1km north of Waiwera ☎ 09 366 2000. Large, new *Schischka* campsite with flush toilets and potable water but little shade, beside the estuary plus self-contained campervan parking for one night in the main car park (access only when park gates are open). Per person: camping **$13**, campervans **$6**

Puhoi

A pale blue wayside crucifix marks the entrance to tiny **PUHOI**, 6km north of Waiwera, a bucolic place settled by staunchly Catholic Bohemian migrants who arrived in 1863 from what is now the Czech Republic. The land was poor, and settlers were forced to eke out a living by cutting the bush for timber. They stuck with it, though, and Mass is still held in the 1881 weatherboard Saints Peter and Paul **church**.

Puhoi Bohemian Museum

Christmas–Easter daily 1–4pm; Easter–Christmas Sat, Sun & school holidays 1–4pm • $3.50 • ☎ 09 422 0472, ⓦ puhoihistoricalsociety .org.nz

Most visitors to Puhoi get no further than the pub, but try to look in at the **Puhoi Bohemian Museum**, in the former Convent School. The model of the village as it was in 1900 is a gem and really comes alive if you engage the interest of one of the volunteers on duty.

ACTIVITIES   PUHOI

Puhoi River Canoe Hire ☎ 09 422 0891, ⓦ puhoirivercanoes.co.nz. Rents kayaks for a gentle, unguided 2hr trip to or from Wenderholm, always going with the tide. $50 including pick-up; booking essential. Daily Sept–June.

EATING AND DRINKING

Puhoi Pub Puhoi Rd ☎ 09 422 0812. Iconic 1879 Kiwi pub festooned with photos and pioneering paraphernalia including the horns of famed bullock teams that once helped clear the dense bush hereabouts. The drinks and food are barely average but tourists, motorbike groups and Auckland weekenders all enjoy

1

chilling in the beer garden. Daily 10am–7pm, later at weekends.

★ **Puhoi Valley Café & Cheese Store** 275 Ahuroa Rd, 3km north ☎ 09 422 0670, ⓦ puhoivalley.co.nz. Pop in for free samples of the delicious cheeses, super-rich ice cream (the hokey pokey is locally famous) and sorbets such as forest berry, all made on the premises, but plan to stick around for something like an aged cheddar Welsh rarebit and bacon ($15) or a cheese platter ($18–45). It's all elegantly served inside or on the terrace overlooking lawns with bush-clad hills behind. Mon–Fri 10am–4pm, Sat & Sun 9am–5pm.

Southeast of Auckland

Most southbound travellers hurry along Auckland's southern motorway to Hamilton or turn off to Thames and the Coromandel Peninsula at Pokeno – either way missing out on the modest attractions of the **Firth of Thames**, a sheltered inlet of the Hauraki Gulf separating south Auckland from the Coromandel Peninsula. Its frequently windswept western littoral comprises land built up from successive deposits of shell banks; much has been converted to farmland but newer shell banks in the making can be seen, along with flocks of feeding birds, on what is known as the **Seabird Coast**.

GETTING AROUND

By bike Cyclists will find that the coast road to the southeast is an excellent way into and out of Auckland, following Tamaki Drive from the city centre through Panmure and Howick to Clevedon and the coast.

Kaiaua

The tiny village of Kaiaua comprises little more than a pub, a fish and chip shop and a tiny marina where half a dozen boats squeeze in between the mangroves. It is like much of New Zealand was half a century ago.

Miranda Shorebird Centre

283 East Coast Rd, 7km south of Kaiaua • Daily 9am–5pm, and often later in the summer • Free • ☎ 09 232 2781, ⓦ miranda-shorebird .org.nz

In the peak January-to-March season the modest **Miranda Shorebird Centre** is often full of twitchers who can point you in the direction of the best hide (1hr return) and fill you in on the current hot sightings. Almost a quarter of all known species of migrating shore birds visit the region, and 30,000-strong flocks of **wrybill plover** avoid the northern winter by spending it at this internationally significant site. During the southern summer (Sept–March) you'll see arctic migrants – notably bar-tailed **godwits** and **lesser knots** – who fly 15,000km from Alaska and Siberia. Viewing is optimal two hours either side of high tide; the centre also has a good stock of natural history books and a sunny deck.

Miranda Hot Springs

Front Miranda Rd, 10km south of Kaiaua • Daily 9am–9.30pm • General entry $14, private spa $15/person for 30min, combo $24 each • ☎ 07 867 3055, ⓦ mirandahotsprings.co.nz

Just twenty minutes' drive short of Thames, the slightly alkaline **Miranda Hot Springs** is an open-air affair with an Olympic-size warm pool kept at 36–38°C, a cooler children's pool and private kauri spa tubs (40–41°C).

ACCOMMODATION AND EATING   MIRANDA SEABIRD COAST

Kaiaua Fisheries 939 East Coast Rd, Kaiaua ☎ 09 232 2776. You can sit in at the small fish restaurant, but the real pleasure here is to order fish and chips to go (around $8), buy a couple of takeaway beers from the pub and sit by the water watching the world go by. Daily 9am–8.30pm.

Miranda Holiday Park Miranda Hot Springs ☎0800 833 144, ⓦmirandaholidaypark.co.nz. Very high quality campsite with separate tent area, a wide range of cabins, a tennis court and delightful landscaped, hot mineral pools. Camping $23, cabins $149

Miranda Shorebird Centre 283 East Coast Rd, 7km south of Kaiaua ☎09 232 2781, ⓦmiranda -shorebird.org.nz. Keen birders can stay here in

4–6-person bunk rooms or self-contained units. There's a good kitchen and a sunny veranda. Bring food and bedding (or rent for $5). Dorms $25, units $95

Rays Rest 5km south of Kaiaua. A line of campervans is normally parked on the shoreline where self-contained vans can stay for up to two nights. When it is full, some people camp outside the designated area (though you shouldn't). Public toilets are available in Kaiaua. **Free**

Islands of the Hauraki Gulf

Auckland's greatest asset is the island-studded **Hauraki Gulf**, a 70km-square patch of ocean to the northeast of the city. In Maori, Hauraki means "wind from the north" – though the gulf is somewhat sheltered from the prevailing winds and ocean swells by Great Barrier Island, creating benign conditions for Auckland's legions of yachties. Most just sail or fish, but those who wish to strike land can visit some of the fifty-odd islands, administered by the Department of Conservation, designated either for recreational use with full access, or as sanctuaries for endangered wildlife, requiring permits.

Auckland's nearest island neighbour is **Rangitoto**, a flat cone of gnarled and twisted lava that dominates the harbourscape. The most populous of the gulf islands is **Waiheke**, with sandy beaches and classy wineries. Wine was definitely verboten at nearby **Rotoroa Island**, once a Salvation Army detox centre and now open for day-visits.

Waiheke's sophistication is a far cry from laidback **Great Barrier Island** with its sandy surf beaches, hilly tramping tracks and exceptional fishing. The Department of Conservation's policy of allowing access to wildlife sanctuaries is wonderfully demonstrated at **Tiritiri Matangi**, where a day-trip gives visitors an unsurpassed opportunity to see some of the world's rarest birds.

Rangitoto and Motutapu islands

The low, conical shape of **Rangitoto**, 10km northeast of the city centre, is a familiar sight to every Aucklander. Yet few set foot on the island, missing out on a freakish land of fractured black lava with the world's largest pohutukawa forest clinging precariously to its crevices. Alongside lies the much older **Motutapu** or "sacred island", linked to Rangitoto by a narrow causeway.

A **day-trip** is enough to get a feel for Rangitoto, make the obligatory hike to the summit (from where there are magnificent views of the city and Hauraki Gulf) and tackle a few trails, but **longer stays** are possible if you pitch your tent at the simple campsite at Home Bay on Motutapu – though this is a 3hr walk from Rangitoto Wharf. Currently, separate ferry operators run to the two islands; inconveniently, neither offers one-way fares.

Brief history

Rangitoto is Auckland's youngest and largest **volcano**, its birth witnessed around six hundred years ago by Motutapu Maori, who apparently called the island "blood red sky" after the spectacle that accompanied its creation.

The government purchased Rangitoto for £15 in 1854, putting it to use as a military lookout point and a work camp for **prisoners**. From the 1890s, areas were leased for camping and unauthorized **baches** were cobbled together on the sites. Over 100 *baches* had sprouted by the late 1930s when legislation stopped any new construction. In

1

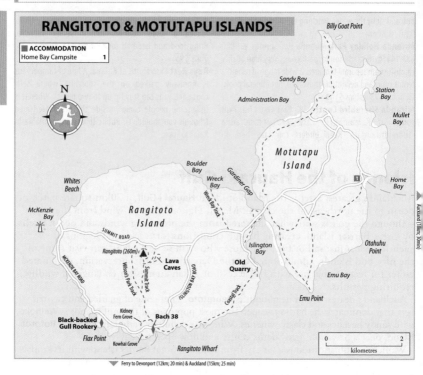

RANGITOTO & MOTUTAPU ISLANDS

■ **ACCOMMODATION**
Home Bay Campsite 1

Billy Goat Point

N

Sandy Bay

Administration Bay

Station Bay

Mullet Bay

Motutapu Island

Boulder Bay

Wreck Bay

Gardiner Gap

Home Bay

Whites Beach

Wreck Bay Track

McKenzie Bay

Rangitoto Island

SUMMIT ROAD

Rangitoto (260m)

Lava Caves

Islington Bay

Otahuhu Point

MCKENZIE BAY ROAD

Wilson's Park Track

Summit Track

ISLINGTON BAY ROAD

Old Quarry

Emu Bay

Coastal Track

Kidney Fern Grove

Bach 38

Emu Point

Black-backed Gull Rookery

Flax Point

Kowhai Grove

Rangitoto Wharf

0   2
kilometres

Auckland (18km; 30min)

▼ Ferry to Devonport (12km; 20 min) & Auckland (15km; 25 min)

recent years, the cultural value of this unique set of 1920s and 1930s houses has been appreciated and the finest examples of the remaining 34 are being preserved for posterity, their corrugated-iron chimneys and cast-off veranda-railing fenceposts capturing the Kiwi make-do spirit.

Flora and fauna

Rangitoto's lack of soil and porous rock have created unusual conditions for **plant life**, though the meagre supply of insects attracts few birds, making it eerily quiet. Pohutukawa trees seeded first, given a head start by their roots, which are able to tap underground reservoirs of fresh water up to 20m below the surface. Smaller and fleshier plants then established themselves under the protective canopy. Harsh conditions have led to some strange **botanical anomalies**: both epiphytes and mud-loving mangroves are found growing directly on the lava, an alpine moss is found at sea level, and the pohutukawa has hybridized with its close relative, the northern rata, to produce a spectrum of blossoms ranging from pink to crimson. Successful eradication of wallabies, possums and even rats has allowed pohutukawa to rebound with vigour as DOC have introduced takahe, saddleback and whiteheads to Motutapu. Native parakeets (*kakariki*) have also self-introduced and bred here for the first time in a century.

Bach 38

Near Rangitoto Wharf • Generally only open by appointment • Free • ☎ 09 445 1894, ⓦ rangitoto.org

Bach 38 has been restored to its 1930s condition and you're free to look around the outside. If you're lucky you might strike one of the days when the Rangitoto Island Historic Conservation Trust opens it up for inspection. Several more *baches* are being preserved by the trust, though it is slow work.

Motutapu

The landscape of **Motutapu** is more typical rural New Zealand – grassy paddocks, ridge-top fencelines and macrocarpa windbreaks – but DOC's plan is to re-vegetate a third of the island with natives. It is early days yet and the only moderately mature section is the **Rotary Centennial Walkway** (2km one way; 40min) through bush first planted in 1994. Continue beyond the end of the walkway to see the remains of World War II gun emplacements, and long views of some beautiful coastline.

ARRIVAL AND DEPARTURE   RANGITOTO AND MOTUTAPU

By ferry Fullers (☎09 367 9111, ⚲fullers.co.nz; 2–4 daily; $29 return) takes 25min to reach Rangitoto Wharf. Crossings also call at Devonport. Catch the 7.30am ferry on Sat or Sun and the round-trip is just $18. Explore (☎0800 397 567, ⚲exploregroup.co.nz) operate between the Ferry Building and Motutapu's Home Bay (Dec 1–21 Sat & Sun 1–2 daily, Dec 22–Jan 1–2 daily, check website for non-peak services; $32 return).

INFORMATION AND TOURS

Bio-security Check your shoes for seeds and your bags for stray mice – it does happen.

What to bring Apart from a couple of toilets there are no facilities on Rangitoto, so bring everything you need – including strong shoes to protect you from the sharp rocks, weather protection, water, food and a torch for exploring the lava caves.

Volunteering The Motutapu Restoration Trust (⚲motutapu.org.nz) runs volunteer day-trips (usually first, third and fifth Sundays of each month), typically involving 4–5 hours' weed busting and sapling planting. A ferry ($21 return) takes you direct to Home Bay.

Fullers Volcanic Explorer Tour Save yourself the slog and catch this tractor-drawn buggy tour (daily; 2hr; $60 including cost of ferry) to the summit with full commentary; the final 900m is on foot along a boardwalk.

ACCOMMODATION

Home Bay Campsite Eastern side of Motutapu ⚲doc.govt.nz. The only place to stay on the twin islands is this primitive, but pleasant and spacious beachside DOC campsite, with toilets and water. Access is by Explore ferry in season or a 3hr walk from Rangitoto Wharf. Booking is essential Christmas to Jan. **$6**

Waiheke Island

Pastoral **WAIHEKE**, 20km east of Auckland, is the second largest of the gulf islands and easily the most populous, particularly when summer visitors quadruple its population of around 8000. The traffic isn't all one way, though, as fast and frequent ferry services allow islanders to commute to the city, a trend that has turned the western end of Waiheke into a suburb. But, with its chain of sandy beaches along the north coast, a climate that's less humid than Auckland's and some great wineries, Waiheke is popular

---

RANGITOTO SUMMIT WALK

The way to really appreciate Rangitoto Island is on foot, best along shady paths away from sun-baked black lava. A favourite is the **Summit/Coastal Loop Track** (12km; 5–6hr; 260m ascent) around the southeast of the island. Turn left just past the toilets at Rangitoto Wharf and follow signs for the **Kowhai Grove**, ablaze with yellow blooms in September. Turn right onto the coastal road from Rangitoto Wharf then left into **Kidney Fern Grove**, which is packed with unusual miniature ferns that unfurl after rain. From here, the well-worn **Summit Track** winds through patches of pohutukawa forest. Around three-quarters of the way to the summit, a side track leads to the lava caves (20min return) that probe deep into the side of the volcano. Further along the main track a former military observation post on the summit provides views out across Auckland city and the Hauraki Gulf.

Continue northwards to the east–west road across the island and follow it towards Islington Bay; from there, pick up the **coastal track south**, initially following the bay then cutting inland through some little-frequented forests back to Rangitoto Wharf.

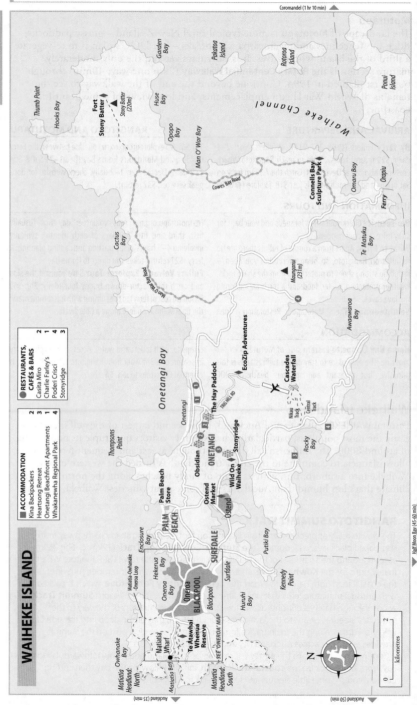

WAIHEKE ISLAND

■ ACCOMMODATION	
Kina Backpackers	2
Heartsong Retreat	3
Onetangi Beachfront Apartments	1
Whakanewha Regional Park	4

● RESTAURANTS, CAFÉS & BARS	
Casita Miro	2
Charlie Farley's	1
Poderi Crisci	4
Stonyridge	3

Coromandel (1 hr 10 min)

Thumb Point
Hooks Bay
Garden Bay
Huse Bay
Opopo Bay
Man O'War Bay
Fort Stony Batter
Stony Batter (220m)
Pakatoa Island
Rotoroa Island
Ponui Island

Waiheke Channel

Cowes Bay Road
Connells Bay Sculpture Park
Omaru Bay
Orapiu
Ferry
Te Matuku Bay

Cactus Bay
Man O'War Bay Road
Maunganui (231m)
Awaawaroa Bay

Onetangi Bay
Onetangi
Thompsons Point
The Hay Paddock
Tiri Hill Rd
EcoZip Adventures
Cascades Waterfall
Nikau Track
Central Track
Rocky Bay

Obsidian
ONETANGI
Stonyridge
Wild On Waiheke
Ostend
Ostend Market
Palm Beach Store
PALM BEACH
Enclosure Bay
Putiki Bay
SURFDALE

Hekerua Bay
Oneroa Bay
Oneroa
BLACKPOOL
Blackpool
Surfdale
Huruhi Bay
Kennedy Bay

Matiatia-Owhanake-Oneroa Loop
Owhanake Bay
Te Atawhai Whenua Reserve
Matiatia Wharf
Matiatia B05
Matiatia Headland: North
Matiatia Headland: South

SEE 'ONEROA' MAP

N

0   2
kilometres

Auckland (35 min)
Auckland (50 min)
Half Moon Bay (45–60 min)

1

with international visitors in search of a peaceful spot to recover from jet lag or to idle away a day or two before flying home. The island is **busiest** on summer weekends and throughout January, when Aucklanders descend en masse and there's often live music.

People, cafés and restaurants mostly cluster around **Oneroa**. You can go for a swim here, but most people head elsewhere: to the almost circular **Enclosure Bay** for snorkelling, **Palm Beach** for swimming, and the more surf-oriented **Onetangi**. All over the island, the bays and headlands lend themselves to short, often steep walks, wineries tempt, and if you're still restless, there's kayaking or sailing.

Brief history

Waiheke Maori trace their lineage back to the Tainui canoe that landed at Onetangi and gave the island its first name, Te Motu-arai-Roa, "the long sheltering island". Waiheke, or "cascading waters", originally referred to a particular creek but was assumed by **Europeans** to refer to the entire island. Among the first **settlers** to set foot on Waiheke was Samuel Marsden, who preached here in 1818 and established a mission near Matiatia. The island then went through the familiar cycle of kauri logging, gum digging and clearance for farming. Gradually, the magnificent coastal scenery gained popularity as a setting for grand picnics, and hamper-encumbered Victorians, attired in formal dress, arrived in boatloads.

Development was initially sluggish, but the availability of cheap land amid dramatic landscapes drew painters and **craftspeople**; others followed as access from Auckland became easier and faster.

Oneroa

Most ferries arrive at **Matiatia Wharf**, a 2km uphill walk or bus ride from the main settlement of **ONEROA**, whose main street hugs a ridge-top from the library and cinema, past a bunch of cafés, restaurants and the island's i-SITE. There are accommodation and wineries close by. To the south is the silty sweep of Blackpool Beach while to the north the hill drops steeply down to the sandy sweep of Oneroa Bay. It is a great spot to swim, but if the summer crowds get to you head to the eastern

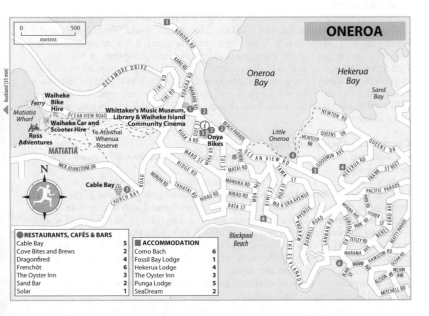

RESTAURANTS, CAFÉS & BARS	
Cable Bay	5
Cove Bites and Brews	2
Dragonfired	4
Frenchôt	6
The Oyster Inn	3
Sand Bar	2
Solar	1

ACCOMMODATION	
Como Bach	6
Fossil Bay Lodge	1
Hekerua Lodge	4
The Oyster Inn	3
Punga Lodge	5
SeaDream	2

1

end where, at anything other than high tide, you can access some quieter nooks between the rocks.

Whittaker's Music Museum

2 Korora St • Daily: 1–4pm; performances Sat 1.30pm • Free; performances $12.50 • ☎ 09 372 5573, ⓦ musicalmuseum.org

Oneroa's only real sight is this slightly eccentric museum full of flageolets, piano accordions, player pianos, xylophones and even a very well-restored 1896 Steinway and one owned by Paderewski. Incredibly, you're allowed to play most of them, and all are ably demonstrated during the occasional musical performances.

Ostend Market

Ostend Hall, corner of Ostend Rd and Belgium St • Sat 7.30am–noon • ⓦ ostendmarketwaiheke.co.nz

What passes for a main road on Waiheke winds east from Oneroa through the contiguous settlements of Little Oneroa, Blackpool and Surfdale to light-industrial **Ostend**. Ignore the place except for its **market** when the island's neo-hippies come out to offer organic produce, arts and crafts, food stalls, massage, iridology readings and entertainment. Take cash.

Palm Beach and Onetangi

Palm Beach is 4km east of Oneroa • Onetangi is 9km east of Oneroa

Palm Beach takes a neat bite out of the north coast, with houses tumbling down to a small sandy beach separated by a handful of rocks from the nude bathing zone at its western end.

Waiheke's longest and most exposed beach is **ONETANGI**, popular in summer with surfers, board riders and swimmers, and the venue for beach horse races (ⓦ onetangibeachraces.co.nz; usually early March) along with sandcastle building, tug-o-war etc.

Stony Batter Historic Reserve and Fort Stony Batter

Stony Batter Historic Reserve Open 24hr • Free • Fort Stony Batter generally daily 10am–3pm but call ahead • Entry $8, guided tours $15, cash only • ☎ 021 043 8821

There's very little habitation east of Onetangi, just tracts of open farmland, vineyards and **Stony Batter Historic Reserve**, a mass of abandoned World War II defences at the northeastern tip of the island, 23km from Matiatia wharf. It is a twenty-minute walk from the car park to the site where you can wander around topside, or head into **Fort Stony Batter**, a labyrinth of dank concrete tunnels and gun emplacements built to protect Auckland from a feared Japanese attack during World War II. The attack never came and after the war the guns and equipment were removed. Bring or rent ($5) a torch to explore on your own, or join one of the guided tours that bring the place to life.

Connells Bay Sculpture Park

142 Cowes Bay Road, 20km east of Oneroa • Late Oct to late April daily on pre-booked guided tours only • $30 • ☎ 09 372 895, ⓦ connellsbay.co.nz

Book ahead and set a couple of hours aside to visit this wonderful, private contemporary **sculpture trail** typically guided in small groups by one of the instigators and owners, John and Jo Gow. As pasture has been turned into immaculate regenerating bush the Gows have commissioned the cream of New Zealand sculptors – Michael Parekowhai, Jeff Thompson, Chris Booth, Fatu Feu'u – to produce site-specific works, often the largest they've undertaken. The commissioning and development process comes alive with videos and working models, but the stars are the works themselves – a massive tree stump turned into what looks like an Easter Island *moai*, an organically sculpted steel wall and a stainless-steel limpet, fern and leaf delicately beautifying a small wetland.

WALKS ON WAIHEKE

Sometimes it is nice to feel like you've earned your extended winery lunch, or work it off afterwards. A series of leaflets (free from the i-SITE) expand on our suggested walks.

Matiatia Headland North (2–3hr loop; undulating). One of the island's finest walks visiting secluded beaches and windswept headlands, both peppered with some of New Zealand's finest modern mansions, many with sculptures visible in the grounds. Walk from Oneroa to Matiatia then complete the loop using the Te Atawhai Whenua Reserve (see below).

Matiatia Headland South (3–4hr loop; undulating). Easily combined with its northern counterpart, this walk follows the clifftops south of Matiatia and loops back passing close to three wineries open for tasting, including Cable Bay (see p.127).

Nikau Track (4km loop; 2hr; 100m ascent). Starting at Whakanewha Regional Park (see p.127) this track runs past wetland and through mature native forest to the pretty tumbling Cascades Waterfall. Return via Central Track.

Onetangi Wine Trophy Trail (1–4hr). Short field and vineyard walk that's really an excuse to taste wine at *The Hay Paddock* (451b Seaview Rd) and *Obsidian* (22 Te Makiri Rd) and eat and taste at *Casita Miro* (see p.128). Park at *The Hay Paddock*, walk past *Casita Miro* to *Obsidian* then turn round and taste and dine on the way back. Open Nov–March 11.30am–3.30pm.

Te Atawhai Whenua Reserve (30min). Great bushwalk alternative to the roadside footpath when walking between the Matiatia ferry and Oneroa. Pick it up at the southern end of Matiatia beach.

ARRIVAL AND DEPARTURE WAIHEKE ISLAND

By passenger ferry Fullers (📞 09 367 9111, 🌐 fullers .co.nz; roughly hourly 6am–10pm or later; 35min; $36 return, bikes free) and Explore (📞 0800 397 567, 🌐 exploregroup.co.nz; roughly hourly; $36 return) operate from the Ferry Building in Auckland to Matiatia Wharf, just over 1km from the main settlement of Oneroa with times staggered so that in effect there is a ferry every half-hour. At weekends Sealink (📞 0800 732 546, 🌐 sealink.co.nz; late Oct–Feb roughly hourly 9am–6pm; 40min; $15 each

way) plies the same route and adds a free shuttle service between Matiatia and Oneroa.

By car ferry If you're staying more than a couple of days it becomes cost-effective to bring your vehicle over using the Sealink car ferry (📞 0800 732 546, 🌐 sealink.co.nz) from Half Moon Bay in Auckland's eastern suburbs to Kennedy Point, 4km south of Oneroa (roughly hourly; 45min; car only $152 return, each person $36.50 return), or less frequently from Wynyard Wharf in Auckland.

INFORMATION

Visitor information i-SITE (118 Ocean View Rd, Oneroa; Mon–Sat 9am–5pm, Sun 9.30am–4pm; 📞 09 372 1234, 🌐 waiheke.aucklandnz.com). Pick up the free *Island of Wine* map and guide and the *Waiheke Art Map*, which details over 30 galleries and artists' studios you can visit.

Newspaper The weekly *Gulf News* ($2; 🌐 waihekegulfnews .co.nz) is published on Thurs and has details of what's on.

Services Free internet access is available at the wonderful new library, 131 Ocean View Rd (Mon–Fri 9am–6pm, Sat &

Sun 10am–4pm). There are a couple of banks on the main street.

Events The highlights of Waiheke's summer season are the annual Jazz Festival (Easter weekend; 🌐 waihekejazz festival.co.nz) and, in odd-numbered years, the free Headland Sculpture on the Gulf (late Jan to mid-Feb; 🌐 sculptureonthegulf.co.nz) when the headland south of Matiatia and down to Church Bay is festooned with mostly wonderful, contemporary sculptures.

GETTING AROUND

By bus Ferry arrivals connect with Fullers buses, which run to Onetangi via Oneroa, Surfdale and Ostend, and to Rocky Bay via Oneroa, Little Oneroa and Palm Beach. Tickets ($2–4.50/ride, $9 all day) are available on the bus. Use 🌐 at.govt.nz for times.

By car Waiheke Car and Scooter Hire, Matiatia Wharf (📞 09 372 3339, 🌐 rentmewaiheke.co.nz), are cheapest renting scooters ($59/day), cars (from $69) and 4WDs ($79). They charge by the calendar day, though if you get the vehicle back before 10am they'll only charge a $15 overnight fee for that day.

By bike Waiheke is constantly undulating, so you might want to rent an electric-assist bike from Onya Bikes of Waiheke, Matiatia Wharf and 124 Ocean View Rd (📞 09 372 4428, 🌐 ecyclesnz.com). They have short-range machines ($50/day), and longer-range ($60/day) models which will get you right round the island, just. They also rent fully-human-powered bikes for $35/day, as do Waiheke Bike Hire at Matiatia Wharf (📞 09 372 7937, 🌐 waihekebike hire.co.nz).

By taxi Waiheke Independent Taxis (📞 0800 300 372, 🌐 waihekeindependenttaxis.co.nz).

WAIHEKE ISLAND TOURS AND ACTIVITIES

Unless you've got transport, tours can be the most effective way to see something of the island, particularly the wineries.

TOURS

Ananda Tours ✆09 372 7530, ⓦananda.co.nz. Personalized wine, eco, art and scenic tours around the island from around $110/person (minimum numbers apply). Trips are timed to ferry arrivals; try the Gourmet's Food and Wine Tour ($120), particularly on Saturday, when they take in Ostend Market.

Fullers ✆09 367 9111, ⓦfullers.co.nz. The ferry company runs a bunch of tours, all timed with boat arrivals. The Explorer Tour (daily year-round departing Auckland 10am, 11am & noon; $52) includes an open-dated return ferry trip from Auckland, an hour-and-a-half island tour, plus an all-day bus pass so you can explore further on your own. Their Wine on Waiheke tour (departing Auckland Wed–Sun at 1pm; $119, without lunch $89) has the same benefits but spends three hours visiting three top vineyards.

Hike Bike Ako ✆021 465 373, ⓦhikebikeako .co.nz. Ako means "learn" in Maori and you'll certainly get a far greater understanding of both the Maori world and Waiheke's place in it on these academic-led half-day (3hr; $99) and full-day (5hr; $159 including lunch) trips which combine easy walking and cruisey biking in whatever combination suits the group. There's usually a bit of wine tasting. Trips start at the Matiatia ferry terminal (bookings essential; daily 9.50am & 1.50pm).

KAYAKING

Ross Adventures ✆09 372 5550, ⓦkayakwaiheke .co.nz. Guided paddling trips from Matiatia including half-day trips ($125), full-day trips with the wind behind you plus a shuttle back to your starting point ($195 including a good lunch), plus kayak rentals including sit-on-tops ($50 for 3hr), proper sea kayaks (from $110/half-day) and even kayaks set up for fishing ($90/half-day).

ZIPLINES

EcoZip Adventures 150 Trig Hill Rd, 2km south of Onetangi ✆09 372 5646, ⓦecozipadventures .co.nz. You get a great view right over Waiheke Island from the end of Trig Hill Road even before you enter EcoZip Adventures, where you're harnessed up and guided down a trio of increasingly steep and fast 200m-long ziplines. It is a pleasant way to spend a couple of hours, complete with a well-paced and informative bushwalk back to base. $99; includes free pick-ups from Matiatia Wharf. Daily 9am–5pm.

ACCOMMODATION

Accommodation is generally plentiful except for the three weeks after Christmas and all summer weekends. While Oneroa is convenient for buses, restaurants and shops, many prefer the more relaxing **beaches** such as Palm Beach and Onetangi. There's often a two-night minimum at weekends.

ONEROA, LITTLE ONEROA AND BLACKPOOL

Como Bach 30 The Esplanade ⓦvisitwaiheke.co.nz; map p.123. One of the more convenient (and reasonably priced) holiday homes rented through this website, this small sunny beachfront house is priced for up to 4 people in two bedrooms. $250

Fossil Bay Lodge 58 Korora Rd, Oneroa ⓦfossilbay .net; map p.123. A very chilled collection of two-person huts and "glamping" tents 1km from town on an organic farm. Lovely communal spaces and lots of privacy, with a 5min walk to an all-but-private beach. Various cabins (one a single; $50). Two-night minimum (three Christmas–Jan). Cabins $80, tents $90

Hekerua Lodge 11 Hekerua Rd, Little Oneroa ✆09 372 8990, ⓦhekerualodge.co.nz; map p.123. Fun and often very lively backpackers peacefully set in the bush 10min walk from Oneroa. There's a small swimming pool, table tennis, a volleyball court often almost surrounded by tents (per person $18) and some en suites ($120). Two-night minimum. Dorms $30, doubles $90

The Oyster Inn 124 Ocean View Road ✆09 372 2222, ⓦtheoysterinn.co.nz; map p.123. Like the namesake restaurant the three luxurious rooms here are all white with an elegant stripped-back beachy feel. You're right in the heart of Oneroa and breakfast and ferry transfers are included. Two-night minimum at weekends. $285

★**Punga Lodge** 223 Ocean View Rd, Little Oneroa ✆0800 372 6675, ⓦpungalodge.co.nz; map p.123. Delightful and hospitable B&B, well located in the bush close to Oneroa beach, with tea and muffins available from the helpful hosts. Accommodation consists of a range of comfortable and spacious en-suite doubles with verandas (breakfast included), and four self-catering apartments of different sizes. There's a free spa pool, and good-value off-season deals. They also run the nearby *Tawa Lodge*, which has well-priced shared-bathroom B&B doubles ($110) and a very comfortable "cottage" with wonderful sea views ($285). Free wi-fi. Shared bath $120, B&B rooms $145

SeaDream 35 Waikare Rd ☏09 372 8991, ⓦseadream .co.nz; map p.123. These two comfortably appointed and very peaceful self-contained units are perfectly sited just steps from Oneroa's restaurants and with long bay views from the terrace. $200

ONETANGI

Kina Backpackers 421 Sea View Rd, Onetangi ☏09 372 8971, ⓦkinabackpackers.co.nz; map p.122. Relaxed hostel on a headland just above Onetangi beach, with long views over the sea from the hammocks and bean bags on the lawn. Accommodation is a little rustic with 14 two-bunk rooms and a couple of larger dorms, plus good bathrooms, cheap wi-fi and free ferry pick-ups and drop-offs. Look for leaflets (try the i-SITE) to claim a 10 percent discount. Dorms $28, twins per person $35

Onetangi Beach Apartments 5 Fourth Avenue ☏0800 663 826, ⓦonetangi.co.nz; map p.122. Only a road separates these upscale motel apartments from Onetangi beach. All are self-contained, with Sky TV and DVD players, access to a free sauna and spa pools, plus kayaks and paddleboards for rent. Apartments $190, "beachfront" $215

ROCKY BAY

Heartsong Retreat 8 Omiha Rd ☏09 372 2039, ⓦheartsongretreat.co.nz; map p.122. Tranquil bush-girt eco-retreat with sea views and a choice of two elegantl. B&B suites in the house, a self-contained cabana and a lovely separate cottage, and everyone has access to a beautiful hot pool, boathouse and kayaks. Massage and assorted holistic treatments are available. Suites & cabana $395, cottage $450

Whakanewha Regional Park ☏09 366 2000; map p.122. The island's only official campsite is simple but attractively sited on a tidal bay. It has flush toilets, potable water and free gas barbecues but no showers. The nearest bus stop is over 2km away. Self-contained campers can stay for a night in summer, 3 in winter. Reserve in Jan & Feb. Per person: vans $6, camping $10

EATING, WINE TASTING AND ENTERTAINMENT

To Aucklanders, Waiheke is all about long winery lunches, and we've listed some of the best, all also doing tastings. The bulk of the rest of the restaurants are in Oneroa, with additional spots at the various beaches. Live music mostly happens at weekends, with *Sand Bar* in Ostend being a worthy bet.

ONEROA AND SURFDALE

★**Cable Bay** 12 Nick Johnstone Drive, 1km west ☏09 372 5889, ⓦcablebay.co.nz; map p.123. Starkly modern winery with magnificent views across the beanbag-dotted lawns to Auckland from two restaurants. The linen-tableclothed *Dining Room* has à la carte (mains around $38) and degustation (8-course dinner $110, $160 with wine matches), while the *Verandah* is more for casual drinking and sharing plates from its outdoor kitchen. Wine tasting costs $2 per sample (their rosé and Syrah are superb) and the winery is an easy 15min uphill bushwalk from the Matiatia ferry terminal. Daily: tasting 11am–5pm; Verandah 11am–late; Dining Room noon–3pm & 6–10pm.

Cove Bites and Brews 149 Ocean View Rd ☏09 372 8209, ⓦdcbrewing.co.nz; map p.123. Cruisey spot with a great seaview terrace that's perfect for sampling their Deep Creek Brewing Co beers and one of their surf and turf "paddles" ($35) laden with ribs, calamari, lamb skewers and dipping sauces. Daily 11am–11pm.

Dragonfired Little Oneroa Beach ☏021 922 289, ⓦdragonfired.co.nz; map p.123. Very Waiheke, this beachside caravan contains a wood-fired oven that's

perfect for creating thin-based organic margherita pizza ($12, extra toppings $2 each) and polenta squares with salad ($12). Grab a drink from the nearby shop and head for the beach. Summer only, daily 10.30am–8pm.

Frenchôt 8 Miami Ave, Surfdale ☏09 372 3400, ⓦfrenchot.com; map p.123. A welcome find, this traditional French bakery and crêperie where you can perch on stools overlooking the street or head to the spacious courtyard for a coffee and a *pain aux raisins*, Petit Dej galette ($13) or an apple, caramel and almond crêpe ($10). The upstairs bistro serves classic French dishes such as canard confit and bouillabaisse (both $32). Café Tues–Sun 8am–4pm, bistro Wed–Sat 6–10pm.

The Oyster Inn 124 Ocean View Rd ☏09 372 2222, ⓦtheoysterinn.co.nz; map p.123. Grab a people-watching spot on the veranda at this chic beach restaurant and bar, whose prices are pretty reasonable (for Waiheke). Local oysters ($5–6 each) might be followed by a crayfish and watercress risotto ($28) or a battered fish with triple-cooked chips ($26). There's plenty of island wine and classic cocktails to help it down. Mon–Fri noon–10pm or later, Sat & Sun 11am–10pm or later.

Sand Bar 153 Ocean View Rd ☏09 372 9458,

ⓦ sandbar.co.nz; map p.123. Chic little bar, great for a cocktail on the deck as the sun goes down and frequently hosting DJs at the weekend. Burgers ($17), pizzas ($12–19) and salt-and-pepper squid provide an excuse to stay longer. Daily noon–10pm or later, closed Mon & Tues in winter.

★**Solar** 139 Ocean View Rd ⓣ09 372 2133, ⓦ solarwaiheke.co.nz; map p.123. A chilled place to hang out and watch an endless parade of local characters call in for coffee or something from their menu of staunchly free-range and predominantly local and organic fare. Drop into a retro armchair or head out into the garden with sea views for Kiwi breakfasts (around $18), beef burger and chips ($15) and one of the Waiheke Island Brewing Co beers they have on tap. Free wi-fi. Mon–Thurs & Sun 8.30am–3pm, Fri & Sat 8.30am–9pm.

Waiheke Island Community Cinema 2 Koroka Rd ⓣ09 372 4240, ⓦ waihekecinema.co.nz; map p.123. Screens recent movies 3–4 times a day in a room full of old sofas.

ONETANGI AND BEYOND

★**Casita Miro** 3 Brown Rd ⓣ09 372 7854, ⓦ casitamiro.co.nz; map p.122. Come to sample their excellent wines (5 for $15) but mainly to dine on Iberian- and Mediterranean-inspired dishes like *harira* ($8), lamb and fig tajine with pistachio ($26), 18-month-aged serrano ham ($20) and Cloudy Bay clams with pearl barley and fino ($17). You've a choice of the rustic glass pavilion overlooking the vines or at the mosaic outdoor bar styled like Gaudí's Parc Güell. Both are delightful. Daily except Tues & Wed noon–3pm plus Fri & Sat 6–10pm.

Charlie Farley's 21 The Strand ⓣ09 372 4106, ⓦ charliefarleys.co.nz; map p.122. Casual licensed café serving the usual Kiwi breakfasts ($16–20) and the likes of squid with wasabi and lime mayo ($20) and fish of the day ($29), best served with a sundowner or two overlooking the sea. Free wi-fi. Daily 8.30am–10pm or later.

★**Poderi Crisci** 205 Awaawaroa Rd, Awaawaroa Bay, 7km southeast of Onetangi ⓣ09 372 2148, ⓦ podericrisci.co.nz; map p.122. Set a few hours aside to dine at this family-run vineyard restaurant at the far end of the island. The large kitchen garden is used to great effect in traditionally inspired, modern Italian dishes such as octopus carpaccio with broad beans and chilli citrus salsa ($21) and skewer of lamb with sautéed artichokes ($34). The degustation dinners ($120–135 including wine matches) and the leisurely Sunday "long lunch" (from $70) are exemplary. Also does wine tasting. Bookings highly recommended. Check website for winter hours; late Oct–Easter Mon–Wed & Sun noon–sunset, Thurs–Sat noon–11pm.

★**Stonyridge** 80 Onetangi Rd ⓣ09 372 8822, ⓦ stonyridge.co.nz; map p.122. None of Waiheke's wineries is more highly regarded than *Stonyridge*, whose organic, hand-tended vines produce Larose, one of the world's top Bordeaux-style reds. Vintages are often sold out (at over $250 a go) before they're even bottled, so there are limited cellar-door sales. Come to taste ($7 for 3 of their less pricey wines, $30 for their 3 premiums including Larose), for the tour and tasting (Sat & Sun 11.30am; $10), to sample olive oil from some of NZ's oldest olive trees (though only from the 1980s), or for a casual alfresco lunch overlooking the vines. Expect tasting platters on the deck, or the likes of scallops with pea purée ($18) or herb-crusted rack of lamb ($39) in the restaurant. Glasses of Larose are $46. Daily 11.30am–5pm.

Rotoroa Island

ⓦ rotoroa.org.nz

To cruise a fair bit of the Hauraki Gulf, swim off a gorgeous beach and experience something of Auckland's social history all in one compact day out, visit **Rotoroa Island**, off Waiheke's eastern tip. For over a hundred years this was a Salvation Army alcohol and drug rehab centre, off-limits except to detoxing residents; now it's something of an environmental restoration project, the residual grassland gradually being replanted with native saplings. The island has also been rendered pest-free and, in collaboration with Auckland Zoo, native species are being introduced, including tieke (saddleback), popokotea (whitehead) and, in summer, juvenile kiwi.

You can walk around the island in an hour or so, stopping off at beaches, headland viewpoints graced with sculptures and several buildings left from its working days: a chapel, diminutive jail and an 1860s-era schoolhouse. There's no food for sale but there are free barbecues, so take picnic supplies.

ARRIVAL AND INFORMATION ROTOROA ISLAND

By ferry 360 Discovery (☎ 0800 360 3472, ⓦ 360discovery .co.nz) ferries call in to Rotoroa (late Sept–early April 3–7 weekly; bookings essential; $50 return) on the way to Coromandel. The journey takes 1hr 15min, giving you about 4hr on the island.

Information The island's story is told in the superb Exhibition Centre (generally daily 10am–5pm).

ACCOMMODATION

Superintendent's House ☎ 0800 768 676 ⓦ rotoroa .org.nz. Smart and well-equipped hostel-style accommodation in an old villa with great views. Bring a sleeping bag or bedding and all your food. There are also three super-stylish homes sleeping 6–13. Dorms $\overline{\$35}$, homes $\overline{\$375}$

Great Barrier Island

Rugged and sparsely populated, **Great Barrier Island** (Aotea) lies 90km northeast of Auckland on the outer fringes of the Hauraki Gulf and, though only 30km long and 15km wide, packs in a mountainous heart which drops away to deep harbours in the west and golden surf beaches in the east. It's only a half-hour flight from the city but exudes a tranquillity and detachment that makes it seem a world apart. There is no mains electricity or water, no industry, no towns to speak of and only limited public transport.

Much of the pleasure here is in lazing on the **beaches**, ambling to the **hot springs** and striking out on foot into the **Aotea Conservation Park**, a compact and rugged chunk of deer- and possum-free bush between Port FitzRoy and Whangaparapara that takes up about a third of the island. In no time at all you can find yourself climbing in and out of little subtropical gullies luxuriant with nikau palms, tree ferns, regenerating rimu and kauri, and onto scrubby manuka ridges with stunning coastal and mountain views. Many of the tracks follow the routes of mining and kauri-logging tramways. Tracks in the centre of the island converge on 621m **Hirakimata** (Mount Hobson), which is surrounded by boardwalks and wooden steps designed to keep trampers on the path and prevent the disturbance of nesting **black petrels**. If you're looking for more structure to your day, a few small-time tour and activity operators can keep you entertained (see p.134).

The vast majority of visitors arrive from Auckland **between Boxing Day and the middle of January**, many piling in for the New Year's Eve party at the sports club at Crossroads. The rest of the year is pretty quiet.

Brief history

Great Barrier is formed from the same line of extinct **volcanoes** as the Coromandel Peninsula and was one of the places first populated by **Maori**, who were occupying numerous *pa* sites when Cook sailed by in 1769. Recognizing the calming influence of Aotea on the waters of the Hauraki Gulf, Cook renamed it Great Barrier Island. From 1791, the island's vast stands of kauri were seized for ships' timbers, and kauri **logging** didn't cease until 1942, outliving some early copper mining and sporadic attempts to extract gold and silver. Logging and gum digging were replaced by a short-lived whale-oil extraction industry at Whangaparapara in the 1950s, but the Barrier soon fell back on tilling the poor clay soils and its peak population of over 5000 has now dropped to around 900.

Back to the land

Alternative lifestylers arrived in the 1960s and 1970s, and while 1970s idealism has largely been supplanted by modern pragmatism, **self-sufficiency** remains. People grow their own vegetables, everyone has their own water supply and wind-turbines and solar panels reduce the strain on diesel generators. **Agriculture** takes a back seat

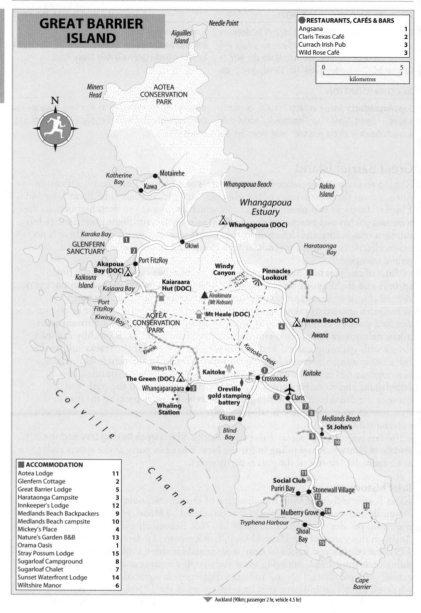

GREAT BARRIER ISLAND

RESTAURANTS, CAFÉS & BARS
Angsana	1
Claris Texas Café	2
Currach Irish Pub	3
Wild Rose Café	3

0 — 5 kilometres

Needle Point
Aiguilles Island
Miners Head
AOTEA CONSERVATION PARK
N
Katherine Bay
Kawa
Motairehe
Whangapoua Beach
Rakitu Island
Whangapoua Estuary
Whangapoua (DOC)
Karaka Bay
GLENFERN SANCTUARY
Okiwi
Harataonga Bay
Akapoua Bay (DOC)
Port FitzRoy
Kaikoura Island
Kaiaara Bay
Kaiaraara Hut (DOC)
Windy Canyon
Pinnacles Lookout
Port FitzRoy
Kiwiriki Bay
Hirakimata (Mt Hobson)
AOTEA CONSERVATION PARK
Mt Heale (DOC)
Awana Beach (DOC)
Awana
Kiwiriki
Kaitoke Creek
Withey's Tk
The Green (DOC)
Kaitoke
Kaitoke
Whangaparapara
Oreville gold stamping battery
Crossroads
Claris
Whaling Station
Okupu
Blind Bay
Medlands Beach
St John's
Colville Channel

ACCOMMODATION
Aotea Lodge	11
Glenfern Cottage	2
Great Barrier Lodge	5
Harataonga Campsite	3
Innkeeper's Lodge	12
Medlands Beach Backpackers	9
Medlands Beach campsite	10
Mickey's Place	4
Nature's Garden B&B	13
Orama Oasis	1
Stray Possum Lodge	15
Sugarloaf Campground	8
Sugarloaf Chalet	7
Sunset Waterfront Lodge	14
Wiltshire Manor	6

Social Club
Puriri Bay
Stonewall Village
Mulberry Grove
Tryphena Harbour
Shoal Bay
Cape Barrier

Auckland (90km; passenger 2 hr, vehicle 4.5 hr)

to **tourism**, however, and wealthy second-home owners are moving in. Islanders have resisted this trend but as land prices rocket, some on low incomes are forced to leave, while others head out when their kids reach high-school age. Indeed, a dropping population and the need to cater for visitors means there's often **casual work** available in the summer.

Tryphena

Pretty **Tryphena** (Rangitawhiri) is the southernmost harbour, where the Great Barrier's main settlement is spread over four bays: **Shoal Bay** (where ferries arrive), **Mulberry Grove**, **Stonewall Village** (the largest settlement) and **Puriri Bay** (a short walk along the coast from Stonewall Village). Tryphena has good accommodation and places to eat, but activities are limited to swimming, renting a kayak and tackling a few short walks.

Medlands Beach

Most people head straight for **Medlands Beach** (Oruawharo), a long sweep of golden sand on the east coast broken by a sheltering island and often endowed with some of the Barrier's best (unpatrolled) surf. The pretty blue and white **St John's Church** looks suitably out of place, having only been moved here from the mainland by barge in 1986 before being dragged over the dunes.

Claris

Most flights arrive at **CLARIS** (Kaitoke), just north of Medlands, where the post office is called Pigeon Post in honour of Great Barrier's original airmail service, said to be the world's first. The story goes that when the SS *Wairarapa* was wrecked on the northwest coast of Great Barrier in 1898, the news took a sobering three days to get to Auckland. In response the island set up a **pigeon-gram** mail service that was used until 1908, when a telephone was installed.

Milk, Honey and Grain Museum

47 Hector Sanderson Rd • Open most days • Donation • ☎ 09 429 0773

The **Milk, Honey and Grain Museum** does what it says on the box, thanks to a neatly organized collection of memorabilia, but also ranges far wider, covering odd aspects of the island's development. It's a worthwhile stop if the weather's bad.

Crossroads, Whangaparapara and the road north

Crossroads, 2km north of Claris, is just that – the junction of roads to Okupu, Port FitzRoy and Whangaparapara. The Whangaparapara road runs past the scant roadside remains of the **Oreville gold stamping battery** (unrestricted entry) and the start of a path to **Kaitoke Hot Springs** (see box, p.134). At **WHANGAPARAPARA**, a short stroll around the bay brings you to the foundations of a whaling station built here in the 1950s.

North of Crossroads, the Port FitzRoy road passes the lovely surf and swimming beach of **Awana Bay** and the roadside **Pinnacles Lookout** before reaching the start of a track to **Windy Canyon** (see p.134).

Port FitzRoy

The harbour at **PORT FITZROY** remains remarkably calm under most wind conditions, a quality not lost on yachties who flock here in summer. They're served by a shop, burger bar and the *Port FitzRoy Boat Club*. Port FitzRoy also makes a good jumping-off point for tramps in the Aotea Conservation Park, though the huge Kaiaraara kauri dam that was once the main destination was swept away by floods in 2014.

Glenfern Sanctuary

Glenfern Rd • Guided tour by appointment $40 • ☎ 09 429 0091, ⊚ glenfern.org.nz

The northern shore of Port FitzRoy's harbour is formed by the Kotuku Peninsula, which since 2008 has been separated from the rest of the island by a 2km-long predator-proof fence forming the 2.3-square-kilometre **Glenfern Sanctuary**. Rats have been virtually eliminated, North Island robins have been reintroduced and other birdlife is slowly returning. Highly informative guided tours include a lovely kauri tree canopy walkway.

ARRIVAL AND DEPARTURE
GREAT BARRIER ISLAND

BY FERRY
SeaLink ☎ 0800 732 546, ⓦ sealink.co.nz. The sedate year-round car and passenger ferry leaves Brigham Street in Auckland's Wynyard Quarter for Tryphena (3–7 weekly; 4hr 30min). Infrequent services also visit Whangaparapara and Port FitzRoy. Return fares: passengers $95 ($140 in Dec & Jan); cars $325 ($410 in Dec & Jan); bikes $21. They also run a fast ferry (20 Dec–4 Jan most days, then weekends until late April; 2hr; $90 each way).

BY PLANE
Claris Airport Most flights from Auckland International Airport arrive at Claris, the island's administrative centre

and convenient for the best beaches at Medlands and Awana Bay. Companies do fly/ferry combos and, if they get numbers, Great Barrier Airlines also flies to Whangarei and Whitianga, allowing you to use Great Barrier as a stepping stone.

AIRLINES
FlyMySky ☎ 0800 222 123, ⓦ flymysky.co.nz. Flights from Auckland (3–4 daily; $118 if booked online 3 days ahead).
Great Barrier Airlines ☎ 0800 900 600, ⓦ great barrierairlines.co.nz. Flights from Auckland (3–4 daily; $114 each).

INFORMATION
Visitor information i-SITE is at Claris Airport (daily Dec & Jan 10am–5pm; Feb–Nov 10am–2pm, ☎ 0800 468 822, ⓦ thegreatbarrier.co.nz). Info on all things Barrier, including DOC huts, tracks and campsites.
Services There are no banks or ATMs on the island. Most places accept credit and debit cards, but bring plenty of cash. Mobile coverage is patchy at best; Tryphena and Port FitzRoy have reasonable Spark coverage (from

Auckland) while Vodafone and 2Degrees pick up the island's only repeater around Claris, Medlands and Kaitoke. Internet access is limited but there's free wi-fi at the Claris Airport and free internet at the library, 75 Hector Sanderson Road, Claris (Mon–Fri 8.30am–5pm). Tryphena's *Curragh Irish Pub* has free wi-fi for customers, *Claris Texas Café* is online and a few other places offer access.

GETTING AROUND
Great Barrier has just one scheduled bus service plus several on-demand shuttle buses; they generally meet all ferries and flights, but it's better to book in advance. It is often more convenient to rent a car, or even a bike, though the hills are steep and the more interesting roads are dusty in summer.

By bus Great Barrier Buses (☎ 0800 426 832, ⓦ greatbarriertravel.co.nz) operate daily (except Sat & Sun in winter) from Tryphena (9.40am) via Claris (10am) to Port FitzRoy (11am) and back to Claris (noon) and Tryphena (12.20pm). Tryphena to Port FitzRoy costs $35. They also run on-demand shuttle services, as do GBI Shuttle Buses (☎ 09 429 0062, ⓦ greatbarrierisland.co.nz). From

Tryphena, fares are around $20 to Medlands, $25 to Claris and $35 to Whangaparapara.
By rental car Aotea Rentals (☎ 0800 426 832, ⓦ aoteacarrentals.co.nz) in Tryphena has cars from $60/day. GBI Rent A Car in Claris (☎ 09 429 0062, ⓦ greatbarrierisland.co.nz) has basic cars from $40/day.

ACCOMMODATION
Along with plush lodges and hostels Great Barrier has some lovely **self-catering cottages**, many listed on ⓦ greatbarrierislandtourism.co.nz and ⓦ thegreatbarrier.co.nz. The owners often live close by and can arrange breakfast and sometimes dinner. **Book well ahead** from Christmas to mid-January when the island is packed. There are numerous, simple DOC **campsites** ($10; book at peak periods; ⓦ doc.govt.nz), all with toilets, water and cold showers (except *The Green*) and marked on our map.

AROUND THE ISLAND
Kowhai Glamping ☎ 09 429 0700, ⓦ facebook.com /GreatBarrierIslandEcoExperiences. Make the most of the wonderful DOC campsites without having to worry about a tent. Comfy bell tents with mattresses can be

erected wherever you want them. They can include cooking gear, will even supply food and bike rental (they're the same folk as Paradise Cycles) and can even organize a hiking or biking package with tents where you need them. Tent for 2 from **$120**

OPPOSITE MEDLANDS BEACH, GREAT BARRIER ISLAND (P.131) >

GREAT BARRIER ISLAND WALKS AND ACTIVITIES

A couple of days **hiking** in the Aotea Conservation Park is a great way to experience the Barrier: the i-SITE's leaflets and maps will do for most hikers. Either tackle the walks separately or piece together a loop using *Kaiaraara Hut* and the lovely modern *Mount Heale Hut* (see opposite). Shuttle operators offer trailhead transport from the airport or Tryphena.

Great Barrier also has an enviable reputation for the quality of its **fishing** and several operators vie for your business. Alternatively, opt for something altogether more sedate – **golf**.

WALKS AND TRAMPS

Harataonga/Okiwi Coastal Track (12km one way; 5hr; undulating). Superb coastal views and easy walking along an old coast road that passes through some private property. Get one of the shuttle companies to pick you up at the far end, or just walk partway and back.

Hirakimata via Windy Canyon (6km return; 3hr; 400m ascent). The easiest way to get to the highest point on the island is via Windy Canyon (see below). Beyond, you follow a broad ridge with long coastal views, then hike boardwalks and climb stairs up through lovely, mature kauri and rimu forest to the summit.

Kaitoke Hot Springs (6km return; 1hr 30min; flat). Gentle, wheelchair-accessible path that skirts the attractive wetlands of Kaitoke Swamp en route to the Kaitoke Hot Springs, where a couple of dammed pools in a stream make a great place for a soak. The best spot is 50m upstream (follow the path) where a pool is tucked into a small chasm.

Windy Canyon (1km return; 20–30min; 50m ascent). An easy walk to a narrow passage that gets its name from the eerie sounds produced by certain wind conditions. The narrow path winds through nikau palms and tree ferns to a viewpoint that gives a sense of the island's interior, as well as coastal views. Starts 4km northwest of Awana Bay.

GEAR RENTAL

Hillary Outdoors Karaka Bay, at the end of the road 4km north of Port FitzRoy ☎ 0800 688 843, ⊛ hillaryoutdoors.co.nz. For an easy introduction to what the island waters offer, this place rents various aquatic gear (double sea kayak $70/day, dinghy $40/half-day, snorkelling gear $20).

BIKING

Paradise Cycles ☎ 09 429 0700, ⊛ facebook.com /ParadisecyclesAotea. There's enough worthwhile riding here to justify renting a bike for a day or two from this Whangaparapara-based company who deliver all over the island, run bike workshops, and are a mine of information. Tackle Te Ahumata Track, the Harataonga Coastal Track, Kowhai Track and Forest Road between Whangaparapara and Port FitzRoy. Short rentals from $25, but best deals for multi-day rentals for several people.

KAYAKING

Rent kayaks from the Mulberry Grove store at Tryphena or Hillary Outdoors at Karaka Bay.

FISHING AND SCUBA DIVING

Freedom Fishing Charters Medlands ☎ 09 429 0861, ⊛ freedomfishingcharters.co.nz. Ivan "Skilly" McManaway has been fishing the island for approaching fifty years and will take you out for $125 a head for half a day (minimum 2 people). He's also equipped for scuba diving, with gathering crayfish the main goal.

GOLF

Claris Golf Club Whangaparapara Rd, Claris ☎ 09 429 0420. Odd-ball nine-hole par-three course surrounded by bush with pukeko strutting across the fairways. Green fees are $20, club rental is from $5 and there's a lively bar with cheap drinks and decent meals (Thurs & Sun noon–7pm).

TRYPHENA AND AROUND

Aotea Lodge 41 Medland Road, almost opposite Barrier Oasis Lodge ☎09 429 0628. Three one- and two-bedroom self-contained units in pleasant grounds 600m inland from Tryphena Harbour. Rates are $40 higher for single nights but their ferry and car rental deals are worth exploring and there's free wi-fi. $120

★ **Innkeeper's Lodge** Stonewall, Tryphena ☎09 429 0211, ⓦcurrachirishpub.co.nz. The pick of the places around Tryphena – homely, small and welcoming, with a great pub and restaurant spilling out onto the veranda, all conveniently close to the shop. There are attractive rooms plus a single four-bed backpacker room that can be noisy with pub patrons leaving. Good-value flight, transport and accommodation packages available. Dorm $35, doubles $130

Nature's Garden B&B Rosalie Bay Rd ☎09 429 0494, ⓦnaturesgardenbandb.co.nz. You'll need a vehicle to stay at this B&B on an organic, bio-dynamic macadamia orchard with lily ponds and native bush in the grounds. The two rooms are only for single-party bookings as they share a bathroom and living area. A delicious continental breakfast is included. $150

Stray Possum Lodge 64 Cape Barrier Rd ☎0800 767 786, ⓦstraypossum.co.nz. A little out on a limb, this bush-girt hostel has six-bed dorms, doubles, cabins and lovely self-contained chalets ideal for groups of up to six ($155). There's also a licensed pizza restaurant though this is mainly open for group bookings. Linen $5 for your stay, or bring a sleeping bag. Camping $15, dorms $27, doubles $79

Sunset Waterfront Lodge Mulberry Grove, Tryphena ☎09 429 0051, ⓦsunsetlodge.co.nz. Motel-style accommodation in grassy grounds that aren't really waterfront but have close sea views. Choose from A-frames sleeping four and several smaller studios. Studio $195, A-frames $245

MEDLANDS

Medlands Beach Backpackers and Villas 9 Mason Rd ☎09 429 0320, ⓦmedlandsbeach.com. Basic, low-key backpackers with four-bed dorms, a secluded chalet ($80) and a couple of self-contained villas ($120) on a small farm a 10min walk from Medlands Beach – making it popular with surfers. There are bodyboards for guests' use, but there are no meals and no shops nearby, so bring your own food. Dorms $35, room $70

CLARIS, CROSSROADS AND AROUND

★ **Sugarloaf Chalet** Sugarloaf Rd, Kaitoke ☎09 429 0229. A gorgeous, rustic-chic self-catering cottage with barbecue area, fire pit and solar power, just steps from a lovely beach and with a real outdoors flavour (complete with external shower and toilet). $150

Wiltshire Manor 47 Hector Sanderson Rd ☎021 138 7293 ⓔjacqui@islandaccommodation.co.nz. Well-sited just 400m from the airport, this simple hostel is really just a basic house with one double and two twin rooms. $35

WHANGAPARAPARA

Great Barrier Lodge Whangaparapara Harbour ☎09 429 0488, ⓦgreatbarrierlodge.com. This harbour-side lodge is pretty much all there is at Whangaparapara, and also serves as the local grocery and dive shop. Accommodation is in rooms with access to a shared kitchen, and self-catering cottages and suites. The main building houses a bar/restaurant and there are free kayaks for guests. Rooms $99, cottages and suites $149

PORT FITZROY

Glenfern Cottage Glenfern Rd, Port FitzRoy ☎09 429 0091, ⓦfitzroyhouse.co.nz. Stay inside Glenfern Sanctuary at this wood-floored self-contained cottage sleeping six, with views over the harbour and free access to the sanctuary and to canoes and a dinghy. Two-night min; $50-a-night discount for 3 nights or more. $225

Orama Oasis Karaka Bay ☎09 429 0063, ⓦwww .orama.org.nz. Welcoming Christian camp that also operates as a waterfront holiday park, with bunkrooms ($33), lodges ($52) and self-contained cottages ($195). There's a swimming pool, basic shop and access to magnificent bushwalks, fishing and diving. Camping $25, cabins $90

CAMPSITES AND HUTS

Harataonga Campsite Harataonga. Excellent, shady DOC site 300m back from the beach and very popular with families in the fortnight after Christmas. $10

Kaiaraara Hut Near Port FitzRoy ⓦdoc.govt.nz. Longstanding 28-bunker huddled in the bush with a wood stove for heating. Book through DOC and take pots, utensils and all food. $15

Medlands Beach Campsite Medlands Beach. Attractive DOC site beside an estuary and just over the dunes from an excellent beach. Very crowded for most of Jan but at other times you'll have it to yourselves. $10

Mickey's Place Awana ☎09 429 0140. Hospitable but primitive campsite 25km north of Tryphena that's less well located than the nearby DOC site but has hot showers, toilets and a basic cookhouse. $7

Mount Heale Hut Superb new 20-bunk hut set in a saddle below Mt Heale with great views across the Hauraki Gulf to Little Barrier Island. There's a gas cooking stove but take pots, utensils and food. No bookings. $15

Sugarloaf Campground Sugarloaf Rd, Kaitoke ☎ 09 429 0229. A great private campsite overlooking the southern end of Kaitoke beach. It has water, toilets and showers. Ask about exploring the Mermaid Pool at low tide. $10

EATING AND DRINKING

The limited number of stand-alone **restaurants** encourages lots of accommodation operators to offer meals, and those that don't will almost certainly have self-catering facilities. Restaurants often close early (or don't open at all) if business is slow, so **book ahead**. There are also **shops** in Tryphena, Claris, Whangaparapara and Port FitzRoy, where you can pick up picnic provisions. **Drinking** tends to happen in bars attached to accommodation establishments or in the social clubs at Tryphena and Claris.

Angsana 63 Grays Rd, just north of Crossroads ☎ 09 429 0272. A quality Thai restaurant seems incongruous for the Barrier, but the island is a better place for it. The menu features all the Thai favourites (mains around $30) with friendly service. Oct–May Thurs–Sun 6–9pm.

Claris Texas Café 129 Hector Sanderson Rd, Claris ☎ 09 429 0811. Reliable café with a sunny courtyard and a grassy patch for the kids. Visit for a full range of breakfasts, fish burger and chips ($14), soups and great desserts. Internet available. Daily 8am–4pm.

★ **Currach Irish Pub** Stonewall, Tryphena ☎ 09 429 0211, ⓦ currachirishpub.co.nz. An Irish pub that's about as traditional as you can get on a South Pacific island – a lot of the paraphernalia came from the owner's grandmother's pub in County Kerry, which closed in 1950. There's Guinness plus local craft beers on tap and hot bar meals served in the evening (crumbed scallops and chips $27). There's also often live acoustic music, especially on Thurs when anyone is welcome to jam. Daily noon–10pm or later.

Wild Rose Café Stonewall, Tryphena ☎ 09 429 0905. Sit on the veranda or in the garden at this daytime café specializing in organic products, fine teas and juices. Also does a good range of breakfasts, burgers ($13) and nachos. Mon–Sat 8am–5pm, Sun 9am–5pm.

Tiritiri Matangi

Tiny **Tiritiri Matangi** island (roughly 2km by 1km) just off the tip of the Whangaparaoa Peninsula and 30km north of Auckland, is a wonderful "open sanctuary" where visitors are free to roam through the predator-free bush. Within a couple of hours, it's possible to see rarities such as takahe, saddlebacks, whiteheads, red-crowned parakeets, North Island robins, kokako and brown teals, though to stand a chance of seeing the little-spotted kiwi and tuatara, you'll have to stay overnight.

Four of the species released here are among the rarest in the world, with total populations of around a couple of hundred. The most visible are the flightless **takahe**, lumbering blue-green birds the size of a large chicken and long thought to be extinct (see p.757); the birds were moved here from Fiordland, have bred well and are easily spotted as they are unafraid of humans and very inquisitive. **Saddlebacks**, **kokako** and **stitchbirds** stick to the bush and its margins, but often pop out if you sit quietly for a few moments on some of the bush boardwalks and paths near feeding stations. **Northern blue penguins** also frequent Tiritiri and can be seen all year round, but are most in evidence in March, when they come ashore to moult, and from September to December, when they nest in specially constructed viewing boxes located along the seashore path west of the main wharf.

The standard loop along the east coast then back via the central Ridge Track passes **Hobbs Beach**, where you can swim from the island's only sandy strand.

Brief history

Tiritiri Matangi was first populated by the Kawerau-A-Maki **Maori** and later by Ngati Paoa, both of whom are now recognized as the land's traditional owners. They partly **cleared the island** of bush, a process continued by Europeans who arrived in the mid-nineteenth century to graze sheep and cattle. Fortunately, **pests** such as possums, stoats, deer and cats failed to get a foothold, so since farming became uneconomic in the early 1970s Tiritiri has been **reforested** with 300,000 saplings. Though the rapidly regenerating bush is far from mature, the **birds** seem to like it and the cacophony of birdsong in the bush is stark evidence of just how catastrophic the impact of these predators has been elsewhere.

ARRIVAL AND DEPARTURE

TIRITIRI MATANGI

By ferry 360 Discovery Cruises (daily Christmas to mid-Jan, 9am; rest of year Wed–Sun and public holidays, 9am; Auckland $70; Gulf Harbour $55; ☎0800 360 3472, ⓦ360discovery.co.nz) do day-trips giving five hours on the island.

INFORMATION AND TOURS

Tourist information ⓦ tiritirimatangi.org.nz.
Food There is no food on the island. Bring your own lunch.
Guided walks Ferry passengers can join a guided walk (1.5hr; $5) from the wharf, led by enthusiastic volunteers steeped in bird lore. They typically finish near the lighthouse at the modern interpretation centre.

ACCOMMODATION

Tiritiri Matangi Island Bunkhouse ⓦdoc.govt.nz/tiritiribunkhouse. The island's only accommodation is this communal bunkhouse near the lighthouse. Book as far in advance as you can (months ahead for weekends), and bring a sleeping bag and food in sealed rodent-proof containers. **$30**

Northland

CAPE REINGA

Northland

2

Thrusting 350km from Auckland into the subtropical north, Northland separates the Pacific Ocean from the Tasman Sea. The two oceans swirl together off Cape Reinga, New Zealand's most northerly road-accessible point, which tourists often approach via the sands of Ninety Mile Beach. Kiwis regularly describe this staunchly Maori province as the "Winterless North", a phrase that evokes the citrus trees, avocado plantations, vineyards, warm aquamarine waters and beaches of white silica or golden sand. These attractions have increasingly made the upper reaches of the region a magnet for discerning tourists and holidaying Kiwis, keen to escape the hullabaloo of Auckland traffic. Increased tourism has, in turn, slowly brought back some prosperity and a more positive and welcoming attitude to a region once noted for its ambivalence to visitors.

Scenically, Northland splits down the middle. The **east coast** is a labyrinth of coves hidden between plunging headlands. Beaches tend to be calm and safe, with the force of occasional Pacific storms broken by clusters of protective barrier islands. There could hardly be a greater contrast than the long, virtually straight, **west coast** pounded by powerful Tasman breakers and broken only by occasional harbours. Tidal rips and holes make swimming dangerous, and there are no lifeguard patrols. Some beaches are even designated as roads but are full of hazards for the unwary – and rental cars aren't insured for beach driving, so don't risk it. Exploration of the undulating **interior** involves long forays down twisting side roads.

Beyond Auckland's extended suburbs, on the east shore, is the rural **Matakana Coast**, popular with yachties circumnavigating Kawau Island and snorkellers exploring the underwater world of the **Goat Island Marine Reserve**. The broad sweep of **Bream Bay** runs to the dramatic crags of Whangarei Heads at the entrance to Northland's major port and town, **Whangarei**. Off the coast here lie the **Poor Knights Islands**, one of the world's premier scuba spots with a multitude of unique dives around the islands. Tourists in a hurry tend to make straight for the **Bay of Islands**, a jagged bite out of the coastline that is steeped in New Zealand history and dotted with islands suitable for cruising, diving and swimming (some of the time) with dolphins. Everything north of here is loosely referred to as **The Far North**, a region characterized by the quiet remoteness of the **Whangaroa Harbour**, **Doubtless Bay**, and the **Aupori Peninsula**, which backs **Ninety Mile Beach** and leads to **Cape Reinga**.

WAIPOUA KAURI FOREST

Highlights

❶ The Arts Factory, Te Hana Offers the chance to see the work of a Kiwi icon and his team sculpting beautiful and enormous jewellery-like pieces out of massive lumps of swamp kauri that are thousands of years old. **See p.146**

❷ Poor Knights Islands World-class scuba diving and snorkelling in caves, along walls and under rock arches, all abundant with beautiful and unusual sea life. **See p.157**

❸ Bay of Islands Sail, kayak and soak up the history and scenery of Northland's tourism hotspot and – if you're lucky – swim with dolphins. **See p.161**

❹ Ninety Mile Beach and Cape Reinga Journey the length of one of the country's best-known beaches, stopping to sandboard giant dunes along the way, before taking in views of the Pacific Ocean and Tasman Sea meeting in a swirling mass. **See p.185**

❺ Hokianga Harbour Settle in to watch the sun set in a fiery rainbow of orange, fuchsia and indigo, or explore the wind-sculpted dunes that overlook this scenic, laidback harbour. **See p.190**

❻ Kauri forests Marvel at New Zealand's largest tree, the majestic 2000-year-old Tane Mahuta, and the other ancient kauri in the same stand. **See p.195**

HIGHLIGHTS ARE MARKED ON THE MAP ON P.142

2

The west coast is clearly discernable from the east, marked by the struggle out of economic neglect caused by the cessation of kauri logging and establishment of farming and tourism in its stead, both of which are finally beginning to alter the landscape and create a more positive atmosphere. First stop on the way back south from Ninety Mile Beach is the fragmented but alluring **Hokianga Harbour**, one of New Zealand's largest, with spectacular sand dunes gracing the north head. South of here you're into the **Waipoua Forest**, which is all that remains after the depredations of the kauri loggers – a story best told at the excellent Kauri Museum at Matakohe.

GETTING AROUND

By car With no trains and few airports, you'll be hitting Northland's roads. Driving is the only sensible option as there is little public transport. Road choices are limited to the state highways running up each side of the peninsula. These form a logical loop formalized as the Twin Coast Discovery Highway: there's no need to follow

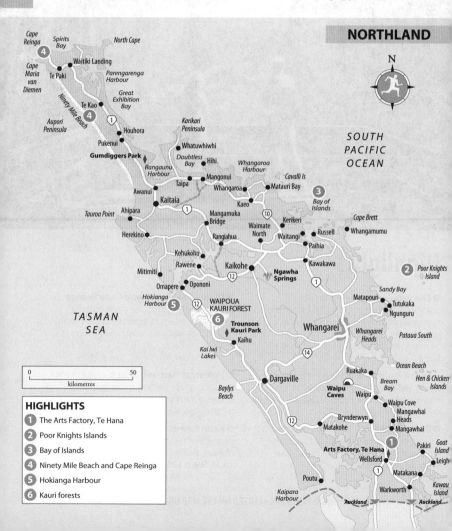

NORTHLAND

N

SOUTH PACIFIC OCEAN

TASMAN SEA

0   50
kilometres

HIGHLIGHTS

1. The Arts Factory, Te Hana
2. Poor Knights Islands
3. Bay of Islands
4. Ninety Mile Beach and Cape Reinga
5. Hokianga Harbour
6. Kauri forests

Cape Reinga · Spirits Bay · North Cape · Waitiki Landing · Cape Maria van Diemen · Te Paki · Parengarenga Harbour · Great Exhibition Bay · Ninety Mile Beach · Te Kao · Aupori Peninsula · Houhora · Pukenui · Gumdiggers Park · Whatuwhiwhi · Karikari Peninsula · Doubtless Bay · Hihi · Rangaunu Harbour · Whangaroa Harbour · Cavalli Is · Awanui · Taipa · Mangonui · Whangaroa · Mauri Bay · Bay of Islands · Kaitaia · Kaeo · Tauroa Point · Ahipara · Mangamuka Bridge · Waimate North · Kerikeri · Cape Brett · Herekino · Rangiahua · Waitangi · Russell · Whangamumu · Kohukohu · Paihia · Mitimiti · Rawene · Kaikohe · Kawakawa · Poor Knights Island · Omapere · Opononi · Ngawha Springs · Sandy Bay · Hokianga Harbour · Matapouri · Tutukaka · Ngunguru · WAIPOUA KAURI FOREST · Trounson Kauri Park · Whangarei · Kaihu · Whangarei Heads · Pataua South · Kai Iwi Lakes · Ocean Beach · Baylys Beach · Dargaville · Ruakaka · Hen & Chicken Islands · Waipu Caves · Waipu · Bream Bay · Brynderwyn · Waipu Cove · Mangawhai Heads · Matakohe · Mangawhai · Arts Factory, Te Hana · Pakiri · Goat Island · Wellsford · Leigh · Poutu · Matakana · Kawau Island · Kaipara Harbour · Warkworth · Auckland · Auckland

HIGHLIGHTS
1. The Arts Factory, Te Hana
2. Poor Knights Islands
3. Bay of Islands
4. Ninety Mile Beach and Cape Reinga
5. Hokianga Harbour
6. Kauri forests

it slavishly, but the brown signs emblazoned with a dolphin and curling wave make a good starting framework.

By bus The main bus line is InterCity (☎ 09 583 5780, ⓦ intercity.co.nz), running multiple routes. Nakedbus (premium charged ☎ 0900 62533, ⓦ nakedbus.com) and Kiwi Experience (☎ 09 336 4286, ⓦ kiwiexperience .com) also run around the region and can be a very affordable option.

By plane Northland has a limited number of flights and since distances are relatively short you're unlikely to need them, except perhaps for flights from Whangarei to Great Barrier Island with Great Barrier Airlines (☎ 0800 900600, ⓦ greatbarrierairlines.co.nz) or a flightseeing trip from Paihia to Cape Reinga via the Bay of Islands (see p.171).

INFORMATION

Websites The Northland website is ⓦ northlandnz.com. The Far North region of Northland has regional i-SITE offices in Paihia, Kaitaia and Opononi; see ⓦ topofnz.co.nz for more information.

Brief history

Northland was the site of most of the early contact between Maori and European settlers, and the birthplace of New Zealand's most important document, the **Treaty of Waitangi**. Maori legend tells of how the great Polynesian explorer Kupe discovered the Hokianga Harbour and, finding the climate and abundance of food to his liking, encouraged his people to return and settle there. It was their descendants in the Bay of Islands who had the dubious honour of making the first contact with white men, as European whalers plundered the seas and missionaries sought converts. Eventually, the northern chiefs signed away their sovereignty in return for assurances on land and traditional rights, which were seldom respected. There is still a perception among some Maori in the rest of the country that the five northern *iwi* gave Aotearoa away to the Pakeha.

As more fertile farmlands were found in newly settled regions further south, rapacious **kauri loggers** and **gum diggers** cleared the bush, and later, as extractive industries died away, pioneers moved in, turning much of the land to **dairy country**. Local dairy factories closed as larger semi-industrial complexes centralized processing, leaving small towns all but destitute, though the planting of fast-growing exotic trees and sporadic horticulture keep local economies ticking over.

The Matakana Coast to Bream Bay

ⓦ matakanacoast.com

Around 50km north of central Auckland the city's influence begins to wane, heralding the **Matakana Coast**, a 30km stretch of shallow harbours, beach-strung peninsulas and small islands. Its individual character becomes apparent once you pass pretty **Warkworth** and head out either to **Kawau Island**, or up the coast to the village of **Matakana** and the snorkelling and diving nirvana of **Goat Island**.

The journey from Auckland to Warkworth has been made quicker, though less scenic, by the introduction of a 7km stretch of toll road ($2.20/car, payable online within five days). It's worth sticking to the old route though, if you have time, as there are great views via Orewa on the Hibiscus Coast Highway.

Other than the excellent woodcarving on display at **Te Hana**, there's little to detain you on SH1 between Warkworth and Waipu as it passes the road junction at **Brynderwyn**, where SH12 loops off to Dargaville, the Waipoua kauri forest and the Hokianga Harbour. If you're heading north and want a scenic route, it's better to stay on the coast and follow **Bream Bay**, named by Cook when he visited in 1770 and his crew hauled in tarakihi, which they mistook for bream. There are no sizeable towns here, only the small beach communities of **Mangawhai Heads** and **Waipu Cove**, looking out to the **Hen and Chicken Islands**, refuges for rare birds such as the wattled saddleback.

Warkworth

The peaceful and slow-paced rural town of **WARKWORTH** only really comes to life in high summer when thousands of yachties moor their boats in the numerous estuaries and coves nearby. From the late 1820s for about a century, the languid stretch of river behind the town seethed with boats shipping out kauri: a boardwalk now traces its shores past the *Jane Gifford* (Ⓦjanegifford.org.nz), a rebuilt scow which once worked the tidal waterways and now runs occasional trips (1hr; $20).

Warkworth and Districts Museum

Tudor Collins Drive, 3km south of Warkworth off the SH1 • Daily 9am–3pm • $8 • Ⓦ wwmuseum.orconhosting.net.nz

Spend a few minutes at the **Warkworth and Districts Museum**, which explores the region's history through re-created rooms, and a 5m-long, 130-link chain carved from a single piece of kauri. The two ancient kauri outside mark the start of two well-presented twenty-minute boardwalk nature trails through the preserved bush of the **Parry Kauri Park** (9am–dusk; donation). A free leaflet at the museum's entrance explains the trees in detail.

Brick Bay Sculpture Trail

Arabella Lane, 6km east of Warkworth off SH1 • Daily 10am–5pm, last entry 4pm • $12; wine tastings $5; olive oil tastings $8 • ☏ 09 425 4690, Ⓦ brickbaysculpture.co.nz

For a combination of outdoor sculpture and striking architecture, try the **Brick Bay Sculpture Trail**. An hour wandering the 2km-long bush, vines and parkland trail past the art – fifty plus sculptures mostly by New Zealand artists and all for sale (and likely to remain so, given the prices) – gets you back to the predominantly glass café, where wine tastings, olive oil tastings and platters (for two) of local-ish produce ($27) may slow you down further.

Kawau Island

With a resident population of around seventy (plus lots of weekenders), **KAWAU ISLAND** is chiefly given over to holiday homes, each with its own wharf. For information on how to get to the island, see p.147.

Mansion House

Sept–May Mon–Fri noon–2pm, Sat & Sun noon–3.30pm • $4

The only sight of note on Kawau Island is the grand, kauri-panelled **Mansion House**, the former private home of George Grey – then doing his second stint as New Zealand's governor – and furnished much as it would have been in the late 1880s, including with Grey's writing desk.

Grey's pursuit of the Victorian fashion for all things exotic resulted in **grounds** stocked with flora and fauna from all over the world, such as Chilean wine palms and coral trees. He also brought in four species of **wallaby**, which have overtaken the island and have to be regularly culled. You might even see Australian kookaburras and a white peacock.

A path runs through the gardens to the tiny beach at **Lady's Bay** and on to a network of short tracks that weave through pine forest and kanuka scrub. The most popular destination is the ruins of the island's old **copper mine** (40min each way). The on-site **café** (see p.149) provides sustenance.

Matakana and around

Over the last decade or so, **MATAKANA**, 9km northeast of Warkworth, has transformed itself from an inconsequential crossroads to the heart of an aspiring **wine** region, and minor Slow Food centre. It is close enough to Auckland to attract weekenders who arrive for the **farmers' market** (Sat 8am–1pm) and stick around to visit the local boutique cinema (2 Matakana Valley Rd; ☏09 422 9833, Ⓦmatakanacinemas.co.nz), browse the shops – which include a heritage butchers, a quality bookshop and an excellent deli (see p.149) – and stop in at the wineries (see p.149 & p.150).

Morris & James Pottery & Tileworks

2km west of Matakana at Tongue Farm Rd · Daily 9am–5pm; café/bar 9am–4pm; free tour daily 11.30am · Free · ☎ 09 422 7116, ⓦ morrisandjames.co.nz

The catalyst for the region's development was the **Morris & James Pottery & Tileworks**, which has been producing vibrant, handmade terracotta tiles and bright, large garden pots from local clay since the late 1970s. You can catch a free thirty-minute tour of the pottery and visit the café/bar.

Tawharanui Regional Park

10km southeast of Matakana, along Takatu Rd · Gates open daily 6am–dusk · Free

Tawharanui Regional Park has great beaches and swathes of regenerating bush, and makes for a pleasant spot to visit before leaving the Matakana area. Predators have been eradicated and native birds are returning to this designated **open sanctuary**: come to swim, snorkel, picnic and walk or bike the easy trails, but you'll have to bring everything with you. You can also camp here (see p.148).

Leigh and Goat Island

The village of **LEIGH**, 13km northeast of Matakana, holds a picturesque harbour with bobbing wooden fishing boats. Heading a further 4km northeast brings you to the **Cape Rodney–Okakari Marine Reserve**, usually known simply as **Goat Island** since the bush-clad islet is 300m offshore. In 1975, this became New Zealand's first marine reserve, with no-take areas stretching 5km along the shoreline and 800m off the coast. Some 35 years on, the undersea life is thriving, with large rock lobster, huge snapper and rays. Feeding has been discouraged since blue maomaos developed a taste for frozen peas and began to mob swimmers and divers. Easy beach access (from the road-end parking area), clear water, rock pools on wave-cut platforms, a variety of undersea terrains and relatively benign currents combine to make this an enormously popular year-round diving spot, as well as a favourite summer destination for families: aim to come midweek if you value tranquillity.

GOAT ISLAND TOURS AND ACTIVITIES

The waters surrounding Goat Island have good visibility, making them perfect for snorkellers and scuba divers who can enjoy a lush world populated by kelp forest and numerous multicoloured fish, while deeper still are more exposed seascapes with an abundance of sponges. Because of the clarity of the water this is also an excellent spot for the less adventurous who want to observe from glass-bottom boats or kayaks.

Glass Bottom Boat ☎ 09 422 6334, ⓦ glassbottomboat.co.nz. Tours on the *Aquador* depart from the beach (3 trips daily in winter, more in the summer; $28), last about 45min and are best in fine, calm weather. Phone ahead to check conditions and make bookings.

Goat Island Dive 142a Pakiri Rd, Leigh ☎ 09 422 6925, ⓦ goatislanddive.co.nz. A highly professional outfit that rents mask, snorkel and fins ($25), and wetsuits (from $15) plus offers a 2hr guided snorkel ($75). They also run scuba courses and trips to Goat Island Marine Reserve and beyond. They'll also rent scuba gear (full set from $90) if you want to go independently, assuming you have the relevant qualification. Open daily in summer, and on weekends in winter.

Goat Island Beach Hire On the beach, opposite the island ☎ 021 460 121, ⓦ goatislandbeachhire.co.nz. Rents glass-bottomed (double $45/hr) and traditional kayaks (double; $35/hr, single $25/hr), mask, snorkel and fins ($25), and do a combo of glass-bottom boat tour, kayak and snorkel ($66).

Pakiri

There's not much to **PAKIRI**, 10km north of Leigh, except for a beautiful, lon, deserted white surf beach, backed by farmland, dunes and stands of mature pohutukawa trees that bloom with vibrant red flowers in December (hence their nickname: Christmas trees). This is a perfect setting for leisurely beachcombing, birdwatching, sunset gazing and **horseriding** (see p.148).

Te Hana

Spread out along either side of SH1 is the small roadside settlement of **TE HANA**, 4km north of Wellsford. It's your next chance to turn off towards the coast and a settlement which, until recently, most people have passed through without pause. This does Te Hana an injustice, as it is home to one of New Zealand's most adventurous and spectacular woodcarvers.

The Arts Factory

Behind the *Te Hana Café* · Summer daily 9am–5pm; winter Mon–Fri 9am–5pm, Sat & Sun by appointment · ☎ 09 423 8069, ⓦ strongmanishere.com

Te Hana is home to **The Arts Factory**, where unique and iconic artist Kerry Strongman and his team carve breathtaking "jewellery for giants" – massive pieces of swamp kauri that are thousands of years old. The pieces are innovatively and experimentally carved (sometimes as interpretations of traditional Maori and/or other ancient peoples' designs) and all are supersized to fill and enhance large spaces. Most of the pieces go to galleries and commissioners in New Zealand and abroad, but other, smaller pieces are on sale in the gallery shop. Best of all, you get to wander round the expansive studio, inside and out, and watch the works being created.

Te Hana Cultural Experience

317 SH1 · Guided tour Wed–Sun on the hour 9am–5pm; multicultural package daily 11.30am (booking essential) · Guided tour $36; multicultural package $145 · ☎ 09 423 8701, ⓦ tehana.co.nz

On the opposite side of SH1 is the newly constructed *pa* and Maori village, all part of the Te Hana cultural experience. The originally flat site needed 250 lorry-loads of mud to create a hill for the *pa*, and the money and effort that went into building this authentic and thoughtful Maori experience is clear to see. There's a 60-minute guided tour during which you'll hear Maori stories and beat the war drum, and a "cultural experience" package which includes a welcome ceremony, buffet lunch or traditional *hangi* dinner, a guided tour and cultural concert over 2.5 hours, day or night.

Mangawhai

Tiny **Mangawhai**, 20km northeast of Te Hana, is a commercial farm supply settlement that has transmogrified into a weekend village for holidaying Aucklanders. It has a few restaurants, a chic farmers' market at the weekends and access to the infinitely more scenic Mangawhai Heads.

Mangawhai Heads

On the coast 3km north of Mangawhai sits **Mangawhai Heads**, at the mouth of the Mangawhai Harbour, marked by holiday homes straggling over the hillsides behind a fine surf beach. Long a Kiwi summer-holiday favourite, Mangawhai Heads is relaxed outside the peak summer blitz and is chiefly of interest for the extraordinary views on the scenic **Mangawhai Cliffs Walkway** (2–3hr; year-round). Walk north along the beach for fifteen minutes then follow the orange markers up through bush-backed farmland along the top of the sea cliffs until the path winds back down to the beach. Provided the tide is below half, you can return along the beach through a small rock arch.

Mangawhai Museum

Molesworth Drive • $10 • ☎ 09 431 4663, ⓦ mangawhai-museum.org.nz

The new **Mangawhai Museum** is home to exhibitions charting human habitation of the area around this natural harbour, stretching from Maori settlement to the present day – "from building ships to building sandcastles". Follow the strands of 11 different stories through the stingray-shaped contemporary building, discovering everything from the great Maori battle between the Ngapuhi and Ngati Whatua groups to the ongoing struggle to save the critically endangered Fairy Tern.

Waipu and around

An Aberdeen granite monument topped by a Scottish lion rampant dominates the quirky village of **WAIPU**, 25km north of Mangawhai. It's a nod to the nine hundred Scottish settlers who followed charismatic preacher, the Reverend Norman McLeod, here in the mid-1800s. On New Year's Day, Waipu hosts its **Highland Games** (ⓦ highlandgames.co.nz), in which competitors heft large stones and toss cabers and sheaves in Caledonian Park.

Waipu Museum

36 The Centre • Tues–Sat 10am–4.30pm, Sun & Mon 10am–4pm • $8 • ☎ 09 432 0746, ⓦ waipumuseum.com

The excellent **Waipu Museum** tells the tale of Scottish settlers and their journey via Nova Scotia where famine and a series of harsh winters drove them on to form a strict, self-contained Calvinist community. All is admirably illustrated, with everything from McLeod's old pocket watch to genealogical records that are regularly consulted by Kiwi Scots tracing their ancestry. Also worth a look are the various Caledonian-themed rotating exhibitions.

Waipu Caves

Just past the Waipu Caves Estate gate, about 16km from town (signposted) via Shoemaker and Waipu Caves roads

Waipu Caves is a popular local excursion, and in among its many limestone formations is one of the longest stalagmites in New Zealand, in a 200m glowworm-filled passage. Obtain a free map from the visitor centre in the Waipu Museum, wear old clothes and good footwear, and take a couple of reliable torches. The cave is impenetrable after heavy rain; even when it's dry you'll get muddy, so use the cold shower, located on the wall away from the road, or the public toilets on the site.

ARRIVAL AND DEPARTURE

MATAKANA COAST TO BREAM BAY

WARKWORTH

By bus InterCity, Northliner and NakedBus buses stop outside the i-SITE on Baxter St.

Destinations Auckland (4 daily; 1hr 20min); Whangarei (4 daily; 2hr).

KAWAU ISLAND

By boat All boats to Kawau Island leave from the wharf (parking $10/24hr) at Sandspit, a small road-end community on the Matakana Estuary, 8km east of Warkworth. Kawau Cruises (☎ 0800 111 616, ⓦ kawaucruises.co.nz) run one or two trips direct to Mansion House Bay daily ($55 return), which allow for roughly twice the time ashore as the Royal Mail Run

(see p.148), which also takes you to the island.

LEIGH AND GOAT ISLAND

By taxi Without your own vehicle, the only way to get to Leigh is via taxi from Matakana. Matakabs (☎ 0800 522743) cost around $40 one way.

WAIPU

By bus InterCity/Northliner and NakedBus drop off and pick up on request outside the Pear Tree gift shop, 13 The Centre (☎ 09 432 0046), which also acts as a ticket agent.

Destinations Auckland (4 daily; 2hr 30min); Whangarei (4 daily; 40min).

2

INFORMATION AND TOURS

WARKWORTH

Information i-SITE, 1 Baxter St (Nov–Easter Mon–Fri 8.30am–5pm, Sat & Sun 9am–4pm; Easter–Oct Mon–Fri 8am–5pm, Sat & Sun 9am–3pm; ☎09 425 9081, ⓦwarkworthnz.com). The office can help with travel bookings and has free internet access.

KAWAU ISLAND

Royal Mail Run ☎0800 111616, ⓦkawaucruises .co.nz. Kawau Cruises (see p.147) operates the mail run service (daily 10.30am; 4hr; $68 return; $90 with BBQ lunch), delivering mail, papers and groceries to all the wharves on the island and giving you around an hour and a half ashore at Mansion House Bay – plenty of time to enjoy the native bush and beach, take a swim or have a look around the house before meeting the boat for the return.

Lunch is served on board on the outward leg of the trip.

Blue Adventures Sandspit Wharf ☎022 630 5705, ⓦblueadventures.co.nz. Offers rentals and lessons for stand-up paddleboarding ($40/person/hr), wakeboarding ($100/person/2hr; minimum three people) and kitesurfing ($50/person/hr).

MATAKANA

Winery information The widely available *Matakana Wine Trail* leaflet details eighteen wineries and wine-related sites that offer tastings, mostly for a small charge.

WAIPU

Visitor information 36 The Centre (daily 9.30am–4.30pm; ☎09 432 0746). Located in the museum, and run by volunteers.

ACCOMMODATION

WARKWORTH

★ **Sandspit Holiday Park** 1334 Sandspit Rd ☎09 425 8610, ⓦsandspitholidaypark.co.nz. Set among mature trees and situated next to the ferry landing for Kawau Island, the camp offers free use of canoes and paddleboats, safe swimming, proximity to surf beaches and an internet kiosk. Camping $20, cabins $70

Warkworth Country House 18 Wilson Rd, 300m north of Warkworth and Districts Museum (see p.144) ☎09 422 2485, ⓦwarkworthcountryhouse.co.nz. Two cosy en suites with their own private patio entrances that overlook an acre of well-tended garden, with a further acre of native bush full of birds nearby – all run efficiently by a friendly ex-school teacher. $120

LEIGH AND GOAT ISLAND

Goat Island Camping & Backpackers 123 Goat Island Rd ☎09 422 6185, ⓦgoatislandcamping.co.nz. A welcoming site about 500m back from the reserve on the way to Goat Island, with four simple cabins and nine basic caravans nestled among the trees. The bay views are great, plus there's snorkel gear rental. Cash only. Camping $20, cabins $80

PAKIRI

Pakiri Beach Horse Rides Rahuikiri Rd ☎09 422 6275, ⓦhorseride-nz.co.nz. Has a range of wonderfully atmospheric accommodation: riverside backpacker cabins; self-contained, beachside *baches* for two with a bed, stove and loo; a family cabin for seven; and the luxurious Ngapeka four-bedroom beach house ($600, 2-night minimum stay) sleeping up to eight. The café, at the stables, is a one-room supply store and eatery serving basic food at basic prices from around 9am until 5pm. The horse-riding part of the operation runs year-round and offers

some stunning trips. Rides ($65/hr, $135/2hr, $175/half day, $299/full day with lunch) go along the beach, among the dunes, across streams and through a pohutukawa glade. Cabins $70, beachside cabins $155

MANGAWHAI

Coastal Cow Backpackers 299 Molesworth Drive ☎09 431 5246, ⓦmangawhaibackpackers.com. Hostel accommodation in a pleasant, modern house with all the usual facilities, run by a helpful and informative host. Choose from either dorms or rooms, and be sure to make use of the deck and BBQ area. Dorms $28, rooms $66

★ **Milestone Cottages by the Sea** 27 Moir Point Rd ☎09 431 4018, ⓦmilestonecottages.co.nz. This cluster of six lovingly constructed timber and mud-brick cottages is divided into studio and family units, all luxurious but still extremely good value. Two of the cottages overlook the sea, while the other four sit amid sumptuous organic gardens and coastal bush. A short walk down a private track leads to a secluded estuary beach where kayaks are available (free) to transport you along the river or over to the bird reserve on a sand dune, for a glimpse of dotterels and fairy terns. All units are self-catering and include a BBQ deck, plus there's a saltwater lap pool for guests' use. Studio $135, cottages $180

TAWHARANUI REGIONAL PARK

Campsite ☎09 366 2000, ⓦregionalparks .aucklandcouncil.govt.nz. Beautiful and very low key tents-only campsite with simple toilet blocks set back behind the sand dunes on the northern coast. $13

WAIPU COVE

Camp Waipu 869 Cove Rd, Waipu Cove ☎09 432 0410, ⓦcampwaipucove.com. Beachside accommodation is extensive at the southern end of Bream Bay north of Lang's Beach, but packed in January. Most cabins are pretty basic but there are a few high-end self-contained units. Camp facilities are clean and there's access to the beach on foot. Camping $23, self-contained units $220

★**Waipu Cove Cottages and Camping** 685 Cove Rd, Waipu Cove ☎09 432 0851, ⓦwaipucovecottages .co.nz. Adjacent to *Camp Waipu*, this is a smaller establishment with a more exclusive feel and modern cottages ($155). The grounds contain well-spaced camping sites, plus there's free use of dinghies. Camping $21, doubles $54

WAIPU
Uretiti Beach campsite 6km north of Waipu, signposted on SH1. The wonderful long white beach at Uretiti is backed by a basic DOC camping area with running water, toilets, cold showers and an adjacent (and unofficial) naturist beach. $10

Waipu Wanderers 25 St Mary's Rd ☎09 432 0532, ⓔwaipu.wanderers@xtra.co.nz. Offers cosy, homey, welcoming budget accommodation in a separate house with its own kitchen and bathroom, as well as one double, a twin and a three-share. About a 2min walk from the town centre. Dorms $30, room $66

EATING AND DRINKING

WARKWORTH
You can eat well enough in town – there's a New World supermarket for those wanting to stock up – or at a price in the surrounding vineyards; check the *Matakana Wine Trail* leaflet (see opposite).

Ginger Café 21 Queen St ☎09 422 2298. Has good coffee and they bake their own bagels and bread (which they stuff with lots of goodies), as well as offering an impressive breakfast menu and veggie meals (mains around $20). They specialize in gluten- and dairy-free. Mon–Fri 6.45am–4pm, Sat & Sun 7.30am–4pm.

Quince Café 10 Elizabeth St ☎09 442 2555. A local favourite, serving up dishes such as lamb shanks with pea and lentil gravy and mint jelly pistachio mash (mains around $26). It's licensed, but you can also bring your own booze. Wed–Sun 9am–late.

★**Tahi** 1 Neville St ☎09 422 3674, ⓦtahibar.com. Located in an alley opposite the i-SITE, this craft beer bar stocks a good range of boutique NZ beers and dishes up a number of booze-soaking favourites, including decent fish and chips ($17.50). Daily noon–late.

WINERIES
Ransom Wines 46 Valerie Close, 1.5km off SH1, south of Warkworth ☎09 425 8862, ⓦransomwines.co.nz. Take in the vineyard views over a wine tasting at the cellar door ($5 donation) or do a full tour and tasting for $20. The wine bar has platters ($20) and a full wine list. Feb–Dec Tues–Sun and public holidays 10am–5pm; Jan daily 10am–5pm.

KAWAU ISLAND
Café Sandspit The wharf at Sandspit, 8km east of Warkworth. A pleasant, licensed café in a wooden shed offering passable nosh, specializing in seafood, such as chowder ($13), fish and chips ($17), and burgers ($14.50), and serving up post-cruise liquid restoratives. Daily 9am–3.30pm.

Mansion House Bay Café ☎09 422 8903. Licensed café open for lunches as well as snacks and light meals ($10–30), including the likes of all-day breakfast, seared beef on noodles, or seared salmon. Most people visit as part of one of the guided trips so lunch is your most likely option, but a water taxi from Kawau Cruises (see p.147) will get you there and back for dinner. Open weekends and most days in summer; call ahead for exact hours.

MATAKANA
Black Dog Café 23 Matakana Valley Rd ☎09 422 9130. A local favourite for coffee, chocolate cake, breakfasts, big juicy burgers ($12.50) with beetroot, and bagels with a variety of good-quality fillings. Mon–Fri 7.30am–3.30pm, Sat & Sun 8am–4pm.

Matakana Market Kitchen 2 Matakana Valley Rd ☎09 423 0383, ⓦmatakanamarketkitchen.com. Expect classy and expensive dining at this designer restaurant with schist rock walls, wooden furniture and a big shiny bar. Dishes include avocado on toast ($13), brunches made with free-range eggs ($16.50–18), and dinner mains such as scallop and snapper risotto ($28). Gluten-free options also available. Daily 9am–late.

★**Nosh Food Market** 2 Matakana Valley Rd ☎09 422 9534, ⓦnoshfoodmarket.com. Great nosh for less dosh in the form of a substantial deli that has something to tempt everyone, including local meats and cheeses and some stunning imports from Italy and France. Mon–Fri 9am–7pm, Sat & Sun 7.30am–7pm.

Oob Organic Café 2 Matakana Valley Rd ☎09 422 7797, ⓦblue.co.nz. Traditional parlour serving organic ice creams ($6), sorbets and great smoothies ($7), using blueberry flavours from their renowned orchard. If you're after something more substantial they also have good sandwiches and coffee. Mon–Fri 10am–5pm, Sat 8am–5pm, Sun 10am–5pm.

Plume 49a Sharp Rd ☎09 422 7915, ⓦplume restaurant.co.nz. A stylish, expensive vineyard restaurant (at *Heron's Flight*, see p.150) with an open kitchen, serving classy dishes such as venison medallions with cassis juniper ($37.50) and tempura prawn tails with dipping sauce ($35). Tues–Sun 11am–3.30pm, Fri & Sat 6pm–late.

2

2

WINERIES

Heron's Flight 49 Sharp Rd ☎ 09 950 6643, ⓦ heronsflight.co.nz. Italian Sangiovese and Dolcetto have been planted at this Tuscan-influenced vineyard and olive grove with considerable success. It's a slick operation, but tastings are by appointment only. Daily from 11am.

Hyperion 188 Tongue Farm Rd, off Leigh Rd ☎ 09 422 9375, ⓦ hyperion-wines.co.nz. Compared with *Heron's Flight*, this is more in the Kiwi tradition of a passionate personal quest, with the only decent Cabernet Sauvignon north of Auckland, as well as other delicious wines, all sampled in a small shed surrounded by moss-covered trees and fences. Tastings are free, but you'll need to call and make an appointment if you want to visit outside of weekends and public/summer holidays. Sat & Sun 10am–5pm.

LEIGH AND GOAT ISLAND

Leigh Fish and Chip Shop 18 Cumberland St ☎ 09 422 6035. Legendary (locally) for tasty fish and chips, mussel fritters and gourmet burgers, this is a traditional takeaway serving fresh fish, mostly cooked to order with nothing on the menu over $15. April–Dec Thurs–Sun 11am–7pm, Fri & Sat 11am–8pm; Dec–Easter 11am–8pm, Fri & Sat 11am–9pm.

★**The Leigh Sawmill Café** 142 Pakiri Rd ☎ 09 422 6019, ⓦ sawmillcafe.co.nz. This converted former sawmill is now a smart café/bar with an abundance of historic milling paraphernalia (closed Mon–Wed in winter) and is the premier gig venue in these parts. They do excellent gourmet pizzas ($25) and there is a good wine list, plus tasty beers from the excellent microbrewery next door, which does takeaway sales. Live music is usually at weekends in the massive beamed area in front of the bar. Also has five spacious en-suite doubles, a self-contained cottage and two dorms. March–Dec Thurs noon–late, Fri–Sun 10am–late; Dec–Feb daily 10am–late.

MANGAWHAI AND MANGAWHAI HEADS

Bennetts Café 52 Moir St, Mangawhai ☎ 09 431 5072. Specializes in imaginative breakfasts and lunches such as chocolate pancakes with their own hazelnut spread ($18) and mussel fritters ($20.50) using quality ingredients in a pseudo-Tuscan setting. There's also a wonderful chocolatier just across the courtyard. Daily 9am–5pm.

★**Frog and Kiwi** 6 Molesworth Drive, Mangawhai ☎ 09 431 4439. As the name suggests, the food here is of the Franco-New Zealand fusion variety. Particular treats include a bowl of coffee, snails and *sauté de lapin* (rabbit with Dijon mustard, gherkins and olives), and a six-course degustation menu with drinks ($116). Most dishes cost around $25. Licensed. Daily 9am–2.30pm & 6pm–late.

Harvest Café 5 Molesworth Drive, Mangawhai Heads, ☎ 09 431 4111. Lively, ultra-friendly little café, much loved by locals, serving home-made pies and cakes before switching to a tapas evening menu ($8–13). Daily 8am–5.30pm, Thurs–Sat also 6–11pm.

Mangawhai Tavern 2 Moir St, Mangawhai ☎ 09 431 4505, ⓦ mangawhaitavern.co.nz. This traditional Kiwi pub serving traditional Kiwi grub would have little to recommend it except a beautiful location were it not a world-famous (in Northland, at least) venue for live music. Every weekend, summer and winter, Kiwi favourites and touring international acts strut their stuff in front of up to 1200 whooping drinkers. Daily 11am–1am.

★**Sail Rock Café** 12a Wood St, Mangawhai Heads ☎ 09 431 4051, ⓦ sailrockcafe.co.nz. This fabulous bistro-bar-restaurant serves fresh seafood, Angus steaks, salt-and-pepper squid and delicious carrot cake (mains start at $22.50). Check out the live music on Saturdays, including solo piano and guitar workshops, and say hi to the landlady, one of the friendliest this side of the dateline. Licensed. Daily 8.30am–11pm or later.

WAIPU

Pizza Barn 2 Cove Rd ☎ 09 432 1011. The tastiest fare is traditional pub food or pizza in Waipu's former post office. Well-priced lunches and dinners (mains $15–25) vie with pizzas sporting elaborate toppings. You can either eat in the cosy corrugated iron, timber and McLeod tartan bar, or the garden room, which is filled with surfboards and a massive stuffed fish. Take a minute to peek at the toilets, a veritable art installation of 1950s kitsch. Dec–March daily 11.30am–late; April–Nov Wed–Sun same hours; closed in June.

Whangarei

Despite its prime gateway location to Whangarei Heads' sweeping beaches and world-class diving around the Poor Knights Islands, Northland's capital, **WHANGAREI** (pronounced Fahn-ga-ray), has never had the wherewithal to slow down tourists on their mad dash up to the Bay of Islands. But things are changing. The newly developed **Town Basin marina** provides a focal point for visitors, with a few restaurants overlooking the sleek yachts dotted along the river and a landscaped

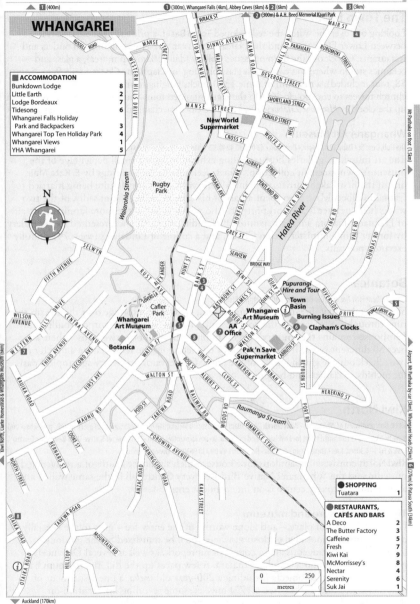

① (300m), Whangarei Falls (4km), Abbey Caves (6km) & ② (6km)

② (300m) & A.H. Reed Memorial Kauri Park

③ (3km)

WHANGAREI

ACCOMMODATION

Bunkdown Lodge	8
Little Earth	2
Lodge Bordeaux	7
Tidesong	6
Whangarei Falls Holiday Park and Backpackers	3
Whangarei Top Ten Holiday Park	4
Whangarei Views	1
YHA Whangarei	5

SHOPPING

Tuatara	1

RESTAURANTS, CAFÉS AND BARS

A Deco	2
The Butter Factory	3
Caffeine	5
Fresh	7
Kiwi Kai	9
McMorrissey's	8
Nectar	4
Serenity	6
Suk Jai	1

New World Supermarket

Rugby Park

Cafler Park

Whangarei Art Museum

Botanica

Pupurangi Hire and Tour

Town Basin

Whangarei Art Museum

Burning Issues

Clapham's Clocks

AA Office

Pak 'n Save Supermarket

N

0   250
metres

Mt Parihaka on foot (1.5km)

Airport, Mt Parihaka by car (3km); Whangarei Heads (25km); ⑥ (27km) & Pataua South (34km)

Kiwi North, Clarke Homestead & Whangarei Museum (6km)

Auckland (170km)

boardwalk along the water's edge. There are sculptures by local artists arranged along here, plus a series of easy walks within a few minutes of the town, the best of which are outlined in the free *Whangarei Walks* leaflet. Married with Whangarei's state-of-the-art Kiwi House, the peaceful parks, and the scenic track to Whangarei Falls, Whangarei may finally be able to persuade tourists to stick around, for a day or so at least.

2

The Town Basin

Looking out over the water, the redeveloped **Town Basin**, a primarily pedestrian area between Lower Dent Street and the Hatea River, is an attractive hub of retail outlets and restaurants. Check out the **Burning Issues Gallery** (daily 10am–5pm; free), a glass and ceramics studio where you can watch glass-blowing, or **Clapham's Clocks** (daily 9am–5pm; $8, tour included), a museum of some 1300 clocks ranging from mechanisms taken out of church towers to cuckoo clocks. On the regular guided tours you'll learn why the mouse ran up the clock in *Hickory, Dickory, Dock* and see clock mechanisms put through their paces.

Whangarei Art Museum

The Hub, Dent St · Daily 10am–4pm · Donation · ☎ 09 430 4240, ⓦ whangareiartmuseum.co.nz

The art museum's galleries host travelling exhibitions and a small percentage of the museum's own excellent collection. Worth seeking out are paintings by **E. Kate Mair**, one of the first Pakeha artists to paint Maori sympathetically despite being married to Captain Gilbert Mair, who spent a part of his career fighting them; sadly, of the two works held, neither is a Maori portrait. Also worth a look is the more familiar portrait of Harataori Harota Tarapata, painted by Goldie (see p.79) and presented to the gallery by former prime minister Helen Clarke, and a couple of Lindauer's (see p.79) skilfully executed portraits.

Botanica

Entrance from First Ave or Cafler Park · Daily 10am–4pm · Free

Should a rainy day threaten your equilibrium, cross the footbridge over the stream that runs through Cafler Park to the cool, restful **Botanica**, where the purpose-built Filmy Fernhouse contains the country's largest public collection of native ferns – there are over 80 different types. If you don't mind ratcheting up the temperature a notch or two, check out the garish glories of the Snow Conservatory, a sweaty subtropical oasis for orchids, cyclamen and begonias.

Kiwi North

SH14, 6km southwest of Whangarei · **Kiwi North** Daily 10am–4pm; steam locomotive rides third Sunday of every month, plus school and bank holidays · $15 combined ticket for kiwi house and museum; steam locomotive $2.50 · **Whangarei Native Bird Recovery Centre** Mon & Fri 1–4.30pm, Tues–Thurs 10am–4.30pm · Donation · ☎ 09 438 9630, ⓦ kiwinorth.co.nz

Kiwi North consists of a fabulous kiwi house, which sits at the centre of a rejuvenated museum and the Whangarei Native Bird Recovery Centre, all in the same walled area, although the recovery centre is an independent entity.

The kiwi enclosure and museum

Undoubted pride of place – and alone worthy of the entry fee – goes to the specially designed and spacious **kiwi enclosure**, where you'll be transfixed by the glorious, long-beaked curmudgeons and a couple of morepork, as well as several Duvaucel's gecko, some skink and a couple of tuatara. A few paces up the hill, the **museum** has an intriguing selection of objects including a 200-year-old *waka*, a fine assortment of Maori cloaks, Hone Heke's (see p.172) musket, some revealing information on Ruapekapeka Pa – including some of the cannon balls from the battle (see p.158) – and photographic collections that include images of Maori and early settlers.

Heritage Park and Native Bird Recovery Centre

Surrounding the two central attractions is the **Heritage Park**, at the heart of which is the **Clarke Homestead**, a rare example of an original unrestored homestead, built in 1886 for Scottish doctor Alexander Clarke. Also of note are the restored **steam locomotives** running through the compound.

A must-see for all twitchers is the **Native Bird Recovery Centre**, which attempts to rehabilitate injured birds. This collection of walking and hopping wounded is a mixture of temporary and permanent residents, among which you are almost certain to find a talking tui.

Mount Parihaka

1.5km northeast of the town centre

Extensive views over the harbour and town are the reward for climbing to the sheet-metal war memorial atop **Mount Parihaka**, which can be approached by car along Memorial Drive and then by clambering up the steps or by negotiating the steep Ross Track (40min ascent). Pick up the track from the end of Dundas Road, head through Mair Park past its selection of native and imported trees, the views improving as you climb, and ascend to the memorial, an ugly metallic obelisk to World War I and World War II – more rewarding are the *pa* remnants and interpretive boards.

Whangarei Falls

5km northeast of the town centre

A broad curtain of water cascades over a 26m-high basalt ridge into a popular swimming hole at **Whangarei Falls**. The nicest way to get here is to walk along a bushland trail, which winds up at a bridge overlooking the falls after following the Hatea River (90min one way) from the Parihaka Scenic Reserve on the opposite shore from the Town Basin; the i-SITE has a route map.

A.H. Reed Memorial Kauri Park

Northeast of the town centre, 1.5km down Whareora Rd

The **A.H. Reed Memorial Kauri Park** holds shady paths that weave through native bush, passing 500-year-old kauri trees; look out for the ten-minute Alexander Walk, which links with a short, sinuous **canopy boardwalk** high across a creek before reaching some fine kauri. From the lower car park, it's possible to take the Elizabeth track and link up with the trail along the Hatea River to Whangarei Falls (30min one way).

Abbey Caves

6km east of the town centre on Abbey Caves Rd, accessed via Whareora Rd

The fluted and weather-worn limestone formations of **Abbey Caves** have stalactites and stalagmites in abundance, as well as glowworms. Armed with a torch plus a moderate level of fitness you can explore them at leisure. A little scrambling is required to get into the first, Organ Cave, where you can walk a couple of hundred metres along an underground stream, although it's best avoided after heavy rain. Middle Cave and Ivy Cave are badly signposted but, once found, are worth exploring.

ARRIVAL AND DEPARTURE   WHANGAREI

By bus InterCity/Northliner and NakedBus pull up on Bank St. Destinations Auckland (4 daily; 3hr); Paihia (4 daily; 1hr 15min); Warkworth (4 daily; 2hr).

By plane Onerahi Airport, which is served by Air New Zealand and Great Barrier Airlines, is 5km east of town. Get into town on the City Link bus or with Kiwi Cabs (☎ 09 438 4444; around $25).

Destinations Auckland (7–9 daily; 35min); Great Barrier Island (1–2 weekly; 30min); Wellington (1 Mon–Fri; 1hr 40min).

GETTING AROUND

By bus Bank St is the hub of the skeletal local town bus service (City Link; ⓦ citylinkwhangarei.co.nz) that runs frequently on weekdays, slightly less so on Saturday, and not at all on Sunday.

2

WHANGAREI TOURS AND ACTIVITIES

In and around Whangarei there are a number of tours taking in the various parks, riverside walks and areas of interest, including Whangarei Heads and the Abbey Caves. Most sights can be managed as well and more cheaply independently, but a tour will introduce you to experiences and places that you would be unlikely to find for yourself.

Ballistic Blondes ☎ 0800 695 867, ⊛ skydive ballisticblondes.co.nz. Great panoramic views of Whangarei Heads, via a tandem skydive (from $275) with this Paihia-based outfit – the only skydiving business to currently offer beach landing at Paihia. They'll pick you up from accommodation around Whangarei.

Pupurangi Hire and Tour Jetty One, opposite side of the sail bridge from Town Basin ☎ 09 438 8117, ⊛ hirentour.co.nz. Runs more formal and better-

informed tours than most but minimum numbers apply, so call to make a booking. All the trips are steeped in Maori history, nature and stories, including a basic walking *pa* tour (1–4hr; $35–65) and a flora and fauna tour (1hr; $35). They also offer river trips in a *waka ama* (an outrigger canoe) with the same level of cultural input (1hr; $35; maximum five people). You can also rent paddlebikes and kayaks (double kayaks $22/hr; paddlebikes $12/30min).

INFORMATION

Tourist information There are two i-SITE offices in Whangarei: 92 Otaika Rd, 2km south of town (Nov–Easter daily 9am–5pm; Easter–Oct Mon–Fri 9am–5pm, Sat &

Sun 9am–4.30pm; ☎ 09 438 1079, ⊛ whangareinz.com); and a satellite branch in The Hub, within the Town Basin complex (same hours; ☎ 09 430 1188).

ACCOMMODATION

Bunkdown Lodge 23 Otaika Rd ☎ 09 438 8886, ⊛ bunkdownlodge.co.nz. Ageing, low-key, small hostel with dorms and rooms in and around a pretty 1903 villa. There are two kitchens, a bath, piano, heaps of DVDs, and the owners go out of their way to help with local information. Linen rental $3. Dorms $25, rooms (linen included) $55

★ **Little Earth Lodge** 85 Abbey Caves Rd ☎ 09 430 6562, ⊛ littleearthlodge.co.nz. Tucked into a pastoral valley 7km northeast of Whangarei beside Abbey Caves, this hostel has three-bed shares and a range of singles, doubles and twins, some with garden views. There's also wi-fi, gear to hire to explore the caves, and free-range eggs – but be quick, as the latter get snapped up fast. Dorms (no bunks) $30, rooms $72

Lodge Bordeaux 361 Western Hills Drive ☎ 09 438 0404, ⊛ lodgebordeaux.co.nz. Elegant modern motel with a summer-only heated outdoor pool. All rooms come with a/c, heated tile floors, spa bath and DVD players, and some have dishwashers. Studios $195, suites $230

Whangarei Falls Holiday Park & Backpackers Ngunguru Rd at Tikipunga, 5km from town near Whangarei Falls ☎ 0800 227 222, ⊛ whangareifalls .co.nz. On the edge of the countryside and within walking distance of the falls, this basic site has a small pool, hot tub and a comfy lounge with wi-fi. The dated units provide

good value for money. Camping $20, dorms $27, cabins $60

Whangarei Top 10 Holiday Park 24 Mair St ☎ 0800 455 488, ⊛ whangareitop10.co.nz. Small, tranquil and friendly site in a pretty setting 2km north of town with a range of accommodation. Camping $26, cabins (without linen) $82

Whangarei Views 5 Kensington Heights Rise ☎ 09 437 6238, ⊛ whangareiviews.co.nz. Great views over the town from modern accommodation kept tidy by a well-travelled Swiss–British couple who share their passion for the area and offer guided tours. Choose from a comfortable en-suite room with deep bath or a self-contained two-bedroom apartment with a deck and BBQ (minimum two-night stay). Breakfast can be served in your room. Apartment $159, room $120

★ **YHA Whangarei** 52 Punga Grove Ave ☎ 09 438 8954, ⊛ yha.co.nz. Intimate, sociable hostel, a steep 15min walk from the centre of Whangarei with expansive views over town from the BBQ and deck area and glowworms illuminating the bush just a short walk away (torches available). Accommodation is in rooms or four- and six-bed dorms, all in a glass-fronted lodge below the house. Reception is manned by friendly, helpful and knowledgeable staff, but is closed 1–5pm. Free wi-fi. Dorms $27, rooms $58

EATING AND DRINKING

Cafés, **bars** and **restaurants** are spread through the town and the Pak 'n Save supermarket is on the corner of Robert and Carruth sts. Also in town is a vibrant **farmers' market** (6–10.30am) every Saturday, in Water St, opposite the Shell station.

★**À Deco** 70 Kamo Rd ☎09 459 4957, ⓦfacebook .com/aDeco.restaurant. Probably Northland's finest restaurant, set in an elegant Art Deco home 2km north of the centre. Exquisite evening meals full of complex flavours and textures include the like of grilled hapuku with seared king prawn tails and crisp shallots (mains $37–40; full degustation with wine $145). Fri from noon, Tues–Sat from 6pm.

The Butter Factory 8 Butter Factory Lane ☎09 430 0044, ⓦthebutterfactory.co.nz. Whangarei's liveliest bar/restaurant caters to a slightly older crowd and serves the likes of tapas and stone-baked pizza ($14–17). There are often DJs and live acts, as well as more relaxed jazz evenings. Drinks run the gamut from Kiwi beers and wines to cocktails with names like Purple Death. Daily 10am–1pm.

Caffeine 4 Water St ☎09 438 6925, ⓦcaffeinecafe .co.nz. Relaxed café with wi-fi, serving tasty omelettes ($16.80) and eggs Benedict ($16.50) for breakfast, and lunch mains such as seared scallop salad ($16.50) in hearty portions, plus good strong coffee. Daily 7am–3pm.

Fresh 12 James St ☎09 438 2921. Airy, licensed, daytime café with a great range of panini, pasta, frittata and salads – roasted vegetable and quinoa, for example – with lunch specials from $15–20. Mon–Fri 8am–4pm, Sat 8am–2pm.

Kiwi Kai 68a Cameron St ☎09 430 2931. Cheap takeaway for all things Kiwi. Expect big portions of hangi-roast meat, Maori bread, burgers, fritters and seafood, all of it rib-sticking stuff (under $15). Mon–Fri 9am–6pm, Sat 8am–3pm.

McMorrissey's 7 Vine St ☎09 430 8081, ⓦmcmorrisseys.co.nz. Irish bar that's primarily for drinking but also serves simple and hearty meals such as fish and chips, bangers and mash or stew (all around $20) to soak up the beer. Live music at weekends. Daily 11am–11pm or later.

Nectar 88 Bank St ☎09 438 8084, ⓦnectarcafe.co.nz. Contemporary café/restaurant with big windows overlooking the town's rooftops, serving up classy breakfasts ($13–20) and healthy lunch such as Thai salad ($16.50) and corn fritters ($15.50). Gluten free and vegan available. Mon–Fri 7am–3.30pm, Sat 8am–2.30pm.

★**Serenity Café** 6, 45 Quay St, Town Basin ☎09 430 0841. Pick of the Town Basin cafés, this local favourite serves excellent and generous breakfasts ($9–23), including a monster steak breakfast that would stop an All Black forward, and lunch dishes such as burgers ($9) and BLTs ($12). Mon–Sat 7am–3pm, Sun 8am–3pm.

★**Suk Jai** 93 Kamo Rd ☎09 437 7287. Authentic Thai restaurant where attention to detail and good service complement tasty Thai favourites such as fish cakes ($7), gang massaman ($15.50) and pad thai ($14.50). Mon–Sat 11.30am–2.30pm & 5–10pm.

SHOPPING

Tuatara 29 Bank St ☎09 430 0121, ⓦtuatara designstore.co.nz. Small design store and gallery near the centre of town focusing on works by emerging Maori artists. The inventive shop stocks Maori-designed goods from contemporary clothing to fine jewellery and greenstone carving. Tues–Fri 10am–4pm, Sat 8am–2pm, and by appointment.

Around Whangarei

It's worth hanging around Whangarei to explore the surrounding area, particularly to the east and north of the town where craggy, weathered remains of ancient volcanoes abut the sea. Southeast of the town, **Whangarei Heads** is the district's volcanic heartland, where dramatic walks follow the coast to calm harbour beaches and windswept coastal strands; a kayak trip is a great way to get the best views of a landscape built from often-violent activity. To the northeast, **Tutukaka** acts as the base for dive trips to the undersea wonderland around the **Poor Knights Islands**. Many **regional w**alks are described in DOC's *Whangarei District Walks* leaflet, available from the i-SITE in Whangarei.

Whangarei Heads

Whangarei Heads, 35km southeast of Whangarei, is a series of small, residential beach communities scattered around jagged volcanic outcrops that terminate at Bream Head, the northern limit of Bream Bay. About the best way to see the area is from the sea, more specifically from the quiet, low viewpoint of a kayak, and one of the most accessible trips is a paddle over to, or around, Limestone Island.

2

Limestone Island

Just off the coast of Onerahi, a waterside suburb, Limestone Island (Matakohe) is a microcosm of New Zealand history. Now managed by DOC, it was originally home to part of the Ngaitahuhu *iwi*, and various tribes vied for control before European settlers established a flax pressing plant. Thereafter, settlers fleeing Hone Heke (see p.172) used the island as a refuge, before it became a farm and then a lime works until 1918. In 1989 it was gifted to the Whangarei District for ecological restoration. These days the process is well under way and fifty kiwi chicks have been raised on the island before being released on the mainland; there are interpretive boards at various sites across the island. Visiting the island (see below) – you can land on or circumnavigate it – is best done on an organized trip or with a DOC ranger.

Mount Manaia and around

For safe swimming stop at **McLeod Bay**, or continue until the road leaves the harbour and climbs to a saddle at the start of an excellent, signposted **walk** (3km return; 2hr–2hr 30min; 200m ascent) up the 403m **Mount Manaia**, crowned with five eroded pinnacles shrouded in Maori legend – the rocks are said to be Chief Manaia, his children and the last, facing away, his unfaithful wife. The pinnacles remain *tapu*, but you can climb to their base through native bush, passing fine viewpoints.

Beyond Mount Manaia, the road runs for 5km to **Urquharts Bay**, where a short walk (20min each way) leads to the white-sand **Smugglers Cove**.

Pataua South and Pataua North

Pataua South is 30km east of Whangarei

There's a gorgeous surf beach at the holiday community of **Pataua South**, backed by the simple *Treasure Island Motor Camp* (see below). A footbridge over the estuary leads to another sweeping surf beach at Pataua North. *Tidesong* B&B (see below) is 6km to the southeast and serves tea, coffee and cakes to passers-by.

ARRIVAL AND DEPARTURE   **WHANGAREI HEADS**

By bus City Link buses run (Mon–Sat; every hour) as far as Onerahi, a beachside community on the way to the Heads.

If you want to get further on to the Heads you'll need a car.

GETTING AROUND

By boat Pacific Coast Kayaks (☏09 436 1947, ⓦ nzseakayaking.co.nz) run trips to Limestone Island ($90/ half-day; $130/full day), leaving from the Onerahi Yacht Club.

ACCOMMODATION

★**Tidesong** Beasley Rd, Onerahi ☏09 436 1959, ⓦ tidesong.co.nz; map p.151. Very welcoming B&B set in a peaceful spot on the mangrove-filled Taiharuru Estuary, a twitcher's paradise with 25 species on view in the extensive bush and gardens surrounding the property. On offer are a great-value self-contained apartment or smaller room, free kayaks, a putting course round the gardens and the chance to take a guided ride in the estuary on a small sailing boat. Home-cooked meals are available (lunch $20; dinner $30–35) and there's an outdoor pizza oven, which is also used for baking. Look out for a bit of family history in the hall – a picture of former prime minister Thomas McKenzie. Apartment **$145**, room **$145**

Treasure Island Motor Camp ☏09 436 2390, ⓦ treasureislandnz.co.nz. Treasured by in-the-know Kiwis as a secluded and picturesque spot with access to some even prettier areas and good fishing. There's a kitchen, TV room and BBQ area, plus an on-site general takeaway and bakery (Dec–Feb) serving coffee and croissants. Camping **$18**

Tutukaka and the Poor Knights Islands

Boats set out from tiny **TUTUKAKA** – set on a beautiful, deeply incised harbour 30km northeast of Whangarei – for one of the world's premier dive locations, the **Poor Knights Islands Marine Reserve**, 25km offshore.

Poor Knights Islands Marine Reserve

The warm East Auckland current and the lack of run-off from the land combine to create visibility approaching 30m most of the year, though in spring (roughly Oct–Dec) plankton can reduce it to 10–15m. The clear waters are home to New Zealand's most diverse and plentiful range of sea life, including a few subtropical species found nowhere else, as well as a striking underwater landscape of near-vertical **rock faces** and arches that drop almost 100m. One dive at the Poor Knights, the Blue Mao Mao Cave, was rated by Jacques Cousteau as one of the top ten dive sites in the world. The Poor Knights lie along the migratory routes of a number of **whale** species, so blue, humpback, Bryde's, sei and minke whales, as well as dolphins, are not uncommon sights on the way to the islands. The waters north and south of Tutukaka are home to two navy **wrecks**. The survey ship HMNZS *Tui* was sunk in 1999 to form an artificial reef, and it was so popular with divers and marine life that the obsolete frigate *Waikato* followed two years later.

2

ARRIVAL AND DEPARTURE   TUTUKAKA

By shuttle bus The only public transport from Whangarei to Tutukaka is with Tutukaka Shuttle ($25 one way, $40 return, to coincide with dive times; $55 one way at other times; ☎ 021 901 408, ⓦ coastalcommuter.co.nz).

ACCOMMODATION AND EATING

★**Sands Motel** Tutukaka Block Rd, Whangaumu Bay ☎ 09 434 3747, ⓦ sandsmotel.co.nz. There's a retro feel to this establishment, with comfortable, well-equipped and spacious two-bedroom units beautifully set beside a nice beach 4km off the highway. It's quiet (but within the sound of the crashing waves) and well run with friendly hosts. Units **$180**

Schnappa Rock Café Marina Rd ☎ 09 434 3774, ⓦ schnapparock.co.nz. The most notable of the restaurants around the harbour, this groovy bar-restaurant turns out a tempting range of meat and vegetarian dishes such as lamb back strap ($32.50) and potato gnocchi ($27), as well as bar snacks. It's buzzing with divers and serves good coffee. Book ahead for dinner in summer. Daily 8am–late.

★**Tutukaka Holiday Park** Matapouri Rd ☎ 09 434 3938, ⓦ tutukaka-holidaypark.co.nz. An ever-expanding and improving site a 2min walk from the harbour that is very busy in Jan and Feb. It's also simply awash with pukeko (see p.813), who are not averse to panhandling. The self-contained cabins are spacious and the standard cabins adequate, while the en suites are great value. The camp kitchen and laundry are clean and well equipped. Camping **$20**, dorms **$27**, cabins **$75**

ACTIVITIES AT THE POOR KNIGHTS

The Poor Knights is a big draw for scuba divers (novices and experts), snorkellers and, outside the Marine Reserve, fishermen, primarily because of great visibility, the broad range of wildlife and the spectacular nature of the underwater environment. You'll get the most out of the area by scuba diving, as you'll be able to inspect the wildlife and scenery more closely.

Dive Tutukaka Marina Rd, Tutukaka ☎ 0800 288 882, ⓦ diving.co.nz. The largest, best and most flexible operator leaves from Tutukaka (with pick-ups from Whangarei at no extra charge) several times a day from Nov–April, and usually offers at least one trip a day for the rest of the year. It has several boats, so you are typically with similarly skilled divers. Two-dive trips ($169; including gear $269) also carry snorkellers and sightseers ($169) and everyone can use the on-board kayaks. Those with significant dive experience and the right qualifications can explore the two wrecks, nearby and deeper, on two-dive trips ($199 for tanks and weights), while first-timers can try a Discover Scuba dive ($299 with full gear and one-to-one instruction). A five-day PADI open-water dive qualification costs $799.

Whangarei Deep Sea Anglers Club Marina Rd, Tutukaka ☎ 09 434 3818, ⓦ sportfishing.co.nz. Fishing for marlin, shark and tuna outside the Poor Knights Reserve (Dec–April) can be done by taking a quarter-share of a charter game-fishing boat for the day, which will cost around $250–350. The club (daily 8am–6pm during fishing season) can provide a list of operators who run fishing charters.

Matapouri and Whale Bay

MATAPOURI, 6km north of Tutukaka, is a lovely holiday settlement which backs onto a curving white-sand bay. At low tide, you can swim in safe, clear-blue rock pools (locally known as the Mermaid Pools) just above the sea. Bushy headlands separate Matapouri's beach from the pristine **Whale Bay**, signposted off Matapouri Road 1km further north and reached by a twenty-minute bushwalk. There are virtually no facilities along this stretch, apart from a shop and takeaway at Matapouri.

2

North of Whangarei to the Bay of Islands

The roads that access the coast around Tutukaka and Matapouri rejoin SH1 at **Hikurangi** 16km north of Whangarei. About 6km further north you have a choice of routes: both go to the Bay of Islands but approach from different directions: carry straight on and you go direct to Paihia with opportunities for side trips to the Maori redoubt of Ruapekapeka Pa, and the **Hundertwasser toilets** at Kawakawa; turn right along Old Russell Road and you twist towards the coast on the tar-sealed but narrow and winding back-road to Russell. The latter route is the most scenic way to approach the Bay of Islands, along a 70km narrow, winding road that takes about two hours. You can spin the drive out by admiring the wonderful coastline around the **Whangaruru Harbour**, stopping for swims in numerous gorgeous bays, and perhaps a short walk in the mixed kauri forest of the **Ngaiotonga Scenic Reserve**.

Ruapekapeka Pa

17km north of Hikurangi on SH1 then 5km east on a signposted road · Free

Ruapekapeka Pa is the site of the final battle in the War of the North in 1846, a grassy hilltop with a few earthworks, a commemorative wooden pole, one of the original cannons and stunning views of the surrounding countryside. Hone Heke's repeated flagpole felling in Russell (see p.168) precipitated nine months of fighting during which Maori learnt to adapt their *pa* defences to cope with British firepower. The apotheosis of this development is Ruapekapeka, the "Bat's Nest". Its hilltop setting, double row of totara palisades and labyrinth of trenches and interconnecting tunnels helped Hone Heke and his warriors defend the site, despite being heavily outgunned and outnumbered three to one. Signs explain the full story, and trench lines and bunkers are clearly visible.

Kawakawa

The small town of **KAWAKAWA**, 15km north of Ruapekapeka, would be otherwise unremarkable if it wasn't known for being the home of the celebrated **Hundertwasser toilets** on the town's main drag, Gillies Street. These works of art were created in 1997 by the reclusive Austrian painter, architect, ecologist and philosopher, **Friedrich Hundertwasser**, who made Kawakawa his home from 1975 until his death in 2000, aged 71. The ceramic columns supporting the entrance hint at the interior's complex use of broken tiles, coloured bottles and found objects such as the old hinges on the wrought-iron doors. A steady trickle of visitors takes a peek in both the Gents and the Ladies after suitable warning. The local council is planning a Hundertwasser Visitor Centre in the Bay of Islands but it's dependent on donations mounting up. To learn more meanwhile, pop along to the **Kawakawa Museum**, 3 Wynyard St (Mon–Sat 11am–3pm; $3; ☎09 404 0406), where two DVDs on Hundertwasser run on request.

FROM TOP OMAPERE PIER (P.191); SCUBA DIVING, POOR KNIGHTS ISLANDS (P.157) >

Vintage Railway

Fri, Sat & Sun 10.45am, noon, 1.15pm & 2.30pm, daily during school holidays • $12 • ☎ 09 404 0684, Ⓦ bayofislandsvintagerailway.org.nz

Kawakawa is New Zealand's only town with a rail track running down its main street. Ride the rails on the Bay of Islands **Vintage Railway**, whose steam- and diesel-hauled 1930s carriages trundle 5km north to Taumarere and back. The line will eventually extend further north to Opua (30km return), but the work is progressing at an agricultural Northland pace.

Oakura

Leaving SH1, you travel through 14km of farmland along Old Russell Road before reaching Helena Bay, where's there's a gallery-café (see opposite), which is a good spot to stop for a bite (there's little else between here and Russell) before continuing north to **OAKURA**. Oakura itself is not much more than an island-studded bay backed by a gently curving beach and a cluster of holiday homes. Its primary appeal is that not a great deal ever happens, though there are plenty of places to swim and walk, and one decent place to stay (see opposite).

Whangaruru North Head Scenic Reserve

10km from Ngaiotonga

At Ngaiotonga, a sealed side-road runs through hilly farmland to the broad sweep of **Bland Bay** with great beaches on both sides of an isthmus. Continue beyond Bland Bay to reach **Whangaruru North Head Scenic Reserve**, with yet more lovely beaches, fine walks around the end of the peninsula and a DOC campsite (see opposite).

Rawhiti

Back on the coast road it is 7km north to a junction where you turn left for Russell (25km further) and continue straight on for the scattered and predominantly Maori village of **Rawhiti**, the start of the Cape Brett Track (see box below). Just 1km along the Rawhiti road there's shorter, easier walking in the form of the **Whangamumu Track** (4km each way; 1hr; 150m ascent), a forest path that crosses the base of the Cape Brett Peninsula to a lovely beach. Here you can see the remains of a whaling station, which closed in 1940.

Following the Manawaroa Road back to the Russell Road and on toward Russell for 11km you'll come across a signposted side road to some fine stands of kauri. These can be visited on the **Twin Bole Track** (around 200m; 5min) and the **Kauri Grove Walk** (1km; 20min).

THE CAPE BRETT TRACK

Northland's best overnight tramp is the challenging but rewarding **Cape Brett Track** (20km each way; 6–8hr) which follows the hilly ridge along the centre of the peninsula with sea occasionally visible on both sides: a route outlined in DOC's *Cape Brett* leaflet. The former lighthouse keeper's house at the tip of the peninsula is now a DOC **hut** (23 bunk beds; $15; backcountry hut pass not valid) and the only place to **stay** on the track itself, in a fabulous location surrounded by sea and views out to the Hole in the Rock. There are gas cooking stoves but no utensils, and camping is not allowed.

The track starts in Rawhiti (see above) and crosses private land, so all walkers must pay a **track fee** ($30; day-walkers $10). The Russell Booking & Information Centre is the place to pay this, book the DOC hut and ask about secure parking in Rawhiti. You might also enquire about a **water taxi** from Russell to Rawhiti (around $170 for up to six people), Deep Water Cove, three-quarters of the way along the track ($190), or Cape Brett ($230; conditions permitting). Secure parking is available at *Hartwells* in Kaimarama Bay, at the end of Rawhiti Road, for a small fee.

Coast Road Farm Russell Rd, 12km north of Oakura ☎ 09 433 6894, ⓦ thefarm.co.nz. Along the Russell Road you can get involved with dairy farm life, ride horses ($50/2hr trek), go kayaking ($15/person/day), fishing ($39) and much more, while staying in the dorm room, one of three doubles (one en suite), one of four cabins, or camping. Meals (breakfast $5; lunch $8; dinner $15) are by arrangement. Camping $̶1̶3̶, dorms $̶2̶0̶, doubles $̶6̶0̶

Puriri Bay campsite Whangaruru North Rd, Whangaruru North Head Scenic Reserve ⓔ whangareiao@doc.govt.nz. DOC site overlooking Puriri Bay and Whangaruru Harbour, with 93 sites, running water, toilets and cold showers. The camp office is open 7.30am–8pm, and bookings are essential in the summer. $̶1̶0̶

EATING AND DRINKING

The Gallery & Café Helena Bay Hill Old Russell Rd, Helena Bay ☎ 09 433 9616, ⓦ galleryhelenabay.co.nz. An imaginative gallery coupled with a great German-run daytime café with views across bush-clad hills down to Helena Bay. Stop for a coffee or a snack: schnitzel and strudel alongside more traditional Kiwi fare. Café daily 10am–5pm; gallery October–Easter daily 10am–5pm, Easter–Sept Thurs–Sun 10am–5pm.

Railway Station Café Gillies St, Kawakawa ☎ 09 404 1110. You can watch the trains from the comfort of the café or the outdoor seating on the platform of the station itself. Simple food is served, including toasties for just $4. The boat marooned here was once Hundertwasser's studio. Tues–Sun 9am–4pm.

The Bay of Islands

THE BAY OF ISLANDS, 240km north of Auckland, lures visitors to its beautiful coastal scenery, scattered islands and clear blue waters. There are other equally stunning spots along the Northland coast, such as the Whangaroa and Hokianga harbours, but what sets the bay apart is the ease with which you can get out among the islands, and its pivotal history. This was the cradle of European settlement in New Zealand, a fact abundantly testified to by the bay's churches, mission stations and orchards. It's also a focal point for Maori because of the **Treaty of Waitangi** (see box, p.165), still New Zealand's most important legal document.

Perhaps surprisingly, much of your time in the Bay of Islands will be spent on the mainland, as there are no settlements on the islands. Most visitors base themselves in beachside **Paihia**, which is set up to deal with the hordes who come here for the various cruises and excursions, as well as being the closest town to the Treaty House at **Waitangi**. The compact town of **Russell**, a couple of kilometres across the bay (though still on the mainland) by passenger ferry, is prettier and almost equally convenient for cruises. To the northwest, away from the bay itself, **Kerikeri** is intimately entwined with the area's early missionary history, while **Waimate North**, inland to the west, was another important mission site and Mission House.

In 1927 American Western writer **Zane Grey** came here to fish for striped and black marlin, making the area famous with his book *The Angler's El Dorado*. Every summer since, the bay has seen game-fishing tournaments and glistening catches strung up on the jetties.

Brief history

A warm climate, abundant seafood and deep, sheltered harbours contributed to dense pre-European **Maori settlement** in the Bay of Islands, with many a headland supporting a *pa*. The bay also appealed to **Captain Cook**, who anchored here in 1769. Cook landed on Motuarohia Island at what became known as Cook's Cove, where he forged generally good relations with the inhabitants. Three years later the French sailor **Marion du Fresne**, en route from Mauritius to Tahiti, became the first European to have sustained contact with Maori, though he fared less well when a misunderstanding, probably over *tapu*, led to his death, along with 26 of his crew. The French retaliated, destroying a *pa* and killing hundreds of Maori.

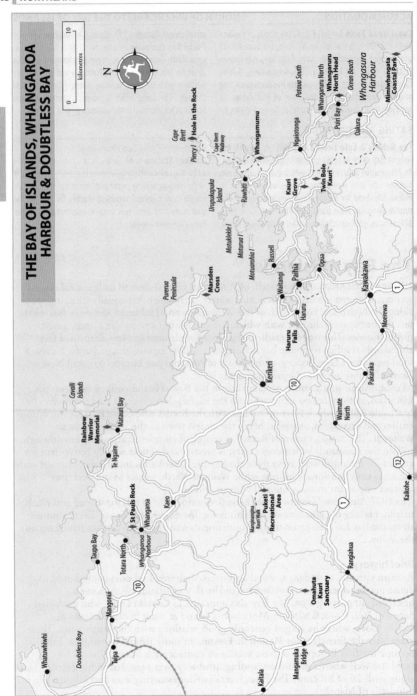

THE BAY OF ISLANDS, WHANGAROA HARBOUR & DOUBTLESS BAY

2

N

0   10
kilometres

Whatuwhiwhi

Doubtless Bay

Taipa

Kaitaia

Mangamuka Bridge

Mangonui

Taupo Bay

Totara North

Whangaroa

Whangaroa Harbour

Kaeo

Matauri Bay

Te Ngaire

St Pauls Rock

Rainbow Warrior Memorial

Cavalli Islands

Rangiahua

Omahuta Kauri Sanctuary

Mangapunga Kauri Walk

Puketi Recreational Area

Kaikohe

Kerikeri

Waimate North

Pakaraka

Moerewa

Kawakawa

Purerua Peninsula

Marsden Cross

Waitangi

Paihia

Haruru

Haruru Falls

Opua

Russell

Motuarohia I

Motuarua I

Motukiekie I

Urupukapuka Island

Rawhiti

Kauri Grove

Twin Bole Kauri

Cape Brett Walkway

Cape Brett

Piercy I   Hole in the Rock

Whangamumu

Whangamumu

Ngaiotonga

Oakura

Puiri Bay

Whangaruru North

Whangaruru North Head

Ocean Beach

Patawa South

Whangasura Harbour

Mimiwhangata Coastal Park

Missionaries and treaties

Despite amicable relations between the local Ngapuhi Maori and Pakeha whalers in the early years of the nineteenth century, the situation gradually deteriorated. With increased contact, firearms, grog and Old World diseases spread and the fabric of Maori life began to break down, a process accelerated by the arrival in 1814 of Samuel Marsden, the first of many **missionaries** intent on turning Maori into Christians. In 1833, James Busby was sent to secure British interests and prevent the brutal treatment meted out to the Maori by whaling captains, but lacking armed backup or judicial authority, he had little effect. The signing of the **Treaty of Waitangi** in 1840 brought effective policing yet heralded a decline in the importance of the Bay of Islands, as the capital moved from its original site of Kororareka (now Opua, although many claim it was Russell), first to Auckland and later to Wellington.

2

Paihia and Waitangi

PAIHIA is the place where things kick off, mostly on the 2km-long string of waterside motels, restaurants and holiday homes lined with trip operators, backpacker hostels, party-oriented bars and hotels. Fortunately, Paihia's low-rise development is sympathetic to its three beautiful, flat bays looking towards Russell and the Bay of Islands, encircled by forested hills. A plaque outside the current **St Paul's Anglican Church** on Marsden Road marks the spot where, in 1831, the northern chiefs petitioned the British Crown for a representative to establish law and order. In 1833 King William IV finally addressed their concerns by sending the first British resident, James Busby. Busby built a house on a promontory 2km north across the Waitangi River in **WAITANGI** – the scene some seven years later of the signing of the **Treaty of Waitangi**, which ceded the nation's sovereignty to Britain in return for protection.

Paihia is primarily a base for exploring the bay, and there are no sights in town itself. Fans of mangroves and estuarine scenery can tackle the gentle **Paihia–Opua Coastal Walkway** (6km; 90min–2hr one way), which wanders along the wave-cut platforms and the small bays in between.

Waitangi Treaty Grounds
Tau Henare Drive

Crossing the bridge over the Waitangi River you enter the Waitangi Treaty Grounds, where in 1840 Queen Victoria's representative William Hobson and nearly fifty Maori chiefs signed the Treaty of Waitangi (see box, p.165).

Waitangi Visitor Centre and Treaty House
Tau Henare Drive • **Visitor Centre and Treaty House** Daily: Jan & Feb 9am–7pm; March–Dec 9am–5pm • $25 (valid for two consecutive days); $15 for NZ citizens; cultural performance $10; guided tour $10; combo ticket $40, $25 for NZ residents • **Culture North Night Show** 4–6 nights/week • $60 • Book ahead on ☎ 09 402 5990, ⓦ culturenorth.co.nz • ☎ 09 402 7437, ⓦ waitangi.net.nz

The **Waitangi Visitor Centre and Treaty House** is the single most symbolic place in New Zealand for Maori and Pakeha alike, and a focal point for the modern nation's struggle for identity. You can easily spend half a day here, taking in an audiovisual presentation that sets the historical framework, bolstered by a small exhibition of Maori artefacts, and perhaps a short daytime cultural performance or a guided tour, though most people give it around two hours then perhaps return for the **Culture North Night Show**, an excellent contemporary approach to presenting Maori culture conducted inside the traditional meeting house. Over an hour and a quarter you're introduced to an extended family as the stories of Maori life from the arrival of Kupe to the present day are enacted with verve, mixing drama, song and dance with storytelling. Free pick-ups are available from Paihia.

2

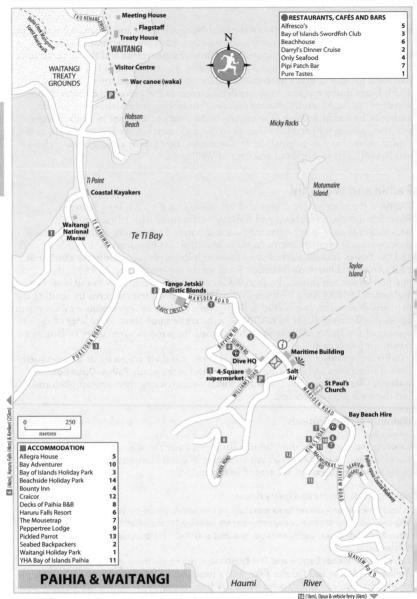

RESTAURANTS, CAFÉS AND BARS
Alfresco's	5
Bay of Islands Swordfish Club	3
Beachhouse	6
Darryl's Dinner Cruise	2
Only Seafood	4
Pipi Patch Bar	7
Pure Tastes	1

■ ACCOMMODATION
Allegra House	5
Bay Adventurer	10
Bay of Islands Holiday Park	3
Beachside Holiday Park	14
Bounty Inn	4
Craicor	12
Decks of Paihia B&B	8
Haruru Falls Resort	6
The Mousetrap	7
Peppertree Lodge	9
Pickled Parrot	13
Seabed Backpackers	2
Waitangi Holiday Park	1
YHA Bay of Islands Paihia	11

PAIHIA & WAITANGI

The Treaty House

The **Treaty House** was built in Georgian colonial style in 1833–34. Its front windows look towards Russell over sweeping lawns, where marquees were erected on three significant occasions: in 1834, when Maori chiefs chose the Confederation of Tribes flag, which now flies on one yardarm of the central flagpole; the meeting a year later at which northern Maori leaders signed the

Declaration of Independence of New Zealand; and, in 1840, the signing of the Treaty of Waitangi itself.

The northern side of the lawn is flanked by the *whare runanga*, or **Maori meeting house**, built between 1934 and 1940 as a cooperative effort between all Maori. The richly carved interior panels represent all *iwi* (rather than the usual single tribe).

Housed in a specially built shelter in the Treaty House grounds is the world's largest **war canoe** (*waka*), the 35m-long *Ngatoki Matawhaorua*, named after the vessel navigated by Kupe when he discovered Aotearoa, and built from two huge kauri. It has traditionally been launched each year on Waitangi Day, propelled by eighty warriors.

2

THE TREATY OF WAITANGI

The Treaty of Waitangi is the **founding document** of modern New Zealand, a touchstone for both Pakeha and Maori, and its implications permeate New Zealand society. Signed in 1840 between what were ostensibly two sovereign states – the United Kingdom and the United Tribes of New Zealand, plus other Maori leaders – the treaty remains central to New Zealand's **race relations**. The Maori rights guaranteed by it have seldom been upheld, however, and the constant struggle for recognition continues.

THE TREATY AT WAITANGI

Motivated by a desire to staunch French expansion in the Pacific, and a moral obligation on the Crown to protect Maori from rapacious land-grabbing by settlers, the British instructed naval captain William Hobson to negotiate the transfer of sovereignty with "the free and intelligent consent of the natives", and to deal fairly with the Maori. Hobson, with the help of James Busby and others, drew up both the English Treaty and a Maori "translation". On the face of it, the treaty is a straightforward document, but the complications of having two versions (see p.791) and the implications of striking a deal between two peoples with widely differing views on land and resource ownership have reverberated down the years.

The treaty was unveiled on February 5, 1840, to a gathering of some 400 representatives of the five northern tribes in front of Busby's residence in Waitangi. Presented as a contract between the chiefs and Queen Victoria – someone whose role was comprehensible in chiefly terms – the benefits were amplified and the costs downplayed. As most chiefs didn't understand English, they signed the Maori version of the treaty, which still has *mana* (authority or status) among Maori today.

THE TREATY AFTER WAITANGI

The pattern set at Waitangi was repeated up and down the country, as seven copies of the treaty were dispatched to garner signatures and extend Crown authority over parts of the North Island that had not yet been covered, and the South Island. On May 21, before signed treaty copies had been returned, Hobson claimed New Zealand for Britain: the North Island on the grounds of cession by Maori, and the South Island by right of Cook's "discovery", as it was considered to be without owners, despite a significant Maori population.

Maori fears were alerted from the start, and as the settler population grew and demand for land increased, successive governments passed laws that gradually stripped Maori of control over their affairs – actions which led to the New Zealand Wars of the 1860s (see p.792). Over the decades, small concessions were made, but nothing significant changed until 1973, when **Waitangi Day** (February 6) became an official national holiday. Around the same time, Maori groups, supported by a small band of Pakeha, began a campaign of direct action, increasingly disrupting commemorations, thereby alienating many Pakeha and splitting Maori allegiances between angry young urban Maori and the *kaumatua* (elders), who saw the actions as disrespectful to the ancestors and an affront to tradition. Many strands of Maori society were unified by the *hikoi* (march) to Waitangi to protest against the celebrations in 1985, a watershed year in which Paul Reeves was appointed New Zealand's first Maori Governor General and the **Waitangi Tribunal** for land reform was given some teeth.

Protests have continued since, as successive governments have vacillated over whether to attend the commemorations at Waitangi.

Haruru Falls

4km west of Waitangi, accessed from the main road

At **Haruru Falls**, the Waitangi River drops over a basalt lava flow, and though they're not that impressive by New Zealand standards, there's good swimming at their base. Haruru Falls are also reached from the Treaty House grounds via the very gentle **Hutia Creek Mangrove Forest Boardwalk** (2hr return) or on a guided **kayak** trip up the estuary and among the mangroves (see p.171).

ARRIVAL AND DEPARTURE — PAIHIA AND WAITANGI

By bus InterCity/Northliner and NakedBus arrive on Marsden Rd, outside the Bay of Islands' main i-SITE.
Destinations Auckland (4–6 daily; 4hr); Kaitaia (1 daily; 2hr 15min); Kerikeri (3 daily; 30min); Mangonui (1 daily; 1hr 50min); Whangarei (4–6 daily; 1hr 15min).

By plane Flights from Auckland arrive at the Bay of Islands airport (☏09 407 6133, ⓦ bayofislandsairport.co.nz), 22km northwest, near Kerikeri, and are met by the Super Shuttle bus ($60 to Paihia).
Destinations Auckland (5–6 daily; 45min).

By vehicle ferry A small vehicle ferry runs between Paihia and Russell (daily 6.50am–9.50pm; every 20min or so; car & driver $11 each way, foot/additional passengers $1; buy ticket on board; 10min), crossing the Veronica Channel at Opua, 6km south of Paihia. Taking the ferry shortens the 100km drive between Paihia and Russell to 15km.

By passenger ferry Foot passengers can use one of the three frequent passenger ferries (Oct–May 7am–10pm; June–Sept 7am–8pm; every 30min or so; $7 one way, $12 return; 15min) between Paihia and Russell.

GETTING AROUND

By car Paihia isn't big, and everywhere is within walking distance, but if you do have a car, note that parking is tight in the high season; your best bet is the pay-and-display car park opposite the 4-Square supermarket on Williams Rd.

By shuttle bus Paihia Tuk Tuk Shuttle Service (☏027 486 6071), based outside the i-SITE, will pick up and drop off two to six people pretty much anywhere in town for around $5 each, run joy rides for $7, or run up to Haruru Falls for a bit more.

By bike Rent good-quality mountain bikes from Bay Beach Hire (☏09 402 6078, ⓦ baybeachhire.co.nz; $10/hr; $35/day) at the south end of Paihia Beach.

INFORMATION

Tourist information i-SITE is at The Wharf, 101 Marsden Rd (daily 8am–5pm; ☏09 402 7345, ⓦ northlandnz.com).

The office here – one of three for the Far North region of Northland – has internet access and books tours.

ACCOMMODATION

Paihia abounds in accommodation for all budgets, though rates can be stratospheric during the couple of weeks after Christmas. B&Bs and homestays vary their prices less than motels, and hostels mostly maintain the same prices year-round. Kings Road is a veritable backpackers' village with a selection of generally good places, noisy in the height of summer.

★**Allegra House** 39 Bayview Rd ☏09 402 7932, ⓦ allegra.co.nz. A choice of luxury B&B or self-contained apartment in a big, light and modern house at the top of a hill, and all with stupendous views right out over the Bay of Islands. All are a/c, sport their own balconies and have access to a hot tub in native bush. B&B $230, apartment $285

Bay Adventurer 26–28 Kings Rd ☏09 402 5162, ⓦ bayadventurer.co.nz. Upmarket backpackers resort with apartments, an attractive pool, free bikes, kayaks and access to the nearby tennis courts (free in winter). It's particularly good for its rooms and fully self-contained studio apartments. Dorms (some female only) $22, rooms $85

Bounty Inn 42 Selwyn Rd ☏09 402 7088, ⓦ www.bountyinn.co.nz. Pleasant, central yet quiet motel, 100m from the beach and with ample off-street parking. Rooms without cooking facilities, and fully equipped motel units all come lined in timber with a sundeck or balcony. Unrestricted free wi-fi. $140

Craicor 49 Kings Rd ☏09 402 7882, ⓦ craicor-accom.co.nz. A couple of excellent-value self-catering apartments, both spacious, well kept and with limited sea views, plus an attractive double room. Continental breakfast can be supplied for $12. $180

Decks of Paihia B&B 69 School Rd ☏09 1402 6146, ⓦ decksofpaihia.co.nz. Welcoming three-room B&B in a comfortable, tastefully decorated modern house with swimming pool set into a large, sunny deck high on the hill above Paihia. $265

The Mousetrap 11 Kings Rd ☏0800 402 8182, ⓦ mousetrap.co.nz. Welcoming, nautically themed, wood-panelled hostel that sets itself apart from the other backpackers on this lively street. Rooms are scattered all over the site, there are three small kitchens, a BBQ area, free bike use and a decent sea view. Dorms $29, rooms $69

Peppertree Lodge 15 Kings Rd ☎09 402 6122, ⓦpeppertree.co.nz. Very clean, central hostel with spacious eight-bunk dorms, four-bunk en-suite dorms, great en-suite doubles and a self-contained flat with kitchenette ($110). Guests can make use of a tennis court, free good-quality bikes and kayaks, and there's an excellent DVD library. Be sure to book ahead Oct–April. Dorms $25, rooms $72

Pickled Parrot Grey's Lane, off MacMurray Rd ☎09 402 6222, ⓦpickledparrot.co.nz. One of Paihia's smaller, more relaxed hostels, tucked away in a peaceful spot with a lovely courtyard. Secluded tent sites ($16); four- and six-bed dorms as well as singles, doubles and twins, all with free continental breakfast, plus free pick-ups, bikes and tennis racquets. Dorms $26, doubles $66

★**Seabed Backpackers** 46 Davis Crescent ☎09 402 5567, ⓦseabeds.co.nz. The best-value backpackers in town: grown-up accommodation with proper facilities in a one-time motel, with extremely reasonable rates, run by a friendly professional with abundant local knowledge. Dorms $28, en-suite doubles $85

YHA Bay of Islands Paihia Corner of Kings and MacMurray rds ☎09 402 7487, ⓦyha.co.nz. Well-maintained and -run hostel with well-informed staff and a good kitchen, attracting a friendly mix of travellers and families. Most rooms and dorms are ensuite. Dorms $25, rooms $99

CAMPSITES

Bay of Islands Holiday Park 52 Puketona Rd ☎09 402 6601 ⓦboihacvp.co.nz. Small, super-friendly site with modern toilets and showers ($2 for 4min), a pleasant BBQ area next to a lilypad pond and unlimited free wi-fi. It's a 15min walk to town. Camping $20, luxury holiday flats $350

Beachside Holiday Park SH11, 3km south of Paihia ☎09 402 7678, ⓦbeachsideholiday.co.nz. Small and peaceful, beautifully situated waterside site with a range of cabins and units, good kitchen and laundry, as well as dinghies and kayaks for rent. Camping $26, cabins $85

★**Haruru Falls Resort** Puketona Rd, 4km north of Paihia ☎0800 757 525, ⓦharurufalls.co.nz. Fabulous location by the river with commanding views of Haruru Falls, offering riverside campsites and recently refurbished hotel rooms around a pool. The resort has outdoor games such as pétanque and volleyball, a BBQ, and its own restaurant bar, plus kayaks and paddle bikes for rent. Camping $22, rooms $120

Waitangi Holiday Park 21 Tahuna Rd, Waitangi ☎09 402 7866, ⓦwaitangiholidaypark.co.nz. The closest campsite to Waitangi and a 20min walk to Paihia, this simple site has pitches overlooking the Waitangi River and four spacious kitchen cabins. Camping $22, cabins $8

EATING, DRINKING AND ENTERTAINMENT

Paihia's range of places to eat is plentiful but, with a few notable exceptions, all are sort of similar; competition keeps prices reasonable and many spots specialize in seafood. The restaurants also tend to be good places to stick around for postprandial drinking in the summer and there are several raucous bars along Kings Road.

★**Alfresco's** 6 Marsden Rd ☎09 402 6797, ⓦalfrescosrestaurantpaihia.com. Relaxed café and bar that's excellent for a coffee, breakfasts (including great corn fritters), lunchtime paninis ($17) and some fine dining in the evening (mains from $27.50). Daily 7.30am–late.

★**Bay of Islands Swordfish Club** Marsden Rd ☎09 403 7857, ⓦswordfish.co.nz. Private club, overlooking the bay and welcoming visitors outside the peak summer season: just get the bar staff to sign you in. The great views are accompanied by ample, good-value food such as fish and chips or steak and chips (mains $18–25). "Swordy's" also has some of the cheapest drinks in town. Sun–Thurs from 4pm, Fri & Sat from noon.

Beachhouse 16 Kings Rd ☎09 402 6063. All-day café and juice bar better known for its *Sand Pit* bar with pool tables round the back, where live music clashes with the next-door *Pipi Patch Bar* (run by *Base Backpackers*) most nights in the summer. Daily 10am–late.

Darryl's Dinner Cruise Paihia Wharf ☎0800 334 6637, ⓦdinnercruise.co.nz. Convivial and leisurely cruise (2hr 30min; $95) leaving from the wharf around 6.30pm and heading up the Waitangi River to Haruru Falls, where you tuck into prawns and mussels followed by T-bone steak, lamb and fish. There's a cash bar on board or BYO wine. If you catch it during a good sunset it's a great way to spend the evening. Trips are subject to minimum numbers.

Only Seafood ☎09 402 6066 ⓦonlyseafood.co.nz. Fish-focused restaurant serving up the catch of the day ($29.50), oysters several ways and tasty king prawns ($31.50), all washed down with a 100% Kiwi wine list.

Pure Tastes 116 Marsden Rd ☎09 402 0003, ⓦpaihiabeach.co.nz. Fine-dining restaurant at the *Paihia Beach Resort*. Breakfasts will see you through to intricately prepared lunches (mains around $25), but the dinners are more memorable, including lamb rump ($34), caramelized pork belly ($32) and a tasting menu of six courses with wine to match for $150. Daily 8am–late.

The islands

The Bay is aptly named, with six large, and around 140 small, islands. Many are subject to the DOC-led **Project Island Song**, which aims to rid many islands of introduced predators and turn them into wildlife havens. Assorted birds have been reintroduced to many islands, notably **Urupukapuka Island**, which can be explored in a few hours using DOC's *Urupukapuka Island Archeological Walk* leaflet highlighting Maori *pa* and terrace sites.

Of the other large islands, by far the most popular is **Motuarohia** (**Roberton Island**), where DOC manages the most dramatic central section, an isthmus almost severed by a pair of perfectly circular blue lagoons. Snorkellers can explore an undersea nature trail waymarked by inscribed stainless-steel plaques.

Other sights that often feature on cruise itineraries include the **Black Rocks**, bare islets formed from columnar-jointed basalt – these rise only 10m out of the water but plummet a sheer 30m beneath. At the outer limit of the bay is the craggy peninsula of **Cape Brett**, named by Cook in 1769 after the then Lord of the Admiralty, Lord Piercy Brett. Cruises also regularly pass through the **Hole in the Rock**, a natural tunnel through Piercy Island, which is even more exciting when there's a swell running.

ACCOMMODATION THE ISLANDS

Urupukapuka Island ⓦ doc.govt.nz. This is the only island in the Bay of Islands that accommodates overnight guests, with DOC managing three basic sites: *Cable Bay*, with running water, showers and toilets, and *Sunset Bay*, with running water and toilets, are both on the south shore; *Urupukapuka Bay*, with running water, toilets and showers, is the island's easternmost campsite. Book your site well in advance. $10

Russell

The isolated location of **RUSSELL** – on a narrow peninsula with poor road but good sea access – gives this small hillside settlement an island ambience. In summer, however, the place is often full of day-trippers who pile off passenger ferries from Paihia and vehicle ferries from nearby Opua to explore the village's historic buildings and stroll along its quaint waterfront.

Brief history

Modern-day Russell is a far cry from the 1830s when **Kororareka**, as it was then known, was a swashbuckling town full of whalers and sealers with a reputation as the "Hell Hole of the Pacific". Savage and drunken behaviour served as an open invitation to **missionaries**, who gradually won over a sizeable congregation and left behind Russell's two oldest buildings, the church and a printing works that produced religious tracts.

After the Treaty of Waitangi

By 1840, Kororareka was the largest settlement in the country, but after the signing of the Treaty of Waitangi, Governor William Hobson fell out with both Maori and local settlers and moved his capital progressively further south.

Meanwhile, initial Maori enthusiasm for the Treaty of Waitangi had faded: financial benefits had failed to materialize and the Confederation of Tribes flag that flew from Flagstaff Hill between 1834 and 1840 had been replaced by the Union Jack. This came to be seen as a symbol of British betrayal, and as resentment crystallized it found a leader in **Hone Heke Pokai**, Ngapuhi chief and son-in-law of Kerikeri's Hongi Hika. Between July 1844 and March 1845, Heke and his followers cut down the flagstaff no fewer than four times, the last occasion sparking the first **New Zealand War**, which raged for nearly a year, during which Kororareka was destroyed. The settlement rose from the ashes under a new name, Russell, and grew slowly around its beachfront into the tranquil village of today.

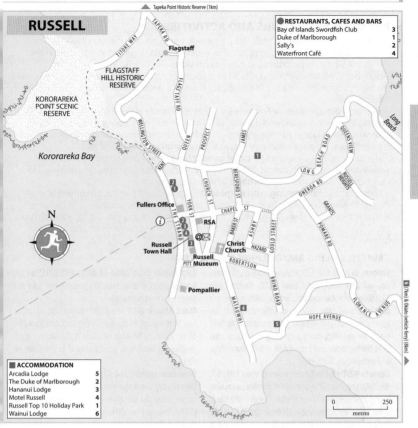

RUSSELL

FLAGSTAFF HILL HISTORIC RESERVE

KORORAREKA POINT SCENIC RESERVE

Kororareka Bay

RESTAURANTS, CAFES AND BARS

Bay of Islands Swordfish Club	3
Duke of Marlborough	1
Sally's	2
Waterfront Café	4

ACCOMMODATION

Arcadia Lodge	5
The Duke of Marlborough	2
Hananui Lodge	3
Motel Russell	4
Russell Top 10 Holiday Park	1
Wainui Lodge	6

0 — 250 metres

Pompallier

The Strand • Daily: Nov–April 10am–5pm; May–Oct 10am–4pm • $10 • ☎ 09 403 9015, ⊕ historicplaces.org.nz

Russell's most striking building is the fascinating **Pompallier**, the last survivor of Russell's Catholic mission, and once the headquarters of Catholicism in the western Pacific. Pompallier was built in 1842 as a printing works for the French Roman Catholic bishop Jean Baptiste François Pompallier. He had arrived three years earlier to find the Catholic word of God under siege from Anglican and Wesleyan tracts, translated into Maori. The missionaries built an elegant rammed-earth structure in a style typical of Pompallier's native Lyon. The press and paper were imported, and a tannery installed to make leather bookbindings. During the next eight years over a dozen titles of Catholic teachings were printed, comprising almost forty thousand volumes, which were some of the first books printed in Maori.

In a building now restored to its 1842 state, artisans again produce handmade books, all best understood on the **free tours**, which explain the production processes in each room. You can even get your hands dirty in what is New Zealand's only surviving colonial tannery.

Christ Church

Robertson Rd

New Zealand's oldest church, the cream, weatherboard **Christ Church** was built in 1836 by local settlers – unlike most churches of similar vintage, which were mission

2

BAY OF ISLANDS TOURS AND ACTIVITIES

Unless you get out onto the water you're missing the essence of the Bay of Islands. The majority of yachting, scuba diving, dolphin-watching, kayaking and fishing trips start in Paihia, but all the major **cruises** and bay **excursions** also pick up in Russell. From December to March everything should be booked a couple of days in advance. Hotels and motels can book for you; hostels can usually arrange a discount of around ten percent for backpackers.

The two main operators are Fullers Great Sights and Explore NZ/Dolphin Discoveries, both offering sightseeing, sailing and dolphin trips. There are also numerous **yachts** that usually take fewer than a dozen passengers and go out for around six hours: competition is tight and standards vary. Most operators give you a chance to **snorkel**, **kayak** and **fish**.

The Bay of Islands is excellent for **dolphin watching**; there's an eighty percent chance of seeing bottlenose and common dolphins in almost any season, as well as orca from May to October, and minke and Bryde's **whales** from August to January.

Your chances of **swimming with dolphins** are about 35–40 percent. Swimming is forbidden when there are juveniles in the pod, and only 18 people are allowed in the water with dolphins at any time. There's usually a money-back offer if you miss out (check when you book); your best chance is on a cruise with companies licensed to search for and swim with dolphins.

CRUISES, SAILING AND DOLPHIN ENCOUNTERS

Ecocruz ☏ 0800 432 627, ⊛ ecocruz.co.nz. A three-day sail (Oct–April; dorm bunk $650, double cabin $1500) on the *Manawanui*, which takes up to ten people around the bay, with the emphasis on appreciation of the natural environment. Excellent meals are included, along with use of kayaks, snorkel gear, fishing tackle and a good deal of local knowledge and enthusiasm. Book early.

Explore NZ/Dolphin Discoveries ☏ 0800 397 567, ⊛ explorenz.co.nz. The pioneers of dolphin swimming in this area operate a range of trips. Discover the Bay is a 4hr cruise including a spin through the Hole in the Rock, a stop at Otehei Bay on Urupukapuka and dolphin viewing ($115); the Swim with Dolphins trip prioritizes getting in the water with bottlenose dolphins (4hr; $95); and the full-day (10hr) Dune Rider travels up to Cape Reinga along the "sand highway" of 90 Mile Beach ($150).

Fullers Great Sights ☏ 0800 653 339, ⊛ dolphincruises.co.nz. The Cream Trip (a.k.a. "Day in the Bay"; Oct–April daily; 7hr; $125) is the best all-round option, with a visit to the Hole in the Rock, a stop on Urupukapuka, a chance to get wet boom-netting and a look around as the boat delivers groceries and mail. You'll probably see dolphins and may have the chance to swim with them. There's also a dedicated dolphin-swimming cruise (2 daily; 4hr; $115) on the bay's smallest dolphin boat (35 passengers). Save ten percent by booking online.

Mack Attack ☏ 09 402 8180, ⊛ mackattack.co.nz. Fast boat trip out to the Hole in the Rock and back (1hr 30min; $99), with stops en route if the skipper spots dolphins or whales. A good choice if you're short on time.

Phantom ☏ 0800 224 421, ⊛ yachtphantom.com. Only ten can board this excellent, Russell-based ocean-racing sloop for six glorious hours around the bay ($110), relaxing on deck or taking the helm. Lunch included. Oct–April only.

R. Tucker Thompson ☏ 0800 882 537, ⊛ tucker .co.nz. Day-trips into the islands on a beautiful Northland-built schooner (daily Nov–April; 6hr; $145) with morning tea and freshly baked scones and cream before anchoring for a swim and BBQ lunch. Two-hour late-afternoon sails (Nov–March Wed, Fri & Sun; $65) including an antipasto platter are also available.

★**The Rock** ☏ 0800 762 527, ⊛ rocktheboat.co.nz. Backpacker-style accommodation and group activities aboard a converted former car ferry, with a great range of ages and a real sense of kicking back. Board in the late afternoon and chug out to some gorgeous bays for fishing, swimming, snorkelling and night kayaking

churches. In the mid-nineteenth century the church was besieged during skirmishes between Hone Heke's warriors and the British, leaving several still-visible bullet holes.

Russell Museum

2 York St • Daily: Jan 10am–5pm; Feb–Dec 10am–4pm • $10 • ☏ 09 403 7701, ⊛ russellmuseum.org.nz

The small **Russell Museum** shows a video telling the town's history and contains

– which usually includes the chance to experience phosphorescence – and then feast on a big BBQ before a walk on an island the next day and 3pm

KAYAKING

Coastal Kayakers ☎09 402 8105, ⓦcoastal kayakers.co.nz. Operates from the Paihia wharf and runs a variety of trips, from half-day paddles in the bay or upstream to Haruru Falls ($85) to three-day guided camping excursions (Nov–May; $685). Also offers kayak hire ($15/hr, $40 half-day).

FLIGHTS AND PARASAILING

Flying Kiwi Paihia Wharf ☎0800 359 691, ⓦparasailnz.com. Offers ten- to fifteen-minute parasail flights from the back of a speedboat to a height of 1200ft, NZ's highest parasail. Single, tandem and triple parasails available (from $95).

Salt Air Marsden Rd, near the Maritime Building ☎09 4028 338, ⓦsaltair.co.nz. Runs chopper

JET-SKI AND SKYDIVE

★**Ballistic Blondes** 1 Davis Cresent ☎0800 695 867, ⓦskydiveballisticblondes.co.nz. Offers tandem jumps of 12,000ft ($380) and all manner of other deals (see Whangarei, p.150) as well as the opportunity, unique in New Zealand, of landing on the beach after getting an eyeful of the Bay of Islands.

SCUBA DIVING

Dive HQ Williams Rd ☎0800 107 551, ⓦdivenz .com. Will take you out in the Bay of Islands or to the wrecks of the *Rainbow Warrior* (see p.178) and the scuttled navy frigate *Canterbury*. Two-tank dives including gear cost $239 for those with Advanced Open Water certification or higher, $289 for those with Open Water

arrival back at Paihia. Six-berth dorms ($221) and private cabins ($396) all have sea views. Dinner and breakfast included, but not drinks. Take a sleeping bag.

Pacific Coast Kayaks ☎09 436 1947, ⓦnzseakayaking.co.nz. Runs a number of wonderful short and multi-day guided trips in the outer reaches of the Bay of Islands and slightly further afield (from 2hr/$40).

flights ($230/20min to the Hole in the Rock; $315/30min up the coast) along with awesome fixed-wing flights to Cape Reinga (see p.188). A new tour in conjunction with the Motu Kōkako Ahu Whenua Trust offers the chance to land atop the Hole in the Rock, with guided tour of the island with a Maori guide ($595).

★**Tango Jetski Adventure** 1 Davis Cresent ☎0800 253 8754, ⓦtangojetskitours.co.nz. The self-drive, speed-lover's way to see the seascape can cover a lot of ground in a relatively short period of time. Try the one-hour Island Blaster ($180).

status and $250 for the beginners' Discover Scuba Diving. **Dive North** ☎09 402 5369, ⓦdivenorth.co.nz. This professional outfit has dive options including a trip to the *Rainbow Warrior* or *Canterbury* wrecks ($235 with gear, $150 if you have your own), or to both for $325 ($285 with own gear).

TRIPS FROM THE BAY OF ISLANDS

As the main tourist centre in Northland, the Bay of Islands acts as a staging post for forays further north, in particular for day-long bus tours to **Cape Reinga** and **Ninety Mile Beach** (see p.185) – arduous affairs lasting eleven hours, most of them spent stuck inside the vehicle. You're better off making your way up to Mangonui, Kaitaia or Ahipara and taking a trip from there, or taking Salt Air's fixed-wing Cape Reinga Flight (see above), which takes in the beach, Bay of Islands, and includes a field landing and short run to the cape itself.

Fullers Great Sights (see opposite) also runs Discover Hokianga (daily; 8hr; $115), another epic tour visiting the **Hokianga Harbour**, taking a Footprints Waipoua tour to the giant **kauri trees**, and taking a look at the **Wairere Boulders**. Again you are better off getting closer independently and spending more time at the actual attractions.

---

great exhibits, including an impressive one-fifth scale model of Cook's *Endeavour*, which called in here in 1769. From the museum, a stroll along The Strand passes the prestigious *Bay of Islands Swordfish Club*, which was founded in 1924, and the *Duke of Marlborough Hotel* – the original building on this site held New Zealand's first liquor licence.

Flagstaff Hill and Tapeka Point Historic Reserve

30–40min return

At the end of The Strand, a short track climbs steeply to **Flagstaff Hill** (Maiki). The current flagpole was erected in 1857, some twelve years after the destruction of the fourth flagpole by Hone Heke, as a conciliatory gesture by a son of one of the chiefs who had ordered the original felling. The Confederation of Tribes flag, abandoned after the signing of the Treaty of Waitangi, is flown on twelve significant days of the year, including the anniversary of Hone Heke's death and the final day of the first New Zealand War. From Flagstaff Hill it's a further kilometre to the **Tapeka Point Historic Reserve**, a former *pa* site at the end of the peninsula – a wonderfully defensible position with great views and abundant evidence of terracing.

ARRIVAL AND DEPARTURE   RUSSELL

By ferry and car Most visitors reach Russell by ferry, but it's also accessible along the back road described on p.160. Foot passengers can take one of the three frequent passenger ferries (Oct–May 7am–10pm; June–Sept 7am–7pm; $7 one way, $12 return) between the main wharves in Paihia and Russell, a fifteen-minute journey.

INFORMATION AND TOURS

Tourist information Russell Booking & Information Centre is located at the end of the wharf (daily: Sept–May 7.30am–8pm; June–Aug 8.30am–4pm; ☎0800 633 255, ⓦrussellinfo.co.nz). Makes bookings for local trips and accommodation. Also stocks the *Russell Heritage Trail* and *Bay of Islands Walks* leaflets.

Tours Most of the bay's cruises and dolphin trips are based in Paihia but also pick up at Russell wharf (with prior reservation) around 15min later. Occasionally there are no pick-ups available, but you can catch the frequent, inexpensive passenger ferry between Paihia and Russell. Fullers Russell Mini Tour (☎0800 646 486, ⓦrussellminitours.com) offers a locals' view on the area's history and the town (six daily Oct–April, four daily May–Sept; $29).

ACCOMMODATION

Accommodation in Russell is much more limited than in Paihia and tends to be more upmarket, mostly B&Bs and lodges.

Arcadia Lodge 10 Florance Ave ☎09 403 7756, ⓦarcadialodge.co.nz. Stylish B&B in a historic wooden house encircled by decks on a quiet hill overlooking cottage gardens and the bay. Five of the wooden-floored suites and rooms (one not en-suite) enjoy sea views and much of the produce is organic and grown in the garden, or locally. Free wi-fi. No under-15s. Two-night minimum in summer. Rooms $210, suites $325

★**The Duke of Marlborough** 35 The Strand ☎09 403 7829, ⓦtheduke.co.nz. New owners have renovated and modernized to create a beating heart in the centre of the town. The ambience is of an old colonial hotel until you get into your room, at which point it becomes modern with a hint of romance. Some rooms have sea views ($360), others sundecks ($290), and there are a few cosy options with neither. $165

Hananui Lodge 4 York St ☎09 403 7875, ⓦhananui .co.nz. Well-run, modernized motel-style place by the water. The waterfront suites have the best views but even the standard units are comfortable, with sea glimpses, and all get spa access. There are also new apartments across the road with big-screen TV and a/c. Units $185, apartments $210

Motel Russell 16 Matauwhi Rd ☎0800 240 011, ⓦmotelrussell.co.nz. Choose one of the comfortable, recently modernized units in an acre of well-tended subtropical garden full of birds surrounding this simple motel with an attractive pool. Studios $118, one-bedroom units $159

Russell Top 10 Holiday Park Long Beach Rd ☎09 403 7826, ⓦrusselltop10.co.nz. Central, well-ordered and spotless campsite with tent and campervan sites and an extensive range of high-standard cabins (from $85) and motel units. Campervans $52, motel units $175

Wainui Lodge 92d Wahapu Rd, 7km south of Russell ☎09 403 8278, ⓦwainuilodge-russell-nz.com. Excellent, tiny two-room backpackers with morning birdsong and kayaking from its own mangrove-lined beach. Full kitchen and wi-fi. Dorm $28, room $66

EATING AND DRINKING

Russell has a limited range of restaurants and prices are fairly high, but quality is good. For drinking the best bets are often the cheap private clubs – the *RSA* on Chapel Street and *Bay of Islands Swordfish Club* – which both welcome visitors.

Bay of Islands Swordfish Club 25 The Strand ☎09 402 7773, ⓦ swordfish.co.nz. Technically a private club, much the same as the one in Paihia (see p.167), so you just sign yourself in or get the bartender to do it. Always a winner for cheap beer, fish and chips, simple bar meals (mains around $25) in big portions, and great sunset views from the veranda. Daily 4pm–late.

★**Duke of Marlborough** 35 The Strand ☎09 403 7829, ⓦ theduke.co.nz. Waterside bar seating, a pub bar at the back and a restaurant all serving a broad range of wine and beer. Best of all is the food, stunningly presented in imaginative combinations and generous portions. King on the menu is the 8hr cooked shoulder of lamb on the bone ($49 for two), which melts in the mouth and could feed a coach party. Daily 7.30am–late.

★**Sally's** 25 The Strand ☎09 403 7652, ⓦ sallysrestaurant.co.nz. Convivial, unpretentious and always busy licensed restaurant that's strong on seafood, and especially seafood chowder ($14). It's worth booking ahead in peak season. Mains around $32. Daily 10.30am–9pm.

Waterfront Café 23 The Strand ☎09 403 7589, ⓦ waterfrontcafe.co.nz. Simple café with waterfront seating, and great coffee, home-made muffins, cakes, pies and scones ($5–15), as well as all-day breakfasts and hearty lunches. Daily 8am–4pm.

Kerikeri

KERIKERI, 25km north of Paihia, is central to the history of the Bay of Islands and yet geographically removed from it, strung out along the main road and surrounded by the orchards that form Kerikeri's economic mainstay. Two kilometres to the east of town, the thin ribbon of the Kerikeri Inlet forces its way from the sea to its tidal limit at **Kerikeri Basin**, the site chosen by Samuel Marsden for the Church Missionary Society's second mission in New Zealand.

For most of the year it's possible to get **seasonal work** weeding, thinning or picking in the subtropical orchards among citrus, tamarillos, feijoas, melons, courgettes, peppers and kiwifruit. Work is most abundant from January to July, with so-called "silly season" from mid-March to mid-June. The best contacts are the managers of the hostels and campsites, many of which also offer good weekly rates. In recent years Kerikeri has earned itself a reputation for its high-quality **craft shops** dotted among the orchards.

Kerikeri's past importance is evident at peaceful Kerikeri Basin, nearly 2km northeast of the current town where a few buildings have stood the test of time.

Kerikeri Mission House

246 Kerikeri Rd • Daily: Nov–April 10am–5pm; May–Oct 10am–4pm (café closed); entry by guided tour only, minimum of four; call ahead for tour times, $10 • ☎09 407 9236, ⓦ historicplaces.org.nz

It was here, in 1821, that mission carpenters started work on what is now New Zealand's oldest European-style building, **Kerikeri Mission House**, a restrained, two-storey Georgian colonial affair. The first occupants, missionary John Butler and family, soon moved on, and by 1832 the house was in the hands of lay missionary and blacksmith James Kemp, who extended the design. Since the last of the Kemps moved out in 1974 it has been restored, furnished in mid-nineteenth-century style, and surrounded by colonial-style gardens. There's also an on-site café in summer.

Old Stone Store

246 Kerikeri Rd • Daily: Nov–April 10am–5pm; May–Oct 10am–4pm (café closed) • Free; upper floors $10 • ☎09 407 9236, ⓦ historicplaces.org.nz

Mission House guided tours start next door at the **Old Stone Store**, the only other extant building from the mission station and the country's oldest stone building, constructed mostly of local stone, with keystones and quoins of Sydney sandstone. Completed in 1836 as a central provision store for the Church Missionary Society, it successively served as a munitions store for troops garrisoned here to fight Hone Heke,

2

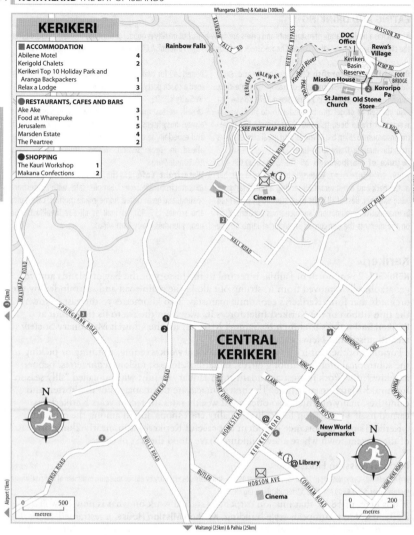

KERIKERI

■ ACCOMMODATION

Abilene Motel	4
Kerigold Chalets	2
Kerikeri Top 10 Holiday Park and Aranga Backpackers	1
Relax a Lodge	3

● RESTAURANTS, CAFES AND BARS

Ake Ake	3
Food at Wharepuke	1
Jerusalem	5
Marsden Estate	4
The Peartree	2

● SHOPPING

The Kauri Workshop	1
Makana Confections	2

CENTRAL KERIKERI

then a kauri-trading store and a shop, before being opened to the public in 1975.

The ground-floor **store** (free) sells some goods almost identical to those on offer almost 180 years ago, most sourced from the original manufacturers. You can still buy the once-prized Hudson Bay trading blankets, plus copper and cast-iron pots, jute sacks, gunpowder tea, old-fashioned sweets, and preserves made from fruit grown in the mission garden next door. The two **upper floors** admirably outline the history of Maori and European contact and the relevance of Kerikeri Basin, aided by old implements, including a hand-operated flour mill from around 1820, thought to be the oldest piece of machinery in the country.

From opposite the Old Stone Store, a path along the river leads to **Kororipo Pa**, which commands a hill on a prominent bend in the river from where local chief Hongi Hika launched attacks on other tribes using newly acquired firearms.

Rewa's Village

1 Landing Rd • ⓦ rewasvillage.co.nz, ☏ 09 407 6454 • Daily: Dec & Jan 9am–5pm; late Oct–April 9.30am–4.30pm; May–late Oct 10am–4pm • $5

A footbridge across the creek leads to **Rewa's Village**, a reconstruction of a fishing village where you'll get a better appreciation of pre-European Maori life. It comes complete with *marae*, weapons and *kumara* stores, as well as an authentic *hangi* site with an adjacent shell midden.

Kerikeri Basin Reserve

Opposite Rewa's Village

The **Kerikeri Basin Reserve** marks the start of a track past the site of Kerikeri's first hydroelectric station (15min each way) and the swimming holes at Fairy Pools (35min each way) to the impressively undercut **Rainbow Falls** (1hr each way). The latter are also accessible off Waipapa Road, 3km north of the Basin.

2

Steam Sawmill

Inlet Rd, 4km east of town • Mon–Fri 9am–4pm; tours Mon–Fri 10.30am & 1.30pm; closed from Christmas to New Year • $7.50 • ☏ 09 407 9707, ⓦ steam.co.nz/collins.html

The **Steam Sawmill** is a working steam-driven mill powered by secondhand equipment garnered from all over the country. You can take a look anytime, but it is best to join one of the tours when the steam whistle is blown.

ARRIVAL AND DEPARTURE KERIKERI

By plane Air New Zealand flights from Auckland arrive at the Bay of Islands airport (☏ 09 407 6133, ⓦ bayofislandsairport.co.nz), 6km southwest of town and are met by the Super Shuttle bus ($12 into town).

Destinations Auckland (5–6 daily; 45min).
By bus InterCity/Northliner buses stop on Cobham Rd. Destinations Auckland (4 daily; 5hr); Kaitaia (1 daily; 1hr 45min); Paihia (4 daily; 30min).

INFORMATION

Tourist information There's no official visitor centre, but you can pick up leaflets inside the foyer of the library on Cobham Rd (Mon–Fri 8am–5pm, Sat 9am–2pm, Sun 9am–1pm), which also has free wi-fi.

DOC 34 Landing Rd (Mon–Fri 8am–4.30pm; ☏ 09 407 8474). Advises on local walks and more ambitious treks into the Puketi Forest (see p.177).

ACCOMMODATION

Kerikeri has a good selection of accommodation in all categories, particularly budget places – a consequence of the area's popularity with long-stay casual workers. Seasonal price fluctuations are nowhere near as marked as in Paihia, though it's still difficult to find accommodation in January.

Abilene Motel 136 Kerikeri Rd ☏ 0800 224 536, ⓦ abilenemotel.co.nz. Centrally located, older-style, ten-unit motel (some of which are for families) in a garden setting with a solar-heated pool, spa and Sky TV and run by a couple of country and western fans. Free wi-fi. **$130**

Kerigold Chalets 326 Kerikeri Rd ☏ 0800 537 446, ⓦ kerigoldchalets.co.nz. Modern, spacious and spotless one-bedroom stand-alone wooden chalets with kitchens and access to a communal pool and barbecue area. Breakfast available on request and courtesy car to the airport. **$225**

★**Kerikeri Top 10 Holiday Park and Aranga Backpackers** Kerikeri Rd ☏ 0800 272 642, ⓦ aranga .co.nz. Large, beautiful streamside site on the edge of town

with a spacious camping area, well-equipped standard cabins with good weekly rates, comfortable self-contained units and a separate backpackers section (prices vary depending on length of stay with most stays at least a week). There's the occasional sound of kiwi in the night, and free kayaks to paddle up the river. Dorms per week **$125**

Relax A Lodge SH10, 5km west of Kerikeri ☏ 09 407 6989, ⓦ relaxalodge.co.nz. Top-class rooms and cottages on an organic citrus orchard, with comfortable, shared-bathroom rooms in the lovely wooden house and gorgeous cottages scattered around the orchard. The owners speak German, there's free wi-fi, an outdoor pool and free-range eggs are available. **$110**

2

EATING, DRINKING AND ENTERTAINMENT

★**Food at Wharepuke** 190 Kerikeri Rd ☎09 407 8936, ⓦfoodatwharepuke.co.nz. Stunning Thai-European fusion garden café serving high-quality nosh ($14–39) including crispy pork-belly salad, aged Angus eye fillet and *tom yum* with tiger prawns, to name but a few. Also plays some lounge-like live music to entertain diners. Three-course Thai banquet ($47.50) served every Friday. Tues–Sat 10am–3pm & 5–10pm, Sun 9am–3pm.

Jerusalem Cobblestone Mall ☎09 407 1001, ⓦcafejerusalem.co.nz. Small, friendly, licensed Israeli café beloved by Northlanders for its authentic, low-cost and wonderfully aromatic Middle Eastern dishes to eat in or take away, including falafel, *levivot* and *metuvlum* ($4–18). Mon–Sat 10am–late, Sun (summer only) 5pm–late.

The Peartree 215 Kerikeri Rd ☎0508 732 78733, ⓦthepeartree.co.nz. With a fabulous setting by Kerikeri Basin this spot is best used for midday tipples or sun-downers, but if you're too lazy to get lunch or dinner elsewhere you can eat here in a semiformal atmosphere, inside or on the veranda. Typical menu items are twice-baked *kumara* soufflé and tempura-battered fish and chips (mains around $32). Daily 10am–late.

WINERIES

Ake Ake Vineyard 165 Waimate North Rd ☎09 407 8230, ⓦakeakevineyard.co.nz. Vineyard producing intriguing wines (including Chambourcin, which has become a favourite with Northland grape growers) that's open for tastings ($5, or free with lunch), vineyard tours ($5, refunded with any purchase) and for lunch or dinner (mains $27–35), including the likes of chargrilled venison steak and fish of the day. Tastings Wed–Sun 10.30am–4.30pm; vineyard tours daily in summer 11.30am.

Marsden Estate Wiroa Rd ☎09 407 9398, ⓦmarsdenestate.co.nz. A medium-sized winery producing a broad variety of excellent reds and whites sampled through free tastings, or in larger quantities in the moderately priced lunch restaurant. Well worth a taste are the French onion tart, the Basque seafood stew and the marinated Vietnamese beef salad (mains $18–32). Daily: Aug–May 10am–5pm; June & July 10am–4pm.

CINEMA

Cathay Cinemas Hobson Avenue ☎09 407 4428, ⓦcathaycinemas.co.nz. Entertainment is thin on the ground in Kerikeri, so thank goodness for this lovingly restored cinema showing mainstream and more off-beat movies, with three screens and a licensed café.

SHOPPING

You could easily spend a couple of hours pottering around the **craft outlets** that dominate the Kerikeri hinterland, guided by the free and widely available *Kerikeri Art & Craft Trail* leaflet: most places are open daily from 9am–5pm.

The Kauri Workshop 500 Kerikeri Rd ☎09 407 9196. Stocks anything you might hope to make from kauri, including spoons, bowls and carvings. Open daily.

Makana Confections 504 Kerikeri Rd ☎09 407 6800, ⓦmakana.co.nz. Boutique shop produces handmade chocolates, which you can see being made and then, of course, sample. It's hard not to leave with your wallet a little lighter. Daily 9am–5.30pm.

Around Kerikeri

At first glance the area around Kerikeri isn't the most inspiring part of Northland, but it is characterized by a few historic locations, some good walks and one magical tour that reveals bubbling mud beneath the otherwise peaceful surface of the earth.

Te Waimate Mission House

344 Te Ahu Ahu Rd, 15km southwest of Kerikeri • Nov–April daily 10am–5pm; May–Oct Sat–Mon 10am–4pm • $10 • ☎09 405 9734, ⓦheritage.org.nz

WAIMATE NORTH is home to the colonial Regency-style **Te Waimate Mission House**, New Zealand's second-oldest European building. Now virtually in the middle of nowhere, in the 1830s this was the centre of a vigorous **Anglican mission**. Missionaries were keen to add European agricultural techniques to the literacy and religion they were teaching the Maori, and by 1834 locally grown wheat was milled at the river, orchards were flourishing and crops were sprouting – all impressing Charles Darwin, who visited the following year. The house, built by converts from local kauri in 1832, has been restored as accurately as possible to its original design. Guided tours highlight prize possessions.

Kaikohe and the Hidden Walk

SH12, southwest of Waimate North • Hidden Walk by appointment only; phone or stop in at Kaikohe Photographic Centre, 89 Broadway • $28 • ☎ 021 277 7301, ⓦ hiddenwalks.com

The primary reason to stop in **KAIKOHE**, almost equidistant from both coasts, is the magical **Hidden Walk**, a guided tour through a section of the Ngawha Valley. The tour begins inauspiciously with a meeting in the car park of the local golf club, but after that it just gets better and better. Situated on private land is a large thermally active area of bubbling mud and springs, where ancient kauri lay scattered by the extraordinary natural forces unleashed over thousands of years. Among the various bubbling pools are examples of everything you will see in Rotorua (see p.265), just on a smaller scale and in a situation that enables you to get closer and lacks the commercialism of New Zealand's most famous thermal town. The trip then moves on to the remaining bones of a mercury extraction plant, some intermingled in native regrowth, the remainder in ghostly clearings full of rusty, calcified and broken remnants of human occupation. Trying to unravel how the various ruins fit together and how the workers went about their tasks is an archeological puzzle that will have you scratching your head for days after the tour.

Ngawha Springs

7km southeast of Kaikohe • Daily 9am–9pm • $4

If you have time and the need of some relaxation, soak your bones at **Ngawha Springs** (pronounced "Naf-fa"), where eight individual pools (all with different mineral contents and at different temperatures) are enclosed by native timber, but otherwise uncluttered by tourist trappings or, for the most part, other people.

Puketi Kauri Forest

20km north of Kaikohe

The **Puketi Kauri Forest** comprises one of the largest continuous tracts of kauri forest in the north. Signposted routes from Kaikohe and Kerikeri lead to the **Manginangina Kauri Walk** where a five-minute boardwalk through lush forest brings you to a stand of good-sized kauri.

ACCOMMODATION AND TOURS

Puketi Recreation Area Campsite 2km south of Puketi Kauri Forest ⓦ doc.govt.nz. A wee, bog-standard DOC campsite in the Puketi Forest about 20km north of Kerikeri, with running water, long-drop toilets, cold showers, BBQs and picnic tables. No bookings; leave the fee in the honesty box. $6

AROUND KERIKERI

Adventure Puketi 476 Puketi Rd ☎ 09 401 9095, ⓦ forestwalks.com. Runs a number of walks, one of which takes place at night (2hr; $75), along the Manginangina Kauri Walk (see above), with the hope of encountering kiwi, morepork and other night owls.

Matauri Bay to the Karikari Peninsula

North of the Bay of Islands everything gets a lot quieter. There are few towns of any consequence along the coast and it is the peace and slow pace that attract visitors to an array of glorious beaches and the lovely Whangaroa Harbour. The first stop north of Kerikeri is tiny **Matauri Bay**, where a hilltop memorial commemorates the Greenpeace flagship, *Rainbow Warrior*, which now lies off the coast. A sealed but winding back road continues north, offering fabulous sea views and passing gorgeous headlands and beaches before delivering you to **Whangaroa Harbour**, one of the most beautiful in Northland, and an excellent place to go sailing or kayaking. Further north is the idyllic surfing and fishing hideaway of **Taupo Bay**.

2

FRENCH NUCLEAR TESTING IN THE PACIFIC

Claiming that nuclear testing was completely safe, the French government for decades conducted tests on the tiny Pacific atolls of **Mururoa** and **Fangataufa**, a comfortable 15,000km from Paris, but only 4000km northeast of New Zealand.

In 1966 France turned its back on the 1963 Partial Test Ban Treaty, which outlawed atmospheric testing, and relocated Pacific islanders away from their ancestral villages to make way for a barrage of tests over the next eight years. The French authorities claimed that "Not a single particle of radioactive fallout will ever reach an inhabited island" – and yet radiation was routinely detected as far away as Samoa, Fiji and even New Zealand. Increasingly antagonistic public opinion forced the French to conduct their tests underground in deep shafts, where another 200 detonations took place, threatening the geological stability of these fragile coral atolls.

In 1985, Greenpeace coordinated a New Zealand-based protest flotilla, headed by its flagship, the **Rainbow Warrior**, but before the fleet could set sail from Auckland, the French secret service sabotaged the *Rainbow Warrior*, detonating two bombs below the waterline. As rescuers recovered the body of Greenpeace photographer Fernando Pereira, two French secret service agents posing as tourists were arrested. Flatly denying all knowledge at first, the French government was finally forced to admit to what then Prime Minister David Lange described as "a sordid act of international state-backed terrorism". The two captured agents were sentenced to ten years in jail, but France used all its international muscle to have them serve their sentences on a French Pacific island; they both served less than two years before being honoured and returning to France.

In 1995, to worldwide opprobrium, France announced a further series of tests. Greenpeace duly dispatched *Rainbow Warrior II*, which was impounded by the French navy on the tenth anniversary of the sinking of the original *Rainbow Warrior*. In early 1996 the French finally agreed to stop nuclear testing in the Pacific.

Continuing north brings you to the huge bite out of the coast called **Doubtless Bay**, which had two celebrated discoverers: Kupe, said to have first set foot on Aotearoa in **Taipa**; and Cook, who sailed past in 1769 and pronounced it "doubtless, a bay". Bounded on the west and north by the sheltering **Karikari Peninsula**, the bay offers safe boating and is popular with Kiwi vacationers. In January you can barely move here and you'll struggle to find accommodation, but the shoulder seasons can be surprisingly quiet, and outside December, January and February room prices drop considerably. Most of the bay's facilities cluster along the southern shore of the peninsula in a string of beachside settlements – **Coopers Beach**, **Cable Bay** and **Taipa Bay** – running west from picturesque **Mangonui**.

Matauri Bay

A high inland ridge provides a dramatic first glimpse of the long, Norfolk-pine-backed **MATAURI BAY**, 20km north of Kerikeri, and the **Cavalli Islands** just offshore. At the northern end of the main bay a well-worn path (20min return; 70m ascent) climbs to Chris Booth's distinctive **Rainbow Warrior Memorial**, which remembers the Greenpeace flagship (see box above), now scuttled off the Cavalli Islands. The memorial comprises a stone arch (symbolizing a rainbow) and the vessel's salvaged bronze propeller. Paihia-based dive operators (see p.171) run trips out to the wreck, ten minutes offshore from Matauri Bay. The best visibility is in April; from September to November plankton sometimes obscure the view, but it's still pretty good.

Samuel Marsden Memorial Church

Matauri Bay Rd, just before the beach

Missionary Samuel Marsden first set foot in Aotearoa in 1814 at Matauri Bay, where he mediated between the Ngati Kura people – who still own the bay – and some Bay of

Islands Maori, a process commemorated by the quaint wooden **Samuel Marsden Memorial Church**. The Ngati Kura tell of their ancestral *waka*, *Mataatua*, which lies in waters nearby. It was the resonance of this legendary canoe that partly led the Ngati Kura to offer a final resting place to the wreck of the *Rainbow Warrior*.

Whangaroa Harbour

West of Matauri Bay, the virtually landlocked and sheltered **Whangaroa Harbour** is the perfect antidote to Bay of Islands' commercialism. The scenery, albeit on a smaller scale, is easily a match for its southern cousin and, despite the limited facilities, you can still get out on a cruise or to join the big-game fishers. Narrow inlets forge between cliffs and steep hills, most notably the two bald volcanic plugs, **St Paul and St Peter**, which rise behind the harbour's two settlements, **WHANGAROA** on the south side, and **TOTARA NORTH** opposite.

Brief history

Whangaroa Harbour was among the first areas in New Zealand to be visited by European pioneers, most famously those aboard the *Boyd*, which called here in 1809 to load kauri spars for shipping to Britain. A couple of days after its arrival, all 66 crew were killed and the ship burned by local Maori in retribution for the crew's mistreatment of Tara, a high-born Maori sailor who had apparently transgressed the ship's rules. A British whaler avenged the incident by burning the entire Maori village, sparking off a series of skirmishes that spread over the north for five years. Later the vast stands of kauri were hacked down and milled, some at Totara North. Even if you're just passing through, it's worth driving the 4km along the northern shore of the harbour to Totara North, passing the remains of this historic community's last sawmills, which ceased operation in 2004.

Taupo Bay

A sealed 13km road from SH10 brings you to **TAUPO BAY**, a blissfully undeveloped holiday community with a smattering of beach shacks, and some of the best surfing and rock and beach fishing in Northland.

Mangonui and around

With its lively fishing wharf and a traditional grocery perched on stilts over the water there's an antiquated air to **MANGONUI**, strung along the sheltered Mangonui Harbour off Doubtless Bay. A handful of two-storey buildings with wooden verandas have been preserved, some operating as craft shops or cafés, but this is still very much a working village. To get a feel for the layout of Mangonui Harbour, take in the views at **Rangikapiti Pa Historic Reserve**, off Rangikapiti Road, between Mangonui and Coopers Beach.

Mangonui also makes a good base for organized trips to **Cape Reinga** and **Ninety Mile Beach** (see p.185).

Brief history

Mangonui means "big shark", recalling the legendary chief Moehuri's *waka* which was supposedly led into Mangonui Harbour by such a fish. But it was whales and the business of provisioning **whaling** ships that made the town: one story tells of a harbour so packed with ships that folk could leap between the boats to cross from Mangonui to the diminutive settlement of Hihi on the far shore. As whaling diminished, the kauri trade took its place, chiefly around Mill Bay, the cove five minutes' walk to the west of Mangonui.

2

WHANGAROA HARBOUR AND DOUBTLESS BAY TOURS AND ACTIVITIES

If you can't afford to charter a boat to take you to the rugged, uninhabited and beautiful **Cavalli Islands**, ask at the wharf or the local dairy (☎09 405 0230). In Whangaroa Harbour, you will find a limited number of distractions – unless you are an angler, fancy a solitary hike or a peaceful kayak paddle.

WALKS

St Paul hike (30min return; 140m ascent). One of the most immediately rewarding walks is the hike up the volcanic dome of St Paul from the top of Old Hospital Rd in Whangaroa. The final few metres involve an easy scramble with fixed chains to assist.

Wairakau Steam Track (6km each way; 90min–2hr). Located on the harbour's north side, this DOC track runs from Totara North, past freshwater pools, mangroves and viewpoints to Pekapeka Bay.

FISHING

Whangaroa Big Gamefish Club ☎09 405 0399, ⓦwhangaroasportfishingclub.co.nz. The people you want to see if you want to go game fishing are listed on the website, or you can phone them, but don't just rock up to the bar and expect to go out that day.

Charter rates typically kick off at around $1000/day, with bait and ice costing extra. Expect mostly marlin off the Cavalli Islands and more modest edible domestic fish closer to shore.

KAYAKING AND DIVING

Northland Sea Kayaking ☎09 405 0381, ⓦnorthlandseakayaking.co.nz. Located on the northeastern flank of Whangaroa Harbour, this knowledgeable operator arranges local kayak trips in the summer ($90 half-day; no credit cards).

A to Z Diving Whatuwhiwhi ☎09 408 7077, ⓦatozdiving.co.nz. Offers diving off the Karikari Peninsula (two-tank dive $185), plus trips to the *Rainbow Warrior* wreck, including gear.

Coopers Beach

While ships were repaired and restocked at Mangonui, barrels were mended a couple of kilometres west at **COOPERS BEACH**, a glorious and well-shaded sweep of sand backed by a beautiful stand of red-flowering pohutakowa trees and, less elegantly, by a string of motels. The beach is popular in January and at weekends, but at other times you may find you have it pretty much to yourself.

Cable Bay

About 3km west of Coopers Beach, the smaller swimming and surfing settlement of **CABLE BAY** is separated by the Taipa River from the beachside village of **TAIPA**. This pleasant stretch of pink coral sand is now the haunt of sunbathers and swimmers, but it's also historically significant as the spot where Kupe, the discoverer of Aotearoa in Maori legend, first set foot on land. There's a concrete memorial to him near the Shell station by the Taipa River.

The Karikari Peninsula

Doubtless Bay to the east and Rangaunu Harbour to the west are bounded by the crooked arm of the **Karikari Peninsula**, which strikes north swathed in unspoiled golden- and white-sand beaches. Outside Christmas to mid-February, they have barely a soul on them. Apart from the large and modern **Karikari Estate** golf resort, vineyard and winery, facilities remain limited, though there's the usual scattering of motels and cheap places to eat. There's no public transport, and without diving or fishing gear, you'll have to resign yourself to lazing on the beaches and swimming from them.

Puheke Scenic Reserve

About 15km from SH10 via Inland Rd

The initial approach across a low and scrubby isthmus is less than inspiring, but 10km on, a side road leads to the peninsula's west coast and the **Puheke Scenic Reserve**, a gorgeous, dune-backed beach that's usually deserted. Another fine white strand spans the nearby hamlet of **RANGIPUTA**.

The peninsula's main road continues past the Rangiputa junction to the community of **TOKERAU BEACH**, a cluster of houses and shops at the northern end of the grand sweep of Doubtless Bay.

2

Karikari Estate winery

1km north of Tokerau Beach • Daily summer 11am–4pm • $15 for five tastings • ☎ 09 408 7222, ⓦ karikariestate.co.nz

Passing between an international-standard golf course and a hillside swathed in vines you soon reach **Karikari Estate winery**, situated in a monstrous resort estate, the northernmost in New Zealand. The winery produced its first vintage in 2003, has lovely views and you can, of course, sample the wares; the café serves a great beef pie, which goes down well with a glass of Syrah.

Maitai Bay

6km north of of Karikari Estate winery

The Karikari Peninsula saves its best until last: **Maitai Bay**, a matchless double arc of golden sand split by a rocky knoll, encompassed by a campsite (see p.182). Much of the site is *tapu* to local Maori, and you are encouraged to respect the sacred areas. A walking track (3.5km) runs out from here to the rugged headland and fantastic views over the sea, though the path can be dangerously slippery in wet weather.

ARRIVAL AND INFORMATION

MATAURI BAY TO THE KARIKARI PENINSULA

By bus There is little public transport so your own wheels are recommended if not essential. InterCity/Northliner buses serve the Mangonui waterfront, running once a day in each direction between Paihia and Kaitaia.
Destinations Kaitaia (1 daily; 55min); Paihia (1 daily; 1hr 50min).

Tourist information 118 Waterfront Drive, Mangonui (Nov–Easter daily 10am–4pm; Easter–Oct Tues–Sat 10am–3pm; ☎ 09 406 2046). The volunteer-staffed visitor centre can point you to accommodation, both here and along the coast, and has wi-fi.

ACCOMMODATION

WHANGAROA HARBOUR

Kahoe Farms Hostel SH10, 1.5km north of the Totara North turn-off ☎ 09 405 1804, ⓦ kahoefarms .co.nz. A small and extremely hospitable backpackers on a working cattle farm with a dorm and rooms in a house with polished wood floors and more rooms (some en-suite) in a separate villa on the hill behind. The owner whips up superb home-made pizza, pasta and farm steak dinners, generous breakfasts and a fine espresso, plus there's kayak rental and hiking trails to some lovely swimming holes. The daily InterCity/Northliner bus passes the farm and will drop up/pick up on request. Dorm **$32**, doubles **$86**

TAUPO BAY

Taupo Bay Holiday Park 1070 Taupo Bay Rd ☎ 09 406 0315, ⓦ taupobayholidaypark.co.nz. One of the few places worth staying at in the area, much beloved by Kiwi holiday-makers for its ample camping, good communal

facilities and modern but no-frills cabins sleeping up to five. Camping **$16**, cabins **$140**

MANGONUI

★**Beach Lodge** 121 SH10, Coopers Beach ☎ 09 409 0068, ⓦ beachlodge.co.nz. Five breezy yet elegant water-view apartments, on the beachfront at Coopers Beach and within the sound of the waves, each with its own deck, full kitchen and free wi-fi. No under-8s. **$400**

Carneval 360 SH10, Cable Bay ☎ 09 406 1012, ⓦ carneval.co.nz. Perched high on a hill overlooking the sea is this relaxed, Swiss-run house with comfortable spacious rooms and a stunning view of the coastline, plus a full Swiss breakfast if you can handle it. Rooms **$200**

★**Driftwood Lodge** SH10, Cable Bay ☎ 09 406 0418, ⓦ driftwoodlodge.co.nz. Great lodge right beside the beach with views of the Karikari Peninsula

2

from the broad deck where everyone gathers for sundowners and perhaps a BBQ. Accommodation is in fully self-contained units and there's free access to dinghies, kayaks and boogie boards. It's popular, so book well ahead. Free wi-fi. $285

Mangonui Hotel Waterfront Drive/Beach Rd, Mangonui ✆ 09 406 0003, ⓦ mangonuihotel.co.nz. Century-old, traditional hotel opposite the harbour with an upstairs veranda. Dorms, singles ($45) and en-suite doubles are cheerfully decorated in bright colours and those with harbour views go quickly, so book ahead or arrive early. Dorms $30, doubles $100

Puketiti Lodge 10 Puketiti Drive, 7km south of Mangonui ✆ 09 406 0369, ⓦ puketitilodge.co.nz. There's a rural feel to this modern lodge with three en-suite rooms, sleeping up to three, and a deluxe dorm all with long views to the coast. Everyone has access to the huge

deck and well-equipped kitchen and lounge. Dorm $40, rooms $150

KARIKARI PENINSULA

Maitai Bay Campground Maitai Bay Rd ⓦ doc.govt .nz. Northland's largest DOC campsite has cold showers, toilets and drinking water, as well as campervan access. DOC rangers service the site daily in the high season. Ideal for birdlife and wildlife watching. Camping $10

Whatuwhiwhi Top 10 Holiday Park Whatuwhiwhi Rd, 18km off SH10 ✆ 0800 142 444, ⓦ whatuwhiwhitop10.co.nz. Within easy walking distance of a picturesque bay and beach, this is a quiet, basic and traditional Kiwi campsite with a spa pool and good communal facilities. It gets very busy in the summer. Camping $31, cabins $85

EATING AND DRINKING

MATAURI BAY

Matauri Top Shop Top of Matauri Bay Rd ✆ 09 405 1040. A combined store and good-value café, this is the only place to stop for a bite in town, serving sandwiches, rolls and ice cream (nothing over $12), as well as offering a few supplies for you to make up a picnic, which might be preferable. Daily from 8am (9am public holidays) until it's not busy.

WHANGAROA HARBOUR

Whangaroa Big Gamefish Club ✆ 09 405 0399, ⓦ whangaroasportfishingclub.co.nz. Overlooking the yacht harbour, the café here serves adequate snacks and lunches (around $15) when the club bar upstairs opens. Both are pleasant enough, only ever crowded at the height of the summer or on Friday nights or Saturdays. Daily noon–8.30pm.

MANGONUI

Committed drinking mostly happens at the *Mangonui Hotel*, which often has bands at weekends.
The Bakerman 118 Waterfront Rd ✆ 09 406 1233.

A cheap and cheerful café offering breakfasts and lunches, burgers and fresh baked bread, with none of it costing over $20. Daily 7am–4pm.

Fresh & Tasty Inside the Mangonui Hotel, Waterfront Drive ✆ 09 406 0082. Rival chippy to neighbouring *Mangonui Fish Shop*, and much frequented by locals happy to trade location for lower prices (under $15), less waiting time and equally good tucker, plus roast dinners if you can't stand fish. Open daily 11am–8pm.

Mangonui Fish Shop 137 Waterfront Drive ✆ 09 406 0478. Famed fish and chip restaurant idyllically set on stilts over the water, and a regular afternoon stop for returning Cape Reinga buses. Expect fresh-cooked fish, buckets of chips and some more healthy seafood-oriented salads and seafood chowder (all under £21). Licensed and BYO. Daily 8.30am–9pm.

★ **Waterfront Café** Waterfront Drive ✆ 09 406 0850. Decent café/bar with harbour views, good coffee, breakfasts, light lunches, a wide range of dinner mains including fine pizzas, seared scallops and fresh oysters (mains $30–38). Occasional live music. Daily 8am–late.

NIGHTLIFE, ENTERTAINMENT AND SHOPPING

Bush Fairy Dairy 1195 Oruru Rd, Peria, 12km south of Taipa ✆ 09 408 5508. An authentic hippie-style commune that hosts Sunday bazaars every few weeks throughout the summer, complete with poetry readings and acoustic jam sessions around a bonfire. It's also brimming with art, crafts, clothing, organic produce, plus standard dairy items. Call ahead for dates and times.

Far North Wine Centre 60 Waterfront Drive, Mangonui ✆ 09 406 2485. You can sample – and purchase – wines from throughout Northland at this shop, which has a good selection and a knowledgeable staff.

Daily 11am–4pm, closed Sundays in the winter.

Flax Bush 50 Waterfront Drive, Mangonui ✆ 09 406 1510, ⓦ flaxbush.co.nz. Carries reasonably priced woven flax items and other locally made crafts; the deals on woven baskets (*kete*) are worth it. Mon–Sat 9.30am–4.30pm.

Swamp Palace Oruru Rd, 7km south of Taipa ✆ 09 408 7040. A quirky cinema located in the Oruru Community Hall. It caters to an eclectic mix of tastes – cult and classic movies, as well as the very latest releases. Call ahead for show times.

Kaitaia and around

KAITAIA, 40km west of Mangonui, is the Far North's largest commercial centre, situated near the junction of the two main routes north. It makes a convenient base for some of the best trips to Cape Reinga and Ninety Mile Beach (see p.185), far preferable to the longer trips from the Bay of Islands. As a farming service town you'd expect there'd be little to detain you, but these days Kaitaia boasts a rather fine museum, built in 2011. If you have your own transport, however, you might want to base yourself at the magnificent beach in nearby **Ahipara** (see below), to sand-toboggan the giant dunes, surf or explore the old gumfields.

2

Brief history

A Maori village already flourished at Kaitaia when the first missionary, Joseph Matthews, came looking for a site in 1832. The protection of the mission encouraged European pastoralists to establish themselves here, but by the 1880s they found themselves swamped by the gum diggers who had come to plunder the underground deposits around Lake Ohia and Ahipara. Many early arrivals were young Croats fleeing tough conditions in what was then part of the Austro-Hungarian Empire, though the only evidence of this is a Serbo-Croat welcome sign at the entrance to town, and a cultural society that holds a traditional dance each year.

Te Ahu Far North Regional Museum

Corner of Matthews Ave and South Rd • Mon–Fri 10am–4pm, Sat 10am–3pm • $4 • ☎ 0800 920 029, ⓦ teahuheritage.co.nz

The best place to gain a sense of the area is the recently extended **Te Ahu Far North Regional Museum**. The museum showcases the best of the extensive local archive including the massive anchor from the *De Surville*, wrecked in 1769, considered to be the first European object left in New Zealand. Look too for the copy of the twelfth- or thirteenth-century Kaitaia Carving (the original is in the Auckland Museum), a fine example of the transitional period during which Polynesian art began to take on Maori elements. The museum also houses temporary exhibitions, a cinema and the local i-SITE.

Ahipara

The southern end of Ninety Mile Beach finishes with a flourish at **AHIPARA**, 15km west of Kaitaia, a secluded scattered village that grew up around the Ahipara gumfields. A hundred kilometres of sand recede into sea spray to the north, while to the south the high flatlands of the Ahipara Plateau tumble to the sea in a cascade of golden dunes. Beach and plateau meet at **Shipwreck Bay**, a surf and swimming beach with an underground following with surfers for its long tubes (sometimes 400m or more). The bay is named after the 1870 wreck of the *Favourite*, its paddle-shaft still protruding from the sand. At low tide you can pick mussels off the volcanic rocks and follow the

---

KAITAIA FESTIVALS AND EVENTS

If you're in the area around the third weekend of March, you can catch competitors from around the world taking part in a series of running events on Ninety Mile Beach, including the **Te Houtaewa Challenge** (ⓦ tehoutaewachallenge.com), named after the tale of a great Maori athlete. The races are preceded by the **Te Houtaewa Waka Ama Surf Challenge**, a series of six-man outrigger *waka* races at Ahipara, and the five-day **Kai Maori Food Festival** and **Te Houtaewa Arts & Crafts Festival**, both held in Kaitaia. Around the same time, the **Snapper Classic** (ⓦ snapperclassic.co.nz) is among the world's biggest **surfcasting** competitions, with a $30,000 prize for the largest snapper.

wave-cut platform around a series of bays for about 5km to the dunes – about an hour's walk – although most do it by quad bike or mountain bike.

The gumfields

On a sandy dune plateau to the south of town

At their peak in the early twentieth century, the now barren **gumfields** supported three hotels and two thousand people. Unlike most gumfields, where experimental probing and digging was the norm, here the soil was methodically excavated, washed and sieved to extract the valuable **kauri gum** (see box, p.194). None of the dwellings remain on the plateau, and the gumfields are an eerie, desolately beautiful spot.

ARRIVAL AND DEPARTURE

By bus The daily InterCity/Northliner bus service pulls up behind the Te Ahu Centre on the corner of South Rd and Matthews Ave.

Destinations Kerikeri (1 daily; 1hr 40min); Paihia

(1 daily; 2hr 15min).

By plane Kaitaia's airport is 9km north of town, near Awanui, and is serviced by taxi shuttle ☏ 09 408 0116.

Destinations Auckland (1–4 daily; 40min).

INFORMATION

Tourist information i-SITE are at the corner of Matthews Ave and South Rd, in the Te Ahu Centre, Kaitaia (daily 8.30am–5pm; ☏ 09 408 9450, ⓦ northlandnz.com). The office – one of three for the Far North region of Northland

– stocks DOC leaflets such as *Kaitaia Area Walks* and *Cape Reinga and Te Paki Walks*, sells bus tickets, rents sand toboggans ($10/day), and has internet access.

ACCOMMODATION

Outside the post-Christmas peak, rooms are plentiful and prices are generally lower than at the coastal resorts to the east. Ahipara is a more appealing place to stay than Kaitaia, though there is little public transport (just a local bus to and from Kaitaia), supermarket or bank here.

KAITAIA

Loredo 25 North Rd ☏ 0800 456 733, ⓦ loredomotel

.co.nz. Clean, well-maintained and ever-popular motel 1km north of the town centre with a pool, spa and

---

AHIPARA TOURS AND ACTIVITIES

The **dunes** and **gumfields** are best approached on foot or via a guided quad bike tour. There have been access problems of late across Shipwreck Beach, due to disagreements between operators and the local *iwi*; check with the tour guides listed below for the latest information.

WALKS

Foreshore Road Walk (500m; 10min return) A short but worthwhile walk on a track that begins at the end of Foreshore Road. It takes you to the western end of the beach to a lookout giving spectacular views all the way to Cape Reinga.

Gumfields Walk (12km loop; free maps and tide times from the Ahipara Adventure

Centre and Kaitaia i-SITE) Keen hikers might fancy tackling a 6hr section of this tide-dependent walk, which begins at the bridge at Shipwreck Bay and takes you into an eerie and desolate landscape of wind-sculpted dunes before heading back along the beach. Let someone know where you're going and take plenty of water.

TOUR OPERATORS

Tua Tua Tours ☏ 0800 494 288, ⓦ ahipara.co.nz /tuatuatours. Runs a variety of quad biking tours around the gumfields and dunes, including the chance to try sand-boarding. From $100.

Ahipara Adventure Centre 15 Takahe St ☏ 09 409 2055, ⓦ ahiparaadventure.co.nz. Rents single-rider quad bikes ($95/hr; $150/2hr) heading north of the

settlement along the beach. They also rent surfboards ($30/half-day) and kayaks ($25/hr), and blo-karts for use on the beach ($45/30min).

Ahipara Horse Treks Foreshore Rd ☏ 09 409 4122 or ☏ 027 333 8645. Saddle up for two-hour rides ($60) along the beaches and across some of the local farmland.

barbecue area, run by an ageing biker couple and boasting some simple but comfortable units. $120

★**Mainstreet Lodge** 235 Commerce St ☎09 408 1275, ⓦmainstreetlodge.co.nz. A welcoming, well-equipped and deceptively large hostel that's alive with folk headed for the Cape (tours pick up from the hostel). The doubles are spacious and there are a number of dorm rooms. You can also do half-day bone-carving sessions here. Dorms $27, rooms $72

Waters Edge 25b Kitchener St ☎09 408 0870, ⓦwatersedgebandbkaitaia.co.nz. An attractive B&B – owned by the last lighthouse keeper at Cape Reinga – in a modern suburban house with lush gardens, a pool and cosy rooms. You can have dinner, too, by prior arrangement. $120

AHIPARA

Ahipara Bay Motel 22 Reef View Rd ☎09 408 2010, ⓦahiparabaymotel.co.nz. A choice of pleasant older motel units, or six excellent luxury versions with tremendous sea and beach views. There's a decent on-site

restaurant – useful if you arrive late or on Sunday. $110

★**Ahipara Holiday Park** 164 Takahe St ☎09 409 4864, ⓦahiparaholidaypark.co.nz. The area's best camping option, just 300m from the sea, offering YHA discounts across the accommodation range, which includes good-value cabins, en-suite doubles and well-equipped self-contained cabins. Camping $21, cabins $70

Beach Abode 11 Korora St ☎09 409 4070, ⓦbeachabode.co.nz. The three well-appointed (and serviced) beachfront apartments here each come with free wi-fi, full kitchen, BBQ, deck, great sea views and a private path to the sand. Not recommended for children. Apartments $145

★**Endless Summer Lodge** 245 Foreshore Rd ☎09 409 4181, ⓦendlesssummer.co.nz. Well-managed hostel in an atmospheric 1880 timber homestead with kauri floors, right across the road from the beach; choose from comfortable doubles, twins or two four-bed dorms. There's also a BBQ, free boogie boards, and surfboard rental; surfing instruction can be arranged. Bookings by phone only. Dorms $28, rooms $66

EATING AND DRINKING

KAITAIA

★**Beachcomber** 222 Commerce St ☎09 408 2010, ⓦbeachcomber.net.nz. Probably Kaitaia's best restaurant, serving a fairly standard range of meat and fish dishes (lunches $19; dinner mains from $28), which all come with a visit to the salad bar. Try the prawn, chilli and lemon pasta or the lamb rump with roasted garlic and herbs. Mon–Fri from 11am, Sat from 5pm.

★**Birdie's** 14 Commerce St ☎09 408 4935. Fantastic old-school café with inventive modern touches, which is open for breakfast until 3.30pm and serves up huge portions of hearty Kiwi food at modest prices (mains $15–25), including some rib-sticking chilli beef nachos and good eggs Benedict. Daily 8am–3.30pm & from 6pm–late in the summer.

AHIPARA

Bayview Restaurant and Bar Ahipara Bay Motel, 22 Reef View Rd ☎09 408 2010, ⓦahiparabaymotel.co.nz. Decent (for these parts) licensed restaurant that benefits from sea views and serves traditional dishes, including seafood chowder ($12.50), lamb rump with mint sauce ($26.50) and fish of the day ($25). Daily 11.30am–11pm.

Gumdiggers Café Takahe Rd ☎09 409 2012. Café and takeaway, serving good coffee, cakes and snacks, as well as some truly mammoth breakfasts. All the food is $22 and under. Daily 7am–2pm; opens in the evening from Christmas–Feb.

Ninety Mile Beach and Cape Reinga

Northland's exclamation mark is the **Aupori Peninsula**, a narrow, 100km-long finger of consolidated and grassed-over dunes ending in a lumpy knot of 60-million-year-old marine volcanoes. To Maori it's known as Te Hika o te Ika ("The tail of the fish"), recalling the legend of Maui hauling up the North Island ("the fish") from the sea while in his canoe (the South Island).

The most northerly accessible point is **Cape Reinga**, where the spirits of Maori dead depart this world. Beginning their journey by sliding down the roots of an 800-year-old pohutukawa into the ocean, they climb out again on Ohaua, the highest of the Three Kings Islands, to bid a final farewell before returning to their ancestors in Hawaiiki. The spirits reach Cape Reinga along **Ninety Mile Beach** (actually 64 miles long), which runs straight along the western side of the peninsula. Most visitors follow the spirits, though they do so in modern buses specifically designed for belting along

2

GOING IT ALONE ON NINETY MILE BEACH

Rental cars and private vehicles are not insured to drive on Ninety Mile Beach and for good reason. Vehicles frequently get bogged in the sand and abandoned by their occupants. As there are no rescue facilities near enough to get you out before the tide comes in, and mobile phone coverage is almost nil, you could end up with a long walk. Even in your own vehicle, **two-wheel-drives** aren't recommended, regardless of weather conditions, which can change rapidly.

If you are determined to take your own vehicle for the 70km spin along the beach, seek local advice and prepare your car by spraying some form of water repellent on the ignition system – CRC is a common brand. Schedule your trip to coincide with a receding tide, starting two hours after high water and preferably going in the same direction as the bus traffic that day; drive on dry but firm sand, avoiding any soft patches, and keep your speed down. The main reason for this is the gutters and streamlets running over the beach, which pop up out of nowhere; they might look fairly insignificant but their banks can be surprisingly steep – you definitely don't want to negotiate one at high speed. Slow down too when turning on sand, otherwise your front wheels can dig in to any unexpectedly soft patches, flipping the vehicle over. Another hazard is pedestrians, should you encounter any, who won't be able to hear you coming from behind against the noise of the surf (even if it's far away); give them a wide berth. If you get stuck in a soft drift at any stage, don't sit there revving the engine – all that will happen is your rapidly spinning wheels will dig the car down into the sand. The first thing to do is to stop, then attempt to reverse out slowly in low range; if this doesn't work you need to dig out behind each wheel to make a ramp and try again. If you still have no luck, then deflate tyres to about 10psi, which will give the vehicle far more traction, and try once more. Don't forget to pump your tyres up again as soon as you are off the beach, as they can easily overheat or simply slip off the wheel on solid roads.

There are several access points along the beach, but the only ones realistically available to ordinary vehicles are the two used by the tour buses: the southern access point at **Waipapakauri Ramp**, 6km north of Awanui, and the more dangerous northern one along **Te Paki Stream**, which involves negotiating the quicksands of a river – start in low gear and don't stop, no matter how tempting it might be to ponder the dunes.

---

the hard-packed sand at the edge of the surf – officially part of the state highway system – then negotiating the quicksands of Te Paki Stream to return to the road; for many, the highlight is **sandboarding** on a boogie board (or in a safer but less speedy toboggan) down the huge dunes that flank the stream. The main road runs more or less down the centre of the peninsula, while the western ocean is kept tantalizingly out of sight by the thin pine ribbon of the **Aupori Forest**. The forests, and the **cattle farms** that cover most of the rest of the peninsula, were once the preserve of gum diggers, who worked the area intensively early last century.

Awanui

The eastern and western roads around Northland meet at **AWANUI**, 8km north of Kaitaia, Maori for "Big River" – though all you'll find is a bend in a narrow tidal creek that makes a relaxing setting for the daytime *Big River Café*, serving a range of light meals.

Ancient Kauri Kingdom

229 SH 1F, 1km north of Awanui • Daily 8.30am–5.30pm; later in summer • Free • ☏ 09 406 7172, ⓦ ancientkauri.co.nz

Almost all buses to Cape Reinga stop at the **Ancient Kauri Kingdom**, a defunct dairy factory now operating as a sawmill, cutting and shaping huge peat-preserved kauri logs hauled out of swamps where they have lain for around 45,000 years. You can watch slabs of wood being fashioned into bowls, sculptures and breadboards but the emphasis is on the shop. Be sure to climb up to the mezzanine on the spiral staircase hewn out of the centre of the largest piece of swamp kauri trunk ever unearthed, a monster 3.5m in diameter.

Gumdiggers Park Ancient Buried Kauri Forest

171 Heath Rd, 3km off SH1 • Daily summer 9am–5pm • $12 • ☎ 09 406 7166, ⓦ gumdiggerspark.co.nz

The delightfully low-key **Gumdiggers Park Ancient Buried Kauri Forest** is the pick of the local attractions. It features an easy thirty-minute nature trail through shady manuka forest and includes a gum diggers' camp, holes that have been excavated to show the methods used for gum digging, huts illustrating the living conditions and a small kauri gum collection. There's a longer trail through the bush with information boards speculating on what knocked over the two giant kauri forests thousands of years ago: tidal wave, meteor or earthquake. Be sure to check out the monstrous section of a kauri dating back 100,000 years. The main southern entrance to Ninety Mile Beach, the **Waipapakauri Ramp**, is just south of the park's turn-off.

Houhora and Pukenui

The Aupori Peninsula's two largest settlements, 30km north of Awanui, are scattered **HOUHORA** and the working fishing village of **PUKENUI**, 2km to the south, where good catches are to be had off the wharf. At Houhora, a 3km side road turns east to **Houhora Heads**. A further 10km north is the turn-off for Rarawa Beach, home to a great DOC campsite (see p.189).

Te Kao

The Maori Ngati Kuri people own much of the land and comprise the bulk of the population in these parts, particularly around **TE KAO**, 20km north of Houhora. Beside SH1, you'll spot the twin-towered Ratana Temple – one of the few remaining houses of the Ratana religion, which combines Christian teachings with elements of Maori culture and spiritual belief.

Parengarenga Harbour

12km north of Te Kao on SH1, then follow the Paua Rd

Straggling **Parengarenga Harbour** was the drop-off point for the limpet mines (delivered by yacht from New Caledonia) that were used in the 1985 sabotage of the *Rainbow Warrior*. Bends in the road occasionally reveal glimpses of the harbour's southern headland. In late February and early March, hundreds of thousands of bar-tailed godwits turn the silica sands black as they gather for their 12,000km journey to Siberia. Insect repellent is a must here.

Waitiki Landing to Spirits Bay

The last place of any consequence before the land sinks into the ocean is **WAITIKI LANDING**, 21km from Cape Reinga. If you are heading to Spirits Bay this is your last chance to buy petrol and milk. From Waitiki Landing a dirt road twists 15km to the gorgeous and usually deserted 7km sweep of **Spirits Bay** (Kapowairua), where you'll find a DOC campsite (see p.189).

Te Paki

The main road (SH1) continues towards Cape Reinga. After 4km you pass a turn-off to the **Te Paki Stream entrance** to Ninety Mile Beach, where there's a small picnic area and

2

CAPE REINGA WALKS

A couple of worthwhile short **walks** radiate from the Cape Reinga car park: both form part of the much longer Cape Reinga Coastal Walkway. All are described in the DOC leaflet *Cape Reinga and Te Paki Walks*, containing a useful map of the area, and are available at Kaitaia and elsewhere. Beware of **rip tides** on all the beaches hereabouts and bear in mind the wild and unpredictable nature of the region's weather. Arrange with one of the more local bus tours (see opposite) for pick-up.

Cape Reinga Coastal Walkway (38km one way; 2 days; constantly undulating). This spectacular and increasingly popular coastal hike starts at Kapowairua (Spirits Bay), heads west to Cape Reinga, continues to Cape Maria van Diemen, swings southeast to the northernmost stretch of Ninety Mile Beach, and then finally past the impressive dunes of Te Paki Stream. You need to be fit and self-sufficient: the only facilities are a couple of DOC campsites, and some ad hoc camping spots with no guaranteed water.

Fresh water from streams is limited and you'll need mosquito repellent.
Sandy Bay (3km return; 200m ascent on the way back; 50–90min). Eastbound walk through scrub and young cabbage trees to a pretty cove. You can continue to the lovely Tapotupotu Bay (a further 3km one way; 1–2hr).
Te Werahi Beach (2.5km return; 200m ascent on the way back; 40min–1hr). A gradually descending westbound walk that keeps Cape Maria van Diemen in your sights as you go.

---

parking, plus a twenty-minute **hike** to huge sand dunes ideal for **sandboarding** or **tobogganing**. Equipment can be rented at several places from Kaitaia northwards; and also by calling ahead to Ahikaa Adventures (☎09 409 8228, ⓦahikaa-adventures.co .nz), who often rent boards from the Te Paki road end, right by the dunes.

Cape Reinga

The last leg to **Cape Reinga** (Te Rerenga Wairua: the "leaping place of the spirits") runs high through the hills before revealing magnificent views of the Tasman Sea and the huge dunes that foreshadow it. At road-end there's just a car park with toilets and a 800m-long interpretive trail to the Cape Reinga **lighthouse**, dramatically perched on a headland 165m above Colombia Bank, where the waves of the Tasman Sea meet the swirling currents of the Pacific Ocean in a boiling cauldron of surf. On clear days the **view** from here is stunning: east to the Surville Cliffs of North Cape, west to Cape Maria van Diemen, and north to the rocky **Three Kings Islands**, 57km offshore, which were named by Abel Tasman, who first came upon them on the eve of Epiphany 1643.

GETTING AROUND   NINETY MILE BEACH AND CAPE REINGA

You can explore **Ninety Mile Beach** and **Cape Reinga** independently if you have your own vehicle. If you don't, then the best way to see the region is on one of the many tours listed below.

By plane The best (and easiest) way to experience the phenomenal length of Ninety Mile Beach and the wild beauty of Cape Reinga is to take the Salt Air plane trip (see p.171).

By bus Bus tours all make a loop up the Aupori Peninsula, travelling SH1 in one direction and Ninety Mile Beach in the other, the order being dictated by the tide. Trips start from Kaitaia, Mangonui and Paihia in the Bay of Islands. Those from Paihia are the most numerous but far too long (11hr), most leaving daily at around 7.30am. They go via Kerikeri, Mangonui and Awanui in one direction and pass Kaitaia and the kauri trees of the Puketi Forest in the other, with pick-ups along the way, but there is little time for sightseeing. Tours starting further north give you less time in the bus and more for exploring.

By 4WD A few operators offer a somewhat more personalized experience than bus trips, via tours in 4WD vehicles, usually for anywhere from two to six people.

By car You can drive yourself along Ninety Mile Beach, although doing so is fraught with potential difficulties (see box, p.186).

TOURS

FROM KAITAIA AND AHIPARA

Far North Outback Adventures Kaitaia ☎ 09 408 0927, ⊛ farnorthtours.co.nz. Exclusive 4WD custom tours (8hr; $650 for up to two passengers; $700 for three to six passengers) that include morning tea and lunch. They go off the beaten track, taking in the white sands of Great Exhibition Bay to explore flora, fauna and archeological sites.

Harrisons Cape Runner Kaitaia ☎ 09 408 1033, ⊛ ahipara.co.nz/caperunner. Bargain, basic coach tour (8hr; $50) including the Cape, beach, Kaitaia pick-up and a light lunch.

Sand Safaris Kaitaia ☎ 0800 869 090, ⊛ sandsafaris .co.nz. Good-value tour (8hr; $50) that's similar to Harrisons but with Ahipara pick-ups (extra $5) and a Maori welcome. A light lunch is included.

FROM PAIHIA

Awesome NZ ☎ 0800 653 339, ⊛ awesomenz.com. Cape bus trip ($124) aimed at those with an adventurous spirit, with maximum sandboarding time. The cost of a lunch stop at Mangonui for fish and chips comes out of your own pocket.

Dune Rider ☎ 09 402 8681, ⊛ explorenz.co.nz. Upscale Cape and beach trips ($150) in a comfortable high-clearance bus with just 36 reclining seats. Included in the cost are a stop at and guided tour of Gumdiggers Park, plus a lunch.

Salt Air ☎ 0800 475 582, ⊛ saltair.co.nz. Fly to the Cape, landing at Waitiki, then cover the last section to Cape Reinga by 4WD ($425). Includes refreshments at Tapotupotu Bay and sandboarding, as well as a flight across the Bay of Islands.

INFORMATION

Tourist information The Far North region's i-SITE offices are in Paihia (see p.166), Kaitaia (see p.184) and, if you're coming via Hokianga, in Opononi (see p.192). They should be able to answer all your questions, including those pertaining to Ninety Mile Beach and Cape Reinga.

Services As with the rest of rural Northland, there is a paucity of facilities here. You can refuel at Houhora; petrol isn't always available in Waitiki.

ACCOMMODATION

There's sporadic accommodation along the Aupori Peninsula, ranging from some beautifully sited DOC campsites to motels, lodges and hostels. Most are reasonably priced, reflecting the fact that many visitors pass through without stopping; however, all are very busy immediately after Christmas.

PUKENUI

Rarawa Beach Campsite 10km north of Pukenui, down a signposted side road ⊛ doc.govt.nz. The pure white silica sand at this shady, streamside DOC campsite is beautiful, and a great place for birdwatching and swimming in the lagoon – although abundant mosquitoes temper its paradisiacal appeal. Amenities include running water, toilets and cold showers. No bookings: first come, first served. $\overline{\underline{\$6}}$

★**Wagener Holiday Park** 3km south of Pukenui, off SH1 ☎ 09 409 8511, ⊛ wagenerholidaypark .co.nz. A beautifully located, traditional, council-run campsite with great-value accommodation under canvas or in cabins, all nestled among tall trees with great views of the sea and just 500m from the Houhora Wharf. Camping $\overline{\underline{\$20}}$, cabin $\overline{\underline{\$58}}$

SPIRITS BAY

Kapowairua (Spirits Bay) campsite Spirits Bay Rd, 16km from Waitiki Landing ⊛ doc.govt.nz. A simple DOC site with pitches in manuka woods, and campervan access. It has cold showers, running water and toilets, and is also ideal for fishing, swimming and walking. $\overline{\underline{\$6}}$

CAPE REINGA

Tapotupotu Bay campsite Tapotupotu Rd, 3km south of Cape Reinga ⊛ doc.govt.nz. A serene DOC site with toilets, cold showers, running water and lots of mosquitoes in the summer. It's beautifully sited where the beach meets the estuary and is a popular lunchtime picnic stop for tour buses. $\overline{\underline{\$6}}$

EATING

Houhora Tavern Saleyard Ave, just off SH1, Pukenui ☎ 09 409 8805, ⊛ houhoratavern.co.nz. New Zealand's northernmost pub, dating from the 1800s, with lawns beside the harbour and great views, as well as one room with stuffed fish beside a saltwater aquarium. Basic meals that come with chips for the most part, fish and-, burger and-, as well as home-made pies and sausage rolls and decent coffee, all for under $25. Daily 9am–11pm, meals 9am–4pm & 5–8pm.

★**Pukenui Pacific Bar and Café** 816 Far North Rd (SH1), Pukenui ☎ 09 409 8816. Diners are often defeated by the huge burger known as PukuNui (Maori for "big stomach") at this good-value café/bar, the only takeaway north of Kaitaia (mains $10–25). Daily 7am–9pm.

Hokianga Harbour

South of Kaitaia, the narrow, mangrove-flanked fissures of the **Hokianga Harbour** snake deep inland past tiny and almost moribund communities. For a few days' relaxation, the tranquillity and easy pace of this rural backwater are hard to beat. From the southern shores, the harbour's incredible, deep-blue waters beautifully set off the mountainous **sand dunes** of North Head. The dunes are best seen from the rocky promontory of South Head, high above the treacherous Hokianga Bar, or can be reached by boat for sandboarding or the fantastic Sandtrails Hokianga tours. The high forest ranges immediately to the south make excellent hiking territory, and the giant kauri of the Waipoua Forest are within easy striking distance.

Note that there are **no banks** between Kaitaia and Dargaville, 170km away to the south. The ATMs in Rawene and Omapere accept a limited range of cards so bring cash.

Brief history

According to legend, it was from here that the great Polynesian explorer **Kupe** left Aotearoa to go back to his homeland in Hawaiiki during the tenth century, and the harbour thus became known as Hokianganui-a-Kupe, "the place of Kupe's great return". Cook saw the Hokianga Heads from the *Endeavour* in 1770 but didn't realize what lay beyond, and it wasn't until a missionary crossed the hill from the Bay of Islands in 1819 that Europeans became aware of the harbour's existence. Catholics, Anglicans and Wesleyans soon followed, converting the local Ngapuhi, gaining their trust, intermarrying with them and establishing the well-integrated Maori and European communities that exist today. The Hokianga area soon rivalled the Bay of Islands in importance and notched up several firsts: European boat building began here in 1826; the first signal station opened two years later; and the first Catholic Mass was celebrated in the same year.

With the demise of kauri felling and milling (see p.194), Hokianga became an economic backwater, but over the last couple of decades, city dwellers, artists and craftspeople have started creeping in, settling in **Kohukohu** on the north shore, **Rawene**, a short ferry ride away to the south, and the two larger but still small-time settlements of **Opononi** and **Omapere**, opposite the dunes near the harbour entrance. Note though, that this is still the sort of place where businesses close at 7pm, taking your chance of a cooked meal with them.

Kohukohu

Heading south from Kaitaia, the hilly SH1 twists its way through the forested Mangamuka Ranges for 40km to reach **Mangamuka Bridge** from where an equally tortuous road heads to **KOHUKOHU**, a waterside cluster of century-old wooden houses on the northernmost arm of Hokianga Harbour. Kohukohu was once the hub of Hokianga's kauri industry, but the subsequent years of decline have only partly been arrested by the recent influx of rat-race refugees.

Village Arts Gallery

1376 Kohukohu Rd • Daily 10am–4pm • Free • ✆ 09 405 5827, Ⓦ villagearts.co.nz

Check out the community-run **Village Arts Gallery**, which promotes Hokianga's artistic community, with exhibitions of sculpture, painting, photography, steampunk models and textiles at a much higher standard than you might expect for such a backwater.

Four kilometres further east, Narrows Landing is the northern terminus of the **Hokianga Vehicle Ferry** (see p.192).

Rawene and around

Delightfully situated **RAWENE** occupies the tip of Herd's Point, a peninsula roughly halfway up the harbour. Though almost isolated by the mudflats at low tide, Rawene's strategic position made it an obvious choice for the location of a timber mill, which contributed material for the town's attractive wooden buildings, some perched on stilts out over the water.

Clendon House

Clendon Esplanade • Nov–April Sat & Sun 10am–4pm; May–Oct Sun 10am–4pm; more extensive hours during school holidays • $10

2

Clendon House is Rawene's only significant distraction, and was the last residence of British-born US Consul James Clendon, a pivotal figure in the early life of the colony. Starting life as a ship-owner transporting convicts to Australia, Clendon settled in New Zealand, befriended local Maori and was instrumental in the negotiations which culminated in the Treaty of Waitangi. The house itself is mostly pit-sawn kauri construction. Downstairs, one room beside the veranda has been retained as the post office it once was.

Clendon Esplanade leads to the **Mangrove Walkway**, a pleasant fifteen-minute return boardwalk through the coastal shallows with boards telling of intertidal life and the sawmill, which once operated here.

Wairere Boulders

70 McDonnell Rd, signposted 14km north off SH12; 40km northeast of Rawene • Daily during daylight hours • $15 • ☏ 09 401 9935, ⓦ wairereboulders.co.nz

Wairere Boulders is a privately run park encompassing huge 2.8-million-year-old basalt rocks with natural fluting that makes them appear like carved corrugated iron. The main self-guided loop (40min) follows a narrow path weaving among boulders and across a stream with signs turning it into a kind of nature trail. There are several additional loops plus a spur trail leading through the rainforested valley and up to a good viewpoint. Wairere is a bit out of the way, so bring supplies and make an afternoon of it.

Opononi and Omapere

The two small villages of **OPONONI** and **OMAPERE**, 20km west of Rawene, comprise little more than a roadside string of houses running seamlessly for 4km along the southern shore of the Hokianga Harbour, with great views across to the massive sand dunes on the north side. If you decide to break your journey in this area it will be because you want to explore the dunes, either on foot or by beach buggy (see p.192), or by viewing them from afar; the Arai te Uru Reserve is a wonderful viewpoint reached along Signal Station Road, 1km south of Omapere. The only other reason to stop in either settlement is to hook up with a guided tour of the Kauri forests to the south (p.193).

OPONONI THE DOLPHIN

If you didn't know about Opononi's moment of fame in the summer of 1955–56 when a wild bottlenose dolphin, dubbed "Opo", started playing with the kids in the shallows and performing tricks with beach balls, you will by the time you leave.

Christmas holiday-makers jammed the narrow dirt roads; film crews were dispatched; protective laws drafted; and Auckland musicians wrote and recorded the novelty song *Opo The Crazy Dolphin* in a day. Their tape arrived at the radio station for its first airing just as news came in that Opo had been shot under mysterious circumstances. The i-SITE shows a short video in classic 1950s-documentary style, which gives a sense of the frenzied enthusiasm for Opo.

Waiotemarama Bush Walk

647 Waiotemarama Gorge Rd, 8km southeast of Opononi • 2km loop

Labyrinth Woodworks (see p.193) marks the start of the **Waiotemarama Bush Walk**, the best and most popular of the short walks in the district, running through a lovely fern-, palm- and kauri-filled valley. A ten-minute walk leads you to a waterfall with a small swimming hole, and after a further ten minutes you reach the first kauri.

2

GETTING AROUND   HOKIANGA HARBOUR

By bus To properly explore the Hokianga and Waipoua region you will need your own vehicle, though Northliner Express (wnorthliner.co.nz) do run some services through here.

By ferry Apart from a lengthy drive around the head of the harbour, the only way around the Hokianga is on the Hokianga Vehicle Ferry (car and driver $20 one way;

campervan and driver $40; car passengers and pedestrians $2 each way), which shuttles from Narrows Landing, 4km east of Kohukohu on the northern shores, to Rawene in the south, a journey of 15min. Departures (around 7am–8pm) are on the hour southbound and on the half-hour northbound.

INFORMATION

Tourist information i-SITE are at 29 SH12, just outside Opononi (daily: Nov–April 8.30am–5pm; May–Oct 9am–5pm; **t** 09 405 8869, w hokianga.co.nz). The office

— one of three for the Far North region of Northland — has information for the Hokianga area and Waipoua Forest (see p.195), can book accommodation, and has internet access.

ACCOMMODATION

KOHUKOHU

★ **The Tree House** 168 West Coast Rd, 2km west of the car ferry terminus **t** 09 405 5855, w treehouse.co.nz. Accommodation is scattered among the trees in two spacious dorms, double and twin cabins with sundecks ($88) and a well-equipped house bus in a macadamia orchard. There's also a self-contained cottage in Kohukohu

itself, sleeping five. Bedding is provided, towels are $3 to hire. Camping $20, dorms $32

RAWENE

Rawene Holiday Park 1 Marmon St, 1.5km from the ferry landing **t** 09 405 7720, w raweneholidaypark .co.nz. A low-key site with hilltop harbour views,

---

OPONONI AND OMAPERE TOURS AND ACTIVITIES

Motoring over the magnificent sand dunes in a beach buggy on a cultural, historic and adventure tour is one way to spend time hereabouts, but you may also find yourself hurtling down the dunes on a plastic tray, trying desperately to stop before you hit the water. Alternatively, try your hand at Maori-style bone carving or visit the nearby kauri trees.

CRAFTS

Hokianga Bone Carving Studio 15 Ahika St, Omapere **t** 09 405 8061, **e** hokiangabonecarving studio@gmail.com. Spend an entertaining and fruitful day making a Maori bone carving with Maori

carver, Jim Taranaki. Book ahead, have a design in mind and be prepared to spend as much of the day as you need to complete your carving: you'll be well fed while you're at it.

TOUR OPERATORS

Hokianga Express **t** 09 405 8872 or **t** 021 405 872, w hokiangaexpress.webs.com. Operating from 10am daily, this charter service ($25) leaves from Opononi wharf and will drop you off at the dunes with sandboards (after a modicum of instruction) and pick you up a couple of hours later.

Footprints Waipoua 334 SH12, Omapere **t** 09 405 8207, w footprintswaipoua.co.nz. Runs excellent guided walks to the kauri trees in Waipoua Forest

(see p.195). The pick of the tours is the four-hour Twilight Encounter ($95) through the forest to the two largest trees. You might see giant kauri snails, eels and ruru (native owl), but the emphasis is more on listening to and sensing the forest under the cover of darkness leavened with a strong Maori spiritual component – story, song and music. They pick up from accommodation in Opononi and Omapere.

sheltered areas for tents and good-value, spacious, well-kept cabins in bush enclaves. The views from the swimming pool and shared kitchen are fabulous, especially at sunset. Camping $\overline{\$16}$, cabins $\overline{\$40}$

OPONONI AND OMAPERE

Copthorne Hotel & Resort SH12, Omapere ☎09 405 8737, ⓦ**milleniumhotels.co.nz**. The best of the hotels in town, set opposite the dunes, with a solar-heated pool, nice bar and licensed restaurant and a range of accommodation including some beautifully appointed waterside rooms with all the usual big hotel touches. $\overline{\$240}$

★**Globetrekkers Lodge** SH12, Omapere ☎09 405 8183, ⓦ**globetrekkerslodge.com**. Relaxing and very well-kept hostel with some harbour views. The five- and six-bed dorms and doubles are all spacious and airy. TV is intentionally absent and the evening BBQ usually brings everyone together. Dorms $\overline{\$29}$, doubles $\overline{\$67}$

★**Hokianga Haven** 226 SH12, Omapere ☎09 405 8285, ⓦ**hokiangahaven.co.nz**. The owner only takes single-party bookings for her two attractively furnished beachside B&B rooms with private bathrooms, opposite the harbour entrance with fabulous views of the dunes and the sea. Two-night minimum. $\overline{\$180}$

McKenzie's Accommodation 4 Pioneers Walk, Omapere ☎09 405 8068, ⓦ**mckenziesaccommodation .co.nz**. Excellent beachside options in either a spacious room rented as a B&B double or a twin, with a separate bathroom and private entrance, or the self-contained two-bedroom cottage rented as accommodation only. Room $\overline{\$120}$, cottage $\overline{\$110}$

Opononi Beach Holiday Park SH12, Opononi ☎09 405 8791, ⓦ**opononibeachholidaypark.co.nz**. Spacious, very basic harbour-side campsite with facilities for laundry and a camp kitchen. You're better off with the self-contained cabins unless you're in a campervan. Camping $\overline{\$17}$, cabins $\overline{\$60}$

EATING AND DRINKING

KOHUKOHU

The Koke Pub 1372 Kohukohu Rd ☎09 405 5808. The best place to eat in town serves up a friendly welcome, not to mention tasty breakfasts, snacks and lunches. It also has great coffee, pork loin roast dinners and local seafood. Live music every Thursday. Food served Sun–Wed 8am–8pm, Thurs–Sat 8am–late. Pub open daily 11am–late.

RAWENE

★**Boatshed Café** 8 Clendon Esplanade ☎09 405 7728. A daytime, licensed establishment built out over the water, offering magazines to read on the sunny deck as you tuck into gourmet pizza slices or home-made muffins and soups, and espresso from just $5. Daily 8.30am–4.30pm.

OPONONI AND OMAPERE

Copthorne Hotel & Resort SH12, Omapere ☎09 405 8737, ⓦ**milleniumhotels.co.nz**. The best dining

hereabouts, in both the elegant *Bryers Room* restaurant (mains around $40) and the *House Bar Bistro* (mains around $30). Both have great views over the lawns and harbour to the sand dunes. Look out for dishes with a Maori influence, such as local seafood or *rawena* bread and butter pudding with *titoki* liqueur. Daily 8am–late.

Opononi Hotel SH12, Opononi ☎09 405 8858, ⓦ**opononihotel.com**. Lively pub offering good-value eating, both bar food and à la carte. Try the surf and turf ($29.50). Regular Kiwi touring bands stop by in summer when 1200-odd people can crowd in. Daily 11am–11pm.

Opo Takeaways SH12, Opononi. Known locally as the best fish and chip takeaway, it also serves generous, well-stuffed burgers, mussel and *paua* fritters, battered sausages and other deep-fried delights. Fish is usually $4–6 a piece, depending on type. Daily 10am–7pm, until 9pm in summer.

SHOPPING

Hoki Smoki Signposted on SH12 1km south of Omapere. An excellent fish and seafood smokery – drop in and buy some to take on the road with you or for a picnic. It's only open for business if the sign is out.

Labyrinth Woodworks 647 Waiotemarama Gorge Rd, 8km southeast of Opononi ☎09 405 4581, ⓦ**nzanity .co.nz**. One of the region's better craft shops, with wares

including carved kauri pieces and excellent woodblock prints. Pride of place, however, goes to the mind-bending puzzles in the puzzle museum, which include the smallest puzzles in the world, and a maturing hedge maze with an anagram problem that stumps many a visitor – it's great fun. Daily 9am–5pm.

The kauri forests and around

Northland, Auckland and the Coromandel Peninsula were once covered in mixed forest dominated by the mighty kauri (see box, p.194), the world's second-largest

2

THE KAURI AND ITS USES

The **kauri** (*agathis australis*) ranks alongside the sequoias of California as one of the largest trees in existence. Unlike the sequoias, which are useless as furniture timber, kauri produce beautiful wood, a fact that hastened its demise and spawned the industries that dominated New Zealand's economy in the latter half of the nineteenth century.

The kauri is a type of pine that now grows only in New Zealand, though it once also grew in Australia and Southeast Asia, where it still has close relations. Identifiable remains of kauri forests are found all over New Zealand, but by the time humans arrived on the scene its range had contracted to Northland, Auckland, the Coromandel Peninsula and northern Waikato. Individual trees can live over two thousand years, reaching 50m in height and 20m in girth, finally toppling over as the rotting core becomes too weak to support its immense weight.

KAURI LOGGERS

Maori have long used mature kauri for dugout canoes, but it was the "rickers" (young trees) that first drew the attention of **European loggers** since they formed perfect spars for sailing ships. The bigger trees soon earned an unmatched reputation for their durable, easy-to-work and blemish-free wood, with its straight, fine grain. Loggers' ingenuity was taxed to the limit by the difficulty of getting such huge logs out of the bush. On easier terrain, bullock wagons with up to twelve teams were lashed together to haul the logs onto primitive roads or tramways. Horse-turned winches were used on steeper ground and, where water could be deployed to transport the timber, dams were constructed from hewn logs. In narrow valleys and gullies all over Northland and the Coromandel, loggers constructed kauri dams up to 20m high and 60m across, with trapdoors at the base. Trees along the sides of the valley were felled while the dam was filling, then the dam was opened to flush the floating trunks down the valley to inlets where the logs were rafted up and towed to the mills.

GUM DIGGERS

Once an area had been logged, the **gum diggers** typically moved in. Like most pines, kauri exudes a thick resin to cover any scars inflicted on it, and huge accretions form on the sides of trunks and in globules around the base. Maori chewed the gum, made torches from it to attract fish at night and burned the powdered resin to form a pigment used for *moko* (traditional tattoos). Once Pakeha got in on the act, it was exported as a raw material for furniture varnishes, linoleum, denture moulds and the "gilt" edging on books. When it could no longer be found on the ground, diggers – mostly Dalmatian, but also Maori, Chinese and Malaysian – thrust long poles into the earth and hooked out pieces with bent rods; elsewhere, the ground was dug up and sluiced to recover the gum. Almost all New Zealand gum was exported, but by the early twentieth century synthetic resins had captured the gum market. Kauri gum is still considered one of the finest varnishes for musical instruments, and occasional accidental finds supply such specialist needs.

THE FUTURE

In recent years the kauri have been further threatened by a new disease known as PTA or **kauri dieback** (W kauridieback.co.nz) with symptoms including yellowed leaves, dead branches and resinous lesions close to the ground, eventually leading to the tree's death. The disease is transmitted through soil and water, so always keep to the tracks and boardwalks and clean your footwear after visiting a kauri forest.

tree. By the early twentieth century, rapacious Europeans had nearly felled the lot, the only extensive pockets remaining in the **Waipoua and Trounson kauri forests** south of the Hokianga Harbour. Though small stands of kauri can be found all over Northland, three-quarters of all the surviving mature trees grow in these two small forests, which between them cover barely a hundred square kilometres. Walks provide access to the more celebrated examples, which dwarf the surrounding tataire, kohekohe and towai trees.

Just south of the Trounson forest are the **Kai Iwi Lakes**, a trio of popular dune lakes that get busy in the summer season.

Brief history

This area is home to the Te Roroa people who traditionally used the kauri sparingly. Simple tools made felling and working these huge trees a difficult task, and one reserved for major projects such as large war canoes. Once the Europeans arrived with metal tools, bullock trains, wheels and winches, clear felling became easier, and most of the trees had gone by the end of the nineteenth century. The efforts of several campaigning organizations eventually bore fruit in 1952, when much of the remaining forest was designated the Waipoua Sanctuary. It's now illegal to fell a kauri except in specified circumstances, such as culling a diseased or dying tree, or when constructing a new ceremonial canoe.

Waipoua Kauri Forest

SH12, 15km south of Omapere

Heading south from the Hokianga Harbour area, you pass through farmland and arrive at Waimamaku. The highway then twists and turns through nearly 20km of mature kauri in the **Waipoua Kauri Forest**. Eight kilometres south of Waimamaku you reach a small car park, from where it's a three-minute walk to New Zealand's mightiest tree, the (estimated) 2500-year-old **Tane Mahuta**, "God of the Forest". A vast wall of bark 6m wide rises nearly 18m to the lowest branches, covered in epiphytes. A kilometre or so further south on SH12, a ten-minute track leads to a clearing where three paths split off to notable trees: the shortest (5min return) runs to the **Four Sisters**, relatively slender kauri all growing close together; a second path (30min return) winds among numerous big trees to **Te Matua Ngahere**, the "Father of the Forest", the second-largest tree in New Zealand – shorter than Tane Mahuta but fatter and in some ways more impressive. The third path, the **Yakas Track** (3km return; 1hr), leads to Cathedral Grove, a dense conglomeration of trees, the largest being the **Yakas Kauri**, named after veteran bushman Nicholas Yakas.

Trounson Kauri Park

Signposted off SH12, 7km down an unsealed side road

Trounson Kauri Park is a small but superb stand of kauri where the **Trounson Kauri Walk** (40min loop) weaves though lovely rainforest. In 1997, Trounson was turned into a "mainland island" in order to foster North Island brown kiwi survival. Numbers are up significantly, and you've a good chance of seeing them – along with weta and glowworms – if you stay over. A **tour** of the kauri stands is easy enough to do on your own, but *Kauri Coast Top 10 Holiday Park* offers a guided night walk (see p.196).

Kai Iwi Lakes

11km west off SH12, 20km south of Trounson

The **Kai Iwi Lakes** are a real change, with pine woods running down to fresh, crystal-blue waters fringed by silica-white sand. All three are dune lakes fed by rainwater and with no visible outlet. Though the largest, **Taharoa**, is less than 1km across, and **Waikere** and **Kai Iwi** are barely 100m long, they constitute the deepest and some of the largest dune lakes in the country. People flock here in the summer to swim, fish and waterski, but outside the first weeks in January you can usually find a quiet spot. Shallow and consequently warmer than the sea, they're good for an early-season dip.

2

INFORMATION

Tourist inforamtion Te Roroa Waipoua Visitor Centre (SH12, 9km south of Tane Mahuta; daily 8.30am–4.30pm) has displays and information on the Waipoua Kauri Forest and its past.

ACCOMMODATION AND EATING

WAIPOUA KAURI FOREST

Kaihu Farm Hostel 3344 SH12, Kaihu, 23km south of the visitor centre ☎09 439 4004. The budget accommodation here – in clean, homey and cosy rooms – is appealingly rural, and really more of a farm stay than a hostel. There are glowworms in the surrounding bush, and it's also just an atmospheric 7km tree-lined walk from the magnificent Trounson kauris (see p.195) or a 10min drive from the beach. Dorms $23, rooms $56

Morrell's Café 7235 SH12, Waimamaku ☎09 405 4545. The best café in the area cooks up all-day breakfasts (under $25), light meals such as gourmet burgers, wraps and salads (all under $12), mussel chowder ($10) and excellent coffee. Daily 9am–4pm.

TROUNSON KAURI PARK

★ **Kauri Coast Top 10 Holiday Park** Trounson Park Rd, off SH12 ☎09 439 0621, ⓦkauricoasttop10 .co.nz. A traditional Kiwi campsite with tidy communal areas, clean toilets and showers and well-tended campsites. There are also small but adequate basic cabins (add $10 for a kitchen) and roomy motel units. You can join the site's two-hour guided night walk ($25, non-guests $30) which explores the kauri forest. Camping $21, cabins $85

Trounson Kauri Park Campground Signposted off SH12, 17km south of Waipoua Forest. A simple but popular DOC campsite with sites by a small stand of kauri, and equipped with kitchen, toilets, tap water and hot showers. No bookings: first come, first served. $10

KAI IWI LAKES

Kai Iwi Lakes ☎09 439 4757. Comprised of two locally run sites: the *Pine Beach* site on the gently shelving shores of Taharoa Lake, with running water, toilets and cold showers; and the intimate but primitive *Promenade Point* site, with just long-drop toilets. An attendant shows up once a day in the summer. Pay your fee to the honesty box. Camping $12, campervans $20

SHOPPING

Katui Kauri Gum Store SH12, 9km south of the Te Roroa Waipoua Visitor Centre ☎09 439 4733. This charmingly eccentric shop provides a little welcome relief from the rigours of the road, offering cheap bits of kauri gum, carved kauri gum, polished gum and wood with gum inlays, all at rather reasonable prices. Daily 8.30am–late.

The northern Kaipara Harbour

South of the kauri forests are the muddy, mangrove-choked shores of the **Kaipara Harbour**, New Zealand's largest. The harbour once unified this quarter of Northland, with sailboats plying its waters and linking the dairy farming and logging towns on its shores. Kauri was shipped out from the largest northern town, **Dargaville**, though the fragile boats all too often foundered on the unpredictable Kaipara Bar. Many eventually washed up on **Ripiro Beach**, which just pips Ninety Mile Beach to the title of New Zealand's longest, running for 108km.

Dargaville and around

The sleepy dairying and *kumara*-growing town of **DARGAVILLE**, 30km south of Kai Iwi Lakes, was founded as a port in 1872, on the strongly tidal but navigable Northern Wairoa River, by Australian Joseph McMullen Dargaville. Ships came to load kauri logs and transport gum (see box, p.194) extracted by Dalmatian settlers who, by the early part of the twentieth century, formed a sizeable portion of the community.

Dargaville Museum

Harding Park, 2km west of town • Daily: Oct–March 9am–5pm; April–Sept 9am–4pm • $15 • ☎09 439 7555, ⓦ dargavillemuseum.co.nz

Two masts rescued from the *Rainbow Warrior* (see box, p.178) mark the surprisingly good **Dargaville Museum**. It contains extensive displays of artefacts recovered from the shifting dunes, which occasionally reveal old shipwrecks. The only pre-European artefact is the Ngati Whatua *waka*, which lay buried under the sands of the North Head of the Kaipara Harbour from 1809 until 1972, and is a rare example of a canoe hewn entirely with stone tools. A fine collection of kauri gum gives pride of place to an 84kg piece – reputedly the largest ever found – and there is an ancient heated oil Blackstone engine-powered gum washer that they occasionally run to the delight of visitors.

Woodturners Kauri Gallery & Working Studio

4 Murdoch St (SH12) • Daily 9am–dark • ☏ 09 439 4975, ⓦ thewoodturnersstudio.co.nz

At the western end of town, at the **Woodturners Kauri Gallery & Working Studio**, leading woodturner Rick Taylor demonstrates what can be done with the extraordinarily varied grains and colours of kauri, sells all manner of kauri products, and runs courses for those prepared to dedicate a day or more.

Baylys Beach and Ripiro Beach

14km west of Dargaville, along a minor road

BAYLYS BEACH is a conglomeration of mostly holiday homes on a central section of 100km-long **Ripiro Beach**, a strand renowned for its mobility, with several metres of beach often being shifted by a single tide, and huge areas being reclaimed over the centuries; the anchors or prows of long-lost wrecks periodically reappear through the sand. As elsewhere on the West Coast, tidal rips and holes make swimming dangerous and there are no beach patrols. Beach driving is no less fraught with danger and shouldn't be undertaken without prior local consultation; vehicles frequently get stranded. Nevertheless, it's a fine place for long walks, and spotting **seals** and **penguins** in winter. When easterlies are blowing the coastline is adorned with kites, flown out from the shore and drawing fishing lines for anything up to 1km. They're left for twenty minutes or so then hauled in, often heavy with fish.

ARRIVAL AND DEPARTURE
DARGAVILLE AND AROUND

There is no longer a bus service to Dargaville so you will need your own transport.

INFORMATION AND TOURS

Tourist information There is no official tourist office in Dargaville, but stop in at Woodturners Kauri Gallery & Working Studio (see above) for advice.

The Kumara Box 503 Pouto Rd, just south of Dargaville ☏ 09 439 7018, ⓦ kumarabox.co.nz. Low-key tours of a *kumara* farm, in the heart of *kumara*-growing country, would seem like a bit of a spud, but these are so full of charm, enthusiasm and ingenuity

that you cannot fail to be captivated. A *kumara* train takes you past the smallest church in Northland, and through a variety of minor hazards before depositing you in a barn where you see the home-made video about *kumara* and the area. It's all great fun and you won't be reaching for the *kumara* vodka, though you might get home-made *kumara* soup or a *kumara* muffin before you leave.

ACCOMMODATION

★ **Baylys Beach Holiday Park** 22 Seaview Rd, Baylys Beach ☏ 09 439 6349, ⓦ baylysbeach.co.nz. A well-run and tidy park with charming *bach*-style cabins just a short walk from the beach, good camping, clean cabins and some spacious units. You can rent quad bikes for a gentle putter up the beach to see the wind-crafted sand sculptures, and lines of burned kauri captured in sand banks. Camping $16, cabins $65

★ **Commercial Hotel** 75 River Rd, Dargaville ☏ 09 439

0878, ⓦ commercialhotel.co.nz. Recently renovated former colonial-style hotel that is now a very comfortable homestay overlooking the river. Accommodation is spacious, with polished kauri floors and large windows, though many rooms share bathrooms. They whip up good breakfasts and have lots of local knowledge. Shared bathroom $85, en suite $135

Dargaville Holiday Park 10 Onslow St, Dargaville ☏ 0800 114 441, ⓦ dargavilleholiday.co.nz. A large traditional Kiwi campsite set in park-like grounds a 10min walk from town, with well-kept but simple cabins and comfortable units. There's lots to keep the kids happy, too, including the large community swimming pool right next door. Camping **$21**, cabins **$55**

Greenhouse Hostel 15 Gordon St, Dargaville ☎ 09 439 6342, ⊜ greenhousebackpackers@ihug.co.nz. Centrally located in a 1920s former school, this hostel is old-fashioned but clean and well run, with simple rooms,

great-value doubles, bedding and a communal kitchen. Closed May–Aug. Dorms (no bunks) **$28**, doubles **$70**

★ **Kauri House Lodge** 60 Bowen St, Dargaville ☎ 09 439 8082, ⓦ kaurihouselodge.co.nz. Dargaville's grandest accommodation option is contained within an engagingly low-key yet vast and magnificent kauri villa. The large rooms are all en-suite, and there's a billiard room, library and swimming pool. Free wi-fi. **$250**

EATING AND DRINKING

★ **Blah Blah Blah** 101 Victoria St, Dargaville ☎ 09 439 6300. A licensed café specializing in dishes featuring Dargaville's famed *kumara*; try the *kumara* and mussel chowder ($15). They also serve tasty coffee and a selection of home-made cakes, plus great breakfasts. Tues–Sat 9am–late; kitchen closes at 9pm.

Shiraz 17 Hokianga Rd, Dargaville ☎ 09 439 0024, ⓦ shiraz-nz.co.nz. Restaurant and takeaway specializing in north Indian dishes, seafood and pizza – not a combination forged in heaven but there isn't much in the way of competition in town so it can get quite busy. The curries are pretty fair and there is nothing on the menu

more than $25. Try the tandoori or the Amritsari fish, but give the pizza a miss. Mon–Sat 8am–3pm.

★ **The Funky Fish** 34 Seaview Rd, Baylys Beach ☎ 09 439 8883, ⓦ thefunkyfish.co.nz. Modern café and bar where you'll find great fish and chips, a speciality beer-battered dory with chargrilled lemon and salad, plus a range of burgers, baguettes and a varied à la carte evening menu. Prices range from $10–35. The great garden bar is the icing on the cake. Reserve for dinner in summer and for Sun lunch year-round. Summer Wed–Sun 11am–late; Winter Tues & Wed 5pm–late, Thurs–Sun 11am–late.

Tokatoka Peak

SH12, 17km southwest of Dargaville

SH12 zips through flat farmland before reaching the knobby 180m **Tokatoka Peak**. Panoramic views unfold from the summit of this extinct volcanic plug, reached in ten breathless minutes from a trailhead 1km off SH12 near the *Tokatoka* pub.

Matakohe and the Kauri Museum

30km south of Tokatoka Peak, on SH12 • Kauri Museum • Church Rd • Daily 9am–5pm • $25 • ☎ 09 431 7417, ⓦ kaurimuseum.com

If there's one museum you must see in the north it's the **Kauri Museum** at tiny **MATAKOHE**. One of the best museums in the country, and deserving at least three hours, it explains the way the kauri's timber and its valuable gum shaped the lives of pioneers in Northland. The displays focus on the makeshift settlements around logging camps, the gumfields, and the lives of merchants who were among the few who could afford to buy the fine kauri furniture or beautifully carved gum on show. Diagrams show how even Tane Mahuta is a midget compared to the giants of yore, and the smell of the freshly sawn timber lures you to the replica steam sawmill. There is also a stunning collection of kauri furniture, boats and gum (in the basement), and plenty more to keep you occupied for an afternoon.

ACCOMMODATION AND EATING   MATAKOHE

Gumdiggers Café Church Rd, opposite the museum ☎ 09 431 7075. Owned by the museum, the café makes a welcoming spot to rest before, during and after your meanderings round the galleries. Daytime food includes gumdiggers' pasties, excellent wraps, pies, burgers, sandwiches, chips and cakes, all freshly made or cooked to order, with nothing over $20. Daily 8.30am–5pm.

Matakohe Holiday Park ☎ 0800 431 6431,

ⓦ matakoheholidaypark.co.nz. A well-kept small hillside campsite 500m beyond the museum offering great harbour views and a broad range of accommodation including decent well-spaced camping, cabins and comfortable motel units. Camping **$19**, cabins **$65**

★ **Petite Provence** 703c Tinopai Rd, 9km south of Matakohe ☎ 09 431 7552, ⓦ petiteprovence.co.nz. A lovely Kiwi-French-run B&B amid rolling farmland with views of the Kaipara Harbour. Rooms are nicely decorated and comfortable, and wonderfully tasty evening meals ($45, BYO wine) are available. The host also makes beautiful, handcrafted metal and wood furniture, featured in some rooms, which is stunningly comfortable and quite captivating. **$160**

2

Western North Island

MOUNT TARANAKI (EGMONT) AND DAIRY COWS

Western North Island

The western North Island is wetter than the east, the prevailing westerlies dropping rain on a land that's lush with remote bush and plains given over to dairy cattle. Moisture erodes gorgeous limestone caverns around Waitomo, falls as snow on the high peak of Taranaki, and works its way to the sea through roadless tracts along the Whanganui River. The region's waterways empty into the Tasman Sea where huge rollers and magical surf have sculpted a coastline of rugged headlands and sea stacks. Much of the region's appeal is tied to its extraordinary history: it was on the west coast, at Kawhia, that the Tainui people first landed in New Zealand; the canoe in which they arrived is buried here, and the waterside tree it was moored to lives on. Kawhia was also the birthplace of Te Rauparaha, the great Maori chief who led his people down the coast to Kapiti Island and on to the South Island, to escape the better-armed tribes of the Waikato.

Approaching the region from the north, the farming country of the **Waikato** centres on the workaday provincial capital, **Hamilton**, which won't detain you long, but has enough to soak up a couple of days' exploration in the immediate vicinity. The nearby surfers' paradise of **Raglan** has world-class waves as well as some great places to stay, eat or just unwind. Southeast of Hamilton on SH1, there's a genteel English charm to **Cambridge**, while at Matamata, **Hobbiton** tours are an essential stop for *Lord of the Rings* and *The Hobbit* film fans.

South of the Waikato, the highlight is **Waitomo**, where fabulous adventure trips explore otherwordly glowworm-filled limestone caverns. The adjacent **King Country** took its name from the King Movement (see p.217), and was the last significant area in New Zealand to succumb to European colonization. Further south, the giant thumbprint peninsula of **Taranaki** is dominated by the symmetrical cone of **Mount Taranaki**, within the **Egmont National Park**. At its foot, **New Plymouth** warrants a visit for its excellent contemporary art gallery and access to a multitude of **surf beaches**.

Inland from Egmont National Park, the farming town of **Taumarunui** is one of the main jumping-off points for multi-day canoe trips along the **Whanganui River**, through the heart of the verdant **Whanganui National Park**. The river bisects **Wanganui**, a small, gracious and creative city whose river-port past can be relived on a restored paddle steamer. Some 60km to the southeast, the university city of **Palmerston North** lies at the

Highlights

❶ Raglan Surf New Zealand's finest waves, kayak around the harbour or just soak up the laidback atmosphere of this hypnotic harbourside town. **See p.212**

❷ Waitomo Abseil, squeeze or blackwater raft into labyrinthine caves on some of the world's best adventure caving trips, often illuminated by a glittering canopy of glowworms. **See p.218**

❸ Egmont National Park Scale the conical summit of the North Island's second-highest peak, Mount Taranaki, or get great views of the mountain from the less committing Pouakai Circuit. **See p.232**

❹ Forgotten World Highway Take the slow road through pristine countryside and get your passport stamped at the self-declared village republic of Whangamomona. **See p.239**

❺ Whanganui River Spend three chilled days far from roads, canoeing through verdant canyons and tackling the gentle rapids of the country's longest navigable river. **See p.240**

❻ Kapiti Island Marvel at what birdsong in the Aotearoa bush used to be like on this pest-free island full of rare native birds. Go for the day or stay overnight to go kiwi spotting. **See p.256**

HIGHLIGHTS ARE MARKED ON THE MAP ON P.204

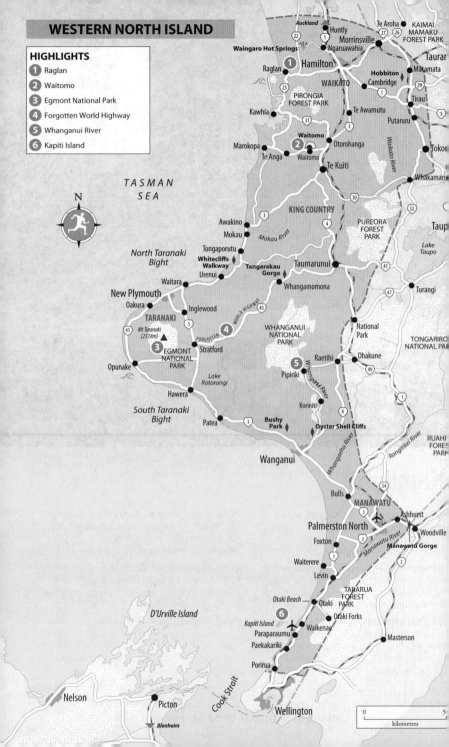

WESTERN NORTH ISLAND

HIGHLIGHTS
1. Raglan
2. Waitomo
3. Egmont National Park
4. Forgotten World Highway
5. Whanganui River
6. Kapiti Island

TASMAN SEA

N

North Taranaki Bight

New Plymouth
Oakura
TARANAKI
Mt Taranaki (2518m)
EGMONT NATIONAL PARK
Opunake
Hawera
South Taranaki Bight
Patea
Bushy Park
Oyster Shell Cliffs

Waitara
Inglewood
Stratford
Lake Rotorangi

Waingaro Hot Springs
Auckland
Huntly
Morrinsville
Ngaruawahia
Raglan
Hamilton
WAIKATO
Hobbiton
Cambridge
PIRONGIA FOREST PARK
Te Awamutu
Kawhia
Te Aroha
KAIMAI MAMAKU FOREST PARK
Taurar
Matamata
Tirau
Putaruru
Tokor
Whakamaru

Marokopa
Te Anga
Waitomo
Otorohanga
Te Kuiti
Waikato River

KING COUNTRY
Awakino
Mokau
Mokau River
Tongaporutu
Whitecliffs Walkway
Urenui
Tangarakau Gorge
Taumarunui
PUREORA FOREST PARK
Taup
Lake Taupo

Whangamomona
WORLD HIGHWAY
FORGOTTEN
WHANGANUI NATIONAL PARK
National Park
TONGARIRO NATIONAL PA
Turangi

Raetihi
Ohakune
Pipiriki
Whanganui River
Koriniti
Wanganui
Whangaehu River
Rangitikei River
RUAHI FORES PARK

Bulls
MANAWATU
Ashhurst
Palmerston North
Woodville
Foxton
Manawatu River
Manawatu Gorge
Waiterere
Levin
TARARUA FOREST PARK

Otaki Beach
Otaki
Otaki Forks
Kapiti Island
Waikanae
Paraparaumu
Paekakariki
Masterton
Porirua

D'Urville Island

Nelson
Picton
Blenheim
Cook Strait
Wellington

0   5
kilometres

centre of the rich farming region of **Manawatu**. A cluster of rural communities lines the highway south to the **Kapiti Coast**, where laidback beachside **Paraparaumu** is the launch point for boat trips to the paradisiacal bird sanctuary of **Kapiti Island**.

GETTING AROUND

By train The main Auckland–Wellington rail line runs partly through the region, with a single service in each direction (Oct–April daily; May–Sept Fri, Sat & Sun only). Frequent commuter rail services also run between Wellington and Waikanae.

By bus Most long-haul bus services are run by InterCity/Newmans/Great Sights and NakedBus (who use a number of local operators).

Hamilton

On the banks of the languid green Waikato River, New Zealand's fourth-largest city, **HAMILTON**, functions as a regional hub rather than a major tourist destination, but it's within striking distance of some of the North Island's top spots, such as the surf beaches of Raglan and Waitomo Caves, as well as Auckland, 127km north. There's not much to detain you in town but it is worth devoting some time to the excellent **Waikato Museum** and the tranquil **Hamilton Gardens**, and, during term-time at least, there's a reasonable nightlife thanks to the city's university. Consider also making time for tea at **Zealong Tea Estate**.

3

In mid-June, the annual four-day **Fieldays festival** (ⓦ fieldays.co.nz) is held at Mystery Creek Events Centre just outside the city. The largest agricultural field day in the southern hemisphere, it's a quintessentially Kiwi event with everything from sheep shearing to ploughing contests plus lots of entertainment, mostly with a rural tenor.

Victoria Street

Everything of interest in Hamilton is either along or just off the main drag, **Victoria Street**, which parallels the west bank of the tree-lined Waikato River. One of the more striking buildings is the 1924 **Wesley Chambers** (now *Hamilton City Oaks* hotel) on the corner of Collingwood Street, influenced by the buildings of boomtime Chicago. Diagonally opposite, a small open space is graced by a statue of the English-born *Rocky Horror Show* creator, **Richard O'Brien** – decked out as Riff Raff, the role he played in the film of the show – who spent his teens and early twenties in Hamilton watching science-fiction double features.

Waikato Museum

1 Grantham St · Daily 10am–4.30pm · Free · ☏ 07 838 6606, ⓦ waikatomuseum.co.nz

Set in a modern building that steps down to the river, the excellent **Waikato Museum** takes an imaginative approach to local history but really excels with its section devoted to **Tainui culture**, much of it curated by the local Maori community. Of course there are tools, ritual artefacts, woven flax and carvings, but the displays give a real sense of the living culture of the four main Tainui subtribes along with insights into tribal leaders, and there's frequently changing art. The magnificent *Te Winika* war canoe is housed beside a window where you can look out over the river at the mouldering hulk of the paddle steamer *Rangiriri*, which worked the river in early colonial times.

Hamilton Gardens

Cobham Drive (SH1), 4km southeast of the city centre · Gardens daily 7.30am–dusk; visitor centre daily 9am–5pm · Free · ☏ 07 838 6782, ⓦ hamiltongardens.co.nz · Bus #10 (#17 on Sat & Sun) from the Transport Centre

From Memorial Park, a riverside path follows the bends in the river to the huge, unfenced **Hamilton Gardens**, with extensive displays of roses, tropical plants, rhododendrons, magnolias and cacti.

Pick up a free map from the gardens' visitor centre then duck next door to the inner sanctum of the **Paradise Gardens Collection**, six beautiful enclosures each planted in a different style from around the world. Wander through an uninspiring archway to be dazzled by the stunning colours of the Indian Char Bagh Garden, stroll and smell the

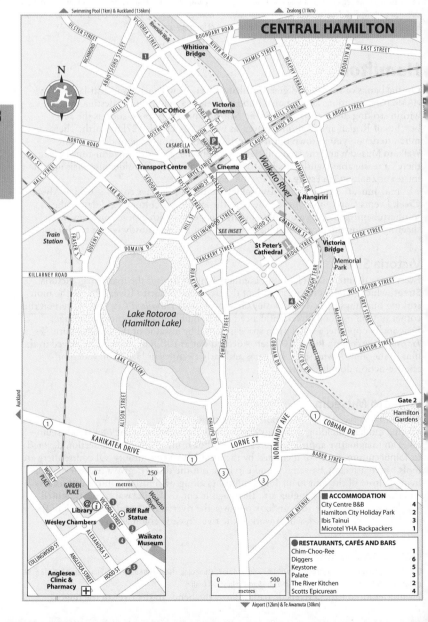

CENTRAL HAMILTON

Swimming Pool (1km) & Auckland (136km)

Zealong (11km)

Whitiora Bridge

Victoria Cinema

DOC Office

Transport Centre

Cinema

Rangiriri

Train Station

St Peter's Cathedral

Victoria Bridge

Memorial Park

Lake Rotoroa (Hamilton Lake)

Gate 2
Hamilton Gardens

KAHIKATEA DRIVE

LORNE ST

Airport (12km) & Te Awamutu (30km)

GARDEN PLACE

Library

Riff Raff Statue

Wesley Chambers

Waikato Museum

Anglesea Clinic & Pharmacy

■ ACCOMMODATION	
City Centre B&B	4
Hamilton City Holiday Park	2
Ibis Tainui	3
Microtel YHA Backpackers	1

● RESTAURANTS, CAFÉS AND BARS	
Chim-Choo-Ree	1
Diggers	6
Keystone	5
Palate	3
The River Kitchen	2
Scotts Epicurean	4

flowers in the English Garden and take in the idealized Chinese Scholar's Garden, complete with red pavillion where you can sit and catch a view of the Waikato River. A surprise highlight is the American Modernist Garden, with aloe-and-grass mass plantings around a shallow pool, ringed with bright yellow loungers and a huge Marilyn Monroe screenprint.

The rest of the gardens are also well worth a stroll – even packing a picnic. The **Rose Garden** is especially popular, featuring a wide range of different colours and cultivars, arranged to tell the story of the development of the modern rose, including some of the latest hybrids.

Zealong

495 Gordonton Rd, 13km north of the city centre • Tours Tues–Sun 9.30am & 2.30pm; Camellia Teahouse Tues–Sun 10am–5pm • Tours $18 (bookings essential); tea with as many infusions as you wish $8; signature tea $39 for one • ☏ 07 853 3018, ⓦ zealong.com

The flat, low-lying sheep and cattle country of the northern Waikato seems an unlikely place to find rows of neatly tended *Camellia sinensis*, but in the late 1990s Taiwanese immigrant Vincent Chen pioneered growing tea in New Zealand – and very fine it is, too. They concentrate on **oolong tea** (partly fermented, somewhere between green and black tea), best experienced as part of the **90-minute guided tour**, which involves a video explaining the history and process, a walk among the tea plants and an elaborate tea ceremony.

Alternatively, just drop in to the fabulous *Camellia Teahouse* for a leisurely (and informative) tea or settle in for the signature high tea ($39) with delicious savouries and exquisite cakes. They also serve lunches and individual cakes.

ARRIVAL AND DEPARTURE · HAMILTON

By plane Hamilton's airport is 15km south of town. Super Shuttle (☏ 0800 748 885) does the run to and from there from $23 each way.

Destinations Auckland (3 daily; 30min); Christchurch (2 daily; 1hr 45min).

By train The station is on Fraser St in the suburb of Frankton, almost 2km west of the city centre. Bus #3 runs to the Transport Centre in town, where you can also buy train tickets.

Destinations Auckland (3–7 weekly; 2hr 30min); Wellington (3–7 weekly; 9hr 30min).

By bus The Transport Centre, 373 Anglesea St (Mon–Thurs 7am–6pm, Fri 7am–7pm, Sat 9am–4.30pm, Sun 9am–4pm), is the hub for local and long-haul buses and has left-luggage lockers ($4). An office here sells tickets for InterCity and NakedBus.

Destinations Auckland (16–19 daily; 2hr); Cambridge (12 daily; 30min); Matamata (4 daily; 1hr); New Plymouth (4 daily; 4hr); Ngaruawahia (14–16 daily; 15min); Otorohanga (5 daily; 1hr); Paeroa (2 daily; 1hr 30min); Raglan (2–3 daily; 1hr); Rotorua (8 daily; 1hr 45min); Taupo (6 daily; 2–3hr); Tauranga (4 daily; 1hr 45min); Te Aroha (3 daily; 1hr); Te Awamutu (8 daily; 30min); Te Kuiti (4 daily; 1hr–1hr 50min); Thames (2 daily; 1hr 45min); Tirau (11 daily; 35–55min); Wanganui (2 daily; 6–8hr); Wellington (7 daily; 9hr).

GETTING AROUND

By bus Busit (☏ 0800 428 75463, ⓦ busit.co.nz) run services around town and to Cambridge, Te Awamutu, Raglan and Paeroa from the Transport Centre. Pick up the free timetable there or at the i-SITE. One-way fares within the city limits are $3.10 including free transfers for two hours.

By taxi There's a taxi rank at the Transport Centre, or call Hamilton Taxis on ☏ 0800 477 477.

INFORMATION

Visitor information i-SITE is at 5 Garden Place (Mon–Fri 9am–5pm, Sat & Sun 9.30am–3.30pm; ☏ 07 958 5960, ⓦ visithamilton.co.nz).

DOC Level 5, 73 Rostrevor St (Mon–Fri 8.30am–4.30pm; ☏ 07 858 1000, ⓦ doc.govt.nz). Come here for hiking information and hut passes.

Services Free wi-fi around Garden Place and free computers (and wi-fi) in the Central Library, 9 Garden Place (Mon–Fri 9.30am–8pm, Sat 9am–4pm, Sun noon–3.30pm; ☏ 07 838 6826).

ACCOMMODATION

Hamilton specializes in business accommodation for farm company reps in motels, mostly lining Ulster St, but there are also several B&Bs and hostels.

City Centre B&B 3 Anglesea St ☎07 838 1671, ⓦcitycentrebnb.co.nz. There's a relaxed homey feel to the two spacious and good-value rooms with kitchenettes, both opening out to a courtyard garden with swimming pool. Generous breakfast ingredients are supplied, and extra nights are cheaper. $165

Hamilton City Holiday Park 14 Ruakura Rd ☎07 855 8255, ⓦhamiltoncityholidaypark.co.nz. Well-tended grassy campsite amid mature trees 2km east of the centre with a full range of cabins and units. Bedding extra. Camping $19, cabins $48

Ibis Tainui 18 Alma St ☎07 859 9200, ⓦibishotel .com/hamilton. Smart eight-storey hotel with river views from many rooms and the restaurant terrace. Rooms are fairly high standard considering the rates, which are modest, especially at weekends. $89

Microtel YHA Backpackers 140 Ulster St ☎07 957 1848, ⓦmicrotel.co.nz. Compact and contemporary urban associate YHA with Sky TV in its private rooms (some of which are en-suite) and plenty of singles. Mixed dorms $29, doubles $69

EATING AND DRINKING

The city's food and drink scene is concentrated along the southern end of Victoria Street and around the corner on Hood Street, where places start off as cafés and become restaurants/bars as the day wears on. Hamilton's sizeable student population ensures lively term-time nightlife – *Digger's* is the place of choice.

Chim-Choo-Ree 14 Bridge St ☎07 839 4329, ⓦchimchooree.co.nz. A bare concrete floor and a cluster of 1930s and 1940s lampshades greet you at this bustling bistro where bentwood chairs hang on the walls until needed. Nip in for a glass or two of wine or tuck into entrees such as roast tuna tartare with miso mayo ($19) and mains like snapper with pomme purée ($37). Alternatively, settle in for the five-course tasting menu ($85; $115 with wine). Mon–Fri 11.30am–2pm & 5pm–late, Sat 5pm–late.

Diggers 17 Hood St ☎07 834 2228 ⓦdiggersbar.co.nz. Down-to-earth drinkers' den (that also serves pizzas) with a long kauri bar and live music most nights, though it is liveliest at weekends when there's a great atmosphere. Tues–Sun 3–10pm or later.

Keystone 150 Victoria St ☎07 839 4294, ⓦkeystonebar.co.nz. Hamilton's only Monteith's craft bar serves a wide range of beers as well as a menu of pub grub-style meals such as hanger steak ($16) and meatballs ($14). Daily 11.30am–midnight.

Palate 20 Alma St ☎07 834 2921, ⓦpalaterestaurant.co.nz. Hamilton's finest dining, done in a relaxed but professional style by people who really know what they're doing. Try the pork belly, seared scallop and apple salad ($19), followed by wagyu ravioli with beetroot purée on dauphinoise potatoes ($35). Mon–Sat 6–11pm.

The River Kitchen 237 Victoria St ☎07 839 2906. Sit in the window that opens out onto the street and try the breakfast of Spanish beans with smoked ham hock and poached eggs ($17.50) or some of the superb sandwiches and salads from the cabinet. They make a fine coffee, too. Mon–Fri 7am–4pm, Sat 8am–4pm, Sun 8am–3pm.

★**Scotts Epicurean** 181 Victoria St ☎07 839 6680, ⓦscottsepicurean.co.nz. Bustling daytime café/restaurant with stacks of inviting sandwiches, cakes and muffins in the cabinet, great coffee and beautifully presented breakfasts, brunches and lunches such as *kumara* cakes with sour-cream dressing ($14). Mon–Fri 7am–3pm, Sat & Sun 8.30am–4pm.

ENTERTAINMENT

Victoria Cinema 690 Victoria St ☎07 838 3036, ⓦnzcinema.co.nz. Screens the latest and best in art-house films.

Around Hamilton

As the hub for the region, Hamilton makes a good base for exploring the Waikato region and its cluster of modest sights. Heading south from Auckland, the first place of real interest is the important Maori town of **Ngaruawahia**, though if you are headed for Raglan you may skip Ngaruawahia and follow the back roads past **Waingaro Hot Springs**. Art-lovers will want to nip east to the **Wallace Gallery** while Hobbit fans shouldn't miss **Hobbiton**, on the outskirts of Matamata. Southeast of Hamilton, Cambridge and Tirau are really just waystations on the route to Taupo, while to the south, **Te Awamutu** celebrates its Maori, Pakeha and Finn brothers heritage.

Waingaro Hot Springs

Waingaro Rd, 40km northwest of Hamilton • Daily 9am–9.30pm • $11; hot-water slide extra $6 for all day • ☎ 07 825 4761, ⓦ waingarohotsprings.co.nz

If you're working your way on the back roads between Auckland and Raglan consider stopping off at the old-fashioned (some might say dated) **Waingaro Hot Springs**, which offer a real slice of Kiwi family life with three hot-water pools and New Zealand's longest open hot-water slide.

Ngaruawahia

The Waikato and Waipa rivers meet at the historically and culturally significant farming town of **NGARUAWAHIA**, 18km northwest of Hamilton on SH1. Both rivers were important Maori canoe routes and the **King Movement** (see p.217) has its roots here. Home to the Maori king, the town was the scene of the signing of the Raupatu Land Settlement (1995), whereby the government agreed to compensate Tainui for land confiscated in the 1860s.

The Maori heritage is most evident on **Regatta Day** (the closest Saturday to March 17). Watched by the Maori king, a parade of great war canoes takes place along the two rivers, with events such as hurdle races at the **Turangawaewae Marae** on River Road, off SH1 just north of the river bridge. The *marae* is only open to the public on Regatta Day; the rest of the year you can view it through the perimeter fence made of the dead trunks of tree ferns interspersed with robustly sculpted red posts and a couple of finely carved entranceways.

Wallace Gallery

167 Thames St, Morrinsville, 33km northeast of Hamilton • Tues–Sun 10am–4pm • Free • ☎ 07 889 7791, ⓦ morrinsvillegallery.org.nz

The nondescript farming service town of **MORRINSVILLE** seems an unlikely location for this small but classy gallery that's a rural offshoot of Auckland's Wallace Arts Centre (see p.90). It is housed in the town's mid-century former post office building where the old radiators have been put to imaginative use as doors and gallery seating. Changing exhibitions draw from the wider Wallace collection of contemporary New Zealand art.

Matamata

The dairy-farming and racehorse-breeding town of **MATAMATA**, 63km east of Hamilton, shot to prominence just after the millennium as the location of **Hobbiton** from the *Lord of the Rings* trilogy. Lifelike *Lord of the Rings* character **statues** have since been installed in the town centre but the only way to visit the Hobbiton location (on a working sheep farm 15km southwest of town) is on a tour.

Hobbiton Movie Set and Farm Tours

501 Buckland Rd, 16km southeast of Matamata • Tours daily every 15–30min • $75 • ☎ 07 888 9913, ⓦ hobbitontours.com • Drive straight there, get the free shuttle from Matamata i-SITE, or do the tour from Rotorua (2 daily; $110)

Between the filming of Peter Jackson's three *Lord of the Rings* films in the early 2000s and the master's return a decade later to shoot the two films of *The Hobbit*, there really wasn't much to see at Hobbiton. The set was mostly dismantled and early visitors just got to see a handful of hobbit-hole facades amid the rolling hills of a working sheep farm. Interiors for all films were done in Wellington.

Since the shooting of *The Hobbit* in late 2011, however, almost all sets have been left intact. You can wander over a hillside of 42 hobbit-hole facades, some small, some large (to help give the sense of perspective when filming) and all superbly rendered to look old and hobbit-like. Chimneys appear to have soot on them, the fake lichen on fences looks totally authentic and there's an orchard of apple and pear trees (one of which was turned into a plum tree for the filming to satisfy a single line in the book). Across the lake the film-makers have created two of New Zealand's very few thatched buildings, a water mill connected by a "stone" bridge to *The Green Dragon* inn. Die-hard fans will revel in the chance to wander around real-life Hobbiton, but the less ardent may find the whole experience overlong – and overpriced.

ARRIVAL AND INFORMATION   MATAMATA

By bus InterCity and NakedBus Auckland–Rotorua runs stop outside the i-SITE.
Destinations Auckland (1 daily; 3hr); Hamilton (4 daily; 1hr); Rotorua (1 daily; 50min); Tauranga (3 daily; 1hr).

Visitor information i-SITE, 45 Broadway (Mon–Fri 9am–5pm, Sat & Sun 9am–2.30pm; ☎07 888 7260, ⓦmatamatanz.co.nz). Useful for Hobbit-related information and has internet access.

EATING

★**Workman's Café & Bar** 52 Broadway ☎07 888 5498. Funky, licensed café with more of a free spirit than you would expect to find in a place such as Matamata.

Great for coffee, cakes and snacks but also full meals such as beef salad with baby beets ($22). Tues 4–9pm, Wed–Sun 7am–9pm or later.

Cambridge

CAMBRIDGE, 24km southeast of Hamilton, was founded as a militia settlement at the navigable limit of the Waikato River in 1864, and today is surrounded by stud farms. Mosaics of Cambridge-bred winners are embedded in the pavements along the town's **Equine Stars Walk of Fame**; of these Zabeel stands out for having sired winners of prestigious races in Hong Kong, Dubai and Australia – including the Melbourne and Caulfield cups.

The town's collection of elegant **nineteenth- and twentieth-century buildings** is mapped on a heritage trail brochure (free from the i-SITE), making for a pleasant hour-long stroll.

ARRIVAL AND INFORMATION   CAMBRIDGE

By bus InterCity and NakedBus stop on Lake St, 50m from the i-SITE, on their Auckland–Wellington routes. BusIt (☎0800 287 5463, ⓦbusit.co.nz) runs a local service from Hamilton that stops outside 36 Victoria St.
Destinations Hamilton (12 daily; 30min); Matamata (1–2

daily; 30min); Tauranga (1–2 daily; 1hr 30min).
Tourist information i-SITE, cnr of Queen and Victoria sts (Mon–Fri 9am–5pm, Sat & Sun 10am–4pm; ☎07 823 3456, ⓦcambridge.co.nz). Located in the gracious former library building and has internet access.

EATING

The Deli on the Corner 48 Victoria St ☎07 827 5370. The pick of Cambridge's cafés is located in the airy 1920s Triangle Building, with a nice little corner seat for two in the apex. The sandwiches, pies and wraps are excellent, as are brunch dishes such as creamy mushrooms on toast

($14), which are served until 2pm. Or just stop in for great coffee, a pear and ginger muffin, bread and butter berry pudding ($6) or an ice cream. Mon–Fri 8am–5pm, Sat 8am–4pm, Sun 9am–3pm.

Tirau

Almost everyone seems to stop for a coffee in the farming settlement of **TIRAU**, 55km southeast of Hamilton, its highwayside strip completely taken over by corrugated iron.

It kicked off with a corrugated-iron sheep housing a woolshop and followed with a sheepdog containing the **i-SITE**. The corrugated-iron constructions have attained iconic status and spawned a rash of sheet-metal structures and signs, including a biblical shepherd in the grounds of a church.

INFORMATION AND EATING — TIRAU

Visitor information i-SITE, SH1 (daily 9am–5pm; ☎07 883 1202, ⓦ tirauinfo.co.nz).

Beanz & Machines 1 Hillcrest St ☎07 883 1146. The range of food is limited so focus on the coffee at this small roastery, where you can drink top-class espresso. They also sell all sorts of coffee-making paraphernalia. Daily 7am–4pm.

Te Awamutu

TE AWAMUTU, 30km south of Hamilton, is renowned for its musical and military history. The birthplace of fraternal Kiwi music icons Tim and Neil Finn, of **Split Enz** and **Crowded House** fame, "TA", as it's dubbed by locals, is surrounded by rolling hills and dairy pasture, and overlooked by Mount Pirongia. During the 1863 **New Zealand Wars**, Te Awamutu was a garrison for government forces and site of one of the most famous battles of the conflict, fought at the hastily constructed Orakau *pa*, where three hundred Maori held off two thousand soldiers for three days.

Immediately across the road from the i-SITE you'll find Te Awamutu's extensive **rose gardens** (open access; free), at their best between November and May. The i-SITE also holds the key to the 1854 garrison church, **St John's**, just across Arawata Street. Inside is a tribute from the British regiment, written in Maori, honouring Maori who crawled, under fire, onto the battlefield to give water to wounded British soldiers.

Te Awamutu Museum

135 Roche St • Mon–Fri 10am–4pm, Sat 10am–2pm • Free • ☎07 872 0085, ⓦ tamuseum.org.nz

The **Te Awamutu Museum** punches above its (admittedly modest) weight with interesting displays about European settlers and the New Zealand Wars, and a "*True Colours*" exhibit devoted to the Finn brothers, complete with home movies, newspaper clippings from the early days, an interview with the boys and assorted artefacts.

The room of Maori artefacts is notable chiefly for **Uenuku**, a 2.7m-high wooden representation of an important Maori god. It looks quite unlike almost any other Maori carving you'll see, something that supports the contention that it was made before 1500 AD. No one really knows why it spent decades (perhaps centuries) in a lake near Te Awamutu where it was found in 1906.

ARRIVAL AND DEPARTURE — TE AWAMUTU

Buses InterCity and NakedBus stop at the i-SITE. BusIt (ⓦ busit.co.nz) runs to Hamilton.

Destinations Hamilton (8 daily; 30min); Otorohanga (5 daily; 20min).

INFORMATION AND TOURS

Visitor information i-SITE, 1 Gorst Ave (Mon–Fri 9am–5pm, Sat & Sun 10am–4pm; ☎07 871 3259, ⓦ teawamutuinfo.com). All the information you need, plus free hot showers.

Finn Tour Fans of the brothers Finn can take a self-guided jaunt around (the frankly fairly dull) places of significance from the brothers' formative years by buying the "Finn Tour" booklet ($5) from the i-SITE.

EATING AND DRINKING

Empire Espresso Bar 65 Sloane St ☎07 871 2095, ⓦ facebook.com/EmpireEspressoEatery. Smart little café in the entrance to a 1915 former cinema with great counter food (roast vegetable filo), a light breakfast of German rye

with honeycomb and lemon crème ($5.50), and lunches such as Cajun chicken with hummus and salad ($16). Try their passionfruit and macadamia macaroon with a long black. Mon–Fri 6am–3.30pm, Sat 6am–2.30pm.
Fahrenheit 13 Roche St ☎07 871 5429,

ⓦfahrenheitrestaurant.co.nz. Find a sunny afternoon seat on the terrace overlooking the main street for a beer, fish and chips ($18) or tapas ($12) such as duck rillette or salt-and-pepper calamari. Tues–Sun 11am–10pm or later.

Raglan

Visitors often linger far longer than they intended to in **RAGLAN**, 48km west of Hamilton, which hugs the south side of the large and picturesque Whaingaroa Harbour. They're lured by the town's bohemian arts and crafts tenor and the laidback spirit of the **surfing** community – the waters here feature some of the best left-handed breaks in the world.

Cafés, banks and pubs line palm-shaded **Bow Street**, whose western end butts against the harbour, spanned by a slender footbridge where kids are always egging each other to jump off. Apart from wandering the foreshore, there are few sights as such, so you'll soon want to head 8km south of town to the surf beaches.

There's good **hiking** and **horseriding** both here and further south at **Bridal Veil Falls**. Sweeping views of Raglan Harbour and along the coast unfurl from the **summit** of **Mount Karioi** (755m), reached on a winding gravel-road loop around the Karioi Mountain.

Brief history

The horizon to the south is dominated by **Mount Karioi**, which according to Maori legend was the ultimate goal of the great migratory canoe Tainui. On reaching the mouth of the harbour a bar blocked the way, hence the name Whaingaroa ("long pursuit"). The shortened epithet, Whangaroa, was the name used for the harbour until 1855, when it was renamed Raglan after the officer who led the Charge of the Light Brigade.

Raglan Museum

15 Wainui Rd • Nov–March Mon–Sat 9am–7pm, Sun 9.30am–6pm; April–Oct Mon–Fri 9.30am–5.30pm, Sat–Sun 9.30am–5pm • $2 • ☎ 07 825 0556, ⓦraglanmuseum.co.nz

The i-SITE provides access to this small museum with modest displays on the area's history including the original telephone exchange and an apothecary chest. Alongside the usual run of old photos and paraphernalia, surf fans should check out the short film on 1970s attempts to use early computers to predict ocean wave patterns and hence the best day to head to the coast at a time when high petrol prices limited the transport options of impecunious surfers.

Old School Arts Centre

5 Stewart St • ☎ 07 825 0023, ⓦraglanartscentre.co.nz

Raglan is home to dozens of **artists** and a handful of **galleries** including the Old School Arts Centre, housed in a heritage building and run by the town's creative community. It hosts a funky **market** (second Sun of each month 10am–2pm; ⓦraglanmarket.com) with everything locally produced. They also publish the free *Raglan Arts Trail* leaflet.

Te Kopua and Ocean beaches

The safest **swimming beach** is **Te Kopua**, in the heart of town, reached via the footbridge from lower Bow Street or by car along Wainui Road and Marine Parade.

RAGLAN TOURS AND ACTIVITIES

There are great waves all around the country but Raglan is New Zealand's finest **surfing** destination – the lines of perfect breakers appear like blue corduroy southwest of town. The best place for inexperienced surfers is the rock-free **Ngarunui Beach**, 5km south of Raglan. For the experienced, the main breaks, both around 8km south of town, are **Whale Bay** and **Manu Bay** (Waireki), which featured in the cult 1960s surf film *Endless Summer*.

For non-surfers, Raglan is mostly about doing not much at all, but there is plenty to keep you occupied. You really should spend some time on the water, particularly exploring the horizontally jointed **Pancake Rocks** forming low cliffs just across Raglan's Whaingaroa Harbour. Kayaking is a perfect way to see them at their best.

Inland, saddles are the way to go, either on horseback or mountain bike.

SURFING AND BOARD SPORTS

GAgRAglan Volcom Lane ☎07 825 8702, ⓦgagraglan.com. Kitesurf lessons starting at $60/hour for beginners, rising to $80 once boat-assisted.

Raglan Kitesurfing Lost Lane ☎07 825 8402, ⓦraglankitesurfing.com. Beginners can take one-on-one intro sessions for $80/hr.

Raglan Surfing School Whale Bay ☎07 825 7873, ⓦraglansurfingschool.co.nz. The main surf school with rentals (half-day from $35) and assorted packages including starter lessons (3hr; group $89; private $149) using soft boards.

EXPLORING THE HARBOUR

Raglan Backpackers ☎07 825 0515, ⓦraglanbackpackers.co.nz. Rent sit-on-tops (singles $35/3hr; doubles $45/4hr) then launch them from right next to the hostel and explore the harbour, particularly the Pancake Rocks over the far side, easily reached in 15–20min. $5 discounts for hostel guests.

Raglan Kayak ☎07 825 8862, ⓦraglaneco.co.nz.

Join their guided "Kayak 'n' Coffee" tour (3hr; $75) across the harbour to Pancake Rocks or rent a kayak (singles: $40/half-day; $50/full day).

Wahine Moe Raglan Wharf ☎07 825 7873, ⓦraglanboatcharters.co.nz. Delightful 2hr sunset cruises ($49) on Raglan Harbour aboard a powerful cruiser. A barbecue sandwich is included and there's a bar on board. Operated Dec–March Thurs–Sun.

HORSERIDING

Extreme Horse Adventures Ruapuke, 20km southwest of Raglan ☎07 825 0059, ⓦwildcoast.co.nz. Get almost 3hr of horseriding on this farm, through native bush and on to Ruapuke Beach ($120/person). They'll provide low-cost transport out there if you get a group of four or more together.

Magic Mountain Horse Treks 334 Houchen Rd,

15km south of Raglan ☎07 825 6892, ⓦmagicmountain.co.nz. Ride an hour across farmland ($50) or take a two-hour trek to Bridal Veil Falls ($100; advance bookings essential, two riders minimum). To get there, head 8km east of Raglan on SH23, then 6km up Te Mata Rd, and 3km up Houchen Rd.

CYCLING

Cyclery Raglan 24b Stewart St ☎07 825 0309, ⓦcycleryraglan.co.nz. There's great riding in the countryside all around Raglan (some of it quite challenging) and these guys know it best. They specialize in self-guided tours including bike rental

($20/4hr) and plenty of local knowledge. Go for the Round Mt Karioi (45km; $30), a sunset descent known as Ruapuke Thunder ($40 including car transfer), or a two-day tour to some limestone caves with B&B in a nearby cabin ($180).

The black sand can make it look a little dowdy, but it's popular enough and there are barbecue sites and a children's play area.

Ocean Beach, just outside the town off Wainui Road on the way to Whale Bay, gives great views of the bar of rock and sand that stretches across the mouth of the harbour and is a fine picnic spot, but strong undertows make swimming unsafe. For Raglan's renowned **surf beaches**, see box above.

Te Toto and Mount Karioi tracks

Both start 12km south of Raglan along Whaanga Rd • Te Toto 2km return; 1hr; 200m ascent on way back • Karioi 8km return; 5–6hr; 650m ascent; not to be attempted in bad weather

For a short walk head to **Te Toto Track** which heads down steeply from an obvious car park through coastal forest to the grassy margins of Te Toto Stream. From there it is easy enough to access the stony beach.

The same car park is the start of the much more arduous **Mount Karioi Track**, which follows a ridge through manuka with rapidly improving views along the coast. A walk through dense forest and a short descent using a ladder brings you to the final hand-over-hand ascent using fixed chains.

Bridal Veil Falls

20km southeast of Raglan

Bridal Veil Falls hides in dense native bush just off the Kawhia Road. Water plummets 55m down a sheer rock face into a green pool where rainbows appear in the spray in the sunshine. From the car park it's a ten-minute walk down to the bottom of the falls; allow twice that for the walk back up.

ARRIVAL AND INFORMATION   RAGLAN

By bus The #23 Hamilton city Busit (Ⓦ busit.co.nz) bus arrives outside the i-SITE.
Destinations Hamilton (2–3 daily; 1hr).
i-SITE 13 Wainui Rd (Nov–April Mon–Sat 9am–7pm, Sun 9.30am–6pm; April–Nov Mon–Fri 9.30am–5.30pm, Sat &

Sun 9.30am–5pm; ☎ 07 825 0556, Ⓦ raglan.org.nz). Can help with booking accommodation, including holiday cottages and apartments.
Services There's wi-fi internet access at the library, 7 Bow St (Mon–Fri 9.30am–5pm, Sat 9.30am–12.30pm).

ACCOMMODATION

Bow Street Studios 1 Bow St ☎ 07 825 0551, Ⓦ bowstreet.co.nz. All seven one-bedroom units have harbour views from the upstairs bedroom and a subtropical terrace accessed from the kitchen/lounge. Everything is well thought out, including New Zealand art and good magazines. There's also a pretty two-bedroom cottage. **$230**

Harbourview Hotel 14 Bow St ☎ 07 825 8010, Ⓔ harbourviewhotel@vodafone.co.nz. A stay at Raglan's centrepiece old hotel comes with verandas overlooking the main street, pleasant rooms and an on-site sports bar and à la carte restaurant. **$80**

Karioi Lodge 5 Whaanga Rd, Whale Bay ☎ 07 825 7873, Ⓦ karioilodge.co.nz. Pleasant hostel in native bush 8km southwest of Raglan, with four-bed dorms and doubles and hillside campervan sites. Amenities include a communal kitchen, sauna, cheap bike rental, mountain tracks to explore and free pick-up from Raglan. Also runs Raglan Surfing School. Dorms **$30**, doubles **$75**

★**Raglan Backpackers** 6 Nero St ☎ 07 825 0515, Ⓦ raglanbackpackers.co.nz. Wonderfully relaxed hammock-strewn backpackers in the town centre, laid out around a courtyard that backs onto the estuary. There's free use of kayaks, bikes, golf clubs, fishing gear, spa and sauna. Also offers cheap surfboard rental ($25/half-day including wetsuit) and lessons. Dorms **$27**, doubles **$72**

Raglan Kopua Holiday Park Marine Parade ☎ 07 825 8283, Ⓦ raglanholidaypark.co.nz. Central but somewhat raucous and overpacked campsite with a wide range of cabins, 1km by road from town and also accessible by a short footbridge. It is well sited next to Te Kopua, the harbour's safest swimming beach. Camping **$23**, cabins **$100**

Sleeping Lady Lodgings 5 Whaanga Rd, Whale Bay ☎ 07 825 7873, Ⓦ sleepinglady.co.nz. *Karioi Lodge* (see above) also has half a dozen delightful self-contained holiday homes scattered through coastal bush 8km south-west of Raglan, sleeping from two to twelve (minimum two-night stay in peak season); prices can range as high as $260/night for two, and it's $35 for each additional person. **$99**

★**Solscape Eco Retreat** Wainui Rd, Manu Bay, 6km south of Raglan ☎ 07 825 8268, Ⓦ solscape.co.nz. Wonderfully idiosyncratic accommodation (and associate YHA) in imaginatively converted train carriages and cottages (from $180) set on top of a hill with panoramic views. Ecofriendly initiatives include a home-made solar water-heating system, solar LED lights, tipi-style accommodation and individual earth-wood units (timber frames and roofs with mud walls). There are also free pick-ups from Raglan, and surf lessons. Camping **$16**, tipis per person **$34**

EATING AND DRINKING

One of Raglan's charms is the relaxed café-style places that make for a great post-surf breakfast or laidback meal. Most places are around the intersection of Bow Street and Wainui Road, and generally run considerably shorter hours in winter and close when they feel like it.

Food Department Raglan Roast 45 Wainui Road ☏ 07 282 0248. Laidback pizza joint with a pleasant terrace on which to sit and carve up the large inventive pizzas with friends (from $18). Also has accommodation in lovingly furnished units complete with upcycled wooden furniture out the back ($110). Daily 7am–8.30pm.

Harbourview Hotel 14 Bow St ☏ 07 825 8010. This reliable hotel/pub has good-value meals (mains $23–30), a bar menu of burgers, nachos and seafood chowder (all around $15) and draught beer and wine by the glass. Mon–Sat 10am–midnight, Sun 10am–10pm.

Orca Restaurant & Bar 2 Wallis St ☏ 07 825 6543, ⓦ orcarestaurant.co.nz. Raglan's best restaurant, serving casual brunches and standout modern Kiwi evening meals with a seasonal slant (most mains $20–30). The attached bar opens onto a deck overlooking the estuary, and has regular live bands (Fri free, Sat $5–10). Mon–Fri 10am–10pm, Sat & Sun 9am–10pm. Bar stays open until 1am when busy.

★**Raglan Roast** Volcom Lane ☏ 07 825 8702, ⓦ raglanroast.co.nz. Tucked down a laneway next to GAgRAglan surf shop, this tiny, daytime hole-in-the-wall spills out to a clutch of tables and roasts its knockout coffee on site. There's no food except a cookie jar, but you're welcome to bring your own. Mon–Sat 7.30am–5pm, Sun 8am–5pm.

★**The Shack** 19 Bow St ☏ 07 825 0027, ⓦ theshackraglan.com. Contemporary café/bar with a laidback vibe, a steady flow of interesting locals and an extensive range of imaginative food such as creamy balsamic mushrooms with thyme on sourdough ($13). Free (very limited) wi-fi with purchase. Mon–Wed 8am–5pm, Thurs & Sun 8am–9pm, Fri & Sat 8am–10pm.

Kawhia

Museum, Kaora St • Oct–March daily 11am–4pm; April–Nov Wed–Sun noon–3pm • Free

Far-flung **KAWHIA**, 55km south of Raglan and a similar distance northwest of Otorohanga, slumbers on the northern side of Kawhia Harbour but wakes up when its population of around five hundred people is joined by over four thousand holidaying Kiwis flocking to **Ocean Beach**, where **Te Puia Hot Springs** bubble from beneath the black sand. At peak time, many come to witness the annual **whaleboat races** (Jan 1), when 11m-long, five-crew whaling boats dash across the bay. The only other site of note is the modest **Kawhia Museum**, covering the region's rich Maori heritage with some good carved pieces, a fine modern flax-and-feather cloak and an 1880s-era kauri whaleboat.

The village centre is strung along Jervois Street, where there's a petrol station and a handful of combined shop/cafés.

Brief history

Legends tell of the arrival of the **Tainui** in 1350, in their ancestral **waka** (canoe), and of how they found Kawhia Harbour so bountiful that they lived on its shores for three hundred years. Tribal battles over the rich fishing grounds eventually forced them inland, and in 1821, after constant attacks by the better-armed Waikato Maori, the Tainui chief, Te Rauparaha, finally led his people to the relative safety of Kapiti Island.

When the original *waka* arrived in Kawhia, it was tied to a pohutukawa tree, Tangi te Korowhiti, still growing on the shore on Kaora Street, near the junction with Moke Street, 800m west of the museum, and reached along the waterside footpath. The Tainui canoe is buried on a grassy knoll above the beautifully carved and painted **meeting house** of the **Maketu Marae**, further along Kaora Street at Karewa Beach, with Hani and Puna stones marking its stern and prow. The arrival of **European** settlers and missionaries in the 1830s made Kawhia prosperous as a gateway to the fertile King Country, though its fortunes declined in the early years of the twentieth century, owing to its unsuitability for deep-draught ships.

Te Puia Hot Springs

Accessed 4km along the Tainui–Kawhia Forest Rd

It isn't easy to find **Te Puia Hot Springs**, and they're at their best an hour either side of low tide: check times and ask for detailed directions at the museum or any of the local stores. Park at the road-end car park and follow a track over the dunes to where you may find others have already dug shallow holes in the sand. Be warned: the black sand can scorch bare feet and dangerous rip tides make swimming unsafe.

ARRIVAL AND INFORMATION   KAWHIA

By car There is no public transport of any kind to Kawhia, so you'll have to use your own wheels to get here.
Tourist information There's a small visitor centre located inside the museum (Oct–March daily 11am–4pm;

April–Nov Wed–Sun noon–3pm; Ⓦ kawhiaharbour.co.nz). This is the best place to enquire about harbour cruises that usually run through the summer months.

ACCOMMODATION AND EATING

Quintessential eating Kawhia-style is fish and chips from one of the town takeaways, eaten on the wharf overlooking the harbour, followed with a beer in the very traditional *Kawhia Hotel* on Jervois St.

Annie's 146 Jervois St ☎ 07 871 0198. The best of Kawhia's limited selection of cafés, with seating on the back lawn and on the front deck with its distant harbour views. Expect espresso, milkshakes, toasted sandwiches and the likes of fish, chips and salad ($18). Internet available. Daily 9am–4pm or later.
Kawhia Camping Ground 73 Moke St ☎ 07 871 0863, Ⓦ kawhiacampingground.co.nz. Shady and fairly basic

family campsite one block back from the beach with simple but adequate facilities. Camping $̲18, cabins $̲60
Kawhia Beachside S-cape 225 Pouewe St (SH31) ☎ 07 871 0727, Ⓦ kawhiabeachsidescape.co.nz. Water-side campsite where, a couple of hours either side of high tide, you can launch kayaks ($10/hr). The cabins are a bit scruffy but the cottages are modern. Camping sites $̲30, cabins $̲60

The King Country

The rural landscape inland from Kawhia and south of Hamilton is known as the **King Country**, because it was the refuge of **King Tawhiao** and members of the **King Movement** (see box opposite), after they were driven south during the New Zealand Wars. The area soon gained a reputation among Pakeha as a Maori stronghold renowned for difficult terrain and a welcome that meant few, if any, Europeans entered. However, the forest's respite was short-lived: when peace was declared in 1881, loggers descended in droves.

Tourist interest focuses on **Waitomo**, a tiny village at the heart of a unique and dramatic landscape, honeycombed by limestone caves ethereally illuminated by glowworms, and overlaid by a geological wonderland of karst. North of Waitomo is the small dairy town of **Otorohanga**, with a kiwi house and Kiwiana displays. To the south of Waitomo, **Te Kuiti** provided sanctuary in the 1860s for Maori rebel Te Kooti, who reciprocated with a beautifully carved meeting house.

From Te Kuiti, SH4 runs south to **Taumarunui**, with access to the Whanganui River and the start of the **Forgotten World Highway** (see p.239).

Otorohanga

Surrounded by sheep and cattle country some 30km south of Te Awamutu, **Otorohanga** celebrates all things archetypally Kiwi with street signs bearing kiwi-bird icons and a series of glassed-in shrines to **Kiwiana icons** along the **Ed Hillary Walkway**, off Maniapoto Street next to the ANZ bank. Exhibits include Marmite, pavlova, the farm dog and Hillary himself. A few more displays spill over onto Maniapoto Street, where John Haddad Menswear Store, at no. 65, sells classic Kiwi menswear such as hats and oilskins.

THE KING MOVEMENT

Before Europeans arrived, Maori loyalty was solely to their immediate family and tribe, but wrangles with acquisitive European settlers led many tribes to discard age-old feuds in favour of a common crusade against the Pakeha. **Maori nationalism** hardened in the face of blatantly unjust treatment and increasing pressure to "sell" land.

In 1856, the influential Otaki Maori sought a chief who might unite the disparate tribes against the Europeans, and in 1858 the Waikato, Taupo and other tribes, largely originating from the Tainui canoe (see p.215), chose **Te Wherowhero**. Taking the title of **Potatau I**, the newly elected king established himself at Ngaruawahia – to this day the seat of the **King Movement**. The principal tenet of the movement was to resist the appropriation of Maori land and provide a basis for a degree of self-government. Whether out of a genuine misunderstanding of these aims or for reasons of economic expediency, the settlers interpreted the formation of the movement as an act of rebellion – despite the fact that Queen Victoria was included in the movement's prayers – and tension heightened. The situation escalated into armed conflict later in 1858 when the Waitara Block near New Plymouth was confiscated from its Maori owners. The fighting spread throughout the central North Island: the King Movement won a notable victory at Gate Pa, in the Bay of Plenty, but was eventually overwhelmed at Te Ranga.

Seeing the wars as an opportunity to settle old scores, some Maori tribes sided with the British and, in a series of battles along the Waikato, forced the kingites further south, until a crushing blow was struck at Orakau in 1864. The king and his followers fled south of the Puniu River into an area that, by virtue of their presence, became known as the **King Country**.

There they remained, with barely any European contact, until 1881, when **King Tawhiao**, who had succeeded to the throne in 1860, made peace. Gradually the followers of the King Movement drifted back to Ngaruawahia. Although by no means supported by all Maori, the loose coalition of the contemporary King Movement plays an important role in the current reassessment of Maori–Pakeha relations, and the reigning Maori King is the recipient of state and royal visits.

Otorohanga Kiwi House & Native Bird Park

20 Alex Telfer Drive, off Kakamutu Rd • Daily: Sept–May 9am–4.30pm; June–Aug 9am–4pm; kiwi feeding daily 1.30pm and 3.30pm • $24 • ☎ 07 873 7391, ⓦ kiwihouse.org.nz

Otorohanga prides itself on having one of the best kiwi houses in the country. The grumpy little bird's lifestyle is explained in the well-laid-out nocturnal enclosure where you really feel close to the birds. Outdoor enclosures contain the lizard-like tuatara and most species of the New Zealand native bird, many in a walk-through aviary. You can catch a kiwi feeding and there are also guided twilight tours with plenty of explanation and a chance to see the birds at their most active.

ARRIVAL AND INFORMATION OTOROHANGA

By train The station is centrally located on Wahanui Crescent.

Destinations National Park (3–7 weekly; 2hr 20min); Wellington (3–7 weekly; 9hr).

By bus InterCity and NakedBus both stop on SH3 in the middle of town.

Destinations Hamilton (5 daily; 1hr); Te Kuiti (5 daily; 15–50min); Waitomo (5 daily; 15min).

Visitor information i-SITE, 27 Turongo St (Mon–Fri 9am–5pm, Sat & Sun 10am–2pm; ☎ 07 873 8951, ⓦ otorohanga.co.nz).

Services You can pick up free wi-fi from the library, adjacent to the i-SITE.

ACCOMMODATION AND EATING

Otorohanga Holiday Park 20 Huiputea Drive ☎ 07 873 7253, ⓦ kiwiholidaypark.co.nz. Well-equipped central campsite in the centre of town with modern facilities including wi-fi throughout. Can also book Waitomo tours. Camping __$17.50__, cabin __$64__

The Thirsty Weta 57 Maniapoto St ☎ 07 873 6699, ⓦ theweta.co.nz. This is your best bet for a beer in the sun – or try one of their hearty meals, such as a pot of greenshell mussels in chilli and coconut ($18). There's live music on Friday nights and free wi-fi. Daily 10am–1am.

Origin Coffee Station 7 Wahanui St ⊕ 07 873 8550, ⓦ origincoffee.co.nz. The old Otorohanga Railway Station is the venue for the best coffee in town, directly imported from Malawi, where the owner, Roger, once grew the stuff.

It is roasted on the premises to produce mild but complex flavours. If you want to eat you'll need to BYO food. Mon–Fri 8.30am–4.30pm.

Waitomo

Some 16km southwest of Otorohanga (8km west of SH3), **WAITOMO** is a diminutive village of under fifty inhabitants with an outsize reputation for incredible **cave trips** and magnificent **karst features** – streams that disappear down funnel-shaped sinkholes (Waitomo means "water entering shaft" in Maori), craggy limestone outcrops, fluted rocks, potholes and natural bridges caused by cave ceiling collapses. Below ground, seeping water has sculpted the rock into eerie and extraordinary shapes. The ongoing process of **cave creation** involves the interaction of rainwater and carbon dioxide from the air, which together form a weak acid. As more carbon dioxide is absorbed from the soil the acid grows stronger, dissolving the limestone and enlarging cracks and joints, eventually forming the varied caves you see today. Each year a further seventy cubic metres of limestone (about the size of a double-decker bus) is dissolved. Many of the caves are dazzlingly illuminated by **glowworms**, not in fact a worm but really an insect – see the box opposite.

Only a fraction of the 45km of cave passages under Waitomo can be visited on **guided tours**. Operators lease access from farmers, so each offers the chance to explore different caves. The get-wet active caving trips are listed in the "Adventure caving" box (see p.221). In all cases, **heavy rain** can lead to cancellations if water levels rise too high. This happens perhaps ten days a year, so it pays to check weather forecasts and plan accordingly.

Brief history

Local chief **Tane Tinorau** introduced Waitomo's underground passages to English surveyor **Fred Mace**, in 1887. The pair explored further, building a raft of flax stems and drifting along an underground stream, with candles their only source of light.

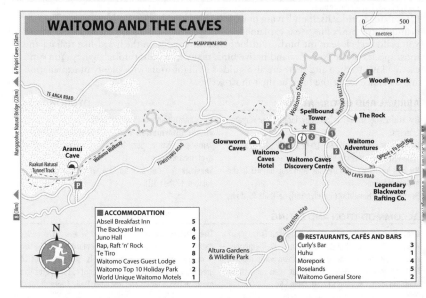

WAITOMO AND THE CAVES

■ ACCOMMODATTION	
Abseil Breakfast Inn	5
The Backyard Inn	4
Juno Hall	6
Rap, Raft 'n' Rock	7
Te Tiro	8
Waitomo Caves Guest Lodge	3
Waitomo Top 10 Holiday Park	2
World Unique Waitomo Motels	1

● RESTAURANTS, CAFÉS AND BARS	
Curly's Bar	3
Huhu	1
Morepork	4
Roselands	5
Waitomo General Store	2

GLOWWORMS

Glowworms (*Arachnocampa luminosa*) are found all over New Zealand, mostly in caves but also on overhanging banks in the bush where in dark and damp conditions you'll often see the telltale bluey-green glow. A glowworm isn't a worm at all, but the matchstick-sized larval stage of the fungus gnat (a relative of the mosquito), which attaches itself to the cave roof and produces around twenty or thirty mucus-and-silk threads or "fishing lines", which hang down a few centimetres. Drawn by the highly efficient chemical light, midges and flying insects get ensnared in the threads and the glowworm draws in the line to eat them.

The six- to nine-month larval stage is the only time in the glowworm **life cycle** that it can eat, so it needs to store energy for the two-week pupal stage when it transforms into the adult gnat that has no mouthparts. The gnat only lives a couple of days, during which time the female has to frantically find a mate in the dark caves (the glow is a big help here) and lay her batch of a hundred or so eggs. After a two- to three-week incubation, they hatch into glowworms and the process begins anew.

Within a year, the enterprising Tane was guiding tourists to see the spectacle. The government took over in 1906 and it wasn't until 1989 that the caves were returned to their Maori owners, who receive a percentage of all revenue generated and participate in the site's management.

Waitomo Caves Discovery Centre

At the i-SITE, 21 Waitomo Caves Rd • Daily: Dec 26–Jan 8.30am–6.45pm; Feb 8.30am–6pm; March & April 8.45am–5.30pm; April–Oct 9am–5pm; Oct–Dec 24 9am–5.30pm • $5, though free or discounted with many caving trips • ☎ 07 878 7640, Ⓦ waitomocaves.com

Your underground experience will be enhanced by a prior visit to this small museum with informative exhibits on the geology and history of the caves, interactive displays on the life cycle of glowworms and **cave wetas** (prehistoric grasshopper-like creepy crawlies) and a free eighteen-minute multimedia show, screened on request. If you're worried about tight underground passages, test out your nerve (and girth) on the cave crawl.

Waitomo Glowworm Caves

39 Waitomo Caves Rd • Daily 9am–5pm plus additional summer twilight tours; 45min tours depart every 30min • $49; combination ticket available: with Aranui cave $70; with Ruakuri cave $85; all 3 caves $93 • ☎ 0800 456 922, Ⓦ waitomo.com

Bus tours all stop at Waitomo's original cave experience, **Waitomo Glowworm Caves**, 500m west of the i-SITE. Paved walkways and lighting pick out the best of the stalactites and stalagmites and there's a boat ride through the grotto, where glowworms form a heavenly canopy of ghostly pale-green pinpricks of light.

The fairly steep price is offset by combos with Ruakuri and Aranui caves (see below), and a ten percent online discount when booked 48 hours in advance. To avoid the crowds and have the best experience, try and get on to either the first or last tour of the day.

Ruakuri and Aranui caves

Ruakuri Scenic Reserve, 3.5km west of the i-SITE • **Ruakuri** Tours daily 9am, 10am, 11am, 12.30pm, 1.30pm, 2.30pm & 3.30pm; 2hr with 90min underground • $69 **Aranui** Tours daily 9.30am, 11am, 1pm, 2.30pm & 4pm; 1hr • $49 • ☎ 0800 782 587, Ⓦ waitomo.com

You descend into a vast, theatrically lit void to access the "The Den of the Dogs" as **Ruakuri Cave**'s name translates. Waitomo's longest guided underground walking tour follows suspended walkways linking spectacular, subtly-lit cavern passages as guides thread the practicalities of cave creation and the glowworm life cycle with Maori stories. The whole trip is wheelchair accessible.

The Glowworm Caves office also sells tickets for tours around the **Aranui Cave**, which, although only 250m long, is geologically spectacular, with high-ceilinged chambers and magnificent stalactites and stalagmites. You'll see cave wetas here but no glowworms.

Spellbound
10 Waitomo Caves Rd • Tours July–May 2–6 daily • 3hr • $75 • ☎ 0800 773 552, ⊛ glowworm.co.nz

For a gentle but impressive underground experience it is hard to beat this two-cave combo starting off with a peaceful drift along a subterranean stream under a canopy of magnificent glowworms. The second cave has the pick of the limestone formations, a moa skeleton and expert explanation of the processes that create the weird forms and force the passages to cross a natural faultline.

Woodlyn Park
1177 Waitomo Valley Rd, 1km north of Waitomo • Show daily at 1.30pm • $27 • ☎ 07 878 6666, ⊛ woodlynpark.co.nz

If the rain hits and caving is a washout, head for **Woodlyn Park**, where a rustic barn hosts the entertaining hour-long **Billy Black's Kiwi Culture Show**, an offbeat look at the history of logging and farming, with loads of audience participation such as helping shear sheep or chop wood, always with a dollop of rural Kiwi humour. Even if this is normally the sort of thing you'd run a mile from, take a chance on this – it's good fun.

ARRIVAL AND DEPARTURE

WAITOMO

By train and bus The nearest trains, InterCity and Naked buses stop 15km away in Otorohanga, from where the Waitomo Shuttle ($12 one way; bookings essential; ☎ 0800 808 279) ferries people to Waitomo. Great Sights buses (run by InterCity) run daily to Waitomo on their Auckland–Rotorua run. The Waitomo Wanderer (☎ 0800 000 4321, ⊛ travelheadfirst.com) runs daily from Rotorua (and Taupo by prior booking). Tickets for trains and buses are available at the i-SITE.

Bus destinations Auckland (1 most days; 4hr 20min); Otorohanga (5 daily; 15min); Rotorua (2 daily; 2hr–2hr 30min).

INFORMATION

Visitor information i-SITE, 21 Waitomo Caves Rd, inside the Waitomo Caves Discovery Centre (daily 8.45am–5.30pm; ☎ 07 878 7640, ⊛ waitomodiscovery.org). This mine of information acts as a booking agent for cave trips; pick up the free *Waitomo Caves* map, which shows local walks.

Services Though there is an ATM, there is no bank, petrol or supermarket at Waitomo; the nearest are 15km away at Otorohanga and Te Kuiti. The i-SITE has a post office and internet access.

ACCOMMODATION

Backpackers are well provided for but other accommodation is fairly limited so **book in advance**, particularly between November and January.

Abseil Breakfast Inn 709 Waitomo Caves Rd, 400m east of the museum ☎ 07 878 7815, ⊛ abseilinn.co.nz. Charge up the very steep drive to this relaxing and stylish B&B on top of a hill with great views from the four

---

WAITOMO WALKS

Ruakuri Bushwalk (2km return; 45min). Tumutumu Road takes you 3.5km west to this wonderful track, one of the most impressive short walks in the country. Starting from the car park for the Aranui Cave, the track follows the Waitomo Stream on boardwalks and walkways past cave entrances. Ducking and weaving through short tunnel sections, you eventually reach a huge cave where the stream temporarily threads underground. The walk is especially magical at night when lit by glowworms in the bush, so head out there around dusk for the best of both worlds.

Waitomo Walkway (4km each way; 1hr). Waitomo village and the Ruakuri Bushwalk are linked by this pleasant track that starts opposite the i-SITE, disappears into the bush then follows the Waitomo Stream to the Aranui Cave car park. They make a great 3hr combo.

ADVENTURE CAVING

Waitomo excels at adrenaline-fuelled **adventure-caving trips**, which need to be booked in advance, especially for the November to January period. Most trips involve getting kitted out in a wetsuit, rubber boots and a caver's helmet with lamp, and combine two or more adventure elements. Kids under 12 (or under a minimum weight) are not usually allowed on adventure trips, and the wilder trips are for those 16 and over.

Access to some caves is by **abseiling**. Some trips feature **cave tubing** (also known as blackwater rafting), generally involving wedging your derrière inside a rubber ring for a (usually) gentle float through a pitch-black section of cave gazing at a galaxy of glowworm light overhead.

OPERATORS

★ **The Legendary Black Water Rafting Co** 585 Waitomo Caves Rd ☎0800 228 464, ⓦwaitomo .com. A range of trips in Ruakuri Cave, the easiest being the Black Labyrinth (3hr; 1hr underground; $128), which includes scrambling through the caves, an idyllic float through a glowworm-clad tunnel on a cave tube and two short jumps from underground waterfalls. The more adventurous Black Abyss (5hr; 2–3hr underground; $231) kicks off with a 35m abseil down a narrow *tomo* followed by an eerie flying-fox ride into darkness, some floating among glowworms and an exciting scramble back to the surface up two short waterfalls. If you'd rather not get wet, but still fancy working up some adrenalin, the Black Odyssey tour (5hr; $179) takes you through the caves on a series of high wires, featuring spider walks and flying foxes to really test that head for heights.

Rap, Raft 'n' Rock 95 Waitomo Caves Rd/SH37, 8km east of the i-SITE, 1km from the junction with SH3 ☎0800 228 372, ⓦcaveraft.com. Budget, do-everything-in-one, small-group trips starting with

a 27m abseil into a glowworm-filled cave explored partly on foot and partly floating on a tube, and ending with a rock climb out to the starting point (5hr; $250).

Waitomo Adventures Waitomo Caves Rd ☎0800 924 866, ⓦwaitomo.co.nz. Professional outfit offering five trips, including its signature Lost World (4hr; $360) – a glorious, spine-tingling 100m abseil into the gaping fern-draped mouth of a spectacular pothole, followed by a relatively dry cave walk before climbing out on a seemingly endless ladder. Cave junkies should go for the Lost World Epic (7hr; $515, including lunch underground and BBQ dinner above), where an abseil is followed by several "wet" hours, navigating upstream through squeezes, behind a small waterfall and into a glittering glowworm grotto. There's also an abseil-free cave tubing trip (4hr; $190), the active abseil-heavy Haggas Honking Holes (4hr; $275) and St Benedict's Cavern (3hr 30min; $190), a dry trip with abseils and a flying fox. Save twenty percent on either trip if you book more than 12hr ahead.

individually styled rooms and the lovely BBQ deck. Your enthusiastic host will keep you entertained, and there's free wi-fi. Excellent breakfasts. **$180**

The Backyard Inn School Rd ☎07 347 0931, ⓦthebackyardinn.co.nz. Purpose-built and slightly soulless 120-guest hostel in the heart of Waitomo with beds and rooms in a lodge, separate chalets with private bathrooms, and an on-site café (see p.222). There's space to camp too ($20pp). Dorms **$29**, chalets **$87**

Juno Hall 600 Waitomo Caves Rd, 1km east of Waitomo ☎07 878 7649, ⓦjunowaitomo.co.nz. Cosy, well-equipped associate YHA hostel in a timber-lined building set on a low hill by a pool, BBQ deck and a tennis court, with the chance to hand-feed baby animals. Some powered sites ($19pp). Dorms **$30**, doubles **$74**

Rap, Raft 'n' Rock 95 Waitomo Caves Rd/SH37, 8km east of the i-SITE, 1km from the junction with SH3 ☎0800 228 372, ⓦcaveraft.com. Homey backpacker digs attached to an adventure-caving operator with

brightly painted dorms sleeping ten, a cosy lounge, kitchen and sunny courtyard. Dorms **$30**, doubles **$70**

Te Tiro 9km west of Waitomo ☎07 878 6328, ⓦwaitomocavesnz.com. Cosy self-contained cottages with fabulous views and a glowworm grotto. Breakfast goodies are included, but if you're cooking, bring food or something for the BBQ. **$140**

Waitomo Caves Guest Lodge 7 Te Anga Rd, 100m east of the museum ☎07 878 7641, ⓦwaitomocaves guestlodge.co.nz. Eight comfortable, good-value rooms (some in cabins with good views) perched on a hillside in a lovely garden. Continental breakfast included. **$110**

Waitomo Top 10 Holiday Park 12 Waitomo Caves Rd ☎07 878 7639, ⓦwaitomopark.co.nz. Well-equipped campsite in the heart of town, with lots of new cabins and a swimming pool and spa for soaking after your underground adventure. Camping **$12**, cabins **$95**

★**World Unique Waitomo Motels** 1177 Waitomo Valley Rd, 1km north ☏ 07 878 6666, ⊛ woodlynpark .co.nz. Ingenious motel-style accommodation on the site of Billy Black's Kiwi Culture Show (see p.220). Sleep in a Bristol freighter aircraft converted into two comfortable self-contained units; a 1914 railway carriage containing a three-room unit; two hobbit holes with circular entrances sunk into a hillside; and a converted World War II patrol boat. Book at least a month ahead for Dec–Feb. Self-contained campervans can park here for free. **$175**

EATING AND DRINKING

Curly's Bar School Rd ☏ 07 878 8448. Almost everyone eventually ends up at this unreconstructed Kiwi pub, either for convivial boozing or good-value meals in the steak, seafood and burger tradition (mains mostly $15–25). Occasional live music. Daily 11am–2am.

★**Huhu** 10 Waitomo Caves Rd ☏ 07 878 6674, ⊛ huhucafe.co.nz. Classy restaurant dining with a short lunch menu including soup with soft, chewy *rewana* (Maori bread) with herb butter. Dinner dishes include bacon-wrapped pork loin ($31) and lamb curry ($28). Reservations are recommended in the evenings. King Country Brewing Company beer is on tap and there's a newly opened bar dedicated to these local brews downstairs. There's also accommodation in the self-contained Huhu Tower out front, which sleeps two ($130). Daily 4–9pm or later.

Morepork School Rd ☏ 07 878 3395, ⊛ waitomokiwipaka.co.nz. Licensed café open from breakfast, serving made-to-order breakfasts, lunches and evening meals such as fettucini, Thai curry and pizzas ($18–22). Daily 8am–10pm.

Roselands 579 Fullerton Rd, 3km south of the i-SITE ☏ 07 878 7611, ⊛ roselands-restaurant.co.nz. Fish or meat (or vegetarian options by prior arrangement) sizzles on the barbecue on the deck of this garden-set restaurant in a beautiful hillside location. Fixed-priced menu $30. Daily for lunch 11.30am–3pm and dinner.

★**Waitomo General Store** 15 Waitomo Caves Rd ☏ 07 878 8613. A modern take on the classic general store with groceries, organic meat and cone ice-cream, plus excellent espresso, great pies and a range of breakfasts, including eggs Benny ($16). Daily 7.30am–6pm or later.

Mangapohue Natural Bridge

Te Anga Rd, 24km west of Waitomo

The finest free limestone sight hereabouts is the **Mangapohue Natural Bridge**, an easy fifteen-minute loop trail through forest to a riverside boardwalk leading into a narrow limestone gorge topped by a double bridge formed by the remains of a collapsed cave roof. It's especially dazzling at night when the undersides glimmer with constellations of glowworms. In daylight, don't miss the rest of the walk, through farmland past fossilized examples of giant oysters, 35 million years old.

Piripiri Caves and Marakopa Falls

Te Anga Rd, 4km west of Mangapohue Natural Bridge

A five-minute walk through a forested landscape full of weathered limestone outcrops brings you to **Piripiri Caves**. Inside the cavern you'll need a decent torch (and an emergency spare) to explore the Oyster Room, which contains giant fossil oysters, though there are no glowworms.

A kilometre or so on, a track (15min return) accesses one of the area's most dramatic waterfalls, the multitiered 30m **Marakopa Falls**, through a jungle-like rainforest of tawa, pukatea and kohekohe trees.

Te Kuiti

The "Shearing Capital of the World", **TE KUITI**, 19km south of Waitomo, greets visitors with a 7m-high statue of a man shearing a sheep at the southern end of Rora Street, and hosts the annual New Zealand **Shearing and Wool Handling Championships** in late March or early April; get details from the **i-SITE**.

OPPOSITE MARAKOPA FALLS (P.220) >

At the south end of Rora Street on Awakino Road is a magnificently carved **meeting house**, Te Tokanganui-a-noho, left by Maori rebel Te Kooti in the nineteenth century in thanks for sanctuary.

INFORMATION
TE KUITI

i-SITE Rora St (Mon–Fri 9am–5pm, Sat & Sun 10am–2pm; ☎ 07 878 8077, ⓦ waitomo.govt.nz). Can arrange accommodation, and has information on activities and

transport requirements within the Waitomo region and beyond.

EATING AND DRINKING

★ **Bosco Café** 57 Te Kumi Rd (SH3), 1km north of town ☎ 07 878 3633, ⓦ boscocafe.me. Hip daytime café in an airy pine-and-plywood building, serving sensational

Fairtrade coffee, smoothies, home-made pies and a range of breakfasts and lunches. Eggs Benedict is $21.50, the Kiwi burger $22.50. Daily 8am–5pm.

Towards the Taranaki Peninsula

Southwest of Te Kuiti, **SH3** makes a beeline for the Tasman Sea and the small coastal town of **Mokau**, noted for its run of whitebait from mid-August to November, when there are plenty of opportunities to sample it in the local cafés. The highway then twists its way through tiny communities, sandwiched between spectacular black beaches and steep inland ranges. Opportunities for exploration focus on the wonderful **Whitecliffs Walkway**; eventually the scenery opens out onto the Taranaki Plains just north of New Plymouth.

Whitecliffs Walkway

Starts on Pukearuhe Rd, off SH3, 11km northwest of Mimi, itself 47km south of Mokau • 5km return; 4–7hr; flat

Though billed as a 4–7hr loop walk over the hills and back along the beach, it is the beach section that really makes this special, and that's the walk described here. If you want to do the whole thing, start 2hr before low tide, but it is worth coming down for a short walk at any time. Start by the steep Pukearuhe boat ramp then simply follow the beach north with the Tasman breakers sweeping up the beach towards high, off-white sandstone cliffs. Calm pools, boulder fields and the odd stream-crossing keep it interesting until you reach the **Te Horo Stock Tunnel**, a 80m-long passage bored through the cliff in the 1870s to allow stock to be driven along the beach, on up to the clifftops and then beyond to market. The tunnel itself is crumbling and is officially closed, though repairs are planned. Return along the beach or follow the Walkway signs back across the bush-clad hills following the route of a buried gas pipeline.

EATING AND DRINKING
SH3 TOWARDS TARANAKI

Mike's Organic Brewery 487 Mokau Rd (SH3), 48km south of Mokau ☎ 05 0846 4537, ⓦ organicbeer .co.nz. Stop by this craft brewery of international standing which produces eight organic brews using rainwater – including Strawberry Blonde, made from

whole organic strawberries. Buy to take away or sit in the garden over a beer flight (4 small glasses for $12), a gourmet pie and chips ($14) or a pizza. Daily 10am–6pm.

The Taranaki Peninsula

The province of **Taranaki** (nicknamed "The 'naki") juts out west from the rest of the North Island forming a thumbprint peninsula centred on **Maunga Taranaki** (aka **Mount Egmont**), an elegant conical volcano rising 2500m from the subtropical coast to its icy summit. Taranaki means "peak clear of vegetation", an appropriate description of the upper half of "the mountain", as locals simply refer to it.

The mountain remains a constant presence as you tour the region, though much of the time it is obscured by cloud. The summit is usually visible in the early morning and just before sunset, with cloud forming through the middle of the day – the bane of summit aspirants who slog for no view.

Taranaki's vibrant provincial capital and largest city, **New Plymouth**, makes a good base for day-trips into the **Egmont National Park**, surrounding the mountain. It is

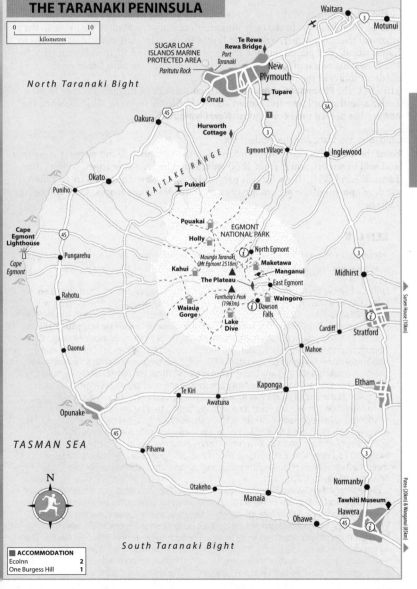

THE TARANAKI PENINSULA

0 _____ 10
kilometres

North Taranaki Bight

Waitara
Motunui

SUGAR LOAF
ISLANDS MARINE
PROTECTED AREA
Port
Taranaki
Paritutu Rock
Te Rewa
Rewa Bridge
New
Plymouth

Omata
Tupare

Oakura

Hurworth
Cottage

Egmont Village
Inglewood

K A I T A K E   R A N G E

Okato
Pukeiti

Puniho

Pouakai
EGMONT
NATIONAL PARK

Cape
Egmont
Lighthouse
Holly

Cape
Egmont
Pungarehu

North Egmont
Maunga Taranaki
(Mt Egmont 2518m)
Maketawa
Manganui

Kahui
The Plateau
East Egmont

Rahotu
Fanthams Peak
(1963m)
Waingoro

Waiaua
Gorge
Dawson
Falls

Lake
Dive

Cardiff
Stratford

Oaonui
Mahoe

Midhirst

Kaponga
Eltham

Te Kiri
Awatuna

Opunake

TASMAN SEA
Pihama

N

Otakeho
Normanby

Manaia
Tawhiti Museum
Hawera

Ohawe

South Taranaki Bight

Sarjeant House (10km)

Patea (20km) & Wanganui (85km)

■ ACCOMMODATION
EcoInn   2
One Burgess Hill   1

also very convenient for short forays to the surfing and windsurfing hotspot of **Oakura**.

Rural Taranaki's attractions, including the **Surf Highway**, are best sampled on a one- or two-day loop around the mountain.

Brief history

According to Maori, the mountain-demigod Taranaki fled here from the company of the other mountains in the central North Island. He was firmly in place when spotted by the first European in the area, **Cook**, who named the peak Egmont after the first Lord of the Admiralty. In the early nineteenth century few **Maori** were living in the area as annual raids by northern tribes had forced many to migrate with Te Rauparaha to Kapiti Island. This played into the hands of John Lowe and Richard Barrett who, in 1828, established a trading and whaling station on the Ngamotu Beach on the northern shores of the peninsula.

In 1841, the **Plymouth Company** dispatched six ships of English colonists to New Zealand, settling at Lowe and Barrett's outpost. Mostly from the West Country, the new settlers named their community **New Plymouth**.

Land disputes, wars, and the modern era

From the late 1840s many Maori returned to their homeland, and disputes arose over land sold to settlers, which from 1860 culminated in a ten-year armed conflict, the Taranaki Land Wars. These formed part of the wider New Zealand Wars and slowed the development of the region, leaving a legacy of **Maori grievances**, some still being addressed.

LEN LYE

All of a sudden it hit me – if there was such a thing as composing music, there could be such a thing as composing motion. After all, there are melodic figures, why can't there be figures of motion?   Len Lye

Until fairly recently, New Zealand-born sculptor, film-maker and conceptual artist **Len Lye** (1901–80) was little known outside the art world, but his work is now earning well-deserved recognition. Born in Christchurch, Lye developed a fascination with movement, which expressed itself in his late teens in early experiments in **kinetic sculpture**. His interest in Maori art encouraged him to travel more widely, studying both Australian Aboriginal and Samoan dance. Adapting indigenous art to the precepts of the Futurist and Surrealist movements coming out of Europe, he experimented with sculpture, batik, painting, photography and animated **"cameraless" films** (he painstakingly stencilled, scratched and drew on the actual film). Lye spent time working on his films in London, but towards the end of World War II he joined the European artistic exodus and ended up in New York. Here he returned to sculpture, finding that he could exploit the flexibility of stainless-steel rods, loops and strips to create abstract "tangible motion sculptures" designed to "make movement real". The erratic movements of these motor-driven sculptures give them an air of anarchy, which is most evident in his best-known work, 1977's *Trilogy* (more commonly referred to as "Flip and Two Twisters"), three motorized metal sheets that wildly shake and contort until winding down to a final convulsion.

Lye envisaged his works as being monumental and set outdoors, but was always aware of the technical limitations of his era and considered his projects to be works of the twenty-first century. Just before his death in New York in 1980, friend, patron and New Plymouth resident, John Matthews, helped set up the Len Lye Foundation, which brought most of Lye's scattered work to New Plymouth's Govett-Brewster Art Gallery. The foundation has been instrumental in furthering Lye's work. The *Wind Wand* is the most visible and largest product of their work, though the foundation has also been instrumental in creating Lye's *Water Whirler* on the Wellington waterfront (see p.422).

Once hostilities were over, the rich farmlands were primarily used as grazing grounds for dairy cattle. As economies of scale became increasingly important, most dairy complexes closed down, finally leaving just one huge complex outside Hawera.

The discovery in the early 1970s of large deposits of **natural gas** off the Taranaki coast diverted attention towards petrochemical industries, but supplies have dwindled as prospectors seek new finds.

New Plymouth

The small but bustling city of **New Plymouth**, on the northern shore of the peninsula, is the commercial heart of Taranaki and renowned New Zealand-wide for its concerts and arts festivals. **Port Taranaki**, at the edge of the city, serves as New Zealand's western

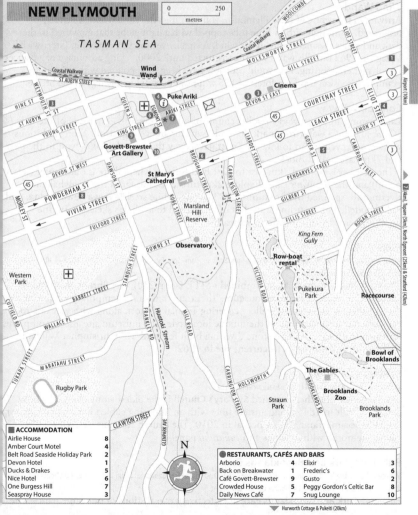

NEW PLYMOUTH

0 — 250 metres

3

TASMAN SEA

Coastal Walkway

Wind Wand

Puke Ariki

Cinema

Govett-Brewster Art Gallery

St Mary's Cathedral

Marsland Hill Reserve

Observatory

Western Park

King Fern Gully

Row-boat rental

Pukekura Park

Racecourse

Bowl of Brooklands

The Gables

Rugby Park

Straun Park

Brooklands Zoo

Brooklands Park

Airport (10km)

(4km), Tupare (5km), North Egmont (25km) & Stratford (40km)

■ ACCOMMODATION

Airlie House	8
Amber Court Motel	4
Belt Road Seaside Holiday Park	2
Devon Hotel	1
Ducks & Drakes	5
Nice Hotel	6
One Burgess Hill	7
Seaspray House	3

N

● RESTAURANTS, CAFÉS AND BARS

Arborio	4	Elixir	3
Back on Breakwater	1	Frederic's	6
Café Govett-Brewster	9	Gusto	2
Crowded House	5	Peggy Gordon's Celtic Bar	8
Daily News Café	7	Snug Lounge	10

Hurworth Cottage & Pukeiti (20km)

gateway and is the only deep-water international port on the west coast. There's a strong **arts** and **gardens** bias to its attractions, though it is a pleasure just to walk around the town. Just offshore is the **Sugar Loaf Islands Protected Area**, a haven for wildlife above and beneath the sea.

Govett-Brewster Art Gallery

42 Queen St • Daily 10am–5pm • Free • ☎ 06 759 6060, ⓦ govettbrewster.com

The **Govett-Brewster** is one of the country's finest contemporary art galleries. It owns a huge permanent collection of works by **Len Lye** (see box, p.226), and at the time of writing a smart new Len Lye gallery was mushrooming beside the original building. When this opens it will allow visitors access to a large collection of this visionary artist's work for the first time. There's also a good art and design bookshop and an excellent café (see p.231).

Wind Wand

Arriving in the centre of New Plymouth, you can't miss the **Wind Wand**, a slender, bright-red, 45m-high carbon-fibre tube topped with a light globe that glows red in the dark and sways mesmerizingly in the wind. A smaller version was erected in Greenwich Village in 1962 but this wand wasn't constructed until 2000, taking advantage of advances in polymer engineering. Lye would probably have been disappointed with this single example: his vision was for a forest of 125 wind wands swaying together in the breeze.

Coastal Walkway

Landscaping and pathways stretch a couple of hundred metres either side of the *Wind Wand*, making a **waterfront park** that's pleasant for an evening stroll. More ambitious walkers and cyclists can follow the **Coastal Walkway** that stretches 3km west to the port and 7km east to Bell Block.

The best bet is to head 2km east to East End Reserve where there is bike rental (see p.230) and the *Big Wave Café*. Explore 2km further east as far as the Waiwhakaiho rivermouth, spanned by the stunning, 83m-long, white steel **Te Rewa Rewa Bridge**, said to be modelled on a curling wave but often likened to a whale's skeleton. In fine weather there's usually a coffee cart nearby.

Puke Ariki

1 Ariki St • Mon, Tues, Thurs, Fri 9am–6pm, Wed 9am–9pm, Sat & Sun 9am–5pm; Richmond Cottage Sat & Sun 11am–3.30pm • Free • ☎ 06 759 6060, ⓦ pukeariki.com

The city's hub is **Puke Ariki**, a combined i-SITE (see p.230), city **library**, **exhibition space** and interactive **regional museum**. The strength is in the temporary exhibitions, though there is an extensive gallery covering Taranaki Maori, along with volcanic rock carvings and woodcarvings in the unique local style. The museum site also encompasses **Richmond Cottage**, an 1854 stone dwelling built for local MP Christopher William Richmond, and moved to its current site in 1962.

St Mary's Cathedral

37 Vivian St • Free • ☎ 06 758 3111, ⓦ taranakicathedral.org.nz

The Frederick Thatcher-designed **St Mary's Church** is the oldest stone church in New Zealand. Built in 1845 along austere lines with an imposing gabled dark-wood interior, it finally became Taranaki's cathedral in 2010. The church contains a striking 1972 Maori memorial with carvings and *tukutuku* panels.

Pukekura Park and Brooklands Park

Main entrances on Liardet St and Brooklands Park Drive • Daily dawn–dusk • Free **Gables** Sat & Sun 1–4pm • Free **Rowboats** Dec–Feb daily 11am–4pm & 7–10pm • $10 for 30min • ⓦ pukekura.org.nz

Pukekura Park and Brooklands Park are effectively two sections of one large park – one of New Zealand's finest city parks and setting for both the Festival of Lights and WOMAD (see box, p.230). Pukekura is mostly semiformal, with glasshouses, a boating lake and a cricket pitch. The more freely laid out Brooklands occupies the grounds of a long-gone homestead and includes the **Bowl of Brooklands** outdoor amphitheatre, attracting big-name artists, as well as numerous mature trees, among them a 2000-year-old puriri and a big ginkgo. Nearby, a former colonial hospital from 1847 is now the **Gables**, containing an art gallery and small medical museum. Near the renovated Pukekura Teahouse you can rent **rowboats**.

Paritutu Rock

4km west of the city centre

New Plymouth's port sprawls out from the foot of the 200m-high **Paritutu Rock**, a feature of great cultural significance to Maori and a near-perfect natural fortress that still marks the boundary between Taranaki and Te Atiawa territories. You can ascend it from a car park on Centennial Drive, signposted off Vivian Street. It's a steep scramble (20–50min return) with a steel rope providing support, but the reward is a great view along the coast.

Sugar Loaf Islands Marine Protected Area

1hr boat trips • 2–3 daily, weather permitting • $40 • ☎ 06 758 9133, ⓦ chaddyscharters.co.nz

A few hundred metres off the north Taranaki coast, a cluster of rocky islands is the eroded remnant of ancient volcanoes, a sanctuary for rare plants, little blue penguins, petrels and sooty shearwaters. The surrounding waters form the DOC-administered **Sugar Loaf Marine Reserve**, which harbours some 89 species of fish and a wealth of multicoloured anemones, sponges and seaweeds in undersea canyons. Humpback whales (Aug & Sept) and dolphins (Oct–Dec) migrate past, and the tidal rocks are populated by New Zealand's northernmost breeding colony of fur seals. Although the islands themselves are off-limits, Chaddy's Charters run entertaining **trips** around them.

Tupare

487 Mangorei Rd, 6km southeast of the city centre • Daily 9am–8pm; house tours Oct–March Fri–Mon 11am • Free • ☎ 0800 736 222, ⓦ tupare.info

Taranaki's fertile volcanic soils and moist climate make for some great gardens, and there are few better than **Tupare**, developed since the1930s. There's pleasure in just wandering round the maples, azaleas and rhododendrons, and learning a little of the history in the pretty **Gardener's Cottage**, but it all makes more sense when combined with a tour of the quirky **Arts & Crafts house** designed by prominent Kiwi architect James Chapman-Taylor.

Hurworth Cottage

906 Carrington Rd, 9km south of the city centre • Sat & Sun 11am–3pm and by appointment • $5 • ☎ 06 753 3593, ⓦ historicplaces .org.nz

The charming and historic **Hurworth Cottage** was built in 1856 for Harry Atkinson, four times prime minister of New Zealand and famous for advocating women's suffrage and introducing welfare benefits. The plain two-room cottage is the only one to have survived the New Zealand Wars of the 1860s and is now furnished as it would have been in the mid-nineteenth century. Check out the ancient charcoal graffiti, one section depicting a Maori warrior with full-face *moko*.

Pukeiti

2290 Carrington Rd, 23km southwest of the city centre • Daily 9am–5pm; café Wed–Sun 10am–4pm • Free • ☎ 0800 736 222, ⓦ pukeiti.org.nz

Carved out of the bush 370m up on the northern slopes of the Pouakai Range,

Pukeiti are Taranaki's finest public gardens. They were established in 1951 by Douglas Cook, founder of Gisborne's Eastwoodhill Arboretum (see p.377), who needed a cooler, damper climate to grow New Zealand's largest collection of rhododendrons and azaleas. The result is a wild array of superb blooms, with bush paths linking up grassy avenues lined with fine specimens. The on-site *Founders Café* provides sustenance.

ARRIVAL AND DEPARTURE   NEW PLYMOUTH

By plane From the airport, 12km northeast of town, Scott's Airport Shuttle Service can drop you anywhere in the city (from $18 for 1 and $22 for 2; ☎ 06 769 5974 or ☎ 0800 373 001, ⓦ npairportshuttle.co.nz). Shuttles meet all flights, but reserve ahead to guarantee a seat.
Destinations Auckland (5–8 daily; 45min); Nelson (1 daily; 1hr); Wellington (4–5 daily; 55min).

By bus InterCity/Newmans and NakedBus stop at the bus station at 19 Ariki St, just along from the i-SITE.
Destinations Auckland (3 daily; 6hr–6hr 30min); Hamilton (4 daily; 4hr); Hawera (3 daily; 50min–1hr 15min); Te Kuiti (4 daily; 2hr 30min); Wanganui (2 daily; 2hr 30min); Wellington (2 daily; 7hr).

GETTING AROUND

By bus CityLink (☎ 0800 872 287, ⓦ trc.govt.nz/bus-routes) run local services. The limited routes may be useful for Tupare and Oakura, but services are infrequent.
By bike Cycle Inn, 133 Devon St East (☎ 06 758 7418, ⓦ cycleinn.co.nz; Mon–Fri 8.30am–5pm, Sat 9am–4pm,

Sun 10am–2pm) rent city bikes for $20/day or $10/2hr. Wind Wanderers, East End Reserve (☎ 027 358 1182, ⓦ windwanderer.co.nz), rent cruiser bikes ($15/hr then $5/hr) and 4-wheeled, pedal-powered buggies ($15/20min) for exploring the Coastal Walkway.

INFORMATION AND TOURS

Visitor information i-SITE, 65 St Aubyn St, in the foyer of Puke Ariki (Mon–Fri 9am–6pm, Wed till 9pm, Sat & Sun 9am–5pm; ☎ 06 759 6060, ⓦ taranaki.co.nz). Excellent visitor centre with touch screens to access local

info, and plenty on Egmont National Park, including hut tickets.
Services The library, 1 Ariki St, has free internet access (Mon–Fri 9am–6pm, Wed till 9pm, Sat & Sun 9am–5pm).

ACCOMMODATION

New Plymouth has a range of modestly priced accommodation, as well as options close to the city at the surf beach town of Oakura (see p.236), or on the flanks of the mountain (see p.235). Motels are strung along the approach roads into the city centre.

Airlie House 161 Powderham St ☎ 06 757 8866, ⓦ airliehouse.co.nz; map p.227. Gracious B&B in a large villa dating from the turn of the last century, with crisp modern decor. The "drawing room", with a bay-window seat, and studio apartment (with kitchen) are both en-suite, while the "garden room", overlooking the

flowering front garden, has a private bathroom with a claw-foot bath. There are hundreds of DVDs and excellent breakfasts. $180
Amber Court Motel 61 Eliot Street ☎ 0800 654 800, ⓦ ambercourtmotel.co.nz; map p.227. Bargain of a motel, complete with indoor swimming pool, in a

---

NEW PLYMOUTH FESTIVALS

Festival of Lights (mid-Dec to Jan nightly dusk–10.45pm; free; ⓦ festivaloflights.co.nz). On summer evenings, stroll the gorgeously lit pathways of Pukekura Park between illuminated trees, then rent a rowboat festooned with lights. There's live music most nights.
Taranaki Garden Spectacular (late Oct to early Nov; ⓦ taft.co.nz). Ten-day celebration of the region's fine gardens, timed to when the rhododendrons are at their best.

Taranaki International Arts Festival (two weeks in Aug; ⓦ taft.co.nz). This biennial festival (odd-numbered years) features a wide range of music, films and plays in venues all over town.
WOMAD (mid-March; ⓦ taft.co.nz). Superb annual three-day festival of world music that takes place in Brooklands Park. Hundreds of international artists performing on six stages, workshops, and a "global village" market.

central location, just off the highway but easy walking distance to the CBD. Rooms are spacious with separate kitchen and bathroom, and there's an on-site laundry. $118

Belt Road Seaside Holiday Park 2 Belt Rd ☎0800 804 204, ⓦbeltroad.co.nz; map p.227. A scenic, seaside site that's a 25min walk along the coastal path from the city centre, with camping and cabins (some en-suite) in a tidy area mostly sheltered from the otherwise exposed clifftop location. The three-night minimum stay in high season is inconvenient. Camping $20, cabins $70

Devon Hotel 390 Devon St East ☎0800 843 338, ⓦdevonhotel.co.nz; map p.227. A smart business hotel with a heated pool and spa, room service, buffet restaurant, free bikes and a range of rooms, including some spacious suites. Free wi-fi and complementary use of off-site gym. $149

Ducks & Drakes 48 Lemon St ☎06 758 0403, ⓦducksanddrakes.co.nz; map p.227. Choose to stay in the charming 1920s house (from $130), with a roomy kitchen and book-filled lounge, or the bright, airy backpackers next door, opening onto a communal lawn.

There's also a sauna ($5/person) and some tent sites ($22). Dorms $32, hostel rooms $88

★**Nice Hotel** 71 Brougham St ☎06 758 6423, ⓦnicehotel.co.nz; map p.227. Book in advance to ensure you get one of the seven unique rooms in this intimate *pied-à-terre*, with designer bathrooms, contemporary artworks and luxurious fittings. Its on-site restaurant, *Table* (dinner only; mains around $35), is renowned for its French-accented cuisine. $250

One Burgess Hill 1 Burgess Hill Rd, 5km south of the city centre ☎06 757 2056, ⓦoneburgesshill.co.nz; map p.225. Set on a high promontory with great views across the cascading Waiwhakaiho River to a giant vertical garden of bush and tree ferns, these fifteen apartments (many with log fires) have state-of-the-art decor and furnishings including sleek self-catering kitchens and decadent bathrooms. Studio $140, one-bedroom $175

★**Seaspray House** 13 Weymouth St ☎06 759 8934, ⓦseasprayhouse.co.nz; map p.227. With no bunks, no TV and shoes off inside, you soon relax at this central hostel that sleeps just 14, excluding the cat and the dog. Towels available for hire. Closed June–August. Dorms $33, doubles $78

EATING AND DRINKING

The majority of the cafés, restaurants, bars and clubs are on the so-called "**Devon Mile**", along Devon St between Dawson and Eliot sts. In recent times a second culinary hotspot has sprung up at Port Taranaki overlooking the water.

★**Arborio** St Aubyn St, inside Puke Ariki ☎06 759 1241, ⓦarborio.co.nz; map p.227. A brilliant, licensed, modern café overlooking the *Wind Wand*, for contemporary dinners of spicy fried calamari ($19) followed by pan-roasted lamb back-strap ($39) or house hot smoked salmon (37). Or just come for one of their thin-crust pizzas, served evenings only (around $23). Reservations recommended, as are seats on the outdoor terrace overlooking the water (it can be very dark inside). Daily 9am–10pm or later.

Bach on Breakwater Ocean View Parade, Port Taranaki ☎06 769 6967, ⓦbachonbreakwater.co.nz; map p.227. Rustic *bach*-style licensed café opening to a timber deck overlooking the port, dishing up moderately priced daytime favourites such as nachos ($16) and traditional evening meals including homebaked pies ($27) and lamb shank ($28). Wed & Thurs 9.30am–4pm, Fri–Sun 9.30am–10pm.

★**Café Govett-Brewster** Queen St ☎06 759 2038, ⓦgovettbrewster.com; map p.227. This airy café attached to the art gallery is a work of art in itself – specifically in the form of Sara Hughes' *The Golden Grain*, an installation piece that includes everything from the white banquettes and pie chart discs on the ceiling to the tables and crockery. None of it distracts from the

excellent food and coffee, either, whether you opt for the great muffins, a breakfast of eggs Benedict ($17.50), or salads of roast beetroot, mint, almonds and grilled haloumi. Mon–Fri 8am–2.30pm, Sat & Sun 9am–2.30pm.

Crowded House 93 Devon St East ☎06 759 4921, ⓦcrowdedhouse.co.nz; map p.227. Fairly formulaic downtown bar that's often busy, particularly if there's a big game on TV. Monteith's beers are on tap and you can eat well on a chicken and bacon burger and chips or Thai green curry (both $19.50). Daily 10am–10pm or later.

Daily News Café Level 1 in the library, 1 Ariki St; map p.227. Small, tranquil café, stocked with newspapers from across the country and around the world, serving coffee and snacks. Daily 9.30am–3.30pm.

Elixir 117 Devon St East ☎06 769 9902, ⓦelixircafe .co.nz; map p.227. Chilled café plastered with posters of upcoming festivals and gigs, serving freshly baked muffins, panini, bagels and wraps, as well as delicious mains ($17–24) such as Szechuan pepper prawns and calamari. Licensed; also BYO after 6pm. Mon 7am–4.30pm, Tues–Thurs 7am–9.30pm, Fri & Sat 7.30am–10pm, Sun 8am–4pm.

Frederic's 34 Egmont St ☎06 759 1227, ⓦfrederics .co.nz; map p.227. This welcoming pub-style bar serves a range of craft beers and ciders and a solid Kiwi-focused wine list. Generally a chilled atmosphere though things can get lively later in the week. Mon–Sun 11am–late.

Gusto Ocean View Parade, Port Taranaki ☎06 759 8133, Ⓦgustotaranaki.co.nz; map p.227. This minimalist-chic harbour-view fine-diner, hidden away in a semi-industrial marina area, is a winner for its classy, contemporary fare such as local mussels ($13) and queen scallops wrapped in pancetta ($23) to start and mains that range from fish of the day to sautéed lamb rump ($28–42). Mon–Fri 10am–10pm, Sat 9am–10pm, Sun 9am–3pm.

Peggy Gordon's Celtic Bar 58 Egmont St ☎06 758 8561, Ⓦpeggygordons.com; map p.117. With an extensive range of whiskies, twelve beers on tap, inexpensive meals – BBQ Guinness ribs ($15.50), Kilkenny battered blue cod ($18.50) – and regular live Irish music, it's no surprise that this is a popular haunt for both locals and travellers. The *Basement Bar* showcases alternative bands. Daily 10am–10pm or later.

Snug Lounge 134 Devon St West ☎06 757 9130, Ⓦsnuglounge.co.nz; map p.227. Stylish reinvention of the corner bar at the classic *White Hart Hotel*, all plush seating, deer antler cushions and walls of ancient wallpaper stripped partly back to reveal the changing tastes over the decades. Come for the delectable cocktails and the ambience, though they also serve decent *yakitori*. Daily 3pm–late.

ENTERTAINMENT

Arthouse Cinema 73 Devon St West ☎06 757 3650, Ⓦnzcinema.co.nz. Grown-up films with a glass of wine.

Event Cinema 119–125 Devon St East ☎06 759 9077, Ⓦeventcinemas.co.nz. Screens mainstream films.

New Plymouth Observatory Robe St, Marsland Hill Reserve. Members of the Astronomical Society volunteer to point out highlights in the night sky for visitors ($5). Tues summer 8–10pm; winter 7.30–9.30pm.

Egmont National Park

Taranaki (Mount Egmont), a dormant volcano that last erupted in 1755, dominates the entire western third of the North Island. Often likened to Japan's Mount Fuji, its profile is a cone rising to 2518m, though from east or west the profile is disturbed by the satellite **Fantham's Peak** (1692m). In winter, snow blankets the mountain, but as summer progresses only the crater rim remains white. The mountain is the focal point for **Egmont National Park**, the boundary forming an arc with a 10km radius around the mountain, interrupted only on its north side where it encompasses the **Pouakai Range** and **Kaitake Range**, older, more weathered cousins of Taranaki.

Surrounded by farmland, the mountain's lower slopes are cloaked in native bush that gradually changes to stunted flag-form trees shaped by the constant buffeting of the wind. Higher still, vegetation gives way to slopes of loose scoria (a kind of jagged volcanic gravel) – hard work if you're hiking.

Three sealed roads climb Taranaki's eastern flanks, each ending at a separate car park a little under halfway up the mountain from where the park's 140km of walking tracks spread out. **North Egmont** is the most easily accessible from New Plymouth but you can get higher up the mountain at **East Egmont**, and there are particularly good short walks around **Dawson Falls**. The i-SITE in New Plymouth has extensive **information** on the park.

All three trailheads are under an hour's drive from New Plymouth, but with accommodation close to all of them, avid hikers may choose to base themselves inside the park. Gung-ho hikers go for the summit (not a trivial ascent by any means; deaths do occur). If you want to spend longer than a day on the mountain, the varied **Pouakai Circuit** or the testing **Around the Mountain Circuit** might fit the bill.

North Egmont

From New Plymouth, the easiest access point to the park is tiny **Egmont Village**, 13km to the southeast on SH3. From here, the 16km sealed but winding Egmont Road runs up the mountain to **North Egmont** (936m), the starting point for the Pouakai Circuit, summit ascents and several easier walks.

SAFETY ON THE MOUNT TARANAKI SUMMIT ROUTE

The hike to the **summit** is possible in a day for anyone reasonably fit, but shouldn't be underestimated; expect to take a full day (setting off before 7.30am). The hiking season normally runs from Jan to mid-April.

The upper mountain is off-limits to ordinary hikers in winter, but even during the hiking season **bad weather**, including occasional snow, sweeps in frighteningly quickly, and hikers starting off on a fine morning frequently find themselves groping through low cloud before the day is through. Deaths occur far too often: consult the **hiking advice** in Basics (see p.48), get an up-to-date **weather forecast** (ⓦmetservice.com/mountain/egmont-national-park) and obtain further information from the nearest DOC office or visitor centre in New Plymouth or North Egmont. Climb with at least one companion or a mountain guide, and leave a **record of your intentions** with your accommodation or at ⓦadventuresmart.org.nz.

Take **warm clothing** at any time of year and, except for Jan and Feb, you should carry (and know how to use) an **ice axe and crampons**; if you don't have your own, rent equipment (from $55) at Kiwi Outdoors, 18 Ariki St, in New Plymouth (☎06 758 4152, ⓦoutdoorgurus. co.nz; Mon–Fri 9am–5pm, Sat 9.30am–2.30pm, Sun in summer 10am–2pm).

3

The Taranaki summit route

10km return; 7–10hr; 1560m ascent

Poled all the way, the route to the summit of Taranaki begins at North Egmont and initially follows the gravel Translator Road (the appropriately dubbed "Puffer") to *Tahurangi Lodge*, a private hut run by the Taranaki Alpine Club. A wooden stairway leads to North Ridge, and after that you're onto slopes of scoria up the Lizard Ridge leading to the crater. Crossing the crater ice and a short scoria slope brings you to the summit and, hopefully, magical views over the western third of the North Island.

Pouakai Circuit

Year-round, but expect snow from May–Sept; get advice from DOC before embarking • 24km loop; 2–3 days; track varies in altitude from 700–1300m

For exposed wetlands, subalpine tussock, steep fern-draped gullies, cliffs of columnar basalt and superb views of Taranaki make straight for this delightful loop tramp. Much of it is above the bushline, giving long views over the flatlands and the coast. It is steep in places and the tracks are never as groomed as the Great Walks, making the rewards well earned. There are two huts with camping outside (see p.235).

Veronica Loop Track

2.5km loop; 2hr; 200m ascent

A fairly stiff walk which initially climbs steps along a ridge through mountain forest and scrub past a monument to Arthur Ambury, a climber who died trying to save another man. Continue uphill (go past the sign that points you back downhill to the car park) to a great lookout with fine views of the ancient lava flows known as Humphries Castle, and beyond to New Plymouth and the coast, before retracing your steps and continuing with the loop. This is a good route for hikers with little time but plenty of energy.

East Egmont

East Egmont is accessed through Stratford (see p.235), from where Pembroke Road runs 14km west to the *Stratford Mountain House* hotel then a further 3km to a rugged and windswept spot known as **The Plateau**. At 1172m this is the highest road-accessible point on Taranaki's flanks. As well as being on the upper route of the Around the Mountain Circuit (see p.234), this acts as the wintertime parking area for the tiny **Manganui Ski Area** (ⓦskitaranaki.co.nz).

Curtis Falls Track

3.5km return; 2–3hr; 120m ascent

A fairly tough, short walk from the *Mountain House* hotel, crossing numerous deep gorges via steps and ladders, to the Manganui River Gorge, where you can follow the riverbed (no track or signs) to the base of a waterfall. This is part of the lower Around the Mountain Circuit (see box below).

Enchanted Track

3km oneway; 3hr return; 300m ascent

Park at the *Mountain House* hotel then hike up the road to The Plateau before heading south and cutting down onto the Enchanted Track, named for the fabulous views to the east. Note how the vegetation gradually changes as you descend.

Dawson Falls

Visitor centre Thurs–Sun & public holidays 8am–4.30pm

The most southerly access up Taranaki follows Manaia Road to **Dawson Falls** (900m), roughly 23km west of Stratford. Here you'll find the **Dawson Falls visitor centre** outside of which stands an impressive 8m-high *pou whenua* (carved pole) depicting famous Maori associated with the area.

Kapuni Loop Track

2km loop; 1hr; 100m ascent

A delightful walk through the twisted and stunted kamahi trees of the so-called "Goblin Forest", gnarled trunks hung with ferns and mosses. You soon reach Dawson Falls, where the Kapuni Stream plummets 17m over the end of an ancient lava flow. On the way back, call at the shed that houses the tiny **Dawson Falls Power Station**, a historic hydro plant built in 1935 to provide power for the *Dawson Falls Mountain Lodge* (see opposite).

Wilkies Pool Loop Track

2.3km loop; 1hr; 100m ascent

This walk from the Dawson Falls visitor centre heads uphill through more "Goblin Forest" to a series of pretty pools carved out by the Kapuni Stream. Take your time on the wet rocks and pause occasionally to appreciate the lush bush all around.

ARRIVAL AND DEPARTURE

EGMONT NATIONAL PARK

By shuttle bus Cruise New Zealand (☎ 0800 688 687, ✉ kirkstall@xtra.co.nz) run shuttles that pick up at accommodation around New Plymouth around 7am, dropping you off at North Egmont before 8am; the pick-up at North Egmont for the return journey to New Plymouth accommodation is around 4pm and they charge $50 return.

AROUND THE MOUNTAIN CIRCUIT

Dedicated hikers might consider tackling the testing Around the Mountain Circuit (44km; 3–5 days), an irregular loop around Taranaki varying in altitude from 500m to 1500m. The track is not fully maintained, so check conditions with DOC and obtain a detailed Topomap. From December through to February, the snow melts enough for hikers to occasionally loop off the main track onto the more strenuous **high-level route**, essentially making a few short cuts by heading higher up the slopes, shaving a day off the lower circuit.

ACCOMMODATION

DOC huts There are six well-spaced huts along the way. Backcountry hut passes (see p.50) are valid, or buy tickets from DOC visitor centres. Camping is only allowed alongside the huts, and is free outside Kahui hut. Huts $\overline{\$15}$, Kahui hut $\overline{\$5}$

INFORMATION AND GUIDES

North Egmont Visitor Centre End of Egmont Rd (daily 8am–4.30pm; ☎ 06 756 0990, ⓦ doc.govt.nz). This is the park's main information source, and has displays about the mountain, (not particularly detailed) maps of all the tracks for purchase, good viewing windows, weather updates and a decent café (daily 9am–4pm).

Mountain guides Several guides offer bushwalking, guided summit treks and a range of more technical stuff.

They generally take up to six clients for summer hiking and summit attempts but perhaps only two for winter expeditions, rock climbing or instruction. Guiding rates are around $300 a day for two, plus around $50 for each extra person. Try Top Guides (☎ 0800 448 433, ⓦ topguides .co.nz) or Adventure Dynamics (☎ 06 751 3589, ⓦ adventuredynamics.co.nz).

ACCOMMODATION AND EATING

NORTH EGMONT

The Camphouse North Egmont ☎ 06 278 6523 or ☎ 06 756 9093, ⓦ doc.govt.nz. This large mountain hut, built in 1891, now operates as a basic but comfy backpackers, with a heated communal lounge, full kitchen and hot showers. Check-in is at the *Mountain Café*. Dorms **$25**

The Pouakai Circuit Hikers on the Pouakai Circuit have access to two huts: the 32-bunk Holly Hut and the 16-bunk Pouakai Hut. Both operate on a first come, first served basis and backcountry hut passes are valid. **$15**

Mountain Café North Egmont, inside the visitor centre. Warm café with good views that's perfect for all-day breakfast ($14–19), soup ($12), burgers ($18) or just a post-hike coffee. Daily 9am–3pm.

EAST EGMONT

Stratford Mountain House Pembroke Rd, 14km west of Stratford ☎ 06 765 6100, ⓦ stratfordmountainhouse .co.nz. Beautifully sited and revamped lodge 4km inside the national park boundary and 850m above sea level. Birds chirp in the bush outside the windows of the ten very

comfortable rooms, all with spa bath. Alongside the spacious lounge there's a café and restaurant with fine views of the tip of Taranaki. Typical lunch dishes include chicken salad ($17) while the quality dinner menu features items including pork belly on Asian greens or steak frites (mains around $32). Restaurant Wed–Sun 9am–9pm or later. Room-only **$195**

DAWSON FALLS

Dawson Falls Mountain Lodge ☎ 06 765 5457, ⓦ dawsonfallsmountainlodge.kiwi.nz. Drive through a tunnel of native forest to reach this alpine-style lodge and find simple en-suite rooms and a cosy restaurant (Fri & Sat from 5pm) serving dishes such as grilled snapper ($35) and bacon-wrapped venison ($45). **$190**

Konini Lodge ☎ 06 756 0990, ⓦ doc.govt.nz. Essentially a DOC-run oversized hikers' hut sleeping 38, with three- and eight-bed bunkrooms, hot showers and a kitchen equipped with stoves and fridges. Bring your own sleeping bag, towel, food, pans and eating utensils and be sure to clean up after yourself. **$25**

Stratford

Just over halfway between New Plymouth and Hawera, **STRATFORD** celebrates its name with a its kitsch mock-Elizabethan **clock tower** (built in 1996 to hide the 1920s version), from which a life-size Romeo and Juliet emerge to mark the hour (at 10am, 1pm, 3pm and 7pm), accompanied by recordings of Shakespearean quotes. Every street name is a character from the bard's plays.

If you're bound for the central North Island, Stratford marks the start of the scenic **Forgotten World Highway** (p.239).

ARRIVAL AND INFORMATION   STRATFORD

By bus Stratford provides direct access to the slopes of Mount Taranaki, particularly East Egmont and Dawson Falls. Eastern Taranaki Experience (☎ 06 765 7482, ⓦ eastern -taranaki.co.nz) operates a 4WD mountain transport to The Plateau ($40–60 for a group of 1–5 people).

Visitor information i-SITE, Prospero Place (Mon–Fri 8.30am–5pm, Sat & Sun 10am–3pm; ☎ 0800 765 6708, ⓦ stratford.govt.nz). The office is in an alley opposite the clock tower.

The Surf Highway

The best route around Taranaki is the **Surf Highway** (SH45) from New Plymouth to Hawera, mostly travelling about 3km inland, with roads leading down to tiny uninhabited bays. It runs for only about 100km, but its beachy charms can consume half a day, longer if you want to surf its consistent glassy, even breaks. **Windsurfing** and **kiteboarding** are good too, with near constant onshore winds. Surf beaches are everywhere, but facilities are concentrated in the towns of **Oakura** and the quieter **Opunake**. Between the two towns is **Cape Egmont**, with its picturesque lighthouse.

Oakura

OAKURA is basically a commuter suburb for New Plymouth, 17km away, wedged between the highway and the surf beach. It has managed to retain a hint of counter-cultural spirit thanks to its board-rider residents and a handful of funky **craft shops** and **cafés** that cluster along SH45.

Cape Egmont

At Pungarehu, about 25km southwest of Oakura, Cape Road cuts 5km west to the cast-iron tower of **Cape Egmont Lighthouse**, moved here in 1877 from Mana Island, north of Wellington. It perches on a rise on the westernmost point of the cape overlooking Taranaki's windswept coast, a great spot around sunset with the mountain glowing behind.

Opunake

Opunake, 20km south of Cape Egmont, is a large village with a golden beach and little to do but swim, surf and cast a line. The beach is patrolled in summer (Jan daily 10am–6pm; Feb & March Sat & Sun 10am–5pm). The Opunake Surf Co (Dreamtime), at the corner of Havelock and Tasman streets, arranges **surfboard rental**.

INFORMATION AND ACTIVITIES   THE SURF HIGHWAY

Tourist information Oakura Library, 16 Donnelly St, Oakura ☏ 06 759 6060 (Mon, Wed & Fri noon–6pm, Tues, Thurs & Sat 9am–1pm). In the absence of a visitor centre, the library has the best local information.

Surf tuition Vertigo, 605 Main St, Oakura ☏ 06 752 7363, ⓦ vertigosurf.com. Offers stand-up paddle-board lessons starting with theory and finishing in the water, hopefully on two feet ($80/hr)!

ACCOMMODATION AND EATING

OAKURA

Ahu Ahu Beach Villas 321 Ahu Ahu Rd ☏ 06 752 7370, ⓦ ahu.co.nz. The four gorgeous and luxurious self-contained villas here are fashioned from wharf piles, French clay tiles and all manner of salvaged architectural pieces. The three family villas sleep four and the studio sleeps a couple; all overlook the ocean. Their new *Oraukawa Lodge* has two bedrooms, two bathrooms and bi-fold doors that bring the outdoors indoors ($650). <u>$295</u>

Butlers Reef 1133 South Rd (SH45) ☏ 06 752 7765, ⓦ butlersreef.co.nz. This lively pub is the centre of Oakura action, with hearty meals such as beer-battered fish and chips ($20), regular events and loads of concerts through the summer. There's also a bottle shop. Daily 11am–10pm or later.

Oakura Beach Holiday Park 2 Jans Terrace ☏ 06 752 7861, ⓦ oakurabeach.com. Perfectly sited

campsite with ageing but good facilities. Some tent sites are just two steps from the black-sand beach and there are cabins on a rise with awesome bay views. Camping <u>$22</u>, cabins <u>$120</u>

OPUNAKE

Opunake Beach Holiday Park Beach Rd ☏ 0800 758 009, ⓦ opunakebeachnz.co.nz. A golden beach with good surf pretty much right on your doorstep is the main lure of this welcoming campsite. Camping <u>$20</u>, units <u>$120</u>

Sugar Juice Café 42 Tasman St ☏ 06 761 7062. Considerable care goes into everything at this brightly decorated, licensed café serving up huge breakfasts such as field mushroom, spinach, bacon and egg ($18), an old-school counter selection of quiches, sausage rolls, filo wraps and carrot cake, and large pizzas ($26). Tues 9am–3pm, Wed–Sun 9am–9pm or later.

Hawera

Surrounded by gently undulating dairy country, **HAWERA** is the meeting point of the eastern and western routes around Taranaki. A service and administration centre for the district's farmers, Hawera is also home to the world's largest **dairy complex**, just south of town, which handles twenty percent of the country's milk production, mostly gathered from the rich volcanic soils of Taranaki but also brought by rail from other parts of the North Island. The town's dominant feature is the concrete former **Hawera Water Tower** (55 High St; Mon–Fri 8.30am–5.15pm, Sat & Sun 10am–3pm; $2.50), which was built in 1914 and soars 54m above town, offering fabulous views over South Taranaki; ask at the i-SITE for the key.

Morrieson's Café and Bar

58 Victoria St • Daily 11am–9pm or later

A working bar is an appropriate location for the town's ad hoc memorial to one of New Zealand's most celebrated authors, **Ronald Hugh Morrieson** (see p.817 & p.822). He spent his entire life in Hawera, wrote well-observed and amusing Gothic novels about small-town life, and loved jazz (and a drink or three). The house where he once lived was demolished to make way for a *KFC*, but his fireplace and staircase were relocated here, the bar's tabletops are made of timbers salvaged from the house, a few of his books lie stacked on the mantelpiece, and there's a short biography of the man himself on the bar.

Elvis Presley Museum

51 Argyle St • Visits by appointment • Donation • ☏ 06 278 7624, ⓦ elvismuseum.co.nz

Kevin Wasley loves Elvis Presley and, wanting to share that love around, opens up his garage-shrine to the King. Call ahead and walk the ten minutes from the i-SITE to see thousands of rare recordings, photographs and memorabilia amassed since his boyhood spent trading goods with his Memphis-based pen pal. Much is from the 1950s era Kevin so admires – ask him and you'll hear a tale or two.

Tawhiti Museum and Bush Railway

401 Ohangai Rd, 4km northeast of Hawera • **Museum** Boxing Day–Jan daily 10am–4pm; Jan–May Fri–Mon 10am–4pm; June–Aug Sun 10am–4pm • $15 • **Bush railway** First Sun of the month, plus most public holidays; every Sun during school holidays • $6 • ☏ 06 278 6837, ⓦ tawhitimuseum.co.nz

Unique and ever-expanding exhibits at the absorbing **Tawhiti Museum and Bush Railway** explore the social and technological heritage of both Maori and Pakeha using a multitude of life-size figurines modelled on local people. Other highlights include a diorama of 800 miniatures depicting the 1820s musket wars; an extraordinary account of the 1860s New Zealand Wars, seen through the eyes of a deserter from the British Army who lived out his days with the Ngati Ruanui tribe; and a small-scale **bush railway** that trundles 1km through displays recounting Taranaki's logging history, as well as a good on-site **café**.

ARRIVAL AND DEPARTURE   HAWERA

By bus InterCity and NakedBus services stop outside the i-SITE.

Destinations New Plymouth (3 daily; 50min–1hr 15min); Wanganui (2 daily; 1hr 15min).

INFORMATION

Visitor information i-SITE, 55 High St, at the base of the water tower (Mon–Fri 8.30am–5pm, Sat & Sun

10am–3pm; ☏ 06 278 8599, ⓦ southtaranaki.com).

ACCOMMODATION AND EATING

Il Chefs 47 High St ☏ 06 278 4444, ⓦ twochefs.co.nz. Hawera's top restaurant places the emphasis on locally sourced ingredients and freshly prepared dishes. Lunch might be sweet and spicy pulled pork belly spring-rolls ($19.50), while steak lovers shouldn't pass up a dinner of

ribeye fillet on garlic and rosemary fondant potato ($39). Mon 5–10pm, Tues–Sat 11am–2pm & 5–10pm or later, Sun 11am–2pm & 5–10pm.

Marracbo Down the alley at 172 High St ☏ 06 278 5334. The pick of Hawera's cafés has a wide range of breakfasts, counter food and more substantial mains (around $20). Mon–Thurs 8.30am–4pm, Fri & Sat 8.30am–10pm or later, Sun 9am–4pm.

Tairoa Lodge 3 Pouawai St ☎06 278 8603, ⓦtairoa-lodge.co.nz. B&B in a gorgeous 1875 two-storey house set by a swimming pool in mature grounds on the edge of town. There are three tastefully appointed en suites in the main house, a self-catering cottage sleeping six and the

more modern three-bedroom Gatehouse. B&B $195, cottage & gatehouse $245

Wheatly Downs Farmstay 484 Ararata St, 5km past the Tawhiti Museum ☎06 278 6523, ⓦmttaranaki .co.nz. A great opportunity to stay out of town in a backpacker-style place on a peaceful and charming sheep and cattle farm with views of Mount Taranaki. There are also campsites for $20pp/pn. Dorms $30, doubles $75

Patea

Cutting through heavily cultivated farmland, SH3 splits **PATEA**, the only major community between Hawera and Wanganui. The township has a model of the Aotea canoe at the western end of the main street, commemorating the settlement of the area by Turi and his *hapu*; a good **surfing beach** at the mouth of the Patea River (unsafe for swimming); and a safe freshwater **swimming hole**, overlooked by the Manawapou Redoubt and *pa* site.

Museum of South Taranaki

127 Egmont St • Daily 10am–4pm • Donation • ☎06 273 8354

For an insight into the town, visit the **Museum of South Taranaki**, known as Aotea Utangunui in Maori. It features displays on the town and its freezing works (abattoir) that closed in 1982, spawning the creation of the Patea Maori Club, whose 1984 hit single *Poi-E* was imaginatively repurposed in Taika Waititi's 2010 film *Boy*. The original *Poi-E* video was shot around the town's Aotea canoe.

Check out the **Waitore artefacts**, early fifteenth-century wooden tools and carvings found in a local swamp between 1968 and 1978; the canoe prow, bow cover and bailer are the oldest wooden pieces found in New Zealand, their patterns showing clear Polynesian stylings predating the later, specifically Maori, patterns.

Bushy Park

791 Rangitatau East Rd, 47km southeast of Patea, 16km northwest of Wanganui • Daily 10am–5pm • $6 • ☎03 342 9879, ⓦ bushyparksanctuary.org.nz

A well-signposted side road runs 8km northeast off SH3 to **Bushy Park**, a charming historic homestead in native bush threaded by tracks. Encircled by a 5km fence, it's now a protected **bird sanctuary** with native birds including North Island robins, moreporks, saddlebacks, flocks of kereru and North Island brown kiwi.

Taumarunui

At the confluence of the Ongarue and Whanganui rivers, **TAUMARUNUI**, 83km south of Te Kuiti, is a little down on its luck. Still, it is well located at the northern end of the Forgotten World Highway (with its associated cycle trail) and is a base for canoe trips on the Whanganui River (see p.240).

Taumarunui was one of the last towns in New Zealand to be settled by Europeans, who arrived in large numbers in 1908, when the railway came to town.

Raurimu Spiral

Visible from a signposted viewpoint 37km south of Taumarunui on SH4 • Departures daily in summer at noon • $48 one way; $96 return

Finding a suitable route for the railroad on its steep descent north towards Taumarunui from the area around the Tongariro National Park proved problematic, but surveyor R.W. Holmes' ingenious solution, the **Raurimu Spiral**, is a remarkable feat of engineering combining bridges and tunnels to loop the track over and under itself. The cost may make riding the spiral from Taumarunui to National Park unappealing, especially if you've got to come back again, but it's an interesting ride.

ARRIVAL AND DEPARTURE
TAUMARUNUI

By train and bus The train station is on Hakiaha St; buses stop outside the train station.
Train destinations Auckland (3–7 weekly; 5hr); National Park (3–7 weekly; 50min); Wanganui (1 daily; 2hr 40min);

Wellington (3–7 weekly; 7hr 30min).
Bus destinations Hamilton (1 daily; 2hr 20min); National Park (1 daily; 30min); Te Kuiti (1 daily; 1hr); Wanganui (1 daily; 2hr 40min).

INFORMATION

Visitor information i-SITE, 116 Hakiaha St (daily 8.30am–5.30pm; ☎ 07 895 7494, ⓦ visitruapehu.com). Located at the train station, it has a model train replica of the Raurimu Spiral, internet access, books accommodation and sells Whanganui National Park Hut and Camp passes.

ACCOMMODATION AND EATING

Jasmine's 43 Hakiaha St (SH4) ☎ 07 895 5822. Slightly odd synthesis of a traditional Thai restaurant and a standard Kiwi café. Come for decent coffee and cakes, bacon and egg breakfasts, a seafood *pad thai* lunch ($12.50) or a hot jungle curry dinner ($16). BYO wine. Daily 7am–9pm.
Kelly's Motel 10 River Rd ☎ 07 895 8175, ⓦ kellysmotel .co.nz. A modest and ageing – but still comfortable – motel off the highway at the western end of town with studios, two-bedroom units and breakfast on request. $80
Taumarunui Holiday Park SH4 3km east ☎ 0800 473 281, ⓦ taumarunuiholidaypark.co.nz. Small, well-run site wedged between the Whanganui River and a grove of native bush at the start of the riverside Mananui Walkway (3km). There are simple but attractive wood-lined cabins, a self-contained cottage sleeping seven and a nice kids' play area. Camping $18, cabins $55

The Forgotten World Highway

For a taste of genuinely rural New Zealand, follow the **Forgotten World Highway** between Taumarunui and Stratford (SH43), a rugged 155m road that twists through the hills west of Taumarunui. All but a 12km stretch through the Tangarakau Gorge is sealed, but allow at least three hours for the journey, and be sure to fuel up beforehand as there's **no petrol** along the route. Much of the route is covered on the Whanganui National Park map (see p.240).

Tangarakau Gorge

58km west of Taumarunui

Leaving behind the farmland around Taumarunui, SH43 snakes through the sedimentary limestone of the **Tangarakau Gorge**, possibly the highlight of the trip, with steep bush-draped cliffs rising up above the river. At the entrance to the gorge, a small sign directs you along a short trail to the picturesque site of **Joshua Morgan's grave**, the final resting place of an early surveyor. At the crest of a ridge you pass through the dark, narrow **Moki Tunnel** before reaching Whangamomona.

Whangamomona

A steady descent brings you alongside a little-used rail line that runs parallel to the road as far as tiny **WHANGAMOMONA**, 88km southwest of Taumarunui, with just ten residents. The population is boosted in late January of every odd-numbered year during celebrations of the village's independence, declared on October 28, 1989, after the government altered the provincial boundaries, removing it from

Taranaki. The **republic** swears in a president and in full party mood hosts whip-cracking and gumboot-throwing competitions, amid much drinking, eating and merriment. Celebrations revolve around the 1911 *Whangamomona Hotel*, where year-round you can get your passport stamped or buy a Whangamomonian version ($1).

Leaving Whangamomona, SH43 climbs beside steep bluffs and passes a couple of saddles with views down the valley and across the **Taranaki Plains**. It then descends to flat dairy pasture, eventually rolling into **Stratford** as the permanently snowcapped Mount Taranaki looms into view, if the weather allows.

ACCOMMODATION AND EATING

THE FORGOTTEN WORLD HIGHWAY

Ohinepane campsite 21km west of Taumarunui, ⓦ doc.govt.nz. For a peaceful night beside the Whanganui River, stop at this grassy DOC campsite with water and long-drop toilets and possibly the company of canoeists stopping for their first night downstream from Taumarunui. **$10**

Whangamomona Domain Camp Whangamomona Rd ☏ 06 762 5822, ⓦ whangamomonacamp.webs .com. Simple campsite in a peaceful setting with campervan hook-ups, basic cabins (bring your own bedding) and showers ($2), all an easy wander from the *Whangamomona Hotel*. Camping **$10**, cabins for two **$20**

Whangamomona Hotel Ohura Rd ☏ 06 762 5823, ⓦ whangamomonahotel.co.nz. Classic country pub/ hotel that has been refurbished without losing any of its character. Airy guest rooms share bathrooms and a continental breakfast is included. The hotel serves basic pub meals (mains $10–20). **$150**

Whanganui National Park

The emerald-green Whanganui River tumbles from the northern slopes of Mount Tongariro to the Tasman Sea at Wanganui, passing through the **Whanganui National Park**, a vast swathe of barely inhabited and virtually trackless bush country east of Taranaki. The park contains one of the largest remaining tracts of lowland forest in the North Island, growing on a bed of soft sandstone and mudstone (*papa*) that has been eroded to form deep gorges, sharp ridges, sheer cliffs and waterfalls. Beneath the canopy of broad-leaved podocarps and mountain beech, an understorey of tree ferns and clinging plants extends down to the riverbanks, while abundant and vociferous **birdlife** includes the kereru (native pigeon), fantail, tui, robin, grey warbler, tomtit and brown kiwi.

The best way to explore the Whanganui National Park is on a multi-day **canoe trip** into the wilderness mostly stopping at riverside campsites. The most popular exit point for canoe trips is the small settlement of **Pipiriki**, where jetboat operators run trips upstream to the **Bridge to Nowhere**.

If you're not taking a river trip, you can explore the **roads** that nibble at the fringes of the park: the Forgotten World Highway (SH43) provides limited access to the northwest, but only the slow and winding **Whanganui River Road** stays near the river for any length of time.

Brief history

At 329km, the Whanganui is New Zealand's longest navigable river. It plays an intrinsic part in the lives of local **Maori**, who hold that each river bend had a *kaitiaki* (guardian) who controlled the *mauri* (life force). The *mana* of the old riverside settlements depended upon the maintenance of the food supplies and living areas: sheltered terraces on the riverbanks were cultivated and elaborate weirs constructed to trap eels and lamprey.

European missionaries arrived in the 1840s, traders followed, and by 1891 a regular boat service carried passengers and cargo to settlers at Pipiriki and Taumarunui. In the early twentieth century **tourist-carrying** paddle steamers plied the waters to reach elegant hotels en route to the central North Island.

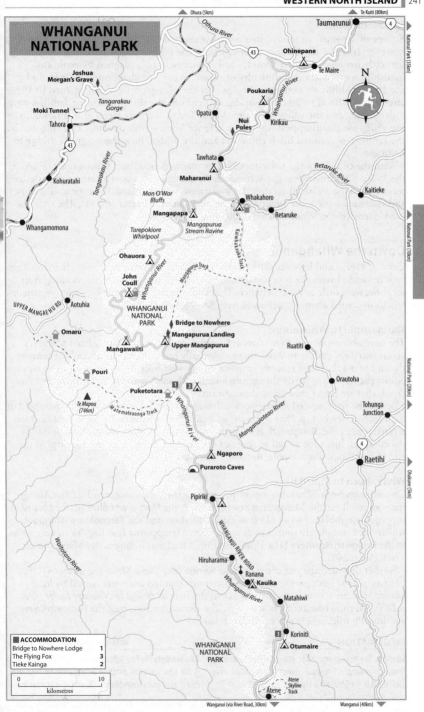

WHANGANUI NATIONAL PARK

3

ACCOMMODATION
Bridge to Nowhere Lodge 1
The Flying Fox 3
Tieke Kainga 2

0 ————— 10
kilometres

Failed settlements

European attempts to stamp their mark on this wild landscape have been ill-fated, however. In 1917 the **Mangapurua Valley**, in the middle of the park, was opened up for settlement by returned World War I servicemen, but, plagued by economic hardship, remoteness and difficulty of access, many had abandoned their farms by the 1930s. Although a concrete bridge over the Mangapurua Valley opened in 1936, after a major flood in 1942 the bridge was cut off, the three remaining families were ordered out, and the valley officially closed. Today, the only signs of habitation in the valley are the disappearing road, old fence lines, stands of exotic trees planted by the farmers, occasional brick chimneys and the bridge, now the poignant **Bridge to Nowhere**.

With the coming of the railway and better roads, the riverboat tourist trade ceased in the 1920s but farms along the Whanganui continued to support a cargo and passenger service until the 1950s; thereafter the wilderness reclaimed land. This attracted recluses and visionaries, the most celebrated being poet **James K. Baxter** (p.245). The river was used extensively in Vincent Ward's 2005 film *River Queen*.

Down the Whanganui

Canoes, kayaks and jetboats work the river, tailoring trips to your needs. The rapids are mostly Grade I with the occasional Grade II, making this an excellent paddling river for those with little or no experience. That said, the river shouldn't be underestimated: talk to operators about variations in river flows before embarking.

Taumarunui to Whakahoro

The navigable section of river starts at Cherry Grove in **Taumarunui**, from where it's about two days' paddle to **Whakahoro**, essentially just a DOC hut and a boat ramp at the end of a 45km road (mostly gravel) running west from SH4. Between these two points the river runs partly through farmland with roads nearby, and throws up a few rapids that are larger than those downstream.

Beside the river, several kilometres southwest of Cherry Grove, a former stronghold of the *Hauhau* (see box, p.358) is the site of a couple of **nui poles**. In 1862 the Hau Hau erected a war pole, **Rongo-nui**, here, with four arms indicating the cardinal points of the compass, intended to call warriors to their cause from all over the country. At the end of hostilities, a peace pole, **Rerekore**, was erected close by.

Whakahoro to Pipiriki

Downstream from Whakahoro most people take three days to get to Pipiriki. Along the way you'll see the Mangapapa Stream Ravine, the **Man-o-war Bluff** (named for its supposed resemblance to an old iron-clad battleship) and the **Tarepokiore Whirlpool**, which once completely spun a river steamer. At Mangapurua Landing it's an easy walk to the **Bridge to Nowhere** (1hr 15min return), a trail that becomes the Mangapurua Track (see p.244).

Further downstream you come to **Tieke Kainga** (aka Tieke Marae), a former DOC hut (see p.244) built on the site of an ancient *pa* that has been reoccupied by local Maori; you can stay or camp here or across the river at *Bridge to Nowhere Lodge* (see p.244), a terrific base for river activities. The last stretch runs past the **Puraroto Caves** and into Pipiriki, where most paddlers finish.

INFORMATION	WHANGANUI RIVER TRIPS
Seasons The river is accessible year-round but paddling season is generally Oct–April, when all overnight river users must buy a Great Walk Ticket (see p.244).	**DOC leaflets** The free *Whanganui Journey* leaflet and map is the best source of practical information for river trips. Pick it up at visitor centres and DOC offices in Taumarunui or

Wanganui, or download it from ⓦ doc.govt.nz.

Supplies There are no shops along the river, so you need to take all your supplies with you: the nearest large supermarkets are in Taumarunui and Wanganui.

TOURS

Most tour operators and accommodation options operating on the river can be accessed through ⓦ whanganuiriver.co.nz.

Awa Tours ⓣ 02 7895 5261, ⓦ awatours.co.nz. Excellent three-day guided canoe tours ($770) from Whakahoro on the scenic middle reaches, during which you learn about the river environment from a Maori perspective in an effort to engender a true cultural exchange, take bushwalks and stay at *marae*.

Blazing Paddles 1033 SH4, 10km south of Taumarunui ⓣ 0800 252 946, ⓦ blazingpaddles.co.nz. Good-value gear rental for self-guided trips, with prices including drop-off, pick-up and the DOC Great Walk Ticket, with options ranging from one hour to five days.

Bridge to Nowhere ⓣ 0800 480 308, ⓦ bridgetonowhere.co.nz. Popular and frequent jetboat tours from Pipiriki, principally to the Bridge to Nowhere (4hr; $130 return). They have an excellent option allowing you to canoe the last 10km downstream to Pipiriki ($145) taking an hour or two. Also has Mangapurua mountain-bike options (see below).

Wades Landing Outdoors ⓣ 0800 226 631, ⓦ whanganui.co.nz. Whakahoro-based operator offering one-day jetboat and kayak trips ($165) as well as three-day self-guided canoe and kayak trips from Whakahoro to Pipiriki ($170) and a five-day DOC "Great Walk" tour along the entire navigable length of the river ($190).

Whanganui Scenic Experience ⓣ 0800 945 335, ⓦ whanganuiscenicjet.com. Range of jetboat and canoeing tours including an eight-hour tour to the Bridge to Nowhere ($195) and a thrilling 20min jetboat ride through Wanganui ($65).

Yeti Tours ⓣ 0800 322 388, ⓦ yetitours.co.nz. Ohakune-based guided trips on the river from two to six days ($420–895), including transport to launch points or for the tracks, a plethora of rental gear for self-guided trips (canoes/kayaks from $175 for two days, camping equipment packages from $35 for one person for 3 days) and lots of help and advice.

ACCOMMODATION

Great Walks Ticket ⓦ doc.govt.nz. Whanganui River canoeists stay at huts and campsites dotted along the riverbank. In summer (Oct–April) you must obtain a Great Walk Ticket, available online (where you can check hut and campsite availability and adjust your plans accordingly) or at DOC offices and i-SITEs for a small fee. The price depends on the number of places you book, and under-18s go free at both. Backcountry hut passes are valid in winter. Many operators offer canoe rental, transport and accommodation packages that include the Great Walks Ticket. Summer: huts $32, campsites $14. Winter: huts $15, campsites $10

Bridge to Nowhere Lodge 20km upstream from Pipiriki ⓣ 0800 480 308, ⓦ bridgetonowhere.co.nz; map p.241. The only comfortable accommodation beside the river is this boat-accessed lodge offering shared-bathroom doubles, twins and simple bunkrooms

(bring a sleeping bag), all with great bush or river views. Either self-cater (bring all your food) or go for the home-cooked dinner, bed and buffet breakfast deal ($145/ person); there's also a bar. Non-canoeists can get a package that includes a return jetboat (30min each way) transfer from Pipiriki, plus a Bridge to Nowhere tour, as well as accommodation and meals ($245). People taking packages get precedence for double rooms. Dorms $50, doubles $100

Tieke Kainga 20km upstream from Pipiriki; map p.241. Relaxing former DOC hut where you can stay in big sleeping huts for a small donation, or camp on terraces by the river (no alcohol allowed); if any of the Maori care-takers are about, you'll be treated to an informal cultural experience. You can just turn up, or prearrange through the *Bridge to Nowhere Lodge*.

HIKING AND BIKING THE MANGAPURUA TRACK

One of the few tracks that investigates the deep, rugged valleys and bush-clad slopes is the wonderful **Mangapurua Track** (40km one way; 3 days; 660m ascent), passing through semi-open former farmland. It can certainly be hiked but works better as a superb and moderately tough **mountain-bike trip**. Contact Bridge to Nowhere (ⓣ 0800 480 308, ⓦ bridgetonowhere.co.nz) whose Mangapurua Trail Package ($285) includes road transport, jetboat pick-up at Mangapurua Landing, a night at their riverside lodge and then canoeing back downstream. Conditions are best from October to April.

The Whanganui River Road

The outlying sections of the park to the south can be accessed along the **Whanganui River Road**, from either **Raetihi**, a small town on SH4 near Ohakune, or Wanganui (see p.246). The River Road hugs the river's left bank from the riverside hamlet of **Pipiriki** 79km downstream to **Upokongaro**, just outside Wanganui. It's a winding road and only fully sealed since 2014. Even in the best conditions the route takes a minimum of two hours.

Opened in 1934, the road is wedged between river, farmland and heavily forested outlying patches of the Whanganui National Park, and forms the supply route for the four hundred people or so who live along it. **Facilities** along the way are almost nonexistent: there are no shops, pubs or petrol stations, and only a handful of places to stay. If you don't fancy the drive, consider joining one of the Wanganui-based bus tours.

The road is detailed in the free *Whanganui River Road* leaflet (readily available from i-SITE and DOC offices and downloadable from ⓦwanganui.com), which highlights points of interest and lists their **distance from Wanganui**.

Pipiriki

The southern reaches of the Whanganui National Park are accessed from Raetihi along the winding 27km Pipiriki–Raetihi Road, meeting the river at **PIPIRIKI**, 76km north of Wanganui. It is little more than a bend in the road, the finishing point for canoe journeys and the start of jetboat trips upstream. A couple of operators run snack bars that are open whenever there's enough business.

Hiruharama

HIRUHARAMA (Maori for Jerusalem), 13km south of Pipiriki and 64km north of Wanganui, was originally a Maori village and Catholic mission but is now best known as the site of the **James K. Baxter commune** that briefly flourished in the early 1970s. Baxter, one of New Zealand's most (in)famous poets, attracted hundreds of followers to the area. A devout Roman Catholic convert, but also firm believer in free love in his search for a "New Jerusalem", he became father to a flock of his own, the *nga moki* (fatherless ones), who soon dispersed after his death in 1972. The main commune house is situated high on a hill to the northeast of the church, and Baxter is buried just below. Ask for directions from the remaining Sisters of Compassion, who still live beside the 1892 **church** (from the north head up the first driveway, with a mailbox marked "The Sisters"), which features a Maori-designed and -carved altar.

Moutoa Island and Ranana

Moutoa Island, 59km north of Wanganui, was the scene of a vicious battle in 1864 when the lower-river Maori defeated the rebellious Hauhau warriors, thus protecting the *mana* of the river and saving the lives of European settlers downstream at Wanganui. A cluster of houses 1km on marks **RANANA** (London), where there's a Roman Catholic mission church that's still in use today.

WHANGANUI RIVER ROAD MAIL TOUR

If you have neither the time nor inclination to spend a few days canoeing in the Whanganui National Park, consider taking the **Whanganui River Road Mail Tour** (daily; $63; ☎06 345 3475, ⓦwhanganuitours.co.nz), a genuine mail-delivery service stopping frequently at houses along the way as well as points of interest. The trip starts early (accommodation pick-up can be arranged from Wanganui city) and doesn't return until mid- to late afternoon, so bring your own food or take up the $12 home-made lunch option, as there's nowhere to buy refreshments en route. Canoeing from Pipiriki, trampers' transport and jetboating can also be arranged.

Koriniti

The only real settlement of note in these parts is **KORINITI** (Corinth), 45km north of Wanganui, home to a lovely small church and a trio of traditional Maori buildings, the best being a 1920s **meeting house**, all down a side road. It's a private community, so while you can enter the church, the rest you should view from the road, unless you're invited into the compound. A *koha* of a couple of dollars is appropriate.

Atene and the Oyster Shell Cliffs

Atene 35km north of Wanganui • Oyster Shell Cliffs 8km south of Atene

The **Atene Viewpoint Walk** (5km return; 2hr; 100m ascent) affords great views of Puketapu, a hill that was once on a peninsula almost entirely encircled by the river. Riverboat owner Alexander Hatrick saw an opportunity to shave some time off his trips and blasted through the isthmus to leave the hill surrounded by a dried-out oxbow. The Viewpoint Walk comprises the first few kilometres of the **Atene Skyline Track** (18km loop; 6–8hr), making a wide loop following a gently ascending ridgeline that ends with a 2km walk along the road back to the start.

Further downriver are the **Oyster Shell Cliffs**, roadside bluffs with oyster-shell deposits embedded in them.

Aramoana Summit

17km northwest of Wanganui

Soon the winding climb begins to the summit lookout of **Aramoana**, giving a last look at the river below. On a clear day you can enjoy views of the northeast horizon, dominated by Mount Ruapehu. From the junction of the River Road and SH4, it's 14km to Wanganui.

ACCOMMODATION   **WHANGANUI RIVER ROAD**

★**The Flying Fox** Koriniti ☏06 342 8160, ⓦtheflyingfox.co.nz; map p.241. At this wonderfully remote and romantic hideaway, accessible only by boat or aerial cableway (prior booking essential), an eclectic range of found objects and scavenged pieces of old buildings have been imaginatively combined to create three separate self-contained buildings which encourage outdoor living amid the organic gardens and bush. Wood-fired bush baths, solar-heated showers, odourless composting toilets and a few spiders keeping the mosquitoes at bay add to the appeal. Browse through a fascinating range of books, old vinyl and CDs in the James K (self-catering, sleeping five), the Brewers Cottage (self-catering, sleeping three), or the Glory Cart (modelled on a gypsy caravan; $100), or camp. You can self-cater or prearrange predominantly organic breakfasts, and book canoeing trips (from $85/3hr). Free wi-fi. Camping **$20**, Brewers Cottage & James K **$200**

Wanganui

There's an old-fashioned charm to **WANGANUI**, the slow pace mirroring the speed of the river that bisects it. Founded on the banks of the **Whanganui River**, New Zealand's longest navigable watercourse, Wanganui is one of New Zealand's oldest cities and was

WANGANUI OR WHANGANUI?

Unlike the Whanganui National Park and Whanganui River, the city of Wanganui has long been spelt without an "h". The pronunciation of both is the same, deriving from the local Maori dialect, pronouncing the "wh" prefix phonetically (as opposed to elsewhere in the country, where the "wh" is pronounced "f"). The spelling quirk results from a direct transcription of the Maori name (*whanga nui* translates as "big harbour"). Most locals opposed any streamlining of the spelling, but in 2009 authorities ruled that the "h" is optional. For consistency with the majority of current usage, the city spelling "Wanganui" has been retained in this guide.

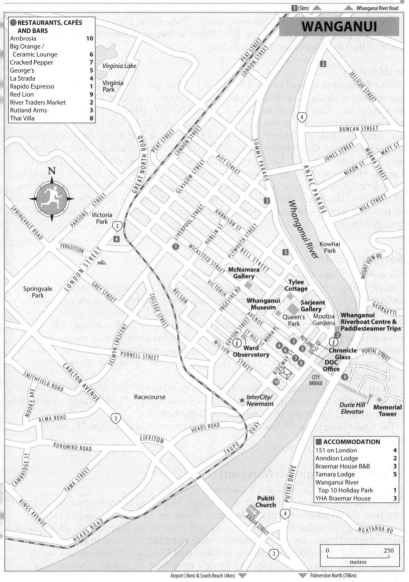

WANGANUI

RESTAURANTS, CAFÉS AND BARS	
Ambrosia	10
Big Orange / Ceramic Lounge	6
Cracked Pepper	7
George's	5
La Strada	4
Rapido Espresso	1
Red Lion	9
River Traders Market	2
Rutland Arms	3
Thai Villa	8

ACCOMMODATION	
151 on London	4
Anndion Lodge	2
Braemar House B&B	3
Tamara Lodge	5
Wanganui River Top 10 Holiday Park	1
YHA Braemar House	3

Airport (3km) & South Beach (4km) ▽   ▽ Palmerston North (70km)

the hub of early European commerce because of its access to the interior, and coastal links with the ports of Wellington and New Plymouth. The river traffic has long gone and the port is a shadow of what it was, leaving a city that feels too big for its 42,000 people – it even has a small opera house. Still, it's a manageable place that exudes civic pride, both for its quality museums and well-tended streetscape. The low cost of living has seen a thriving **arts community** spring up here, and it's a pleasant place to idle away some time in the renowned **art gallery**, watch a **glass-blowing** demonstration or take a class, and to ride on a restored **river steamer**.

The cultural heart of Wanganui beats around Pukenamu, a grassy hill that marks the site of Wanganui's last tribal war in 1832. Now known as **Queens Park**, it contains three of the city's most significant buildings.

Brief history

When **Europeans** arrived in the 1830s, land rights quickly became a bone of contention with the local Maori population. Transactions that Maori perceived as a ritual exchange of gifts were taken by the New Zealand Company to be a successful negotiation for the purchase of Wanganui and a large amount of surrounding land. Settlement went ahead regardless of the misunderstanding, and it was not until the **Gilfillan Massacre** of 1847 that trouble erupted – when a Maori was accidentally injured, his tribesmen massacred four members of the Gilfillan family. Further violent incidents culminated in a full-scale but inconclusive **battle** at St John's Hill. The next year the problems were apparently resolved by a payment of £1000 to the Maori. In the 1990s, the central Moutoa Gardens became the focus of renewed tensions, while the **spelling** of the city's name also creates divisions – see box, p.246.

Sarjeant Gallery

Queens Park • Daily 10.30am–4.30pm • Free • ☎ 06 349 0506, ⓦ sarjeant.org.nz

The gleaming hilltop **Sarjeant Gallery** is housed in one of Wanganui's most impressive buildings, a 1919 Oamaru stone structure boasting a magnificent dome that filters natural light into the exhibition space. Rotating quarterly exhibitions partly draw on the highly regarded permanent collection that is strong on both colonial and contemporary New Zealand art and photography. One artist to look out for is the underrated Edith Collier, a local painter whose career was overshadowed by that of her contemporary, Frances Hodgkins. All this is augmented by various strong touring exhibitions.

Much of the contemporary collection is the product of regular artist residencies at one of Wanganui's oldest buildings, the 1853 weatherboard **Tylee Cottage**, immediately to the north at the corner of Cameron and Bell streets.

The Quay Gallery, an offshoot of the Sarjeant, is upstairs at the i-SITE, and has quality exhibitions.

Whanganui Regional Museum

Watt St • Daily 10am–4.30pm • Free • ☎ 06 349 1110, ⓦ wrm.org.nz

Southwest of the Sarjeant Gallery, the Veteran Steps lead towards the centre of the city past the **Whanganui Regional Museum**. Founded in 1892, it contains an outstanding collection of Maori artefacts and three impressive canoes, all displayed in the central court. In smaller galleries hang portraits of Maori in full ceremonial dress and *moko* (traditional tattoos) by Gottfried Lindauer. Look out too for the photos of Whanganui river life, and models of ancient Maori methods of trapping eels and lampreys.

Moutoa Gardens

Moutoa Gardens, where the river kinks around the central city on Somme Parade, is little more than a small patch of grass imbued with history. Traditionally Maori lived at Moutoa during the fishing season, until it was co-opted by Pakeha settlers, who renamed the area Market Square. It was here that Maori signed the document agreeing to the "sale" of Wanganui, an issue revisited on Waitangi Day 1995, when simmering old grievances and one or two more recent ones reached boiling point. Maori occupied

GLASS-BLOWING AND PHOTOGRAPHY IN WANGANUI

New Zealand's only **glass-blowing** school is based in Wanganui, and the city is home to around three dozen glass-blowing artists brought together as the Wanganui Glass Group (ⓦwanganuiglass.com). Many work out of private studios, which open their doors to the public during March as part of the Whanganui Artists Open Studios programme – dates and trails are listed at ⓦopenstudio.co.nz. The annual Wanganui **Festival of Glass** takes place from late September to early October. Wanganui also has one of New Zealand's very few galleries totally dedicated to **photography**.

Chronicle Glass Studio 2 Rutland St ☎06 347 1921, ⓦchronicleglass.co.nz. You can see glass-blowing demonstrations – and some superb pieces – year-round here, the workshop/gallery of acclaimed glass-blowers Katie Brown and Lyndsay Patterson. You can also make your own paperweight during a forty-minute course ($100, by appointment), or book in for a weekend-long glass-blowing course ($390).

McNamara Gallery 190 Wickstead St ☎06 348 7320, ⓦmcnamara.co.nz. Paul McNamara's gallery is New Zealand's only dedicated photographic gallery, really just a couple of rooms in a house, though always with something challenging on show. Generally open Tues–Sat 11am–3pm, call to check.

3

Moutoa Gardens, claiming it as Maori land, for 83 days. This ended peacefully in the High Court, but created much bitterness on both sides. By 2001 a more conciliatory atmosphere prevailed, and the government, city council and local *iwi* agreed to share management of the gardens.

Waimarie paddle steamer

1a Taupo Quay • Daily 11am • $39 • ☎06 347 1863, ⓦriverboats.co.nz

Wanganui's history is inextricably tied with the Whanganui River, and though commercial river traffic has virtually stopped, you can still ride the *Waimarie* **paddle steamer**. New Zealand's last surviving paddle steamer, it makes a two-hour run up a tidal stretch of the river. The huffing of the coal-fired steam engine and the slosh of the paddles make for a soothing background to an afternoon's sunning on deck, or you can retire to the wood-panelled saloon for scones and tea (or a glass of wine).

Yarrow and Company of London built the *Waimarie* in 1899 to a shallow-draught design with a tough hull, making it suitable for river work. It was transported to New Zealand in kit form, then put to work on the Whanganui River, where it saw service during the pre-Great War boom in tourism, when thousands from all over the world came to travel up the Whanganui River and stay at the hotel at Pipiriki. In 1949 the *Waimarie* made her last voyage and three years later sank at her moorings. It wasn't until 1993 that the boat was salvaged, and it returned to the river in 1999.

Whanganui Riverboat Museum

1a Taupo Quay • Mon–Sat 9am–4pm, Sun 10am–2pm • Free • ☎06 347 1863, ⓦriverboats.co.nz

The restoration of the *Waimarie* took place at the **Whanganui Riverboat Museum**, adjacent to the cruise departure docks and flanked by old warehouses and stores. Housed in an 1881 two-storey timber-framed building, the museum concentrates on the river and its history in relation to the town and includes the partly restored MV *Ongarue*, which worked the river from 1900 to 1957.

Durie Hill Elevator and Memorial Tower

Elevator Mon–Fri 8am–6pm, Sat & Sun 10am–5pm • $2 each way **Tower** Daily 8am–dusk • Free

City Bridge takes you from downtown to the east bank of the river and the **Durie Hill**

Elevator. A Maori carved gateway here marks the entrance to a 213m tunnel, at the end of which a historic 1919 elevator carries passengers 66m up through the hill to the summit. At the top of the hill two excellent vantage points grant extensive views of the city, beaches and inland. The viewpoint atop the elevator's machinery room is the easy option, but the best views are 176 steps up at the top of the 33.5m-high **Memorial Tower**. Head back to town using the 191 steps to the river – it only takes about ten minutes, and provides additional satisfying views.

Putiki church

Anaua St • Often locked; contact the i-SITE for access • $2 donation

It's about 2km south along Putiki Drive to the small, whitewashed **St Paul's Memorial Church**, which contains magnificent Maori carvings adorned with paua, a painted rib ceiling (as in Maori meeting houses), two beautiful etched-glass windows and some intricate *tukutuku* panels.

ARRIVAL AND DEPARTURE WANGANUI

By plane Flights from Auckland arrive at the airport (ⓦwanganuiairport.co.nz), 7km southwest of the city; a taxi into town costs around $25.
Destinations Auckland (3–4 daily; 1hr).
By bus InterCity buses drop off at the Wanganui Travel Centre, 156 Ridgway St (ⓣ06 345 4433). NakedBus stop

outside the i-SITE.
Destinations Auckland (1 daily; 8hr 30min); Hamilton (2 daily; 5hr 40min); New Plymouth (2 daily; 2hr 30min); Palmerston North (3 daily; 1hr 15min); Taumarunui (1 daily; 2hr 40min); Wellington (3 daily; 4hr 10min).

GETTING AROUND

By bus Tranzit buses (ⓣ06 345 4433, ⓦhorizons.govt .nz) run a limited Mon–Sat bus service round the city

(flat fare $2).
By taxi Wanganui Taxis (ⓣ0800 343 5555).

INFORMATION

Tourist information i-SITE, 31 Taupo Quay (Mon–Fri 8.30am–5pm, Sat & Sun 9am–4pm; ⓣ06 349 0508, ⓦwanganui.com). Has free internet access and wi-fi, timetables for the local buses and sells Whanganui

National Park hut and camping passes.
DOC 35 Taupo Quay (Mon–Fri 8am–5pm; ⓣ06 348 8475). Sells Whanganui National Park hut and camping passes.

ACCOMMODATION

151 on London 151 London St ⓣ0800 151 566, ⓦ151onlondon.co.nz. Contemporary motel, with a range of studios and suites, sleek TVs, broadband, a/c, a small gym and even an on-site café. (Limited) free wifi. **$120**

Anndion Lodge 143 Anzac Parade ⓣ0800 343 056, ⓦanndionlodge.co.nz. Professional combination of an upmarket backpackers and a very comfortable lodge spread over three suburban houses. There are no dorms, just comfortable shared-bath rooms, en-suite rooms and one- and two-bedroom suites, all done out in slightly tacky black-and-crimson colour schemes. There is a communal kitchen complete with bread maker and dishwasher, plus a lovely BBQ area, swimming pool, spa and sauna, free wi-fi, courtesy city transport and even a restaurant. Double **$88**, en-suite double **$130**

Braemar House B&B 2 Plymouth St ⓣ06 348 2301, ⓦbraemarhouse.co.nz. Bathrooms are shared in this

excellent-value budget B&B situated in a lovely 1895 homestead surrounded by lawns. Some rooms front onto a sun-drenched veranda and there's a YHA hostel out back (see opposite). Add $20 a head for continental breakfast. **$100**

Tamara Lodge 24 Somme Parade ⓣ06 347 6300, ⓦtamaralodge.com. A large and well-kept historic building with pretty gardens and a sociable vibe that makes it popular with younger backpackers. Offers free bikes, musical instruments, neat comfortable four-bed dorms, doubles and twins (some en-suite, $84), plus a balcony with a river view, and a trampoline in the large garden. Unlimited free fast wi-fi. Dorms **$28**, rooms **$70**

Wanganui River Top 10 Holiday Park 460 Somme Parade ⓣ0800 272 664, ⓦwrivertop10.co.nz. Well-tended site 6km northeast of the city centre, beside the river in the shade of giant trees. There's kayak and jet ski rental too. Camping **$48**, cabins **$70**

YHA Braemar House 2 Plymouth St ☎ 06 348 2301, ⓦ braemarhouse.co.nz. Welcoming backpackers attached to *Braemar House B&B* with separate male and female dorms, private rooms out back, a kitchen and cosy lounge and a peaceful atmosphere. Dorms $̄30, hostel rooms $̄60

EATING AND DRINKING

Ambrosia 63 Ridgway St ☎ 06 348 5524. Great little deli stocking all manner of gourmet and artisan goodies from New Zealand and around the world, including organic meats, cheeses and Wanganui olive oil, plus top-notch bagels, pastries and excellent coffee to go. Mon 8.30am–4pm, Tues–Fri 8.30am–5pm, Sat 9am–2pm.

Big Orange/Ceramic Lounge 51 Victoria Ave ☎ 06 348 4449. Two names, same place: this buzzing café (*Big Orange*) transforms into the hip restaurant/cocktail bar *Ceramic Lounge*, where you might expect roast pork medallion on gnocchi ($27) followed by piña colada sago ($13). Mon & Tues 7am–5pm, Wed–Fri 7.30am–8.30pm or later, Sat 8.30am–8.30pm or later, Sun 8.30am–5pm.

Cracked Pepper 21 Victoria Ave ☎ 06 345 0444. Licensed café serving gourmet twists on old favourites, including lamb's fry and bacon, calamari risotto, and good chicken Caesar salad, all under $20. A good choice for breakfast, with delicious eggs Benedict ($18). Mon–Sat 7.30am–4.30pm.

George's 40 Victoria Ave ☎ 06 345 7937. A local institution, this old-fashioned fish and chip shop has an attached dining room and also sells good-value wet fish. Mon–Sat 8.30am–7.30pm, Fri to 8.30pm.

★**La Strada** 13 Victoria Ave ☎ 06 345 9797, ⓦ lastradarestaurant.co.nz. Italian/Spanish-influenced restaurant serving tapas-style dishes and freshly baked pizzas. Take a table out on the main street or in the funky interior with its bare-brick walls and cosy corners. Sun–Thurs 11am–2pm and 5pm–late, Fri & Sat 11am–late.

Rapido Espresso 71 Liverpool St ☎ 06 347 9475. Sink into a sofa in this chilled villa café that focuses on its superb organic coffee, though they sell a few muffins, cake slices and lunchtime veggie and meaty sandwiches ($6–7.50). Mon–Fri 7.30am–6pm, Sat 9am–3pm.

Red Lion 45 Anzac Parade ☎ 06 348 4080, ⓦ redlioninn .co.nz. Atmospheric pulse-of-the-town pub overlooking the river with meal deals and a lively atmosphere as the weekend approaches. Visit for happy hour on Friday or on Monday or Tuesday for $8 burger night. Daily 11am–10pm or later.

River Traders Market On Taupo Quay, behind the i-SITE ⓦ therivertraders.co.nz. Come the weekend, get yourself along to this hugely popular market where local artisans and growers set up their stalls, rain or shine. Sat 9am–1pm.

The Rutland Arms Cnr Victoria Ave & Ridgway St ☎ 06 347 7677, ⓦ rutlandarms.co.nz. Slap bang in the centre of the city this friendly pub is a relaxed place for a drink at any time of day. There's also a simple menu of pub meals including NZ lamb rump ($33.50) and chicken supreme ($29.50). Daily 9am–late.

Thai Villa 7 Victoria Ave ☎ 06 348 9089. Quality Thai place with all your favourite curries and stir-fries ($18–21) along with hot plate options such as Weeping Tiger, a dish of marinated beef and vegetables. ($23). Licensed and BYO. Tues–Sat 5–10.30pm.

ENTERTAINMENT

Embassy 3 Cinema 34 Victoria Ave ☎ 06 345 7958, ⓦ embassy3.co.nz. Mainstream films at Wanganui's only cinema, an Art Deco affair from the early 1950s.

Ward Observatory Hill St. Every clear Friday evening you can look through the 24cm refractor at this wonderful 1901 observatory ($2 donation). To arrange a viewing outside of the hours listed here, contact the i-SITE. Oct–March Fri 8.30pm; April–Sept Fri 8pm.

Palmerston North and around

One of New Zealand's largest landlocked cities, **PALMERSTON NORTH** (as opposed to Palmerston near Dunedin, and known as "Palmy") is the thriving capital of the province of Manawatu, with around 80,000 residents, including a lively student population attending **Massey University**. After the arrival of the rail line in 1886, Palmerston North flourished, thanks to its pivotal position at the junction of road and rail routes, reflected today by some fine civic buildings, notably an excellent **museum** and **gallery** and a stunning **library**. Nonetheless, an unimpressed John Cleese famously claimed, "If you want to kill yourself but lack the courage, I think a visit to Palmerston North will do the trick." The town responded by naming the local rubbish dump after him.

The city's main cultural event, the Festival of Cultures (ⓦfoc.co.nz), takes place around The Square in late March with a Friday-night lantern festival and a Saturday craft, food and music fair. Artists who recently played at WOMAD in New Plymouth often turn up on the bill.

The Square

Palmerston North centres on **The Square**, a smart, grassy expanse with an elegant clock tower. The adjacent **Te Marae o Hine**, or the Courtyard of the Daughter of Peace, is graced by a couple of 5m-high Maori figures carved by renowned artist **John Bevan Ford**. The Maori name is the one suggested for the settlement's central square by the chief of the Ngati Raukawa in 1878, in the hope that love and peace would become enduring features in the relationship between the Manawatu Maori and incoming Pakeha.

The most striking of the surrounding buildings is the **City Library**, a postmodern reworking of the original 1927 department store by Kiwi star architect, Ian Athfield.

Te Manawa

326 Main St • Daily 10am–5pm • Free • ☎ 06 355 5000, ⓦtemanawa.co.nz

The city's main cultural focus is **Te Manawa**, with well-laid-out galleries covering Maori heritage and life in the Manawatu once Europeans arrived. Some of the best material is in the Te Awa section, covering all aspects of the Manawatu River from geology and ecology to bug life (there's a weta cave) and a tank of native fish (effectively grown-up whitebait). The stunning carpet is an aerial view of the entire region. Throughout the galleries there's masses of hands-on stuff for kids.

The adjacent **Art Gallery** displays Pakeha and Maori art from its permanent collection, alongside touring exhibitions.

New Zealand Rugby Museum

Upstairs at Te Manawa • Daily 10am–5pm • \$12.50 • ☎ 06 358 6947, ⓦrugbymuseum.co.nz

Knock down a tackle bag, try to move a scrum machine or kick goals better than Piri Weepu at the small **New Zealand Rugby Museum**, where the interactive area is surrounded by an excellent decade-by-decade social history of rugby in New Zealand including games played by soldiers in Egypt during World War II. There's everything from old leather shoulder-pads and footage of the 1905 All Black "originals" tour, to cartoons lampooning rugby selectors and the coin tossed at the start of each Rugby World Cup final.

Manawatu Gorge

15km northeast of Palmerston North

Heading northeast from Palmerston North the skyline above the semirural town of **Ashhurst** is broken by the southern hemisphere's largest **wind farms**, draped across the Ruahine and Tararua ranges. These hills are separated by the Manawatu Gorge (Te Apiti in Maori), a narrow 10km-long defile through which a rail line, SH3 and the Manawatu River squeeze. The gorge can be explored on foot along the **Manawatu Gorge Track** (3–4hr one way; contact the i-SITE for gorge transport options), or you can see it on a jetboat tour (see opposite).

| ARRIVAL AND DEPARTURE | PALMERSTON NORTH AND AROUND |

By train The train station is on Matthews Ave, about 1500m northwest of the city centre.

Destinations Auckland (3 weekly; 8hr 50min); Hamilton (3 weekly; 6hr 30min); Wellington (3–8 weekly; 2hr 10min).

By bus InterCity buses stop at the Palmerston North Travel

Centre, at the corner of Pitt and Main sts, while NakedBus stops outside the i-SITE.

Destinations Auckland (3 daily; 9hr); Hastings (2 daily; 2hr 30min); Napier (2 daily; 3hr); Paraparaumu (6 daily; 1hr 30min); Rotorua (2 daily; 5hr 30min); Taupo (3 daily; 4hr); Wanganui (3 daily; 1hr 45min); Wellington (6 daily; 2hr 30min).

By plane The airport (⊛ pnairport.co.nz) is 3km northeast of the city. SuperShuttle (☎ 0800 748 885) runs into town ($18 for one, $22 for two).

Destinations Auckland (5 daily; 1hr); Christchurch (4 daily; 1hr 15min); Wellington (2 daily; 30min).

GETTING AROUND

By bus A series of loop services ($2.50 single) runs from Main St, near the i-SITE, where you can pick up timetables.

By taxi Palmerston North Taxis (☎ 06 355 5333).

INFORMATION AND TOURS

Visitor information i-SITE, The Square (Mon–Fri 9am–5pm, Sat & Sun 9am–3pm; ☎ 06 358 8414, ⊛ manawatunz.co.nz). Good for DOC leaflets and hut tickets plus showers ($2; $4 with towel). Parking is tricky here though.

Services Downtown Palmerston North has free wi-fi (limited to 100Mb per month).

Manawatu Gorge Jet ☎ 0800 945 335, ⊛ manawatugorgejet.com. Take a hair-raising 25min jetboat ride through Manawatu Gorge ($75).

ACCOMMODATION

Palmerston North has more motels than you could ever imagine the town might need, so turning up and simply driving along Fitzherbert Avenue until you see one that takes your fancy is always an option.

Acacia Court Motel 374 Tremaine Ave ☎ 0800 685 586, ⊛ acaciacourtmotel.co.nz. Friendly, older-style motel with good prices for spotlessly clean if slightly dowdy self-contained units (some sleeping up to five) with Sky TV and off-street parking. $98

Arena Lodge 74 Pascal St ☎ 0800 881 255 or 06 357 5577, ⊛ arenalodge.co.nz. Smart, modern motel in a quiet location 1km west of the Square with a range of deluxe rooms, some with barbecue area and spa bath. $140

Palmerston North Holiday Park 133 Dittmer Drive ☎ 06 358 0349, ⊛ palmerstonnorthholidaypark.co.nz. Quiet (sometimes almost eerily so), shady campsite with basic facilities, 2km south of the city centre and close to the Manawatu River. Camping per site $35, cabins $58

Pepper Tree 121 Grey St ☎ 06 355 4054, ⊛ peppertreehostel.co.nz. The best of the city's limited range of hostels, located in a welcoming and comfortable villa within easy walking distance of the central square. Dorms $30, doubles $74

Plum Trees Lodge 97 Russell St ☎ 06 358 7813, ⊛ plumtreeslodge.co.nz. Lovely and tastefully decorated self-catering loft in a quiet suburban street, with a leafy deck where you can pick your own plums. An extensive breakfast hamper is supplied. $155

★ **Rose City Motel** 120–122 Fitzherbert Ave ☎ 06 356 5388, ⊛ rosecitymotel.co.nz. Pick of the motels along a street full of them, with contemporary and surprisingly spacious rooms with kitchens. Some have spa baths and there's free wi-fi. $128

EATING AND DRINKING

Thanks to its term-time student population, Palmerston North supports a vibrant restaurant scene, with almost everything close to the Square.

Barista 59 George St ☎ 06 357 2614, ⊛ barista .co.nz. Minimalist espresso bar in a stripped industrial space of exposed pipes and concrete where they grind their own coffee and serve great cakes, snacks and full meals such as salmon fillet and fish of the day (both $30), along with an excellent range of New Zealand wines. There's a Sunday high tea (3–5pm; $24), and Saturday-night live jazz and standards. Daily 8am–10pm or much later.

Brewers Apprentice 334 Church St ☎ 06 358 8888, ⊛ brewersapprentice.co.nz. Lively, modern Monteith's pub with plenty of open-air drinking space, and a good

range of quality pub meals including pan-fried market fish with boulangère potatoes ($31). Mon–Wed 4–10pm, Thurs–Sun 10am–10pm or later.

★ **Café Cuba** 236 Cuba St ☎ 06 356 5750, ⊛ cafecuba .co.nz. Funky day/night café that's a local institution for breakfast, all-day brunch and lunch (under $20) and dinners such as parmesan crumbled lamb cutlets ($31). Lots of vegetarian fare, hip staff and usually live music on Friday or Saturday nights. Licensed & BYO. Daily 7am–10pm.

Café Express 41 The Square ☎ 06 353 8440, ⊛ cafeexpress.net.nz. The perfect place to start the day in

Palmy, overlooking the Square as it comes to life. Order the eggs Benedict ($15.90) or buttermilk pancakes ($15.40) washed down with strong coffee, or visit at lunchtime for risotto, pasta and steak (around $23). Mon–Fri 7am–4pm, Sat & Sun 8am–4pm.

The Fish Regent Arcade, 57 Broadway Ave ☎ 06 357 9845. Cool little cocktail and wine bar with DJs on Thursday and Friday nights. Wed 4–11pm, Thurs 4pm–1am, Fri & Sat 4pm–3am.

Thai House 84 Fitzherbert Ave ☎ 06 357 0885. Friendly Thai restaurant with all the standard fare, including fiery curries. Daily 4.30–10pm.

Tomato 72 George St ☎ 06 357 6663. Faded Kiwi landscapes and a paua-shell counter give this relaxed café a retro vibe. Tuck into a breakfast of Avo smash ($15.90) or gumbo ($16.90), or mains such as rabbit pie ($24.90) or pizza (from $12.90) from 5.30pm. And don't miss the bathroom decor of 1970s women's magazine advertising. Mon–Wed 7am–3pm, Thurs & Sat 7am–9pm, Sun 7am–4pm.

Yeda 78 Broadway Ave ☎ 06 358 3978, ⓦ yeda.co.nz. Pan-Asian restaurant and cocktail bar with a good line in the likes of steamed fish with ginger and soy ($17.50) and barbecue pork buns ($5). Daily 11am–9pm.

NIGHTLIFE AND ENTERTAINMENT

Centrepoint 280 Church St ☎ 06 354 5740, ⓦ centre point.co.nz. New Zealand's only professional provincial theatre is a 135-seater with shows from April to Christmas.

Downtown Cinemas 70 Broadway Ave ☎ 06 355 5655, ⓦ dtcinemas.co.nz. Screens both mainstream and art-house films.

Foxton and around

Horowhenua's most interesting town is **FOXTON**, 38km southwest of Palmerston North, where the old-style shop facades line the broad main street bypassed by SH1. Archeological evidence suggests that there was a seminomadic **moa-hunter** culture in this area between 1400 and 1650, predating larger tribal settlements. **Europeans** arrived in the early 1800s and settled at the mouth of the Manawatu River, subsequently founding Foxton on a tributary. It quickly became the **flax-milling** capital of New Zealand, the industry only finally dying in 1985. A **historic walk** tells the tale through 28 plaques around town.

Progress has been slow on the proposed new cultural precinct next to the windmill, known as **Te Awahou–Nieuwe Stroom**. Check ⓦ tans.org.nz for updates on this new facility designed to celebrate local Maori and the strong New Zealand–Dutch heritage, along with a visitor centre and library.

The long, sandy **Foxton Beach** is 5km away on the coast, where there's good surfing, safe swimming areas and abundant birdlife around the Manawatu river estuary.

De Molen

Main St · Daily 10am–4pm · Tours $5 · ☎ 06 363 5601, ⓦ demolenfoxton.org.nz

Low-rise Foxton is dominated by **de Molen**, a modern, full-scale **replica** of a classic seventeenth-century **Dutch windmill**. Self-guided tours visit the inner workings, and on three to four days a month you'll see it producing stoneground wholemeal flour. On the ground floor, you can buy Dutch groceries and the town's local soft drink, **Foxton Fizz**, in old-fashioned flavours such as creaming soda.

Flax Stripper Museum

Main St · Daily 1–3pm · $5 · ☎ 06 363 6846

A broad history of Foxton's flax industry is recounted in the **Flax Stripper Museum**, which shows examples of the handmade flax (*harakeke*) baskets and cloaks perfected by local Maori. But the real emphasis is on European operations, cultivating flax near swamps and on riverbanks in Manawatu and Horowhenua then exporting flax fibre around the country and abroad for binder twine, fibrous plaster and carpet.

Subsequently, woolpacks were made in Foxton. The staff put the loud mechanical flax stripper through its paces, explain the history in fascinating detail and point out the benefits of various flax varieties planted outside.

Papaitonga Scenic Reserve

Off SH1, 23km south of Foxton

The main southbound road routes converge at the workaday town of **LEVIN**, the administrative centre of the Horowhenua region. Just south of town at the **Papaitonga Scenic Reserve**, a boardwalk leads to the Papaitonga Lookout (20min return) and great **views** of Lake Papaitonga. The surrounding wetlands provide a refuge for many **rare birds**, including the spotless crake, Australasian bittern and New Zealand dabchick.

The Kapiti Coast

3

The narrow plain between the rugged and inhospitable **Tararua Range** and the Tasman breakers is known as the **Kapiti Coast**, effectively part of Wellington's commuter belt, peppered with dormitory suburbs and golf courses. Still, it has sweeping beaches, a few minor points of interest and provides access to **Kapiti Island**, 5km offshore, a magnificent bush-covered sanctuary where birdlife thrives.

Otaki

OTAKI, 20km south of Levin, sits beside a broad, braided section of the Otaki River, surrounded by market gardens. For most of the year, this is a quiet place with strong Maori heritage (it was the first town in New Zealand to have bilingual road signs), but, like other towns along this coast, it swells to bursting point for the month or so after Christmas when Kiwi holiday-makers descend en masse.

Otaki comes in three parts: the train station and i-SITE on SH1; Otaki township 2km towards the sea along Mill Road; and the **beach**, a further 3km along Mill Road, safe to swim at in summer thanks to a surf patrol. Self-contained campervans can freedom-camp here on the north bank of the river.

Along SH1 are around twenty **designer outlet stores**, mostly women's clothing but also outdoors shops such as Kathmandu and Icebreaker.

Rangiatea Church

33 Te Rauparaha St, 200m west of SH1 • Casual visits Mon–Fri 9.30am–1.30pm; guided tours Mon–Sat 10am & 2pm • Free; guided tours $35 • ☎ 06 364 6838

Rangiatea Church is an exact replica of the 1849 original that was widely regarded as the finest Maori church in New Zealand. The church was consecrated in 2003, eight years after the original was razed in an arson attack. Inside, the building is simple, with *tukutuku* panels on the walls, the pattern representing both the stars and the departed.

The rafters are painted in Maori designs representing hammerhead sharks (symbols of power and privilege), and the exquisite model of the Tainui *waka*, which escaped the blaze. Outside, the simple, grey-slate headstone of the Maori chief Te Rauparaha can be found in a row of three by a decapitated Norfolk pine. Opposite the church is a memorial to the great chief.

Waikanae

WAIKANAE, 14km south of Otaki, is divided between the highwayside settlement and a beach community, 4km away along Te Moana Road, where the broad, dune-backed **beach** has safe swimming.

Nga Manu Nature Reserve

Ngarara Rd; Take Te Moana Road off SH1 for just over 1km and turn right at Ngarara Road; the sanctuary is a further 3km • Daily 10am–5pm • $15 • ☎ 04 293 4131, ⓦ ngamanu.co.nz

To see native wildlife in its more-or-less natural habitat, stop at the **Nga Manu Nature Reserve**, a large man-made bird sanctuary with easy walking tracks and some picnic spots. A circular track (1500m) cuts through a variety of habitats, from ponds and scrubland to swamp and coastal forest, which attract all manner of birds. There is also a nocturnal house containing kiwi, morepork and tuatara, plus eels, fed at 2pm daily, and some walk-in aviaries where kea and kaka strut their stuff.

Southward Car Museum

Otaihanga Rd, 3km south of Waikanae • Daily: Nov–April 9am–5pm; May–Oct 9am–4.30pm • $10 • ☎ 04 297 1221, ⓦ southwardcarmuseum.co.nz

With over 250 vehicles in a specially built showroom, the **Southward Car Museum** contains one of the largest collections of cars, fire engines and motorbikes in Australasia. Well-kept examples of mundane models from the 1960s, 1970s and 1980s might strike older readers as barely museum-worthy, but there's no shortage of exotica, all in mint condition. Gems include Marlene Dietrich's Rolls-Royce, a 1915 Stutz Racer and a 1955 gull-winged Mercedes Benz. Look out, too, for one of the futuristic white cars used in Woody Allen's 1973 film *Sleeper*, and half a dozen hand-built models that were the product of assorted Kiwi back sheds.

Paraparaumu

The burgeoning dormitory community of **PARAPARAUMU** (aka "Paraparam"), 7km south of Waikanae and 45km from Wellington, is the Kapiti Coast's largest settlement. It is primarily of interest as the only jumping-off point to Kapiti Island, which faces the long and sandy **Paraparaumu Beach**, 3km to the west along Kapiti Road. With safe swimming, accommodation and a few restaurants, this is the place to hang out.

Kapiti Island

Kapiti Island is one of the best and most easily accessible island **nature reserves** in New Zealand, a 15min boat ride offshore from Paraparaumu Beach. This magical spot, just 10km by 2km, was once cleared for farmland but is again cloaked in bush and home to birdlife that has become rare or extinct on the mainland. Much of New Zealand's bush is now virtually silent but here it trills to the sound of chirping birds – much as it did before the arrival of humans.

In 1824, famed Maori chief **Te Rauparaha** (original composer of the *haka*) captured the island from its first known Maori inhabitants and, with his people the Ngati Toa, used it as a base until his death in 1849. The island is considered extremely spiritual by Maori, and was designated a reserve in 1897.

Late January and February are the best months to visit, when the **birdlife** is at its most active, but at any time of the year you're likely to see kaka (bush parrots that may alight on your head or shoulder), weka, kakariki (parakeets), whiteheads (bush

---

WALKING AROUND KAPITI

The island can be explored on two fairly steep **walking tracks**, the **Trig Track** and the **Wilkinson Track**, which effectively form a loop by meeting near the island's highest point, Tuteremoana (521m). There are spectacular views from the summit, though the widest variety of birdlife is found along the lower parts of the tracks – take your time, keep quiet and stop frequently (allow about 3hr for the round trip).

canaries), tui, bellbirds, fantails, wood pigeons, robins and a handful of the 300 takahe that exist in the world.

The **North End** of the island (about a tenth of its total area) is also part of the Kapiti Nature Reserve, though it's managed and accessed separately. The **Okupe Lagoon** has a colony of royal spoonbills, and there are plenty of rare forest birds and kiwi.

A wedge of sea between Kapiti Island and Paraparaumu has been designated a **marine reserve**, and its exceptionally clear waters make for great **snorkelling** around the rocks (bring your own gear, or rent it from the *Kapiti Nature Lodge*). You'll need your own gear for **scuba diving**, which is particularly good to the west and north of the island.

Paekakariki and around

At the southern extent of the Kapiti Coast, the village of **Paekakariki** has a tiny but vibrant beach community. Families should make straight for the 6.5-square-kilometre **Queen Elizabeth Park** (daily 8am–8pm), which has entrances at MacKays Crossings on SH1, and off the Esplanade in Raumati. At the former entrance is the **Tramway Museum** (Sat & Sun 11am–4.30pm; daily in Jan; tram rides $8; ☎04 292 8361, ⓦwellingtontrams.org.nz), which runs restored Wellington trams along 2km of track to the beach. The adjacent **Stables on the Park** (Sat & Sun 10.30am–3.30pm; horse treks and pony rides from $25; ☎04 298 4609, ⓦstablesonthepark.co.nz) offers horse treks and pony rides for kids.

Pataka Museum of Arts and Cultures

22km south of Paekakariki, corner of Norrie and Parumoana sts • Mon–Sat 10am–4.30pm, Sun 11am–4.30pm • Free • ☎04 237 1511, ⓦpataka.org.nz

Just 20km north of Wellington, the expanding satellite city of **Porirua** is worth a brief stop for the excellent **Pataka Museum of Arts and Cultures**, which hosts local and touring exhibitions by leading contemporary New Zealand artists, plus regular Maori dance performances.

ARRIVAL AND DEPARTURE

THE KAPITI COAST

PARAPARAUMU

By train The *Overlander* and Wellington's TranzMetro commuter trains stop opposite the Coastlands shopping centre.

Destinations Paekakariki (every 30min; 17min); Plimmerton (every 30min; 30min); Porirua (every 30min; 45min); Wellington (every 30min; 1hr 10min).

By bus InterCity and NakedBus stop at the train station. Destinations Wellington (every 1hr; 1hr).

By plane Paraparaumu's airport (ⓦkapiticoastairport .co.nz), midway between SH1 and the beach, is served by Air New Zealand and Air2There (ⓦair2there.com).

Destinations Auckland (2–3 daily; 1hr 10min); Blenheim (1–3 daily; 40min); Nelson (1–3 daily; 45min).

KAPITI ISLAND

By boat DOC-approved operators Kapiti Marine Charter (☎0800 433 779, ⓦkapitimarinecharter.co.nz) and Kapiti Tours (☎0800 527 484, ⓦkapititours.co.nz) both run boat trips to the island from $75, including a tour when you get there. Boats generally leave from the beach beside Kapiti Boating Club around 9am and return around 3.30pm, with the option of a transfer to the North End (extra $10).

GETTING AROUND

By train The Auckland–Wellington rail line serves the coastal towns; services are much more frequent in the commuter belt from Waikanae south.

By bus The main bus companies serve the coastal towns, but off SH1 options are severely limited.

INFORMATION AND TOURS

OTAKI

i-SITE 239 SH1 (Mon–Fri 9am–5pm, Sat 10am–3pm, Sun 10am–2pm; ☎06 364 7620). This twice-relocated 1891-built wooden courthouse is the place to come for hut passes for tracks in the Tararua Forest Park

and the picturesque gorge of the Otaki River to the east.

PARAPARAUMU

i-SITE 134 Rimu Rd (Mon–Fri 9am–5pm, Sat & Sun

10am–2pm; ☎04 298 8195). Has local and DOC information and can help with permits for Kapiti Island.

KAPITI ISLAND

Bio-security DOC is understandably wary about the reintroduction of pests, so your bags are checked for any stray mammals.

Facilities On the island you'll find toilets and a shelter at the landing point: take your own food and water, and bring back all rubbish.

Tours See p.257 for how to get to Kapiti Island. Companies include a tour by foot on the island in their rates.

ACCOMMODATION

PARAPARAUMU

There's an adequate range of accommodation, and freedom campers in self-contained vans can park up opposite nos. 54 62 & 69 Marine Parade beside Paraparaumu Beach.

Barnacles Seaside Inn 3 Marine Parade, Paraparaumu Beach ☎04 902 5856, ⓦseasideyha .co.nz. This associate YHA in a rambling 1923 wooden hotel across the road from the beach has comfortable antique-furnished, shared-bath rooms and dorms. Dorms **$29**, doubles **$72**

Earthbush 197 Main North Rd, 3km north of town ☎04 298 7224, ⓦearthbushbedandbreakfast.co.nz. The owners built this ecofriendly, modern, rammed-earth home with very comfortable rooms, both opening out onto delightful gardens. There is a strong emphasis on organics, and free-range eggs get turned into delicious breakfasts. **$150**

Kapiti Court Motel 341 Kapiti Rd ☎0800 526 683, ⓦkapiticourtmotel.co.nz. Beside the shops and a 2min walk from the beach, quiet with outdoor pool and pleasant twin- and king-bed rooms, some with self-contained kitchens. **$120**

KAPITI ISLAND

Kapiti Nature Lodge Waiorua Bay ☎06 362 6606, ⓦkapitiislandnaturetours.co.nz. At the northern reserve, private land owned by the descendants of Te Rauparaha is the setting for the island's only accommodation and the most rewarding way to experience Kapiti. There's a simple, comfortable lodge and an intimate communal feel running through to the all-inclusive, family-style meals (which might include fresh seafood). Rates are per person and dependent on the type of accommodation, which is made up of cabins sleeping up to five. There are two excellent daytime walks (one beach, including spoonbills at certain times of the year, and one bush) and the night-time kiwi-spotting walks have a high success rate – there are estimated to be more than 1200 on the island. Alternatively, the day-tour ($165) includes the ferry, DOC permit, lunch and hour-long guided walk. Transfers can be arranged from Wellington. Per person **$355**, en suite **$405**

PAEKAKARIKI AND AROUND

Hilltop Hideaway 11 Wellington Rd, Paekakariki ☎04 902 5967, ⓦwellingtonbeachbackpackers.co.nz. Former backpackers close to the train station now offering just two budget en-suite doubles. Both have a kitchenette and a small terrace, one with great sunset views to the ocean. Discounts for longer stays. **$80**

★ **Moana Lodge** 49 Moana Rd, Plimmerton ☎04 233 2010, ⓦmoanalodge.co.nz. Superb bunk-free hostel that consistently ranks as one of New Zealand's best, set in a beautifully sited Edwardian villa with sea views from many rooms and four-bed dorms. There's free wi-fi and kayaks and a very friendly atmosphere. Dorms **$34**, doubles **$86**

Paekakariki Beachfront B&B 136 The Parade, Paekakariki ☎04 905 8595, ⓦpaekakarikibnb.co.nz. Just one large self-contained studio (containing a queen and a single bed) with great sea views and mere steps from the beach. Free pick-up from the train station on request. **$120**

Paekakariki Holiday Park 180 Wellington Rd, Paekakariki ☎04 292 8292, ⓦpaekakarik holidaypark.co.nz. Very popular and well-appointed family holiday park on the southern fringe of QE Park with good access to a safe swimming beach. Camping **$16**, units **$90**

EATING AND DRINKING

OTAKI

River Cottage SH1, 1km south ☎06 364 6359. Drop into this relaxed roadside stop with plenty of cottage garden seating for coffee and cake, a pesto-filled cheese Danish or a pumpkin, spinach and olive pizza ($16). Daily 8.30am–4pm.

PARAPARAUMU

Fed Up Fast Foods 40 Marine Parade ☎04 902 6686. Simple but stylish fresh fare including the area's best fish and chips and Kapiti ice cream, to eat in or take away. Daily blackboard combos under $10. Daily 11am–8.30pm.

Kapiti Cheeses & Ice Cream Lindale Centre, SH1, 2km north of town ☏ 04 298 1352, ⊛ kapiticollection.co.nz. Sample ice cream (in rich flavours such as gingernut and fig-and-honey) or some of the cheeses – among New Zealand's finest – at this shop in the Lindale shopping centre. Daily 9am–5pm.

Muang Thai 22 Maclean St ☏ 04 902 9699. Small, reliable spot serving quality Thai favourites such as *pad thai* and curries (all around $15). Mon–Thurs 5–10pm, Fri & Sat 5–11pm.

PAEKAKARIKI AND AROUND

The Beach Store 104 The Parade, Paekakariki ☏ 04 292 8330, ⊛ thebeachstore.co.nz. Essentially a cool design store with a kind of eclectic, *bach*-like, surf-shack feel, looking out across the water to Kapiti Island. Stop in for a coffee or a juice as you browse their goodies. Thurs–Sat 9.30am–5pm, Sun 10am–5pm.

3

Central North Island

EMERALD LAKES, TONGARIRO ALPINE CROSSING

Central North Island

The Central North Island contains some of New Zealand's star attractions, many the result of its explosive geological past. It's dominated by three heavyweight features: Lake Taupo, the country's largest; Tongariro National Park, with its trio of volcanoes; and the volcanic field that feeds colourful and fiercely active thermal areas, principally around Rotorua, where boiling mud pools plop next to spouting geysers fuelled by super-heated water, drawn off to fill hot pools around town. Accessible Maori cultural experiences abound here, with highly regarded Arawa carvings and groups who perform traditional dances and *haka* before a feast of fall-off-the-bone meat and succulent vegetables cooked in a *hangi* underground steam oven. The dramatic volcanic scenery of Rotorua is striking for its contrast with the encroaching pines of the Kaingaroa Forest, one of the world's largest plantation forests, with serried ranks of fast-growing radiata (Monterey) relishing the free-draining pumice soils. In recent years, high international milk-powder prices have fuelled a large-scale conversion to dairying, but silviculture remains the area's chief earner.

The rest of the region is loosely referred to as the **Volcanic Plateau**, high country overlaid with a layer of rock and ash expelled two thousand years ago, when a huge volcano blew itself apart, the resultant crater and surrounds filled by expansive **Lake Taupo**. This serene lake, and the streams and rivers feeding it, have long lured anglers keen to snag brown and rainbow trout, while visitors flock to diverse sights and activities located near the thundering rapids on the Waikato River, which drains the lake. South of Lake Taupo rise three majestic volcanoes in **Tongariro National Park**, created in 1887 – a winter playground for North Island skiers and a summer destination for trampers drawn by spectacular walking trails.

The altitude of the Volcanic Plateau lends Taupo, the Tongariro National Park and environs a crisp **climate**, even in high summer. Spring and autumn are tolerably warm and have the added advantage of freedom from the summer hordes, though the freezing winter months from May to October are mainly the preserve of winter-sports enthusiasts. Rotorua is generally balmier but still cool in winter, making the thermal areas steamier and hot baths even more inviting.

HUKA FALLS, TAUPO

Highlights

❶ Kaituna River Raft this excellent short river and shoot its spectacular 7m Tutea Falls. **See p.272**

❷ Maori cultural performance A delectable *hangi* feast wraps up an evening of chants, dance, songs, stories and insight into the Maori world-view. **See p.275**

❸ Wai-O-Tapu Luminous pools, bubbling mud and a spurting geyser make this the best of Rotorua's thermal areas. **See p.281**

❹ Lake Taupo Cruise, windsurf or kayak on New Zealand's largest lake, haul trout out of it,

or approach at dizzying speed while skydiving. **See p.282**

❺ Huka Falls For volume and power alone – some three hundred tonnes of water per second plunging into a maelstrom of eddies and whirlpools – this is the country's finest waterfall. **See p.290**

❻ Tongariro Alpine Crossing Quite simply the best and most popular one-day hike in New Zealand, climbing over lava flows, crossing a crater floor, skirting active geothermal areas, and passing emerald and blue lakes. **See p.300**

HIGHLIGHTS ARE MARKED ON THE MAP ON P.264

GETTING AROUND

By bus Public transport around the Central North Island is limited to buses, mostly run by InterCity and NakedBus who ply routes from Rotorua through Taupo and on south to Turangi, Waiouru and Taihape. A bunch of minor companies service the small towns and trailheads around the Tongariro National Park (see p.293).

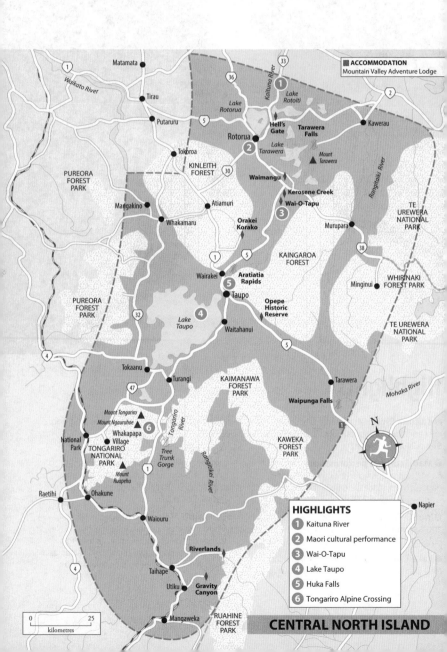

■ **ACCOMMODATION**
Mountain Valley Adventure Lodge

HIGHLIGHTS

1 Kaituna River
2 Maori cultural performance
3 Wai-O-Tapu
4 Lake Taupo
5 Huka Falls
6 Tongariro Alpine Crossing

CENTRAL NORTH ISLAND

Rotorua

You smell **Rotorua** long before you see it. Hydrogen sulphide drifting up from natural vents in the region's thin crust means that a whiff of rotten eggs lingers in the air, but after a few hours you barely notice it. The odour certainly doesn't stop anyone from visiting this small city on the southern shores of **Lake Rotorua**. Indeed, this is the North Island's tourist destination *par excellence* – so much so that locals refer to the place (only half-jokingly) as Roto-Vegas.

A big part of the appeal is that Rotorua is one of the world's most concentrated and accessible geothermal areas, where 15m geysers spout among kaleidoscopic mineral pools, steam wafts over cauldrons of boiling mud and terraces of encrusted silicates drip like stalactites. Everywhere you look there's evidence of volcanism: birds on the lakeshore are relieved of the chore of nest-sitting by the warmth of the ground; in churchyards tombs are built topside as digging graves is likely to unearth a hot spring; and hotels are equipped with geothermally fed hot tubs, perfect after a hard day's sightseeing. Throughout the region, sulphur and heat combine to form barren landscapes where only hardy plants brave the trickling hot streams, sputtering vents and seething fumaroles. There's no shortage of colour, however, from iridescent mineral deposits lining the pools: bright oranges juxtaposed with emerald greens and rust reds. The underworld looms large in Rotorua's lexicon: there's no end of "The Devil's" this and "Hell's" that, prompting George Bernard Shaw to quip that the Hell's Gate thermal area "reminds me too vividly of the fate theologians have promised me".

But constant hydrothermal activity is only part of the area's appeal. The naturally hot water lured **Maori** to settle here, using the hottest pools for cooking and bathing, and building their *whare* (houses) on warm ground to drive away the winter chill. Despite the inevitably diluting effects of tourism, there's no better place to get an introduction to Maori values, traditions, dance and song than at a concert and *hangi* evening.

The lake's northern and southern boundaries are marked by two ancient villages of the Arawa subtribe, Ngati Whakaue: lakeshore **Ohinemutu** and inland **Whakarewarewa**. The original **Bath House** is now part of **Rotorua Museum**, set in the grounds of the oh-so-English **Government Gardens**, which successfully and entertainingly puts these early enterprises into context. Half a day is well spent on foot visiting the museum's fine collection of Maori artefacts and bathhouse relics, and strolling around the lakeshores to Ohinemutu, the city's original Maori village with its neatly carved church. Afterwards, you can ease your bones with a soak in the hot pools set in a native bird sanctuary by catching a boat out to **Mokoia Island**.

At the southern end of town, Maori residents still go about their daily lives amid the steam and boiling pools at **Whakarewarewa Thermal Village**, while the adjacent **Te Puia** offers the region's only natural geysers, plopping mud and a nationally renowned Maori carving school.

Where Rotorua's northwestern suburbs peter out, Mount Ngongotaha rises up, providing the necessary slope for a number of gravity-driven activities at the **Skyline Skyrides**. In its shadow, **Rainbow Springs Kiwi Wildlife Park** provides a window into the life cycle of trout, and an excellent **Kiwi Encounter**, while the nearby **Agrodome** fills the prescription for adrenaline junkies.

Some of the region's finest geothermal areas lie outside the city – see p.276.

Brief history

The Rotorua region is the traditional home of the **Arawa** people. According to Maori history, one of the first parties to explore the interior was led by the *tohunga* (priest), **Ngatoroirangi**, who made it as far as the freezing summit of Mount Tongariro, where he feared he might die from cold. His prayers to the gods of Hawaiki were answered with fire that journeyed underground, surfacing at White Island in the Bay of Plenty, then at several more points in a line between there and the three Central North Island volcanoes. Ngatoroirangi was saved, and he and his followers established themselves around Lake Rotoiti ("small lake") and Lake Rotorua ("second lake").

Battles and bloodshed

In revenge for an earlier raid, the Northland Ngapuhi chief, **Hongi Hika**, led a war party here in 1823, complete with muskets traded with Europeans in the Bay of Islands. The Arawa retreated to Mokoia Island, in the middle of Lake Rotorua; undaunted, Hongi Hika and his warriors carried their canoes overland between lakes (the track between

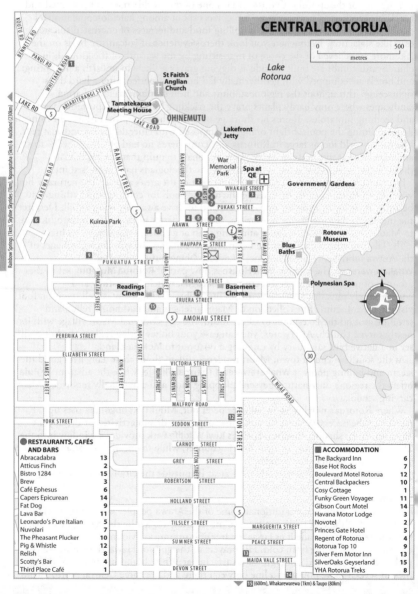

CENTRAL ROTORUA

0 — 500 metres

● RESTAURANTS, CAFÉS AND BARS	
Abracadabra	13
Atticus Finch	2
Bistro 1284	15
Brew	3
Café Ephesus	6
Capers Epicurean	14
Fat Dog	9
Lava Bar	11
Leonardo's Pure Italian	5
Nuvolari	7
The Pheasant Plucker	10
Pig & Whistle	12
Relish	8
Scotty's Bar	4
Third Place Café	1

■ ACCOMMODATION	
The Backyard Inn	6
Base Hot Rocks	7
Boulevard Motel Rotorua	12
Central Backpackers	10
Cosy Cottage	1
Funky Green Voyager	11
Gibson Court Motel	14
Havana Motor Lodge	3
Novotel	2
Princes Gate Hotel	5
Regent of Rotorua	4
Rotorua Top 10	9
Silver Fern Motor Inn	13
SilverOaks Geyserland	15
YHA Rotorua Treks	8

ROTORUA SAFETY

A continuing problem in and around Rotorua is **theft from cars**, with thieves targeting those parked near hostels, as well as cars left at trailheads, tourist attractions and other unguarded areas (Kerosene Creek is a particular hotspot for break-ins). Take any valuables into your room or ask to use a safe. The general rate of crime in Rotorua is also higher than the national average; keep your wits about you. On the upside, the local police (p.276) are friendly and efficient at assisting visitors.

Lake Rotoiti and Lake Rotoehu still bears the name Hongi's Track) and defeated the traditionally armed Arawa. In the New Zealand Wars of the 1860s the Arawa supported the government. In return, colonial troops helped repulse **Te Kooti** (see box, p.383) and his people a decade later.

The birth of tourism

A few **Europeans** had already lived for some years in the Maori villages of Ohinemutu and Whakarewarewa, but it wasn't until Te Kooti had been driven off that Rotorua came into existence. **Tourists** began to arrive in the district to view the Pink and White Terraces, and the Arawa, who up to this point had been relatively isolated from European influence, quickly grasped the possibilities of tourism, helping make Rotorua what it is today. Set up as a **spa town** on land leased from the Ngati Whakaue, by 1885 the fledgling city boasted the Government Sanatorium Complex, a spa designed to administer the rigorous treatments deemed beneficial to the "invalids" who came to take the waters.

Government Gardens

With their juxtaposition of the staid and the exotic, **Government Gardens**, east of the town centre, are a bizarre vision of an antipodean little England. White-clad croquet players totter round sulphurous steam vents and palm trees loom over rose gardens centred on the Elizabethan-style **Bath House**, built in 1908. Heralded as the greatest spa in the South Seas, it was designed to treat patients suffering from just about any disorder – arthritis, alcoholism, nervousness – and offered ghoulish treatments involving electrical currents and colonic irrigation as well as the geothermal baths. The bathhouse limped along until 1963, although the era of the grand spas had come to a close long before. For a contemporary, altogether more luxurious version of the experience, head to the nearby **Polynesian Spa** or the **Spa at QE**.

The Rotorua Museum

Queens Drive, Government Gardens • Daily: Dec–Feb 9am–6pm; March to Nov 9am–5pm; free guided tours on the hour • $20 • ⓦ rotoruamuseum.co.nz

The old bathhouse is now home to the wonderful **Rotorua Museum of Art and History**, which was reopened after extensions, in part to the original plans of 1908. The spa's history is told through the "Taking the Cure" exhibit, set around the old baths themselves, complete with gloomy green and white tiling and exposed pipes. Several rooms have been preserved in a state of arrested decay while an entertaining film re-creates some of the history of both the area and baths. To see more of the inner workings of the building, head for the basement – all old pipes, foundations and mud baths – which gets hotter as you walk further south, closer to the geothermal source. The remains of the original ventilation system (which quickly proved inadequate for dealing with the high humidity and hydrogen sulphide gas in the bathhouse) are on show in the roofspace, on the way up to a great rooftop viewing platform. Apart from the displays listed below, make sure to catch the small but moving section on

---

THE LOVE STORY OF HINEMOA AND TUTANEKAI

The Maori love story of **Hinemoa and Tutanekai** has been told around the shores of Lake Rotorua for centuries. It tells of the illegitimate young chief Tutanekai of Mokoia Island and his high-born paramour, Hinemoa, whose family forbade her from marrying him. To prevent her from meeting him they beached their *waka* (canoe), but the strains of his lamenting flute wafted across the lake nightly and the smitten Hinemoa resolved to swim to him. One night, buoyed by gourds, she set off towards Mokoia, but by the time she got there Tutanekai had retired to his *whare* (house) to sleep. Hinemoa arrived at the island but without clothes was unable to enter the village, so she immersed herself in a hot pool. Presently Tutanekai's slave came to collect water and Hinemoa lured him over, smashed his gourd and sent him back to his master. An enraged Tutanekai came to investigate, only to fall into Hinemoa's embrace.

---

the **Maori battalion**, an infantry battalion of the New Zealand Army that served during World War II, with an evocative half-hour video.

The Te Arawa display

Don't miss the small but internationally significant **Te Arawa** display showcasing the long-respected talents of Arawa carvers who made this area a bastion of pre-European carving tradition. Many pieces have been returned from European collections, and the magnificent carved figures, dog-skin cloaks, *pounamu* (greenstone) weapons and intricate bargeboards are all powerfully presented. Prized pieces include the flute played by the legendary lover Tutanekai (see box above), an unusually fine pumice goddess, and rare eighteenth-century carvings executed with stone tools.

The Tarawera eruption display

Extensive displays covering the dramatic events surrounding the **Tarawera eruption** include an informative relief map of the region, eyewitness accounts and reminiscences, an audiovisual presentation and photos of the ash-covered hotels at Te Wairoa and Rotomahana, both now demolished.

The Polynesian Spa

Hinemoa St, lake end • Daily 8am–11pm; spa therapies daily 10am–7pm • Adult pools $27; private pools $18 each/30min, lake view $27/30min; adult spa $45; family spa $39 for up to two adults and four kids; spa therapies from $130/45min available daily in Lake Spa and include Lake Spa entry • ☎ 07 348 1328, ⓦ polynesianspa.co.nz

A mostly open-air complex landscaped for lake views, the **Polynesian Spa** comprises four separate areas. Most people head straight for the **Adult Pools**, a collection of seven pools (36–42°C) ranged around the historic Radium and Priest pools. These are off-limits, but the Priest water (claimed to ease arthritis and rheumatism) is fed into three of the pools. If you only want half an hour in the water, you're probably better served by the **Private Pools** where two or three of you can soak in a shallow rock-lined pool. For a little exclusivity opt for the adjacent **Lake Spa**, with landscaped rock pools along with private relaxation lounge and bar or book ahead for massages, mud wraps and general pampering. Kids are catered for in the **Family Spa**, with one chlorinated 33°C pool, a couple of mineral pools and a waterslide.

The Blue Baths

Queens Drive, Government Gardens • Daily: Nov–March 10am–6pm; April–Oct noon–6pm • $11 • ⓦ bluebaths.co.nz

While the main bathhouse promoted health, the adjacent **Blue Baths** promised only pleasure when it opened in 1933. Designed in the Californian Spanish Mission style, this was one of the first public swimming pools in the world to allow mixed bathing. It closed in 1982, but has since partly reopened to allow swimming in an outdoor pool (29–33°C) and soaking in two smaller pools (38–40°C). The water is fresh, not mineral. Most of the building is given over to private functions so it's often closed at weekends.

The Spa at QE

1073 Whakaue St • Mon–Fri 9am–9pm, Sat 9am–5pm • Public pool $6; private pool $12; treatments $35–150 • ☎ 07 343 1665, ⓦ spaatqe.co.nz

The spirit of the original bathhouse lives on at the **Spa at QE**, where the emphasis is on cures and therapeutic treatments. It has a clinical, slightly scruffy feel, but there's increasing sophistication in the areas devoted to pampering. Soak in a private pool filled with alkaline water from the Rachel Spring or book in for treatments such as a soothing mud bath or an Aix massage – like being rubbed down while under a horizontal hot shower.

Ohinemutu

On the lakeshore, 500m north of Rotorua • $2 donation • ☎ 07 348 0189 or ☎ 0800 527 8767

Before Rotorua the principal Maori settlement in the area was at **Ohinemutu**. Ohinemutu remains a Maori village centred on its hot springs and the small half-timbered neo-Tudor **St Faith's Anglican Church** built in 1914 to replace its 1885 predecessor. Within, there's barely a patch of wall that hasn't been carved or covered with *tukutuku* (ornamental latticework) panels. The main attraction is the window featuring the figure of Christ, swathed in a Maori cloak and feathers, positioned so that he appears to be walking on the lake. Outside is the grave of Gilbert Mair, a captain in the colonial army who twice saved Ohinemutu from attacks by rival Maori, becoming the only Pakeha to earn full Arawa chieftainship.

At the opposite end of the small square in front of the church stands the **Tamatekapua Meeting House**, again beautifully carved, though the best work, some

4

LAKE ROTORUA AND MOKOIA ISLAND TOURS AND ACTIVITIES

Rotorua meets the water at the Lakefront Jetty, at the northern end of Tutaneka Street, where you can rent kayaks, pedalboats and the like. This is the starting point for trips to **Mokoia Island**, 7km north of the jetty, a predator-free bird sanctuary where a breeding programme supports populations of saddlebacks and North Island robins (often spotted at the feeder stations) and kokako. The island is better known, however, for the story of **Hinemoa and Tutanekai** (see box opposite); the site of Tutanekai's *whare* and Hinemoa's Pool can still be seen on guided island visits.

All sixteen lakes around Rotorua, but especially Lake Rotorua, given its proximity to the city, have a reputation for **trout fishing**. The angling is both scenic and rewarding, with waters stocked with strong-fighting rainbow trout.

CRUISES

Lakeland Queen ☎ 0800 572 784, ⓦ lakeland queen.com. For a leisurely cruise on the lake, try the *Lakeland Queen*, a replica paddle steamer that runs a series of trips including meals (breakfast $40; lunch $50; coffee $25; BBQ dinner $49).

FISHING

O'Keefe's 1113 Eruera St ☎ 07 346 0178, ⓦ okeefes fishing.co.nz. Has up-to-date information on lake and river conditions, and stocks the free *Lake Rotorua & Tributaries* leaflet published by Fish & Game New Zealand, explaining the rules of the fishery, and will provide contacts for fly-fishing guides, generally around $500 for

a day. For information on fishing licences, see p.54. Mon–Thurs 8.30am–5pm, Fri 8.30am–5.30pm, Sat 9am–2pm.

JETBOATING

Kawarau Jet ☎ 07 343 7600, ⓦ nzjetboat.co.nz. Runs high-octane spins around the lake ($85/30min) and trips across the lake to the Ohau Channel and Lake Rotoiti ($125/2hr 30min), giving an hour at Manupirua Hot Springs, which can only be accessed by boat.

TOURS

Mokoia Island WaiOra ☎ 07 345 7456, ⓦ facebook .com/Mokoialsland. Offers guided visits ($69/2hr 30min) of Mokoia Island, with the emphasis on Maori cultural interpretation and conservation.

dating back almost two hundred years, is inside and inaccessible. Call for details of guided tours.

Whakarewarewa Thermal Reserve

17 Tryon St, 3km south of the centre • Daily: Nov–March 9am–5pm; April–Oct 9am–4pm; free hour-long guided tours on the hour • $49.90; daytime cultural show with *hangi* $98; evening show with *hangi* $151 • ☎ 07 348 9047, ☏ tepuia.com

Rotorua's closest geothermal attractions, Te Puia and the Whakarewarewa Thermal Village, share the **Whakarewarewa Thermal Reserve**. Around two-thirds of the active thermal zone is occupied by **Te Puia**, a series of walkways past glooping pools of boiling mud, sulphurous springs and New Zealand's most spectacular geysers, the 7m **Prince of Wales' Feathers** and the granddaddy of them all, the 15m **Pohutu** ("big splash"). The latter performed several times a day until 2000, when it surprised everyone by spouting continuously for an unprecedented 329 days. It has since settled back to jetting water into the air two to three times an hour, immediately preceded by the Prince of Wales' Feathers.

The geothermal wonders are certainly impressive, but Te Puia is also home to a **nocturnal kiwi house**, a replica of a traditional **Maori village** that's used on ceremonial occasions, and an **Arts and Crafts Institute** where skilled artisans produce flax skirts and some enormous carvings. More portable (though expensive) examples can be bought in the gift shop.

Whakarewarewa Thermal Village

9a Tukiterangi St • Daily 8.30am–5pm • Guided tours hourly: $35; *hangi* (served noon–2pm) $31; free cultural performance at 11.15am and 2pm • ☎ 07 349 3463, ☏ whakarewarewa.com

The rest of the thermal area falls under the auspices of **Whakarewarewa: The Thermal Village**, a living village founded in pre-European times and undergoing continual, though sympathetic, modernization. The focus here is not on geysers but on how Maori interact with this unique environment. You can stroll at leisure around the village, attend the free **cultural performance**, and partake in a **hangi**. You can even buy corn cobs ($2) boiled in one of the natural cauldrons.

Northwest Rotorua

Aside from visits to the thermal areas, much of Rotorua's daytime activity takes place around the flanks of **Mount Ngongotaha**, 5–10km northwest of the centre, which is increasingly being overtaken by the city's suburbs.

Skyline Skyrides

185 Fairy Springs Rd, 4km northwest of the centre • Daily 9am–late • Gondola $27; gondola and luge packages $38–59; gondola, 3 luge rides and Zoom Zipline $75 • ☎ 07 347 0027, ☏ skylineskyrides.co.nz/rotorua

At **Skyline Skyrides**, gondolas whisk you 200m up to the station on the mountain for views across the lake and town and for lunch or dinner in the buffet restaurant (see p.275). Once you're up above Rotorua you can zip around the hillside, trying out adventure activities including the **luge** and the adjacent **Zoom Zipline**, which whizzes down the side of Mount Ngongotaha for 383m. There are two parallel lines so you can zip with a friend, and at the end there's the chance to finish with a leap of faith, falling backwards off the 10metre-high **Quickjump** freefall. A taller Quickjump is being planned too.

Rainbow Springs Kiwi Wildlife Park

Fairy Springs Rd, 4km from the centre • **Wildlife Park** Daily 8am–9.30pm; to 10.30pm in summer • $40 • **Kiwi Encounter** Daily 10am–4pm; guided tour on the hour from 10am • Combo ticket with Rainbow Springs $50 • ☎ 07 350 0440, ☏ rainbowsprings.co.nz

At the foot of Mount Ngongotaha lies **Rainbow Springs Kiwi Wildlife Park**, a series of pools where you can view massive rainbow, brown and North American brook trout. These are linked by nature trails which visit several free-flight bird enclosures, a tuatara, a talkative kea and a nocturnal kiwi house. Your ticket gives you access for 24 hours, so come back after dark when the trees and pools are colourfully lit and kiwi are out and about in a naturalistic enclosure with little separating you from the birds.

Also here is the excellent **Kiwi Encounter**, giving visitors an insight into the conservation work supporting the country's icon in the battle against extinction. A heart-warming 30-minute guided tour demonstrates egg incubation and ends with a kiwi viewing.

Paradise Valley Springs

467 Paradise Valley Rd, 11km west of the centre • Daily 8am–5pm • $30 • ☎ 07 348 9667, Ⓦ paradisev.co.nz

Trout share billing with lions at **Paradise Valley Springs**, a patch of mature bush where manicured pathways weave between pools of trout, an attractive wetland area, a walk-in aviary with kea, and paddocks containing tahr, wallabies and wild pigs. An elevated boardwalk nature trail gives a great introduction to New Zealand's trees, but the big draw is the breeding pride of lions which are fed daily at 2.30pm. At times they have lion cubs which, between the ages of four weeks and one year, can be petted.

The Agrodome

Western Rd, Ngongotaha, 10km north of the centre • Shows at 9.30am, 11am & 2.30pm • Show $32.50; organic farm tour and show $62 • ☎ 07 357 1050, Ⓦ agrodome.co.nz

Just about every bus touring the North Island stops at the **Agrodome**, where the star attraction is an hour-long **sheep show**. Though undoubtedly corny, this popular spectacle is always entertaining: rams representing the nineteen major breeds farmed in New Zealand are enticed onto the podium, a sheep is shorn, lambs are bottle-fed and there's a sheepdog display. Afterwards, the dogs are put through their paces outside and you can watch a 1906 industrial carding machine turn fleece into usable wool. There's also a one-hour farm tour complete with honey tasting, a visit to an organic orchard, deer viewing and, between April and June, kiwifruit picking.

Agroventures

1335 Paradise Valley Rd, 10km from the centre • Daily 9am–5pm • Bungy jump $109; Swoop swing, Agrojet, Freefall Extreme and Shweeb one for $49, two for $79, all four $109; all four plus bungy $189 • ☎ 0800 949 888, Ⓦ agroventures.co.nz

Adrenaline junkies can get a hit at **Agroventures**, where attractions include a 43m **bungy jump**, the **Swoop** swing ride, and the **Agrojet** where you're piloted around a short course at breakneck speed in a three-seater jetboat (purportedly New Zealand's fastest). The **Freefall Extreme** simulates a freefall skydive using a powerful vertical fan above which you hover (or at least try to). The **Shweeb** offers a chance to race recumbent bicycles encased in clear plastic fairings and slung from an overhead monorail. Either race the clock or your mates around the undulating track. It's nowhere near as geeky as it sounds, particularly if you can get two teams together. Assorted Agroventures combo deals get you more bang for your buck.

Zorb

SH5, at Western Rd, 10km from the centre • Daily 9am–5pm • $39/ride • ☎ 0800 227 474, Ⓦ zorb.com

Another Kiwi-pioneered nutter ride is the **Zorb**. You dive into the centre of a huge clear plastic ball and roll down a 200m hill or the slower but wilder zigzag course; you can choose from wet and dry rides, the former being the more fun.

Canopy Tours

SH5, at Western Rd, 10km from the centre • Daily 9am–5pm • $45/ride • ☎ 0800 227 474, Ⓦ zorb.com

For an adventure that gives something back, head out to the evergreen native forests of the Mamaku Plateau with **Canopy Tours**. The three-hour ziplining tour runs through a beautiful tract of rare virgin native forest with platforms high in the rimu trees with the indigenous birds (listen out for robins and morepork) and zipwires swooping at great heights (up to 44 metres) over fern-packed gullies looked down upon by moss-covered trunks. The company have spent thousands in trapping to rid the forest of pests such as possums and rats, giving rare native birds a fighting chance and returning this gorgeous area to its former pre-European glory. Though the moa and Haast's eagle will never return, many native birds have, and future plans include fencing a large area to keep all pests out – and possibly reintroduce the kiwi.

ARRIVAL AND DEPARTURE   ROTORUA

By plane Rotorua's lakeside airport is 8km northeast of town on SH30 (ⓦrotorua-airport.co.nz). In addition to domestic flights, there are also direct services to/from Sydney, Australia. Rotorua Taxi (ⓣ07 348 1111) charges around $40 to the city centre; Grumpy's Tours & Transfers (see opposite) have airport transfers from $30.
Destinations Auckland (2–4 daily; 40min); Christchurch (3 daily; 1hr 40min); Queenstown (3 daily; 3hr 15min, via

Christchurch); Wellington (2 daily; 1hr 10min).
By bus InterCity and NakedBus long-distance buses stop outside the i-SITE on Fenton St.
Destinations Auckland (5 daily; 4hr 20min); Gisborne (1 daily; 5hr 10min); Hamilton (5 daily; 2hr 5min); Opotiki (1 daily; 2hr 30min); Palmerston North (2 daily; 5hr 40min); Taupo (5 daily; 1hr 10min); Tauranga (2 daily; 1hr 40min); Waitomo (1 daily; 2hr 40min); Whakatane (1 daily; 1hr 50min).

RAFTING, KAYAKING AND SLEDGING AROUND ROTORUA

Rotorua has a considerable reputation for its nearby **whitewater rivers**, which you can tackle aboard rafts, kayaks (usually tandems) or, more in-your-face, by "sledging" – floating down rapids clinging to a buoyant plastic sledge (really only for good swimmers). There's no shortage of operators willing to take you out (usually from September to May); the most popular rivers are listed below, along with recommended outfitters.

Other options include renting kayaks or undertaking kayaking courses and guided trips on several of the larger lakes in the region, with the emphasis on scenic appreciation, soaking in hot pools and a little fishing. With more time and money, it's worth considering a multi-day wilderness rafting trip on the East Cape's Motu River (see box, p.359).

RIVERS

Kaituna River Much of the hype is reserved for this Grade IV river, or at least the 2km section after it leaves Lake Rotoiti 20km north of Rotorua, which includes the spectacular 7m Tutea Falls (sledgers walk around the falls).
Wairoa River If you can get the timing right, this Grade IV+ river, 80km by road from Rotorua, on the outskirts of Tauranga, is the one to go for. It relies on dam-releases for raftable quantities of whitewater

(Dec–March every Sun; Sept–Nov, April & May every second Sun). This is one of the finest short trips available in New Zealand, negotiating a hazardous but immensely satisfying stretch of water.
Rangitaiki River If your tastes lean more towards appreciation of the natural surroundings with a bit of a bumpy ride thrown in, opt for this Grade III river, which also shoots Jeff's Joy, a Grade IV drop that's the highlight of the trip.

OUTFITTERS

Kaitiaki Adventures ⓣ0800 338 736, ⓦkaitiaki .co.nz. Rafting and sledging trips with a cultural dimension – explaining the significance of the river to Maori. Along with trips down the Kaituna (rafting $95; sledging $109) they do summer Sunday trips down the Wairoa (rafting $99; sledging $299) with sledgers getting one-on-one guiding down this tricky river. They also do trips on the gentler Rangitikei River ($125 including hot pools).

Kaituna Kayaks ⓣ07 362 4486, ⓦkaitunakayaks .co.nz. Tandem kayaking on the Kaituna River, including Tutea Falls ($199) plus whitewater kayak courses.
Raftabout/Sledgeabout ⓣ0800 723 822, ⓦraftabout.co.nz. Mostly trips down the Kaituna either on rafts ($105) or sledges ($129), plus summer Sunday rafting trips down the Wairoa ($129 including lunch), some trips down the Rangitikei ($139) and a variety of combo deals with other adventure activities.

GETTING AROUND

By bike *Lady Jane's Ice Cream Parlour* (☎07 347 9340), centrally located at 1092 Tutanekai St, rents bikes for $30/day.

By bus Cityride (☎0800 422 928, ⌨baybus.co.nz) is an urban bus system centred on Pukuatua St between Tutanekai and Amohia streets; its most useful services are #1 (to Skyline Skyrides, Rainbow Springs and the Agrodome) and #2 (to Te Puia); both run daily from roughly 6.30am–6.30pm every 30min (hourly on Sun, none on public holidays). Timetables are available at the i-SITE. Tickets are $2.50 each way, or $7.80 for a day-pass.

By car Most of the majors are represented but the best deals and service are generally with Pegasus (☎0800 803 580, ⌨rentalcars.co.nz), based at the airport, which delivers and charges from $45/day. Shorter and one-way rentals can cost significantly more.

INFORMATION AND TOURS

Visitor information i-SITE, 1167 Fenton St (daily 7.30am–6pm, until 7pm in summer; ☎07 343 1730, ⌨rotoruanz.com). Handles local, DOC and New Zealand-wide travel enquiries, and offers copies of the free weekly visitor's guide.

Tours Geyser Link (☎0800 004 321, ⌨travelheadfirst.com) have tours to Waimangu and Wai-O-Tapu (full day $125) as well as packages including Hobbiton and Whakarewarewa Thermal Village. Grumpy's Tours & Transfers (☎07 348 2229, ⌨grumpys.co.nz) has entertaining tours to everywhere from Wai-O-Tapu ($70) to Hawkes Bay ($700 for up to six people) as well as tours around town. Tim's Thermal Shuttle (☎0274 945 508, ⌨thermalshuttle.co.nz) runs to Waimangu, Wai-O-Tapu and Te Puia from $17.50.

ACCOMMODATION

There's a wide range of accommodation in Rotorua, and almost everywhere, no matter how low-budget, has a **hot pool**, though genuine mineral-water pools are less common. **Hostels** are all within walking distance of the city centre, while **motels** mostly line Fenton Street, which runs south towards Whakarewarewa. Competition is fierce and off-peak prices plummet. **B&Bs** and **guesthouses** are thinner on the ground, and the **hotels**, while plentiful, generally cater to bus-tour groups and have high "walk-in" rates.

CENTRAL ROTORUA

The Backyard Inn 60 Tarewa Rd ☎07 347 0931, ⌨thebackyardinn.co.nz; map p.266. This well-organized complex is only a 10min walk from the town centre (on the far side of Kuirau Park), yet it's far enough away to avoid late-night party noise. There's also an excellent low-cost, licensed café/restaurant and a small hot pool. Dorms **$29**, chalets **$87**

Base Hot Rocks 1286 Arawa St ☎0800 227 396, ⌨stayatbase.com; map p.266. Large, lively hostel that's a perennial favourite of the backpacker tour buses, with heated outdoor spa and swimming pool and the *Lava Bar* next door. Accommodation is mostly eight-bunk en-suite dorms; girls can check into the female-only Sanctuary dorm ($29). Dorms **$24**, doubles **$38**

Boulevard Motel Rotorua 265 Fenton St ☎07 348 2074, ⌨boulevardrotorua.co.nz; map p.266. Smartly appointed, well-run motel with a range of room sizes and some of the best on-site mineral pools in town, as well as a heated swimming pool, spa and free wi-fi. **$128**

Central Backpackers 1076 Pukuatua St ☎07 349 3285, ⌨bbh.co.nz; map p.266. Small, homey hostel, with beds rather than bunks in the four- and six-bed dorm rooms, plus a spa pool. Dorms **$25**, twins & doubles **$59**

★**Cosy Cottage** 67 Whittaker Rd ☎07 348 3793, ⌨cosycottage.co.nz; map p.266. Friendly holiday park 2km from town with an extensive range of comfortable cabins, self-contained cottages, powered and tent sites, some geothermally heated – great in winter. There's a swimming pool, a couple of pleasant mineral pools, naturally-fed steam boxes for *hangi*-style cooking, city bikes and direct access to a lake beach where you can dig your own hot pool. Camping **$42**, cabins **$75**, cottages **$105**

Funky Green Voyager 4 Union St ☎07 346 1754, ⌨bbh.co.nz; map p.266. Relaxed, eco-conscious hostel in a pair of suburban houses a 10min walk from the centre, with an easy-going communal atmosphere. Some doubles have en-suite bathrooms. Cooking facilities in particular are excellent and there's a cosy TV-less lounge. Dorms **$25**, doubles **$61**

★**Gibson Court Motel** 10 Gibson St ☎07 346 2822, ⌨gibsoncourtmotel.co.nz; map p.266. Welcoming motel in a quiet area with ten one-bedroom units that are showing their age but are great value, particularly since most come with a private mineral-water pool in a secluded, leafy courtyard and free wi-fi. **$95**

Havana Motor Lodge 1078 Whakaue St ☎0800 333 799, ⌨havanarotorua.com; map p.266. Quiet motel, close to the lakefront with spacious grounds, a heated pool and two small mineral pools. **$150**

Novotel Lake end of Tutanekai St ☎07 3463 888, ⌨novotelrotorua.co.nz; map p.266. Although it's part of a world-wide chain, and lacks unique character, this top-line hotel has a great location close to the lakeshore and restaurants, as well as a pool, gym and business centre. Rates vary wildly; check the website for deals. **$179**

Princes Gate Hotel 1057 Arawa St ☎ 0800 500 705, ⓦ princesgate.co.nz; map p.266. Historic 1897-built wooden wide-verandahed hotel that's the sole survivor from the days when all of Hinemaru St was lined with places catering to folk taking the waters at the bathhouse. Lounges and bar are delightfully creaky (serving high tea), while the rooms and suites have been modernized. **$165**

★ **Regent of Rotorua** 1191 Pukaki St ☎ 0508 734 368, ⓦ regentrotorua.co.nz; map p.266. Accommodation at this revamped 1950s motel is in immaculate all-white studio suites that come with a pristine bathroom, stylish wallpaper and furnishings straight out of the style mags. Naturally, wi-fi and iPod docking stations are standard and you can lounge next to the heated outdoor pool. There's also a mineral pool and small gym, and a stylish restaurant and bar. **$200**

Silver Fern Motor Inn 326 Fenton St ☎ 0800 118 808, ⓦ silverfernmotorinn.co.nz; map p.266. Knockout modern motel with spacious, refurbished studios and one-bedroom units, all with spa pools, Sky TV, sunny balconies, oodles of space and helpful staff. Free city bikes and wi-fi. Studios **$145**, one-bedroom **$180**

SilverOaks Geyserland 424 Fenton St ☎ 0800 881 882, ⓦ silveroaks.co.nz; map p.266. Comfortable-enough business hotel where you should book early to get a third- or fourth-floor room with unsurpassed views of the Whakarewarewa thermal area. **$82**

YHA Rotorua Treks 1278 Haupapa St ☎ 07 349 4088, ⓦ yha.co.nz; map p.266. This sparkling, purpose-built, 180-bed hostel comes with spacious communal areas including a big timber deck plus a well-equipped kitchen and exemplary enviro credentials. Most dorms shun bunks; a female-only dorm is available. Dorms **$26**, rooms **$81**

CAMPING

Rotorua Top 10 1495 Pukuatua St ☎ 07 348 1886, ⓦ rotoruatop10.co.nz; map p.266. This is the closest campsite to the city, with good facilities including a small outdoor pool and two hot tubs. Camping **$44**, cabins **$100**

AROUND ROTORUA

Aroden 2 Hilton Rd, just off the Tarawera Rd 4km from Rotorua ☎ 07 345 6303, ⓦ babs.co.nz/aroden; map p.277. Comfortable suburban homestay B&B in a rambling timber house, with two nicely appointed, flower-filled queen-size rooms, books and games in the guest lounge, lush gardens and tasty cooked-to-order breakfasts, plus complimentary New Zealand wine on arrival. **$145**

Blue Lake Top 10 723 Tarawera Rd, Blue Lake, 9km southeast of Rotorua ☎ 0800 808 292, ⓦ bluelaketop10.co.nz; map p.277. A well-organized rural site, just across the road from Blue Lake, featuring a games room and spa pool. Camping **$18**, cabins **$75**

Koura Lodge 209 Kawaha Point Rd, 5km north of central Rotorua ☎ 07 348 5868, ⓦ kouralodge.co.nz; map p.277. Go for a lakeside room in the main building at this stylish lodge equipped with secluded sauna and hot tub right on the water's edge, kayaks, tennis court and even a jetty for direct access to floatplane sightseeing. Understated rooms are tastefully furnished and well equipped, and there's a comfy guest lounge where a buffet breakfast is served. **$345**

The Lake House 6 Cooper Ave, Holdens Bay, 7km northeast of town ☎ 07 345 3313, ⓦ thelakehouse .co.nz; map p.277. This luxurious but understated house filled with fresh flowers opens out on a sunny veranda with only lawns separating you from the lake. There's a big spa pool and free use of sit-on-top kayaks. Kids can be accommodated in the built-in bunks of the Ship's Cabin ($50) providing no other guests are booked in. Minimum stay is two nights. Free wi-fi. **$225**

EATING, DRINKING AND NIGHTLIFE

Head to the short strip at the lake end of Tutanekai Street (known as "Eat Streat") for the greatest concentration of international cuisine – from Korean to Tunisian – and a few quality restaurants. Lots of great cafés enliven the town centre and there are several good bars, but otherwise nightlife is limited. Most visitors spend one evening of their stay at a combined *hangi* and **Maori concert** in either a tourist hotel or, preferably, one of the outlying Maori *maraes*. Rotorua's night market takes place on Thursday from 5pm on Tutanekai Street, with lots of food stalls plus arts and crafts.

RESTAURANTS AND CAFÉS

Abracadabra 1263 Amohia St ☎ 07 348 3883, ⓦ abracadabracafe.com; map p.266. Maghrebi music provides a suitable accompaniment in this loosely Moroccan café and restaurant strung with filigree lamps and divided into intimate rooms. Come for coffee and almond cake, a falafel burger, tapas ($9–14) or dinner dishes such as mushroom chicken or seafood tagine (mains

$22.50–30). Tues–Sat 10.30am–11pm, Sun 10.30am–3pm.

Atticus Finch Eat Streat ☎ 07 460 0400, ⓦ atticusfinch .co.nz; map p.266. This newly opened, informal restaurant is the pick of Eat Streat, serving sharing plates and wines by the glass in casual surroundings. Order a range of dishes, such as baked salmon sharing plank ($18), skirt steak ($19) and roasted beetroot salad ($10). Daily 9am–late.

Bistro 1284 1284 Eruera St ☎07 346 1284, ⓦbistro1284.co.nz; map p.266. Rotorua's best fine-dining restaurant has a relatively relaxed atmosphere despite the white-linen tablecloths. Classy mains ($35–39) include market fish and Hawkes Bay lamb rack. Tues–Sat 5pm–late.

Café Ephesus 1107 Tutanekai St ☎07 349 1735; map p.266. Unassuming and cheap, dishing up generous portions of Turkish, Mediterranean and Middle Eastern fare. Traditional delights include pastas, *dolmades*, *güveç* and kebabs (around $15). Tues–Sun lunch & dinner.

Capers Epicurean 1181 Eruera St ☎07 348 8818, ⓦcapers.co.nz; map p.266. Large, airy, licensed café/deli serving up wonderful breakfasts, healthy salads, overstuffed panini, and a great range of dinner mains such as twice-cooked duck breast ($29.90) or South Island salmon with sticky rice ($31.90). Daily 7am–9pm.

Fat Dog 1161 Arawa St ☎07 347 7586, ⓦfatdogcafe.co.nz; map p.266. Heaped portions of robust food are served at mismatched tables at this relaxed café/bar. The Fat Dog Works breakfast should sort out hangovers; lunches span salads and panini and huge burgers ($18.60–19.90), while more substantial evening mains include seared swordfish ($29) and Scotch fillet ($30). Sun–Wed 7am–9pm, Thurs–Sat 7am–9.30pm.

★**Leonardo's Pure Italian** ☎07 347 7084; map p.266. Book ahead to eat at this diminutive Italian, widely regarded as the best restaurant in the town centre. Hosts Leonardo and Yuka treat guests like friends and serve a limited but excellent range of expertly prepared Italian dishes such as sirloin steak served the Italian way with provolone and rocket ($12.50 per 100g) and Leonardo's chicken ($35.50), which comes wrapped in pancetta. Sun–Wed 5–9.30pm, also Thurs–Sat 11.30am–2pm.

Nuvolari 1122 Tutanekai St ☎07 348 1122, ⓦnuvolari.co.nz; map p.266. Lunch specials ($9.20) span the globe – from Australia to the Netherlands, Malaysia and Qatar – but evening pizzas, antipasti platters and pastas and mains such as pan-seared scallops on pumpkin risotto ($29.90) are in keeping with its "Italiano Ristorante Bar" tagline. Daily 11.30am–late.

Okere Falls Store 757a SH33, 15km northeast of town ☎07 362 4944, ⓦokerefallsstore.co.nz; map p.277. A rambling beer garden (which hosts winter bonfire nights from 5–9pm on Friday, Saturday and Sunday) surrounds this fabulous gourmet and general store and café, while the big timber deck out front is also a choice spot for tucking into roast veggie frittata, ricotta-stuffed baked potatoes or beef lasagne ($9). Daily 7am–7pm.

Relish 1149 Tutanekai St ☎07 343 9195, ⓦrelishcafe.co.nz; map p.266. Excellent licensed café covering the bases from quality counter food, delicious cakes and coffee to dinners including calamari ($15) and smoked chicken fettucine ($24) plus a changing roster of tapas and a short

menu of wood-fired pizza. Mon & Tues 7am–4pm, Wed–Fri 7am–9pm, Sat 8am–9pm, Sun 8am–4pm.

★**Stratosfare** Skyline Rotorua ☎07 347 0037, ⓦskyline.co.nz; map p.277. This classy buffet restaurant reclines at the top of the Skyline gondola (see p.270), ranging across the hillside with great views of Rotorua. Not to mention great steak and seafood cooked to order, abundant salads and a dessert buffet that will keep kids of all ages happy for hours. There's also wine from on-site winery Volcanic Hills. Lunch and gondola $54, dinner and gondola $76. Daily: lunch 11.30am–2pm, dinner 5.30pm–late.

Third Place Café 35 Lake Road ☎07 349 4852, ⓦthirdplacecafe.co.nz; map p.266. Buzzing café popular with locals and with views of the lake. Fill up with an all-day breakfast ($16.50) or call in for brunch of Moroccan chicken salad or steak sammie and fries ($18.50). Mon–Fri 7.30am–4pm, Sat & Sun 7.30am–3.30pm. Closed public holidays.

BARS AND CLUBS

Brew Eat Streat ☎07 346 0976, ⓦbrewpub.co.nz; map p.266. For the discerning beer drinker, this craft beer pub has the full range of their own Croucher Brewing beers on tap and an ever-changing line-up of Kiwi craft brews. There's also an after-10pm menu of dishes like pizza if you've left it too late for dinner. Daily 11am–late.

Lava Bar Base Hot Rocks hostel (see p.273); map p.266. A pool table, discount drinks, budget meal deals and theme nights (Sunday pyjama party, Thursday ladies' night etc), are sure-fire winners with assorted backpackers, rafting guides and locals. Daily 5.30pm–3am.

The Pheasant Plucker 1153 Arawa St ☎07 343 7071; map p.266. Convivial bar chiefly notable for its nightly live music – open mic on Tues, covers bands Fri & Sat. Tues–Sat 5pm–3am.

Pig & Whistle Corner of Haupapa and Tutanekai sts ☎07 347 3025, ⓦpigandwhistle.co.nz; map p.266. Lively but laidback pub in a redbrick former police station with a garden bar, and live bands Thurs–Sat. There's also a wide range of bar meals including burgers (around $20) and fish and chips ($23.70), served until 10pm. Daily 11.30am–late.

Scotty's Bar 1104 Tutanekai St ☎07 348 1810; map p.266. There are just a few leaners and the bar itself in this intimate cocktail and wine bar among the restaurants. Daily noon–3am.

HANGI AND MAORI CONCERTS

Rotorua provides more opportunities than anywhere else to sample food steamed to perfection in the Maori earth oven or *hangi* and watch a Maori concert, typically an hour-long performance of traditional dance, song and chants. The bigger hotels all put on somewhat forced extravaganzas, so go for the "Maori experiences" below instead (daily, by reservation). All have buses picking up at hotels and hostels ready for a start around 6pm, then run for three to four hours. They follow largely the same format, giving instruction on *marae* customs and protocol (see the "Experiencing Maori culture" box in Contexts, p.806) followed by a formal welcome, concert and *hangi*.

Mitai ✆07 343 9132, ⍟mitai.co.nz. All the standard elements are very well done, the excellent *hangi* is cooked in the ground, plus the events are conveniently sited beside Rainbow Springs, giving a chance of a night-time walk through the bush past a beautiful clear spring which feeds a stream where a fully manned *waka* arrives in flaming torchlight. $116.

Tamaki Maori Village ✆07 349 2999, ⍟maoriculture .co.nz. You, and several busloads, are driven out to a specially built "Maori village" south of town for a spine-chilling welcome and tales of early Maori–European interaction. Everything is so professionally done that it is hard to quibble, but its popularity has become its biggest downfall and sightlines can be restricted. The *hangi* is good, though, and the overall experience memorable. $110.

Te Po ✆07 348 9047, ⍟tepuia.com. Wear clean socks as it is shoes off (and men to the front) for the thoroughly professional performance in a traditional meeting house at Te Puia (p.270). The *hangi* is top-class, and the night is rounded off with a tour of the geothermal valley, and hopefully a sight of a floodlit geyser performing. $115; $151 combined with daytime entry to Te Puia.

CINEMAS

Basement Cinema 1140 Hinemoa St ✆07 350 1400, ⍟basementcinema.co.nz. Intimate, two-screen art-house theatre with a licensed café.

Readings Cinema 1263 Eruera St ✆07 349 0061, ⍟readingcinemas.co.nz. The local multiplex showing the latest mainstream releases.

DIRECTORY

Library 1127 Haupapa St (Mon–Wed & Fri 9.30am–6pm, Thurs 9.30am–8pm, Sat 9.30am–4pm; ✆07 348 4177, ⍟rotorualibrary.govt.nz). Unlimited free wi-fi and free use of computers for up to 30min.

Medical treatment For emergencies and urgent health care go to Lakes Care, at Arawa and Tutanekai sts (daily 8am–10pm; ✆07 348 1000).

Pharmacy Lakes Care Pharmacy is at 1155 Tutanekai St (daily 8.30am–9.30pm; ✆07 48 4385).

Police 1190–1214 Fenton St ✆07 348 0099.

Post office The main post office, with poste restante facilities, is on the corner of Pukuatua and Tutanekai sts.

Around Rotorua

Many of the best attractions in the area lie outside the city itself but shuttles and tours (see p.273) mean that just about every combination of sights can be packed into a day, as well as all manner of **adventure activities** – from rafting to skydiving.

Travellers can quickly dispatch minor sights along the eastern shore of Lake Rotorua, leaving time for the seldom-crowded **Hell's Gate** thermal area and the opportunity to watch terrified rafters plunging over **Tutea Falls**. Rewards are more plentiful to the east and south especially around the shattered 5km-long massif of **Mount Tarawera**. During one cataclysmic night of eruptions in 1886 this chain split in two, destroying the region's first tourist attraction (the beautiful Pink and White Terraces), entombing the nearest settlement, Te Wairoa, now known as the **Buried Village**, and creating the **Waimangu Volcanic Valley**. It now ranks as one of the finest collections of geothermal features in the region alongside kaleidoscopic **Wai-O-Tapu**, with its daily triggered **Lady Knox Geyser**, boiling mud, and brilliantly coloured pools. Other magnificent geothermal areas around Rotorua include **Kerosene Creek**, which has the best free hot pools hereabouts, and **Orakei Korako**, which offers a peaceful geothermal experience. Meanwhile, the **Whirinaki Forest Park** presents great hiking and biking opportunities on the road to Lake Waikaremoana (p.381).

Te Ngae 3D Maze

On SH30, 10km northeast of the centre • Daily 9am–5pm • $12 • ✆07 345 5275, ⍟3dmaze.co.nz

Scenery aside, there isn't a great deal to stop for along the shoreline, apart from this huge **wooden maze**, in a cleared section of beautiful bushland (bring a picnic; snacks

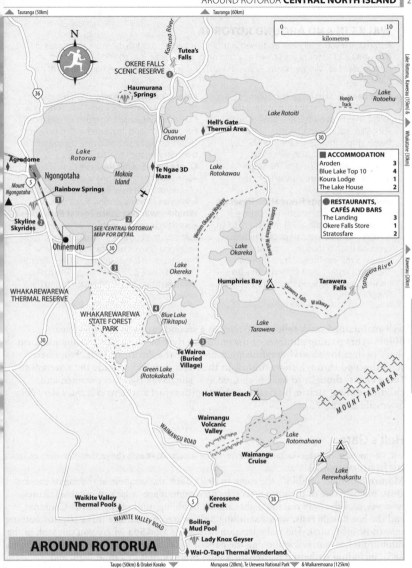

Tauranga (50km)

Tauranga (60km)

Lake Rotoma, Kawerau (15km) &

Whakatane (30km)

Kaweka (20km)

N

Kaituna River

Tutea's Falls

OKERE FALLS SCENIC RESERVE

Haumurana Springs

Hongi's Track

Lake Rotoehu

Hell's Gate Thermal Area

Lake Rotoiti

Ouau Channel

36

Lake Rotorua

Lake Rotokawau

Agrodome

Ngongotaha

Mokoia Island

Te Ngae 3D Maze

Mount Ngongotaha

5

Rainbow Springs

1

Skyline Skyrides

2

Lake Rotokawau

Western Okataina Walkway

Eastern Okataina Walkway

Tarawera River

Ohinemutu

SEE 'CENTRAL ROTORUA' MAP FOR DETAIL

2

30

3

■ ACCOMMODATION
Aroden	3
Blue Lake Top 10	4
Koura Lodge	1
The Lake House	2

● RESTAURANTS, CAFÉS AND BARS
The Landing	3
Okere Falls Store	1
Stratosfare	2

Lake Okareka

Lake Okereka

Humphries Bay

Tarawera Falls

Tarawera Falls

Tarawera Falls Walkway

WHAKAREWAREWA THERMAL RESERVE

WHAKAREWAREWA STATE FOREST PARK

4

Blue Lake (Tikitapu)

Lake Tarawera

30

Te Wairoa (Buried Village)

3

Green Lake (Rotokakahi)

Hot Water Beach

M O U N T   T A R A W E R A

Waimangu Volcanic Valley

Lake Rotomahana

WAIMANGU ROAD

Waimangu Cruise

Lake Rerewhakaaitu

Waikite Valley Thermal Pools

5

Kerosene Creek

38

WAIKITE VALLEY ROAD

Boiling Mud Pool

AROUND ROTORUA

Lady Knox Geyser

Wai-O-Tapu Thermal Wonderland

0 ——————— 10
kilometres

Taupo (50km) & Orakei Korako

Murupara (20km), Te Urewera National Park & Waikaremoana (125km)

and drinks are also available on site). Bridges link separate sections that complicate things immeasurably: set an hour aside to navigate the maze's 1.7km of pathways.

Okere Falls Scenic Reserve

Trout Pool Rd, off SH33, 21km from central Rotorua

SH33 continues north towards Tauranga. Signs 6km north point down Trout Pool Road to **Okere Falls Scenic Reserve**, which surrounds the popular rafting destination of the Kaituna River. From the first car park, 400m along Trout Pool Road, a broad,

4

WALKS IN AND AROUND ROTORUA

Rotorua isn't especially well endowed with serious tramps, though there are several good day-walks and Rotorua works well as a staging post for forays into the Whirinaki Forest and further afield to Waikaremoana. Rotorua's i-SITE and DOC visitor centres have details of the following:

Blue Lake (5.5km loop; 2hr; 500m ascent) This moderate loop around the Blue Lake starts by the *Blue Lake Holiday Park*, 9km southeast of Rotorua, and heads through regenerating bush, Douglas firs and past some sandy beaches perfect for a dip. The single major climb takes you away from the lake to a viewpoint.

Hamurana Springs Recreation Reserve (1.5km loop; 45min; mostly flat) On the shores of Lake Rotorua, 24km north of town, an easy trail meanders through a redwood grove to the North Island's largest spring. Almost 5 million litres an hour flow out, creating a crystal-clear stream with a faint tinge that's like looking through a bottle of Sapphire gin.

Lake Okareka Walkway (5km return; 1hr plus; mostly level) Located 12km southeast of Rotorua, this lakeside interpretive trail mostly borders farmland, leavened with patches of regenerating bush and a nice boardwalk through wetlands to a bird hide.

Okere Falls Scenic Reserve (2.5km return; 40min–1hr) An easy stroll starting 18km north of Rotorua, with river views and spectacular angles on rafters shooting Tutea Falls.

Whakarewarewa State Forest Park Several easy trails meander through an experimental forest on the edge of Rotorua. The impressive Redwood Grove contains trees that grow three times as fast as in their native California. The i-SITE (see p.273) has maps. The park is also renowned for its mountain-biking trails (see opposite).

---

well-maintained track follows the river to a second car park (2.5km return; 40min–1hr) passing glimpses of the churning river below, and a viewing platform that's perfect for observing rafters plummet over the 7m **Tutea Falls**. From here, steps descend through short tunnels in the steep rock walls beside the waterfall to **Tutea Caves**, thought to have been used as a safe haven by Maori women and children during attacks by rival *iwi*. Afterwards refuel at the wonderful *Okere Falls Store* café (see p.275).

Hell's Gate

SH30, 14km northeast of the centre • **Geothermal walk** Daily 8.30am–8.30pm • $35 • **Mud Spa** Daily 8.30am–10pm • Hot pools $20 • ☎ 07 345 3151, ⊛ hellsgate.co.nz

Most traffic sticks to SH30, the route to **Hell's Gate**, the smallest of the major thermal areas, but also one of the most active. Its fury camouflages a lack of notable features, however, and the only real highlights are the bubbling mud of the Devil's Cauldron and the hot **Kakahi Falls**, whose soothing 38°C waters once made this a popular bathing spot (now off-limits). The real attraction here is the **Mud Spa** where you can soak in the sulphurous hot waters overlooking the park or sign up for mud-based treatments (from $85), including slathering rejuvenating mud over yourself in a mud bath, and massages. There are a number of combination packages including bus transfers from central Rotorua.

The northern lakes

Lake Rotoiti translates as "small lake", though it is in fact the second largest in the region, and is linked to Lake Rotorua by the narrow Ohau Channel. This passage, along with the neighbouring **Lake Rotoehu** and **Lake Rotoma**, traditionally formed part of the canoe route from the coast. A section of this route, apparently used on a raid by the Ngapuhi warrior chief Hongi Hika, is traced by **Hongi's Track** (3km return; 1hr), a pretty bushwalk which runs through to Lake Rotoehu.

Whakarewarewa State Forest

Free entry but you'll need to buy the waterproof trail map ($5) or book ($10) from the visitor centre and from bike shops in town; ⓦ riderotorua.com and ⓦ redwoods.co.nz for more information • Southstar Shuttles (ⓦ southstaradventures.com) operate a shuttle service to the top of the hill ($10) • Bike rental from Mountain Bike Rotorua ⓔ mtbrotorua@gmail.com • Access is from the car park on Waipa Mill Rd, 5km south of the centre, off SH38

The North Island's best accessible **mountain biking** lies fifteen minutes' ride southeast of central Rotorua, with large areas of the **Whakarewarewa Forest**'s redwoods, firs and pines threaded by single-track trails especially constructed with banked turns and drops. Altogether there's around 70km of track, divided into over a dozen circuits graded from 1 (beginner) to 6 (death wish).

The Blue and Green lakes

Around 10km southeast of Rotorua, Tarawera Road reaches the iridescent waters of **Blue Lake** (Tikitapu) with its campsite, easy circuit walk (see box opposite) and safe swimming beach. A little further on, a ridge-top viewpoint overlooks both Blue Lake and **Green Lake** (Rotokakahi), whose name means "freshwater mussel lake", although because it's privately owned, no fishing or boating activity is allowed here. Tarawera Road then reaches the shores of Lake Tarawera 15km southeast of Rotorua.

The Buried Village and Lake Tarawera

Buried Village 1180 Tarawera Rd • Daily: Nov–March 9am–5pm; April–Oct 9am–4.30pm • $32.50 • ☎ 07 362 8287, ⓦ buriedvillage.co.nz

Just before the Tarawera lakeshore, the **Buried Village** kicks off with a **museum** that captures the spirit of the village in its heyday and the aftermath of its destruction, through photos, fine aquatints of the Pink and White Terraces and ash-encrusted knick-knacks. The Maori and European settlement here was larger than contemporary Rotorua until the Tarawera eruption when numerous houses collapsed under the weight of the ash; others were saved by virtue of their inhabitants hefting ash off the roof to lighten the load. From the museum, either opt for a free **guided tour** with period-costumed guides (available throughout the day; call for seasonal hours) or make your own way through the grounds.

What you see today is the result of 1930s and 1940s excavations plus some substantial reconstructions. The village itself is less an archeological dig than a manicured orchard: half-buried *whare* and the foundations for the Rotomahana Hotel sit primly on mown lawns among European fruit trees gone to seed, marauding hawthorn and a perfect row of full-grown poplars fostered from a line of fenceposts. Many of the *whare* house collections of implements and ash-encrusted household goods, and contrast starkly with the simplicity of other dwellings such as **Tohunga's Whare**, where the ill-fated priest lay buried alive for four days (see box, p.280). Look out too for the extremely rare, carved-stone *pataka* (storehouse) and the bow section of a *waka* once used to ferry tourists on the lake and allegedly brought to the district by Hongi Hika, when he invaded in 1823. Beyond the formal grounds a steep staircase and slippery boardwalk dive into the hill alongside **Te Wairoa Falls**, then climb up through dripping, fern-draped bush on the far side. If that's worked up an appetite, stop by the on-site café.

ROTORUA SCENIC FLIGHTS

The scenery around Rotorua is breathtaking from the air, particularly the region's volcanic spine centred on Mount Tarawera.

Volcanic Air Safaris ☎ 0800 800 848, ⓦ volcanicair .co.nz. Offers all manner of flight options from floatplane flights over Tarawera and Orakei Korako ($455/2hr15min) and helicopter flights to land on White Island ($835).

THE MOUNT TARAWERA ERUPTION

Volcanic activity provides the main theme for attractions southeast of Rotorua, most having some association with **Lake Tarawera** and the jagged line of volcanic peaks and craters along the southeastern shore, collectively known as **Mount Tarawera**, which erupted in 1886.

Prior to that eruption Tarawera was New Zealand's premier tourist destination, with thousands of visitors every year crossing lakes Tarawera and Rotomahana in whaleboats and *waka*, frequently guided by the renowned Maori guide Sophia, to the **Pink and White Terraces**, two separate fans of silica that cascaded down the hillside to the edge of Lake Rotomahana. Boiling cauldrons bubbled at the top of each formation, spilling mineral-rich water down into a series of staggered cup-shaped pools, the outflow of one filling the one below. Most visitors favoured the Pink Terraces, which were prettier and better suited to sitting and soaking. All this came to an abrupt end on the night of June 10, 1886, when the long-dormant Mount Tarawera erupted, creating 22 craters along a 17km rift, and covering over 15,000 square kilometres in mud and scoria. The Pink and White Terraces were shattered by the buckling earth, covered by ash and lava, then submerged deep under the waters of Lake Rotomahana.

The cataclysm had been foreshadowed eleven days earlier, when two separate canoe-loads of Pakeha tourists and their Maori guides saw an ancient *waka* glide out of the mist, with a dozen warriors paddling furiously, then vanish just as suddenly; the ancient *tohunga* (priest) Tuhoto Ariki interpreted this as a sign of imminent disaster. The fallout from the eruption buried five villages, including the staging post for the Pink and White Terrace trips, **Te Wairoa**, where the *tohunga* lived. In a classic case of blaming the messenger, the inhabitants refused to rescue the *tohunga* and it wasn't until four days later that they allowed a group of Pakeha to dig him out. Miraculously he lived, for a week.

In 2011, scientists discovered that rather than being completely destroyed, parts of the Pink Terraces appear to have survived the 1886 eruption (the White Terraces are thought to have been more likely to have been affected). The gas and hot water vents discovered on the lake floor indicate rare active underwater geothermal systems, which scientists are continuing to research.

Tarawera Road ends 2km further on at the shore of **Lake Tarawera** with the mountain rising beyond. Contact staff at *The Landing* café if you fancy getting out on the water; in the warmer months you can paddle sit-on-top kayaks ($25/hr).

Waimangu Volcanic Valley

587 Waimangu Rd, 5km east off SH5 • Daily: Jan 8.30am–6pm (last admission 4.40pm); Feb–Dec 8.30am–5pm (last admission 3.40pm) • Walking and hiking $36; 45min lake cruises $42.50; combo package $78.50 • ☏ 07 366 6137, ⓦ waimangu.co.nz

Head 19km south of Rotorua on SH5 towards Taupo and you'll soon reach the southern limit of the volcanic rift blown out by Mount Tarawera, the **Waimangu Volcanic Valley**. This is one of the world's youngest geothermal areas, created in 1886 when a chain of eruptions racked the Mount Tarawera fault line. Pick up the comprehensive self-guided walking tour leaflet at the visitor centre then head downhill along a streamside path, which cuts through a valley choked with scrub and native bush that has regenerated since 1886. This process has been periodically interrupted by smaller eruptions, including one in 1917 that created the magnificent 100m-diameter **Frying Pan Lake**, the world's largest hot spring. Massive quantities of hot water well up from the depths of the **Inferno Crater**, an inverted cone where mesmerizing steam patterns partly obscure the stunning powder-blue water and are stirred and swirled by breezes across the lake. The water level rises and falls according to a rigid 38-day cycle – filling to the rim for 21 days, overflowing for two then gradually falling to 8m below the rim over the next fifteen. Steaming pools and hissing vents line the path, which passes the muddy depression where, from 1900 to 1904, the **Waimangu Geyser** regularly spouted water to 250m (and occasionally to an astonishing height of 400m), carrying rocks and black mud with it.

The path through the valley ends at the wharf on the shores of Lake Rotomahana, where the rust-red sides of Mount Tarawera dominate the far horizon. From here, free buses run back up the road to the visitor centre and **cruises** chug around the lake past steaming cliffs, fumaroles, and over the site of the Pink and White Terraces.

Kerosene Creek

1km south of SH38 junction turn east from SH5 along Old Waiotapu Rd and follow the gravel 2km to the parking area

If you're looking for free, hot soaking in natural surroundings, make straight for **Kerosene Creek**, 27km south of Rotorua, a stream that's usually the temperature of a warm bath and plunges over a metre-high waterfall into a nice big pool. It's always open and sometimes attracts a party crowd at weekends. Camping in the area is banned and there have been thefts from vehicles in the car park – see box, p.267.

Wai-O-Tapu

201 Waiotapu Loop Rd, just off SH5 • April–Oct 8.30am–5pm, last entry 3.45pm; Nov–March 8.30am–6pm, last entry 4.45pm • $32.50 • ☎ 07 366 6333, ⊛ waiotapu.co.nz

Wai-O-Tapu Thermal Wonderland, 10km south of Waimangu, is the area's most colourful and varied geothermal site. At 10.15am daily, the 10m **Lady Knox Geyser** is ignominiously induced to perform by a staff member who pours a soapy surfactant into the vent. If you miss the geyser your ticket allows you to come back next morning.

Everyone then drives 1km to the main site where an hour-long walking loop wends its way through a series of small lakes which have taken on the tints of the minerals dissolved in them – yellow from sulphur, purple from manganese, green from arsenic and so on. The gurgling and growling black mud of the **Devil's Ink-Pots** and a series of hissing and rumbling craters pale beside the ever-changing rainbow colours of the **Artist's Palette** pools and the gorgeous, effervescent **Champagne Pool**, a circular bottle-green cauldron wreathed in swirling steam and fringed by a burnt-orange shelf. The waters of the Champagne Pool froth over **The Terraces**, a rippled accretion of lime silicate that glistens in the sunlight.

As you drive back to the main road, follow a short detour to a huge and active **boiling mud pool** which plops away merrily, forming lovely concentric patterns.

Orakei Korako

494 Orakei Korako Rd • Daily: Oct–March 8am–4.30pm; April– Sept 8am–4pm • $36, shuttle-boat journey included • ☎ 07 378 3131, ⊛ orakeikorako.co.nz

Diverting from either SH1 (14km) or SH5 (21km) and about 60km southwest of Rotorua is the atmospheric thermal area of **Orakei Korako**, characterized by its belching fumaroles, gin-clear boiling pools and paucity of tourists. A short shuttle-boat journey across the Waikato River (on demand throughout the day) accesses an hour-long trail which visits Ruatapu Cave, once used by Maori women to prepare themselves for ceremonies – hence Orakei Korako, "a place of adorning".

Orakei Korako can also be reached by **jetboat** along the Waikato River with NZ Riverjet (☎0800 748 375, ⊛ riverjet.co.nz), based beside SH5, at Tutukau Road, 44km south of Rotorua and almost 20km south of Wai-O-Tapu. Its Riverjet Thermal Safari (3hr; $169) includes a jetboat ride and entry.

Te Urewera

Midway between Waimangu and Wai-O-Tapu, 25km south of Rotorua, SH38 spurs southeast through the regimented pines of the Kaingaroa Forest towards the jagged peaks of **Te Urewera** (see p.380), a vast tract of untouched wilderness separating the

Rotorua lakes from Poverty Bay and the East Cape. The Kaingaroa Forest finally relents 40km on, as the road crosses the Rangitikei River by the predominantly Maori timber town of **MURUPARA**.

INFORMATION   TE UREWERA NATIONAL PARK

Te Urewera Area DOC 1km southeast of Murupara, on SH38 (Nov–April Mon–Fri 8am–5pm, Sat & Sun 9am–3pm; May–Oct Mon–Fri 8am–5pm; ☏ 07 366

1080). Has stacks of information on the park and Lake Waikaremoana (see p.381).

Whirinaki Forest Park

Adjoining Te Urewera National Park to the southeast is the wonderful but little-visited **Whirinaki Forest Park**, around 30km south of Murupara, which harbours some of the densest and most impressive stands of bush on the North Island: podocarps on the river flats, and native beech on the steep volcanic uplands between them, support a wonderfully rich birdlife with tui, bellbirds, kereru and kaka. The forest is now protected, after one of the country's most celebrated environmental battles, and is a wilderness paradise for hikers and mountain-bikers.

You can sample some of the best of the forest on a stretch of the well-formed **Whirinaki Track** (4hr return) which passes magnificent podocarps, the Whaiti-nui-a-tio Canyon where the river cascades over an old lava flow, and Whirinaki Falls. Go as far as you like and turn back, but the track system continues, allowing tramps of up to five days.

INFORMATION AND TOURS   WHIRINAKI FOREST PARK

Tourist information DOC offices (the closest is at Murupara) in the region carry the *Ride Whirinaki* leaflet ($2), which details a couple of great mountain-bike rides in the area (2hr–2 days), but you'll need to have your own bike or rent one in Rotorua (see p.279).

Whirinaki Rainforest Experiences ☏ 0800 869 255, ⓦ whirinaki.com. Explore Whirinaki Forest Park on a friendly and involving day-long guided tour ($155) that offers a Maori perspective on the forest and its history.

ACCOMMODATION

Huts If you're planning a multi-day tramp through Whirinaki you can either camp or stay in the basic DOC huts

that pepper the park. Camping $\overline{\$5}$, huts $\overline{\$10}$

Taupo

The burgeoning resort town of **TAUPO**, 80km south of Rotorua and slap in the centre of the North Island, is strung around the northern shores of **Lake Taupo**, the country's largest lake, which is the size of Singapore. Views stretch 30km southwest towards the three snowcapped volcanoes of the Tongariro National Park, the reflected light from the lake's glassy surface combining with the 360m altitude to create an almost alpine radiance. Here, the impossibly deep-blue waters of the Waikato River ("flowing water" in Maori) begin their long journey to the Tasman Sea, and both lake and river frontages are lined with parks.

For decades, Kiwi families have been descending en masse for a couple of weeks' holiday, bathing in the crisp waters of the lake, and lounging around holiday homes that fringe the lakeshore. But there's no shortage of things to see and do, from the spectacular rapids and geothermal badlands north of town to **skydiving** – this is New Zealand's freefall capital – and **fishing**. The Taupo area is a most fecund trout fishery, extending south to Turangi and along the Tongariro River, with an enviable reputation for the quality of its fish. Year-round, you'll see boats drifting across the lake with lines

trailing and, particularly in the evenings, rivermouths choked with fly-casters in waist-high waders.

Nowhere in **Taupo**'s compact low-rise core is more than five minutes' walk from the waters of the Waikato River or Lake Taupo, which jointly hem in three sides. The fourth side rises up through the gentle slopes of Taupo's suburbs. Most of the commercial activity happens along Tongariro Street and the aptly named Lake Terrace.

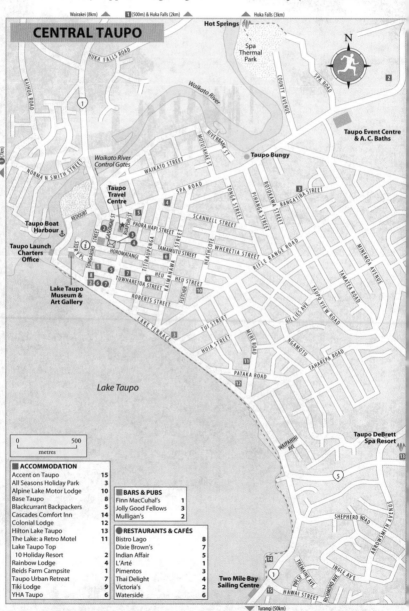

CENTRAL TAUPO

Taupo also makes a great base for exploring the surrounding area (see p.290), where highlights include Huka Falls, Aratiatia Rapids, Wairakei Terraces and the Craters of the Moon geothermal area.

Brief history

The Tuwharetoa people had lived in the area for centuries, but it wasn't until the New Zealand Wars that Europeans took an interest with the Armed Constabulary trying to track down **Te Kooti** (see box, p.383). They set up camp one night in June 1869 at Opepe, 17km southeast of Taupo (beside what is now SH5), and were ambushed by Te Kooti's men, who killed nine soldiers. Garrisons were subsequently established at Opepe and Taupo, but only Taupo flourished, enjoying a more strategic situation and being blessed with hot springs for washing and bathing. By 1877, Te Kooti had been contained, but the Armed Constabulary wasn't disbanded until 1886, after which several soldiers and their families stayed on, forming the nucleus of European settlement.

Taupo didn't really take off as a domestic resort until the prosperous 1950s, when the North Island's roads had improved to the point where Kiwi families could easily drive here from Auckland, Wellington or Hawke's Bay.

Lake Taupo Museum and Art Gallery

Story Place, Tongariro Park, off SH1 · Daily 10am–4.30pm · $5 · ⓦ taupodc.govt.nz

Set aside at least half an hour for the **Lake Taupo Museum and Art Gallery**, if only for the beautiful Reid Carvings, created in 1927–28 by the famous master carver Tene Waitere and exhibited in the form of a meeting house. They're as fine as you'll see anywhere and are supplemented with modern *tukutuku* panels and a lovely flax rain-cape probably from the 1870s or earlier. Interesting displays on the geology of the area, fly-fishing and the logging industry line the way to the Tuwharetoa Gallery ranged around the decayed hull of a 150-year-old 14.5m *waka*, found in the bush in 1967. Paintings around the room include two of Ngati Tuwharetoa chiefs by local polymath Thomas Ryan, who was also a lake steamer captain and an All Black. The watercolours show the unmistakeable influence of the artist's great friend Charles Goldie. Outside, the stunning **Ora Garden**, a 2004 Chelsea Flower Show winner, has been re-created in all its geothermal glory.

LAKE TAUPO: GIANT SPIRIT

Lake Taupo (616 square kilometres, 185m deep) is itself a geological infant largely created in 186 AD when the Taupo Volcano spewed out 24 cubic kilometres of rock, debris and ash – at least ten times more than was produced by the eruptions of Krakatoa and Mount St Helens combined – and covered much of the North Island in a thick layer of pumice. Ash from the eruption was carried around the world – the Chinese noted a blackening of the sky and Romans recorded that the heavens turned blood-red. As the underground magma chamber emptied, the roof slumped, leaving a huge steep-sided **crater**, since filled by Lake Taupo. It's hard to reconcile this placid and beautiful lake with such colossal violence, though the evidence is all around: entire beaches are composed of feather-light pumice which, when caught by the wind, floats off across the waters. Volcanologists continue to study the Taupo Volcano (currently considered dormant) and treat the lake as a kind of giant spirit-level, in which any tilting could indicate a build-up of magma below the surface that might trigger another eruption.

The local Tuwharetoa people ascribe the lake's formation to their ancestor, Ngatoroirangi, who cast a tree from the summit of Mount Tauhara, on the edge of Taupo, and where it struck the ground water welled up and formed the lake. The lake's full name is Taupo-Nui-A-Tia, "the great shoulder mat of Tia" or "great sleep of Tia", which refers to an explorer from the Arawa canoe said to have slept by the lake.

Taupo DeBrett Spa Resort

3km southeast on SH5 • Daily 8.30am–9.30pm • $22 • ☎ 07 377 6502, ⓦ taupohotsprings.com

Geothermal bathing is best at the family-oriented **Taupo DeBrett Spa Resort**, which has a couple of large outdoor pools filled with natural mineral water plus private mineral pools in a range of temperatures; an additional $7 buys as many descents as you like on the hot-water hydroslide.

A.C. Baths and Taupo Events Centre

A.C. Baths Ave • **Baths** Daily 6am–9pm • Swimming $7; private hot pools $10/person/30min • **Climbing wall** Timetable varies monthly • Harness and shoes $8, plus $10 entry • A.C. Baths ☎ 07 376 0350, Events Centre ☎ 07 376 0350, ⓦ taupodc.govt.nz.

Even without your own vehicle it's easy to reach the **A.C. Baths and Taupo Events Centre**, a sparkling sports hall and 12m climbing wall, alongside the longstanding **A.C. Baths**, a well-maintained complex of thermally heated swimming and hot pools.

Spa Thermal Park and Hot Stream

County Ave, 1km northeast of the centre • 24hr • Free

A small hot creek cascades through a series of wonderful soaking pools then mixes with the cool waters of the Waikato River at the **Spa Thermal Park and Hot Stream**. The stream is around 400m along the riverside walkway which continues downstream (2.8km one way; 45min) to Huka Falls (see p.290).

4

ARRIVAL AND DEPARTURE   TAUPO

By plane Taupo's little airport (ⓦ taupoairport.co.nz), 10km south of the centre, has Air New Zealand flights to Auckland and Wellington.

Destinations Auckland (2 daily; 50min); Wellington (2 daily; 1hr).

By bus InterCity and Newmans buses stop at the Taupo Travel Centre bus station, 16 Gascoigne St (☎ 07 378 9005), in the middle of town. NakedBus stops outside the i-SITE on Tongariro St.

Destinations Auckland (4 daily; 5hr 20min); Hamilton (4 daily; 3hr); Hastings (2 daily; 2hr 50min); Napier (2 daily; 2hr 15min); Palmerston North (2 daily; 4hr 10min); Rotorua (4 daily; 1hr 15min); Taihape (4 daily; 2hr 5min); Tauranga (2 daily; 3hr 10min); Turangi (4 daily; 55min); Wellington (4 daily; 6hr 30min).

GETTING AROUND

By shuttle For visiting the surrounding sights (and airport transfers), Shuttle 2U (daily 24hr; ☎ 07 376 7638) does a hop-on-hop-off circuit of all the main attractions and will even pick up from your accommodation.

By car Pegasus Rental Cars (☎ 0800 803 580, ⓦ rentalcars .co.nz) generally have the best deals, from $45/day, but check the fine print, as shorter and one-way rentals can cost significantly more.

By bike Most hostels have basic bikes for guests' use. Pack & Pedal, 5 Tamamutu St (☎ 07 377 4346, ⓦ skiandbiketaupo.wix.com/pack-and-pedal), rents MTBs from $40/4hr, $60 all day. Rapid Sensations, 413 Huka Falls Rd (☎ 0800 35 34 35, ⓦ rapids.co.nz), run guided bike tours in Wairakei Forest (see box, p.288), but also rent mountain bikes from $40/2hr or $60/day.

By taxi Call Top Cabs (☎ 07 378 9250) or Taupo Taxis (☎ 07 378 5100).

INFORMATION

Visitor information i-SITE, 30 Tongariro St (daily 8.30am–5pm; ☎ 0800 525 382, ⓦ greatlaketaupo.com).
Experience Taupo 29 Tongariro St (daily: Oct–April 9am–7pm; May–Sept 9am–6pm; ☎ 0800 368 775, ⓦ experiencetaupo.com). Provides good information and promotes its sponsor's adventure companies.

ACCOMMODATION

Taupo maintains a high standard of accommodation for all budgets, but given its proximity to Tongariro National Park and host of events, it's worth booking ahead whatever the time of year. Much of the lakefront is taken up with **motels**, and grassy spots on the fringes of town are given over to **campsites**, while **hostels** are abundant in the town centre.

ccent on Taupo 310 Lake Terrace ☎ 0800 222 368, ⓦ accentontaupo.com; map p.284. Stylishly appointed hotel with super-king-size beds, timber decks, a spa, trampoline and BBQ and attractive taupe-toned decor right down to the fan-folded flannels). Fantastic value for money. **$120**

ll Seasons Holiday Park 16 Rangatira St ☎ 0800 77 272, ⓦ taupoallseasons.co.nz; map p.284. ituated 1.5km east of town, with thermal mineral pool, edged tent sites scattered among cabins, some with itchens, and a range of self-contained units ($5 for nen) plus budget rooms in a lodge. Camping **$24**, abins **$82**

lpine Lake Motor Lodge 141 Heu Heu St ☎ 0800 400 41, ⓦ alpinelake.co.nz; map p.284. One of Taupo's ewer motels, the luxurious *Alpine Lake* comes with nderfloor heating, DVD players, free broadband and spa aths in most units. Most units also have hobs, and some ave their own BBQs in private courtyards. **$135**

ase Taupo 7 Tuwharetoa St ☎ 07 377 4464, ⓦ stayatbase.com; map p.284. Secure 120-bed ostel in the heart of Taupo's bar zone and with a good ake-view deck, all the expected facilities (including vi-fi in the lobby), the women-only Sanctuary section $30) and a lively bar, *Element*. Dorms **$25**, en-suite ooms **$76**

★ Blackcurrant Backpackers 20 Taniwha St ☎ 07 378 292, ⓦ blackcurrantbp.co.nz; map p.284. Bright, ontemporary hostel arranged around a courtyard garden, vith about the best kitchen you'll ever find in a hostel, no unk beds, and a friendly welcome. There are great views rom the veranda over to the lake – settle in and watch the unset. Dorms **$27**, en-suite double **$78**

ascades Comfort Inn 303 Lake Terrace, SH1, Two lile Bay ☎ 0800 996 997, ⓦ cascades.co.nz; map .284. Ideally sited with direct access to an attractive eated pool and the lake. Units are spacious with a ull kitchen, a mezzanine sleeping area, a patio and a spa ath. **$89**

olonial Lodge 134 Lake Terrace ☎ 0800 353 36, ⓦ colonial.co.nz; map p.284. Double spas in he bathrooms, kitchenettes, huge TVs and fast, free vi-fi are among the highlights of this efficient motel. o for the upstairs rooms, opening to a sunny alcony. **$100**

Hilton Lake Taupo 80 Napier–Taupo Hwy ☎ 07 378 080, ⓦ hilton.com/laketaupo; map p.284. This Hilton hotel combines the beautifully restored 1889 riginal hotel with heritage rooms and distant lake iews, and a modern wing with suites and apartments. With the classy *Bistro Lago* (see p.288) and a hot prings next door, you've got all you need for a relaxed tay. **$179**

★ The Lake: a Retro Motel 63 Mere Rd ☎ 07 378 4222, ⓦ thelakeonline.co.nz; map p.284. Taupo's first ever motel has gone back to its roots, from its striking black exterior to rooms fitted out with funky 1960s and 70s decor (with touches like shag-pile rugs, red-leather and moulded white-plastic chairs and Noddy and Big Ears egg cups), most opening to black-and-white-furnished gardens. Free wi-fi in all rooms. Studio **$125**, one-bedroom units **$145**

Lake Taupo Top 10 Holiday Resort 28 Centennial Drive, 2km northeast of town ☎ 0800 322 121, ⓦ taupotop10.co.nz; map p.284. Large, super-organized site with free activities including swimming pool, volleyball, tennis, games room, kids' playground, giant chessboard and New Zealand's largest jumping pillow. The bathrooms even have heated floors. Camping **$25**, cabins **$100**

Rainbow Lodge 99 Titiraupenga St ☎ 07 378 5754, ⓦ rainbowlodge.co.nz; map p.284. Spacious, relaxed backpackers spread over three buildings with a comfortable lounge, sauna, safe parking and bike rental ($20/day). A stack of local information and little touches create a homey atmosphere. Dorms have six to nine beds (female-only available on request) and there are some particularly good-value en-suite doubles and twins with TV and patio. Free pick-ups from the bus station. Dorms **$24**, rooms **$62**

Reids Farm Campsite 3km north of Taupo on Huka Falls Rd; map p.291. Spacious free campsite right by the Waikato River just 1km upstream of the exclusive *Huka Lodge*, left to the world by a previous owner who liked backpackers. The makeshift slalom course makes it a popular spot with kayakers. Maximum stay of 7 nights in any 14; closed April to late Oct. **Free**

Taupo Urban Retreat 65 Heu Heu St ☎ 0800 872 261, ⓦ tur.co.nz; map p.284. A 96-bed oasis in the heart of town, this hostel comes with its own house bar, small garden, 1hr free internet, discounted gym passes, bike rental ($20/day) and off-street parking. Popular with the backpacker bus crowd, it has great four-bunk dorms with lake views, though others are windowless. Dorms **$25**, en-suite doubles **$75**

Tiki Lodge 104 Tuwharetoa St ☎ 0800 845 456, ⓦ tikilodge.co.nz; map p.284. The best of the flashpacker-style hostels, purpose-built with a spacious kitchen and 24-hour lounge area plus a great balcony with lake views, and a spa. Dorms **$25**, en-suite doubles with kitchenettes **$80**

YHA Taupo 56 Kaimanawa St ☎ 07 378 3311, ⓦ yha .co.nz; map p.284. Welcoming modern YHA hostel, close to town and with good lake and mountain views from the kitchen and BBQ balcony. There's a spa pool, volleyball court and a garden with hammocks. Dorms either have eight bunks or four beds. Dorms **$26.70**, rooms **$77.80**

4

EATING, DRINKING AND NIGHTLIFE

Taupo is loaded with good **cafés** and restaurants, including plenty of Asian restaurants. **Nightlife** almost all happens along the westernmost block of Tuwharetoa Street through to the wee hours. Alternatively head out to Wairakei Terrace for a **Maori cultural experience** (p.291).

CAFÉS AND RESTAURANTS

Bistro Lago *Hilton Lake Taupo* (see p.287) ☎ 07 377 1400, ⓦ bistrolago.co.nz; map p.284. Taupo's finest dining in the beautifully modernized old wing of the hotel. Great service, immaculate presentation and delectable food that's similarly priced (fish and chips $32, Taupo beef eye fillet $42) to far inferior places. Daily 9am–late.

Dixie Browns ☎ 07 378 8444, ⓦ dixiebrowns.co.nz. The

pick of the lakeshore restaurants for a laidback lunch. High quality mains include butter chicken ($16.90) and gourmet pizzas (from $14.90), and there's plenty of seating outside and friendly efficient service. Ask for free wi-fi. Daily 6am–10pm.

Indian Affair 34 Ruapehu St ☎ 07 378 2295, ⓦ indianaffair.co.nz; map p.284. Smart, modern surroundings and the best curries in town. There's a great vegetarian selection, including a rich *malai kofta* ($17.90).

TAUPO TOURS AND ACTIVITIES

Taupo offers a huge range of air-, land- and water-based activities to relieve you of your holiday money. There's great **mountain biking** around Taupo, much of it maintained by Bike Taupo (ⓦ biketaupo.org.nz). With great scenery and very competitive prices, Taupo is claimed to be the busiest tandem **skydiving** drop zone in the world; all operators offer jumps from 12,000ft (45 seconds of freefall; $249) and 15,000ft (60 seconds of freefall; $339). **Cruises** visit striking, modern Maori **rock carvings** that can only be seen from the water at Mine Bay, 8km southwest of town. The 10m-high carvings date from the late 1970s and depict a stylized image of a man's face heavy with *moko*, together with *tuatara* (lizard-like reptiles) and female forms draped over nearby rocks. All cruise trips operate two or three times daily, weather permitting; they can be booked through the Taupo Charters Office (☎ 07 378 9794) at the boat harbour. Several **kayaking** trips also visit the carvings. New Zealand's **fishing** rules dictate that trout can't be sold, so if you've got a taste for them you'll need to catch them yourself. The easiest way is to fish the lake from a charter boat. Rivers flowing into Lake Taupo are the preserve of fly-fishers. The Taupo Launch Charters Office, by the boat harbour (☎ 07 378 3444), can hook you up with something suitable. Although minimum numbers don't apply, the more on the boat the cheaper it is – book in advance from mid-December to February. Boat operators supply tackle and will organize the mandatory Taupo District Fishing Licence ($17/24hr). The charters office also has a list of fishing guides (about $300 for half a day).

MOUNTAIN BIKING

Huka Falls Walkway A scenic ride best reached by heading north from Spa Thermal Park to Huka Falls (4km one-way) and on to Aratiatia Dam (additional 8km one-way).

W2K This challenging single-track route (16km one way, with an additional 10km loop) starts at Whakaipo Bay, 20km west of

Taupo, and finishes at Kinloch. Either plan to ride it both ways or arrange transport – it's around 40km by road.

Wairakei Forest Excellent loop riding: start by the Helistar Helicopter, 3km north of Taupo. Rapid Sensations (see opposite) does guided rides of the forest ($90/2hr). For bike rental, see p.286.

SKYDIVING

Taupo Tandem Skydiving ☎ 0800 826 336, ⓦ tts .net.nz. Skydiving trips with this operator have been running since 1992.

Skydive Taupo ☎ 0800 586 766, ⓦ skydivetaupo .co.nz. Skydives with expert instructors and including a stretch-limo pick-up service.

BUNGY JUMPING

Taupo Bungy 202 Spa Rd ☎ 0800 888 408, ⓦ taupobungy.co.nz. The river swirls right past one of New Zealand's finest bungy sites, cantilevered 20m out from the bank with a 47m drop and an optional

dunking. Bungy $169, swing solo/tandem $119/238, swing/bungy combo $238. Daily summer 9.30am–6.30pm, winter weekdays until 4pm, weekends until 5pm.

a sublime *paneer makhani* (home-made cottage cheese in creamy tomato sauce, $16.90), and a renowned Goan fish curry ($22.90). Daily 11.30am–2pm & 5pm–late.

★**L'Arté** 255 Mapara Rd, Acacia Bay ☎07 378 2962, ⓦlarte.co.nz; map p.284. A pretty 8km drive around the head of Lake Taupo to this rural sculpture gallery and garden of quirky mosaics, including some arranged as an outdoor living room. Great food, such as corn fritter stacks layered with crispy bacon and avocado or eggs Benedict with home-made potato cakes and hollandaise ($13), and drinks including a wonderful hot lemon, honey and ginger, are served inside or on a shady deck. Licensed. Wed–Sun 8am–4pm, also open most public holidays.

Pimentos 17 Tamamutu St ☎07 377 4549; map p.284. Fairly casual, central restaurant specializing in modern takes on classic dishes, such as coconut-coated fresh fish on Asian-dressed green vegetables, or marinated pork loin on roasted *kumara*. Mains around $30. Daily noon–3pm & 6–11pm.

Thai Delight 19 Tamamutu St ☎07 378 9554, ⓦthaidelight.co.nz; map p.284. Delights at this spacious Thai restaurant include curries, beef, pork, duck and seafood dishes; try the crisp taro cone filled with chicken, vegetables and Thai-style sweet and sour sauce ($24.90). Tues–Sun lunch from 11.30am, dinner from 5pm.

Victoria's 127 Tongariro St ☎07 376 7310, ⓦvictorias .co.nz; map p.284. Take a booth for breakfast of eggs

SCENIC FLIGHTS AND HELICOPTER TRIPS

Taupo's Float Plane ☎07 378 7500, ⓦtauposfloatplane.co.nz. Scenic flights over the lake and its surrounds ($105/10min; Mount Ruapehu $395/60min).

Helistar Helicopters ☎0800 435 478, ⓦhelicoptertours.co.nz. Runs the best helicopter trips, from a 10-minute flight over Huka Falls ($99) to a 90min voyage over the Tongariro World Heritage Park ($740).

LAKE CRUISES

★**The Barbary** Entertaining cruises (2hr 30min; $40), aboard a 1926 ketch allegedly once owned by Eroll Flynn (who, it's claimed, won it in a card game), including up-close viewing of the Mauri rock carvings and the chance to swim. Thanks to its electric engine, this is the quietest boat on the lake, so enjoy the peace and quiet.

Ernest Kemp A replica 1920s steamboat that chugs to the carvings and back (2hr; $40).

Fearless Relaxed sailing trips on the comfortable *Fearless* (2hr; $40) include a swimming stop at the Maori rock carvings and a drink served by the friendly skipper.

KAYAKING AND WATERSPORTS

Rapid Sensations ☎0800 353 435, ⓦrapids .co.nz. Runs a kayaking trip to the carvings ($98/3hr on the water), and offers rafting trips ($129) on the Tongariro River.

Taupo Kayaking Adventures ☎027 480 1231, ⓦtka.co.nz. Does half-day kayak trips to the carvings ($100) and various other trips including

fishing tours by kayak on request.

2MileBay Watersports Centre Two Mile Bay ☎07 378 3299, ⓦsailingcentre.co.nz. Rents catamarans ($60/hr), windsurfing boards ($30/hr) and other sailboats (from $50/hr). Daily 9am–5pm in summer, otherwise sporadically.

JETBOATING

Huka Falls Jet ☎0800 485 2538, ⓦhukafallsjet .com. The peace at Huka Prawn Park (see p.291) is periodically shattered by one of this company's jetboats ($115/30min) roaring along the river and doing 360-degree spins on the way to the base of Huka Falls.

Rapids Jet Rapids Rd, 3km beyond Aratiatia Dam ☎0800 727 437, ⓦrapidsjet.com. The North Island's only true whitewater jetboating run gives you plenty of bang for your buck ($105), taking you down and up Nga Awapura rapids, during which the entire boat gets airborne. Listen closely to the safety spiel, hang on and prepare to get wet.

FISHING

White Striker ☎07 378 2736, ⓦtroutcatching.com. Has a good strike rate and a wealth of local knowledge. Their smallest charter holds up to four ($110/hr).

Taupo Rod & Tackle 7 Tongariro St ☎07 378 5337,

ⓦtauporodandtackle.co.nz. You can rent all manner of tackle here and pick your own spot to cast from – but average catches are much larger if you engage the services of a fishing guide.

HORSERIDING

Taupo Horse Treks Karapiti Rd ☎0800 244 3987, ⓦtaupohorsetreks.co.nz. Offers one-hour ($70) and

two-hour ($140) jaunts through the pine forests around the Craters of the Moon.

4

Benedict, served on potato cakes ($17) or come in the evening for small plates and platters, such as the local cheeseboard ($16) and Taupo beef meatballs ($9). Either way you're sure to find the cakes cabinet a tempting finish. Mon 7.30am–5pm, Tues–Fri 7.30am–late, Sat 8.30am–late, Sun 8.30am–5pm.

Waterside 3 Tongariro St ☎ 07 378 6894, ⓦ waterside .co.nz; map p.284. Big cooked breakfasts, beer-battered fish and chips ($23.90) and seafood chowder ($11.90) for lunch and evening meals such as roast chicken ($26.90) and surf 'n' turf (from $27.50), topped off with a cheeseboard, keep appetites in check from morning to night. Daily 11am–late.

BARS AND PUBS

Finn MacCuhal's Corner of Tongariro and Tuwharetoa sts ☎ 07 378 6165, ⓦ finns.co.nz; map p.284. Large Irish bar popular with both backpackers and locals; most come

for the Guinness, but they also do good-value steaks and fish and chips (mains $19.90–29.90) and will cook your catch for you for $20. Daily 5pm–late.

Jolly Good Fellows 76–80 Lake Terrace ☎ 07 378 0457, ⓦ jollygoodfellows.co.nz; map p.284. The nearest Taupo gets to a British pub, not in style but for its excellent range of draught ales (most of which have travelled well) and lively community feel. Pub meals are also in the English tradition, with mains including lamb shank and fish and chips (around $20). Lots of diners early on followed by revellers for the late shift. Daily 10am–late.

Mulligan's 15 Tongariro St ☎ 07 376 9100, ⓦ mulligansbar.co.nz; map p.284. Dimly lit, Irish-style spot with stout on tap, mischievous Kiwi bar staff, live music, pool table, quiz nights and massive plates of bar food (mains $19–25) including Irish stew and steak-and-stout pie. Popular with both locals and tour buses. Daily 4pm–late.

DIRECTORY

Medical treatment Taupo Health Centre, 113 Heu Heu St (Mon–Fri 8am–5.30pm; ☎ 07 378 7060, ⓦ taupohealth .co.nz).

Pharmacy Unichem Mainstreet Pharmacy, at Tongariro & Heuheu sts (daily 8.30am–8.30pm; ☎ 07 378 2636).

Police 21 Story Place, by the museum and art gallery (☎ 07 378 6060).

Post office At Horomatangi & Ruapehu sts, with poste restante facilities (☎ 07 378 9093).

Around Taupo

On the town's outskirts is a concentration of natural wonders, all within a few minutes of one another. Here you'll find boiling mud, hissing steam harnessed by the Wairakei power station, and the clear-blue Waikato River, which cuts a deep swirling course north over rapids and through deep-sided gorges.

The majority of sights and activities are within 10km of Taupo, flanking the Waikato River as it wends its way north, and are accessible through Taupo's tour companies.

Huka Falls Road

Huka Falls Road loops off SH1 a couple of kilometres north of Taupo and passes the *Reids Farm* (see p.287) free campsite and *Huka Lodge* (one of New Zealand's most exclusive luxury retreats) en route to the first port of call, the magnificent **Huka Falls** (*hukanui*, or "great body of spray"). Here the Waikato, one of New Zealand's most voluminous rivers, funnels into a narrow chasm before plunging over a 9m shelf into a seething maelstrom of eddies and whirlpools; the sheer power of some three hundred tonnes of water per second makes it a far more awesome sight than the short drop would suggest. A footbridge spans the channel, providing a perfect vantage point for watching the occasional mad kayaker making the descent, usually on weekend evenings. The car park is only open until 6pm but you can park outside the barriers and walk in at any time.

Honey Hive

65 Karetoto Rd, off Huka Falls Rd · Daily 9am–5pm · Free · ☎ 07 374 8553, ⓦ hukahoneyhive.com

Continuing along Huka Falls Road, a large Russian helicopter marks the launch pad for Helistar flights (see box, p.289) en route to the cutaway hives and educational video at the **Honey Hive**, 1km further north, where you can buy products from jars of the sweet stuff through to skin-care products and meads and wines.

Volcanic Activity Centre

Corner of Karetoto Rd and Huka Falls Rd • Mon–Fri 9am–5pm, Sat & Sun 10am–4pm • $12 • ☎ 07 374 8375, ⓦ volcanoes.co.nz

The **Volcanic Activity Centre** is an instructional museum where the dense text is alleviated by striking photos and interactive computer displays on all things tectonic. Watch one of several films run continuously then check out the seismograph linked to sensors on Mount Ruapehu, an earthquake simulator and a large relief map of Taupo Volcanic Zone, which extends from Mount Ruapehu to White Island.

Huka Prawn Park

Karetoto Rd • Daily: Dec & Jan 9am–4pm; Feb–Nov 9.30am–3.30pm • $28 • ☎ 07 374 8474, ⓦ hukaprawnpark.co.nz

The new Taupo bypass road separates you from the Wairakei geothermal power station from where excess heat is channelled into the family-oriented **Huka Prawn Park**, large open ponds where tropical prawns are raised. Stroll around the ponds and nature walk, spend as long as you like fishing for prawns or combine the two. If learning about a day in the life of "Shawn the Prawn" doesn't fire your imagination, dine on some of Shawn's delicious little friends in the adjacent riverside restaurant.

Craters of the Moon

Karapiti Rd, off SH1 • Daily Dec–April 8.30am–6pm; April–Nov 8.30am–5.30pm, dependent on daylight • $8 • ⓦ cratersofthemoon.co.nz

The Huka Falls loop road rejoins SH1 near Karapiti Road which runs west to **Craters of the Moon**, a lively geothermal area that sprang to life in the 1950s, after the construction of the Wairakei geothermal power station drastically altered the underground hydrodynamics. While it lacks geysers and colourful lakes, the area is so vigorous that you must wear closed footwear to walk the 3km of trails among roaring fumaroles and rumbling pits belching out a pungent rotten-egg stench.

The Wairakei Terraces

SH1, 3km north of Craters of the Moon • Daily 8.30am–5pm • Walkway $18; thermal pools $25; Maori cultural experience from 6pm, with reservation, $104 • ☎ 07 378 0913, ⓦ wairakeiterraces.co.nz

The Wairakei power station is supplied by shiny high-pressure steam pipes that

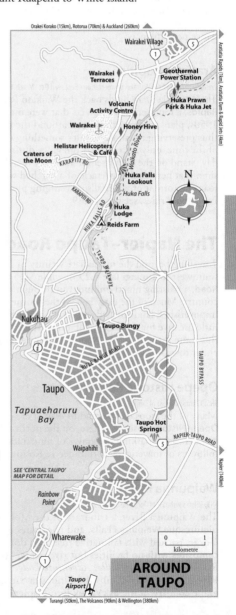

Orakei Korako (15km), Rotorua (70km) & Auckland (260km)

Aratiatia Rapids (1km), Aratiatia Dam & Rapid Jets (4km)

Wairakei Village

Wairakei Terraces

Geothermal Power Station

Volcanic Activity Centre

Huka Prawn Park & Huka Jet

Wairakei

Honey Hive

Waikato River

Helistar Helicopters & Café

Craters of the Moon

KARAPITI RD

KARAPITI RD

HUKA FALLS RD

Huka Falls Lookout

Huka Falls

Huka Lodge

Reids Farm

N

TAUPO BYPASS

Nukuhau

Taupo Bungy

RIFLE RANGE ROAD

Taupo

Tapuaeharuru Bay

Taupo Hot Springs

NAPIER-TAUPO ROAD

Napier (140km)

Waipahihi

SEE 'CENTRAL TAUPO' MAP FOR DETAIL

Rainbow Point

Wharewake

0 ——— 1 kilometre

AROUND TAUPO

Taupo Airport

Turangi (50km), The Volcanos (90km) & Wellington (380km)

cross under SH1, twisting and bending like a giant ball-bearing racetrack. The power of mineral-laden steam is harnessed nearby at **Wairakei Terraces**, where a vigorously boiling cauldron feeds an artificial cascade of silica terraces and pools. It mimics the process that created Rotorua's Pink and White Terraces, and has grown since the late 1990s. Paths lead through the surrounding model Maori village that comes alive for a **Maori cultural experience**, where you can see weaving, tattooing, and stick games in action. The hot pools here are adults only and a blissfully quiet place for a soak. The evening is an engagingly low-key affair (a world away from Rotorua's extravaganzas) with a good introduction to Maori culture and a *hangi* meal followed by the *haka* and dance performance.

Aratiatia Rapids

2km downstream from Wairakei power station • Best seen Oct–March 10am, noon, 2pm & 4pm; April–Sept 10am, noon & 2pm

The Aratiatia Dam holds back the Waikato River immediately above the **Aratiatia Rapids**, a long series of cataracts that were one of Taupo's earliest attractions. In the 1950s, plans to divert the waters around the rapids were amended by public pressure, thus preserving them, though it's something of a hollow victory since they are dry most of the time, only seen in their full glory during three or four thirty-minute periods each day. Stand on the dam itself or at one of two downstream viewpoints, and wait for the siren that heralds the spectacle of a parched watercourse being transformed into a foaming torrent of waterfalls and surging pressure waves, before returning to a trickle. For jetboat rides, see box, p.289.

The Napier–Taupo Road

Travelling beyond the immediate vicinity of Taupo, SH1 hugs the lake as it heads southwest to Turangi (see p.295), while SH5 veers southeast along the **Napier–Taupo Road**, a twisting ninety-minute run through some of the North Island's remotest country. Much of the early part of the journey crosses the Kaingaroa Plains, impoverished land cloaked in pumice and ash from the Taupo volcanic eruption and of little use save for the pine plantations which stretch 100km to the north. The history of this route is traced by the **Napier–Taupo Heritage Trail**; pick up a free booklet from either town's i-SITE.

Opepe Historic Reserve

SH5, 17km southeast of Taupo

Many of the stops on the road to Napier are of limited interest, but be sure to call in at **Opepe Historic Reserve**, where, on the north side of the road, a cemetery contains white wooden slabs marking the graves of nine soldiers of the Bay of Plenty cavalry, killed by followers of maverick Maori leader Te Kooti in 1869.

Waipunga Falls

SH5, 35km southeast of Opepe Historic Reserve

The Waipunga River, a tributary of the Mohaka, plummets 30m over the picturesque **Waipunga Falls**, and continues beside SH5 through the lovely Waipunga Gorge, packed with tall native trees and dotted with picnic sites which double as **campsites** with no facilities but river water. The highway descends to the Mohaka River and *Mountain Valley Adventure Lodge* (see opposite). Beyond the Mohaka River, the highway climbs the Titiokura Saddle before the final descent through the grape country of the **Esk Valley** into Napier.

Mountain Valley Adventure Lodge 408 McVicar Rd, 5km south of SH5 ☎06 834 9756, ⓦmountainvalley .co.nz; map p.264. A little slice of rural New Zealand with a riverside bar and restaurant and the opportunity to fish the river (rod hire from $15), mountain bike (bike hire from $35/half-day), go on a farm and forest horse trek (from

$65/hr), or do some scenic rafting and kayaking on Grade I–II stretches of the Mohaka River (from $65). Accommodation includes powered campsites, a bunkhouse (dorms $22), chalets and cottages. Camping $16, lodge rooms $75

Tongariro National Park and around

New Zealand's highly developed network of national parks owes much to Te Heu Heu Tukino IV, the Tuwharetoa chief who, in the Pakeha land-grabbing climate of the late nineteenth century, recognized that the only chance his people had of keeping their sacred lands intact was to donate them to the nation – on condition that they could not be settled or spoiled. His 1887 gift formed the core of the country's first major public reserve, **Tongariro National Park**, which became a **UNESCO World Heritage Site** in 1991 due to its unique landscape and cultural significance (see box below). In the north a small, outlying section of the park centres on **Mount Pihanga** and the tiny **Lake Rotopounamu**, but most visitors head straight for the main body of the park, dominated by the three great volcanoes which rise starkly from the desolate plateau: the broad-shouldered ski mountain, **Ruapehu** (2797m); its squatter sibling, **Tongariro** (1968m); and, wedged between them, the conical **Ngauruhoe** (2287m).

Within the boundaries of the park is some of the North Island's most striking scenery – a beautiful mixture of semi-arid plains, steaming fumaroles, crystal-clear lakes and streams, virgin rainforest and an abundance of ice and snow. The more forbidding volcanic areas were used as locations for Mordor and Mount Doom in the *Lord of the Rings* trilogy. All of this forms the backdrop to two supremely rewarding tramps, the

4

THE MAORI MOUNTAIN LEGENDS

When Te Heu Heu Tukino donated Tongariro's central volcanoes to the Crown (see above), he was motivated by a deep spiritual need for their protection. According to Maori, the mountains at the heart of the park have distinct personalities that symbolize the links between the community and its environment. This significance was recognized in 1991 when the park became the first UNESCO World Heritage Site included as a **cultural landscape**.

Legends tell of a number of smaller mountains clustered around the dominating **Ruapehu**, **Tongariro**, **Ngauruhoe** and **Taranaki**. Among these was the beautiful **Pihanga** in the northern section of the park, whose favours were widely sought. Pihanga loved only Tongariro, the victor of numerous battles with her other suitors, including one that had brought him to his knees, striking off the top of his head, giving him his present shape. Taranaki, meantime, defeated Ngauruhoe, but when he came to face Ruapehu, he was exhausted and badly wounded. He fled, carving out the Whanganui River as he made for the west coast of the North Island. Meanwhile the smaller **Putauaki** got as far north as Kawerau; but **Tauhara** was reluctant to leave and continually glanced back, so that by dawn, when the mountains could no longer move, he had only reached the northern shores of Lake Taupo, where he remains to this day, "the lonely mountain".

To the local Tuwharetoa people these mountains were so sacred that they averted their eyes while passing and wouldn't eat or build fires in the vicinity. The *tapu* stretches back to legendary times when their ancestor **Ngatoroirangi** came to claim the centre of the island. After declaring Tongariro *tapu*, he set off up the mountain, but his followers broke their vow to fast while he was away and the angry gods sent a snowstorm in which Ngatoroirangi almost perished, before more benevolent gods in Hawaiki saved him by sending fire to revive his frozen limbs.

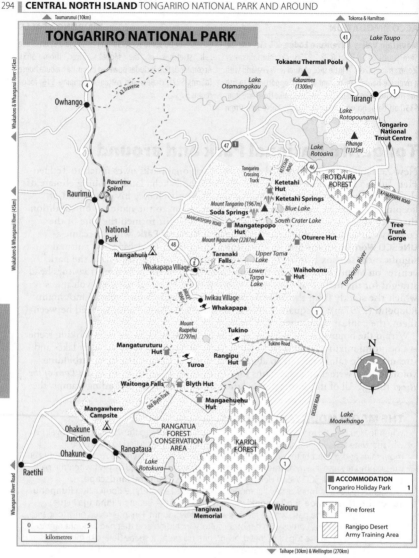

one-day **Tongariro Alpine Crossing** and the three- to four-day **Tongariro Northern Circuit**, one of New Zealand's Great Walks. The undulating plateau to the west of the volcanoes is vegetated by bushland and golden tussock, while on the eastern side the rain shadow of the mountains produces the **Rangipo Desert**. Although this is not a true desert, it is still an impressively bleak and barren landscape, smothered by a thick layer of volcanic ash from the 186 AD Taupo eruption. **Mount Ruapehu** frequently bursts into life (most recently 1995, 1996 and 2007), occasionally emptying its crater lake down the side of the mountain in muddy deluges known as lahars. In 2011 Mount Ruapehu's Volcanic Alert Level was elevated to level 1 (signs of volcanic unrest), but at the time of writing it was not affecting visitors. Keep tabs on its status with DOC and the local i-SITE office.

The northern approach to the region is through **Turangi**, which – though it lacks the mountain feel of the service town of **National Park** and the alpine **Whakapapa Village**, 1200m up on the flanks of Ruapehu – makes a good base both for the Tongariro tramps and for rafting and fishing the Tongariro River. The southern gateway is **Ohakune**, a more aesthetically pleasing place than National Park but distinctly comatose outside the ski season. Heading south, the Army Museum at **Waiouru** marks the southern limit of the Volcanic Plateau, which tails off into the pastoral lower half of the region set around the agricultural town of **Taihape**, home to the North Island's highest bungy jump.

Pretty much everyone comes to the park either to **ski** or to **tramp**, staying in one of the small towns dotted around the base of the mountains. Note that this region is over 600m above sea level, so even in the height of summer you'll need **warm clothing**.

Turangi

The small town of **Turangi**, 50km south of Taupo, was planned in the mid-1960s and built almost overnight for workers toiling away at the tunnels and concrete channels of the ambitious Tongariro Power Scheme (see box, p.297). It's legendary among trout fishermen but otherwise is relatively quiet and a non-touristy alternative to Taupo, with Lake Taupo just 4km to the north.

Many people also stay in Turangi to hike the Tongariro Alpine Crossing (see p.300), 40km to the southwest, but there are less daunting alternatives (see p.296); the i-SITE (see p.296) has details of these and other walks in the area.

4

Tongariro National Trout Centre

SH1, 4km south of Turangi • Daily: Dec–April 10am–4pm; May–Nov 10am–3pm • $10 • ☎ 07 386 8085, ⓦ troutcentre.com

The massive amount of trout fishing around Turangi makes it essential that rivers are continually restocked from hatcheries such as the **Tongariro National Trout Centre**, set amid native bush between the Tongariro River and one of its tributaries, the Waihukahuka Stream. With an **aquarium** filled with native species such as eels, a chance to see fingerlings being raised and lots of material on water conservation, biodiversity protection and how to fish, it's a great place to spend an hour, especially if you've got kids in tow.

FISHING AND WATERSPORTS IN TURANGI

Turangi is famed internationally for the quality of its **trout fishing**, both on the lake and in the Tongariro River. If you're keen to haul a trout from Lake Taupo or one of the local rivers, the i-SITE will help pair you with a **fishing** guide to match your experience and aspirations as well as a licence ($17/24hr); expect to pay around $300 for a half-day with gear and guiding. Alternatively, Sporting Life, The Mall (☎ 07 386 8996, ⓦ sportinglife-turangi.co.nz), sells and rents gear and has a huge amount of info on its website.

Rotorua and Taihape offer wilder **rafting** rivers, but for beautiful gorge scenery, the chance to see the endangered blue duck (*whio*) and fun rapids without the white knuckles, **rafting** the Tongariro River is unbeatable. Young families should opt for the Grade II lower section but most will want to try the Grade III Access 10 section upstream.

Rafting New Zealand 41 Ngawaka Place ☎ 0800 865 226, ⓦ raftingnewzealand.com. Local operators who throw in a waterfall jump on their White Water tour, and have plenty of cultural interpretation ($129/4hr).
Tongariro River Rafting Atirau Rd, near Firestone Tires ☎ 0800 101 024, ⓦ trr.co.nz. Runs an equally good Grade III trip ($125), a family float down the Grade II section (1hr 15min on the water; $85), and raft fishing (Dec–May only), only, which involves rafting the Tongariro and stopping off at the otherwise inaccessible pools to cast a fly. Rates are $700/day for a maximum of three – little more than you'd pay for a fishing guide alone. The company also rents mountain bikes ($50/day).

Tokaanu Thermal Pools

Mangaroa Rd, 5km west of Turangi • Daily 10am–9pm • $6; private pools $10/20min, including public pool access • ☎ 07 386 8575

If you want to wallow in hot water, head for **Tokaanu Thermal Pools** in tiny **Tokaanu**, which was the main settlement hereabouts in pre-European times. There's an open-air public pool and hotter, partly enclosed and chlorine-free private pools.

Tongariro River Loop Track

Starts at end of Koura St • 4km

The pleasant **Tongariro River Loop Track** is well worth the hour it takes to complete, starting from the Major Jones footbridge at the end of Koura Street on the edge of town. It follows the true right bank of the river north past a couple of viewpoints and over a bluff, then crosses the river and returns along the opposite side.

Lake Rotopounamu Circuit

Off SH47, 10km south of Turangi • 5km

A local favourite, the **Lake Rotopounamu Circuit** (90min) encircles the pristine "Greenstone Lake" surrounded by bush alive with native birds such as the kaka, robin, fantail, kakariki, whitehead, long-tailed cuckoo, kereru, grey warbler, bellbird and tui. The easy path is well graded and suitable for prams.

ARRIVAL AND DEPARTURE

TURANGI

By bus InterCity buses drop off at the i-SITE visitor centre, Ngawaka Place. Tongariro Expeditions (see p.303) also stop when taking Taupo hikers to the Tongariro Alpine Crossing, although not if the weather is bad.

Destinations Auckland (3 daily; 6hr); Wellington (4 daily; 5hr 40min).

GETTING AROUND

By car and shuttle While a car makes life easier, there's a reasonable network of shuttles plying the more useful routes and providing trailhead transport for trampers (see p.302).

INFORMATION

i-SITE Ngawaka Place (daily 8.30am–5pm; ☎0800 288 726, ⓦlaketauponz.com). Offers a more personalized service than the busy offices in Taupo and Rotorua and sells bus tickets, Taupo fishing licences, maps, DOC tramping brochures and hut tickets. It also books accommodation for free and has wired and wi-fi internet access.

ACCOMMODATION

Turangi has a pretty good spread of **accommodation**; the budget places are congregated in the town centre, while plusher lodges and B&Bs line the Tongariro River to the east.

Club Habitat 25 Ohuanga Rd ☎07 386 7492, ⓦclubhabitat.co.nz. Vast complex over 9.5 acres fashioned from a former workers' camp that's cheap and fairly faded with the exception of the refurbished "executive" units ($125). There's also a spacious games bar, dining complex, spa and sauna. Camping $15, dorms $25

Creel Lodge 183 Taupahi Rd ☎07 386 8081, ⓦcreel .co.nz. A simple and well-run fishing-oriented motel comprising a cluster of self-contained one- and two-bedroom units in grounds running down to the river edge with barbecuing facilities. $135

Extreme Backpackers 26 Ngawaka Place ☎07 386 8949, ⓦextremebackpackers.co.nz. Amenable hosts take good care of guests at this purpose-built backpackers with simply decorated rooms set around a central courtyard. There's also a climbing wall ($15; $10 for guests) and an amiable café. Dorms $26, rooms $64

Parklands Corner of SH1 and Arahori St ☎0800 456 284, ⓦparklandsmotorlodge.co.nz. Extensive motor lodge with pine-lined studios and spacious modernized units plus an outdoor pool, games room and a small restaurant serving home-style dinners. Studios $115, units $140

Riverstone Backpackers 222 Tautahanga Rd ☎07 386 7004, ⓦriverstonebackpackers.com. Lovely purpose-built boutique backpackers in a converted house with lots of communal living space, both inside and out, a well-equipped modern kitchen, herbs from the garden, bike and walking-pole rentals. Dorms $35, rooms $74

Tongariro Holiday Park SH47 ☎07 386 8062, ⓦthp .co.nz. The most convenient base for doing the Tongariro Alpine Crossing (see p.300) has powered sites and a range of cabins as well as a camp kitchen and a newly refurbished shower room. They can also book transport with Tongariro Expeditions, who pick up and drop off here daily. Camping $44, cabins $60

Tongariro River Motel Corner of SH1 and Link Rd ☎0800 187 688, ⊛tongarirorivermotel.co.nz. Homey, comfortable motel that is hugely popular with anglers, partly for its rod racks and smoker, but mainly because of its "manager", a lovable boxer named Boof. The friendly owner runs a lively website on everything to do with Turangi, and trout fishing in particular. $90

EATING AND DRINKING

Eating options in Turangi have improved in recent years, with some smart cafés and restaurants serving modern New Zealand cuisine providing visitors with better choice. The well-stocked New World supermarket in the centre of town is useful for self-caterers.

Oreti 88 Pukawa Rd, Pukawa ☎07 386 7070, ⊛oretivillage.co.nz. Angus ribeye fillet with *vigneronne* sauce ($37.50), seared lamb rump ($34), and a warm chocolate and toffee fondant star on the dinner menu of this romantic spot 8km northwest of Turangi on the shores of Lake Taupo. Sat and Sun breakfast from 9am, Thurs–Sun noon–3pm, Tues–Sun 6pm–late.

River Vineyard Restaurant 134 Grace Rd, 4km north of town off SH1 ☎07 386 6704, ⊛riverwines.co.nz. Fuel up for mountain treks with brunches featuring items such as muesli with yoghurt or brioche French toast; snack on caramelized onion and blue cheese filo tarts or burgers with honey-cured bacon; or relax over a dinner of braised beef cheek with warm celeriac ($16) followed by baked regal salmon with lemon *buerre blanc* ($32). Tues–Sun 10am–late.

Tongariro Lodge 83 Grace Rd ☎07 386 7946, ⊛tongarirolodge.co.nz. Mushroom and tofu dumplings, a duo of Hawke's Bay lamb and rack of venison with seasonal vegetables are among the inventive mains ($24–40) at the restaurant of the *Tongariro Lodge*, which also has pricey but luxurious chalets and villas (from $392/person). Daily 6–10pm.

Turangi Bridge Motel SH1, 800m north of Turangi ☎07 386 8804, ⊛bridgefishinglodge.co.nz. Take a seat in front of the big fireplace for heart-warming meals such as garlic prawns ($29) or lamb shanks ($27). Mon–Sat 6–9pm.

Turangi Tavern Pihanga Road ☎07 386 6071. Classic Kiwi pub complete with Tab, beers on tap and pub meals served from the counter. Try the pig and slaw ($16) or fill up with bangers and mash ($17). Daily 11am–late.

Whakapapa

Tiny **WHAKAPAPA**, 45km south of Turangi on SH48, is the only settlement set firmly within the boundaries of Tongariro National Park and hugs the lower slopes of Mount Ruapehu. Approaching from the north, an open expanse of tussock gives distant views of the imposing *Chateau Tongariro* hotel, framed by the snowy slopes of the volcano behind and overlooked by the arterial network of tows on the Whakapapa ski-field.

THE TONGARIRO POWER SCHEME

The **Tongariro Power Scheme** provides an object lesson in harnessing the power of water with minimal impact on the environment. Its two powerhouses produce around seven percent of the country's electricity, while the outflows that feed into Lake Taupo add flexibility to the much older chain of eight hydroelectric dams along the Waikato River. Some argue it is unacceptable to tamper with such a fine piece of wilderness, but, while there have been some minor environmental impacts, it is surely better than a nuclear power station.

In fact, if it weren't for the scale models in visitor centres and the ugly bulk of the Tokaanu power station, only astute observers would be aware of the complex system of tunnels, aqueducts, canals and weirs unobtrusively going about their business of diverting the waters of the Tongariro River and myriad streams running off the mountain slopes, back and forth around the perimeter of the national park, using modified natural lakes for storage. Mount Ruapehu poses its own unique problems: the threat of **lahars** (mud- and debris-flows) is ever-present and, after the 1995 eruption, abrasive volcanic ash found its way into the turbines of the Rangipo underground powerhouse, causing an unscheduled seven-month shutdown.

Swarms of trampers use Whakapapa as a base for short walks or long tramps. The Tongariro Northern Circuit and the Round the Mountain track (see p.302) can both be tackled from here, but there are also easier strolls covered by DOC's *Walks in and around Tongariro National Park* leaflet (download at ⓦ doc.govt.nz). Three of the best of these are the **Whakapapa Nature Walk** (1km; 20–30min), highlighting the unique flora of the park; the **Taranaki Falls Walk** (6km; 2hr), which heads through open tussock and bushland to where the Wairere Stream plunges 20m over the end of an old lava flow; and the **Silica Rapids Walk** (7km; 2hr 30min), which follows a stream through beech forests to creamy-coloured geothermal terraces.

Ruapehu Crater Rim hike

5–8hr return **From Iwikau Village car park** 15km return; 1000m ascent • **From top of Waterfall Express chairlift** 9km return; 650m ascent • Chairlift Nov–April, depending on weather, 9am–4pm • $30 return

There's much more of a vertical component to the **Ruapehu Crater Rim hike**, a tough, steep slog made worthwhile by the dramatic silhouettes of Cathedral Rocks and the views west to Mount Taranaki. The walk can be done from the car park at Iwikau Village but is much more appealing from the top of the Waterfall Express chairlift,

---

MOUNT RUAPEHU SKI-FIELDS

Mount Ruapehu is home to the North Island's only substantial **ski-fields**, **Whakapapa** and **Turoa**, which attract around two-thirds of the nation's skiers. Every weekend from **late June to mid-October**, cars pile out of Auckland and Wellington (and everywhere in between) for the four-hour drive to Whakapapa, on the northwestern slopes of Mount Ruapehu, or Turoa, on the south side. Both have excellent reputations for pretty much all levels of skier and the orientation of volcanic ridges lends itself to an abundance of dreamy, natural half-pipes for snowboarding.

TICKETS AND EQUIPMENT

Mt Ruapehu (ⓦ mtruapehu.com) manages both fields, sells lift passes ($99/day) and rents gear (skis, boots and poles from $39, boards and boots from $47). For beginners there's a Discover package ($112) including ski or snowboard rental, 1hr 50min lesson and a learners' area lift pass. Several places in National Park, Ohakune and Turangi also offer competitive rates and a wide selection of equipment.

ACCOMMODATION

Neither field has public **accommodation** on site. Ski clubs maintain dozens of chalets at the foot of the main lifts in Whakapapa's Iwikau Village, but casual visitors (unless invited as a guest) have to stay 6km downhill at Whakapapa Village or 22km away at National Park (see p.304). Almost everyone skiing Turoa stays in Ohakune.

SKI AREAS

Whakapapa New Zealand's largest and busiest ski area, with over sixty runs (two beginner, forty intermediate, twenty advanced), a dozen major chairlifts and T-bars and the dedicated learners' area of Happy Valley. It offers 675 vertical metres of piste, plus snow-making equipment, ski schools, a huge gear-rental operation and some café/bars. Access is along the toll-free, sealed Bruce Road. Tyre chains are not available (see opposite). Shuttle buses run regularly from Whakapapa Village, National Park, Turangi and Taupo. Typically open late June to mid-Oct.

Turoa The country's greatest vertical range of piste (720m) and a skiable area almost as extensive as Whakapapa's, with wide, groomed trails (three beginner, eleven intermediate, over a dozen advanced) particularly aimed at intermediate skiers; it also offers the region's best après-ski at Ohakune. It's usually possible to drive straight up the sealed, toll-free, 17km access road from Ohakune without chains, and park for nothing, but the ski-field operators will fit chains ($30; cash only) when needed. Several shuttle buses run up from Ohakune, charging around $30 return. Typically open mid- to late June to mid-Oct.

thereby avoiding a long trudge through a barren, rocky landscape. From the top of the **chairlift** the route is unmarked, but from Christmas until the first snows, the ascent can usually be made in ordinary walking boots without crampons. Guided crater walks are also available (see below).

Iwikau Village
From Whakapapa, SH48 continues as Bruce Road 6km uphill to **Iwikau Village** (known locally as the "Top o' the Bruce"), an ugly jumble of ski-club chalets which from late June through to mid-October becomes a seething mass of wraparound shades and baggy snowboarders' pants. Outside the ski season, the village dies, leaving only a couple of **chairlifts** to trundle up to the shiny-new *Knoll Ridge Café* (see p.300), from where you can take **guided walks** on the mountain.

ARRIVAL   WHAKAPAPA

By bus The only bus services to Whakapapa are the shuttle buses from Turangi (twice daily) and National Park (3–5 daily), which drop off close to the DOC, plus NakedBus (1 daily).

GETTING AROUND

By car and shuttle No snow chains are available in Whakapapa, so you'll need to bring your own or use one of the shuttle services, which operate from accommodation in the area, or with the hourly-or-better mountain shuttle (❶0800 117 686).

INFORMATION AND TOURS

Visitor information DOC, SH48 (daily: Dec–Feb 8am–6pm; March–Nov 8am–5pm; ❶07 892 3729, ❸tongarirovc@doc.govt.nz). Contains all the maps and leaflets you'll need, plus has extensive displays on the park, including the tiny Ski History museum and a couple of audiovisual presentations (one for $3, both for $5) shown on demand – one on volcanism hereabouts, the other combining Maori legends surrounding Tongariro with impressive footage of the landscape through the seasons.
Mt Ruapehu guided tours ❶07 892 4000, ❿mtruapehu.com. Guided crater walks (mid-Dec to May weather dependent daily 8.30am, returns by 4pm; $99 including the chairlift) providing a commentary on geology, flora and more.

ACCOMMODATION

Whakapapa has limited places to stay, which are often booked out well in advance. Reserve as far ahead as possible through the ski season and over the Christmas and January school holidays.

Chateau Tongariro SH48 ❶0800 242 832, ❿chateau .co.nz. Whakapapa's most prominent building is this 1929 brick edifice with gracious public areas including a huge lounge with full-size snooker table and great mountain views; it's worth a visit for a Devonshire tea even if you're not staying. Guests have use of the highest nine-hole golf course in New Zealand, tennis courts, gym and a small indoor pool, and stay in fairly anodyne rooms modernized to international hotel standard. If you're after space and good views you'll need one of the premium rooms, mostly in the new wing sympathetically added in 2004. The website often advertises significant discounts in spring and autumn. Standard rooms $195, premium rooms $280
Discovery SH47, 1.1km south of the SH48 turn-off ❶07 892 2744, ❿discovery.net.nz. A five-minute drive northwest of Whakapapa Village, this 10-acre site with views of the Tongariro volcanoes has a wide range of accommodation options including one-bedroom chalets with self-contained kitchen and bathroom ($285). Camping $22, backpacker double $115
Mangahuia Campsite Off SH47, close to the foot of the Whakapapa access road. Simple, seventeen-pitch streamside DOC campsite with toilets, running water, picnic tables and sheltered cooking area. Operates on a first-come, first-served basis; deposit fee at site registration stand. $6
Skotel 100m up the hill beside the *Chateau Tongariro* ❶0800 756 835, ❿skotel.com. Hotel with woodsy, three-bunk rooms, en-suite doubles, a sauna and a restaurant/bar. There are also some cabins with full cooking facilities, sleeping up to six ($225). Note that rates are hiked considerably in the ski season. Backpacker rooms $65, standard rooms $140
Whakapapa Holiday Park Opposite the DOC office ❶07 892 3897, ❿whakapapa.net.nz. The budget option, set in a pretty patch of beech forest with tent and powered sites, plus self-contained units with bathrooms ($109) and cabins without. Camping $19, dorms $25

4

EATING AND DRINKING

Fergusson's Café Opposite the DOC office, ⓦ chateau .co.nz/fergussons-cafe. Start your day with egg-laden breakfasts, fill up on cheap snacks or tuck into filled (and filling) sandwiches for lunch (dishes $6.50–16.50). Daily 7am–6pm.

Knoll Ridge Café ⓦ mtruapehu.com. This shiny-new café has a very modern design and is New Zealand's highest, perched at 2020m, serving up long views and typical mountain fare such as ham and cheese toasties, panini and caramel slices (dishes $5.50–10.50). Daily winter and Dec–Easter 9.30am–3.30pm.

Lorenz's Café 5km up the hill from Whakapapa Village ⓦ mtruapehu.com. Basic café with a range of snacks (pies et al), as well as larger meals (mains $12–25). It's at the base of the chairlift that whisks you up to *Knoll Ridge Café*. Daily breakfast and lunch.

Pihanga Café & T Bar Chateau Tongariro ☎ 0800 242 832, ⓦ chateau.co.nz. The *Chateau's* budget option, serving pub-style meals that are a cut above: rare roasted beef salad for $15.50; home-made

venison sausages for $22. Daily 11.30am–late.

Ruapehu Room Chateau Tongariro ☎ 0800 242 832, ⓦ chateau.co.nz. If you want to reward yourself for the successful completion of a major tramp, it has to be the *Chateau's Ruapehu Room*, where elegant à la carte meals with an emphasis on high-quality meat (Chateaubriand, lamb rack, and pâté of venison and wild boar), at à la carte prices (mains $30–38), are served. You'll need to reserve ahead for dinner and Sunday lunch, and to dress for the occasion (no jeans or T-shirts). Daily breakfast 6.30–10am, dinner from 6.30pm, Sun lunch from noon.

The Terrace Restaurant & Bar Skotel ☎ 0800 756 835. Serves good-value bistro meals spanning burgers ($22.50) and grilled polenta to porterhouse steak ($31.50), and has a lively bar. Dinner daily 6pm–9pm.

Tussock Pub At the base of the village ☎ 07 892 3809, ⓦ chateau.co.nz. The cheapest booze and food (burgers $18, pizzas $17) is at the village pub, where the few locals tend to drink and catch sports on the big-screen TV. Daily 3pm–late.

4 Tramping in Tongariro National Park

Tongariro National Park contains some of the North Island's finest walks, all through spectacular and varied volcanic terrain. The **Tongariro Alpine Crossing** alone is often cited as the best one-day tramp in the country, but there are many longer possibilities, notably the three- to four-day **Tongariro Northern Circuit**. Mount Ruapehu has the arduous but rewarding **Crater Rim Hike** (see p.298) and the **Round the Mountain Track**, a circuit of Ruapehu offering a narrower variety of terrain and sights than the Tongariro tramps, but consequently less used; both are best accessed from Whakapapa.

Tongariro Alpine Crossing

19.4km; 6–8hr; 750m ascent • All shuttles drop off at Mangatepopo Rd End car park between 6–9am and pick up at Ketetahi Rd around 3–4.30pm

During the summer season (typically mid-Nov to April) the **Tongariro Alpine Crossing** is by far the most popular of the major tramps in the region, and for good reason. Within a few hours you climb over lava flows, cross a crater floor, skirt active geothermal areas, pass beautiful and serene emerald and blue lakes and have the opportunity to ascend the cinder cone of Mount Ngauruhoe. Even without this wealth of highlights it would still be a fine tramp, traversing a mountain massif through scrub

---

TRAMPING IN WINTER

Once the autumn snows arrive (typically in late April) ordinary tramping gear becomes inadequate for doing the Tongariro Alpine Crossing or any of the longer tramps. If you have crampons and an ice axe (and know how to use them) then winter is a great time to get out into the mountains: there are far fewer people, and while the Great Walk huts along the Tongariro Alpine Crossing and Tongariro Northern Circuit lose their cooking facilities they become cheaper ($15.30, instead of $31). Huts along the Round the Mountain Track are the same price year-round. For more information on weather and equipment, see p.303.

For those less experienced, there are **guided walks** (generally June–Oct) along large sections – though not all – of the Tongariro Alpine Crossing, which include basic instruction on how to use the ice axe and crampons provided (see p.303).

and tussock before descending into virgin bush. On weekends and through the height of summer up to seven hundred people per day complete the Crossing: aim for spring or autumn and stick to weekdays. Another way to **avoid the crush** is to get the earliest possible shuttle, though you'll have to go at a fast pace to keep ahead of the crowds.

Mangatepopo car park to Mangatepopo Saddle

Almost everyone walks west to east, saving 400m of ascent. The first hour is gentle, following the Mangatepopo Stream through a barren landscape and passing the Mangatepopo Hut (with toilets). The track steepens as you scale the fractured black lava flows towards the **Mangatepopo Saddle**, passing a short side track to the **Soda Springs**, a small wildflower oasis in this blasted landscape. There are also toilets here, though bring your own toilet paper. The Saddle marks the start of the high ground between the bulky and ancient Mount Tongariro and its youthful acolyte, **Mount Ngauruhoe** (aka Mount Doom of *Lord of the Rings* fame) which fit walkers can climb (additional 2km return; 2–3hr; 600m ascent) from here and still make the shuttle bus at the end of the day. The two-steps-forward, one-step-back ascent of this 35-degree cone of red and black scoria is exhausting but the views from the toothy crater rim and the thrilling headlong descent among a cascade of tumbling rocks and volcanic dust make it a popular excursion.

Mangatepopo Saddle to Ketetahi Hut

From the Mangatepopo Saddle, the main track crosses the flat pan of the **South Crater** and climbs to the rim of **Red Crater**, with fumaroles belching out steam, which often obscures the banded crimson and black of the crater walls. The track from here down to the **Emerald Lakes** is by far the toughest, steepest section of the descent and sees trepidatious trampers gingerly sliding down the scree slope while more gung ho hikers run down past them at a rate of knots. It's a relatively short section though and the colours around you get more vibrant still as you reach the Emerald Lakes at the bottom, where opaque pools shading from jade to palest duck-egg herald the start of the long but easy downhill hike. You'll make a short climb to the crystal-clear Blue Lake before sidling around Tongariro's **North Crater**, and enjoying the view over golden tussock slopes as you descend on well-made paths to **Ketetahi Hut**, a rest stop with views of Lake Rotoaira and Lake Taupo – and toilets.

Ketetahi Hut to Ketetahi car park

From Ketetahi Hut you make your final descent through cool streamside bush. This is a pleasant forested walk that comes as a relief to tired limbs, especially on hot days. Note, though, that there is a short (700m) section with a higher than average risk of lahars; no stopping is advised here so keep up the pace all the way to the car park on Ketetahi Road.

Tongariro Northern Circuit

42km; 3–4 days at a gentle pace • Whakapapa is the main point of access

If the Tongariro Alpine Crossing appeals, but you're looking for something more challenging, the answer is the **Tongariro Northern Circuit**, one of New Zealand's Great Walks. In summer (roughly Oct–April), the huts – Mangatepopo, Ketetahi, Waihohonu and Oturere – are classed as **Great Walk huts** and come with gas cooking stove but not pans or crockery. Campers can use the hut facilities. The circuit is usually done clockwise.

Whakapapa to Mangatepopo

9km; 2–3hr; 50m ascent

This section can be skipped by getting a shuttle to Mangatepopo car park. The track undulates through tussock and crosses numerous streams before meeting the Tongariro

Alpine Crossing track close to Mangatepopo Hut. The track can be boggy after heavy rain but is usually passable.

Mangatepopo Hut to Emerald Lakes

6km; 3–4hr; 660m ascent

Follow the Tongariro Alpine Crossing (see p.300); you then have the choice of continuing on the Crossing to Ketetahi Hut (4km; 2–3hr; 400m descent) and returning to this point the next day, or continuing to the right. The track passes black lava flows from Ngauruhoe's eruptions in 1949 and 1954. From the top of Red Crater a poled route (to the left) leads to Tongariro Summit, while the main track continues on past the crater rim.

Emerald Lakes to Oturere Hut

5km; 1–2hr; 500m descent

There are spectacular views of the Oturere Valley, the Kaimanawa Ranges and the Rangipo Desert as you descend steeply through fabulously contorted lava formations from Red Crater's eruptions towards the desert and Oturere Hut.

Oturere Hut to Waihohonu Hut

8km; 2–3hr; 250m descent

You begin this leg by crossing open, rolling country over gravel fields – plant regeneration after volcanic eruptions is a lengthy process – before fording a branch of the Waihohonu Stream. You then descend into the beech forests before a final climb over a ridge brings you to the hut, where you can drop your pack and press on for twenty minutes to the cool and clear Ohinepango Springs.

Waihohonu Hut to Whakapapa

14km; 5–6hr; 200m ascent

The final day cuts between Ngauruhoe and Ruapehu, passing the Old Waihohonu Hut (no accommodation), which was built for stagecoaches on the old road in 1901. The path then continues alongside Waihohonu Stream to the exposed Tama Saddle and, just over 1km beyond, a junction where side tracks lead to Lower Tama Lake (20min return) and Upper Tama Lake (1hr return), both water-filled explosion craters, where you can swim, if you don't need your water warm. It is only around a two-hour walk from the saddle back to Whakapapa, so you should have time to explore Taranaki Falls before ambling back through tussock to the village.

Round the Mountain Track

71km; 4–5 days • Whakapapa is the main point of access

The challenging **Round the Mountain Track** loops around Mount Ruapehu and is most easily tackled from Whakapapa. The track can also be combined with the Northern Circuit to make a mighty five- or six-day **circumnavigation** of all three mountains.

ARRIVAL AND DEPARTURE   TONGARIRO PARK TRAMPS

By car Most visitors access both the Tongariro Alpine Crossing and the Tongariro Northern Circuit from the car park at the end of Mangatepopo Rd, off SH47. Car parks at both ends of the Alpine Crossing track have a reputation for break-ins so it's a good idea to leave your vehicle in Ohakune, Turangi, National Park or Whakapapa and make use of the shuttle buses (see below).

GETTING AROUND

By bus and shuttle bus A couple of InterCity bus routes pass through Tongariro National Park but most services are run by smaller companies, many associated with backpacker hostels. If you're staying in any of the towns listed below there'll be a choice of operators offering basically the same service (often with an early bus getting you to the trailhead before the masses). The larger, reliable operators are listed below: your accommodation and the various visitor centres can flesh out the options. Companies generally charge around $35 for combined Tongariro Alpine Crossing drop-off and pick-up.

FROM NATIONAL PARK

Numerous shuttle buses serve the trailheads in summer and ski-fields in winter. Try *Howard's Lodge*, *The Park* and *YHA National Park Backpackers* (see p.305), who all run their own services.

FROM OHAKUNE

Ruapehu Connexions ⓣ 0800 462 824, ⓦ ruapehuconnexions.co.nz. Shuttle services for the Tongariro Alpine Crossing, the ski-fields and into Ohakune town centre for nightlife. Pick-ups on request from Turoa and Whakapapa and others.

FROM TAUPO

Tongariro Expeditions ⓣ 07 377 0435, ⓦ thetongarirocrossing.co.nz. Good for getting to the park generally, but to attempt the Crossing from Taupo involves a ridiculously early start and puts you on it at its busiest.

FROM TURANGI

Mountain Shuttle ⓣ 0800 117 686, ⓦ tongarirocrossing.com. Runs Alpine Crossing and ski-field shuttles year-round. The earliest of the several crossing shuttles available is around 6am.

Extreme Backpackers ⓣ 07 386 8949 (see p.296). Also offers Alpine Crossing and ski-field shuttles year-round.

FROM WHAKAPAPA

Several shuttles stop on their way to the Tongariro Alpine Crossing. The most frequent is Mountain Shuttle (see above).

INFORMATION AND TOURS

Visitor information DOC leaflets from i-SITEs in Taupo and Turangi covering the tramps are informative and adequate for most purposes though map fans will want the region's *Parkmap* ($19).

Weather Mountain weather (ⓦ metservice.com) is extremely changeable, and the usual provisos apply. Even on scorching summer days, the increased altitude and exposed windy ridges produce a wind-chill factor to be reckoned with, and storms roll in with frightening rapidity. From the end of March through to late November there can be snow on the tracks, so check current conditions.

Equipment Any time of year, it's essential to take warm clothing and rain gear – and if you plan to scramble up and down the steep volcanic cone of Mount Ngauruhoe, take gloves and long trousers for protection from the sharp scoria rock. Water is also scarce on most tracks so carry plenty. For information on tramping in winter, see box, p.300.

GUIDED WINTER WALKS

Adrift Outdoors ⓣ 07 892 2751, ⓦ adriftnz.co.nz. National Park-based operator that offers a winter Alpine Crossing for $175 and short walks in summer from $95.

Tongariro Expeditions ⓣ 07 377 0435, ⓦ thetongarirocrossing.co.nz. Charge $175 from National Park, Turangi and Taupo for trips across the sections of the Alpine Crossing that are open. You don't really need a guide in summer; in winter (June-Oct) they are essential.

ACCOMMODATION

Other than accommodation in Whakapapa (see p.299), the only places to stay are trampers' huts, all of which have adjacent campsites. Hut tickets can be bought in advance from DOC offices in Whakapapa and Ohakune, or the i-SITE in Turangi; if bought from a hut warden you pay an extra $5.

Round the Mountain Track The Backcountry hut pass is not valid at Waihohonu Hut (Great Walk Hut) but the hut is bookable online. Backcountry hut passes are valid for all other huts. Under-18s free. Huts $15, Waihohonu Hut $32, camping $5, Waihohonu camping $14

Tongariro Northern Circuit Mangatepopo, Ketetahi, Waihohonu and Oturere are all Great Walk huts and are bookable online. Under-18s free. Huts $32, winter $15

National Park

The evocative moniker attached to **National Park**, 15km west of Whakapapa Village, belies the overwhelming drabness of this tiny settlement – a dispiriting collection of A-frame chalets sprouting from a scrubby plain with only the views of Ruapehu and Ngauruhoe to lend it grace. Comprised of a grid of half a dozen streets wedged between SH4 and the parallel rail line, the place owes its continued existence to skiers and trampers bound for the adjacent Tongariro National Park, and paddlers

THE 42 TRAVERSE

Near the town of National Park, the **42 Traverse** (46km one way; 4–6hr) **mountain-bike ride** – often wrongly called the 42nd Traverse – has long been popular with Kiwi riders and is gaining a wider following. It mostly follows a narrow 4WD road through some fairly remote country with great downhills (500m net descent), a couple of stream crossings and lashings of atmospheric native bush.

It isn't a particularly technical ride, but there are 300m of climbing and it will take moderately experienced and fit riders four to six hours to complete. The traverse is best done from National Park where all lodgings will help organize pick-up and drop-off (usually $35 in total). Some lodgings have bike rental.

BIKE RENTAL

Kiwi Mountain Bikes ☎0800 562 4537, ⓦ kiwimountainbikes.co.nz. If you don't – or can't – rent a bike from where you're staying, try here; they charge $65 for the 42 Traverse and do guided rides on the mostly downhill Fishers Track (17km; 520m descent; $99) with van pick-up from the bottom.

---

heading for **Whanganui River trips**. With limited accommodation at Whakapapa Village, visitors often stay here, using shuttle buses (see p.302) to get to the slopes and the tramps.

Tupapakurua Falls Track
4–5hr return

When wind and rain tempt you to stay indoors, consider the **Tupapakurua Falls Track** which winds through the bush protected from the worst of the weather. It initially follows the gravel Fisher Road from near the train station then, at a small parking area after 2km (30min), you branch left onto a track to a bench seat (additional 20min) with great views west to Mount Taranaki. A further hour's walk brings you to a small canyon with views of the slender, 50m Tupapakurua Falls.

ARRIVAL AND DEPARTURE NATIONAL PARK

By train and bus Trains stop beside Station Road. InterCity buses from Taumarunui, Turangi and Ohakune pull up nearby on Carroll Street close to the *National Park Hotel*. Both bus and train tickets can be bought at *Howard's Lodge* (see below).

Train destinations Auckland (3–7 weekly; 5hr 30min); Ohakune (3–7 weekly; 35min); Palmerston North (3–7 weekly; 3hr 40min); Wellington (3–7 weekly; 5hr 30min). **Bus destinations** Auckland (2 daily; 7hr).

INFORMATION

Tourist information National Park has no i-SITE but visitor information is available from the *Macrocarpa Café*, which also has postal facilities.

Services There's an ATM in the petrol station on SH4 (generally daily 7.30am–7pm); *Schnapps Bar* also has an ATM.

ACCOMMODATION

Accommodation is plentiful except over weekends and school holidays during the **ski season** – when prices generally rise – and from Christmas to the end of January. Half a dozen places have a mixture of backpacker dorms and doubles (some en suite) and everywhere either has its own **track transport** (typically around $40 for drop-off and pick-up) or works closely with someone who does.

Howard's Lodge Carroll St ☎07 892 2827, ⓦ howardslodge.co.nz. High-standard lodge where those in the en-suite rooms get access to a plusher kitchen and lounge. There's also a spa, and a wide range of rentals including mountain bikes ($60/day), skis ($33) and snowboards ($40). Transport to the Tongariro Crossing is free on some rates and

there's a two-night minimum stay. Dorms $30, rooms $75
The Park Corner of SH4 and Millar St ☎07 892 2748, ⓦ the-park.co.nz. The town's largest lodge is a well-organized 82-room complex with a bar, restaurant and spa pool, though no mountain views from rooms. Dorms $35, rooms $79

Plateau Lodge Carroll St ☎0800 861 861, ⓦplateaulodge.co.nz. There's a relaxed ski-chalet feel to this wood-panelled lodge with a broad range of accommodation including en suites ($115), a hot tub, and freebies including wi-fi and a guest phone. Dorms $30, rooms $75

Tongariro Crossing Lodge Carroll St ☎07 892 2688, ⓦtongarirocrossinglodge.co.nz. This quaint, colonially furnished, former stagecoach inn has a more private feel than most of the lodges hereabouts, with just six rooms, all of which are en suite. Breakfast (at an extra charge) is available. $140

YHA National Park Backpackers Findlay St ☎07 892 2870, ⓦnpbp.co.nz. Fairly basic associate YHA with its own indoor climbing wall ($15, including harness and instruction). Dorms $26, rooms $62

EATING AND DRINKING

All the lodges mentioned above offer **self-catering** facilities, and *The Park* has an on-site **restaurant** serving good, pub-style meals.

Macrocarpa Café 3 Waimarino Tokaanu Rd ☎07 892 2911, ⓦmacrocarpacafe.co.nz. Busy café that serves as the village's post office, visitor centre and general gathering point, dishing up filling fare including breakfast for $9 and lunch packs designed with trampers in mind. Daily 7am–6pm.

Schnapps Bar SH4 ☎07 892 2788, ⓦschnapps barruapehu.com. Braised lamb shanks in mint jus is the perennially popular choice at this big, orange pub at the entrance to town, which also serves mountain burgers ($18.50) and huge portions of fish and chips ($20.50). Breakfast is also served on weekends during winter, when, of an evening, there's often live entertainment, quizzes and sport on the big screen. Daily noon–late.

★**The Station** At the train station ☎07 892 2881, ⓦthestationcafe.co.nz. Worth a trip to National Park in its own right for its big cooked breakfasts, photo-worthy counter food (also available to take away) or hot lunches such as seafood chowder. Exquisite evening meals include dill and lemon marinated salmon and beef eye fillet with a French mustard jus (mains average $30), topped off with scrumptious desserts ($14) such as sweet spring rolls (banana and macadamia nuts in crispy pastry with butterscotch sauce) and chocolate parfait (creamy frozen mousse with espresso jelly), paired with suggested wines. Daily 9am–late.

4

Ohakune

Ohakune, 35km south of National Park, welcomes you with a giant fibreglass carrot, celebrating its position at the heart of one of the nation's prime market-gardening regions. This is easily forgotten once you're in town among the chalet-style lodges and ski-rental shops geared to cope with the influx of winter-sports enthusiasts who descend from mid-June to around the end of October for the ski season. Outside these months Ohakune has traditionally been quiet, but restaurants and bars are increasingly open year-round to cater to summer visitors here to **hike** the Old Coach Road, get bussed to the Tongariro Alpine Crossing or prepare for the Whanganui River journey (see p.242).

ARRIVAL AND DEPARTURE   OHAKUNE

By train The Auckland–Wellington rail line passes through Ohakune Junction, at the town's northern edge. The train station is on Thames St.

Destinations Auckland (3–7 weekly; 6hr 30min); Wellington (3–7 weekly; 5hr 30min).

By bus InterCity buses on the Hamilton–Taumarunui–Wanganui run stop close to the i-SITE in Central Ohakune, 2km to the southwest of the train station.

Destinations Auckland (1 daily; 6hr 30min); Wellington (1 daily; 5hr 15min).

GETTING AROUND

By shuttle bus Ruapehu Connexions (☎0800 462 824, ⓦruapehuconnexions.co.nz) provides transport around town, including a night shuttle during the ski season between Ohakune town centre and Ohakune Junction (daily 6pm until the last bar shuts; $5 one way).

INFORMATION

i-SITE & DOC 54 Clyde St (i-SITE daily 9am–5pm; DOC hours vary but it's open at least Wed–Sun 9am–5pm; ☎06 385 8427, ⓦvisitruapehu.com).

OHAKUNE OUTDOOR ACTIVITIES

During winter, the most popular activity is **skiing** and **snowboarding** at Turoa (see box, p.298). There are numerous **walks** around Ohakune, most listed in the *Walks in and around Tongariro National Park* brochure (🌐download from doc.govt.nz); the best are detailed below. Tracks can be slippery, so check conditions in advance, especially in winter. Most tracks are off-limits for **mountain biking**, although you can coast down Ohakune Mountain Rd (1000m descent in 17km).

WALKS

Lake Surprise (9km return; 5hr) Tackle an undulating section of the Round the Mountain track (see p.302) to a shallow lake, from the trailhead at the 15km mark on Ohakune Mountain Road. The hike passes evidence of volcanic debris which swept down the mountain during the 1975 and 1995 eruptions.

Mangawhero Forest Walk (3km loop; 1hr) The pick of Ohakune's shorter trails following a well-marked loop through the bush from the bottom of Ohakune Mountain Road.

Old Coach Road (11km; 3hr one way) Excellent easy walking and mountain-bike path that combines beautiful native bush, long views over farmland and a disused tunnel with a good deal of history, all explained on wayside panels. From the end of Marshalls Rd, 2km northwest of Ohakune Junction, the route partly follows a track which, for a couple of years from 1906, allowed Auckland–Wellington rail passengers to link up the then incomplete line. Today, a highlight of the road is the spindly 290m-long Hopruwhenua Viaduct (part of the original rail route but abandoned by line straightening in the 1980s), which was briefly the site of A.J. Hackett's first commercial bungy operation in 1987. The website 🌐ohakunecoachroad.co.nz has background information, including some great historic photos. DOC also has information on the route.

Waitonga Falls Walk (4km return; 1hr 20min) Moderate bushwalk to a spectacular 39m waterfall, starting 11km up Ohakune Mountain Road.

HORSERIDING

Ruapehu Homestead 4km east of town on SH49 ☎027 267 7057, 🌐ruapehuhomestead.co.nz. If the area's more strenuous activities aren't to your taste, then let horses do the work on rides lasting anywhere from one to two and a half hours. Riders can choose from forest or open farmland routes. Rates start at $40 for a 45min trek around the village.

MOUNTAIN BIKING

TCB 27 Ayr St ☎06 385 8433, 🌐tcbskiandboard .co.nz. Rents mountain bikes from $50/day. Ruapehu Connexions (see p.305) will take you and your bike to the top of the old Coach Road for $15.

ACCOMMODATION

Ohakune has stacks of **places to stay**, though several of them close outside the ski season and are packed once the snows arrive; prices get hiked up by around thirty percent more than those quoted here. Many places have a minimum two-night stay, especially during weekends. Those arriving by bus will find it more convenient to stay in the main town rather than Ohakune Junction.

Hobbit Motor Lodge 80 Goldfinch St ☎06 385 8248, 🌐the-hobbit.co.nz. Situated midway between the town and Ohakune Junction, with motel-style amenities, including an outdoor spa. Bed down in backpacker dorms, basic through to en-suite studios, or self-contained units from $189. Dorms $25, studios $99

Ohakune Top 10 Holiday Park 5 Moore St ☎06 385 8561, 🌐ohakune.net.nz. A well-kept and central campsite with a pleasant bush-girt setting and a range of basic cabins, some with their own kitchen ($90). Camping $21, cabins $71

Powderhorn Chateau 194 Mangawhero Terrace, at base of Ohakune Mountain Rd, Ohakune Junction ☎06 385 8888, 🌐powderhorn.co.nz. Hotel in an immense log cabin, with spacious, cosy rooms (the best with balcony and forest views), plus a large indoor hot pool. $240

★ **Rimu Park Lodge** 27 Rimu St, Ohakune Junction ☎06 385 9023, 🌐rimupark.co.nz. One of the most comprehensive choices, this 1914 villa contains six-bunk dorms and doubles. Along with a hot tub, the grounds are dotted with simple cabins, en-suite units (studios $90, one-bedroom $140), two railway carriages ($120) fitted out as self-contained units with separate lounge and sleeping quarters, some classy modern apartments and a fully self-contained chalet. Dorms $20, rooms $80

The River Lodge 206 Mangawhero River Rd ☎ 06 385 4771, ⓦ theriverlodge.co.nz. Appealing lodge rooms and two cabins in a wonderfully peaceful parkland setting with mature native beech trees beside a small trout river. Well-appointed rooms (most with mountain views) are complemented by lounge areas, DVDs, books and games, and an outdoor spa pool. Look for signs 5km out on the road to Raetihi. Lodge rooms $195, chalets $225

Station Lodge 60 Thames St ☎ 06 385 8797, ⓦ stationlodge.co.nz. In the heart of the wintertime action at Ohakune Junction, this popular, well-equipped lodge has backpacker dorms through to chalets, and great facilities including an outdoor spa and free town bikes, plus on-site mountain-bike, ski and snowboard rental. Dorms $27, doubles $65

Whare Ora 1 Kaha St, Rangataua ☎ 06 385 9385, ⓦ whareoralodge.co.nz. Lovely, woodsy B&B with amiable hosts, in a large house 5km east of Ohakune. The downstairs room has a spa bath and overlooks a lovely garden while the immense attic suite ($325) comes with unsurpassed mountain views. Delicious three-course dinners are available on request ($80 including wine). $255

YHA LKNZ Backpackers 1 Rata St, Ohakune Central ☎ 06 385 9169, ⓦ localknowledgenz.com. Decent YHA-affiliated hostel with all manner of rooms and games areas. The owners are full of enthusiasm for the outdoors and run shuttles to help you access it. Dorms $30, en-suite doubles $89

EATING, DRINKING AND NIGHTLIFE

During the ski season, Ohakune Junction is *the* happening place to spend your evenings, with a string of busy bars, while in summer the focus switches to central Ohakune.

The Bearing Point 55 Clyde St, central Ohakune ☎ 06 385 9006. The locals' hangout, favoured for its internationally inspired dishes such as vegetarian *korma*, *dukkah*-coated chicken with couscous and Thai seafood curry (mains average $30), and its relaxed bar. Tues–Sun 6pm–late.

Cyprus Tree 77 Clyde St, central Ohakune ☎ 06 385 8857, ⓦ cyprustree.co.nz. Leather sofas and a roaring fire set the tone for this café/bar/restaurant doing a modern take on classic Italian dishes – antipasto platters and bruschetta followed by pasta, risotto, pizza, plus a couple of steak and fish dishes and desserts. Fish of the day is $28, Scotch fillet $32. Brunch daily from 10am; dinner from 5pm–late.

Matterhorn Powderhorn Chateau (see opposite). The chateau's fine-dining option has beamed ceilings and delivers superb food such as five-spice duck breast (mains $27–36) in a refined but relaxed atmosphere. Seasonally by reservation.

Misha's Italian Café & Restaurant 55 Clyde St, central Ohakune ☎ 06 385 8346. Dishes up authentic Italian cuisine, from pastas including cannelloni, linguini and traditional lasagne to *scaloppine masala* (finely sliced pork flambéed in Marsala wine), chicken cacciatore and daily changing, home-made desserts. Daily 5pm–late.

Powderkeg Powderhorn Chateau (see opposite). With a woodsy après-ski feel, this casual (and usually jumping) brasserie/bar is always good for burgers and pizzas, as well as a short but stellar selection of mains including burgers ($20) and pizzas ($22), many of which are vegetarian. Daily 7am–late.

Utopia 47 Clyde St, central Ohakune ☎ 06 385 9120. There's a European theme at this casual daytime spot for an extensive range of breakfasts, light lunches such as Portuguese-style sardines and the town's best espresso (mains $9.50–19.50). Free wi-fi. Daily 8am–3pm.

The Desert Road

South of Turangi, SH1 sticks to the east of the Tongariro National Park running roughly parallel to the Tongariro River. This is the eerily scenic **Desert Road** (SH1), which traverses the exposed and barren Rangipo Desert – not a true desert (it gets too much rainfall), but kept arid by the free-draining blanket of volcanic ash and pumice. Road cuttings slice through several metres of the stuff, leaving a timeline of past eruptions. Snow can close the road in winter – keep tabs on the weather before you set out. The Desert Road and the roads flanking the western side of Ruapehu, Ngauruhoe and Tongariro meet at **WAIOURU**, an uninspiring row of service stations and tearooms perched 800m above sea level on the bleak tussock plain beside New Zealand's major **army base**, home to New Zealand's National Army Museum.

Tree Trunk Gorge

14km south of Turangi, down Tree Trunk Gorge Rd

Tree Trunk Gorge Road leads down to the Tongariro River at a spot where it squeezes and churns through a narrow fissure known as **Tree Trunk Gorge**. Back on the highway you soon climb out of the pine forest for great views of the three volcanoes off to the west and the blasted territory ahead. It is a dramatic scene, somehow made even more elemental by the three lines of electricity pylons striding off across the bleak tussock towards Waiouru.

The National Army Museum

SH1, at Hassett Drive, Waiouru • Daily 9am–4.30pm • $15 • ☎ 06 387 6911, ⓦ armymuseum.co.nz

Concrete bunkers house the **National Army Museum**, where the *Roimata Pounamu* ("Tears on Greenstone") **wall of remembrance** comprises water (symbolizing mourning and cleansing) streaming down a curving bank of heavily veined greenstone tiles while a recorded voice recites the name, rank and place of death of each of the roughly 33,000 New Zealanders who have died in various wars. The chronologically arranged exhibits are manageable in scale but detailed enough to give coverage of the campaigns, the affecting human stories behind them and the smaller details such as the display on the warrior flags Maori fought under during the New Zealand Wars of the 1860s. Accounts of the bungled Gallipoli campaign of World War I come complete with an instructive model of Anzac Cove. Nursing during World War II gets equal billing with coverage of POWs incarcerated not just in Germany but also Singapore as New Zealand's world focus begins to shift towards Asia, and eventually the Vietnam War. Allow around an hour and a half to take it all in.

There's also an interesting **discovery centre** for the kids, and the museum **café** is about the best around.

Taihape and around

In the 30km south of Waiouru you drop down off the volcanic plateau into the farming service town of **TAIHAPE** in the heart of the Rangitikei District. The main reason to stop is its proximity to the hilly country to the east, which hides one of New Zealand's most thrilling whitewater-rafting trips and the North Island's highest bungy jump.

Taihape promotes itself as "New Zealand's Gumboot Capital" with a corrugated iron boot sculpture and an annual **Gumboot Day** (mid-March), a tongue-in-cheek celebration of this archetypal Kiwi footwear with a gumboot-throwing competition.

Gravity Canyon

332 Mokai Rd; turn off SH1 at Utiku and follow signs east; or follow gravel backroads from River Valley • Daily 10am–4pm • Bungy jump $179; flying fox $155; bridge swing $159 • ☎ 0800 802 864, ⓦ gravitycanyon.co.nz

Some adventure seekers may want to skip the rafting thrills nearby and instead head straight to Gravity Canyon. Here you'll find an 80m **bungy jump**, the country's longest and fastest **flying fox** (175m high, 1km long), on which you reach speeds of up to 160km/hr, and a **bridge swing** offering 50m of freefall. The bungy has a unique and rather pleasant water-powered lift to get you back to the bridge.

ARRIVAL AND DEPARTURE   TAIHAPE

By bus InterCity buses stop on Kuku St, around the corner from the Information Centre, while NakedBus stops at *Gumboot Manor* restaurant at the northern end of town. Destinations Auckland (3 daily; 7hr 10min); Taupo (4 daily; 2hr); Turangi (4 daily; 1hr 15min); Wellington (4 daily; 4hr 20min).

By train The train station is one block west of the Information Centre on Robin St. Destinations Auckland (3–7 weekly; 7hr 50min); Wellington (3–7 weekly; 4hr 50min).

RAFTING THE RANGITIKEI RIVER

The Grade V gorge section of the **Rangitikei River** is one of the toughest **whitewater-rafting** rivers in the country, with ten major rapids packed into a two- to three-hour run. Trips are run from Mangaweka (see below), or more directly from *River Valley*, an adventure lodge beside the river.

OUTFITTERS

Mangaweka Adventure Company SH1, Mangaweka village ☎0800 655 747, ⓦmangaweka .co.nz. Offers a number of whitewater-rafting and kayaking trips including the Rangitikei Grade V Gorge trip ($175), a couple of family-oriented rafting trips (from $90) and two-day trips from $469 including meals, with camping beside the river. For more information on camping here, see below.

River Valley 30km east of Taihape ☎06 388 1444, ⓦrivervalley.co.nz. Morning, and occasionally afternoon, trips ($175) are run throughout the year. There are also scenic rafting trips ($175) down the quieter Grade II section immediately downstream of the lodge, plus a range of multi-day trips. For information on accommodation at River Valley, see below.

INFORMATION AND TOURS

Tourist information 90–92 Hautapu St (daily 9am–5pm; ☎06 388 0604, ⓦtaihape.co.nz). The Information Centre is inside the library; information on the region is also available at ⓦrangitikei.com.

River Valley ☎06 388 1444, ⓦrivervalley.co.nz. Offers excellent horse-trekking trips ($109/2hr) which head over farmland and provide great views across the rugged country hereabouts.

ACCOMMODATION

★ **River Valley** Pukoekahu ☎06 388 1444, ⓦrivervalley.co.nz. Visitors to the adventure lodge best known for its rafting trips (see box above) camp ($18), stay in six-bunk dorms (linen provided), or the pleasant rooms. Kiwi Experience buses call nightly. There's a self-catering kitchen or straightforward low-cost meals (using organic produce from the garden) and a bar. Everyone also has free access to pétanque and volleyball and (for a small fee) a wood sauna, an infrared sauna (with coloured lighting and music), a spa pool with views of the river and massage in summer. Dorms $31, rooms $169

Safari Motel 18 Mataroa Rd ☎06 388 1116, ⓦsafarimotel.co.nz. The NakedBus stops opposite this clean, uncluttered motel 1km north of town on SH1, but they'll also pick up from the visitor centre. Larger studios have kitchenettes, as do the one-bedroom apartments. Rooms $80, apartments $120

Taihape Motels Kuku St, at Robin St ☎0800 200 029, ⓦtaihapemotels.co.nz. Spotless rooms at this bargain-priced central motel have comfy queen- or king-size beds; there are also three holiday flats sleeping up to eight people (call for rates). Rooms $70

EATING AND DRINKING

Brown Sugar Café Huia St ☎06 388 1886. Cottage-like café with a tempting blackboard menu of grilled brie and chicken, vegetable samosas and big Greek salads (dishes $12–19). Daily 7am–3.30pm.

Soul Food Café 69 Hautapu St ☎06 388 0176. Big

breakfasts – including pancakes, corn fritters and a "farmers brekkie" of mince meat on grain toast with relish ($11) – are served all day at this popular spot; lunch could be an open steak sandwich ($17.50) or butter chicken ($16.50). Friday night is pizza night. Sat–Thurs 8am–4pm, Fri 8am–8pm.

Mangaweka

SH1, 24km south of Taihape

A DC3 aeroplane (and sign reading "Mangaweka International Airport") marks the dilapidated hamlet of **MANGAWEKA**, headquarters of the Mangaweka Adventure Company, which offers a number of **whitewater-rafting** and **kayaking** trips (see box above).

ACCOMMODATION

MANGAWEKA

Mangaweka Adventure Company 1km east of SH1 ☎0800 655 747, ⓦmangaweka.co.nz. A lovely, simple campsite with some riverside pitches, swimming and $2

showers, with accommodation and a bar in the works – check the website for updates. Camping $9

The Coromandel, Bay of Plenty and the East Cape

CATHEDRAL COVE, COROMANDEL PENINSULA

5

The Coromandel, Bay of Plenty and the East Cape

The long sweep of bays and peninsulas that forms the east coast of the North Island is split into three distinct areas, some of the most beguiling coastal strips in the country. Visitors and locals flock to the jagged Coromandel Peninsula, a volcanic spine cloaked in rainforest with edges nibbled into countless rugged coves and sweeping golden beaches. Its coast smooths into the Bay of Plenty, strung by yet more beaches and dotted with islands, notably the fuming, volcanic White Island. Further east, the East Cape is one of the least-visited parts of the country where time virtually stands still and life is measured by the rhythm of the land. This is the most intensely Maori part of New Zealand, but as far away from the performance-and-*hangi* shtick of Rotorua as you could imagine.

Coromandel-bound from Auckland you'll cut across the dairy country of the **Hauraki Plains** at the foot of the Coromandel Peninsula, with a few pleasant surprises. In the spa town of **Te Aroha** you can luxuriate in a private soda bath, while near **Paeroa** there are walks in the lush **Karangahake Gorge**, once the scene of intensive gold mining.

Jutting north, the only half-tamed **Coromandel Peninsula** is an area of spectacular coastal scenery, offering walks to pristine beaches and tramps in luxuriant mountainous rainforest. Its two coasts are markedly different. The west has a more rugged and atmospheric coastline, and easier access to the volcanic hills and ancient kauri trees of the **Coromandel Forest** – best explored from historic **Thames**, and from quaint **Coromandel**, set in rolling hills beside a pretty harbour. On the east coast, **Whangamata** and **Whitianga** offer a plethora of water activities and long sandy beaches. Whitianga is also handy for **Hot Water Beach**, where natural thermal springs bubble through the sand, and the vibrant **Cathedral Cove Marine Reserve**, ideal for dolphin spotting and snorkelling.

From the open-pit gold-mining town of **Waihi**, at the base of the Coromandel Peninsula, the **Bay of Plenty** sweeps south and east to **Opotiki**, traced along its length by the Pacific Coast Highway (SH2). The bay earned its name in 1769 from **Captain Cook**, who was impressed by the Maori living off its abundant resources and by the generous supplies they gave him – an era of peace shattered by the **New Zealand Wars** of the 1860s, when fierce fighting led to the establishment of garrisons at **Tauranga** and **Whakatane**.

DRIVING CREEK RAILWAY

Highlights

❶ Te Aroha Rejuvenate in the geyser-fed hot soda springs in this charming Edwardian spa town at the foot of Mount Te Aroha. **See p.317**

❷ Kauaeranga Valley Hike past gold-mining remains as you work your way through a jagged landscape of bluffs and gorges to the Pinnacles overlooking both Coromandel Peninsula coasts. **See p.325**

❸ Driving Creek Railway One man's passion for pots created this modern narrow-gauge railway, now moving not clay but visitors through rich Coromandel bush to a wonderful viewpoint. **See p.327**

❹ Hot Water Beach Grab a shovel, find your spot and dig into the sand to wallow in surfside hot springs. **See p.336**

❺ Mataatua Wharenui Be introduced to one of the most beautiful meetinghouses returned to its rightful home after more than a century. **See p.354**

❻ White Island Visit the otherworldly moonscape and sulphur deposits of New Zealand's most active volcano. **See p.356**

❼ The East Cape Rugged, isolated and solidly Maori, this little-visited region is the place to connect with the land and its people. **See p.360**

HIGHLIGHTS ARE MARKED ON THE MAP ON P.314

5

The Bay of Plenty has the best **climate** on the North Island, making it a fertile fruit-growing region (particularly citrus and kiwifruit). The coast, though popular with Kiwi holiday-makers, has remained relatively unspoiled, offering great surf beaches and other offshore activities. The western bay is home to one of the country's fastest-growing urban areas, centred on Tauranga and the contiguous beach town of **Mount Maunganui**. The east revolves around Whakatane, the launching point for boat excursions to active **White Island**, as well as dolphin swimming, and wilderness rafting on the **Motu River**.

Contrasting with these two regions is the rugged and sparsely populated **East Cape**. With a dramatic coastline backed by the **Waiapu Mountains**, a rich and varied Maori history and great hospitality, this isolated region provides a taste of a more traditional way of life.

The Hauraki Plains

The fertile **Hauraki Plains** stretch southeast from the Coromandel Peninsula forming a low-lying former swamp-turned-farming region which, in typically laconic Kiwi fashion, describes itself as "flat out and loving it". The Firth of Thames, the final destination for a number of meandering rivers, borders it to the north.

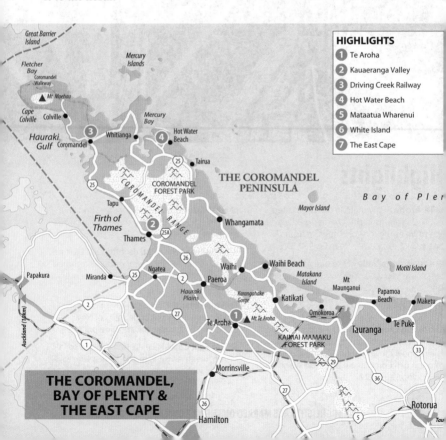

HIGHLIGHTS
1. Te Aroha
2. Kauaeranga Valley
3. Driving Creek Railway
4. Hot Water Beach
5. Mataatua Wharenui
6. White Island
7. The East Cape

THE COROMANDEL, BAY OF PLENTY & THE EAST CAPE

The hub of the plains is **Paeroa**, not much in itself but handy for walks in the magnificent **Karangahake Gorge**, running almost to **Waihi**.

The real gem hereabouts is **Te Aroha**, a delightful Edwardian spa town (little more than a village) at the southern extremity of the plains, where you can hike Mount Te Aroha and soak afterwards in natural hot soda springs.

Paeroa

PAEROA, 120km southeast of Auckland, is "World Famous in New Zealand" as the birthplace of **Lemon and Paeroa** (L&P), an iconic home-grown soft drink founded in 1907 using the local mineral water (though it is now made elsewhere by Coca-Cola). It's pretty artificial-tasting but more lemony than Sprite and the likes. The L&P logo is emblazoned on shopfronts throughout town and there's a giant brown L&P bottle at the junction of SH2 and SH26.

ARRIVAL AND DEPARTURE   PAEROA

By bus InterCity and NakedBus both stop outside the Information Centre on their Auckland–Tauranga run. Services on Hamilton's Busit network (☎0800 428 748, ⓦbusit.co.nz) go between Hamilton and Paeroa via Te Aroha, and from Coromandel to Hamilton via Thames, Paeroa and Te Aroha.

Destinations Auckland (3 daily; 2hr 20min); Hamilton (daily; 1hr 30min); Te Aroha (daily; 20min); Thames (daily; 30min).

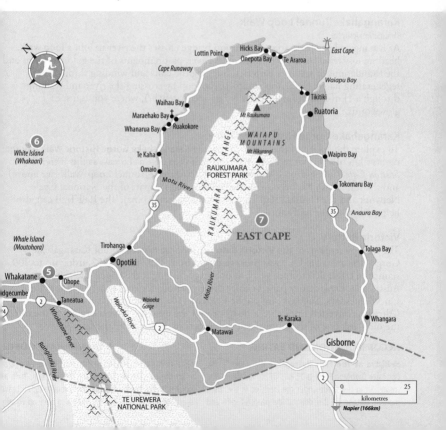

5

INFORMATION

Tourist information The Paeroa Information Centre (☎ 07 862 8636) is on the corner of SH2 and Seymour St (daily 9am–3pm). Apart from telling you how you can spend your time in Paeroa, the information centre also sells L&P souvenirs.

EATING AND DRINKING

L&P Café & Bar Corner of SH2 and Seymour St ☎ 07 862 7773, ⓦ lpcafe.co.nz. Sells L&P-flavoured ice cream as well as filling breakfast, lunch and dinner highway-stop fare such as chicken pie and salad ($7.50), corned beef and mash ($22.50) and L&P-battered gurnard and chips ($19.50). Mon–Wed 8am–3pm, Thurs–Sun 8am–7.30pm.

Karangahake Gorge

SH2, 8km east of Paeroa

Karangahake Gorge was the scene of the Coromandel's first gold rush, though in this leafy cleft it's hard to envisage the frenetic activity that took place around the turn of the twentieth century. The steep-sided gorge snakes along SH2 as it traces the Ohinemuri River to Waihi.

The largest (though still tiny) settlement is **KARANGAHAKE**, where a car park marks the start of several excellent walks along the rivers and around old gold-mining ruins. They range from twenty minutes to several hours and are detailed in DOC's *Karangahake Gorge* leaflet. Beyond, minuscule **Waikino** is the western terminus of the Goldfields Railway (see p.342).

Karangahake Tunnel Loop Walk

3km; 45min; mostly flat

At Karangahake, a pedestrian suspension bridge crosses the river to join a **loop walk**, heading upstream beside the Ohinemuri River, past remnants of the gold workings and the foundations of stamper batteries, hugging the cliffs and winding through regenerating native bush. You complete the loop by crossing the river and walking through a 1km-long tunnel (partially but adequately lit), where you can spot glowworms.

Karangahake Gorge Historic Walkway

To explore the length of the gorge, follow the **Karangahake Gorge Historic Walkway** that covers 7km of a former rail line right through the gorge as far east as the *Waikino Station Café*. One section is shared by the Karangahake Tunnel Loop Walk (see above) and the full length has been made suitable for **bikes** as part of the National Cycle Network and the Hauraki Rail Trail (ⓦ haurakirailtrail.co.nz). The Rail Trail can also help with bike hire and shuttles.

Victoria Battery

The stumpy remains of the **Victoria Battery** mark the eastern end of Karangahake Gorge. The area's gold ore was processed here from 1897 until 1952, using up to 200 stamps to crush 800 tonnes a day, at one stage making it the largest such site in Australasia. Explanatory panels clarify the mysterious-looking concrete foundations. On Wednesdays, Sundays and public holidays (10am–3pm) you can ride a tram (Alfred is converted from a milk float) or visit the museum (ⓦ vbts.org.nz) at the top of the hill – ask one of the enthusiastic volunteers to demonstrate the stamper.

ACCOMMODATION AND EATING

KARANGAHAKE GORGE

★**Bistro at The Falls Retreat** 25 Waitawheta Rd, opposite Owharoa Falls ☎ 07 863 8770, ⓦ fallsretreat .co.nz. Sit in the shade under the trees, or in the rustic modern cottage at this delightfully peaceful café and restaurant that whips up a fine thin-crust, wood-fired pizza – try the cured duck ($25) – and dinner mains such as porchetta with twice-cooked *kumara* souffle ($32). Leave space for a delectable dessert. They also have an equally peaceful self-catering cottage (☎ 07 212 8087; $150). Jan–Feb daily 11am–10pm; March–Dec Wed–Sun 1am–8.30pm.

Ohinemuri Estate Winery and Café 21 Moresby St ☎ 07 862 8874, ⓦ ohinemuri.co.nz. Peaceful winery, restaurant and lodging where you can sample the wines made here with grapes grown elsewhere), tuck into café fare including Vintner's platters ($48), and then stay in a self-contained hayloft under a 300-year-old totara ($135;

sleeps four; the rate drops if you stay a couple of nights). Daily 10am–5pm; closed Mon & Tues in winter.

Waikino Station Café SH2, 13km east of Paeroa ☎ 07 863 8640. The original Waikino train station (still served by the Goldfields Railway from Waihi) makes a superb setting for this good café with great old photos and a roaring fire in winter. Expect breakfasts and burgers ($13.50–18.50) plus cakes and coffee. Daily 9.30am–4pm (a bit earlier if they're quiet).

Te Aroha

On the fringes of the Hauraki Plains, the small town of **TE AROHA**, 21km south of Paeroa, is home to New Zealand's only intact **Edwardian spa**. In a quiet way it is a delightful spot, hunkered beneath the imposing bush-clad slopes of the **Kaimai-Mamaku Forest Park**. The 952m **Mount Te Aroha** rears up immediately behind the neat little town centre, providing a reasonably challenging goal for hikers. The town itself is a good base for the relaxing Hauraki Rail Trail.

Everything of interest – banks, post office, library – is on or close to Whitaker Street, the old-fashioned feel enhanced by an old air-raid **siren** which sounds daily at 8am, 1pm (midday in winter) and 5pm: some people still measure their day by it.

Brief history

The town was founded in 1880 at the furthest navigable extent of the Waihou River. A year later, rich deposits of gold were discovered on Mount Te Aroha, sparking a full-scale **gold rush** until 1921. Within a few months of settlement, the new townsfolk set out the attractive **Hot Springs Domain**, 44 acres of gardens and rose beds around a cluster of **hot soda springs** which, by the 1890s, had become New Zealand's most popular mineral spa complex. Enclosures were erected for privacy, most rebuilt in grand style during the Edwardian years. The fine suite of original buildings has been restored and integrated with more modern pools fed by the springs and nearby **Mokena Geyser**.

Te Aroha Mineral Spas

Hot Springs Domain • Mon–Thurs 10.30am–9pm, Fri–Sun 10.30am–10pm • $18/person for 30min, minimum 2 people; advance bookings essential • ☎ 07 884 8717, ⓦ tearohamineralspas.co.nz

Te Aroha's centrepiece is the well-signposted **Mineral Spas** where the silky-smooth mineral waters of the Mokena Geyser are channelled into private, enclosed pools, usually kept at 40°C though you can adjust the temperature. Choose a king-size claw-foot slipper bath if you fancy adding aromatherapy oils; otherwise go for one of the six, bubbling cedar tubs, good for up to eight people. A half-hour soak in the hot, naturally carbonated water is plenty. Not only will your skin feel gloriously soft (don't shower directly afterwards), but it's claimed that the alkaline waters extract polluting heavy metals from your system and ease arthritis. Fear of people fainting and drowning means you're not allowed to bathe alone. Assorted pampering and massage treatments are also available.

Te Aroha Leisure Pools

Hot Springs Domain • Mon–Fri 10am–5.45pm, Sat & Sun 10am–6.45pm • Spa pool daily 11am–4pm • $7 all day plus $2 for the spa • Café Tues–Sun 9am–3pm • ☎ 07 884 4498, ⓦ tearohaleisurepools.co.nz

There's a family feel to the outdoor **Te Aroha Leisure Pools**, where regular town water is chlorinated and kept at around 32°C in the 20m-long main pool and around 38°C in the spa. There's also a toddlers' pool and, nearby, a free 36°C **foot-spa** that's perfect for a bit of pampering at the end of a Mount Te Aroha hike. A decent **café** occupies the adjacent timber cottage with views over the Domain.

5

Mokena Geyser

Hot Springs Domain

Just uphill from the Mokena Spa Baths is the erratic **Mokena Geyser** (said to be the world's only hot soda geyser), which goes off roughly every forty minutes to a height of four metres – on a good day. Due to its spa-feeding duties it doesn't always spurt to an impressive height, so take a coffee and perhaps a book while you wait.

Te Aroha and District Museum

Daily: Nov–Easter 11am–4pm; Easter–Oct noon–3pm • $4 • ☏ 07 884 4427, ⊕ tearoha-museum.com

An old sanatorium, just below the spa baths in front of the croquet lawn, houses the exhibit-packed town **museum**. Highlights include two finely decorated Royal Doulton Victorian lavatories, a chemical analysis of the local soda water, the remains of Pelton power station, and over three hundred pieces of souvenir porcelain from Te Aroha and around the world.

St Mark's Anglican Church

Corner of Church and Kenrick sts • Often open during the day; call ahead • ☏ 07 884 9292

By the Boundary Street exit from the Domain you'll find the 1926 **St Mark's Anglican Church**, insignificant but for the incongruous 1712 organ, brought to New Zealand in 1926 and said to be the oldest in the southern hemisphere. Organ demonstrations can be arranged if you can rustle up another nineteen listeners ($10pp); ask at the i-SITE or call.

Mount Te Aroha

Immediately east of the Hot Springs Domain

The town edges up onto the lower slopes of **Mount Te Aroha** (952m), which, legend has it, was named by a young Arawa chief, Kahumatamomoe, who climbed it after losing his way in the region's swamp while making for Maketu in the Bay of Plenty. Delighted to see the familiar shoreline of his homeland, he called the mountain Te Aroha, "love", in honour of his father and kinsmen. There are some great new mountain-bike tracks and enough **trails** to keep you entertained for a day or so; two of the best walks are Bald Spur Track and Summit Track.

Bald Spur Track

3km return; 1hr 30min; 900m ascent

The most rewarding short hike is the there-and-back tramp from the Hot Springs Domain up through a lovely puriri and fern grove, climbing fairly steeply to a bench and lookout point known as Whakapipi or **Bald Spur**. With great views across the town and farmland beyond, it is particularly good before breakfast or towards sunset.

Summit Track

8km return; 4–6hr; 900m ascent

This thigh-burning ascent builds on the Bald Spur walk, continuing steeply up into the Kaimai-Mamaku Forest Park and gradually getting rougher to the TV transmitter at the top. The reward (at least on a fine day) is a 360-degree view, as far as Ruapehu and Taranaki. Return by the same route or the longer **Tui Mine Track** (extra 1–2hr) via old mine workings.

ARRIVAL AND INFORMATION
TE AROHA

By bus Services on Hamilton's Busit network (☏ 0800 428 748, ⊕ busit.co.nz) stop at Kenrick St on SH26.
Destinations Hamilton (2 daily; 1hr 5min); Paeroa (1 daily; 20min).
Visitor information i-SITE is at 102 Whitaker St, by the

Domain (Mon–Fri 9.30am–5pm, Sat & Sun 9.30am–4pm ☏ 07 884 8052, ⊕ tearohanz.co.nz). This is New Zealand' oldest information centre (since 1894), handing out loca and DOC information along with leaflets on day-walks in the area. They can also advise on bike hire for the cycle trail

ACCOMMODATION

Aroha Mountain Lodge 5 Boundary St ☎ 07 884 8134, ⊚ arohamountainlodge.co.nz. Opt for comfortable rooms in a pair of villas right next to the Hot Springs Domain, or one of the self-contained cottages sleeping up to eight nearby. Go out for breakfast or pay an extra $20 a head to eat in. Doubles $145, cottages $295

The Nunnery 16 Burgess St ☎ 07 884 4436, ⊚ thenunnery.co.nz. Air-conditioned rooms in a quiet, brick-built converted convent close to the town and attractions, with friendly hosts. Doubles $85, studio $105

Te Aroha Holiday Park 217 Stanley Rd, 3km south, off the road to Hamilton ☎ 07 884 9567, ⊚ tearohaholiday

park.co.nz. Traditional site set among shady oaks, with a flying fox, mineral water rock pool (open evenings), large summer-only swimming pool, free wi-fi and a haphazard range of mismatched buildings that have accumulated over the decades. Bring your own linen. Camping $18, cabins $53

★ **Te Aroha Landing** 29 Terminus St ☎ 0800 002 990, ⊚ talanding.co.nz. This small, brand-new development is right by the river (ask about kayaks or a licence to catch the trout), with beautifully equipped houses (usb charging points, free wi-fi), a spacious studio and a couple of funky chalets. Check the website for good-value packages including Hobbiton tours. Chalet $150, house $170

EATING

Banco 174 Whitaker St ☎ 07 884 7574. This gracious former bank is an intriguing amalgam of café, secondhand clothing shop and art gallery. It's always interesting and there's an attractive, sunny courtyard out back. Try smoked chicken salad ($14.50) or opt for coffee and cake. Wed–Sun 9am–3pm.

Ironique 159 Whitaker St ☎ 07 884 8489, ⊚ ironique .co.nz. This friendly all-rounder is a good bet for breakfast, lunch (soup $13), snacks, and evening meals such as burger and chips ($17.50) or lamb and mint winter hotpot ($17.50). Or just go for a beer. The pub quiz is on Tuesdays. Tues–Sat 5.30am–8pm, Sun 9am–4.30pm.

★ **Organic Health Shop** 9 Lawrence Avenue ☎ 07 884 9696. Pretend you've chosen this spot just for the health benefits of its scrumptious cakes (try a caramel slice or the raw banana chocolate tart $6.50) and imaginative mains (asparagus and lemon frittata $6.90). Mon–Fri 8am–4.30pm, Sat 8am–4pm.

Palace Hotel 165 Whitaker St ☎ 07 884 4536, ⊚ palacehoteltearoha.co.nz. Typical NZ local, with pokies, live music on Fridays, and main meals for $12 (dinner Wed–Mon). Mon–Thurs 9am–8pm, Fri & Sat 9am–late, Sun 11am–late.

The Coromandel Peninsula

The Hauraki Gulf is separated from the Pacific Ocean by the mountainous, bush-cloaked **Coromandel Peninsula**, fringed with beautiful surf and swimming beaches and basking in a balmy climate.

Along the **west coast**, cliffs and steep hills drop sharply to the sea, leaving only a narrow coastal strip shaded by **pohutukawa** trees that erupt in a blaze of red from mid-November to early January. The beaches are sheltered and safe but most are only good for **swimming** when high tide obscures the mudflats. Most people prefer the sweeping white-sand beaches of the **east coast**, which are pounded by impressive but often perilous **surf**.

At the base of the peninsula, **Thames** showcases its gold-mining heritage and is the most convenient place from which to explore the forested **Kauaeranga Valley**'s walking tracks. Further north, **Coromandel town** offers the opportunity to ride the narrow-gauge **Driving Creek Railway** and is close to the scenic trans-peninsular 309 Road. For really remote country, however, head to **Colville** and beyond, to the peninsula's northern tip. The sealed SH25 continues east to **Mercury Bay**, centred on more populous **Whitianga**, near which you can dig a hole to wallow in the surfside hot springs that lure hundreds to **Hot Water Beach**, or snorkel in a gorgeous bay at **Cathedral Cove Marine Reserve**. Yet more beaches string the coast further south around **Whangamata** and **Waihi Beach**, which is separated from nearby **Waihi** by about 10km of farms and orchards.

If you're here between mid-November and early December you'll come across the **Pohutukawa Festival** (⊚ pohutukawafestival.co.nz), during which the whole peninsula marks the crimson blooms of these distinctive coastal trees with picnics, wearable art competitions and music: look for posters and leaflets.

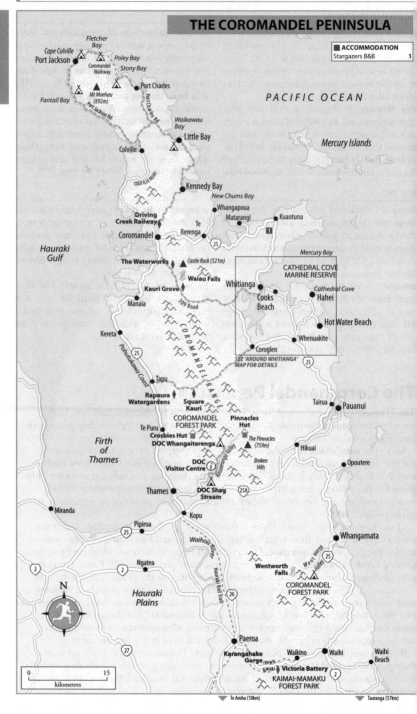

THE COROMANDEL PENINSULA

ACCOMMODATION
Stargazers B&B   1

Fletcher Bay
Cape Colville
Port Jackson
Poley Bay
Coromandel Walkway
Stony Bay
Mt Moehau (892m)
Port Charles
Fantail Bay
Port Jackson Rd
Port Charles Rd

PACIFIC OCEAN

Waikawau Bay
Little Bay
Mercury Islands
Colville
COLVILLE ROAD
Kennedy Bay
New Chums Bay
Whangapoua
Driving Creek Railway
Kuaotunu
Matarangi
Te Rerenga
Coromandel
25

Hauraki Gulf

Mercury Bay
The Waterworks
Castle Rock (521m)
Waiau Falls
CATHEDRAL COVE MARINE RESERVE
Whitianga
Kauri Grove
Cathedral Cove
Cooks Beach
Hahei
309 Road
Manaia
Hot Water Beach
Kereta
COROMANDEL RANGE
Whenuakite
Pohutukawa Coast
Tapu
Coroglen
SEE 'AROUND WHITIANGA' MAP FOR DETAILS
25

Rapaura Watergardens
Square Kauri
Tairua
Pauanui
Te Puru
COROMANDEL FOREST PARK
Pinnacles Hut
Crosbies Hut
DOC Whangaiterenga
The Pinnacles (759m)
Hikuai
Firth of Thames
Kauaeranga Valley
Broken Hills
Opoutere
DOC Visitor Centre
Thames
DOC Shag Stream
25A
Miranda
Kopu
Pipiroa
Waihou River
Whangamata
25
Wentworth Valley
Ngatea
2
Wentworth Falls
COROMANDEL FOREST PARK
2
Hauraki Plains
Haurakai Rail Trail
26
N
0   15
kilometres
Paeroa
27
Karangahake Gorge
Waikino
Waihi
Waihi Beach
Victoria Battery
2
KAIMAI-MAMAKU FOREST PARK

Te Aroha (10km)   Tauranga (57km)

Brief history

The peninsula is divided lengthwise by the **Coromandel Range** – sculpted millions of years ago by volcanic activity, its contorted skyline clothed in dense rainforest. Local Maori interpret the range as a canoe, with **Mount Moehau** (the peninsula's northern tip) as its prow, and Mount Te Aroha in the south as its sternpost. The summit area of Mount Moehau is sacred, Maori-owned land, the legendary burial place of Tama Te Kapua, the commander of one of the Great Migration canoes, *Te Arawa*.

Except for the gold-rush years, the peninsula largely remained a backwater, and by the 1960s and 70s, the low property prices in declining former gold towns, combined with the juxtaposition of bush, hills and beaches, lured hippies, **artists** and New Agers. Most eked out a living from organic market gardens, or holistic healing centres and retreats, while painters, potters and **craftspeople**, some very good, hawked their work (i-SITEs have details of rural craft outlets all over the peninsula). These days much of the peninsula is a more commercial animal: increasingly Aucklanders are finding ways to live here permanently or commute, and are converting one-time *baches* into expensive designer properties, raising both the area's profile and the cost of living.

GETTING AROUND

By car Your own vehicle gives the most flexibility, and though many of the more remote roads are gravel, few pose any real danger. Just take it steady.

By bus The main services are: InterCity (☎ 09 583 5780, ⊕ intercity.co.nz), which runs two routes: Thames north to Coromandel, across to Whitianga (2 daily) and another from Coromandel through Thames and down to Hamilton (daily); NakedBus ($2/min charge to call ☎ 0900 62533, ⊕ nakedbus.com), which runs from Whitianga to Ngatea

(1 daily) where it connects with their Auckland–Tauranga service; and Whitianga-based Go Kiwi (☎ 866 0336, ⊕ go -kiwi.co.nz) who run Whitianga to Auckland Airport and Auckland via Hahei, Tairua, Whangamata and Thames, and Whitianga (1 daily) then back again.

By bike An excellent (if tiring) way to explore the Coromandel Peninsula is by bike, making a 3–4-day loop taking plenty of rests for swims. Try Paki Paki Bike Shop for rentals (see p.324).

ACCOMMODATION

Seasons and reservations As one of the North Island's principal holiday spots, the Coromandel Peninsula becomes the scene of frenetic activity from late Dec–Jan with little real relief until the end of March. Finding accommodation can become impossible – book as far ahead as you can, never less than a couple of days. Numbers are more manageable for the rest of the year (though long weekends fill quickly), and in winter much

of the peninsula is deserted, though the climate remains mild.

Camping The whole issue of limiting freedom camping really came to a head on the Coromandel Peninsula and rules are stricter here than elsewhere – and enforced. You can only legally freedom-camp in a certified self-contained vehicle, and only in a very few places: search for freedom camping at ⊕ tcdc.govt.nz for the latest.

Thames

The Coromandel's gateway and main service hub, the historic former gold town of **THAMES** is packed into a narrow strip between the Firth of Thames and the Coromandel Range. It retains a refreshingly down-to-earth sense of community, and its range of accommodation, eateries, transport connections and generally lower prices make it a good starting point for forays further north.

Its gold legacy forms the basis of Thames' appeal and you can spend half a day visiting the several museums, though they're all volunteer-run and, frustratingly, open at different times – summer weekends are best. Fans of Victorian **architecture** can spend a happy couple of hours wandering the streets aided by the maps in two free leaflets *Historic Grahamstown* and *Historic Shortland & Tararu*.

Inland, the industrial heritage is all about kauri logging in the **Kauaeranga Valley**, a popular destination for hikers visiting the Coromandel Forest Park and easily accessible from town.

5

Brief history

Thames initially evolved as two towns: **Grahamstown** to the north and **Shortland** to the south. The first big discovery of gold-bearing quartz was made in a creek-bed in 1867, and by 1871 Grahamstown had become the largest town in New Zealand with a population of around 20,000 and over 120 pubs, only a handful of which remain today. Due to the reliance on machinery (rather than less costly gold-panning), gold mining tailed off during the 1880s and had mostly finished by 1913. Little of significance has happened since.

Goldmine Experience

Corner SH25 and Moanataiari Creek Rd · Dec 26–March daily 10am–4pm; April–Dec 24 Sat & Sun 10am–1pm · $15 · ⓦ goldmine -experience.co.nz

The only way to really get a sense of what it was like to be a miner in Thames is to visit the **Goldmine Experience**, built around an informative 40-minute tour underground along a narrow horizontal shaft originally cut by hand by Cornish miners. Topside, gold ore is crushed and the gold extracted when a stamper battery kicks into deafening gear. You can also pan for gold, while the historically inclined can watch a great video of miners at work, played in the 1914 office building.

School of Mines & Mineralogical Museum

Corner of Cochrane and Brown sts · Jan & Feb daily 11am–3pm; March–Dec Wed–Sun 11am–3pm · $10 · ☎ 07 868 6227, ⓦ thamesschoolofmines.co.nz

Adults with little or no mining experience flocked to Thames, and the more ambitious among them attended this **School of Mines**, which operated from 1886 until 1954 and was one of the most important in the country. Enthusiastic volunteers will show you around the ancient chemistry lab with its lovely precision balance and the public assay room – all crucibles, glass jars and a furnace – where miners could bring their ore for quality assessment. Most of what's here has been on-site since the glory days, including the vast collection of geologic samples in rows of glass cases.

Museum of Technology and Thames Historical Museum

Museum of Technology Cnr of Bella St and Waiokaraka Rd · Generally Sat & Sun 10am–3pm · $5 · ☎ 07 868 8696, ⓦ bellastreetpumphouse.com **Thames Historical Museum** · Corner of Cochrane and Pollen sts · Daily 1–4pm · $5

The vast machinery may be gone but this 1898 building (aka the Bella Street Pumphouse Museum) remains largely unchanged from when its pump helped keep most of Thames' mines dry. Excellent models and photos help interpret its pivotal role. Just up the road is the Thames Historical Museum, which covers the town's social history. Rooms in the old schoolhouse are set up as old miners' huts, there are tales of logging days, and a nice 1925 Simplex movie projector.

Butterfly and Orchid Garden

Dickson Holiday Park, 115 Victoria St, just off SH25, 3.5km north · Sept–May daily 9.30am–4.30pm · $12 · ☎ 07 868 8080, ⓦ butterfly.co.nz

Spend a tranquil half-hour or so inside a tropical hothouse at the magical **Butterfly and Orchid Garden** amid the acrobatics of hundreds of butterflies. At any one time there are around twenty to thirty species here; because of the insects' short lifespan (roughly 2–3 weeks), the garden cycles through over a thousand of these exquisite winged creatures each month, about half imported as pupae, and half bred on-site.

ARRIVAL AND DEPARTURE   THAME

By bus NakedBus, Go Kiwi and InterCity buses stop outside the i-SITE.

Destinations Auckland (5 daily; 2hr); Coromandel (2 daily; 2hr); Tauranga (3 daily; 2hr); Whitianga (2 daily; 2hr 15min;

THAMES

1 (1.5km), 2 (2.5km), Butterfly & Orchid Garden (2.5km), Coromandel (55km) & Whitianga (100km)

COROMANDEL FOREST PARK

Goldmine Experience

WW1 Memorial & lookout

Historical Museum

Museum of Technology

School of Mines & Mineralogical Museum

Organic Co-op

Karaka Bird Hide

Embassy Cinema

Pak 'n Save

Paki Paki

Goldfields Mall

Hauraki Rail Trail Base

Firth of Thames

ACCOMMODATION

Coastal Motor Lodge	1
Cotswold Cottage	7
Cruz 'n' Stop	4
Dickson Holiday Park	2
Gateway Backpackers	5
Rolleston Motel	6
Sunkist	3

EATING & DRINKING

Brew	5
Café Melbourne at The Depot	1
Food for Thought	4
Grahamstown Bar & Diner	3
Kopu Station Hotel	6
Organic Co-op	2
Sola Café	2

7 (2km) & 6 (4km)

INFORMATION AND ACTIVITIES

Visitor information i-SITE is at 206 Pollen St (Nov–April Mon–Fri 8.30am–5pm, Sat & Sun 9am–4pm; May–Oct Mon–Fri 9am–5pm, Sat 9am–1pm, Sun noon–4pm; 07 868 7284, thamesinfo.co.nz). Sells bus tickets and has AA services.

Canyoning 0800 422 696, canyonz.co.nz. To really get off the beaten track, head down the fabulous Sleeping God Canyon with Canyonz. These experts will get you abseiling, jumping and sliding your way out, with free photos to prove to yourself you really did it. Pick-up at the i-Site ($360).

Embassy Cinema 708 Pollen St 07 868 6602, cinemathames.co.nz. Three screens showing a huge range of films (twenty different titles in a week) with discounts on Wednesdays.

5

GETTING AROUND

By bike Paki Paki Bike Shop, 535 Pollen St (☎07 867 9026, ⓦpakipakibikeshop.co.nz; Mon–Fri 9am–5pm, Sat 9am–1pm), have trail bikes and a couple of hybrid touring bikes (all $30/day) ideal for getting around town or further afield (see p.321).

By bus *Sunkist* (see below) run a shuttle service to the Kauaeranga Valley road end ($39 return; minimum 2 people).

By car Davy Rentals, 731 Pollen St (☎07 868 7152, ⓦdavyrentals.co.nz; Mon–Fri 7.30am–5pm), has budget cars for $55–65/day and allows them onto the peninsula's roughest roads. *Sunkist* rent RAV4s for $85/day or $55/day if you rent for a fortnight.

By taxi Thames Taxis ☎07 868 3100 (closed Sun).

ACCOMMODATION

Coastal Motor Lodge 608 Tararu Rd (SH25), 2.5km north of town ☎07 868 6843, ⓦstayatcoastal.co.nz. Well-equipped "cottage" family units and streamlined, spacious black A-frame chalets (all self-contained and designed for two) set in spacious grounds, some with views over the firth. Free wi-fi. Cottages $145, chalets $190

★**Cotswold Cottage** 46 Maramarahi Rd, 3km south of town off SH25 ☎07 868 6306, ⓦcotswoldcottage.co.nz. Restored 1920s villa in mature grounds on the outskirts of Thames with beautiful views of the adjacent river and hills, a guest spa, and three renovated en-suite rooms (one with a four-poster). Rates include delicious cooked breakfasts (great coffee and pancakes); evening meals are available on request for around $45. $200

Cruz 'n' Stop 309 Mary St ☎07 868 9833, ⓦcampervancruznstopcom.com. Basic, paved parking lot right in the centre of town with no dump station but with power hook-ups, a shower, toilets and a small lounge with TV and magazines. Per van $30

Dickson Holiday Park 115 Victoria St, off SH25, 3.5km north of town ☎07 868 7308, ⓦdicksonpark.co.nz. Large, friendly campsite ($37 for two) in a pretty valley with good facilities including a pool. There's free pick-up from Thames. Dorms $25, motel units $136

Gateway Backpackers 209 Mackay St ☎07 868 6339. You'll be well looked after at this intimate hostel just a few paces from the i-SITE and bus stop, housed in two wooden buildings linked by a central courtyard with facilities including free bikes. Dorms $27, doubles $66

Rolleston Motel 105 Rolleston St ☎07 868 8091, ⓦrollestonmotel.co.nz. Classic 1970s motel (recently remodelled) on a quiet backstreet. Each unit has its own little courtyard and everything is beautifully maintained including the outdoor pool, hot tub and barbecue area. $125

Sunkist 506 Brown St ☎07 868 8808, ⓦsunkistbackpackers.com. Atmospheric 1860s former pub, with a wide balcony and hammocks in the garden. Excellent facilities include on-site 4WD rental. InterCity buses stop out front on request; free pick-ups can be arranged from the bus station. Dorms $26, doubles $75

EATING AND DRINKING

Brew 200 Richmond St ☎07 868 5558. Casual daytime café that becomes gastropub at night. Their own Foundry Pale Ale goes nicely with the hearty slow-cooked pork belly ($26). Occasional live music and poetry readings. Mon–Fri 8am–10pm or later, Sat & Sun 9am–10pm or later.

Café Melbourne at The Depot 715 Pollen St ☎07 868 3159, ⓦcafemelbourne.co.nz. The ladies who lunch like the urban industrial vibe of this café, or maybe they're just here for the imaginative breakfasts (mince jaffle, tapioca porridge), tasty fish curry ($19), flat whites and wicked cabinet food (try the double lemon tart $4.50). Next door there's *Bite*, a great deli with fresh bread. Mon–Thurs 8am–5pm, Fri 8am–9pm, Sat & Sun 9am–4pm.

Food for Thought 574 Pollen St ☎07 868 6065. This budget café has taken numerous New Zealand-wide awards for its home-made pies (especially its vegetarian version; $4) and also has a mouthwatering range of cakes, plus excellent coffee. Mon–Fri 6am–3.30pm, Sat 6am–2pm.

Grahamstown Bar & Diner 700 Pollen St ☎09 868 6008. Popular, polished-wood bar that's fine for a pint or generous meals such as nachos ($15), roasted vegetable salad ($18.50), or lamb rack with mash ($29.50). Mon–Wed 11am–9pm, Thurs & Fri 11am–9.30pm, Sat 8.30am–9.30pm, Sun 8.30am–9pm.

Kopu Station Hotel 1 Kopu Rd, Kopu, 5km south of town ☎07 868 7916. "Te Kopu" is a favourite local watering hole, popular for its regular live bands, great range of drinks, stone grills, grassy beer garden and laidback attitude. Daily 10am–11pm or later.

Organic Co-op 736 Pollen St ☎07 868 8797. Community-run nonprofit place that's good for organic supplies, veggies, eggs and frozen organic meat. Mon–Fri 9am–5pm, Sat 9am–noon.

★**Sola Café** 720b Pollen St ☎07 868 8781, ⓦsolacafe .co.nz. Relaxed bohemian café serving cakes, stellar coffee, salads and vegetarian dishes, from breakfasts and frittatas to wraps and enchiladas (mostly $12.50); some vegan and gluten-free options are available. There's courtyard seating out back. Sun–Fri 8am–4pm, Sat 7.30am–4pm.

Kauaeranga Valley

The steep-sided **Kauaeranga Valley** stretches east of Thames towards the spine of the Coromandel Peninsula, a jagged landscape of bluffs and gorges topped by **the Pinnacles** (759m), with stupendous views to both coasts across native forest studded with rata, rimu and kauri. It's reached along the scenic and mostly sealed Kauaeranga Valley Road making 21km beside the river, providing access to some of the finest walks in the Coromandel Range. The road winds through regenerating bush containing scattered "pole stands" of young kauri that have grown since the area was logged a century ago: only a handful in each stand will reach maturity.

The ease of access to these tracks can lead trampers not to take them as seriously as other tramps, but in bad weather the conditions can be treacherous, so go properly prepared (see p.50).

Note that the soil-borne **kauri dieback** (see box, p.194) was recently found in the Coromandel. Be extra vigilant about cleaning your footwear before and after trips, especially if you've recently visited the Auckland or Northland forests (where the disease is widespread).

INFORMATION
KAUAERANGA VALLEY

DOC visitor centre 14km along Kauaeranga Valley Rd (Dec 26–April daily 8.30am–5pm; May–Dec 8.30am–4pm; closed in severe weather; ☏ 07 867 9080). Superb visitor centre with great displays on early kauri logging in the valley, big maps of the area and a 20min DVD on the history of logging. Pick up the *Kauaeranga Valley & Broken Hills Recreation* booklet ($2) that details walks or buy the 1:50,000 *Hikuai Topo50* map BB35 ($9). Buy hut tickets via the on-site computer.

ACCOMMODATION

The DOC campsites (⊕ doc.govt.nz) listed here are the best of eight very similar options, all dotted along Kauaeranga Valley and 14–23km east of Thames. The two huts are only accessible on foot on the Kauaeranga walks (see box below).

Crosbies Hut Pretty new, ten-bunk hut best accessed on the Wainora–Booms Flat circuit. It comes equipped with mattresses and a wood store but no gas rings. If you're looking for a quieter alternative to the Pinnacles Hut, this is it. **$15**

KAUAERANGA WALKS

Cookson Kauri Track (6km return; 3–4hr). Moderate, well-formed track to a couple of large kauri – pretty much the only accessible ones left standing hereabouts. Starts from the Wainora campsite, 7km beyond the DOC office.

Kahikatea Walk (900m return; 20min). Flat walk from the DOC office to a scale model of a kauri driving dam, a type once used extensively in this forest.

Nature Walk to Hoffman's Pool (1.5km loop; 30min). A short, easy loop beginning 1.5km beyond the DOC office. Information panels help make it a classic introduction to the valley's native forest. The track leads to a tranquil sand-edged pool in a river bend, an ideal picnic and swimming spot with a lovely deep swimming hole. You return the same way or in a loop along the road.

Pinnacles Hut–Billygoat Basin Walk (18km loop; 8hr). Typically done as a two-day hike with a night spent at the Pinnacles Hut (see p.326), this is a great way to get a taste of the region. It starts at the road-end and spends the first 2–3hr following Webb Creek along an old packhorse route used by kauri bushmen in the 1920s (steep in places) up to Pinnacles Hut. From the hut there's a steep 50min climb, including some short ladders, to the jagged teeth of the Pinnacles themselves, and wonderful views. On the return, head south from the Hydro junction via Billygoat Basin, where panels give the loggers' story. At the time of writing, you need to ford the river to get back, so check before you start and watch the weather.

Wainora–Booms Flat circuit (15km loop; 7hr). Excellent full-day outing starting along the Cookson Kauri Track then topping out at 549m with great views all around. After following an undulating track to Orange Peel Corner you can descend on the track to Booms Flat or turn this into a two-day walk by overnighting at Crosbies Hut (see above) which adds 4hr to the total length. In wet weather, avoid the Booms Flat track.

5

Pinnacles Hut and campsite ⓦ doc.govt.nz. This large and relatively plush eighty-bunk place is one of the most popular of all DOC huts, especially on Saturday nights and during school holidays. It is beautifully sited atop the range, around a 3hr walk from the road end, and there's always a warden present. You can camp here, too, in a wooded streamside setting beside the hut. Book online; backcountry hut passes not valid. Hut $15, camping $5

Shag Stream 14km along Kauaeranga Valley Rd fro Thames. The nearest DOC campsite to Thames is a simpl bush-girt affair right by the DOC visitor centre. It's equippe with vault toilets and has access to stream water (whi should be treated). $10

Whangaiterenga 19km along Kauaeranga Valley R from Thames. Marginally the nicest of the roadsic campsites and the only one with flush toilets. Water gathered from the stream and should be treated. $10

The Pohutukawa Coast

From Thames, SH25 snakes 58km north to Coromandel town, tracing the grey rocky shoreline of the "**Pohutukawa Coast**" (so called for its abundance of these blazing nativ trees) past a series of tiny, sandy bays, most with little more than a few houses and the occasional campsite.

Tapu–Coroglen Road

Hills and sand-coloured cliffs rise dramatically from the roadside for the first 19km until you reach **Tapu**, where the **Tapu–Coroglen Road** peels off to the peninsula's east coast. It is a wonderfully scenic 28km run of narrow, unsealed yet manageable driving, leaving behind the marginal farmland on the coast and climbing over the peninsula's mountainous spine. You eventually drop down to Coroglen, linking with the main road between Whitianga and Whangamata.

Rapaura Watergardens

586 Tapu–Coroglen Rd · Daily 9am–5pm · $15 · ☎ 07 868 4821, ⓦ rapaurawatergardens.co.nz

Even if you aren't driving the whole Tapu–Coroglen Road, it's worth making a detour 6km along to **Rapaura Watergardens**, a landscaped "wilderness" of bush and blooms, lily ponds and a trickling stream, threaded by paths, with philosophical messages urging you to stop and think. There are a few picnic areas, an excellent summer-only **café** and accommodation (see below).

Square kauri

Tapu–Coroglen Rd, 3km east of Rapaura Watergardens

Near the road's summit, an easily missed signpost points to the "**square kauri**", opposit a rough lay-by and just before a small bridge. Steep steps through bush (175m; 10min) lead to this 1200-year-old giant of a tree (41m high and 9m wide), whose unusual, angular shape saved it from loggers.

Manaia-Kereta Lookout

SH25, 12km north of Tapu

The road lurches inland soon after Kereta, snaking over hills to the roadside **Manaia-Kereta Lookout** (206m), which has great views of the northern peninsula, the majestic Moehau Range and Coromandel Harbour. Beyond, the vertical cliffs of Great Barrier Island may be visible on a clear day. Along the rocky shoreline and blue-green Firth of Thames, SH25 continues for 23km before reaching Coromandel.

ACCOMMODATION POHUTUKAWA COAST

Rapaura Watergardens 586 Tapu–Coroglen Rd ☎ 07 868 4821, ⓦ rapaurawatergardens.co.nz. Choose from an enchanting luxury cottage for two or a serene two-bedroom lodge lined with rimu. Once the

day-visitors have gone you have the watergardens t yourself. Cottage $165, lodge $285

Coromandel

5

The peninsula's northernmost town of any substance is charming little **COROMANDEL**, 58km north of Thames, huddling beneath high, craggy hills at the head of Coromandel Harbour.

From the south, SH25 becomes Tiki Road and then splits into two: Wharf Road skirts the harbour while Kapanga Road immediately enters the heart of town, which is made up of photogenic wooden buildings, where you'll find supermarkets, petrol stations, a bank and a cluster of cafés and arty shops. A couple of blocks further on, it becomes Rings Road, before heading northwards out of town towards the main attractions, the **stamper battery** and the **Driving Creek Railway**.

Brief history

The town and peninsula took their name from an 1820 visit by the British Admiralty supply ship *Coromandel*, which called into the harbour to obtain kauri spars and masts. A more mercenary European invasion was precipitated by the 1852 discovery of **gold**, near Driving Creek.

Driving Creek Railway and Potteries

380 Driving Creek Rd, 3.5km north of town · **Train trips** Daily 10.15am & 2pm plus up to four extra trips per day during school holidays; 1hr return , booking advised · $30 **Pottery** Daily 10am–4pm · Free · ☏ 07 866 8703, ⊛ drivingcreekrailway.co.nz

The ingenious **Driving Creek Railway** is the country's only narrow-gauge hill railway. It was built mostly by hand and is the brainchild of Barry Brickell, an eccentric local potter and rail enthusiast who wanted to access the clay-bearing hills. The track is only 381mm wide and climbs 105m over a distance of about 3km, rewarding you with spectacular views, extraordinary feats of engineering and quirky design; at the end of the line panoramas extend from a specially constructed wooden lodge, the Eyefull Tower. The journey starts and ends at the **workshops**, where you can see various types of **pottery**: stoneware, bricks and earthenware items, and terracotta sculptures.

Coromandel Goldfields Centre & Stamper Battery

410 Buffalo Rd, 2km north of town · Summer daily 10am–3pm; Winter by arrangement · 1hr guided tours available; check times with the i-SITE · $15 · ⊛ coromandelstamperbattery.weebly.com

To get the most from this fascinating site, take the enthusiastic and expert guided tour (on the hour, every hour in summer – plus a spooky evening tour) which brings to life Coromandel's gold-mining history, explains how gold ore was extracted and refined, and includes a demo of New Zealand's biggest water wheel which runs the fully functional 1899 stamper battery. It makes quite a racket.

Long Bay Kauri Grove

Wharf Rd, 3km west of town · 40min loop

The attractive beach at **Long Bay** marks the start of a pleasing **walk** through a scenic reserve winding through bush to an ancient kauri tree and on to a small grove of younger ones. Beyond, at the junction with a gravel road, turn right to Tucks Bay to follow the coastal track back. The track starts 100m inside the *Long Bay Motor Camp* where a signpost marks the track.

ARRIVAL AND INFORMATION

COROMANDEL

By bus InterCity buses pull into the car park opposite the i-SITE.

Destinations Thames (2 daily; 1hr 15min); Whitianga (2 daily; 1hr).

By ferry 360 Discovery (☏ 09 307 8005, ⊛ 360discovery .co.nz) operate a passenger ferry between Auckland and

Hannafords Wharf, 7km south of Coromandel. The $55 one-way fare includes a bus into town.

Destinations Auckland (3–7 weekly; 2hr).

Information Centre 8 Kapanga Rd (daily 10am–4pm; ☏ 07 866 8598, ⊛ thecoromandel.co.nz). Carries DOC leaflets and Hot Water Beach tide times.

5

GETTING AROUND

By car Car rental outlets in town include the Coromandel service station at 226 Wharf Rd (☎07 866 8736; $65/24hr), which allows its cars onto the unsealed roads north of Colville.

By shuttle bus There are two tour and shuttle bus operators offering trips to the must-see spots and up north so you can enjoy the view rather than worry about the road. Both also run trips for the Coromandel Walkway (see p.331), dropping off walkers at one end, and picking up at the other before returning to Coromandel. Coromandel

Discovery starts at Fletcher Bay ($125 return, complimentary tea, coffee and biscuits; ☎0800 668 175, ⊚coromandeldiscovery.co.nz). Coromandel Adventures starts at Stony Bay, which means you can tack on the Muriwai walk if you're still lively at the end ($115 return, stop to brew hot drinks and nibble biscuits; ☎0800 462 676, ⊚coromandeladventures.co.nz).

By taxi Coromandel Cabs will also drop you off for walks (☎07 866 8927, ⊚coromandelcabs.co.nz).

ACCOMMODATION

Anchor Lodge 448 Wharf Rd ☎07 866 7992, ⊚anchorlodgecoromandel.co.nz. Modern, well-run motel with heated pool, free spa and a wide range of accommodation including a backpacker hostel section and some nice two-bedroom units nestled in the bush. Dorms $29, motel units $145

Buffalo Lodge 860 Buffalo Rd ☎07 866 8960, ⊚buffalolodge.co.nz. Artist Evelyne's architect-designed home is perched high up in the bush north of town, with dizzying gulf views from its three guest rooms (all with private deck). If she can find them, you'll have free-range eggs for breakfast (GF pancakes on request). Not suitable for children. Closed May–Sept. $220

Coromandel Colonial Cottages 1737 Rings Rd ☎07 866 8857, ⊚corocottagesmotel.co.nz. Eight well-kept whitewashed wooden cottages (some sleeping six) neatly arranged in tranquil gardens 1.5km north of town with a big solar-heated swimming pool, a kids' playground and a BBQ area. $170

Coromandel Top 10 Holiday Park 636 Rings Rd ☎0800 267 646, ⊚coromandelholidaypark.co.nz. Sprawling over 3.5 acres a 3min walk north of town, this all-purpose spot combines camping ($22) and campervan facilities with a comprehensive range of cabins and well-equipped motel units. All guests have access to the heated swimming pool and facilities including bike rental. Cabins $75, motel units $140

★ **Hush** 425 Driving Creek Rd ☎07 866 7771, ⊚hushaccommodation.co.nz. These aren't any cabins: these are stylish modern Hush cabins, with eating nooks, fridges, the occasional TV, crisp cotton sheets and thoughtful touches like umbrellas. Each is discreetly nestled in native bush, so you'll be woken by tui and kereru before you make breakfast in the shared open-air kitchen. There's also a self-contained Petite house ($140). Cabin

$120, en suite $145

Jacaranda Lodge 3195 Tiki Rd (SH25) ☎07 866 8002, ⊚jacarandalodge.co.nz. Set in farmland 3km south of town offering B&B accommodation in five immaculate and thoughtfully styled rooms (most en-suite), a stellar collection of New Zealand films on DVD, and delicious continental breakfasts including home-made muesli and juices and jams from the orchards outside. $150, en suite $190

Lion's Den 126 Te Tiki St ☎07 866 8157, ⊚lionsdenhostel.co.nz. Small, funky hostel beloved by backpackers for its cosy, colourful common areas, tropical gardens, sociable shared-house-style atmosphere and proximity to town and bushwalks. Check out the outdoor shower. There's beauty therapy on site (facials from $35). Dorms $27, doubles $62

★ **Long Bay Motor Camp** 3200 Long Bay Rd ☎07 866 8720, ⊚longbaymotorcamp.co.nz. Laidback beachfront campsite 3km west of town with great sunset views, safe swimming, bushwalks and kayak rental ($10/hr). There are additional unpowered sites at the secluded Tucks Bay, a 1km drive through the bush or a 5min walk around the headland. Camping $20, cabins $65

Tidewater Tourist Park 270 Tiki Rd ☎07 866 8888, ⊚tidewater.co.nz. Comfortable motel and attached associate YHA, 200m from town near the harbour, with BBQ area, free guest bikes and kayaks and spacious cabin-style units sleeping up to six people ($160). You can pitch a tent too ($15). Dorms $30, doubles $60

Tui Lodge 60b Whangapoua Rd, just off SH25 ☎07 866 8237, ⊚coromandeltuilodge.co.nz. Good-value hostel a 10min walk south of town (and on the InterCity bus route), set in a big rambling house surrounded by an orchard and tranquil garden with a large chill-out gazebo. Free perks include laundry, tea and coffee, fruit (in season), a BBQ and bike use. Dorms $28, doubles $70

EATING AND DRINKING

Little Coromandel has a disproportionate number of places to **eat** and some great seafood vendors for essential supplies.

Coromandel Hotel 611 Kapanga Rd ☎07 866 8760, ⊚coromandelhotel.co.nz. Even farmers and fishermen can

barely finish the meals at this traditional boozer known locally as the "Top Pub". Expect typical bar meals, and go for chicken

FROM TOP WHITE ISLAND (P.356); RUAKOKORE CHURCH, EAST CAPE (P.362) >

5

and banana curry ($22) in the dining room, or grab a drink and sit out in the beer garden. Daily 11am–10pm or later.

Coromandel Mussel Kitchen Corner of SH25 and 309 Rd, 4km south ☎07 866 7245, ⓦmusselkitchen.co.nz. They cultivate and cook their own premium mussels at this roadside café specializing in mussel pots ($19.50) with sourdough bread to dunk into a broth of Thai green curry or cream and garlic. They also dish up mussel chowder and other regular café fare. Daily 9.30am–4pm and until 9pm in summer.

Coromandel Oyster Company 1611 Tiki Rd (SH25), 5km south of town ☎07 866 8028. Buy mussels, scallops and, of course, oysters fresh out of the water. They also sell oyster or mussel chowder ($7). Daily 8am–6pm.

Coromandel Smoking Company 70 Tiki Rd ☎0800 327 668, ⓦcorosmoke.co.nz. Great shop selling their own smoked fish (hot- and cold-smoked salmon) and shellfish, and particularly notable for kahawai and mussels. A perfect spot to stop for picnic supplies. Daily 9am–5pm.

★**Driving Creek Café** 180 Driving Creek Rd, 3.5km north of town ☎07 866 7066, ⓦdrivingcreekcafe.com. Classic Coromandel: a laidback and welcoming vegetarian

(and mostly organic) café that's perfect for great coffee rich fruit smoothies, banana pancake breakfasts ($15) an(lunch. There are beautiful hill views from the veranda an(garden, occasional acoustic music, and a great secondhan(bookshop. Fri–Tues 9.30am–4pm.

Peppertree 31 Kapanga Rd ☎07 866 8211 ⓦpeppertreerestaurant.co.nz. Coromandel's finest dining, serving either indoors – there's an open fire in winter – or in the garden. Pop in for a zucchini curry burge(and chips ($17) or dinner of fillet steak with bacon wrapped scallops ($37). Daily 10am–9pm.

Star and Garter 5 Kapanga Rd ☎07 866 8503 ⓦstarandgarter.co.nz. Airy wood-lined 1873-built ba(and covered beer garden in the centre of town, popula(with an urbane, mixed-age crowd for the full range o(Monteith's brews and wine specials. Daily 11am–1am.

Umu 22 Wharf Rd ☎07 866 8618. Popular for its pizza((try Graeme's special) but worth returning for thei(imaginative meals: breakfast on Umu baked beans with egg and bacon ($16); pop in for Asian chicken slaw ($18.50(or come back at dinner (if only for the coconut sago brûlée) Daily 8.30am–10pm or later.

Northern Coromandel Peninsula

The landscape at the tip of the Coromandel is even more rugged than the rest of the peninsula, its green hills dropping to apparently endless beaches, clean blue sea and frothing white surf. The roads are lined with ancient pohutukawa trees, blazing red from early November until January. It's virtually uninhabited and there are **few facilities** except for some superb basic camping; replenish supplies in Coromandel.

The only real settlement is tiny **Colville**. North of there the road turns to gravel, becoming narrower, rougher and dustier the further north you go. Three kilometres beyond Colville the road splits, the right fork heading east over the hills to **Stony Bay** and the southern end of the Coromandel Walkway. The left fork runs 35km north to **Port Jackson** and **Fletcher Bay** at the very tip of the peninsula, following the coast all the way. In fine weather, allow an hour to reach Fletcher Bay from Colville.

Colville

From Coromandel town, the road is sealed to just beyond the tiny settlement of **COLVILLE**, a quiet valley comprising little more than a post office, a petrol pump, a café and the **Colville General Store** (☎07 866 6805), where you can stock up on provisions before heading to points north.

Port Jackson

An abandoned **granite wharf** 19km northwest of Colville marks the halfway point on the road to the peninsula tip. The road then cuts inland, over hills rising straight from the shore, to reach **PORT JACKSON**, just two houses and a 1km sandy crescent of beach. It's safe for swimming and is backed by a grassy DOC reserve (ideal for a picnic) and campsite.

Fletcher Bay

From Port Jackson the road deteriorates on the final 6km stretch to **FLETCHER BAY**, probably the best beach of all, with safe swimming and backed by another DOC campsite and a backpackers. The eastern end of the beach marks the start of the **Coromandel Walkway**.

Stony Bay

Stony Bay, at the southern end of the Coromandel Walkway, is reached by two perilously narrow and twisty gravel roads – one, via Little Bay, across the Coromandel Range from just beyond Coromandel, the other traversing the Moehau Range from just beyond Colville. The latter runs 14km from Colville to the small holiday settlement of **Port Charles**, and a further 6km to Stony Bay, where there's another beautiful DOC campsite.

INFORMATION AND ACTIVITIES

Visitor information Before heading out, check on the road conditions at the Coromandel information centre (8 Kapanga Rd; daily 10am–4pm; ☏ 07 866 8598, ⟲ thecoromandel.co.nz), fill up with petrol and be prepared to drive slowly and take your time. There's no hurry up here.

NORTHERN COROMANDEL PENINSULA

Horse trekking Colville Farm (2140 Colville Rd, 1.5km south of Colville ☏ 07 866 6820, ⟲ colvillefarmholidays .co.nz) offers guided horse trekking with short rides on a sheep and cattle farm. Longer treks head into native bush or out along the beach ($40/hr; $150/5hr).

ACCOMMODATION

With a few exceptions, accommodation is limited to camping. To help deter illegal freedom camping, DOC has opened five waterside campsites around the northern peninsula (see map p.320): three of the best are listed below. For the two weeks after Christmas the campsites are full, but for most of the rest of the year you'll have this unspoilt area to yourself. Expect toilets, cold showers and not much else.

Colville Farm Colville Rd, 1.5km south of Colville ☏ 07 866 6820, ⟲ colvillefarmholidays.co.nz. Great rural bolt-hole with spots for tents ($12; pay $2 extra to use the backpacker facilities), backpacker beds in a cottage, a couple of rustic bush lodges and two self-contained houses with fabulous views ($120). Dorm $25, lodge $85

Fantail Bay campsite 22km north of Colville ⟲ doc .govt.nz. Fairly small beachfront DOC site surrounded by farmland. There's room for just 100 people, sharing flush toilets, stream water and cold showers. Booking is essential in the summer. $10

Fletcher Bay Backpackers Fletcher Bay, 34km north of Colville ☏ 07 866 6685, ⟲ doc.govt.nz. Fairly basic hostel in a superb location on a hill 400m from the beach overlooking the campsite. The four rooms have two bunk beds in each and bedding is provided. $25

Fletcher Bay campsite 34km north of Colville ⟲ doc .govt.nz. The most remote of the DOC sites, with views across to Great Barrier and Little Barrier islands. It comes with flush toilets, stream water and cold showers, and, despite its 250-person capacity, booking is essential for the two weeks after Christmas. $10

Coromandel to Whitianga

The drive east from Coromandel to Whitianga can be done in under an hour, but you could easily stretch it out longer on either of two highly **scenic roads** that cross the mountains: the snaking **309 Road** (33km, of which 14km are gravel; no public transport) spends much of its time in the bush, twisting across the peninsula's spine and topping out at the 306m-high saddle before descending to Whitianga; the main **SH25** climbs through forested hills before zigzagging down to the coast past the deserted beaches of Whangapoua and Kuaotunu.

THE COROMANDEL WALKWAY

If you're after more exertion than swimming, fishing or lolling about on the beaches, consider hiking from Fletcher Bay to Stony Bay (or vice versa) along the easy **Coromandel Walkway** (11km one way; 3hr). The walk starts at the far end of the beach in Fletcher Bay and first follows gentle coastal hills that alternate between pasture and bush, before giving way to wilder terrain as you head further south past a series of tiny bays. Several hilltop **vantage points** provide spectacular vistas of the coast and Pacific Ocean beyond. **Stony Bay** is a sweep of pebbles with an estuary that's safe for swimming. The DOC leaflet *Coromandel Recreation Information* briefly describes the walk and shows a map, but the path is clearly marked.

For information on how to reach the walkway via shuttle bus from Coromandel town, see p.328.

5

Along the 309 Road

Keep an eye out for Stu's pigs (about 3km along the 309). These friendly, free-roaming Captain Cookers, and the character who owns them, are world famous in Coromandel.

The Waterworks

471 The 309 Rd · Daily: Nov–April 10am–6pm; May–Oct 10am–4pm · $24 · ☎ 07 866 7191, ⓦ thewaterworks.co.nz

Set at least a couple of hours aside to visit **The Waterworks**, 5km along the 309 Road, an eccentric garden carved from the bush where you can do fun stuff with water. The tone is set with a waterwheel built from construction helmets, teapots and gumboots. Play an elaborate form of pooh sticks on the raised waterway or try one of many devices designed to splash the unsuspecting. The highlight is a huge clock powered by jets: apparently it keeps remarkably good time unless the wind blows the pendulum off kilter. Have a snack in the café, and bring a swimsuit for a dip in the natural swimming hole. There's no electricity – everything's powered by the on-site spring (make sure you find it before you leave).

Castle Rock

100m past The Waterworks · 2km return; 40min–1hr 30min

A rough access road to the north crosses a ford and climbs steeply for 3km to the trailhead for the track to **Castle Rock**, the most easily accessible peak on the Coromandel Peninsula. The climb gets steeper towards the final tree-root claw onto the 521m summit of this old volcanic plug, but your efforts are rewarded by fantastic views to both coasts: the Whangapoua Peninsula and the Mercury Islands on the east, and Coromandel and the Firth of Thames on the west.

Waiau Falls and the "Siamese" Kauri

309 Rd, 2.5km southeast of Castle Rock

Though of modest height, **Waiau Falls** still crash over a tiered rock-face into a pool below, making this a gorgeous spot to cool off right next to the road. Half a kilometre on, a car park heralds the easy bush track to the towering, magnificent **Kauri Grove** (1km return; 30min) and the so-called "**Siamese**" Kauri a little further; this is one of the best places in the country to appreciate their immense size.

Along the SH25

Whangapoua and New Chums Beach

From Coromandel, **SH25** traverses lush native forest, passing a couple of isolated but pretty beachside settlements with campsites. About 14km from Coromandel is the 5km turn-off to the secluded village and white-sand beach of **WHANGAPOUA**. At the end of the road (along the right fork into town) a pretty bushwalk over a headland brings you to **New Chums Beach** (accessible at low tide only; 4km return; 1hr), one of New Zealand's finest beaches.

Stargazers Astronomy Tours

392 SH25 · Advance booking essential · 1–1hr 30min · $50 · ☎ 07 866 5343, ⓦ stargazersbb.com

With so little light pollution the New Zealand night sky can be amazing, but to be really wowed let Alastair Brickell (cousin of the more famous Barry Brickell; see p.327) show you around the universe. He's got great kit, but it's his enthusiasm, humour and clear explanations that really delight. If you can't drag yourself away from the stars, stay the night (see opposite).

Kuaotunu

Continuing along SH25, about 30km from Coromandel, you descend to diminutive **KUAOTUNU**, beside a lovely white-sand beach. There's not much to it, but the village is an alluring spot with a few places to stay and a great pizza joint. From here, SH25 continues through farmland to Whitianga and Mercury Bay.

Kuaotunu Bay Lodge B&B SH25 ☎07 866 4396, ⍟kuaotunubay.co.nz. Understated luxury in a modern house with amazing views from private decks. Everything is beautifully appointed and there's free wi-fi. Two-night minimum stay Dec–March. **$295**

Kuaotunu Camp Ground 33 Bluff Rd ☎07 866 5628, ⍟kcg2008.co.nz. Decent campsite with kayak rental and an on-site fish and chip shop. The beach is just across the road but most sites don't have great views. Camping **$20**, cabins **$65**

★ **Luke's Kitchen** 20 Blackjack Rd, off SH25 ☎07 866 4480, ⍟lukeskitchen.co.nz. The only place to eat in Kuaotunu. Fortunately, it's great. There's a bar, café,

outdoor seating, and new gallery of local art. Come for a coffee and savoury scone while you enjoy the view, or a superb pizza (try the Never Fail, with fresh fish, courgette and aioli; $28). Live music most summer evenings. Daily in summer 8am–9pm; winter Fri–Sun 8.30am–3pm.

Stargazers B&B 392 SH25 2km south of Kuaotunu ☎07 866 5343, ⍟stargazersbb.com. Only one booking a night at this beautiful home in the bush. You have your own separate lounge, breakfast is served on the spacious deck, and binoculars are provided to spot birds or stars. They've also restored the self-contained *Miner's Cottage* down the hill, with modern bathrooms and the chance to spot glowworms. **$250**

Whitianga and around

Pretty **WHITIANGA** clusters where Whitianga Harbour meets **Buffalo Beach**, a long curve of surf-pounded white sand on the broad sweep of **Mercury Bay**. The town is a relaxed place to chill for a day or two, perhaps trying **bone carving** or getting pampered at The Lost Spring **hot pools**. It also makes a central base from which to make a series of half-day and **day-trips** to some of the Coromandel's top spots.

A short passenger ferry ride across the narrow harbour mouth to **Ferry Landing** opens up a bunch of **gorgeous beaches** such as Lonely Bay. They're often deserted out of season, though from December to February you'll have to work harder to find tranquillity. By taking a bus from Ferry Landing (or driving south via Whenuakite) you can access **Cathedral Cove**, a stunning geological formation with great swimming, and magical **Hot Water Beach**, where natural hot springs bubble up through the sand.

Offshore, the protected waters of **Te Whanganui-A-Hei (Cathedral Cove) Marine Reserve** offer superb snorkelling and scuba diving, where bottlenose **dolphins** and **orca** are often seen. These, and an extraordinary array of volcanic island and sea caves, are the main focus of a range of **boat tours** and **kayak trips** from Hahei and Whitianga.

Mercury Bay Museum

1 The Esplanade • Daily 10am–4pm • $7.50 • ☎07 866 0730, ⍟mercurybaymuseum.co.nz

An old butter factory on the Esplanade houses the **Mercury Bay Museum** with plenty on kauri logging, early settlers and big game fishing. The highlight is the coverage of early explorers, particularly Maori pioneer Kupe, who is thought to have landed near here up to a thousand years ago. Don't miss the moa or the reconstructed 1960s *bach*.

The Lost Spring

121a Cook Drive • Daily 10.30am–7pm (9pm on Sat) • $36 for 1hr, $60 all day • ☎07 866 0456, ⍟thelostspring.co.nz • foot pamper $70; decadent full-body pamper, including glass of bubbly $370

A nondescript patch of suburban Whitianga is the unlikely location for **The Lost Spring**, a series of hot pools set among lavishly landscaped grounds, where cocktails are

---

COOK PLANTS THE FLAG

James Cook effectively claimed New Zealand for King George III, planting the British flag at Cooks Beach in November 1769. Cook spent 12 days anchored here – the longest he spent anywhere on his first voyage around Aotearoa – observing the **transit of Mercury** across the sun on November 9; in doing so he established the exact latitude and longitude of the new-found land and named (or rather renamed) both Mercury Bay and, of course, Cooks Beach.

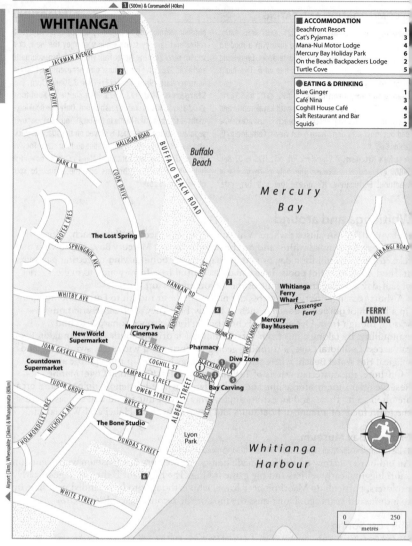

▲ 🚌 (500m) & Coromandel (40km)

WHITIANGA

delivered by staff with frangipani flowers behind their ears. The complex is the brainchild of Alan Hopping, who believed in, searched for, and finally found and tapped a local hot spring to create this extraordinary oasis. Ranging from 33°C–40°C, the pools combine spa kitsch with re-created natural bush splendour. You can dine at the classy on-site **café** and should book ahead for all manner of decadent pampering opportunities.

Shakespeare Lookout

1.5km east of Ferry Landing and another 1km uphill • Free

The cliffs below **Shakespeare Lookout** apparently once resembled the Bard's profile, though it is hard to imagine today. It is better to admire the panoramic views from the lookout, which stretch east to Cooks Beach and across Mercury Bay, west to Buffalo Beach, and north towards Mount Maungatawhiri. Signposted tracks (2km one way; 30min) lead from the car park to the secluded Lonely Bay and on to the popular family holiday spot of **Cooks Beach**, also accessible from the main road 2km further east.

Hahei

The small beachside community of **HAHEI**, 6km east of Cooks Beach (10km by road), has a store, a few places to stay and eat, and is the launch site for boat, kayak and dive trips into **Te Whanganui-A-Hei (Cathedral Cove) Marine Reserve** (see box, p.337), also accessible via the Cathedral Cove Walk.

Cathedral Cove Walk

5km return; 1hr 30min; 300m ascent on the way back

Almost everybody does the **Cathedral Cove Walk**, a hilly coastal track from a car park on Grange Road. Although steep in places, the route affords great views out to sea. The reward is a perfect pair of beaches backed by white cliffs and separated by an impressive rock arch that vaults over the strand like the nave of a great cathedral.

Steps bring you down onto **Mare's Leg Cove**, a gorgeous swimming beach with composting toilets offering a seat with a view. You need to walk through the arch to reach the second fine beach, **Cathedral Cove**. **Rockfalls** from the ceiling have made DOC jittery, so there are warning signs – and if the arch is roped off, stay well back.

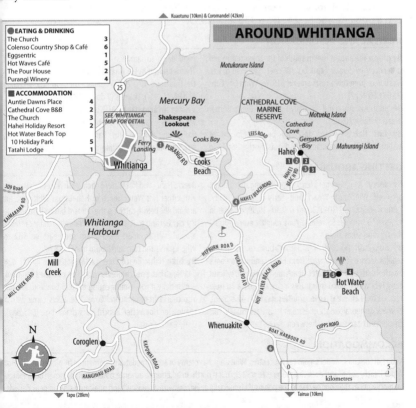

AROUND WHITIANGA

EATING & DRINKING
The Church	3
Colenso Country Shop & Café	6
Eggsentric	1
Hot Waves Café	5
The Pour House	2
Purangi Winery	4

ACCOMMODATION
Auntie Dawns Place	4
Cathedral Cove B&B	2
The Church	3
Hahei Holiday Resort	2
Hot Water Beach Top 10 Holiday Park	5
Tatahi Lodge	1

Kuaotunu (10km) & Coromandel (42km)

Motukorure Island

Mercury Bay

CATHEDRAL COVE MARINE RESERVE

Motueka Island

Cathedral Cove

Gemstone Bay

Mahurangi Island

Shakespeare Lookout

SEE 'WHITIANGA' MAP FOR DETAIL

Cooks Bay

LEES ROAD

Hahei

Ferry Landing

PURANGI RD

Whitianga

Cooks Beach

HAHEI BEACH ROAD

309 Road

KAIMARAMA RD

Whitianga Harbour

HEPBURN ROAD

PURANGI ROAD

Mill Creek

MILL CREEK ROAD

HOT WATER BEACH ROAD

Hot Water Beach

N

Whenuakite

BOAT HARBOUR RD

CUPPS ROAD

Coroglen

KAPOWAI ROAD

RANGIHAU ROAD

Tapu (28km)

Tairua (10km)

0   5
kilometres

5

To walk from Hahei Beach follow the step at the northern end of the beach: you'll reach the car park at the start of the walk in around twenty minutes.

Gemstone Bay and Stingray Bay

A short way along the Cathedral Cove Walk, a five-minute track descends to the rocky **Gemstone Bay**, which is great for snorkelling. DOC has set up buoys in different marine environments between 50m and 150m offshore with panels explaining the undersea wonders. Rent gear from Cathedral Cove Dive (see box opposite).

Stingray Bay, signposted further along the Cathedral Cove Walk, is a perfect cove of white sand that's often deserted when Cathedral Cove is packed.

Hot Water Beach

15km southeast of Whitianga, but over 30km by road

With the opportunity to dig your own hot pool in the sands next to the breakers, **Hot Water Beach** is understandably one of the most popular destinations on the Coromandel Peninsula. The hot springs which bubble up beneath the sand can only be exploited two hours either side of **low tide** (less in rough weather; check tide times at the Whitianga i-SITE). Wander 100m across the sands to the rocky outcrop that splits the beach in two, dig your hole and enjoy the hot water, refreshed by waves. You'll need a spade to dig your "spa": rent one from your accommodation, the local café or *Hot Waves Café* (see p.339) for $5, plus $20 deposit.

The springs have become so popular – up to five hundred people crowd the beach at peak times – that some prefer to come at night: bring a torch. The beach here has a dangerous **tidal rip**, so take care when swimming (see box, p.63). For accommodation and a café near the beach, see p.338 and p.339.

ARRIVAL AND INFORMATION

WHITIANGA AND AROUND

By plane The airport is 4km south of the town centre and is serviced by Sunair (☎ 0800 786 247, ⓦ sunair.co.nz). A cab to or from town costs around $15; try Whiti City Cabs (☎ 07 866 4777).

Destinations Auckland (2 daily; 30min); Great Barrier Island (1 daily; 30min).

By bus NakedBus and InterCity buses drop off at accommodation around town and outside the i-SITE. To

head down to Tauranga you'll need to change at either Thames (InterCity) or Ngatea (NakedBus).

Destinations Ngatea (1 daily; 1hr 15min); Tauranga (2 daily; 2–3hr); Thames (2 daily; 1hr 40min).

Visitor information i-SITE is at 66 Albert St (Christmas–Jan daily 9am–5pm; Feb–Christmas Eve Mon–Fri 9am–5pm, Sat & Sun 9am–4pm; ☎ 07 866 5555, ⓦ thecoromandel.com). Internet service is available here.

GETTING AROUND

By ferry A passenger ferry (ⓦ whitiangaferry.co.nz) between Whitianga Wharf and Ferry Landing (daily: 7.30am–6.30pm, 7.30–8.30pm & 9.30–10.30pm, later in summer; $3 single, $5 return) runs roughly every 10min; the crossing takes 3min.

By bus BusIt (☎ 0800 427 546, ⓦ busit.co.nz) runs a regular service ($3 one way) from Ferry Landing to Cooks Beach, Hahei and Hot Water Beach from Boxing Day until early Feb, with around four buses a day and extra on New Year's Eve. Cathedral Cove Shuttles (☎ 027 422 5899, ⓦ www.cathedralcoveshuttles.co.nz) is essentially an on-demand taxi service between Ferry Landing, Cooks

Beach, Hahei and Hot Water Beach. With NakedBus you can visit either Hot Water Beach or Hahei from Whitianga for around 4hr before catching the onward bus to Tairua.

By car Getting to Hahei and Hot Water Beach by car takes around half an hour: head 25km southeast on SH2 to Whenuakite and turn north onto minor roads.

By bike Hahei Beach Bikes (2 Margot Place ☎ 021 028 64594, ⓦ haheibeachbikes.co.nz). Best call ahead to book – especially if you want meeting at Ferry Landing. You can also collect from Cathedral Cove Dive. Bikes come with a spade (for Hot Water Beach) or storage box ($45/day). Daily 8am–6pm.

ACCOMMODATION

As one of the Coromandel's main tourist centres, Whitianga has plenty of accommodation, augmented by places around Hot Water Beach, Hahei and even Kuaotunu (see p.332), 16km north. In addition to advance bookings in summer, be prepared for higher prices than on the rest of the peninsula (especially anywhere with a sea view) and minimum stays in peak periods.

TOURS AND ACTIVITIES AROUND WHITIANGA AND MERCURY BAY

BONE CARVING

Bay Carving 5 Coghill St ☎021 105 2151, ⓦbaycarving.com. German carver Roland Baumgart offers short (1.5–2hr) carve-your-own sessions (from $45) based on set patterns using cattle bone blanks.
The Bone Studio 6b Bryce St ☎07 866 2158,

ⓦcarving.co.nz. Master carver Ian Thorne's beautiful pieces are sold in galleries across NZ. He takes only a couple of budding carvers at a time, giving just the right amount of guidance and encouraging self-expression to produce your own art. Bookings essential. $120/full day.

KAYAKING

Cathedral Cove Kayak Tours 88 Hahei Beach Rd, Hahei ☎0800 529 258, ⓦseakayaktours.co.nz. Hahei Beach is the launch pad for professional, guided sea-kayak half-day trips ($105) either to Cathedral Cove

and the islands offshore, or into the sea caves to the south. Full-day trips ($170) combine the two, and they offer shorter but wonderful dawn and sunset trips (Dec–Feb only; $105). Pick-ups available from Ferry Landing.

BOAT TRIPS

All trips cover pretty much the same territory, between Whitianga and Hot Water Beach, including Cathedral Cove and its marine reserve.

Cave Cruzer Adventures Whitianga Wharf ☎0800 427 893, ⓦcavecruzer.co.nz. RIB tours past Shakespeare Cliff to Cathedral Cove and beyond. The Express tour departs 9am & 4.30pm (1hr plus; $50); an extended and more leisurely variation departs 10.30am & 1.30pm (2hr plus; $75).
Glass Bottom Boat Whitianga Wharf ☎07 876 1962, ⓦglassbottomboatwhitianga.co.nz. Two-hour trips ($95) with the chance to see what's below

the surface. Departures daily at 10.30am & 1.30pm, and more in summer.
Hahei Explorer Hahei ☎07 866 3910, ⓦhaheiexplorer.co.nz. A rigid-hull inflatable that takes small groups on exhilarating hour-long sea-cave trips (2–4 departures daily; call ahead for times; $75), visiting Cathedral Cove and an amazing blowhole, with an entertaining commentary.

DIVING

Scuba diving and snorkelling in Cathedral Cove Marine Reserve and along the coast can be arranged through a couple of companies, both offering first-time dives and full instruction courses.

Cathedral Cove Dive 48 Hahei Beach Rd, Hahei ☎07 866 3955, ⓦcathedralcovedive.co.nz. Perfectly located to get you quickly into the marine reserve, come to this friendly, family-run business to rent snorkelling gear for Gemstone Bay ($20), opt for a boat-based snorkelling trip ($85 with all gear) or take a dive trip (single dive $120; 2 dives $225; all gear

included). If you've never dived before, take their Discover Scuba dive ($195).
Dive Zone 7 Blacksmith Lane, Whitianga ☎07 867 1580, ⓦdivezonewhitianga.co.nz. A wide range of snorkelling and dive trips ($225 for 2 dives with all gear) plus snorkelling or diving from sit-on-top kayaks. It's great fun and prices are usually cheaper than a boat dive.

WHITIANGA

Beachfront Resort 113 Buffalo Beach Rd ☎07 866 5637, ⓦbeachfrontresort.co.nz; map p.334. Luxurious yet kid-friendly motel, right on the beach, with eight spacious units with sea views and private balconies. Guests can use the spa pool, BBQ, kayaks, and boogie boards. $200
Cat's Pyjamas 12 Albert St ☎07 866 4663, ⓦcats-pyjamas.co.nz; map p.334. Cosy central hostel a 2min walk from the town centre and beach, with graffitied common areas, and a sunny courtyard. Corrugated plastic walls give some privacy in the largest (10-bed) dorm. Dorms $25, double $60
Mana-Nui Motor Lodge 20 Albert St ☎07 866 5599, ⓦmananui.co.nz; map p.334. A centrally located,

comfortable motel with twelve fully self-contained ground-floor units (some of which have two bedrooms), plus a pool and spa. The owners are lovely. $130
Mercury Bay Holiday Park 121 Albert St ☎07 866 5579, ⓦmercurybayholidaypark.co.nz; map p.334. Sheltered, award-winning site about 700m from the town centre with barbecues, a pool and free spades for Hot Water Beach. Camping $20, motel units $135
★**On the Beach Backpackers Lodge** 46 Buffalo Beach Rd ☎07 866 5380, ⓦcoromandelbackpackers.com; map p.334. Whitianga's best hostel, this associate YHA is a 10min walk north of town and just across the road from the beach and a grassy reserve. A couple of the dorms are en-suite and most of the doubles and twins are in self-contained

5

apartment-style units with barbecues. Kayaks, boogie boards and spades for Hot Water Beach are all free, and bike rentals are available. Dorms $26, doubles $80

Turtle Cove 14 Bryce St ☎07 867 1517, ⓦturtlecove .co.nz; map p.334. Just a 5min walk from the beach and town. There are stylish rooms (some en-suite) in the main building (the doubles next to the lounge can get noisy) and garden-set cabins. The facilities are good and include free local calls, free pool table and free breakfast. Dorms $27, doubles $70

HAHEI

Cathedral Cove B&B 14 Cathedral Court ☎021 722 402, ⓦcathedralcovebandb.co.nz; map p.335. With spades and torches for Hot Water Beach, umbrellas for the local beach, a book exchange and all manner of caring touches, the owners of this modern, sustainably minded B&B seem to have thought of everything. Pine-panelled rooms are very comfy and the breakfasts are excellent. $230
★**The Church** 87 Beach Rd ☎07 866 3533, ⓦthechurchhahei.co.nz; map p.335. Lovely array of handcrafted cottages in a garden setting, all facing the sun, most with leadlight windows and some with wood fires. Continental breakfast trays available ($12). Studios $140, self-contained cottages $215

Hahei Holiday Resort 41 Harsant Ave ☎07 866 3889, ⓦhaheiholidays.co.nz; map p.335. Located on half a kilometre of beachfront an easy walk from Cathedral Cove and close to restaurants so popular with the buses, the

options here include powered sites right on the beach (2 people $40), dorms in a basic backpacker lodge, and luxurious self-contained beachfront villas ($260). Cabins $80, cottages $170

Tatahi Lodge 13 Grange Rd ☎07 866 3992, ⓦtatahilodge.co.nz; map p.335. Tranquilly set in bush and gardens, just footsteps from cafés and shops and with easy access to Cathedral Cove, your options here comprise self-contained timber-lined units ($220), airy backpacker accommodation, and a tucked-away cottage that sleeps five ($260). Free spades. Dorms $32, studios $155

HOT WATER BEACH

★**Auntie Dawns Place** 15 Radar Rd ☎07 866 3707, ⓦauntiedawn.co.nz; map p.335. This hillside house overlooking the beach offers true Kiwi hospitality. They've been welcoming guests here for decades, and the home brew (which is regularly shared) is better than ever. There are two simple yet comfortable self-contained apartments for two, and a caravan just a 3min walk along a hidden track from Hot Water Beach. $120

Hot Water Beach Top 10 Holiday Park 790 Hot Water Beach Rd, Hot Water Beach ☎800 246 823, ⓦhotwaterbeachtop10.co.nz; map p.335. Friendly owners and modern amenities, plus a sunny glassed-in guest lounge and an on-site shop serving fresh fish and chips in summer. Family campers have a separate area to the under-25s, so the Kiwi Experience bus shouldn't disturb you. Camping $21, cabins $80, en-suite chalets $150

EATING AND DRINKING

WHITIANGA

★**Blue Ginger** 10 Blacksmith Lane ☎07 867 1777, ⓦblueginger.co.nz; map p.334. Great little eat-in or takeaway spot serving delectable morsels such as *banh mi* ($12.50) and beef *rendang* ($22). On Fridays there are doughnuts. Summer daily 10.30am–10pm (closed for an hour each afternoon); winter Tues–Fri 11am–2pm, Sat 5.30pm–late.

Café Nina 20 Victoria St ☎07 866 5440; map p.334. Café in one of Whitianga's oldest cottages serving made-to-order dishes such as chicken Caesar salad ($16), or vegetarian, vegan and gluten-free options including *spanakopita* ($8.50). They also do great coffee and home-made carrot cake. There's a sweet patio on the edge of the Reserve. Daily 8am–3pm or later.

Coghill House Café 10 Coghill St ☎07 866 0592, ⓦthecog.co.nz; map p.334. Relaxing café that's good for breakfast ($10–18), as well as snacks such as sausage rolls. Daily 7am–4.30pm.

Salt Restaurant and Bar Whitianga Marina Hotel, The Esplanade ☎07 866 5818, ⓦsalt-whitianga.co.nz; map p.334. Beachy-chic lunch and dinner café/bar with decking onto the marina, serving à la carte evening mains (under

$36) such as goat's cheese and leek ravioli. Bands sometimes play here in summer. Daily 11.30am–10pm or later.

Squids 15/1 Blacksmiths Lane ☎07 867 1710; map p.334. Wine bar, good for a few drinks and good-value portions (most evening mains under $30) such as 1kg mussel pots with fries. Winter Mon–Sat noon–2pm & 5.30–9pm; summer daily 3.30–9pm or later.

FERRY LANDING

★**Eggsentric** 1049 Purangi Rd, Flaxmill Bay, 1km west of Ferry Landing ☎07 866 0316, ⓦeggsentriccafe.co.nz; map p.335. Quirky place where the tables are scattered among the sculpture-strewn gardens and the colourful interior comes alive in the evenings with acoustic music and poetry readings, particularly on Fridays. Simple but superb dishes might include macadamia-crumbed scallops ($20). Try the home-made ice cream. Tues–Sun 9am–10pm.

HAHEI

★**The Church** 87 Beach Rd ☎07 866 3797, ⓦwww .thechurchhahei.com; map p.335. A wooden former Methodist church, trucked here from Taumarunui, makes a lovely setting for this classy tapas restaurant (plates

$6–26). Best to grab a friend or two so you can enjoy the chef-patron's selection ($42pp; min 2). The wines are excellent, too. Daily 5.30–10pm, but often closed in winter if it is quiet.

The Pour House 7 Grange Rd ☎07 866 3354, ⓦcoromandelbrewingcompany.co.nz; map p.335. Coromandel Brewing Company bar and restaurant, offering their finest beer alongside generous portions of burgers, fish and chips, and gourmet pizzas ($20–25). Winter Mon–Fri 3–10pm, Sat & Sun noon–late; summer daily 11am–late.

HOT WATER BEACH

Hot Waves Café 8 Pye Place ☎07 866 3887; map p.335. Stylish licensed café with airy dining areas and an attractive garden setting, serving light meals such as Greek salad or breakfast burrito ($12–16), snacks and excellent coffee. Book exchange too. Daily 8.30am–4pm.

PURANGI

★**Purangi Winery** 450 Purangi Road ☎07 866 3724; map p.335. Rustic bar with foosball, snooker and table tennis plus great gardens for lounging, wood-fired pizzas (including a banana-berry-chocolate-dessert-pizza for $20). There's a great range of drinks too: try the feijoa and apple cider, lemon gin, or Sauvignon blanc from their 60-acre vineyard. Daily wine-tasting 10am–6pm, food noon–8pm, bar 10am–late.

WHENUAKITE

★**Colenso Country Shop & Café** SH25, 2km south of Whenuakite ☎07 866 3725, ⓦcolensocafe.co.nz; map p.335. Sit in the delightful gardens, on the sunny deck or inside this excellent café where great care is taken preparing the likes of olive and sundried tomato tarte with salad ($15), lamb pie ($6.50), toothsome cakes and great coffee. Daily Oct–April 10am–5pm, May–July & Sept 10am–4pm.

Tairua

Diminutive and pretty **TAIRUA**, 22km south of Hot Water Beach and 44km from Whitianga, nestles between pine-forested hills and the estuary of the Tairua River. Mostly popular with holidaying Kiwis, it's separated from the crashing Pacific breakers by two opposing and almost touching peninsulas: one is covered by the exclusive suburban sprawl of anodyne **Pauanui**; the other is crowned by the impressive volcanic **Mount Paku**, which can be climbed (10min ascent from car park, 30min ascent from beach) for spectacular views over the town, its estuary and beaches.

ARRIVAL AND INFORMATION

TAIRUA

By bus Daily NakedBus and InterCity buses from Auckland, Thames and Whitianga stop at the information centre.
Tourist information 223 Main St (Mon–Fri 9am–5pm,

Sat & Sun 9am–4pm; ☎07 864 7575, ⓦtairua.info). Tairua's information centre can organize accommodation and sells bus tickets.

GETTING AROUND

By ferry A five-minute passenger ferry ride links Tairua and Pauanui (Dec–Easter 9am–5pm every 2hr; $8 return,

$5 one way). Check updated schedules with the information centre.

Opoutere

Around 20km south of Tairua, a 5km side road leads to **Opoutere**, a tiny harbourside retreat at the foot of a mountain with a gorgeous, wild sweep of white-sand **surf beach** backed by pines. The pohutukawa-fringed road hugs the shores of the Wharekawa Harbour where wetlands make good birdwatching spots, mudflats yield shellfish and the calm waters are good for kayaking.

Opoutere Beach

1km east of Opoutere

At the junction of Opoutere and Ohui roads, Opoutere Beach car park has a footbridge leading to two paths, both reaching the beach in ten minutes or so. The left fork runs straight through the forest to the usually deserted **beach**, while the right-hand track follows the estuary to the edge of the **Wharekawa Harbour Sandspit Wildlife Refuge**, where endangered New Zealand **dotterels** breed from November to March. Opoutere Beach can have a strong undertow and there are no lifeguards, so don't swim. It's an

5

unofficial nudist beach, but even if you're clothed, be sure to bring repellent to guard against sandflies.

Mount Maungaruawahine

2km return; 40–50min

For a wider view over the estuary and the coastline, tackle the track up **Mount Maungaruawahine**, climbing through gnarled pohutukawa and other native trees to the summit where there are sweeping vistas of the estuary and out towards the coast. The summit track begins just before the gate to the *YHA* (see below).

ARRIVAL AND INFORMATION OPOUTERE

By bus There's no regular bus service, but drop-offs can be arranged with Go Kiwi (see p.321).

Groceries You'll need to bring all your food as there is no shop, and lodgings offer only basic provisions.

ACCOMMODATION

Opoutere Coastal Camping 460 Ohui Rd, 700m beyond the YHA ☎07 865 9152, ⊛opouterebeach.co.nz. There's direct beachfront access from this well-maintained campsite in a secluded setting amid pines and pohutukawas. There are also rustic cabins with limited facilities but great views, and some more sophisticated chalets ($140). Closed May–late Oct. Camping **$23**, cabins **$100**

YHA Opoutere Opoutere Rd ☎07 865 9072, ⊛yha.co.nz. Old-school in both senses, this traditional YHA beside the estuary occupies a 1908 schoolhouse and surrounding wooden buildings amid mature bush alive with the calls of native birds. There's free use of kayaks and the chance for nocturnal glowworm spotting. Look out for the kaka. Closed Sun–Thurs between May and late Oct. Dorms **$27**, rooms **$80**

Whangamata

The summer resort town of **WHANGAMATA**, 15km south of Opoutere, is bounded on three sides by estuaries and the ocean, and on the fourth by bush-clad hills. **Ocean Beach**, a 4km-long crescent of white sand, curves from the harbour to the mouth of the **Otahu River**. The sandbar at the harbour end has an excellent left-hand break that's sought after by **surfers**.

The main drag, Port Road, runs straight through the small town centre, linking it with SH25.

Wentworth Falls

The track starts at the DOC campsite (see opposite) 5km down Wentworth Valley Rd, which is off SH25 about 2km south of town • Walk 10km return; 2hr

One of the best ways to pass a couple of hours is to **walk** to **Wentworth Falls** in the Wentworth Valley which cuts into foothills of the Coromandel Range, 7km southwest of town. It is a lovely walk on well-maintained paths winding gradually uphill through regenerating bush past numerous small swimming holes. The route continues into the heart of the mountains, but most turn around at the pretty two-leap 50m falls, best viewed from a small deck.

ARRIVAL AND DEPARTURE WHANGAMATA

By bus Go Kiwi (☎0800 446 549, ⊛go-kiwi.co.nz) run from Auckland via Thames to Whangamata (change at Hikuai).

Destinations Auckland (1 daily; 3hr 10min); Thames (1 daily; 1hr).

INFORMATION AND TOURS

Visitor information i-SITE is at 616 Port Rd (Mon–Sat 10am–5pm, Sun 9am–2pm; until 5pm Sun, Oct–March; ☎07 865 8340, ⊛thecoromandel.com/whangamata).

Whangamata Surf Shop 634 Port Road ☎07 865 8252, ⊛whangamatasurfschool.co.nz. There are a number of surf shops along Port Rd which will rent you a

board or arrange a lesson, but only one run by the parents of a world champion surfer (Ella Williams). A one-to-one lesson is $80/hr. Mon–Sat 9am–5pm.

Pedal and Paddle 100 Hunt Rd ☎07 865 8096, ⊛pedalandpaddlenz.com. Huge range of bikes, kayaks and SUPs from the experts. Check the website for the full range (even hiring fat bikes), call in for gossip and advice on trips to the islands or to Whangamata Ridges mountain bike park. Double kayak $70/day; SUP $20/hr, $70/day; road bike $30/day; mountain bike $50/day.

Kiwi Dundee Adventures ☎07 865 8809, ⓦ kiwidundee.co.nz. Dedicated conservationist Doug Johansen (aka "Kiwi Dundee") runs a variety of day- and multi-day ecotours incorporating wildlife experiences and paths off the beaten track. Full-day trips, including lunch and pick-ups from accommodation in Tairua, Pauanui and Whangamata, cost $245; book well in advance.

ACCOMMODATION

Breakers Motel 318 Heatherington Rd ☎0800 865 8464, ⓦ breakersmotel.co.nz. Modern motel with spacious units, many of which have spa pools and views over the marina. There's also a large swimming pool and breakfast is available. $175

★**Brenton Lodge** 2 Brenton Place ☎07 865 8400, ⓦ brentonlodge.co.nz. A garden-set retreat with sea views on the edge of Whangamata, with two beautifully decorated cottages (sleeping two) and two suites, as well as a sparkling swimming pool, spa, fresh flowers, home-made chocolates and delicious breakfasts. Three-course dinner on request ($75). $435

Southpacific Accommodation Corner of Port Rd and Mayfair Ave ☎07 865 9580, ⓦ thesouthpacific.co.nz. An immaculate motel (with full kitchens in some rooms) and conference centre. Guests have free use of kayaks and surfboards. Units $150

Wentworth Valley Campground Wentworth Valley Rd, 7km southwest of Whangamata ☎07 865 7032, ⓦ wentworthvalleycamp.co.nz. Chilled DOC campsite with streamside pitches, BBQs, ice cream for sale in the office and coin-operated hot showers, right by the start of the track to Wentworth Falls. $10

EATING

Argo 328A Ocean Rd ☎07 865 7157, ⓦ argorestaurant .co.nz. Whangamata's finest dining spot has a reassuringly short menu (mains $33, though you'll probably want an extra side for $8), and great selection of NZ wines and craft beers. Jan–March daily 8.30am–11.30pm, April–Dec 5.30pm–10pm.

Minato Sushi 713 Port Rd ☎07 865 8680. Wonderful sushi spot, with meticulously prepared fish; platters ($38) to share are a speciality. Mon–Sat 8.30–2pm.

Six Forty Six 646 Port Rd ☎07 865 6117. Contemporary café serving a range of breakfasts, cakes and good coffee. Try the king prawn taco ($14). Daily 8am–4pm, Fri & Sat 8am–9pm in the summer.

Waihi and around

SH25 and SH2 meet at the southernmost town on the Coromandel Peninsula, **WAIHI**, 30km south from Whangamata. The small town merits a quick stop to sample its gold mining, both past and present.

Brief history

Gold was first discovered here in a reef of quartz in 1878, but it wasn't until 1894 that a boom began with the first successful trials in extracting gold using cyanide solution. Workers flocked, but disputes over union and non-union labour ensued, and the violent **Waihi Strike** of 1912 helped galvanize the labour movement and led to the creation of the Labour Party.

Although underground mining stopped in 1952, extraction was cranked up again in 1987 in the open-pit but well-hidden Martha Mine. As the open-pit mine slowly winds down (possibly closing around 2020), recent finds of deep veins have refocused mining minds on tunnel mining.

Cornish pumphouse

Seddon St • Free

In the last few years, the hollow concrete shell of a three-storey 1904 **Cornish-style pumphouse** has become the town's icon and most prominent feature. It once kept the mine dry by pumping 300 tonnes of water an hour, then languished in an increasingly precarious position on the edge of the open-cast mine. Then, over a period of three months in 2006, hydraulic rams slid the building 296m on teflon pads and steel

5

runners to its current central location. The move was ostensibly to save the historic building, but also allowed the mine to expand into new territory.

Mine viewpoint and the Pit Rim Walkway

Walk behind the Cornish pumphouse to the **mine viewpoint**, where you can peer 260m down into the abyss where 85-tonne dump trucks look like toys. For more pit views follow the **Pit Rim Walkway** (4km loop; 1hr), an almost level track which circumnavigates the mine past a number of explanatory panels and one of the huge dump trucks.

Waihi Arts Centre & Museum

54 Kenny St • Jan Sat–Mon noon–3pm, Thurs & Fri 10am–3pm ; Feb–Dec Thurs–Mon noon–3pm • $5 • ☎ 07 863 8386, ⓦ waihimuseum.co.nz

Mining life, including the 1912 strike, is conjured up evocatively in displays at the **Waihi Arts Centre & Museum**. Check out the diorama of the Victoria Battery and the ants' nest-like model of the original fifteen-level-deep Waihi mine; only the uppermost eight levels have been chewed out by the current open-cast incarnation. There's also a small-scale stamper battery, a model of the Cornish pumphouse, a re-created gold mine tunnel, and a couple of **thumbs** preserved in formaldehyde. Miners once deliberately chopped off a thumb to get £500 compensation – enough to buy a small cottage they'd otherwise never be able to afford on miners' wages.

Gold Discovery Centre

126 Seddon St • Daily 9am–5pm • $25 ($46 incl. mine tour) • ☎ 07 863 9015, ⓦ golddiscoverycentre.co.nz

Well-presented, if a little glossy, with an emphasis on participation – try your hand with the pneumatic drill, set off dynamite, gamble at cards and pick up a gold ingot. There are also a fair few facts, and a great Lego model.

Goldfields Railway

End of Wrigley St • Weekends, public holidays and school holidays daily 10am, 11.45am & 1.45pm; rest of year Mon–Fri 11.45am • $12 single, $18 return • ☎ 07 863 9020, ⓦ waihirail.co.nz

The 1930s diesel engine of the **Goldfields Railway** runs scenic 6km rail trips west to Waikino in the nearby **Karangahake Gorge** (see p.316) along tracks built by a mining company. The return trip takes about an hour, provides attractive views of the Ohinemuri River and allows a few minutes at the far end to inspect the displays on local history. Hire a bike and cycle back.

Waihi Beach

11km east of Waihi

The 9km-long golden-sand surf beach of **WAIHI BEACH**, 11km east of Waihi, is one of the safest ocean beaches in the country. Although the area has something of a suburban feel, there's an excellent campsite that justifies the detour off SH2.

ARRIVAL AND DEPARTURE **WAIHI AND AROUND**

By bus InterCity and NakedBus buses on their Auckland–Tauranga runs stop outside the visitor centre in Waihi.

Destinations Auckland (4 daily; 3hr); Tauranga (4 daily; 1hr).

INFORMATION AND TOURS

Information The i-SITE is at 126 Seddon St (daily 9am–5pm; ☎ 07 863 6715, ⓦ waihi.org.nz), in the same building as the mine tour office and mining display. Pay internet available.

Waihi gold-mine tours Pick-up from i-SITE (Mon–Sat 10.30am & 12.30pm; $29, $46 incl. Discovery Centre; ☎ 07 863 9015, ⓦ waihigoldminetours.co.nz). As a complement

to the Discovery Centre, the mine company offers a 1.5-hour guided tour to the mine rim, and then to the other end of the 2.7km conveyor belt where the ore is processed. It's partly to demonstrate how environmentally friendly they are (dotterel nest at the waste dump), but even grown-ups will be thrilled by the size of the machinery here.

ACCOMMODATION AND EATING

Bowentown Beach Holiday Park 510 Seaforth Rd, Bowentown Beach ☎ 0800 143 769, ⌨ bowentown .co.nz. A secluded site right at the southern end of the beach with lots of water activities available, new showers, an adult TV room plus bike and kayak rental for guests. Camping $26, cabins $75, apartments $160

The Porch 23 Wilson Rd, Waihi Beach ☎ 07 863 1330, ⌨ theporchwaihibeach.co.nz. Waihi Beach's dining mainstay for everything from chilli hot chocolate and cake to a sundowner dinner mains such as chicken breast with roast *kumara* ($28). Winter Mon–Thu & Sun 8am–4pm, Fri & Sat 8am–11pm; summer daily 8am–11pm.

Ti-Tree Café 14 Haszard St, Waihi ☎ 07 863 8668. Grab a coffee at this great little café with a wood-floored interior

and a garden out back. Food spans the likes of pumpkin feta frittata ($16.50) and "world famous" chowder to evening wood-fired pizzas ($18–26). Gluten-free options available, occasional live music. Mon–Sat 6.30am–3pm, Thurs & Fri also 5.30–8.30pm.

Waitete Restaurant 31 Orchard Rd, 1.5km west of Waihi ☎ 07 863 8980, ⌨ waitete.co.nz. Combined restaurant, café and ice creamery that serves superb natural ice creams and fat-free sorbets made in the small on-site factory. Lunch is a relaxed affair with dishes such as samosa and salad ($17), while dinner is more linen-and-candles formal and features the likes of grilled pork belly with blueberry sauce and pumpkin purée ($32). Daily 11am–4pm & 6–10pm.

Katikati

South of Waihi, the coast begins to curl eastwards into the Bay of Plenty, leaving the bush-clad mountains behind to take on a gentler, more open aspect, with rolling hills divided by tall evergreen shelter belts that protect the valuable kiwifruit vines. In summer, numerous **roadside fruit stalls** spring up, selling ripe produce straight from the orchards, often at knockdown prices.

Some 20km after leaving Waihi you pass **KATIKATI**, an otherwise ordinary town but for the colourful and well-painted **murals** that have sprung up in the last couple of decades to catch passing traffic, many reflecting the heritage of the original Ulster settlers.

The Bay of Plenty

The **Bay of Plenty** occupies the huge bite between the Coromandel Peninsula and the East Cape, backed by rich farmland famous for its **kiwifruit orchards**. Its western end centres on the prosperous and fast-growing port city of **Tauranga** and its beachside neighbour **Mount Maunganui**. These amorphous settlements essentially form a single small conurbation sprawled around the glittering tentacles of Tauranga Harbour. A combination of warm dry summers and mild winters initially attracted retirees, followed by telecommuters and home-based small businesses.

Both towns have a thriving **restaurant** and **bar** scene, and a number of boats help you get out on the water to **sail**, or **swim with dolphins**. On land, make for Tauranga's modern **art gallery**, or head inland to picnic beside the swimming holes at **McLaren Falls** or paddle to see **glowworms**. With all this, it comes as no surprise that the area is a big draw for Kiwi summer holiday-makers.

Heading southeast along the Pacific Coast Highway (SH2), the urban influence wanes, the pace slows and the landscape becomes more rural, with orchards gradually

---

KIWIFRUIT-PICKING

Tauranga is a major centre for **kiwifruit-picking**, a tough and prickly task that generally requires a commitment of at least three weeks. The picking season is late April to mid-June, but pruning and pollen collection also take place from mid-June to early September and again from the end of October to January. You're usually paid by the bin or by the kilo, so speed is of the essence. If this doesn't put you off, you'll find up-to-date information at the backpacker hostels, which will often help you arrange work.

5

giving way to sheep country. You'll also find a gradual change in the racial mix, for the eastern Bay of Plenty is mostly **Maori** country; appropriate since some of the first Maori to reach New Zealand arrived here in their great *waka* (canoes). In fact, **Whakatane** is sometimes known as the birthplace of Aotearoa, as the Polynesian navigator **Toi te Huatahi** first landed here. Whakatane makes a great base for forays to volcanic **White Island** or the bird reserve of **Whale Island**. Further east, **Opotiki** is the gateway to the East Cape and to Gisborne, as well as trips on the remote and scenic **Motu River**.

Tauranga

Once you're through the protecting ring of suburbs, it's apparent that rampant development hasn't completely spoilt central **TAURANGA** ("safe anchorage" in Maori), huddled on a narrow peninsula with city parks and gardens backing a lively waterfront area. You can easily spend half a day here, checking out the art gallery, strolling along the waterfront or lingering in the shops, restaurants and bars in the compact **city centre**, concentrated between Tauranga Harbour and Waikareao Estuary. Come summer, though, you'll soon want to head over to Mount Maunganui (see p.349).

Brief history

In 1864 the tiny community of Tauranga became the scene of the **Battle of Gate Pa**, one of the most decisive engagements of the **New Zealand Wars**. In January the government sent troops to build two redoubts, hoping to prevent supplies and reinforcements from reaching the followers of the Maori King (see p.216), who were fighting in the Waikato. Most of the local Ngaiterangi hurried back from the Waikato and challenged the soldiers from a *pa* they quickly built near an entrance to the mission land, which became known as Gate Pa. In April, government troops surrounded the *pa* in what was New Zealand's only naval blockade, and pounded it with artillery. Despite this, the British lost about a third of their assault force and at nightfall the Ngaiterangi slipped through the British lines to fight again in the Waikato.

The Rena oil spill

In October 2011, the area became the focus of attention when the MV *Rena* container ship grounded on the **Astrolabe Reef**, 20km northeast of Mount Maunganui. Images of crazily tilted stacks of containers on the back of the severely listing ship zipped around the world as rescue crews tried to save the local beaches and birds from the slick of leaking fuel oil. All appears back to normal today, though the ship (now in two parts) remains on the reef.

Tauranga Art Gallery

108 Willow St • Daily 10am–4.30pm • Free • ☏ 07 578 7933, ⓦ artgallery.org.nz

After a determined fifteen-year campaign to give the city a contemporary cultural attraction, the **Tauranga Art Gallery** opened in 2007. A former bank building has been so transformed with layered metal sheets that it has been dubbed "the armadillo". There's no permanent display inside, but its series of clean-lined display spaces over two floors are a great blank canvas for excellent national and international travelling exhibitions.

Te Awanui and Robbins Park

The Strand • Free

A protective awning on the Strand shelters *Te Awanui*, the carved traditional **war canoe** that is still used on ceremonial occasions on the harbour. The Strand continues north to **Robbins Park**, a swathe of green adorned by a rose garden and begonia house with fine views of Mount Maunganui. This was the site of Monmouth Redoubt from the New Zealand Wars (see p.792).

CENTRAL TAURANGA

■ ACCOMMODATION

Harbour View Motel	5
Harbourside City Backpackers	2
Hotel on Devonport	4
Loft 109	3
Strand Motel	1

● EATING & DRINKING

Bahama Bar	1
Bravo	5
Brew Bar	4
Café Mediterraneo	6
Café Versailles	8
Cornerstone	2
Crown & Badger	3
Grindz	9
Harbourside Brasserie & Bar	7

The Elms Mission House

Mission St • Public holidays, Wed, Sat & Sun 2–4pm, and by appointment • $5 • ☎ 07 577 9772, ⓦ theelms.org.nz

The Elms Mission House, at the northern end of town, is one of the country's oldest homes, built from kauri between 1835 and 1847 by an early missionary, Archdeacon A.N. Brown, who tended the wounded of both sides during the **Battle of Gate Pa** (see p.344). The house has maintained its original form complete with dark-wood interior

5

TUHUA (MAYOR ISLAND)

The ecotourism-geared **Tuhua (Mayor Island)** is a cone-shaped, dormant volcano protruding from the Bay of Plenty and accessed by boat from Tauranga, 40km to the south. Its crater is virtually overgrown and the whole place is threaded with great **walking tracks** that open up a landscape thick with healthy populations of bellbird, tui, wood pigeon, fantail, grey warbler, waxeye, kingfisher, pied tit, kaka, morepork, shining cuckoo and harrier hawk. As there are no natural predators on the island, the birds are quite fearless and can be viewed at close range. **Wasps** are abundant, however, and anyone allergic to stings should pack medication or stay away. A third of the island's coast has been designated as a **marine reserve**, making for excellent **snorkelling**: many boats will rent snorkelling gear (around $20/day).

TOURS AND ACCOMMODATION

Blue Ocean Charters (☎0800 224 278, ⓦblueocean.co.nz) run day-trips to the island several times a week in summer (7am–5.30pm; $130), giving you around 8hr on land. That's just about enough to fully explore the place, though you'll appreciate it more if you stay overnight in simple cabins ($35; ☎07 578 7677, ⓔtaurangainfo@doc.govt.nz) or camping ($15/person) at Opo, the bay where you land. Blue Ocean don't charge any extra for overnight stays. To preserve Tuhua's pest-free status, all luggage must be thoroughly checked for stowaways.

and a dining table at which Brown entertained several British officers on the eve of the battle, little suspecting that over the next few days he would bury them all. Other buildings in the beautiful grounds include a Fencible Cottage (given to retired British soldiers).

ARRIVAL AND DEPARTURE
TAURANGA

By plane The airport lies midway between Tauranga and Mount Maunganui (around 3km from each). Bus #2 goes to both towns but there are few evening services, so you may want to catch a cab: the fare to either is around $15.
Destinations Auckland (5 daily; 35min); Christchurch (2 daily; 1hr 50min); Wellington (4 daily; 1hr 15min).

By bus InterCity and NakedBus long-distance buses stop outside the Tauranga i-SITE.
Destinations Auckland (9 daily; 3hr 40min); Hamilton (4 daily; 2hr); Napier (2 daily; 2hr 45min); Rotorua (4 daily; 1hr 30min); Taupo (5 daily; 2hr 50min); Thames (4 daily; 1hr 45min); Wellington (daily; 8hr 30min).

GETTING AROUND

Tauranga and Mount Maunganui are 6km apart, separated by the 3.5km-long Tauranga Harbour Bridge and an industrial estate linked to the Port of Tauranga.

By bus Bayhopper (☎0800 422 928, ⓦbaybus.co.nz) operates the services around Tauranga and Mount Maunganui, covering most places in the immediate vicinity. Routes #1 and #2 run between Tauranga and Mount Maunganui. Single fares are $3; all-day passes are $7.
By taxi Try Tauranga Mount Taxis (☎07 578 6086). There's

a cab rank in Hamilton St (between the Strand and Willow St) in Tauranga. The fare between Tauranga and Mount Maunganui is around $30.
By bike Cycle Tauranga, 50 Wharf St (☎0800 253 525, ⓦcycletauranga.co.nz), rent hybrids good for town and around ($20/2hr; $49/day).

INFORMATION

Visitor information i-SITE is at 95 Willow St (daily 8.30am–5pm; ☎07 578 8103, ⓦbayofplentynz.com).
DOC 253 Chadwick Rd, Greerton, 6km south of central Tauranga (Mon–Fri 8am–4.30pm; ☎07 578 7677). They have details of charter operators for Mayor Island.

Services Free internet at the library, corner of Wharf and Willow sts (Mon–Fri 9.30am–5.30pm & Wed to 7pm, Sat 9.30am–4pm, Sun 11.30am–4pm). The Gateway Cyber Café, 50 Devonport Rd (Sat–Tues 9am–6pm, Wed–Fri 9am–10pm), charges $1/30min, $15/day.

ACCOMMODATION

Tauranga has numerous hostels and motels within walking distance of the centre, and plenty more out in the suburbs. A plethora of motels line 15th Avenue, some offering good deals at slack times of year.

★**Ambassador Motor Inn** 9 15th Ave ☎07 578 5665, ⓦambassador-motorinn.co.nz; map p.345. A 6min drive from the city centre, near the estuary, this has popular, well-equipped budget units and more luxurious options. There's a heated pool, some rooms have a spa bath, while others have river views. $110

★**Arthouse** 11 Beach Road, Otumoetai ☎07 578 0560; map p.345. Clean, modern and funky homestay with three rooms and a studio suite. Bright art, retro styling, continental breakfasts (home-made fruit salad) and great uninterrupted views across the bay to the Mount. About half an hour's walk from central Tauranga. Oh, and the owner's very helpful. $100

Bell Lodge 39 Bell St, off Waihi Rd (take Otumoetai exit off SH2) ☎07 578 6344, ⓦbell-lodge.co.nz; map p.351. Clean, modern and comfortable hostel with mostly en-suite rooms and bargain motel units ($95). It's well set up for job seekers, particularly those after long, hourly paid contracts. It's in a peaceful spot 4km from the centre, with free pick-up and a free daily shuttle to Mount Maunganui on request. Dorms $28, doubles $74

Harbourside City Backpackers 105 The Strand ☎07 579 4066, ⓦbackpacktauranga.co.nz; map p.345. Large hostel bang in the middle of the action. The waterfront views and tranquil atmosphere of the roof terrace make up for the basic rooms and noise on Fri and Sat nights (soundproofing from neighbouring bars and rooms at the rear of the building also help). Popular with workers who appreciate the management's good kiwifruit contacts. Dorms $32, doubles $74

Harbour View Motel 7 Fifth Ave East ☎07 578 8621, ⓦharbourviewmotel.co.nz; map p.345. Quiet and homey, recently upgraded units, just a 15min walk from town and a stone's throw from the bay. Free use of wi-fi, bikes and kayaks. Ideal for families. $125

Hotel on Devonport 72 Devonport Rd ☎07 578 2668, ⓦhotelondevonport.net.nz; map p.345. Sleek, modern boutique hotel with 38 rooms, all in muted tones with black-and-white photos on the walls and most with super-king-size beds and a minibar. Breakfast adds another $30. Higher-priced rooms ($240–300) have city and/or harbour views. $200

Just the Ducks Nuts 6 Vale St ☎07 576 1366, ⓦjusttheducksnuts.co.nz; map p.351. A small, family-run hostel 1.5km from the city centre up a very steep driveway. It's popular with workers, has great views of the harbour and the Mount, a piano and free pick-ups. Dorms $27, doubles $66

Loft 109 109 Devonport Rd ☎07 579 5638, ⓦloft109 .co.nz; map p.345. Slightly cramped but central and friendly hostel in a trendy townhouse-style building with a roof deck and nautical decor. Separate women's dorm. Dorms $30, doubles $74

Strand Motel 27 The Strand ☎07 578 5807, ⓦstrandmotel.co.nz; map p.345. Ageing budget motel that's central and near the waterfront, but on a fairly noisy corner. Most of the fully equipped units offer sea views from their front decks. $95

CAMPING

Silver Birch Family Holiday Park 101 Turret Rd ☎07 578 4603, ⓦsilverbirch.co.nz; map p.351. Fairly central campsite right on the river's edge with a family atmosphere, playground and hot mineral pools. Camping (2 people) $30, cabins $60

EATING

Most of Tauranga's cafés and restaurants are in the centre, notably along Devonport Road and the Strand. Fresh produce is sold at the Saturday-morning farmers' market (8am–noon) at the Tauranga Primary School at 31 5th Ave.

Bravo Red Square ☎07 578 4700, ⓦbravocafe.co.nz; map p.345. Cool, minimalist café and restaurant that spills onto the pedestrianized Red Square. Great counter food, or try the French toast with caramelized apple ($17) or calamari curry ($18.50). Winter Mon–Thurs 8am–4.30pm, Fri 8am–5pm, Sat & Sun 8.30am–5pm. Stays open for dinner until 9pm Tues–Sat Nov–Feb.

Café Mediterraneo 62 Devonport Rd ☎07 577 0487; map p.345. Also known as *The Med*, this popular café has good breakfasts, such as rhubarb compote and porridge ($9.50), tempting counter food, and specials (written on a giant wall-mounted roll of brown paper) including smoked salmon and capers in wine and cream sauce (dishes $9–19). Mon–Fri 7am–4pm, Sat 7.30am–4pm, Sun 8am–4pm.

★**Café Versailles** 107 Grey St ☎07 571 1480, ⓦwww .cafe-versailles.net; map p.345. If it wasn't for the super-helpful staff, you might almost believe you were in France. This award-winning authentic restaurant serves a wonderful range of traditional Gallic fare from snails ($18) to *boeuf bourguignon* ($29) and conversation-stopping crêpes suzette. Mon–Sat 3.30–9pm or later.

★**Grindz** 50 First Ave ☎07 579 0017; map p.345. Laidback Tardis-like neighbourhood café, with free wi-fi, zingy flat whites, cakes to die for, the biggest "mini" sausage rolls, and a ridiculous range of milks (soy, rice, almond, gluten-free, coconut). Mon–Fri 7am–4pm, Sat 8am–3.30pm, Sun 8.30am–3pm.

Harbourside Brasserie & Bar Under the railway bridge at the southern end of the Strand ☎07 571 0520, ⓦharboursidetauranga.co.nz; map p.345. Tucked under the rail bridge in a former dinghy storage shed, this fine-dining restaurant presents a short, stellar menu which might include half a dozen oysters with *yuzu kosho* ($24) followed by Chinese roast duck ($36). Daily 11.30am–10pm.

5

ACTIVITIES AROUND TAURANGA AND MOUNT MAUNGANUI

The Tauranga and Mount Maunganui region is great for getting out **on the water**. There's a full range of boats to take you cruising, fishing, sailing, swimming with dolphins and even out to Tuhua (Mayor Island). Tauranga Wharf has recently been overhauled, with a barge converted into a finger pier from which a number of trips depart. Others leave from Tauranga Bridge Marina, over on the Mount Maunganui side of the harbour.

DOLPHIN WATCHING

Dolphin Seafaris ☎ 0800 326 8747, ⊛ nzdolphin .com. Five-hour trips ($140) in a powerful cruiser with committed anti-whaling crew. Trips generally run

Nov–May (weather permitting), leaving at 8am. There's a repeat trip for dolphin no-shows.

FISHING

Blue Ocean Charters Tauranga Bridge Marina ☎ 0800 224 278, ⊛ blueocean.co.nz. Game fishing for marlin, tuna and kingfish (Dec–April), which involves chartering the boat (from $1250/day), but you can sometimes join an existing charter. Reef fishing for snapper and tarakihi goes for $100/person, with an extra $30 for tackle.

Deep Star Charters ☎ 07 575 8917, ⊛ deepstarcharters.co.nz. Regular reef-fishing trips ($80/day plus $30 for tackle and bait), plus overnight hapuku trips ($140 breakfast included, tackle $30) which involve reef fishing in the morning then seeking hapuku, blue nose and bass around Mayor Island later on.

SURFING

Discovery Surf 167 Marine Parade, Mount Maunganui ☎ 027 632 7873, ⊛ discoverysurf.co.nz. One of several outfits offering surfing lessons at the

Mount, with 2hr starter and improver group sessions ($90) and 2hr private lessons ($160 for one, $210 for two).

KAYAKING AND GLOWWORM KAYAKING

Canoe & Kayak 5 MacDonald St, Mount Maunganui ☎ 07 574 7415, ⊛ canoeandkayak.co.nz. Budget, guided kayak trips taking you either round the Mount (3–4hr; $129), or into a beautiful canyon overhung with trees on Lake McLaren (3hr; 1hr 30min paddling; $99). At the time of writing, a landslip prevented their

glowworm tours – contact them to check.
Waimarino 36 Taniwha Place, Bethlehem ☎ 07 576 4233, ⊛ waimarino.com. Offers kayak trips and unguided exploration of the placid sections of the Wairoa River ($65), and to the glowworm canyon on Lake McLaren, if running ($120, $190 with gourmet dinner).

DRINKING, NIGHTLIFE AND ENTERTAINMENT

Tauranga nights have two very different crowds – the early evening strollers and then the partygoers from 11pm onwards. Summer revelry continues into the wee hours along the Strand.

CLUBS AND BARS

Bahama Bar 10 Harington St; map p.345. Yes it's cheesy (surfboards, palm trees), yes it's been around for years, but it's still the best place to party and, er, play beer pong. Best walk on by if you're over 30. Wed 9pm–late, Thurs–Sat 10pm–3am.
Brew Bar 107 The Strand ☎ 07 578 3543, ⊛ brewpub .co.nz; map p.345. The craft beer, friendly staff, relaxed vibe, and live music at weekends would be enough. But add dirty food done well (try the pork belly with fried coleslaw $27) and tutored beer tastings (first Wednesday of the month, 6pm, $20), and this bar is just great. Mon & Tues 4pm–late, Wed–Sun 11am–late.
Cornerstone 55 The Strand ☎ 07 928 1120, ⊛ cornerstonepub.net.nz; map p.345. The live music, mostly cover bands, starts around 10pm nightly in summer,

and you should catch a few sessions per week at other times. Visit Sunday afternoons for jamming. Mon–Fri 10am–late, Sat & Sun 8.30am–late.
Crown & Badger Corner of the Strand and Wharf St ☎ 07 571 3038, ⊛ crownandbadger.co.nz; map p.345. Lively and sometimes frenetic English-style pub with decent enough beer and great-value meals such as pepper steak ($27). Daily 9am–10pm or later.

CINEMAS

Bay City Cinemas 45 Elizabeth St ☎ 07 577 0800, ⊛ baycitycinemas.co.nz; map p.345. Smart, multi-screen cinema showing mostly mainstream films, with discounts all day Tues.
Rialto Tauranga 21 Devonport Rd ☎ 07 577 0445, ⊛ rialtotauranga.co.nz; map p.345. Boutique

three-screener showing mostly art-house films in lush environs. Also has discounts before 5pm and all day Tues.

Mount Maunganui

Habitually sun-kissed in summer, Tauranga's neighbouring beach resort, **MOUNT MAUNGANUI**, huddles under the extinct volcano of the same name, a modest cone that's a visible landmark throughout the western Bay of Plenty. It was once an island but is connected to the mainland by a narrow neck of dune sand (a tombolo) now covered by "The Mount", as the town is usually known. The sprawl of apartment blocks, shops, restaurants and houses isn't especially pretty but is saved by the 20km-long golden strand of **Ocean Beach**, itself enhanced by a couple of pretty islands just offshore and lined by Norfolk pines. It's wonderful for swimming, surfing and beach volleyball, and there are good restaurants and bars nearby where everyone gravitates for sundowners. Naturally, it is a big draw for Kiwi holiday-makers, some of whom give it a party-town reputation, especially at New Year when the place can be overwhelming and accommodation hard to come by.

Exploring the Mount

Walking track 3km; 45min • Summit hike 2km one way; 1hr

The grassy slopes of the Mount (Mauao in Maori) rise 232m above the golden beach and invite exploration. A mostly level **walking track** loops around the base of the mountain, offering a sea and harbour outlook from under the shade of ancient pohutukawas. The base track links with a **hike to the summit** that is tough going towards the top but well worth the effort for views of Matakana Island and along the coast.

Hot Saltwater Pools

Adams Ave • Mon–Sat 6am–10pm, Sun 8am–10pm • public pool $10.80; private spa, not including public pool $15.60/30min • ☎ 07 577 8551, ⓦ tcal.co.nz

Wedged between the shopping strip

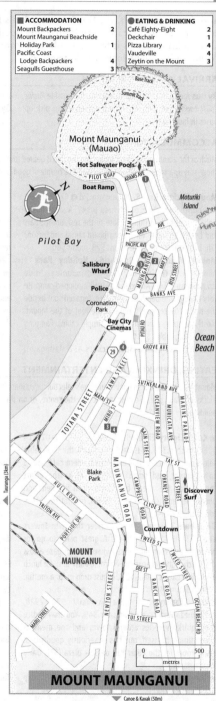

■ ACCOMMODATION	
Mount Backpackers	2
Mount Maunganui Beachside Holiday Park	1
Pacific Coast Lodge Backpackers	4
Seagulls Guesthouse	3

● EATING & DRINKING	
Café Eighty-Eight	2
Deckchair	1
Pizza Library	4
Vaudeville	4
Zeytin on the Mount	3

MOUNT MAUNGANUI

▼ Canoe & Kayak (50m)

5

and the Mount itself, the **Hot Saltwater Pools** harness deep geothermal groundwater to heat seawater, creating family-friendly open-air pools ranging from 33°C–39°C. Chlorination makes it feel more like a swimming pool, but after a stroll around the Mount a luxuriant soak is well deserved.

ARRIVAL AND INFORMATION   MOUNT MAUNGANU

By bus A couple of NakedBus services stop outside *Pacific Coast Lodge*, but it is often more convenient to pick up buses in Tauranga.

Destinations Auckland (2 daily; 3hr 45min).
By plane Mount Maunganui shares an airport with Tauranga (see p.346).

ACCOMMODATION

Much of the accommodation at Mount Maunganui is geared towards long-staying Kiwi holiday-makers, but you'll also fine short-stay apartments and motels, as well as a couple of good hostels.

Mount Backpackers 87 Maunganui Rd ☎07 575 0860, ⓦmountbackpackers.co.nz; map p.349. A small hostel right in the thick of things, close to the restaurants, bars and beach, and with on-site surfboard rental and lessons (2hr beginner lesson $75). Dorms $28, rooms $80
Mount Maunganui Beachside Holiday Park 1 Adams Ave ☎0800 682 3224, ⓦmountbeachside .co.nz; map p.349. An extensive, well-equipped campsite very close to the beach in a pleasant, terraced spot beside the hot saltwater pools, right at the foot of the Mount. Mostly camping spots plus a few simple cabins. Camping per site $63, cabins $130
Pacific Coast Lodge Backpackers 432 Maunganui

Rd ☎07 574 9601, ⓦpacificcoastlodge.co.nz; map p.349. Vast hostel with spacious dorms, plus a large kitchen and BBQ area. Nakedbus stops outside. The only downside is that it's about a 25min walk from the restaurants and the fashionable end of the beach. Dorm $28, doubles $82
★**Seagulls Guesthouse** 12 Hinau St ☎07 574 2099 ⓦseagullsguesthouse.co.nz; map p.349. Clean, nea and immaculately maintained upscale backpackers wit well-appointed kitchen, bike and surfboard rental ($25 day) and continental breakfast ($8). Almost everyone get a double or twin as there is just one three-bed dorm. Dorm $30, doubles $74

EATING, DRINKING AND ENTERTAINMENT

Mount Maunganui doesn't have Tauranga's selection or culinary hotspots, but there are plenty of places on the half-doze blocks of Maunganui Road that make up the centre, or on the waterfront strip by the Mount in the lee of apartmen buildings.

★**Café Eighty-Eight** 88 Maunganui Rd ☎07 574 0384; map p.349. It is hard to go past the delectable selection of cakes at this excellent modern café with a cosy interior and small courtyard. Make the effort though for the great breakfasts or a chicken and pineapple Jamaican burger ($19.50). Top hot chocolate, too. Daily 7am–4pm.
Deckchair 2 Marine Parade, under the Twin Towers ☎07 572 0942; map p.349. A great place to go for breakfast and morning coffee (when you can gaze across the beach to the ocean in the warming early sun), for lunch of chicken Caesar salad ($21), or just drop in for a muffin. Daily 6.30am–4pm.
Pizza Library 314 Rata St ☎07 574 2928, ⓦthepizzalibrary.co.nz; map p.349. You may notice their quirky vehicles around town, and the menu is entertaining in itself, but this is seriously good pizza. Leave room for the Peter Pan dessert pizza ($7). Daily 11am–late.
★**Vaudeville** 314 Rata St ☎07 575 0087; map

p.349. Owned by the same people who run the *Pizza Library*, the delightfully alternative *Vaudeville* bar i the best place to hang out in the Mount whether you want to gossip with the locals, enjoy an awesome cocktail (ask for a Carey Martin) or grab som entertainment – it might be a singing poet, Jimbob th resident pianist, or a fire-eater. Mon–Thurs 4pm–late Fri–Sun 1pm–late.
Zeytin on the Mount 118 Maunganui Rd ☎07 57 3040; map p.349. Relaxed Turkish restaurant with wide Mediterranean influences, dishing up a meze board ($28 kebabs ($25), a delicious chicken, date and almond tagin ($25), or feta, spinach and roasted veggie pizza ($23 Tues–Sun 9am–9pm.

CINEMAS
Bay City Cinemas 249 Maunganui Rd ☎07 577 0900 ⓦbaycitycinemas.co.nz; map p.349. Mainstream films i a more laidback environment than the sister location i Tauranga.

Around Tauranga and Mount Maunganui

The fertile countryside inland from Tauranga and Mount Maunganui is backed by the angular peaks of the Kaimai-Mamaku Forest Park. Rivers cascade down the slopes and across the coastal plain, along the way creating **McLaren Falls** on the Wairoa River, which eventually reaches the sea near the adventure park of Waimarino.

Waimarino

36 Taniwha Place, Bethlehem, 8km west of town • Day-pass $42; under-16s $32 • ☎ 07 576 4233, ⓦ waimarino.com

This fun **adventure park** beside a tidal section of the Wairoa River is great for kids of all ages with opportunities to swim, work out on an outdoor climbing wall, plummet down New Zealand's only kayak slide, muck around in kayaks and pedalos and get jettisoned off The Blob, a kind of massive cushion that lets you launch your mates sky high. They also run a variety of kayak trips (see box, p.348) and offer kayak rentals.

McLaren Falls

McLaren Falls Rd, off SH29, 18km southwest of Tauranga • Waters released on Sundays weekly from late Dec–early April; and every second week Sept–early Dec & late April–May • ⓦ kaimaicanoeclub.org.nz

A dam normally diverts water away from the 15m **McLaren Falls**, but thanks to Kaimai Canoe Club the waters are released on selected Sundays, firing up the falls – check their website to be sure of the dates. The **Wairoa River** downstream then becomes the scene of frenetic activity as hundreds of **rafters and kayakers** congregate to run the Grade IV–V rapids (see box, p.272). On other days the place is the preserve of locals who flock here to soak in a series of shallow pools hewn out of the bedrock. A few minutes' rock hopping should secure you a pool to yourself; bring a picnic and sunscreen.

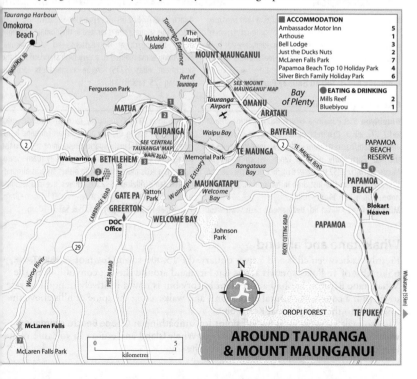

■ ACCOMMODATION	
Ambassador Motor Inn	5
Arthouse	1
Bell Lodge	3
Just the Ducks Nuts	2
McLaren Falls Park	7
Papamoa Beach Top 10 Holiday Park	4
Silver Birch Family Holiday Park	6

● EATING & DRINKING	
Mills Reef	2
Bluebiyou	1

AROUND TAURANGA & MOUNT MAUNGANUI

5

McLaren Falls Park

Daily Oct–April 7.30am–7.30pm; May–Sept 7.30am–5.30pm

Just upstream from McLaren Falls, 190 hectares have been turned into a pretty waterside park around **Lake McLaren**, most notable for its campsite (see below), the easy Waterfall Track through a glowworm dell, and excellent glowworm kayak tours (see box, p.348).

Papamoa Beach

Blokart Heaven 176 Parton Rd • $30/30min; tuition available • ☎ 07 572 4256, ⓦ blokartrecreationpark.co.nz

Mount Maunganui's Ocean Beach stretches 20km southeast to **Papamoa Beach**, which is great for surfing and swimming away from the glitz of the Mount.

Papamoa is also home to the world's original purpose-built **blokart speedway track** at Blokart Heaven: think go-kart with a sail. With a fair wind you can get up to 60km/hr; if there's no wind try a drift kart instead.

Te Puke

Kiwi360 daily: summer 9am–6pm; winter 9am–5pm; Café daily 9am–3pm • 45min guided tours $20 • ☎ 07 573 6340, ⓦ kiwi360.com

Te Puke, 12km southeast of Papamoa Beach, is New Zealand's kiwifruit capital, as evidenced by **Kiwi360**, 6km east of the town centre. Graced by a surreal giant kiwifruit slice, this massive **orchard and processing plant** operates as a kind of horticultural theme park, running informative tours as well as a souvenir emporium offering tastings of dried kiwifruit, kiwifruit liqueur, kiwifruit wine, and a café serving kiwifruit muffins, kiwifruit biscuits and kiwifruit pancakes.

ACCOMMODATION   AROUND TAURANGA AND MOUNT MAUNGANUI

McLaren Falls Park McLaren Falls Rd, 11km south of Tauranga ☎ 07 577 7000, ⓦ tauranga.govt.nz; map p.351. Simple grassy camp sites in a wooded, lakeside park (see above) with water, toilets and free showers. Three-night maximum stay. **$5**

Papamoa Beach Top 10 Holiday Park 535 Papamoa Beach Rd ☎ 07 572 0816, ⓦ papamoabeach.co.nz; map p.351. This spotless site is located in the domain and right beside the beach at the eastern end of Papamoa. Everything is maintained to a very high standard and the beachfront villas ($215) are in a matchless location. Camping **$25**, cabins **$88**

EATING AND DRINKING

Bluebiyou 559 Papamoa Beach Rd, Papamoa Beach ☎ 07 572 2099, ⓦ bluebiyou.co.nz; map p.351. Smart and airy café/bar/restaurant with views over the dunes to the sea. Particularly nice for lunch, which might be Moroccan chicken ($23) followed by choc berry cheesecake ($12.50). You can also just drop in for a drink. Wed–Sat noon–10pm, Sun 11am–10pm.

Mills Reef 143 Moffat Rd, Bethlehem, 8km southwest of Tauranga ☎ 07 576 8800, ⓦ millsreef.co.nz; map p.351. Come during the day and you can combine lunch (platter for two $45) in the spacious restaurant or out on the terrace with a free tasting of their wines (daily 10am–5pm). Dinner is a little more formal with dishes such as almond-crusted lamb rillettes ($32.50). There's live music some summer Sunday lunchtimes. Mon–Wed 11.30am–3pm, Thurs–Sat 10.30am–3pm and Fri & Sat 5–10pm.

Whakatane and around

Prettily set between cliffs and a river estuary, the 13,000-strong town of **WHAKATANE**, 65km east of Te Puke, sprawls across flat farmland around the last convulsions of the Whakatane River. It has had a turbulent history but is now a relatively tranquil service town with a couple of cultural attractions, and walks along the spine of hills above the town and to the viewpoint at **Kohi Point**.

It also makes a great jumping-off point for sunbathing at **Ohope Beach**, **swimming with dolphins**, visits to the bird sanctuary of **Whale Island** and cruises to volcanic **White Island**, which billows plumes of steam into the sky.

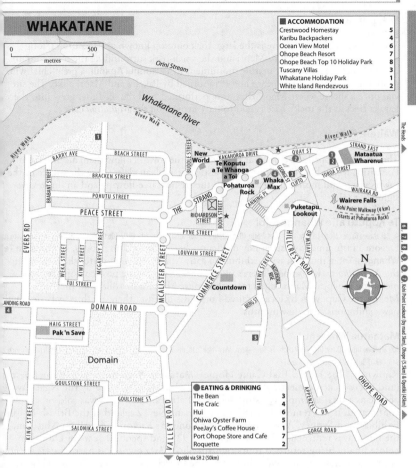

Opotiki via SH 2 (50km)

Brief history

The area has had more than its fair share of dramatic events. The **Maori** word *Whakatane* ("to act as a man") originated when the women of the *Mataatua* canoe were left aboard while the men went ashore; the canoe began to drift out to sea, but touching the paddles was *tapu* for women. Undeterred, Wairaka, the teenage daughter of a chief, led the women in paddling back to shore, shouting *Ka Whakatane Au i Ah au* ("I will deport myself as a man"); a statue at Whakatane Heads commemorates her heroic act.

Apart from a brief sortie by Cook, the first Europeans were flax traders in the early 1800s. In March 1865, missionary **Carl Völkner** was killed at Opotiki and a government agent, **James Falloon**, arrived to investigate. Supporters of a fanatical Maori sect, the Hauhau (see box, p.358), attacked Falloon's vessel, killing him and his crew. In response, the government declared **martial law**, and by the end of the year a large part of the Bay of Plenty had been confiscated and Whakatane was a military settlement. **Te Kooti** (see box, p.383) chose Whakatane as his target for a full-scale attack in 1869 before being driven back into the hills of Urewera.

5

Pohaturoa

The Strand

Whakatane's defining feature is the large rock outcrop known as **Pohaturoa** ("long rock"). The place is sacred to Maori and the small park surrounding the rock contains carved benches and a black marble monument to **Te Hurinui Apanui**, a great chief who propounded the virtues of peace and is mourned by Pakeha and Maori alike. The site was once a shrine where Maori rites were performed, and the seed that grew into the karaka trees at the rock's base is said to have arrived on the *Mataatua* canoe.

Wairere Falls

Wairaka Rd

The sea once lapped the cliffs that now hem in the town. Follow them around from Pohaturoa to the base of **Wairere Falls**, nestled in a sylvan cleft. Once the source of the town's water and motive power for mills, they're now free-flowing and an impressive sight after rain.

Te Koputu a Te Whanga a Toi

49 Kakahoroa Drive • Mon–Fri 9am–5pm, Sat & Sun 10am–2pm • $5 donation requested • ☎ 07 306 0509, ⓦ whakatanemuseum.org.n

Devote a little time to Eastern Bay of Plenty's brand-new cultural focus, **Te Koputu a Te Whanga a Toi**, a museum with exhibits on early Maori settlement after their arrival in the *Mataatua waka* (canoe). There's plenty of material on the post-colonial era too, including the local Maori rugby team that toured Britain in 1888, and the 1954 Melbourne Cup, won by locally raised horse, Rising Fast. There are three galleries, with new exhibitions every few months.

Mataatua Wharenui

105 Muriwai Drive • Daily: Dec–April Mon–Fri 9am–4pm; May–Nov 9.30am–3.30pm • Visitor centre free; tour $29.50, with *hangi* lunch $45 • ☎ 07 308 4271, ⓦ mataatua.com

Known as "The House That Came Home", **Mataatua Wharenui** is one of the finest (and largest) carved meetinghouses you'll see. Built here in 1875 by the Ngati Awa people as a final attempt to restore self-belief after all their land was sold or confiscated, it was removed in 1879 to represent New Zealand at the British Empire Exhibition in Sydney. After a long stint at London's Victoria and Albert Museum, the house was returned to New Zealand in 1925 and spent 70 years in Dunedin before finally being returned to its rightful Ngati Awa owners as part of a Treaty of Waitangi settlement in 1996. Don't miss the brief but emotional film showing the house's history, before participating in the cultural tour. This is very intimate and engaging, greetings are given in Maori and English, and your guide will explain what some of the beautiful carvings of ancestors mean to them before the effective light show brings the images to life.

River Walk

A walking path follows the levee along the south side of the Whakatane River for 4km to its mouth. The most interesting section runs two kilometres from the city centre to the heads and makes for a lovely late-afternoon stroll that passes two replicas of the *Mataatua waka* in a reserve, Muriwai's cave and views across the river to the sprightly bronze statue of Wairaka on a rock. You can also reach the heads by car along Muriwai Drive.

Kohi Point and Ohope Walk

5.5km one way; 2hr • Details in a free leaflet from i-SITE

The best of the local walks starts in the centre of town and follows the Nga Tapuwae o Toi ("Sacred Footsteps of Toi") Walkway, which traverses the domain of the great chieftain Toi and continues to **Kohi Point**, giving panoramic views of Whakatane,

Whale and White islands and Te Urewera. From Kohi Point, continue through Otarawairere Bay (no passage for an hour either side of high tide) and on to Ohope Beach, from where you can return to Whakatane by the Bayhopper bus (see below).

Ohope

The tiny settlement of **OHOPE**, 7km east of Whakatane, extends along the beach in a thin ribbon to the entrance of **Ohiwa Harbour**. Ohiwa ("a place of watchfulness") is the site of a natural shellfishery for pipi and cockles, and a place of numerous *pa* sites, signifying the importance of a convenient and renewable food source to the Maori way of life.

Otherwise, this is very much a surf-and-sand beach resort, though it makes a pleasant base from which to explore Whakatane (just $3 one-way on the Bayhopper bus) and its surroundings.

ARRIVAL AND DEPARTURE WHAKATANE AND AROUND

By bus InterCity and NakedBus buses running along SH2 between Rotorua and Gisborne stop twice daily in each direction outside the Whakatane i-SITE. The local Bayhopper (☎0800 422 928, ⊛baybus.co.nz) serves Tauranga, Ohope ($3 one way) and Opotiki (Mon & Wed). **Destinations** Gisborne (2 daily; 3hr); Ohope (Mon–Sat 4–6 daily; 30min); Opotiki (2 daily; 40min); Rotorua (2

daily; 1hr 30min); Tauranga (Mon–Sat 1 daily; 2hr).

By plane At the time of writing it was unclear whether flights to Auckland would resume from Whakatane airport, about 10km west of the centre, connected by the Dial-A-Cab shuttle (around $25; ☎0800 308 0222). Check with the i-SITE.

Destinations Auckland (45min).

INFORMATION AND TOURS

Visitor information The i-SITE (corner of Quay St and Kakahoroa Drive; Mon–Fri 8am–5pm, Sat & Sun 10am–4pm; ☎07 306 2030, ⊛whakatane.com) is well-stocked with DOC leaflets and other information including walks for the local area. Also offers rental bikes, free internet and wi-fi.

Kiwi Jet Tours ☎0800 800 538, ⊛kiwijetboattours.com. Zoom around on the Rangitikei River with an

ex-world champion jetboat racer, who will take you from the Matahina Dam, 25km south of Whakatane, to the beautiful Aniwhenua Falls via a number of modest whitewater sections ($95).

Services The library (49 Kakahora Drive; Mon–Fri 9am–5pm, Sat & Sun 10am–2pm) offers 30min free internet.

ACCOMMODATION

Whakatane has a sizeable stock of accommodation, with an emphasis on mid-range motels. Also consider Ohope Beach, just over the hill.

Crestwood Homestay 2 Crestwood Rise ☎07 308 7554, ⊛crestwood-homestay.co.nz. Attractive, friendly B&B in a quiet hilltop setting with scenic views to the islands and a 20min walk from the town centre. Evening meals ($50 including wine) are available by arrangement. The owner is a radio operator for the Whakatane Coastguard and is happy to show guests around its headquarters. **$160**

Karibu Backpackers 13 Landing Rd, 1.5km southwest of the centre ☎07 307 8276, ⊛karibubackpackers.co.nz. Suburban house converted into a big, well-maintained and welcoming hostel with an attractive garden for camping ($16). There's off-street parking and free pick-up from the bus stop. Dorms **$27**, rooms **$74**

Tuscany Villas 57 The Strand ☎07 308 2244, ⊛tuscanyvillas.co.nz. Top-of-the-line motor inn with a range of recently-renovated studios and suites, all fitted

out to a high standard with kitchenette and free wi-fi. The one-bedroom suites all have a spa bath or hot tub. Studio **$145**, suite **$195**

Whakatane Holiday Park McGarvey Rd ☎07 308 8694, ⊛whakataneholidaypark.co.nz. A sheltered campsite a 10min walk along the levee from the Strand, with a summertime outdoor pool and basic but well-maintained facilities. Rates rise by a quarter from Christmas to early Feb. Camping **$15**, self-contained units **$85**

White Island Rendezvous 15 The Strand East ☎07 308 9588, ⊛whiteisland.co.nz. Spotless, Mediterranean-style multi-level motel opposite the wharf. Some rooms have spa baths, and all are equipped with Sky TV, free wi-fi and microwave. Next door is a beautiful kauri villa that provides B&B with breakfast from the café. There's also a popular on-site café, *PeeJay's Coffee House* (see p.357). **$140**

OFFSHORE WHAKATANE

WHALE ISLAND

Whale Island (Moutohora), 10km offshore from Whakatane, is a 2km-by-1km DOC-controlled haven where considerable efforts were made decades ago to eradicate goats and rats. Native bush is rapidly returning and the island has become a bird reserve and safe environment for saddlebacks, grey-faced petrels, sooty shearwaters, little blue penguins, dotterels and oystercatchers, as well as three species of lizard – geckos and speckled and copper skinks – and the reptilian tuatara; occasional visits are made by the North Island kaka and falcon, as well as fur seals. In the breeding season (May–Dec) over 100,000 muttonbirds return to the island, a spectacular sight made comical by their lousy landing skills.

Access to the island itself is only by a limited number of **guided tours**. Expect to pay around $95 for a 3hr trip.

WHITE ISLAND

Whakatane's star attraction is **White Island** (Whaakari), named by Cook for its permanent shroud of mist and steam. Roughly circular and almost 2km across, White Island lies 50km offshore, sometimes a rough ride. Neither this nor its seething volcanism deters visitors, who flock to its desolate, other-worldly landscape, with billowing towers of gas and steam spewing from a crater lake 60m below sea level. Smaller fumaroles come surrounded by bright yellow and white crystal deposits that re-form in new and bizarre shapes each day. The crystal-clear and abundant waters around the island make this one of the best **dive** spots in New Zealand.

Whaakari embodies the ongoing clash between the Indo-Australian Plate and the Pacific Plate that has been driven beneath it for the last two million years. This resulted in the upward thrust of super-heated rock through the ocean floor, creating a massive **volcanic** structure. **Sulphur**, for use in fertilizer manufacture, was sporadically mined on the island from the 1880s, but catastrophic eruptions, landslides and economic misfortune plagued the enterprise. The island was abandoned in 1934, and these days it is home only to 60,000 grey-faced **petrels** and 10,000 **gannets**. You can only land on the island via a guided boat tour or by helicopter.

TOURS AND ACTIVITIES ON AND AROUND THE ISLANDS

Easily the most popular way to experience the islands is with White Island Tours, who get out to White Island whenever the weather plays ball. You can also get out there by helicopter or explore below the surface on dive trips. Head out dolphin watching and swimming from December to March: anybody offering to take you outside those months is either wildly optimistic or less than scrupulous.

Whakatane's numerous **fishing** guides predominantly work on a charter basis from the local marina; the i-SITE has a list of operators doing half-day and full-day trips and they can usually hook you up with a boat to suit your needs.

Dive Works Charters 96 The Strand ☏0800 354 7737, ⓦwhaleislandtours.com. Excellent dolphin and seal swimming (3–4hr; $160) around Whale Island and White Island, plus ecotours onto Whale Island ($120 with about 3 hours on the island) and dive and snorkelling trips.

Frontier Helicopters ☏0800 804 354, ⓦvulcanheli.co.nz. See White Island from the air on flights (2hr; $650/person for 2 passengers) that leave from Whakatane airport and include a 1hr walking tour of the island visiting the crater rim, fumaroles and the old sulphur works.

White Island Tours (aka **"Pee Jay"**) 15 The Strand East ☏0800 733 529, ⓦwhiteisland.co.nz.

Book at least a couple of days in advance for the 6hr trip ($199) out to White Island, which offers two hours on the island – including standing on the edge of the crater (with a gas mask on) amid pillars of smoke and steam looking down into the steaming crater lake. You also visit the site of a 1923 sulphur-processing factory that is being gradually eaten away by the corrosive atmosphere. Whale Island is much closer to the mainland, so trips will often run when it's too rough to get to White Island; tours last about 3hr ($95) and are dependent on numbers, so book in advance. They run in the morning all year round; dusk trips operate May–Dec when hard hats are provided to protect you from crashing muttonbirds.

OHOPE

Ocean View Motel 18/2 West End, Ohope Beach ☎ 07 312 5665, ⓦ oceanviewmotel.co.nz. Very relaxing motel at the western end of the beach, with safe swimming, bushwalks and free use of bikes, kayaks, boogie boards, surfboards, wi-fi and laundry facilities. All of its self-contained units have sea views. $160

Ohope Beach Resort 307 Harbour Rd, 10km east of Whakatane ☎ 0800 464 673, ⓦ ohopebeachresort.net. 21 classy apartments with balconies and views across the water. Each is fully equipped with dishwasher, washing machine, wi-fi and a/c. Shared facilities include sauna, pétanque, gym, tennis court and three pools. 2-bedroom $220, penthouse $320

★**Ohope Beach Top 10 Holiday Park** 367 Harbour Rd, 10km east of Whakatane ☎ 0800 264 673, ⓦ ohopebeach.co.nz. Upmarket holiday park right behind Ohope Beach, with a pool complex including a waterslide and a free summertime kids' programme. Higher rates apply from Christmas to early Feb. Camping $24, motel units $144

EATING, DRINKING AND NIGHTLIFE

The Bean 72 The Strand East ☎ 07 307 0494, ⓦ thebeancafe.co.nz. Laidback daytime café and coffee roastery, so you can be sure of a whizzy coffee hit to go with your breakfast, sandwich or home-style baking. Free wi-fi. Mon–Fri 7am–4pm, Sat 8am–3pm, Sun 9am–3pm.

The Craic Whakatane Hotel, 79 The Strand ☎ 07 307 1670. Atmospheric Irish bar furnished in mellow dark wood and serving inexpensive fare. Live bands on Friday night and some Sunday afternoons, and dancing in the bar. Daily noon–9pm or a lot later.

★**PeeJay's Coffee House** 15 The Strand, inside the White Island Rendezvous Motel ☎ 07 308 9589, ⓦ whiteisland.co.nz. A good spot for breakfast, snacks and lunch. If you've got an early boat ride, you may just want a decent espresso; others should relax, make use of the free wi-fi, try the mushroom and chorizo-slathered ciabatta ($15.50) and perhaps a glass of something – they're licensed. Daily 6.30am–2pm.

Roquette 23 Quay St ☎ 07 307 0722, ⓦ roquette -restaurant.co.nz. Whakatane's best restaurant and bar features dishes such as salt-and-pepper calamari with lemon aioli ($18.50) and seafood pappardelle ($34). Mon–Sat 10am–10pm.

OHOPE

Hui 19 Pohutukawa Ave ☎ 07 312 5623, ⓦ huibarandgrill.com. Polished concrete floors mean sandy beach bums are welcome at this restaurant and bar with a deck out back overlooking Ohope Beach. Come for a coffee, a beer or anything from chipotle mussels ($16) to venison shanks with blackberry jus ($30). Occasional acoustic acts. Daily 8.30am–10pm or later.

Ohiwa Oyster Farm 11 Wainui Rd, 1km south of Ohope Beach on the road to Opotiki ☎ 07 312 4565. Pick up cheap supplies of fresh seafood, including mussels, oysters and smoked fish, from this shack beside Ohiwa Harbour, or tuck into some fish and chips at one of the picnic tables at the water's edge. Daily 9am–9.30pm.

Port Ohope Store and Café 311 Harbour Rd ☎ 07 312 4707. Licensed café overlooking the harbour and the surf. Go for breakfast or great fish and chips after you've hired one of their SUPs ($45/90min). Daily 7.30am–10pm.

Opotiki

The small settlement of **OPOTIKI**, 46km east of Whakatane (via the Ohope Road), is the easternmost town in the Bay of Plenty and surrounded by lush countryside and beaches. Opotiki also acts as the gateway to (and final supply stop for) the wilds of the East Cape and trips on the remote and scenic Motu River.

The town has few notable sights to delay your departure. From Opotiki, SH2 strikes inland to the more citified opportunities of **Gisborne** (see p.372), while SH35 meanders around the perimeter of the **East Cape** (see p.360), never straying far from its rugged and windswept coastline.

Opotiki Museum

123 Church St • Mon–Fri 10am–4pm, Sat 10am–2pm • $10

All Opotiki's significant historic buildings cluster around the junction of Church and Elliot streets, including the **Opotiki Museum**, which occupies the whole block between Elliot and Kelly streets. Much of the content is typical small-town museum fare (agricultural implements, display rooms), boosted by the Tanewhirinaki Carvings, a fine collection of Maori sculptures from this area that spent many years as part of the Auckland Museum collection. After you leave, be sure to stroll along to the *Shalfoon &*

5

THE HAUHAU

Zealous missionaries encouraged many Maori to abandon their belief structure in favour of **Christianity** but, as land disputes with settlers escalated, the Maori increasingly perceived the missionaries as agents for land-hungry Europeans.

When **war** broke out and the recently converted Maori suffered defeats, they felt betrayed not only by the Crown but also by their newly acquired god, and some formed the revivalist **Hauhau** movement, based on the Old Testament. It started peacefully, to spread Te Hau (the breath of God), but disciples became dedicated to routing the interlopers, dancing around *niu* **poles**, chanting for Pakeha to leave the country. The name is derived from the **battle cry** of the warriors, who flung themselves at their enemies with their right arms raised to protect them from bullets, believing that true faith prevented them from being shot. The movement began in 1862 and by 1865, having capitalized on widespread Maori unrest, there was a *niu* pole in most villages of any size from Wellington to the Waikato. The Hauhau were some of the most feared **warriors** and involved in the bloodiest and most bitter battles, but the movement began to fade after their **leader** and founder, Te Ua Haumene, was captured in 1866. Some of the sect's ideas were **revitalized** when the rebel **Te Kooti** (see p.383) based parts of his **Ringatu** movement on Hauhau doctrine.

Francis section at 129 Church St, a nostalgic 1890s-established grocery and hardware store that revels in its uncatalogued collections of old typewriters, biscuit tins and just about anything you might find in such a shop.

St Stephen's Church

Church St, opposite the museum • Mon–Fri 10am–4pm, Sat 10am–2pm; get key from the museum if it isn't open • Free

The innocent-looking white clapboard **St Stephen's Church** was once the scene of a notorious murder. In March 1865, following incitement by the Hauhau (see box above) prophet Kereopa Te Rau, local missionary **Carl Völkner** was killed here. The case is far from clear-cut: it appears that Völkner had written many letters to Governor Grey espousing the land-grabbing ambitions of settlers, and local Maori claim Völkner was justly executed. Settlers used the story as propaganda, fuelling intermittent skirmishes over the next three years. Nip in and see the gorgeous *tukutuku* panels around the altar. Völkner's gravestone is slotted into the wall of the church around the back.

Hukutaia Domain

Daily dawn–dusk

A welcome retreat into the bush is given by the small and unspoiled **Opotiki (Hukutaia) Domain**, with its understorey of nikau and a grand puriri tree thought to date from 500 BC and once used as a burial tree by local Maori. The bush also contains a good lookout over the Waioeka Valley and a series of short yet interesting rainforest tracks. To get here, head south from the centre of town on Church Street as far as the Waioeka River Bridge, cross it and bear left along Woodlands Road for 7km.

ARRIVAL AND DEPARTURE

OPOTIKI

By bus InterCity and NakedBus buses between Whakatane and Gisborne stop outside the *Hot Bread Shop Café* at the corner of Bridge and St John sts. Bayhopper buses to Whakatane (Mon & Wed) and Potaka via Omaio, Te Kaha and Waihau Bay (Tues & Thurs only) leave from the corner of Elliot and St John sts in the centre of town.

Destinations Gisborne, via SH2 (2 daily; 2hr 30); Hicks Bay via SH35 (1 weekly; 3hr); Rotorua (2 daily; 2hr 30min); Whakatane (2–4 daily; 1hr).

GETTING AROUND

By bike Travel Shop, 104 Church St (☎07 315 8881, ✉travelshop@xtra.co.nz). This travel agent rents bikes (including trail bikes), surfboards and kayaks (all $30/half day, $40/day) with drop-offs arranged. Internet is $2 for 30 minutes.

INFORMATION

Visitor information The i-SITE/DOC is at 70 Bridge St (Christmas–Jan daily 8am–5pm; Feb–Christmas Mon–Fri 9am–4.30pm; Sat & Sun 9am–1pm; ☎ 07 315 3031, ✇ opotikinz.com). The combined i-SITE and DOC office has loads of information about the East Cape, plus pay showers.

Services Free wi-fi or 30min on a terminal at the library, 101 Church St (Mon–Fri 9am–5pm & Sat 9am–1pm).

ACCOMMODATION

★**Aurum** 213 Ohiwa Beach Rd, 13km west of town ☎ 07 315 4737, ✇ aurumretreat.co.nz. Beautifully appointed self-contained rooms (with full kitchens), tucked under pohutukawas and with fabulous sea views. The Sufi architecture gives a wonderful serenity. There's even an outdoor wood-fired bath. Breakfast ($15) can be arranged on request. __$160__

Beyond the Dunes 12 Wairakaia Rd, 5km east of town

OPOTIKI TOURS AND ACTIVITIES

Opotiki is about getting away from it all – out on the water, either fishing offshore, or exploring the rivers on kayaks, whitewater rafting or cycling the Motu trails.

FISHING AND KAYAKING

Marine Life Tours 16 Wharf St ☎ 027 350 4910, ✇ marinelifetours.com. Runs simple surfcasting trips ($80 2hr trip for two people, with all gear), but they also organized the construction of the Opotiki Community Reef, designed to maintain fish stocks. Learn about it on a 1hr tour ($20). Best of all, there's also a self-guided 10km drift down an easy section of the Waioeka River (3–4hr; $80).

Travel Shop 104 Church St ☎ 07 315 8881, ✉ travelshop@xtra.co.nz. Rents kayaks ($30 half-day, $40/day) for self-guided tours with drop-offs arranged.

WILDERNESS RAFTING ON THE MOTU RIVER

Some of the best **wilderness rafting** trips in New Zealand are on the Grade III–IV **Motu River**, hidden deep in the mountain terrain of the remote Raukumara Ranges, with long stretches of whitewater plunging through gorges and valleys to the Bay of Plenty coast. In 1981, after a protracted campaign against hydro-dam builders, the Motu became New Zealand's first designated "wild and scenic" river. Access by 4WD, helicopter and jetboat makes one- and two-day trips possible, but to capture the essence of this remote region you should consider one of the longer trips in which you'll see no sign of civilization for three days – a magical and eerie experience.

Wet 'n' Wild Rafting ☎ 0800 462 7238, ✇ wetnwildrafting.co.nz. Rotorua-based company starting trips from Opotiki that range from two days ($1095, with helicopter access), to the full five-day adventure ($995, with no helicopter access) from the headwaters to the sea. In all cases transport and meals are provided; you can bring your own tent and sleeping bag or rent them from Wet 'n' Wild.

MOUNTAIN BIKING THE MOTU TRAILS

These three new trails (✇ motutrails.co.nz) can be linked together for a challenging 2-day loop ride, or separated according to your ability and enthusiasm. Most popular is the level 11km **Dunes trail**, with its fantastic views. The **Motu road trail** (67km, usually ridden from Matawai) is a good challenge (rated intermediate) with a few uphill sections following the old coach road. The 44km **Pakihi track** through the bush will really get your heart racing (despite being downhill all the way). It's rated advanced, mainly because it runs along some sheer drops, so take your time and don't be embarrassed to get off and walk. Both companies offer packages and, with enough notice, may be able to group you with other riders to reduce costs.

Motu Trails Ltd ☎ 07 315 5864, ✇ motucycletrails .com. Ngaio and her team will do their best to ensure your ride matches your experience and enthusiasm. Hire bikes for the Pakihi track ($65/day), or Dunes trail ($50/day). The shuttle to Matawai is $50 and minimum numbers apply. They also have a bunkhouse (dorm $30) and secure parking near the centre of Opotiki.

Bushaven ☎ 07 929 7564, ✇ hireandshuttle.co.nz. A range of accommodation (cabin $90) and services from this outfit based at the bottom of the Pakihi track. Their shuttle fares to Matawai are broadly the same as Motu Trails (from $50, minimum numbers apply), and mountain-bike hire is from $50/day.

5

☎021 123 0789, ⓦbookabach.co.nz/13241. Simple, modern, self-contained, pine-lined *bach* just over the dunes from a sweeping swimming beach. A great spot to hole up for a day or two. $90

Capeview Cottage Tablelands Rd, 8km southeast of town ☎0800 227 384, ⓦcapeview.co.nz. Very comfortable rimu-lined, fully self-contained cottage on a kiwifruit orchard with long coastal views, outdoor hot tub and a small library. The hosts are eco-minded and very knowledgeable about the area. $145

Central Oasis Backpackers 30 King St ☎07 315 5165, ⓔcentraloasis@hotmail.com. Friendly German-run hostel in a higgledy-piggledy villa right in the centre of town, with one double, one twin and a three-bed

dorm. Dorm $23, double $56

Ohiwa Beach Holiday Park 380 Ohiwa Harbour Rd, off SH2, 15km west of town ☎07 315 4741, ⓦohiwaholidays.co.nz. Little-known gem of a campsite right on the beach, with safe swimming, glowworms, kayaks for rent and a "jumping pillow" – massively popular with kids (and a few adults). Camping $19, cabins $65, motels $120

★**Opotiki Beach House** 7 Appleton Rd, off SH2, 5km west of town ☎07 315 5117, ⓦopotikibeachhouse .co.nz. The pick of Opotiki's hostels is this laidback beach-side hangout with free use of kayaks and bodyboards. Dorms $30, doubles $66

EATING AND DRINKING

1759 Masonic Hotel, 121 Church St ☎07 315 8284. Huge, great-value meals – steak, fish and chips – in the raw brick backroom of an Irish pub. The brandy snaps ($6.50) are pretty good too. Daily 10am–10pm.

Beyond the Bean Waiotahi Beach Rest Area on SH2, 6km west of town. Run by the same people who own *Beyond the Dunes*, this coffee cart serves imported Italian coffee with a small selection of home-made cakes and counter food. Mon 6.30am–noon, Tues–Fri 6.30am–2pm.

Hot Bread Shop & Illy Café 43 St John St ☎07 315 6795. The spot for good coffee, yummy traybakes, pies,

brunch and snacks (BLT $13.90). Daily 5am–5pm.

Ocean Seafoods Fish and Chips 90 Church St ☎07 315 6335. The best chip shop in town, doing fish and chips for around $8, plus burgers and the usual Kiwi chippy staples. In fine weather, grab some and head down to the riverside. Daily 9am–9pm.

★**Two Fish** 102 Church St ☎07 315 5448. Excellent café with mismatched furniture and a dedication to quality, made-on-the-premises foods; stop in for breakfast, a choice of delicious muffins (try raspberry and lemon) or quick bites such as chicken wraps. Also has the best espresso around. Mon–Fri 8am–3pm, Sat 8am–2pm.

The Waioeka Gorge route

From Opotiki, **SH2** strikes out south to **Gisborne**, 137km away. It's one of New Zealand's great scenic drives, dotted with tiny settlements, weaving up and down steep hills cloaked in bush. The route winds gingerly along the Waioeka River for 30km before tracing the narrow and steep **Waioeka Gorge** then emerging onto rolling pastureland and dropping to the plains around Gisborne, all arrow-straight roads through orchards, vineyards and sheep farms.

The **only petrol** along the route is at Matawai, but opening hours are limited: fill up in Opotiki or, if you're coming from the south, in Gisborne.

Waioeka Gorge walks

Break your journey on the first 72km stretch to Matawai by tackling one of the interesting **walks** on either side of the road. Check at the Opotiki i-SITE for details.

The East Cape

Jutting into the South Pacific northeast of Opotiki and Gisborne, the little-visited **East Cape** (also known as Eastland) is an unspoilt backwater that's a reminder of how New Zealand once was. Between Opotiki and Gisborne, the Pacific Coast Highway (SH35) runs 330 scenic kilometres around the peninsula, hugging the rugged coastline much of the way and providing mesmerizing sea views on a fine day.

As soon as you enter the region you'll notice a change of pace, epitomized by the occasional sight of a lone horseback rider clopping along the road. **Maori** make up a significant percentage of the population – over eighty percent of land tenure here is in Maori hands, and locals are welcoming, particularly once you take time to talk to them and adjust to the Cape's slower pace.

The **coast** is very much the focus here but there are also **hiking** opportunities, and just about everywhere you go there will be someone happy to take you **horse trekking**, either along the beach or into the bush. The **towns**, such as they are, don't have much to recommend them and you're better off planning to stay at scattered places in between, perhaps by a rocky cove or wild beach.

Inland, the inhospitable **Waiapu Mountains** run through the area, encompassing the northeastern Raukumara Range and the typical native flora of the Raukumara Forest Park. The isolated and rugged peaks of Hikurangi, Whanokao, Aroangi, Wharekia and Tatai provide a spectacular backdrop to the coastal scenery, but are only accessible through **Maori land** and **permission** must be sought.

GETTING AROUND   THE EAST CAPE

By car Although the road is sealed all the way around the East Cape, it twists in and out of small bays so much that it takes a full six hours from Opotiki to Gisborne without any stops. Pumps around the East Cape are relatively few and far between, and some run out of petrol from time to time. Te Araroa, Ruatoria and Tolaga Bay are your best bets, but fill up before you start.

By bus Public transport is limited to infrequent buses and courier services, which also carry passengers. Currently they don't quite overlap, making it difficult to complete the full journey without resorting to hitching. Tour company buses (see below) are also an option.

BUS COMPANIES

BayHopper ☏ 0800 422 928, ⓦ baybus.co.nz. Runs

from Potaka (just west of Hicks Bay) to Opotiki and back on Tues and Thurs only. No booking needed; pay as you get on. If those don't quite suit, be polite and check where the driver lives – sometimes they might drop people off there at the end of their run.

Cooks Couriers ☏ 06 864 4711. Runs from Te Araroa to Gisborne and back (Mon–Sat only), stopping to pick up parcels.

TOURS

Stray ☏ 09 526 2140, ⓦ straytravel.co.nz. From Nov–April, Stray's hop-on, hop-off East Bro pass (minimum 3 days; $325) covers the cape from Rotorua with stops in Maraehako Bay, Te Araroa and Gisborne.

INFORMATION

Tourist information There are no i-SITE offices or formal visitor centres around the East Cape: pick up information in Opotiki or Gisborne. The annual *Pacific Coast Highway Guide* (ⓦ pacificcoasthighwayguide.co.nz) is a useful resource, though operators pay to be included.

Services The only banking services around here are a bank and ATM at Ruatoria. Mobile phone coverage is limited to around Opotiki and from Te Araroa to Gisborne (Vodafone), and from Tokomaru Bay to Gisborne (Telecom).

ACCOMMODATION AND EATING

Hostels are scattered along the route, with the occasional motel and B&B, but upmarket accommodation is almost nonexistent.

Camping Campsites are an East Cape staple with several good commercial sites. Free beachside camping is prohibited, but there are six designated "freedom camping" sites, from Waipiro Bay down to the outskirts of Gisborne. These operate from mid-Sept to mid-April and require a permit ($16 for 2 consecutive nights; $31 for 10; $66 for 28; valid for up to 6 people), available from the i-SITEs in

Opotiki and Gisborne. Fairly strict (but common sense) rules apply and inspectors periodically enforce them. Fires are not allowed and campers must have an onboard or chemical toilet.

Eating Apart from a couple of steak-and-chips places attached to pubs and motels, there isn't anywhere on the East Cape that you'd describe as a real restaurant. Come prepared for self-catering or accept a diet of toasted sandwiches and fish and chips. Self-caterers will find limited grocery shopping, and many places close as early as 5pm.

Opotiki to Waihau Bay

The road from Opotiki to **Waihau Bay** covers 103km, generally sticking close to the sea, but frequently twisting up over steep bluffs before dropping back down to desolate

5

beaches heavy with driftwood. The logs have been washed down from the Raukumara Range by the numerous rivers that reach the sea here, often forming delightful freshwater swimming holes. This is probably the section of the East Cape where you'll want to spend much of your time. You'll find family campsites every few kilometres, none of them far from the beach, with a wealth of aquatic activities on offer – from boogie boards and canoes to half-day fishing and dive trips – along with horseriding and bikes to search out your own secluded cove.

Omaio

Leaving Opotiki, you first pass Tirohanga, the last of the real swimming beaches for some distance. After 40km you cross the **Motu River** where you can pick up jetboat tours. A further 12km on, **OMAIO** offers a store with a petrol pump and takeaways, and *Hoani Waititi Reserve* (see below), one of the East Cape's few free campsites.

Te Kaha
13km east of Omaio

TE KAHA spreads for 7km along the highway in a beautiful crescent shape, with spectacular headlands and a deserted, driftwood-strewn beach that's safe for swimming. Te Kaha is about the closest land to White Island, 50km offshore, and has some good places to stay.

Whanarua Bay and Maraehako Bay

White Island remains in view as you continue 16km to the twin communities of **WHANARUA BAY** and **MARAEHAKO BAY**, a pair of rock-fringed coves separated by a craggy headland. With a selection of good accommodation, a café at *Pacific Coast Macadamias* (see opposite) and restaurant at *Te Kaha Beach Resort*, this makes one of the best places in these parts to base yourself for a couple of days of swimming and exploring.

Ruakokore Church

Still hugging the coast, SH35 winds 13km to **Ruakokore**, not really a place at all, but the memorable site of a picture-perfect, white clapboard Anglican church which stands on a promontory framed by the blue ocean. The church was built in 1895 and is usually open. It has little blue penguins nesting underneath.

Waihau Bay

From Ruakokore Church it's 5km to **WAIHAU BAY**, another sweeping crescent of sand and grass that's ideal for swimming, surfing and kayaking. The film director Taika Waititi thought it ideal too, and in 2010 shot his film *Boy* in the area. The abundance of shellfish and flatfish here might encourage you to sling a line from the wharf beside the combined store, post office and petrol station.

ACCOMMODATION AND EATING   **OPOTIKI TO WAIHAU BAY**

OMAIO
Hoani Waititi Reserve Omaio Marae Rd, opposite the store. This is a very basic campsite set on a grassy pohutukawa-fringed headland. You'll have to bring your own water and use the public toilets 500m away. **Free**

Oariki Coastal Cottage Maraenui, almost 40km east of Opotiki ☎ 07 325 2678, ⓦ bookabach.co.nz/6515, ⓔ oariki@xtra.co.nz. Relax in front of the log fire at the self-catering cottage, or enjoy B&B (en suite) at the main house. Either way, you'll be surrounded by native bush and overlook the sea. Ask about opportunities for fishing. Call

ahead for directions and to arrange a three-course dinner ($40). Cottage **$140**, B&B **$120**

TE KAHA
Te Kaha homestead SH35 ☎ 07 325 2194, ⓔ paora @hotmail.com. Relaxing hostel at the water's edge with an outdoor spa, access to the beach, and opportunities for kayaking, jetskiing and fishing. There's much singing, music and Maori/Irish festivities. The dorms sleep 6–12 and there's a chance to buy dinner, often with kai moana caught nearby. Dorms **$30**, double **$80**

LEGENDS OF THE EAST CAPE MAORI

According to legend, a great *ariki* (leader) from the East Cape was drowned by rival tribesmen, and his youngest daughter swore vengeance: when she gave birth to a son called **Tuwhakairiora**, she hoped he would make good her promise. As a young man, Tuwhakairiora travelled and encountered a young woman named **Ruataupare**; she took him to her father, who happened to be the local chief. A thunderstorm broke, signalling to the people that they had an important visitor among them, and Tuwhakairiora was allowed to marry Ruataupare and live in Te Araroa. When he called upon all the *hapu* of the area to gather and avenge the death of his grandfather, many warriors travelled to Whareponga and sacked the *pa* there. Tuwhakairiora became renowned as a warrior, dominating the area from **Tolaga Bay** to Cape Runaway, and all Maori families in the region today trace their descent from him.

Ruataupare, meanwhile, grew jealous of her husband's influence. While their children were growing up, she constantly heard them referred to as the offspring of the great Tuwhakairiora, yet her name was barely mentioned. She returned to her own *iwi* in **Tokomaru Bay**, where she summoned all the warriors and started a war against rival *iwi*; victorious, Ruataupare became chieftainess of Tokomaru Bay.

Another legend that has shaped this wild land is one of rivalry between two students – **Paoa**, who excelled at navigation, and **Rongokaka**, who was renowned for travelling at great speed by means of giant strides. At the time, a beautiful maiden, Muriwhenua, lived in Hauraki and many set off to claim her for their bride. Paoa set off early but his rival took only one step and was ahead of him; this continued up the coast, with Rongokaka leaving huge footprints as he went – his imprint in the rock at Matakaoa Point, at the northern end of Hicks Bay, is the most clearly distinguishable. En route, they created the **Waiapu Mountains**: Paoa, flummoxed by Rongokaka's pace, set a snare for his rival at Tokomaru Bay, lashing the crown of a giant totara tree to a hill; recognizing the trap, Rongokaka cut it loose. The force with which the tree sprang upright caused such vibration that Mount Hikurangi partly disintegrated, forming the other mountain peaks. Finally, Rongokaka stepped across the Bay of Plenty and up to Hauraki, where he claimed his maiden.

Te Kaha Beach Resort SH35 ☎07 325 2830, ⓦtekahabeachresort.com. There's a very un-East Cape feel (apart from the dairy) to this modern, streamlined 3-storey complex with apartment-style accommodation featuring state-of-the-art kitchens, as well as a pool, and a restaurant and bar with 180-degree ocean views. Studio $145
Tui Lodge 200 Copenhagen Rd ☎07 325 2922, ⓦtuilodge.co.nz. Set within three acres of gardens, this spacious and supremely tranquil B&B in a purpose-built lodge just inland from the *Te Kaha Beach Resort* has en-suite rooms and offers dinner by arrangement ($37.50). $165

Pacific Coast Macadamias SH35 ☎07 325 2960, ⓦmacanuts.co.nz. Simple café amid the nut orchards where you can feast on delicious home-made macadamia products such as muffins and ice cream, as well as good coffee. Ask for directions to walk up to the waterfall. Oct–April daily 10am–3pm, longer in Jan.
★**The Homestead** SH35 ☎07 325 2071, ⓦhomesteadonthebay.co.nz. An attractive B&B on a sunny clifftop setting with great views. There are only two bedrooms, which share a bathroom, and three-course dinners ($50 with wine) are available on request. $190

WHANARUA BAY AND MARAEHAKO BAY

★**Maraehako Bay Retreat** SH35 ☎07 325 2648, ⓦmaraehako.co.nz. Paradisiacal, rustic waterside hostel in a rocky cove with a safe, private swimming beach, free use of sit-on-top kayaks and the chance for fishing, diving, whale and dolphin watching and horse-trekking expeditions. If you're lucky, you might meet Conrad the eel. Dorms $28, doubles $66
Maraehako Camping Ground SH35 ☎07 325 2901. Simple campsite covering the eastern end of stony Maraehako Bay, with toilets, solar-heated showers and plenty of space to pitch up. Run by the same welcoming Maori family as *Maraehako Bay Retreat*. Camping $16

WAIHAU BAY

Oceanside Apartments Oruaiti Beach, 5km east of Waihau Bay ☎07 325 3699, ⓦwaihaubay.co.nz. Two spacious self-contained units (one sleeping seven) just across the road from a safe, sandy beach. Try to catch your own supper by surfcasting for snapper and kahawai off the beach. Ask about the diving and fishing trips and kayak rental. Two-night minimum from Christmas–Easter. $130
Waihau Bay Holiday Park SH35, 3km east of Waihau Bay ☎07 315 3031. Modest campsite across SH35 from the beach, with reasonable facilities and its own camp store. Camping $16, units $110

5

Cape Runaway to Waipiro Bay

Beyond Waihau Bay the highway continues close to the water for a few more kilometres before veering inland at **Cape Runaway**, the East Cape's northernmost point. For the next 125km you hardly see the coast again, with the significant exceptions of **Hicks Bay**, **Te Araroa** and **East Cape**.

Hicks Bay

Tiny **HICKS BAY** (Wharekahika), 44km east of Waihau Bay, shelters between headlands and coastal rock bluffs almost halfway along SH35. There's a safe swimming beach at **Onepoto Bay** (the southern corner of the larger Hicks Bay), and the area makes a good base from which to visit the East Cape Lighthouse. Hicks Bay was named after Lieutenant Zachariah Hicks, who sighted it on Cook's *Endeavour* expedition in 1769. There are numerous *pa* sites in the area, in varying states of repair, some of which were modified for musket fighting during the 1860 Hauhau uprising.

Entering the community along Wharf Road, off SH35, you'll find a general store and not much else.

Te Araroa

From Hicks Bay, SH35 climbs over a hill and drops back to the coast beside the broad surf-washed shore of Kawakawa Bay. At its eastern end, the small village of **TE ARAROA** ("long pathway") marks the midway point between Opotiki and Gisborne. Te Araroa was once the domain of the famous Maori warrior Tuwhakairiora and the legendary Paikea, who is said to have arrived here on the back of a whale. Ironically, the first Europeans in the area set up a **whaling station** not far from the present township. These days the settlement contains little more than a petrol pump, two stores and a takeaway (daily for lunch and 4–6pm) selling fresh **fish and chips**. In the grounds of the local school on Moana Parade stands a **giant pohutukawa** tree – so giant that it's easy to believe the claims that it's New Zealand's largest.

East Cape Lighthouse

21km east of Te Araroa along an unsealed road • Follow the sign east along the foreshore

The New Zealand mainland's easternmost point is marked by the **East Cape Lighthouse**. The dramatic coastal run from Te Araroa is along a cliff-clinging road that ends in a tiny car park. From there, climb 757 steps to the lighthouse perched atop a 140m-high hill – an atmospheric spot with views inland to the Raukumara Range and seaward towards East Island (a bird sanctuary), just offshore.

St Mary's Church

SH35, Tikitiki • Open most days • Donations requested

From Te Araroa SH35 cuts inland through 24km of sheep-farming country before reaching **TIKITIKI** where you should take a peek inside the Anglican **church**, on a rise as you enter the town. It looks very plain from outside, but within hides a

---

EAST CAPE MANUKA OIL

Australian tea tree oil is famous for its antimicrobial qualities. The oil of the almost identical New Zealand **manuka** is generally just as good, but in 1992 manuka oil from the East Cape was found to have super-strong antibacterial and antifungal properties. The small factory at 4464 Te Araroa Rd, 2km west of Te Araroa (Nov–April Mon–Fri 8.30am–4pm, Sat & Sun 8.30am–2pm; May–Oct Mon–Fri 8.30am–4pm; ☎0508 626 852, ⊛manukaproducts.co.nz), extracts the essential oils by steam distillation from the twigs of manuka trees grown in the surrounding hills. You can't tour the factory, but a wide range of manuka-oil soaps, medicinal creams and aromatherapy potions (all exported around the world) is sold in the shop/café where you can also sample manuka tea and buy local manuka honey.

treasure-trove of elaborate Maori design, *tukutuku* and carving; unusually, the stained glass is also in Maori designs, and the rafters are painted in the colours of a Maori meetinghouse. The memorial to the war dead has a very long list for such a tiny community.

Ruatoria

Inland **RUATORIA**, signposted just off the main highway 19km south of Tikitiki, is the largest town since Opotiki (though that's not saying much), with a bank, petrol, a pub, groceries, and a serviceable daytime café as well as evening takeaways from the roadside *Kai Kart* nearby.

Waipiro Bay

At Kopuaroa, back on SH35 and 17km south of the Ruatoria turning, a loop road (the southern stretch is sealed and in better nick than the north) heads 6km to the broad sweep of **Waipiro Bay**, a busy port in its heyday, but now a beautiful and secluded inlet with just an incongruous brick church, and a few houses. It's a fine spot for a swim, or just sit on the beach watching the breakers.

ACCOMMODATION	CAPE RUNAWAY TO WAIPIRO BAY

HICKS BAY

Hicks Bay Motel Lodge 5198 Te Araroa Rd (SH35), 2km east of Hicks Bay ☎06 864 4880, ⓦhicksbaymotel.co.nz. A complex of comfortably vintage 1960s hotel rooms (some equipped with four bunks, others with motel-style kitchen facilities) set in spacious grounds high on the hill overlooking Onepoto and Hicks bays, with incredible views, good walks and wonderful bird song. There's also a licensed restaurant

(daily 7–8am & 6–7pm), a bar and access to a glowworm grotto. Dorms $50, doubles $110

TE ARAROA

Te Araroa Holiday Park 4814 Te Araroa Rd (SH35), 6km west of town ☎06 864 4873, ⓦteararoaholidaypark .co.nz. Campsite with a handy shop and a takeaway van in summer, plus sea kayaks and mountain bikes for rent. Camping $15, cabins $55, motel $140

CAPE RUNAWAY TO WAIPIRO BAY TOURS AND ACTIVITIES

Spend a little time around the northeastern reaches of the East Cape, either horse trekking, sampling something of the local Maori culture or exploring the slopes of sacred Mount Hikurangi.

Eastender Horse Treks ☎021 0258 0172, ⓦeastenderhorsetreks.co.nz. Book ahead for some of the best trips in the area, including a gallop along the beach ($85/2hr).

Matakaoa Cultural Tours 141 Onepoto Rd, Hicks Bay ☎021 885 602, ✉aniph407@gmail.com. To sample something of what it means to be Maori in Hicks Bay, join this tour which takes you around to points of significance to Maori, and might include a few house calls as well (2–3hr; $50).

MOUNT HIKURANGI TREK

The 1754m-high **Mount Hikurangi**, 25km west of Ruatoria, is the North Island's highest non-volcanic peak and the first place on the New Zealand mainland to see the sunrise. Sacred to Maori as the place where Maui (p.802) beached his *waka* after fishing up the North Island, nine giant **carvings** were installed at 1000m to celebrate the new millennium.

This hill country to the west of Ruatoria comes under the jurisdiction of the **Raukumara Conservation Area**, which includes the upper catchments of several rivers that drain into the Bay of Plenty. The desolate terrain and limited access discourage most visitors from exploring the park but it's possible to tackle the **trek** up Mount Hikurangi (20km return; 8–16hr; 1500m ascent) in one long day, although it's really best done over two days with a night in the rustic Mt Hikurangi Hut ($15) partway up.

The Ngati Porou control the land, so you'll need to contact Te Runanga O Ngati Porou, 1 Barry's Ave, Ruatoria (☎06 864 9004, ✉pbrooking@tronp.org.nz), for access permission and to pay hut fees. For a cultural perspective, ask about customized **guided trips**.

5

Tokomaru Bay to Whangara

At **Tokomaru Bay** the road emerges from inland bush and pastoral country to reveal the North Island's east coast in all its glory. For the remaining 80km to Gisborne you stay mostly inland but catch frequent glimpses of yawning bays and crashing surf, accessed directly on SH35 or short side roads leading to little-visited coves.

Tokomaru Bay

TOKOMARU BAY (or just "Toko"), 40km south of Ruatoria, is a gorgeous spot to idle for a day, exploring the steep green hills, rocky headlands and the broad expanse of **beach**, which is dotted with driftwood, pounded by surf, and provides a good spot to swim. The Maori who settled here trace their descent to Toi te Huatahi, the great navigator and the first to arrive from the ancestral home of Hawaiki. In 1865 the Mawhai *pa* was the scene of several attacks by a party of Hauhau, but a small garrison of old men and women repulsed them.

At the far northern end of the bay, a long wooden wharf and the ruined buildings of the abattoir and freezing works testify to the former prosperity of this once-busy port, which thrived until improved road transport forced the factory's closure in 1953.

Anaura Bay

Some 23km south from Tokomaru, a 7km-long sealed side road runs over the hill to rugged **ANAURA BAY**, a prized **surf** spot with a broad sweep of sand and jagged headlands. At the north end of the bay (4km on a gravel road), the **Anaura Scenic Reserve** harbours a large area of mixed broadleaf bush noted for its large puriri trees and abundance of native birds. Starting near the end of the road, and signposted to the west by the reserve, the **Anaura Bay Walkway** (3.5km loop; 2hr) follows the course of the Waipare Stream into thick green bush, up a gently climbing valley and out into scrubland before turning back towards the bay and a lookout point with magnificent views.

Tolaga Bay

TOLAGA BAY (Uawa), 36km south of Tokomaru, is the first place you reach since leaving Opotiki that feels like a viable town, its eight-hundred-strong population one of the better-serviced communities on the East Cape, with a supermarket, petrol and a clutch of cafés. Once again, rugged headlands enclose the bay, the scene of a 1769 visit by James Cook and his crew. They're commemorated in the town's street names: Banks, Solander, Forester and, of course, Cook. Anchoring to replenish his stocks of food and water, Cook named the bay "Tolaga", a misinterpretation of the Maori name for the prevailing wind (*teraki*).

Tolaga Bay Wharf
Wharf Rd

Tolaga Bay's claim to fame is the 660m-long concrete **Tolaga Bay Wharf**, said to be the longest concrete jetty in the southern hemisphere. Built in the late 1920s to service coastal shipping, it juts out past steep sandstone cliffs into deep water. Its impressive length didn't stop it becoming redundant when coastal shipping ceased here in 1963. Once in a near-ruinous state, some restoration has taken place, and its historic-place ranking has been raised to the highest level, so more will undoubtedly follow. It's no longer strong enough for vehicles, but you can wander to the end for a picturesque picnic.

Cooks Cove Walkway
1km south of town on Wharf Rd • 5.8km; 2hr 30min return

Cooks Cove Walkway is the best of Tolaga Bay's short walks, involving an initial walk across farmland then a steep and often muddy climb through bush and birdlife to a great viewpoint looking down to Cook's Cove. The track heads down to the cove where there's a plaque marking the good captain's visit here in 1769.

Whangara

Guided introduction to the area, including a visit to *a marae*, with Tipuna Tours • from $70 • ☎ 027 240 4493 or ☎ 06 862 6118

The 47km stretch from Tolaga Bay to Gisborne becomes both tamer and bleaker the further south you travel, much of the land cleared for farming. The road climbs in and out of more small bays, occasionally providing panoramic vistas of sea and close-ups of the slate-grey rock shelves that characterize this coast. It passes the turn-off to **Whangara**, where the film *Whale Rider* was shot, but, as there's no direct access, there's little to see from the lookout apart from a sweep of sand and an island said to be the fossilized remains of the whale that the legendary Paikea rode all the way from Hawaiki.

After Whangara there's little to stop you heading straight for Gisborne except to ride the renowned surf at **WAINUI BEACH**, 9km from the city.

ACCOMMODATION AND EATING   TOKOMARU BAY TO WHANGARA

TOKOMARU BAY

★ **Stranded in Paradise** 21 Potae St ☎ 06 864 5870, ⓦ stranded-in-paradise.net. A small, friendly spot with loft-style rooms, dorms with a maximum of three guests, composting toilets, a couple of superb tent sites and some amazing cabins (one of which is a single; $45), all perched on a hillside with great sea views. Borrow a fishing line, rent surfboards or a kayak ($5; free if you stay a second night) or ask them to arrange a horse trek with the local cop. Camping $\overline{20}$, dorms $\overline{30}$, doubles and cabins $\overline{70}$

Te Puka Tavern 153 Beach Road ☎ 06 864 5465, ⓦ tepukatavern.co.nz. Revitalised traditional Kiwi pub with coffee machine, internet and decent grub such as a seafood basket or steak and eggs ($25). It is the only place in town for a drink, so it can get busy at weekends. They also have four brand-new townhouse-style units with awesome sea views. Daily 11am–10pm or later, closed Mon & Tues lunch in winter. $\overline{160}$

ANAURA BAY

Anaura Bay campsite Very basic DOC site wonderfully set beside the beach immediately beyond the start of the Anaura Bay Walkway. There's water but no toilets (you'll need a chemical toilet or holding tank), though there is a dump station on-site from Dec–Feb. Closed Easter–late Oct. $\overline{6}$

Anaura Bay Motor Camp ☎ 06 862 6380. At the south end of the bay, superbly sited beside the beach. Facilities are in the former schoolhouse and there's a store selling essentials. Free wi-fi so you can keep in touch – there's no cellphone coverage. Camping $\overline{16}$, powered sites $\overline{18}$

TOLAGA BAY

Tolaga Bay Holiday Park 167 Wharf Rd ☎ 06 862 6716, ⓦ tolagabayholidaypark.co.nz. Beachfront campsite with a store, barbecue area, kayak rental, great views and a handful of cabins, as well as a few other options. Camping $\overline{16}$, beachfront cabin $\overline{90}$

Tolaga Bay Inn 12 Cook St ☎ 06 862 6856. The Bay's best place to eat, serving muffins, coffee, and the likes of chicken ciabatta open sandwich ($18) or eggs Benedict with salmon ($17.50). 9am–7pm daily.

Poverty Bay, Hawke's Bay and the Wairarapa

VINEYARD AND TE MATA PEAK, HAWKES BAY

Poverty Bay, Hawke's Bay and the Wairarapa

From the eastern tip of the North Island, a mountainous backbone runs 650km southwest to the outskirts of Wellington, defining and isolating the east coast. The Raukumara, Kaweka, Ruahine, Tararua and Rimutaka mountain ranges protect much of the region from the prevailing westerlies and cast a long rain shadow, the bane of local sheep farmers, who watch their land become parched, dusty and brown each summer. Increasingly, these pastures are being given over to viticulture, and the regions of Poverty Bay, Hawke's Bay and the Wairarapa are world-renowned for their wine. Any tour has to take in Poverty Bay, a major grape-growing region, whose main centre, Gisborne, was the first part of New Zealand sighted by Cook's expedition in 1769. Finding little – besides wary Maori – he named it Poverty Bay and sailed south to an area he later named Hawke Bay, after his boyhood hero Admiral Sir Edward Hawke (the name of the surrounding province has since evolved into Hawke's Bay). Here Cook clashed with Maori at Cape Kidnappers, now the site of an impressive gannet colony.

Hawke's Bay has long been dubbed "the fruit bowl of New Zealand" and its orchard boughs still sag under the weight of apples, pears and peaches. The district is best visited from the waterfront city of **Napier**, famed for its Art Deco buildings, constructed after a massive earthquake flattened much of the city in 1931. Nearby **Hastings** suffered the same fate and wove Spanish Mission-style buildings into the resulting Art Deco fabric, though these won't delay you long as you head south to the sheep lands of the **Wairarapa** and the temptingly accessible vineyards surrounding **Martinborough**.

Access to the mountainous **interior** of this region is limited, with only six roads winding over or cutting through the full length of the ranges. The tortuous but scenic SH38 forges northwest from the small town of **Wairoa**, the gateway to the remote wooded mountains of Te Urewera and beautiful **Lake Waikaremoana**, which is encircled by the four-day Lake Waikaremoana Track tramping route.

GETTING AROUND

By train The only passenger trains in the region are Tranz Metro (☎ 0800 801 700, ⓦ metlink.org.nz) linking the main Wairarapa towns (including Masterton, Carterton and Featherston) with Wellington.

By bus InterCity (ⓦ intercity.co.nz) run a daily service between Gisborne and Napier, and two south to Wellington, though these go through Palmerston North, missing the Wairarapa past Dannevirke. NakedBus (ⓦ nakedbus.co.nz) run a twice daily service from Napier and Hastings to Wellington that also routes via Palmerston North.

Highlights

❶ Lake Waikaremoana Take in this picturesque lake on short hikes or while tackling the North Island's most prized multi-day tramp. **See p.381**

❷ Napier Wander through the world's finest collection of small-scale Art Deco architecture to Napier's pine-shaded seafront promenade. **See p.385**

❸ Swim with sharks Take a dip – if you dare – with the sharks in their tank at Napier's National Aquarium. **See p.388**

❹ Cape Kidnappers Come face-to-beak with residents of the world's largest mainland gannet colony on a tour or under your own steam. **See p.392**

❺ Vineyards Sip to your heart's content in Hawke's Bay Wine Country, or stroll to almost a dozen fine wineries from appealing Martinborough. **See p.396 & p.408**

❻ Pukaha Mount Bruce National Wildlife Centre Observe some of the world's rarest birdlife thanks to the conservation heroics performed at this bushland sanctuary. **See p.402**

HIGHLIGHTS ARE MARKED ON THE MAP ON P.372

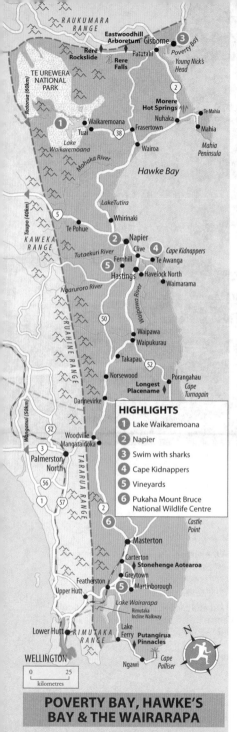

(see box, p.383)

Gisborne

New Zealand's easternmost city, **GISBORNE**, is the first to catch the sun each day, and, thanks to the isolating mountain ranges all about, it has been spared from overdevelopment. Broad straight streets are lined with squat weatherboard houses and shops and interspersed with expansive parkland hugging the Pacific, the harbour and three rivers – the Taruheru, Turanganui and Waimata.

Brief history

Here, in October 1769, **James Cook** first set foot on the soil of Aotearoa, an event commemorated by a shoreside statue. He immediately ran into conflict with local Maori, killing several of them before sailing away empty-handed. He named the landing site **Poverty Bay**, since "it did not afford a single item we wanted, except a little firewood". Despite the fertility of the surrounding lands, the name stuck, though many Maori prefer **Turanganui a Kiwa** – honouring a Polynesian navigator.

Early nineteenth-century Poverty Bay remained staunchly Maori and few Pakeha moved here, discouraged by both the Hauhau rebellion and Te Kooti's uprising (see box, p.383). It wasn't until the 1870s that **Europeans** arrived in numbers to farm the rich alluvial river flats. After a decent port was constructed in the 1920s, sheep farming and market gardening took off, followed more recently by the grape harvest and the rise of plantation forestry. Today Gisborne's Maori and Pakeha population is almost exactly 50:50, and the city's relaxed pace and easy-going beach culture make it appealing to visitors in search of a little sun and surf.

Cook's statue and landing site

Young's and Cook's statues are both in the park on the western side of the river-mouth • Cook's landing site is on the opposite side of the river, on Kaiti Beach Rd

Most of Gisborne's sights are connected in some way to the historical accident of James Cook's landing – and the dynamic between Maori and Pakeha cultures it engendered. The first of Cook's crew to spy the mountains of Aotearoa, a couple of days before the first landing, was 12-year-old

GISBORNE

■ ACCOMMODATION	
Flying Nun	2
Knapdale Eco Lodge	1
Pacific Harbour Motor Inn	4
Waikanae Beach Top 10 Holiday Park	5
Whispering Sands	3
YHA Gisborne	6

● EATING & DRINKING	
Café 84	7
Gisborne Farmers' Market	1
Gisborne Wine Centre	9
Muirs Bookshop Café	4
Off the Hook & Real Fisheries	10
The PBC	6
The Rivers	5
Smash Palace	2
Soho	11
Tatapouri Sports Fishing Club	8
Verve Café	3

surgeon's boy Nick Young. Cook rewarded him by naming the white-cliffed promontory, 10km south of Gisborne across Poverty Bay, on his chart as Young Nick's Head. Young's keen eyes are commemorated by a statue of a youth pointing (hopefully but none too certainly) at the cliffs. Nearby is a **statue of Cook** atop a stone hemisphere. A grey obelisk on the eastern side of the river-mouth marks **Cook's landing site**.

James Cook Observatory

Titirangi Drive • Public stargazing every Tues; non-Daylight Saving Time door closes at 7.30pm; during Daylight Saving Time door closes at 8.30pm • $5 • You can access the observatory from Titirangi Domain via a footpath that leads to Titirangi Drive

Behind Titirangi Domain, Titirangi Drive climbs the side of **Kaiti Hill** to **Cook Plaza**, designed around a sculpture intended to represent Cook. Kaiti Hill's highest point has tremendous views across Poverty Bay to the cliffs of Young Nick's Head, and is occupied by the **James Cook Observatory**, which runs public stargazing nights and amateur research – they discovered an exoplanet a few years back.

Te Poho-o-Rawiri Meeting House

Queens Drive • Visits arranged by calling Mihi Aston at ☎ 06 863 2350 • Donation

On the eastern side of the Kaiti Hill lies **Te Poho-o-Rawiri Meeting House**, one of the largest in the country. The interior is superb, full of fine ancestor carvings interspersed with wonderfully varied geometric *tukutuku* (woven panels). At the foot of the two support poles, ancient and intricately carved warrior statues provide a fine counterpoint to the bolder work on the walls. Like most *marae* it is not easily accessible but you may be able to tag on to large prearranged tours; book in advance.

Te Tauihu Turanga Whakamana

Heipipi Endeavour Park, corner of Customhouse St and Gladstone Rd

Early Maori explorers are honoured with **Te Tauihu Turanga Whakamana** – a striking wooden sculpture in the centre of town, depicting a Maori *tauihu* (canoe prow) carved with images of Tangaroa (god of the sea), the demigod Maui, and Toi Kai Rakau (one of the earliest Maori to settle in New Zealand).

Tairawhiti Museum

10 Stout St • Jan daily 10am–4pm, Feb–Dec Mon–Sat 10am–4pm, Sun 1.30–4pm • $5; free on Mon • ☎ 06 867 3832, ⓦ tairawhitimuseum.org.nz

Across the river at the **Tairawhiti Museum**, the permanent Watersheds exhibit charts the parallel and intertwining lives of Maori and Europeans on the East Coast. There's everything from a whalebone walking stick carved with Maori designs and coverage of Cook's arrival to the vibrant painting of early Ngati Porou leader Hinematioro by renowned painter Robyn Kahukiwa.

A maritime wing incorporates the original wheelhouse and captain's quarters of the 12,000-tonne *Star of Canada*, which ran aground on the reef off Gisborne's Kaiti Beach in 1912, along with exhibits on shipping, and a shrine to local surfing. Several disused buildings from around the region are clustered outside the museum, notably the six-room 1872 **Wyllie Cottage**, the oldest extant house in town, and the **Sled House**, built on runners at the time of the Hauhau uprising so that it could be hauled away by a team of bullocks at the first sign of unrest.

GISBORNE TOURS AND ACTIVITIES

Gisborne offers one of New Zealand's few opportunities for heart-pounding **shark encounters**, thankfully (for some) in the safety of an aquarium. The **reef** is worth a look, too, or you can try your hand at **surfing**. **Wine tours** are also popular, and a good way to see the surrounding countryside.

Blitz Surf 34 Wainui Road ☎ 06 868 4428, ⓦ blitzsurf.co.nz. The helpful guys at this well-stocked store will also advise on local conditions and run classes. Private ($75) and group ($50, maximum six people/group) lessons for SUP or surfing, including gear hire and transport. They'll give you an extra two hours' free hire so you can practise. To hire an SUP is $40/half-day. Mon–Fri 9am–5.30pm, Sat 9am–4pm, Sun 10am–3pm.

Dive Tatapouri Tatapouri, 14km northeast of Gisborne ☎ 06 868 5153, ⓦ divetatapouri.com. Offer a reef ecology tour ($45) on which you don waders, walk onto the reef at low tide and hand-feed stingrays, kingfish and octopus. They also run a snorkel with stingrays session for $70. Book in advance for both.

Gisborne Wine Tours Shed 3, 50 The Esplanade ☎ 06 867 4085, ⓦ gisbornewine.co.nz. This five-hour tour visits three wineries (locations are changed daily) and the price ($110) includes all wine tastings and an antipasto lunch at one of the stops. It departs daily at 11am from the Gisborne Wine Centre, with a maximum of eight people/trip or minimum of two; book in advance.

Surfing With Frank ☎ 06 867 0823, ⓦ surfingwithfrank.com. To take advantage of Gisborne's renowned surf, hit the breaks with Frank Russell and his team. Frank's been doing this for years and can get most anyone standing up on a board (private lesson $90; group lesson $60 including board and wetsuit rental, maximum four people/group).

Tipuna Tours ☎ 027 240 4493 or ☎ 06 862 6118. One of the best ways to explore the region is with this operator, who runs cultural interpretation tours (from $70) which can include a visit to a *marae* or to Whangara (see p.367), visiting some locations where the movie *Whale Rider* was shot.

Next door is a striking new memorial house commemorating the 28th Maori Battalion C Company, a voluntary rifle unit which served in World War II.

Toihoukura

Cobden St, near the corner of Gladstone Rd • Mon–Fri 9am–5pm, but during termtimes by appointment • ☎ 06 898 0847 • Free

A striking modern whale-tail sculpture heralds **Toihoukura**, a school of Maori visual arts and design where existing carvings are restored and students are instructed in the oral history and traditions of Maori design. Interpretations using modern materials and techniques are encouraged, and many vibrant and stunning pieces find their way into the public gallery. Most exhibits are for sale and would make meaningful souvenirs.

Sunshine Brewery

49 Awapuni St • Mon–Wed 3–7pm, Thurs & Fri noon–8pm, Sat noon–8pm, Sun noon–6pm • ☎ 06 867 7777, ⓦ sunshinebrewery.co.nz

If you've worked up a thirst sightseeing, repair here for a peep of the brewhouse and a sampling of Gisborne Gold lager, Pilsner, stout and a delectable English-style ale in their new taproom. The lager is available in bars around town too, but the shop prices are cheaper.

The Cidery

91 Customhouse St • Mon–Fri 9am–4pm • ☎ 06 868 8300

This is Bulmer Harvest's smallest plant, where you can peer at operations through the glass wall. The guys here are friendly and they've been making cider, using apples from local orchards, for the last 25 years. The samples they dish out are splendid; try the zingy ciders (including refreshing watermelon and cucumber), local mead, harvest scrumpy and a non-boozy ginger beer.

ARRIVAL AND DEPARTURE   GISBORNE

By bus NakedBus and InterCity buses converge on the i-SITE. **Destinations** Auckland (1 daily; 9hr 30min); Hastings (1 daily; 5hr); Napier (1 daily; 4hr); Opotiki, via SH2 (2 daily; 2hr); Rotorua (1 daily; 5hr); Wairoa (1 daily; 1hr 30min); Whakatane (2 daily; 3hr).

By plane Direct flights from Auckland and Wellington arrive at Gisborne airport, about 2km west of the town centre, which can be reached by taxi for $20; try Gisborne Taxis (☎ 06 867 2222). There are also flights to Rotorua, Hamilton, Tauranga, Napier and Palmerston North. **Destinations** Auckland (4–5 daily; 1hr); Wellington (3–4 daily; 1hr 15min).

GETTING AROUND

By bike Most of the city is easily covered on foot, though Gisborne Cycle Tour Company (☎ 06 927 7021, ⓦ gisbornecycletours.co.nz) rent bikes and mountain bikes from $50/day, and also put together packages for guided or unguided spins round the wineries (from $100; see p.377). Their bikes can be collected at the i-SITE.

INFORMATION

i-SITE 209 Grey St (daily: Dec to Easter Mon–Sat 8.30am–6pm, Sun 10am–4pm; Easter to Nov Mon–Sat 8.30am–4pm, Sun 10am–4pm; ☎ 06 868 6139, ⓦ gisbornenz.com). Offers internet access, has exhibits on local social and natural history, and a mini-golf course. Hires fishing rods, bikes (see above) and skateboards for the park opposite. Can advise on freedom camping ($16/2 nights to $66/28 nights).

DOC 63 Carnarvon St (Mon–Fri 8am–5pm; ☎ 06 869 0460). Has plenty of information on local walks and tramping outside the immediate Gisborne area; also sells hut passes.

Services Internet terminals and free wi-fi at the library, 35 Peel St (Mon & Wed–Fri 9.30am–5.30pm, Tues 9.30am–8pm, Sat 9.30am–1pm). Free wi-fi in the CBD.

ACCOMMODATION

Despite the huge number of motels – chiefly along the main strip, palm-shaded Gladstone Road, and the waterfront Salisbury Road – accommodation can be hard to come by during the month or so after Christmas.

6

Flying Nun 147 Roebuck Rd ☎ 06 868 0461. This slightly scruffy, hippyish former convent, a 15min walk from town, is where Dame Kiri Te Kanawa first trained her voice. Some of the spacious dorms front onto broad verandas, and although doubles can be a little cramped, singles are good value. Spacious grounds include a BBQ area and games room. Cash only. Dorms $24, doubles and twins $58

★**Knapdale Eco Lodge** 114 Snowsill Rd, Waihirere, 13km northwest of Gisborne ☎ 06 862 5444, ⊛ knapdale .co.nz. Luxurious lodge in a tranquil semi-permaculture farm with chickens, deer and horses. The two rooms are both airy and cosy, and a dawn chorus from the nearby forest alerts you to the sumptuous breakfast. Gourmands should book one of the exquisite dinners ($85/person). Deluxe room $398, "Romance" room $472

Pacific Harbour Motor Inn Cnr of Reads Quay and Pitt St ☎ 06 867 8847, ⊛ pacific-harbour.co.nz. Glass bricks and panoramic windows – some with harbour views – flood this contemporary motel with natural light. The rooms are large and fully equipped, and some come with balconies and spa baths. Units $130

Waikanae Beach Top 10 Holiday Park Grey St ☎ 06 867 5634, ⊛ www.gisborneholidaypark.co.nz. Idyllically sited motor-park right by Gisborne's main beach and a 5min walk from town. Some of the comfortable cabins are en suite ($75), and there are also self-contained ($115) and motel units ($139). Camping $18, standard cabins $65

★**Whispering Sands** 22 Salisbury Rd ☎ 0800 405 030, ⊛ whisperingsands.co.nz. Great-value beachfront motel with fourteen large, modern units, all with full kitchens; those on the upper level have sea views – well worth it for an extra $5. The owners are friendly and very helpful. $150

YHA Gisborne 32 Harris St ☎ 06 867 3269, ⊛ yha.co.nz. Spacious, central hostel in a weatherboard homestead with a sunny deck, barbecue, a cheery paint job and staff switched on to the local surf hotspots. Guests can rent bikes, surfboards or wetsuits for $25/day. There are twins, doubles and one en suite. Ask nicely and the buses may drop you off outside. Dorms $26, rooms $58

EATING

Café 84 14 Childers Rd ☎ 06 868 6516. Licensed, daytime café with free wi-fi and an authentic Hawaiian theme. Good specials, or create your own juice combo or design an omelette ($14 with 3 fillings). Everything's under $20. Tues–Fri 7am–2pm, Sat 8am–2pm.

Gisborne Farmers' Market Army Hall car park, cnr Fitzherbert and Stout Sts ⊛ gisbornefarmers market.co.nz. A bustling market that's great for fruit and vegetables, as well as all manner of meats, cheeses, organic produce and baked goods. Sat 9.30am–12.30pm.

Muirs Bookshop Café 62 Gladstone Rd. Airy café tucked above Gisborne's best bookshop, adjacent to the secondhand section. From a sun-drenched balcony that overlooks the main street, you can tuck into panini, salads, scrumptious cake; most menu items are under $12. Mon–Fri 8.30am–3.30pm, Sat 9am–3pm.

★**Off the Hook & Real Fisheries** The Esplanade, at Crawford Rd ☎ 06 868 1644. The best fish and chip takeaway in town serves cooked-to-order fresh fish, including snapper, moki, trevally and terakihi ($14 with chips). *Real Fisheries* is part of the same operation, and good for those looking for straight-off-the-boat catches.

Tues 10am–5pm, Wed & Thurs 10am–6pm, Fri 10am–8pm; Real Fisheries Mon & Tues 9am–5pm, Wed & Thurs 9am–6pm, Fri 9am–8pm.

Soho 2 Crawford Rd, Wharfside ☎ 06 868 3888. Pretty standard (dark wood and mood lighting) bar that comes alive on Friday and Saturday nights when there are live bands and occasional DJs. The menu is eclectic – they've sourced Wagyu beef (with pumpkin purée; $38) and decided to make a Gizzy carbonara ($20) with risotto. Tues–Fri 11am–late, Sat 9am–late.

Tatapouri Sports Fishing Club 54 The Esplanade ☎ 06 868 4756. Sociable club right on the wharf with veranda seating for seafood, steaks or gourmet burgers (all under $30). Visitors just sign in: ask at the bar. Mon & Tues 11am–10pm, Wed & Thurs 11am–midnight, Fri & Sat 10am–midnight, Sun 10am–11pm.

★**Verve Café** 121 Gladstone Rd ☎ 06 868 9095. With rotating art exhibitions by up-and-coming local artists, this groovy but low-key daytime café and restaurant serves gorgeous, moderately priced food, from the famous chicken sandwiches ($18) to falafel, steak sandwiches and cakes (mains to $25). Mon–Fri 7.30am–5.30pm, Sat & Sun 8am–3pm.

DRINKING AND NIGHTLIFE

Gisborne Wine Centre 50 The Esplanade ☎ 06 867 4085 ⊛ gisbornewine.co.nz. Set up by a co-operative of local winegrowers, you can pick up a map of local wineries, get advice on which cellar doors are open (they'll make appointments too), book a tour, have a tasting, or just buy a glass or bottle of wine to enjoy overlooking the water with one of their local food platters. Winter daily noon–6pm;

summer Mon & Tues noon–6pm, Wed & Thurs noon–8pm, Fri noon–10pm, Sat & Sun noon–8pm.

The PBC (Poverty Bay Club) 38 Childers Rd, at Customhouse St ☎ 06 863 2006, ⊛ thepovertybayclub .co.nz. A cool, intimate bar/club with a great bar, smooth leather sofas and some classy liquids to partake of while listening to mellow sounds. Occasional cover charge

around $5. Wed–Fri 5pm–late, Sat 8pm–late, Sun 5.30pm–late.
The Rivers Cnr Gladstone Rd and Reads Quay ☎ 06 863 3733. Convivial Irish-type bar with Emerson's porter and a range of hearty meals including steaks, pies, chicken and fish ($16–33) that's popular with families. Mon–Sat 11am–late, Sun noon–late.
★**Smash Palace** 24 Banks St ☎ 06 867 7769.

Wonderfully oddball bar in a corrugated-iron barn, where overalls from the surrounding industrial area rub shoulders with suits. Food basically comprises snacks – favourites include flaming pizzas ($20) and nachos flame-toasted with a blowtorch ($15). There's live entertainment, too, from rock to heavy metal, mostly at weekends and in summer. Tues–Thurs 3pm–late, Fri 2pm–late, Sat noon–late, Sun 2.30pm–late.

CINEMAS

★**Dome Cinema** The Poverty Bay Club, 38 Childers Rd ☎ 083 243 005, ⓦ domecinema.co.nz. Fabulous, independent screen with bean-bag seating, a bar and an eclectic mix of must-see films, all shown in the old

billiard room.
Odeon Cinema 79 Gladstone Rd ☎ 06 867 3339. Expect all the usual mainstream blockbusters.

SHOPPING

Stone Studio 237 Stanley Road ☎ 06 867 3900, ⓦ stonestudio.co.nz. Small family-run shop and studio where you can watch the two carvers at work. They only

use New Zealand greenstone, and take commissions. Mon–Fri 8.30am–5pm, Sat 10am–noon.

Around Gisborne

Winery visits, gentle walks and a smattering of specific attractions make a day or so spent in Gisborne's surrounds an agreeable prospect. Occupying a free-draining alluvial valley in the lee of the Raukumara Range and blessed with long hours of strong sun and cooling sea breezes, the wineries (ⓦ gisbornewine.co.nz) have traditionally operated as a viticultural workhorse, churning out vast quantities of gluggable Chardonnay. Many give a personal touch if you call in advance, and a few open for regular tastings in summer. If you don't have a car, your best bet is to hire a **bike** or opt for a wineries tour (see box, p.374).

Bushmere Estate

166 Main Rd South, 6km northwest of Gisborne • Tastings normally Thurs–Sun; call ahead to check • ☎ 06 868 9317 • ⓦ bushmere.com
With a reduced demand for Chardonnay, many smaller producers in the Poverty Bay region are now planting better cultivars (along with Viognier and Gewürtztraminer) and producing boutique wines. One such is **Bushmere Estate**, with a good café in a pretty vineyard setting; it's very popular with locals for Sunday lunch.

Millton

119 Papatu Rd, 11km southwest of Gisborne • Tastings daily 10am–5pm • ☎ 06 862 8680, ⓦ millton.co.nz
Millton is one of New Zealand's few organic wineries to apply biodynamic principles. The timing of planting, harvesting and bottling is dictated by the moon's phases to produce some delicious wines (especially Chardonnay, Chenin Blanc and Viognier) that, it is claimed, can be enjoyed even by those who experience allergic reactions to other wines. Buy a cheese or charcuterie platter to enjoy with your wine.

Eastwoodhill Arboretum

Wharekopae Rd, 35km northwest of Gisborne • Daily 9am–5pm • $15 • ☎ 06 863 9003, ⓦ eastwoodhill.org.nz
A bottle of wine tucked under your arm and a groaning picnic hamper is the way to enjoy New Zealand's largest collection of northern hemisphere vegetation at

6

Eastwoodhill Arboretum. It was the life's work of William Douglas Cook, who grew to love British gardens and parks while recuperating in England during World War I. Concerned that war would break up the great estates of Europe and destroy their genetic stock of trees, he imported the best he could. Cook died in 1967 leaving over 3500 species – magnolia, oak, spruce, maple, cherry – brought together in an unusual microclimate in which both hot- and cold-climate trees flourish.

6

Rere rockslide

12km past Eastwoodhill Arboretum, accessed off Wharekopae Rd

The Wharekopae River plunges 10m over **Rere Falls**, where you can walk behind the curtain of water, but this is easily eclipsed by the **Rere rockslide**, about 2km upstream, where the river cascades down a 20m-wide and 60m-long rock slope that is smooth enough to provide great sport. In summer there's little water and a lot of algae, making for a super-fast ride down to the pool at the bottom. The extra water in winter makes for a slower, less exciting and colder ride. Bring something to slide on – a boogie board, inner tube or old bit of plastic – and ask locals for advice and safety tips.

The road to Napier

At 213km, the road from Gisborne to Napier is easily manageable in a day, allowing plenty of time to take in the at times spectacular scenery and all the worthwhile stops along the way. South of Gisborne, **SH2** leaves the Poverty Bay vineyards behind and traverses the hill country of the Wharerata State Forest before reaching **Morere**. From there it's just a short jaunt down SH2 before you can turn east and access the **Mahia Peninsula**. Continuing west on SH2 brings you to Wairoa, from where you can access Te Urewera (see p.380) and Lake Waikaremoana, or continue on to Napier, stopping off to see the **Boundary Scenic Reserve**.

Morere and Morere Hot Springs

SH2, 50km south of Gisborne • Daily 10am–5pm, later in summer if busy • $10; private pools extra $5 for 30min • ☏ 06 837 8856, ⓦ morerehotsprings.co.nz

Tiny **MORERE** is best known for the highly saline and pleasantly non-sulphurous waters – the result of ancient seawater, warmed and concentrated along a fault line – that well up along a small stream at the **Morere Hot Springs**. The immediate area is also one of the East Coast's last remaining tracts of native coastal forest, and grassy barbecue areas surrounding the pools form the nucleus of numerous trails that radiate out through stands of tawa, rimu, totara and matai; a short streamside walk (10min) takes you to the Nikau Plunge Pools, where soaking tanks are surrounded by nikau palm groves. Also consider the **Mangakawa Track** (3km; 2hr), which loops from the springs through gorgeous virgin bush up to a ridge-top beech forest.

ACCOMMODATION | MORERE

Morere Hot Springs Lodge & Cabins SH2 ☏ 06 837 8824, ⓦ morerehotsprings.co.nz. A wonderfully relaxing spot with self-contained accommodation scattered around the well-kept grassy site, all on a working farm with a good swimming hole. Bring most supplies with you. Cabins **$90**, cottage **$120**

Morere Tearooms & Camping Ground Just west of Nuhaka on SH2 ☏ 06 837 8792. A traditional Kiwi campsite surrounded by trees, with good tent sites, basic cabins and limited communal facilities, but more comfortable self-contained units. Limited supplies are available at the tearooms, at a price. Tearoom open daily 8am–5pm, later after Dec. Camping **$18.50**, cabins **$55**, self-contained units **$95**

Mahia Peninsula

At Nuhaka, 8km south of Morere, the highway flirts briefly with the sea before turning sharp right for Wairoa. Nuhaka–Opoutama Road spurs east to the **Mahia Peninsula**, a distinctive high promontory that separates Hawke Bay from Poverty Bay. Surfers make good use of the rougher windward side, while the calmer beaches on the leeward side offer safe bathing and boating. Outside the mad month after Christmas it makes a relaxing place to break your journey. The peninsula's main settlement, **MAHIA BEACH**, lies 15km further on. It's famous nationally because Moko, a bottlenose dolphin cavorted with swimmers in 2008 and 2009. He's not been back.

6

ACCOMMODATION AND EATING   MAHIA PENINSULA

Café Mahia 476 Mahia East Coast Rd. Licensed café serving tempting hogget rolls and flogging home-made jams and relishes. Nothing on the menu is over $20 – you'll find coffee and cake or a sandwich is ambitious enough. Daily 11am–2pm, later in Dec and Jan.

Mahia Beach Holiday Park 43 Moana Drive, Mahia Beach ☎ 06 837 5830, ⓦ mahiabeach.com. Spacious camping, basic tourist cabins and flashier motel units are the order of the day at this refurbished camp spread out on grassland back from the beach, which gets

absolutely stuffed in the summer. The office shop has a small amount of supplies. Camping $21, cabins $75, motel units $125

Sunset Point Bar and Grill 2 Newcastle St ☎ 06 837 5071. Apart from takeaways, eating in Mahia is limited to this lively spot, which does hearty meals such as steak, crayfish, and fish and chips ($15–34). The bottleshop closes at 10pm, the kitchen at 8pm. They often have live music at weekends during high season. Closed Mon, Tues–Thurs 4pm–late, Fri–Sun noon–late.

Wairoa

Although the official launch pad for trips to Lake Waikaremoana, many trampers prefer to travel from Gisborne or Napier and not disturb the dust at the sleepy farm service community of **WAIROA**, 40km west of the Nuhaka junction. Hugging the banks of the willow-lined Wairoa River a couple of kilometres from its mouth, where ships once entered to load the produce of the dairy- and sheep-farming country all around, the town offers little reason to break your journey, except an intriguing museum and the chance to eat or stock up on provisions for the Waikaremoana Track (see p.381).

Wairoa Museum

142 Marine Parade • Mon–Fri 10am–4pm, Sat 10am–noon • Donation

The **Wairoa Museum** evokes a picture of the town's more lively history through well-presented displays (including one on the devastating cyclone Bola, which swept through the region in 1988) and contains a beautifully carved Maori figure dating back to the early eighteenth century. Also worth checking out is the information on the Wairoa Bar and the river pilot from 1872 who died at sea; no mention is made of whether he had a locker, but he was called Davy Jones.

ARRIVAL AND INFORMATION   WAIROA

By bus InterCity buses pick up daily at the i-SITE.
Destinations Gisborne (1 daily; 1hr 30min); Napier (1 daily; 2hr 30min).

i-SITE Corner of SH2 and Queen St (Mon–Fri 8am–5pm, Sat & Sun 10am–11am & 3.15–4pm to coincide with incoming buses; ☎ 06 838 7440, ⓦ visitwairoa.co.nz). Sells

DOC hut tickets, arranges Lake Waikaremoana shuttle pick-ups, has internet access and can advise on freedom camping sites in the district.

Internet There's free wi-fi in the CBD, charged-for at the i-SITE.

GETTING AROUND

By bus The Big Bush Lake Waikaremoana Shuttle Service (☎ 06 837 3777) picks up on demand for the trip inland to the lake ($50/person, depending on numbers).

6

ACCOMMODATION

Riverside Motor Camp 19 Marine Parade ☎06 838 6301, ⓦriversidemotorcamp.co.nz. Clean and simple but ageing accommodation in on-site vans, slightly more salubrious cabins, plus flat tent pitches ($20) and a very basic backpackers with a wee lounge and deck. It's all on a relatively narrow riverside pitch about a 2min walk from SH2. Dorm $30, kitchen cabins $70

Vista Motor Lodge SH2 north of the Wairoa bridge ☎0800 284 782, ⓦvistamotorlodge.co.nz. The only worthwhile motel in town is showing its age a little but is still essentially good value with a variety of comfy units, well-kept gardens, a heated pool and a startlingly bright reception area redolent of Hawaii in the 1970s. On-site restaurant open Mon–Fri evenings. $120

EATING AND DRINKING

Café 287 3km south of Wairoa on SH2 ☎06 838 6601. Roadside diner with accommodation, dishing up hearty, home-cooked breakfasts, lunches and dinners from fettuccini to steaks ($15–30) – breakfasts seem to be the most popular choice with the passing trade. They also have some cabins ($110). Daily 7.30am–4pm.

Eastend Café 250 Marine Parade ☎06 838 6070. This surprisingly big-town-feeling, sophisticated licensed place is one of the two best spots to eat during the day, serving the likes of BLT and steak burgers ($8–18) along with delicious cakes and coffee. They occasionally have live music. Tues–Fri 7am–4pm, Sat & Sun 8am–4pm.

★ **Osler's Bakery & Café** 116 Marine Parade. Try one of twenty or so sorts of home-made pie at this local

institution. They've gently updated the traditional tearoom. Mon–Fri 4.30am–4.30pm, Sat, Sun and public holidays 6am–3pm.

★ **The Saloon** 248 Marine Parade. Quirky bar currently only open on Fridays for very popular 6.30pm dinners (booking essential, $15 set menu plus $5 drinks) with live music. Inside is a king-size snooker table and Jeff's extensive record collection. In the old Gaiety Theatre out back they occasionally show movies. Fri 6.00pm–late.

Wairoa Home Grown Market The Greenhouse Garden Centre & Café, 21 Mahia Ave (SH2). Wairoa's farmers market sets up in the garden centre's car park, and is a good place to grab a quick snack or stock up on supplies for the trip to Lake Waikaremoana. Sat 8–11am.

Boundary Stream Scenic Reserve

Off SH2 at Tutira and 15km northwest along Pohakura Rd

From Wairoa south to Napier, SH2 becomes considerably steeper and twistier, so take it slowly and allow about an hour and a half. Make time to visit the wonderful **Boundary Stream Scenic Reserve**, a "mainland island" with great examples of a variety of environments from lowland to mountain forest. The reserve contains North Island brown kiwi, kereru, North Island kaka, shining cuckoo and, very occasionally, New Zealand falcon. There are several walks, including one to the Bell Rock viewpoint (5km return; 3hr) and, at the far end of the reserve, to **Shine Falls**, which crashes 58m down onto rocks surrounded by lush vegetation.

Te Urewera

Te Urewera, 65km northwest of Wairoa, was recognized as a legal entity in 2014. This means the area has the same rights as a living person, and is not owned by anyone; it's a first in New Zealand and possibly the world. Te Urewera's needs are now overseen by a guardian Board comprising the Crown and Tuhoe (from each *hapu*). The area straddles the North Island's mountainous backbone and at 2120 square kilometres encompasses the largest untouched expanse of native bush outside Fiordland. Unusually for New Zealand, it is almost completely covered in vegetation; even the highest peaks – some approaching 1500m – barely poke through this dense cloak of primeval forest, whose undergrowth is trampled by deer and wild pigs and whose rivers are filled with trout. One road, SH38, penetrates the interior, but the way to get a true sense of the place is to hike, particularly the celebrated Lake Waikaremoana Track encircling **Lake Waikaremoana**, the "Sea of Rippling Waters" and the area's undoubted jewel. The lake's deep clear waters, fringed by white sandy beaches and rocky bluffs, are ideal for swimming, fishing and kayaking.

Habitation is sparse, but twenty percent of Tuhoe people, the "Children of the Mist", still live here (the largest concentration around the village of **Ruatahuna**). Most visitors make straight for **Waikaremoana**, the visitor centre and motor camp on the lakeshore, but immediately south, the quiet former hydroelectric development village of **Tuai** provides some additional basic services. Otherwise you're on your own.

Lake Waikaremoana

Shrouded by bushland, **Lake Waikaremoana** fills a huge scalloped bowl at an altitude of over 585m, precariously held back by the Panekiri and Ngamoko ranges. The lake came into being around 2200 years ago when a huge bank of sandstone boulders was dislodged from the Ngamoko range, blocking the river that once drained the valleys. The Maori have a more poetic explanation for the lake's creation. Hau-Mapuhia, the recalcitrant daughter of Mahu, was drowned by her father and turned into a *taniwha*, or "water spirit". In a frenzied effort to get to the sea, she charged in every direction, thereby creating the various arms of the lake. As she frantically ran south towards Onepoto, the dawn caught her, turning her to stone at a spot where the lake is said to ripple from time to time, in memory of her struggle. Now two of those peninsulas have been fenced and predator-proofed, and **kiwi** are being reintroduced.

Lake Waikaremoana Track

46km; 3–4 days; 1150m ascent

The **Lake Waikaremoana Track** is one of New Zealand's "Great Walks". As the most popular multi-day tramp in the North Island, it's often compared with the South Island's renowned Routeburn and Milford tracks, although, with the exception of an exhausting climb on the first day, this is a much gentler affair, with plenty of opportunities to fish, swim and listen to the plentiful birdlife. Three days is enough for fit walkers, but it's normally done in four, spending nights in the five Great Walk **huts** or five designated **campsites** scattered around the lakeshore.

Most walkers travel clockwise, as outlined below, where the first leg (up and over the challenging but panoramic Panekiri Bluff) is the toughest. If the

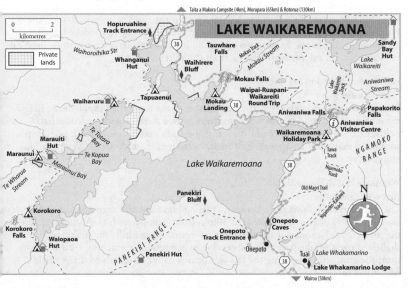

6

LAKE WAIKAREMOANA: SHORT HIKES

The Aniwaniwa Visitor Centre and the *Waikaremoana Holiday Park* are both well set up for helping hikers tackle the Lake Waikaremoana Track. But if you're not up for a three- to four-day trek, the best way to see and get a feel for the place is on one or more of the region's rewarding shorter hikes, detailed in DOC's *Lake Waikaremoana Walks* leaflet.

Kick off with **Papakorito Falls**, a 20m-wide curtain of water 2km east of the visitor centre; the easy **Hinerau Track** (1km; 20min return; 50m ascent), which starts from the visitor centre and leads to the double-drop **Aniwaniwa Falls**; or the **Black Beech Track** (2km; 30min one way; 50m descent), which follows the old highway from the visitor centre to the motor camp.

Allow about 2hr to explore the limestone **Onepoto Caves** (9km south of the *Holiday Park* on SH38), formed by the same landslide that created the lake. Take a torch and wear sensible shoes – caves have holes and slippery rock.

If you've the best part of a day to spare, take on the **Waipai–Ruapani–Waikareiti Round Trip** (17km; 5–6hr; 300m ascent), which starts 200m north of the visitor centre and winds up heading through dense beech forest past the grass-fringed Lake Ruapani to the beautiful and serene **Lake Waikareiti**. You can rent rowboats here (around $20/half-day), though you'll need to plan ahead as the key is held at Aniwaniwa Visitor Centre. Return down the Waikareiti Track (2hr round trip) or head on around to the northern side of the lake (3hr one way) and stay at **Sandy Bay Hut** (18 bunks; $15).

---

weather looks bad, there's no reason why you shouldn't change your bookings (through the Aniwaniwa visitor centre) and go anticlockwise in the hope that it will improve.

Note there's **no mobile phone coverage** on the walk – hire a personal locator beacon at the visitor centre.

Onepoto to Panekiri Hut

9km; 4–5hr; 750m ascent; 150m descent

The track starts at a shelter by the lakeshore close to SH38 and climbs steeply past the site of a redoubt set up by soldiers of the Armed Constabulary in pursuit of Te Kooti (see box opposite). It then undulates along the ridge top, occasionally revealing fabulous lake views. Wonderfully airy steps up a rocky bluff bring you to the Panekiri Hut, magnificently set on the brink of the cliffs that fall away to the lake far below. Camping in this fragile environment is prohibited; committed campers must press on to Waiopaoa, an exhausting 8hr walk from the start.

Panekiri Hut to Waiopaoa Hut

7.5km; 3–4hr; 600m descent

Setting out from Panekiri Hut, the track descends the ridge then rapidly loses height through an often muddy area where protruding tree roots provide welcome hand-holds. Occasional lake views and the transition from beech forest to rich podocarp woodland make this an appealing, if tricky, section of track down to Waiopaoa Hut and campsite.

Waiopaoa Hut to Marauiti Hut

11km; 4–5hr; 100m ascent

The track largely follows the lakeshore, crossing grassland and then kanuka scrub before reaching the Korokoro campsite (1hr 30min from Waiopaoa Hut). A side track leads to the pretty 20m Korokoro Falls (45–60min return). Meanwhile, the main track climbs slightly above the lake past barely accessible bays, eventually reaching the Maraunui campsite and, after ascending the low Whakaneke Spur, descends to the waterside Marauiti Hut.

Marauiti Hut to Waiharuru Hut

7km; 2hr; 150m ascent

From the Marauiti Hut, the track crosses the bridge over the stream that runs into Marauiti Bay, passing the lovely white-sand Te Kopua Bay. It then climbs an easy saddle before dropping down to Te Totara Bay and follows the lake to the large and modern Waiharuru Hut and campsite.

Waiharuru Hut to Whanganui Hut

6.3km; 2–3hr; 100m ascent

It's a short hike across a broad neck of land to the Tapuaenui campsite and beyond. The track follows the lakeshore to the characterful old Whanganui Hut, which is set in a clearing beside a stream and is fitted with built-in three-tier bunks.

Whanganui Hut to Hopuruahine

6km; 2–3hr; 50m ascent

The final leg of the hike is also the shortest and easiest. The track skirts the lake to the point where water taxis pick up (45min), then follows grassy flats beside the Hopuruahine River before crossing a suspension bridge to the access road to a camping area (free).

ARRIVAL AND DEPARTURE   **LAKE WAIKAREMOANA**

Lake Waikaremoana is approached most easily from Wairoa along SH38. This continues through to Murupara and Rotorua, but note that between Lake Waikaremoana and Murupara there is nearly 100km of tortuous gravel road; if you wish to travel this route, take advice, grab the *Te Urewera Rainforest Route* leaflet, and go slow.

By bus The Big Bush Lake Waikaremoana Shuttle Service (☎ 06 837 3777, ⊚ lakewaikaremoana.co.nz) services the lake from Wairoa.

TE KOOTI RIKIRANGI

Te Kooti Rikirangi was one of the most celebrated of Maori "rebels", a thorn in the side of the colonial government throughout the New Zealand Wars of the 1860s and 1870s. An excellent fighter and strategist, Te Kooti kept the mountainous spine of the North Island on edge for half a decade, eluding New Zealand's biggest manhunt.

Born near Gisborne around 1830, Te Kooti was not of chiefly rank but could trace his ancestry back to the captains of several *waka* (canoes) that brought the Maori to New Zealand. By the middle of the 1860s, he was fighting for the government against the pseudo-Christian Hauhau cult that started in Taranaki in 1862. The cult spread to the east coast where, in 1866, Te Kooti was unjustly accused of being in league with its devotees. Denied the trial he demanded, he was imprisoned on the Chatham Islands, along with three hundred of his supposed allies. In 1867, he was brought close to death by a fever, but rose again, claiming a divine revelation and establishing a new religion, **Ringatu** ("the uplifted hand"), which still has some thirteen thousand believers today. Ringatu took its cues from the Hauhau, but developed into a uniquely Maori version of Catholicism, drawing heavily on the Old Testament. Some say Te Kooti saw himself as a Moses figure – apparently given to dousing his uplifted hand in phosphorus so that it glowed brightly in the dim meetinghouses.

After two years on the Chathams, Te Kooti and his fellow prisoners commandeered a ship and engineered a dramatic escape, returning to Poverty Bay. He sought safety in the **Urewera Range**, with the Armed Constabulary in hot pursuit. Te Kooti still managed to conduct successful campaigns, exacting revenge against government troops at Whakatane on the Bay of Plenty, Mohaka in Hawke's Bay and at Rotorua. With the end of the New Zealand Wars in 1872, Te Kooti took refuge in the Maori safe haven of the King Country. He was eventually pardoned in 1883, and in 1891 was granted a plot of land near Whakatane, where he lived the last two years of his life.

INFORMATION AND TOURS

Visitor information Aniwaniwa Visitor Centre is by the lake in the old rangers' house (daily: Oct–April 8am–4.45pm; May–Sept 8am–4.15pm; ☎06 837 3803, ✉ teureweravc@doc.govt.nz). The DOC-operated visitor centre is the place to come for Lake Waikaremoana Track hut bookings and to hire personal locator beacons.

DOC leaflets and maps Comprehensive walking information is covered in the *Lake Waikaremoana Track* leaflet, though map enthusiasts might like the two 1:50,000 Topo50 maps that cover the full circuit.

Services The only place that has petrol between Wairoa and Murupara is the *Waikaremoana Holiday Park*.

Weather The winter months (June–Sept) can be cold and wet, making spring and autumn the best times to undertake the walk, though go prepared as it can snow at any point in the year.

Equipment Each hut is supplied with drinking water, toilets and a heating stove, but a cooking stove, fuel and all your food must be carried. Campsites only have water and toilets.

Pack transport Big Bush (☎06 837 3777; ✇ lakewaikaremoana.co.nz) can organize pack transport between most huts, allowing for a largely luggage-free walk though this is only economical for groups of four or more.

GUIDED HIKES

Walking Legends ☎0800 925 569, ✇ walkinglegends .com. Offers four-day walks ($1450), led by enthusiastic and knowledgeable guides, with accommodation in the same DOC huts used by independent walkers. Trips depart from Rotorua and excellent meals and wine are provided – all you need to carry is a day- or small pack. The longest day is around seven hours and there's usually enough time for a bit of trout fishing

FISHING

David Dods 4939 Main Rd (SH38) ☎06 837 3988, ✇ nztroutfishing.co.nz. Lake Waikaremoana is one of the best places for brown trout in the world. Whether you're an expert or complete novice, David will create a good experience – worth it for the entertaining yarns alone! Trips vary from a straightforward $150 to $750 (for about five hours out, including a lunch of smoked trout with wine) – grab a few mates to share the cost. Also runs a backpackers and B&B.

GETTING AROUND

By car You can drive to the trailheads at either end of the Lake Waikaremoana Track, but there are occasional thefts and most people prefer to park free of charge at the *Waikaremoana Holiday Park* and take a bus or boat out.

By bus and boat Big Bush (☎06 837 3777, ✇ lakewaikaremoana.co.nz) charge around $55 for a joint drop-off and pick-up package, and they'll also run a water-taxi service to anywhere else you might want to start or finish, enabling you to walk shorter sections by means of prearranged pick-ups from specified beaches.

ACCOMMODATION

LAKE WAIKAREMOANA

Lake Whakamarino Lodge Tuai village, off SH38 15km south of the visitor centre ☎0800 837 387, ✇ lakelodge .co.nz. Converted construction workers' quarters wonderfully sited beside the trout-filled Lake Whakamarino. Accommodation is in basic rooms and more upmarket self-contained units; book ahead, as it fills up quickly. Dinner can be booked two days ahead for $30. Dorms $40, unit $140

Mokau Landing campsite SH38, 11km northwest of the visitor centre. A large, grassy DOC site that sits between the bush and the lake, with running water and toilets. Mokau Falls is just 1.5km away. $7

Te Taita O Makora campsite SH38, 22km northwest of the visitor centre. Very basic ten-pitch DOC site with toilets and a water supply from a nearby stream; it's best to take the necessary precautions in treating any drinking water. **Free**

Waikaremoana Holiday Park SH38, 2km south of the visitor centre ☎06 837 3826, ✇ waikaremoana.info. A well-equipped establishment with camping sites, wooden cabins, larger semidetached tourist flats and wee individual chalets ($100). There is also a store, a reasonably sized communal kitchen and dining room. Showers are available for non-guests ($5). Camping $15, cabins $65

LAKE WAIKAREMOANA TRACK

DOC huts and campsites ✇ doc.govt.nz. Panekiri, Waiopaoa, Marauiti, Waiharuru and Whanganui are all Great Walk huts and must be booked in advance, as must the campsites; you can do so online, although you'll need to call in at the Aniwaniwa Visitor Centre to pick up your Great Walk Ticket. Your chances of getting a place are much better outside Christmas and Easter. Backcountry Hut Pass not valid. Under-18s free. Huts $32, camping $14

EATING

Groceries and meals on request The nearest full-time restaurant is over 60km away in Wairoa, so you'll largely have to fend for yourself when it comes to food. There's a reasonable range of groceries at the *Waikaremoana Holiday Park*, and you might get signed into the district club at Tuai (☎06 837 3885). Meals are sometimes available on request at the *Lake Whakamarino Lodge* (mains around $25), but you're better off relying on your own supplies.

Napier

Laidback, seaside **NAPIER** is Hawke's Bay's largest city (population 54,000) and one of New Zealand's most likeable regional centres, thanks to its Mediterranean climate, affordable prices and the world's best-preserved collection of small-scale Art Deco architecture, built after the earthquake that devastated the city in 1931 (see p.387).

Thanks to the whim of mid-nineteenth-century Land Commissioner Alfred Domett, the grid of streets in the city's Art Deco **commercial centre** bears the names of British literary luminaries – Tennyson, Thackeray, Byron, and more. Bisecting it all is the

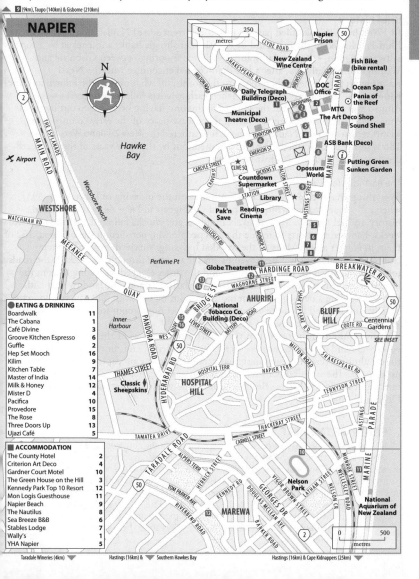

NAPIER

9 (9km), Taupo (140km) & Gisborne (210km)

Hawke Bay

✈ Airport

WESTSHORE

CLYDE ROAD

Napier Prison 50

New Zealand Wine Centre

Fish Bike (bike rental)

SHAKESPEARE RD

CAMERON

Daily Telegraph Building (Deco)

DOC Office

Ocean Spa

Pania of the Reef

Municipal Theatre (Deco)

MTG

The Art Deco Shop

Sound Shell

TENNYSON STREET

EMERSON ST

ASB Bank (Deco)

Putting Green

Sunken Garden

CARLYLE STREET

CLIVE SQ

DICKENS ST

Opossum World

Countdown Supermarket

STATION

Library

Pak'n Save

Reading Cinema

Perfume Pt

Globe Theatrette

HARDINGE ROAD

BREAKWATER RD

WAGHORNE STREET

QUAY

BRIDGE ST

AHURIRI

BLUFF HILL

Centennial Gardens

Inner Harbour

National Tobacco Co. Building (Deco)

LEVER STREET

COOTE RD

SEE INSET

PANDORA ROAD

WEST QUAY

BATTERY RD

THAMES STREET

HYDERABAD RD

HOSPITAL TERR

NAPIER TERR

Classic Sheepskins

HOSPITAL HILL

TAMATEA DRIVE

THACKERAY STREET

CARNELL STREET

TARADALE ROAD

ALPERS TERR

HERRICK STREET

KENNEDY RD

Nelson Park

VIGOR BROWN STREET

MUNROE STREET

WELLESLEY ROAD

MARINE PARADE

National Aquarium of New Zealand

TOM PARKER AVE

RIVERBEND ROAD

MAREWA

DOUGLAS MCLEAN AVE

GEORGES DR

BARKER ROAD

● EATING & DRINKING

Boardwalk	11
The Cabana	1
Café Divine	3
Groove Kitchen Espresso	6
Guffle	2
Hep Set Mooch	16
Kilim	9
Kitchen Table	7
Master of India	14
Milk & Honey	12
Mister D	4
Pacifica	10
Provedore	15
The Rose	8
Three Doors Up	13
Ujazi Café	5

■ ACCOMMODATION

The County Hotel	2
Criterion Art Deco	4
Gardner Court Motel	10
The Green House on the Hill	3
Kennedy Park Top 10 Resort	12
Mon Logis Guesthouse	11
Napier Beach	9
The Nautilus	8
Sea Breeze B&B	6
Stables Lodge	7
Wally's	1
YHA Napier	5

Taradale Wineries (4km) ▼   Hastings (16km) & ▼ Southern Hawke's Bay   Hastings (16km) & Cape Kidnappers (25km) ▼

partly pedestrianized main thoroughfare of Emerson Street, whose terracotta paving and palm trees run from Clive Square – one-time site of a makeshift "Tin Town" while the city was being rebuilt after the earthquake – to the Norfolk pine-fringed **Marine Parade**, Napier's main beach.

Around the northeastern side of Bluff Hill (Mataruahou), about 5km from the city centre, lies the original settlement site of **Ahuriri**, now home to trendy restaurants, cafés, bars and boutiques.

Napier makes a perfect base from which to visit the gannet colony at Cape Kidnappers (see p.392) as well as the vat-load of **wineries** on the surrounding plains (see p.392).

Brief history

In 1769, James Cook sailed past **Ahuriri**, the current site of Napier, noting the sea-girt Bluff Hill linked to the mainland by two slender shingle banks and backed by a superb saltwater lagoon – the only substantial sheltered mooring between Gisborne and Wellington. Nonetheless, after a less-than-cordial encounter with the Ngati Kahungunu people he anchored just to the south, off what came to be known as Cape Kidnappers. Some thirty years later, when early whalers followed in Cook's wake, Ahuriri was all but deserted, the Ngati Kahungunu having been driven out by rivals equipped with European guns. During the uneasy peace of the early colonial years, Maori returned to the Napier area, which weathered the **New Zealand Wars** of the 1860s relatively unscathed. The port boomed, but by the early years of the twentieth century all the available land was used up.

The earthquake

Everything changed in two and a half minutes on the morning of February 3, 1931, when a 7.9 magnitude **earthquake**, one of the biggest in New Zealand's recorded history, rocked the city. More than six hundred aftershocks followed over the next two weeks, hampering efforts to rescue the 258 people who perished in the bay area, 162 of them in Napier alone. Many of the wooden buildings survived, except for their chimneys; but the rest was destroyed by fires that swept through unchecked (the roads too badly damaged for the fire engines, and the hoses clogged with shingle from the beach) – a sea breeze saved the Six Sisters on Marine Parade. The land twisted and buckled, finding a new equilibrium more than 2m higher, with 300 square kilometres of new land wrested from the grip of the ocean – enough room to site the Hawke's Bay airport and expand the city.

Napier embraced the opportunity to start afresh: out went the trams, telephone wires were laid underground, the streets were widened and, in the spirit of the times, almost everything was designed according to the precepts of the **Art Deco** movement. The simultaneous reconstruction gave Napier a rare stylistic uniformity, ranking it alongside Miami Beach as one of the world's largest collections of Art Deco buildings.

PANIA OF THE REEF

Just south of Ocean Spa (see opposite) is a bronze cast of the curvaceous **Pania of the Reef**, a siren of local Maori legend. **Pania** was a beautiful sea-maiden who would swim from the watery realm of Tangaroa, the god of the ocean, each evening to quench her thirst at a freshwater spring close to the base of Bluff Hill before returning to her people each morning. One evening, she was discovered by a young chief who wooed her and wanted her to remain on land. Eventually they married, but when Pania went to pay a farewell visit to her kin they forcibly restrained her in the briny depths and she turned to stone, forming what is now known as **Pania Reef**. Fishers and divers still claim they can see her with arms outstretched towards the shore.

Marine Parade

Napier's most striking feature is **Marine Parade**, a dead-straight 2km of boulevard lined with stately Norfolk pines, bordered on one side by hotels, motels, B&Bs, hostels, shops and restaurants and by a dark grey stony beach on the other. The latter is Napier's main beach, but it's unsafe for swimming – better head 30km north to Waipatiki or 35km south to Waimarama or Ocean Beach. A popular walking and cycling path links a string of attractions along the seaward edge of Marine Parade, starting by Napier's port at the northern end of town and passing the foot of Bluff Hill before arriving at the Ocean Spa.

6

Ocean Spa

42 Marine Parade • Mon–Sat 6am–10pm, Sun 8am–10pm • $10.70 • ☎ 06 835 8553, ⓦ oceanspa.co.nz

A large glass and concrete beachside complex, **Ocean Spa** houses a gym and salt-chlorinated, lido-style complex of hot pools (36–38°C) with bubbles, jets, spouts, steam room, sauna, massages ($40/30min), beauty treatments and a lap pool (26°C),

---

ART DECO NAPIER

The 1931 earthquake saw Napier rebuilt in line with the times. Although **Art Deco** embraced modernity, glorifying progress, the machine age and the Gatsby-style high life, the onset of the Great Depression pared down these excesses, and Napier's version was informed by the privations of an austere era. At the same time, the architects looked for inspiration to California's Santa Barbara – which, just six years earlier, had suffered the same fate and risen from the ashes. They adopted fountains (a symbol of renewal), sunbursts, chevrons, lightning flashes and fluting to embellish the highly formalized but asymmetric designs. In Napier, what emerged was a conglomeration of early twentieth-century design, combining elements of the Arts and Crafts movement, the Californian Spanish Mission style, Egyptian and Mayan motifs, stylized floral designs and even Maori imagery. For the best part of half a century, the city's residents merely daubed the buildings in grey or muted blue paint. Fortunately, this meant that when a few savvy visionaries recognized the city's potential in the mid-1980s and formed the **Art Deco Trust**, everything was still intact. The trust continues to promote the preservation of buildings and provides funding for shopkeepers to pick out distinctive architectural detail in pastel colours similar to those originally used.

You can get a sense of Art Deco Napier by wandering along the half-dozen streets of the city centre, notably **Emerson Street**. Worth special attention here is the **ASB Bank**, on the corner of Hastings Street. Its exterior is adorned with fern shoots and a mask from the head of a *taiaha* (a long fighting club), while its interior has a fine Maori rafter design. On Tennyson Street, look for the flamboyant **Daily Telegraph** building, with stylized fountains, and the **Municipal Theatre**, built in the late 1930s in a strikingly geometric form.

ART DECO NAPIER TOURS AND TRAILS

Keen observers will find classic Art Deco everywhere but for a systematic exploration of Napier's Art Deco revival, try any or a combination of the options listed below.

The Art Deco Shop 7 Tennyson St ☎ 06 835 0022, ⓦ artdeconapier.com. Apart from all the merchandise it sells, the shop also shows a 20min introductory video ($5) and sells a leaflet ($9) for the self-guided Art Deco Walk, which outlines a stroll (1.5km; 1hr 30min–2hr) through the downtown area. Most staff (and guides) are volunteers; everyone enjoys dressing up in period clothes.

Art Deco Afternoon Walking Tour Dedicated Deco buffs, and anyone wanting some gossip, should meet at the Art Deco Shop for the 2pm tour (April–Sept daily 2pm; 2hr; $20), which brings 1930s Napier to life through anecdotal patter and gives you the chance to gaze around the interiors of shops and banks without feeling too self-conscious. There are additional shorter tours in the busier months: 5pm (Oct–March; 1.5hr; $19) and 10am (Jan–March; 1hr; $17, from the i-SITE).

Vintage Deco Car Tours and Deco Tour 7 Tennyson St ☎ 06 835 0022, ⓦ artdeconapier.com. The Art Deco Trust operates both these tours. The vintage car tour (1hr 15min; $160 for a maximum of four people) is subject to availability, while the Deco Tour (daily 11.30am; 1hr 15min; $40) involves a minibus jaunt around Art Deco attractions outside the city centre.

all overlooking the sea. The long hours and warm waters make it a great place for a relaxed summer evening.

MTG

1 Tennyson St • Daily 10am–6pm • $10 • ☎ 06 835 7781• ⓦ mtghawkesbay.com

Opposite Pania (see box, p.386) stands **MTG**, the stylishly revamped Hawke's Bay museum and art gallery. It's light and spacious and has some good views across the town and bay. There's a moving permanent exhibition on the earthquake in the basement with stories from survivors (sailors were spooked by the appearance of a ghost ship thrown from the sea bed). The rest of the space is given to temporary exhibitions, with an emphasis on design and decorative arts.

Opossum World

157 Marine Parade • Mon–Fri 9.30am–5pm, plus Sat & Sun in the summer 10am–3pm • Free • ☎ 06 835 7697, ⓦ opossumworld.co.nz

You won't really get a sense of what so incenses Kiwis about these seemingly cute animals until you walk through the display in this shop, which touts itself as a "unique shopping and educational experience". New Zealand's 70 million possums – originally introduced from Australia – eat 21,000 tonnes of vegetation every night, and if they weren't controlled, they'd turn the country into a desert. The displays here cover the lives of the old possum trappers such as Barry Crump (see p.821) and the controversial use of 1080 poison – used to control numbers; it also has a devastating effect on native wildlife. Possum fur has great insulating properties, so much so that it was used to protect the wiring on some of the Apollo Space Program's equipment; the shop sells possum fur hats, gloves, scarves and more.

National Aquarium of New Zealand

546 Marine Parade • Daily 9am–5pm; check website for various feeding times; behind-the-scenes tour daily by reservation • $20; animal close encounters $65; snorkelling with sharks $82/30min (incl. gear); scuba diving (qualified divers only) with sharks $82, or $127 with all gear • ☎ 06 834 1404, ⓦ nationalaquarium.co.nz

The **National Aquarium of New Zealand** is one of the finest in the country, with distinct marine environments from around the globe. The most spectacular section is the **ocean tank**, its walk-through tunnel giving intimate views of rays and assorted sharks, with which you can swim by arrangement. Hand feeding the fish happens at the **reef tank**, plus there's a new pool for rescued little penguins, with live video feeds from their burrows and windows to watch them swimming. Non-aquatic sections include one for New Zealand's reptilian tuatara, and a nocturnal **kiwi house**.

Bluff Hill

The city centre's northern flank butts up against the steep slopes of **Bluff Hill**, a 3km-long hummock of winding streets, home to some of Napier's more desirable suburbs. The primary reason for negotiating the hill is the **Bluff Hill Domain Lookout** (daily 7am–dusk) at the eastern summit, which offers views of Cape Kidnappers to the west and across to the Mahia Peninsula in the east.

Napier Prison

55 Coote Rd • Daily 9am–6pm; R16 night tour monthly • $20 (incl. self-guided audio tour); R16 night tour $25 • ☎ 06 835 9933, ⓦ napierprison.com

Immediately south of Bluff Hill, **Napier Prison** is an imposing sandstone ex-clink, built in 1862 and decommissioned in 1993. This is no Alcatraz but a very Kiwi jail – all weatherboard and corrugated iron – that, like its inmates, had a chequered career, housing women, children and lunatics as well as hardened male inmates. Several cells are intact, complete with gang graffiti and, reputedly, the ghosts of former inmates.

If you book in advance, and are flexible on dates, you may be able to join a guided tour ($25), otherwise do the one-hour audio tour, or join the monthly R16 night tour, which includes spooky interaction.

New Zealand Wine Centre

1 Shakespeare Rd, Napier • Daily: Dec–Feb 10am–7pm; March–Nov 10am–6pm • $29; $14 for tasting only • ☎ 06 835 5326, ⓦ nzwinecentre.co.nz

Before heading out to the wineries themselves (see p.392), visit **New Zealand Wine Centre** to learn how to identify wine flavours, then sit in a small cinema sampling six wines as winemakers on screen enthuse about them. There's also a museum and aroma room. It's in a fine Art Deco building with the original doors now restored from a chook shed.

Ahuriri

5km northwest of the city centre

Napier's European foundations are in harbourside **Ahuriri**. James Cook found shelter for the *Endeavour* in the estuary here and the fledgling town grew up around the harbour. When the industrial port moved round the headland Ahuriri languished, but in recent years the old wool stores and warehouses around the inner harbour (also known as the Iron Pot) and the waterfront strip stretching back to town, have been reborn as home to cavernous bars, cafés and restaurants, all buzzing from Thursday evening through the weekend.

National Tobacco Company Building

Corner of Bridge and Ossian sts

During the day the Ahuriri district makes for a pleasant place to stroll beside the yachts or peek in to the boutiques. The only real sight, however, is the **National Tobacco Company Building**. Its exterior is the most frequently used image of Art Deco Napier and exhibits a decorative richness seldom seen on industrial buildings, including Art Nouveau motifs of roses and raupo (a kind of Kiwi bulrush).

Sheepskin Tannery

22 Thames St • Tours Mon–Fri 11am & 2pm • Free • ☎ 06 835 9662, ⓦ classicsheepskins.co.nz

Classic Sheepskins offer unique behind-the-scenes twenty-minute tours of their **tannery**. You can also buy factory-priced products including Thor boots (the Kiwi equivalent of Ugg boots).

ARRIVAL AND DEPARTURE   **NAPIER**

By plane Regular direct flights from Auckland, Wellington and Christchurch, as well as Rotorua, Tauranga and Gisborne arrive at Hawke's Bay Airport, 5km north of town on SH2, where they are met by the Super Shuttle (☎ 0800 748 885, ⓦ supershuttle.co.nz), which charges $20 to get into town.
Destinations Auckland (5–8 daily; 1hr); Christchurch (2–3 daily; 1hr 35min); Wellington (3–5 daily; 1hr).

By bus InterCity and NakedBus buses stop on Carlyle St by Clive Square.
Destinations Auckland (1 daily; 6hr); Dannevirke (5 daily; 2hr); Gisborne (1 daily; 4hr); Hastings (7 daily; 30min); Norsewood (4–5 daily; 1hr 40min); Palmerston North (4–5 daily; 2hr 45min); Taupo (4 daily; 2hr); Wellington (4–5daily; 5hr 15min).

GETTING AROUND

By bike Napier's central sights are easily covered on foot, but cycling along the 130km of paths in and around the city is a pleasant way to see the area; try Fish Bike, 26 Marine Parade (daily 9am–5pm; ☎ 06 833 6979, ⓦ fishbike.co.nz), who rent out an assortment of bikes (including electric) from $50/day.

By bus The GoBay local bus services (☎ 06 878 9250, ⓦ hbrc.govt.nz/Services/Transport) from Dalton St are of use primarily for visits to Hastings and Havelock North. In addition, the #13 stops by the Church Road and Mission Estate wineries.

By car Auto Rental (☎ 06 834 0045, ⓦ autorentalvehicles

.co.nz) and Pegasus (☎ 06 843 7020, ⓦ rentalcars.co.nz) both have short-lease vehicles from $40/day.

By taxi Napier Taxis (☎ 06 835 7777).

INFORMATION

Visitor information i-SITE, 100 Marine Parade (daily 9am–5pm; ☎ 06 834 1911, ⓦ hawkesbaynz.com). Can advise on tide times for gannet visits, book travel and track/hut tickets and has internet access.

DOC 59 Marine Parade (Mon–Fri 9am–4.15pm; ☎ 06 834 3111). Has information about walks into the remote Kaweka and Ruahine ranges to the west.

ACCOMMODATION

Apart from the usual shortage of rooms during the month or so after Christmas and the February festivals (see box opposite), you should have little trouble finding accommodation in Napier. There are dozens of **motels** around town, many concentrated in Westshore, a beachfront suburb a couple of kilometres from the centre beside SH2. Right in the thick of things, Marine Parade has low-cost backpacker **hostels**, plush **motels** and classy **B&Bs**.

The County Hotel 12 Browning St ☎ 06 835 7800, ⓦ countyhotel.co.nz. One of the few 1931 earthquake survivors, this elegant, period-decorated business and tourist hotel (in the Edwardian former council offices) has only 18 luxurious rooms (some with clawfoot baths), a posh restaurant and tiny cocktail bar. Check for special offers. **$315**

Criterion Art Deco 48 Emerson St ☎ 06 835 2059, ⓦ criterionartdeco.co.nz. Central, well-organized 60-bed hostel in an Art Deco building, formerly a hotel. The dorms (some single-sex) and doubles (some en suite) are good value and there are large communal areas (and a pool table), but a small kitchen. Continental breakfast included. Dorms **$28**, doubles **$66**

★**Gardner Court Motel** 16 Nelson Crescent ☎ 0800 000 830, ⓦ gardnercourtmotel.co.nz. Exceptionally welcoming, quiet, clean and reasonably central old-school motel with a solar-heated pool and simple motel rooms at bargain prices. The place is made by the enthusiasm and friendliness of the long-term owners. **$110**

The Green House on the Hill 18b Milton Oaks, Bluff Hill ☎ 06 835 4475, ⓦ the-green-house.co.nz. You'll get a warm welcome in this vegetarian homestay, surrounded by trees halfway up a hidden urban hill and at the end of a steep drive. Choose from the en suite or two-room suite with a private bathroom. Free wi-fi. **$135**

Kennedy Park Top 10 Resort 11 Storkey St, off Kennedy Rd ☎ 0800 457 275, ⓦ kennedypark.co.nz. This organized and ultra-efficient campsite, just 2km from the city centre, has acres of powered sites ($48 for two people), a pool, BBQ area, kids' playground, restaurant and a huge range of cabins. Basic cabin **$63**, units **$121**

Mon Logis Guesthouse 415 Marine Parade ☎ 06 835 2125, ⓦ monlogis.co.nz. Four rooms sharing a balcony with sea views in a century-old wooden house. The friendly and knowledgeable Gallic owner makes every effort to look after you and provides delicious breakfasts. **$180**, sea view **$240**

Napier Beach 10 Gill Rd, Bay View, 9km north of Napier ☎ 0800 287 275, ⓦ napierbeach.co.nz. Welcoming, with a jazzy reception, wi-fi access and summer-only café, this beachfront campsite provides an antidote to *Kennedy Park*'s gulag ambience. An extra couple of dollars gets a beach site with great views (usual rates: camping $22, powered sites $24), or splash out on a beach motel unit ($179). Cabins **$109**, units **$159**

The Nautilus 387 Marine Parade ☎ 0508 628 845, ⓦ nautilusnapier.co.nz. Large, modern motel in which all rooms offer sea views, a hot tub or spa bath, balcony and room service. There is also a small on-site restaurant and wi-fi. Studios **$175**, apartments **$225**

★**Sea Breeze B&B** 281 Marine Parade ☎ 06 835 8067, ⓦ seabreezebnb.co.nz. Unique, seafront Victorian villa with just three flamboyantly decorated themed rooms; India and China have en suites, Turkish has its own separate bathroom. The owners go to great lengths to ensure you enjoy your stay and provide a guest kitchenette and a lounge with sea views. Breakfast is a generous, self-service continental. **$130**

Stables Lodge 370 Hastings St ☎ 06 835 6242, ⓦ stableslodge.co.nz. Rooms ranged around a central courtyard give this 34-bed hostel an intimate feel and it is all pretty friendly and relaxed. Free internet, hammocks, a book exchange and a BBQ that takes the pressure off the small but well-equipped kitchen add to the communal atmosphere. Dorms **$25**, rooms **$64**

Wally's 7 Cathedral Lane ☎ 06 833 7930, ⓦ wallysbackpackers.co.nz. Central hostel in a pair of 1920s villas, plus a cottage used as an eight-bed dorm. Reasonably comfortable, huge DVD collection and some off-street parking. Dorms **$21**, rooms **$56**

★**YHA Napier** 277 Marine Parade ☎ 06 835 7039, ⓦ yha.co.nz. Spacious hostel spread across three airy historic weatherboard houses on the waterfront. Some rooms have sea views, there's free wi-fi, a just-about-adequate kitchen and a sunny courtyard at the back with a BBQ. Dorms **$26**, doubles **$69**

EATING, DRINKING AND ENTERTAINMENT

Both Central Napier and the suburb of Ahuriri both boast decent eating options, but Ahuriri's large bars are a cut above for drinking. There are two large, central **supermarkets** on Munroe St: Countdown (daily 7am–10pm) at no. 1, and Pak 'n Save (daily 7am–10pm) at no. 25. It's rare to find any really exciting entertainment, unless you hit town at **festival time** (see box below), but a couple of the **bars** host live music at weekends and when touring bands pass through. Entertainment listings are covered in the Thursday and Friday edition of *Hawke's Bay Today* newspaper.

CITY CENTRE

★**The Cabana** 11 Shakespeare Rd ☎06 835 1102, ⓦcabana.net.nz. Venue for travelling bands and shows that's the envy of many larger towns; a visit to Napier is not complete without at least poking your head round the door. Occasional cover charge applies, depending on the acts (usually $10). Thurs–Sat 8pm–1am; sometimes Sun–Wed 8pm–midnight.

Café Divine 53 Hastings St ☎06 835 6218. Licensed spot popular with locals and travellers alike, living up to its name with enormous slices of healthy home-made quiches, veggie bakes, filos and wraps, delicious seafood chowder ($13.50), and other inexpensive breakfasts and lunches. Daily 6.30am–5pm.

★**Groove Kitchen Espresso** 112 Tennyson St ☎06 835 8530. Cool café with irresistible coffee, great sounds and lovely food – try the Jammin' salmon ($17.50) of hash cakes, spinach, fresh pesto, poached eggs, or hope they have sweetcorn stack on special ($16). There's a dance party on the last Saturday of every month ($10). Mon–Fri 8am–2pm, Sat & Sun 9am–3pm.

★**Guffle** 29a Hastings St ☎06 835 8847. Dress up just a little or not at all (depending on your sense of occasion) when you visit this ultra-cool cocktail and wine bar, which serves the best drinks in town and has great tunes anytime, plus occasional movie classics and live music. They can rustle up some chips if you need them (and pizzas on occasional Sundays in summer) but their specialities are the phenomenally good cocktails. Mon–Sat 4pm–midnight.

Kilim 193 Hastings St ☎06 835 9100. BYO wine without corkage and cheap Turkish grub to eat in or take away make this a local favourite. Mains (around $16.50) include grilled *kofte*, falafel and spinach *börek*. Service is haphazard but the staff are keen and the food is tasty and filling. Sun–Thurs 11am–9pm, Fri & Sat 11am–9.30pm.

Kitchen Table 138 Tennyson St ☎06 835 8142. Embracing a small photography gallery, this not-for-profit family-owned licensed café is a kitsch fifties antidote (knitted tea cosies and lurid wallpaper) to Napier's Art Deco austerity. Sofas are scattered through a large hall, with live music on the stage about once a month. Buzzy coffee, fruit crumble ($13) and meals such as sweetcorn stack ($18). Mon–Sat 9am–3pm.

★**Mister D** 47 Tennyson St ☎06 835 8530, ⓦwww .misterd.co.nz. Great ingredients prepared lovingly. If you eat meat, don't leave Napier without trying the bone-marrow ravioli ($24.50), while anyone with a sweet tooth should get their fix of home-made doughnut plus filling to inject (custard, jelly or chocolate $6). Sun–Wed 7.30am–4pm, Thurs–Sat 7.30am–11pm.

Pacifica 209 Marine Parade ☎06 835 5022, ⓦpacificarestaurant.co.nz. A bit too sophisticated for its own good, this restaurant concentrates on fish and seafood dishes, mixed in a confusing consommé of *nouvelle cuisine* (such as greenlip mussel sago). There's just the $50 degustation menu, though the suggested wines will double that. In fine weather, head for the driftwood-screened garden. Mon–Fri 6pm–late.

The Rose 72 Hastings St ☎06 835 8689. Large boozer with sports screens, live music on Thursdays and Sundays, a regular quiz and good-value pub meals (mostly $15–20). Daily 11am–late.

Ujazi Café 28 Tennyson St ☎06 835 1490. Napier's oldest café serving good breakfasts (including vegetarian) and lunch: quiches, salads, fruit sorbets, strong Fairtrade coffee and particularly good custard squares; dishes around $15–25. Daily 8am–5pm.

AHURIRI

★**Boardwalk** 8 Hardinge Rd ☎06 834 1168, ⓦboardwalknapier.co.nz. From the outside it looks like a

---

NAPIER FESTIVALS AND EVENTS

The Mission Concert ⓦmissionconcert .co.nz. An outdoor concert at the *Mission Estate Winery* featuring an internationally famous vocalist – past luminaries include Ronan Keating, Eric Clapton and Rod Stewart – and drawing crowds of around 25,000. Usually sometime between January and March.

Art Deco Weekend ⓦartdeconapier.com. A celebration of all things Art Deco-related, featuring guided walks, open-house tours of domestic architecture, vintage cars, 1930s-dress picnics, champagne breakfasts, Depression dinner, silent movies and the like. Usually the third weekend in February.

bog-standard beachside bar and café, with patio seating next to the pavement. But walk through to a lovely outdoor bar area and covered deck for the restaurant, both with great views across the sea. The menu's set by price ($21–32) and surprisingly reasonable given the view and vibe, though you could spend more on a "surf and turf" blow-out. Mon–Fri 9am–late, Sat & Sun 8am–late.

Hep Set Mooch 58 West Quay ☎ 06 833 6332, ⊛ shed2 .co.nz/hep_set_mooch. Gaudy, relaxed daytime café in a vast warehouse. Friendly staff serve a range of breakfasts (such as porridge with stewed apple), great muffins and a healthy selection of salads, frittatas and filo pies (nothing over $25). Daily 8am–3pm.

Master of India 79 Ahuriri Shopping Centre ☎ 06 834 3440, ⊛ masterofindia.co.nz. Atmospheric licensed curry house with ornate gilded decor and a broad menu of vegetarian delights and goat specialities, all mostly under $25; takeaways available. Thurs–Sat 11.30am–2pm & 5.30pm–late.

Milk & Honey Crown Hotel, Corner of Bridge St and Hardinge Rd ☎ 06 833 6099, ⊛ themilkandhoney.co.nz. Polished boards, concrete beams and fold-back windows with sea views make this smart restaurant/bar a popular spot, aided by the Mediterranean menu (mains around $30) and considerate service. Try the tuna starter with wasabi

and sesame ($15) or the slow roast lamb shank with blue cheese gnocchi ($27), or drop in to browse the foodie books while sipping a Syrah or fine espresso. Daily 7am–10pm.

Provedore 60 West Quay ☎ 06 834 0189. Popular café/bar with a sophisticated, European edge, serving tapas ($7–16.50) and playing some nice DJ sounds plus occasional live music – it all adds up to a fine place to while away an evening. Wed & Thurs 4–10pm, Fri 4pm–1am, Sat noon–1am & Sun noon–10pm.

Three Doors Up 3 Waghorne St ☎ 06 834 0835, ⊛ three doorsup.co.nz. A licensed fine-dining restaurant with a cosy atmosphere and affordable prices, hence very popular with the locals. Some of the Italian-influenced dishes can be a little overloaded (scallops with blue cheese and cream) but everything is tasty (mains $22–36). Their neighbouring bar *Four Doors Down* (open Wed–Sun) has live music on Friday evenings and Sunday afternoons. Daily 5.30pm–late.

CINEMAS

Reading Cinema 154 Station St ☎ 06 831 0600, ⊛ readingcinemas.co.nz. Screens all the latest first-release mainstream films.

Globe Theatrette 15 Hardinge Rd, Ahuriri ☎ 06 833 6011, ⊛ globenapier.co.nz. Tiny cinema with leather seats showing a mix of mainstream and art movies.

Cape Kidnappers

After James Cook's ill-starred initial encounter with Maori at Gisborne (see p.372), he sailed to the southern limit of Hawke's Bay and anchored off the jagged peninsula known to the Ngati Kahungunu as Te Matua-a-maui, "the fishhook of Maui" – a reference to the origin of the North Island, which was, as legend has it, dragged from the oceans by Maui. Here, Maori traders noticed two young Tahitian interpreters aboard the *Endeavour*, believing them to be held against their will, the traders captured one of them and paddled away. The boy escaped back to the ship but Cook subsequently marked the point on his chart as **Cape Kidnappers**.

Neither Cook nor Joseph Banks, both meticulous in recording flora and fauna, mentioned any **gannets** on the peninsula's final shark-tooth flourish of pinnacles. However, a hundred years later, twenty or so pairs were recorded, and now there are 16,000 birds – no visit to Napier and Hastings is complete without a visit to this, the world's most accessible mainland gannet colony (see box, p.395).

Hawke's Bay Wine Country

Napier and Hastings are almost entirely encircled by the **Hawke's Bay's Wine Country**, one of New Zealand's largest and most exalted grape-growing regions. Largely the province of boutique producers, it is threaded by the **Hawke's Bay Wine Trail** linking 30-odd wineries, some offering free tastings and many with a restaurant, or at least the chance to picnic in landscaped grounds.

With a climatic pattern similar to that of the great Bordeaux vineyards, Hawke's Bay produces fine **Chardonnay** and lots of **Merlot**. **Cabernet Sauvignon** is also big

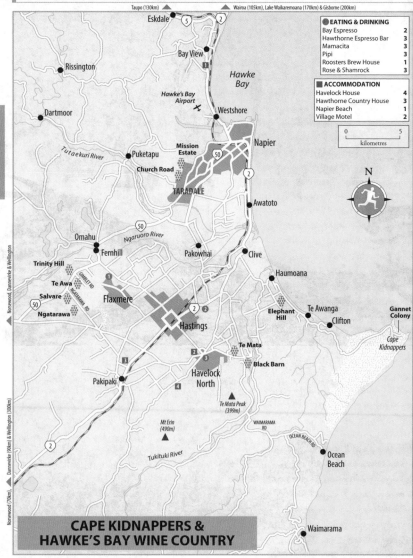

CAPE KIDNAPPERS &
HAWKE'S BAY WINE COUNTRY

but struggles to ripen in cooler summers. Many winemakers are now setting Hawke's Bay up to become New Zealand's flagship producer of **Syrah**, a subtler version of the Aussie Shiraz (though it is made from the same grape) that utilizes the original European name.

Much of the country covered by the wine trail is also part of the region's **art and food trails** (see p.397).

Brief history

Hawke's Bay is New Zealand's longest-established wine-growing region: French Marist missionaries planted the first vines in 1851, ostensibly to produce sacramental wine.

6

THE CAPE KIDNAPPERS GANNETS

Gannets are big birds that can live for up to thirty years. They're distinguished by their gold-and-black head markings and fearlessness round humans. The birds at Cape Kidnappers start nesting in June, laying their eggs from early July through to October, with the chicks hatching six weeks later. Once fledged, at around fifteen weeks, the young gannets embark on their inaugural flight, a marathon, as-yet-unexplained 3000km journey to Australia, where they spend a couple of years before flying back to spend the rest of their lives in New Zealand, returning to their place of birth to breed each year. It is thought that the birds mate for life, using the same or an adjacent nest each year, but recent observation indicates that adultery does occur – usually because of mistaken identity.

During the **breeding season** (July–mid-Oct), the cape is closed to the public. One of the three colonies, the Saddle, is reserved for scientific study and allows no public access. The remaining two colonies, Plateau and Black Reef, are open outside the breeding season, and at the former you will get within a metre or so of the birds. When pairs reunite, after a fishing or nest-material-gathering trip, you can get close enough to hear their beaks clack together in greeting.

VISITING THE GANNETS

There are three ways to visit the gannets – on foot and with two tours – all starting from Clifton, 20km southeast of Napier, though the tours can pick you up for an additional cost. Most tours are tide-dependent and travel to the colony along the beach below rock-fall-prone 100m-high cliffs.

Walking (late Oct–April; roughly 6hr return) The most strenuous but least expensive way to get to the gannets is to walk the 11km along the beach from Clifton. No permits are needed, but you'll need to check tide tables and pick up DOC's useful *Guide to Cape Kidnappers* leaflet either from DOC or the Hastings or Napier i-SITEs. You set off from Clifton about three hours after high tide; head back no more than ninety minutes after low tide. Once at the access point on the beach it's a strenuous 25min climb to the Plateau Colony across private land, though the track is well marked.

Gannet Beach Adventures ☎ 0800 426 638, ⓦ gannets.com. The traditional gannet trip, aboard tractor-drawn trailers along the beach. The pace and approach give plenty of opportunities to appreciate the

geology along the way and observe the birds at close quarters. Tours end near a DOC shelter from where it's a 25min uphill slog to the Plateau, where you'll have half an hour to admire the birds. For an extra $45 they'll pick you up from Napier, Havelock North or Hastings i-SITEs. (daily late Oct–early May; 4hr; $42).

Gannet Safaris ☎ 06 875 800 0888, ⓦ gannetsafaris.com. If you don't fancy the uphill walk, want more time with the birds and the chance to see and learn about the spectacular *Summerlee Station* luxury accommodation complex, this is the tour for you. You travel overland by minibus, passing through *Summerlee Station*, and continue through some stunning scenery and great views to the colonies, where you have 55 minutes or so to gander at the gannets (3hr; $75, or $105 with pick-up from Napier or Hastings).

The excess was sold, and the commercial aspect of the operation continues today as the *Mission Estate Winery*. Some fifty years later, other wineries began to spring up, favouring open-textured gravel terraces alongside the Tutaekuri, Ngaruroro and Tukituki rivers, which retain the day's heat and are free from moist sea breezes. In this arena the vineyards of the **Gimblett Road** – the so-called **Gimblett Gravels** – produce increasingly world-renowned wines.

GETTING AROUND   HAWKE'S BAY WINE COUNTRY

By car You can easily drive yourself around and visit the wineries, but taking a tour obviates the need to find a designated driver.

Wine tours At least half a dozen tours are on offer, most visiting four or five wineries over the course of a morning or afternoon. They're mainly Napier-based but will pick up in Hastings and Havelock

North, usually for free. Self-guided bike tours are also available.

TOUR OPERATORS

Grape Escape ☎ 0800 100 489, ⓦ grapeescape.net.nz. Runs half-day trips ($70), visiting four to five wineries and tasting about thirty different wines – and some cheese.

6

HAWKE'S BAY WINERIES

There are over seventy **wineries** in the entire region. Those listed below are recommended, either because they stand out for some particular reason other than wine tastings or because they make good lunch spots. You may find it cheaper to buy the same bottle of wine at a local supermarket than at the cellar door.

Napier's closest wineries are 8km to the southwest in the suburb of **Taradale**. Closer to Hastings, there are clusters outside **Havelock North**, 5km southeast of Hastings, and 10km northwest near **Fernhill** – the fastest-growing wine district in Hawke's Bay. Winery **opening hours** are generally daily 10am–5pm in summer, but they are sometimes closed on Monday, Tuesday and even Wednesday when things are quiet – if there's somewhere you must visit, phone first.

The best of the winery restaurants are those at *Black Barn, Elephant Hill, Mission Estate* and *Te Awa*.

★ **Black Barn** Black Barn Rd, Havelock North ☏ 06 877 7985, ⊛ blackbarn.com. Designer winery complex with free cellar-door tastings, a lunch bistro and café (mains around $35) that also opens for dinner on Fridays, an art gallery and a growers' market. The amphitheatre hosts a number of outdoor events, including cinema, through the summer. Tastings daily 10am–5pm; bistro and café closed Mon & Tues; growers' market Dec–Feb 9am–noon.

Church Road 150 Church Rd, Taradale ☏ 06 833 8324, ⊛ churchroad.co.nz. Renowned winery with an interesting guided tour ($15), which visits their museum, fashioned from old underground vats. There's also a behind-the-scenes tour, which advises on food-matching for $35 (advance booking essential). Tastings are free and often include their famed Church Road Chardonnay. Platters for one or two cost $45, cheese boards $36. Tour daily 11am & 2pm; tastings daily Oct–April 10am–5pm; May–Sept 10.30am–4pm.

Elephant Hill 86 Clifton Rd, Te Awanga ☏ 06 872 6060, ⊛ elephanthill.co.nz. Architecturally dramatic winery with an infinity pool, single vineyard wines and award-winning restaurant/bar open for lunch and dinner (mains around $39). Best known for its Chardonnay, Rose and Syrah; tastings are $5 redeemable on purchase of a bottle. Tastings: daily April–Sept 11am–4pm; Oct–April 11am–5pm.

Mission Estate 198 Church Rd, Taradale ☏ 06 845 9350, ☏ 06 845 9354 for restaurant bookings, ⊛ missionestate.co.nz. Noted for its pivotal role in the development of the Hawke's Bay wine industry, New Zealand's oldest winery offers well-organized, free historic tours that culminate in a tasting; tastings only are also free. The à la carte restaurant serves lunch and dinner on the terrace or in the old seminary building; expect dishes such as molasses-cured salmon ($20) and herb-crusted lamb loin with harissa ($38.50). Tours daily 10.30am & 2pm; tastings Mon–Sat 9am–5pm, Sun 10am–4.30pm.

Ngatarawa 305 Ngatarawa Rd, Bridge Pa ☏ 06 879 7603, ⊛ ngatarawa.co.nz. Dependable small winery

with educational tastings ($3 service charge) of quality tipples in a century-old racing stables overlooking attractive picnic areas and a pétanque pitch. Tastings daily summer 10am–5pm, winter 11am–4pm.

★ **Salvare** 403 Ngatarawa Rd, Bridge Pa ☏ 06 874 9409, ⊛ salvare.co.nz. Tiny two-person operation, this is the place to come for passion and personal service as well as great wines (Chardonnay, Viognier and lighter, French-style reds), ridiculously good wine slushies, plus olive oils, mustards and suchlike. Tastings may be $5 and are usually outside among the vines – perfect with a platter (from $29). They don't sell anywhere else. Tastings: summer daily 10.30am–4.30pm; winter Thurs–Mon 10.30am–4pm, Tues & Wed 10.30am–3pm.

Te Awa 2375 SH50, Fernhill ☏ 06 879 7602, ⊛ teawa.com. This winery near the famed Gimblett Road produces exceptional reds (Merlot and Cabernet Merlot) that are more aromatic and livelier than many of their Hawke's Bay rivals; tastings are $5. Treat yourself to lunch in one of New Zealand's finest winery restaurants, dining inside or out on dishes such as the charcuterie board ($45) or braised beef cheek with smoked beetroot purée ($27). Tastings daily 10am–4pm.

Te Mata 349 Te Mata Rd, Havelock North ☏ 06 877 4399, ⊛ temata.co.nz. New Zealand's oldest winery on its existing site, making a notable Bordeaux-style Coleraine, one of New Zealand's top reds. Free tastings – try the Syrahs and Sav' Blancs – with the added bonus of Ian Athfield's controversial house among the grapes. Tastings Mon–Fri 9am–5pm, Sat 10am–5pm, Sun (Nov–May) 11am–4pm.

Trinity Hill 2396 Roy Hills Rd (SH50), Fernhill ☏ 06 879 7778, ⊛ trinityhill.com. Strikingly modern winery in the Gimblett Road area, producing excellent reds and Chardonnay and leading New Zealand's experimentation with the likes of Montepulciano and Tempranillo; they even make a port blended from Touriga Nacional. Tastings are $5, cheese platters $20. Tastings daily 10am–5pm.

Picks up and drops off at accommodation in Napier, Hastings and Havelock.

On Yer Bike 12543 SH50, Hastings ☎06 650 4627, ⓦonyerbikehb.co.nz. A great alternative to a driven tour, with a series of easy routes from five wineries in 5km to nine in 23km. All-day bike rental (tandems available),

route map, roadside support and a packed lunch are included ($60).

Vince's World of Wine ☎06 836 6705. Great fun, with an entertaining, knowledgeable guide and a flexible schedule. A half-day trip fits in four to five wineries ($65) and will pick you up from Napier.

INFORMATION

Wine leaflets The region's i-SITE offices carry the free *Hawke's Bay Wine Trail* leaflet, which outlines the wineries – for the pick of the bunch, see box opposite.

Arts and crafts leaflets The free *Hawke's Bay Art Guide* directs you to studios, workshops and galleries of painters, sculptors, potters and craftspeople in the region.

Food leaflets The free *Hawke's Bay Food Trail* includes a map showing the location of all manner of quality foodstuffs – everything from chocolate and olive oil to cheese and pepper sauce – along with gourmet cafés and restaurants.

6

Hastings

Inland **HASTINGS**, 20km south of Napier, was once a rival to its northern neighbour as Hawke's Bay's premier city, buoyed by the wealth generated by the surrounding farmland and orchards. Napier's ascendancy as a tourist destination put Hastings firmly in second place, though it does have an attractive core of buildings, erected after the same 1931 earthquake that rocked Napier. Hastings was saved from the worst effects of the ensuing fires, which were quenched before they could take hold using the artesian water beneath the city.

After the earthquake, Hastings embraced the Californian-inspired **Spanish Mission** style of architecture: roughcast stucco walls, arched windows, small balconies, barley-twist columns and heavily overhung roofs clad in terracotta tiles. The finest examples can be seen in an hour or so, using the self-guided *Art Deco Hastings* walk leaflet ($1 from the i-SITE). If time is short, limit your wanderings to Heretaunga Street East, taking in the gorgeous bronzework and sumptuous lead lighting of the **Westerman Building** or, at the corner of Hastings Street, the **Hawke's Bay Opera House** – built fifteen years before the earthquake, but remodelled to create the region's finest Spanish Mission facade.

The city is mostly an alternative to Napier as a base for touring the wonderful Hawke's Bay Wine Country, with many of the vineyards within easy reach. Apples, pears and peaches also continue to be grown in huge quantities, and the harvest provides work (see p.398).

Te Mata Peak

Te Mata Peak Rd • ⓦtematapark.co.nz

Driving from Hastings to the satellite suburb of Havelock North, the long ridge of limestone bluffs which make up the 399m **Te Mata Peak** looms into view. The ridge is held to be the supine form of a Maori chief, Rongokako, who choked on a rock as he tried to eat through the hill – one of many Herculean feats he attempted while wooing the daughter of a Heretaunga chief; according to legend, overcome with grief at her father's death, Rongokako's daughter threw herself off the peak.

Te Mata Peak Road winds up the hill to a wonderful vantage point that's great towards sunset. Views stretch over the fertile plains, north across Hawke's Bay and Cape Kidnappers, and east to surf-pounded Ocean Beach and Waimarama, the main swimming **beaches** for Hastings and Havelock North. A parking area partway up Te Mata Peak Road marks the start of moderate **walking tracks** through groves of native trees and redwoods and a wetland area before reaching the summit (2–3hr return).

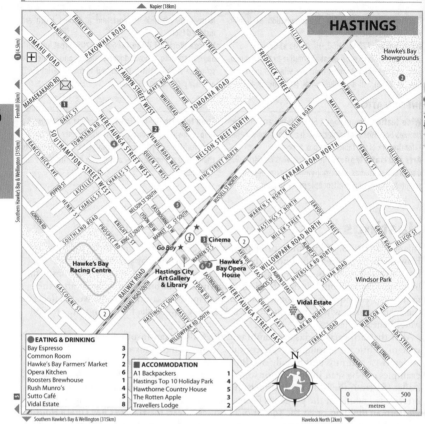

HASTINGS

Napier (18km)

Hawke's Bay Showgrounds

Hawke's Bay Racing Centre

Hastings City Art Gallery & Library

Hawke's Bay Opera House

Cinema

Go Bay

Vidal Estate

Windsor Park

Southern Hawke's Bay & Wellington (315km)

Havelock North (2km)

● EATING & DRINKING
Bay Espresso	3
Common Room	7
Hawke's Bay Farmers' Market	2
Opera Kitchen	6
Roosters Brewhouse	1
Rush Munro's	4
Sutto Café	5
Vidal Estate	8

■ ACCOMMODATION
A1 Backpackers	1
Hastings Top 10 Holiday Park	4
Hawthorne Country House	5
The Rotten Apple	3
Travellers Lodge	2

0 — 500 metres

ARRIVAL AND DEPARTURE

HASTINGS

By bus Long-distance buses stop at Russell Street North, a few steps from the i-SITE. Local operator GoBay (☎ 06 878 9250) runs to Napier (1 daily, roughly 2/hr 8am–6pm) and Havelock North (Mon–Fri; 4 daily) from the Library.

Destinations Auckland (1 daily; 8hr); Dannevirke (5 daily; 1hr 30min); Gisborne (1 daily; 5hr); Napier (7 daily; 30min); Norsewood (4 daily; 1hr); Taupo (4–5 daily; 2hr 30min); Wellington (4 daily; 4–5hr).

By plane Regular direct flights from Auckland, Wellington and Christchurch, as well as Rotorua, Tauranga and

Gisborne arrive at Hawke's Bay Airport, which is about 20km north of town on SH2. The airport is served by Super Shuttle (☎ 0800 748 885, ⓦ supershuttle.co.nz) which charges $43 to Hastings ($45 to Havelock North); and Village Shuttle (☎ 0800 777 796, ⓦ villageshuttle.co.nz) who charge about $5 less.

Destinations Auckland (5–8 daily; 1hr); Christchurch (2–3 daily; 1hr 35min); Wellington (3–5 daily; 1hr).

By taxi Hastings Taxis (☎ 06 878 5055).

INFORMATION AND ACTIVITIES

Visitor information Hastings i-SITE, 100 Heretaunga St East (Mon–Fri 9am–5pm, Sat 9am–3pm & Sun 10am–2pm; ☎ 06 873 5526, ⓦ visithastings.co.nz), has wineries leaflets, a gift shop and keen staff will help with bookings and sell bus tickets. Havelock North's i-SITE (cnr Middle and Te Aute rds; Mon–Fri 10am–5pm, Sat 9am–4pm & Sun 9am–3pm; ☎ 06 877 9600,

ⓦ visithastings.co.nz) can also help with bookings and rent bikes.

Fruit-picking work The fruit harvest begins in February and lasts three or four months, providing casual, hard-going, low-paid orchard work for those willing to thin, pick or pack fruit. The hostels are a good source of work and up-to-the-minute information though you'll be competing with locals and itinerant old fruit-picking hands; for more information on working in the region, see p.58.

Services Hastings Library, cnr Eastbourne and Warren streets (Mon 10am–5pm, Tues 9am–8pm, Wed–Fri 9am–5pm, Sat 10am–4pm, Sun 1–4pm) offers wi-fi

($2.50/30min or 15mb) and internet terminals ($1/15min). There's free wi-fi in the CBD.

Cinema Focal Point, 126 Heretaunga Street East; ☏ 06 871 5418, ⊛ hastings.focalpointcinema.co.nz. Three screens mostly showing mainstream movies.

ACCOMMODATION

Availability of budget accommodation in Hastings is affected by the fruit-picking season: from mid-February to May you'll struggle to find cheap rooms, especially if you're looking for self-catering or a long-stay, so book well ahead. Nearby Napier (see p.390) makes a good alternative base if you're able to commute. For more luxurious accommodation, head for Havelock North, where **B&Bs** and swanky self-catering predominate.

6

HASTINGS

A1 Backpackers 122 Stortford St ☏ 06 873 4285, ⊛ a1backpackers.co.nz; map p.398. Less of a work-camp feel than Hastings' other backpackers, set in a well-kept peaceful villa whose helpful owner offers free local pick-up for two-night stays. The dorms are adequate but the doubles more comfortable. Off-street parking. Dorms $\overline{\underline{\$26}}$, rooms $\overline{\underline{\$60}}$

Hastings Top 10 Holiday Park 610 Windsor Ave ☏ 06 878 6692, ⊛ hastingstop10.co.nz; map p.398. Appealing campsite on the edge of Windsor Park, with tent sites ($22) and a range of modern units (the more expensive of which are quite swish) and good facilities, though it does get busy in the fruit-picking season. Cabins $\overline{\underline{\$80}}$, serviced apartment $\overline{\underline{\$160}}$

Hawthorne Country House 1420 Railway Rd South (SH2), 6km southwest of Hastings ☏ 06 878 0035, ⊛ hawthorne.co.nz; map p.398. Beautiful and very welcoming B&B in a grand Edwardian villa surrounded by croquet lawns and farmland. The four en-suite rooms are decorated with understated elegance, while good breakfasts, afternoon teas and drinks with canapés all make for a relaxed atmosphere. $\overline{\underline{\$350}}$

★ **The Rotten Apple** 114 Heretaunga St East ☏ 06 878 4363, ⊛ rottenapple.co.nz; map p.398. Central hostel with lots of long-stayers, assistance for would-be fruit workers and low weekly rates for the same, all in an old

hotel with basic rooms and facilities that just about stand up when the place is full. Enough free wi-fi to email your mum. Dorms $\overline{\underline{\$26}}$, rooms $\overline{\underline{\$70}}$

Travellers Lodge 608 St Aubyn St West ☏ 06 878 7108, ⊛ tlodge.co.nz; map p.398. Hostel in three suburban houses, with bike rental, charged-for wi-fi and off-street parking. There is a range of rooms, all pretty basic, but with lots of beds, mostly seeing an uneven mix of Kiwi labourers and touring foreigners from Nov–May. Facilities are limited. Dorms $\overline{\underline{\$26}}$, rooms $\overline{\underline{\$60}}$

HAVELOCK NORTH

★ **Havelock House** 77 Endsleigh Rd, 3km southwest off Middle Rd ☏ 06 877 5439, ⊛ havelockhouse.co.nz; map p.394. Three large guest rooms (two with deep baths) occupy this spacious house in a quiet, woodsy setting. Guests can access a vast lounge equipped with full-size snooker table, a tennis court and an outdoor pool, plus there's a separate two-bedroom house with deck and barbecue. Room $\overline{\underline{\$180}}$, with spa bath $\overline{\underline{\$255}}$

Village Motel Cnr Te Aute and Porter ☏ 06 877 5401, ⊛ villagemotel.co.nz; map p.394. Centrally located motel run by friendly owners. The rooms have been recently renovated, so all have air-conditioning and spa pools. Breakfast is available. Studio $\overline{\underline{\$165}}$, Apartment $\overline{\underline{\$185}}$

EATING, DRINKING AND ENTERTAINMENT

For a town of its size, Hastings is relatively poorly supplied with good places to eat, though an ever-expanding selection of places in neighbouring Havelock North bumps up the quota, and lunches at the region's wineries are a good if pricey option (see box, p.396).

HASTINGS

Bay Espresso 141 Karamu Rd, 3km east of Hastings ☏ 06 876 5782, ⊛ www.bayespresso.co.nz; map p.394. A rustic café with plenty of garden seating that's a locals' weekend home-from-home. Superb coffee and breakfasts are supplemented by lunch specials ($14–20). If you're hungry, try the Orchardists Big Breakfast, which boasts chorizo and black pudding ($18.50). Mon–Fri 7am–4pm, Sat & Sun 8am–4pm.

Common Room 227 Heretaunga St East ☏ 027 656 8959, ⊛ commonroombar.com; map p.398. Wine bar

with threadbare sofas and a straightforward admissions policy: no idiots. Occasional DJs, but mainly live bands playing anything from electronica to country, usually only for a little *koha*. Good drinks deals and tasty paella. Wed & Thurs 4pm–late, Fri 3pm–late, Sat 4pm–late, summer Sun 1–7.30pm.

Hawke's Bay Farmers' Market Hawke's Bay Showgrounds, Kenilworth Rd; map p.398. On a fine weekend morning, skip breakfast and head straight to this excellent market, where innumerable stalls introduce you to fresh local produce, coffee and pastries while a local musician or two entertains. It's held indoors in winter. Sat 7–10.30am, Sun 8.30am–12.30pm; Oct–April also Thurs 5–9pm.

★**Opera Kitchen** 312 Eastbourne St East ☎06 870 6020, ⓦoperakitchen.co.nz; map p.398. Classy licensed café showcasing local produce through simple but delicious dishes (under $25) served in stripped-back surroundings. Worth checking out if just for the knitted hats they put on boiled eggs ($8.50 with Marmite soldiers). Mon–Fri 7.30am–4pm, Sat & Sun 9am–3pm.

Roosters Brewhouse 1470 Omahu Rd, 7km northwest ☎06 879 4127; map p.394. Micro-brewery offering traditional natural brews best supped in its pleasant café or outdoors at garden tables while tucking into straightforward dishes at reasonable prices. There's free tasting of its English ale, lager and dark beers, and you can buy a flagon to take away – a wise move considering the prices elsewhere. Occasional live music. Mon–Fri 10am–7pm, Sat 2–7pm.

Rush Munro's 704 Heretaunga St West; map p.398. A small ice-cream garden that's been packing in the locals for 80 years – even Bill Clinton once stopped in. For the retro experience go for an ice cream soda ($4). Mon–Fri 11am–5pm, Sat & Sun 11am–6pm.

Sutto Café 103-5 King St ☎06 878 4163; map p.398. Popular with local workers, *Sutto's* has the usual range of counter food plus some interesting specials. Lunch might be warm beef salad with "tropical oils" ($17.80). Mon–Fri 7am–4.30pm, Sat & Sun 8am–3pm.

Vidal Estate 913 Aubyn St East ☎06 872 7440, ⓦvidal .co.nz; map p.398. Ingredients are mostly local and organic in this popular semiformal restaurant attached to

an award-winning winery and specializing in pricey nosh (dinner mains $27–40); go for the set menus ($29 for 3 course lunch, $63 for dinner). Book ahead at weekends. Mon–Sat 11.30am–late, Sun 11.30am–3pm.

HAVELOCK NORTH

Hawthorne Espresso Bar 23 Napier Rd ☎06 877 1113; map p.394. Coffee roastery and tiny café serving perfect drinks and the best scones for miles around. There's a craft market on the first Saturday of the month. Mon–Fri 8.30am–4pm, Sat 9am–12.30pm.

Mamacita 12 Havelock Rd ☎06 877 6200, ⓦmamacita .co.nz; map p.394. Short menu (the drinks list is as long) covering tacos, quesadillas and specials such as pork braised in coffee ($15). No reservations. Tues–Sun 4.30–10pm.

Pipi 16 Joll Rd ☎06 877 8993, ⓦpipicafe.co.nz; map p.394. Impressive in its pinkness, this casual and very popular café and pizza restaurant exudes casual style. Nothing matches but everything fits, and you help yourself from the drinks fridge and tell them what you've had when you pay. The food's great too, offering the likes of fishcakes with rocket and white bean mash ($22), great pizzas (from $16) and a slew of local wines. Tues–Sun 4–10pm.

Rose & Shamrock 15 Napier Rd ☎06 877 2999, ⓦroseandshamrock.co.nz; map p.394. Popular for Sunday roasts with the agricultural and blue-rinse gangs, this fair attempt at a pub has 24 Irish, English and Kiwi beers on tap, plus well-priced bar meals ($18–30), including fish and chips and old Irish sausages with gravy. Tripe nights, quiz nights and occasional live Irish folk music. Daily 10.30am–late.

OPERA

Hawke's Bay Opera House 101 Hastings St South ☎06 871 5280, ⓦhawkesbayoperahouse.co.nz; map

p.398. Currently closed as it fails the latest earthquake regulations. A review was due at the time of writing.

Southern Hawke's Bay

South of Hastings, the main road (SH2) runs through the relentless sheep stations of **Southern Hawke's Bay**, a region uncluttered by places of genuine interest. Small farming towns stand as fitting memorials to the pioneers who tamed the region, particularly Danes and Norwegians who stepped in when the New Zealand Wars of the 1860s discouraged immigration from Britain.

Norsewood

If time isn't too pressing, make a fleeting stop at the "**Scandinavian**" **settlements** such as the village of **NORSEWOOD**, 45km south of Hastings, little more than a quiet street (west of SH2) which runs from a replica Norwegian-style stave church, past *Café Norsewood* to a glassed-in boathouse containing the fishing boat *Bindalsfaering*, a gift from the Norwegian government commemorating Norsewood's centenary in 1972.

Dannevirke

The Danish heritage of the farming town of **DANNEVIRKE**, 20km south of Norsewood, is flagged by a modern windmill in Copenhagen Square on the main street, along with cut-out signs of smiling Vikings greeting and farewelling visitors. If you're after sustenance, try the licensed *Black Stump* café, 21 High Street (Tues–Fri 10am–late, Sat 9am–late & Sun 10am–3pm).

South of Dannevirke, SH2 runs 25km to Woodville, where SH3 strikes west through the Manawatu Gorge to Palmerston North and SH2 heads south into the Wairarapa.

6

The Wairarapa

Most of the **Wairarapa** region is archetypal Kiwi sheep country, with wool-flecked green hills stretching into the distance. In recent years, however, the southern half of the region has increasingly benefited from free-spending weekenders from Wellington visiting the boutique hotels, innovative restaurants and many wineries surrounding **Martinborough**, the region's current wine capital and, along with **Greytown**, its most appealing settlement.

North of **Masterton**, the region's main commercial centre, the **Pukaha Mount Bruce National Wildlife Centre** provides a wonderful opportunity to witness ongoing bird conservation work; to the south, **Featherston** is a base for walks up the bed of the Rimutaka Incline Railway.

Back on the coast, the laidback holiday settlement of **Castlepoint** is good for swimming and surfing, and **Cape Palliser** is the ideal spot for blustery mind-clearing walks and dramatic coastal scenery.

Cross the **Rimutaka Range** towards Wellington and you're into the Hutt Valley, full of commuter-belt communities, none of which really warrants a stop until you reach Petone, on the outskirts of the capital.

Brief history

The establishment of New Zealand's earliest sheep station in the 1840s on rich alluvial lands close to present-day Martinborough paved the way for development by the progressive **Small Farm Association** (SFA). This was the brainchild of Joseph Masters, a Derbyshire cooper and longtime campaigner against the separation of landowner and labourer, who sought to give disenfranchised settlers the opportunity to become smallholders. Liberal governor George Grey supported him and in 1853 suggested the SFA should persuade local Maori to sell land for the establishment of two towns – Masterton and Greytown.

Initially Greytown prospered, and it retains an air of antiquity rare among New Zealand towns, but the routing of the rail line favoured Masterton, famed chiefly today for the annual Golden Shears sheepshearing competition.

LONG NAMES AND FAMOUS FLUTES

Visitors in search of the esoteric might want to stray along SH52, which makes a 120km tar-sealed loop east towards the rugged coastline from dull Waipukurau, 50km south of Hastings, re-emerging at Dannevirke. Almost 50km south of Waipukurau (and 6km south of Porangahau, where there is rare coastal access), a sign marks the hill known as aumatawhaka-tangihangakoauauotamateaturipukakapikimaungahoronukuupokaiwhenuakitanatahu, which, unsurprisingly, rates as one of the world's longest place names; roughly, this mouthful translates as "the hill where Tamatea, circumnavigator of the lands, played the flute for his lover".

Tui Brewery

SH2 Mangatainoka, 10km south of Woodville • Mon–Thurs 10am–4pm, Fri–Sun 10am–5pm; tours daily 11am & 2pm (bookings essential) • Museum free; beer sampling $20; tours $25 • ☎ 06 376 0815, ⓦ tui.co.nz

The northern half of the Wairarapa is very much a continuation of southern Hawke's Bay, but make a brief stop at the **Tui Brewery**, which brews cheap consistent beer that has built an enthusiastic following with its "Yeah. Right" billboard advertisements, seen all over the country. The small light-hearted museum (their founder, Henry Wagstaff, was apparently a "useless cheesemaker") is adjacent to their bar serving good Kiwi tucker matched to their beers. You can sample several beers and keep the glass or join one of the **tours**, which include a visit to the distinctive seven-storey brick brewery, tastings and, again, a glass to keep.

Ekehatuna

Information Centre 23 Main Street, 30km south of the Tui Brewery • Daily 10am–4pm • ☎ 06 375 8545, ⓦ eketahunakiwicountry.co.nz

Ekehatuna accepts its national reputation as the back of beyond, and there's not much to see except the large model kiwi, but *Lazy Graze* on the main street is a good spot for a coffee, and it's worth a stop to experience small-town rural NZ.

Pukaha Mount Bruce National Wildlife Centre

SH2, 10km south of Ekehatuna • Daily 9am–4.30pm; check website for feeding and talk times • $20 • Guided tour daily 11am & 1pm ($45 incl. entry); night walks Sat 2.5hr/$35; Look-out lunch $60 (incl. picnic); behind the scenes $125 • ☎ 06 375 8004, ⓦ pukaha.org.nz

Pukaha Mount Bruce National Wildlife Centre is one of the best places in the country to view endangered native birds, and is staffed by people engaged in bringing them back from the edge. Kokako, whio, kakariki, hihi, kiwi, takahe (a "rainbow couple") and more can be found in aviaries set along the trails through lowland primeval forest. The nocturnal **kiwi house** houses Manukura, a rare white kiwi, and there's also a **kiwi breeding facility** (ask about chicks). Beyond the aviaries, several thousand acres of forest have been set aside for reintroducing birds to the wild. Bring a packed lunch for the picnic area, or support the on-site café (no refunds if a kaka spills your coffee).

ACCOMMODATION   PUKAHA MOUNT BRUCE

★**The Hut** SH2, first house on the right north of the Wildlife Centre ☎ 06 375 8681, ⓦ thehut.co.nz. Stay in this traditional *bach* high above the wildlife centre, with an outdoor tub for a romantic bath under the stars and a log burner to cook meals. It's a steep 40min walk, or arrange four-wheeler transport for an additional charge. **$100**

Masterton and around

Though it is Wairarapa's largest town, workaday **MASTERTON**, crouched at the foot of the Tararua Range some 30km south of Pukaha Mount Bruce, is of only passing interest, with a commercial heart strung along the parallel Chapel, Queen and Dixon streets. On the town's eastern side **Queen Elizabeth Park** provides a pleasant opportunity to stroll through formal gardens.

GOLDEN SHEARS

The town's major event is the annual **Golden Shears** competition (ⓦ goldenshears.co.nz), effectively the Olympiad of all things woolly, held on the three days leading up to the first Saturday in March. Contestants flock from around the world to demonstrate their prowess with the broad-blade handpiece; a top shearer can remove a fleece in under a minute, though for maximum points it must be done with skill as well as speed, and leave a smooth and unblemished, if shivering, beast. For a few bucks you can just walk in on the early rounds, but to attend the entertaining finals on Friday and Saturday nights you'll need to book well in advance.

Aratoi
Corner of Bruce and Dixon sts, opposite Queen Elizabeth Park • Daily 10am–4.30pm • Donation • ☏ 06 370 0001, ⓦ aratoi.co.nz

This museum-gallery gives a good insight into the history of the Wairarapa region, along with hosting some excellent art exhibitions. Among the subjects are the **oldest Maori house site** (1180 AD) in New Zealand, part of an archeological exhibition based around findings at Omoekau, Palliser Bay. From the gallery collection the most interesting exhibits are early Lindauer portraits of local Maori (ask to see them if they're not on display), kinetic sculpture by Tony Nicholls in the style of Len Lye, and a Barbara Hepworth copper and bronze from 1956.

Wool Shed (National Museum of Sheep and Shearing)
12 Dixon St • Daily 10am–4pm • $8 • ☏ 06 378 8008, ⓦ thewoolshednz.com

An excellent museum on all things woolly; there's even weaving on Wednesdays. Housed in two century-old shearing sheds relocated from rural Wairarapa, it's filled with everything from sheep pens and shearing handpieces to pressed bales of wool stencilled with the marks of sheep stations, and a replica cloak from LOTR. Classic 1957 footage of Kiwi shearing hero Godfrey Bowen shows how it should be done, and there's usually footage of recent Golden Shears finals, perhaps showing the super-fast handiwork of David Fagan, New Zealand's five-time world champ and record-breaking sixteen-time Golden Shears winner.

Tararua Forest Park
Accessed from SH2, 25km west of Masterton

Draped over the hills to the west of town, the **Tararua Forest Park** offers excellent tramping through beech and podocarp forest to the subalpine tops, but be aware that the notoriously fickle weather in this area can be dangerous. Serious walkers should consider the **Powell–Jumbo Tramp**, a worthwhile twelve-hour circuit that can be broken down into two or more manageable days by staying at **huts** ($15) evenly spaced along the route. The track starts at the backcountry hut-style *Holdsworth Lodge* (see below). Day-trippers can undertake easy riverside walks (1–2hr) or head three hours across easy ground to the cosy Atiwhakatu Hut ($5), which has bunks.

ARRIVAL AND DEPARTURE   MASTERTON AND AROUND

By train Tranz Metro (☏ 0800 801 700, ⓦ metlink.org.nz) runs commuter services from Wellington. The train station is a 15min walk from the centre at the end of Perry St; call Rideshop (☏ 06 377 4231) for a taxi.
Destinations Carterton (Mon–Fri 5 daily, weekends 2 daily; 20min); Featherston (Mon–Fri 5 daily, weekends 2 daily; 45min); Wellington (Mon–Fri 5 daily, weekends 2 daily; 1hr 40min).

By bus Tranzit buses (☏ 0800 471 227) run north to Palmerston North, stopping at 316 Queen St, a short walk from the i-SITE.
Destinations Carterton (7 Mon–Fri, 3 Sat; 15min); Featherston (7 Mon–Fri, 3 Sat; 40min); Greytown (7 Mon–Fri, 3 Sat; 25min); Palmerston North (1 Sun and Tues–Thurs, 2 Fri; 1hr 35min).

INFORMATION

i-SITE Corner of Bruce and Dixon sts (Mon–Fri 9am–5pm, Sat & Sun 10am–4pm; ☏ 06 370 0900, ⓦ wairarapanz.com). Enthusiastic staff can give information on local hikes as well as the usual services.

ACCOMMODATION

Cornwall Park 119 Cornwall St, 2km west of the town centre ☏ 06 378 2939, ⓦ cornwallparkmotel.co.nz. A clean, peaceful old-style motel with a pool, spa and free wi-fi. It's all a bit dated-looking, but everything works perfectly well and units are undoubtedly great value. **$104**
Holdsworth Lodge 25km west of Masterton at the end of Norfolk Rd, off southbound SH2 ⓦ doc.govt.nz.

Only those taking on the Powell–Jumbo Tramp (see above) will likely be interested in staying at this backcountry hut-style accommodation. Booking in advance with DOC is essential. Tent sites **$12**, lodge **$25**
Mawley Park Motor Camp 55 Oxford St ☏ 06 378 6454, ⓦ mawleypark.co.nz. Masterton's best budget accommodation is this riverside spot, which offers decent

flat campsites ($15) interspersed with trees, backpacker accommodation ($25), some new en-suite units and a

range of the more traditional cabins and motel units. Cabins $60, en suites $85

EATING, DRINKING AND ENTERTAINMENT

★**Café Strada** 232 Queen St ☎06 378 8450, ⓦcafestrada.co.nz. The best eating and drinking option in town provides tasty meals and counter grub during the day and stays open for quality, moderately priced dinners (under $30) featuring dishes such as crispy-skinned South Island salmon. Licensed. Free wi-fi. Daily 8am–8.30pm.

Clareville Bakery 3340 SH2, Clareville ☎06 379 5333. Converted church where everything's made on the (licensed) premises, from award-winning pies (lamb cutlet and *kumara*) and great counter food to good café dishes (Basque eggs $18). Wednesday evenings feature more

formal dinners with live music. Mon & Tues 7am–4pm, Wed 7am–11.30pm, Thurs–Sat 7am–4pm.

Entice At Aratoi, corner of Bruce and Dixon sts ☎06 377 3166, ⓦentice.co.nz. Licensed café at the museum-gallery serving delicious counter food including monster savoury muffins, sandwiches and great coffee, with nothing over $20. Daily 8am–4pm.

King Street Live 21 King St ☎06 370 4332, ⓦkingstreetlive.co.nz. Unexpectedly great live venue, with bar serving local wine and interesting nibbles (paua wontons). Tickets $5–35. Thurs–Sat 5pm–late.

Castlepoint

The 300km of coastline from Cape Kidnappers, near Napier, south to Cape Palliser is bleak, desolate and almost entirely inaccessible – except for **CASTLEPOINT**, 65km east of Masterton, where early explorers found a welcome break in the "perpendicular line of cliff". A lighthouse presides over the rocky knoll, which is linked to the mainland by a thin hourglass double **beach** that encloses a sheltered **lagoon** known as the Basin. Wairarapa families retreat here for summer fun and surfers ride the breakers, though when the weather turns it is a wonderfully wild bit of coastline. Unless you are a keen surfer, a day-visit will suffice; if you do decide to stay, take all your provisions with you.

ACCOMMODATION   CASTLEPOINT

Castlepoint Holiday Park & Motels ☎06 372 6705, ⓦcastlepoint.co.nz. Wonderfully situated, traditional Kiwi holidaymaker campsite, in the middle of nowhere and within

earshot of the crashing waves. The broad range of reasonably kept accommodation also includes cottages and motel units ($140–200). Camping for 2 people $36, kitchen cabins $85

Carterton

The service town of **CARTERTON**, 15km south of Masterton, has but one thing to offer: **Paua World**, 54 Kent St (Mon–Fri 8am–5pm, Sat & Sun 9am–5pm; free; ⓦpauaworld .com), an Aladdin's Cave of objects fashioned from this beautiful rainbow-swirled seashell – pick up anything from wonderfully kitsch fridge magnets to elegant jewellery. The factory supplies just about every tourist knick-knack shop in the country and there's a free self-guided tour to see how the stuff is made.

Stonehenge Aotearoa

51 Ahiaruhe Rd, 12km southeast of Carterton • Sept–May Wed–Sun 10am–4pm (daily Christmas to mid-Jan), May–Aug weekends 10am–4pm; • $8 • Guided tours Sat & Sun 11am, and daily Dec 27–Jan 19 (bookings recommended); $16 • ☎06 377 1600, ⓦstonehenge-aotearoa.co.nz

Stonehenge Aotearoa, 12km southeast of Carterton, appears like some vision of Neolithic Britain on a hill amid Wairarapa farmland. Though built on the same scale as its kin on Salisbury Plain, there the similarity ends. This is a modern wood and concrete edifice, technically classed as a garden ornament by the local council when planning permission was sought. The resulting "open-sky observatory" is primarily educational and best experienced on the detailed hour-and-a-half tours, which cover a fascinating array of information ranging from pure astronomy through Maori star stories and navigation to astrology and myth-busting comparative religion.

Some 5km south of Carterton, a rough road runs 15km west into the foothills of the Tararua Range to **Waiohine Gorge**, a picturesque chasm ideal for picnics.

Greytown

Laid out in 1853, the genteel settlement of **GREYTOWN**, 9km south of Carterton, retains something of its original Victorian feel. Once Wairarapa's main settlement, it declined when the railway bypassed the town and revived only when it became the favoured getaway for weekending Wellingtonians. The two-storey wooden buildings either side of the highway house assorted art galleries, "collectibles" shops, boutiques, excellent cafés and stylish B&Bs, as well as a great traditional butcher (67 Main St).

6

Cobblestones Early Settlers Museum

169 Main St • Thurs–Mon 10am–4pm; printing works in action at weekends 1–4pm • $5 • ☎ 06 304 9687, ⓦ cobblestonesmuseum.org.nz

Local historical buildings (one containing Schoc, a chocolate shop worth entering for the smell alone) have been resited here next to the original Greytown stables and surrounded by pleasant gardens. It's entertaining to wander round for an hour or two, peering through windows, trying to identify farm implements and admiring the room reconstructions. There's a **printing works**, and a smart new entrance building containing carriages and a *waka*.

ARRIVAL AND INFORMATION
GREYTOWN

By bus and train Tranzit buses (☎ 0800 471 227) shuttle between Greytown, Martinborough and Featherston station for the Tranz Metro commuter trains (☎ 04 801 7000) from Wellington. They drop off by the Four Square.

Information Centre 115 Main St (staffed Fri 2–4pm, Sat & Sun 11am–3pm). Masses of neatly organized information on things to do locally. Also open outside the staffed hours for browsing.

ACCOMMODATION

Much accommodation is targeted at the smart set, but there's more choice for the budget traveller here than in Martinborough.

Greytown Camp Ground Kuratawhiti St ☎ 06 304 9387, ⓦ greytowncampground.co.nz. Basic campsite with two amenity blocks right next door to a large children's playground, the town swimming pool and tennis courts. **$14**
Oak Estate 2 Hospital Rd ☎ 0800 843 625, ⓦ oakestate .co.nz. Smart motel units, each with its own deck under the shady trees, less than ten minutes' walk into the town centre. The studios are nicely spacious and all have flatscreen TV and free wi-fi. There's even pétanque. **$130**
★ **Saddlery** 17 Main St ☎ 06 304 7228, ⓦ thesaddlery .co.nz. Just three en-suite rooms in this stylishly restored,

luxurious B&B, with friendly, helpful hosts. The downstairs room was the old store, now transformed with a clawfoot bath. Breakfast on fresh fruit, home-made muesli and jams from their garden or, for an additional $25, enjoy an authentic German breakfast (including pickles, boiled eggs and cheese). **$185**
TurkeyRed 53 Main St ☎ 06 304 9569, ⓦ turkey redhotel.co.nz. Cheerfully decorated rooms upstairs in the old hotel (so they can get noisy) with shared facilities. Out back is a small, slightly cramped backpackers. Dorm **$35**, double **$95**

EATING AND DRINKING

The town's dining leans towards the upmarket, though there are some good down-to-earth places as well.

★ **Cahoots Café** 97 Main St ☎ 06 304 8480. Not as cool and stylish as some of the newer competition, this small neighbourhood café serves great coffee and produces generous meals from a tiny kitchen. The staff welcome visitors and throw friendly abuse at their regulars. Mon–Fri 7am–3pm, Sat & Sun 8am–4pm.
Cuckoo 128 Main St ☎ 06 304 8992. Funky pizza and pasta joint (try the Kiwi, with *kumara* and lamb chorizo, for

$23.50) that even does pizza for breakfast. If you still have room, tuck in to one of their cheesecakes. Wed–Sun 10am–8.30pm.
The French Baker 81 Main St. Delectable breads, sandwiches, pastries, smoked fish pies and cakes (all under $18). Mon–Fri 7.30am–3pm, Sat & Sun 7.30am–4pm.
Main Street Deli 88 Main St ☎ 06 304 9022. Reliable café good for soups and sandwiches (all under $18) as well

as larger, moderately priced meals. They sell a good range of cheeses, which make for a nice combination with bread from the *French Baker*. Daily 8am–5pm.

Salute 83 Main St ☏ 06 304 9825. Popular spot offering

imaginative tapas ($9–17), such as *ras el Hanout* chicken wings or crispy lamb with quince. Wed–Sat noon–10pm, Sun 10.30am–3pm.

Featherston

Locomotive Museum Mon–Fri 10am–2.30pm, Sat & Sun 10am–4pm • $5 • ☏ 06 308 9379, �𝗪 fellmuseum.org.nz

The last of the Wairarapa towns before SH2 climbs west over the Rimutaka range, **FEATHERSTON**, 13km south of Greytown, is for steam-train buffs, who come from across the country to visit the **Fell Locomotive Museum** on Lyon Street. This contains the last surviving example of the locos that, for 77 years (until the boring of a new tunnel in 1955) climbed the 265m, one-in-fifteen slope of the Rimutaka Incline.

Rimutaka Rail Trail

Trail starts 10km south of Featherston at Cross Creek • 18km; 4–5hr; 265m ascent • ⟨ rimutakacycletrail.com

The rails of the Rimutaka Incline have long been pulled up, but you can follow the trackbed on the **Rimutaka Rail Trail**, which passes old shunting yards and steams through the 576m summit tunnel before descending to Kaitoke. To save a long shuttle ride back, most just walk up to the summit and back (4–5hr return), or do the same trip by bike (3hr return).

The trail has now been extended as part of Nga Haerenga, the New Zealand Cycle Trail. You could start in Petone, and loop back round to Wellington over 4–5 days, or continue to the coast from the Incline, past Lake Wairarapa and down to Ocean Beach (36km). The final section (18km) is off-road through Orongorongo Station.

INFORMATION   **RIMUTAKA RAIL TRAIL**

Transport If you want to just do a stretch, contact Rimutaka Shuttles (☏ 06 308 9007 ⟨ rimutakashuttles .com) about transport.

Bike hire Green Jersey Cycle Tours (☏ 021 074 6640,

⟨ greenjersey.co.nz) can hire you a bike ($85/day for the Incline) or arrange your entire trip – including transport, bikes and accommodation – for around $1000.

Martinborough

Little **MARTINBOROUGH**, 18km southeast of Featherston, has been transformed into the centre of a compact wine region synonymous with some of New Zealand's finest reds. It's within easy striking distance of Wellington, and weekends see the arrival of the smart set to load up their shiny 4WDs at the cellar doors. On Mondays and Tuesdays much of the town simply shuts down to recover. Other busy times include **Toast Martinborough** (⟨ toastmartinborough.co.nz), a wine-oriented affair in November with international live acts; and the two **Martinborough Fairs** (first Saturday in February and March; ⟨ martinboroughfair.org.nz) – huge country fêtes during which the central streets are lined with art and craft stalls.

Brief history

Martinborough was initially laid out in the 1870s by landowner John Martin, who named the streets after cities he had visited on his travels and arranged the core, centred on a leafy square, in the form of a Union Jack. For over a century the town languished as a minor agricultural centre until the **first four wineries** – Ata Rangi, Dry River, Chifney and Martinborough (all of which produced their first vintages in 1984) – reinvented it as the coolest, driest and most wind-prone of the North Island's grape-growing regions. With the aid of shelterbelts, strategically planted trees and hedges that splice the vineyards, the wineries produce some outstanding Pinot Noir, notable Cabernet Sauvignon, rich Chardonnay and richly aromatic Riesling.

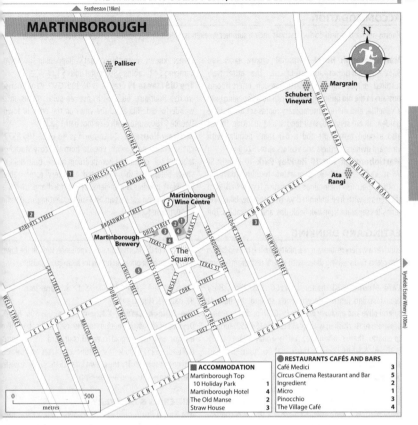

Martinborough Wine Centre

6 Kitchener St • Daily 10am–5pm, summer Fri & Sat 10am–7pm • $2–5 per tasting • ☎ 06 306 9040, Ⓦ martinboroughwine
centre.co.nz

Outside the festival times, your best starting point is the **Martinborough Wine Centre**, which offers free tastings from a different local winery every month, and a taste of fifteen other local wines "on tap". You can quaff a full glass at their seats in the square.

ARRIVAL AND INFORMATION   MARTINBOROUGH

By bus and train Tranzit buses (☎ 0800 471 227) shuttling between Greytown, Featherston, Masterton and Martinborough meet the Tranz Metro commuter trains (☎ 04 801 7000) from Wellington and drop off diagonally opposite the i-SITE and at the Martinborough Wine Centre.

Visitor information i-SITE, 18 Kitchener St (Tues–Sat 9am–5pm, Sun & Mon 10am–4pm; ☎ 06 306 5010, Ⓦ wairarapanz.com), carries loads of information on the surrounding vineyards, including the *Wairarapa Wine Trail* sheet. They also book accommodation and hire bikes.

Winery information Over a dozen wineries (see p.408) are accessible on foot or by bike, guided by the free and widely available *Wairarapa Wine Trail* sheet. During the summer, places generally open from 11am–4pm at weekends and have shorter hours midweek. They usually charge $5 entry, often refunded with any wine purchase.

Bike hire To rent a bike for a spin round the vineyards try Christina Estate (28 Puruatanga Rd ☎ 06 306 8920; $25/day), the Martinborough Wine Centre ($40/day), or March Hare (at the i-SITE ☎ 027 515 3780, Ⓦ march -hare.co.nz; $40/day).

ACCOMMODATION

Rooms are hard to find during festivals and on summer weekends: weeknights are often a happier hunting ground.

Martinborough Hotel Memorial Square ☎ 06 306 9350, ⓦ martinboroughhotel.co.nz. The attractively restored *grande dame* of Martinborough offers rooms upstairs in the old building with French doors opening onto a veranda, and more contemporary rooms set around the garden; all are serviced, well tended and spacious. There's also a good restaurant and a bar that's popular with vineyard owners, farmers and visitors alike. __$200__

Martinborough Top 10 Holiday Park 10 Dublin St West ☎ 06 306 8946, ⓦ martinboroughholidaypark .com. Impeccably maintained campsite a 10min walk from the centre, with free unlimited wi-fi, pétanque, bike hire, tent sites separate from van hook-ups, and cosy cabins. The

owner knows everything that's happening in town Camping __$42__, cabins __$80__, motel units __$129__

The Old Manse 19 Grey St ☎ 06 306 8599, ⓦ oldmanse .co.nz. Boutique B&B with five en-suite rooms in a wonderful old villa amid the vines on the edge of town Double __$180__, suite (with clawfoot bath) __$225__

★ **Straw House** 22–24 Cambridge Rd ☎ 06 306 8577, ⓦ thestrawhouse.co.nz. Choose from the cosy studio or fabulous self-contained two-bedroom house, both built of straw bales, stylishly decorated and very comfortable. Breakfast goodies are generously provided and there's a small reduction for second and subsequent nights. Studio __$150__, house __$270__

EATING AND DRINKING

Lunch at a winery restaurant or a platter among the vines is an essential part of the Martinborough experience, though the town also caters to discerning diners with several restaurants charging moderate to high prices, in return for high-quality dishes.

Café Medici 9 Kitchener St ☎ 06 306 9965. Busy breakfast and lunch café efficiently serving the likes of salami olive and anchovy *pizzette* ($16.50) or dinner mains of whole roast chicken with goat's cheese ($49.50) for two to share. There's often jazz on a Friday night. Daily 8.30am–4.30pm, plus Thurs–Sat 6.30pm–late in summer.

★ **Circus Cinema Restaurant and Bar** 34 Jellicoe St ☎ 06 306 9442, ⓦ circus.net.nz. Wonderful coffee in the atmospheric bar, plus an unpretentious restaurant serving meze platters, movie-themed pizza – a Dr Evil is chorizo, bacon, black olive and chilli – and delicious desserts (under $34). The place also happens to be a bijou HD cinema with two screens and a penchant for showing art-house classics. Sit watching the film, sipping your wine, and a tap on the shoulder announces your dessert. Wed–Mon 4pm–late.

Ingredient 8 Kitchener St ⓦ ingredient.co.nz. One of the best places to stock up on gourmet local produce such as olives, cheese and charcuterie. Or sit down and enjoy a glass of wine and a ploughman's platter ($40). Mon–Fri 8am–4pm, Sat & Sun 8am–4.30pm.

Micro 14c Ohio St ☎ 06 306 9716. Unsurprisingly tiny wine bar with equally wee courtyard out the back that only serves small plates (obviously) but somehow manages to squeeze in a couple of dozen craft beers as well as fine local wines. If they're not too busy, you can get a flight of wines to taste (Pinot Noir $22). Mon, Thurs & Fri 4pm–late, Sat & Sun 3–9pm.

★ **Pinocchio** 3 Kitchener St ☎ 06 306 6094. Wonderful, unassuming restaurant that produces classy evening meals (try confit duck leg on *kumara* gratin for $30), as well as tempting brunch in the courtyard out front (informed by seasonal Kiwi produce; $16–21). Worth booking. Wed &

Thurs 11am–late, Fri & Sat 8.30am–late, Sun 8.30am–7.30pm.

The Village Café 6 Kitchener St ☎ 06 306 8814. Daytime café with seating in the rustic-chic barn-like interior and the pergola-covered courtyard. Menu items (all under $25) include tasty brunches, pizzas and salads, and good espresso. Try the prawn *laksa* ($15.50). Free wi-fi. Daily 8am–4pm, Sun also 6–9pm.

WINERIES & BREWERY

Ata Rangi Puruatanga Rd ☎ 06 306 9570, ⓦ atarangi .co.nz. One of New Zealand's finest Pinot Noir producers also does the excellent Célèbre Merlot/Syrah blend and a couple of lovely steely Chardonnays. A great place to start. Service charge for tastings $5 (not refunded). Mon–Fri 1–3pm, Sat & Sun noon–4pm.

Margrain Vineyard Cnr Huangarua and Ponatahi rds ☎ 06 306 9292, ⓦ margrainvineyard.co.nz. Good-quality wine from the relaxed cellar door plus the great little *Old Winery Café* (generally open for lunch Fri–Sun, also summer Wed & Thurs lunch) overlooking the vines with well-priced dishes (nothing over $20). The most entertaining tasting notes you will ever read. Tastings $5. Labour Day weekend–Easter Fri–Sun 11am–5pm; Jan 1–Feb 6 daily 11am–5pm; Easter–Labour Day weekend Sat 11am–5pm, Sun 11am–4pm.

Martinborough Brewery 8 Ohio St ☎ 06 306 6249, ⓦ martinboroughbeer.com. New boutique brewery and tasting room. Try their Black Nectar, an oyster stout which, like traditional beers, makes the most of the local water. Thurs–Sat 11am–7pm, Sun & Mon 11am–4pm.

Palliser Kitchener St ☎ 06 306 9019, ⓦ palliser.co.nz. Pioneering Martinborough winery which limits its impact n the environment while producing premium wines and unning cooking classes. $5 information charge with astings. Daily 10.30am–4pm.

Schubert 57 Cambridge Rd (entrance on Huaranga Rd) ☎06 306 8505, ⓦschubert.co.nz. Kai and Marion researched worldwide before settling here to grow their beloved Pinot Noir. Small, enthusiastic team. $5 service

charge. Daily 11am–3pm.
Vynfields 22 Omarere Rd ☎06 306 9901, ⓦvynfields .com. Choose from open lawns, shady bowers or the elegant villa interior to sample flights of five wines (quarter glasses $15; half glasses $20) accompanied by antipasto platters ($32) and terrines ($18) to share. Tastings free. Wed–Mon 11am–4pm.

6

Cape Palliser

Cosmopolitan Martinborough stands in dramatic contrast to the stark, often windswept coast around **Cape Palliser**, 60km south. The southernmost point on the North Island, the cape was named in honour of James Cook's mentor, Rear Admiral Sir Hugh Palliser. Apart from a few gentle walks and the opportunity to observe **fur seals** at close quarters, there's not a lot to do out here but clear your head, as swimming is unsafe and the weather changeable.

Lake Ferry

From Martinborough, a sealed road leads 35km south to **Lake Ferry**, a tiny, comatose surfcasting settlement on the sandy shores of Lake Onoke. There's little to do here but kick back and recharge your batteries, either by staying the night or stopping off for some food and drink at the *Lake Ferry Hotel* (see below).

Putangirua Pinnacles

13km south of Lake Ferry

The Cape Palliser road then twists through the coastal hills until it meets the sea near the **Putangirua Pinnacles**, dozens of grey soft-rock spires and fluted cliffs up to 50m high, formed by wind and rain selectively eroding the surrounding silt and gravel. From the parking area, where there are BBQ areas and a DOC campsite (see below), allow a couple of hours to wander up the easy streambed to the base of the pinnacles, up to a viewpoint and then back along a pretty, ridge-top bush track.

Ngawi

Beyond the pinnacles, the sealed road hugs the rugged, exposed coastline for 15km to **Ngawi**, a small fishing village where all manner of colourful **bulldozers** grind out their last days, hauling sometimes massive fishing boats up the steep gravel beach. It is five rough kilometres on to the cape proper, where a resurgent **fur seal colony**, right beside the road, is overlooked by the century-old Cape Palliser **lighthouse**, standing on a knoll 60m above the sea at the top of a long flight of some 250 steps. It's easy enough to get within 15m of the seals, but they can become aggressive if they feel threatened, and move surprisingly quickly, given their bulk – keep your distance from pups or their parents will bite you, and don't get between any seal and the sea.

ACCOMMODATION AND EATING   CAPE PALLISER

Lake Ferry Hotel 2 Lake Ferry Rd, Lake Ferry ☎06 307 7831, ⓦlakeferryhotel.co.nz. The southernmost motel on the North Island is a great spot for fish and chips on a sunny afternoon on your way back to Martinborough. There's a traditional Kiwi public bar and garden, overlooking the water, and a slightly more formal restaurant; arrive early to grab a table on fine weekends. Dorms $30, rooms $75

Lake Ferry Holiday Park Lake Ferry ☎06 307 7873, ⓦlakeferryholidaypark.co.nz. Dirt-cheap and a little

more cramped than the *Lake Ferry Hotel*, but still handy for the latter's pub. Accommodation options here include camping, cabins and one self-contained unit ($85), and there are kitchen facilities, showers, TV and laundry. Camping $15, cabins $60

Putangirua Pinnacles campsite Halfway between Lake Ferry and Cape Palliser. A view of the Cook Strait and a pebbly beach across the road are all you get at this DOC site that's within walking distance of the Pinnacles. It can get windy. There's tap water and toilets. Camping $6

Wellington
and around

HILLSIDE HOMES IN WELLINGTON

Wellington and around

Understandably, many people visiting New Zealand often reject its cities in favour of scenic splendour – with the exception of Wellington. The urban jewel in the country's otherwise bucolic crown, Wellington is by far New Zealand's most engaging and attractive metropolis, a buzzing, cosmopolitan capital worthy of any visitor's attention. With a population of around 190,000 (450,000 in the wider region), Wellington is New Zealand's third most populous centre, but while Auckland grows more commercially important (and self-important in the eyes of its residents), Wellington reaches for higher ground as the nation's cultural capital: as the country's only city with a beating heart, it warrants a stay of at least a couple of days – more if you can manage it. Wellingtonians have cultivated the country's most sophisticated café society, nightlife and arts scene, especially in late summer when the city hosts a series of arts and fringe festivals (see box, p.441). More prosaically, the city is also the principal departure point for the South Island.

7

Wedged between glistening Wellington Harbour (technically Port Nicholson) and the turbulent Cook Strait, tight surrounding hills restrict Wellington to a compact core, mostly built on reclaimed land. Distinctive historical and modern architecture spills down to the bustling waterfront with its beaches, marinas and restored warehouses, overlooked by Victorian and Edwardian weatherboard villas and bungalows that climb the steep slopes to an encircling belt of parks and woodland, a natural barrier to development. Many homes are accessed by narrow winding roads or precipitous stairways flanked by a small funicular railway to haul groceries and just about anything else up to the house. What's more, "Welly", as it's locally known, is New Zealand's **windy city**, buffeted by chilled air funnelled through Cook Strait, its force amplified by the wind-tunnelling effect of the city's high-rise buildings.

Central Wellington is easily walkable; the heart of the **city centre** stretches south from the train station to Courtenay Place along the backbone of the central business and shopping district, **Lambton Quay**. The main areas for eating, drinking and entertainment are further south around Willis Street, Courtenay Place, arty Cuba Street, and down to the waterfront at Queens Wharf. From the central **Civic Square**, points of interest run both ways along the waterfront, including the city's star attraction, **Te Papa**, the ground-breaking national museum. Also worth a look is the revamped **Museum of Wellington City and Sea**, which recounts the city's development, Maori history and seafaring traditions. Politicians and civil servants populate the streets of the **Parliamentary District**. Nearby, you can visit **Katherine Mansfield's Birthplace**, the period-furnished childhood home of New Zealand's most famous short-story writer.

WELLINGTON CABLE CAR

Highlights

❶ Te Papa The striking and inventive national museum showcases New Zealand's natural and bicultural history through intriguing exhibits, interactive technology and the nation's premier art collection. **See p.418**

❷ Cuba Street People-watching, café-hopping and window-shopping along the city's hip "alternative" strip give a taste of its divergent lifestyles. **See p.421**

❸ Parliamentary District Visit the country's seat of power and associated national institutions, and view documents highlighting milestones on the country's road to nationhood – including the original Treaty of Waitangi. **See p.423**

❹ Zealandia: the Karori Sanctuary Experience Native birds once again flock around Wellington, thanks to the predator-free environment and regenerating native bush at this unique wildlife sanctuary. **See p.425**

❺ Weta Workshop A genuine behind-the-scenes tour with one of the model or prop makers working for this global special-effects company. **See p.430**

❻ Nightlife Wellington's nightlife surpasses that of anywhere else in New Zealand – from atmospheric theatres and stylish cinemas to cool cocktail bars, bouncy pubs and edgy clubs, alternatives abound. **See p.439**

HIGHLIGHTS ARE MARKED ON THE MAP ON P.414

The city centre is also the jumping-off point for ambling or cycling along **Oriental Parade** and up to one of the hilltop viewpoints, such as **Mount Victoria**, or catching the stately **Cable Car** to Kelburn. From Kelburn, you can either wander down through the formal **Botanic Gardens** or continue further out to see the ambitious and important conservation work at **Zealandia: the Karori Sanctuary Experience**, and **Otari-Wilton's Bush**, the only public botanic garden in the country dedicated solely to native plants. Zealandia and Otari-Wilton's Bush form part of the **Town Belt**, a band of greenery across the hills that encircles the city centre containing several good walks and many of the city's best lookout points. To the east of the city are the quiet suburbs and beaches of the **Miramar Peninsula**, now best known as the home of "Wellywood", the heart of the city's film industry; you can't miss it, thanks to the new Hollywood-style Wellington sign, with the letters symbolically blown along by the wind.

Superb **hiking** opportunities include the seal colony at Red Rocks, or the city's many trails, notably the **Southern Walkway**. And at some point during your stay in this harbour city, you really should get out on the water to the serene wildlife sanctuary of **Matiu/Somes Island**.

Wellington also makes a good base to explore **Kapiti Island** (p.256) and the **Wairarapa** wine district; see box, p.406 and the box opposite for wine tours from Wellington.

Brief history

Maori oral histories tell of the demigod **Maui**, who fished up the North Island, with Wellington Harbour being the mouth of the fish; and of the first Polynesian navigator, **Kupe**, discovering Wellington Harbour in 925 AD and naming the harbour's islands Matiu (Somes Island) and Makaro (Ward Island) after his daughters (see box, p.431). Several *iwi* settled around the harbour, including the Ngati Tara people, who enjoyed the rich fishing areas and the protection the bay offered.

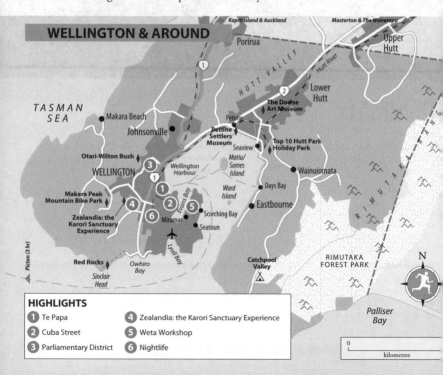

WELLINGTON & AROUND

HIGHLIGHTS

1 Te Papa
2 Cuba Street
3 Parliamentary District
4 Zealandia: the Karori Sanctuary Experience
5 Weta Workshop
6 Nightlife

CITY TOURS

An ever-increasing number of clued-up local outfits offer entertaining and informative tours of the city; the best are listed below.

Flat Earth ⊤ 0800 775 805, ⓦ flatearth.co.nz. Upmarket outfit which takes very good care of you on its range of tours (from $175), including Wellington city highlights, nature and eco tours, and several specialist film tours.

Movie Tours ⊤ 027 419 3077, ⓦ adventuresafari.co.nz. Dedicated movie-theme tour options such as the half-day Wellington Movie Tour, including Weta ($70).

Tranzit Tours ⊤ 06 370 6600, ⓦ tranzittours.co.nz. Popular day-tours of the Wairarapa (p.401), including a Martinborough Wine Tour ($197).

Wellington Rover ⊤ 0800 426 211, ⓦ wellingtonrover.co.nz. Half-day minibus tours ($95, twice daily) of the city's sights which includes a ride on the Cable Car, the seals and windfarm, or LOTR locations (and to Weta). There's also a full-day LOTR tour ($190) that includes a themed lunch and more locations in the Hutt Valley.

Zest Food Tours ⊤ 04 801 9198, ⓦ zestfoodtours.co.nz. Gourmet tours (Mon–Sat; from $169) taking in coffee roasteries, chocolate producers, cheese and honey tastings and more.

Both Abel Tasman (in 1642) and Captain Cook (in 1773) were prevented from ntering Wellington Harbour by fierce winds and, apart from a few sealers and whalers, wasn't until 1840 that the first wave of **European settlers** arrived. They carved out a iche on a large tract of harbourside land, purchased by the New Zealand Company, vho set up their initial beachhead, named Britannia, on the northeastern beaches at etone. Shortly afterwards, the Hutt River flooded, forcing the settlers to move around ne harbour to a more sheltered site known as Lambton Harbour (where the central city as grown up) and the relatively level land at Thorndon, at that time just north of the noreline. They renamed the settlement after the Iron Duke and began **land eclamations** into the harbour, a process that continued for more than a hundred years.

In 1865, the growing city succeeded Auckland as the **capital** of New Zealand, and by ne turn of the twentieth century the original shoreline of Lambton Harbour had been eplaced by wharves and harbourside businesses, which formed the hub of the city's oastal trade; Wellington has prospered ever since.

Civic Square and around

popular venue for outdoor events, **Civic Square** was extensively revamped in the early 990s by New Zealand's most influential and versatile modern architect, **Ian Athfield**, vho juxtaposed old and new, regular and irregular forms and incorporated artwork. he open space is full of interesting sculptures, including Neil Dawson's *Ferns* – metal ronds linked into a ball that appears to float above the square.

Central Library

5 Victoria St • Mon–Fri 9.30am–8.30pm, Sat 9.30am–5pm, Sun 1–4pm

he most arresting building on Civic Square is Athfield's magnificent 1991 **Central ibrary**, a spacious high-tech statement in steel, stone, glass and timber with its inner vorkings – air ducts, water pipes – exposed. Athfield also created the supporting steel ikau palms, which ring the building and provide a link to the rest of Civic Square by ontinuing out beyond the building.

City Gallery Wellington

01 Wakefield St • Daily 10am–5pm • Donation • ⊤ 04 801 3021, ⓦ citygallery.org.nz

he impressive 1939 Art Deco **City Gallery Wellington** hosts touring shows of national

Matiu/Somes Island ▲

CENTRAL WELLINGTON

Town Belt

■ ACCOMMODATION

Apollo Lodge Motel &	9
Majoribanks Apartments	14
Austinvilla B&B	8
Base Wellington	15
Booklovers B&B	10
Cambridge Hotel	12
CQ Hotels	13
Gourmet Stay	11
Halswell Lodge	1
Hotel Waterloo	5
Museum Hotel	3
Nomads Capital	6
Ohtel	4
Trinity Hotel	2
Waterfront Motorhome Park	7
YHA Wellington City	

● RESTAURANTS

Floriditas	12
Logan-Brown	17
MariLuca	1
Masala	11
Matterhorn	8
Oriental Kingdom	9
Ortega	16
Sweet Mother's Kitchen	14
Wellington Trawling	
Sea Market	20

● CAFÉS / DELIS

Aro Coffee	18
Beach Babylon	7
Ekim	23
Fidel's	22
Hangar	6
L'affare	25
Lamason	4
Midnight Espresso	15
Mojo	2
Moore Wilson's	24
Nikau Gallery Café	3
Olive	13
Plum	10
Poneke	5
Prefab	21
Trisha's Pies	19

● CLUBS AND LIVE MUSIC VENUES

Bodega	7
Boogie Wonderland	12
San Francisco Bathhouse	15
Valhalla	17

● PUBS AND BARS

Alice	16
The Backbencher	5
Crumpet	3
Fork and Brewer	2
Foxglove	8
Goldings Free Dive	18
Hawthorne Lounge	20
Hopgarden	11
The Library	4
Little Beer Quarter	9
The Malthouse	6
Matterhorn	13
Motel	10
Rogue & Vagabond	14
S&M	19
Southern Cross	

7

N

Katherine Mansfield Birthplace (100m), Interislander Ferry Terminal (700m) & Otari-Wilton Bush (6km)

Westpac Stadium

Container & Cruise Terminal

WATERLOO QUAY

THORNDON QUAY

DIXON ST

HOBSON STREET

MULGRAVE ST

PIPITEA ST

MURPHY ST

MOLESWORTH STREET

HAWKESTONE STREET

AITKEN ST

KATE SHEPPARD RD

PARK ST

GRANT ROAD

GEORGE

HARRIET ST

HILL STREET

BOWEN ST

THE TERRACE

WELLINGTON MOTORWAY

THORNDON

Thorndon Pool

Old St Paul's Cathedral

Archives New Zealand

National Library

St Paul's Cathedral

Parliamentary Library

Parliament House

The Beehive

Old Government Buildings

Lambton Interchange

THORNDON QUAY

BUNNY ST

STOUT ST

WHITMORE ST

FEATHERSTON STREET

KINGSTON ST

GREY ST

LAMBTON QUAY

Long Distance Buses

Train & Bus Station

Bluebridge Ferry Terminal

Queens Wharf

Fergi's Kayaks

Wildwinds Windsurfing

Dominion Post Ferry Terminal

Museum of

Cable Car Lower Terminal

Saddon Memorial

Bolton Street Memorial Park

BOLTON STREET

AURORA TERRACE

CLIFTON TERRACE

EVERTON

WESLEY ROAD

GLENMORE STREET

CLERMONT STREET

Begonia House

Lady Norwood Rose Garden

Botanic Gardens

Carter Observatory

Cable Car Museum

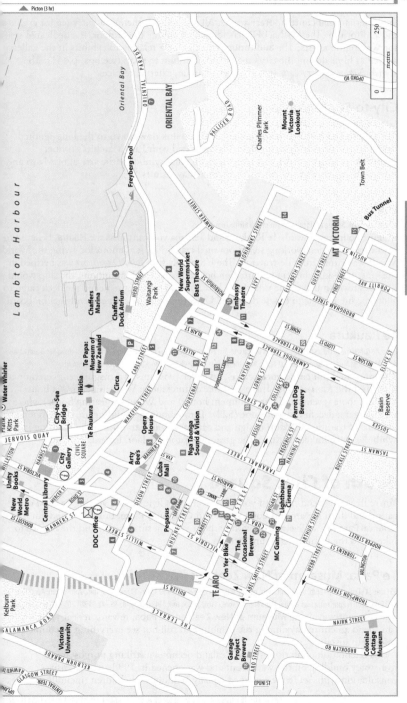

Picton (3 hr)

Oriental Bay

ORIENTAL BAY

Charles Plimmer Park

Mount Victoria Lookout

Town Belt

Lambton Harbour

MT VICTORIA

Bus Tunnel

Basin Reserve

Water Whirler

Frank Kitts Park

City-to-Sea Bridge

City Gallery

CIVIC SQUARE

Te Papa: Museum of New Zealand

Hikitia

Te Raukura

Circa

Chaffers Marina

Chaffers Dock Atrium

Waitangi Park

New World Supermarket

Bats Theatre

Embassy Theatre

Opera House

Arty Bee's

Cuba Mall

Nga Taonga Sound & Vision

Pegasus

On Yer Bike

The Occasional Brewer

MC Gaming

Lighthouse Cinema

Parrot Dog Brewery

Garage Project Brewery

Colonial Cottage Museum

Victoria University

Kelburn Park

New World Metro

Unity Books

Central Library

DOC Office

Freyberg Pool

TE ARO

7

0   250
metres

and international contemporary works. All are free, but there's an entry fee for events at the auditorium. The Michael Hirscheld Gallery, on the upper floor, is a dedicated space for Wellington artists. The **auditorium** screens works relating to exhibits in the gallery, as well as films during the city's many specialist film festivals (see box, p.441). The stylish *Nikau Gallery Café* (p.437) opens onto an external terrace.

City-to-Sea Bridge

Just east of Civic Square, across Jervois Quay

The **City-to-Sea Bridge** is intentionally broad to link downtown to the long-ignored waterfront as seamlessly as possible. It's decorated with Para Matchitt's timber sculptures of birds, whales and celestial motifs that symbolize the arrival of Maori and European settlers and, by extension, present-day visitors.

Hikitia

Southeast of Civic Square along the waterfront • Ⓦ hikitia.com

Making your way towards Te Raukura and Te Papa you can't miss the **Hikitia**, believed to be the world's oldest working steam-powered crane ship. It's famous for saving the World War II waterfront from destruction. The US supply ship *John Davenport* was berthed in the inner harbour when a fire started on board. Loaded with munitions, the ship would have destroyed much of the waterfront had *Hikitia*'s crew not removed the deck cargo to allow the fire brigade to dowse the blaze. Unfortunately you can't currently get on board.

Te Raukura

Opposite the *Hikitia* in Odlins Square, between the City-to-Sea Bridge and Te Papa • Oct–April Mon–Fri 7.30am–dusk, Sat & Sun 8am–dusk; May–Sept Mon–Fri 8am–dusk, Sat & Sun 9am–dusk • Free • ☎ 0508 386 2846, Ⓦ wharewakaooponeke.co.nz

This purpose-built conference centre and gallery contains two magnificent ceremonial *waka* and the *Karaka Café*. There are three distinct areas: Wharewaka (*waka* house), Whare Tapere (events and entertainment house) and Wharekai (eating house) where you can get a decent *hangi* for one ($22). Throughout the building are contemporary versions of traditional Maori design and carvings, which transform the building into a symbolic *waka* linked to Kupe, the great navigator of Maori legend.

South of Civic Square

You're likely to spend much of your time south of Civic Square visiting **Te Papa** or eating and drinking around **Cuba Street** and **Courtenay Place**, but don't miss out on **Oriental Parade** – a lovely stroll with harbour views, a small beach and the chance to hike up to the summit of **Mount Victoria**.

Te Papa: Museum of New Zealand

55 Cable St • Daily 10am–6pm, until 9pm Thurs; guided tours daily: Nov–March 10.15am, 11am, noon, 1pm, 2pm & 3pm; April–Oct 10.15am, noon & 2pm; extra tour at 7pm Thurs both seasons • Free; guided tour $14; audioguide $5 • ☎ 04 381 7000, Ⓦ tepapa.govt.nz

The constantly evolving **Museum of New Zealand, Te Papa**, rewards repeat visits – you can spend an entire day among the exhibits and still not see everything. A couple of **cafés** help sustain visitors.

This celebration of all things New Zealand occupies a striking purpose-built five-storey building on the waterfront and was opened in 1998 after extensive consultation with *iwi* (tribes). Aimed equally at adults and children (including

hands-on kids' activities in dedicated "discovery" spaces), it combines state-of-the-art technology and dynamic exhibits.

Well worth $3 is the *Te Papa Explorer* guide, outlining routes such as "Te Papa Highlights" or "Kids' Highlights". Alternatively, book one of the amazing **guided tours**

Level 2

The hub of Te Papa is **Level 2**, with its interactive display on earthquakes and volcanoes where you can experience a realistic quake inside a shaking house, see displays on the fault line that runs right through Wellington, watch Mount Ruapehu erupt on screen and hear the Maori explanation of the causes of such activity. You can also find out more about New Zealand's ecosystems, and see the colossal squid. Level 2 provides access to the outdoor **Bush City**, a synthesis of New Zealand environments complete with native plants, caves and swingbridge.

Level 4

The main collection continues on **Level 4**, home to the excellent, main Maori section including a thought-provoking display on the Treaty of Waitangi, dominated by a giant glass image of this significant document. There's also an **active marae** with a symbolic modern meetinghouse quite unlike the classic examples found around the country, protected by a sacred boulder of *pounamu* (greenstone); check behind the cupboard doors at the back for some imagery that shows both a sense of humour and the incredible significance of the place. Temporary exhibitions include displays by different *iwi* showcasing that particular *iwi*'s art and culture.

Adjacent to the *marae*, look out for displays on New Zealand's people, land, history, trade and cultures including Michel Tuffery's bullock made from corned beef cans, and Brian O'Connor's paua-shell surfboard.

Level 5

Level 5 is the home of New Zealand's **national art collection**, a changing display of works on paper, oils and sculpture representing luminaries of the New Zealand art world past and present; Colin McCahon, Rita Angus, Ralph Hotere, Don Binney, Michael Smither and Shane Cotton are just a few names to watch for.

Oriental Parade

Immediately east of Te Papa, **Waitangi Park** is named after a long culverted stream that has been restored to its natural course, creating a small urban wetland. At the end of Herd Street, the **Chaffers Dock** development incorporates cafés and an atrium where Wellington's Sunday-morning farmers' market (see p.436) sets up. The park marks the start of **Oriental Parade**, Wellington's most elegant section of waterfront. Skirting **Oriental Bay**, this Norfolk-pine-lined road curls past some of the city's priciest real estate and even flanks a **beach** installed here in 2003 with sand brought across Cook Strait from near Takaka. Apart from the Freyberg pool (see p.441) and a few restaurants, there are no attractions as such, but you can extend a stroll into a full afternoon by continuing to Charles Plimmer Park and joining the Southern Walkway (see box, p.428) to the summit of **Mount Victoria**.

Mount Victoria

At 196m, **Mount Victoria Lookout** is one of the best of Wellington's viewpoints, offering sweeping views of the city, waterfront, docks and beyond to the Hutt Valley, all particularly dramatic around dusk. If you don't fancy the steep but rewarding walk, you can also reach the summit on the #20 bus (Mon–Fri only) or by car following Hawker Street, off Majoribanks Street, then taking Palliser Road, which twists uphill to the lookout.

FOODIE WELLINGTON

The founders of the well-established restaurant and café scene are now so established that they're taking on new challenges, and a new breed of coffee makers has emerged who are less concerned with espresso techniques than the beans and flavours. Brewing institutions such as Macs aren't just being challenged by craft beer behemoths like Tuatara and Emersons, but quirky newcomers (check ⓦcraftbeercapital.com for the latest listings) including *The Garage Project* and *Fork and Brewer* (p.437) who have the flexibility to keep creating new batches. Food trucks are springing up (like *Ekim*, p.436), while the Eva St enclave is home to *Fix & Fogg*, whose small-batch peanut butter is fought over, and the *Wellington Chocolate Factory*, who are building links with individual cocoa estates (taste their untempered hot chocolate to discover flavours as complex as fine wine). If sampling artisan produce whets your appetite, try making it yourself. For tours, see box, p.415.

COURSES

L'affare 27 College St ☎04 385 9748, ⓦlaffare .co.nz. A two-hour class ($140) to improve your technique making espresso-based drinks at home. The cost includes a copy of *How to Make Really Good Coffee.*
Flight School ☎04 212 4547, ⓦflightcoffee.co.nz. Half-day courses, teaching you how to brew coffee in three different ways ($60), or how to enhance your drinking experience by exploring taste and aroma ($80).
Mojo Shed 13, 37 Customhouse Quay ☎04 385 3001, ⓦmojocoffee.co.nz. A three-hour one-to-one ($175) where you'll learn what's needed for that

perfect flat white. You can then move on to latte art ($175/2hr). They also run NZ's only City and Guilds barista course ($595/3 days).
The Occasional Brewer 211 Victoria St ☎04 384 8268, ⓦtheoccasionalbrewer.co.nz. Only really worth it if you know you'll be round Wellington for a month – plus drinking time. Make 40 litres of your own craft beer ($149 plus $55–$100 for the bottles) in an evening, leave it fermenting under the brewers' watchful eyes for a couple of weeks, then come back for bottling. It'll need another couple of weeks to settle.

FOOD

Wellington Chocolate Factory 3 Eva St ☎04 385 7555. Irresistible small-batch bars and hot chocolate. Check in advance for a tour. Mon–Sat 10am–6pm, Sun 11am–4pm.

Fix & Fogg 5 Eva St ⓦfixandfogg.co.nz. Tap on the window to sample their wares, or nip over the lane to buy from the *Chocolate Factory*.

CRAFT BEER

Garage Project 68 Aro St ☎04 384 3076, ⓦgarageproject.co.nz. Queues now form at this old, barely modernized, petrol station to fill up bottles with delightful Venusian pale ale, or taste the chilli kick of Day of the Dead lager. Sun & Mon noon–6pm, Tues–Thurs noon–8pm, Fri & Sat noon–9pm.

Parrot Dog 29 Vivian St ☎04 384 3076, ⓦparrotdog.co.nz. Small central brewery where you can sample (free) their latest brews, buy take-out flagons and peep at the process. Their classic is the refreshing Bitter Bitch, a 5.8% IPA. Mon–Thurs 10am–6pm, Fri 10am–8pm, Sat noon–6pm.

Nga Taonga Sound and Vision

84 Taranaki St, at Ghuznee St · Mon & Tues 9.30am–5pm, Wed–Fri 9.30am–7pm, Sat 4.30–7pm; evening screenings Wed–Sat 7pm · Free; evening screenings $8–10 · ☎04 384 7647, ⓦngataonga.org.nz

The excellent **New Zealand Film Archive** has small film-themed exhibits though the main attraction is the ability to watch just about any New Zealand movie ever made, plus TV programmes, old commercials and assorted home movies on monitors in the media library or in the small viewing room (all free). There are also evening screenings in the cinema. They sell the cheapest good coffee in town, and if you rustle up a group of around ten, you can book the viewing room for free – the perfect spot for a *LOTR* marathon.

Courtenay Place and Cuba Street

Wellington's entertainment heartland is centred on **Courtenay Place** and adjacent **Cuba Street**. Named after an emigrant ship (not the island after which the ship was christened, despite the Cuban-themed establishments in this part of town), Cuba Street and its offshoots comprise Wellington's "alternative" district, with secondhand bookshops, vintage record stores, retro and emerging-designer fashion outlets, quirky cafés, and hip bars and restaurants. Between Dixon and Ghuznee streets, Cuba Street's colourful and iconic **Bucket Fountain** was installed in 1969 and still splashes unsuspecting passers-by.

Colonial Cottage Museum

68 Nairn St • Christmas to mid-Feb daily noon–4pm; mid-Feb to Christmas Sat & Sun noon–4pm; guided tours hourly noon–3pm • $8 • Ⓦ colonialcottagemuseum.co.nz

Heritage fans may be keen to see the twee **Colonial Cottage Museum**, central Wellington's oldest building. Though dating from 1858 (two decades into Queen Victoria's reign), it's built in late Georgian style, and its decor gives the impression the family has just left for church and will be back for Sunday lunch.

7

North of Civic Square

As the city nears the harbour, there's plenty of action around **Queens Wharf**, home to expensive harbour-view apartments, the Museum of Wellington City and Sea and a variety of bars and restaurants, as well as the *Mojo* coffee roastery (see p.437).

The business heart of Wellington beats along Lambton Quay, which runs north to the **Parliamentary District**, the city's administrative and ecclesiastical hub. Parliament marks the southern edge of **Thorndon**, Wellington's oldest suburb and home of the **Katherine Mansfield Birthplace**.

Frank Kitts Park and around

Water Whirler hourly 10am–3pm and 6–10pm but not 2pm; 5–10min • Plimmer's Ark Mon–Fri 9am–6pm, Sat & Sun 11am–3pm; free

Just north of the Civic Square lies **Frank Kitts Park**, where the mast of the *Wahine* (see below) stands poignant sentinel on the waterfront. A few metres further along is the *Water Whirler*, a kinetic sculpture designed by Len Lye (see box, p.226) and opened in 2006, a quarter of a century after the artist's death. Roughly every hour, it erupts into a sequence of complex and increasingly energetic gyrations with jets spewing water. Between the sculpture and the Museum of Wellington (see below), in the Old Bank Arcade, is **Plimmer's Ark**, the resting place of what's left of the *Inconstant*, a wooden sailing ship that was beached and converted to a trading wharf in 1850 by John Plimmer, the father of commercial activity in the burgeoning city.

Museum of Wellington City and Sea

3 Jervois Quay • Daily 10am–5pm; free 30min tours Sun 2pm • Free; Ship 'n Chip tour (5hr) $39 • ☏ 04 472 8904, Ⓦ museumswellington .org.nz

Near lively **Queens Wharf**, a Victorian former bond store houses the absorbing **Museum of Wellington City and Sea**. The city's social and maritime history unfolds through well-executed displays on early Maori and European settlement and the city's seafaring heritage. The ground floor offers a straightforward chronicle of key events, while the main focus of the first floor is the **Wahine disaster**, the inter-island ferry that sank with the loss of 52 lives on April 10, 1968. When the new attic floor opens, virtually all of the museum's exhibits will be on display, telling many more stories. There are also museum tours, including the popular **Ship 'n Chip tour** which involves a ferry trip to Matiu/Somes Island (see box, p.431) and fish and chips for lunch.

Lambton Quay

Now Wellington's main commercial street, **Lambton Quay** formed the original waterfront but was cut off by the docks formed by reclamation. Head straight along Lambton Quay to the Parliamentary District, or detour up the **Cable Car** (see box below) and back down through the Botanic Gardens.

The Botanic Gardens

Entrances on Glenmore St, Salamanca Rd, Upland Rd and on the Cable Car • Daily dawn–dusk • Free

A lookout at the top of the Cable Car provides spectacular views over the city. Here, you're also at the highest point of Wellington's **Botanic Gardens**, a huge swathe of green with numerous paths that wind down towards the city. Pick up the free map from the Cable Car Museum.

Lady Norwood Rose Garden and Begonia House

Begonia House daily Oct–April 9am–5pm; May–Sept 10am–3pm, closed Tues • Free

The star in the Botanic Garden's firmament is the fragrant **Lady Norwood Rose Garden**, where a colonnade of climbing roses frames beds of over three hundred varieties set out in a formal wheel shape. The adjacent **Begonia House** is divided into two areas: the tropical, with an attractive lily pond, and the temperate, which has seasonal displays of begonias and gloxinias in summer, changing to cyclamen, orchids and impatiens in winter.

7

Carter Observatory

Mon, Wed, Thurs & Fri 10am–5pm, Tues & Sat 10am–11pm, Sun 10am–5.30pm • Planetarium shows: Mon–Fri 11am, 12.30pm, 3pm, Sat & Sun 10.15am and then on the hour; night shows Tues & Sat 6pm, 7pm & 8pm (book ahead) • Exhibition $10; 45min planetarium shows (incl. exhibition) $18.50 • ☎ 04 910 3140, ⓦ carterobservatory.org

Two minutes' walk from the upper Cable Car terminus is the fabulous 1941 **Carter Observatory**, which has illuminating displays on the New Zealand angle on the exploration of the southern skies, from Maori and Pacific Island astronomy and astronavigation through to recent planet searches. Of particular note are a telescope from Captain Cook's era, a piece of moon rock you can touch and a rocket-launching simulator. Make time to catch one of the jaw-dropping planetarium shows that include a tour of that night's sky. Telescope viewings on late nights, weather permitting.

Parliamentary District

The northern end of Lambton Quay marks the start of the **Parliamentary District** – keep an eye out for the Kate Sheppard-themed pedestrian crossings. The district is dominated by the grandiose **Old Government Buildings**, which at first glance appear to be constructed from cream stone, but are really wooden. Designed by colonial architect

---

RIDING THE CABLE CAR

Even if you never use the rest of Wellington's public transport system, don't miss the short scenic ride up to the leafy suburb of Kelburn and the upper section of the Botanic Gardens on the **Cable Car** (Mon–Fri 7am–10pm, Sat 8.30am–10pm, Sun 9am–9pm; $4 one way, $7.50 return), installed in 1902. Its shiny red railcars depart every ten minutes from the lower terminus on Cable Car Lane, just off Lambton Quay, and climb a steep, one-in-five incline, making three stops along the way and giving great views over the city and harbour. At the upper terminus on Upland Road, the **Cable Car Museum** (daily: 9.30am–5pm; free) contains the historic winding room with the electric drive motor and a cat's cradle of cables. Two century-old cars are on display along with plenty of background on cable cars around the world. Take time to catch the short movies, particularly the one about the 400-plus mini cable cars people still use to access their properties locally.

William Clayton (1823–77) to mark the country's transition from provincial to centralized government, the intention was to use stone but cost-cutting forced a rethink. When completed in 1876, it was the largest building in New Zealand, and except for an ornamental palace in Japan, remains the largest timber building in the world. It's currently occupied by Victoria University's Law Faculty, but you can usually duck inside, nip up the rimu staircase and see the series of photos of the building as a backdrop to various historical demonstrations and protests.

The Parliament Buildings

Daily 10am–4pm • Free 1hr guided tours on the hour • ☎ 04 817 9503, ⓦ parliament.nz

Visible across Lambton Quay are the **Parliament Buildings**, the seat of New Zealand's government, a trio of highly individual structures that nonetheless sit harmoniously together. Most distinctive is the modernist **Beehive**, a seven-stepped truncated cone that houses the Cabinet and the offices of its ministers. Designed by British (and Coventry Cathedral) architect Sir Basil Spence in 1964, it was finally completed in 1982, six years after Spence's death. The Beehive is connected directly to the Edwardian Neoclassical **Parliament House**, a grand authoritarian seat of government that stands in stark contrast to the Gothic Revival **Parliamentary Library**, all high church, pomp and whimsy.

Hour-long guided tours start from a visitor centre on the Beehive's ground floor. Highlights include the decorative **Maori Affairs Select Committee Room** with its specially commissioned carvings and woven *tukutuku* panels from all the major tribal groups in the land, and the beautifully restored 1899 Victorian Gothic library. You're led through the Debating Chamber when Parliament's not sitting; when it is, check with your guide about watching proceedings from the public gallery. You might also find MPs gathering across Molesworth Street in the **Backbencher Pub** (see p.439).

Archives New Zealand

10 Mulgrave St • Mon–Fri 9am–5pm • Free • ☎ 04 499 5595, ⓦ archives.govt.nz

The **national archives**' prize exhibit is the original Maori-language **Treaty of Waitangi** (see box, p.165 & p.791) in the Constitution Room – a dimly lit, climate-controlled vault. The original barely survived a long spell lost in the bowels of the Old Government Buildings, suffering water damage and gnawing by rodents before it was rescued in 1908. Various copies did the rounds of the country collecting Maori chiefs' signatures, giving a sense of how haphazard the whole process was. There's still talk that the Treaty might move over the road to the National Library, but don't hold your breath.

Other key documents here include the 1835 Declaration of Independence of the Northern Chiefs, and Maori petitions dating back to 1909 complaining of broken treaty promises. Look also for the **1893 petition for women's suffrage**, put together by New Zealand's iconic suffragette, Kate Sheppard, who features on the $10 note. At this third attempt she managed to amass 32,000 signatures, a quarter of the adult female population, ushering in legislation which made New Zealand the first country to give women the vote.

KATHERINE MANSFIELD

Katherine Mansfield Beauchamp (1888–1923) is New Zealand's most famous short-story writer. During her brief life, she revolutionized the form, eschewing plot in favour of poetic expansiveness. Virginia Woolf claimed Mansfield's work to be "the only writing I have ever been jealous of".

Mansfield lived on Tinakori Road for five years with her parents, three sisters and beloved grandmother, and the place is described in some of her works, notably "Prelude" and "A Birthday". The family later moved to a much grander house in what is now the western suburb of Karori until, at 19, Katherine left for Europe, where she lived until dying of tuberculosis in France, aged 34.

Old St Paul's Cathedral

Corner of Mulgrave and Pipitea sts • Daily 9.30am–5pm • Free; guided tours $5 (45min) • ☎ 04 473 6722, ⓦ oldstpauls.co.nz

From 1866 to 1964 the modest **Old St Paul's** operated as the parish church of Thorndon, but after the houses of the Parliamentary District were taken over by government departments and foreign delegations it was only saved from demolition by sustained public protest. Among the finest European timber churches in the country, its interior is beautiful, lit by stained-glass windows and crafted in early English Gothic style from native timbers that progressively darken with age. The church was the major work of an English ecclesiastical architect, Reverend Frederick Thatcher.

St Paul's Cathedral

Corner of Molesworth and Hill sts • Daily 8.30am–4.30pm • Services daily • Free • ⓦ wellingtoncathedral.org.nz

Old St Paul's could hardly stand in greater contrast to its modern successor, **St Paul's Cathedral**. A mix of Byzantine and Santa Fe styles, it was designed in the 1930s by renowned ecclesiastical architect Cecil Wood of Christchurch. Queen Elizabeth II laid the foundation stone in 1954 but the cathedral wasn't complete until 1998. The cavernous interior dwarfs the dark-wood choir stalls, which look out of place among all the powder-pink concrete. The distinctive pipe organ, built in London, was originally installed in Old St Paul's.

The Katherine Mansfield Birthplace

25 Tinakori Rd • Tues–Sun 10am–4pm • $8 • ☎ 04 473 7268, ⓦ katherinemansfield.com • Bus #14 stops on nearby Park St

A ten-minute walk north from the cathedrals through Thorndon gets you to the **Katherine Mansfield Birthplace**, a modest wooden house with small garden that was Mansfield's (see box opposite) childhood abode. The house has a cluttered Victorian/Edwardian charm and avant-garde decor for its time, inspired by Japonisme and the Aesthetic Movement. There's more on the author's life and career in an upstairs room, with black-and-white photos and videos including the excellent *A Woman and a Writer*.

The suburbs

Wellington's suburbs are within easy reach of the city centre and contain the groundbreaking **Zealandia: the Karori Sanctuary Experience**, complemented by a fine stand of native bush a few kilometres north at **Otari-Wilson's Bush**. A number of good walks thread through the greenery of the Town Belt or head beyond to the quiet pleasures of **Scorching Bay** on the **Miramar Peninsula**, the hub of Wellington's film industry.

Zealandia: Te Mara a Tane

Waiapu Rd • Daily: Nov–March 9am–5pm; April–Oct 10am–5pm; 2hr 30min guided night tours daily in summer (April–Oct Wed, Fri–Sun only) 30min before sunset • $17.50; night tour $85 including admission (book ahead) • ☎ 04 920 9200, ⓦ visitzealandia.com • Walk

---

THE BEST VIEW IN WELLINGTON

If the city panorama from Mount Victoria isn't enough for you, head west to **Brooklyn Hill**, easily identified by its crowning 32m-high **wind turbine**. Fantastic views unfold across the city and south towards the South Island's Kaikoura Ranges as the giant propeller blades whirr overhead. This demonstration turbine has been harnessing Wellington's wind since 1993, providing energy for up to a hundred homes. To reach the turbine by car, take Brooklyn Road from the end of Victoria Street and turn left at Ohiro Road, then right at the shopping centre up Todman Street and follow the signposts (the road up to the turbine closes at 8pm Oct–April and 5pm May–Sept). Bus #7 runs up Victoria Street in town and drops you 3km from the summit.

7

WELLINGTON

OTARI-WILTON'S BUSH

▲ Matiu/Somes Island (20 min)   ▲ Picton (3 hr)

● RESTAURANTS, CAFÉS AND BARS	
Chocolate Fish	1
CoCo at the Roxy	2
Maranui Surf Club Café	3

● ACCOMMODATION	
Catchpool Valley	2
Koromiko Homestay	3
Top 10 Hutt Park Holiday Park	1

Scorching Bay

Weta Workshop

SCORCHING BAY

Propeller Studios

Shelly Bay

Point Halswell

Wellington Harbour

Point Jerningham

Kio Bay

SEE 'CENTRAL WELLINGTON MAP'

Westpac Stadium

Container Terminal

Bluebridge Ferry terminal

Interislander Ferry Terminal

AOTEA QUAY

Katherine Mansfield Birthplace

Tinakori Hill

THORNDON

Train Station

Lambton Harbour

Oriental Bay

ORIENTAL PARADE

Charles Plimmer Park

MT VICTORIA TUNNEL

Town Belt

Basin Reserve

TARANAKI STREET

WALLACE ST

MOUNT COOK

Cable car

Town Belt

Botanic Gardens

KELBURN

UPLAND RD

GLENMORE ST

NORTHLAND

CURTIS ST

KARORI

Zealandia Entrance

Lower Reservoir

ARO VALLEY

ZEALANDIA: TE MARA A TANE

Upper Reservoir

KARORI ROAD

Otari-Wilton Visitor Centre

WILTON ROAD

❶ (13km), The Hutt Valley, Lower Hutt (14km) & Porirua (15km)

❷ (23km)

❸

▲ Makara Peak (5km)

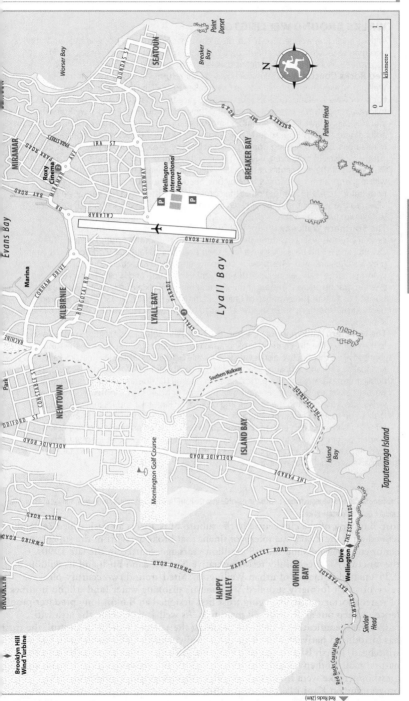

7

7

WALKS AROUND WELLINGTON

With its encircling wooded Town Belt, great city views from nearby hills and the temptation of watching seals along the southern coast, Wellington offers some excellent and easily accessible walking. Pick up free detailed leaflets from the i-SITE (see p.434).

Red Rocks Coastal Walk (4km each way; 2–3hr return). An easy walk that traces Wellington's southern shoreline from Owhiro Bay to Sinclair Head, where a colony of bachelor New Zealand fur seals takes up residence from May–Oct each year. The walk follows a rough track, passing a quarry and the eponymous Red Rocks – well-preserved volcanic pillow lava, formed about 200 million years ago by underwater volcanic eruptions and coloured red by iron oxide. Maori variously attribute the colour to bloodstains from Maui's nose, blood dripping from a paua-shell cut on Kupe's hand, or that Kupe's daughters cut themselves in mourning, having given up their father for dead. The track starts around 7km south of the city centre at the quarry gates at the western end of Owhiro Bay Parade, where there's a car park. To get here by bus, head east from Courtenay Place on the frequent #1 to Island Bay (get off at the corner of Reef Street and the Parade and walk 2.5km to the start of the walk) or catch #4 (peak times only), which continues to Happy Valley, 1km from the track.

The Southern Walkway (11km; 4–5hr). Offering excellent views of the harbour and central city, this walk cuts through the Town Belt to the south of the city centre, between Oriental and Island bays. Despite a few steep stretches it's fairly easy going overall. Fantails, grey warblers and wax-eyes provide company, and Island Bay offers some of the city's best swimming. The walk can be undertaken in either direction and is clearly marked by posts bearing orange arrows. To start at the city end, simply walk along Oriental Parade (or take bus #14 or #24) to the entrance of Charles Plimmer Park, just past 350 Oriental Parade. To begin at the southern end, take the #1 bus to Island Bay and follow the signs from nearby Shorland Park.

The Northern Walkway (16km; 4–5hr). Extending through tranquil sections of the Town Belt to the north of the city centre, this panoramic walk stretches from Kelburn to the suburb of Johnsonville, covering five distinct areas – Botanic Gardens, Tinakori Hill, Trelissick Park, Khandallah Park and Johnsonville Park – each accessible from suburban streets and served by public transport. Highlights are the birdlife on Tinakori Hill (tui, fantails, kingfishers, grey warblers, silver-eyes); the regenerating native forest of Ngaio Gorge in Trelissick Park; great views across the city and the harbour and over to the Rimutaka and Tararua ranges from a lookout on Mount Kaukau (430m); and, in Johnsonville Park, a disused road tunnel hewn through solid rock. Start at the top of the Cable Car and head north through the Botanic Garden, or join the walk at Tinakori Hill by climbing St Mary Street, off Glenmore Street, and following the orange arrows through woodland. To begin at the northern end, take a train to Raroa station on the Johnsonville line.

2km from the Cable Car upper terminus, catch the free shuttle from the i-SITE (from 9.45am, roughly every hour; 10min), or #3 bus from Lambton Quay or Courtney Place

Just 3km west of the city centre in the suburb of Karori is an oasis called **Zealandia**, named after the Zealandia microcontinent that broke away from the super-continent of Gondwana some 85 million years ago. Started in the late 1990s, the sanctuary is successfully restoring native New Zealand bush and its wildlife to 2.25 square kilometres of urban Wellington. Sited around two century-old reservoirs that formerly supplied Wellington's drinking water (and still do in times of water shortage), the managing trust first designed an 8.6km-long **predator-proof fence** to keep out all introduced mammals. As well as restocking the area with native trees, eradicating weeds and fostering the existing morepork and tui, the trust has introduced native birds – little spotted kiwi, weka, saddleback, kaka, bellbird, whitehead, North Island robins, takahe and kakariki – plus tuatara (back in a natural mainland environment for the first time in over two hundred years) and the grasshopper-like weta from the overspill of the conservation and restocking programme on Kapiti Island (see p.256).

This far-reaching project won't be entirely complete until the forest has matured – in another five hundred years. You can already walk the 32km of paths (some almost flat, others quite rugged) listening to birdsong heard almost nowhere else on the mainland, making it easy to understand why early arrivals to New Zealand were so impressed with the avian chorus.

The sanctuary grounds

It's worth spending at least half a day here wandering past viewing hides, areas noted for their fantails or saddleback, and even the first few metres of a gold-mine tunnel from the 1869 Karori gold rush. Join a free day-tour to get help spotting birds (11.15am and 1.15pm weekdays, also 12.15 and 2.15pm on weekends and holidays). Night tours give you a chance to watch kaka feeding, see banks of glowworms and hear kiwi foraging for their dinner – there's a good chance you'll even see one or two. The sanctuary is already having a wider effect, with increasing numbers of tui, bellbirds and kaka spotted in neighbouring suburbs.

Admission includes entry to Zealandia's state-of-the-art visitor centre. Spending around an hour touring its interactive exhibits before exploring the sanctuary puts Zealandia's evolution into context. There's also an on-site café serving sustainable, sustaining deli-style food.

Otari-Wilton's Bush

160 Wilton Rd, 5km northwest of the city centre • Daily dawn–dusk; visitor centre 9am–4pm • Free • Walk 3km from Zealandia or take the #14 bus from the Lambton Interchange (every 30min)

For a glimpse of New Zealand bush as it was before humans arrived, head to **Otari-Wilton's Bush**. The remains of the area's original podocarp-northern rata forest (including an 800-year-old rimu) were set aside in 1860 by one Job Wilton and form the core of the lush 0.8 square kilometres preserved here.

At the unstaffed visitor centre you'll find a map of the walks (all 30min–1hr), which initially follow a 100m **Canopy Walkway** of sturdy decking high in the trees across a gully. This leads to the **Native Botanic Garden**, laid out with plants from around the country, and the informative **Nature Trail** (30min), a good introduction to New Zealand forest plants.

Wellington Harbour

The sight of multicoloured sails scudding across the water should convince you Wellington is at its best when seen from the water. **Wellington Harbour** offers some excellent water-based activities (see box, p.432) that can help you do so, although at the time of writing there were very few sailing opportunities. However, you can hop on the ferry to **Matiu/Somes Island** for a good look around.

The Hutt Valley

15km northeast of the city centre along SH2 • Information from Hutt Valley i-SITE, 25 Laings Rd (Mon–Fri 9am–5pm, Sat & Sun 10am–2pm; ☎ 04 560 4715, ⓦ huttvalleynz.com)

At the northern end of the harbour commuter-land spreads along the **Hutt Valley**, the largest tract of flat land in these parts, accessible along SH2 and by suburban trains and buses. The original founding of Wellington is remembered in **Petone's Settlers Museum**, while nearby **Lower Hutt** has Wellington's closest campsite (see p.436), a great art gallery, and is on the way to the rugged **Rimutaka Forest Park**.

"WELLYWOOD" AND WETA WORKSHOP

Wellington is the capital of **New Zealand's film industry**, which is centred on the Miramar Peninsula, some 12km southeast of the centre. During World War II, defence bases were set up here, and the large, long-abandoned buildings were prime for conversion into production company studios. The stunning natural setting has also been used as **locations** for numerous films including the *Lord of the Rings*, *King Kong*, and *The Hobbit*.

Peter Jackson still lives out this way, and his special effects and entertainment company, Weta, which he co-owns with Richard Taylor, Tania Rodger and Jamie Selkirk, has its base in Miramar. It's refreshingly low-key for the second largest **digital workshop** in the world.

Visit the workshop's **Weta Cave**, on the corner of Camperdown Road and Weka Street (daily 9am–5.30pm; free; ☎04 909 4000, ⓦwetanz.co.nz; bus #2 from the city) – look for the King Kong footprint in the concrete out front – to watch an engaging twenty-minute film on their work, peek at the small museum, and browse hand-crafted figurines and limited-edition collectibles at its shop, which also sells movie location guides (from $45). To get the stories behind the sets, go on a **workshop tour** with a member of their crew ($24). A new Thunderbirds experience was due to be unveiled at the time of writing, but details were a secret almost as closely guarded as Tracy Island's location. Peninsula parking is difficult, so take Weta's There and Back Again tour ($65 including pick-up from the i-Site, DVD introduction and some site-spotting en route), or a **movie tour** such as those listed on p.415.

To learn more about New Zealand's film industry – and to watch New Zealand films on demand for free – stop by **Nga Taonga Sound and Vision** (p.440) in the city centre.

Petone Settler Museum

The Esplanade, 2.5km east of the Petone train station • Wed–Sun 10am–4pm • Free • ☎04 568 8373, ⓦpetonesettlers.org.nz • Buses #81, #83, #84 or the orange Flyer (#91) from Courtenay Place and Lambton Quay

The suburb of Petone is the site of the first, short-lived European settlement in the Wellington region. The **Petone Settlers Museum**, in a striking old bathing pavilion built to commemorate the centenary of the arrival of the first British immigrants, and decorated with beautiful mosaics, tells the tale of the early Maori life in the region, the subsequent colonial settlement and relationships between the peoples.

The Dowse Art Museum

45 Laings Rd, 2km west of the Waterloo train station • Daily 10am–5pm; café Mon–Thurs 8am–4.30pm, Fri 8am–7.30pm, Sat 9am–4.30pm, Sun 10am–4.30pm, plus open til 9pm first Thurs of each month for live jazz • Donation • ☎04 570 6500, ⓦdowse.org.nz • Bus #81, #83 or the orange Flyer from Courtenay Place and Lambton Quay

Six kilometres north of Petone sprawls **Lower Hutt**, home to the **Dowse Art Museum**, a progressive institution stunningly redeveloped by **Ian Athfield**. The well-conceived space is filled with travelling shows and occasionally challenging arts and crafts rotated from its permanent collection, as well as a beautiful pataka. While there you'd be wise to visit the on-site licensed café, *Reka*.

Rimutaka Forest Park

Main entrance due south of Lower Hutt and 20km from Wellington along the Coast Rd • 8am–dusk • Pick up the *Catchpool Valley/ Orongorongo Valley* leaflet from DOC in Wellington • No convenient bus service, so drive or arrange a lift/taxi

The **Rimutaka Forest Park** is popular among city-dwellers for its series of easy, short and day- **walks** in the attractive Catchpool Valley; there are also picnic and barbecue facilities, and a well-maintained DOC **campsite** (see p.436). From the signposted main entrance Catchpool Road winds a further 2km up the valley to the car park, the starting point for most of the walks. Keen hikers and campers will want to get as far as the braided Orongorongo River, from where a startlingly grand landscape opens out; camping is free at Graces Stream.

MATIU/SOMES ISLAND

One of Wellington's best day-trips is to **Matiu/Somes Island**, in the northern reaches of the harbour. Legendary navigator Kupe is said to have named it Matiu (meaning "peace") in the tenth century and his descendants lived on the island until deposed by European settlers in the late 1830s. They renamed the island after Joseph Somes, then deputy governor of the New Zealand Company that had "bought" it. For eighty years it was a quarantine station where travellers carrying diseases such as smallpox were held until they recovered or died. During both world wars anyone in New Zealand considered even vaguely suspect – Germans, Italians, Turks, Mexicans and Japanese – was interned on the island until the end of the war, after which it became an animal quarantine station for a number of years.

In the early 1980s its conservation value was recognized, and it is now managed by DOC, which oversees continued efforts to revitalize **native vegetation** and restore the historic buildings. All introduced mammalian predators have been eradicated and threatened native species are being introduced. Already there are seven different reptiles, kakariki (the red-crowned parakeet), North Island robins, little blue penguins, the cricket-like weta and the ancient reptilian tuatara. They seem to like it, as numbers are increasing.

ACCESS, INFORMATION AND ACCOMMODATION

Access is on the **Dominion Post Ferry** (3–4 services weekdays, more at weekends; 20min each way; $22 return; ☎04 499 1282, ⊛eastbywest.co.nz) which stops at the island on its cross-harbour journey to Days Bay, enabling you to explore for up to five hours before catching a ferry back to Wellington. Sailings are weather-dependent, so call ahead to confirm departures. From the wharf at the island's northeastern end, a surfaced road runs uphill for 400m to the **DOC field centre** in an old hospital, which has maps of the island (also available at the city DOC office, p.434). A popular option is to take a picnic lunch onto the island. Note that this is a protected reserve; smoking and fires are not allowed, and access may be restricted in summer months to reduce fire risk. The Museum of Wellington City and Sea (p.422) and Flat Earth (p.415) also run tours here. For information on camping on the island, see p.436.

ARRIVAL AND DEPARTURE   WELLINGTON

BY PLANE

Wellington International Airport (⊛wellington airport.co.nz), about 10km southeast of the city centre, is an important domestic hub, linking around fifteen airports across New Zealand and handling international flights from Australia. Flying avoids the potentially choppy ferry crossing (see below), but you miss cruising through Marlborough Sound. Soundsair (☎0800 505 005, ⊛soundsair.com) flies from Wellington to Picton and Blenheim ($109 one way) and Nelson ($130).

Destinations Auckland (14–20 daily; 1hr); Blenheim (10–14 daily; 25min); Christchurch (14 daily; 45min); Dunedin (3–5 daily; 1hr 15min); Gisborne (2–4 daily; 1hr); Hamilton (4–7 daily; 1hr 10min); Napier/Hastings (5–7 daily; 55min); Nelson (3–5 daily; 40min); New Plymouth (4 daily; 55min); Palmerston North (1–3 daily; 35min); Picton (4–6 daily; 25min); Rotorua (3 daily; 1hr 10min); Tauranga (3–5 daily; 1hr 15min); Timaru (2–4 daily; 1hr 20min).

Getting to/from town Green Cabs (☎0508 447 336) use hybrids; Wellington Combined Taxis (☎04 384 4444) are carbon zero-certified; both will cost about $35. The Airport Flyer bus (daily 6.30am–9.25pm; Mon–Fri every 10–20min, Sat & Sun 7am–8.45pm every 20–30min) costs $9 for the 15min journey to the city centre. Super

Shuttle (☎0800 748 885 or ☎09 522 5100, ⊛supershuttle .co.nz) charges from around $20 for the first person to a city centre destination, plus $5 for each extra person travelling to the same place.

BY FERRY

The Interislander terminal (☎0800 802 802, ⊛inter islander.co.nz) is 1km north of the train station; the Bluebridge terminal (☎0800 844 844, ⊛bluebridge.co.nz) is opposite the train station. Both companies offer year-round services across the Cook Strait to Picton (6–9 daily; 3hr). The crossing can be choppy, but does afford the chance to see the Marlborough Sounds. Both companies have different fare categories with varying flexibility – check the cancellation policy prior to booking. Interislander fares are around $65–75 one-way for a single passenger, $208–318 for a car and driver, and $15 for bikes. Interislander's *Kaitaki* and *Aratere* ferries offer the Plus service ($45 extra, over-18s only), which includes private lounge, complimentary food, newspapers and internet. Get to the Interislander terminal on the shuttle bus ($2) from the train station (by Platform 9) 50min before each sailing, or with the backpacker bus ($3) from *Base* and the *YHA* for the 8.30am sailing (book through the hostels).

7

WELLINGTON TOURS AND ACTIVITIES

Wellington harbour's brisk winds make it ideal for **windsurfing** and **kiteboarding** (most of the action centres on Kio and Evans bays), while kayaking and diving are also popular.

On a fine day there's little to beat **cycling** around the coastal roads that follow the bays east of the city. Start by heading east along Oriental Parade and follow the coast as far as you want; even right past the airport and around the northern tip of the Miramar Peninsula to Scorching Bay and Seatoun (25–30km one way). There is also stacks of **off-road riding**, much of it outlined in the *Mountain Biking in Wellington* leaflet (available free from the i-SITE), which contains maps of key areas a short ride from the city. Highlights include the coastal track out to Red Rocks (see box, p.428) and the single-track trails around Mount Victoria (see p.420).

Other dry-land pursuits include quadbiking, in-line skating and climbing. Ferg's Kayaks (see below) rents **in-line skates** ($20/2hr; $25/3hr), perfect for use in nearby Frank Kitts Park or around Oriental Parade. Ferg's also offers an excellent and very popular **indoor climbing** wall ($15; harness and shoes $4 each).

For information on **walks in Wellington**, see box, p.428.

WATERSPORTS

Dive Wellington 432 The Esplanade, Island Bay ⊕04 939 3483, ⊛divewellington.co.nz. Scuba-diving charters to the frigate *Wellington*, scuttled a 5min boat ride off the coast in 21m of water in 2005 ($120 for two dives with gear rental), or just walk across the road and straight into the marine reserve ($40/day). There are options for people only qualified to 18m, and courses for all levels including beginners. One of the few activities that isn't weather or wind dependent.

Ferg's Kayaks Shed 6 Queens Wharf ⊕04 499 8898, ⊛fergskayaks.co.nz. Rents SUPs ($25/hr), single ($30/2hr) and double ($40/2hr) sit-on-tops, plus single ($35/2hr) and double ($50/2hr) sea kayaks. They also run some fun guided trips, the best being the Lights at Night, a city-illuminated paddle round the bay with great views, lots of photograph opportunities and a light supper (Tues 5.30–9pm weather permitting; four or more $85 each, $105 each for 2; book in advance).

Wildwinds 36 Customhouse Quay ⊕04 473 3458, ⊛wildwinds.co.nz. Offers a two-hour taster windsurf lesson ($110) or a series of two three-hour sessions ($295).

CYCLING AND QUAD BIKING

Makara Peak Mountain Bike Park 116–122 South Karori Rd, about 8km west of the city centre ⊛makara peak.org; map p.426. Committed mountain-bikers should head to this two-and-a-half-square-kilometre area of forest and farmland centred on the 412m Makara Peak, up behind Karori. There's no entry fee and you'll have the run of some 40km of tracks suitable for all abilities.

Mud Cycles 421 Karori Rd, 2km short of the Makara Peak Mountain Bike Park ⊕04 476 4961, ⊛mudcycles.co.nz. Rents hard tail ($35/half-day; $60/day) and full suspension mountain bikes ($50/half-day, $70/day). You can also rent for longer periods. Helmet and trail maps are included.

Wellington Adventures 1051 Coast Rd, Wainuiomata ⊕0800 948 6386, ⊛wellington adventures.co.nz; map p.426. If you have the urge to push the limit and rack up the kilometres with a few jaw-dropping views along the way, this is the outfit for you. They run one of the best-value, most enjoyable and technically challenging quad-bike trips in the country. The views from the farm where it all kicks off are spectacular, but it keeps getting better as you head through a mixture of coastal scrub, farmland, forest, riverbed and beach (half-day $229, full day $329).

Bluebridge fares are generally $53–73 one-way for a single passenger, $173–245 for a car (up to 5.5m) and driver, and $10 for bikes. Car rental companies that permit their vehicles on the ferries include Ace, Apex, Maui and Jucy (see p.33).

BY TRAIN AND BUS

Train The main train station is on Bunny St; the Auckland–Wellington *Northern Explorer* train (see p.31) runs once daily, arriving from Auckland Mon, Thurs & Sat, and heading back Tues, Fri & Sun.

Destinations Auckland (Tues, Fri & Sun 1 daily; 11hr); Hutt Central/Waterloo (every 30min; 20 min); Masterton (1–6 daily; 1hr 30min); National Park (Tues, Fri & Sun 1 daily; 5hr 20min); Otaki (Mon–Fri 1 daily; 1hr 10min); Otorohanga (Tues, Fri & Sun 1 daily; 8hr); Paekakariki (every 30min; 50min); Palmerston North (Sun–Fri 1–2 daily; 2hr); Paraparaumu (every 30min; 1hr).

Bus Nakedbus and InterCity buses terminate at the train station, alongside Platform 9.

Destinations Auckland (6 daily; 11hr); Napier (5 daily; 5hr 15min); New Plymouth (1–2 daily; 6hr 30min); Palmerston

North (12–14 daily; 2hr 15min); Paraparaumu (13–15 daily; 50min); Rotorua (4–5 daily; 7hr); Taupo (8–9 daily; 6hr).

BY CAR
From the north, both the SH1 through Porirua and SH2

(part of the grape-signed Classic New Zealand Wine Trail) via Lower Hutt turn into short urban motorways that merge, running scenically along the harbourside to the city centre. For details of parking, see below. Coming from or heading to the South Island, see p.431 for details of crossing Cook Strait.

GETTING AROUND

BY BUS

Wellington's extensive network of buses and trolley buses operates from Lambton Interchange, just west of the train station.

Bus tickets and passes All tickets and day-passes can be bought direct from the bus driver. One-way fares are $2 within the inner city, beyond which a zone system comes into operation: each extra zone costs an extra $1.50. For heavy use it's worth getting a Stored Value Card on the first bus you board – it knocks about twenty percent off each journey. The After Midnight service (Sat & Sun hourly midnight–3am), designed to get the party crowd home safely, is centred on Courtenay Place and costs $6–13.

BY TRAIN

Tranz Metro (☎0800 801 700, ☻tranzmetro.co.nz) run suburban train services from the station on Bunny Street. Trains to the Hutt Valley (see p.429) and the Kapiti Coast (see p.255) leave the train station roughly every half-hour for Waterloo (for Lower Hutt; 20min; $5.50); Porirua (20min; $6.50); Plimmerton (30min; $8); and Paraparaumu (1hr; $11.50). The Johnsonville line (Raroa; 20min; $5) provides handy access for hiking the Northern Walkway (see p.428). You save a dollar or two if you travel outside peak hours (usually not before 9am or from 4–7pm).

Train tickets and passes A one-day Rover ticket ($14) gives you the run of the train network after 9am weekdays and all weekend; up to four people travelling together can save with a group Rover ticket ($40). A three-day weekend Rover ($21) is valid from 4.30am Fri–midnight Sun. Bicycles are free. Tickets can be bought at the Tranz Rail Travel Centre at the main train station or on the train.

BY CAR

Making your way around the inner city is simple enough once you get used to the extensive one-way system.
Parking There is no free weekday parking in the city centre,

but parking is free for up to 2hr at a time on Sat and all day Sun. Car parks are plentiful, council ones charging around $4/ hr during weekdays (generally cheaper at night and on weekends), often with a one-day maximum of $15, assuming you park before 9am. The car park by the Te Papa museum is suitable for campervans, and there are several others nearby. If you don't want to bother with moving your vehicle all the time, some places charge $25–50 for a full 24hr.

Parking meters and coupon parking Most inner-city streets have parking meters (usually Mon–Thurs 8am–6pm & Fri 8am–8pm $4/hr; otherwise free) that limit you to a 2hr stay during the metered hours and weekends 8am–6pm. Slightly further out you get coupon parking (Mon–Fri 8am–6pm) where the first 2hr are free, but to stay longer you have to display a coupon ($7.50 for all day), available from dairies and petrol stations. These areas are also free outside the set hours.

Car rental As well as the companies covered in Basics (see p.33), local firms offering good deals include Rent-a-Dent, 24 Tacy St, Kilbirnie ☎04 387 9931, ☻rentadent .co.nz; and Ace Rental Cars, 126 Hutt Rd ☎0800 535 500, ☻acerentalcars.co.nz.

BY TAXI

You can hail one almost anywhere in town, but there are authorized stands at: the train station; on Whitmore St between Lambton Quay and Featherston St; outside the *James Smith Hotel* on Lambton Quay; off Willis St on the Bond St corner; at the corner of Courtenay Place and Taranaki St; and at the junction of Willis & Aro sts. Try Green Cabs (☎0508 447 336) or Wellington Combined Taxis (☎04 384 4444).

BY BIKE

On Yer Bike (181 Vivian St ☎04 384 8480) has mountain, road and city bikes for $40 a day, plus some good tips on where to go. For information on mountain bike rental and Makara Peak Mountain Bike Park, see box, p.432.

7

WELLINGTON TRANSPORT INFORMATION AND PASSES

The useful **Metlink Explorer** ($21) gives one day of unlimited bus and train travel throughout the Wellington region from 9am on weekdays and all day at weekends. You can buy the pass from bus drivers, train staff and from Tranz Metro ticket offices.

For region-wide **train and bus information**, pick up the free *Metlink Network Map* or any of the individual timetables at the visitor centre or train station, or call Metlink (☎0800 801 700, ☻metlink.org.nz).

INFORMATION

i-SITE Corner of Wakefield and Victoria sts (daily 8.30am–5pm, public holidays 11am–4pm; ☎0800 933 536, ⊛wellingtonnz.com). Has all the usual leaflets and maps, plus the handy and free *Wellington: Official Visitor Guide* booklet. There are also internet terminals ($8/hr).

DOC 18 Manners St (Mon–Fri 9am–5pm, Sat 10am–3.30pm; ☎04 384 7770). Has stacks of information on walks in the Wellington region and sells hut tickets and issues permits for Kapiti Island (both also available online).

ACCOMMODATION

Wellington has plenty of accommodation in the city centre, including some excellent **backpacker hostels**. **B&Bs** are becoming less common, but there's an increasing number of stylish self-catering serviced **apartments**. Breakfasting (or brunching) out is a quintessential Wellington experience, so you might not want a place where breakfast is included. Central **motels** are in short supply, but many business-oriented **hotels** offer good-value deals, especially at weekends. For a little peace and quiet, you might want to stay outside the city centre (see p.258), and drive or take public transport into town.

Apollo Lodge Motel & Majoribanks Apartments 49 Majoribanks St ☎0800 361 645, ⊛apollolodge.co.nz; map pp.416–417. Appealing medium-sized renovated motel with modern rooms (some decorated in Edwardian style) 200m from Courtenay Place with off-street parking. Its adjacent apartments are well set up for longer stays; call ahead for prices. $150

Austinvilla B&B 11 Austin St, Mount Victoria ☎04 385 8334, ⊛austinvilla.co.nz; map pp.416–417. Two lovely and very private self-contained apartments (one a studio, the other with a separate bedroom and a small garden), both with bathtubs, continental breakfast and off-street parking, in an elegant villa with leafy surrounds a 10min walk from Courtenay Place. Not suitable for young children. Studio $205, one-bedroom $245

Base Wellington 21–23 Cambridge Terrace ☎04 801 5666, ⊛stayatbase.com; map pp.416–417. Slick, well-organized 280-bed hostel converted from an office building. Facilities include cheap internet, lockable cupboards, parking ($15/night) and *Basement* bar with theme nights. Women-only "Sanctuary" rooms ($3/night extra) includes free sparkling wine. Dorms $24, en suite $110

★ **Booklovers B&B** 123 Pirie St, Mount Victoria ☎04 384 2714, ⊛booklovers.co.nz; map pp.416–417. For charm and comfort you can't do better than this three-bedroom literary B&B in an unfussy Victorian villa a 10min walk from Courtenay Place and Mount Victoria Park. There are books in every room and a full cooked breakfast is served any time within reason. $240

Cambridge Hotel 28 Cambridge Terrace ☎0800 375 021, ⊛cambridgehotel.co.nz; map pp.416–417. Renovated 1930s hotel that operates partly as a backpackers and partly as accommodation for long-stay residents and workers. There's a popular, inexpensive bar and restaurant, the four- to eight-bed dorms are spacious and the hotel rooms, while smallish, are good value. Dorms $26, en suites $99

★ **CQ Hotels** 223 Cuba St ☎04 385 2156, ⊛hotelwellington.co.nz; map pp.416–417. Two hotels run to a high standard by the same family, and sharing the same facilities (swimming pool, café, bar, gym, restaurant, free wi-fi, charged-for off-street parking) in the heart of Cuba St. Rooms at the *Comfort* can be small but they are all en suite, stylish and great value, while the *Quality* is more luxurious and includes lavish apartments with kitchenettes ($409). *Comfort* $139, *Quality* $219

Gourmet Stay 25 Frederick St ☎04 801 6800, ⊛gourmetstay.co.nz; map pp.416–417. Modern flashpackers at the groovy end of town, that uses every inch of space to squeeze in three-share dorms and doubles (some en suite). There are also three motel units across the courtyard. There's free wi-fi, a café downstairs and off-street parking ($10/night) for residents. Dorm $45, motel units $195

Halswell Lodge 21 Kent Terrace ☎04 385 0196, ⊛halswell.co.nz; map pp.416–417. Comfortable, central and welcoming establishment with simple but good-value hotel rooms, relatively pricey motel units and lovely deluxe rooms (some with spa $165) in a lodge set back from the street. Free off-street parking. Rooms $105, motel units $145

Hotel Waterloo 1 Bunny St ☎04 473 8482, ⊛downtownbackpackers.co.nz; map pp.416–417. Large hostel in the Art Deco *Waterloo Hotel*, convenient for train, bus and ferry arrivals. Dorms and rooms (some en suite) are adequate, and there's a cheap bar and a café in this once-grand hotel's former ballroom. Dorms $29, en suites $115

Koromiko Homestay 11 Koromiko Rd, Aro Valley ☎04 938 6539, ⊛koromikohomestay.co.nz; map pp.426–427. This homestay for "gay men and their friends" is on a quiet street overlooking the harbour, with two doubles and one single that share a bathroom. There's a double outdoor "garden bath" with views of the city, and meals ($25 including wine) are available on request. $135

Museum Hotel 90 Cable St ☎0800 994 335, ⊛museumhotel.co.nz; map pp.416–417. Big, black business hotel with an intimate feel and contemporary New Zealand art on show, nicknamed the Museum Hotel de Wheels for having been trundled across the street from

the Te Papa construction site on rail tracks. Rates are reasonable for the high standards – check their website for deals. **$229**, harbour view **$270**

Nomads Capital 118 Wakefield St ☎0508 666 237, Ⓦnomadscapital.com; map pp.416–417. Comfy 180-bed hostel (with vertigo-inducing top bunks) in the city centre with a backpacker bar/café *Blend* attached. Women-only dorms available ($7 extra) as well as "elite" en-suite doubles ($110). Dorms **$29**, standard doubles **$95**

★**Ohtel** 66 Oriental Parade ☎04 803 0600, Ⓦohtel .com; map pp.416–417. Chic, sophisticated boutique hotel opposite Waitangi Park at the city end of Oriental Parade, with valet parking, free wi-fi, gym and sauna. Each of its ten rooms has a decadent bathroom (some have two-person baths, not all have doors), high-tech entertainment systems and hand-picked mid-century vintage furniture and designer furnishings. **$295**

Trinity Hotel 166 Willis St ☎04 801 8118, Ⓦtrinityhotel.co.nz; map pp.416–417. A comfortable and well-run budget hotel with sixty rooms, all with free wi-fi and Sky TV. There's an on-site restaurant-bar, plus parking ($15; book ahead). Weekend deals ($200) include a bottle of bubbly, cooked breakfast and late checkout. **$130**

★**YHA Wellington City** 292 Wakefield St ☎04 801 7280, Ⓦyha.co.nz; map pp.416–417. This award-winning 320-bedder is one of the best – and greenest – hostels, right in the heart of the city with great harbour views from some of the upper-floor rooms. Spacious common areas include a foosball table and projector-screen TV room, well-equipped kitchens, bike storage, espresso bar, an info and travel desk and social events such as regular meal nights ($7–10). Many of the doubles, twin, four- and six-share dorms have en suites. Dorms **$30**, rooms **$95**

CAMPSITES

Catchpool Valley Rimutaka Forest Park, 30km northeast of Wellington; map p.414. Pleasant drive-in DOC campsite beside the Catchpool stream with hot showers, toilets, water supply and barbecues. The 150 sites are scattered among tall trees. **$10**

★**Matiu/Somes Island** Twelve-person DOC campsite on the Matiu/Somes Island wildlife reserve (see p.414) in the middle of Wellington Harbour with great city views. There are flush toilets, tap water and a camp kitchen with gas oven, but you need to bring everything else. Book in advance through DOC or contact the Wellington i-SITE for more information. **$10**

Top 10 Hutt Park Holiday Park 95 Hutt Park Rd, Lower Hutt ☎0800 948 686, Ⓦwellingtontop10.co.nz; map p.414. The capital's closest campsite, 12km north of Wellington on the harbour's northeastern shore. It's near beaches, shops and bushwalks and can be accessed on buses #81 and #83 from Courtenay Place and Lambton Interchange. There's a good range of accommodation, from camping ($45 per site) to motel units with Sky TV ($130). Kitchen cabins **$80**, self-contained units **$115**

Waterfront Motorhome Park Waterloo Quay ☎0800 948 686, Ⓦwwmp.co.nz; map pp.416–417. Basically, a small (30 powered sites) council-run parking lot with an ablution block. The manager's on site during the day, or you pay at the machine. **$50**

EATING

Wellington has more places to eat per capita than New York and the standard is impressively high, whatever the budget. There's little need to venture much beyond the bounds of the city centre, though a couple of reasons to stray are listed below. As the country's self-professed **coffee** capital (Wellington has nearly twenty independent roasteries), you'll find the good stuff served up everywhere from cosy spots through to the *très chic*. Gastronomes might want to join a gourmet tour (see box, p.415). If you want to head off the beaten track, local neighbourhoods worth scouting out include Newtown and the Aro Valley. In the streets around **Courtenay Place** and **Cuba Street** there's a plethora of local and international restaurants – from cheap curry joints and bohemian cafés through to award-winning establishments headed up by some of New Zealand's finest. During the day many restaurants offer bargain lunch specials. Many pubs and bars (p.438) also serve impressive and generally inexpensive fare.

For **groceries** try **Moore Wilson's** or the three central New World supermarkets: at 68 Willis St; inside the railway station; and the largest, at the eastern end of Wakefield Street. If you're here on a weekend, head down to the car park near Te Papa to the Saturday morning gourmet market, or Sunday morning **fruit and vegetable market** and the nearby **farmers' market** in the Chaffers Dock Atrium, with stalls of artisan goods from local producers.

CENTRAL WELLINGTON

★**Aro Coffee** 90 Aro St ☎04 384 4970; map pp.416–417. The pick of a village-like cluster of cafés in weatherboard buildings in the Aro Valley, serving its own hand-blended coffee roasted on the premises, along with a short, smart menu of brunch fare such as their own baked beans with fried eggs and chorizo ($17). Mon–Fri 7.30am–4pm, Sat & Sun 9am–5pm.

Beach Babylon Ground floor, 232 Oriental Parade ☎04 801 7717; map pp.416–417. Done out like a *bach*, and serving casual brunches to stylish dinners with a retro twist: chicken Kiev ($28), meatloaf ($26), fondue for two ($15) and banana splits ($10) for dessert. Good cocktails, too. Licensed and BYO. Daily 8am–late.

Ekim 257 Cuba St; map pp.416–417. Caravan and (licensed) bus selling milkshakes and burgers to take away or eat in their urban garden (occasional DJs and bands). There's an incredible six veggie options if you don't want meat, and everything is transformed by Mike's secret sauce. Daily 11am–9pm.

Fidel's 234 Cuba St ☎04 801 6868, ⓦfidelscafe.com; map pp.416–417. At the offbeat southern end of Cuba St, this eternally funky, always busy café is plastered with revolution-era pictures of Castro, and extends into the former barber's next door and camouflage-netted courtyard. Come for locally roasted Havana coffee, vegan muffins, booze, milkshakes, or excellent-value meals (mains $10–24). Mon–Fri 7.30am–10pm, Sat 8am–10pm, Sun 9am–10pm.

Floriditas 161 Cuba St ☎04 381 2212; map pp.416–417. This light, airy and stylish café is always busy. Wonderful breakfasts range from $13–24 and its limited but clever menu includes lunches such as smashed pea risotto ($23.50), dinners of char-grilled lamb ($32.50) or the house speciality amaretto *affogato* ($15). Mon–Sat 7am–10pm, Sun 7.30am–9.30pm.

Fork and Brewer 14 Bond St ☎04 472 0033, ⓦforkand brewer.co.nz; map pp.416–417. Brave the unprepossessing staircase and you'll enter beer heaven – just smell the hops. With around thirty regularly changing beers and two ciders on tap, including their own, you better have a tasting tray (4 beers/$15). Beers are matched to the decent pub grub if you're dining (most items under $25). Their flagship beer is the malty APA Base Isolator (6.3%), but they may have a special like Tainted Love (with yoghurt culture). Mon–Thurs 11.30am–10.30pm, Fri & Sat 11.30am–1.30am.

Hangar 171-7 Willis St (cnr Dixon & Willis, entrance on Dixon) ☎04 830 0909; map pp.416–417. Come for a long black or espresso and test your palate as each single-origin roast comes with a tasting card. There's also cold brew and drip coffee. Eggs Benjamin ($18) are their own take on eggs Bene: poached eggs served with hollandaise and black pudding or *kimchi*. Licensed. Mon & Tues 7am–5pm, Wed–Fri 7am–1am, Sat 8am–1am, Sun 8am–5pm.

★**Lamason** Cnr Lombard & Bond sts ☎04 473 1632; map pp.416–417. Technically on the corner, but wander up Lombard St to this unprepossessing coffee bar hidden under a car park and run by friendly but madly obsessive coffee makers who specialize in smooth subtle vacuum pot and filter (v60) coffee. Mon–Fri 7am–4.30pm, Sat 9.30am–3pm.

Logan-Brown 192 Cuba St ☎04 801 5114; map pp.416–417. Though no longer the domain of Al Brown (Steve Logan and Brown were Kiwi TV chefs), this Wellington icon of fine dining has hung on to its reputation as one of the best places to spend great wedges of cash in the pursuit of a culinary thrill. Mains include lamb rack with broad beans ($49), accompanied by a bottle of Central Otago Pinot Noir that at $80 provides more of a shock than a thrill. On Saturdays it's tasting menus only ($95–125 excl. wine). Fri & Sat noon–3pm for lunch and high tea, Tues–Sat dinner from 5.30pm.

MariLuca 55–57 Mulgrave St ☎04 499 5590, ⓦmariluca.co.nz; map pp.416–417. High-quality, well-priced Italian food to meet Grandpa's Sicilian maxims: "meat makes meat, bread makes belly, wine makes dance". The menu varies seasonally, almost everything is cooked from scratch using mostly organic ingredients and the wine list extends beyond the horizon. Stop in while touring the Parliamentary District. Lunch Tues–Fri 11.30am–2.30pm; dinner Mon–Sat 5.30pm–midnight.

Masala 2 Allen St ☎04 385 2012; map pp.416–417. Sleek banquettes and an ambient soundtrack offer a stylish, retro-contemporary alternative to most of Wellington's Indian restaurants. Curries (lunch mains under $13, dinner mains under $20), from the classic to the innovative, are cooked to perfection. Licensed & BYO. Lunch Mon–Sat 11am–2.30pm, dinner daily 5pm–late.

Matterhorn 106 Cuba St ☎04 384 3359, ⓦmatterhorn .co.nz; map pp.416–417. At the end of a long timber-lined corridor in a 1960s coffee house, this establishment is a successful merger of glam bar (see p.439) and fancy restaurant. The slightly overcomplicated food (evening mains $28–34) includes coddled egg with chicken wing bacon, and plate of pig; the Sunday-night roast ($25) has cult status. Mon–Sat 3pm–late, Sun 1pm–late.

★**Midnight Espresso** 178 Cuba St ☎04 384 7014; map pp.416–417. Looking like a bohemian artists' squat, with posters and flyers pinned to the community notice board, artwork and murals covering the walls, a pinball machine and frogger, this caffeine junkie's heaven serves Havana coffee along with lovely breakfasts, counter food and tasty hot dishes (many veggie or vegan), all under $18. Mon–Fri 7am–3am, Sat & Sun 8am–3am.

Mojo 37 Customhouse Quay ☎04 385 3001, ⓦmojocoffee.co.nz; map pp.416–417. Most days you can watch the hand-blending and roasting at the HQ of one Wellington's most successful coffee roasteries. Beans are sold at the shop while the building directly opposite houses *Mojo*'s flagship café. Café Mon–Fri 7am–5pm, Sat & Sun 9am–4pm; shop Mon–Fri 7.30am–3.30pm.

★**Moore Wilson's** Corner of Tory and College sts; map pp.416–417. Tucked under a parking station opposite the historic Thompson Lewis spring, this superb deli, charcuterie and bakery is the place to come for top-quality picnic supplies, including its own aged cheese. Fill your water bottle from the spring water fountain. Mon–Fri 7.30am–7pm, Sat 7.30am–6pm, Sun 9am–5pm.

★**Nikau Gallery Café** City Gallery Wellington, Civic Square ☎04 801 4168, ⓦnikaucafe.co.nz; map pp.416–417. A stylish, contemporary daytime café with an airy setting and outdoor terrace, plus excellent coffee and a high-quality yet reasonably priced menu that makes the most of seasonal produce: try the kedgeree with house-smoked fish ($23.50) with a home-made soda or a glass from their fine selection of wines. Mon–Fri 7am–4pm, Sat 8am–4pm.

7

Olive 170 Cuba St ☎04 802 5266; map pp.416–417. Elegant but relaxed bare-boards, licensed café that sticks mainly to organic produce and is popular with the natives. Great for coffee and cake throughout the day, as well as for delicious breakfasts such as their own granola, lunches such as sweetcorn baked custard and evening meals (mains $27–38) – try the pan-roasted fish. Mon–Fri 8am–9.30pm, Sat 9am–9.30pm, Sun 9am–4.30pm.

Oriental Kingdom Left Bank ☎04 381 3303; map pp.416–417. A large, simple café beloved by young in-the-know Wellingtonians. All of its pan-Asian fare is fresh, cheap (mains $9–11) and filling, particularly the *laksas* and *roti*. Licensed & BYO. Daily 11am–10pm.

Ortega 16 Marjoribanks St ☎04 382 9559, ⓦortega .co.nz; map pp.416–417. This self-titled "fish shack" with the feel of a classy neighbourhood bistro, concentrates on superb seafood served with relaxed panache. Book for dinner (mains around $38), a dessert matched to a sticky, or just drop in for an Oloroso sherry at the bar. Tues–Sat 5.30pm–late.

Plum 103 Cuba St ☎04 384 8881, ⓦplumcafe.co.nz; map pp.416–417. Elongated dark-timber, licensed café perfect for cocooning over the paper and a post-hangover "Plumster" breakfast of eggs, sausages, bacon, slow-roasted tomatoes, grilled field mushrooms and more ($22), or a veggie Plumster including home-made hash browns ($22). Open Tues–Sat 9am–10pm, Sun & Mon 9am–6pm.

Poneke 1 Clyde Quay Wharf ☎04 979 9283; map pp.416–417. Martin Bosley's closed his eponymous fine-dining restaurant and is now running a café – but what a café. Worth a trip just for the delicious pastries, there are also fine mains ($20–27 excl. sides) such as whole baked flounder and "ridiculously sticky" ribs. Mon–Fri 7am–10pm, Sat & Sun 8am–10pm.

Prefab 14 Jessie St ☎04 385 2263, ⓦpre-fab.co.nz; map pp.416–417. Sit at the counter to watch Jeff (the godfather of NZ espresso) roasting the beans in this airy, industrial-style café. Efficient service, fresh bread, and lovely seasonal food (lunch $16–25). They're such perfectionists, they even make the best coffee cups. Open Mon–Fri 7am–4pm, Sat 8am–3.30pm.

★**Sweet Mother's Kitchen** 5 Courtenay Place ☎04 385 4444, ⓦsweetmotherskitchen.co.nz; map pp.416–417. Breakfast on beignets ($5.50), tuck into a Po' Boy baguette ($12.50), warm up with a bowl of gumbo

($16.50) or blackened terakihi and hush puppies ($27) and finish with a pecan and bourbon pie ($8). Rightly popular. Licensed. Daily 8am–late.

Trisha's Pies 32 Cambridge Terrace ☎04 801 5506; map pp.416–417. A traditional Kiwi pie shop and a Wellington institution, serving a vast array of wonderful home-made pies. Particular favourites are the steak and cheese, pepper steak, steak and mushroom and veggie, all under $6. Mon–Fri 6am–3.30pm, Sat 9am–2pm.

Wellington Trawling Sea Market 220 Cuba St ☎04 384 8461; map pp.416–417. The best fish and chip shop in the city (eat in or takeaway) also sells wet fish. The fish is cooked to order, and you can complement it with Paua fritters or oysters. Fish dinners under $15. Mon–Thurs & Sat 7am–8.30pm, Fri 7am–9.30pm, Sun 8am–8pm.

THE SUBURBS

Chocolate Fish Café 100 Shelly Bay Rd, opposite Propeller Studio, Shelly Bay ⓦchocolatefishcafe.co.nz; map pp.426–427. In its previous Scorching Bay location, the *Chocolate Fish* was famously the *Lord of the Rings* cast and crew hangout. Now at the former Shelly Bay air force base, it has transformed into a barbecue with alfresco and indoor seating, sandwiches hot off the grill ($10–20), and delicious home-made muffins, slices and biscuits. Licensed. Daily 8.30am–5pm.

★**CoCo at The Roxy** 5 Park Road, Miramar ☎04 388 5555, ⓦcocoattheroxy.co.nz; map pp.426–427. Classy bar and dining room in the grand foyer of *The Roxy* cinema (see p.440). The food (mains $15–25) almost manages to outshine its stunning surroundings. The focus is seasonal ingredients from local suppliers, so cross your fingers they're still making the eight-hour braised beef cheek burger ($19.50) – heaven. Daily 9am–10.30pm.

★**Maranui Surf Club Café** Maranui Surf Life Saving Club, The Parade, Lyall Bay ☎04 387 4539, ⓦmaranuicafe.co.nz; map pp.426–427. Situated on the top floor, with a balcony overlooking the beach, sea and approaches to Wellington airport, this licensed café is an established locals' favourite, with colourful retro beachside decor, generous breakfasts, great salads and chocolate coconut cakes (all under $20). There are few better places to sit and watch the planes go by, particularly at weekends. Daily 7am–5pm.

DRINKING AND NIGHTLIFE

Most **pubs** and **bars** are open daily, from around eleven in the morning until midnight or later. The distinction between bars and **clubs** is often blurred, with many bars hosting free live music and dancing in the evenings, especially at weekends. Resident and guest DJs mix broad-ranging styles to create a party- or club-style atmosphere. Cuba Street is home to some of New Zealand's best **nightlife**, with a huge array of late-night cafés, bars and clubs within walking distance of each other.

Wellington's **gay and lesbian scene** is focused in the inner city, but for the most part it's woven seamlessly into the general café/bar mainstream. In the centre, at least, gay people openly express affection in public, and gays, lesbians, transgender and bi-folk mix freely together. For the latest information, check out ⓦgaynz.com, or pick up the free, monthly *Express* (ⓦgayexpress.co.nz). There's an annual Out in the Park festival (ⓦoutinthepark.co.nz), usually around Valentine's Day.

Alice Forresters Lane, off Tory St; map pp.416–417. At the far end of the same laneway as *Motel*, a neon-lit rabbit disappearing down a hole leads you into this Lewis Carroll-inspired fantasyland where cocktails such as the Mad Hatter's Tea Party (vanilla vodka and iced peppermint tea) are served in teapots and china cups. An internal door connects *Alice* with *Boogie Wonderland*. Wed–Sat 5pm–3am.

The Backbencher Pub 34 Molesworth St, at Kate Sheppard St ☎ 04 472 3065, ⓦ backbencher.co.nz; map pp.416–417. A favourite with MPs and civil servants for the satirical cartoons and the convivial pub ambience. Try one of the dozen or more draught beers and the hearty meals named after current MPs. Daily 7am–11pm.

★ **Crumpet** 109 Manners St ☎ 04 803 3846; map pp.416–417. It looks like an English tea shoppe, and it does indeed serve tasty crumpets ($8) and sterling coffee, but the real reason to come is alcoholic reinvigoration. Try their gin shrubb ($10.50), or just tell one of the "brothers" what mood you're in, and they will create something wonderful to suit. Sun–Thurs 10am–11pm, Fri & Sat 10am–3am.

Foxglove 33 Queens Wharf ☎ 04 460 9410, ⓦ foxglovebar.co.nz; map pp.416–417. *Foxglove* is a popular locals' bar serving decent food with harbour views. What makes it different is the wardrobe on the first floor – when you walk through you enter a cosy little cocktail bar with DJs (though sadly no lion or witch). Daily 11.30am–late.

Goldings Free Dive 14 Leeds St ☎ 04 381 3616, ⓦ goldingsfreedive.co.nz; map pp.416–417. Small bar with even smaller balcony packed with office workers, families and hipsters. Short solid selection of craft beers, ciders, NZ wines and 6 barrel sodas, but apparently some people come just for their authentic Italian pizza. Mon–Thurs noon–10.30pm, Fri & Sat noon – "when it dies down".

Hawthorn Lounge 82 Tory St ☎ 04 890 3724; map pp.416–417. Spot the inconspicuous staircase up to this cocktail bar that's all dark wood and upholstered chairs. Their drinks menu changes frequently, entertainingly daft names undermining the skilled mixology. Tues–Fri 6pm–the early hours, Sat 7pm–3am.

Hopgarden 13 Pirie St ☎ 04 801 8807, ⓦ thehopgarden .co.nz; map pp.416–417. Get through the Hobbit-hole entrance and you're in a sheltered open-air bar, with smart dining room at the back. There's a good range of craft beers, some very good snacks (from pork scratchings to arancini) and fancy meals (all mains under $30) – leave room for the beignets ($14). Mon & Tues 3pm–late, Wed–Fri 11.30am–late, Sat & Sun 10.30am–late.

★ **The Library** Level 1, 53 Courtenay Place ☎ 04 382 8593, ⓦ thelibrary.co.nz; map pp.416–417. Ultra-cool book-lined cocktail bar with separate rooms (including one that looks like your granny's lounge with a bath in it) and a cornucopia of nooks and crannies where you can sip on excellent drinks and listen to the live music. Service can be famously slow. Sun–Thurs 5pm–late, Fri & Sat 4pm–late.

Little Beer Quarter 6 Edward St ☎ 04 803 3304, ⓦ littlebeerquarter.co.nz; map pp.416–417. A suitably dingy bar where you can nibble on a pint of sausage rolls ($11) while you browse the craft beer menu. Tues–Sat noon–3am, Mon 3.30pm–3am, Sun 3pm–late.

★ **The Malthouse** 48 Courtenay Place ☎ 04 802 5484, ⓦ themalthouse.co.nz; map pp.416–417. In a lounge setting with low sofas, high stools and sleek glossy timber tables, this drinker's paradise has around thirty different brews on tap plus some 150 varieties by the bottle. The choice includes some of New Zealand's finest craft brews described in detailed tasting notes by top Kiwi beer commentator Neil Miller. There's a great selection of malt whiskies too. Sun & Mon 3–11pm, Tues & Wed 3pm–late, Thurs noon–late, Fri & Sat noon–3am.

Matterhorn 106 Cuba St ☎ 04 384 3359, ⓦ matterhorn .co.nz; map pp.416–417. Uber-stylish cocktail bar and restaurant (see p.437) with regular live and electronic music. Try the basil and manuka honey Martini at the long bar. Pricy but worth it. Mon–Sat 3pm–late, Sun 1pm–late.

Motel Bar Foresters Lane ☎ 04 384 9084; map pp.416–417. Accessed off an atmospheric back alley, this New York-style, first-floor bar with a tiny sign, surveillance camera and an intercom to buzz visitors up was once so exclusive it famously turned away Liv Tyler when she was shooting *Lord of the Rings*. It still cuts it, with semi-private booths, cool sounds and serious cocktails. Mon–Thurs 5pm–3am, Fri & Sat 6pm–3am.

Rogue and Vagabond 18 Garrett St ☎ 04 381 2321, ⓦ rogueandvagabond.co.nz; map pp.416–417. It might not look much, but they dish up a good choice of craft beers, filling bar grub and there's live music (jazz, blues, funk) at least four nights a week. Plus it's on Glover Park, which they've annexed with bean bags. And there's Bruce himself... Open daily 11am–late.

S&M's 176 Cuba St ☎ 04 802 5335, ⓦ scottyandmals .co.nz; map pp.416–417. A stylish, alternative bar that is friendly and happening. Features DJs on Fri and Sat, plus the occasional live show on the corner stage, or private events downstairs. They'll order in food from *Midnight Espresso*. Tues–Thurs, Sun 5pm–midnight, Fri 5pm–3am, Sat 7pm–3am.

Southern Cross 39 Abel Smith St ☎ 04 384 9085, ⓦ thecross.co.nz; map pp.416–417. Cavernous bar divided into some cosy spaces with a heated Balinese-style outdoor garden (and hot water bottles and blankets in winter), this charming local hosts everything from a knitting circle (Mon) to music quiz nights (Thurs) and dancing classes (Sun), plus live music on Wednesdays and weekends. New Zealand beers are well represented on tap, and the great pub grub includes snacks such as bowls of cheerios (not the breakfast cereal but Kiwi cocktail sausages). Daily 9am–late.

7

CLUBS AND LIVE MUSIC VENUES

Live bands are a regular fixture across town, so check out the bars listed above as well as the clubs below, dedicated smaller venues or bigger halls such as the TSB Bank Arena and occasionally free concerts at the waterfront Frank Kitts Park or Civic Square.

Bodega 101 Ghuznee St ☎ 04 384 8212, ⓦ bodega .co.nz; map pp.416–417. New Zealand's longest-running music venue hosts cutting-edge Kiwi bands and the odd offbeat international act. Usually Tues–Fri 4pm–3am, Sat 8pm–3am.

Boogie Wonderland 25 Courtenay Place; map pp.416–417. Wild and wonderfully cheesy, so if you love flares, disco and mirror balls then this retro joint is for you. Free entry

through *Alice*. Cover typically $10–20. Wed–Sat 10pm–2am. **San Francisco Bathhouse** 171 Cuba St ☎ 04 801 6797, ⓦ sanfran.co.nz; map pp.416–417. Not a bathhouse and, obviously, not San Franciscan, but the city's main indie, alternative rock and reggae venue, with a balcony looking out on the assorted life passing along Cuba St. First-rate Kiwi bands are occasionally joined by international acts. Most gigs $15–60, though some are free. Thurs–Sat 3pm–late, Tues & Wed 3pm–1am.

Valhalla 154 Vivian St; map pp.416–417. A lively, well-respected venue with a tradition of metal gigs plus everything from hardcore and goth to ukeleles, from emerging and established artists. Occasional cover $5–10. Wed–Sat 5pm–late (bands on at 8pm)

ENTERTAINMENT

Performing arts are strong in Wellington, which is home to several professional theatres, the Royal New Zealand Ballet, the New Zealand Symphony Orchestra and assorted opera and dance companies. In addition to its quota of multiplexes, Wellington also has a smattering of art-house cinemas: you can usually save a couple of dollars by going during the day or any time early in the week.

ESSENTIALS

Listings The best introduction is the *Wellington – What's On* booklet, free from the i-SITE and from accommodation around the city. There are also listings in the *Dominion Post* (ⓦ dompost.co.nz) on weekends.

Tickets Book tickets direct at venues or, for a small fee, through Ticketek (☎ 0800 842 538, ⓦ ticketek.co.nz) which has an outlet at the Michael Fowler Centre, 111 Wakefield St.

THEATRES AND CONCERT HALLS

Bats Theatre 1 Kent Terrace ☎ 04 802 4175, ⓦ bats .co.nz. Lively theatre (recently saved from demolition by Peter Jackson) that concentrates on developmental works served up at affordable prices (usually under $20), with discounts for backpacker card-holders.

Circa 1 Taranaki St, at Cable St ☎ 04 801 7992, ⓦ circa .co.nz. One of the country's liveliest and most innovative professional theatres, which has fostered the skills of some of the best-known Kiwi directors and actors.

Michael Fowler Centre 111 Wakefield St ☎ 04 801 4231, ⓦ pwv.co.nz. Award-winning building showing touring comedy, classical music, and ballet.

Opera House 111–113 Manners St ☎ 04 801 4231, ⓦ pwv.co.nz. Hosts touring opera, ballet and musicals. Sneak from the foyer into *Crumpet*.

St James Theatre 77–87 Courtenay Place ☎ 04 801 4231, ⓦ pwv.co.nz. This refurbished theatre in a fine 1912 building is the major venue for the Royal New Zealand Ballet and hosts opera, dance, musicals and plays. It also has a licensed café for pre- and post-performance drinks.

Westpac Stadium (Wellington Regional Stadium) Featherston St ☎ 04 473 3881, ⓦ westpacstadium .co.nz. Dubbed "the cake tin" by its detractors for its iron-clad

design, this modern purpose-built stadium is the venue for rugby and cricket as well as occasional rock concerts.

CINEMAS

Embassy 10 Kent Terrace ☎ 04 384 7657, ⓦ deluxe .co.nz. Mainstream and independent movies are shown on a single giant screen at this city-centre cinema.

Lighthouse 29 Wigan St ☎ 04 385 3337, ⓦ lighthouse cuba.co.nz. Plush modern cinema with three small screens, some rather fine pies and a programme mixing relayed theatre and opera, as well as mainstream and art-house films.

Nga Taonga Sound and Vision 84 Taranaki St, at Ghuznee St ☎ 04 384 7647, ⓦ ngataonga.org.nz. Cheap coffee, knowledgeable staff, evening screenings. For more information, see p.421.

Paramount 25 Courtenay Place ☎ 04 384 4080, ⓦ paramount.co.nz. Central 1917-established multi-screen showing art and mainstream films with the added indulgence of being able to watch while sipping a beer or wine.

Reading Cinemas 100 Courtenay Place ☎ 04 801 4600, ⓦ readingcinemas.co.nz. Shows mostly main-stream movies with the option of going for their plush Gold Lounge seats (from $20) which come with an in-seat food and drink service.

The Roxy 5 Park Rd, Miramar ☎ 04 388 5555, ⓦ roxycinema.co.nz. The Roxy has been lovingly refurbished and redesigned in 1930s style. Apart from its two screens, it boasts a glorious cocktail bar and restaurant, *CoCo* (p.438), where jazz bands re-create the feel of a premier on Sundays (5pm). Check out the details, the bronze of Gollum, the light fittings, pillars, door pulls and toilets – a positive Weta dream for anybody who is a fan. Daily 9am–10pm or so.

WELLINGTON FESTIVALS

Whenever you visit Wellington there's a good chance there'll be some sort of festival happening. The visitor centre has full details; the following are the biggest occasions, listed chronologically.

Summer City Festival (ⓦwellington.govt .nz) A council-sponsored series of free concerts, cultural events and performances around town. January–March.

Wellington Fringe Festival (ⓦfringe.co.nz) Vibrant affair run as a separate and roughly concurrent event to the International Arts Festival, filling the inner city with street and indoor theatre. Usually held in late February or early March.

New Zealand International Arts Festival (ⓦfestival.co.nz) The country's biggest cultural event lasts a full month and draws top performers from around the world. Fashioned along the lines of the Edinburgh Festival, it celebrates the huge diversity of the arts: classical music, jazz and pop, opera, puppet shows, cabaret, poetry readings, traditional Maori dance, modern ballet and

experimental works. Most venues are in the city centre. Usually held in February and March in even-numbered years.

Wellington International Film Festival (ⓦnzff.co.nz) The Wellington leg of the nationwide film tour screens less mainstream offerings at cinemas around town. Tickets around $18. Usually late July to early August.

Wellington on a Plate (ⓦwellingtonona plate.com) Celebrates the capital's cuisine through tastings, talks and behind-the-stoves tours as well as discounted menus at top restaurants. Last two weeks of August.

World of WearableArt (WOW) (ⓦworldofwearableart.com) Tickets go like hot cakes for this glorious spectacle of weird costumes which runs like a bizarre fashion show. Usually last two weeks of September.

7

SHOPPING

Bookshops Unity Books (57 Willis St; Mon–Thurs 9am–6pm, Fri 9am–7pm, Sat 10am–6pm, Sun 11am–5pm; ☎04 499 4245, ⓦunitybooks.co.nz) has the best selection of New Zealand and special interest titles, plus more mainstream titles. For mainstream titles, try Whitcoulls, with locations at 226 Lambton Quay and 91

Cuba St; for secondhand books, try Pegasus at 204a Left Bank Cuba Mall, or Arty Bee's Books, 106 Manners St.

Camping and outdoor equipment Several good shops – Bivouac, Macpac and Kathmandu – cluster around the junction of Willis and Mercer sts.

DIRECTORY

Automobile Association 342–352 Lambton Quay ☎04 931 9999.

Banks and foreign exchange Banks are dotted all over the city centre CBD. To change money head to ANZ at 215–229 Lambton Quay, BNZ at 38 Willis St and Travelex at 120 Lambton Quay.

Embassies and consulates Australia, 72–76 Hobson St, Thorndon ☎04 473 6411; Canada, 125 The Terrace ☎04 473 9577; UK, 44 Hill St ☎04 924 2888; US, 29 Fitzherbert Terrace, Thorndon ☎04 462 6000. For other countries, check online.

Emergencies Police, fire and ambulance ☎111. Wellington Central Police Station is on the corner of Victoria and Harris sts (☎04 381 2000).

Internet Plenty of places, many along Courtenay Place, generally charge $4–8/hr. There's free access at the library.

Library Central Library, 65 Victoria St ☎04 801 4040. Mon–Fri 9.30am–8.30pm, Sat 9.30am–5pm, Sun 1–4pm.

Medical emergencies For emergency treatment try the After Hours Medical Centre, 17 Adelaide Rd, Newtown, near Basin Reserve (daily 8am–11pm; ☎04 384 4944). Wellington Hospital is on Riddiford St, Newtown (☎04 385 5999).

Pharmacy Urgent Pharmacy, 17 Adelaide Rd, Newtown (Mon–Fri 9am–11pm, Sat, Sun & public holidays 8am–11pm; ☎04 385 8810), is open late.

Post office Several throughout the city centre; for poste restante go to 2 Manners St.

Swimming Freyberg Pool and Fitness Centre, 139 Oriental Parade (daily 6am–9pm; ☎04 801 4530), has a 33m indoor pool ($5.90 to swim), plus gym, spas, saunas, steam room, fitness classes and massage therapy. Thorndon Pool, 26 Murphy St (Oct–April Mon–Thurs 6.30am–8pm, Fri 6.30am–7pm, Sat & Sun 7.30am–7pm; $5.90) is a 30.5m heated outdoor pool near Parliament.

Marlborough, Nelson and Kaikoura

SEAWARD KAIKOURA RANGE, KAIKOURA

Marlborough, Nelson and Kaikoura

The South Island kicks off spectacularly in a blaze of indented bays and secluded hideaways along the northern coast, then descends in a sweep of golden beaches to an impressive array of national parks, sophisticated wineries and natural wonders. Most visitors arrive by ferry, striking land at Picton – drab in the winter, lively in the summer and surrounded by the beautiful Marlborough Sounds. Here, bays full of unfathomably deep water lap at tiny beaches, each with its rickety boat jetty, and the land rises steeply to forest or stark pasture. To the west, lively Nelson is the springboard for forays into the wilds of Abel Tasman National Park, with the country's most gorgeous walking tracks and dazzling golden beaches; while further north the relatively isolated Golden Bay offers peaceful times with uniformly decent weather. The curve of the bay culminates in a long sandy bar that juts into the ocean – Farewell Spit, an extraordinary and unique habitat bordering Kahurangi National Park, through which the rugged and spectacular Heaphy Track forges a route to the West Coast.

The least visited of the region's well-preserved areas of natural splendour is the sparsely populated **Nelson Lakes National Park**, principally a spot for tramping to alpine lakes or fishing, though the nearby **Buller River** also attracts raft and kayak rats.

South of **Picton**, slurp your merry way through **Marlborough**, New Zealand's most feted winemaking region centred on the modest towns of **Blenheim** and **Renwick**. A night or two in one of the rural B&Bs and some time spent around the wineries happily balances the more energetic activities of the national parks, and sets you up nicely for a few days of ecotourism in **Kaikoura** where **whale watching** and **swimming with dolphins** and **seals** are the main draws.

The region's **weather** is some of the sunniest in the land, particularly around Blenheim and Nelson, which regularly compete for the honour of the greatest number of sunshine hours in New Zealand.

LAKE ROTOITI, NELSON LAKES NATIONAL PARK

Highlights

① The Queen Charlotte Track This beautiful multi-day hike is made all the more manageable by staying in great backpackers and B&Bs, and having your bags carried for you. **See p.456**

② Nelson A vibrant arts community, vineyards on the doorstep, a laidback atmosphere and great weather combine to make Nelson an essential stop. **See p.459**

③ Abel Tasman National Park Crystal-clear water and golden beaches are rewards for hiking the lush Coast Track or kayaking the myriad inlets and islands. **See p.472**

④ Farewell Spit tours The original Farewell Spit Safari is the only way to access this unique place. **See p.486**

⑤ Heaphy Track The huge range of dramatic scenery and final sense of achievement puts this Great Walk up with the best. **See p.488**

⑥ Marlborough Wine Country No trip to this area is complete without supping Sauvignon Blanc in New Zealand's most famous wine region. **See p.496**

⑦ Kaikoura Whale-watching and dolphin-swimming trips from this pretty town are the highlight of many a visitor's trip. **See p.499**

HIGHLIGHTS ARE MARKED ON THE MAP ON P.446

GETTING AROUND

By ferry and train Cross Cook Strait by ferry (see p.431) and link up with the region's only train, from Picton to Christchurch (Oct–April;1 daily).

By bus Buses fill in the gaps, doing the Picton–Christchurch run via Kaikoura and to Blenheim and Nelson where there are connections for the Abel Tasman National Park and Golden Bay. The main operators running between Picton and Christchurch are Atomic Shuttles (☏03 349 0697, ⊛atomictravel.co.nz), Nakedbus (⊛nakedbus.com), and InterCity (☏09 583 5780, ⊛intercitycoach.co.nz).

MARLBOROUGH, NELSON & KAIKOURA

HIGHLIGHTS
1. The Queen Charlotte Track
2. Nelson
3. Abel Tasman National Park
4. Farewell Spit tours
5. Heaphy Track
6. Marlborough Wine Country
7. Kaikoura

The Marlborough Sounds

The **Marlborough Sounds** are undeniably picturesque, a stimulating filigree of bays, inlets, islands and peninsulas rising abruptly from the water to rugged, lush green wilderness and open farmland. Large parts are only accessible by sea, which also provides the ideal vantage point. The area is part working farms, including salmon or mussel farms, and part reserve – a mixture of islands, sections of coast and land-bound tracts. The Sounds' nexus, **Picton**, is the jumping-off point for **Queen Charlotte Sound** where cruises and water taxis provide access to the undemanding, varied and scenic **Queen Charlotte Track**. Heading west, Queen Charlotte Drive winds precipitously to the small community of **Havelock**, New Zealand's green-lipped mussel capital; turn off to explore the spectacular vistas of Pelorus Sound and take the back roads or a boat to view the rich, swirling waters of French Pass.

Picton

Cook Strait ferries from Wellington arrive in **Picton**, a small harbour and tourist town sandwiched between hills and Queen Charlotte Sound. Many people stop only for a coffee, looking out over the water before pressing on, but Picton is the best base for exploring the **Queen Charlotte Track**, serviced by several water taxis, and a good spot for getting into the Sounds on **cruises and kayak trips**. The town itself has a few noteworthy attractions and it also makes a decent base for exploring the **wine region** around Blenheim, half an hour's drive to the south.

8

Brief history

There was a European settlement in the region as early as 1827 when John Guard established a whaling station, but Picton itself didn't come into being until the New Zealand Company purchased its site for £300 in 1848. Picton flourished as a port and **service town** for the Wairau Plains to the south but developed predominantly as the most convenient port for travel between the islands.

The Edwin Fox

Close to the ferry terminal • Daily: Dec–March 9am–5pm; April–Nov 9am–3pm • $10

At its western end of Picton's phoenix-palm-lined waterfront, close to the ferry terminal, the hulk of the 1600-tonne, Calcutta-built **Edwin Fox** is the last of some four thousand "East Indiamen" that once brought migrants to New Zealand. This 1853 example operated as a troop carrier in the Crimean War, transported convicts to Australia and helped establish New Zealand's frozen meat trade before being towed to Picton in 1967. A small but well-designed museum prepares you for the age-blackened

---

HIKING AROUND PICTON

The best of the local trails run through Victoria Domain, a mostly bush-clad peninsula immediately east of Picton. Many of the trails link, so pick up one of the several widely available free maps in town.

Bob's Bay Track (1km one way; 30min; gently undulating). Starting at Shelly Beach, this extends along the shoreline to a safe swimming and picnicking beach providing great views across the water to the ferry terminal and up Queen Charlotte Sound. From Bob's Bay a short steep path climbs away to the Harbour View parking area.
The Snout (5km one way; 1hr 15min; 200m

ascent on return). From Harbour View parking area follow the top of the ridge past Queen Charlotte View to the tip of the promontory, whose evocative Maori name, Te Ihumoeone-ihu, translates as "the nose of the sand worm".
Tirohanga Track (3km one way; 1hr 15min; 300m ascent). Starting on Newgate Street this is a fairly strenuous walk up the hills behind Picton, passing the lovely Hilltop Viewpoint.

hull of the ninth-oldest ship in the world. Standing on the small part of the lower deck that remains gives a sense of what it must have been like to sail, but the best bit is in the large open hold, all heavy planking and teak ribs.

Eco World

Next to the *Edwin Fox* • Daily: Dec–Feb 9.30am–7pm; March–Dec 9.30am–5.00pm; feeding at 11am & 2pm • $22 • W ecoworldnz.co.nz

Eco World offers an insight into the flora and fauna of the Marlborough Sounds with local marine life (including little blue penguins), a few small sharks, a preserved giant

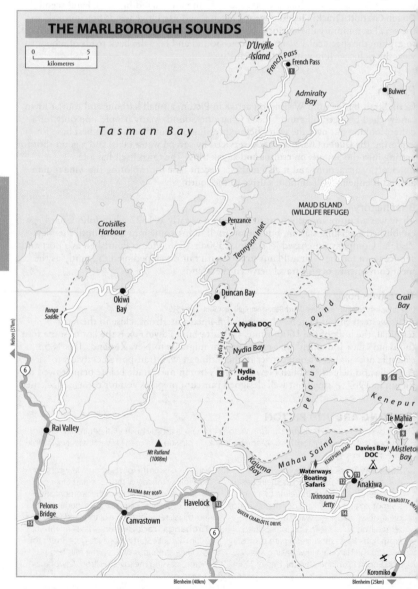

THE MARLBOROUGH SOUNDS

quid plus tuatara, including babies, giant weta, and a breeding programme for
yellow-crowned kakariki. It is best visited at feeding time. They also have the only
cinema in town.

Picton Community Museum

London Quay • Daily 10am–4pm • $5

At the end of the High Street, the **Picton Community Museum** uses photos, a harpoon
gun and some excellent examples of carved whalebone (scrimshaw) to illustrate the

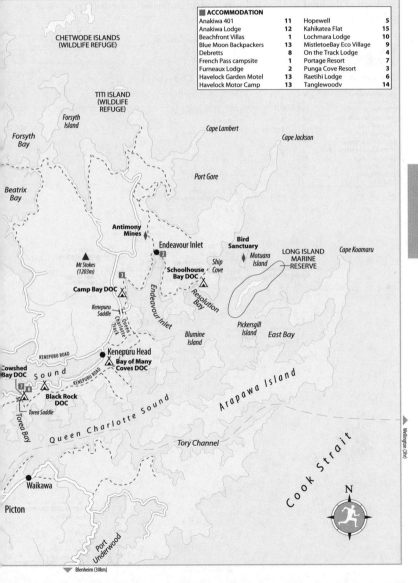

ACCOMMODATION			
Anakiwa 401	11	Hopewell	5
Anakiwa Lodge	12	Kahikatea Flat	15
Beachfront Villas	1	Lochmara Lodge	10
Blue Moon Backpackers	13	MistletoeBay Eco Village	9
Debretts	8	On the Track Lodge	4
French Pass campsite	1	Portage Resort	7
Furneaux Lodge	2	Punga Cove Resort	3
Havelock Garden Motel	13	Raetihi Lodge	6
Havelock Motor Camp	13	Tanglewoodv	14

8

working life of the Perano Whaling Station, which operated in Queen Charlotte Sound until 1964. Recently extended, there are also displays of Maori *taonga*, and the scarred chair of a whale lookout, each notch showing a kill.

National Whale Centre

London Quay • Tues–Sun 11am–6pm • Free • Ⓦ aworldwithwhales.com

Formerly a virtual museum, this newly-opened waterfront centre aims to share all aspects of current research on international biodiversity and cetacean protection. There's material on the history of Maori and Pakeha relations with whales, including a rundown of the local whaling industry, and an emphasis in the displays towards new technology and modern art.

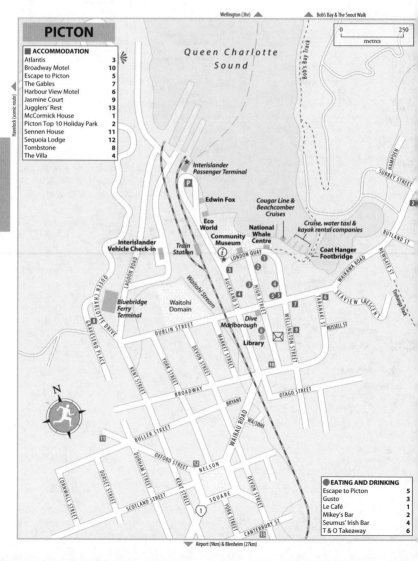

PICTON

ACCOMMODATION	
Atlantis	3
Broadway Motel	10
Escape to Picton	5
The Gables	7
Harbour View Motel	6
Jasmine Court	9
Jugglers' Rest	13
McCormick House	1
Picton Top 10 Holiday Park	2
Sennen House	11
Sequoia Lodge	12
Tombstone	8
The Villa	4

● EATING AND DRINKING	
Escape to Picton	5
Gusto	3
Le Café	1
Mikey's Bar	2
Seumus' Irish Bar	4
T & O Takeaway	6

ARRIVAL AND DEPARTURE PICTON

By ferry Interislander ferry foot passengers disembark close to the town centre, while Bluebridge foot passengers and all vehicles disembark on the western side of town about 1km from the centre; Bluebridge operates a free shuttle bus to the i-SITE.

Destinations Wellington (6–9 daily).

By train Interislander ferry schedules work in with the summer-only *TranzCoastal* train to Christchurch (one-way fares from $75).

Destinations Christchurch, via Blenheim and Kaikoura

(daily Oct–April; 1 daily).

By bus Buses stop outside the Interislander ferry terminal and again at the i-SITE.

Destinations Blenheim (8 daily; 30min); Christchurch (4–5 daily; 5hr–5hr 30min); Kaikoura (4–5 daily; 2hr 15min); Nelson (5 daily; 2hr).

By plane Picton airport, 9km south of town, is served by Soundsair (☎0800 505 005, ⊛soundsair.com). A bus ($7 one way) meets flights and runs into Picton.

Destinations Wellington (6 daily).

GETTING AROUND

By bus Ritchies (☎03 578 5467) and InterCity go to Blenheim. The half-hour run costs $10–16.

By mail bus The Rural Mail Bus Service (☎027 255 8882) is a minivan serving remote spots linking the main post offices in Havelock and Picton, and the southern end of the Queen Charlotte Track at Anakiwa. There are several runs each day. Fares start at $15.

By car Most major international and domestic companies

have offices at the ferry terminal or around town. The i-SITE has a freesheet listing them.

By taxi Picton Shuttles ☎027 696 5207.

By water taxi A number of companies run services around the sound, as well as cruises (see box, p.454), including: Beachcomber Fun Cruises (☎0800 624 526, ⊛beachcomber cruises.co.nz); Cougar Line (☎0800 504 090, ⊛cougarline .co.nz); Arrow (☎03 573 8229, ⊛arrowwatertaxis.co.nz).

INFORMATION AND ACTIVITIES

Visitor information The combined i-SITE and DOC office is on the foreshore, a 5min walk from the ferry terminal (Mon–Fri 9am–5pm, Sat & Sun 8am–4pm, an hour later every day in the summer; ☎03 520 3113, ⊛marlboroughnz .com). It's packed with leaflets on the town and the rest of the South Island, including a free *Picton and Blenheim* map and DOC's free *Queen Charlotte Track* visitor guide.

Scuba diving Dive Marlborough (59 High St; ☎03 573 7831, ⊛godive.co.nz) offers scuba discovery dives in the

reserve ($225), two-tank guided days ($185) and 24hr liveaboard trips ($330 incl. transport and gear) diving the *Mikhail Lermontov*, a Soviet cruise ship that became the southern hemisphere's largest diveable wreck when it hit rocks in 1986. For the latter you'll need experience at 30m in cold water. They also organize trips to Abel Tasman and off Kaikoura.

Winery tours Tours of the Marlborough Wine Country are covered in detail on p.496. Most pick up from Picton.

ACCOMMODATION

Atlantis London Quay ☎03 573 7390, ⊛atlantishostel .co.nz. Central hostel, close to the ferry, with a variety of colourfully decorated dorms (some without windows), cosy doubles and free breakfasts in an old diving school, though the communal facilities need a little TLC. Dorms $23, doubles $58

Broadway Motel 113 Picton High St ☎0800 101 919, ⊛broadwaymotel.co.nz. Attractive, relatively modern motel units with large windows and all the usual mod-cons, including Sky TV and wi-fi. Everything is clean and well-kept and they have a good recycling policy. $149

Escape to Picton 33 Wellington St ☎03 573 5573, ⊛escapetopicton.com. Chic, tiny boutique hotel finished to the highest standard (including freestanding baths in two of the three suites) and authentic Thai massage treatments. Rates vary widely so it pays to check their website. $350

The Gables 20 Waikawa Rd ☎03 573 6772, ⊛thegables.co.nz. Pleasant and welcoming B&B with three rooms in the house (one with en suite) and two self-contained cottages out back where breakfast can be

provided. Children and dogs welcome. Rooms $160, cottages $175

Harbour View Motel 30 Waikawa Rd ☎0800 101 133, ⊛harbourviewpicton.co.nz. Twelve spacious and tastefully appointed self-contained units, each with a balcony and great views over the harbour. Guests are treated to a variety of well-kept clean units with a communal laundry and luggage storage if you're going on the Queen Charlotte Track. $165

★**Jasmine Court** 78 Wellington St ☎0800 421 999, ⊛jasminecourt.co.nz. Top-of-the-line medium-sized motel with luxury units, recently extended and revamped, professionally run by a couple prepared to go that extra mile. Rooms include DVD and CD players, and some have spa baths and verandas. Free wi-fi. Standard $165, with spa $185

Jugglers' Rest 8 Canterbury St ☎03 573 5570, ⊛jugglersrest.com. Small, very welcoming and relaxed shoes-off hostel about a 10min walk from the ferries, with spacious dorms (no bunks) and a couple of quiet rooms in the grounds. There's a strong recycling ethic and the

8

vegetable garden is open to all. You can book breakfast of home-made jam and fresh bread. Closed June–Sept. Dorms $33, rooms $70

McCormick House 21 Leicester St ☎03 573 5253, ⓦ mccormickhouse.co.nz. Situated in a half acre of native garden, this atmospheric Edwardian villa has an original rimu-panelled staircase, at the top of which are three luxurious, individually decorated rooms. The indulgent breakfasts are made from local produce, and there's a good stock of Kiwi movies and music in the lounge. $350

Picton Top 10 Holiday Park 78 Waikawa Rd ☎0800 277 444, ⓦ pictontop10.co.nz. Centrally located campsite with swimming pool, children's playground, cabins ($78–98, bedding $5) and motel-style self-contained units in a pleasant spot with sheltering trees. Camping $22, units $128

Sennen House 9 Oxford St ☎03 573 5216, ⓦ sennenhouse.co.nz. Just a 10-minute walk from town, this gorgeous, grand 1886 villa has been tastefully converted into a B&B with three suites, all with kitchen facilities. A welcome wine and a breakfast hamper are supplied. $319

Sequoia Lodge 3 Nelson Square ☎0800 222 257, ⓦ sequoialodge.co.nz. Very popular, well-organized

hostel shoehorned onto a site 10min walk from the town centre; make use of the free ferry pick-ups. Beds and bunks come with lights and side tables, rooms have heated towel rails, and there's a separate, en-suite female dorm. Breakfast, hammocks, spa, nightly pudding and ice cream, wi-fi and home cinema are all free. Dorm $27, en suites $8?

★**Tombstone** 16 Gravesend Place ☎0800 573 7116, ⓦ tombstonebp.co.nz. Wonderfully friendly, well-run hostel right by the town cemetery, and an easy walk from the port. The purpose-built accommodation has great views of the water and is carpeted and double-glazed, making it super-quiet. The barbecue area, piano, table tennis, gym machines, hot tub, wi-fi, bikes and fresh breakfast scones come at no extra charge. Dorms can be single-sex, private rooms come with electric blankets and a balcony, and there's a one-bedroom self-contained flat ($118). Dorms $27, rooms $82

The Villa 34 Auckland St ☎03 573 6598, ⓦ thevilla.co.nz. Central associate YHA set in two houses, and a more modern cottage. When busy it is cramped, but there are all manner of free inducements such as bikes, wi-fi, outdoor spa (with rubber ducks), gym and apple crumble in winter. There's also a women-only 6-bed dorm ($29). Dorms $27, rooms $72

EATING, DRINKING AND ENTERTAINMENT

Escape to Picton 33 Wellington St ☎03 573 5573. You can pop in to this former bank for a beer (the only Heineken on tap in the town) or bistro fare ($17.50–32.50) such as gourmet fish and chips. Live music on Fridays and Saturdays. Mon–Fri 10am–2.30pm & 5pm–late, Sat & Sun 11am–late.

★**Gusto** 33 High St ☎03 573 7171. Cosy and popular, this daytime café opens up onto the street and dishes up delicious breakfasts along with a short menu of daily specials, including marinated lamb couscous with yoghurt ($19), cakes and good coffee. Summer daily, closed Sat in winter, 7.30am–2.30pm.

Le Café 14 London Quay ☎03 573 5588, ⓦ lecafepicton .co.nz. Bustling, popular and stylish café and bar with pavement seating just across from the Sounds, serving mouthwatering steaks with home-made chilli jam and all sorts of fresh seafood. Lunch mains around $20, dinners

$30. Bands play regularly in the summer. Daily 7.30am–late.

Mikey's Bar 18 High St ☎03 573 5164. Modern bar with very cheap food (all under $27, most around $15), a pool table, and a barn-like nightclub out back where DJs and bands trying to scrape together enough money to play somewhere bigger perform at the weekends. Daily 11.30am–11pm.

Seumus' Irish Bar 25 Wellington St. Poky Irish bar popular with backpackers for their inexpensive drinks and food (pizzas under $21). There's outdoor seating and live music on Fridays. Daily 3pm–1am.

T & O Takeaway 85 High St ☎03 573 6115. Serves the freshest and best fish and chips in town, plus a variety of other fruits of the sea, all under $10 and usually cooked to order. Mon 4.30–7.30pm, Tues–Fri 10.30am–1.30pm & 4.30–7.30pm, Sat & Sun 11am–1.30pm & 4.30–8pm.

DIRECTORY

Internet Free access during opening hours at the library and free wi-fi in the centre of town.
Library 67 High St (Mon–Fri 8am–5pm, Sat 10am–1pm, Sun 1.30–4.30pm).

Luggage storage Most lodgings store luggage while you walk the Queen Charlotte Track. The i-SITE has large luggage lockers ($4/day).

Queen Charlotte Sound

Picton is a pretty spot, but you've barely touched the region's beauty until you've explored **Queen Charlotte Sound**. This wildly indented series of drowned valleys encloses moody picturesque bays, small deserted sandy beaches, headlands with

BIKING THE QUEEN CHARLOTTE TRACK

Though the Queen Charlotte Track (see box, pp.456–457) is primarily for hikers, **mountain-bikers** can ride the whole thing in a day or two. There are two steep ascents but nothing overly technical, and with pack transfers and abundant accommodation you won't need to lug heavy panniers. Most of the track is open to bikers year-round, though the northern quarter (Ship Cove–Camp Bay) is off-limits from December to February.

Marlborough Sounds Adventure Company (see box, p.454) operates a three-day Freedom Bike Ride ($605–685) with bike rental, transfers and comfortable accommodation at *Punga Cove* and *Portage Resort*. Alternatively, you cant rent a mountain bike ($60/day) from either Marlborough Sounds Adventure or Sea Kayak Adventures (see box, p.454) and organize your own trip, either camping or staying in cheaper accommodation.

panoramic views and cloistered islands, while grand, lumpy peninsulas offer shelter from the winds and storms, and solitude for the contemplative fisherman or kayaker. For a taste of these labyrinthine waterways, take one of the many **day-cruises** from Picton, but to really appreciate the tranquil beauty you're better off **kayaking** round the bays or **tramping** the Queen Charlotte Track (see box, pp.456–457). The relatively calm and warm waters of the Sounds also give the opportunity for **scuba diving**, checking out the rich marine life of the huge wreck of a Soviet cruise ship, the *Mikhail Lermontov* (see p.451).

Motuara Island

A couple of sights at the far end of Queen Charlotte Sound crop up on most itineraries, including the DOC-managed **Motuara Island**, a predator-free wildlife sanctuary that is home to the saddleback, South Island bush robin, bellbird and a few Okarito brown kiwi. All the birds are quite fearless and will rest and fly startlingly close to you. Throughout the island, little blue penguins choose to nest in boxes provided, rather than build their own, and in spring (Oct–Dec), you can gently lift the top of the box and see the baby penguins.

Just across a channel from Motuara Island, **Ship Cove** marks the bay where Captain Cook spent a total of 168 days during his three trips to New Zealand. A large concrete monument – a disappointingly dull block surrounded by cannon – commemorates his five separate visits to the cove.

Queen Charlotte Drive

The 35km Queen Charlotte Drive between Picton and Havelock is a picturesque and spectacular back road, which slides past the flat plain at the head of Queen Charlotte Sound and climbs into the hills overlooking Pelorus Sound before descending to SH6 and Havelock itself. It is a slow and winding drive, but you may want to take it even slower by stopping to wander down to a couple of sheltered coves or up the **Cullen Track** (a 10min walk with spectacular views). With water taxis providing convenient access to fabulous out-of-the-way spots, it may seem a little perverse to try to see the Marlborough Sounds by car – doubly so when you start weaving your way around the slow, narrow roads – but ultimately it is well worth the effort as the views of turquoise bays, seen through the ponga, are magical.

Around 18km west of Picton, a narrow road heads north to **Anakiwa**, the southern end of the Queen Charlotte Track. Here you'll find a wharf used by water taxis taking hikers back to Picton, *Anakiwa Lodge* and *Anakiwa 401* (see box, pp.456–457), the latter with its coffee caravan.

QUEEN CHARLOTTE SOUND CRUISES AND TOURS

Water taxis (see p.451) are always flitting about Queen Charlotte Sound taking hikers to the Queen Charlotte Track, or delivering guests to swanky lodges. If you just want to get out on the water this may be all you need, but several companies also run excellent **cruises**.

Beachcomber Cruises ☎0800 624 526, ⊛beachcombercruises.co.nz. Although there are many other cruising options for the Sounds, there is still something unique about the Rural Mail Runs, pulling up at a lonely wharf to deliver the post. The journey includes golden beaches with bush-clad shorelines and dolphins sometimes escort the boat. The downside is that you can't get off for a walk or jump off for a swim. The four-hour Magic Mail Run (Mon–Sat 1.30pm; 4hr; $97) leaves from Picton. Three routes are plied on different days of the week, but there's little to choose between them. In summer, all call into Endeavour Inlet, pass a salmon farm and allow fifteen minutes ashore at Ship Cove. Alternative postal routes explore Pelorus Sound from Havelock (see p.455). This operator also offers trips to Ship Cove (3hr; $81) and to Motuara Island (3hr; $85).

Cougar Line ☎0800 504 090, ⊛cougarline.co.nz. The direct competition to Beachcomber Cruises run similar trips, including a Ship Cove Cruise ($85) and scheduled as well as on-demand water taxi services.

Dolphin Watch Nature Tours London Quay ☎0800 945 354, ⊛naturetours.co.nz. Some of the most sympathetic wildlife trips in the Sounds, including dolphin swimming (2–4hr; $165 to swim; $99 to watch) with dusky, common or bottlenose dolphins, as well as sightings of the endemic Hector's dolphins. To combine dolphin-watching with the Sounds' other sights, join their trips to either Motuara Island (45min, guided; $99) or Ship Cove (45min, unguided; $99), both of which can also be used as a drop-off for Queen Charlotte Track walkers. The Birdwatchers Expedition (daily 1.30pm; $99) gives you the chance to tick many New Zealand species off your list – if you're lucky you may get to see an extremely rare king shag. Oct–April only.

Myths and Legends Eco Tours ☎03 573 6901, ⊛eco-tours.co.nz. Run by a sixth-generation local Pakeha and his Maori wife, who tour the bays in their 1930s kauri launch explaining the history and culture of the region ($200/4hr; $250/8hr and lunch; all tours have a two-person minimum).

Queen Charlotte Steam Ship Company ☎03 573 7443, ⊛steamshipping.co.nz. A variation on the standard cruise, with hour-long cruises (on the hour from Short Finger Jetty; $30) puttering about the Sound immediately adjacent to Picton in a small, replica 1920 steel-hull steamboat.

Waterways Boating Safaris 7km along the Kenepuru Rd ☎03 574 1372, ⊛waterways.co.nz. Explore the Sounds in the best drive-it-yourself traditions of New Zealand, via guided flotillas of two-person motorboats on amazing excursions round Kenepuru Sound (half-day $110; full day $150). Follow Leicester, your guide, to out-of-the-way bays and bushwalks, as well as getting a view of a local mussel farm.

KAYAKING

Visitors dashing straight to Abel Tasman National Park sadly overlook the breathtaking views to be had kayaking Queen Charlotte Sound, where other floating traffic is virtually nonexistent by comparison.

Marlborough Sounds Adventure Company London Quay ☎0800 283 283, ⊛marlboroughsounds .co.nz. Friendly and professional outfit offering a huge range of guided kayaking trips including half-day paddles from Picton (Oct–April daily; 4hr; $95), a gentle one-day trip (7hr; $130), a two-day trip, initially guided then camping out by yourselves and paddling home the next day ($190); and a fully guided three-day trip in the outer sounds ($595). Rentals are $60 for one day, $100 for two.

Sea Kayak Adventures At the turn-off for Anakiwa ☎03 574 2765, ⊛nzseakayaking.com. Well-run, enthusiastic and intimate, with half-day ($85) and full-day ($125 with lunch) guided trips, a two-day guided and catered trip ($295) and various paddle and walk or bike options. These guys will help you experience the silence of the Sounds. Independent rentals are $60/day, $100/two days and $125/three days.

Kenepuru Road

A couple of kilometres further along Queen Charlotte Drive, **Kenepuru Road** cuts right and begins its 75km journey out along the shores of Kenepuru Sound. There are many picturesque bays and views along the way and the road provides access to several points along the Queen Charlotte Track, running past a handful of DOC campsites and several places to stay before ending at *Hopewell* backpackers.

Debretts Backpackers Kenepuru Rd, Km51 ☎03 573 2522, ⒲stayportage.co.nz. Tranquil hostel sleeping fifteen, with great views of Portage Bay and Kenepuru Sound. It's a 30min walk from Torea Bay or get them to arrange a taxi. Dorms (linen $5) $45, doubles $100

★ **Hopewell** Double Bay, Kenepuru Sound ☎03 573 5341, ⒲hopewell.co.nz. Gorgeous hostel in a dreamy setting where even a couple of nights isn't enough to fully appreciate the relaxing surroundings. The hosts are welcoming, there's a waterside hot tub, plus kayaks ($20), fishing, mountain bikes, the occasional free evening meal with *kai moana* and opportunities to visit the local mussel farm or go sailing. Access is either on a tortuous 2–3hr drive along Kenepuru Road, or by a sequence of water taxis from Picton ($65/person each way): call the hostel for details. Closed June–Aug. Dorms $40, en suites $140

Raetihi Lodge Double Bay, Kenepuru Sound ☎03 573 4300, ⒲raetihilodge.co.nz. New owners are transforming this small lodge with international beach chic. Borrow a fishing rod, SUP or kayak, go mountain-biking, play croquet on the lawn or have a relaxing massage before a gourmet dinner (mains $26–35). Hill-view room $227, sea view $333

Havelock and Pelorus Sound

The sleepy town of **HAVELOCK**, 35km west of Picton, is primarily of interest for cruising the stunning **Pelorus Sound**, an intricate maze of steep-sided bays, crescent beaches and sunken sea passages surrounded by forested peaks – the largest sheltered waterway in the southern hemisphere. Almost every bay has a farm for green-lipped mussels, making Havelock the world capital for these choice bivalves: you simply can't leave without tucking into a plateful. Self-caterers can buy fresh mussels from the Four Square supermarket.

8

Pelorus Mail Boat

Departs Tues, Thurs and Fri 9.30am • $128; under-16s free • ☎03 574 1088, ⒲mail-boat.co.nz • Can pick up from Blenheim or Picton

To see an extensive section of Pelorus Sound, get aboard the **Pelorus Mail Boat**, which follows a different route each day. All the trips are a scenic delight, dropping in on a mussel farm and delivering mail, perishable groceries and even correspondence-school papers to the far-flung residents. Friday's outer-sounds trip is the most comprehensive, but the schedule on other days gives more flexibility for dolphin watching and a brief time ashore. The trips return late in the afternoon so bring lunch.

THE NYDIA TRACK

If you are looking for excellent bushwalking with few fellow travellers, consider the **Nydia Track** (27km one way; 2 days), preferably tackled from Havelock and explained on DOC's *The Nydia Track* leaflet. It follows a series of bridle paths, passing through pasture, regenerating woodland and beech forest, with great views from the Kaiuma Saddle (387m) and Nydia Saddle (347m), as well as along the head of Nydia Bay. The first day (5–6hr) is pleasant, but the second (4–5hr) is the real gem.

If walking, **start** at Kaiuma Bay, most easily accessed by water taxi from Havelock (from $30), but driveable in around an hour and a half: turn off SH6 12km west of Havelock onto Daltons Road. The track **finishes** at Duncan Bay, in Tennyson Inlet, about an hour's drive from Havelock. Mountain biking (best starting at Duncan Bay) is allowed all year round, though it's a tough proposition in the dry, and near impossible when wet.

PACKAGES AND CAMPSITES

The best value and most convenient approach is to buy a **package** ($150) from *On the Track Lodge* (see p.458; ☎03 579 8411, ⒲nydiatrack.org.nz) that includes one night's accommodation in a private room, water taxi or shuttle to the start, and pick-up from the end back to Havelock. Large groups are best served by DOC's *Nydia Lodge* ($15 per person). There are also **campsites** ($6) at the northern end of Nydia Bay, and at Harvey Bay, 3km from the Duncan Bay terminus.

THE QUEEN CHARLOTTE TRACK

The **Queen Charlotte Track** (71km one way; 3–5 days; open year-round) is a stunning walk partly tracing skyline ridges with views across coastal forest to the waters of Queen Charlotte and Kenepuru sounds. It is broad, relatively easy-going and distinguished from all other Kiwi multi-day tramps by the lack of DOC huts, replaced by some lovely **accommodation**. Access is generally by boat from Picton, and water taxis can **transport your bags** to your next destination each day. Boats call at numerous bays along the way, so less-ambitious walkers can tackle shorter sections, do day-hikes from Picton or take on the track as part of a guided walk.

INFORMATION, COSTS AND ACCESS

The Picton i-SITE can help organize your trip and has the free *Queen Charlotte Track Visitor Guide*; check ⓦ doc.govt.nz or ⓦ qctrack.co.nz for more information. Parts of the track cross private land and there is a **fee** for anyone over 15 hiking or biking these sections: Queen Charlotte Track Land Cooperative Passes are sold by Picton and Blenheim i-SITEs and a number of accommodations on the track. A one-day pass costs $10; a pass for up to five consecutive days is $18; an annual pass is $25.

Trampers normally **travel north to south** from Ship Cove to Anakiwa, using **water taxis** to drop them off and pick them up. Sections of the track are accessible from Kenepuru Road, but there is no public transport. There is no overnight parking at Anakiwa, although the Rural Mail Bus Service (see p.451) can take you there.

Water taxi companies (see p.451) all offer a standard package with drop-off at Ship Cove, bag transfers and pick-up at Anakiwa for about $100 – pick whoever has the most convenient schedule. Bikes cost $5/journey, double kayaks $30.

GUIDED WALKS, COMBOS AND DAY-TRIPS

Marlborough Sounds Adventure Company (see box, p.454) offers **freedom walks** (4-day from $745; 5-day from $875; packed lunch each day), with nights spent at *Furneaux Lodge*, *Punga Cove Resort* and *Portage Resort*. Fully catered **guided walks** (4-day $1795; 5-day $2250) include a visit to Motuara Island and an optional day spent paddling. To pack in a day each of hiking, biking and paddling, go for the three-day Ultimate Sounds Adventure ($1060). Beachcomber Fun Cruises (see p.454) offer a series of one-day walks ($67–77), while the Cougar Line has walks from one to five hours ($80).

ACCOMMODATION

Booking is essential. Some smaller places don't accept debit or credit cards, so **take plenty of cash**. The six DOC **campsites** cost $6 and have water and toilets but only four have water taxi access. The accommodation below is listed from north to south, with hiking distances measured from Ship Cove.

★**Anakiwa 401** Anakiwa, Km71 ☎ 03 574 1388, ⓦ anakiwa401.co.nz. Great, sparkling, renovated hostel, with hammocks in the garden, a small orchard, free kayaks, a windsurfer ($25), an espresso machine and a coffee caravan directly below (open afternoons). It makes a great base for walking the southern end of the track or just hanging out. There's a two-bed share, doubles, and a self-contained apartment sleeping four. Bed $40, rooms $85

Anakiwa Lodge 9 Lady Cobham Grove, Anakiwa ☎ 03 574 2115, ⓦ anakiwa.co.nz. Around 400m from the end of the track, this comfortable associate YHA

Pelorus Bridge Scenic Reserve

18km west of Havelock

The **Pelorus Bridge Scenic Reserve** is a gorgeous forested spot run through by the crystal-clear Pelorus River with abundant swimming holes and verdant bush enlivened by tui, bellbirds and rare native long-tailed bats. The place is understandably popular in summer; there's a revamped but still basic DOC camping area (see p.458) and a DOC office adjoining a modest daytime-only café.

The **walking tracks** in the reserve are well maintained, fairly flat and clearly marked and there's a swingbridge to add a little extra excitement: the **Totara Walk** (1.5km return; 30min) and **Circle Walk** (1km return; 30min) routes pass through the low-lying

sleeps ten and offers internet and wi-fi, pre-prepared dinners ($16, book ahead for pizza), free kayaks and a spa pool. Dorm $35, deluxe $136

Furneaux Lodge Endeavour Inlet, Km14 ☎ 03 579 8259, ⦿ furneaux.co.nz. One of the region's bigger lodges built in attractive grounds around a century-old homestead, with a convivial bar and an excellent restaurant. Rooms range from basic bunk rooms to self-contained cottages ($336). Internet access and phone available. Hikers cabin (per person) $54, en suite $305

Lochmara Lodge Lochmara Bay, Km58 ☎ 03 573 4554, ⦿ lochmaralodge.co.nz. Beautiful ecolodge with its own café, bar, and art gallery overlooking Lochmara Bay. There are also free kayaks, a bathhouse ($60 for two for 1hr), and massage available. All rooms are en-suite and have free wi-fi. The lodge is almost an hour's walk off the QCT or a 20min water-taxi ride from Picton ($45; Picton departures daily 9am, 12.30pm, 3.15pm & 5.30pm). Closed June–Aug. Units $130, chalets $280

Mistletoe Bay Eco Village Mistletoe Bay, Km65 ☎ 03 573 4048, ⦿ mistletoebay.co.nz. Family-oriented, road-accessible rustic luxury in either the Whare (eight cabins with a communal kitchen), Jo House (a self-contained cottage) or the backpackers and campsite ($32 per couple) with a camp kitchen and coin-op showers ($2). A small store sells home-grown organic produce, meats, eggs and fresh coffee. Backpackers $30, Whare or Jo House $140

Portage Resort Kenepuru Rd, Km51 ☎ 0800 762 442, ⦿ portage.co.nz. Resort hotel with range of accommodation, swimming pool, restaurant and bar overlooking the Sound. It's a 30min walk from Torea Bay or get them to arrange a taxi. Double en suite $195, suite $299

Tanglewood 1744 Queen Charlotte Drive, Anakiwa ☎ 03 574 2080, ⦿ www.tanglewood.net.nz. Just four en-suite rooms in this family B&B, nicely surrounded by woodland (with some massive tree ferns next to the house) and popular with kereru. $155

THE ROUTE

The track passes through grassy farmland and open gorse-covered hills, but both ends are forest reserves. **Detours** off the main track include a short walk from Ship Cove to a pretty forest-shrouded waterfall, a scramble down to the Bay of Many Coves, or a foray to the Antimony Mines (beware of exposed shafts – stick to the marked tracks). To do the whole track in three days, get an early start from Ship Cove and plan to hike to Camp Bay. From there you have a fairly long day to Portage, then a relatively easy finish.

Ship Cove to Resolution Bay (4.5km; 1–2hr; 200m ascent). The track climbs steeply away from the shore through largely untouched forest to a lookout with great views of Motuara Island, before dropping down to Resolution Bay, where there's a DOC campsite.

Resolution Bay to Endeavour Inlet (11km; 3–5hr; 200m ascent). Follows an old bridle path over the ridge to *Furneaux Lodge* and *Endeavour Resort*.

Endeavour Inlet to Camp Bay (11.5km; 3–4hr; 100m ascent). Coastal track through regenerating forest packed with birdlife. There's a DOC campsite and several lodges.

Camp Bay to Portage (24.5km; 6–8hr; 650m ascent). The longest stretch without convenient roofed accommodation (just two DOC campsites) is also the most rewarding, mostly following a ridge with views down to the Sounds on both sides.

Portage to Mistletoe Bay (7.5km; 3–4hr; 450m ascent). A steep initial climb is followed by a pleasant ridge walk through manuka, gorse and shrubs with the chance to break the journey at the *Lochmara Lodge*, some 2km off the track.

Mistletoe Bay to Anakiwa (12.5km; 3–4hr; 100m ascent). Follows an old bridle path well above the water with great views, then finishes off through some lovely beech forest.

8

woodland for which the area is famous, while the **Trig K Track** (2.5km one way; 2hr), after a steady climb to 417m, offers stunning views of the whole area. For a different perspective, join Pelorus Eco Adventures barrelling down the river.

SH6 continues west past the turn-off to French Pass at the small settlement of **Rai Valley** and climbs the hills towards Nelson past Happy Valley Adventures (see box, p.462).

French Pass

Narrow winding roads head north from Rai Valley towards French Pass, a two-hour, 60km drive through pockets of bush locked in sheep country and pine plantations.

After tantalizing glimpses of inaccessible bays and coves you're finally rewarded with French Pass itself, a narrow channel between the mainland and D'Urville Island where nineteenth-century French explorer Dumont d'Urville was spun by tumultuous whirlpools. If you're here at mid-tide it is easy to understand why these seething waters were so feared. The maelstrom is best seen from a couple of short tracks in **French Pass Scenic Reserve**, 1km before the road end at **FRENCH PASS**. This tiny settlement is little more than a wharf, a shop, DOC's basic **campsite** and *Beachfront Villas* (see below).

ARRIVAL AND DEPARTURE

By bus and water taxi Buses between Picton and Nelson all stop at Havelock, while local bus and water taxi operators offer services to Kenepuru and Pelorus sounds.

HAVELOCK AND PELORUS SOUN

ACTIVITIES

Foxy Lady Havelock ☎0508 428 35625, ⓦ pelorussoundwatertaxis.co.nz. Bruce runs water taxi services, fishing charters and some lovely multi-day trips to get you away from the crowds aboard the 60ft *Foxy Lady* (sleeps 9), in conjunction with *On the Track Lodge* and Sea Kayak Adventures (p.454). The Pelorus Loop ($850) includes walking the Nydia Track, one night on board *Foxy Lady* and one night at *On the Track Lodge*, plus cruising Pelorus Soun and Tennyson Inlet and a couple of short hikes.

Pelorus Eco Adventures 48 Main Rd, Havelock ☎ 080 252 663, ⓦ kayak-newzealand.com. Trips down th Pelorus River in inflatable kayaks. It's a fun, undemandin trip with stops to explore the scenery, and imagine th famous Hobbit scene, before exiting at Totara Flats ($165)

ACCOMMODATION

HAVELOCK

Blue Moon Backpackers 48 Main Rd ☎03 574 2212, ⓦ bluemoonhavelock.co.nz. Rooms are small but comfortable, and there are good communal facilities in this intimate hostel right in the centre of town, with friendly, helpful hosts. Dorms $25, rooms $76

★**Havelock Garden Motel** 71 Main Rd ☎03 574 2387, ⓦ gardenmotels.com. Slightly older, fully self-contained units that are well kept and clean and set in a beautiful green garden with mature trees. The hosts are very helpful. Studio $125, motel unit $140

Havelock Motor Camp 24 Inglis St ☎03 574 2339, ⓦ havelockmotorcamp.co.nz. Simple, traditional Kiwi campsite with good communal facilities and a good location near the centre of the community, just off Main Road. You'll need to book in the summer. Camping $30 (for 2), cabins $50

PELORUS BRIDGE SCENIC RESERVE

Kahikatea Flat campsite ☎03 571 6019. Basic DOC camping area that has a fabulously-sited kitchen block, plus toilets, hot showers and tap water. Camping $15

PELORUS SOUND

★**On the Track Lodge** Nydia Bay, Pelorus Soun ☎03 579 8411, ⓦ nydiatrack.org.nz. Right on th Nydia Track and only accessible by boat, foot or bike (se box, p.455), but well worth visiting in its own right - you'll get a genuine Kiwi welcome, scrumptious cakes revamped accommodation in a yurt dorm, chalets c railway carriage, with endless hot water and wood-fire central heating. The spa bath, kayaks, fishing rods, an dinghies are all free. Home-cooked meals are availabl (mains $20); breakfast ($15) includes fresh croissants and they provide a generous packed lunch ($20). Dorr $60, double $130

FRENCH PASS

Beachfront Villas ☎03 576 5204, ⓦ seasafaris.co.nz B&B beachfront accommodation in self-contained units, a of which have a BBQ and patio. Meals available on reques ($42). Closed June–Sept. $162

French Pass campsite A basic 16-pitch DOC site with ta water, toilets and cold showers. Booking required Dec 1– Feb 28. $10

EATING AND DRINKING

Havelock Hotel 54 Main Rd, Havelock ☎03 574 2412. Serves simple cuisine for under $30, including steak and chips, fish and chips, burger and chips, plus mussel dishes. Daily 11am–late, kitchen closes at 9pm.

Mussel Pot 73 Main Rd, Havelock ☎03 574 2824, ⓦ themusselpot.co.nz. Popular for selfies with the outsize green-lipped mussels, and for the choice of steamed, smoked, marinated, grilled, battered or chowder-ed shellfish. Share a platter to taste the range ($46). Sept–June daily 10.30am–2.45pm & 5.30–9pm.

Slip Inn Havelock Marina ☎03 574 2345, ⓦ slipinn .co.nz. Marina-side establishment with big windows an decks does good mussel dishes ($16.50 for a kilo in whit wine sauce), plus slightly fancier dishes including the ubiquitous pizza ($18–30). It's also fine for coffee or a sundowner. Daily 8am–late.

Nelson

The thriving city of **Nelson**, set on the coast in a broad basin between the Arthur and Richmond ranges, is beguiling. Low rent and low rise, it is not much to look at, but the location – perfect for accessing Golden Bay and a raft of national parks – warm climate, good beaches and a cluster of worthwhile wineries pulls in all manner of tourists and artists, and the city has become one of the most popular visitor destinations in New Zealand.

Within central Nelson itself the **Suter Gallery** and the lively **Saturday market** are good diversions, but you'll soon want to venture further, perhaps to **Tahunanui Beach** or the suburb of **Stoke** for the fascinating **World of WearableArt** museum. You can even do an **Abel Tasman day-trip** from town using early buses, which give you enough time for a water taxi ride and a few hours' walking along the Coast Track.

Brief history

Nelson is one of the oldest settlements in New Zealand. By the middle of the sixteenth century it was occupied by the Ngati Tumatakokiri, some of whom met **Abel Tasman**'s longboats at Murderer's Bay (now Golden Bay) and killed four of his sailors.

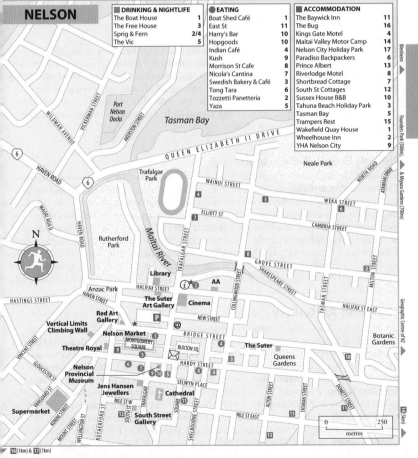

NELSON

DRINKING & NIGHTLIFE	
The Boat House	1
The Free House	3
Sprig & Fern	2/4
The Vic	5

EATING	
Boat Shed Café	1
East St	11
Harry's Bar	10
Hopgoods	10
Indian Café	4
Kush	9
Morrison St Cafe	8
Nicola's Cantina	7
Swedish Bakery & Café	3
Tong Tara	6
Tozzetti Panetteria	2
Yaza	5

ACCOMMODATION	
The Baywick Inn	11
The Bug	16
Kings Gate Motel	4
Maitai Valley Motor Camp	14
Nelson City Holiday Park	17
Paradiso Backpackers	6
Prince Albert	13
Riverlodge Motel	8
Shortbread Cottage	7
South St Cottages	12
Sussex House B&B	10
Tahuna Beach Holiday Park	3
Tasman Bay	5
Trampers Rest	15
Wakefield Quay House	1
Wheelhouse Inn	2
YHA Nelson City	9

8

NELSON'S MARKETS

Saturday morning should involve a pilgrimage to the renowned **Nelson Market** (8am–1pm), which takes over Montgomery Square. Artists are flushed out of their rural boltholes and stalls groan with hand-dipped candles, turned wooden bowls, bracelets made from forks and all manner of crafts. Food stalls with mounds of fruit, endless varieties of fresh bread and fish, Thai and vegetarian dishes, preserves, coffee and cakes will sustain you. On Wednesdays (11am–4pm) there's also a **farmers' market** at the corner of Morrison and Hardy sts.

By the time Europeans arrived in earnest, Maori numbers had been decimated by internecine fighting and the nearest *pa* site to Nelson was at Motueka, though this did little to prevent land squabbles, culminating in the **Wairau Affray** in 1843. Despite assurances from chiefs Te Rauparaha and Te Rangihaeata that they would abide by the decision of a land commissioner, the New Zealand Company pre-emptively sent surveyors south to the Wairau Plains, the catalyst for a skirmish during which Te Rangihaeata's wife was shot. The bereaved chief and his men slaughtered 22 Europeans in retaliation but the settlers continued their land acquisition after numbers were boosted by immigrants from Germany.

Christ Church Cathedral

Trafalgar St • Daily 9am–5pm (services permitting) • Donation requested

The glowering, grey-stone Christ Church Cathedral, perched on a small hill, and unusually facing north (towards the sea), dominates the grid-pattern streets of Nelson. English architect Frank Peck's original 1924 design was gradually modified over many years due to lack of money; World War II intervened further, and even now the cathedral tower still looks as if it's under construction. The interior is illuminated by dazzling stained-glass windows with ten particularly noteworthy examples in a small chapel to the right of the main altar.

Nelson Provincial Museum

Corner of Hardy and Trafalgar sts • Mon–Fri 10am–5pm, Sat & Sun 10am–4.30pm • $5 • ☎ 03 548 9588, ⓦ nelsonmuseum.co.nz

The **Nelson Provincial Museum** takes a fresh, multimedia approach to local exhibits and then draws strands from them to the rest of New Zealand and the wider world. The Maori displays are each curated by the various local *iwi* with their choice of treasures from their own *marae*; witness the fine bone club, delicate flax and feather cloak, and interpretation of the designs in *tukutuku* panels. The death masks from the Maungatapu Murders near Canvastown highlight a grisly tale of robbery, murder and betrayal from 1866, and there's a collection of traditional Maori musical instruments whose sounds echo throughout the galleries. Upstairs, there's an exhibition on the First World War and the locals it affected.

The Suter Art Gallery

28 Halifax St • Daily 10.30am–4.30pm • $3; free on Sat • ⓦ thesuter.org.nz

The original **Suter Art Gallery** is just east of the centre, in the pretty Victorian **Queens Gardens**. It's currently being modernized to provide more gallery space, so for now they've relocated part of the collection, the café and the shop to Halifax Street. On show are some fine **watercolours**, especially those of John Gully; also look for oils by **Toss Woollaston**, a founder of the modernist movement in New Zealand and one of a group of artists and writers who, during the 1930s and 1940s, began exploring notions of a New Zealand culture independent of colonial Britain. Another must is Gottfried Lindauer's painting of Huria Matenga, a Maori woman who helped save many lives from the wreck of the *Delaware* in 1863.

Botanical Reserve

Accessed from the corner of Milton and Hardy sts • Open access • Free

At the east end of Bridge Street is the **Botanical Reserve**, where New Zealand's first ever rugby game was played in 1870. The hill behind commands a good view over the town and, it is claimed, marks the **geographical centre** of New Zealand.

Founders Park and Miyazu Gardens

87 Atawhai Drive • Daily 10am–4.30pm; Miyazu Gardens daily 8am–dusk • $7; gardens free

About 1km north of the Botanical Reserve, **Founders Park** offers a somewhat sanitized version of early colonial history through relocated and replica buildings. Next door, the delightful Japanese-style **Miyazu Gardens** celebrate the relationship between Nelson and its sister city Miyazu. The gardens are a quiet oasis of reflective pools, ornamental cherry trees and traditional bridges.

Tahunanui Beach

4km northwest of central Nelson • Buses run here frequently along SH6 from the city

Haven Road (SH6) runs northwest out of central Nelson and, after 1km, becomes **Wakefield Quay**, a popular spot for strolling along the waterfront but primarily known for the *Boat Shed Café* jutting picturesquely over the water. Continue 3km along SH6 to reach **Tahunanui Beach Reserve**, a long golden strand backed by grassland and drifting dunes. This is where Nelson comes to relax on sunny weekends, with safe swimming, a fun park, zoo and children's playgrounds.

8

World of WearableArt (WOW)

95 Quarantine Rd • Daily 10am–5pm • $24 • Ⓦ wowcars.co.nz

About 3km out of Nelson on SH6, follow signs off the roundabout to the **World of WearableArt and Classic Cars** for a unique theatrical experience. It is primarily a purpose-built showcase for the best designs from the annual WearableArt Show, a fashion show with a difference first put on by Suzie Moncrieff in Nelson in 1987 and now held annually in Wellington. Participants from around the world submit

---

NELSON ARTS AND CRAFTS

Many of the region's artists and craftspeople display at galleries outside Nelson (see p.466) but you can get an idea of what's in store by visiting galleries in town. Good starting points are listed below.

Craig Potton Gallery 255 Hardy St ☎ 03 548 9554. The emphasis here is on Craig's well-known landscape photography, but there are also some paintings. Mon–Fri 10am–5pm, Sat 10am–2pm.

Jens Hansen 320 Trafalgar Square Ⓦ jenshansen .com. *Lord of the Rings* fans will want to visit the jeweller's Jens Hansen, who made "The one ring to rule them all", and a few dozen more of them to suit various cast members. Replicas are available. They also design their own, more individual jewellery. Mon–Fri 9am–5pm, Sat 9am–2pm, Sun in summer 10am–1pm.

Red Art Gallery 1 Bridge St ☎ 03 548 2170, Ⓦ redartgallery.com. Very friendly gallery with café attached, selling contemporary New Zealand fine art,

design, prints and jewellery. Mon–Fri 8am–4pm, Sat & Sun 9am–2pm.

South Street Gallery 10 Nile St West ☎ 03 548 8117, Ⓦ nelsonpottery.co.nz. Standing on the corner of South Street, one of Nelson's oldest with a row of pretty workers' cottages, this gallery specializes in local pottery. Mon–Fri 8.30am–4.30pm, Sat 9.30am–4pm, & Sun 10am–4pm.

Stephan Gillberg Bone Carving 87 Green St ☎ 03 546 4275, Ⓦ carvingbone.co.nz. Put your creativity to work by bone carving; one-day workshops will see you complete an attractive pendant, have a reasonable understanding of how the process works and know a bit about what the traditional symbols mean. $79 with pick-up from your accommodation at 9.30am.

NELSON ACTIVITIES

Nelson is the sort of place where sunbathing at Tahunanui might be as active as you want to get, though there is no shortage of energetic diversions. In additon to the following, you might want to catch the Nelson Arts Festival (twelve days in mid-Oct; ⊕nelsonartsfestival.co.nz), which includes theatre, music, readings and street entertainment, much of it either free or costing just a few dollars. The city also hosts the Nelson Jazz & Blues Festival (five days in early January; ⊕nelsonjazzfest.co.nz) at venues around the city.

QUAD BIKING AND THE SKYWIRE

Happy Valley Adventures 194 Cable Bay Rd, 17km northeast of Nelson off SH6 ☎03 545 0304, ⊕happyvalleyadventures.co.nz. Explore up to 40km of track on a large forested farm, climbing hills, passing monstrous matai trees, stopping to learn a little about the forest and its stories and eventually reaching a high spot with expansive views of Cable Bay. The most popular trips are the Bayview Circuit (2hr; rider $130; passenger $35), and the Blue Hill Ride (3hr; $180; no passengers) designed for the more skilled and ambitious rider. Happy Valley Adventures also operates the Skywire ($85), a four-seater cable-car chair that swoops almost 1km across a forested valley at speeds of around 80kmph then back to the excellent hilltop café with its panoramic deck. The bird's-eye view is spectacular though many people find the return, with your back to the action, a little unnerving.

TANDEM PARAGLIDING

Nelson Paragliding ☎03 544 1182, ⊕nelson paragliding.co.nz. A hair-raising drive up the hill to the launch site reveals a spectacular landscape, before you run like hell then glide off into the quiet updraft for 15–20min of eerily silent flight. Tandem flights go for $180 and a half-day introductory lesson costs $250.

KAYAKING AND SAILING

Cable Bay Kayaks ☎03 545 0332, ⊕cablebaykayaks.co.nz. Paddling with this outfit makes a refreshing change from the mayhem around Abel Tasman. They do a half-day trip ($85) and a full-day tour ($145; bring your own lunch) which gives more time for exploring the caves of this beautiful and intricate coastline and doing a little snorkelling. They're based near Happy Valley. **Sail Nelson** ☎03 546 7275, ⊕sailnelson.co.nz. Great, fully-catered sailing courses (two-day beginner $695; five-day RYA course $1845) living aboard a 10m yacht, typically around D'Urville Island and Abel Tasman. Courses run on fixed dates for two to four people.

ROCK CLIMBING

Vertical Limits 34 Vanguard St ☎0508 837 842, ⊕verticallimits.co.nz. Indoor rock climbing is ideal for a wet day ($17 entry and harness), and when the weather improves ask to join their full-day climbing trips. Mon–Thurs 3–9pm, Fri noon–5pm, Sat noon–6pm, Sun noon–4pm.

sculptures or pieces of art that can be worn as clothes – many made from unusual materials such as household junk, food, metal, stone, wood and tyres. Attached is an exhibition of cars from the past half-century, including the world's fastest mini.

ARRIVAL AND DEPARTURE

By plane Flights arrive at Nelson airport, 8km west of the centre. Super Shuttle (☎0800 748 885; $19 one person; $23 for two) meets most flights, or you can grab a taxi (☎03 548 8225; $27).
Destinations Auckland (9–11 daily; 1hr 25min); Christchurch (5–7 daily; 50min); Wellington (13–17 daily; 35min).
By bus Long-distance buses drop you near the centre of the city, within easy walking distance of most accommodation. Abel Tasman Coachlines pull in at 27 Bridge St, while the other companies all stop outside the i-SITE.
Destinations Blenheim (3–4 daily; 1hr 15min); Collingwood (1 daily; 3hr); Fox Glacier (1–2 daily; 10hr 30min); Franz Josef (1–2 daily; 9hr); Greymouth (1–2 daily; 6hr); Heaphy Track (1 daily; 3hr 30min); Kawatiri Junction, for Nelson Lakes (1–2 daily; 1hr 5min); Motueka (3 daily; 1hr); Murchison (1–2 daily; 2hr); Picton (3–4 daily; 2hr 15min); Punakaiki (1–2 daily; 4hr 40min); Takaka (1 daily; 2hr 30min); Westport (1–2 daily; 3hr 30min).

GETTING AROUND

By bike Aurora Bike Barn, 114 Hardy St (☎03 548 1666), rents bikes from $20/half-day depending on the type. Ask the guys about local tracks and hire a mountain bike for £50. A2B Ecycle, 8a Nile St (☎021 222 7260,

W a2b-ecycle.co.nz), have electric bikes for $45/ half-day.

By car Daily rates start at about $80, or $40/day for week-long rentals. Try: Nelson Car Hire (**☎** 0800 283 545, **W** nelsoncarhire.co.nz); Apex (**☎** 03 546 9028); Hardy Cars (**☎** 03 548 1681); Rent-a-Dent (**☎** 03 546 9890); and Thrifty (**☎** 03 547 5563).

By taxi Nelson City Taxis **☎** 03 548 8225.

By bus SBL buses (**☎** 03 548 3290, **W** nelsoncoaches.co.nz)

run local routes to Tahunanui Beach and Stoke from the terminal at 27 Bridge St, while Abel Tasman Coachlines (**☎** 03 548 0285, **W** abeltasmantravel.co.nz) leaves Nelson at 7.45am daily in summer for Mapua ($10) and Marahau ($20) via Motueka ($12), connecting with launch services deeper into the Abel Tasman National Park. Goldenbay Coachlines (**☎** 03 525 8352, **W** goldenbaycoachlines.co.nz) also run a service to Takaka ($37) in Golden Bay, with links to the Heaphy Track ($57).

INFORMATION

Visitor information i-SITE is at the corner of Trafalgar and Halifax streets (Mon–Fri 8.30am–5pm, Sat & Sun 9am–4pm; **☎** 03 548 2304, **W** nelsonnz.com), where you'll also find the DOC (same hours; **☎** 03 546 9339), which handles track bookings and has lots of details on the local

national parks and tracks – including Abel Tasman tide tables.

Cycling information Check out **W** heartofbiking.org.nz on the Great Taste Trail, Dun Mountain and the cycleway to Abel Tasman National Park.

ACCOMMODATION

There's a broad range of accommodation, much of it in the centre of town within reach of cultural diversions and nightlife. Classy **B&Bs** and excellent **hostels** are abundant, and there are a couple of campsites close to town, but you may want to save your camping for the prettier areas around Motueka, the national park or Golden Bay.

★ **The Baywick Inn** 51 Domett St **☎** 03 545 6514, **W** baywicks.com. Lovely, renovated two-storey 1885 villa, overlooking the Maitai River with luxuriously appointed rooms, two in a new cottage out back ($225 for a room, $450 to take as a self-catering unit). An enthusiastic welcome includes afternoon tea. Platters of local antipasti by arrangement ($50). Free wi-fi. **$165**

★ **The Bug** 226 Vanguard St **☎** 03 539 4227, **W** thebug .co.nz. Welcoming 46-bed hostel about 1km from the centre of Nelson adorned with VW Beetle paraphernalia. Along with free bikes, wi-fi and local pick-ups they have a hammock, table football and a female dorm, and make a point of lacking a TV. Dorms **$28**, rooms **$80**

Kings Gate Motel 21 Trafalgar St **☎** 0800 104 022, **W** kingsgatemotel.co.nz. Close to the town centre with spacious, comfortable and well-kept studios and units complete with full kitchens, spa baths and free wi-fi. There's also a pool. **$149**

Maitai Valley Motor Camp 472 Maitai Valley Rd **☎** 03 548 7729, **W** maitaivalleymotorcamp.co.nz. Basic camping in a quiet, lovely wooded section beside the Maitai River (with good swimming holes), 7km southeast of Nelson. Camping **$8**, cabins **$50**

Nelson City Holiday Park 230 Vanguard Rd **☎** 0800 778 898, **W** nelsonholidaypark.co.nz. Small and well-managed campervan park with limited tent space ($42/2 people) but various grades of accommodation from simple cabins to more salubrious kitchen cabins ($85) and one-bed units. Bike rental available for $35/day. Cabins **$60**, units **$150**

Paradiso Backpackers 42 Weka St **☎** 03 546 6703, **W** backpackernelson.co.nz. A big hostel set in a converted villa with purpose-designed outbuildings, sleeping around

140. The outdoor pool, spa, sauna, volleyball and free wi-fi attempt to make up in shiny things what it lacks in space, peace and privacy; the slightly more expensive motel units next door offer more of the last two. Packed in the summer. Dorms **$26**, rooms **$66**

Prince Albert 113 Nile St **☎** 03 548 8477, **W** theprincealbert.co.nz. Traditional neighbourhood pub providing backpacker accommodation. All rooms are en suite, there's a small courtyard with hammocks, and the owners are keen to make your visit fun. Free off-road parking, breakfast, bikes, and wi-fi allowance. Dorms **$27**, doubles **$80**

Riverlodge Motel 31 Collingwood St **☎** 03 548 3094, **W** riverlodgenelson.co.nz. One of the better motels in town, giving good value for money across a range of clean and comfortable units. All have Sky TV, access to a guest laundry, good showers and some have spa baths. Continental breakfast available. Studio **$130**, unit **$150**

★ **Shortbread Cottage** 33 Trafalgar St **☎** 03 546 6681, **W** www.shortbreadcottage.co.nz. Lovely boutique hostel with polished-wood floors, only thirteen comfy beds, free internet and breakfast, loads of peace and quiet and lots of home comforts (including shortbread sold for charity). Best to book ahead. Dorms **$38**, rooms **$64**

South St Cottages South St **☎** 0800 292 535, **W** cottageaccommodation.co.nz. A gorgeous 1860s cottage in Nelson's prettiest street let on a nightly, self-catering basis with breakfast provisions supplied by the knowledgeable hosts. The accommodation is charmingly old-fashioned but with all mod cons. **$230**

Sussex House B&B 238 Bridge St **☎** 03 548 9972, **W** sussex.co.nz. Charming, recently refreshed (new beds) five-room B&B in a central, 1880s villa featuring

8

honey-coloured rimu floors and welcoming owner. All rooms are en-suite, except for one with a private bathroom, and two of the rooms open onto a veranda. The extensive continental breakfasts are great and there's free internet too. **$170**

Tahuna Beach Holiday Park 70 Beach Rd, Tahunanui ☎ 0800 500 501, ⊛ tahunabeach.co.nz. Absolutely enormous, sometimes overwhelming, estuary-side campsite a 5min walk from Tahunanui Beach. Abundant facilities include mini-golf and kids' playground. Book far in advance for the summer. Camping **$18**, self-contained units **$120**

Tasman Bay 10 Weka St ☎ 0800 222 572 ⊛ tasmanbaybackpackers.co.nz. Comfortable purpose-built hostel a few minutes from the town centre, with clean, spacious rooms (some en-suite) and enthusiastic, friendly management who ensure you always get more than you pay for. Free bikes, and free chocolate pudding nightly. Dorms **$26**, doubles **$85**

Trampers Rest 31 Alton St ☎ 03 545 7477. Lovely and cosy backpackers with only eight beds in comparatively small rooms. TV watching is by consensus only, there's free wi-fi, a tuned piano, and the wee garden boasts a hammock, avocado tree and bike storage. There are also free bikes, and the owner, a real tramping enthusiast, is an absolute mine of information. Dorms **$29**, doubles **$70**

★ **Wakefield Quay House** 385 Wakefield Quay ☎ 03 546 7275, ⊛ wakefieldquay.co.nz. Great B&B with stupendous sea views over Haulashore Island. The house is up a steep rise from the busy road. Both rooms are beautifully turned out, drinks are served at 6pm, plus there's a tasty breakfast available. Minimum 2-night stay. **$350**

★ **Wheelhouse Inn** 41 Whitby Rd ☎ 03 546 8391, ⊛ wheelhouse.co.nz. The bay views are magical from the picture windows of these five upgraded, nautically themed, self-catering apartments high on the hill, 2km west of central Nelson. All are very private and come with full kitchen, laundry, TV/DVD, internet and BBQ, but you'll need to book well in advance. **$180**

★ **YHA Nelson City** 59 Rutherford St ☎ 03 545 9988, ⊛ yha.co.nz. Purpose-built, this is the best hostel in Nelson, whose generous facilities include two kitchens, plenty of communal space, informed staff, foosball, table tennis, and an infrared sauna. There's a wide range of accommodation, including connecting rooms for families and two disabled-access units. Dorms **$31**, double **$88**

EATING

Nelson's enviable lifestyle is reflected in the broad choice of eating options within easy reach of the town centre. And when you tire of these, there's always fine food on the waterfront, at Mapua Wharf or at the wineries. Nelson's pubs and bars (see opposite) are also good for a quick snack.

Boat Shed Café 350 Wakefield Quay ☎ 03 546 9783, ⊛ boatshedcafe.co.nz. Fine views over Tasman Bay make this converted boat shed hanging out over the water a hit, but you also get fabulous fresh seafood and great concoctions from the best local producers. Perfect for romantic sunset dinners and relaxed lunches. Trust the Chef menu features four small courses ($65; add a dessert $77.50). Mon–Fri 9.30am–late, Sat & Sun 10am–late.

East St 335 Trafalgar Square East ☎ 03 970 0575. Funky vegetarian café and bar, with outdoor seating, in the basement of a hostel. This helps guarantee generous portions and good value (everything under $23), occasional live music, and cheap drinks, so the clientele includes locals as well as backpackers. Daily noon–11pm.

★ **Harry's Bar** 296 Trafalgar St ☎ 03 539 0905, ⊛ harrysnelson.nz. Smooth cocktail bar and Asian restaurant, known these days primarily for good-quality, well-priced food, including particularly fine crispy duck, chilli salt squid, and kaffir lime tart. At weekends it can also get a bit lively after the plates are stacked. Tues–Sat 4pm–late.

Hopgoods 284 Trafalgar St ☎ 03 545 7191, ⊛ hopgoods.co.nz. Some of Nelson's finest dining is found in this airy restaurant with outdoor streetside tables. Locally sourced, organic produce informs a range of seasonal dishes fashioned by a perfectionist chef into traditional European-influenced gastronomy. Expect the likes of beef fillet with mushroom crumble, polenta and nettle salsa ($37.50). Mon–Sat 5.30–9.30pm, also Fri 11.30am–2pm.

★ **Indian Café** 94 Collingwood St ☎ 03 548 4089. The town's best curry house is set in a historic villa and dishes up all your favourites, plus one or two highly imaginative variations, for around $18, as well as offering a takeaway menu ($10–20). Mon–Fri noon–2pm & daily 5pm–late.

Kush 5 Church St ☎ 03 394 793, ⊛ kush.co.nz. Funky, licensed coffee house named after the eponymous kingdom in Ethiopia thought to be populated by the world's first coffee drinkers. They may have calmed down the 1970s kitsch decor but not the coffee. There's a great selection of organic beans with each duty manager roasting their own *in situ*, keeping bug-eyed caffeine addicts fuelled on double shots. The counter food is simple but tasty, there's free wi-fi, they do legendary brunches on Sundays, and the notice board is full of local gossip. Mon–Thurs 7.30am–4pm, Fri & Sat 7.30am–2pm, Sun 9am–2pm.

Morrison St Cafe 244 Hardy St ☎ 03 548 8110, ⊛ morrisonstreetcafe.co.nz. Smart café serving extremely good-quality brunches, lunches and snacks, with many dishes dairy or gluten free. Along with the liberal sprinkling of local art adorning the walls there is outdoor seating, newspapers and magazines, but don't let anything distract you from the food ($11–22), which is rightly popular with the natives, including home-made muesli, Nelson tasting platters and excellent coffee. Mon–Fri 7.30am–4pm, Sat 8.30am–4pm & Sun 9am–4pm.

Nicola's Cantina 6 Church St ☎03 548 8761. Short menu of Mexican standards (tacos, burrito, *quesadillas*, *huevos rancheros*). Everything is under $22 and there are some fun cocktails. Tues–Sat 11.30am–2pm & 5–9pm.

★**Swedish Bakery & Café** 54 Bridge St ☎03 546 8685, ⓦtheswedishbakery.co.nz. So small you could blink and miss it, but if you do you'll kick yourself. Swedish marzipan treats and sandwiches (including Swedish meatball and beetroot combos) sit beside some classic bakery favourites including a passion fruit and lemon tart that is quite literally the taste of summer. Mon–Fri 8.30am–3.30pm, Sat 9.30am–1.30pm.

Tong Tara 142 Hardy St ☎03 548 8997,

ⓦtongthai.co.nz. Top traditional Thai, relaxed and well run and dishing up all your perennial favourites – including fiery *moo kum wan*, or local mussels *tom yum* – for around $20. BYO. Tues–Sun 11am–late.

Tozzetti Panetteria 41 Halifax St. Wonderful little bakery serving freshly cut sandwiches, great pies, muffins, delicious cakes and stupendous bread (all under $15). Go early to get the pies – particularly the fish – and don't be surprised if you leave with more than you intended to buy. Tues–Fri 7am–4pm, Sat 7.30am–noon.

★**Yaza** Montgomery Square. So hip it'll never need a replacement, this cool licensed café is the epitome of laidback. They serve excellent breakfasts, lunches, coffees and the cheesiest cheese scones around (most items $5–20). Occasional evening entertainments too, including poetry, music and talks. Mon–Fri 8am–5pm, Sat 7am–4pm & Sun 8am–4pm.

DRINKING, NIGHTLIFE AND ENTERTAINMENT

While most of its suburban neighbours retire early to sip cocoa, Nelson stays up and parties – at least on Friday and Saturday. For raucous boozing and some dancing head for Trafalgar Street or the half-dozen bars on Bridge Street between Trafalgar and Collingwood streets. Pubs and **bars** of all stripes often have **live music**, karaoke and DJ **nights**; pick up the *Star Times* gig guide flyer to find out **what's on**.

The Boat House 326 Wakefield Quay ☎03 548 7646. Just down the road – on the Nelson side – from the more famous *Boat Shed Café* (see opposite), with equally fine views over Tasman Bay is this private licensed club, set up in the 1980s to save the 1906 rowing club building – a large stilted boat shed and ramp hanging over the waves. Open to the public and now a highly regarded live-music venue (cover charges $10–20), it's a fabulously atmospheric place to enjoy a gig, a drink or some home-made, high-end bar food (mains $16–22). Wed–Fri 11am–2pm & Fri 5pm–late.

★**The Free House** 95 Collingwood St ☎03 548 9391, ⓦthefreehouse.co.nz. Brilliant pub in a former church fitted with the only hand pumps in town, perfect for their selection of the best local microbrews. They do some food, but better ask at the bar and order in a curry from across the *Indian Café*. Frequent movies and live music in the Bedouin-style tent out front. Mon–Thurs 3–10.30pm, Fri 3pm–midnight, Sat noon–midnight, Sun noon–10.30pm.

★**Sprig & Fern** 280 Hardy St ⓦsprigandfern.co.nz. Central incarnation of this local institution, set in a double-fronted shop with LED light decoration at the top of the front windows and a large outdoor courtyard at the back. Great beer on tap (tasting racks of six beers cost $17), good pub surroundings and you can order takeaway to eat in.

Popular with the locals, who come along for the chat, the pub quiz and because it's slightly less expensive than *The Free House*. Daily 11am–10pm.

Sprig & Fern 134 Milton St ⓦsprigandfern.co.nz /taverns. Suburban villa converted into a cosy bar with open fires and a selection of twenty locally brewed, unpasteurized Sprig & Fern beers – crisp lagers and wheat beers to a ruby porter and a delicious pale ale – plus berry cider and a selection of local wines. Grab fish and chips from next door and bring them over. Daily 10am–10pm.

The Vic 281 Trafalgar St ⓦvicbrewbar.co.nz. Quality version of the Mac's brewery pubs that have sprung up all over the country, with a lively atmosphere, decent beer, good-value pub grub ($16–29) and mostly iffy live music (Fri & Sat) – with the occasional good band thrown in. Mon–Fri 11am–11pm, Sat & Sun 9am–11pm.

CINEMA AND THEATRE

State Cinema 6 91 Trafalgar St ☎03 548 0808, ⓦstatecinemas.co.nz. Screens all the latest mainstream films.

Nelson Theatre Royal 78 Rutherford St ☎03 548 3840. Recently renovated, showing traditional touring productions, local dramatics and vaudeville/cabaret-style shows.

DIRECTORY

Internet Free at the library plus good rates at Aurora, 161 Trafalgar St.

Library 27 Halifax St (Mon–Fri 10am–6pm, Sat 10am–1pm, Sun 1–4pm).

Left luggage Lockers at the i-SITE ($6/12hr) and Aurora ($5/day).

Medical treatment Nelson Region After Hours and Duty Doctor, 96 Waimea Rd ☎03 546 8881 (daily 8am–10pm).

Pharmacy Prices Pharmacy, corner of Hardy & Collingwood sts. (Mon–Fri 8am–8pm, Sat 9am–8pm, Sun 10am–6pm).

Post office 209 Hardy St (Mon–Fri 8am–5.30pm, Sat 9am–1pm).

The road to Abel Tasman

A great part of Nelson's charm lies on its doorstep, particularly the excellent **wineries** to the west. Here the vines appreciate the combination of New Zealand's sunniest climate and either the free-draining alluvial gravels of the Waimea Plains or the clay gravels of the Moutere Hills. Wineries are interspersed with the **studios** of contemporary artists, many of whom exhibit in their own small **galleries**, showcasing ceramics, glass-blowing, woodturning, textiles, sculpture, installations and painting.

Almost everywhere of interest is located on or just off the much straightened SH60, which runs north from Richmond towards Motueka through rural scenery and sea views. A couple of kilometres north along SH60, the Moutere Highway cuts left for **Upper Moutere**, while Redwood Road turns right past the *Seifried* winery (see p.471) and on to the picture-book-pretty **Rabbit Island**, one of Nelson's most popular beaches.

You can sample the best of the region on an extended drive from Nelson to Motueka, but there's enough on offer to warrant spending a couple of leisurely days in the region. Equip yourself with the *Nelson Wine Guide, Nelson Craft Beer Trail, Art & Craft Nelson* and *Nelson's Creative Pathways* leaflets, all free and available from visitor centres. A few kilometres further north, **Motueka** is the most practical base and provides the easiest access for trips into the Abel Tasman National Park.

Waimea Inlet and around
Höglund Art Glass
Lansdowne Rd • Daily 10am–5pm • ☎ 03 544 6500, ⓦ hoglundartglass.com

Highway 6 runs 15km southwest of Nelson to Richmond where SH60 cuts straight north towards Motueka while its old route runs closer to the shores of **Waimea Inlet**. Roughly 5km along SH60, **Höglund Art Glass** is an international-standard glass gallery displaying a vast array of Scandinavian-influenced work. The bold bright designs work best on bigger pieces with clean lines, but prices start around $49 before swiftly entering the stratosphere. A glass museum introduces you to the history and techniques of handblown glass manufacture through works by the Swedish owners Ola and Marie Höglund, and from December to April you can watch live glass-blowing.

Playhouse Café and Theatre
171 Westdale Rd • Summer Tues–Sun 11am–11pm; mainly only weekends in winter (check the website) • Cover charge for live music $5–15 • ☎ 03 540 2985, ⓦ playhousecafe.co.nz • The management offers free pick-up and drop-off from Mapua

Continuing north on SH60, follow the signs from the right-hand turn into Westdale Road and you'll end up at a curiosity worth at least an hour of your time. The straw-house **Playhouse Café and Theatre** is a live, licensed venue serving interesting daytime grub and hosting an extraordinary array of performances at night. Popular with live music acts, the grotto-like interior and Hundertwasser-esque decor plays host to lectures, talks, themed nights, plays, cabaret and travelling shows.

Bronte Gallery
122 Bronte Rd East • Daily 9am–5.30pm • ⓦ brontegallery.co.nz

Back on SH60, head north for Bronte Road East and signs to the **Bronte Gallery** about 1.5km off the highway. On display and for sale are highly individual works by internationally recognized ceramic artist Darryl Robertson and intriguing abstract oils by Lesley Jacka Robertson.

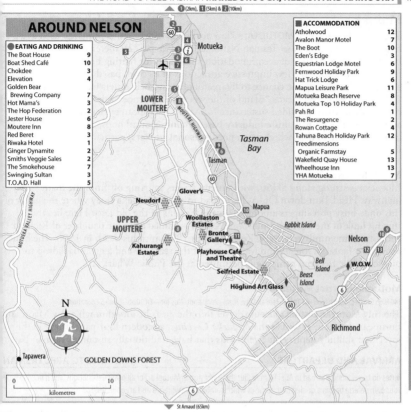

AROUND NELSON

● EATING AND DRINKING

The Boat House	9
Boat Shed Café	10
Chokdee	3
Elevation	4
Golden Bear	
Brewing Company	7
Hot Mama's	3
The Hop Federation	2
Jester House	6
Moutere Inn	8
Red Beret	3
Riwaka Hotel	1
Ginger Dynamite	2
Smiths Veggie Sales	2
The Smokehouse	7
Swinging Sultan	3
T.O.A.D. Hall	5

■ ACCOMMODATION

Atholwood	12
Avalon Manor Motel	7
The Boot	10
Eden's Edge	3
Equestrian Lodge Motel	6
Fernwood Holiday Park	9
Hat Trick Lodge	6
Mapua Leisure Park	11
Motueka Beach Reserve	8
Motueka Top 10 Holiday Park	4
Pah Rd	1
The Resurgence	2
Rowan Cottage	4
Tahuna Beach Holiday Park	12
Treedimensions	
Organic Farmstay	5
Wakefield Quay House	13
Wheelhouse Inn	13
YHA Motueka	7

The Upper Moutere wine region

A rewarding day can be spent touring Nelson's wineries (see p.471). The free *Nelson Wine Guide* includes a map and lists opening hours, typically daily 10am to 4.30pm in summer. The region is centred on the village of **Upper Moutere**, where you'll find locally produced preserves, cheeses and the like inside the Old Post Office at Moutere Gold, 1381 Moutere Hwy (daily 10am–4pm, closed Saturdays in winter).

Mapua

On a sunny late afternoon, tiny **MAPUA**, a couple of kilometres off SH60 and some 34km from Nelson, is an idyllic spot to stop for a stroll and a bite or a drink, while the sun catches the boats moored in the picturesque Waimea Estuary with the pines of Rabbit Island as a backdrop.

Rabbit Island

The Mapua Ferry, Mapua Wharf (☏ 03 540 3095) runs daily from 10am every hour until 5pm Sept–April & 10am–4pm on winter weekends and Wednesdays ($8 single; $12 return) • Trail Journeys (Ⓦ trailjourneys.co.nz) will rent you a bike for $45/day to explore the island

Before or after a munch in Mapua, take a **ferry** to Rabbit Island (Moturoa). The crossing involves a tour of the channel, and if you just go for the ride and don't disembark at the island it costs just $5. The ferry was introduced as part of the Nelson Tasman Cycle Trail, and there are 14km of cycle track round the island.

Motueka

The expanding town of **MOTUEKA**, 47km northwest of Nelson, is primarily used as a base for exploring the Abel Tasman National Park (see p.472): there's a complete booking service, a range of accommodation and places for renting hiking gear. Recently, the town has sprouted a few impressive attractions of its own, based largely around its airfield and including the chance to **fly** microlights and helicopters (see box, p.470).

The name Motueka means "island of the weka", a reference to the abundance of these edible birds, which provided sustenance for Maori. European settlers arrived in 1842 and established a horticulture industry based mainly around hops, since supplemented by pip fruit and grapes, which often need **seasonal workers**, particularly from December to March.

Motueka Quay

Motueka is strung along SH60, with quieter streets spurring off from the main highway. Head 1km down Old Wharf Road to reach **Motueka Quay** where the ghost of this once-busy port lingers among the scant remains of the old jetty. Here lies the rusting hulk of the Scottish-built *Janie Seddon* – named after the daughter of Richard Seddon, prime minister of New Zealand from 1893 until his death in 1906. The hulk provides a fantastic foreground for pictures of the seascape and a great backdrop for picnics, while freedom camping is permitted at the Public Wharf.

Motueka District Museum

140 High St • Dec–March Mon–Fri 10am–3pm and Sun 10am–2pm; April–Nov Tues–Fri 10am–3pm • $2 donation

The tiny **Motueka District Museum** delves into the area's history through a few Maori and European artefacts, as well as the *Motueka Carvings*, a modern four-panel frieze in the foyer that skilfully depicts the livelihoods that have traditionally sustained Tasman Bay.

ARRIVAL AND DEPARTURE THE ROAD TO ABEL TASMAN

Buses do travel along the road to Abel Tasman, but they only stop in Motueka. For all other destinations, you'll need to have your own vehicle or join a guided tour, some of which combine the wineries and art galleries.

By bus Buses pick up and drop off on Wallace St in Motueka, close to the i-SITE.

Destinations Kaiteriteri (1 daily; 25min); Marahau (1 daily; 50min); Nelson (3 daily; 1hr); Takaka (1 daily; 1hr 10min).

INFORMATION & GETTING AROUND

The only i-SITE along the road to Abel Tasman is in Motueka, but you can also check in at the office in Nelson for information on the area before you begin your journey.

Visitor information Motueka's i-SITE (Wallace St; Dec–March Mon–Fri 8.30am–5.30pm, Sat & Sun 9am–5pm; April–Nov Mon–Fri 9am–5pm, Sat & Sun 9am–4.30pm; ☎ 03 528 6543, ✆ abeltasmanisite.co.nz) has wi-fi ($5/24hr), a jobs notice board, and staff can assist in organizing Abel Tasman National Park and Heaphy Track trips. You can also get an hour's free wi-fi in the centre of Motueka.

By bike Trail Journeys, Mapua Wharf (☎ 03 540 3095, ✆ trailjourneys.co.nz), rents a comprehensive range of bikes ($45/day); or try Wheelie Fantastic, Mapua Wharf (☎ 03 543 2245, ✆ wheeliefantastic.co.nz; $30/day). Both companies

can help plan routes and advise on the Taste Trail.

By tour Bay Tours (☎ 0800 229 868, ✆ baytoursnelson .co.nz) offer a range of options, including afternoon winery trips (2–4 vineyards; $98) or full-day tours (3–4 wineries plus visits to artists; $238).

Tramping supplies You might be able to rent tramping gear from hostels. Coppins, 255 High St (Labour weekend to Easter Mon–Fri 8.30am–5.30pm, Sat 9am–4pm, Sun 10am–4pm; winter Mon–Fri 9am–5.30pm, Sat 9am–2pm; ☎ 03 528 7296), can sell you everything you need, including topo maps, and have great knowledge of the area.

ACCOMMODATION

MAPUA

Atholwood 118 Bronte Rd East ☎ 03 540 2925,

✆ atholwood.co.nz. Luxurious accommodation next door to the Bronte Gallery (see p.466), with comfortable rooms,

MOTUEKA TOURS AND ACTIVITIES

There are some great **hikes** around the Motueka area, but **airborne** activities such as skydiving and tandem paragliding are also very popular.

HIKING

In the hills to the west of Motueka is some of the best subalpine hiking in the north of the South Island, around the 1795m **Mount Arthur** and the associated uplifted plateau, the **Mount Arthur Tablelands**, all detailed in DOC's *The Cobb Valley, Mount Arthur and the Tablelands* leaflet available from the Motueka i-SITE. Traditionally, few visitors have bothered coming up this way, so what company you find will mostly be Kiwis and wildlife.

The principal starting point is the Flora car park, 930m up at the end of Graham Valley Road that leads off SH61 30km southwest of Motueka. A good 2–3hr loop heads up an easy path (1hr) to the Mount Arthur Hut ($15), from where the lowlands spread before you with Mount Arthur dominating the southern skyline. Continue along a ridge and down to Flora Hut (free) then back along a gravel road to the car park. The summit of Mount Arthur can be reached in three hours from the Mount Arthur Hut.

SKYDIVING

Skydive Abel Tasman Motueka airport, 3km southwest of town ☎0800 422 899, ⓦskydive.co.nz. Regarded as one of the ten best drop zones in the world, primarily because it offers jumps from 16,500ft (75 seconds freefall; $399) and 13,000ft (50 seconds freefall; $299), which is currently longer than most companies, with a backdrop of stunning scenery.

FLYING STUNTS

Uflyextreme Hangar 2, Motueka airport, 3km southwest of town ☎0800 360 180, ⓦuflyextreme.co.nz. Fly a Pitts Special in a 15min aerobatic display including four point rolls, loops and a Cuban eight without any previous training (allow an hour at the airport). In terms of an adrenaline rush, it makes skydiving look like afternoon tea with your granny. You can also take flights with the instructor, who lets you take control soon after takeoff (15min $395; 15min plus video $455; 20min $495; $850/day, two 20min flights plus 1.5hr school). It is money well spent.

HELICOPTER FLIGHTS, MICROLIGHTS AND TANDEM HANG-GLIDING

Uflyheli Queen Victoria St, Motueka airport, 3km southwest of town ☎0800 835 943, ⓦuflyheli.co.nz. After a short briefing you take the controls of an R22 two-seater, entry-level helicopter (30min $350; 1hr $650), practising simple forward flight, auto rotation and hovering.

Tasman Sky Adventures College St, Motueka airport, 3km southwest of town ☎0800 114 386, ⓦskyadventures.co.nz. Take the passenger seat in a microlight for some pulse-quickening thrills, buzzing above the region's glorious scenery (15min $105; 30min taking in parts of Abel Tasman National Park $205). They also offer tandem hang-gliding, towing the rig by microlight to a pre-appointed height before cutting you and your pilot loose (15min $195; 30min $330).

8

a swimming pool, spa, mature gardens and bush running down to Waimea Inlet. B&B $425, self-contained $350
The Boot 320 Aporo Rd, 7km north of Mapua at Tasman ☎03 526 6742, ⓦtheboot.co.nz. Attached to the *Jester House* café (see p.472) is *The Boot*, an enormous red fairy-tale boot with a luxurious lounge area, romantic bedroom and a little garden patio. B&B $300
Mapua Leisure Park 33 Toru St ☎03 540 2666, ⓦmapualeisurepark.co.nz. A variety of accommodation options, some recently refurbished, including cabins and motel units (from $138), in wonderful surroundings. Stop in at the summer-only *Boatshed Café* and bar. In Feb and March the place is

clothing-optional, though plenty of non-nudists still visit. Beachside camping $28, kitchen cabins $99

MOTUEKA

Avalon Manor Motel 314 High St ☎0800 282 566, ⓦavalonmotels.co.nz. A well-equipped 16-unit motel with spacious and comfortable units that come with Sky TV, a well-tended garden, plus free movies and wi-fi. $160
★**Eden's Edge** 137 Lodder Lane, Riwaka ☎03 528 4242, ⓦedensedge.co.nz. Located on an apple orchard 4km north of town, this purpose-built great-value hostel has a rural but very comfortable feel. There's a garden, pool, bike storage, nicely appointed rooms (some en-suite) and four-share dorms. Dorms $29, en suites $82

Equestrian Lodge Motel Tudor St ☎0800 668 782, ⓦequestrianlodge.co.nz. Well-kept upscale motel in a suburban area, only 5min from the centre of town, with comfy units backing onto a large grassy area with a solar-heated pool. **$170**

Fernwood Holiday Park 519 High St South ☎03 528 7488, ⓦfernwoodholidaypark.co.nz. Small, traditional tree-lined site with free wi-fi, swimming pool, TV room, aviary, herb garden, bike rental, small shop, and strong recycling ethos. Camping **$17**, cabins **$65**

Hat Trick Lodge 25 Wallace St ☎03 528 5353, ⓦhattricklodge.co.nz. Conveniently located opposite the i-SITE, this purpose-built hostel has high standards, a spacious and well-equipped kitchen and lounge, bike rental and free gear storage, as well as a separate women's dorm and a family room with its own bathroom and kitchen. Dorms **$27**, rooms **$62**

Motueka Beach Reserve Wharf Rd, 4km southeast of town. Council-run waterside parking for self-contained campervans only, with toilets and cold showers nearby, plus BBQs and picnic tables. Maximum two nights. **Free**

Motueka Top 10 Holiday Park 10 Fearon St ☎03 528 7189, ⓦmotuekatop10.co.nz. Range of accommodation at this leafy site with well-kept facilities, including heated swimming pool, spa pool, just 1km north of the town centre. Camping/site **$45**, units **$125**

★**Pah Rd B&B** 83 Riwaka Kaiteriteri Rd ☎03 528 5410, ⓦpahrd.co.nz. Two private units hidden in the family garden and only minutes from the beach. Go for the straw-bale studio, with its open-air bathroom, fire bath and kitchen, or the slightly more conventional cottage.

Continental breakfasts with home-made ingredients (yoghurt, muesli, bread and eggs) are provided. **$150**

The Resurgence Riwaka Valley Rd, 12km northwest of town ☎03 528 4664, ⓦresurgence.co.nz. A relaxing boutique lodge tucked away near the resurgence of the Riwaka River from below Takaka Hill. The attention to detail is staggering, from sound eco-credentials to the well-planned meals ($90). Facilities include an outdoor pool and spa, gym and bushwalks. Rooms are in the house or cabins. **$545**

Rowan Cottage 27 Fearon St ☎03 528 6492, ⓦrowancottage.net. Tastefully styled, small cottage with a lovingly tended garden that holds a self-contained guest room with a private entrance and en suite. Continental breakfasts are available ($20) and everyone can use the barbecue. **$130**

★**Treedimensions Organic Farmstay** Shaggery Rd, 10km west of town ☎03 528 8718, ⓦtreedimensions .co.nz. Wake up to birdsong and breakfast on the deck of the attractive, great-value self-contained rooms with comfy beds. Sit overlooking an amazing certified organic orchard with 45 types of fruit and 700 species (you can usually try whatever's ripe), explore the grounds on foot or have a chat with the welcoming host, who is the Gandalf of all things organic. **$135**

YHA Motueka 310 High St ☎03 528 9229, ⓦlaughingkiwi.co.nz. Friendly, central backpackers spread over three houses, with spacious dorms and rooms, a self-contained cottage ($130), plus plenty of outdoor seating, barbecues, free wi-fi and free hot tub. Dorms **$28**, rooms **$66**

EATING, DRINKING AND ENTERTAINMENT

UPPER MOUTERE

★**Moutere Inn** 1406 Moutere Hwy ☎03 543 2759, ⓦmoutereinn.co.nz. Established in 1850, the inn has claims as New Zealand's oldest pub and now expertly balances being a local boozer, brewer and shrine to fine beverages. Alongside the quality pub snacks and main meals ($15–25) you can sip a tasting tray of four beers or a glass of wine – they have sixteen taps (including proper handpulls), around thirty different wines as well as thirteen single malts and six brands of tequila. Thurs–Sun noon–9pm or later.

UPPER MOUTERE WINERIES

★**Glover's** Gardner Valley Rd ☎03 543 2698, ⓦglovers-vineyard.co.nz. A wonderful small-output, one-man-and-his-cats winery run by the slightly eccentric Dave Glover, once renowned for tucking a Wagner CD into every package destined for overseas. Wagner usually plays in the background while you taste (free) European-structured wines crafted to produce highly tannic reds (Pinot Noir and Cabernet Sauvignon) and acidic whites

(Sauvignon Blanc and Riesling) that stand up for themselves. Daily 10am–5pm.

Kahurangi Sunrise Rd ☎03 543 2983, ⓦkahurangiwine.com. Respected winery, offering tastings ($2 for four wines) from some of the South Island's oldest commercial vines (though that's only 1973), as well as the estate's own-brand olive oil and a café, popular for wood-fired pizza ($10–25). Daily 10am–4.30pm.

Neudorf Neudorf Rd, Upper Moutere ☎03 543 2643, ⓦneudorf.co.nz. Relaxed winery in a low-slung wooden building covered by vines with simple outdoor seating in the shade of tall ancient trees. It is a lovely spot for tastings (free), some from the 30-year-old vines on site – splash out ($2.50) to sample the Moutere Chardonnay and the Pinot Noir, two of the country's best. Everything is available by the bottle and glass. Daily 10am–5pm; closed weekends May, June & Sept, and all through July & Aug.

Seifried Corner of SH60 and Redwood Rd ☎03 544 1600, ⓦseifried.co.nz. The area's largest winery offering a wide range of wines to taste ($6); try the Austrian Würzer and Zweigelt varietals, unique within New Zealand. The

8

separately run restaurant fancies itself as fine dining, reflected in the high-end pricing. Daily 10am–4.30pm.

Woollaston Estates 243 Old Coach Rd ☎ 03 543 2817, ⓦ woollaston.co.nz. Swish, fascinating, certified organic winery landscaped into the Moutere Hills with tussock-roofed buildings where operations are all gravity-fed. Try the restaurant, enjoy a platter ($35) or just a tasting (free) with great views over the vines to the coast. A huge steel sculpture welcomes visitors and the art collections include works by relative Toss Woollaston (see p.460). Daily 11am–4.30pm.

MAPUA

Golden Bear Brewing Company 12 Aranui Rd ☎ 03 540 3210, ⓦ goldenbearbrewing.com. Top-class microbrews: elegant lagers and super-hoppy pale ales to take away (grab a Fat Toad to enjoy with fish and chips from the *Smokehouse*), or drink in with the brewing tanks as a backdrop. They also dish up some US versions of Mexican food to soak up the ale. There's often live music on Sunday afternoons. Wed–Fri 4–8pm, Sat & Sun noon–8pm(ish).

★**Jester House** 7km north of Mapua at Tasman ☎ 03 526 6742, ⓦ jesterhouse.co.nz. A rewarding licensed daytime café popular for its tasty food, garden seating, rose arbours, giant chess set and tame eels to keep the kids entertained. The food is all home-baked and reasonably priced, and the coffee is strong. Sept–May daily 9am–5pm; May–Aug Thurs–Sun 9am–4.30pm.

★**The Smokehouse** Shed 2 & 3, Aranui Rd ☎ 03 540 2280, ⓦ smokehouse.co.nz. Sells delicious manuka-smoked fish and mussels, widely acclaimed fish pâtés and lovely traditional fish and chips. Bring along a loaf of bread and some wine and enjoy a picnic on a bench at one of the uncluttered ends of the wharf. Sun–Thurs 11am–7.30pm, Fri & Sat 11am–8pm.

MOTUEKA

Chokdee 109 High St ☎ 03 528 0318. Reliable Thai cuisine to eat in or take away, with all the usual soups, curries and noodle dishes at modest prices ($9–29). Licensed. Daily 11am–2pm & 5pm–late.

Elevation 218 High St. Licensed café with the best food in town, including some great breakfasts, mains like house honey-smoked pork – none of it over $25. Daily 8am–8pm.

★**Ginger Dynamite** Cnr School and Main roads, 7.5km from town. Sit among the 50s kitsch in the old Great Universal Store, and have a paper cup of the fantastic coffee, a cake from the counter, or – if you're lucky – one of

their home-made pies. Daily 8am–3pm.

The Hop Federation 483 Main Rd, Riwaka ☎ 03 528 0486 ⓦ hopfederation.co.nz. A small craft brewery open for tastings and takeaways of their lovingly produced beers – the Red IPA is a real treat. Daily 11am–6pm.

Hot Mama's 105 High St ☎ 03 528 7039, ⓦ hotmamas .co.nz. After years of being the coolest place in town, they've had to cut back the number of gigs but have also increased the specials: pasta, fish, eye fillet and game dishes ($19–28 or so) on a regularly changing menu that concentrates on locally sourced ingredients. Daily 8.30am–9.30pm.

★**Red Beret** 147 High St ☎ 03 528 0087. Excellent café that draws in locals for a wide range of all-day breakfasts and lunches, from filo wraps and pasta dishes to gourmet burgers, steak sandwiches, excellent balsamic mushrooms ($16) and delicious monster slices of cake. Daily 7.30am–4pm.

Riwaka Hotel Main Rd, Riwaka ☎ 03 528 7110, ⓦ riwaka hotel.co.nz. Traditional locals' bar with pub grub, which also books NZ's top bands and has a high-class restaurant tucked out back serving the likes of lamb cutlets with smoked paprika polenta ($33). Daily noon–late; restaurant 5.30pm–late, daily in summer, April–Dec Wed–Sun.

Smiths Veggie Sales 524 Main Rd, Riwaka. The Smiths still grow their own veg to sell here, but now you can get breakfast, cake or a toasted sammie too (everything's under $20). Mon–Sat 7am–5.30pm, Sun 7am–4pm.

Swinging Sultan 172 High St ☎ 03 528 8909. Kebab takeaway with just a couple of tables on the pavement, where you can tuck into chicken and beef kebabs or falafel ($9–12). Daily 8.30am–8pm.

★**T.O.A.D. Hall** 502 High St, 3km south of town ⓦ toadhallmotueka.co.nz. Organic fruit-and-veg vendor and café with a flower-filled garden that's perfect for imbibing delicious made-to-order ice cream, gourmet pies, bagels, great coffee and decent breakfasts. Live music on Friday and Saturday summer evenings. Daily 8am–5pm, closes 10pm Thurs–Sun in summer.

CINEMA AND THEATRE

Gecko 23b Wallace St ☎ 03 528 9996, ⓦ geckotheatre .co.nz. Two small cinemas, two discount days (Tuesday and Wednesday), comfy seats and a mix of art-house and the mainstream.

State Cinema Old Wharf Rd ☎ 03 528 8648, ⓦ statecinemas.co.nz. Screens all the latest mainstream films.

Abel Tasman National Park and around

Abel Tasman National Park, 60km north of Nelson, is stunningly beautiful with golden sandy beaches lapped by crystal-clear waters and lush green bush, interspersed with granite outcrops and inhabited by many birds. Deservedly it has an international

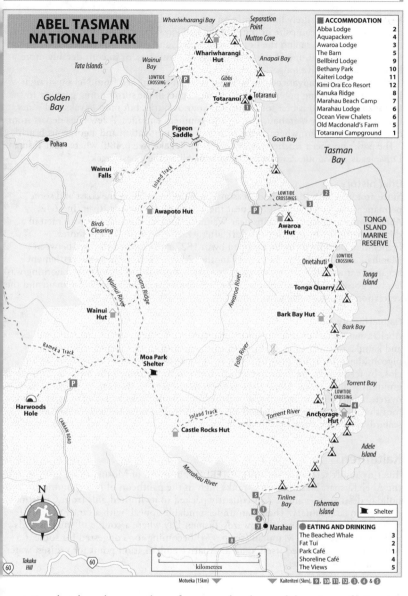

ABEL TASMAN NATIONAL PARK

■ ACCOMMODATION	
Abba Lodge	2
Aquapackers	4
Awaroa Lodge	3
The Barn	5
Bellbird Lodge	9
Bethany Park	10
Kaiteri Lodge	11
Kimi Ora Eco Resort	12
Kanuka Ridge	8
Marahau Beach Camp	7
Marahau Lodge	6
Ocean View Chalets	6
Old Macdonald's Farm	5
Totaranui Campground	1

● EATING AND DRINKING	
The Beached Whale	3
Fat Tui	2
Park Café	1
Shoreline Café	4
The Views	5

reputation that draws large numbers of trampers, kayakers and day-trippers from November to March. But despite being New Zealand's smallest national park – just 20km by 25km – the Abel Tasman absorbs crowds tolerably well and compensates with scenic splendour on an awesome scale.

Most visitors come to see the coastline. Some come to hike the **Abel Tasman Coast Track** with its picturesque mixture of dense coastal bushwalking, gentle climbs to lookouts and walks across idyllic beaches. Abundant water taxis mean you can pick the sections to hike and get a lift back when you've had enough. Others come to

kayak, spending leisurely lunchtimes on golden sands before paddling off in the late afternoon sun to a campsite or hut. Hiking and kayaking can be combined, and you might even tack on **sailing** the limpid waters to round off the experience. You can stay in the park, either at one of the DOC huts and campsites, or in considerably more luxury at an attractive lodge.

With **guided and advanced trip booking** you can be whisked from Nelson straight into the park, missing potentially fascinating nights in the surrounding gateway towns. **Motueka** (see p.468) is best for organizing your own trip, but most kayaks and water taxis leave from tiny **Marahau**, at the park's southern entrance. A few trips depart from diminutive **Kaiteriteri**, where there's plenty of accommodation and a gorgeous beach.

The park's northern reaches are accessed from **Takaka** (see p.480) where Abel Tasman Drive leads to Wainui, Awaroa and **Totaranui**, all on the Coast Track.

Brief history

Since around 1500, Maori made seasonal encampments along the coast and some permanent settlements flourished near the mouth of the Awaroa River. In 1642, **Abel Tasman** anchored two ships near Wainui in Golden Bay and lost four men in a skirmish with the Ngati Tumatakokiri, after which he departed these shores. Frenchman **Dumont d'Urville** dropped by in 1827 and explored the area between Marahau and Torrent Bay, but it was another 23 years before **European settlement** began in earnest. The settlers chopped, quarried, burned and cleared until nothing was left but gorse and bracken. Happily, few obvious signs of their invasion remain and the vegetation has vigorously regenerated.

Natural history

Abel Tasman is full of rich and varied **plant life** with beech trees in the damp gullies and kanuka tolerating the wild and windy areas. **Bird** species include tui, native pigeons, bellbirds (their presence betrayed by a distinctive call), fantails that flutter close by feeding off the insects you disturb as you walk through the bush, and bobbing, ground-dwelling weka. Along the coast you might see the distinctive orange-beaked oystercatchers picking their way along the beaches and shags that dive to great depths for fish. Offshore, the **Tonga Island Marine Reserve** is famous for its **fur seal colony**, seabirds, and varied and bountiful fish.

Kaiteriteri

The tiny resort settlement of **KAITERITERI**, 15km north of Motueka and just south of the Abel Tasman National Park, ranks high in the pantheon of Kiwi summer-holiday destinations and is consequently packed to its limited gills from Christmas through to late January. There's an understandable appeal, with a sandy arc of safe swimming beach looking out towards Tasman Bay where a couple of small islands add perspective. With Marahau (see p.474) becoming too congested for some, Kaiteriteri has fashioned itself as an alternative embarkation point for cruises, water taxis and kayaking trips.

Marahau

About 8km north of Kaiteriteri, tiny **MARAHAU** is poised at the southern entrance to the Abel Tasman National Park. All the tours, water taxis and kayak operators not working out of Kaiteriteri or Motueka are based here, making this a very popular last or first night of civilization for park users.

The beach road runs through the settlement to the **park entrance**, marked by an unstaffed DOC display shelter. A long boardwalk across marshland then leads into the national park.

Inside the national park

There are a plethora of **ways to explore** Abel Tasman National Park – no matter what combination of activities you'd like to try, there's almost bound to be an obliging operator. Relatively few people tramp the **Inland Track**, and most are keen to stick to the **Coast Track**, with its long golden beaches, and the constant temptation to snorkel in some of the idyllic bays. Unsurprisingly, the coast is where you'll find most of the **accommodation**, ranging from beachside campsites to swanky lodges. **Water taxis** take you virtually anywhere along the coast and as far north as the lovely beach at Totaranui. They usually give a commentary along the way, though there are also dedicated **cruises**, some visiting the seal colony on the **Tonga Island Marine Reserve** and **Split Apple Rock**, a large boulder that has split and fallen into two halves, like an upright, neatly cleaved Braeburn.

The intricate details of the coast are best explored by **kayak** (see box, pp.476–477), either on a guided trip or by renting kayaks and setting your own itinerary. Better still, combine kayaking with walking a section of the Coast Track. Water taxi drop-offs and guided kayaking are banned in the section of park north of Totaranui, making this a much **quieter area** to hike and hang out.

Abel Tasman Coast Track

The **Abel Tasman Coast Track** (60km; 3–5 days) is one of the **easiest** of New Zealand's Great Walks, one for people who wouldn't normally think of themselves as trampers, but you should still get DOC's *Abel Tasman Coast Track* leaflet. Lack of fitness is no impediment as huts are never more than four hours apart (campsites 2hr) and you can use water taxis to skip some sections or just to pick the bits you fancy walking. In dry conditions you don't even need strong boots – trainers will do. All this makes the Coast Track extremely popular, especially from December to the end of February when some sections seem like a hikers' highway, although heading for the section north of Totaranui will often deliver a less frenetic experience.

The **route** traverses broad golden beaches lapped by emerald waters, punctuated by granite pillars silhouetted against the horizon and zigzagging gentle climbs through valleys. The main planning difficulty is coping with the **tide-dependent** section across the Awaroa Estuary. Tide times will help you decide which way you're going to do the track – if there are low tides in the afternoon you'll probably want to head south, if they're in the morning, head north. Even at low tide you can still expect to get your feet wet. Before setting off you should also arrange your transport drop-offs and pick-ups with a water taxi or cruise company (see pp.476–477). In winter (May–Sept) you can mountain bike from Totaranui to Wainui Bay.

For accommodation along the track, see p.478.

Marahau to Anchorage
12.4km; 4hr

Direct access from Marahau makes this section popular. The bush isn't the most beautiful but the beaches are unparalleled. The track follows a wooden causeway across the estuary to Tinline Bay before rounding a point overlooking Fisherman and Adele islands. As the track winds in and out of gullies the coastal scenery is obscured by beech forest and tall kanuka trees until you emerge at Anchorage, with its shiny new hut, campsite and summertime offshore backpackers.

Anchorage to Bark Bay
8.7km; 3hr

Cross Torrent Bay two hours either side of low tide, or be prepared to skirt the bay (adding an hour) to reach the few dozen houses that constitute **Torrent Bay**. Climb out of the bay through pine trees to the gorgeous Falls River, crossed by a 47m-long swingbridge. Bark Bay hut and campsites are 1hr ahead.

Bark Bay to Awaroa

11.5km; 4hr

After crossing (or skirting) Bark Bay Estuary, cut away from the coast to return at Tonga Quarry where there's a campsite and views out to Tonga Island and the Marine Reserve. You soon reach the beach at Onetahuti with its new walkway and bridge. The track then climbs to the Tonga Saddle and descends to Awaroa Inlet, its small settlement and a DOC hut with a campsite alongside; *Awaroa Lodge* is within easy walking distance and has a restaurant and bar.

Awaroa to Totaranui

7.1km; 2hr 30min

You must cross the Awaroa Estuary (1.5hr either side of low tide) to reach Goat Bay then up to a lookout above Skinner Point before reaching Totaranui, with its great arc of beach and extensive campsite.

Totaranui to Whariwharangi

9.8km; 3hr 30min

After rounding the Totaranui Estuary, press on over and around rocky headlands as far as Mutton Cove then wander through alternating shrubland and beaches, preferably making a side trip to Separation Point with its lookout and fur seal colony. Continue to the hut at Whariwharangi, a former homestead.

8

ACTIVITIES AND TOURS IN ABEL TASMAN NATIONAL PARK

Although there are a number of operators offering activities such as **scuba diving**, **scenic cruises** and guided **walks**, one of the best ways to explore the park's more remote shores is by **sea-kayak**. Some of the best operators for these activities are listed below.

KAYAKING

It's hard to beat gently paddling along, exploring little coves (and possibly being accompanied by seals or dolphins), stopping on a golden beach for a dip and then continuing to a campsite where you can cool a beer in a stream.

Marahau, at the southern end of the park, is the kayaking hotspot for many operators. Most companies offer a broadly similar range of one- to five-day guided trips and freedom rentals. The stretch north of Marahau is known as the "Mad Mile", because that's where you'll see the largest concentration of paddlers, but congestion eases further north.

Guided trips typically combine paddling, water taxis, visiting seals and walking, while **multi-day** guided trips include all that plus accommodation, food and extra time to explore.

For **freedom rentals** you are typically given shore-based instruction then let loose in a double kayak. You are not allowed to venture north of Abel Head at the north end of the Tonga Island Marine Reserve nor paddle solo. Conditions are generally benign and suitable for relative beginners, though if you've any doubts about your ability, opt for a guided trip. Rental **prices** are around $80 per person for your first day, dropping to $120 for two days, and you can get one-way deals, catching a water taxi back ($200 for 3 days). Most companies have a range of camping **gear rental**, will store your vehicle while you're away and operate year-round, though the range of trips is reduced in winter.

ADVENTURE OPERATORS

Abel Tasman Canyons ☎ 0800 863 472, ⓦ abel tasmancanyons.co.nz. Get away from everyone else by abseiling and hurling yourself down waterfalls. Torrent River ($259 with lunch and water taxis) is a great overall introduction (including an optional 8m jump) that can be combined with a night at *Aquapackers* before walking and kayaking out ($415). All gear provided.

Abel Tasman Charters ☎ 0800 223 522, ⓦ abeltasmancharters.co.nz. Operates a small cruise boat from near Kaiteriteri, with a flexible itinerary partly determined by the guests. Usually there's seal viewing, a visit to Split Apple Rock, time ashore and a good picnic lunch. Nov–April only ($245).

Abel Tasman Kayaks 273 Sandy Bays Rd, Marahau

Whariwharangi to Wainui

5.5km; 1hr 30min

It is an easy walk to the road on the eastern side of Wainui Bay, where buses pick up, but it is also possible to cross Wainui Bay (2hr either side of low tide), or follow the road round the bay. If you follow the road, you can also take in the short hike up to the Wainui Falls, which heads off the road at the base of Wainui Bay.

The Inland Track

The strenuous **Inland Track** (41km; 3 days) between Marahau and Totaranui is far less popular than the Coast Track, and requires moderate fitness and decent tramping gear. The track can be combined with the Coast Track to make a six- to seven-day loop.

The route climbs from sea level to **Evans Ridge** past granite outcrops and views of the coast: highlights include the **Pigeon Saddle**, the moorlands of Moa Park and the moon-like Canaan landscape, with an optional side-trip to Harwood's Hole (see p.480).

Camping is not recommended on the Inland Track, but there are two, small, first-come, first-served **DOC huts** ($5; backcountry hut passes valid), with water and toilets but no cooking facilities.

ARRIVAL AND DEPARTURE   **ABEL TASMAN NATIONAL PARK AND AROUND**

Access into the park proper is generally on foot or by boat, but a couple of roads extend to the park entrances – principally Marahau in the south and Totaranui in the north.

☎0800 732 529, ⊚abeltasmankayaks.co.nz. Guided kayak trip specialists based in Marahau offering half-day ($130) and full-day ($110–225) trips, plus a half-day seal sanctuary tour ($199) – all of which include a water taxi ride around much of the park. They also do catered overnight trips (from $220), and rent freedom kayaks.
Abel Tasman Sailing ☎0800 467 245, ⊚sailingadventures.co.nz. Offers trips on one of three catamarans, combining sailing with walking, seal watching and kayaking, or you can just sail. They also do overnight trips ($94–219) and boat charters.
Abel Tasman Sea Shuttle ☎0800 732 748, ⊚abeltasmanseashuttles.co.nz. Kaiteriteri-based water taxis and scenic cruises (half-day $45; full day $76), with cruise and walk options (from $66). If you get up to Tonga Island, you can add a side trip ($35) in their semi-submersible to peep at the sealife.
Aquataxi ☎0800 278 282, ⊚aquataxi.co.nz. Water taxis from Marahau and Kaiteriteri, plus scenic cruises ($67–82).
★**Golden Bay Kayaks** ☎03 525 9095, ⊚goldenbaykayaks.co.nz. Highly recommended Pohara-based company who are the only ones to operate in the beautiful, quieter northern end of the park. Offers guided trips (half-day $85) and an unguided overnight trip ($90). Also rents double (half-day $90; full day $110) and sit-on-top kayaks ($25/1hr), plus stand-up paddleboards ($15–20/hr).
Kahu Kayaks ☎03 527 8300, ⊚kahukayaks.co.nz. Marahau-based kayak rentals and guided trips that

often come in fractionally cheaper than the opposition. A good trip is the Swingers Delight ($160), which gives you three hours paddling the Mad Mile followed by a visit to the seal colony, a coastal walk (2.5hr) and a water taxi back to Marahau.
Kaiteriteri Kayaks ☎0800 252 925, ⊚seakayak.co.nz. Guided trips from Kaiteriteri, including a half-day paddle to Split Apple Rock ($80); or a full-day with a water taxi ride to Onetahuti Beach, paddle to Tonga Island and the seals, lunch, and paddle to Anchorage Bay for water taxi pick-up ($199). Assorted combos also available.
The Sea Kayak Company 506 High St, Motueka ☎0508 252 925, ⊚seakayaknz.co.nz. Family-owned and -operated Motueka-based business offering half-day trips (Tonga Island $190), multi-day excursions (three days $540) and rentals ($65/person/day; reducing on subsequent days), with free hot showers, wi-fi, parking and transport from Motueka.
Wilsons ☎0800 223 582, ⊚abeltasman.co.nz. Long-standing operator, offering all manner of trips including: a half-day Split Apple Rock kayak ($85); a five-day walking trip with three days walking and two days loafing at luxury beachfront lodges ($2100, all food included); cruises from Kaiteriteri to Totaranui and back on a spacious and stable catamaran (1–2 daily; 4hr; $78); and a Seals and Beach trip (6–8hr; $68), cruising around the Tonga Island seal colony with plenty of time to walk from Tonga Quarry to Medlands Beach and get in a swim.

8

By bus The best bus service in the region is Abel Tasman Coachlines (Nelson; ☎ 03 548 0285, ⓦ abeltasmantravel .co.nz), which runs two to three times daily between Motueka, Kaiteriteri and Marahau. One service runs from Nelson (7.45am) for Motueka (1hr; $12 one way) and Marahau (1hr 50min; $20), connecting with launch services deeper into the park. Golden Bay Coachlines (☎ 03 525 8352, ⓦ goldenbaycoachlines.co.nz) connects Takaka and Motueka (7.45am in summer; $28) and Totaranui ($38).

GETTING AROUND

By water taxi Water taxis based in Kaiteriteri and Marahau give you the chance to walk a particular section of coast or simply ride to any of six beaches along the coast – Anchorage, Torrent Bay, Bark Bay, Onetahuti, Awaroa and Totaranui. Three main companies do two to five scheduled runs from the south of the park to Totaranui and back, charging virtually the same price – just book whichever is going the right way at the right time, or call Aquatax (☎ 0800 278 282, ⓦ aquataxi.co.nz). Typical one-way fares from Marahau are to Anchorage ($35), Torrent Bay ($35), Bark Bay ($40), Onetahuti ($42), Awaroa ($45) and Totaranui ($47).

INFORMATION

Abel Tasman National Park The main sources of information are the i-SITE offices in Nelson, Motueka and Takaka, all of which will book boats, kayaks, hut and camping tickets, transport and accommodation. There are also unmanned DOC display shelters at the Marahau and Totaranu park entrances, with tide times and safety precautions.

ACCOMMODATION

KAITERITERI

★**Bellbird Lodge** Sandy Bay Rd ☎ 03 527 8555, ⓦ bellbirdlodge.com. Offers two comfortable suites, great views, first-class care and welcoming hosts, all in the family home where the peace and quiet is only shattered by the inconsiderate local birds. **$350**

Bethany Park 88 Martin Farm Rd ☎ 03 527 8014, ⓦ bethanypark.co.nz. Set slightly back from the centre, convenient for the mountain bike tracks, and with a good choice of accommodation. Upgraded ablutions and kitchen blocks, water slide, and play areas. Camping/2 people **$25**, en-suite cabins **$85**

Kaiteri Lodge Inlet Rd, just back from the beach ☎ 03 527 8281, ⓦ kaiterilodge.co.nz. Something between a motel and backpackers, with eight-bed dorms and en-suite doubles. It's the primary stop for all the tour buses, including Kiwi Experience, and is right by *The Beached Whale* (see opposite). Dorms **$35**, en-suite rooms **$160**

Kimi Ora Eco Resort 99 Martin Farm Rd, signposted 1km back from the beach road ☎ 0508 546 4672, ⓦ kimiora.com. A genuine European spa complex, set in native bush, with heated indoor and outdoor pools. You can just stay, but the emphasis is on fitness (the mountain-bike park skirts the property), therapy and indulgent massage sessions. Studio **$179**, suites **$219**

MARAHAU

The Barn Harvey Rd ☎ 03 527 8043, ⓦ barn.co.nz. A lively backpackers near the park entrance with an outdoor fireplace and baths in the grounds. Well set up for campers with an outdoor cooking area, the site also has dorms, twins and doubles ($80), mostly in basic cabins. Camping **$20**, dorms **$32**

★**Kanuka Ridge** 21 Moss Rd ☎ 03 527 8435, ⓦ abeltasmanbackpackers.co.nz. Peaceful hostel set on a hill back from the beach with a dedicated walking track just one dorm, several bush-backed rooms, plenty o birdsong, free wi-fi, free bike rental, and the owner can direct you to great tracks and all manner of other cool stuff Closed June–Sept. Dorms **$30**, en suites **$91**

Marahau Beach Camp Franklin St ☎ 0800 808 018 ⓦ abeltasmancentre.co.nz. Unpretentious, well-kept campsite with tent sites, backpackers accommodation and a variety of cabins ($70) on a site with good communal facilities (coin showers) and their own bus service to Nelson and Motueka. Camping **$35**, dorms **$22**,

★**Marahau Lodge** Beach Rd ☎ 03 527 8250, ⓦ abeltas manmarahaulodge.co.nz. Tastefully refurbished studio and larger chalets scattered about the lawns, each with private deck, give a relaxed feel to this upmarket lodge with outdoor spa, sauna, and breakfast delivered to you room (on request). **$175**

Ocean View Chalets Beach Rd ☎ 03 527 8232 ⓦ accommodationabeltasman.co.nz. Open year-round these ten timber chalets set on a hillside contain spacious comfortable rooms, all with balconies and distant sea views from the beds, which are soft and welcoming. Studio **$145**, self-contained unit **$185**

Old Macdonald's Farm Harvey Rd, by the park entrance ☎ 03 527 8288, ⓦ oldmacs.co.nz. Family-run farm with cabins, cottages and a self-contained studio ($80–150), plus camping and a huge wooded area next to a couple of swimming holes. There's also secure parking ($6/night), a well-stocked shop and gear storage. Camping **$16**, dorms **$28**

ABEL TASMAN NATIONAL PARK

Unlike many of New Zealand's national parks, Abel Tasman

ffers a range of accommodation, accessed either by boat or he Abel Tasman Coast Path. Most people stay at the four DOC uts, spaced around four hours' walk apart along the coast, while hardened trampers will want to camp at some of the eighteen DOC campsites strung along the coast, all either eside beaches or near the DOC huts (whose facilities you are ot supposed to use). Bookings are required year-round for ll huts and campsites and should be made at least a week in dvance in summer. Book online (w doc.govt.nz) or at an -SITE. There are also private accommodation options and multi-day all-inclusive trips to consider; Wilsons (see box, .477) run three- to five-day guided walking and kayaking olidays with comfortable accommodation at their two rackside lodges at Torrent Bay and Awaroa.

Huts These come with water, heating, good toilets, basic ut comfortable bunks, but there are no cooking facilities: ring a sleeping bag, cooking stove, pans, utensils, food nd a torch. Two-night maximum stay in summer. $32

Campsites All eighteen DOC sites have a water supply and oilets, but it means carrying more gear and you'll need lots f sandfly repellent. Only the Anchorage and Bark Bay ampsites allow campfires. Two-night maximum stay in ummer for all campsites. $14

Abba Lodge Awaroa Bay ☏ 03 528 8758, w abbalodge hostel.com. Newest backpacker accommodation in the ark, with its own pizzeria and close to the *Awaroa Lodge*

restaurant and bar. Closed May–Sept. Dorms $50, doubles $125

Aquapackers Anchorage ☏ 0800 430 744, w aquapackers.co.nz. Expensive backpacker accommodation in made-up dorms and doubles aboard two converted boats moored for the summer just off the beach in Anchorage Bay: there's a free ferry from beach to boat. The package includes BBQ dinner, basic breakfast and access to a pay bar. It can feel cramped but the stillness of the park at night and sounds of lapping water make it worthwhile. Sept–May only. Dorms $75, doubles $199

Awaroa Lodge Awaroa ☏ 03 528 8758, w awaroalodge.co.nz. Nestled in the bush with great wetland views, this upmarket lodge uses ingredients from its organic garden in its classy restaurant (mains around $40). Hikers and casual visitors can drop in for a coffee or a drink by the enormous fireplace, but it is really aimed at the well-heeled arriving by water taxi or helicopter to stay in the plush en-suite rooms or suites. Closed May–Sept. $290

★ **Totaranui Campground** Totaranui w doc.govt.nz. The only car-accessible accommodation on the Abel Tasman coast, this huge campsite (there's room for 850 people) is so busy in summer that it's online booking-only for Christmas to the end of January. A separate section for track hikers usually has space (one night only), though you might want to press on. $14

EATING AND DRINKING

KAITERITERI

The Beached Whale Inlet Rd ☏ 03 527 8114. Party bar specializing in booze deals, cheap food and live music. Mon–Sat 3–11pm in summer, 5–11pm in winter.

Shoreline Café Corner of Inlet Rd and Kaiteriteri–Sandy Bay Rd ☏ 03 527 8507. Beach views from the terrace and pretty decent meals (including Golden Bay clams), all ranging from $18–28. Daily 9am–10pm in summer, 9am–6pm in winter.

The Views 99 Martin Farm Rd ☏ 0508 546 4672, w kimiora.com. The resort's restaurant serves tasty vegetarian dinners (such as tofu red coconut curry for $24) with a selection of local wines, beers and juices. Nov–Easter Mon–Sat 6–9pm.

MARAHAU

★ **Fat Tui** 11 Marahau Valley Rd, at Kahu Kayaks. A van selling wonderful takeaway fish and chips ($9.50), salads and gourmet burgers (try the Moroccan lamb $14), all to restaurant standard. Sept–Dec Wed–Sun noon–8pm, Jan–April daily 8am–8pm.

★ **Park Café** 1 Harveys Rd ☏ 03 527 8270, w parkcafe .co.nz. Located at the hiking trailhead, this place is legendary among appreciative walkers emerging from the park. Famed for its signature beef goulash with potato gnocchi ($26), wholesome lunches, good coffee, restorative beers and a range of delicious dinner mains ($19–32). Don't miss dessert ($12). Daily 8am–8pm.

Golden Bay

Occupying the northwestern tip of the South Island, **GOLDEN BAY** curves gracefully from the northern fringes of Abel Tasman National Park to the encircling arm of **Farewell Spit**, backed by the magnificent Kahurangi National Park. With bush-clad mountains on three sides and waves lapping at the fourth, Golden Bay's inaccessibility has helped foster the illusion that if it is not a world apart it is certainly otherworldly.

Wainui Bay, just east of the main town of **Takaka**, is most likely the spot where Abel Tasman first anchored, guaranteeing his place in history as the first European to encounter Aotearoa and its fierce inhabitants. The apparently isolating presence of

Takaka Hill keeps today's bayside communities from growing virally, though the area has attracted a cross section of immigrants, alternative lifestylers, craftspeople, businessmen and artists, which goes some way to explaining the population's perceived spirit of **independence**. The area has been particularly popular with German-speakers who constitute almost four percent of the five thousand residents. Sunny, beautiful and full of fascinating sights, Golden Bay deserves a couple days of your time and has a knack of inducing you to stay longer.

Takaka Hill

Ngarua Caves Oct–April daily 10am–4pm • $15 • 45min guided tours on the hour

Unless you'd prefer to fly, the only way to get to Golden Bay is on SH60, a sealed but very twisty road over **Takaka Hill** that skirts the inland border of the Abel Tasman National Park. Take it slow and stop frequently at viewpoints with glorious mountain views and seascapes stretching from Nelson north to D'Urville Island.

Atop Takaka Hill, some 20km north of Motueka, you can be guided through **Ngarua Caves**, a pleasing show cave with illuminated stalactite formations and skeletons of moa which fell through holes in the cave roof.

Harwoods Hole

Accessed along Canaan Rd, 500m north of Ngarua Caves

The twisting, unsealed Canaan Road runs 11km to a car park with access to **Harwoods Hole**, a huge vertical shaft 176m deep and over 50m in diameter, which links up to a vast cave system below. Reached by an enchanting trail (6km return; 1hr 30min; mostly level) through beech forest that follows a dry rock-strewn riverbed, the lip has no viewing platform, so don't go crashing about or you'll end up in it before you see it. About 30min along the trail, a side track (20min return) leads to a **clifftop viewpoint** with stunning views down towards the Takaka Valley and the coast. A spot beside Canaan Road 3km back from the car park was one of several sites in the area used by the **Lord of the Rings** crew and featured again in *The Hobbit* films.

Rameka Track

5km; 3hr one way; 750m descent

Mountain-bikers are spoilt for choice here, with the excellent new Canaan Downs tracks leading off from the road-end car park, and the clearly signposted **Rameka Track**, which follows one of the earliest surveyed routes down into the Takaka Valley. Along the way it includes Great Expectations, a section of single-track designed and built by Jonathan Kennett, co-author of New Zealand's mountain-bikers' bible (see p.823), on land being planted out in native trees. Find an amenable driver who can meet you at the bottom, thus avoiding the slog back up SH60 and Canaan Road.

Takaka and around

The small town of **TAKAKA**, almost 60km north of Motueka, is Golden Bay's largest settlement, and one that has increasingly set its cap at the summer tourists, while continuing to cater for the local farming community and barefoot crusties who emerge from their shacks and tipis to sell home-made crafts and natural healing services. Immediately north, **Te Waikoropupu Springs** emerge from their underground lair, while to the north yawns a considerable stretch of beautiful bay, running parallel to SH60 as it rolls into Collingwood and Farewell Spit. To the east, Abel Tasman Drive winds past the safe swimming beach at **Pohara** and a few minor sights before heading into the northern section of the Abel Tasman National Park (see p.472). Most of the action in Takaka takes place along Commercial Street (SH60 as it passes through town), where you can quickly get a handle on the spirit of the place by visiting **Golden Bay Organics**, at no. 47, and the **Monza Gallery**, at no. 25.

Golden Bay Museum

73 Commercial St • Mon–Fri 10am–4pm, Sat & Sun 10am–1pm • Donation

The **Golden Bay Museum** has a detailed diorama depicting Abel Tasman's ill-fated trip to Wainui Bay in 1642 plus all manner of historic bits and bobs, from terrifying 1950s contact lenses to the skeleton of a pilot whale. There's coverage of local Maori and the area's industries, and some interactive displays.

Te Waikoropupu Springs

4km north of Takaka, off SH60

One sight not to miss is **Te Waikoropupu Springs**, the largest in the southern hemisphere, set amid old gold workings and regenerating forest. Vast quantities of fresh water well up through crystal-clear vents, one creating the Dancing Sands (where the sands, pushed by the surging water, appear to perform a jig). They're an easy walk along an accessible track (1km return, 30min).

Wild Earth

McCallum Rd, 6km southeast of Takaka • Late Sept–April Wed–Sun and school holidays 10am–5pm • $10 (free if you caught a salmon next door) • ☎ 03 525 8261, ⓦ wildearthnaturepark.co.nz

Even if you don't have kids, follow the families flocking to the banks of the Anatoki River, specifically to this farm park where you can feed and pet the llamas, donkeys, emus, piglets, rabbits and yak (among others). Also up for a free lunch are the Anatoki eels, who live wild in the river but have been fed here since 1914. Put some meat (provided) on a stick and the thick black eels will rise out of the water. There's also a café serving lovely organic treats.

Anatoki Salmon

230 McCallum Rd, 6km southeast of Takaka • Christmas–Feb daily 9am–6pm; March–Dec Mon–Sun 9.30am–4pm • Free • ☎ 03 525 7251, ⓦ anatokisalmon.co.nz

You can catch your own hatchery-raised fish at **Anatoki Salmon**. They'll provide you with tackle and you only pay for bait and what you catch ($21/kg of live Chinook or King salmon). They'll prepare your catch as sashimi, smoke or barbecue it; you can eat there or pop it in a pizza box and go somewhere more scenic. There's also a licensed café selling all things salmon-based if, weirdly, you have no luck.

Abel Tasman Drive

East of Takaka, **Abel Tasman Drive** threads its way past the small waterside settlement of Pohara then splits into three, each road ending at a trailhead for the Abel Tasman Coast Track: Awaroa, Totaranui and Wainui Bay – see map on p.473.

Rawhiti Cave

3hr return • Instruction sheet available from DOC

Just off Abel Tasman Drive, a poorly signed rough track, which can be perilously slippery in wet weather and crosses a riverbed, leads to a viewing platform over **Rawhiti Cave**, its cavernous mouth hung with myriad pendulous stalactites, transparent stone straws and a discarded billy, now encrusted in rock deposited from the dripping ceiling. Wear hiking shoes, take a torch and spare batteries.

Grove Scenic Reserve

7km from Takaka • Unrestricted access • Free

From Takaka, follow signs to the wonderful **Grove Scenic Reserve**, a mystical place that could have been transplanted straight from Arthurian legend. Massive rata trees sprout from odd and deformed limestone outcrops, and a ten-minute walk takes you to a narrow slot between two enormous vertical cliffs where a lookout reveals expansive views of the coast and beaches around Pohara. Take your camera.

Pohara

Espresso Ship Nov–May Tues–Sat 10am–4.30pm, but a bit random; check if the sign's out

POHARA, 10km east of Takaka, has a couple of places to stay and eat, a relaxing sandy beach and a working jetty opposite the jarring site of a former cement factory. Among the moored fishing and pleasure boats is *The Espresso Ship*, which roasts, brews and serves excellent organic coffee and an intriguing dandelion espresso. It's actually Jacques Cousteau's old dive ship, the *Physalie* (ask and you might be able to stay on board overnight; $25). At 2pm they feed the stingray.

Just round the corner is pretty **Tata Beach** and the trailhead for **Wainui Falls** (40min return), where Nikau palms shade the banks of the river, and a curtain of spray swathes the rather lovely falls.

Tui Community

The gravel Wainui Bay road runs past the **Tui Community** (one of the last of several spiritual and educational trusts started in Golden Bay in the 1970s), and ends at the northernmost access point to the Coast Track. Other roads go to the Awaroa Estuary, and the wonderful golden arc of **Totaranui Beach**. This is a common place to finish the Coast Track, right by the *Totaranui Campground* (see p.479).

ARRIVAL AND DEPARTURE

TAKAKA AND AROUND

By plane Golden Bay Air (☎ 03 525 8725, ⓦ goldenbayair .co.nz) fly from Wellington.
Destinations Wellington (1–4 daily; 50min).
By bus Golden Bay Coachlines (☎ 03 525 8352, ⓦ goldenbay coachlines.co.nz) run from Nelson and continue north to Collingwood and the Heaphy Track, and east to Totaranui. Both drop off outside the Takaka i-SITE on SH60.
Destinations Collingwood (2 daily; 20min); Heaphy Track (2 daily; 1hr); Motueka (1 daily; 1hr 15min); Nelson (1 daily; 2hr 15min); Totaranui (1 daily; 1hr).

GETTING AROUND

By bike Most of the hostels in Takaka have free bikes for guests, and The Quiet Revolution, 11 Commercial St (closed Sat afternoon & Sun; ☎ 03 525 9555), rents bikes ($25/day; $65/day for full suspension off-road use) and sells the *Fat Tyre Fun* leaflet ($2), containing over a dozen great mountain-bike rides in Golden Bay.
By taxi You don't really need one within town, but to get further out try MaxiCab Shuttles ☎ 03 525 7365.

INFORMATION

Golden Bay Visitor Centre SH60, as you enter Takaka from the south (daily 9am–5pm; ☎ 03 525 9136, ⓦ goldenbaynz.co.nz). Handles bookings, hut tickets for the national parks and rental cars.
DOC 62 Commercial St (Mon–Fri 10.30am–12.30pm and 1.30–3pm, Dec–Easter 9am–4pm; ☎ 03 525 8026). Has the information and expertise to meet your hiking, biking, fishing and ecology needs, including track forecasts and suggestions on getting away from the crowds.
Internet Free wi-fi for an hour plus terminals at the library, 3 Junction St (Mon–Thurs 9.30am–5pm, Fri 9.30am–6pm, Sat 9.30am–12.30pm), and several commercial outlets on Commerce St.

ACCOMMODATION

Golden Bay is a popular holiday spot for both Kiwis and foreign visitors; as a result there is plenty of good-quality accommodation, from backpackers to swanky lodges. Camping ranges from the enormous DOC campsite at Totaranui to wayside spots where you can park your campervan overnight.

TAKAKA

Annie's Nirvana Lodge 25 Motupipi St ☎ 03 525 8766, ⓦ nirvanalodge.co.nz. Enthusiastically-run associate YHA right in town with a homey atmosphere, two kitchens, a female-only dorm, nice garden with lots of seating and a record player, free bikes, and private rooms (including three attractive garden doubles). Dorms $28, rooms $65

★ **Autumn Farm Lodge** 3km south of Takaka, off

SH60 ☎ 03 525 9013, ⊛ autumnfarm.com. Charming gay-friendly lodge, on a sizeable plot with comfortable rooms, a big bathhouse and a laidback (clothing optional) atmosphere. Also hosts an eight-day annual gay summer camp over New Year. Reservations essential. Backpackers $40, B&B $140

Golden Bay Motel 132 Commercial St ☎ 0800 401 212, ⊛ goldenbaymotel.co.nz. Well-kept little motel with off-street parking, limited free wi-fi, and incredibly good-value, spacious, clean, comfy rooms about a 5min walk from the centre of town. Studio $125, motel unit $130

Kiwiana 73 Motupipi St ☎ 03 525 7676, ⊛ kiwianabackpackers.co.nz. Beautifully kept and well-run hostel in a large villa where the Kiwiana theme runs to the labelling of the airy rooms. In the games room they have pool and table tennis. There's a hot tub and BBQ in the well-tended garden, plus free bikes. Closed July & Aug. Dorms $28, rooms $66

Mohua Motels SH60 ☎ 03 525 7222, ⊛ mohuamotels.com. Takaka's newest motel is located at the southern entrance to town and has attractive, well-appointed units, Sky TV and in-room internet. It's all part of a plush package set around a car park about a 5min walk from the local shops. $155

★**Shady Rest** 139 Commercial St ☎ 03 525 9669, ⊛ shadyrest.co.nz. Lovely central B&B in a historic former doctor's house with comfortable, wood-panelled rooms that are either en suite or have a private bathroom. A generous breakfast, solar-heated outdoor bath and a lovely garden that runs down to a peaceful creek make this a treat. $150

AROUND TAKAKA

★**Adrift** Tukurua Rd, 17km north of Takaka ☎ 03 525 8353, ⊛ adrift.co.nz. Five gorgeous, self-contained cottages (and one studio) decorated in chic, modern style and all with direct access across lawns to the beach. All rooms have a sea view, making them perfect for a leisurely breakfast in bed. With double spa baths, free use of kayaks and a small penguin colony on site you may never want to leave. Studio $260, cottages $360

Golden Bay Hideaway 220 McShare Rd, Wainui Bay, 23km east of Takaka ☎ 03 525 7184, ⊛ goldenbayhideaway.co.nz. Wonderful spot, close to the northern end of the Abel Tasman Coast Track, comprising two eco-efficient houses and a "hippie house" (sleeping 4), plus a beautifully crafted house truck. Great views, an outdoor bath and cook-your-own-dinner/breakfast supplies complete the package. Truck $170, houses $225

Laidback Lodge 23 Ironworks Rd, 13km north of Takaka ☎ 03 525 6244, ⊛ laidbacklodge.co.nz. A vibrant, kiwiana *bach* set in the middle of a meadow, surrounded by ponga trees and birds. Enjoy a bush bath under the stars before sleeping in the dinky caravan, or stroll down to the *Mussel Inn* for a few beers. $160

★**Pohara Beach Top 10 Holiday Park** 809 Abel Tasman Drive ☎ 0800 764 272, ⊛ poharabeach.com. A popular, well-equipped traditional Kiwi beachfront holiday park with a broad range of accommodation including cabins ($61–101), excellent communal facilities and very helpful owners. Camping $20, motel $132

★**Sans Souci Inn** 11 Richmond Rd, Pohara Beach, 10km east of Takaka ☎ 03 525 8663, ⊛ sanssouciinn.co.nz. Endearing Swiss-run inn with a communal feel, set in a mud-brick building with sod roof and handmade floor tiles. The six rooms share one large bathroom with shower stalls, bath and composting toilets, though there's also a self-contained cottage sleeping four and an excellent restaurant (see p.484). Guests can use the kitchen or go for the delicious breakfasts ($9–15). Closed July to mid-Sept. Rooms $120, cottage $160

★**Shambhala** SH60, 16km north of Takaka at Onekaka ☎ 03 525 8463, ⊛ shambhala.co.nz. Welcoming shoes-off backpackers located 2km down a track almost opposite the *Mussel Inn*, from where free pick-up can be arranged. There's lovely native gardens, beach access and a slightly spiritual bent, including free daily meditation sessions and yoga classes. Dorms ($28) are in the main house, or there are spacious twins and doubles with lovely sea views in a separate block, with solar-heated showers and composting toilets. Closed June–Oct. Camping and campervans $20, double $68

Totaranui Campground 26km east of Takaka (see p.480). Large and popular beachside campsite within Abel Tasman National Park, with a shop, running water, toilets, picnic tables and cold showers. Book in advance. $15

Waitapu Bridge 4km north of Takaka on SH60. Riverside freedom site for self-contained campervans only. Maximum two-night stay. Free

8

EATING, DRINKING AND ENTERTAINMENT

Takaka has some good places to eat and there are more a few kilometres out that justify the journey. Drinking and music are best in the *Wholemeal Café*, *Roots*, *The Brigand* and the *Mussel Inn*.

TAKAKA

The Brigand 90 Commercial St ☎ 03 525 9636. Relaxed restaurant-bar serving burgers, ribs, and salmon (mains $24–34) – with lots of outdoor seating and live music several nights a week plus open mike on Thurs. Daily 11am–late.

Dangerous Kitchen 46a Commercial St ☎ 03 525 8686 for takeaway orders. Large, good-value café that's very popular with locals for watching the world pass by, or takeaway grub. Exotic pizzas ($15–28) are the mainstay, though they do tasty wraps, good breakfasts (under $20) and salads. Licensed. Mon–Sat 9am–8.30pm (later in summer).

Infusion 30 Commercial St. The only German-run teahouse on the South Island, dishing up the best bread (the flour is freshly stone-ground) and pastries in the bay and thirty varieties of loose tea. Mon–Fri 9am–5pm, Sat 9am–3pm, 8am–6pm in summer.

★**Roots Bar** 1 Commercial St. Hang out around the open fire tucking into lovingly prepared Kiwi-style tapas (nothing over $16) and sipping Nelson-brewed Sprig & Fern beers and ciders as reggae, roots or drum'n'bass music floats by. DJs and bands often play at the weekends until late (occasional $10 cover charge). Tues–Sun 4pm–late.

Schnapp Dragon 1 Hoody Alley, off Commercial St in the town centre ☎03 525 9899, ⓦschnappdragon.co.nz. Takaka's only distillery has an insanely enthusiastic owner who creates world-class whisky, a rum that beats most in the Caribbean, extraordinary liqueurs and champagne from honey. Mon–Fri 9am–5pm, Sat 10am–5pm.

TLC (The Little Café) 65A Commercial St. Tiny coffee house with outdoor seating under a pin oak overlooking the main road, serving the best coffee in the bay and some counter nosh. Mon–Fri 9.30am–4pm.

Village Theatre 32 Commercial St ☎03 525 8483, ⓦvillagetheatre.org.nz. Small not-for-profit cinema screening play, opera and blockbusters.

★**Wholemeal Café** 60 Commercial St. A Takaka institution that's endearingly sloppy at times, but it's always good value and makes a decent spot to hang out over a good coffee and large cake. Return for pizza, colourful and healthy salads, and assorted fish, meat and veggie dishes ($10–22) in the cavernous interior or on the back deck. Licensed. Daily 7.30am–4pm, later for events (such as Friday curry nights in winter) or concerts and during summer.

AROUND TAKAKA

★**Mussel Inn** SH60, 18km north of Takaka ⓦmusselinn.co.nz. Do not miss this place – whether you want to eat, enjoy wine, cider or ale (they brew many varieties of their own, including the manuka-infused "Captain Cooker"), sit and read, play chess or soak up the lively atmosphere of a live band or local event. The building is adorned with Estuary Art and clumpy, but comfortable, wooden furniture. You can always get a simple, fresh and wholesome meal; try a plate of the local mussels ($18), pie, open burger (fish, meat or falafel) or some excellent cake. Daily 11am–late, closed Aug & Sept.

Penguin Café 822 Abel Tasman Drive, Pohara ⓦpenguincafe.co.nz. Spacious café/restaurant and bar that's worth the drive out from Takaka if only to sip a beer or coffee on the roadside deck which catches the sun most of the day, and has a water sculpture to keep you amused. Well-presented dishes include salmon and seafood pizza (mains $22–36). Tues–Sun 11am–late, Mon 4pm–late.

Sans Souci Inn Richmond Rd, Pohara Beach, 10km east of Takaka ☎03 525 8663, ⓦsanssouciinn.co.nz. Simple licensed restaurant with a daily set menu of freshly prepared, imaginative food that can include Anatoki salmon, beef fillets and veggie options (around $35). There's also a choice of sumptuous desserts. Booking essential. Oct–Easter; dinner served at 7pm unless specified.

★**Toto's Cafe** Totoranui Rd, Wainui Bay, 20km east of Takaka and 2km along a gravel road ☎027 800 8476. Earth-built pizza oven, cob café and gallery, with hydropower, amazing views and extremely fine pizza (small $12, large $22). You could also try the Anatoki smoked salmon, finished with fresh oregano from their flowerbed. Summer daily 10am–5pm; weekends only in winter.

Collingwood and around

Collingwood Museum and Aorere Centre daily 9am–6pm • Donation

Golden Bay's northernmost settlement of any consequence is laidback **COLLINGWOOD**, the base for tours to **Farewell Spit** (see p.486). The town occupies a thread of land wedged between the sea and Ruataniwha Inlet, a location which was briefly championed in the 1850s as the site for the nation's new capital; street plans were drawn up, but as the gold petered out, so did the enthusiasm. The details are spelled out in the diminutive **Collingwood Museum** and **Aorere Centre**, in adjoining buildings, the former a traditional museum, the latter using multimedia to present information on natural history and cultural heritage and links with various plaques around the town.

Devil's Boots

7km southwest of Collingwood

Aorere Valley runs southwest of Collingwood towards the start of the Heaphy Track. Call briefly at the **Devil's Boots**, bulbous limestone overhangs on either side of the gravel road that look like two feet protruding from the ground, with shrubs sprouting from their soles.

THE ROAD TO COLLINGWOOD: ARTS AND CRAFTS

Many of the region's best **artists and craftspeople** live and work between Takaka and Collingwood, so the winding roads offer endless opportunities for mooching around country galleries, usually daily between 10am and 4.30pm, armed with the free, widely available *Golden Bay Arts Trail* leaflet. Two of the best are listed below.

Onekaka Arts 13km north of Takaka ☎ 03 525 7366, ⓦ onekakaarts.co.nz. Hand-crafted silver jewellery by Peter Meares and Grant Muir and jade carved by Geoff Williams. Call ahead for hours.
Estuary Arts 22km north of Takaka ☎ 03 524 8466, ⓦ estuaryarts.co.nz. Rosie Little and Bruce Hamlin produce strikingly original kiln-formed glass, art tiles and sculptural ceramics as well as more traditional evocative landscape paintings. Oct to mid-April Wed–Sun 9am–5pm, plus Mon & Tues during January.

About 4km on, follow signs to the *Naked Possum* café (see below) and the beginning of the lovely **Kaituna Track** (2hr return), a bushwalk past old gold workings to the river confluence at Kaituna Forks.

Langford's Store

Bainham, 18km southwest of Collingwood • Boxing Day–Easter daily 9am–6pm, other times Sat–Thurs 8.30am–4.30pm; closed July & Aug

The wonderful **Langford's Store** is a combined general store and post office built in 1928 by ancestors of the current owners and seemingly little changed. They've decided the hand-cranked adding machine is too new-fangled so your bill will be tallied on paper. Be sure to stop for coffee and cake – you can sit out back in the garden, or in the storeroom packed with memorabilia. Five kilometres further on is **Salisbury Falls**, a popular swimming spot.

ACCOMMODATION	COLLINGWOOD AND AROUND

Collingwood Motor Camp 6 William St, Collingwood ☎ 03 524 8149. Traditional but basic campsite, stuffed to the gills in the summer (make sure you book ahead) with a few wooden cabins ($56) and some much more swanky self-contained units. Camping $15, units $70
Collingwood Park Motel 1 Tasman St, Collingwood ☎ 0800 270 520, ⓦ collingwoodpark.co.nz. Good-value units on a small, modern, central site that backs onto the river estuary. They've also got a "pod" ($95/2 people). The

rooms are comfortable, clean and run by friendly people. Free wi-fi. $130
Somerset House 12 Gibbs Rd, Collingwood ☎ 03 524 8624, ⓦ backpackerscollingwood.co.nz. A low-key backpackers with decent, clean and comfortable rooms in a house with reasonable communal facilities, sea and estuary views, kayaks, free breakfast and free bikes. Arrange pick-ups or drop-offs for the Heaphy or Abel Tasman with the owners, who can also help with car hire. Dorms $31, rooms $76

EATING

Courthouse 11 Elizabeth St, Collingwood ☎ 03 524 8025. Small selection of counter food and some tasty specials (grilled halloumi with caper salsa; $18) in this tiny café, popular with locals and visitors alike. In the evenings they do gourmet pizza takeaways. Thurs–Tues 8am–4pm, plus Thurs & Sat 5pm–8pm.
The Naked Possum 14km southwest of Collingwood, signposted 2km along an unsealed road from the Kaituna bridge turn-off ☎ 03 524 8433,

ⓦ nakedpossum.com. Daytime café set on the edge of the bush with stacks of outside seating, some under cover around an always-lit roaring fire. High-quality café food is supplemented by wild bush tucker; try a tahr burger ($21) or a goat curry pie ($25) washed down with a handle of beer from the *Mussel Inn* (see opposite). The wild berry tart is also famed. Make sure to check out the cushions made from local possum skins. Daily 10am–4pm, later on Fri evening; closed on Mon & Tues in winter.

The road to Farewell Spit

North of Collingwood the road skirts Ruataniwha Inlet, and, after 10km, passes *The Innlet* (see p.488). The road now follows the coast 11km to **Puponga**, at the northern tip of the South Island, where you can stay at the *Farewell Gardens Motor*

8

FAREWELL SPIT TOURS

The trip to Farewell Spit, some 22km north of Collingwood, is an iconic New Zealand journey and shouldn't be missed – if you do nothing else but this in Golden Bay your time will not have been wasted. At the time of writing, only one tour company merited inclusion.

Farewell Spit Eco Tours Tasman St, Collingwood ☎0800 808 257, ⓦfarewellspit.com. In operation since 1946, this outfit runs the Farewell Spit Eco Tour (6hr 30min; $150) which heads out along the sands of the spit to its historic lighthouse in a purpose-built 4WD. The trip comes with a bright commentary, peppered with local lore. During the day you'll see vast numbers of birds, seals (plus the occasional sea lion) and fossils, climb an enormous sand dune and maybe see the skeletons of wrecked ships if the sands reveal them. Their more eco-oriented Gannet Colony Tour (6hr 30min; $160) includes most of the above plus a 20min walk to the massive gannet colony towards the very end of the spit. Trips operate year-round with departure times dependent on tides: check the website. On both trips, light refreshments are provided.

Camp (see below). Around 2km on is Puponga Farm Park, a coastal sheep farm open to the public; check out the visitor centre for more information.

Farewell Spit

From Puponga Farm Park, there are great views right along **Farewell Spit** – named by Captain Cook at the end of a visit in 1770 – which stretches 25km east, often heaped with tree trunks washed up from the West Coast. The whole vast sandbank is a **nature reserve** of international importance, with salt marshes, open mudflats, brackish lakes and bare dunes providing habitats for over a hundred **bird species**: bar-tailed godwit, long-billed curlew and dotterel all come to escape the Arctic winter, there are breeding colonies of Caspian terns, and large numbers of black swans. Sadly, the unusual shape of the coastline seems to fool whales' navigation systems and beachings are common.

Short **walks** head to the outer beach (2.5km) and the inner beach (4km); both provide good views of the spit, which is otherwise off-limits except on guided tours from Collingwood (see p.484).

Cape Farewell

Away from Farewell Spit, walks head through the farm park to **Cape Farewell** (the northernmost point on the South Island), the strikingly set **Pillar Point Lighthouse** and to wave-lashed **Wharariki Beach**. Here, rock bridges and towering arches are stranded just offshore, while deep dunes have blocked river-mouths, forming briny lakes and islands where fur seals and birds have made a home. Visit within a couple of hours of low tide to access some sea caves where the seals hang out.

INFORMATION AND ACTIVITIES

Tourist information The *Farewell Spit Café* (daily 9am–5pm; ☎03 524 8454), adjacent to Puponga Farm Park, acts as the visitor centre for Farewell Spit. You can also check ⓦdoc.govt.nz, and download the *Farewell Spit and Puponga Farm Park* leaflet for more information.

THE ROAD TO FAREWELL SPIT

Cape Farewell Horse Treks ☎03 524 8031 ⓦhorsetreksnz.com. Offers some of the most visually spectacular horseriding in the South Island. Trips don't actually go onto Farewell Spit, but visit Pillar Point (90min; $70), Puponga Beach (90min; $80) and Wharariki Beach (3hr; $140).

ACCOMMODATION

Farewell Gardens Motor Camp 37–39 Seddon St, Puponga ☎03 524 8445, ⓦfarewell gardens.co.nz. An idyllic little spot, located beside the sea at the base of Farewell Spit, with a variety of accommodation options for everyone from families to backpackers. Facilities include two camp kitchens, lounge, BBQ, free bikes, and hot showers. Camping $16, en-suite cabin $85

OPPOSITE CROSSING THE KOHAIHAI RIVER ON THE HEAPHY TRACK (P.489) >

KAHURANGI NATIONAL PARK: THE HEAPHY TRACK

The huge expanse of Kahurangi National Park, 4000 square kilometres of the northwestern South Island, lies between the wet and exposed western side of the Wakamarama Range and the limestone peaks of Mount Owen and Mount Arthur. Over half New Zealand's native **plant species** are represented, as are most of its alpine plants, and the remote interior is a haven for wildlife, including rare carnivorous snails and giant cave spiders.

The park's extraordinary landscapes are best seen by walking the **Heaphy Track** (78km; 4–5 days), which links Golden Bay with Kohaihai Bluff on the West Coast. One of New Zealand's Great Walks, it is appreciably tougher than the Abel Tasman Coast Track, though it compensates with beauty and the diversity of its landscapes – turbulent rivers, broad tussock downs, forests, and nikau palm groves at the western end. The track is named after Charles Heaphy who, along with Thomas Brunner, became the first European to walk the West Coast section in 1846, accompanied by their Maori guide Kehu. Maori had long traversed the area heading down to central Westland in search of *pounamu* for weapons, ornaments and tools. In winter (May–Sept) you can mountain-bike it in 2–3 days.

TRAILHEAD TRANSPORT

The western end of the track is over 400km by road from the eastern end, so if you leave gear at one end, you'll have to re-walk the track, undertake a long bus journey, or fly back to your base at Nelson, Motueka or Takaka. Track transport only runs from late October to mid-April: in **winter** everything becomes more difficult, requiring taxis to reach trailheads.

The **east coast end** starts at **Brown Hut**, 28km southwest of Collingwood. Golden Bay Coachlines run there from Nelson (departing 3.15pm; $57), Motueka (4.30pm; $47), Takaka (9.15am; $35) and Collingwood (9.35am; $32). From the **west coast end** of the track, you'll arrive at the **Kohaihai shelter**, 10km north of Karamea. Even with the best connections you'll need to spend nights in both Karamea and Nelson before returning to Takaka. The operators listed below provide services that can help avoid this.

Adventure Flights ☎0800 150 338, ⓦadventureflightsgoldenbay.co.nz. Flying gives you the chance to return to your car the same day you finish. This outfit will pick up and drop off at either end ($200–265; bikes an extra $20).

Trek Express ☎0800 128 735, ⓦtrekexpress.co.nz. They'll run you from one of several start points

(cheapest from Mapua) to Brown Hut, pick you up at Kohaihai Shelter several days later, then run you back that evening ($115).

Heaphy Track Help Takaka ☎03 525 9576, ⓦheaphy trackhelp.co.nz. Takaka-based Derry Kingston will deliver your car to Karamea ($290 plus fuel costs). He then walks the track, meeting you partway to give you the keys.

TRAIL INFORMATION AND GUIDED HIKES

Download DOC's *Heaphy Track* brochure, or buy one at an i-SITE. It includes a **schematic map** that is satisfactory for hiking, though it is helpful to carry the detailed 1:150,000 *Kahurangi Park* map ($19).

The Innlet 839 Collingwood Puponga Rd ☎03 524 8040, ⓦtheinnlet.co.nz. Excellent hostel with delightful garden cottages, several heated outdoor baths in the bush, and plenty of space for camping. Dorms $31, rooms $75

Whararariki Holiday Park Whararariki Beach, Cape

Farewell ☎03 524 8507, ⓦwhararikibeachholidaypar .co.nz. Thirty tent sites, a backpacker lodge, cabins, plus wide range of facilities that includes a communal kitchen BBQ, hot showers (coin-op), laundry, and a coffee an snacks caravan (daily 9am–4pm in summer). Campin $18, cabin $80

Nelson Lakes National Park and around

Two glacial lakes characterize the **Nelson Lakes National Park**, around 120km southwest of Nelson, **Rotoiti** ("little lake") and **Rotoroa** ("long lake"), nestled in the mountains at the northernmost limit of the Southern Alps. Both are surrounded by tranquil mountains and shrouded in dark beech forest and jointly form the headwaters of the

Bush and Beyond Guided Walks ☎021 0270 8209, ⓦnaturetreks.co.nz. Guided walks along the track – and elsewhere in the park – are admirably handled by this ecologically caring operator, who runs five-day trips ($1850).

ACCOMMODATION

Along the route, there are seven **huts** that **must be booked** and paid for year-round ($32; book online at ⓦdoc.govt.nz), with heating, water and toilets (mostly flush). All except Brown and Gouland Downs have cooking stoves, but you need your own pots and pans. There are also nine designated **campsites** that must be booked ($14) and are mostly close to huts, though you can't use hut facilities. There is a two-night limit in each hut or campsite. Take all provisions with you, and go prepared for sudden changes of weather and a hail of sandflies.

THE ROUTE

Ninety percent of hikers walk the Heaphy Track from east to west, thereby getting the tough initial climb over with and taking it relatively easy on subsequent days.

Brown Hut to Perry Saddle Hut (17km; 5hr; 800m ascent). A steady climb all the way along an old coach road, passing the Aorere campsite and shelter, and Flanagans Corner viewpoint – at 915m, the highest point on the track.

Perry Saddle Hut to Gouland Downs Hut (7km; 2hr; 200m ascent). It's a very easy walk across Perry Saddle through tussock clearings and down into a valley (passing the famed pole strung with used tramping boots) before crossing limestone arches to the hut. This is a great little eight-bunk hut where you might hear kiwi.

Gouland Downs Hut to Saxon Hut (5km; 1hr 30min; 200m descent). Crossing Gouland Downs, an undulating area of flax and tussock.

Saxon Hut to James Mackay Hut (12km; 3hr; 400m ascent). Cross the grassy flatlands, winding in and out of small tannin-stained streams as they tip over into the Heaphy River below.

James Mackay Hut to Lewis Hut (12.5km; 3–4hr; 700m descent). If you have the energy it is worth pressing on to a haven of nikau palms – but sadly also less welcome sandflies.

Lewis Hut to Heaphy Hut (8km; 2–3hr; 100m ascent). It is possible to get from Lewis Hut to the track end in a day but it is more enjoyable to take your time and stop at the Heaphy Hut, near where you can explore the exciting Heaphy rivermouth: its narrow outlet funnels the river water, resulting in a maelstrom of sea and fresh water.

Heaphy Hut to Kohaihai (16km; 5hr; 100m ascent). This final stretch is a gentle walk through forest down the coast until you reach Crayfish Point, where the route briefly follows the beach. Avoid this section within an hour of high tide, longer if it's stormy. Once you reach Scott's Beach, you have only to climb over Kohaihai Bluff to find the Kohaihai Shelter car park on the other side – and hopefully your prearranged pick-up from Karamea.

8

Buller River. **Tramping** (see box, p.491) is undoubtedly the main event and you could easily devote a week to some of the longer circuits, though the short lakeside walks are also rewarding.

The park's subalpine rivers, lakes, forests and hills are full of birdlife, but it has offered little solace to humans: Maori passed through the area and caught eels in the lakes, but the best efforts of European settlers and gold prospectors yielded meagre returns. Now, recreation is all, despite the sandflies.

St Arnaud

ST ARNAUD (pronounced Snt-AR-nard) is a speck of a place scattered around the north shore of Lake Rotoiti, with around a hundred residents but over four hundred houses, mostly used by holidaying Kiwis. The town is largely used as a base for anglers, kayakers and yachties.

ARRIVAL AND DEPARTURE

By bus Access to the region is with Nelson Lakes Shuttles (☎ 03 547 6896, ⓦ nelsonlakesshuttles.co.nz) who offer a service to and from Nelson (Dec–April, 3 a week; $45/

person) and also connect St Arnaud with the Mount Robe car park and Lake Rotoroa.

INFORMATION

DOC are on View Rd (daily 8am–4.30pm extended to 5 in summer; ☎ 03 521 1806). Has all the hiking, biking, fishing and ecology information you could need as well as local

accommodation and transport listings. If you're off on hike, they'll store baggage for $1 a day.

GETTING AROUND

By water taxi Rotoiti Water Taxis (☎ 021 702 278, ⓦ rotoitiwatertaxis.co.nz) operate on Lake Rotoiti from St Arnaud to the head of the lake and charge $100 for up to three people, then $30/person, if you fancy sections of

hiking at the southern end of the lake. They also offer scen cruises around the lake by prior arrangement ($40/perso minimum charge $160) and rents kayaks ($50/half-da and canoes ($60/half-day).

ACCOMMODATION AND EATING

★**Alpine Lodge** Main Rd, opposite the Village Alpine Store ☎ 03 521 1869, ⓦ alpinelodge.co.nz. Owned and managed by a family who are passionate about the Lakes. There's a good range of dorms, budget rooms ($69) and hotel rooms in wooden buildings, with an extremely popular licensed restaurant, bar and spa pool, only 10 minutes' walk to Lake Rotoiti. The café provides strong coffee, home-made cakes, all-day snacks and dinners such as steak, fish and burgers. Closed June. Dorms $29, doubles $155

Kerr Bay campsite On the lakeshore, 500m from the Village Alpine Store. Simple DOC site with pay showers ($1), toilets, tap water, and cooking facilities. $10

Nelson Lakes Motels and Travers-Sabine Lodge SH63 ☎ 03 521 1887, ⓦ nelsonlakes.co.nz. About 150m up the street from the *Alpine Lodge*, this is a mid-sized hostel with some doubles, twins and shared rooms, kitchen, TV and a wealth of information. The *Travers-Sabine Lodge* has comfortable, fully self-contained log-built

chalets next door. All have access to a hot tub. Dorms $2 doubles $65, self-contained units $125

St Arnaud Village Alpine Store 74 Main Rd ☎ 03 52 1854. The village hub sells petrol, alcohol, groceries including fresh produce – and fish and chips (Fri & Sat Mon–Sat 8am–6pm, Sun 8.30am–5.30pm.

★**Tophouse** Tophouse Rd, 8km northeast of St Arnau ☎ 0800 544 545, ⓦ tophouse.co.nz. Sitting by the fire this earth-built former drovers' inn and stagecoach hot decorated with Victorian furniture can make you feel lik you've slipped back in time. Accommodation is either shared-bathroom inn rooms or outside in fairly mode motel-style cabins. They serve Devonshire teas, lunche and a set evening meal ($40). Don't miss the country smallest pub – six is a crowd – with excellent local beer Cabin $85, B&B $185

West Bay campsite 3km drive from St Arnaud. A bas DOC site with two separate camping areas with son forested pitches, plus tap water, cold showers and toilet Closed May–Nov. $6

Lake Rotoroa

20km northwest of St Arnaud, approached along the Gowan Valley Rd

Pretty **Lake Rotoroa** feels a good deal more remote than the area around St Arnaud. The lake ends near a DOC **campsite**, from where there are a few short walks. Lake Rotoroa Water Taxis ply the length of the lake ($40/person, minimum $160; ☎ 03 523 9199) to Sabine Hut on the Travers-Sabine Circuit (see box opposite).

Murchison

MURCHISON, 125km southwest of Nelson and 60km west of St Arnaud, is a small former gold town now favoured by hunting and fishing types as well as rafters and rive kayakers. Numerous rivers feed the nearby Buller, providing excellent whitewater and plenty of opportunities for bagging trout. Once clear of Murchison, SH6 shadows the river through the Buller Gorge to the **West Coast** town of Westport, a route covered in Chapter 12.

NELSON LAKES HIKES

With 270km of track served by twenty huts there is no shortage of walking options. For **day-walks**, arm yourself with DOC's *Walks In Nelson Lakes National Park* booklet. The two **multi-day tramps** have their own leaflets supplemented by the 1:100,000 *Nelson Lakes National Park* map ($19). Blue Lake, with reputedly the clearest water in the world, is an overnight trip from West Sabine Hut.

These are alpine tracks so **go equipped** with good boots, and warm, waterproof clothing – it can snow in almost any month up here – and crampons are likely to be needed from April to November. Both tracks start from the upper Mount Robert car park, 7km by road from St Arnaud. There've been some break-ins at the car park so remember the DOC centre will look after bags ($1/day). The following hikes are listed in approximate order of difficulty.

Bellbird Walk Kerr Bay, St Arnaud (10–15min loop; flat). Easy meander through beech forest alive with the sound of tui, bellbirds and fantails thanks to the Rotoiti Nature Recovery Project, an attempt to replicate the successful offshore island pest clearances by concerted trapping and poisoning. Several of these "mainland islands" have been set up across New Zealand since the late 1990s with considerable success. Visit in the early evening when the birds (even reintroduced great spotted kiwi) are particularly noisy and frisky.

Honeydew Walk Kerr Bay, St Arnaud (30–45min loop; flat). An extension of the Bellbird Walk, named for the sweet excretions of the scale insect that burrows into the bark of the beech trees, its produce attracting loads of nectar-loving tui and bellbirds.

Whisky Falls Mount Robert trailhead (10km; 3–5hr return; 100m ascent). From a parking area on the Mount Robert Road, follow the Lakeside Trail to these 40m falls. Often shrouded in mist and fringed by hanging ferns, the falls are particularly grand after heavy rain.

Mount Robert Circuit (9km; 3–4hr loop; 600m ascent). An excellent loop around the visible face of Mount Robert starting at the Mount Robert car park, ascending the steep Pinchgut Track to the edge of the bush then traversing across to Bushline Hut ($15) before zigzagging down Paddy's Track to the start.

Angelus Hut Loop Mount Robert trailhead (28km; 2-day loop; 1000m ascent). One of the most popular overnighters, this loop follows the exposed Robert Ridge to the beautiful Angelus Basin with its shiny new hut (Oct–April bookings required $20, camping $10; May–Sept $15) and alpine tarn. Two common routes complete the loop: the steep Cascade Track and the Speargrass Track, a bad-weather escape.

Travers-Sabine Circuit (80km; 4–7 days; 1200m ascent). This major tramp is the scenic equal of several of the Great Walks, but far less crowded. The track probes deep into remote areas of lakes, fields of tussock, 2000m-high mountains and the 1780m Travers Saddle. At the height of summer its verges are briefly emblazoned with yellow buttercups, white daisies, sundew and harebells. The circuit requires a good level of fitness, but is fairly easy to follow with bridges over most streams. There are 11 huts ($15), all but three serviced ($5; tickets from DOC), and three campsites – fires are not allowed, so carry a stove and fuel.

Murchison museum

0 Fairfax St • Mon–Sat 11am–3pm • Donation

Everything of note is on SH6 (Waller Street) or Fairfax Street, which crosses it, including the **Murchison Museum**. Housed in the 1911 former post office, local history is sketched out in newspaper clippings, photographs and various oddities including Maori axe heads, gold-rush-era Chinese pottery and opium bottles.

ARRIVAL AND DEPARTURE   MURCHISON

By bus Buses stop at the west end of Waller St. Destinations Greymouth (1–2 daily; 4hr); Nelson (1–2 daily; 2hr); Punakaiki (1–2 daily; 2hr 50min); Westport (1–2 daily; 1hr 30min).

INFORMATION AND ACTIVITIES

Tourist information The museum stocks a range of leaflets and has enthusiastic helpers.

Services An ATM has been installed at 32 Waller St, near the bus stop.

RAFTING AND RIVER KAYAKING IN MURCHISON

With its breathtaking scenery and swift (in places) water the Buller River provides an ideal backdrop for **rafting** and **kayak** trips, as do the Mokihinui and Karamea rivers.

Ultimate Descents 38 Waller St ☎ 0800 748 377, ⓦ rivers.co.nz. During early Sept–late May this operator runs sections of the Buller River (Grade III–V; 4hr 30min; $130), spending at least two hours on the water. There are also gentler family trips (Grade II–III; 4hr 30min; $115). Check the website for helicopter-access and multi-day trips on the Mokihinui and Karamea rivers (from $500).

New Zealand Kayak School 111 Waller St ☎ 03 523 9611, ⓦ nzkayakschool.com. Those keen to learn whitewater kayaking or just brush up on some skills should visit this internationally respected school, which offers four-day courses ($895, including lodging at the school's hostel) that are worth every cent. Oct–April.

Gold panning The town is one of the few places in the country with public gold panning. Pick up the *Recreational Gold Panning* leaflet at the museum. For gold pans ($10) and all the other equipment you'll need, head to Hodgson's at 46 Fairfax St (Mon–Fri 8am–5pm, Sat 10am–1pm).

Day-walks When you're in St Arnaud, pick up DOC's

Murchison Day Walks leaflet featuring the Skyline Wa (3km return; 1hr 30min), which climbs through the nativ forest to the skyline ridge above Murchison with views the confluence of the Buller, Matakitaki, Maruia and Mat rivers. The track starts from the junction of SH6 an Matakitaki West Bank Rd.

ACCOMMODATION AND EATING

Commercial Hotel 37 Fairfax St ☎ 03 523 9696, ⓦ thecommercialhotel.co.nz. A transformed Kiwi pub that now concentrates more on eating than session-drinking. There's a zebra-striped dining room and a separate café with children's play area in the old vault. Everything's home-made, from the burgers and pies to the aioli. Closed Mon–Wed in winter, otherwise bar daily 2–10pm, café daily 9am–3.30pm, restaurant daily 5–8pm.

Cowshed 37 Waller St ☎ 03 523 9523. Small BYO café out the back of the *Lazy Cow*, serving fresh, tasty lunches like broccoflower cheese ($10) and set dinners for $38/2 courses – try the venison and chocolate braise. Wed–Sun noon–4pm, Wed–Sat 6–9pm.

Kiwi Park 170 Fairfax St, 1km south of town ☎ 03 523 9248, ⓦ kiwipark.co.nz. Family-run holiday park with farm animals to keep the kids quiet and a range of well-kept cabins ($70) as well as good communal facilities. Camping $36, motel units $135

Lazy Cow 37 Waller St ☎ 03 523 9451, ⓦ lazycow.co.nz. A cosy hostel in the centre of town with a lively atmosphere, clean and snug rooms, bike hire, pizza oven and a spa bath. Dorm $30, doubles $90

Mataki Motel 34 Hotham St ☎ 0800 279 08 ⓦ matakimotel.co.nz. Clean and quiet motel clear signposted about 1km from town, with comfortable an spacious rooms that are reasonably cosy. Some units have full kitchen. $100

Murchison Lodge 15 Grey St ☎ 0800 523 919 ⓦ murchisonlodge.co.nz. Comfortable and convivial eco conscious lodge with airy rooms, welcome drinks and a fu breakfast including eggs laid in the grounds, where you also find a few cows and pigs. Free wi-fi. $150

Rivers Café 51 Fairfax St ☎ 03 523 900 ⓦ riverscafemurchison.co.nz. Serves pretty good coffe and substantial main meals such as burger and chips ($1 or pumpkin and feta salad ($18) in comfortable laidbac surroundings. Licensed. Daily summer 8.30am–9.30pm winter 9am–4pm.

Riverside Holiday Park SH6, 1.5km east of town ☎ 0 523 9591, ⓦ riversidemurchison.co.nz. Simple campsit with lots of pitches, good communal facilities, a variety well-kept, good-value cabins, a café and helpful owner It's all located by the gurgling Buller River and is mu frequented by kayakers and rafters. Camping $20/2, mot double $110

The Marlborough Wine Country

In July 1972, Marlborough County Council Livestock Instructor, S.G.C. Newdick, wrote "Vineyards: in regard to these, as there is a glut on the market of grapes there does not appear to be any likelihood of vineyards starting up in Marlborough in the foreseeable future." In the intervening years **Marlborough Sauvignon Blanc** single-handedly put the New Zealand wine industry on the world map and made the Marlborough Wine Country the largest wine region, now producing almost sixty percent of the national grape crop.

The gravel plains flanking the Wairau River, sheltered by the protective hills of the Richmond Range and basking in around 2500 hours of sunshine a year, are perfect for ripening the Sauvignon Blanc grapes, though Chardonnay and Pinot Noir grapes also grow well (guaranteeing tasty bubbly), as do olives.

Many local wineries go all out to attract visitors, using distinctive architecture, classy restaurants, art and gourmet foodstuffs. The profusion of weekend visitors from Nelson, Wellington and further afield has also spawned a number of smart B&Bs throughout the district, trying to out-luxury one another. If this is what you're after there's little need to bother with **Blenheim** itself, particularly since most of the vineyards are closer to the small, equally unremarkable town of **Renwick**, 10km to the west. The best of the local wineries are listed on p.497.

Blenheim

In the early 1970s, **BLENHEIM**, 27km south of Picton, was a fairly sleepy service town set amid pastoral land: now it is a fairly sleepy service town completely surrounded by some of the most fecund and highly regarded vineyards in the land. Becoming a tourist hub for the region has developed a passable café culture, but most of the attractions of note are beyond its rather conservative town limits.

BLENHEIM

ACCOMMODATION

Bings Motel	4
Blenheim Bridge Top 10 Holiday Park	1
Hotel d'Urville	3
Palms Motel	2

RESTAURANTS, CAFÉS & BARS

Café Home	4
Gramado's	6
Hotel d'Urville	5
Raupo	3
Ritual	7
Rocco's	2
Dodson Street	1

Picton (27km)

Christchurch (300km)

Brayshaw Heritage Park (1km), Hospital (1.5km) & Omaka Aviation Heritage Centre (4km)

Omaka Aviation Heritage Centre

79 Aerodrome Rd, 4km southwest of town • Daily 10am–4pm • $25 • ⓦ omaka.org.nz

Easily the most diverting of Blenheim's sights is the **Omaka Aviation Heritage Centre**, located beside an airfield. Two large hangars contain 21 World War I planes, some original and still airworthy, most authentic replicas, some unique like the German Halberstadt D.IV. Many are set in amazingly realistic dioramas made by film-maker Peter Jackson's Weta Workshop. Indeed, Jackson, a huge World War I buff, owns much of the collection and chairs the trust which set the place up and will guide its growth (they're adding a couple more hangers to cover World War II). Check out the crash-landing scene depicting the death of Manfred von Richthofen complete with an original fabric cross from the plane, and a group of Australian soldiers souveniring his boots. Everything is made more immediate when you chat to the guides and interpreters, who are mostly former aviators.

Omaka Car Collection

79 Aerodrome Rd, 4km southwest of town • Daily 10am–4pm • $10 • ⓦ omakaclassiccars.co.nz

One man's obsession with automobiles, classics and otherwise, from the 1950s to the 1990s, plus a couple of spanky motorbikes. The collection totals around 150 exhibits; just over half are out at any time and all are renovated, taxed and ready to roll.

The Argosy

760 Middle Renwick Rd, at Caldwell • Daily 10am–8pm • $2

The *Argosy* is an Armstrong passenger and freight aircraft, the last of its kind in the world, which flew with the now defunct Safe Air Ltd, servicing the Chatham Islands. Board the plane for a look round and to watch the documentary, and sit in the cockpit to hear the recording of the night the plane encountered a UFO near Kaikoura.

Brayshaw Heritage Park and Marlborough Museum

New Renwick Rd, 2.5km south of Blenheim • Museum daily 10am–4pm • $10 (some vineyards give out complimentary vouchers)

The best bit of the **Brayshaw Heritage Park** is the **Marlborough Museum**, which has a small Maori collection and an interesting wine exhibit, covering the region's wine heritage, *terroir*, and technology. The rest of the park is given over to old buildings, vehicles and equipment that usually come to life at weekends (the forge operates most Saturdays).

ARRIVAL AND DEPARTURE   MARLBOROUGH WINE COUNTRY

By train and bus Trains and long-distance buses stop at the Blenheim i-SITE at the rail station.

Train destinations Christchurch via Kaikoura (Oct–April, 1 daily); Picton (Oct–April 1 daily).

Bus destinations Christchurch (3 daily; 5hr); Nelson (1–2 daily; 1hr 50min); Picton (5 daily; 30min).

By plane The airport is 7km west of town. Marlborough Taxis (ⓣ 03 577 5511) charge $30 into town.

Destinations Auckland (3 daily; 1hr 25min); Christchurch (2–3 daily; 50min); Paraparaumu (1–3 daily; 25min); Wellington (11–13 daily; 25min).

GETTING AROUND

By bike Several hostels rent out bikes, or try AvantiPlus Cycle, 61 Queen St (ⓣ 03 578 0433; $40/day).

INFORMATION

i-SITE Opposite Blenheim train station, 8 Sinclair St (Mon–Fri 8.30am–5pm, Sat & Sun 10am–3pm; ⓣ 03 577 8080, ⓦ marlboroughnz.com). Stocks an assortment of leaflets including the *Marlborough Wine Trail* map and the *Art and*

Craft Trail brochure (both free).

Internet Wi-fi is free in the centre of town and at the library, 33 Arthur St (Mon–Fri 9am–6pm, Sat 10am–1pm, Sun 1.30–4.30pm).

ACCOMMODATION

As befits a major wine region there's an abundance of high-priced luxury accommodation. Budget places mostly cater to seasonal workers, though there is one exceptional hostel in Renwick. During the first full week of February nearly all accommodation is booked far in advance for the festival season (see box, p.497), so either plan well ahead or steer clear of the region.

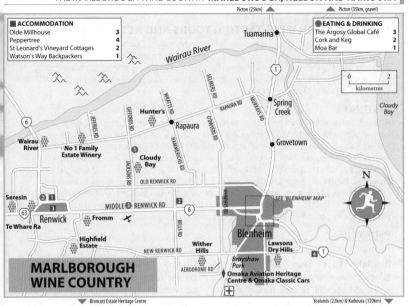

ACCOMMODATION

Olde Millhouse	3
Peppertree	4
St Leonard's Vineyard Cottages	2
Watson's Way Backpackers	1

EATING & DRINKING

The Argosy Global Café	3
Cork and Keg	2
Moa Bar	1

MARLBOROUGH WINE COUNTRY

BLENHEIM

Bings Motel 29 Maxwell Rd ☎03 578 6199, ✉email @bingsmotel.co.nz; map p.493. Classic older-style motel that used to be an old military barracks, close to the centre of Blenheim with plenty of space, low rates and run by a pleasant owner. **$94**

Blenheim Bridge Top 10 Holiday Park 78 Grove Rd ☎0800 268 666, ⓦblenheimtop10.co.nz; map p.493. Sited a little too close to the main road and railway line, but it is central and has all the expected facilities as well as pedal carts, electric bikes, good campsites and comfortable self-contained units and cabins ($78–87). Camping **$38**, units **$120**

Hotel d'Urville 52 Queen St ☎03 577 9945, ⓦdurville .com; map p.493. This former bank right in the centre of town has been turned into a chic and stylish small hotel with a restaurant and cocktail bar. The best – some say the only – place to stay in town, and a good place to eat and party. Free guest wi-fi. **$290**

Palms Motel 78 Charles St (cnr with Henry St) ☎0800 256 725, ⓦblenheimpalmsmotel.co.nz; map p.493. Nicely decorated central motel with free wi-fi, Sky TV and a range of units, most of which are spacious, and some of which come with spa bath. Cooked breakfast available ($19). **$150**

WINE COUNTRY

Olde Millhouse 9 Wilson St, Renwick ☎0800 653 262, ⓦoldemillhouse.co.nz; map p.495. Lovely three-room B&B set among cottage gardens where a continental

breakfast can be served. There is bike rental (also available to non-guests), a spa pool, free wi-fi and free airport transfers. **$175**

★**Peppertree** 3284 SH1 ☎03 520 9200, ⓦthepeppertree.co.nz; map p.495. Luxurious boutique B&B with just five individually styled, generous en suites in a sensitively restored Victorian home surrounded by landscaped gardens with their own orchard, vineyard (Chardonnay), olive grove, pétanque pitch, swimming pool, croquet lawn, and grand duck pond. The Swiss owners couldn't be more helpful. Breakfast includes Bircher muesli, home-made bread and conserves. **$595**

St Leonard's Vineyard Cottages 18 St Leonard's Rd ☎03 577 8328, ⓦstleonards.co.nz; map p.495. A broad range of former farm buildings beautifully converted into five rustically luxurious self-contained quarters (sleeping 2–5), each with fully equipped kitchens, heat pumps, flatscreen freeview TV and free wi-fi. There's access to a heated pool, free bikes, barbecue areas and grounds amid the vines. Breakfast ingredients are supplied, often with home-laid eggs. Old Dairy (sleeps 2) **$120**, Woolshed (sleeps 5) **$320**

★**Watson's Way Backpackers** 56 High St, Renwick ☎03 572 8228, ⓦwatsonswaylodge.co.nz; map p.495. Easily Marlborough's best hostel: a very comfortable spot in the shade of large trees in a wonderful garden, with a public tennis court over the fence, snug rooms, made-up beds, easy access to the wineries, low-cost bikes, an outdoor spa bath, BBQ and owners who can't do enough for you. Closed Sept. Dorms **$30**, en suites **$88**

MARLBOROUGH WINE-TASTING TOURS AND ACTIVITIES

Tastings and tours are the best way to experience the region. Don't be tempted to cram too many tastings into a day; most vineyards are more suited to leisurely sipping than whistle-stop guzzling. Most of the wineries will mail cases of wine anywhere in the world, but shipping costs and high import duties mean it seldom makes financial sense – better just drink the stuff on picnics and at BYO restaurants.

TASTINGS

Around fifty wineries have cellar-door **tastings** (mostly for a small charge, which is deducted from subsequent purchases). Some add a short tour, tack on a restaurant or even link up with outlets hawking olive oil, fruit preserves and the like. Most of the notable wineries are around Renwick or immediately north along Raupara Road, all listed on the free *Marlborough Wine Trail* sheet (along with their opening hours and facilities) and app (ⓦ wine-marlborough.co.nz).

Opening hours are generally 10am to 4 or 5pm daily, though much reduced in winter.

You're now ready for a day among the vines, preferably with lunch at one of the winery restaurants. Few wines are available for much under $20 a bottle, and wineries like to show off with their restaurants, so although it will almost certainly be a pleasurable experience it won't be cheap.

WINE TOURS

To avoid having to designate a driver, take an organized wine tour.

Highlight Wine Tours ☎03 577 9046, ⓦ highlightwinetours.co.nz. A low-key locally owned and operated business, running afternoon ($55), half-day ($65) and full-day ($75, including lunch stop but not the cost of lunch) tours.

Marlborough Wine Tours ☎03 578 9515, ⓦ marlboroughwinetours.co.nz. Offers some of the cheapest tours, including jaunts of three ($55), five ($70) and seven hours ($195), with time for lunch at one of the wineries (not included).

Sounds Connection ☎0800 742 866, ⓦ soundsconnection.co.nz. Specializes in half-day tours visiting four or five wineries ($69), and also offers a full-day circuit of six or seven wineries ($95, excluding lunch).

Wine Tours by Bike ☎03 572 7954, ⓦ winetoursbybike.co.nz. Relatively expensive bike rental ($45/5hr), but the cost includes accommodation pick-ups and they will come and rescue you if you have a mechanical breakdown.

NATURE TOURS

For a different cultural and geological perspective on the landscape, take an ecotour with Driftwood.

Driftwood Retreat and Eco-Tours ☎03 577 7651, ⓦ driftwoodecotours.co.nz. Will is a fount of all knowledge on the Maori and Pakeha history of Blenheim. Join him for an informative, relaxed paddle through the lagoon ($70 to meet the spoonbills), or a comprehensive 4WD tour across a sheep station ($325/8hr) and almost anything in between. Pick-ups available from Blenheim (free) and Picton ($25).

EATING AND DRINKING

A few hours spent visiting vineyards should be accompanied by lunch at one of the wineries – especially *Hunter's*, *Herzog* and *Wairau River*. A few are also open in the evenings, but for dinner you may prefer to head into Blenheim.

BLENHEIM

★**Café Home** 1c Main St; map p.493. Primo espresso alongside fresh sandwiches, frittata slices and cakes in minimalist surroundings ($8–18). Mon–Fri 8am–5pm, Sat 9am–2pm.

Dodson Street 1 Dodson St ☎03 577 8348; map p.493. Convivial bistro, wine and alehouse dishing up tasty pizzas ($20) and regular pub grub. Get a tasting tray, or have a Renaissance beer (brewed next door). Daily 11am–11pm.

★**Gramado's** 74 Main St ☎03 579 1192 ⓦ gramadosrestaurant.com; map p.493. Wonderfully unexpected Brazilian restaurant. The owners have adapted their recipes to take account of Kiwi tastebuds, so you can choose aged Wakanui steak and chips ($36), but if you go for the luscious *feijoada* ($29) you'll be presented with a range of different chillies to enhance and deepen your dish without blowing your socks off. The great customer care includes Saulo's mini wine tastings to ensure you happily match your wine to your meal. Leave room for *pudim*. Tues–Sun 4pm–late.

Hotel d'Urville 52 Queen St ☎03 577 9945, ⓦ durville .com; map p.493. Classy restaurant with stylish modern decor and exemplary cuisine, making the best of seasonal produce (mains $26–34). Book in advance. Daily from 6pm.

Raupo 2 Symons St ☎ 03 577 8822, ⓦ raupocafe.co.nz; map p.493. Great café with a terrace overlooking the Opawa River, serving superb lunches (mostly $22) including hearty steak sandwich, bistro-style dinners ($28–34) and high tea, served morning and afternoon ($17.50). Daily 7.30am–11pm.

★ **Ritual** 10 Maxwell Rd ☎ 03 578 6939; map p.493. Lively, licensed café with booths, serving delights such as herbivore burritos with tempeh and miso ($17), as well as delicious daily $10 "creations" in a bowl. Dinner mains are $20. Mon–Wed 7am–4.30pm, Thurs–Sat 7am–late.

Rocco's 5 Dodson St ☎ 03 578 6940; map p.493. Enjoyable, authentic Italian restaurant that could unabashedly sit on a New York or Rome street. For a blowout, order the awesome chicken Kiev alla Rocco – chicken breast filled with ham, garlic butter and cheese, all wrapped in a veal schnitzel. Fresh pasta is made daily. Licensed or BYO ($10). Mon–Sat 6pm–late.

RENWICK

The Argosy Global Café 760 Middle Renwick Rd, just east of town ☎ 03 572 5034, ⓦ argosy-cafe.co.nz; map p.495. A modern restaurant, next to the *Argosy* plane (p.494) offering a wide range of dishes and special offers such as pizza and a pint for $25. Licensed. Wed–Sat 11am–9pm, Sun 11am–5pm.

Cork and Keg Inkerman St; map p.495. Friendly English-style local with traditional games like dominoes and a good selection of South Island craft beers including those from the local *Moa* stable. All-day pub meals from $12–24. Daily noon–11pm.

Moa Bar 258 Jacksons Rd, a few kilometres northeast of town ☎ 03 572 5149, ⓦ moabeer.com; map p.495. Brilliant little modern bar serving at least twenty beers and two ciders from the *Moa* brewery. Try the Five Hop with a Renwick pie. $5 tastings. Daily 11am–6pm.

THE WINERIES

Brancott Estate 180 Brancott Rd, 5km south of Renwick on SH1 ☎ 03 520 6975, ⓦ brancottestate.com. A good starting point for your exploration of the region. Montana effectively kicked off the wine region in the early 1970s and now operates the country's largest winery, a

favourite with coach parties. Come for free tastings (three wines), a tutored Sauvignon Blanc tasting (daily 11am, 2pm; $18) or a bike tour through the vines (booking essential, 1pm; $35). Also worth a look is the hilltop restaurant and heritage centre, where you can get good food and views. Cellar door daily 10am–4.30pm.

Cloudy Bay Jacksons Rd ☎ 03 520 9197, ⓦ cloudybay .co.nz. Marlborough Sauvignon Blanc put New Zealand on the world wine map in the late 1980s and the Cloudy Bay Sauvignon was its flagship. It is still drinking so well today that they can't keep up with demand; have a taste ($5 for two or $10 for five wines) along with their other top-notch wines. The raw bar is open weekends and daily in summer if you'd like some seafood with your tipple. Daily 10am–5pm.

Fromm Godfrey Rd ☎ 03 572 9355, ⓦ frommwineries .com. A vineyard that is turning winemakers' heads with a very hands-on approach, producing organic, predominantly red, wine, including an excellent Pinot Noir, a peppery Syrah, and a Malbec. Visit if you're serious about the subject and you'll taste ($5) a product that's a match for anywhere in the world. Daily 11am–5pm.

Highfield Estate Brookby Rd ☎ 03 572 9244, ⓦ highfield.co.nz. Easily recognizable by its Tuscan-inspired tower, which you can climb for excellent views, *Highfield* offers free tastings. Daily 10am–5pm (by appointment in winter).

Hunter's Rapaura Rd ☎ 03 572 8489, ⓦ hunters.co.nz. Jane Hunter is recognized as one of the world's top female winemakers. Drop by to taste (free), visit the art gallery, stroll round the gardens or eat in the family-friendly café, which does snack platters ($14.50). Cellar door daily 9.30am–4.30pm.

★ **Lawsons Dry Hills** Alabama Rd ☎ 03 578 7674, ⓦ lawsonsdryhills.co.nz. Established vines produce stunning wines in this multi-award-winning winery, well worth visiting for the Pinot Noir, Pinot Gris, Gewürztraminer and Sauvignon Blanc if nothing else. Tastings are free. Cellar door daily 10am–5pm.

No 1 Family Estate 196 Rapaura Rd ☎ 03 572 9876, ⓦ no1familyestate.co.nz. Home to the area's best-known and most accomplished maker of champagne-style bubbly. Free tastings. Daily 10am–4.30pm.

Seresin Bedford Rd ☎ 03 572 9408, ⓦ seresin.co.nz. Stylish winery with a distinctive primitivist "hand" logo

8

WINE FESTIVAL

Held on the second Saturday in February, the **Marlborough Wine Festival** (ⓦ wine -marlborough-festival.co.nz) is the region's sole big event. Around 8000 people flock to the *Brancott* winery, south of Renwick, where a vast field of marquees contain local wines and food for purchase and consumption and throb with the sound of live music. Tickets are $48, and include a glass. Ritchies (☎ 03 578 5467) run buses to the festival site from the town and the airport ($20 return), as well as from Picton ($30 return).

perched on a rise overlooking the vines. Completely organic, biodynamic, estate-grown grapes interact with wild yeast to create world-class wines (try the Pinot Noir and their soft Chardonnay), and they produce some killer olive oil, jams and even soap. Free tastings. Daily 10am–4.30pm.

Te Whare Ra 56 Anglesea St, Renwick ☎ 03 572 8581, Ⓦ twrwines.co.nz. Great little family-owned and -run vineyard where they still hand-pick and sort the grapes. Free tastings – try their Rieslings and brooding Syrah. Nov–March Mon–Fri 11am–4.30pm, Sat & Sun noon–4pm; April–Oct by arrangement only.

Wither Hills 211 New Renwick Rd ☎ 03 520 8284,

Ⓦ witherhills.co.nz. A striking, roadside winery that's all concrete and tussock. Nip in for tastings ($5) of the popular Chardonnay, Pinot Noir and Sauvignon Blanc (including the fine single-vineyard Rarangi). Vine-to-wine walks at 11.30am, 2.30pm (40min; $20). Daily 10am–4.30pm.

Yealands Awatere Valley ☎ 03 575 7618, Ⓦ yealands .co.nz. Follow the white road to see one Kiwi bloke's vineyard vision, including 1500 babydoll sheep, gangs of chickens, and classical music piped to the vines that fill the valley to the sea. Great story, and the wine's decent too (free tastings, including a port style, and a Tempranillo). Daily 10am–4.30pm.

The road to the Kaikoura Coast

The 130km between the coast and the brooding Seaward Kaikoura Range from Blenheim to Kaikoura is one of the most spectacular coastal roads in New Zealand. It is best to allow plenty of time for frequent stops to soak up the gorgeous scenery.

Around 20km south of Blenheim a sign points inland towards **Molesworth Station** (see box below) and Hanmer Springs. **Lake Grassmere**, 50km south of Blenheim, is a vast, shallow, salt lake, which annually produces 70,000 tonnes a year of table salt. **Cyclists** may want to overnight 20km south of the salt works at *Pedallers Rest Cycle Stop* (see opposite).

From Lake Grassmere, you're now following the coast, with grey gravel beaches all the way and accessible at various points. Almost 90km out of Blenheim, the rocky **Kekerengu Point** juts out and makes a great place to watch the crashing waves while stopping in at *The Store* (see opposite) for a bite to eat.

Ohau Point

35km south of Kekerengu Point

Ohau Point marks the best stretch of coastline – a wonderful rocky, surf-lashed strip that continues for around 30km to Kaikoura then 20km beyond. Ohau Point is home to the South Island's largest **seal colony** with dozens (if not hundreds) of seals lolling on the rocks not more than 20m away. Immediately before Ohau Point, Ohau Stream Walk (15min return) weaves through the bush to a nice waterfall and pool where in October and November seal pups can be seen playing in the pools

---

DRIVING THROUGH MOLESWORTH STATION

Timing is everything if you want to drive (or ride) the Acheron Road through **Molesworth Station**, at 1800 square kilometres New Zealand's largest farm. The central 59km section of road is only open to traffic for a few months each summer (Oct–April). It is an impressive run through New Zealand's most accessible high country, passing historic cob houses with towering mountains all around. The drive from Blenheim to Hanmer Springs (210km) takes over five hours, most of them on gravel. There are no services so make sure your tank is topped up. **Camping** is only permitted at *Molesworth Cob Cottage* and *Acheron Accommodation House* (both $6). For the latest information obtain DOC's *Molesworth* leaflet and check Ⓦ doc.govt.nz.

Molesworth Tour Company ☎ 03 572 8025, Ⓦ molesworthtours.co.nz. If you'd prefer to look at the scenery and not the road, try this operator, which explores the region on one- to four-day trips ($220–1835), as well as cycle tours, which come in a bit cheaper.

during the day. Approach quietly, keep your distance (10m), and don't get between a seal and the water.

The coastline around here is also a perfect habitat for **crayfish**, which are sought by the locals and sold roadside, notably at Rakautara (see below).

ACCOMMODATION AND EATING   **THE ROAD TO THE KAIKOURA COAST**

Cay's Crays and Nin's Bins Rakautara, 3km south of Ohau Point. Two roadside caravans hawking delicious cooked crayfish for around $50–90. Daily, whenever they're in.

Pedallers Rest Cycle Stop Lake Grassmere, 1.5km off SH1 ☏ 03 575 6708, ✉ pedallers@ruralinzone.net. A small, friendly and comfy spot that's frequented by cyclists,

but welcomes most everyone. Linen is included and there's a small on-site shop. To get there, look for the water tank and sign beside the road. Bunks $20, camping $15

The Store Kekerengu Point ☏ 03 575 8600. A great spot to tuck into burgers ($21.50), fish and chips ($20), cakes and coffee. It's licensed, and is popular with the passing tour bus trade. Daily 8am–4pm.

Kaikoura

The small town of **KAIKOURA**, 130km south of Blenheim and 180km north of Christchurch, enjoys a spectacular setting in the lee of the Kaikoura Peninsula, wedged between the mountains and the ocean. Offshore, the seabed drops away rapidly to the kilometre-deep Kaikoura Canyon, a phenomenon that brings sea mammals in large and varied numbers. **Whale watching** and **swimming with dolphins** are big business here, and the presence of expectant tourists has spawned a number of eco-oriented businesses offering **swimming with seals**, **sea-kayaking** and hiking.

Brief history

Kaikoura got its name when an ancient **Maori** explorer who stopped to eat crayfish found it so good he called the place *kai* (food) *koura* (crayfish). Maori legend also accounts for the extraordinary coastline around Kaikoura. During the creation of the land, a young deity, Marokura, was given the job of finishing the region. First, he built the Kaikoura Peninsula and a second smaller peninsula (Haumuri Bluff). Then he set about creating the huge troughs in the sea between the two peninsulas, where the cold waters of the south would mix with the warm waters of the north and east. Realizing the depth of Marokura's accomplishment, the god Tuterakiwhanoa said that the place would be a gift (*koha*) to all those who see its hidden beauty – and it is still known to local Maori as Te Koha O Marokura.

The Ngai Tahu people harvested the wealth of the land and seas until Te Rauparaha and his followers decimated them, in around 1830. The first **Europeans** to settle were whalers who came in the early 1840s, swiftly followed by farmers. The trials and tribulations of their existence are recorded in the **Kaikoura Museum** and the more evocative **Fyffe House**. Kaikoura ticked on quietly until the late 1980s when whale watching really took off and put the place on the tourism map. Since then it has steadily expanded, becoming more commercial, though without losing its small-town feel.

Kaikoura Marine Aquarium

Wakatu Quay • Daily: summer 10am–5pm; winter 11am–4pm • $8

Stocked by the local fishermen, who'll drop off anything interesting they find (and return it to the deep if it begins to seem stressed), managed by a marine biologist and staffed by local volunteers, this small site squeezes in a preserved giant squid and two touch tanks. Live exhibits usually include crayfish, octopus, paua and sea horses, plus there are permanent displays on the local environment and ecology.

WALKS AROUND KAIKOURA

Kaikoura isn't all about spending money watching marine mammals. There's plenty to be seen on foot, best accessed on two local walks and two longer tramps.

DAY-WALKS

Kaikoura Peninsula Walkway (11km loop; 3hr; undulating). A superb circuit of the peninsula covered on DOC's *The Peninsula Walkway* leaflet. Pick it up at the i-SITE and follow the route along the Esplanade past Fyffe House to the seal colony. From here it loops over the grassy cliffs to South Bay, with views down to the seals lolling on the rocks below. Several options follow paths back over the peninsula to the i-start; chances are you'll see red-billed and black-backed gulls, oystercatchers, herons and shags. Be warned that gulls nesting during September and October are likely to attack if they feel that

their nests are threatened, so steer well clear. Also worth a look is the small reserve for Hutton's Shearwaters, set aside behind a predator-proof fence.

Mount Fyffe (16km return; 6–8hr; 1400m ascent). Several walks close to town are outlined in DOC's *Mount Fyffe and the Seaward Kaikoura Range* leaflet. The most immediately appealing is this tough hike to the 1602m summit of Mount Fyffe. Starting at a poorly signposted car park 12km northwest of town, the route climbs steadily up a 4WD road to the summit with its glorious views over the Kaikoura Peninsula and coast.

MULTI-DAY WALKS

Kaikoura Wilderness Walks ☎0800 945 337, ⓦkaikourawilderness.co.nz. Offers a delightful combination of guided walk in gorgeous, wild country up behind Kaikoura and a night in the luxury *Shearwater Lodge* – far from everything on the bushline at 1000m, but with crisp sheets in en-suite rooms and three-course meals. After a Kaikoura pick-up and short drive, day one (8.5km one way; 6hr; 700m ascent) involves a steady ascent to the lodge where you're served refreshments by a roaring fire, followed by dinner. The hills above the lodge are explored on the second day (optional), before wandering back to the valley on the final day ($1795). Oct–March.

Kaikoura Coast Track ☎03 319 2715, ⓦkaikouratrack.co.nz. The mixture of wild beach scenery, farmland and regenerating bush makes for a

pleasant and very manageable walk, but the real pleasure in this self-guided, private walk (37km; 3 days; 600m ascent; $235) is in experiencing country life and chatting to the farming families at the two overnight stops. This walk starts and ends 45km south of Kaikoura at *The Beach House*, 356 Conway Flat Rd, Ngaroma (buses should drop you off at the bridge), then climbs the Hawkeswood Range with spectacular views of the Seaward Kaikoura mountains. Walker numbers are limited, so book in advance. The fee covers bag transport (so you only need carry a daypack), and three nights' accommodation in warm cottages with bunk beds ($20 for linen), fully equipped kitchens and showers as well as fresh farm produce, milk, bread and home-cooked meals by arrangement ($15 for breakfast and $60 for evening meals).

Kaikoura Museum

14 Ludstone Rd • Mon–Fri 10am–4.30pm, Sat & Sun 2–4pm • $5

Kaikoura Museum currently makes the best of its old site, though the bulk of the contents (including the early 1900s jailhouse, in use until 1980 and complete with padded cell) are slowly moving to a new, purpose-built location opposite the i-SITE in the centre of town. Look for a large rock containing the fossilized ribcage of a Cretaceous-period plesiosaur; and the Maori collection, which illustrates the stages needed to convert a mussel shell into an effective fish-hook.

Fyffe House

62 Avoca St • Oct–April daily 10am–5pm; May–Sept Thurs–Mon 10am–4pm • $10

Out on the peninsula, don't miss the town's oldest building, **Fyffe House**, an original whaler's cottage resting on whalebone foundations. The house began life as part of the Waiopuka Whaling Station that was founded by Robert Fyffe in 1842 and was

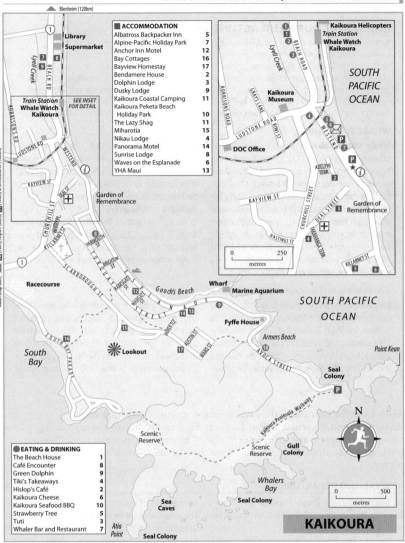

KAIKOURA

ACCOMMODATION

Albatross Backpacker Inn	5
Alpine-Pacific Holiday Park	7
Anchor Inn Motel	12
Bay Cottages	16
Bayview Homestay	17
Bendamere House	2
Dolphin Lodge	3
Dusky Lodge	9
Kaikoura Coastal Camping	11
Kaikoura Peketa Beach Holiday Park	10
The Lazy Shag	11
Miharotia	15
Nikau Lodge	4
Panorama Motel	14
Sunrise Lodge	8
Waves on the Esplanade	6
YHA Maui	13

EATING & DRINKING

The Beach House	1
Café Encounter	8
Green Dolphin	9
Tiki's Takeaways	4
Hislop's Café	2
Kaikoura Cheese	6
Kaikoura Seafood BBQ	10
Strawberry Tree	5
Tuti	3
Whaler Bar and Restaurant	7

originally an unprepossessing two-room cooper's cottage. Extended by George Fyffe in 1860, some rooms look now much as they did then, while others reflect the condition of the place when the last resident moved out in 1980. Avoca Street follows the edge of the peninsula round to a car park (the start of the Kaikoura Peninsula Walkway; see box, p.500) where fur **seals** often lounge on flat, sea-worn rocks watching the plentiful birdlife.

Maori Leap Cave

2km south of town on SH1 · 45min tours daily on the half-hour 10.30am–3.30pm · $15 · ☎ 03 319 5023

The sea-formed **Maori Leap Cave** is named after a Maori warrior who jumped to his

KAIKOURA TOURS AND ACTIVITIES

Just 1km off the Kaikoura Peninsula the seabed plummets into the 1000m-deep Kaikoura Canyon, a network of undersea troughs that funnel warm subtropical waters and cold sub-Antarctic flows. This provides an unusually fecund habitat supporting an enormous variety of marine life, including fourteen species of whale. Marine mammals come for an easy meal, and tourists come to watch. You can expect to see gigantic sperm **whales** (year-round), **dolphins** (year-round), migratory humpback whales (June–July) and **orca** (Dec–Feb). Book well in advance, though rough seas often lead to **cancellations** so allow yourself a couple of days' flexibility.

WHALE WATCHING

Whale Watch Kaikoura The Whaleway Station, Whaleway Rd ☎0800 655 121, ⓦwhalewatch.co.nz. Kaikoura's flagship activity is conducted by this Maori-owned and -operated company. You meet at the office at the train station and are bused around to South Bay where a speedy catamaran whisks you a few kilometres offshore (2hr 30min at sea; $145). There are typically one or two whale sightings along with dolphins and seabirds; if you see no whales there's an eighty percent refund. The office sells pills and bands to alleviate sea sickness – a wise investment, particularly for afternoon trips.

Wings Over Whales ☎0800 226 629, ⓦwhales .co.nz. An alternative to on-the-water viewing is aerial whale watching. This outfit offers 30min flights ($180). There's a shuttle service ($10/person each way) between the town and the airport. Bring binoculars.

Kaikoura Helicopters ☎0800 455 4354, ⓦworldofwhales.co.nz. They offer a 30min and 40min flight (2 people $325/395 each), as well as other helicopter tours. There's an obvious advantage over planes as they can hover to get you the perfect view.

SWIMMING WITH DOLPHINS AND SEALS

Dolphin Encounter 96 Esplanade ☎0800 733 365, ⓦdolphin.co.nz. Runs highly professional trips (5.30am Nov–April, 8.30am & 12.30pm; swimming $170; watching $90), which you'll get the most out of if you're a reasonably confident swimmer; the more you duck-dive the more eager the dolphins will be to hear

you humming through your snorkel – any tune will do. Don't get too carried away: dolphins have a penchant for swimming in ever decreasing circles until lesser beings are quite dizzy and disorientated. Book three to four weeks in advance for the Dec–Feb peak season (though standbys do become available at short notice).

death from the hills above the cave to escape capture by another tribe. Stalagmites and stalactites sprout from the floor and ceiling of the cave, and translucent stone straws seem to defy gravity by maintaining their internal water level. There are also cave corals and algae that survive by turning darkness into energy.

ARRIVAL AND DEPARTURE

KAIKOURA

By bus InterCity and Atomic buses on the Picton–Blenheim–Christchurch run all drop off on Westend, in the town car park near the visitor centre.
Destinations Christchurch (3 daily; 2hr 50min); Picton (3 daily; 2hr 15min).

By train The TranzCoastal train between Picton and Christchurch arrives at the station on Whaleway Station Rd. Destinations Christchurch (Oct–April; 1 daily); Blenheim (Oct–April; 1 daily); Picton (Oct–April; 1 daily).

GETTING AROUND

By taxi Most places in town are within walking distance, though since the town is increasingly spread out you may find use for a taxi; try Kaikoura Shuttles ☎03 319 6166.

By bike Coastal Sport, 24 Westend (☎03 319 5028), charges $30 for a half-day and $40 for a full day.

INFORMATION

Visitor information The i-SITE is on Westend (daily 9am–5pm; ☎03 319 5641, ⓦkaikoura.co.nz). Apart from regular i-SITE duties, the office also handles most DOC enquiries and stores luggage for $2.

Services Internet access at the library, Harakeke Mall, 134 Beach Rd ($6/hr).

Seal Swim Kaikoura 58 Westend ☎ 0800 732 579, ⓦ sealswimkaikoura.co.nz. Seal swimming is just as much fun as dolphin swimming (and some might say equally moving), as seals tend to be even more curious than dolphins. This operator offers shore-based trips ($80) and better, more flexible trips by boat (2–2hr 30min total; $110). There's a fair bit of swimming involved so it helps if you've snorkelled before. Oct–May only.

BIRDWATCHING, SEA-KAYAKING AND SCUBA DIVING

Albatross Encounter 96 Esplanade ☎ 0800 733 365, ⓦ albatrossencounter.co.nz. Travel a kilometre or two offshore in a small boat for the chance to see some endangered seabirds (2–3 trips daily; 2–3hr; $115). Bait is laid to attract all manner of species – shags, mollymawks, gannets, petrels and several varieties of albatross come amazingly close. Relatively sheltered, so often runs when the big boats have to stay in.

Kaikoura Kayaks 19 Killarney St ☎ 0800 452 456, ⓦ kaikourakayaks.co.nz. Operates year-round and often runs trips when others don't because they can take you to sheltered spots. You'll learn most (and probably see more wildlife) on the half-day Seal Kayaking guided trips ($95), though suitably skilled paddlers can rent kayaks ($70/half-day; $85/full day) or mess around on a sit-on-top ($30/hr).

Dive Kaikoura 13 Yarmouth St ☎ 03 319 6622, ⓦ divekaikoura.co.nz. Get a close look at temperate kelp forests, nudibranchs and sponges, plus the odd crayfish and seal on scuba-diving tours run by Go Dive, including two-tank trips for certified divers ($250) and introductory dives for novices.

MAORI CULTURE

Maori Tours Kaikoura ☎ 0800 866 267, ⓦ maoritours.co.nz. Offers emotionally engaging half-day tours ($134), guided by an ex-whale-watch boat driver and his family, that give a real taste of *Maoritanga* and the genuine hospitality it demands.

Tours take in various local sights, storytelling, explanations of Maori ways and medicines, cultural differences, and involve learning a song, that you then surprise yourself by singing.

FLIGHTS

Pilot a Plane Kaikoura Airfield, SH1 ☎ 03 319 6579, ⓦ airkaikoura.co.nz. Aspiring fliers get to take off and then take the controls for 20min ($120). It's a great adrenaline buzz and comes with even better scenery. The company also runs various charter-plane whale-watching options.

ACCOMMODATION

There's a fair range of accommodation, most of it strung out along SH1 (Beach Road) immediately north of the centre, along the Esplanade or on the peninsula east of town.

★ **Albatross Backpacker Inn** 1 Torquay St ☎ 0800 222 247, ⓦ albatross-kaikoura.co.nz. Cool converted post office and telephone exchange with brightly-painted rooms, such as the cute Hobbit dorm. Well-tended grounds and barbecue make it especially good on fine days and they love their music. Dorms $29, rooms $74

Alpine-Pacific Holiday Park 69 Beach Rd ☎ 0800 692 322, ⓦ alpine-pacific.co.nz. This central, shaded park maintains high standards, offers a range of accommodation and has an outdoor pool and hot tubs. Camping $46 (2 people), motel units $130

Anchor Inn Motel 208 Esplanade ☎ 0800 720 033, ⓦ anchorinn.co.nz. Luxurious motel with tastefully decorated, self-contained units that come with every convenience (some with spa bath) plus free wi-fi. $170, sea view $195

★ **Bay Cottages** 29 South Parade, South Bay ☎ 03 319 5506, ⓦ baycottages.co.nz. Purpose-built self-contained motel-style units in a quiet spot 2km from the town centre on the south side of the peninsula. The owner is exceptionally lovely. $130

Bayview Homestay 296 Scarborough St ☎ 03 319 5480, ⓦ bayviewhomestay.wordpress.com. Margaret Woodill, who has lived in this house for almost all of her seventy-odd years, and her daughter really make this traditional B&B homestay a complete delight. Garden and swimming pool are for guests' use and rooms are simple with external access and either an en suite or a private bathroom. It's all that was great about staying with your granny. $130

Bendamere House 37 Adelphi Terrace ☎ 0800 107 770, ⓦ bendamere.co.nz. Five high-standard rooms, in the grounds of a large villa on the hill. There are great sea views, hearty breakfasts, a helpful owner, and it's all within walking distance of the town. Check website for specials. $250

Dolphin Lodge 15 Deal St ☎ 03 319 5842, ⓦ dolphinlodge.co.nz. Small hostel with a garden

8

(complete with spa and hammock) overlooking the sea that offers dorms (with few bunks) and cosy doubles, plus bikes ($5/day). There's no TV, but there is wi-fi and a lovely wood-burning stove. Dorms $28, rooms $62

Dusky Lodge 67 Beach Rd ☎03 319 5959, ⓦduskylodge.com. Well-organized hostel sleeping 120-plus with sauna, spa, swimming pool and a restaurant along with log fires and a big terrace. One level is devoted to deluxe en suites with flat-screen TVs and their own upscale lounge and kitchen. Popular with groups. Book for free pick-ups. Dorms $26, doubles $80

Kaikoura Coastal Camping SH1, 15km south of town ☎03 319 5348, ⓦkaikouracamping.co.nz. A string of appealing, family-oriented campsites, three of which are beachside. The northernmost, Paia Point, has no power, while the others have powered sites and showers. Paia Point $12, other sites $16

Kaikoura Peketa Beach Holiday Park 665 SH1, 8km south of Kaikoura ☎03 319 6299, ⓦkaikoura peketabeach.co.nz. Peaceful beachside campsite that's popular with families and surfers who make use of the excellent waves on the doorstep. The surroundings are quiet (apart from the crashing of waves), there's lots of birdlife, and accommodation is in comfortable cabins. Mini golf, flying fox, wi-fi, and small shop on site. Camping $16, cabins $65

The Lazy Shag 37 Beach Rd ☎03 319 6662, ⓦlazy -shag.co.nz. Purpose-built hostel where guests' comfort is the priority. Rooms are warm and quiet, common rooms are spacious and well equipped, and all dorms, twins and doubles are en suite. Dorms $27, rooms $66

Miharotia 274 Scarborough St ☎03 319 7497, ⓦmiharotia.co.nz. Classy B&B in a plush home with three rooms, all beautifully appointed, with deck access to the outside hot tub. Sea and mountain views are great and the hosts (one a former paua diver) serve an excellent full breakfast. $349

Nikau Lodge 53 Deal St ☎03 319 6973, ⓦnikaulodge .com. Four of the five en-suite rooms in this lovely, wooden, 1925 house have mountain or sea views, plus there's free wi-fi, a hot tub and good breakfasts. Ground floor $220, with view $280

★**Panorama Motel** 266 Esplanade ☎0800 288 299, ⓦpanoramamotel.co.nz. There are superb views from the stripped-pine units with a chalet feel; you'll pay $25 extra for better views from the upper floor, and the whole shebang is run by a helpful owner. $135

Sunrise Lodge 74 Beach Rd ☎03 319 7444, ⓔsunrisehostel@xtra.co.nz. Small hostel, just a 2min walk from Whale Watch, offering a maximum of four to a room (no bunks), plus free wi-fi allowance and bikes. Dorms $28, rooms $79

Waves on the Esplanade 78 Esplanade ☎0800 319 589, ⓦkaikouraapartments.co.nz. Luxurious two-bedroom motel-style apartments with balconies, sea views, full kitchen, laundry and access to a spa pool. Free use of bikes and sit-on kayaks. $270

★**YHA Maui** 270 Esplanade ☎03 319 5931, ⓦyha .co.nz. Comfortable and good-value hostel with renovated bathrooms, four-bed dorms, the best sea and mountain views in town – from the kitchen/diner and lounge – plus well-informed, knowledgeable staff. Dorms $34, rooms $90

EATING AND DRINKING

Kaikoura is small but the steady flow of tourists helps keep a decent selection of cafés and restaurants alive. Prices are a little on the high side, especially if you're keen to sample the local crayfish, though you might prefer to buy them ready-boiled from one of the *kai* caravans north of town (see p.499).

The Beach House 39 Beach Rd ☎03 319 6030. Kaikoura's cool set hangs out here, despite the dreadful service, imbibing coffee over extended breakfasts ($10–20), or lunches, which include seafood chowder and panini from the cabinet. Licensed. Daily 8.30am–4pm.

Café Encounter 96 Esplanade ☎0800 733 365. Possibly the best coffee in town, at a licensed café perfect for treats before or after your dolphin swim, but well worth a visit in its own right – all the baking is done on the premises. Daily 7am–5pm in summer, 7.30am–4pm in winter.

Green Dolphin 12 Avoca St ☎03 319 6666, ⓦgreendolphinkaikoura.com. Large windows and sea views, and food from a short contemporary menu that usually includes a half-crayfish ($60), along with mains for half that price and a fab fish chowder. Daily 5pm–late.

★**Hislop's Café** 33 Beach Rd ☎03 319 6971, ⓦwww.hislops-wholefoods.co.nz. The pick of the

cafés in Kaikoura, a lovely villa that's a must for coffee and cakes, inside or out, as well as wholefood meals (some vegetarian or gluten-free), tasty seafood and toothsome daily fresh-baked bread. Wine by the glass, including vegan and organic varieties. Open for breakfast, lunch (salads and sandwiches) and dinner. Wed–Sun 9am–9pm.

Kaikoura Cheese 45 West End ⓦkaikouracheese .co.nz. Lovely, prize-winning cheeses, such as *labneh* and authentic *fromage blanc*, as well as salami and other picnic essentials. Daily 10am–5.30pm.

Kaikoura Seafood BBQ Armers Beach ☎027 376 3619. A few tables scattered roadside and a takeaway cart make a great setting for simple seafood, all served with salad and rice. Daily 10.30am–dusk.

Strawberry Tree 21 Westend ☎03 319 6451. Convivial Irish-styled bar that's usually busy with a mix of locals and travellers. There is, of course, a seafood-heavy menu. Daily 3–11pm.

Tiki's Takeaways 18 West End. Award-winning fish and crayfish dinners with unforgettably good chips – perfect for sunset on the waterfront or picnics. They also do surprisingly scrumptious chicken nuggets. Daily noon–8.30pm.

Tuti 35 Beach Rd ☏ 03 319 3370, ⓦ tutis.co.nz. Popular modern restaurant serving Kiwi classics (pan-fried Akaroa salmon) alongside authentic Singaporean-Malay dishes, such as prawn satay. Depending on your order, you can get away for under $40 a head. Mon–Sat 5–11pm.

Whaler Bar and Restaurant 49–51 West End ☏ 03 319 3333, ⓦ thewhaler.co.nz. Monteith's bar serving cheap, generous grub (the best deal is their $18.50 steak special), a range of ales and providing live music during the summer. Daily 11am–11pm.

South from Kaikoura

South from Kaikoura, the SH70 slides inland past Mount Lyford ski-field (see box below) to Hanmer Springs; while the SH1 heads along the coast for a delightful 20km, before cutting uneventfully through farmland to Christchurch. Hikers should consider putting three days aside for the Kaikoura Coast Walk (see box, p.500) while wine drinkers will want to stop in the **Waipara Valley**, 130km south of Kaikoura, where the junction with SH7 to Hanmer Springs marks the centre of one of New Zealand's fastest growing viticultural regions, with the focus on quality Pinot Noir and Riesling. As a wine destination it is very much in its infancy, but a dozen places offer tastings and several have restaurants. Some 10km to the south, burgeoning **Amberley** is the largest settlement between Kaikoura and Christchurch, 40km on.

EATING AND DRINKING   **SOUTH FROM KAIKOURA**

The vineyards are all within 5km of Waipara.

★**Black Estate** 614 Omihi Road, just off SH1, 8km north of the junction ☏ 03 314 6085, ⓦ blackestate .co.nz. Welcoming slow-food restaurant in a black shed perched on the hillside overlooking the vines. Expect confit duck leg with warm lentil and baby carrot salad ($38), best washed down with a glass of their bold rosé or single vineyard dry Riesling. Free tastings. Wed–Sun 10am–4pm.

Little Vintage Espresso 20 Markham St, Amberley ☏ 03 314 9580. Virtually everything is made on-site at this welcoming locals' favourite. Drop in for a coffee and a cinnamon scroll, an iced chocolate served in a jar, or perhaps a breakfast burrito. Mon–Sat 7.30am–4pm.

Pegasus Bay 4km south of the junction, then 3km east ☏ 03 314 6869, ⓦ pegasusbay.com. One of the finest winery restaurants in the country with contemporary artworks the backdrop for diners tucking into the likes of venison Denver leg with black pudding, spinach and butternut squash purée ($42). Each course has a recommendation from their superb wines (which can also be sampled). Winery daily 10am–5pm; restaurant Thurs–Mon noon–4pm.

★**Pukeko Junction Café & Deli** 458 Ashworths Rd (SH1), 6km south of Amberley ☏ 03 314 8834, ⓦ pukekojunction.co.nz. Great wayside café. Sit out on the sunny patio and tuck into the likes of bacon and maple syrup pancakes ($18), lamb shank pie ($10), or exemplary fruit muffins ($4). The adjacent wine shop has Waipara wines to sample and buy. Daily 9am–4.30pm.

Waipara Springs 4km north of Waipara ☏ 03 314 6777, ⓦ waiparasprings.co.nz. The oldest surviving winery in the region, but that's only 1982. The family-oriented garden restaurant (mains $22–29; seafood platter for three $60) has wholesome fresh-baked bread to go with the daily specials. Tastings $5. Daily 11am–5pm.

SKI MOUNT LYFORD

In winter, consider following the scenic SH70 inland from Kaikoura and skiing **Mount Lyford** (mid-June to mid-Oct; ⓦ mtlyford.co.nz), which offers some of the best skiing in the upper South Island. It's a small field and has limited lift facilities ($70/day), but caters for a broad range of abilities (3 beginner runs, 11 intermediate, 6 advanced) and is rarely crowded.

Mount Lyford Lodge 10 Mount Lyford Forest Drive ☏ 03 315 6446, ⓦ mtlyfordlodge.co.nz. The best option if you're going to ski at Mount Lyford, with space for campervans, plus dorms and rooms. There's also a welcoming restaurant and bar. Dorms __$30__, rooms __$90__

Christchurch and south to Otago

AKAROA HARBOUR, BANKS PENINSULA

9

Christchurch and south to Otago

In many ways, the South Island's east coast comes closer to expectations of New Zealand than any other part of the country. Huge sweeps of pastoral land come wedged between snowy mountains and a rugged coast. The main hub of the region is New Zealand's third city, Christchurch, stretched out between the Pacific Ocean and the agriculturally rich flatlands of the Canterbury Plains. Tragically, this stately city was severely damaged by a series of devastating earthquakes in 2010 and 2011. The ground has largely stopped moving and the rebuild is now in full swing, but the physical and psychological recovery will take decades. The beach suburb of Sumner, within easy reach of the city, was also badly damaged, as was the port town of Lyttelton, just over the bald Port Hills. However, locals' resilience and initiative have seen some creative innovations. South of Christchurch, the coastline of Banks Peninsula is indented with numerous bays and harbours, best visited from the quaint "French village" of Akaroa.

The main road (SH1) forges south from Christchurch across the Canterbury Plains, a patchwork of fertile fields watered by huge irrigation booms, all bordered by long shingle beaches littered with driftwood. Historic settlements dotted along the coast attest to the wealth that farming brought to the region. The first significant town is the workaday port of **Timaru**, close to a series of Maori rock paintings, evidence of a far longer history than the imposed European feel would have you believe. As you head into the altogether more rugged terrain of North Otago, the countryside again changes character to undulating coastal hills and crumbling cliffs. The region's most beguiling town is **Oamaru**, with wonderfully accessible penguin colonies and an impressive core of nineteenth-century mercantile buildings. Beyond, routes lead on towards Dunedin and the south, passing the unearthly **Moeraki Boulders** – huge, perfectly spherical rocks formed by a combination of subterranean pressure and erosion.

Christchurch

The South Island's largest city, **CHRISTCHURCH** (Otautahi in Maori) is a long way from recovering from the series of devastating earthquakes which struck in 2010 and 2011. Much of the city centre has been demolished, large areas are wasteland and roads are always being diverted, but tower cranes have finally replaced the wrecking balls. As the rebuild picks up, the next few years will be an exciting time for what is one of New Zealand's most fascinating cities.

Most of all it is not a place to avoid: much of what made pre-quakes Christchurch appealing is still here, and the "garden city" moniker is as true today as ever. Strolling

PUNTING ON THE AVON, CHRISTCHURCH

Highlights

❶ **The Christchurch rebuild** Admire the sleek Cardboard Cathedral, the recast Knox Church and lots of great street art as the city puts itself back together. **See p.511**

❷ **Lyttelton** Christchurch's fun and quirky satellite makes a great outing from the city by day and more so for its restaurants and bars at night. **See p.529**

❸ **Akaroa** Stay in a romantic B&B in this French-influenced village on the Banks Peninsula, dine at its excellent restaurants and swim with Hector's dolphins. **See p.533**

❹ **Timaru** Learn about local Maori rock art at the Te Ana Rock Art Centre, or take a fascinating guided tour to see it in its original setting. **See p.540**

❺ **Oamaru** The fine core of Neoclassical buildings in the slowly gentrifying Historic District makes this a perfect base for spotting both blue and yellow-eyed penguins. **See p.543**

❻ **Moeraki Boulders** Watch the surf crash about these extraordinary spherical boulders artfully littering the tide line. **See p.550**

HIGHLIGHTS ARE MARKED ON THE MAP ON P.510

9

(or **punting**) through the **Botanic Gardens** combines well with the **Canterbury Museum** and a visit to the **Art Gallery** and nearby **Arts Centre**. But what's special is the new stuff. Significant new buildings are limited to the wonderful **Cardboard Cathedral** and the inventive **Re-START** mall, but throughout the CBD you'll stumble across curiosities curated by community-minded groups. Empty lots have been turned into imaginative gardens or sculpture installations, walls are graced with beautiful murals and you'll encounter oddball gap-fillers such as astroturf mini-golf holes, an outsize lounge suite

HIGHLIGHTS

1. The Christchurch rebuild
2. Lyttelton
3. Akaroa
4. Timaru
5. Oamaru
6. Moeraki Boulders

CHRISTCHURCH & SOUTH TO OTAGO

r a musical corner where you can bash away to your heart's content on bits of steel. And the city centre is regaining the nightlife it lost to the suburbs; every week sees new openings along Victoria Street, High Street and New Regent Street.

Beyond the open expanse of **Hagley Park**, the sylvan pleasures of **Mona Vale** and the historic **Riccarton Bush** lead you west towards the airport and the fascinating **International Antarctic Centre**. Exotic beasts populate **Orana Wildlife Park** while **Willowbank Wildlife Reserve** concentrates on local creatures. For laidback beach life, head to the Pacific Ocean suburb of **Sumner**.

Christchurch is a **city in flux**: temporary spaces get filled and promised completion dates have a habit of being put back, often by years. More than usually, it pays to double-check opening hours.

Brief history

Maori occupied scattered settlements around the region and worked closely with the Deans Brothers (see p.517) when they arrived in 1843. Neighbouring Lyttelton had already been established as a whaling port in the 1830s and it was here that the **First Four Ships** arrived in 1850 with pilgrims eager to found a new settlement. They were sent by the **Canterbury Association**, formed in 1849 by members of Oxford's **Christ Church** College, and with the Archbishop of Canterbury at its head. The association had the utopian aim of creating a middle-class, Anglican community in which the moralizing culture of Victorian England could prosper.

The millenarian aspirations upon which the city was founded soon faded as people got on with the exhausting business of carving out a new life in unfamiliar terrain. Nevertheless, the association's ideals had a profound effect on the cultural identity of the city, and descent from those who came on the First Four Ships still carries social cachet among members of the Christchurch elite.

Much of the city's most-loved architecture is the work of **Benjamin Mountford**, who fashioned volcanic "bluestone" and creamy Oamaru limestone into his English neo-Gothic creations. Indeed, Christchurch was long regarded as New Zealand's most

---

THE EARTHQUAKES AND THE REBUILD

The absence of really big earthquakes around Christchurch in the latter half of the twentieth century put everyone off their guard, so the 7.1 magnitude quake which hit the city at 4.35am on September 4, 2010, was unexpected. A few chimneys were dislodged but there was no major damage and no one was killed, but unfortunately the 6.3 magnitude aftershock which hit at lunch time on February 22, 2011, was a very different story. It completely devastated the city centre and killed 185 people, mostly in two buildings which collapsed.

Outside the centre, the older, wealthier western suburbs were built on good land and withstood the quakes fairly well, but much of the housing in the eastern suburbs was built on reclaimed swamp that was prone to **liquefaction**: ground that became like quicksand during the quake. Foundations sank, roads buckled and drains gushed a mixture of ground water and waste from broken sewers.

In the aftermath, much of the sludge was initially cleared by some 2500 Canterbury University students. A three-square-kilometre zone enclosing much of the CBD was sealed off for buildings to be demolished and streets made safe; it took over two years for what was left of the centre to be reopened to the public. The government installed heavy-hitting Gerry Brownlee as minister with responsibility for the Canterbury Earthquake Recovery Authority which was charged with the **rebuild**.

Despite broad-ranging powers the city's reconstruction has been frustratingly slow. After extensive public consultation, the plan is to build a greener, smaller and more liveable city centre. Open blocks of land east of Manchester Street and south of Tuam Street will frame a centre anchored by major precincts – Justice, Health, Conventions, Performing Arts, Sports and a bus interchange. The 23-storey pre-quake Pacific Tower still stands as the city's tallest, but new buildings are supposed to be limited to seven storeys.

9

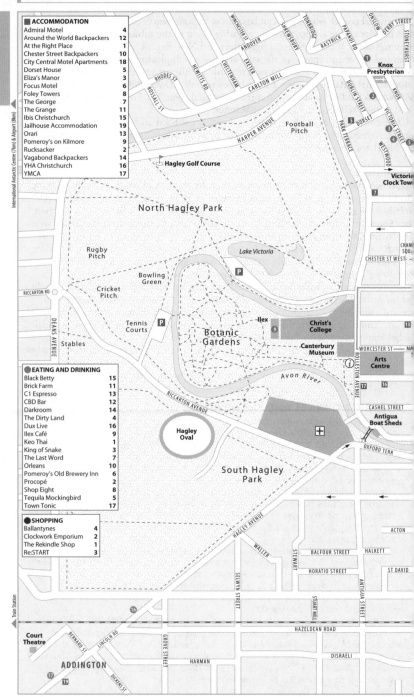

■ ACCOMMODATION

Admiral Motel	4
Around the World Backpackers	12
At the Right Place	1
Chester Street Backpackers	10
City Central Motel Apartments	18
Dorset House	5
Eliza's Manor	3
Focus Motel	6
Foley Towers	8
The George	7
The Grange	11
Ibis Christchurch	15
Jailhouse Accommodation	19
Orari	13
Pomeroy's on Kilmore	9
Rucksacker	2
Vagabond Backpackers	14
YHA Christchurch	16
YMCA	17

■ EATING AND DRINKING

Black Betty	15
Brick Farm	11
C1 Espresso	13
CBD Bar	12
Darkroom	14
The Dirty Land	4
Dux Live	16
Ilex Café	9
Keo Thai	1
King of Snake	3
The Last Word	7
Orleans	10
Pomeroy's Old Brewery Inn	6
Procopé	2
Shop Eight	8
Tequila Mockingbird	5
Town Tonic	17

● SHOPPING

Ballantynes	4
Clockwork Emporium	2
The Rekindle Shop	1
Re:START	3

CENTRAL CHRISTCHRUCH

SPRINGFIELD RD
DURHAM ST NORTH
CALEDONIAN RD
SHERBORNE STREET
Southern Cross
BISHOP ST RD
PACKE ST
GERALDINE ST
CHAMPION ST

BEALEY AVENUE

DOLLANS
OTLEY STREET
AMURI PK
CHURCHILL

PEACOCK STREET
VERIDGE STREET
COLOMBO STREET
MELROSE STREET
MOA PL
ELY STREET

CONFERENCE
GRACEFIELD
MANCHESTER STREET
ABERDEEN STREET
ULSTER
MADRAS STREET
WILLOW
BANGOR

AMREDALE
SALISBURY STREET
HURLEY

PETERBOROUGH LA.
Central Library
Peterborough
DURHAM STREET
PETERBOROUGH STREET

KILMORE STREET

HESTER ST WEST
VICTORIA SQUARE
CAMBRIDGE TERR
OXFORD TERR
CHESTER STREET
DAWSON

ARMAGH STREET

NEW REGENT ST
Isaac Theatre Royal
CHANCERY LA
BARBADOES STREET

GLOUCESTER STREET
LATIMER
WORCESTER STREET
SQUARE

Christchurch Art Gallery
CATHEDRAL SQUARE
Chalice
ChristChurch Cathedral

HEREFORD STREET
LIVERPOOL
WOOLSACK

Quake City
Cardboard Cathedral

CASHEL STREET
185 Chairs
CLARKSON
GILMOUR
FITZGERALD AVENUE

Stranges Lane
BEDFORD ROW
LICHFIELD STREET
POPLAR
ASH
DUKE

Bus Interchange
HIGH ST
TUAM STREET

Alice Cinematheque

MOLLETT STREET
ST ASAPH STREET
ALFRED

WALKER STREET
DURHAM STREET
WINCHCOMBE
WELLES STREET
QUILL
SOUTHWARK
ATLAS
ALLEN STREET
WILLIAMS
COVENTRY
FERRY RD

WILMER STREET
AVCESTER
ROPE

BATH STREET
DUNDAS STREET
EATON
MORTIMER

MOORHOUSE AVENUE

N

CARLYLE

CASS
SANDYFORD
Backpacker Car Market
BYRON

0   250
metres

BATTERSEA ST

▼ Academy Gold Cinema (200m) & Port Hills (5km)

9

English city. With the exception of a few punts on the willow-draped Avon and the Neoclassical stylings of many of the buildings, this tag had outlived its usefulness long before the recent devastation.

Cathedral Square

Food truck market • Nov–March: Fri 4–10pm

The large, open **Cathedral Square** has always been the heart of Christchurch with the former ChristChurch Cathedral (see below) as its focal point. It was closed off for two years after the February 2011 quake and still lacks its old vibrancy but people are slowly returning, encouraged by the **food truck market** on Friday evenings in summer, when a dozen or so mobile kitchens – Sri Lankan, Mexican, Transylvanian, Vietnamese, doughnuts etc – are corralled outside.

Many of the buildings that once surrounded Cathedral Square have gone though you can still see the Italianate 1879 **Old Post Office** which is up for restoration. Outside, the **Memorial of the Four Ships** remembers the city's earliest immigrants and Neil Dawson's 18m-high *Chalice* sculpture marks the Millennium and Canterbury's 150th anniversary.

ChristChurch Cathedral

Closed for the foreseeable future • ⓦ cathedralconversations.co.nz, ⓦ restorechristchurchcathedral.co.nz

In the wake of the 2011 earthquake, the fate of the Gothic Revival Anglican **ChristChurch Cathedral** remains uncertain. The Anglican Church decided the cost of repair was prohibitive and opted to build anew; they got as far as knocking down what remained of the 63m-high tower before heritage buffs used the courts to put a stop to further demolition. Check the websites for both sides of the argument.

The church was designed in 1858 by George Gilbert Scott (architect of London's St Pancras Station) who had intended it to be built of wood. The design was later adapted by Benjamin Mountford, reworked in stone and completed in 1904. Outside, artist Chris Heaphy's 2013 **sculpture**, *Planted Whare* – scaffolding covered in plastic bread baskets filled with foliage – is designed to act as the cathedral's lychgate.

New Regent Street

ⓦ newregentstreet.co.nz

The first real shopping street to reopen in the CBD was little **New Regent Street**, a 1930s Spanish Mission-style strip running north–south along which the heritage Christchurch Tram (see box, p.522) merrily clanks. The neat pastel-painted buildings look pretty lonesome with empty lots all around, but make your way here for the central city's most interesting cluster of cafés and bars, and a few intriguing shops (see p.529).

Cardboard Cathedral

234 Hereford St, overlooking Latimer Square • Daily: Nov–March 9am–7pm; April–Oct 9am–5pm • ☏ 03 366 0046, ⓦ cardboardcathedral.org.nz

The first significant building to rise from the post-quake rubble was the **Transitional Cathedral**, designed pro bono by Japanese "disaster architect" Shigeru Ban. Known as the **Cardboard Cathedral** for its elegant superstructure of 98 industrial-strength cardboard tubes, it replaces St John's parish church, which stood on this site before the quakes. The 700-seat light-filled wedge threw open its doors in August 2013, sending out a message of hope which rippled far beyond the Anglican faithful.

Aside from the superstructure, massive paper tubes also form the cross behind the altar and the front of the pulpit. The walls are made from shipping containers, with timber and steel shoring everything up and clear polycarbonate sheeting as weatherproofing. The overall effect is far more beautiful than it might sound, and the building is intended as more than a short-term fix, with an estimated fifty-year design life.

185 chairs

A bleak street corner immediately south of here is hugely enhanced by Peter Majendie's *185 Chairs*, perhaps the most **poignant memorial** to those lost in the February 2011 quake. The 185 white-painted armchairs, stools, office chairs, etc have been adopted by the community, who replace a chair if one is stolen and whitewash the lot to mark each anniversary. Sit for a moment to remember.

Re:START mall

Cashel St • Daily Mon–Fri 10am–5.30pm, Sat & Sun 10am–5.30pm • ⑩ restart.org.nz

After the February 2011 quake, **shipping containers** quickly became a symbol for the broken city, so it made complete sense when, in late 2011, the first real attempt to bring commerce back to the city centre was created from a brightly-painted cluster of them.

Re:START quickly became a symbol of rejuvenation. Since then it has grown and moved a little down the street to make way for more permanent structures – just as was always intended. With shops, banks, cafés, market stalls, free wi-fi, solar phone-chargers, street performers and buskers, it is usually a pretty lively spot.

Quake City

99 Cashel St • Daily 10am–5pm • $20, children $8 • ⑩ quakecity.co.nz

To capture a sense of Christchurch's spirit during the city's darkest hours, visit Canterbury Museum's **Quake City**, the closest thing Christchurch has to an earthquake museum. Of course all the stats are here – dates, quake magnitudes, measures of destruction – but there's also lots of great photos taken at the time of the quake and soon after, and footage of liquefaction in action. But it is really about the human stories, the dead, the helpless and the helpers who stepped up when the need was greatest.

The Arts Centre

301 Montreal St • ⑩ artscentre.org.nz

The **Arts Centre** fills the entire block once occupied by the University of Canterbury and Christchurch Girls' and Boys' High School from 1874 until the university relocated during the 1970s. It is now one of the largest conservation projects undertaken in New Zealand with most of the 23 heritage buildings here in need of major repair. Over the next few years, the chain-link fencing will gradually come down as more and more of the Centre reopens to the public. Its leafy courtyards, grassy quadrangles and neo-Gothic buildings should once again become the city's cultural heart with performance and exhibition spaces, studios, an arts cinema and a regular food market. Plans also include the restoration of **Rutherford's Den** which honours Nobel Prize-winning atomic nucleus discoverer Ernest Rutherford, commemorated on the $100 banknote.

Christchurch Art Gallery

Corner of Worcester Blvd and Montreal St • Due to reopen in December 2015 • ☎ 03 941 7300, ⑩ christchurchartgallery.org.nz

After 2011, the largely intact **Christchurch Art Gallery** became the Civil Defence base, with its striking frontage of curving glass intersecting at odd angles becoming the backdrop for countless TV interviews. The gallery has been shut since, though the management have remained remarkably active. Their **Outer Spaces** programme has brought art to other public buildings, put on temporary shows, and taken art out onto the streets. Works from the gallery have been painted on walls all over the city centre, often huge and surprising when seen close up – check out Tony Fomison's compellingly dark *No!*, near the corner of Tuam and High streets.

Once the gallery does reopen, new acquisitions will feature alongside works by Christchurch and Canterbury artists. The European landscape tradition comes through

9

forcefully in nineteenth-century paintings by Charles Goldie and Dutch émigré Petrus van der Velden, such as *Mountain Stream Otira Gorge*. More recent works include Rita Angus' *Cass*, depicting a lone customer on the platform of a desolate station (now on the *TranzAlpine* route), and Bill Hammond's primordial works liberally scattered with iconic bird-headed humanoids.

Look, too, for works from the 1930s and 1940s by Frances Hodgkins, superb glass castings by Ann Robinson and Shona Firman, and photographic works by both Neil and Fiona Pardington.

Canterbury Museum

Rolleston Ave • Daily: Oct–March 9am–5.30pm; April–Sept 9am–5pm • Free • ☎ 03 366 5000, ⓦ canterburymuseum.com

Benjamin Mountford's 1870 neo-Gothic **Canterbury Museum** takes a broad-ranging trawl through the history of the province and beyond. Classic dioramas depicting bronzed natives hunting moa, fishing and leaving their marks inside caves set the scene for the superb Maori collection containing fine examples of carving and weaving. Canterbury's links to Antarctica are explored through a flimsy, unreliable motor tractor from Shackleton's 1914–17 expedition, a Ferguson tractor that became the first vehicle to reach the Pole as part of Edmund Hillary's push in 1958, and the far more robust Sno-Cat used by Brit Vivian Fuchs on the same expedition. No one minds the regional connection being stretched by **Fred and Myrtle's Paua Shell House**, a shrine to kitsch Kiwiana modelled on a house in Bluff where the famed Fluteys plastered their home with polished paua shells. After their deaths the contents were shipped here and reassembled.

Botanic Gardens

Main entrance on Rolleston Ave • Daily 7am until 30min after sunset • Free • Visitor Centre daily 8.30am–5pm

The **Botanic Gardens** have helped Christchurch live up to its "Garden City" moniker since1863 and its mature collection of indigenous and exotic plants and trees is unrivalled on the South Island. From summer to autumn, perennials give a constant and dazzling display of colour; the herb garden, containing a variety of culinary and medicinal plants, exudes aromatic scents; and, from December, the rose garden blooms with over 250 varieties. Above all, though, it's just a great place to hang out on a sunny day.

ilex

Daily 8.30am–5pm • Free

Long, low, white and strikingly modern, **ilex** houses a visitor centre, airy café and a plant nursery where everything is visible as you stroll past. The small **museum** explores how the totara and kahikatea forests of the Canterbury Plains were transformed by Maori into flax, kumara and raupo (reed) beds, then by Pakeha into English gardens that struggle to cope with the drying summer winds.

Antigua Boat Sheds

2 Cambridge Terrace • Daily: Oct–April 9am–6pm; May–Sept 10am–4pm • Paddleboat $25/30min for two; single canoe $12/hr; double canoe $24/hr; rowboat $35/hr • ☎ 03 366 5885, ⓦ boatsheds.co.nz

The Botanic Gardens are enclosed by a loop of the River Avon, which you can explore from the **Antigua Boat Sheds** by renting a paddleboat, canoe or rowboat. If you'd rather lie back and enjoy it all, go punting instead (see box, p.522).

Hagley Park

Beyond the Botanic Gardens, the Avon River meanders its way through the trees, lawns and sports grounds of **Hagley Park** which sprawls over two square kilometres immediately vest of the city centre. At weekends it seems like the entire population of Christchurch is here, strolling around, playing some form of sport or attending a cricket match at the new Hagley Oval, which was seen to great effect during the 2015 Cricket World Cup.

Victoria Street

Running northwest from the city centre, **Victoria Street** is one of the city's liveliest, kicking off at Victoria Square and passing the quake-knobbled **Town Hall** and beautifully restored 1860 **Victoria Clock Tower** en route to the restaurant and bar hotspots around the Knox Presbyterian Church.

Knox Presbyterian Church

nr Bealey Ave & Victoria St

One of Christchurch's best syntheses of old and new architecture can be seen by peeking inside what was once a typical Victorian Gothic church. After suitable strengthening with exposed concrete beams, much of the building's structure has been retained, but it now comes wrapped in copper sheeting. The work is beautifully finished, appearing modern on the outside and yet suitably respectful towards what could be saved of the interior.

Mona Vale

3 Fendalton Rd • Grounds open daily 7am–dusk • Free

A picnic hamper and a bottle of rosé are the perfect accompaniment for a visit to these compact and oh-so-English gardens that flank the languid Avon River. Originally part of the Deans' Riccarton Bush estate (see below), the gardens have majestic displays of roses, fuchsias, magnolias and rhododendrons set around the quake-damaged 1897 English Arts and Crafts homestead.

Riccarton Bush

16 Kahu Rd, Riccarton, 3km west of the city centre • Daily dawn–dusk • Free • Bus P runs close by

Twelve hectares of half-millennium-old kahikatea trees rise up 25m in **Riccarton Bush**, a.k.a. **Deans Bush**. This last remnant of Canterbury's original forest was saved from the axe by the Scottish brothers William and John Deans, who came here to farm in 1843 (seven years before the city was founded) and somehow resisted the temptation to put all their property to agricultural use. Protected by a predator-proof fence, it is threaded by a concrete loop path (20–30min) with signs interpreting the various species. On Saturdays the place comes alive with the Farmers' Market (see p.528).

Deans Cottage

Daily 9am–dusk • Free

The tiny black-pine **Deans Cottage** was built nearby by the Deans brothers within a few months of their arrival. The cottage was moved to the entrance to Riccarton Bush in the 1970s and is furnished as it would have been when they lived there.

Riccarton House

Full tours Sun–Fri 2pm; 1hr 15min; $18 • Mini tours Sat 10am–12.30pm; 20min; $5 • ☎ 03 341 1018, ⓦ riccartonhouse.co.nz

John Deans' wife Jane and their son John were largely instrumental in the construction of the grand Victorian **Riccarton House**, next door to Deans Cottage. Started in 1856 on land leased from Ngai Tahu, the building was twice extended and substantially restored after the quakes to produce the grand, three-storey weatherboard homestead you see now – essentially Christchurch's founding family home.

Take one of the two tours to really get a sense of the stoicism required of both men and women in carving out a life here. The short tours visit rooms where wallpaper has

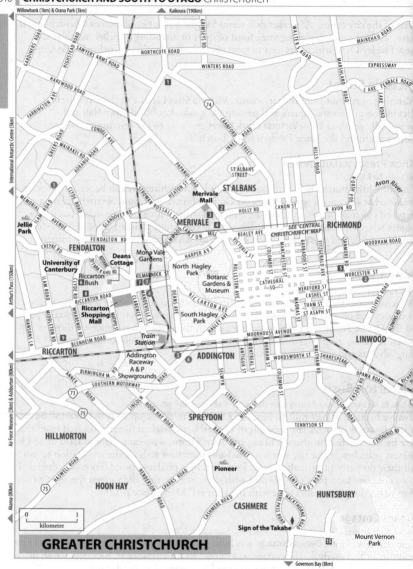

GREATER CHRISTCHURCH

been stripped away in multiple layers to reveal the construction beneath, while the longer tours venture up to the period-furnished bedrooms.

International Antarctic Centre

38 Orchard Rd, an easy ten-minute walk from the airport – follow the penguin footsteps • Daily 9am–5.30pm • General admission $59, Xpress admission $39; discount if bought online • Penguin feedings at 10.30am, 1.30pm & 3.30pm • ☎ 03 357 0519, ⓦ iceberg.co.nz •
Free Penguin Express shuttle bus runs hourly from the city

Christchurch airport is the launchpad for flights to US and New Zealand research bases

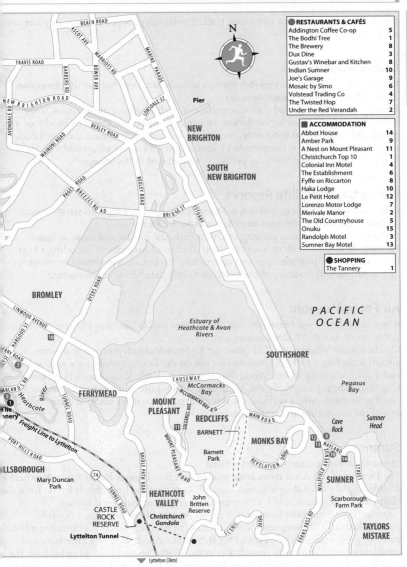

● RESTAURANTS & CAFÉS

Addington Coffee Co-op	5
The Bodhi Tree	1
The Brewery	8
Dux Dine	3
Gustav's Winebar and Kitchen	8
Indian Sumner	10
Joe's Garage	9
Mosaic by Simo	6
Volstead Trading Co	4
The Twisted Hop	7
Under the Red Verandah	2

■ ACCOMMODATION

Abbot House	14
Amber Park	9
A Nest on Mount Pleasant	11
Christchurch Top 10	1
Colonial Inn Motel	4
The Establishment	6
Fyffe on Riccarton	8
Haka Lodge	10
Le Petit Hotel	12
Lorenzo Motor Lodge	7
Merivale Manor	2
The Old Countryhouse	5
Onuku	15
Randolph Motel	3
Sumner Bay Motel	13

● SHOPPING

The Tannery	1

in Antarctica, and if you're interested in all things polar you could easily spend half a day at the **International Antarctic Centre**; it may be pricey but the exhibits are dynamic and well-presented. Don't miss the little blue penguins (which you can see being fed) and the Snow & Ice Experience, where you don a down jacket to endure a (fairly naff) simulated storm and accompanying −18°C Antarctic chill. Another highlight is *Beyond the Frozen Sunset*, a beautifully filmed HD video with great chopper footage of the Dry Valleys and limitless wastes of ice.

The General Admission ticket (but not the Xpress) gives you access to the entertaining 4D theatre show, and unlimited goes at the ten-minute **Hägglund Ride**

9

(every 20min), on which a five-tonne tracked polar buggy is put through its paces over an obstacle course.

Orana Wildlife Park

McLeans Island Rd, 20km west of the city centre • Daily 10am–5pm; lion encounter daily 2.30pm (book ahead) • $28; lion encounter additional $35 • ☎ 03 359 7109, ⓦ oranawildlifepark.co.nz

Feeding times are staggered throughout the day at this well-organized, open-range zoological park that's strong on African savannah animals. You can even hand-feed a giraffe and join the **lion encounter**, touring the big cats' enclosure on the caged back of a truck. New Zealand is represented by kiwi, tuatara, an active aviary and a gecko house where the little critters are perfectly camouflaged in the foliage.

Willowbank Wildlife Reserve

60 Hussey Rd, 10km northwest of the city centre • Daily: Nov–March 9.30am–7pm; April–Oct 9.30am–5pm • $28 • ☎ 03 359 6226, ⓦ willowbank.co.nz • From central Christchurch take the Blue Line bus then transfer to #107

Although nowhere near as exciting as Orana Park, the smaller and more intimate **Willowbank Wildlife Reserve** has some good displays of native birds including a kiwi house where they incubate eggs and raise chicks. Exotics are represented by monkeys, otters, parrots and macaws, all presented in a fairly naturalistic environment.

Air Force Museum

45 Harvard Ave, Wigram, 7km west of the city centre • Daily 10am–5pm; 45min tours daily 11am, 1.30pm & 3pm • Free; flight simulators $5/5min; tours $10 • ☎ 03 343 9532, ⓦ airforcemuseum.co.nz

On the former Wigram RNZAF base, the **Air Force Museum** presents two dozen aircraft including a Dakota converted for use on the British queen's state visit in 1953, and a Spitfire among several World War II veterans. Flight simulators will keep the (big) kids happy, particularly the World War II Mosquito as it engages in combat in the Norwegian fjords, while enthusiastic volunteer guides conduct assorted tours, including one of the restoration and storage hangars.

Sumner

13km southeast of central Christchurch • Bus #3 from the city centre

The Heathcote and Avon rivers estuary opens out into Pegasus Bay at **Redcliffs**, where a double-height row of shipping containers protects the road from debris falling from the cliffs above, once the seat of Christchurch's most spectacularly sited homes.

Around 3km southeast, **Sumner** is the city's premiere beach suburb, a Norfolk pine-backed strip of shops restaurants, cafés, wine bars and surf shacks fronting a broad patch of golden sand. Named after Dr J.B. Sumner, Archbishop of Canterbury and president of the Canterbury Association in the 1850s, Sumner took a big hit from the quakes but has recovered better than elsewhere. The focus is still the beach, marked by the striking **Cave Rock**, peppered with little caves like an enormous Swiss cheese.

Taylor's Mistake

4km southeast of Sumner

The best **surfing** around is at **Taylor's Mistake**, a narrow beach and small community named, according to local lore, after a captain who ran aground here after mistaking the bay for the entrance to Lyttelton Harbour. You can walk here from Sumner via a constantly undulating track around **Scarborough Head** (1hr each way; 3km), with great coastal views – follow The Esplanade south onto Scarborough Road then hug the coast onto Whitewash Head Road.

Godley Head

Evans Pass Road climbs south from Sumner to **Godley Head**, the guardian of the entrance to Lyttelton Harbour. This spectacular DOC-administered piece of land with high cliffs and excellent views is a delightful spot for a picnic. The walkway network is extensive, stumbling across installations left behind after World War II, including dark warren-like tunnels and searchlight emplacements perched like birds' nests on the cliffs – from here, walk down to the tiny coastal settlements of Boulder Bay and Taylor's Mistake.

Christchurch Gondola

10 Bridle Path Rd, Heathcote, 10km southeast of the city centre • Daily 10am–5pm • $25 • ☎ 03 384 0310, ⓦ welcomeaboard.co.nz • served by shuttle from outside the Canterbury Museum ($10 return) and the Lyttelton bus #28

The **Christchurch Gondola** provides the easiest access to great views and easy strolls from the 945m summit of **Mount Cavendish** along the top of the Port Hills. Go early to see the Southern Alps in the best light. Alternatively try a combined gondola ride and mountain bicycle descent with the Mountain Bike Adventure Company (see box, p.522).

Port Hills

10–15km south and southeast of the city centre

Before the quakes, an evening drive along the **Summit Road** of the **Port Hills** was one of the city's pleasures. But the roads, paths and mountain-bike tracks have only partly been reopened and exploration remains limited. The ridge-top Summit Road itself was the passion of public-spirited liberal MP and conservationist Harry Ell who also dreamed of fourteen rest stations between Christchurch and Akaroa. When he died in 1934, only four had been built. Drive over **Dyers Pass Road** (between the city and Governors Bay) and you'll pass the best of these, the quake-damaged **Sign of the Takahe**, a Gothic-style baronial house that is set to reopen in 2016, perhaps once again as a classy restaurant.

ARRIVAL AND DEPARTURE

CHRISTCHURCH

Christchurch is the hub of air, road and rail routes for Canterbury and the rest of the South Island. There are direct **flights** to a dozen cities, but most intercity journeys are best done by **bus**. All depart from central Christchurch, and some also depart directly from the airport.

BY PLANE

Christchurch Airport The airport (☎ 03 358 5029, ⓦ christchurchairport.co.nz) is 10km northwest of the city centre and is open 24hr. It has ATMs, foreign-exchange booths, a Vodafone shop to get your mobile up and running and an i-SITE office open for all arriving international flights. There's also a free-phone board for accommodation and car-rental bookings, plus left luggage at Luggage Solutions (suitcase or backpack $15 for one day, $30 overnight; daily 4.30am–6.30pm; ☎ 03 358 8027, ⓦ luggagesolutions.co.nz). They also do bike boxing for $30.

Destinations Auckland (2 daily; 1hr 20min); Blenheim (1–3 daily; 50min); Dunedin (6 daily; 1hr); Hokitika (2–4 daily; 40min); Invercargill (4–6 daily; 1hr 25min); Napier/Hastings (2 daily; 1hr 30min); Nelson (4–6 daily; 50min); Palmerston North (2–3 daily; 1hr 10min); Queenstown (4 daily; 1hr);

Rotorua (3 daily; 1hr 45min); Wellington (12 daily; 1hr).

TO/FROM AIRPORT

By bus The #29 bus runs direct from the airport to the city (every 30min; 40min journey; $8) while the Purple Line (every 30min; 55min journey; $8) takes a more circuitous route past the university, along Riccarton Road and through Hagley Park.

By shuttle Steve's Airport Shuttles (☎ 0800 101 021; first person $20, additional person $5) operates a frequent door-to-door service. They pick up at most accommodation when heading to the airport; book the evening before.

By taxi Taxis between the airport and central Christchurch charge $50–60.

BY TRAIN

Christchurch train station Two very scenic passenger

TOURS AND ACTIVITIES IN AND AROUND CHRISTCHURCH

Christchurch makes a good base for exploring the immediate vicinity and beyond. Here are some of the more diverting activities and tours.

BALLOONING

Ballooning Canterbury ☎0508 422 556, ⓦballooningcanterbury.com. A romantic and gentle way to get airborne, with peaceful early-morning flights over Christchurch's surrounds and spectacular views from mountains to coast ($320).

CITY, REBUILD, SEGWAY AND BIKE TOURS

Christchurch Rebuild Tour ☎0800 500 929, ⓦredbus.co.nz. Fairly staid but informative 90min bus tour of the CBD ($29). The route changes to visit whatever is currently most interesting, but always includes the Cardboard Cathedral. Daily 11.30am & 1pm.

Christchurch Tram ☎03 366 7830, ⓦwelcome aboard.co.nz. Driver-commentated heritage tramway which weaves a 3km circuit past the Arts Centre, New Regent Street, the Re:START Mall and Cathedral Square every 10min. The tramway was only reinstalled in 1995, but the rolling stock is largely made up of lovingly restored originals built between 1908 and 1925. The $15 ticket allows you to get on and off all day, and kids are free. There's even a restaurant tram (daily 7–9.30pm; $95) which does the circuit as you dine leaving from Cathedral Junction. Oct–March 9am–6pm; April–Sept 10am–5pm.

Discover Christchurch Tours ☎0800 141 149, ⓦhasslefree.co.nz. Fun tours in an open-top double decker bus. Choose from the Central City Tour (2–7 daily; 1hr; $32) which visits the main central city sights, and the Discover Christchurch Tour (2–3 daily; 3hr 30min; $69) which adds Mona Vale, Sumner and the Port Hills.

Mountain Bike Adventure Company ☎0800 424 534, ⓦcyclehire-tours.co.nz. Short-term and touring bike rental company specializing in gondola-assisted downhill rides. Your ticket ($60) gets you a gondola ride, time to look around then either a 16km road ride or a MTB off-road descent. Book ahead.

Rebuild Bike Tour ☎0800 733 257, ⓦchchbiketours .co.nz. Being able to hop off and check out quirky street corner artworks and installations makes cycling the perfect way to explore the rejuvenating city centre. These 2hr small-group tours are supplemented by their Saturday morning tour to the Christchurch Farmers' Market ($50) or the Gourmet Bike Tour (3hr; $160) which includes lunch somewhere interesting. Daily 10am & 2pm.

Urban Wheels ☎03 942 8834, ⓦurbanwheels .co.nz. Segway tours with all the advantages of a bike but faster, more fun and geekier. Go for the Rebuild Zone Tour or the Combo Tour (both 2hr; $109), which wraps in Hagley Park and Mona Vale.

HIGH COUNTRY TOUR

Alpine Safari ☎0800 427 753, ⓦhasslefree.co.nz. A great alternative to a full day on the *TranzAlpine* train spending 10hr jetboating the Waimakariri River, going off-road in a 4WD across a high-country sheep and cattle station and returning by the *TranzAlpine* from Arthur's Pass ($419).

PUNTING

Welcome Aboard ☎03 366 0337, ⓦwelcomeaboard .co.nz. Punters nattily dressed in blazers and straw boaters gently pole you along the river for half an hour, either through the Botanic Gardens from the Antigua Boat Sheds or through the city centre from Worcester St Bridge. Daily: Oct–March 9am–6pm; April–Sept 10am–4pm.

---

trains operate from the station (train information ☎0800 872 467) on Troup Drive, near the corner of Hagley, over 2km southwest of Cathedral Square. The summer-only Coastal Pacific (with panoramic viewing windows) runs to Picton and meets ferries to the North Island, while the *TranzAlpine* does day-returns to Greymouth (see box, p.524). Steve's Airport Shuttles (see p.521) also serve the train station ($7 from the city centre).

Destinations Arthur's Pass (1 daily; 2hr 15min); Blenheim (1 daily in summer; 4hr 45min); Greymouth (1 daily; 4hr 30min); Kaikoura (1 daily in summer; 3hr); Picton (1 daily in summer; 5hr 15min).

BY BUS

Long-distance buses drop off at a confusing array of spots around town, any of which may change at any time. Check the location of stops with your operator.

Destinations Akaroa (2–3 daily; 1hr 30min); Aoraki Mount Cook (1 daily; 5hr 20min); Arthur's Pass (2 daily; 2hr 30min); Blenheim (3–5 daily; 4hr 45min–5hr 30min); Dunedin (6 daily; 6hr); Geraldine (4 daily; 2hr); Greymouth (2 daily; 4hr); Hanmer Springs (2 daily; 2hr); Hokitika (1 daily; 4hr 30min); Kaikoura (3–5 daily; 2hr 30min); Lyttelton (every 15–30min; 35min); Methven (3–7 weekly; 1hr 30min); Oamaru (6 daily; 4hr); Picton (3–5 daily;

nr–5hr 30min); Queenstown (3–4 daily; 7–8hr); Tekapo
4 daily; 3–4hr); Timaru (6 daily; 2hr 30min); Twizel
–4 daily; 4–5hr); Wanaka (1–2 daily; 7–8hr).

US COMPANIES

karoa French Connection ✆ 0800 800 575, ✇ akaroa
us.co.nz. To Akaroa daily at 8.45am (and more in summer).

karoa Shuttle ✆ 0800 500 929, ✇ akaroashuttle
o.nz. To Akaroa 1–3 times daily.

tomic Shuttles ✆ 03 439 0697, ✇ atomictravel.co.nz.
orth to Kaikoura, Blenheim and Picton; south to Timaru,
amaru and Dunedin; west to Greymouth; and inland
hrough Geraldine and Twizel to Wanaka and Queenstown.

lanmer Connection ✆ 0800 242 663,
) hanmerconnection.co.nz. Christchurch to Hanmer
prings and back twice a day.

lanmer Shuttle ✆ 03 315 7418, ✇ hanmertours
co.nz. Hanmer Springs to Christchurch and back daily.

InterCity/Newmans ✆ 03 365 1113, ✇ intercity.co.nz.
North to Kaikoura, Blenheim, Picton and Nelson; south to
Timaru, Oamaru, Dunedin and Invercargill; and inland to
Tekapo, Aoraki/Mount Cook and Queenstown.

Knight Rider ✆ 0800 287 874, ✇ knightrider.co.nz.
Evening trips from Christchurch (3.30pm) via the airport
through Timaru and Oamaru to Dunedin (9.30pm) then
overnight back arriving at Christchurch (3.15am) and the
airport (3.30am). Fares allow stop-offs along the way.

Methven Travel ✆ 0800 684 888, ✇ methventravel
.co.nz. Daily from the city and airport to Methven in winter,
then at odd times in summer. Check the website for
timetable.

NakedBus ✇ nakedbus.com. Daily services to Dunedin,
Picton and Queenstown via Wanaka.

West Coast Shuttle ✆ 03 768 0028, ✇ west
coastshuttle.co.nz. Once daily run from Greymouth to
Christchurch then back in the afternoon.

GETTING AROUND

BY BUS

Bus station By the time you read this, buses should all be
running from the new Bus Interchange on Colombo St
outh of Lichfield St. Services are run by several companies
nified as Metro (Mon–Sat 7am–7pm, Sun 9am–7pm;
) 03 366 8855, ✇ metroinfo.org.nz). The website has good
oute planning.

ares and cards With the exception of trips to and
rom the airport, the fare anywhere in the city's zone
ne, including Sumner and Lyttelton, is $3.50. If you're
ere for a few days, save money by buying a Metrocard
rom the Bus Interchange ($10 fee plus min $10 top-up).
tandard fares drop to $2.30, and once you've paid for
wo fares on a certain day subsequent journeys are free.
Most routes run from 6.30am until around midnight
nd transfers allow you to travel in one direction for up
o 2hr.

BY CAR AND TAXI

riving in Christchurch remains straightforward despite
he quakes, with road closures well signposted.

arking Most central spaces are metered (free on public
olidays). There's convenient parking in the centre of

Hagley Park (Armagh St entrance); it's free for the first
three hours and all day at weekends.

Vehicle rental There are dozens of car and van rental
places in Christchurch, mostly based at the airport. For
more on car rental, see Basics, p.33.

Taxis Try Blue Star (✆ 03 379 9799) or Gold Band
(✆ 03 379 5795).

Backpackers Car Market 33 Battersea St, Sydenham,
1.5km south of Cathedral Square ✆ 03 377 3177,
✇ backpackercarschristchurch.co.nz. A great spot to buy
cars from other travellers with everything made easy. Daily
9.30am–5pm.

BY BIKE

Given Christchurch's relatively quiet roads and flat terrain,
cycling is an ideal way of exploring some of the more out-
of-the-way suburbs.

Antigua Boat Sheds Bike Hire 2 Cambridge Terrace
✆ 03 366 5885, ✇ boatsheds.co.nz. Pootle around town
for two hours ($15) or a full day ($30).

The Vintage Peddler ✆ 03 365 6530, ✇ vintage
peddler.co.nz. Retro bikes for gentle peddling from $15 for
two hours.

INFORMATION

Visitor information The i-SITE is currently on Rolleston
Ave, next to the Canterbury Museum (daily: Nov to mid-Jan
.30am–6pm; mid-Jan to March 8.30am–7pm; April–Oct
.30am–5pm; ✆ 03 379 9629 & ✆ 0800 423 783,
✇ christchurchnz.com), though is likely to move to the Arts
entre. It will handle bookings for much of the South
sland, and should also have a Department of Conservation
desk with stacks of tramping info.

Library A new library is planned on the corner of Colombo

and Gloucester sts, near Cathedral Square, but in the
meantime services are provided by the Central Library
Peterborough, 91 Peterborough St (Mon–Fri 9am–6pm,
Sat & Sun 10am–5pm), which has free wi-fi.

Swimming pools A couple of major pools were lost in the
quakes, so the handiest are Pioneer, 75 Lyttelton St,
Somerfield, 5km southwest, and Jellie Park, 295 Ilam Rd,
Burnside, 7km northwest (both ✆ 03 941 6888).

9

THE TRANZALPINE

One of the most popular day-trips from Christchurch is the tourist-oriented *TranzAlpine* **train** through the Southern Alps to Greymouth on the West Coast (4hr 30min each way; book well ahead for non-changeable half-price fares; full rate $199 each way; ⓦ kiwirailscenic.co.nz). It's a gorgeous 231km journey with braided river valleys, nineteen tunnels and open tussock country all seen from the train's large viewing windows and open-sided observation car. There's a pause at the beech-forest high point of Arthur's Pass before descending through the 8.5km-long Otira Tunnel that burrows under the 920m pass itself.

A good strategy for those with a vehicle is to catch the train at Darfield, 45km west of Christchurch, allowing a later start in return for missing Christchurch's industrial suburbs. It's also worth considering alighting at Moana for a relaxed three-hour lakeside lunch before boarding for the return journey. It beats a hurried snack in Greymouth.

The train leaves Christchurch at 8.15am daily, returns around 6pm and can also form part of a high-country tour (see box, p.522).

ACCOMMODATION

Christchurch is struggling to replace accommodation lost in the quakes, and there's often a shortfall. As a fallback the city has been relying on its **motels**, the majority strung out along Papanui Rd to the northwest of the city centre, and Riccarton Rd to the west of Hagley Park. Most **campsites** are within walking distance of a bus stop and **freedom camping** is permitted in self-contained campervans. Most places (including hostels) accommodate **late arrivals** and early departures: just double-check your date of arrival has been understood, and book ahead, especially Dec–March. Check ⓦ christchurchnz.com for new openings.

CENTRAL CHRISTCHURCH

Admiral Motel 168 Bealey Ave ☎03 379 3554, ⓦ admiralmotel.co.nz; map pp.512–513. Great-value motel with a BBQ, picnic tables and kids' play area in the flowering gardens and spotless rooms. **$115**

★Around the World Backpackers 314 Barbadoes St ☎03 365 4363, ⓦ aroundtheworld.co.nz; map pp.512–513. Well-run compact hostel with shared-bath dorms, doubles and twins plus a "love shack" out the back ($80). There's free wi-fi, cheap bike rental, hammocks in the garden and a free BBQ on Saturdays. Dorm **$31**, doubles **$76**

At the Right Place 85 Bealey Ave ☎0800 778 787, ⓦ atrp.co.nz; map pp.512–513. Set back from the street along a 70m driveway, this quiet budget property has backpacker accommodation with modern kitchen facilities and a Sky TV lounge, and light-filled motel-style studios ($129). Dorms **$30**, doubles **$85**

Chester Street Backpackers 148 Chester St East ☎03 377 1897, ⓦ chesterst.co.nz; map pp.512–513. With just thirteen beds this is the city's smallest hostel and feels more like a shared house with comfy, colourful doubles, a three-bed share and a self-contained cottage ($130). There's limited off-street parking and a pleasant garden; the owner also has a range of campervans for sale. Share **$30**, doubles **$66**

City Central Motel Apartments 252 Barbados St ☎0800 379 0540, ⓦ citycentral.co.nz; map pp.512–513. Modernized motel with flat-screen-TV-equipped, stylish rooms and off-street parking. It's on a busy intersection but the windows are double-glazed. **$145**

★Dorset House 1 Dorset St ☎03 366 8268 & ☎0800 367 738, ⓦ dorset.co.nz; map pp.512–513. Spacious hostel in a nicely renovated 1871 house located in a quiet area, with firm beds (no bunks), a strong eco-consciousness and even bathrobes to rent. There's off-street parking, Sky TV and pool in a huge lounge fitted with stained-glass windows, and free wi-fi. Also self-catering apartments. Dorms **$39**, rooms **$99**

Eliza's Manor 82 Bealey Ave ☎03 366 8584 & ☎0800 366 859, ⓦ elizas.co.nz; map pp.512–513. Luxury B&B in a grand 1861 house with eight rooms, all period furnished and with heat pump temperature control. It's worth splurging on the more spacious Heritage rooms ($345). **$235**

Focus Motel 344 Durham St North ☎0800 943 0800, ⓦ focusmotel.com; map pp.512–513. Stylish, central motel with modern studios and larger units, some with spa baths and all fitted out with leather sofas, classy bed linen with foliage prints and kitchen facilities. **$150**

Foley Towers 208 Kilmore St ☎03 366 9720, ⓦ www .backpack.co.nz/foley.html; map pp.512–513. A Christchurch backpacking original from the mid-1980s, built around a couple of old houses, which manages to maintain an intimate feel thanks to attentive staff, attractive gardens and an abundance of doubles and twins (en-suites $78). Dorms **$30**, doubles **$72**

The George 50 Park Terrace ☎0800 100 220, ⓦ thegeorge.com; map pp.512–513. One of the country's finest urban boutique hotels, renovated with considerable panache. There's great art, a cool bar and the chic *Pescatore* restaurant overlooking Hagley Park. **$450**

The Grange 56 Armagh St ☎03 366 2850, ⓦthegrange.co.nz; map pp.512–513. Classy six-room B&B in a lovely heritage-listed Edwardian home which has a smart eight-room motel annexe out the back with studios and larger apartments all opening onto a sheltered courtyard. Studios $145, B&B $195

Ibis Christchurch 107 Hereford St ☎03 367 8666, ⓦibis.com; map pp.512–513. Modern, no-frills business hotel that was one of the first to reopen in the heart of the city. Rooms are small though they're tastefully decorated and have fridge, tea and coffee and TV, and there's a restaurant and bar on site. $180

★**Jailhouse Accommodation** 338 Lincoln Rd ☎03 982 7777 & ☎0800 524 546, ⓦjail.co.nz; map pp.512–513. This Victorian Gothic prison (operational until 1999) has been imaginatively transformed into an atmospheric hostel with double and twin-bunk rooms plus some bunk-free dorms, all kauri-floored. Staff are super-helpful and the pool table is free. A couple of cells have been left as they were. The Orange bus drops off at the door. Dorms $33, doubles $92

Orari 42 Gloucester St ☎03 365 6569, ⓦorari.net.nz; map pp.512–513. An informally run and art-adorned B&B in a large 1893 home. Ten bright, sunny rooms all have artworks and either en suites or private bathrooms (one with a tub). Rates include off-street parking, wine on arrival, free wi-fi and a full breakfast. $205

Pomeroy's on Kilmore 284 Kilmore St ☎033 374 3532, ⓦpomeroysonkilmore.co.nz; map pp.512–513. Handily sited next to the owners' pub, this comfy B&B has five rooms, some with French doors opening out onto the lovely garden. A continental breakfast is included. $145

Rucksacker 70 Bealey Ave ☎03 377 7931, ⓦrucksacker.com; map pp.512–513. In a century-old traditional timber house, this cheerful hostel has a sociable garden and BBQ area, cheap bike rental and limited off-street parking, as well as the option of female-only dorms. Dorms $27, doubles $66

Vagabond Backpackers 232 Worcester St ☎0800 824 428, ⓦvagabondhostel.co.nz; map pp.512–513. Very friendly place with only thirty beds, some in an annexe at the back of the house; all are well kept, quiet and clean. There's off-street parking, a BBQ and a lovely garden area. There are also two doubles in a self-contained apartment. Dorms $27, doubles $64

YHA Christchurch 35 Hereford St ☎03 379 9536, ⓦyha.co.nz; map pp.512–513. This spic and span 120-bed YHA in a newly-renovated weatherboard building comes with an abundance of 4-shares ($38), 6-bed dorms (including female only) and rooms (some en-suite; $110) plus spacious lounges for reading and TV. Everything is well maintained and there's free wi-fi for members. No parking. *YHA Rolleston House* is around the corner at 5 Worcester Blvd. Dorms $37, doubles $95

YMCA 12 Hereford St ☎03 366 0689, ⓦymcachch.org.nz; map pp.512–513. State-of-the-art YMCA with spartan dorms, singles, basic doubles and deluxe en-suite doubles ($125) with tea, coffee and TV. Guests get significant discounts at the fitness centre, gym, squash courts, climbing wall and sauna, and there's an on-site café. Dorms $33, doubles $85

MERIVALE

Colonial Inn Motel 43 Papanui Rd ☎0800 111 232, ⓦcolonialinnmotel.co.nz; map pp.518–519. Modern motel with clean, comfortable units, including some huge two- and three-bedroom units, and undercover parking. Upper-level units open onto a communal balcony. $130

Merivale Manor 122 Papanui Rd ☎03 667 1554, ⓦmerivalemanor.co.nz; map pp.518–519. Luxurious accommodation based around the 1882 manor with three period-furnished suites and several studio apartments. The spa studios in a separate building have more modern stylings and everything is self-contained and supplied with cereals, milk, bread and spreads – though there are plenty of good breakfast places nearby. Studios $160, suites $235

Randolph 79 Papanui Rd ☎0800 537 366, ⓦrandolph motel.co.nz; map pp.518–519. Excellent modern motel in grounds overshadowed by a huge copper beech tree. Rooms are extremely well equipped with cooking facilities, TV/DVD, stereo and in-room laundry. Deluxe rooms come with double spa baths and there's even a small gym. $170

RICCARTON AND WESTERN CHRISTCHURCH

The Establishment 50 Clyde Rd, Ilam ☎0800 378 225, ⓦtheestablishment.net.nz; map pp.518–519. Chic, modern boutique lodge in the suburbs with three luxuriously-appointed suites all with access to a guest lounge opening out onto a deck. Superb breakfasts too. $395

Fyffe on Riccarton 208 Riccarton Rd ☎0800 341 3274, ⓦfyffeonriccarton.co.nz; map pp.518–519. All rooms at this stylish motorlodge have super-king-size beds, double-glazed windows, DVD players and coffee plungers; higher-priced executive studios also have spas. $140

Lorenzo Motor Lodge 36 Riccarton Rd ☎0800 456 736, ⓦlorenzomotorlodge.co.nz; map pp.518–519. Quality linens, passes to the gym across the road and free wi-fi are among the highlights of this smart motel, which has good-sized studio units plus suites with double spas. $165

PORT HILLS

★**Onuku** 27 Harry Ell Drive, Cashmere, 7km south of the CBD ☎03 332 7296, ⓦonukubedandbreakfast.co.nz; map pp.518–519. Welcoming B&B in a stylish modern house high in the Port Hills, with fab views of the city and access to walking and mountain biking. Rooms are simple but tasteful with comfy beds and there's a full breakfast to set you up for the day. $160

9

EASTERN CHRISTCHURCH AND SUMNER

The beachside suburb of Sumner has a selection of appealing places to stay, all accessible on fast and frequent city buses.

A Nest on Mount Pleasant 24 Toledo Place, Mount Pleasant, 9km southeast of the CBD ☎03 384 9485, ⓦanestbnb.co.nz; map pp.518–519. Welcoming haven that lives up to its name and overlooks a lush glen. The hosts go out of their way to make your stay as comfortable and hassle-free as possible. $135

Abbott House 104 Nayland St, Sumner ☎0800 020 654, ⓦabbotthouse.co.nz; map pp.518–519. Attractively restored 1870s villa set a block back from the beach with accommodation in either a studio with kitchenette, or in a suite with large lounge, kitchen and laundry. Both have TV/DVD, private entrances and continental breakfast ingredients are supplied. Studio $120, suite $140

Haka Lodge 518 Linwood Ave, Woolston ☎03 980 4252, ⓦhakalodge.com; map pp.518–519. Chilled 1970s house that compensates for its poor location with small numbers, a cosy fire in the lounge, an excellent vegie garden, doubles with balconies and even a two-bedroom apartment. Dorms $33, doubles $84

★ Le Petit Hotel 16 Marriner St, Sumner ☎03 326 6675, ⓦlepetithotel.co.nz; map pp.518–519. Boutique B&B with French-themed decor and breakfast (served alfresco in fine weather), airy rooms with balconies or terraces, and facilities including satellite TV and free wi-fi. $149

★The Old Countryhouse 437 Gloucester St, City ☎03 381 5504, ⓦoldcountryhouse.co.nz; map pp.518–519. Top-end, peaceful hostel fashioned from a trio of spacious, wood-floored villas each with their own kitchen and lounges and some en-suite doubles ($145). There's loads of space, nice lawns, free herbs and lemons, solid tables and bunks made by the owners, a spa pool, sauna, free wi-fi and off-street parking. Take bus #60. Dorms $42, doubles $110

Sumner Bay Motel 26 Marriner St, Sumner ☎0800 496 949, ⓦsumnermotel.co.nz; map pp.518–519. Stylish motel a block from the beach, with a range of studios and one- and two- bedroom apartments all with a balcony or courtyard, Sky TV and DVD player; free wi-fi. $159

CAMPSITES

Amber Park 308 Blenheim Rd, Upper Riccarton ☎03 348 3327, ⓦamberpark.co.nz; map pp.518–519. Spacious, grassy site just 4km southwest of the centre with all the expected facilities and en-suite motel units ($128). Handy for the train station; take bus #80 from the city. Camping $42, en-suite cabins $78

Christchurch Top 10 39 Meadow St, Papanui ☎0800 396 323, ⓦchristchurchtop10.co.nz; map pp.518–519. Situated 6km north of central Christchurch on SH74, this large campsite, close to supermarkets and restaurants, has a full range of facilities including self-contained chalets ($105), motel units ($145) and a heated indoor pool. Catch the Blue bus from the city. Camping $42, cabins $83

EATING AND DRINKING

After the quakes many restaurants and bars relocated to the suburbs, but as the rebuild hits its stride the scene is rapidly shifting back to the city. The busiest strip is along Victoria Street, though there is a growing pocket on the opposite side of Cathedral Square along High Street. Casual is the order of the day, with an emphasis on shared plates and quality drinks.

CENTRAL CHRISTCHURCH

Black Betty 165 Madras St ☎03 365 8522, ⓦblackbetty.co.nz; map pp.512–513. The best café in this part of town, all plywood and polished concrete with punchy coffee and the likes of *shakshouka* for brunch ($14.50). Limited free wi-fi. Mon–Fri 7.30am–4pm, Sat & Sun 8am–4pm.

★ Brick Farm 172 High St ☎03 366 5369, ⓦbrickfarm .co.nz; map pp.512–513. A jewel amid the desolation of High Street, this sleek bistro/bar occupies three levels of what used to be a Korean karaoke bar. The menu reflects available fresh produce, the beer is mostly from Christchurch and the wine from Waipara. Expect the likes of lamb *en croute* with cauliflower purée ($30), squid ink risotto with squid rings ($31), or just come for a cocktail on the top floor. Wed–Fri 3pm–late, Sat 10am–late, Sun 10am–5pm.

★C1 Espresso 185 High St ☎03 379 1917, ⓦc1espresso.co.nz; map pp.512–513. Fab licensed café in a grand 1930 former post office with a coffee roaster in the old vault. Get an excellent coffee fix, breakfast on coriander and corn fritters ($18) and return later for their trio of sliders ($20) delivered by pneumatic tube. Daily 7am–10pm.

CBD Bar 208 Madras St ⓦcbdbar.co.nz; map pp.512–513. Can't be bothered heading out to *The Tannery*? Drink Cassels & Sons' beer here accompanied by their crispy wood-fired pizzas ($18–22). Daily 11am–late.

Darkroom 336 St Asaph St ☎03 974 2425, ⓦdarkroom.bar; map pp.512–513. Studenty bar and music venue mostly putting on upcoming bands. Wed 5pm–midnight, Thurs 5pm–1am, Fri & Sat 5pm–3am.

The Dirty Land 131 Victoria St ☎03 365 534, ⓦthedirty land.co.nz; map pp.512–513. Grab a Frangelico sour and settle into the booths in this lively but relaxed and intimate bar where the food is all brought through from the kitchen of *Mexicano's* next door: think pulled pork tacos and tuna tostadas ($8–10). Daily 4pm–2am.

Keo Thai 4 Papanui Rd ☎03 355 6229, ⓦkeothai .co.nz; map pp.512–513. Authentic Thai food is served in an elegant dining room recessed behind a plant- and table-filled courtyard. Mains ($20–29) range from mild *pad thai* to a fearsomely hot *nua narm tok* (traditional beef salad). Great wine list. Mon & Tues 5–10pm, Wed–Sun noon–3pm & 5pm–late.

King of Snake 145 Victoria St ☎03 365 7363, ⓦkingofsnake.co.nz; map pp.512–513. The dark and intimate interior of this frequently-packed joint makes you think bar, and so it is, but the food is superb from the Mt Cook salmon with organic white miso ($21) to the Penang beef cheek curry ($34) and caramelized mango tarte tatin ($13). Mon–Fri 11.30am–late, Sat & Sun 4pm–late.

The Last Word 31 New Regent St ☎03 928 2381, ⓦlastword.co.nz; map pp.512–513. With over 200 single malts and blends (from Wales, Sweden and India as well as the usual sources) at this cosy bar, one visit could never be enough. Mon–Wed 4pm–midnight, Thurs–Sat 4pm–2am, Sun 2pm–midnight.

Orleans 89 Lichfield St ☎03 365 7312, ⓦorleans .co.nz; map pp.512–513. The pick of places around the tight central courtyard of the lively Stranges Lane development. You're normally elbow to elbow in this Louisiana-themed joint trying not to drip sauce from your pulled pork Po Boy ($9) or hoeing into gumbo with a side of cornbread ($24). Music usually spills in from the courtyard. Daily 11.30am–11pm or much later.

Pomeroy's Old Brewery Inn 292 Kilmore St ☎03 365 1523, ⓦpomeroysonkilmore.co.nz; map pp.512–513. There's an English pub feel to this solid brick place that serves its own Four Avenues craft beers, alongside other New Zealand brews – sample four for $17. There are also excellent whiskies, and wines to accompany the great pub food: chicken and pork terrine ($16), rib eye in a peppercorn jus ($34) and fish and chips with pea purée ($24). Bands play several nights a week. Pub Tues–Thurs 3pm–late & Fri–Sun noon–late; restaurant Tues–Thurs 3–10pm, Fri–Sun noon–10pm.

Procopé 165 Victoria St ☎03 379 4299, ⓦprocope .co.nz; map pp.512–513. Smart little café (named after the oldest one in Paris) where you might breakfast on French toast with black Doris plums ($16) or lunch on walnut and rosemary chicken salad ($16). Mon–Fri 7am–5pm, Sat & Sun 8am–4pm.

Shop Eight 8 New Regent St ☎03 390 0199, ⓦshopeight.co.nz; map pp.512–513. There's a dignified cool to this up-to-the-minute restaurant and cocktail bar with tables and chairs from Rekindle (see p.529). Local, organic and biodynamic ingredients are used on a short menu of small plates ($20) perhaps featuring green beans with devilled eel, egg and hazelnuts or goat consommé

with oyster mushrooms and truffle. Tues–Fri 4pm–late, Sat 2pm–late.

Tequila Mockingbird 98 Victoria St ☎03 365 8565, ⓦtequilamockingbird.co.nz; map pp.512–513. Loosely Latin American and Caribbean-themed restaurant and bar where supping on tequila iced tea or a pitcher of sangria is as important as tucking into shared plates of *chilli rellenos* ($12), pork *albondigas* ($14) and Chilean *empanadas* ($10). Later on, drift through to the adjacent *Revival Bar*. Mon–Thurs 4–10pm or later, Fri–Sun 9.30am–10pm or later.

RICCARTON AND WESTERN CHRISTCHURCH

The Bodhi Tree 399 Ilam Rd, Bryndwr ☎03 377 6808, ⓦthebodhitree.co.nz; map pp.518–519. Enormously popular Burmese place. Shared small plates ($14–22) include their locally famed tea-leaf salad along with fish fillet with tamarind, coriander, chilli and tomato, tempura whitebait on mango salad and yellow split-pea tofu salad. Licensed & BYO. Tues–Sat 6–10pm.

Dux Dine 28 Riccarton Rd, Riccarton ☎03 348 1436, ⓦduxdine.co.nz; map pp.518–519. The moneyed "Fendalton lunch set" flock to this delightful café and restaurant in a century-old former stationmaster's house. Lack of meat only enhances the inventiveness of the menu which runs to *huevos rancheros* ($18), pea and haloumi fritters ($27) and pan-fried fish served with polenta fries ($27). Or just come for coffee and excellent cakes out in the garden. Mon–Fri 7am–10pm, Sat & Sun 9am–10pm.

Volstead Trading Co 55 Riccarton Rd, Riccarton ☎03 343 6688, ⓦvolstead.co.nz; map pp.518–519. Sagging sofas and courtyard tables typify this slightly grungy craft beer bar with over a dozen taps offering brews from around the world as well as from the Raindogs and Golden Eagle microbreweries next door. Burgers, burritos and onion rings keep everyone coming back for more. Daily noon–11pm.

ADDINGTON

★**Addington Coffee Co-op** 297 Lincoln Rd ☎03 943 1662, ⓦaddingtoncoffee.org.nz; map pp.518–519. Wonderfully casual café in a former mechanics workshop that withstood the quakes. Sink into old sofas and try their Jailbreaker coffee, perhaps with mushrooms on toast ($16) or poached fruit with banana filo ($15). Cash purchases ensure donations to the company's favoured Fairtrade coffee and cacao suppliers, and you can even clean your smalls while you dine: there's a laundromat at one end. Mon–Fri 7.30am–4pm, Sat & Sun 9am–4pm.

Dux Live 363 Lincoln Rd ☎03 366 6919, ⓦduxlive .co.nz; map pp.512–513. Premiere venue for emerging and smaller touring bands with plenty of sweaty drinking

9

accompanied by a good deal of dubstep and drum 'n' bass. Pizzas and burgers soak up the booze. Wed–Fri 4pm–late, Sun 6pm–late.

Mosaic by Simo 3/300 Lincoln Rd ☎03 338 2882, ⊛simos.co.nz; map pp.518–519. Simple eat-in and takeaway offering dishes bursting with Moroccan and Andalusian flavours. You can select meze, filo parcels and tajines individually but it's best to go for the platters-for-two ($30–50), perhaps choosing Moroccan dips with *dukkah*, beef balls, and lamb *kofta* with sumac. Mon–Sat 9am–9pm.

Town Tonic 335 Lincoln Rd ☎03 338 1150, ⊛facebook .com/thetowntonic; map pp.512–513. Smart, bustling open-kitchen café and restaurant crafting inventive meals from fresh, mostly locally sourced ingredients. Organic grapefruit juice and Bircher muesli give way to a classic Reuben ($16), while shared dishes ($12–24) might include a charcuterie plate or caramelized sweet potato ravioli. The degustation menu (available Wed & Thurs; $85) is superb and they cater to Court Theatre customers with an Express two-course menu (5–6pm; $35). Mon–Fri 7.30am–1am, Sat 11am–1am.

EASTERN CHRISTCHURCH AND SUMNER

★**The Brewery** 3 Garlands Rd, Woolston ☎03 389 5359, ⊛casselsbrewery.co.nz; map pp.518–519. This cornerstone of *The Tannery* (see p.529) is also known as *Cassels & Sons*, the brand of awesome ales, craft beers and lagers made on site using a wood-fired kettle. A few jars perfectly accompany a thin-based wood-fired pizza ($18–22), crumbed pork schnitzel ($25) or beer-battered fish and chips ($26). Quiz night Monday and DJs or live music later in the week. Daily 7am–10pm or later.

Gustav's Winebar and Kitchen 3 Garlands Rd, Woolston ☎03 389 5544, ⊛gustavs.co.nz; map pp.518–519. Top-notch comfort food in fin de siècle European surroundings from another *Tannery* stalwart.

There's plenty of Cassels & Sons beer on tap but they concentrate on excellent wines to complement tapas such as lamb *kofta* or *ceviche* (both $11), or perhaps a shared board of sliders ($24). Mains include their signature rib roast ($44) and seafood en papillote with herb butter and crayfish glaze ($30). Daily 11am–10pm or later.

Indian Sumner 11a Wakefield Ave, Sumner ☎03 326 4777, ⊛indiansumner.com; map pp.518–519. Good name, great curries. Dine outside on the pavement, take away or try to get into the atmospheric interior for something from the small but well-chosen selection of mains ($15–20). Daily 5–10pm.

Joe's Garage 19 Marriner St, Sumner ☎03 962 2233, ⊛joes.co.nz; map pp.518–519. Funky café alive with folk getting their caffeine jolt from great espresso while huddled over a laptop (free wi-fi) or tucking into dishes such as breakfast burrito ($18), beef burger and handcut chips ($18) or Thai beef salad ($19). Pizzas ($20) are available in the evenings. Mon & Tues 7am–5pm, Wed–Sun 7am–8pm or later.

The Twisted Hop 616 Ferry Rd ☎03 943 4681, ⊛thetwistedhop.co.nz; map pp.518–519. CBD refugee now settled in the 'burbs serving their own hand-pumped English-style beers alongside excellent pub food such as Mowbray pork pie ($10) and lamb backstrap salad ($26). Quiz nights, and occasional live music. Mon–Fri 3pm–10 or later, Sat noon–11pm & Sun noon–9pm.

★**Under the Red Verandah** 29 Tancred St, Linwood ☎03 381 1109, ⊛utrv.co.nz; map pp.518–519. Everything is made on-site at this earthquake-survivor that's always popular with the lunching set. Sit in the partly recycled building on the original site or out in the courtyard for great counter food – broccoli and blue cheese tart, *spanakopita* and steak and onion pie (each $9.50, $15 with salad) – or lunches like a corn fritter stack with bacon ($23.50). Mon–Fri 7.30am–4pm, Sat & Sun 8.30am–4pm.

ENTERTAINMENT AND EVENTS

Christchurch Farmers' Market Riccarton House, 16 Kahu Rd, Riccarton ☎03 348 6190, ⊛christchurchfarmersmarket.co.nz; map pp.518–519. The city's original farmers' market where you can buy local produce direct from growers, bakers, brewers and more. Also ready-to-eat gourmet pies, posh porridge and Goan specialities plus bagels, flowers, salami and loads of baked goods. Turn up hungry. Saturday 9am–1pm.

Court Theatre Bernard St, Addington ☎09 963 0870 & ☎0800 333 100, ⊛courttheatre.org.nz; map pp.512–513. Christchurch's premier theatre, moved from the damaged Arts to this warehouse space with a large main stage and studio. There are usually door sales, so just turn up, or at weekends, get along to the improv comedy show

Scared Scriptless (Fri & Sat 10.15pm; $16).

Isaac Theatre Royal 145 Gloucester St ☎03 366 6326, ⊛isaactheatreroyal.co.nz; map pp.512–513. Musicals, ballets, pantomime and live music all get an airing at this magnificent theatre that was rebuilt with support from Sir Ian McKellen. Little except the proscenium arch, an elaborate ceiling dome and the brick-and-Oamaru stone facade are original, but ornate new plasterwork and modern comforts haven't stripped its spirit. Outside on the back of the building, check out Owen Dippie's wonderful *Ballerina* mural.

CINEMAS

Academy Gold Cinema Unit 22, 363 Colombo St,

Sydenham ☎03 377 9911, ⓦartfilms.co.nz. Three-screen complex that's the city's principal art-house movie theatre.

Alice Cinematheque 209 Tuam St, City ☎03 365 0615, ⓦaliceinvideoland.co.nz. Along with their extensive members' DVD library this little two-screener shows the best in art and foreign movies, usually with 3 screenings a day. $16. Shop open daily 9am–10pm.

Hollywood Cinema 28 Marriner St, Sumner ☎03 326 6102, ⓦhollywoodcinema.co.nz. Nice little three-screener with recent releases. Does a $30 movie-and-curry deal with *Indian Sumner*.

SHOPPING

Few shops have returned to the city centre, so everyday shopping for essentials is best done at suburban malls such as Westfield Riccarton, 129 Riccarton Rd.

Ballantynes 43 Lichfield St ☎03379 7400, ⓦballantynes .com; map pp.512–513. Venerable department store in a stylish Modernist building which survived the quakes. Mon–Fri 9am–5.30pm, Sat 9am–5pm, Sun 10am–5pm.

Clockwork Emporium and Café 32 New Regent St ☎03 365 9126, ⓦclockworkcafe.co.nz; map pp.512–513. Steampunk concept store where old world Victorian meets the futuristic age of steam. Expect rayguns, top hats, corsetry, scones and tea. Daily 10am–5pm.

The Rekindle Shop 35 New Regent St ⓦrekindle.org .nz; map pp.512–513. Outlet for a design-forward social enterprise that had its roots in repurposing waste timber from the quake rubble. Beautiful tables, chairs and wooden jewellery. Wed–Sun noon–5pm.

Re:START Cashel St; map pp.512–513. Still the heart of CBD retail with the excellent Johnson's Grocery, an outlet of the independent Scorpio Books, outdoor clothing giant Kathmandu, plus a handful of upscale fashion retailers. Generally daily 10am–5pm.

The Tannery 3 Garlands Rd ⓦthetannery.co.nz; map pp.518–519. Post quakes, Alisdair Cassels (the force behind Cassels & Sons Brewery) converted the long-defunct Woolston Tanneries buildings into a faux-Victorian shopping arcade modelled on Sydney's Strand Arcade. It has quickly grown from a few pop-up shops to over fifty retailers – books, bikes, ethical clothing, a deli, surfboards, shoes, even a spa and modern apothecary – and several good places to eat. Shops generally daily 10am–5pm.

DIRECTORY

Banks and exchange A couple of banks have opened temporary outlets in the new Re:START mall. Most banks have branches in or near suburban malls such as the Riccarton Shopping Mall on Riccarton Rd.

Consulates UK, 46 Hackthorne Rd, Cashmere ☎03 332 5535, ⓔdavid.chris@xtra.co.nz.

Left luggage Most hostels offer a left-luggage facility at usually no more than $5/day. See p.521 for airport storage.

Medical treatment For a doctor at any time call the 24 Hour Surgery (☎03 365 7777; no appointment necessary), at the corner of Bealey Ave and Colombo St. Christchurch Hospital (☎03 364 0640) is at the corner of Oxford Terrace and Riccarton Ave.

Pharmacies The 24 Hour Surgery (☎03 366 4439) stays open daily until 11pm.

Police Central Police Station, 62 St Asaph St (☎03 363 7400) is likely to move to the new Justice Precinct, south of Lichfield St between Durham and Colombo sts.

Post office There's a post office in Re:START.

Lyttelton

Just 12km southeast of central Christchurch, **LYTTELTON** is a wonderful counterpoint to the city. Small and compact, it clings to the steep northern slopes of the Port Hills. Houses tumble down towards the docks on **Lyttelton Harbour**, a deep-water anchorage in a drowned volcanic crater. This working port town's attractive setting drew a coterie of city escapees to its offbeat cafés and restaurants. Sadly, it took a big hit from the quakes, losing much of its infrastructure and historic sites – not least the town's nineteenth-century **Timeball Station**, which awaits reconstruction (see ⓦtimeball.co.nz for the latest). The town's strength of spirit remained, however, and it sometimes seemed everyone was rallying round and opening impromptu cafés in shipping containers.

The shattered buildings have long been removed and while there hasn't been a lot of new construction, permanent businesses are returning to the main drag, **London Street**, and around the newly revamped **Albion Square**.

9

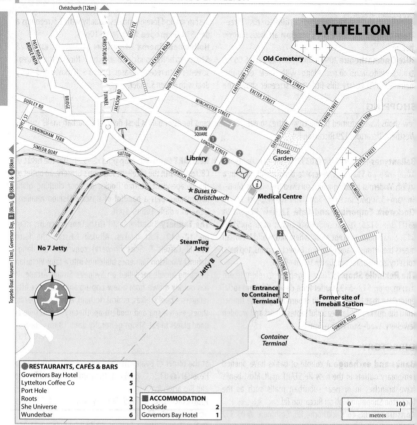

LYTTELTON

RESTAURANTS, CAFÉS & BARS

Governors Bay Hotel	4
Lyttelton Coffee Co	5
Port Hole	1
Roots	2
She Universe	3
Wunderbar	6

ACCOMMODATION

Dockside	2
Governors Bay Hotel	1

Torpedo Boat Museum

Signposted along a five-minute shoreline walk from a car park on Charlotte Jane Quay about 1km west of town • Dec–April Tues, Thurs, Sat & Sun 1–3pm; May–Nov Sat & Sun 1–3pm • $5 • ☎ 03 328 9093, ⓦ lytteltonheritage.co.nz

To get a sense of Lyttelton's maritime importance, visit this small museum in an 1874 former powder magazine building. After the Russian invasion of Afghanistan in 1885, the fear of further Russian expansion spread around the western Pacific. New Zealand responded by building a torpedo boat to protect Lyttelton Harbour. Designed to charge up to an invading ship, detonate a charge below the waterline then scarper before it could be attacked itself, the boat was never used, but its restored remains are here along with an entertaining video.

Steam Tug Lyttelton

No.2 Wharf • Cruises generally Christmas–April Sun 2.30pm • 90min • $25; booking required • ☎ 03 328 8954, ⓦ tuglyttelton.co.nz

To experience a piece of living history, go for a cruise on this beautiful antique boat, the older of just two steam tugs still operating in the country. Built in Glasgow in 1907, it was immediately put to service towing Shackleton's *Nimrod* to the heads on his way to Antarctica. The tug was decommissioned in 1970 but is maintained in full working order by impassioned volunteers who take trips around the harbour. The boiler room is particularly impressive: all burnished brass and oily pistons.

Quail Island

Black Cat Cruises visit the island Oct–April daily 10.20am; additional boat Dec–March at 12.20pm • $25 return; cash only • ☎ 03 384 0621

Set in mid-harbour, kilometre-broad **Quail Island** was, from 1907 to 1925, a small leper colony, though in the early days of Antarctic exploration Shackleton and Scott quarantined and trained their dogs here before venturing towards the South Pole. These days it's a venue for day-trips, swimming and walking: pack food, plenty of drinking water and rain gear. Two circular **walking tracks** (1hr & 2hr 30min) start from the island's wharf and visit safe swimming beaches, along with several shipwrecks that can be seen at low tide.

Diamond Harbour

Ferries every 30–60min; 10min journey • $6.20 each way • ⓦ diamondharbour.org.nz

In bright sunlight the water sparkles like a million gems at **Diamond Harbour**, directly across the water from Lyttelton. The passenger **ferry** makes a nice way to get out on the water, and there are a couple of good cafés a five-minute uphill walk from the Diamond Harbour wharf.

ARRIVAL AND INFORMATION   LYTTELTON

By bus The quickest way from Christchurch to Lyttelton is through the 2km Lyttelton Tunnel. The #28 bus from central Christchurch leaves every 20–60min ($2.50), takes about 30min and stops on Norwich Quay.

Tourist information Lyttelton Harbour Information Centre, 20 Oxford St (Mon–Sat 10am–4pm, Sun 11am–3pm; ☎ 03 328 9093, ⓦ lytteltonharbour.info). Another good source of information on the town is ⓦ lyttelton.net.nz.

ACCOMMODATION

Dockside 22 Sumner Rd ☎ 03 325 5707, ⓦ dockside .co.nz. One very pleasant studio with sky-blue decor, cooking facilities and a private garden, plus two larger apartments with similarly artistic decor, fully equipped kitchens and large decks, all overlooking the docks. Studio $120, apartment $140

Governors Bay Hotel 52 Main Rd, Governors Bay, 8km west of Lyttelton ☎ 03 329 9433, ⓦ governorsbayhotel .co.nz. Renovated colonial hotel with simple bathless rooms above the bar, most with a shared balcony and great harbour views ($130). $110

EATING AND DRINKING

Governors Bay Hotel Main Rd, Governors Bay, 8km west of Lyttelton ☎ 03 329 9433, ⓦ governorsbayhotel.co.nz. Sophisticated pub grub in a historic hotel or with a pint outside looking straight down the harbour. Expect chicken Caesar salad ($23) and eye fillet on herb rosti ($35). Daily 9 am–9pm or later.

Lyttelton Coffee Co 29 London St ☎ 03 328 8096, ⓦ lytteltoncoffee.co.nz. The 2014 return of this Lyttelton institution to its original site brought joy to faithful locals. Great coffee and café food, a lively vibe and always something interesting cranking out of the bank of 1970s hi-fi speakers. Daily 7am–4pm.

Lyttelton Farmers Market London St between Canterbury and Oxford sts. Saturday breakfast and lunch are covered by grazing at this fiesta of local produce. Cars are banned and the music is always good. Farmers Market Sat 10am–1pm; Artisan Market Sun 10am–2pm.

Port Hole 42 London St ☎ 021 328 977, ⓦ portholebar .co.nz. Drink craft beer in this corral of shipping containers that hosts live music (Wed–Sun). There's also a secret garden with table tennis. Daily 11am–1am.

Roots 8 London St ☎ 03 328 7658, ⓦ rootsrestaurant .co.nz. Foodie heaven where nose-to-tail meat cuts and locally foraged ingredients are artfully combined into exquisite small dishes. All meals are degustation ($125 for 8 courses, $205 with wine match) and they'll explain what they've made when it arrives. Wed–Sun noon–3pm, plus Tues–Sat 6–10pm.

She Universe 79 Main Rd, Governors Bay ☎ 03 329 9825, ⓦ shechocolat.com. Eco-chocolate is regarded as a superfood at this café serving decadently thick hot chocolate and chocolates to take away. Its on-site restaurant (mains $17–25) has tables inside and scattered around the deck, all with superb harbour views; and you can even attend a chocolate school (from $275 for a full-day course). Mon, Tues, Thurs & Fri 10am–4pm, Sat & Sun 10am–5pm.

Wunderbar 19 London St ⓦ wunderbar.co.nz. An iron fire escape behind the supermarket leads to this idiosyncratic late-night drinking-hole and club, with decor ranging from crushed velour to a gruesome doll's-head lightshade. The deck overlooking the docks is great for a peaceful drink away from the clamour within, which might be open mike (Tues), poetry, live bands (Wed–Sat), stand-up comics or film-noir evenings. Mon–Fri 5pm–late, Sat & Sun 1pm–even later.

9

Banks Peninsula

Flying into Christchurch you'll be struck by the dramatic contrast between the flat plains of Canterbury and the rugged, fissured topography of **Banks Peninsula**, a volcanic thumb sticking out into the Canterbury Bight. When James Cook sailed by in 1769 he mistakenly charted it as an island and named it after his botanist, Joseph Banks. The fertile **volcanic** soil of the peninsula's valleys sprouted totara, matai and kahikatea trees that, along with the abundant shellfish in the bays, attracted early Maori around a thousand years ago. The trees progressively succumbed to the Maori fire stick and European timber-milling interests, and the peninsula is now largely bald, with patches of tussock grass and small pockets of regenerating native bush.

Banks Peninsula is cut off from the rest of Canterbury by Lyttelton Harbour (see p.529) the first of two drowned craters. The shore of the second is graced by the picturesque, tourist-focused town of **Akaroa**, its refined tone lent a gentle Gallic influence by its French founders. Elsewhere on the peninsula, a network of narrow, twisting roads winds along the crater rims and dives down to gorgeous, quiet bays once alive with whalers, sealers and shipbuilders, but now seldom visited outside of summer. Despite the denuded grassland of much of the landscape, Banks Peninsula is very popular for relatively easy scenic **walks**, with panoramic views, ancient lava flows and relics from the earliest Maori and European settlers.

GETTING AROUND
BANKS PENINSULA

By car and bike To reach the smaller communities tucked into the bays you'll need your own transport. If you're planning on cycling, bear in mind that the peninsula is extremely hilly, and the routes linking the Summit Road with the various bays below can be steep.

Lake Ellesmere and Little River

Half an hour south of Christchurch, SH75 skirts the brackish lagoon of **Lake Ellesmere** (Waihora) and continues past from **Lake Forsyth** (Wairewa) to reach the tiny community of **LITTLE RIVER**, 53km from Christchurch, notable mainly for the *Little River Store* and access to the Little River Railtrail.

GETTING AROUND
LAKE ELLESMERE AND LITTLE RIVER

By bike For a little exercise in these parts, ride a section of the Little River Railtrail (ⓦ littleriverrailtrail.co.nz), which runs 49km from Christchurch past along Lake Ellesmere and Lake Forsyth to Little River. For bike rental, try Natural High in Christchurch (ⓣ 03 982 2966, ⓦ naturalhigh .co.nz), who also operate a one-day Little River Railtrail guided ride ($160).

ACCOMMODATION AND EATING

Little River Store & Gallery SH75, Little River ⓣ 03 325 1944, ⓦ littlerivergallery.com; map p.533. Good little café with attached art gallery and grocery store. Mostly counter food enlivened by imaginative salads (dishes $8–18) eaten inside or in their sunny courtyard. Mon–Thurs 7.30am–4pm, Fri–Sun 7.30am–4.30pm.

Okuti Eco-stay 216 Okuti Valley Rd, 4km southeast of Little River ⓣ 03 325 1913, ⓦ okuti.co.nz; map p.533. Peaceful and welcoming, rural garden with TV-free accommodation in a fairly luxurious yurt, tipi, house truck and earth-brick studio. Everyone shares a garden kitchen (with free home-grown herbs) and the woods, meadows, pond with a dinghy and trampoline keep kids of all ages happy. Save $10 if you bring your own bedding. Per person $50

SiloStay Accommodation 4201 SH75, Little River ⓣ 03 325 1977, ⓦ silostay.kiwi.nz; map p.533. Quirky but very comfortable serviced apartments, each in a corrugated iron silo like those seen on farms all over New Zealand. In this case the two-level wool-insulated silos are beautifully fitted and come with broadband and satellite TV, which is just as well as the views are pretty limited. $220

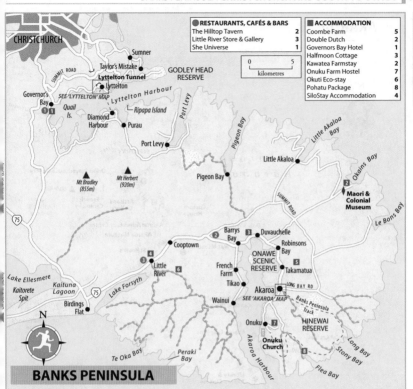

RESTAURANTS, CAFÉS & BARS		ACCOMMODATION	
The Hilltop Tavern	2	Coombe Farm	5
Little River Store & Gallery	3	Double Dutch	2
She Universe	1	Governors Bay Hotel	1
		Halfmoon Cottage	3
		Kawatea Farmstay	2
		Onuku Farm Hostel	7
		Okuti Eco-stay	6
		Pohatu Package	8
		SiloStay Accommodation	4

Barry's Bay

Barry's Bay Cheese daily 9am–5pm • Cheese-making season Oct–May • ☎ 03 304 5809, ⓦ barrysbaycheese.co.nz

From Little River, SH75 climbs over the hills that separate Akaroa Harbour from the rest of Banks Peninsula and down to the tiny community of **BARRY'S BAY**, home to **Barry's Bay Cheese**, where you can tuck into free samples, and watch cheese being made in season or a video presentation on its production.

ACCOMMODATION AND EATING

BARRY'S BAY

Halfmoon Cottage SH75, just east of Barry's Bay ☎ 03 304 5050, ⓦ halfmoon.co.nz; map p.533. A small and wonderfully relaxed hostel in an 1896 villa set in a pretty garden just across from the beach. Often closed June–Aug. Dorm $30, double $78

★**The Hilltop Tavern** 5207 Christchurch Akaroa Rd (SH75) ☎ 03 325 1005, ⓦ thehilltop.co.nz; map p.533. Magical views 450m down to Akaroa Harbour are the big draw to this excellent pub roughly halfway between Little River and Akaroa. In summer, chairs on the deck and bean bags on the grass are full of people tucking into nachos ($18) or wood-fired pizzas ($25), supping on local craft beers or spooning quality ice cream. Weekends bring folk from far and wide for top local bands: check the website. Self-contained campervans can stay overnight in the car park. Daily 10am–7pm, much later for gigs or when busy.

Akaroa

The small waterside town of **AKAROA** ("Long Harbour"), on the eastern shores of Akaroa Harbour, 85km from Christchurch, comes billed as New Zealand's **French settlement**. Certainly the first settlers came from France, some of their architecture survives and the street names they chose have stuck, but that's about as French as it

9

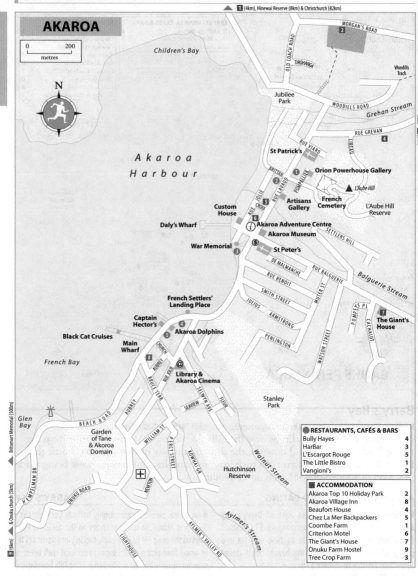

AKAROA

● RESTAURANTS, CAFÉS & BARS	
Bully Hayes	4
HarBar	3
L'Escargot Rouge	5
The Little Bistro	1
Vangioni's	2

■ ACCOMMODATION	
Akaroa Top 10 Holiday Park	2
Akaroa Village Inn	8
Beaufort House	4
Chez La Mer Backpackers	5
Coombe Farm	1
Criterion Motel	6
The Giant's House	7
Onuku Farm Hostel	9
Tree Crop Farm	3

gets. Nonetheless, the town milks the connection with a couple of French-ish restaurants, some French-sounding boutique B&Bs and the tricolour fluttering over the spot where the first settlers landed.

Still, it is a pretty place, strung along the shore in a long ribbon easily seen on foot, with narrow streets, colonial-era cottages and attractive scenery all around. The smattering of low-key activities includes a unique dolphin swim, and easy access to the **Banks Peninsula Track** (see box, p.540). But Akaroa primarily pitches itself to those looking for gentle strolls followed by good food and wine before falling into a comfy bed. These factors make the town a popular Kiwi holiday destination; some two-thirds of its houses are *baches* (holiday homes), leaving only around 600 permanent residents.

Since the earthquakes destroyed the cruise terminal at Lyttelton, Akaroa's daytime peace is regularly shattered by the arrival of cruise ships which spend the day at anchor while passengers get bused to Christchurch, go dolphin watching or just mooch around the galleries and shops.

Brief history

The site of Akaroa was originally the domain of the Ngai Tahu paramount chief, Temaiharanui. In 1838, French Commander Jean Langlois traded goods for what he believed to be the entire peninsula and returned to France to encourage settlers to populate a new French colony. Meanwhile, the British sent William Hobson to assume the role of lieutenant-governor over all the land that could be purchased; and just six days before the French sailed into the harbour, the British flag was raised in Akaroa. Lavaud's passengers decided to stay, which meant that the first formal settlement under **British sovereignty** was comprised of 63 French and six Germans.

Akaroa Museum

71 Rue Lavaud • Daily: Oct–April 10.30am–4.30pm; May–Nov 10.30am–4pm • Free • ☎ 03 304 1013, ⓦ akaroamuseum.org.nz

The **Akaroa Museum** stands head and shoulders above most small-town museums. Several interesting Maori artefacts and a twenty-minute film account of the remarkable history of settlement on the peninsula are backed up by a display illustrating the differences between the English version of the Treaty of Waitangi and a literal English translation of the Maori-language document. Other exhibits deal with the peninsula's whaling history and fascinating albums full of photographs of the original French and German settlers. Look, too, for displays on local son **Frank Worsley**, who captained Shackleton's ship *Endurance* to Antarctica and, after disaster struck, the *James Caird* to South Georgia and safety. His bust surveys the harbour beside the town's main wharf.

The museum incorporates the town's former **Court House**, a tiny **Custom House** and the early 1840s **Langlois-Eteveneaux Cottage**, possibly part-constructed in France before being shipped over, and now filled with nineteenth-century French furniture.

The Giant's House Mosaic & Sculpture Garden

68 Rue Balguerie • Daily: Christmas–March noon–5pm; April–Christmas 2–4pm • $20 • ⓦ thegiantshouse.co.nz

Don't miss **The Giant's House**, home of sculptor Josie Martin and a working testament to her art. Every room, the garden and even the drive to the garage have become a canvas on which she can display her talents. Mosaics, concrete figures and sculpted seats tucked away in garden nooks all have an overriding spirit of fun. In summer there's a small café and Josie exhibits her art from a gallery.

Orion Powerhouse Gallery

1 Rue Pompallier • Daily 10am–4pm during exhibitions • Donation requested • ☎ 03 304 7245, ⓦ akaroagenerator.org.nz

Akaroa became one of the first towns in Canterbury to have a supply of electricity when a small hydro power station was commissioned in 1911. The squat brick building still houses the original Pelton wheel that generated electricity for the town, and has become a venue for local art and craft exhibitions and the occasional acoustic concert.

French Cemetery

The **French Cemetery** at the northern end of town is reached by a footpath that leads from Rue Pompallier into the L'Aube Hill Reserve. The first consecrated burial ground in Canterbury, the cemetery was sadly neglected until 1925, when the bodies were reinterred in a central plot marked by a single monument.

9

Onuku church

Onuku Rd, 5km south of Akaroa • Open daylight hours • Free

The only Maori church left on the peninsula is this little 60-seater surrounded by a neat picket fence. Known locally as The Kaik (probably a corruption of *kainga* or village) it was built in 1876 for the Maori community that once thrived here, but since 1963 has only seen weddings and baptisms. Admire the carved barge boards and then check out the intricate altar inside.

Hinewai Reserve

632 Long Bay Rd, 8km east of Akaroa, with walking access along the Purple Peak Track (see box, p.539) • Open daylight hours • Free

Returning an entire valley to its native state is the sole aim of this 1250-hectare private nature reserve, created from farmland in 1987 and managed by the tireless and dedicated Hugh Wilson. Locals originally dubbed him "The Gorse Farmer" for his then-radical approach, leaving the traditionally-poisoned gorse to grow. This provided shelter for native seedlings which, it was hoped, would eventually form a shady canopy under which the gorse would die off. Thirty years on and this approach is beginning to bear fruit.

Some 16km of tracks weave through patches of mature forest and bush in varying states of regeneration, good for short or lengthy walks. Highlights include small waterfalls, lookout points with sea views, and plenty of birdsong. Bring everything you need and please follow the strict, no-take, no-fire and no-rubbish rules.

ARRIVAL AND DEPARTURE
AKAROA

By car From Christchurch, the main route to Akaroa is SH75, via Little River. It is winding and steep in parts and takes about 90min. You can also follow the long and more tortuous scenic route from *The Hilltop Tavern* along the top of the crater rim to Akaroa.

By bus Akaroa Shuttle (Nov–April three daily; May–Oct

one daily; $50 return; ☎0800 500 929, ⓦakaroashuttle .co.nz) and Akaroa French Connection (one daily; $45 return; ☎0800 800 575, ⓦakaroabus.co.nz) both pick up outside Christchurch's Canterbury Museum for the 90min run to Akaroa. They drop off beside the Akaroa Adventure Centre.

INFORMATION

Tourist information Akaroa Adventure Centre, 74a Rue Lavaud (daily: Nov–April 9am–6pm or later; May–Oct 10am–4pm; ☎03 304 7784, ⓔAkaroaAdventureCentre @gmail.com) is a commercially-run visitor centre promoting the town, selling walking maps and gently pushing their own adventure activities. It shares space with the post office, and

has pack storage ($5/day). Also check out ⓦakaroa.com.
Services There's a BNZ bank (Mon–Fri 9.30am–4.30pm) with an ATM across the street from the Akaroa Adventure Centre. The library, 2 Selwyn Ave (Mon–Fri 10am–4.30pm, Sat 10am–1pm) has free wi-fi which spills over to the adjacent cinema café.

ACCOMMODATION

Akaroa has **accommodation** to suit all budgets, but the best caters to the weekend getaway set with some gorgeous B&Bs, lodges and high-quality hotels and motels. Staying in one of these seems to suit the spirit of Akaroa, and it is worth stretching the budget if you can.

Akaroa Top 10 Holiday Park 96 Morgan's Rd, off the Old Coach Rd ☎0800 727 525, ⓦakaroa-holidaypark .co.nz; map p.534. Sprawling across a terraced hillside overlooking the harbour and the main street, this site has modern facilities, including a swimming pool and self-contained units ($135). Arriving from the north, look for the small, blue caravan sign indicating the turn-off about 500m before you reach the main village. Camping $40, cabins $72

Akaroa Village Inn 81 Beach Rd ☎0800 695 2000, ⓦakaroavillageinn.co.nz; map p.534. A rambling complex with probably the widest range of accommodation in town, a variety of decors and lots of self-catering

apartments, several with two bedrooms and some good harbour views ($350). Studio units $200, apartments $255
★**Beaufort House** 42 Rue Grehan ☎03 304 7517, ⓦbeauforthouse.co.nz; map p.534. Gracious B&B in a fine old home with four antique-decorated rooms, each with en suite or private bath (two with deep tubs). There's a sumptuous guest lounge and breakfast is a major affair often finished with a coffee on the veranda overlooking delightful semiformal grounds. To top it all off, they even have their own small vineyard, the Pinot Noir and Chardonnay usually sampled with canapés on arrival. $350
Chez La Mer Backpackers 50 Rue Lavaud ☎03 304

7024, ⓦchezlamer.co.nz; map p.534. High-quality budget accommodation in a homey 1871 house complete with a lovely garden, hammock and outdoor cooking area. The staff are helpful, and offer free use of bikes and fishing rods and useful maps of local walks and points of interest. Some en suites ($83) and free wi-fi. Dorms $28, rooms $73

★ **Coombe Farm** 18 Old Le Bons Track, 4km north of Akaroa ☎03 304 7239, ⓦcoombefarm.co.nz; map p.533. Though there is a guest lounge stacked with books and DVDs, the farmhouse kitchen is the social hub of this delightful B&B on a working farm. Two very spacious rooms in the farmhouse plus the rustic Shepherd's Hut, with private outdoor bath and shower on the deck overlooking the stream. Make breakfast at your leisure with a hamper supplied. Be sure to take the 5min streamside bushwalk right by the house or a more ambitious hike up to a waterfall. Closed June–Sept. Hut $160, rooms $170

Criterion Motel 75 Rue Jolie ☎0800 252 762, ⓦholidayakaroa.com; map p.534. Assiduously managed, modern motel with spacious rooms each with underfloor heating, double glazing and a balcony. Top-floor rooms ($190) have the best harbour views. Late checkouts and generous free wi-fi make this a good deal. Units $150

The Giant's House 68 Rue Balguerie ☎03 304 7501, ⓦthegiantshouse.co.nz; map p.534. Stay in a living art gallery (see p.535) built in and around this 1881 house. The large rooms (some en-suite) are all wildly decorated as, say, a boat bed or a greenhouse conservatory. A delicious continental breakfast is served and there are big reductions for multi-night stays. $300

★ **Onuku Farm Hostel** 6km south of town on the Onuku Rd ☎03 304 7066, ⓦonuku.co.nz; map p.533. On a hillside sheep farm above a bay, this wonderfully secluded spot centres on the cosy main house where there are doubles (some with a view $80) and dorms (including a 6-bunk girls-only en-suite). There's no TV, and internet access is hidden away. Outside there's a hammock-strung campsite ($15 per person) and another basic dorm equipped with outdoor kitchens and showers, plus several stargazers – rather like wooden tents (BYO sleeping bag; $20 per person), some with magnificent views. The campervan park ($15 per person) has its own kitchen and shower block. There are walks all around, the hostel runs summer dolphin-swimming trips ($110; max 6), and encourages fishing and mussel collecting. Free pick-up around 12.30pm from Akaroa. Cash only. Closed May–Sept. Dorms $28, rooms $66

Pohatu Package Flea Bay ☎03 304 8542, ⓦpohatu .co.nz; map p.533. Not just accommodation but a chance to spend the night at the Pohatu penguin colony (see box, p.539). The 24hr package includes a 4WD transport from Akaroa, their penguin tour, opportunities for walking a section of the Banks Peninsula Track, beach swimming, kayaking in the marine reserve ($20 extra), and fairly rustic but comfy self-catering accommodation. Additional nights $90. $130

Tree Crop Farm 2km up Rue Grehan ☎03 304 7158, ⓦtreecropfarm.com; map p.534. The four "love shacks" are the only place to stay if you're looking for the sort of rustic romance that secluded candle-lit cabins hung with mirrors and supplied with outdoor fire-heated bush baths offer. It's not for everyone but is a unique experience, and checkout isn't until noon or later. The surrounding "farm" is more managed wilderness with tracks throughout. $200

EATING, DRINKING AND ENTERTAINMENT

Akaroa has some outstanding places to eat, with the emphasis towards the upmarket end of things. Many places cut back their hours, or even close completely, during winter. For self-catering, try the old-fashioned Akaroa Butcher & Deli, 67 Rue Lavaud, who make their own sausages and also stock Barry's Bay cheeses and local olive oil.

Bully Hayes 57 Beach Rd ☎03 304 7533, ⓦbullyhayes.co.nz. Named after the eponymous 1800s American pirate who frequented the waters hereabouts, this busy place cooks up big breakfasts and casual lunches, and serves sensational seafood platters (including Akaroa salmon, of course) as well as fancier evening fare like truffle-butter roasted chicken (most mains $35–43). Daily 8am–9pm or later.

HarBar 83 Rue Jolie ☎03 304 8889, ⓦfacebook.com /harbarakaroa. This beach bar in a former women's rest room is the perfect spot to watch the sun go down, craft beer in hand. As the evening cools huddle around the deck fireplace and grab something from their tapas menu. Mon–Fri 11am–10pm, Sat & Sun 10am–10pm.

L'Escargot Rouge 67 Beach Rd ⓦlescargotrouge .co.nz. "Parisian" breakfast choices at this chic spot include a baguette, croissant and pain au chocolat, *croque monsieur* (brioche with Dijon mustard, ham and cheese) and *croque madame* (like a *croque monsieur* but topped with an egg). During the day there's a tempting selection of deli-style counter food (dishes $5–10). Daily 8am–4pm.

★ **The Little Bistro** 33a Rue Lavaud ☎03 304 7314, ⓦthelittlebistro.co.nz. A classic bistro whose thirty seats are packed so tight you eat elbow to elbow. Wonderfully convivial, they use locally-sourced produce to dish up the likes of Canterbury steak with anchovy butter ($39) or a market fish dish of the blackboard, washed down with mostly Canterbury wines. For afters, try their take on an Eton mess ($15). Tues–Sat 5.30–10pm.

Vangioni's 40f Rue Lavaud, entrance on Rue Britain ☎03 304 7714, ⓦvangionis.co.nz. On a Mediterranean-like evening the garden here is a great

AKAROA TOURS AND ACTIVITIES

If you want to do more than sip Pinot Gris and cruise the galleries, you'll find plenty of diversions in Akaroa. The pick is seeing, and even swimming with, **Hector's dolphins**, the world's smallest species at under 1.4m long. They are playful, and small pods are generally happy to approach swimmers, particularly in summer. You may also see them on harbour cruises, and kayaking trips, though probably not on the local mail run. Hector's dolphins are relatively abundant with 7000 animals around New Zealand's east coast, but the western subspecies – Maui's dolphin – is almost extinct.

MAIL RUN

Eastern Bays Scenic Mail Run ☎ 03 304 7784. Hop aboard a minibus (8 passengers max) to twist up and over the crater rim to deliver mail to farms and settlements such as Le Bons Bay and Okains Bay. It is a great way to get the lay of the land, especially if you don't have your own transport. $75 for 5hr; call the night before between 5 and 7pm to confirm.

SWIMMING WITH DOLPHINS, CRUISES AND SAILING

Black Cat Main Wharf, Beach Rd ☎ 03 304 7641, ⓦ blackcat.co.nz. Experienced operator offering 3hr dolphin-swimming trips (Dec–March 8.30am, 11.30am, 1.30pm & 3.30pm; Sept–Nov, April & May 11.30am & 1.30pm; swimming $150, spectators $79; partial refunds if the dolphins don't show). Having cruised out to the dolphins, they watch their behaviour to check that it is okay to get in the water. Their 2hr harbour cruises (year-round at 1.30pm, plus Nov–April 11am; $74) use large boats to visit the mouth of the harbour via a beautiful high-walled volcanic sea cave, colonies of spotted shags and cormorants, and caves where blue penguins reside.

Akaroa Dolphins 65 Beach Rd ☎ 0800 990 102, ⓦ akaroadolphins.co.nz. Smaller number and boats than Black Cat give a more intimate feel to these harbour cruises (daily: Nov–April 10.15am, 12.45pm & 3.15pm; May–Oct 12.45pm; $74). They visit all the same places, usually see dolphins and put an emphasis on the region's history, Maori heritage and spotting black-backed gulls, red-billed gulls, shearwaters, terns, prions and mollymawks.

Fox II Sailing Adventures ☎ 0800 369 7245, ⓦ akaroafoxsail.co.nz. With its red sails catching the breeze, this 1922 kauri-built ketch makes an atmospheric and ecofriendly alternative to the other cruises ($75). They have the sails up whenever conditions permit, generally head out towards Akaroa Heads and will often see dolphins and seals. Late Dec–May daily at 10.30am and 1.30pm from Daly's Wharf.

EcoSeaker ☎ 0800 326 794, ⓦ ecoseaker.co.nz. Intimate, boutique dolphin-swimming operation taking out just six swimmers at a time in a rigid inflatable with over 2hr on the water. Nov–April 1–2 daily. $130 to swim, $70 to watch.

KAYAKING, SUP BOARDING AND BIKING

Akaroa Adventure Centre 74a Rue Lavaud ☎ 03 304 7784, ⓔ AkaroaAdventureCentre@gmail.com. As well as operating as the town's visitor centre, this is the place to organize stand-up paddleboarding rental (1hr for $20, 4hr for $45), bike rental (4hr for $35) with the option of a full-day rental and a drop-off high above town and a cruisey 13km downhill ride back ($65), and even motorized skateboarding (20min for $20).

place to dine on excellent trattoria fare, delicious tapas (including their house-cured meat platter; $26), great pizza ($26–31) and mains like smoked salmon gnocchi with sage cream ($35). When the weather is inclement, retreat to the cosy, casual bar area. Wed–Sun 5pm–late plus lunches in high summer.

CINEMAS

Akaroa Cinema Corner of Rue Jolie and Selwyn Ave ☎ 03 304 7678, ⓦ cinecafe.co.nz. For non-blockbuster movies, check out this boutique cinema, which plays art, foreign, classic and new films. Buy a glass of wine or coffee from the foyer *Ciné Café* and take it in with you. Tickets $15.

East from Akaroa

A day is well spent exploring east from Akaroa via the **Summit Road**, which traces the 600m-high Akaroa crater rim. From here, roads twist down from the open tops (ablaze with gorse in November) to gems of bays with deserted beaches and the remains of once thriving towns where a school or store just about hangs on. With few interconnecting roads, exploring the region is likely to take longer than you might expect.

Captain Hector's Akaroa Kayak, Canoe & Boat Hire 65 Beach Rd ☎0800 990 102, ⓦakaroadolphins.co.nz. If you're just after splashing around in boats, Captain Hector's rents single and double sea-kayaks ($45/person/day), paddleboats, water bikes, canoes and rowboats.

PENGUIN AND SEAL VIEWING

Akaroa Seal Colony Safari ☎03 304 7255, ⓦsealtours.co.nz. Air-conditioned 4WD vehicles from central Akaroa to view fur seals, on the eastern tip of the peninsula. Tours (daily 9.30am & 1pm; $85) last 2hr 30min and are limited to six people.

Pohatu Penguins ☎03 304 8542, ⓦpohatu.co.nz. If you want to see penguins close up, don't miss these tours to the Flea Bay farm on the Banks Peninsula Track (see p.540), where Shireen and Francis Helps have been looking after white-flippered penguins for decades. Their Evening Tour (2–3hr; $75) starts before dusk and

Akaroa Guided Sea Kayaking Safari meets outside The Green Café at 37 Rue Lavaud ☎0800 300 068, ⓦakaroakayaks.com. Provides small-group guided kayaking trips, with swimming and a good chance of encountering dolphins. Three-hour trips ($125) depart at 7.30am and 11.30am. Nov–April only.

gives you plenty of chance to see penguins returning from their day fishing, and your observations contribute to penguin monitoring. On their daytime Nature Tour option (1.30pm; $65) you'll see the penguins in their nesting boxes and learn plenty about a working sheep farm. To see penguins (and probably Hector's dolphins) from the water take their kayaking trips (4hr; daily at noon; $90). All trips involve pick-up from Akaroa and a scenic drive down a 4WD track to the farm; there are cheaper options if you can drive to the farm, but the road is 4WD-only and steep.

WALKING

For those who lack the time or inclination to tackle the Banks Peninsula Track (see box, p.540), there are equally rewarding shorter walks. There's further information at ⓦbankspeninsulawalks.co.nz; detailed maps can be purchased at the Akaroa Adventure Centre.

Skyline Circuit (10km; 4hr return) The best of Akaroa's walks circumnavigates the hills above the town via the Purple Peak Track which gives access to the bush of Hinewai Reserve; get a map from the Akaroa Adventure Centre in town.

Beach Road–Glen Bay–Red House Bay (5km one way; 1hr 15min) Stroll along waterfront Beach Road towards Glen Bay and the wooden lighthouse that used to stand at Akaroa Head before being moved to its current location in 1980. Continue towards Akaroa Head for about fifteen minutes and you'll come to Red House Bay, the scene of a

bloody massacre in 1830, when the great northern chief Te Rauparaha bribed the captain of the British brig *Elizabeth* with flax to conceal Maori warriors about the vessel and then to invite Te Rauparaha's unsuspecting enemies (led by Te Maiharanui) on board, where they were slaughtered. Te Rauparaha and his men then feasted on the victims on the beach.

Onuku Road (5km one way; 1hr 15min) Follow this inland road to Onuku, where you'll find the *Onuku Farm Hostel* (see p.537) and Onuku Marae with the pretty little nineteenth-century Onuku church.

Le Bons Bay and Okains Bay

19km northeast of Akaroa

Verdant **LE BONS BAY** is a small peaceful community with a number of holiday homes ranged behind a gorgeous sandy **beach**, framed on two sides by cliffs. Head here for moody walks along the beach and safe swimming.

   OKAINS BAY has a tiny permanent population but swells with Christchurch family holiday-makers in January. The beach and the placid lagoon formed by the **Opara Stream** are excellent for swimming and boating, but the museum is the real reason to visit.

Okains Bay Maori and Colonial Museum

1146 Okains Bay Rd • Daily 10am–5pm • $10 • ☎ 03 304 8611, ⓦokainsbaymuseum.co.nz

Local collector Murray Thacker has amassed one of the most remarkable collections of Maori artefacts in the South Island, including a great collection of *hei tiki* (a pendant with a design based on the human form) in different styles. There's also a "god stick"

9

dating back to 1400, a war canoe from 1867 and a beautiful meeting house with fine symbolic figures carved by master craftsman John Rua. European-style outbuildings include a "slab" stable and cottage constructed from large slabs of totara wood.

ACCOMMODATION AND EATING	OKAINS BAY

★**Double Dutch** 32 Chorlton Rd ☎03 304 7229, ⓦdoubledutch.co.nz; map p.533. Wonderfully relaxing upscale hostel in a very spacious modern house with just seven beds – which makes it feel more like a friendly share house than a hostel. En suite $86. Closed June–Aug. Dorms $32, doubles $78

Kawatea Farmstay 1048 Okains Bay Rd ☎03 304 8621, ⓦkawateafarmstay.co.nz; map p.533. Century-old homestead set in lush gardens bordered by 5km of scenic coastline, with welcoming hosts, three rooms and a lovely loft. Dinners are available on request. $130

South to Otago

Heading south from Christchurch, SH1 forges straight across the **Canterbury Plains** connecting small farming service towns, many grown rich from the region's intensive dairy farming. Aside from the occasionally magnificent views of the snowcapped **Southern Alps** to the west, the drive south is through a monotonous landscape broken only by the broad gravel beds of braided rivers, usually little more than a trickle spanned by a kilometre-long bridge – check out the longest of them all, just north of Rakaia.

The Canterbury Plains end at mundane **Timaru**, where SH8 strikes inland towards Fairlie, Lake Tekapo and Aoraki/Mount Cook. The coastal highway continues south through rolling hills to the architecturally harmonious city of **Oamaru**, and the unique and fascinating **Moeraki Boulders**. This is **penguin** country, with several opportunities to stop off and spy blue and yellow-eyed penguins.

Timaru

The 28,000-strong port city of **TIMARU**, 100km southwest of Rakaia, is at the end of a straight and flat two-hour drive from Christchurch. The city isn't especially compelling, though the museum, art gallery and **rock art centre** are each worth an hour or so and there's evening penguin viewing.

THE BANKS PENINSULA TRACK

The private **Banks Peninsula Track** (35km; 4-day option $255–295, 2-day option $160–185; closed May–Sept; ⓦbankstrack.co.nz) makes a wonderful alternative to DOC tracks and Great Walks. As well as a lovely combination of coastal cliff walking, volcanic landscapes, sandy swimming beaches, lush native bush and harbour views, you get to meet the locals. Highlights include penguin viewing and kayaking at Pohatu Penguins (see box, p.539), delightfully rustic accommodation at Stony Bay, a night in a farmhouse run by author Fiona Farrell and her husband, and a walk through Hinewai Reserve (see p.536).

It's not a tramp for route-march aficionados, more a social hike best done over four days with friends keen to partake in a little botanizing, some swimming and much lazing around. Both options follow the same route: only twelve people are allowed to start the track each day on the four-day option, and four people on the two-day version, so **book** well in advance.

You need to be reasonably fit, but because you're guaranteed a bed each night you can walk at your own pace. The fee includes transport to the start from Akaroa and accommodation along the way in lodging with showers, full kitchen, electricity and limited food supply. On the 4-day option there is one private double room available each night (additional $75 per night).

You should carry provisions for at least the first two days, although it's possible to buy basic food at small shops at Stony Bay and Otanerito Beach. There's limited scope for having your pack transported to your destination each night: see website for details.

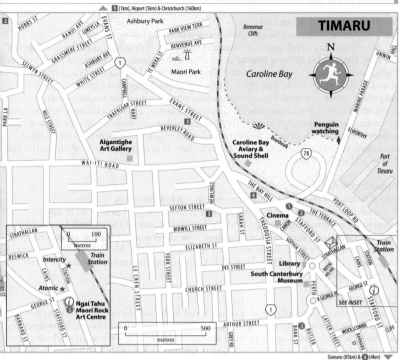

ACCOMMODATION					
1873 Wanderer Backpackers	3	Sefton Homestay	5	Arthur St Kitchen	3
Panorama Motor Lodge	4	Timaru Top 10		Ginger and Garlic	1
Pleasant View	1	Holiday Park	2	Speights Ale House	5

EATING	
Stables Café & Bar	4
Sukhothai	2

Brief history

The name Timaru comes from *Te Maru*, Maori for "place of shelter", as it provided the only haven for *waka* paddling between Banks Peninsula and Oamaru. In 1837 European settlement was founded by Joseph Price, who set up a **whaling** station south of the present city at Patiti Point. Today's commercial and pastoral development was initiated by Yorkshiremen **George and Robert Rhodes**, who established the first cattle station on the South Island in 1839 and effectively founded Timaru. Land reclamation created a harbour in 1877 and helped form the fine sandy beach of Caroline Bay. Once a popular seaside resort, Timaru still packs people in around New Year.

Te Ana: Ngai Tahu Maori Rock Art Centre

2 George St • Daily 10am–3pm • 1hr guided tour $20; 3hr guided tour of rock art sites Nov–April $125 (including transport and refreshments; book ahead) • ☎ 03 684 9141, ⊛ teana.co.nz

Although seeing the rock art *in situ* is a wonderful experience, there's fuller context at this well-planned museum inside the 1876 volcanic "bluestone" **Landing Service Building**. Aerial shots give a sense of location, photos by Fiona Pardington (who has Ngai Tahu roots) show off the paintings themselves, and displays illustrate what life was like at the time they were created. There's even a modern version of the sort of bulrush canoe used to get around the area, and the appropriation of Maori forms is explored through 1960s and 1970s matchboxes, ashtrays and peanut butter jars emblazoned with rock art designs.

9

South Canterbury Museum

Perth St • Tues–Fri 10am–4.30pm, Sat & Sun 1.30–4.30pm • Free • ☏ 03 687 7212, ⓦ museum.timaru.govt.nz

Most come to this small, regional museum to see the flimsy replica of the 1902 **aircraft** used by Temuka lad **Richard Pearse** in his attempt to notch up the world's first powered flight, some months in advance of the Wright brothers. His plane was technically far ahead of that of his rivals, but Pearse himself did not believe his flight – a rather desperate 100m, followed by an ignominious plunge into gorse bushes – was sufficiently controlled or sustained to justify this claim. He was a lifelong tinkerer and inventor, and his drawings are displayed along with rusty engine parts. Elsewhere, the gallery covers the life of local Maori (who lived a much more hunter-gatherer lifestyle than their northern kin), and the whaling station that occupied Patiti Point in the late 1830s and early 1840s.

Aigantighe Art Gallery

49 Wai-iti Rd • Tues–Fri 10am–4pm, Sat & Sun noon–4pm • Free • ☏ 03 688 4424, ⓦ timaru.govt.nz/art-gallery

A grand 1908 house known as Aigantighe (Gaelic for "at home"; their sign's suggested pronunciation is "egg-and-tie") retains many of its original features but now operates as an excellent small gallery. The diverse and rotating permanent collection includes four major works by native son Colin McCahon. Other artists to look out for are Frances Hodgkins, C.F. Goldie and the prolific landscape Realist, Austen Deans.

Caroline Bay

The broad sweep of **Caroline Bay** is much loved by locals, though the looming port cranes detract somewhat. From Boxing Day it hosts the annual two-week **summer carnival** (ⓦ carolinebay.org.nz) centred around a big New Year's Eve fireworks display. At other times, stroll the beach-back **boardwalk** to the low cliffs north past the wooden 1878 **Blackett's Lighthouse** to Dashing Rocks; or, around sunset, find a place along Marine Parade to watch small numbers of **blue penguins** waddle to their nests in the rocks. Follow the posted instructions to avoid disturbing them.

ARRIVAL AND DEPARTURE   TIMARU

By bus InterCity buses stop outside the train station (not served by passenger trains); NakedBus and Atomic buses stop outside the visitor centre.

Destinations Christchurch (5–6 daily; 2hr 30min);

Dunedin (5–6 daily; 3hr 30min); Oamaru (5–6 daily; 1hr).

By plane Timaru's airport is 13km north of the town centre on Falvey Rd.

Destinations Wellington (3–4 daily; 1hr 10min).

GETTING AROUND

By bus Timaru's Metro bus service (☏ 03 688 5544, ⓦ metroinfo.co.nz/timaru) has a flat rate of $2 for all journeys around the city, and $4.80 to Temuka. Tickets are sold in the visitor centre.

By bike Rent bikes from The Cyclery, 106 Stafford St (☏ 03 688 8892), for $35/day.

By taxi Timaru Taxis ☏ 03 688 8899.

INFORMATION

Tourist information The Visitor Centre is at 2 George St, inside the Rock Art Centre (Mon–Fri 10am–4pm, Sat & Sun 10am–3pm; ☏ 03 687 9997, ⓦ southcanterbury.org.nz).

Services The library on Sophia St (Mon, Wed & Fri 9am–8pm, Tues & Thurs 9am–6pm, Sat 10am–1pm, Sun 1–4pm) has free computers and wi-fi.

ACCOMMODATION

1873 Wanderer Backpackers 24 Evans St ☏ 03 688 8795, ⓦ bbh.co.nz. Small, well-run backpackers with mixed and female-only dorms (some of which get a fair bit of road noise) plus a well-equipped kitchen and off-street parking. Dorms $28, doubles $65

Panorama Motor Lodge 52 The Bay Hill ☏ 0800 103 310, ⓦ panorama.net.nz. Striking and hospitable motel with spacious units and all the usual facilities, plus spa pool, spa baths, free wi-fi and one unit with a sauna. There's off-street parking and great views over Caroline Bay. $135

MAORI ROCK ART

Around five hundred years ago, Maori moa hunters visited the South Canterbury and North Otago coastal plain, leaving a record of their sojourn on the walls and ceilings of open-sided limestone rock shelters. There are more than three hundred **rock drawings** around Timaru, Geraldine and Fairlie; the faded charcoal and red ochre drawings depict a variety of stylized human, bird and mythological figures and patterns. The best of the cave drawings can be seen in the region's museums, notably Timaru's Te Ana Maori Rock Art Centre (see p.541) and the North Otago Museum in Oamaru (see p.544). Around 95 percent of those remaining *in situ* are on private land and are often hard to make out, and what is visible is often the misguided result of nineteenth-century repainting. The best destination is **Frenchman's Gully**, where moa and a stylized birdman figure can be seen. Contact the Te Ana Maori Rock Art Centre for guided tours.

Pleasant View 2 Moore St ☎03 686 6651, ⓦpleasantview.co.nz. A stylish, modern house with two en-suite rooms, one of which has great views over Caroline Bay and the docks, plus a living area for all guests. $130

★**Sefton Homestay** 32 Sefton St ☎03 688 0017, ⓦseftonhomestay.co.nz. Great-value B&B in a lovely 1920s house set in leafy grounds. One room is an en suite, while the other is equally attractive with a private guest bathroom fitted with a deep tub. There's free wi-fi plus a dedicated guest lounge and discounts for cyclists. $130

Timaru Top 10 Holiday Park 154a Selwyn St ☎0800 242 121, ⓦtimaruholidaypark.co.nz. Well-kept, very high standard holiday-park offering a range of accommodation, close to the golf course and within walking distance of Maori Park. Camping $39, cabins $69

EATING, DRINKING AND ENTERTAINMENT

Arthur St Kitchen 8 Arthur St ☎03 688 9449, ⓦfacebook.com/arthurstkitchen. Pastel green walls make a backdrop for displays of local art in this relaxed café with plenty of outdoor seating, front and back. Come for coffee and cake, something from their pretty standard breakfast menu or lunches from the counter. Mon–Fri 7am–5.30pm, Sat 9am–3pm.

★**Ginger and Garlic** 335 Stafford St ☎03 688 3981, ⓦgingerandgarlic.co.nz. Timaru's premier fine-dining restaurant is romantically set in a beautiful old building with sweeping views over Caroline Bay. Expect the likes of duck breast with wasabi-spiced onion *bhaji* and honeyed onion broth, followed by caramel *wontons* with vanilla ice cream and chocolate ganache. Mains $30–40. Mon–Fri lunch, Mon–Sat dinner.

Speights Ale House 2 George St ☎03 686 6030, ⓦtimarualehouse.co.nz. Popular, cavernous bar in the Rock Art Centre, offering generous pub-style meals (mains around $25). Daily 11.30am–late.

★**Stables Café & Bar** 253 Beaconsfield Rd, 4km southwest of town ☎03 684 5617, ⓦfacebook.com /stablescafeandbar. Delightful country café with seating in and around converted farm buildings hung with farm implements. Kids will love the chickens, donkeys and budgies and everyone appreciates the excellent coffee and cakes; the menu extends to ribeye with chips and salad ($22). Tues–Sun 9am–5pm.

Sukhothai 303 Stafford St ☎03 688 4843. Good Thai restaurant serving old favourites (most mains $18–25) plus $13 lunch specials. Daily 11.30–3pm & 5–10pm.

Oamaru

The former port town of **OAMARU**, 85km south of Timaru, is one of New Zealand's most alluring provincial cities, and a relaxed place to spend a day or two. The most immediate attraction is the presence of both blue and yellow-eyed **penguin colonies** on the outskirts of town, but Oamaru itself has a well-preserved **Victorian Precinct**, a dense core of grand civic and mercantile buildings built of the distinctive cream-coloured local limestone that earned it the title "The Whitestone City".

The best times to visit Oamaru are from November to January when penguins are in their greatest numbers, and for the **Victorian Heritage Celebrations** (ⓦvhc.co.nz), in November, when the streets of the Victorian Precinct become a racetrack for penny-farthings, cheered on by local residents in Victorian attire. A few rebels hold a competing race on 1970s Raleigh 20s.

9

Brief history

The limestone outcrops throughout the area once provided shelter for Maori and later the raw material for ambitious European builders. As a commercial centre for gold-rush prospectors, and shored up by quarrying, timber and farming industries, Oamaru grew prosperous. The port opened for **migration** in 1874, although many ships foundered on the hostile coastline. After this boom period Oamaru declined, times evocatively recorded in work by local writer **Janet Frame**. It's only in recent years that the town has begun to come alive again.

Thames Street

Thames Street is the more formal face of Oamaru's **Victorian Precinct**, home the majority of civic buildings. One side packs in the 1906 Opera House, the Palladian Courthouse, the classically proportioned Athenaeum building (now home to the North Otago Museum), the First Post Office (see below) and the Former Post Office, whose tower was added by the architect's son, Thomas Forrester, in 1903. Opposite stand two fine buildings by R.A. Lawson: the imposing **National Bank** has perhaps the purest Neoclassical facade in town; while its grander neighbour now operates as the **Forrester Gallery**.

North Otago Museum

60 Thames St • Mon–Fri 10.30am–4.30pm, Sat & Sun 1–4.30pm • Free • ☎ 03 433 0852, ⓦ northotagomuseum.co.nz

The colonnaded 1882 Athenaeum building houses the **North Otago Museum**, where a ten-minute movie introduces a modest selection of displays on North Otago history, Oamaru stone and early Maori rock art. The building was once a subscription library where local novelist Janet Frame spent much of her teenage years. Her typewriter is still here as the centrepiece of a display on her life and works.

First Post Office

12 Thames St

There's something a little incongruous about the Italianate **First Post Office**, which was built in 1864, predating all the other whitestone architecture. It's the town's only remaining example of the work of Australian-born architect W.H. Clayton, who designed Dunedin's All Saints' Church and Edinburgh House before being appointed the country's first – and only – Colonial Architect.

Forrester Gallery

9 Thames St • Daily 10.30am–4.30pm • Free • ☎ 03 433 0853, ⓦ forrestergallery.com

R.A. Lawson's Neoclassical bank building now houses Oamaru's premiere **art gallery**, which runs an impressive programme of touring exhibitions of contemporary and traditional art. There's almost always something fascinating, supplemented by selected works from their own collection. Look out for works by iconic Kiwi artist Colin McCahon and local painter Colin Wheeler, whose cityscapes are dominated by the colour of Oamaru stone.

OAMARU WHITESTONE

The key to Oamaru's distinctive look is **whitestone**, which is still quarried on the outskirts of town. This "free stone" is easily worked with metal hand tools when freshly quarried but hardens with exposure to the elements. While keeping the prevailing Neoclassical fashion firmly in mind, the architects' imaginations ran riot, producing deeply fluted pilasters, finely detailed pediments and elegant Corinthian pillars topped with veritable forests of acanthus leaves. Oamaru was given much of its character by architect **R.A. Lawson** and by the firm **Forrester and Lemon** who together produced most of the more accomplished buildings between 1871 and 1883. Oamaru stone is still used in modern buildings such as the Waitaki Aquatic Centre in Takaro Park.

OPPOSITE STILT WALKERS, HISTORIC PRECINCT, OAMARU (ABOVE) >

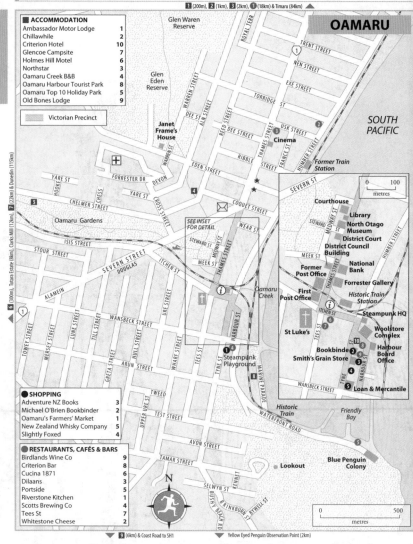

OAMARU

■ ACCOMMODATION

Ambassador Motor Lodge	1
Chillawhile	2
Criterion Hotel	10
Glencoe Campsite	7
Holmes Hill Motel	6
Northstar	3
Oamaru Creek B&B	4
Oamaru Harbour Tourist Park	8
Oamaru Top 10 Holiday Park	5
Old Bones Lodge	9

Victorian Precinct

● SHOPPING

Adventure NZ Books	3
Michael O'Brien Bookbinder	2
Oamaru's Farmers' Market	1
New Zealand Whisky Company	5
Slightly Foxed	4

● RESTAURANTS, CAFÉS & BARS

Birdlands Wine Co	9
Criterion Bar	8
Cucina 1871	6
Dilaans	3
Portside	5
Riverstone Kitchen	1
Scotts Brewing Co	4
Tees St	7
Whitestone Cheese	2

Tyne and Harbour streets

South of Thames Street you nip down Itchen Street into Oamaru's original commercial quarter, full of whitestone solidity. Gentrification is taking its time, but this is gradually becoming the place to hang out, perhaps grabbing a coffee or a beer in between browsing the shops, art galleries and minor museums. Try to come at weekends when there's more happening: there will be little open on a wet Wednesday.

Tyne Street kicks off with the Woolstore Complex (see opposite) and the *Criterion Hotel*, followed by Oamaru's elegant old **Union Offices**, built in 1877. The adjacent **Smiths Grain Store**, built in 1882 by stonemason James Johnson, is considered to be the most ornamental of its kind in the country.

Harbour Street runs parallel to Tyne Street and is lined by more rejuvenated mercantile buildings. The 1876 Venetian Renaissance-style **Harbour Board Office** was one of the first public buildings designed by the prolific Forrester and Lemon. Interpretation panels on the ground floor relate the history of Oamaru Harbour and the architects' influence on Oamaru. The street ends at the massive 1882 **Loan & Mercantile** wool and grain store, once the largest in New Zealand.

Steampunk HQ

Itchen St • Daily 10am–5pm • $10 • ⓦ steampunkoamaru.co.nz

This wonderfully oddball museum has made Oamaru New Zealand's steampunk capital. Outside is a pimped, rakishly perched steam engine which (for $2) provides steam-belching, lights-flashing entertainment; inside is a world – somewhere between dystopian and phantasmagorical – that a modern Jules Verne or H.G.Wells might have created. Much of it is essentially junk reimagined with a welding torch: compressors, divers' helmets, old cathode ray tubes, skulls and much more form a bizarre synthesis of pseudo-Victorian mechanical-style overlaid with retro-futurism. Don't miss the Infinity Portal Experience or the two short movies. Steampunk even informs the design of a **kids' playground** and café at the harbour end of Wansbeck Street.

Woolstore Complex and the Oamaru Auto Collection

1 Tyne St • Daily 10am–4.30pm • Free • Oamaru Auto Collection daily 10am–4.30pm; $10

The **Woolstore Complex** houses the *Woolstore Café* and two floors of boutiques and galleries which are at their liveliest during the Sunday market. Motorsport enthusiasts won't want to miss the **Oamaru Auto Collection**, with some thirty vintage, classic and historic vehicles which might include an Audi Quattro in rally trim and a 1970s Skoda 110 that successfully competed in New Zealand's forest rally stages.

Janet Frame House

56 Eden St • Nov–April daily 2–4pm • $5 • ⓣ 03 434 2300, ⓦ jfestrust.org.nz

The **Janet Frame House** was the modest childhood home of one of New Zealand's greatest writers: "I wanted an imagination that would inhabit a world of fact, descend like a shining light upon the ordinary life of Eden Street…" Restored to 1930s style, you can explore it, get some insight from the custodian and listen to a marvellous recording of the author reading an extract from *Owls Do Cry*, about the very sofa you'll be sitting on. Fans of her work may also want to follow the **Janet Frame Trail** (free leaflet available from the i-SITE), taking you to locations used in varying degrees of disguise in her books.

The penguin colonies

Penguins Crossing: evening (2hr 30min–3hr; $65); morning (1hr; $40) • ⓣ 0800 304 333, ⓦ travelheadfirst.com

Oamaru is unique in having both yellow-eyed and blue **penguin colonies** within walking distance of the town centre. It is usually possible to see both colonies in one evening, since the yellow-eyes tend to come ashore earlier than the blues. Penguins are timid creatures and easily distressed, so keep quiet and still, and do not approach within 10m of the birds. Once disturbed, the penguins may not return to their nests for several hours, even if they have chicks to feed.

To facilitate your penguin watching, use **Penguins Crossing**, a narrated door-to-door bus evening tour that visits the yellow penguins first, getting you to the blue penguins (entry included) in time for their arrival. They also head out before dawn to watch the yellow-eyed penguins head out to sea.

Blue Penguin Colony

2 Waterfront Rd, 1.5km southeast of the town centre • Daily 10am–2hr after dark • Day-tour $10; guided day-tour $16; evening viewing $28; premium evening viewing $40; 15 percent discount for seniors, students etc • ⓣ 03 4331195, ⓦ penguins.co.nz

Blue penguins (a.k.a. little penguins, fairy penguins or korora) are the smallest of their

9

HISTORIC DISTRICT SHOPPING

Adventure NZ Books 7 Harbour St ☎ 03 434 7756, ⓦ adventurebooks.co.nz. Rare, new and out-of-print books about travel, adventure and general derring-do. Daily 10.30am–4.30pm.

Michael O'Brien Bookbinder 7 Tyne St ☎ 03 434 9277, ⓦ bookbinder.co.nz. Watch Michael binding and restoring rare books among the old printing and letterpress machines in the atmospheric old Union offices. New hand-made books are available in various sizes and qualities ($30–700), some leather-bound. If you're captivated, ask about their one-day bookbinding courses ($175). Mon–Fri 2–6pm or by appointment.

Oamaru's Farmers' Market corner of Wansbeck St and Tyne St ⓦ oamarufarmersmarket.co.nz. Two

dozen stalls, a coffee cart and live music bring the Historic District to life. Sunday 9.30am–1pm.

New Zealand Whisky Company 14 Harbour St ☎ 03 434 8842, ⓦ thenzwhisky.com. When New Zealand's southernmost whisky distillery closed in 1997 almost 500 barrels of the good stuff were left in a bondstore in Oamaru's Historic District. Supplies are dwindling but you can still buy a wonderfully diverse range of single malts and blends dating back to 1987, some costing up to $400. Sample individually ($5–7 a dram) or in flights of four ($18–20). Daily 10.30am–4.30pm.

Slightly Foxed 11 Tyne St ☎ 03 434 2155, ⓦ www .slightlyfoxed.co.nz. A wonderful range of quality secondhand and classic books, plus a case of Janet Frame first editions. Mon–Sat 10am–5pm, Sun 10am–4pm.

---

kind. They're found all around the coast of New Zealand, and along the shores of southern Australia, but are most easily seen around Oamaru. Some even nest under waterside buildings, and if you sit along the shoreline just after dark you'll probably see a few waddle past. More formal and informative viewing takes place at the **Blue Penguin Colony**. Visit during the day and you watch videos on little penguins and hopefully see birds on their nests, but you're likely to get far more from an **evening viewing** in the 350-seat grandstand. During the breeding season (June–Dec) you'll see chicks – and hear them calling to their parents out at sea, hunting for food. When the parents return around dusk, travelling in groups known as rafts, they climb the steep harbour banks and cross in front of the grandstand to their nests.

In the peak season (Nov to mid-Feb) you might see two hundred penguins in a night, though this might drop to a dozen or so in March, June and August. If the standard experience seems a bit of a circus, try the daytime **guided tour** (30–40min) or step up to the evening **premium** viewing, where you get more comfortable seats closer to the action, and approach through the penguin colony itself.

Yellow-eyed penguin colony

Bushy Beach, reached along Bushy Beach Rd

The much larger **yellow-eyed penguins** nest in smaller numbers but keep more sociable hours, usually coming ashore in late afternoon or early evening; they're best seen between October and February. The birds mainly arrive 2km south at **Bushy Beach**, where a hide enables you to see them making their way across the beach in the morning and early evening.

ARRIVAL AND DEPARTURE   OAMARU

By bus InterCity and NakedBus drop off at the corner of Eden and Thames sts on their Christchurch–Dunedin runs. Oamaru-based Coastline Tours (☎ 03 434 7744, ⓦ coastline -tours.co.nz) run to Dunedin and will drop off in Moeraki. Destinations Christchurch (6 daily; 4hr); Dunedin (5–6 daily; 2hr); Timaru (6 daily; 1hr).

INFORMATION

Visitor information i-SITE, 1 Thames St (daily 9am–5pm; ☎ 03 434 1656, ⓦ visitoamaru.co.nz), stocks useful free leaflets to self-guided walking tours.

Services There's free wi-fi at the i-SITE and at the Oamaru Public Library, 62 Thames St (Mon–Fri 9.30am–5.30pm,

Sat 10am–12.30pm).

Rentals Oamaru Harbour Tourist Park on The Esplanade rent hybrid bikes ($35/day) along with canoes and paddleboards (both $20/hr).

ACCOMMODATION

Finding accommodation is seldom difficult, but it pays to book a day or two ahead from December to March.

Ambassador Motor Lodge 296 Thames St ☎ 0800 437 214, ⓦ ambassadoroamaru.co.nz. Well-kept and fairly central motel with a range of units including some with spa baths ($149). There are even freshly baked muffins on arrival. **$129**

★ **Chillawhile** 1 Frome St ☎ 03 437 0168, ⓦ chillawhile .co.nz. There's a loose, chilled feel to this arty hostel in a rambling house 2km north of the centre. Rooms are dedicated to playing music (with guitar and organ), painting and drumming workshops. Pot-luck dinners are encouraged and dorms are set up with a small sitting area to encourage sociability. Atomic drop off here. Dorms **$28**, doubles **$72**

Criterion Hotel 3 Tyne St ☎ 03 434 6247, ⓦ criterionhotel.co.nz. This whitestone 1877 hotel is the only place you can stay in the Victorian Precinct. Simple (mostly bathless) rooms above the bar (noisy at weekends) come with a breakfast room where you self-serve cereal and toast. Doubles **$90**, en-suite doubles **$120**

Glencoe campsite Tulliemet Rd, 2km west of Herbert, itself 22km south of Oamaru. Very pleasant and grassy DOC campsite that's fairly handy for Moeraki Boulders and has a track leading down to a swimming hole in the river. In Herbert, take Ord St then follow signs to Glencoe Domain. **$6**

Holmes Hill Motel 92 Wansbeck St ☎ 03 434 7548, ⓦ holmeshillmotel.co.nz. Classic 1960s motel with an open aspect and a series of studios and two-bedroom units ($100) all with full cooking facilities, free wi-fi and access to a garden with kids' play area. **$90**

Northstar 495a SH1 ☎ 03 437 1190, ⓦ northstarmotel .co.nz. Sparkling revamped motel 3km north of the centre with stylish, new units and its own excellent restaurant also open to non-guests. **$140**

Oamaru Creek B&B 24 Reed St ☎ 03 434 1190, ⓦ oamarucreek.co.nz. Warm, friendly homestay B&B in a former maternity home, with spacious rooms, mostly en-suite ($140), great breakfasts and sociable owners who will try to put you on the right trail to a good time. Free wi-fi. **$130**

Oamaru Harbour Tourist Park Esplanade ☎ 03 434 5260, ⓦ oamaruharbour.co.nz. Hardstand campervan parking close to the waterfront, with power, free wi-fi and access to kitchen and showers. Vans **$35**

Oamaru Top 10 Holiday Park 30 Chelmer St ☎ 0800 280 202, ⓦ oamarutop10.co.nz. In a lovely sheltered setting close to Oamaru Gardens with a good range of accommodation including chalets ($125). Camping **$40**, cabins **$73**

★ **Old Bones Lodge** 468 Beach Rd, Kakanui ☎ 03 434 8115, ⓦ oldbones.co.nz. Gorgeous, purpose-built, upscale backpackers on the coast 6km south of town (follow Wharfe Rd) with just eight shared-bath doubles and twins opening onto a spacious, comfortable and TV-free lounge/kitchen. There's free wi-fi and underfloor heating in the bedrooms. They also offer massages and use of the six private hot tubs with waterfall or sea views ($25 a head). Per person: campervan parking **$20**, rooms **$45**

EATING, DRINKING AND ENTERTAINMENT

Most of Oamaru's **eating and drinking** takes place on and around Thames Street. If you're planning an outing to Moeraki Boulders, don't miss dining at the fabulous *Fleur's Place* (p.551); heading north, try lunch at the *Riverstone Kitchen* (below).

Birdlands Wine Co 3 Harbour St ☎ 03 434 2185. This small wine bar with good music, craft beer and wine spills out onto the street and doesn't really get going until 11pm. Fri 4.30pm–2am, Sat 6pm–2am.

Criterion Bar Criterion Hotel, 3 Tyne St ☎ 03 434 6247, ⓦ criterionhotel.co.nz. With the tenor of a Victorian English pub there's a long wooden bar, some good old-fashioned Emerson's Bookbinder or local Scott's beer plus filling, inexpensive food – including bangers and mash ($17). Daily 10am–10pm or later.

Cucina 1871 1 Tees St ☎ 03 434 5696. Fun and buzzing Italian restaurant with a full range of crowd-pleasing pasta, polenta and pizza dishes (mostly $25–35) and a classy wine list. Mon–Sat 4–10pm or later.

Dilaans 263 Thames St. Good-value Turkish takeaway and café. Slather a couple of sauces over the chicken shish and wash it down with an apple tea (dishes $10–17). Daily 11am–10pm.

Portside 2 Waterfront Rd ☎ 03 434 3400. The deck of this casual, airy, harbourside restaurant is a perfect place for a sundowner, or stick around for meals such as grilled sea bass with scallops, prawns and clams in a chilli lime broth ($29). Thurs–Tues 11am–9pm or later.

★ **Riverstone Kitchen** 1431 SH1, 19km north of Oamaru, 66km south of Timaru ☎ 03 431 3505, ⓦ riverstonekitchen.co.nz. Some of the finest meals around are served in an uncluttered country setting with its own produce-filled gardens. They serve sumptuous bistro dinners, but it works best for lunch when you're passing and/or browsing its deli. Expect the likes of slow-cooked pork with wet polenta and wilted greens ($29) perhaps followed by gooseberry tart with elderflower ice cream ($8). Mon 9am–5pm, Thurs–Sun 9am–5pm & 6–10pm.

Scotts Brewing Co 1 Wansbeck St ☎ 03 434 2244, ⓦ scottsbrewing.co.nz. You can grab pizza on the deck with a glass of wine, but this place is really about the

ALPS 2 OCEAN CYCLE TRAIL

If you fancy riding some, or all, of Alps 2 Ocean Cycle Trail (see box, p.586), engage the services of Trail Adventures (☎027 937 447, ⓦtrailadventures.co.nz) who do everything from straight bike rental ($35/day) and day-trips through the Waitaki Valley to fully supported and self-guided tours.

boutique beer, brewed on site and including gluten-free options. Taste ($3), fill a bottle to take away or stick around to work your way through local and quality guest brews. Daily 11am–7.30pm, later on summer weekends.

★**Tees St** 3 Tees St ☎03 434 7004, ⓦfacebook.com /Teesstreet. A great deal of thought and care has gone into both the decor and the food at this modern café where you might brunch on a haloumi and shiitake mushroom stack or mouthwatering fish tacos (around $20). Soft-brew and

espresso coffees, both superb. Mon–Fri 6.30am–4pm, Sat & Sun 7.30am–4pm.

Whitestone Cheese 3 Torridge St ☎03 434 8098, ⓦwhitestonecheese.co.nz. This cheese factory has a viewing gallery at the back (best Mon–Fri before noon) and offers free samples of its daily specials along with a five-cheese tasting platter ($7) which usually includes Whitestone's famed soft, creamy Windsor Blue. Check out the lemon baked cheesecake ($8). Mon–Fri 9am–5pm, Sat & Sun 10am–4pm.

Totara Estate

SH1, 8km south of Oamaru • Sept–May daily 10am–4pm • $10 • ☎03 433 1269, ⓦtotaraestate.co.nz

Set aside an hour to look around **Totara Estate**, the birthplace of the New Zealand meat industry. Until the early 1880s New Zealand was a major wool exporter with surplus meat, while Britain's burgeoning industrial cities starved. The solution came in 1882 when the three-masted *Dunedin* was refitted with coke-driven freezers and filled with UK-bound lamb from Totara Estate. The estate is now a grassy historic park whose solid whitestone buildings contain a small museum along with a harness room, stables, granary barn and blacksmith's forge. The foundations and partial remains of the original slaughterhouse form the basis of a modern reconstruction that gives an idea of what work was like here.

Clarks Mill

SH1, 12km south of Oamaru • Nov–Jan, March & April Sun 1–3pm; Feb daily 10am–4pm • $10; $15 when machinery operating • Machinery operating last Sun of the month plus Thurs 11am and Sun 2pm in Feb • ☎03 433 1269, ⓦhistoricplaces.org.nz

Time it right and you can combine Totara Estate with the farm's four-storey **historic flour mill**, the only remaining, originally water-powered mill in the country. The waterwheel has long gone but otherwise not much has changed since 1866 when its completion finally brought flour to a land drowning in wheat; previously flour had to be imported from Australia. Just touring the belts, pulleys, elevators and wooden chutes with the custodian is wonderfully evocative and informative, but nowhere near as much as when everything is coaxed into flapping and creaking life.

Moeraki Boulders

SH1, 40km south of Oamaru and 3km south of Hampden • Access to the boulders is either by a 300m walk along the beach from a DOC parking area, or more immediately via a short private trail ($2 in the honesty box at any hour), though it's free for patrons of the adjacent café (daily: Nov–March 8am–5.30pm; April–Oct 9am–5pm)

The large, grey spherical **Moeraki Boulders** lie partially submerged in the sandy beach at the tide line, about 2km before you hit Moeraki village. Their smooth skins hide honeycomb centres, which are revealed in some of the broken specimens. They once lay deep in the mudstone cliffs behind the beach and, as these were eroded, out fell the smooth boulders, with further erosion exposing a network of surface veins. The boulders were originally formed around a central core of carbonate of lime crystals that attracted minerals from their surroundings – a process that started sixty million years ago, when muddy sediment containing shell and plant fragments accumulated on the sea floor. They range in size from small pellets to large round rocks (some almost 2m in diameter), though the smaller ones have all been souvenired over the years, leaving only those too heavy to shift.

Maori named the boulders Te Kaihinaki (food baskets), believing them to have been washed ashore from the wreck of a canoe whose occupants were seeking *pounamu*. The seaward reef near Shag Point (see below) was the hull of the canoe, and just beyond it stands a prominent rock, the vessel's petrified navigator. Some of the Moeraki Boulders were *hinaki* (baskets), the more spherical were water-carrying gourds and the irregular-shaped rocks farther down the beach were *kumara* from the canoe's food store. The survivors among the crew were transformed at daybreak into hills overlooking the beach.

Moeraki village

The picturesque and tranquil fishing village of **MOERAKI** offers boulder access along the beach (they're 2km to the north) and a chance to see yellow-eyed penguins up close. Drive to the white wooden **Katiki Point** lighthouse (1km off SH1 then 5km along an unsealed road) then follow signs down a path which leads to a hide, overlooking the beach where yellow-eyed penguins emerge after a hard day's fishing (3.30pm–nightfall), and seals loll. A second path leads to a *pa* site, its importance explained on a panel nearby.

ARRIVAL AND DEPARTURE   MOERAKI VILLAGE

By bus Most bus services don't stop in Moeraki. From Oamaru use Coastline Tours (☎03 434 7744, ⓦcoastline-tours.co.nz) who will drop you in the centre on their Oamaru–Dunedin run (Mon–Fri only) and pick you up about 6hr later on the way back north.

ACCOMMODATION

Moeraki Beach Motels Corner of Cleddy and Haven sts ☎03 439 4862, ⓦmoerakibeachmotels.co.nz. The four units here face the bay, and the owners also manage a number of holiday homes in the village. **$105**

Moeraki Boulders Kiwi Holiday Park 2 Lincoln St, Hampden, 6km north of Moeraki ☎03 439 4439, ⓦmoerakiboudersholidaypark.co.nz. Welcoming, Swiss-run campsite just steps from the beach: you can walk along it to Moeraki Boulders in 30min or ride there on rusty bikes ($5). There are plenty of grassy campsites, a nice range of roofed accommodation (cabins $60, tourist flats and motel units $100), good showers and kayaks ($5/hr) for mucking about in the creek. Camping **$13**, dorm **$25**

Moeraki Village Holiday Park 114 Haven St ☎03 439 4759, ⓦmoerakivillageholidaypark.co.nz. Well located above the boat harbour and just a 50m walk to the beach, this campsite has a range of accommodation options. Camping, per site **$32**, cabins **$60**, motel units **$115**

Three Bays 39 Cardiff St ☎03 439 4520, ⓦthreebays.co.nz. A delightful self-contained unit set high on the hill with great long views over the town towards the Moeraki Boulders and ocean. Unit **$170**

EATING

★Fleur's Place The Old Jetty ☎03 439 4480, ⓦfleursplace.com. Fleur Sullivan lets the freshness of the fish do the talking at this marvellously rustic corrugated-iron shack by the water that attracts sophisticates from Dunedin (plus the likes of Gwyneth Paltrow and Rick Stein). Try the platter for two ($75) with five types of fresh-off-the-boat fish served with your choice of sauces. Dinner bookings are essential and this could be your chance to sample muttonbird. Most mains $35–40. Wed–Sun 9.30am–11pm.

Shag Point and the Matakaea Scenic Reserve

Just over 10km south of Moeraki village, a side road runs 3km to the windswept promontory of **Shag Point** and the **Matakaea Scenic Reserve**, where the rocks are often slathered with fur seals and a viewing platform allows distant views of yellow-eyed penguins, best before 9am and after 3pm.

Central South Island

BOULDERS AT KURA TAWHITI

10

Central South Island

The Central South Island is one of the most varied and visually stunning areas in New Zealand, with expansive pasturelands, dense native forests and a history rich in tales of human endeavour, tinged with the toughness and idiosyncrasies of the area's settlers. The region's defining feature is the icy, white sawtooth ridge of the Southern Alps that forms the South Island's central north–south spine and peaks at New Zealand's loftiest summit, 3754m-high Aoraki/Mount Cook. Summers are generally hot and dry with long days that sear the grasslands tinder-dry. In winter, snow blankets numerous ski-fields. These alpine conditions foster unique plants and wildlife, including the Mount Cook lily – the largest buttercup in the world – and the mischievous kea, the world's only alpine parrot.

Running between Christchurch and Westport, the forested **Lewis Pass** road provides access to the tranquil spa town of **Hanmer Springs** before passing the more rustic hot pools at **Maruia Springs**. Further south, both road and rail head through the spectacular **Arthur's Pass National Park**, with its abundance of day-walks and longer trails.

South of Christchurch, roads lead across the Canterbury Plains towards the small settlement of **Methven**, the base for **Mount Hutt**-bound skiers and summertime walkers exploring **Mount Somers** – often dry when Arthur's Pass is wet and enveloped in cloud.

The southern half of the region spills into the sun-scorched grasslands of the **Mackenzie Country**, an area renowned for vast sheep runs and the unearthly blues of its glacier-fed lakes, **Tekapo**, **Pukaki** and **Ohau**. The mightiest of the Southern Alps form an imperious backdrop. **Aoraki/Mount Cook Village**, huddled at the foot of the mountain, is the starting point of numerous walks, glacial lake trips and heli-trekking and heli-skiing. An alternative base for forays to Aoraki/Mount Cook is the former hydro construction town of **Twizel**, less than an hour's drive south, surrounded by dams, control gates and canals.

Yet further south, the road toward Wanaka and Queenstown passes through New Zealand's gliding capital, **Omarama**, before heading over the dramatic Lindis Pass.

GETTING AROUND

By bus Bus routes centre on Christchurch with services north to Hanmer Springs (though none continue over Lewis Pass to Nelson), west to Arthur's Pass and southwest to Methven.

Atomic, InterCity/Newmans/Great Sights, and NakedBus thread down through the Mackenzie Country to Wanaka and Queenstown. Only Great Sights goes directly to Aoraki/

AMONG THE ICEBERGS AT TASMAN GLACIER

Highlights

❶ Skiing the Central South Island Mount Hutt is a great starting point for some of the country's best, most reasonably priced and least-crowded slopes. **See p.561 & p.570**

❷ Hiking Arthur's Pass Walking in this wild, rugged national park offers a jaw-dropping insight into a uniquely beautiful alpine landscape. **See p.566**

❸ Rafting the Rangitata Raft some of the best and bounciest whitewater in the country on trips from Peel Forest, Geraldine or Christchurch. **See p.572**

❹ Stargazing above Lake Tekapo After taking in the lake's incredible opaque blue waters, gaze up at the astonishingly clear star-filled night sky from Mount John Observatory. **See p.577**

❺ Exploring Aoraki/Mount Cook's glacial lakes Get up close to the icebergs with a boat cruise or closer still on a kayak trip on the glacial lakes beneath the country's highest peak. **See p.582**

❻ Gliding over Omarama Experience the thrill of silent flying at New Zealand's gliding capital, Omarama. **See p.587**

HIGHLIGHTS ARE MARKED ON THE MAP ON P.556

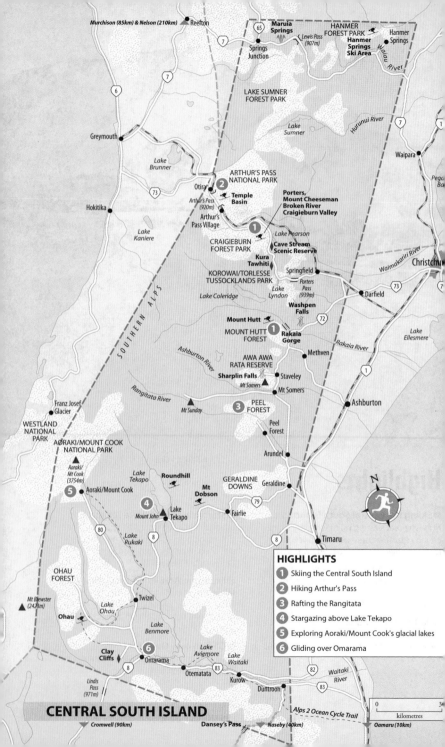

Murchison (85km) & Nelson (210km) Reefton

Maruia Springs
65
Lewis Pass (907m)

HANMER FOREST PARK
Hanmer Springs Ski Area
Hanmer Springs

7

Springs Junction

7

6

LAKE SUMNER FOREST PARK

Lake Sumner

Hurunui River

7

1

Greymouth

Lake Brunner

73

Waipara

Pega Ba

Hokitika

ARTHUR'S PASS NATIONAL PARK

Otira
2
Temple Basin
Arthur's Pass (920m)
Arthur's Pass Village

Porters, Mount Cheeseman Broken River Craigieburn Valley

Lake Kaniere

CRAIGIEBURN FOREST PARK

1

Lake Pearson

Cave Stream Scenic Reserve

Kura Tawhiti

Waimakariri River

Christchu

KOROWAI/TORLESSE TUSSOCKLANDS PARK

Springfield

Lake Coleridge

Lake Lyndon

Porters Pass (939m)

Darfield

73

7

SOUTHERN ALPS

Washpen Falls

Mount Hutt

72

Lake Ellesmere

MOUNT HUTT FOREST

1
Rakaia Gorge

Rakaia River

Methven

AWA AWA RATA RESERVE

Ashburton River

Sharplin Falls

Mt Somers

Staveley

Mt Somers

Rangitata River

Mt Sunday

3
PEEL FOREST

Ashburton

1

Peel Forest

WESTLAND NATIONAL PARK

Arundel

Franz Josef Glacier

AORAKI/MOUNT COOK NATIONAL PARK

Aoraki/ Mt Cook (3754m)

Roundhill

GERALDINE DOWNS

Geraldine

5
Aoraki/Mount Cook

Lake Tekapo

Mt Dobson

79

4
Lake Tekapo

Fairlie

Mount John

8

80

Lake Rukaki

8

Timaru

Lake Ohau

OHAU FOREST

Mt Blewster (2423m)

Twizel

Ohau

Lake Ohau

Lake Benmore

6
Clay Cliffs

Omarama

Lake Aviemore

Lake Waitaki

8

Lindis Pass (971m)

Otematata

83

Kurow

82

Duntroon

83

Waitaki River

CENTRAL SOUTH ISLAND

Alps 2 Ocean Cycle Trail

N

HIGHLIGHTS

1 Skiing the Central South Island

2 Hiking Arthur's Pass

3 Rafting the Rangitata

4 Stargazing above Lake Tekapo

5 Exploring Aoraki/Mount Cook's glacial lakes

6 Gliding over Omarama

0   30
kilometres

Cromwell (90km)   Dansey's Pass   Naseby (40km)   Oamaru (10km)

Mount Cook so it is often more convenient (and usually cheaper) to travel to Tekapo and change onto The Cook Connection (☎0800 266526, ⓦcookconnect.co.nz) which links Aoraki/Mount Cook with Twizel and Lake Tekapo.

By train The wonderfully scenic *TranzAlpine* (see box, p.524) is the only train serving the region. It traverses the mountains daily travelling from Christchurch to Greymouth over Arthur's Pass in 4hr 30min.

Hanmer Springs and the Lewis Pass

10

The most northerly of the cross-mountain roads, SH7, follows an ancient Maori and early Pakeha trade route. A side road leads to the spa town of **Hanmer Springs**, a popular base for summer walks and winter sports at the **Hanmer Springs Ski Area**. Some 60km further west, the SH7 climbs the **Lewis Pass** before dropping down to the steaming thermal waters of **Maruia Springs**.

Hanmer Springs

Around 125km from Christchurch, a spur road branches off the SH7 to **HANMER SPRINGS**, 9km away at the edge of a broad, fertile plain snuggled against the Southern Alps foothills. Rainwater seeps through fractures in the rock of the Hanmer Range, absorbing minerals before being warmed by the earth's natural heat – a process that takes almost two centuries – before surfacing as Hanmer's famous hot springs. Everything centres on oak-lined Amuri Avenue, which runs past the springs, the i-SITE, shops, and the shady park that gives the town its quiet, sheltered feel.

Hanmer Springs Thermal Pools and Spa

42 Amuri Ave • Pools daily 10am–9pm; spa daily 10am–7pm; café daily 10am–5.30pm • Pools $20; towel rental $5; waterslides $10; private pools $30/person for 30min (minimum 2 people, includes general entry) • Pools ☎03 315 0000, spa ☎03 315 0029; ⓦhanmersprings.co.nz

Whatever the weather, it's a pleasure to wallow at this open-air complex where you can soak in twelve landscaped thermal pools ranging from 33°C to 42°C, or cool off in two freshwater swimming pools kept at 29°C. Add in three waterslides (one that swirls you around what looks like a giant toilet bowl), half a dozen private pools and the *Garden House Café* and you could stay all day. It's at its best in the evening when the crowds thin and the sun sets. Next door, the stylish **spa** offers pampering treatments including a good range of massages (from $75).

Queen Mary Hospital Historic Reserve

Main entrance on Amuri Ave • Open access • Free

To older Kiwis "I'm off to Hanmer" may mean a day at the hot pools, but could equally refer to time spent drying out at the Queen Mary Hospital, New Zealand's most famous residential alcohol and drugs rehab centre, which closed in 2003. It started life helping shell-shocked soldiers recuperate during World War I and also spent time as a mental institution. The buildings are closed to the public but you can wander round the leafy grounds admiring well-preserved facades that include the original **Soldiers Block**, where "sunlight and fresh air" were considered key to recovery, the Arts and Crafts **Chisholm Ward** and the 1928 **Nurses' Hostel**, still with an "Out Of Bounds To Clients" sign on the door.

ARRIVAL AND DEPARTURE	HANMER SPRINGS

By bus Two companies, Hanmer Connection (☎0800 242663, ⓦhanmerconnection.co.nz) and Hanmer Tours & Shuttle (☎03 315 7418, ⓦhanmertours.co.nz), run buses between Christchurch and Hanmer, where they arrive and depart from a stop just north of the springs. To reach Kaikoura, you'll need to return to Amberley and catch a northbound bus from there; at the time of writing there was no public transport over the Lewis Pass to Nelson.

Destinations Christchurch (4 daily; 2hr).

INFORMATION

Tourist information i-SITE, 40 Amuri Ave, next to the hot pools (daily 10am–5pm; ☎ 03 315 0020, ⓦ hanmersprings .co.nz). Helpful for local information and bookings, and to obtain the excellent *Hanmer Springs Walks* and *Hanmer*

Springs Mountain Bike Tracks leaflets ($3 each).

Services The i-SITE contains a small bank (Mon–Fri 10am–2pm); there's an ATM outside the Four Square supermarket.

ACCOMMODATION

10

Hanmer has a good spread of accommodation but as a popular weekend getaway it's worth booking ahead year-round. Aside from the campsite, *Hanmer Backpackers* and *Jack in the Green* offer camping.

★**Cheltenham House** 13 Cheltenham St ☎ 03 315 7545, ⓦ cheltenham.co.nz. The best B&B in town, with four large, gracious rooms in a 1930s house with a billiards room, plus two cottages in the lovingly tended garden. Evening drinks, spa and wi-fi are all included; an excellent breakfast is served in your room. They also have two modern self-contained four-bedroom villas. B&B doubles $235, villas $320

Greenacres 84 Conical Hill Rd ☎ 0800 822262, ⓦ greenacresmotel.co.nz. There's a slightly retro quality to this quiet motel at the foot of Conical Hill. One- and two-bedroom chalets come ranged around a central lawn, there's a hot tub ($4/person) and free wi-fi throughout. $135

Hanmer Backpackers 41 Conical Hill Rd ☎ 03 315 7196, ⓦ hanmerbackpackers.co.nz. Heart-warmingly cosy A-frame chalet-style hostel bang in town with a snug,

book-filled, TV-free lounge, hot water bottles, spotless facilities, sociable BBQ patio and lots of free treats such as plunger coffee. It's also possible to camp on a tiny patch of lawn. Dorms $28, doubles $64

★**Jack in the Green** 3 Devon St ☎ 03 315 5111, ⓦ jackinthegreen.co.nz. Relaxed and tastefully decorated BBH hostel, with spacious rooms in a couple of converted houses and chalets a 10min walk from the centre, plus a large garden with a giant swing-sofa. There's plenty of space for tents and campervan parking, and bunk-free dorms. Dorms $29, doubles $70

Rippinvale Retreat 68 Rippingale Rd ☎ 0800 373098, ⓦ hanmersprings.net.nz. Upmarket B&B on the edge of town with just two suites, both beautifully furnished and each with private courtyard and fresh flowers. Breakfast, a gourmet affair with largely home-grown and organic ingredients, is served in your room

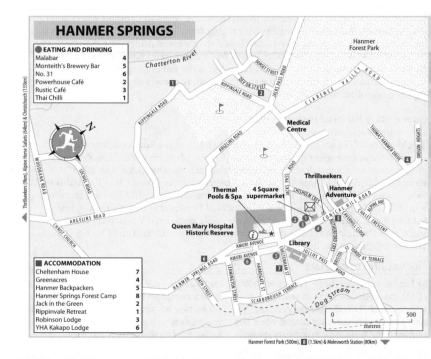

HANMER SPRINGS

● EATING AND DRINKING	
Malabar	4
Monteith's Brewery Bar	5
No. 31	6
Powerhouse Café	2
Rustic Café	3
Thai Chilli	1

■ ACCOMMODATION	
Cheltenham House	7
Greenacres	4
Hanmer Backpackers	5
Hanmer Springs Forest Camp	8
Jack in the Green	2
Rippinvale Retreat	1
Robinson Lodge	3
YHA Kakapo Lodge	6

HANMER SPRINGS OUTDOOR ACTIVITIES

Hanmer has plenty to keep you entertained, most conveniently in the Hanmer Forest Park, where hiking and biking trails wind through groves of black pine, Douglas fir and assorted deciduous trees. Further afield there's a local ski area, plenty of high octane activities on offer at Thrillseekers on SH7, and great horse-trekking outside Hawarden.

SKIING

Tiny **Hanmer Springs Ski Area** lies off Clarence Valley Rd, 17km north of town, and is generally open mid-July to Sept (☎027 434 1806, ⊚skihanmer.co.nz). There's just one rope tow and New Zealand's longest Poma-style lift, with one beginner run, six intermediate and five advanced runs. The access road is notoriously dicey, so take the **shuttle bus** ($40 return) operated by Hanmer Adventure (see below), where you can also rent ski gear; snow chains are essential if you fancy driving yourself. On the mountain, *Robinson Lodge* (see below) has gear rentals and basic accommodation.

HIKING

Conical Hill (2km return; 1hr; 150m ascent). A short, steep and rewarding walk along a switch-backed forest trail to a hilltop pavilion with great views over Hanmer and the surrounding hills.
Waterfall Track (2.5km return; 2hr 30min; 400m ascent). An attractive walk through beech forest that climbs fairly steeply to the 41m-high Dog Stream Waterfall. The path starts from a car park well inside the Forest Park; follow Jollie's Pass Road out of town, after 2km turn left onto McIntyre Road, then follow the road to its end.

BIKING

Hanmer Adventure 20 Conical Hill Rd ☎0800 368 7386, ⊚hanmeradventure.co.nz. Rents out bikes ($60/day) to explore the forest's gravel roads and twisting singletrack. Alternatively, the centre can transport you to the top of Jacks Pass for their self-guided "Twin Passes" ride, a largely downhill trail with a small ascent over Jollies Pass ($125, including a hot pools pass).

BUNGY JUMPING, RAFTING AND JETBOATING

Thrillseekers Near the SH7 junction, 9km south of town and 38 Conical Hill Road ☎03 315 7046, ⊚thrillseekers.co.nz. The Waiau Ferry Bridge is a base for all manner of activities including scenic two-hour rafting trips along the Grade II Waiau River (70–90min rafting, with a jetboat ride back to base; $149), jetboat rides through the steep-sided Waiau River Gorge (30min; $115), bungy jumps ($169 including T-shirt) from a 35m platform on the Waiau Ferry Bridge, and quad biking (2hr; $149), with combo packages available. Book online or visit their office in Hanmer (daily 9am–5pm).

HORSERIDING

Alpine Horse Safaris Hawarden, 65km south of Hanmer ☎03 314 4293, ⊚alpinehorse.co.nz. Short rides are available (2hr for $80, half-day for $120) but this is really a place for serious 3–12-day cross-country trips (from $1090) across high country stations and even down to Tekapo, staying in musterers' huts and eating around camp fires. Check online for schedules.

and there's a spa pool and outdoor fireplace in the grounds. $355
Robinson Lodge Hanmer Springs Ski Area ⊚ski hanmer.co.nz. In season, ski-field visitors can sleep in the simple dorm accommodation. Bring all your food and bedding with you – there's cooking facilities on site. $30
YHA Kakapo Lodge 14 Amuri Ave ☎03 315 7472, ⊚kakapolodge.co.nz. Large, sun-filled associate YHA hostel with modern, roomy dorms and a lovely communal balcony; there's a log-burning stove and a tuck shop in the lobby. Motel units also available ($100). Dorms $28, doubles $66

CAMPING

Hanmer Springs Forest Camp 243 Jollies Pass Rd, 2km east of town ☎03 315 7202, ⊚hanmerforestcamp .co.nz. A community campsite backing onto the Hanmer Forest Reserve with no powered sites, but plenty of well-maintained budget cabins, plus space for tents. Camping $12, cabins $40

EATING AND DRINKING

Malabar 5 Conical Hill Rd ☎ 03 315 7745, ⓦ malabar .co.nz. Modern fusion restaurant with an adventurous menu featuring modern twists on dishes from Asia and the subcontinent such as Canterbury *lamb rogan josh* ($36) and five-spice pork belly ($34). Sun–Fri 5.30–9.30pm, Sat noon–10pm.

Monteith's Brewery Bar 47 Amuri Ave ☎ 03 315 5133, ⓦ mbbh.co.nz. The town's liveliest bar, all timber and river stones fireplaces, with sport on TV and Monteith's on tap, serving reliable meals like pork chops and mash ($27) and pumpkin gnocchi with blue cheese sauce ($24). Daily 9am–10pm or later.

★ **No. 31** 31 Amuri Ave ☎ 03 315 7031. With the kitchen producing beautifully presented, modern Kiwi dishes, and local wines taking pride of place on the wine list, this is fine-dining, Hanmer Springs-style. Mains include Angus beef fillet with black garlic and mushroom glaze ($38), and there are vegetarian options available. Daily dinner only.

★ **Powerhouse Café** 8 Jacks Pass Rd ☎ 03 315 5252. Funky modern café in a 1926 building that once housed a diesel generator, serving Hanmer's best coffee, mouth-watering and often gluten-free counter food, decadent versions of brunch classics including French toast and kedgeree ($16–19), and filling lunches such as pizza verde and *coq au vin* (both $22). Daily 7.30am–3pm.

Rustic Café 8 Conical Hill Rd ☎ 03 315 7274. Great little tapas restaurant with small plates of tasty treats; pan-fried chorizo with roasted capsicum, prawns in coconut panko and halloumi bruschetta ($10–15 each) all feature. Thurs & Fri 9.30am–9.30pm, Sat & Sun 8am–10pm.

Thai Chilli 12a Conical Hill Rd ☎ 03 315 5188. Budget Thai in quantities large enough to take away for later. Mains $18–23, and $12 lunch specials such as Penang curry and jasmine rice. No licence or BYO. Tues–Sun 11am–2.30pm & 4.30–9.30pm.

Lewis Pass

Some 65km to the west of the Hanmer Springs turn-off, SH7 continues its climb towards the 907m-high **Lewis Pass**, the low-yielding grassland studded with broom (blazing yellow each spring), spiky matagouri, manuka and kanuka giving way to red and silver beech forest. To explore the area on foot, pick up DOC's *Lake Sumner and Lewis Pass* leaflet from the Hanmer Springs i-SITE, which outlines a dozen or so day- and multi-day **walks**.

Maruia Springs

SH7, 75km west of Hanmer Springs • Daily 8am–7.30pm • Pools $22; private baths $30/45min; towel rental $6 • ☎ 03 523 8840, ⓦ maruiasprings.co.nz

West of Lewis Pass it's a further 8km to **Maruia Springs**, a blissful riverside spa with Japanese-style men's and women's bathhouses, private spas and natural-rock outdoor **hot pools**, whose steaming mineral-enriched waters range from black to milky white.

ACCOMMODATION   LEWIS PASS

Maruia Springs Resort ☎ 03 523 8840, ⓦ maruiasprings.co.nz. Simple but well-equipped rooms opening to shared or private balconies overlooking the garden and mountains, the hotel's electricity generated by the nearby Maruia River. Access to the springs is included and the restaurant serves good Japanese and European dishes (breakfast $11–19; mains $20–30). **$159**

Porter's Pass and the Craigieburn Range

Both the *TranzAlpine* train and the SH73 (promoted as the Great Alpine Highway) from Christchurch to Arthur's Pass and the West Coast thread across the fertile Canterbury Plains beside the braided Waimakariri River before climbing up through the Torlesse Range and dropping into a beautiful upland region hemmed in by bare-topped hills. The road skirts the otherworldly boulders of **Kura Tawhiti** (Castle Hill Conservation Area) and passes the **Cave Stream Scenic Reserve**, which will attract climbers and spelunkers respectively, while side roads wind up to a series of club-run ski-fields.

Springfield

From Christchurch the route is virtually flat for 65km west to **SPRINGFIELD**, a lowland village that's the main base for four nearby ski-fields (see box below), and high-speed boat trips in the clear waters of the narrow **Waimakariri River**.

Rewi Alley Memorial Park

SH73 • Open access • Free

A vaguely Chinese-style garden **memorial** beside SH73 remembers Springfield's most famous son, writer, social reformer and unofficial ambassador for China, **Rewi Alley** (1897–1987). He spent sixty years in China where he is much revered for starting the Gung Ho ("working together") cooperative movement. His life story is told in a small pavilion.

10

INFORMATION AND ACTIVITIES   SPRINGFIELD

Tourist information The *Station 73 Café* (see p.562) acts as an ad hoc information centre.

Rubicon Valley Horse Treks ☎03 318 8886, ⓦrubiconvalley.co.nz. Offers some of the best-value

---

SKI-FIELDS ALONG THE ARTHUR'S PASS ROAD

The five ski-fields listed below (from east to west along SH73) are easily accessible from the highway, four of them in the Craigieburn Range and one, Temple Basin, around 50km further west, beyond Arthur's Pass. They predominantly offer traditional, inexpensive, Kiwi ski-club-style winter sports with spectacular views, reliable snow and virtually no queues. There are no gondolas or cable cars: T-bars, platter lifts and "nutcracker" rope tows are the order of the day. Most have **equipment rental** and some offer on-field **accommodation**. The season generally runs from July to September, although October is often good; for snow conditions check ⓦsnow.co.nz.

TICKETS, PASSES AND TRANSPORT

All fields offer their own season tickets, though many visitors opt for the multi-mountain Chill11 Pass ($315 for 5 days; ⓦchillout.co.nz), which covers all the mountains below plus Hanmer Springs and five other fields. *Smylies* (see p.562) in Springfield runs **shuttles** to Porters and other fields; check their website for prices.

THE SKI-FIELDS

Broken River 110km from Christchurch, off SH73 at the end of a 6km access road ☎03 318 8713, ⓦbrokenriver.co.nz. An excellent intermediate field with good powder until late in the season, occasional night skiing and fine boarding. A free inclinator (passenger-carrying goods lift) runs from the car park to the ticket office. It's possible to ski between Broken River and Craigieburn Valley (experienced skiers only). Lift passes $75, night pass $40.

Craigieburn Valley 120km out of Christchurch and another 6km up a side road ☎03 318 8711, ⓦcraigieburn.co.nz. This thrill-seeking field has three rope tows accessing the mostly steep runs, including the 600m vertical descent into Middle Basin. No ski hire. Lift passes $72.

Mount Cheeseman 100km from Christchurch along SH73 ☎03 344 3247, ⓦmtcheeseman.co.nz. Well-appointed family-oriented field with good facilities, ski-in ski-out accommodation and a friendly atmosphere, plus an assortment of advanced

and off-piste runs for those with greater experience. Lift passes $79.

Porters 90km west of Christchurch, off SH73 via a 6km access road ☎03 318 4002, ⓦskiporters.co.nz. The region's main commercial field with a wide range of runs, easy access and excellent learners' packages; a shiny new chairlift was being installed at the time of writing. Snow chains are occasionally required for the access road, though a free shuttle (bookings essential) runs from the chain-fitting area to the lifts. Lift pass $85.

Temple Basin SH73, 8km west of Arthur's Pass Village ☎03 377 7788, ⓦtemplebasin.co.nz. Renowned among snowboarders for its 430m drop and great off-piste for those who know their stuff. Floodlit for night skiing, it offers a variety of runs spread across four separate basins and basic, on-field accommodation. From the car park it's an hour's walk up to the ski-field, though there's a goods lift for your gear. Lift passes $68.

horse trekking around, from a gentle farm trek (1hr; $55) to a mountain ride following a musterers' trail (minimum 2 people; 4hr 30min; $285). Heritage-minded visitors can opt for a stagecoach ride and cream tea combo ($50). Pick-ups in Springfield.

Waimak Alpine Jet Rubicon Rd ☎0800 263626, ⓦalpinejet.co.nz. Shallow braided sections, the narrow Waimakariri Gorge, 360-degree spins and a good deal of local lore make these jetboat trips excellent value for money. The route partly follows the *TranzAlpine* train line. Advance bookings essential. The Canyon Safari (1hr; $120) is the one to go for, but the Adventure Tour (30min; $90) covers the essentials.

ACCOMMODATION AND EATING

Kowai Pass Reserve Campground Domain Rd ☎03 818 4887. Basic and peaceful with powered and standard sites in a sheltered spot with coin-operated showers. Sign in with the caretaker signposted on the opposite side of the road. $7

★**Smylies** SH73 ☎03 318 4740, ⓦsmylies.co.nz. Welcoming Japanese/Kiwi-run associate YHA and motel with free Japanese baths (daily in winter, on request in summer), a wood-fire-warmed lounge and comfy but creaky rooms. Delicious Japanese- or Kiwi-style evening meals ($20) and continental or cooked breakfasts ($10–15), plus ski-hire, winter shuttle services (see box, p.561), and bouldering mat rental are also available. Dorms $35, doubles $80

★**Station 73 Café** King St, signposted 500m off SH73 ☎03 318 4000. A slice of ginger crunch and a cuppa seems just about right in this simple but well-kept café in the Springfield train station with mountain views and walls lined with railway ephemera. They also serve toasted sandwiches, gourmet pies and good espresso. Daily 8.30am–3pm, later in summer.

Yello Shack Café SH73 ☎03 318 4880. This cheery café serves wood-fired pizzas on weekend evenings; the rest of the time the menu is focussed on tasty cabinet food and home-made pies, washed down with good coffee (though it's fully licensed too). Daily 8am–8pm.

Porter's Pass

Around 10km west of Springfield, the highway rises dramatically towards the Torlesse Range and neatly bisects the 210-square-kilometre **Korowai/Torlesse Tussocklands Park**, New Zealand's first reserve specifically protecting the eastern South Island's unique and disappearing tussock grasslands. The road peaks at **Porter's Pass**, which at 939m is marginally higher than Arthur's Pass, 65km to the northwest.

Kura Tawhiti (Castle Hill Conservation Area)

SH73 • Open access • Free

Over Porter's Pass, the SH73 drops down into the Castle Hill basin, hemmed in by the ski-field-draped Craigieburn Range. The grassy lower slopes are peppered by clusters of grey limestone outcrops up to 30m high that have become a magnet for **world-class bouldering** and a regular stop for top international rock-climbers.

Boulderers make for scattered locales such as **Flock Hill** (where large portions of *The Lion, the Witch and the Wardrobe* were filmed), Spittle Hill and Quantum Field, but everyone else stops at **Kura Tawhiti**, often known as **Castle Hill** for its resemblance to a ruined fort. This is a place of spiritual significance to Maori – certain boulders are off limits – and home to Castle Hill buttercups and other rare flora; an area has been cordoned off for the plants' protection. From a parking area, a number of easy paths wind among the rocks and tussock-covered hills. Allow an hour or bring a picnic and stay for the afternoon.

Cave Stream Scenic Reserve

SH73, 6km north of Kura Tawhiti • Open access • Free

Cave Stream Scenic Reserve nestles among limestone outcrops with views of the Craigieburn and Torlesse ranges and offers a rare opportunity for an unguided **walk/wade** exploration of a **limestone cave**. Cave art, signs of seasonal camps and the discovery of an ancient wooden-framed flax backpack and other artefacts over 500 years old indicate that Maori visited the area extensively. Today the cave contains bones and provides a home for large but harmless **cave harvestman** spiders – only found here and in one other cave on South Island.

The cave "walk"

The 560m cave traverse takes about an hour: take a companion, dress warmly, be sure to carry at least one good torch each and have something dry to change into afterwards. After entering at the downstream end, you wade through a deep pool. If the water is above waist-high, fast-flowing, foaming or discoloured, do not attempt the walk. As you work your way upstream there are only two major obstacles apart from the dark and cold; a 1.5m rockfall about halfway through that funnels the waterflow and can be quite hard to climb, and a 3m waterfall at the very end. The latter (within sight of the cave exit) is negotiated by climbing a ladder of iron rungs embedded in the rock and crawling along a short, narrow ledge while holding onto an anchored chain.

10

ACCOMMODATION AND EATING	CAVE STREAM SCENIC RESERVE

Craigieburn Shelter campsite SH73, 5km north of Cave Stream Scenic Reserve. A small and pretty DOC site beside a stream with long-drop toilets, tank water (which you'll have to treat), a day-use shelter and a healthy population of sandflies. $6

Flock Hill Lodge SH73, 10km north of Cave Stream Scenic Reserve ☎ 03 318 8196, ⓦ flockhill.co.nz. Accommodation on a high-country sheep station that's handy if you're

bouldering, skiing or tramping hereabouts, set in a gorgeous spot that's popular for weddings. Backpacker bunkrooms sleep four (linen $10 extra) with a separate kitchen/dining room and coin-op internet, plus tent sites, double rooms and attractive wood-panelled self-contained cottages ($155). All options are self-catering; there's also a restaurant serving delicious, upmarket dishes with the menu changing seasonally (mains $26–42). Dorms $31, doubles $90

Craigieburn Forest Park

SH73, 5km north of Cave Stream Scenic Reserve • Open access • Free

The Broken River ski-field road also leads to *Craigieburn Shelter* (see above) and the **Craigieburn Forest Park**. The park is dominated by alpine scrub, tussock grasslands and dense, moss-covered mountain beech forest sprinkled with scarlet mistletoe flowers from December to February. A variety of native birds squawk through the forest, including bellbird, tiny rifleman, silvereye and kea, and, between October and February, long-tailed and shining cuckoos join the throng.

CRAIGIEBURN HIKES

DOC's *Craigieburn Forest Park Day Walks* leaflet, available from the local visitor centres, details half a dozen walks in the park. Some are short and simple while others – particularly those into the neighbouring ski-fields – are for more experienced trampers.

Bealey Spur (14km return; 4–6hr; 500m ascent). When it is too wet to hike up Avalanche Peak in Arthur's Pass, it is often dry on Bealey Spur, a long steady ridge hike through mountain beech forest that rewards with fabulous views of the Waimakariri Basin. It ends at an old sheep musterers' hut (6 bunks; free) set amid subalpine scrub and tussock grasslands. The track starts at the end of Cloudesley Rd, near *Bealey Hotel*, 12km south of Arthur's Pass Village.

Cass–Lagoon Saddle Track (33km; 2 days; 1300m ascent). Rugged hikers might fancy this lovely mountain loop with an overnight

stop at *Hamilton Hut* (20 bunks; $15) almost exactly halfway. It starts at the eastern end of Cass Rd bridge and finishes beside SH73, 11km further west: infrequent buses can be used to complete the loop. DOC publish a handy leaflet (RG12), downloadable from ⓦ doc.govt .nz or available at the Arthur's Pass DOC office.

Lyndon Saddle (6km; 3–4hr; 500m ascent). A fun loop from *Craigieburn Shelter* through regenerating mountain beech to the superb Helicopter Hill (1262m) viewpoint. Continue along glacial terraces to the Broken River ski-field road then follow Cave Stream back to the start.

Arthur's Pass National Park

The most dramatic of the three Southern Alps crossings links Christchurch with Greymouth, via **Arthur's Pass**, traversed by a scenic railway and the equally breathtaking SH73.

The pass is surrounded by the 950-square-kilometre **Arthur's Pass National Park**, a remarkable alpine landscape with some superb easy walks and tough tramps. The park centres on diminutive **Arthur's Pass Village**, nestled along SH73 at 737m above sea level in a steep-sided, forest-covered U-shaped valley. Because the park spans the transition zone between the soggy West Coast and the much drier east, Otira, just west of the pass, gets around 6m of rain a year, while Bealey, 10km to the east, gets only 2m. Consequently, **Arthur's Pass Village** is often shrouded in mist, providing a moody contrast with the rich vegetation of the slopes above. The village offers a slim range of lodging and even more limited eating; stock up beforehand if you're planning to spend time in the area. Nights are often chilly and snow occasionally blocks the pass.

Arthur's Pass

Arthur's Pass itself is 4km west of the village and, at 920m, almost 200m higher. It's marked by an obelisk dedicated to the civil engineer **Arthur Dudley Dobson**, who heard about the route from local Maori, and surveyed it in 1864. By 1886 horse-drawn coaches were using it to access the Westland goldfields. Arthur's Pass Village sprang up in the early 1900s to provide shelter for tunnel diggers and railway workers. The rail line's completion in 1923 coincided with the boom in alpine tourism worldwide, and the village ticks by on summer hikers, winter skiers and the daily *TranzAlpine* train visits. On clear days there are great views here and from the nearby Dobson Nature Walk (see box, p.566).

Immediately west of the pass, the road drops away dramatically across the **Otira Viaduct**, a huge concrete gash completed in 1999 to span the tumbling river below. Side streams carry so much water that one is diverted over the roadway in a kind of artificial waterfall. A small lookout provides the best view.

ARRIVAL AND DEPARTURE | ARTHUR'S PASS

By train The *TranzAlpine* (see box, p.524) stops just south of the village centre; reach the platforms through the underpass opposite the DOC offices.

Destinations Christchurch (1 daily; 2hr 30min); Greymouth (1 daily; 2hr).

By bus West Coast Shuttle (☎03 768 0028,

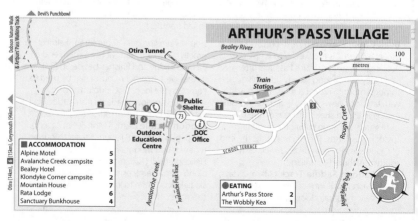

ARTHUR'S PASS VILLAGE

0 — 100 metres

Devil's Punchbowl

Dobson Nature Walk & Arthur's Pass Walking Track

Otira Tunnel

Bealey River

Train Station

Public Shelter

Subway

Otira (14km), ⑥ (15km); Greymouth (96km)

Outdoor Education Centre

DOC Office

SCHOOL TERRACE

Avalanche Creek

Avalanche Peak Track

Rough Creek

Mount Bealey Track

■ **ACCOMMODATION**

Alpine Motel	5
Avalanche Creek campsite	3
Bealey Hotel	1
Klondyke Corner campsite	2
Mountain House	7
Rata Lodge	6
Sanctuary Bunkhouse	4

● **EATING**

Arthur's Pass Store	2
The Wobbly Kea	1

KEA: NEW ZEALAND'S ALPINE TRICKSTER

One of the most enduring memories of a visit to Arthur's Pass and other alpine areas of the South Island is the sight of a bright green **kea** mischievously getting its beak into something, or simply posing for the camera. With their lolloping sideways gait and inexhaustible curiosity, the world's only alpine parrots are endearing; at backcountry huts you might find kea sliding down the corrugated-iron roofing or pulling at the nails holding the roof on. Be careful where you leave your hiking boots – trampers have been known to wake up to a pile of leather strips and shredded laces.

With these playful scavenging tendencies it's hardly surprising kea traditionally got the blame for attacking sheep, and for many years the birds were routinely shot by farmers. Recent research seems to indicate kea only attack already-weakened sheep, and shooting has long since stopped, as the birds are now fully protected.

These days, however, their greatest threat is human food. These kleptomaniacs can be persistent – you'll hear the ruffle of feathers, see the flash of red beneath their wings and they'll be tearing at your lunch just out of reach. But **feeding** them is forbidden as it reduces their ability to forage for themselves in winter when the summertime walkers have left town, and draws them towards the road where many are run over. As a result, the kea population is estimated to be as low as five thousand birds. For more information, visit ⓦ keaconservation.co.nz.

10

ⓦ westcoastshuttle.co.nz) run a daily service from Greymouth to Christchurch and back, stopping in Arthur's Pass mid-morning on the eastbound journey, mid-afternoon on the westbound. Atomic Shuttles (ⓞ 03 349 0697, ⓦ atomictravel.co.nz) does the same journey in reverse, setting out from Christchurch. Both companies stop outside the Arthur's Pass Store.

Destinations Christchurch (2 daily; 2hr 30min); Greymouth (2 daily; 1hr 15min).

INFORMATION

DOC office SH73 (daily: Nov–April 8am–5pm; May–Oct 8.30am–4.30pm; ⓞ 03 318 9211, ⓦ arthurspass.com). Excellent information centre with extensive displays on wildlife, plants, geology and local history; you can watch a video about the trail blazed by the stagecoaches and the railway on request ($2). The latest weather report is posted outside.

Services There is a single ATM in the Arthur's Pass Store which accepts most major cards; the store also operates the only petrol pump between Springfield and the West Coast.

ACCOMMODATION

Good-value accommodation is strung out along the main road; book ahead in high season (Dec–March).

Alpine Motel 52 Main Rd, SH73 ⓞ 0800 900401 or ⓞ 03 318 9233, ⓦ www.apam.co.nz. A short walk south of the village these six aged but well-kept chalet-style motel units come with kitchen, DVD players and electric blankets. There are discounts in low season and wi-fi is free. $125

Bealey Hotel SH73, 10km southeast of Arthur's Pass Village ⓞ 03 318 9277, ⓦ bealeyhotel.co.nz. High on a knoll, this historic hotel has motel-style rooms with great views of the upper reaches of the Waimakariri River. The restaurant/bar is filled with memorabilia of the hotel's early role as a stop-off point for Cobb & Co stagecoaches and of claimed moa sightings hereabouts in recent decades (hence the life-size moa sculptures that dot the grounds). Lodge rooms $80, motel units $155

★**Mountain House** Main Rd ⓞ 03 318 9258,

ⓦ trampers.co.nz. This BBH and associate YHA hostel has the widest range of beds in the village. The neat main hostel is supplemented by a pair of four-bedroom self-contained 1920s railway workers' cottages ($340) and, in summer (normally Dec–March), the owner opens the "Historic Lodge", an original 1950s YHA with bags of old-school character. More upmarket tastes are catered to by two comfortable motel units with kitchenettes, queen beds and satellite TV ($155). Powered sites are also available ($22). Dorms $29, doubles $86

Rata Lodge SH73, Otira, 15km north of Arthur's Pass Village ⓞ 03 738 2822, ⓦ rata-lodge.co.nz. Spacious and chilled forest-girt BBH hostel on the western edge of the national park. There's a four-bunk dorm, two en-suite doubles with TV, and a little bush walk with glowworms. Bring food to self-cater. Dorms $32, doubles $80

10

WALKS AND TRAMPS AROUND ARTHUR'S PASS

Apart from a few easy walks around Arthur's Pass Village, the national park is substantially more rugged than most in New Zealand, making it suitable only for moderately to highly experienced trampers.

SAFETY, INFORMATION AND EQUIPMENT

All multiday walks involve some route finding (bring a compass) and unbridged river crossings; make adequate preparations (see Basics, p.50), and record your intentions through ⓦadventures mart.org.nz. The free *Tramping in Arthur's Pass* National Park leaflet assigns Route Guide numbers (RG) to the major tramps, covered on specific leaflets downloadable from ⓦdoc.govt.nz. You'll also need 1:50,000 topographic maps, available for sale ($9 each) or rent ($2.50 plus $20 deposit for 1–3 days) at the DOC office, which also sells gas canisters, and offers gear storage ($1/item/day).

ACCESS AND ACCOMMODATION

West Coast Shuttles and Atomic (for contacts see p.565) can arrange to drop-off or pick-up from trailheads, if given advance notice. Overnight hikes involve camping or staying in **DOC huts** that can't be booked. Obtain hut tickets from the DOC office in Arthur's Pass or use a Backcountry Hut Pass.

SHORT WALKS

Devil's Punchbowl (2km return; 1hr; 100m ascent). The village's most popular short walk, following an all-weather climb and descent to the base of a 131m waterfall, crossing two footbridges and zigzagging up steps.

Dobson Nature Walk (1km return; 30min). Easy graded walk at the crest of Arthur's Pass with panels explaining subalpine herbs, tussock and shrubs, best seen Nov–Feb when they're in bloom. The nature walk can be reached on foot along the Arthur's Pass Walking Track (see below).

Arthur's Pass Walking Track (6.8km return; 3hr; 200m ascent). A lively bushwalk that links the village to the Dobson Nature Walk and Arthur's Pass. The pretty path winds through beech forest, passing Bridal Veil Falls and Jack's Hut, a green corrugated-iron cabin once used by roading crews during the coaching days, en route.

DAY-WALKS AND MULTI-DAY TRAMPS

Avalanche Peak Track (5km return; 6–8hr; 1100m ascent). Strenuous day-hike that offers wonderful views of the surrounding mountains. Parts of the route are exposed; it should only be attempted by well-equipped, experienced trampers in reasonable weather. The best way is going up the spectacular Avalanche Peak Track and making a circuit by returning on the Scotts Track.

Casey Saddle to Binser Saddle (RG10: 40km; 2 days; 400m ascent). Moderate loop with great views as you cross easy saddles on well-defined tracks through open beech forest, staying overnight in Casey Hut (16 bunks; $15).

Mingha–Deception (RG6: 25km; 2 days; 400m ascent, 750m descent). A great (but demanding) overnighter that traces the route used for the mountain-run stage of the arduous Coast to Coast race (see p.665). The Mingha Valley to Goat Pass section is marked, but the trail down the Deception Valley is unmarked and involves 20–30 river crossings, so watch the water levels. Stay at either the Goat Pass Hut (20 bunks; $5) or the Upper Deception Hut (6 bunks; free) and ponder how mad you'd have to be to run the route competitively.

Sanctuary Bunkhouse 126 Main Rd, SH73 ☎03 942 2230, ⓦthesanctuary.co.nz. Unstaffed dorm-style bunk accommodation with just eight dorm beds and a tiny double. There are adequate kitchen facilities and a day-room, patchwork quilts on the beds and a home-made glass-roofed bathroom for stargazers. Coin-operated hot showers, 24hr internet and laundry facilities are open to the public; payment for everything is via honesty box. Dorms $25, double $50

CAMPING

Avalanche Creek campsite Main Rd. DOC site that's not much more than a patch of grass and a gravel parking lot for campervans directly opposite the DOC office. There's potable water, toilets and a day-use shelter. $6

Klondyke Corner campsite SH73 8km southeast of the village. Basic, grassy DOC site set between the highway and the river with great views, a long-drop toilet and river water (which should be treated). $6

EATING AND DRINKING

Arthur's Pass Store Main Rd ☎ 03 318 9235. The best place to fuel up for a hike or replenish afterwards. It serves breakfasts, pies, sandwiches and excellent coffee, along with limited groceries, a bottle store, ATM and internet access ($2/30min). Daily 8am–5pm, later in summer.

The Wobbly Kea Main Rd ☎ 03 318 9101, ⓦ wobblykea.co.nz. The village linchpin for steaming hot chocolate and coffee, imaginative lunches, and hearty dinners; the $32 pizzas are big enough for two modest appetites. Also doubles as a bar hosting occasional live gigs. Mon–Thurs & Sun 8am–8pm, Fri & Sat 8am–9pm.

10

The South Canterbury foothills

The **South Canterbury foothills** mark the transition from the flat Canterbury Plains to the rugged and spectacular Southern Alps. The main **route** through the area is SH72, dubbed the "Inland Scenic Route" and the region is primarily known for the winter resort town of **Methven**, which serves the ski slopes of **Mount Hutt**. In summer, an array of activities includes skydiving, jetboating and some wonderful **walking** around Mount Somers.

Methven

A hundred kilometres west of Christchurch, **METHVEN** is Canterbury's winter-sports capital and the accommodation and refuelling centre for the busy **Mount Hutt** ski-field during the June to October **ski season**. Outside those months it can be pretty quiet, though summer visitors often base themselves here to explore **Rakaia Gorge** and **Washpen Falls** to the north, and **Mount Somers** to the south. It's not a big place but the small centre has banks, post office, supermarkets and sports supplies.

NZ Alpine & Agriculture Encounter

Methven Heritage Centre, 160 Main St · Daily 9am–5pm · $12.50 · ☎ 03 302 9666

Methven celebrates its position at the intersection of plains and mountains in this interactive museum focussing on winter sports and agriculture. A full-size combine harvester emphasizes the historic importance of arable farming while the cross-section of a model cow celebrates the big bucks that dairying is now bringing in.

A collection of historic skis and some great old film footage herald a section on the development of the Mount Hutt ski-field in the 1970s, including a model of the hut used by Willi Huber to winter on the mountain while assessing its skiing potential – two mice kept him company through the lonely snowy months.

ACTIVITIES AROUND METHVEN

Aoraki Balloon Safaris ☎ 0800 256837, ⓦ nzballooning.com. Hot-air balloon rides above the patchwork quilt of the Canterbury Plains and the magnificent Southern Alps – particularly scenic in winter. The trips start shortly after sunrise (4hr with 1hr flight time; $385) and include bubbly and breakfast back on land.
Braided Rivers Fishing Guides ☎ 022 323 3966, ⓦ salmonfishingguide.co.nz. Professional fishing guide, Ben Haywood, leads salmon and trout fishing trips (from $500, all-inclusive) on the Rakaia and Waimakariri rivers.

Discovery Jet ☎ 0800 538 2628, ⓦ discoveryjet .co.nz. Great-value, high-octane jetboating to the top of the Rakaia Gorge. Go for the full 45min trip ($99), or opt for a 15min spin ($45) with a drop-off at the Rakaia Gorge Walkway and walk back – take a picnic to make an afternoon of it.
Skydiving Kiwis Ashburton Airport, Seafield Road, Ashburton, 35km south of Methven ☎ 0800 359549, ⓦ skydivingkiwis.com. Very professional outfit with an excellent safety record, offering magical mountain views from tandem jumps (from $235).

10

ARRIVAL AND INFORMATION

By bus Methven Travel (☎0800 684888, ✆methventravel .co.nz) runs buses from Christchurch (four weekly in summer; four daily in ski season; 90min; $42 one way) stopping centrally on Main St. Methven Travel and Snowman Shuttles (☎0800 766962, ✆snowmanshuttles .co.nz) serve the ski-field (see p.570).

i-SITE Methven Heritage Centre, 160 Main St (Oct–May Mon–Fri 9am–5pm, Sat & Sun 10am–3pm; June–Oct daily 9am–5pm; ☎03 302 8955, ✆amazingspace.co.nz). Visit for information, internet access ($2/20min) and wi-fi ($5/

hr), plus a "snow desk" run by Mt Hutt staff in ski season.

Ski and bike rental Alpine Sports, 87 Main St (May–Oct daily 7.30am–7pm; ☎03 302 8084, ✆alpinesports .co.nz), rents and sells skis and other equipment. Big Al's, at the corner of Forest Drive and Main St (Nov–May Tues–Fri 9am–1pm & 3–5.30pm, Sat 9am–1pm; June–Oct daily 7.30am–7.30pm; ☎03 302 8003, ✆bigals.co.nz), rents skis, boards and bikes (hardtail $45/day; full suspension $59/day), with information on an easy town loop and the Mount Hutt Bike Park.

ACCOMMODATION

Outside the June–October ski season prices drop significantly from the winter prices shown below.

Abisko Lodge & Campground 74 Main St ☎03 302 8875, ✆abisko.co.nz. Excellent, central establishment incorporating a campsite, en-suite doubles and cosy self-contained apartments ($205), complete with sauna and hot tub (fee charged). Camping/site $30, doubles $145

Big Tree Lodge 25 South Belt ☎03 302 9575, ✆bigtreelodge.co.nz. It's more expensive than the

competition, but laundry and wi-fi are free at this homely snowboarder-run hostel. Rooms in the main house share a kitchen and bathrooms, while the pleasant three-bed cottage is self-contained ($120). Dorms $40, doubles $79

Central Luxury Apartments 6 Methven Chertsey Rd ☎03 302 8829, ✆centralapartmentsmethven.co.nz.

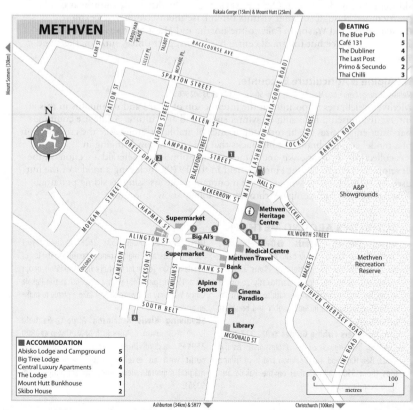

Rakaia Gorge (15km) & Mount Hutt (25km)

METHVEN

Mount Somers (30km)

N

● **EATING**

The Blue Pub	1
Café 131	5
The Dubliner	4
The Last Post	6
Primo & Secundo	2
Thai Chilli	3

FARQUHAR PLACE
CARR ST
TALBOT PL
LILLEY PL
RACECOURSE AVE
MORAN PL
SPAXTON STREET
PATTON ST
ALFORD STREET
ALLEN ST
FOREST DRIVE
LAMPARD STREET
BLACKFORD STREET
STREET
MCKERROW ST
MAIN ST (ASHBURTON–RAKAIA–GORGE ROAD)
HALL ST
LOCKHEAD CRES
BARKERS ROAD
MORGAN STREET
CHAPMAN ST
Supermarket
ALINGTON ST
COLOMBO PL
CAMERON ST
JACKSON ST
THE MALL
Big Al's
Supermarket
MCMILLAN ST
BANK ST
Alpine Sports
SOUTH BELT
Methven Heritage Centre
MACKIE ST
KILWORTH STREET
Medical Centre
Methven Travel
Bank
Cinema Paradiso
Library
MCDONALD ST
METHVEN CHERTSEY ROAD
LINE ROAD

A&P Showgrounds

Methven Recreation Reserve

0   100
metres

■ **ACCOMMODATION**

Abisko Lodge and Campground	5
Big Tree Lodge	6
Central Luxury Apartments	4
The Lodge	3
Mount Hutt Bunkhouse	1
Skibo House	2

Ashburton (34km) & SH77   Christchurch (100km)

These spacious and classy self-contained units come complete with laundry facilities, well-equipped kitchens and proper dining rooms. **$225**

The Lodge 1 Chertsey Rd ☎ 03 303 2000, ⓦ thelodgenz .com. Generously-sized contemporary rooms at very decent prices, some with spa baths, and a popular on-site bistro and bar (see *The Dubliner* below). **$119**

Mount Hutt Bunkhouse 8 Lampard St ☎ 03 302 8894, ⓦ mthuttbunkhouse.co.nz. Comfortable but well-worn

BBH backpackers that's spread over two adjacent houses with a large garden (including volleyball court), BBQ and log fires. Dorms **$30**, doubles **$80**

Skibo House 82 Forest Drive ☎ 03 302 9493, ⓦ skibohouse.com. Friendly B&B in a modern house where most rooms have great mountain views, though they share a bathroom. Excellent breakfasts include Bircher muesli, and eggs and bacon, and there's an outdoor hot tub. B&B **$120**, self-contained units **$140**

10

EATING, DRINKING AND ENTERTAINMENT

The Blue Pub 2 Barkers Rd ☎ 03 302 8046, ⓦ thebluepub.co.nz. Popular with the après-ski crowd, this 1918-built cobalt-painted hotel has a lively bar hosting bands and weekend DJs. The restaurant dishes up hearty meals such as lamb shoulder with potato dumplings ($33) and porterhouse steak with egg and chips ($28). Daily 11am–10pm or later.

Café 131 131 Main St ☎ 03 302 9131. Airy wood-floored Art Deco café that's perfect for people-watching over Methven's best coffee. There's an array of cakes and counter food, all-day breakfasts, filling, inexpensive lunches (BLT and fries $17) and a book exchange. Daily 7.30am–5.30pm.

The Dubliner 1 Chertsey Rd ☎ 03 303 2000 ⓦ thelodgenz.com. Bistro fare, with great pizzas (small $18; large $26) and a few warming Irish dishes, including Irish stew ($28.50), served in a cosy room with a stone fireplace and sports on TV. Daily 5.30–9.30pm or later; closed Mon outside ski season.

The Last Post 116 Main St ☎ 03 302 8259 ⓦ thelastpostrestaurant.co.nz. In a former post office with a roaring open fire, Methven's fanciest restaurant features the likes of home-made cornbread and dips

followed by poached salmon fillet ($32) or venison medallions with *kumara* ($35). You can also just drop in for a cocktail. Tues–Sun 5–10pm or later.

★**Primo & Secundo** 38 McMillan St ☎ 03 302 9060. Wonderfully quirky café in an antique/vintage clothing/ junk shop (everything is for sale), serving breakfast ($10– 16) all day, along with good coffee, delectable home-made cakes and meals including savoury crêpes and shepherd's pie. There's outside seating in the back. Daily 7am–5pm.

Thai Chilli Corner of Main Rd and Forest Drive ☎ 03 303 3038. Enjoy authentic Thai dishes to a soundtrack of old-school tunes in purple-painted surroundings. The short menu is prepared and served with care – try their *pad thai* and green curry – and nothing is over $23, but the $20 Sunday-night buffet is good value in ski season. Daily 5–9pm in ski season; closed Sun & Mon rest of year.

CINEMA

Cinema Paradiso 112 Main St ☎ 03 302 1957, ⓦ cinemaparadiso.co.nz. Wonderful bijou digital cinema, with a licensed bar and two tiny rooms showing a roster of art-house flicks and new releases.

Washpen Falls

590 Washpen Rd, near Windwhistle, 25km northeast of Methven • Self-guided walk $10 • ☎ 03 318 6813, ⓦ washpenfalls.co.nz

One of the area's lesser-known gems, the private family farm of **Washpen Falls** offers a wonderfully diverse meander through native bush and farmland. The **walking track** heads up to a point, and offers spectacular views of the Canterbury Plains. Along the way there's a canyon formed by an ancient volcano (used by Maori to trap moa), great examples of native-bush regeneration and, of course, the cascading falls. The office (a corrugated-iron shed) has leaflets outlining the track's highlights. The walk is short but steep in places; set aside 2hr and take a picnic.

Rakaia Gorge

15km north of Methven

The opaque waters of the Rakaia River spill onto the Canterbury Plains from the **Rakaia Gorge**, created by an ancient lava flow and now lined in many places with regenerating forest. **Maori history** tells how a *taniwha* (water spirit) lived nearby, hunting and eating moa; his possessions, because of his status as a spirit, were *tapu*. One wintry day, while the *taniwha* was away searching for a hot spring, a demon in the form of the northwest wind flattened his property. Once he'd righted the damage, the *taniwha* gathered boulders to block the demon's path, so narrowing the Rakaia River and forcing the demon to blow through the rocky gorge to reach the plains. The heat generated by all this effort melted the mountain snow, and the *taniwha*'s drops of perspiration became crystals in the riverbed.

Today the gorge can be explored on foot and by jetboat (see box, p.567). Downstream, the river fans out into a classic example of the braided rivers so common on the eastern side of the South Island.

10

Rakaia Gorge Walkway
10km; 4hr return

The *taniwha*'s sweaty work can be seen from the **Rakaia Gorge Walkway**, which starts from a carpark on the eastern bank of the river and winds up the wooded riverbank before emerging onto a high gorse-lined track formerly used by ferrymen. This path follows the rim of the gorge, passing hardened lava flows of rhyolite, pitchstone and andesite, and a former coalmine to the upper gorge lookout, forming a loop at its far end. The less committed can walk as far as the lower gorge lookout (3.4km, 1hr return).

ACCOMMODATION   **RAKAIA GORGE**

Rakaia Gorge campsite SH72, 15km north of Methven. Peaceful campsite high on the west bank of the Rakaia with views out across the plains. Equipped with toilets (year-round), hot showers (mid-October–April) and pedestrian access to the river. **$8.50**

Mount Hutt ski-field
25km northwest of Methven • Lift pass $95; ski/board rental $48 • ☎ 03 308 5074, ⓦ nzski.com

Mount Hutt is widely regarded as one of the best and most varied ski-fields in the land, with a vertical rise of 683m, a choice of runs for all talents and, generally, the longest season (roughly June–Oct). All this is served by triple-, quad- and six-seater chairlifts, and plenty of snowmaking. Rentals are available on the mountain, but there's no accommodation, so most people **stay** in Methven, from where there are frequent **shuttle buses** ($20 return; 45min); buy a ticket on board or from the i-SITE, from where the shuttles depart.

Mount Somers and Staveley
The 1687m **Mount Somers** rises from the flatlands above the villages of **Staveley**, 21km southwest of Methven, and **Mount Somers**, 9km further south. The mountain is encircled by the **Mount Somers Track**, which is conveniently in the rain shadow of the Southern Alps and is often above the bushline – when it's raining in Arthur's Pass and Mount Cook is clagged in, there's still a chance you'll be able to get some hiking in here. The terrain, gentle by South Island standards, incorporates patches of beech forest and open tussock pocked by outcrops of rock. Large areas of low-fertility soil subject to heavy rainfall turn to bog, and as a result you'll find bog pine, toatoa, mountain flax and maybe even the rare whio (blue duck).

If you don't fancy a long walk, just go as far as **Sharplin Falls** (about 1hr return from the Sharplin Falls car park, 3km northwest of Staveley along Flynns Road) or go riding with Staveley Horse Treks.

INFORMATION AND ACTIVITIES   **MOUNT SOMERS AND STAVELEY**

Information The stores in Staveley and Mount Somers have good local information, or check out ⓦ mtsomers .co.nz.

Staveley Horse Treks 191 Flynns Rd, 2km from Staveley towards Sharplin Falls ☎ 03 303 0809 ⓔ brucegray@clear.net.nz. Runs some of the South Island's cheapest horse treks across Mt Somers' flanks (from $40/hr; bookings useful but not essential).

MOUNT SOMERS TRACK

The strenuous but exhilarating Mount Somers Track (25km loop; 2–3 days; 1000m ascent) makes a subalpine loop round the mountain, passing abandoned coal mines, volcanic formations and a deep river canyon.

The **entire loop** is best tackled anticlockwise from Staveley. However, roads meet the loop in the west at Woolshed Creek (accessed from Mount Somers) and in the east at Sharplin Falls car park (accessed from Staveley), so if you don't fancy the whole thing you can **walk either half** and get your vehicle shuttled.

TICKETS AND EQUIPMENT

Buy DOC hut tickets ($15 for each hut) before you start at the stores in Staveley or Mount Somers, or from i-SITEs or DOC offices; there is no booking system for the huts. You'll need to carry a cooking stove, pots and all your food; all water should be treated. Marker poles point the way adequately in most conditions but the rolling country on top of the hills is subject to disorientating fog, so bring a map and compass.

TRANSPORT

Staveley Horse Treks (❶03 303 0809, ❷brucegray@clear.net.nz) will shuttle your car for $30. After dropping you at the Woolshed Creek trailhead, they keep your vehicle safe near Sharplin Falls car park ready for your emergence from the wilds. Methven Travel (❶03 302 8106) operates a shuttle service from Methven to the Woolshed Creek or Sharplin Falls car parks ($60 and $45 respectively for one person, plus $20 for each extra person).

THE ROUTE

Sharplin Falls car park to Pinnacles Hut (6km; 3hr 30min; 470m ascent). The most popular section of the track is the first 2km to Sharplin Falls, a modest cascade in a pretty canyon. There are lots of steps but they're even and well cared for. The route then climbs steadily through beech forest, reaching the tree line at *Pinnacles Hut* (19 bunks), nestled below rock monoliths frequently used by climbers.

Pinnacles Hut to Woolshed Creek Hut (6.2km; 3hr; 265m ascent). Climb towards the 1170m saddle, across treeless tussock with open views into the mountains and back to the plains. On the descent, take the 5min side trip to the Water Caves, where a stream courses below a rockfall of house-sized boulders. It is then only 10min to the modern *Woolshed Creek Hut* (26 bunks), a good place to stay a couple of nights, spending the intervening day exploring the little valleys and canyons hereabouts.

Woolshed Creek Hut to the Sharplin Falls car park (13.5km; 8hr; 400m ascent). The tramp around the mountain's south face feels quite different with incredible views across the Canterbury flatlands towards the distant coast. The terrain is a mix of high-country scrub (somewhat exposed at times) and beech forest. Soon after leaving the hut, the Howden Falls side track is worth a quick look. You then climb a ridge before traversing tussock-covered flats, passing a new day-shelter at about the halfway point. After a steep climb up through beech forest you begin the long descent, first on a ridge with great views then down into the bush to Sharplin Falls car park.

ACCOMMODATION AND EATING

STAVELEY

★**Staveley Village Store** 1 Burgess Rd ❶03 303 0859. A local store in the best tradition: a place for great coffee, tasty breakfasts and lunches, ice cream, limited groceries and eight different kinds of superb sausage roll including leek and mushroom. Daily 9am–4pm; closed Mondays in winter.

Topp Lodge 12 Burgess Rd ❶03 303 0955. Lynda Topp, one half of New Zealand's best-known lesbian yodelling cowgirl act, the Topp Twins, runs this quirky B&B in Staveley. The rooms are peaceful

and very comfortable and come with full breakfast; dinner is available ($45) and there's a full liquor licence. $120

MOUNT SOMERS

Mt Somers Domain Hoods Rd, 1km off SH72 ❶021 176 0677. Cheap camping next to the local swimming pool and a historic musterers' hut with a basic toilet and shower block, and a small kitchen and lounge. Camping $15, powered site $20

Mount Somers Holiday Park Hoods Rd, 1km off SH72

10

SEARCHING FOR EDORAS

Go searching for Edoras and you won't find it. Though the crew of *Lord of the Rings: The Two Towers* spent the best part of a year erecting the Rohan capital, everything was removed after filming. What you do get is **Mount Sunday**, a 100m-high glacially levelled outcrop (*roche moutonnée*) surrounded by open river flats a 48km drive west of Mount Somers Village. Over half of the journey is on rough gravel but it is a beautiful drive, bounded by big, grassy, round-shouldered hills sheltering a flat valley, with the main icy backbone of the Southern Alps looming ahead.

You should put an hour aside to wander across the fields (and cross a couple of streams) to get to Mount Sunday. Once you're standing on top surveying the grasslands all about, you can imagine the bleats of the sheep are the battle cries of… well, maybe not.

Hassle-free Tours (☎0800 427753, ⓦhasslefree.co.nz) run fun day-trips here from Christchurch ($235 including a café lunch); departures from Methven and Mount Somers are also possible.

☎03 303 9719, ⓦmountsomers.co.nz. Comfortable tree-filled area with powered sites ($32), simple cabins (and linen for rent) and fully made-up en-suite cabins ($80). Camping **$18**, cabins **$55**

Mount Somers Store 59 Pattons Rd ☎03 303 9831. Another classic country store selling DOC hut tickets, ice cream, sausage rolls and a reasonable range of groceries; there are two fuel pumps outside. Mon–Sat 8am–6pm, Sun 9am–5pm.

Stronechrubie Junction of Hoods Rd and SH72 ☎03 303 9814, ⓦstronechrubie.co.nz. Beautiful modern self-contained chalets in a lovely rural setting, as well as the only real restaurant in these parts: expect local beef ($38) or baked salmon ($34) and an excellent wine selection. Good-value dinner and bed-and-breakfast packages make it popular at weekends. Book for meals Wed–Sat 6.30–10pm, Sun noon–2pm. **$120**

Peel Forest

The tiny hamlet of **PEEL FOREST**, 12km west of SH72 and 45km south of Mount Somers, is the hub of **Peel Forest Park**, one of the eastern South Island's last remaining patches of original native bush, with rare stands of ancient forest trees – including lowland totara and matai – which can be seen from the **walking tracks** that thread through the bush. Come for easy walks, horse trekking and the superb **whitewater-rafting** trips through the Rangitata Gorge.

INFORMATION AND ACTIVITIES
PEEL FOREST

Peel Forest Horse Trekking ☎0800 022536, ⓦpeelforesthorsetrekking.co.nz. Runs excellent treks that range from a stroll along (and occasionally through) the river (1hr; $55) to a full-day trek up Mt Peel ($380 including lunch), plus multi-day trips and accommodation.

Peel Forest Store ☎03 696 3567, ⓦpeelforest.co.nz. Peel Forest revolves around this great old store, which acts as visitor centre (pick up DOC's *Peel Forest Area* leaflet outlining walks from 30min to 6hr), post office, campsite office and takeaway at the adjacent restaurant (see below).

Mon–Sat 9.30am–5pm, Sun 10am–5pm.

Rangitata Rafts 15km north of Peel Forest Store ☎0800 251251, ⓦrafts.co.nz. This highly professional outfit runs some of New Zealand's best whitewater-rafting trips on the Grade IV–V high-sided gorge section of the Rangitata River. Trips (Oct–May daily 11.30am; $208) include three hours on the water – rounded off with a nerve-testing optional 10m cliff jump – plus lunch and a barbecue dinner. Transport from Christchurch (add 2hr at either end) costs just $20 extra. Book well in advance.

ACCOMMODATION AND EATING

Little Mt Peel Restaurant ☎03 696 3567, ⓦpeelforest.co.nz. Attached to the store, this stays open later on Fri & Sat nights to serve meals including Tuscan lamb salad ($23), plus the usual steak and seafood suspects. Mon–Thurs 9.30am–5pm, Fri & Sat 9.30am–9pm, Sun 10am–5pm.

Peel Forest Campground ☎03 696 3567. A lovely wooded DOC-run campsite set beside the Rangitata River, with tent and powered sites and four simple "eco-cabins". Keep an eye peeled for two rare parrots: the drably coloured, bulky kaka and brilliant green kakariki. Camping **$15**, cabins **$50**

Geraldine

The prosperous farming town of **GERALDINE**, 50km south of Mount Somers and 35km north of Timaru, rewards a brief stop for a couple of **attractions** and to browse its smattering of **craft shops**, **galleries**, and **food stores** specializing in gourmet picnic ingredients such as local cheeses, pickles, jams, wine and chocolates.

Giant Jersey and Medieval Mosaic

10 Wilson St • Summer: Mon–Fri 9am–5pm, Sat & Sun 10am–4pm; winter: Mon–Sat 10am–4pm • Giant Jersey donation; tapestry $2 • ☎ 03 693 9820, ⓦ giantjersey.co.nz and ⓦ 1066.co.nz

10

While the whopping 5.5kg jersey on display here ranks among the **world's largest**, you might have more time for the 64m-long **tableau of the Bayeux Tapestry** made entirely from tiny pieces of spring steel broken from the patterning discs of industrial knitting machines. The first 22m reimagine the Battle of Stamford Bridge that immediately preceded 1066's Battle of Hastings, while the last 8m are artists' Michael and Rachael Linton's interpretation of how the missing final section of the original might have looked. Mathematically-minded visitors may want to try decoding the number puzzle hidden in the fragments of metal, which at the time of writing remained unsolved, despite the best efforts of local boffins.

ARRIVAL AND INFORMATION

GERALDINE

By bus InterCity/Newmans stop at the Kiwi Country Tourism Complex (see below), while Atomic and NakedBus pick up and drop off on Cox Street, near Geraldine's i-SITE, as do Budget Shuttles (☎ 03 615 5119, ⓦ budgetshuttles .co.nz) on their Christchurch to Timaru run.

Destinations Aoraki/Mount Cook (daily; 3hr); Christchurch (5–6 daily; 2hr 30min); Queenstown (4 daily; 5–6hr);

Timaru (1–2 daily; 30min).

i-SITE Corner of Talbot and Cox St (Mon–Fri 10am–4pm, Sat & Sun 10am–3pm; ☎ 03 693 1006, ⓦ gogeraldine .co.nz). Information and souvenirs are also available from the Kiwi Country Tourism Complex (daily 8am–5.30pm; ☎ 03 693 1101) on Waihi Terrace, the northern continuation of Talbot St.

ACCOMMODATION

Geraldine KIWI Holiday Park and Motel 39 Hislop St ☎ 03 693 8147, ⓦ geraldineholidaypark.co.nz. Well-tended tree-filled campsite with the usual range of cabins and self-contained units ($82) where guests can rent cheap bikes ($5/hr) for knocking about town. Camping __$34__, cabins __$52__

Rawhiti Backpackers 27 Hewlings St, 1km southwest of the centre ☎ 03 693 8252, ⓦ rawhitibackpackers .co.nz. Peaceful BBH hostel in an artistically decorated 1924 former maternity hospital, with spotless rooms and common areas, and expansive gardens. Dorms __$33__, doubles __$76__

EATING AND ENTERTAINMENT

Café Plums 44 Talbot St ☎ 03 693 9770. Ordinary-looking café that produces delicious made-on-the-premises Swiss chocolates and cakes such as raspberry linzer torte and honey-and-nut cake ($3.50 a slice), plus breakfasts starting from a reasonable $7.50. Mon–Fri 8am–5pm, Sat 9am–2pm.

Verdé Café Deli 45c Talbot St ☎ 03 693 9616. Housed in a secluded rose-clambered cottage set back from the main road, the classy café fare here spans a great selection of counter food plus a tempting brunch menu: think pea,

asparagus and halloumi paella, or salmon on a feta potato cake (both $18). Daily 9am–4pm.

CINEMA

Geraldine Cinema 74 Talbot St ☎ 03 693 8118, ⓦ geraldinecinema.co.nz. Wonderful reinvented movie house with sofas, beanbags and cosy duvets in winter. It occasionally plays host to live bands and even opera. Typically open Thurs–Sun.

The Mackenzie Country

The Canterbury Plains and the central South Island's snow-capped peaks frame the **Mackenzie Country**, a dramatic region of open sheep-grazed grasslands that shimmer golden brown year-round. It is all beautifully set off in November and December by stands of purple, pink and white **lupins** – regarded as weeds but much loved and photographed nonetheless.

10

Light reflected from microscopic rock particles suspended in glacial meltwater lends an ethereal opaque hue to the region's mesmerizingly blue, **glacier-fed lakes**, notably Tekapo, Pukaki and Ohau, which form part of the **Waitaki hydro scheme** (see box, p.585). At 700m above sea level, the region has some of the **cleanest air** in the southern hemisphere, and on a good day the sharp edges and vibrant colours make this one of the best places to stargaze and photograph the Southern Alps, particularly around **Tekapo**.

The region encompasses New Zealand's highest peak, **Aoraki/Mount Cook**, accessed from **Aoraki/Mount Cook Village**, a perfect spot for alpine hiking, scenic flights and glacier skiing.

Sadly, this iconic and beautiful landscape is under threat as high international milk prices are driving the conversion of sheep stations into dairy farms, the necessary lush grass being grown on fields moistened using massive irrigation arms that create kilometre-wide **green patches of grass** amid the otherwise brown landscape.

Tekapo

The **Cass** and **Godley** rivers feed into the 83-square-kilometre **Lake Tekapo** which spills into the **Tekapo River**, wending its way across the Mackenzie Basin. Glacial flour – ultra-fine particles of rock – suspended in the water gives the lake water its milky turquoise hue.

On Lake Tekapo's southern shore, the burgeoning village of **TEKAPO** revolves around a roadside ribbon of cafés and gift shops surrounded by modern housing developments. Its name derives from the Maori *taka* ("sleeping mat") and *po* ("night"), suggesting that this place has long been used as a stopover. It still is, with visitors keen to spend a sunny afternoon picnicking on the lakeshore, enjoying the sunset from a hot pool then stargazing after dark.

Church of the Good Shepherd

Pioneer Drive • Daily 9am–5pm • Donation

Everyone's first stop is the tiny lakeside **Church of the Good Shepherd**, an enchanting little stone church built in 1935 as a memorial to the Mackenzie Country pioneers. Behind the rough-hewn Oamaru stone altar, a window perfectly frames the lake and the surrounding mountains. Fifty metres to the east, the **Collie Dog Monument** was erected in 1968 by local sheep farmers to honour the dogs that make it possible to graze this harsh terrain.

Tekapo Springs

6 Lakeside Drive • Daily 10am–9pm • $22; waterslide & tubing $22; skating $20 • ☎ 03 680 6550, ⓦ tekaposprings.co.nz

To simply unwind, head to this outdoor complex which combines beautiful, state-of-the-art hot pools – each subtly shaped like a local lake, with heated alpine water

10

SKIING IN THE MACKENZIE COUNTRY

Along with the glacier skiing at Aoraki/Mount Cook, the Mackenzie Basin offers club skiing at three fields, all generally open from late June to late September.

Mount Dobson 28km east of Tekapo on SH8 then 15km north along a gravel access road ☏ 03 685 8039, ⓦ dobson.co.nz. Renowned for its powder snow, long hours of sunshine and uncrowded fields, Mt Dobson's four beginner, six intermediate and four advanced runs cater for all levels. There's a platter lift, T-bar and a triple chair, and a weekend and holiday shuttle connects to Fairlie; check online for schedules. Lift pass $78.

Ohau 9km west of Lake Ohau Lodge ☏ 03 438 9885, ⓦ ohau.co.nz. This small, high-country ski-field has reliable powder snow and uncrowded slopes, with

beginner runs, and a range of groomed and off-piste intermediate and advanced runs. Equipment rental and lessons are available at the field. Lift pass $81.

Roundhill 32km northwest of Tekapo along Lilybank Rd ☏ 03 680 6977, ⓦ roundhill.co.nz. Families flock to this relaxed field where you'll find one long T-bar and two learner tows plus the world's longest (1.4km) and steepest rope tow, giving a total vertical of 783m – the greatest in the country. Most of the terrain is gentle and undulating, though the rope tow gives access to four black runs. Lift passes $78.

---

ranging from 36°C to 40°C – with a day-spa (massages from $55 for 30min). Less soothingly, there's also a water slide in summer, an ice rink in winter, and tubing year-round (on snow in winter, carpet in summer).

Mount John

2km on foot, 9km by road northwest of Tekapo • ☏ 03 680 6960, ⓦ earthandsky.co.nz

Minimal light pollution presents perfect conditions for observing the night skies (Tekapo falls inside the **Aoraki Mackenzie International Dark Sky Reserve**), and the 1000m summit of **Mount John**, immediately northwest of Tekapo, has sprouted telescope domes operated by the University of Canterbury and astronomical institutions around the world. There are two excellent hikes up here (see box opposite) and great reward in the form of *Astro Café*, though the star attraction is the range of observatory and night sky tours (see box opposite). Weather conditions occasionally close the access road and café – keep an eye out for the sign at the start of the Mount John Summit walk.

ARRIVAL AND DEPARTURE

By bus Buses linking Christchurch and Queenstown stop in the village centre; NakedBus and InterCity/Newmans/Great Sights outside *Lake Tekapo Tavern*, Atomic outside the Four Square Supermarket. The Cook Connection (☏ 0800 266526,

ⓦ cookconnect.co.nz) pick up from accommodation.
Destinations Aoraki/Mount Cook (1–2 daily; 1hr 30min); Christchurch (4 daily; 3–4hr); Queenstown (4 daily; 3–4hr 30min); Twizel (4 daily; 40min).

INFORMATION

Information The Tekapo i-SITE has closed, leaving tourist information largely in the hands of Tekapo Springs, who run an information centre (daily: 10am–6pm in summer, 9.30am–5pm in winter;

☏ 03 680 6579) next to the Earth and Sky office.
Services Tekapo's sole ATM, outside *Reflections* restaurant, accepts most major cards.

ACCOMMODATION

Most accommodation in this tourist-oriented village is on the expensive side, with the few budget options often oversubscribed – book ahead.

The Chalet Boutique Motel 14 Pioneer Drive ☏ 0800 843242, ⓦ thechalet.co.nz. Seven beautiful individually decorated, self-contained apartments, some overlooking the lake, in a pretty spot 100m along the lakeshore from the Church of the Good Shepherd. $190

Lake Tekapo Motels and Holiday Park 2 Lakeside Drive ☏ 03 680 6825, ⓦ laketekapo-accommodation .co.nz. Situated 1km from the village at Lake Tekapo's southwest corner, this large, well-run holiday park overlooks the lake, and offers a wider-than-usual range of

TOURS AND ACTIVITIES IN TEKAPO

Mount John is the destination for a couple of nice **walks** that can be combined as a loop (probably taking the longer, gentler route up), and for superb skywatching **observatory tours**. The magnificent scenery provides a great backdrop to some fine boat trips, horse rides and flightseeing.

WALKS

Mt John Summit (2km one way; 1hr; 300m ascent). Short, sharp ascent from Tekapo Springs along a switchbacked path that leads through larch forests full of birds.

Mt John Lakeshore & Summit (6km one way; 3hr; 300m ascent). A stroll north along the lakeshore then gradually up a long breezy ridge to the summit with even longer views.

10

OBSERVATORY TOURS

Book early if you don't want to be shunted onto an extra-late tour (there are departures as late as 1.30am in summer), and **dress warmly**: they equip you with enormous red parkas and feed you hot chocolate but it can still be cold. Most tours start from the office in town; a free shuttle bus takes you to the hilltop. Tours usually go ahead even if it's cloudy; you will only qualify for a refund if your tour is cancelled due to wind or rain.

Observatory Day Tour (daily noon–3pm on request; 30min; $20; 2 person minimum). If you've driven or walked to the summit of Mount John, consider this tour, which starts at the *Astro Café*. They'll show you the inside of some of the observatory domes and, if it's clear, you can look at the sun through a solar telescope.

Observatory Night Tour (daily after nightfall, approx 8pm in winter, 10pm in summer; 2hr; $140). Easily the most popular tour, you'll get to look through the largest telescopes available (up to 61cm) at whatever's up: the Southern Cross, the Large Magellanic Cloud, nebulae, and perhaps the glorious Jewel Box. They'll show you how to get the best star photos, and if the night is cloudy you'll delve into the life of an astronomer and the work being done by the universities of Canterbury and Nagoya.

Twilight Tour (daily at dusk; 2hr; $140). If you can't face the late finish of the night tour, go for this option where you'll get a (hopefully) great sunset followed by telescope viewing of the darkening sky.

Cowan's Observatory Star Tour (nightly after dark on clear nights; 75min; $90). A budget tour that doesn't visit Mt John but conducts viewing from a telescope on a hill away from the (admittedly minimal) lights of Tekapo. This is the only tour that offers a full refund if it is cloudy.

BOAT TRIPS

Cruise Tekapo ☎ 027 479 7675, ⊕ cruisetekapo .co.nz. Speedboat lake trips ranging from a spin around the highlights (20min; $40) to a visit to Motuariki Island with a barbecue salmon meal (90min–2hr; $125).

FLIGHTSEEING

Air Safaris ☎ 0800 806880, ⊕ airsafaris.co.nz. Take the "Grand Traverse" (50min; $340) which swoops across the Main Divide to the West Coast, providing views of the Franz Josef and Fox glaciers, the Tasman and Muller glaciers and Aoraki/Mount Cook – luckily every seat is a window seat.

Tekapo Helicopters ☎ 0800 359835, ⊕ tekapohelicopters.co.nz. Various flights (20–60min; prices from $199), all including a snow landing: the most popular flight, the "Mount Cook Adventure", sees you landing on the Liebig Dome, which is covered in snow year-round (40min; $330).

HORSERIDING

Mackenzie Alpine Trekking ☎ 0800 628269, ⊕ maht.co.nz. On one-hour ($60) or 3hr 30min ($140) guided horse rides from Balmoral Station through the dramatic alpine scenery, it's possible to really get a sense of how tough it was to tame this land. **Operates Nov–April.**

accommodation from dorms (housed in the formerly separate *Lakefront Lodge Backpackers*), camping sites $15), cabins and motel rooms ($130). Bike rental available $25/half-day). Dorms $30, standard cabins $85

Peppers Bluewater Resort ☎ 0800 680 7000, ⊕ peppers.co.nz/bluewater. An outpost of the Aussie hotel chain, this collection of small hotel rooms and larger villas (up to three bedrooms) is pleasant but somewhat

10

lacking in atmosphere, though the more expensive rooms compensate with balconies and great lake views. Doubles $179, deluxe doubles $251

★**Tailor-made-Tekapo Backpackers** 9–11 Aorangi Crescent ☎03 680 6700, ⍵tailor-made-backpackers .co.nz. A 5min walk uphill from the bus stop and shops, this friendly BBH hostel lacks views but does have cheerful, comfy rooms and bunk-free dorms, plus well-kept grounds and free-range chickens. Dorms $30, doubles $78

★**YHA Lake Tekapo** 3 Simpson Lane ☎03 680 6857, ⍵yha.co.nz. One of the best YHAs around, full of life and with a common room heated by a log-burner and framed by a floor-to-ceiling lake-view window. Camping too ($18). Dorms $38, double $96

CAMPING

Lake McGregor 1km west of Tekapo then 9km north Simple DOC-style camping in open country beside a pretty lake, with a vault toilet and tap water. Reached along a mostly gravel road. $5

EATING AND DRINKING

Astro Café Mt John summit. With stupendous lake and mountain views, this café atop Mt John serves cakes, sandwiches, soup ($10) and stellar espresso. Daily 10am–5pm.

★**Kohan** SH8 ☎03 680 6688, ⍵kohannz.com. The surroundings are functional, but there's a great view and superb Japanese food that won't break the bank; the bento boxes start from $25, and a plate of "Tekapo rolls" costs $15. BYO & licensed. Daily 11am–2pm & 6–9pm, usually closed Sunday evenings.

Reflections SH8 ☎03 680 6234, ⍵reflectionsrestaurant.co.nz. Local salmon, lamb and beef all get a run on the wide-ranging menu at this reliable restaurant that opens out to a terrace at the lake's edge. Try the unusual burger combinations ($16.50) or salmon with buttered spinach and pumpkin risotto ($29). Free wi-fi. Daily 7am–9pm or later.

Run 77 SH8 ☎03 680 6910. Classy store selling gourmet deli goods and housing the village's best daytime café, though service can be spotty; come here for good coffee, baked treats and hot meals – try the Mackenzie High Country Breakfast ($21.50). Daily 7.30am–4pm.

Lake Pukaki

47km southwest of Tekapo

From Tekapo, SH8 heads to the southern shores of the 30km-long **Lake Pukaki**, another surreally toned glacial lake backed by the glistening peaks of the Southern Alps. A roadside parking area is the spot to pull over and admire fabulous views across the lake to Aoraki/Mount Cook and its icy attendants.

Peters Lookout

A kilometre on from the viewing area, SH80 branches north towards Aoraki/Mount Cook. This good, fast and gently undulating road runs for 55km north of the junction through the tussocklands of Lake Pukaki's western shore, passing, after 12km, **Peters Lookout**, another popular lakeside viewing point.

ACCOMMODATION   LAKE PUKAKI

The Pines SH8, 12km north of Twizel. A vast and unsigned camping area with long-drop toilets, a water tap and fabulous lake and mountain views from spots along the waterfront. **Free**

Aoraki/Mount Cook

New Zealand's highest mountain, the spectacular 3754m **Mount Cook** is increasingly known by its Maori name, **Aoraki**, meaning "cloud piercer" – with the two names often run together as Aoraki/Mount Cook. It commands the 700-square-kilometre **Aoraki/ Mount Cook National Park**, which was designated a UNESCO World Heritage Site in 1986. With 22 peaks over 3000m, the park contains the lion's share of New Zealand's highest mountains, mostly made of greywacke (a type of sandstone common in New Zealand) laid in an ocean trench 250–300 million years ago.

Aoraki/Mount Cook is at the heart of a unique mountain area whose rock is easily shattered in the cold, leaving huge amounts of gravel in the valley floors. The tussock-cloaked foothills, where Mount Cook lilies, celmisia mountain daisies and snow gentians thrive, contrast with the inhospitable ice fields of the upper slopes.

All this is easily accessible on walks to great viewpoints and even to the base of the 27km-long **Tasman Glacier**, fed by icefalls tumbling from the heavily glaciated surrounding peaks.

The **weather** here is highly changeable, often with a pall of low-lying cloud liable to turn to rain, and the mountain air is lung-searingly fresh. On windy days, an atmospheric white dust rises from the plain at the base of the mountain.

Brief history

Maori legends tell that the sky father (Raki) and the earth mother (Papa-tua-nuku) had children by previous unions. After their divine remarriage, the sky father's sons came to inspect their new stepmother. Four brothers, Ao-raki, Raki-roa, Raki-rua and Raraki-roa, circled around her in a canoe, but disaster befell them once they left her shores when their canoe ran aground. The canoe lay tipped on one side, higher in the west than the east, and turned to stone. The brothers climbed to the highest edge of their petrified canoe, where they too were transformed: Ao-raki became Aoraki/Mount Cook, and his three younger brothers formed flanking peaks – Mount Dampier, Mount Teichelmann and Mount Tasman.

Geologists claim that about five million years ago the **Alpine Fault** began to lift, progressively pushing the rock upwards and creating the Southern Alps. These days the process continues at about the same rate as erosion, ensuring that the mountains are at least holding their own – although a massive summit collapse in 1991 took 10m off Aoraki/Mount Cook's peak (an event that registered 3.9 on the Richter scale 70km away in Twizel).

Mount Cook was named in honour of the English sea captain in 1851. It was first summited in 1894 but, due to the peak's sacredness to Maori, climbers are now asked not to step on the summit itself.

Aoraki/Mount Cook Village

The only habitation in the national park is in tiny **AORAKI/MOUNT COOK VILLAGE**, sitting at 760m and encircled by a horseshoe of mountains topped by Aoraki/Mount Cook itself. Almost everything is run by *The Hermitage* hotel (which operates the Sir Edmund Hillary Alpine Centre) or DOC (who run a fascinating visitor centre). Mostly, though, you'll be wanting to get outdoors.

DOC visitor centre

Daily 8.30am–5pm • Free • ☎ 03 435 1186

Not just somewhere to register your intentions, get tramping and weather info and to buy maps, but also a window on the region's wondrous natural and social history – a complement to what's on show at the Sir Edmund Hillary Alpine Centre. Set an hour

AORAKI/MOUNT COOK VILLAGE

■ ACCOMMODATION		● RESTAURANTS, CAFÉS & BARS	
Aoraki/Mount Cook Alpine Lodge	4	Chamois Bar & Grill	3
Glentanner Park Centre	9	The Hermitage	1
The Hermitage	3	The Old Mountaineers	2
Mount Cook Backpacker Lodge	6		
Mueller Hut	2		
Unwin Lodge	8		
White Horse Hill campsite	1/5		
YHA Mount Cook	7		

10

10

SIR EDMUND HILLARY

Sir Edmund Hillary has long been the most famous and admired New Zealander, and his death in 2008, aged 88, probably raised his profile further. His ascent of Mount Everest in 1953 with Sherpa Tenzing Norgay was undoubtedly an impressive achievement, and his humanitarian work in the villages of Nepal was widely lauded, but above all, Hillary embodied the qualities Kiwis hold most dear: hard-working, straight-talking, honest and, most of all, modest. As he famously said on his return from the successful summit attempt, "Well George, we knocked the bastard off". That's what gets your face on every $5 note in the country.

Though he grew up near Auckland, Sir Ed did much of his early climbing around Aoraki/ Mount Cook Village, where a **bronze statue** of a youthful Hillary stands outside *Sir Edmund Hillary Alpine Centre*.

aside to delve into displays spread across two floors exploring climate, glacier dynamics, climbing history, and to flick through four sobering volumes filled with memorials to those who have perished in these mountains. There are wonderful photographs of Victorian climbers posing with their ice axes, a helpful relief model of the mountains, and histories of the mountain huts. Outside, the old six-bunk Empress Hut, relocated from the slopes above, gives a sense of mountain life that isn't much changed today.

Sir Edmund Hillary Alpine Centre
Inside *The Hermitage* • Daily 7am–8.30pm • $20 • ☎ 0800 686800, Ⓦ hermitage.co.nz

The history of *The Hermitage* hotel and its place in Kiwi climbing history is told in this small museum, which also showcases the development of the region and the climbing life of its namesake, including a replica of the tractor Hillary used to get to the South Pole in 1956. It is interesting enough but the emphasis is on a state-of-the-art **3D theatre** and **planetarium** which plays a continuous roster of shows, such as: *Mount Cook Magic*, which whizzes you through the geographical, cultural and sporting evolution of the mountains using a blend of authentic footage and computer graphics; *Hillary on Everest*; and *Tycho to the Moon*, one for the kids. Profits from the centre help fund Hillary's Himalayan Trust.

Tramping and walking in Aoraki/Mount Cook National Park
Scenic **walks** in the park range from gentle day-hikes on the fringes of the village to spectacular alpine treks. DOC's *Walking and Cycling Tracks in Aoraki/Mount Cook National Park* leaflet ($1) lists eleven excellent day-treks (10min–6hr) which can be extended by those with relevant experience. Steer clear of the glaciers unless you know what you're doing, or are in the company of someone qualified.

Governors Bush Walk
1hr return from the village; 2km

The easiest of the local walks, this trail leads through a small stand of silver beech with abundant birdlife. You gradually climb to a lookout with views back towards Aoraki/ Mount Cook. It is sheltered enough to make it viable in poor weather.

Blue Lakes and Tasman Glacier View
1km return; 40min; 100m ascent

A fairly gentle walk with good views of the lower sections of the Tasman Glacier, which is 600m deep at its thickest point, 3km across at its widest and moves at a rate of 20cm a day. The walk starts at the Blue Lakes car park, 8km drive up the Tasman Valley Road, but you'll need your own vehicle as there are no shuttles.

Red Tarns Track
4km return from the village; 2hr; 300m ascent

This excellent and very achievable walk has one short, steep section but rewards with some pretty pools coloured by the red pond weed that gives them their name. From here uninterrupted views stretch across the village towards Aoraki/Mount Cook and along the Tasman Valley.

Kea Point Track

2hr, 7km return from the village or 1hr, 3km return from *Whitehorse Hill* campsite; 200m ascent

For great views with relatively little effort, follow this path through gentle grasslands to a viewpoint on the moraine wall of the Mueller Glacier. Here you can look down into Mueller Lake, up the valley to the Hooker Glacier and above you to the hanging glaciers and icefalls of Mount Sefton.

Hooker Valley Track

9km return from *Whitehorse Hill* campsite; 3hr; 200m ascent

You don't really need to do all of this popular and superb there-and-back hike; just go as far as you want, perhaps to the Alpine Memorial with views of the western side of Aoraki/Mount Cook or across a series of swingbridges to Hooker Lake at the base of the Hooker Glacier. Allow an extra hour if you start from and return to the village.

10

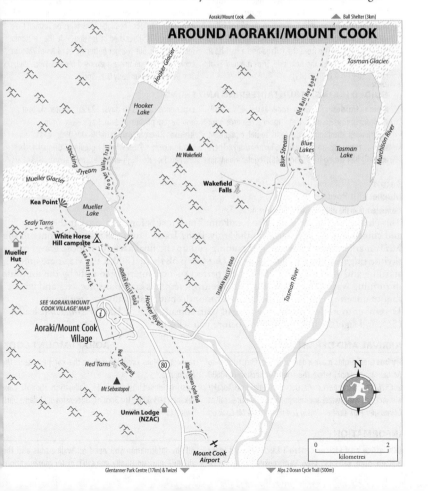

10

AORAKI/MOUNT COOK TOURS AND ACTIVITIES

As long as the weather plays ball, it would be hard to be bored around Aoraki/Mount Cook Village. As well as cruising or paddling a glacier lake you can hike to spectacular viewpoints, ride horses and off-road vehicles through mountain scenery or spend an hour gazing at the night sky. Dress warmly for all activities, and pack waterproofs as well as sunscreen.

Scenic flights offer glimpses of areas you could never dream of reaching on foot. Book a few days ahead, but be prepared to be flexible as flights are cancelled in high winds or poor visibility. The peak season is November–March, but in winter (June & July) the weather is often clearer and the views more dramatic.

There are no developed ski-fields in the Aoraki/Mount Cook area, but choppers open up the Tasman Glacier and surrounding mountains for guided **heli-skiing and heli-snowboarding**. During the **season** (July–Sept or Oct), steep, untouched runs cater for those with strong intermediate skills or better.

BOATING AND KAYAKING

Glacier Explorers ☎0800 686800, ⊛glacierexplorers.co.nz. Spend an eerie hour chugging around on Tasman Lake among detached icebergs turned grey by the presence of ground-down rock that reflects the light. Examining chunks of fallen ice up close reveals beautiful honeycombed cells. Trips incorporate a shuttle from the village and a half-hour moraine walk before the boat ride. Trips run mid-Sept to late May (3–7 days; $145).

Glacier Sea Kayaking ☎03 435 1890, ⊛mtcook .com. There's a real sense of being dwarfed by icebergs when you're at water level on unique and fascinating paddling trips aboard outrigger-stabilized kayaks with enthusiastic guides. The biggest bergs are on Tasman Lake (daily; 4hr; $145), reached by minibus ride then a 30min moraine walk, but you get better views of Aoraki/Mount Cook from trips on the less exposed Mueller Lake (daily; 3hr; $130). Trips run early Oct–April.

GUIDED HIKING, MOUNTAINEERING AND SKIING

Alpine Guides *The Hermitage* ☎03 435 1834, ⊛alpineguides.co.nz. The main resource for experienced climbing guides and rental equipment such as crampons and ice axes ($12/item/day). There are daily heli-hiking trips (3hr; $545), regular mountain experience courses (6 days; $2250), winter ski touring and custom private guiding. Daily 8am–5pm.

Alpine Recreation ☎0800 006096, ⊛alpinerec reation.com. Professional guiding company best known for its high-altitude trek across Ball Pass

Mueller Hut Route

10km return from the village; 6–8hr; 1000m ascent

This challenging route leaves the Kea Point Track just before its arrival at the glacier and climbs steeply westwards up the Sealy Tarns Track. From the tarns, the route to the hut is marked by orange triangles guiding you up the final assault on loose gravel to a skyline ridge and the modern *Mueller Hut* (see p.584). At 1800m the views are quite startling and you're engulfed by almost perfect silence, interrupted only by the murmur of running water and squawking kea. The track requires crampons, ice axes and winter mountaineering experience in the colder months but is generally ice-free from December to mid-April. At any time of year, consult DOC's *Mueller Hut Route* leaflet ($2), and sign the intentions book before you set out.

ARRIVAL AND DEPARTURE   AORAKI/MOUNT COOK

By bus Great Sights make a daily run from Christchurch to Aoraki/Mount Cook, while the Cook Connection (☎0800 266526, ⊛cookconnect.co.nz; Oct–May only) links Aoraki/Mount Cook with Twizel and Tekapo. All bus services call at *Glentanner Park Centre*, *Unwin Lodge* and *YHA Mt Cook* on request, before dropping off at the car park near *The Hermitage*.

Destinations Christchurch (1 daily; 5hr 30min); Lake Tekapo (1–3 daily; 1hr 30min); Queenstown (1 daily; 5hr); Twizel (1–3 daily; 1hr).

INFORMATION

DOC office and visitor centre 1 Larch Grove Rd (daily 8.30am–5pm; ☎03 435 1186, ⊛mtcookvc@doc.govt.nz). All the information you need on walks, huts and the village – plus, unusually, you can register your intentions

($1220) which involves a three-day alpine crossing reaching 2130m close to Aoraki/Mount Cook and staying in the comfortable, private *Caroline Hut*.
Southern Alps Guiding ☎ 03 435 1890, ⓦ mtcook .com. All-day guided ski trips including lunch and two

very long wilderness runs (8–12km; $880), or one run on the Tasman and one on the even less visited Murchison Glacier ($955). Heli-skiing trips to the Ben Ohau range (three runs; $825) and regular mountain guiding also on offer.

SCENIC FLIGHTS

Helicopter Line Glentanner Park, 20km south of the village ☎ 0800 650651, ⓦ helicopter.co.nz. Four scenic helicopter trips with opportunities to hover along the valley walls and peaks, or view the tumbling blocks of the Hochstetter Icefall; all include brief snow landings. Choose from the Alpine Vista (20min; $235), Alpine Explorer (35min; $355), Mountains High (40min; $440) or Mount Cook and Glaciers (50min; $620) which circumnavigates Aoraki and heads over to the West Coast before flying the length of the Tasman Glacier.

Mount Cook Ski Planes ☎ 0800 800702, ⓦ mtcookskiplanes.com. Flights from the company that helped develop the technology for snow landings and has been operating from the Mount Cook Airfield since 1955. Prices are the same for fixed-wing or helicopter flights – from $245 for 25min, up to the Grand Circle (55min; $560), which loops around Aoraki, briefly crossing the Main Divide, hugging the immense valley walls and then landing on the silent Tasman Glacier to wander on the breathtaking footprint-free snow.

FOUR-WHEEL DRIVING

Tasman Valley 4WD & Argo Tours ☎ 0800 686600, ⓦ www.mountcooktours.co.nz. *The Hermitage* operates this good rainy-day alternative

(year-round; 2–5 trips daily; 90min; $79) involving riding around the Tasman moraine in an eight-wheeler Argo, stopping at otherwise inaccessible viewpoints.

HORSERIDING

Glentanner Park Centre SH80, 20km south of the village ☎ 03 435 1855, ⓦ glentanner.co.nz. One-

hour ($70) or two-hour ($90) panoramic horse-trekking tours on easy to moderate terrain. Nov–April only.

STARGAZING

Big Sky *The Hermitage* ☎ 0800 686800, ⓦ bigskystargazing.co.nz. A brief planetarium primer is followed by an outdoor examination of the

southern sky through binoculars or telescope. Departures after dark year-round (2hr; $62).

here if you're heading into the wilds.
Services The unstaffed petrol station accepts some international credit cards (if your card isn't accepted, you can call *The Hermitage* from the station and they'll help out

for a $5 fee). Most accommodation and *The Old Mountaineers* have pay internet. There's no bank or ATM. Basic groceries are available from *The Hermitage*, YHA and *Alpine Lodge*.

ACCOMMODATION

Book early from October to April, when the village often fills to capacity. Prices drop considerably during the rest of the year.

★**Aoraki/Mount Cook Alpine Lodge** 101 Bowen Drive ☎ 0800 680680, ⓦ aorakialpinelodge.co.nz. Great accommodation at realistic prices, with comfy twins and doubles, a lounge with a fantastic view, a fully equipped kitchen and a barbecue deck. You'll pay around $25 more for a room with a view. Doubles $164, family rooms $195
Glentanner Park Centre SH80, 18km south of the village ☎ 03 435 1855, ⓦ glentanner.co.nz. Well-equipped site with sheltered camping ($19), a 10-bed dorm (bring or rent bedding) and cabins with views of the mountains and Tasman Valley, a panoramic sheltered barbecue area and a café. Dorms $28.50, cabins $95
The Hermitage ☎ 0800 686800, ⓦ hermitage.co.nz. Vast hotel and restaurant complex, currently enjoying its

third incarnation since the first premises opened in 1868. Rooms and suites in the high-rise main building (many with fine views; add $100) are supplemented by chalets and motel units scattered nearby and all linked with regular shuttle buses. Breakfast included. Doubles $255, motels & chalets $245
Mount Cook Backpacker Lodge ☎ 0800 100512, ⓦ mountcookbackpackers.co.nz. Smart hostel fashioned from former staff accommodation with a self-catering kitchen and the *Chamois Bar* on site. Quad dorms (all en suite) mostly lack the views and balconies enjoyed by the en-suite doubles and the private units with their own kitchens ($170). Dorms $38, doubles $135
Unwin Lodge Near the airport turn-off, 4km from the

10

10

village **☎**03 435 1100, **⊛**alpineclub.org.nz/hut /unwin. Alpine Club hut that gives priority to NZAC members and climbers but is open to all, with simple bunkroom accommodation and a massive common area with kitchen – you'll need to bring your own linen and food, but laundry and internet are available. **$30**

★**YHA Mount Cook** 1 Bowen Drive **☎**03 435 1820, **ⓔ**yhamtck@yha.co.nz. Excellent if slightly cramped 76-bed hostel in a cosy wooden building with modern well-kept facilities, free evening saunas and a fairly well-stocked shop. Dorms **$38**, doubles **$137**

CAMPSITES AND HUTS

Mueller Hut Only hikers tackling the Mueller Hut Route (see p.582) will want to stay the night at this 28-bunk serviced hut, which can be booked online in summer. Sign in at the visitor centre before you head up here to sign into their intentions system. Hut **$36**, camping **$15**

White Horse Hill campsite Hooker Valley Rd, 2km north of the village. A serene and informal first-come-first-served DOC camping area under Mount Sefton with stony ground and treated water in summer. Accessible by road or a 30min walk from the village along the Kea Point Track. **$10**

EATING AND DRINKING

Groceries don't come cheap here and the range is very limited: bring what you need from Twizel or further afield.

Chamois Bar & Grill Mt Cook Backpacker Lodge. Straightforward boozing bar with pretty ordinary pub meals such as fish and chips, ribs and pizza, with mains around $20–30. Daily 5.30pm–late.

The Hermitage ☎ 0800 686800, **⊛**hermitage.co.nz. The hotel has dining for every taste with the *Sir Edmund Hillary Café & Bar* serving light meals from a deep Mount Cook-view terrace. The *Alpine Restaurant* serves all-you-can-eat buffets for breakfast (continental $19; cooked $29), lunch ($39) and dinner ($62), while the *Panorama Room* offers swanky à la carte dining with matchless views (mains around $40), with priority given to hotel guests. Lastly, the *Snowline Bar* has deep leather

sofas and magic views. Daily: Sir Edmund Hillary Café & Bar 9am–6pm; Alpine Restaurant 6.30–10am, 11.30am–2.30pm & 6–10pm; Panorama Room 6–9.30pm; Snowline Bar 3pm–late.

★**The Old Mountaineers ☎**03 435 1890, **⊛**mtcook.com. A little pricey, but undoubtedly the best place to hang out, with a log fire, real mountain-lodge feel, comfy chairs with wonderful mountain views, vintage mountain photos on the walls and outstanding café-style meals including organic burgers ($24) and scrumptious soups ($13.50) plus great coffee, beer and wine. Daily 10am–9.30pm; winter daily 11am–8pm.

Twizel

TWIZEL (rhymes with bridle), 65km south of Aoraki/Mount Cook and 9km south of the junction of SH8 and SH80, began life in 1968 as a construction village for people working on the **Waitaki hydro scheme** (see box opposite). The town was due to be bulldozed flat after the project finished in 1983. Some think this would have been a kinder fate for the planned community, but enough residents wanted to stay that their wishes were granted, and it's now a low-key summertime base for forays to Aoraki/Mount Cook (a 45min drive away), scenic Lake Ohau and gliding at Omarama.

Kaki/Black Stilt visitor hide

SH8, 3km south of Twizel • Guided tours (book through Twizel Information Centre), daily 10am • $12; min 3 people • **☎** 03 435 3124

Twizel's main attraction is the **Kaki/Black Stilt visitor hide**, which is attempting to save the world's rarest wading bird from extinction by hatching eggs in captivity and raising the chicks before releasing them into the wild. Numbers plummeted thanks to introduced predators and plant species, and habitat loss from the Waitaki hydroelectric project; a low of just 23 birds was reached in 1981. Happily, things are looking up and over a hundred chicks were hatched in 2014 alone.

ARRIVAL AND DEPARTURE

TWIZEL

By bus Atomic, InterCity/Newmans/Great Sights and NakedBus buses stop in the Marketplace car park on their Queenstown–Christchurch runs. Cook Connection links to Tekapo and Aoraki/Mount Cook.

Destinations Aoraki/Mount Cook (2 daily; 1hr); Christchurch (4 daily; 5hr); Omarama (4 daily; 30min); Queenstown (4 daily; 3hr).

THE WAITAKI HYDRO SCHEME

The Waitaki hydro scheme provides a fifth of the nation's power from twelve power stations scattered along the Waitaki River and its headwaters around lakes Tekapo, Pukaki and Ohau. The scheme has its origins in the work of the engineer Peter Seton Hay, who in 1904 submitted a report to the New Zealand government indicating the extraordinary hydroelectric potential of the region. Construction began with the Waitaki power station in 1935 and continued through to 1985, when the commissioning of the Ohau C station completed one of the largest construction projects in New Zealand.

Throughout the region water is diverted along a network of canals to fill a long sequence of storage lakes held back by impressive dams, particularly the 100m-high earth-built **Benmore Dam**, 32km from Omarama in the Waitaki Valley, off SH83 en route to the east coast. You can walk or drive to the top of the dam, or take a short loop track with distant views of Aoraki/ Mount Cook.

10

INFORMATION AND TOURS

Tourist information Marketplace (Mon–Fri 8.30am–5pm, Sat 10.30am–2.30pm; ☎03 435 3124, ⓦtwizel.info). The Twizel information centre has all the local information you need plus bookings for the Black Stilt tours.

Services The post office, bank and ATM are all in the Marketplace Shopping Centre.

The Helicopter Line ☎0800 650652, ⓦhelicopter .co.nz. Does chopper flights over/around Aoraki/Mount Cook ($295–730): they're more expensive than those from Aoraki/Mount Cook Village, but you get more time in the air.

OneRing Tours ☎0800 213868, ⓦlordoftherings tour.com. This outfit gets you out of unlovely Twizel onto the gorgeous surrounding plains which were used for filming the battle scenes on the Pelennor Fields (daily at 9am & 1.30pm; 1hr tour, $64; 2hr tour, $84).

ACCOMMODATION

Twizel has a good range of accommodation but its proximity to Aoraki/Mount Cook means it's essential to book ahead from Christmas to at least the end of February.

Aoraki Lodge 32 Mackenzie Drive ☎03 435 0300, ⓦaorakilodge.co.nz. Tasteful and welcoming B&B in the centre of town with four en-suite rooms, all with separate access, and a pretty rose-filled garden. $220

High Country Lodge & Backpackers 23 Mackenzie Drive ☎03 435 0671, ⓦhighcountrylodge.co.nz. This huge former hydroelectric workers' camp is like a village within a village. It sleeps up to 280 in barrack-style timber buildings and newer motels ($125), but still gets booked solid in summer. Dorms $32, rooms $78

Mountain Chalet Motels Wairepo Rd ☎03 435 0785, ⓦmountainchalets.co.nz. Great-value collection of light-filled, self-contained A-frame chalets and an adjacent lodge offering worn but comfortable backpacker accommodation. Dorms $30, chalets $120

★**Omahau Downs** SH8, 2km north of town ☎03 435 0199, ⓦomahau.co.nz. Lovely combination of four modern en-suite doubles with great Aoraki/Mount Cook views, and three self-catering cottages set on a working family-run farm. All share access to an outdoor wood-fired bath ($20). Closed June–Aug. Doubles $135, cottages $125

Twizel Holiday Park 122 Mackenzie Drive ☎03 435 0507, ⓦtwizelholidaypark.co.nz. Large and fairly typical campsite with powered sites plus a sprinkling of cabins, cottages ($115) and en-suite rooms on the northern edge of town. Powered sites $36, basic cabins $60

EATING AND DRINKING

★**Poppies** 1 Benmore Place ☎03 435 0848, ⓦpoppiescafe.com. Elegant wine-red space with polished concrete floors and shelves of gourmet deli goods, serving classy café fare, as well as beautifully cooked lunches such as venison burgers with beetroot chutney ($18.50) and bean burritos ($14.50), with lots of organic produce straight from the owners' garden. The dinner menu offers the same dishes at higher prices. Daily 9am–late.

Shawty's 4 Market Place ☎03 435 3155, ⓦshawtys .co.nz. Restaurant and bar where tasty breakfasts and sizeable lunches are served with care in the casual interior or overlooking the village green. Dinners include the usual range of meat and fish dishes; more interestingly they do a fine line in creative pizzas including lamb souvlaki ($18) and the delicious "Herbivore" ($16). Daily 8.30am–late.

Lake Ohau

The narrow Lake Ohau Road runs 25km west of Twizel to idyllic **Lake Ohau**, secluded among beech forest with distinctive natural features including kettle lakes (small depressions left when blocks of glacial ice melt) and terracing on its banks that reflects the light of summer sunsets. Northwest of the lake, the **Ohau Forests** are crisscrossed by numerous tracks (30min–4hr), outlined in DOC's *Ruataniwha Conservation Park* leaflet, available from *Lake Ohau Lodge*. In winter, the Ohau ski-field (see box, p.576) is in full swing.

10

ACCOMMODATION AND EATING   LAKE OHAU

Lake Ohau Lodge Lake Ohau Rd ⊙03 438 9885, ⓦohau.co.nz. Though popular on summer tour-bus itineraries, this 62-room hotel is saved by its wonderful setting and super-peaceful evenings. There's no self-catering, but guests and visitors can book ahead for breakfast (continental $16; cooked $22) and dinner ($44) from a set menu, or drop by for a drink at the well-stocked bar. The lodge also has petrol, and organizes a ski-shuttle service ($25 return). Camping/powered sites $15, doubles $109

Omarama

SH8 traverses tussock and sheep country 30km south from Twizel to the junction settlement of **OMARAMA** (Maori for "place of light"), best known for the **Clay Cliffs** just outside town and its wonderful conditions for **gliding**.

Omarama Hot Tubs

25 Omarama Ave (SH8) • Daily 11am–10pm • Hot tubs $90 for two for 90min; hot tub & sauna $140 for two; towel hire $5 • ⊙03 438 9703, ⓦhottubsomarama.co.nz

There are no hot springs at **Omarama Hot Tubs**, just chemical-free mountain water heated in ten exquisitely landscaped private outdoor tubs overlooking the mountains. Though it feels very open, no one can overlook your idyll. Further relaxation is available in the massage rooms, starting from $60 for 30min.

THE ALPS 2 OCEAN CYCLE TRAIL

Stretching over 300km from the Southern Alps to the Pacific Ocean, the **Alps 2 Ocean Cycle Trail** (ⓦalps2ocean.com) is the longest continuous trail in New Zealand's nationwide **Nga Haerenga** network (see p.35). Work on several sections of the track was still under way at the time of writing, but the entire trail is signposted and rideable – even by penny-farthing, as one intrepid group from Timaru proved in 2013.

Cyclists can start either from Mount Cook Village (with a helicopter hop to cross the Tasman River; $125) or from Lake Tekapo. The two trails meet outside Twizel, before looping around Lake Ohau and heading southeast past a series of lakes and dams that form the **Waitaki hydro scheme** (see box opposite), threading through the wine country around Kurow and reaching the coast at Oamaru.

Unless your heart is set on a penny-farthing, it's most comfortable to tackle the frequently bumpy trail on mountain bike. Anyone with a reasonable level of fitness can ride the trail, with the eight stages averaging 30–40km each. Several local operators provide bike hire, portering and transport along different sections of the track, but it's straightforward enough to do the trail independently – just make sure you know how to fix a puncture.

CYCLE HIRE & SUPPORT

Cycle Journeys 2a Wairepo Rd, Twizel ⊙03 435 0578 ⓦcyclejourneys.co.nz. Offers a wide range of services that run the gamut from guided multi-day rides to shuttles, luggage portering ($15/section) and bike hire ($45/day).

The Jollie Biker 193 Glen Lyon Rd, Twizel ⊙03 435 0517 ⓦthejolliebiker.co.nz. Run by a local cyclist and specializing in the first half of the trail from Mt Cook to Omarama, services include bike ($45) and pannier ($15) rental, various transport options and all-inclusive packages, plus they own two wee holiday cottages in Twizel ($150).

GLIDING AROUND OMARAMA

Prevailing westerly winds rising over the Southern Alps create a unique airflow across the Mackenzie Country's flatlands, making Omarama New Zealand's gliding capital. Its airfield was the one-time playground of Dick Georgeson, pioneer of New Zealand aviation and the South Island's first glider pilot, back in 1950. You can follow his lead with Glide Omarama (☎03 438 9555, ⦿glide omarama.com) who let you take the front seat on spectacular two-seater glider flights, with a chance to take the controls and get great views of Aoraki/Mount Cook on a good day. The 30min trip ($335) is a great taster, but if possible, upgrade to the 1hr ($445) or the 2hr ($675), which might head over to the Alps and may require supplementary oxygen. Most trips run October–March.

10

Totara Peak Gallery

Chain Hills Hwy (SH83) • Sept to mid-June daily 9am–5.30pm • Free • ☎03 438 9757, ⦿omaramaantiques.com

It would be easy (but wrong) to pass the Western-style frontage of this movie-museum-cum-collectables-shop. Come to browse the secondhand books, old hand tools, ceramics, jewellery and classic cars (model and full-sized) but mostly to ogle the random collection of original props and costumes from shows such as *Xena: Warrior Princess*.

Clay Cliffs Scenic Reserve

15km from Omarama; turn west off the SH8, 5km north of town • Open access • $5; pay at the Omarama Hot Tubs

A rough side-road leads to the **Clay Cliffs Scenic Reserve** where the braided Ahuriri River provides a picturesque backdrop to eerie badlands of bare pinnacles and angular ridges separated by narrow ravines and canyons. The rock formations were created when a 100m uplift caused by the Ostler Fault exposed layers of gravel and silt that have weathered at different rates. A stony path winds along the bottom of the cliff, with smaller tracks snaking up to the rocks themselves.

The Maori name for the clay cliffs is *Paritea*, meaning white or light-coloured cliff. The cliffs provided natural shelter for moa hunters, with several surviving earth ovens indicative of early Maori settlement.

ARRIVAL AND INFORMATION

OMARAMA

By bus Buses stop near the central crossroads from Christchurch (4 daily; 4–5hr 30min); Queenstown (4 daily; 2hr 30min); and Twizel (4 daily; 30min).

Tourist information Omarama Hot Tubs (daily 11am–10pm; ☎03 438 9703) has a small information centre and does hotel and transport bookings. Hot showers are available for $7/person.

ACCOMMODATION AND EATING

Ahuriri Bridge campsite SH8, 3km north of town. A pretty and peaceful, willow-shaded DOC campsite beside the Ahuriri River that's perfect for tenters and those in campervans. Comes with long-drop toilets and river water. Free

★**Ahuriri Motels** SH83, 500m east of the SH3 junction ☎03 438 9451, ⦿ahuririmotels.co.nz. Well-run complex on the eastern edge of town, with powered sites ($18) and unusually spacious twin and tripled-bedded backpacker rooms, nicely decorated common areas plus a handful of self-contained motel units and the comfiest beds around. Backpackers $30, motel units $100

★**Buscot Station** 1.5km east of SH8, 9km north of town ☎03 438 9646. Peaceful working farm, in a higgledy-piggledy homestead surrounded by vegetable patches. Most rooms overlook the valley; there's a single ten-bed dorm. They'll arrange pick-ups if you book ahead. Dorms $25, doubles $60

Ladybird Hill 1 Pinot Noir Court ☎03 438 9550, ⦿ladybirdhill.co.nz. Off the SH8 on the western edge of town, the "Hill" includes a vineyard, fishponds where you can hook your own salmon ($38/fish) and a licensed restaurant. The menu covers local goats cheese salad ($16.50) and panko-crumbed blue cod with chips and pea purée ($27). Wed & Sun 10am–4pm, Thurs–Sat 10am–late; closed June & July.

Sierra Motels 8 Omarama Ave (SH8) ☎0800 743772, ⦿omarama.co.nz. Popular with cyclists on the Alps-to-Ocean run, this friendly motel has 14 newly renovated units all with Sky TV, kitchenette or full kitchen plus its own fishing tackle shop. $125

The Wrinkly Rams 24–30 Omarama Ave (SH8) ☎03 438 9751, ⦿thewrinklyrams.co.nz. Licensed local landmark that offers Omarama's best café- and pub-style fare, along with live sheep shearing shows. Expect all-day breakfast ($18) and tasty soups ($10). Daily 7am–4pm.

Dunedin
to Stewart
Island

TAIERI GORGE RAILWAY

Dunedin to Stewart Island

The southeastern corner of the South Island contains some of the least-visited parts of New Zealand, and yet still packs in the gems. The darkly Gothic harbourside city of Dunedin is a seat of learning and culture, influenced by the country's oldest university and thriving Scottish immigrant traditions. Once outside the region's main city, however, nature takes precedence over man-made sights. On Dunedin's doorstep, the windswept Otago Peninsula is a phenomenal wildlife haven, fringed with opportunities to see yellow-eyed and blue penguins, fur seals and albatross, all within 5km of each other. South of Dunedin there are yet more exemplary opportunities to see wildlife at its primal best along the dramatic Catlins Coast. Provincial Invercargill is the gateway to Stewart Island, New Zealand's third island, covered in swathes of undisturbed forest and a fantastic place to spot kiwi in the wild.

The "Edinburgh of the South", **Dunedin** takes its name from the Gaelic translation of its Scottish counterpart, with which it shares street and suburb names. Founded by Scottish settlers, its heyday was in the 1860s and 1870s as the commercial centre for the gold-rush towns of inland Central Otago. This left an enduring legacy of imposing **Gothic Revival architecture** fashioned from volcanic bluestone and creamy limestone.

On Dunedin's outskirts, **Port Chalmers** hangs onto a slightly bohemian, rough-around-the-edges feel, repaying a quick visit by combining it with the nearby **Orokonui Ecosanctuary**. Across the harbour, the **Otago Peninsula** is replete with wildlife sanctuaries and penguins, albatross and seals all compete for attention with **Larnach Castle** and its fine grounds.

To the south, the pace slows along the untamed **Catlins Coast**, with yet more wonderful opportunities for spotting marine wildlife, but in an altogether wilder setting. Hills cloaked in native forest come right down to a shoreline indented with rocky bays, long sweeps of sand and spectacular geological formations.

New Zealand's southernmost city is **Invercargill**, bordered by Southland's rich pastureland. The city is the springboard for **Bluff**, the country's oldest European town, and magical **Stewart Island**. Relatively few visit New Zealand's third island, but those who do are rewarded by the extraordinary birdlife, particularly in **Mason Bay** and on **Ulva Island**.

Kiwis from more northern parts delight in condemning the **climate** of the southern South Island, and it's true that the further south you go the wetter and

ROYAL ALBATROSS, OTAGO PENINSULA

Highlights

❶ Dunedin Soak up the Gothic architecture of New Zealand's "Scottish city" while sampling the museums, galleries and frenetic student scene. **See p.592**

❷ Taieri Gorge Combine a train trip winding through the rugged Taieri Gorge with cycling the Otago Central Rail Trail. **See p.606**

❸ Otago Peninsula Whether you choose to paddle, cruise or drive around this stunning coastline you'll get amazingly close to all sorts of wildlife. **See p.607**

❹ Curio Bay Survey a fossilized forest along the shoreline, watch yellow-eyed penguins come ashore and see Hector's dolphins surfing the waves of the wild Catlins Coast. **See p.621**

❺ Invercargill Inspect a tuatara, see Burt Munro's record-breaking motorcycle and sample the fine produce of the Invercargill Brewery. **See p.624**

❻ Stewart Island You'll slip straight into Rakiura's island vibe as soon as you step ashore – but make the effort to rouse yourself for superb birdwatching, great boating and rugged tramps. **See p.630**

❼ Mason Bay Tramp to Stewart Island's windswept west coast for a chance to spot rare kiwis in the wild. **See p.634**

HIGHLIGHTS ARE MARKED ON THE MAP ON P.592

more changeable it gets. Come between November and April and you'll experience daytime highs approaching 20°C and catch the best of the wildlife in breeding season.

Dunedin

The darkly Gothic harbourside city of **DUNEDIN** is the largest city in the southern half of the South Island, its population of around 120,000 bolstered by 25,000 students from the **University of Otago** – New Zealand's oldest tertiary institution

HIGHLIGHTS

1. Dunedin
2. Taieri Gorge
3. Otago Peninsula
4. Curio Bay
5. Invercargill
6. Stewart Island
7. Mason Bay

0		50
	kilometres	

DUNEDIN TO STEWART ISLAND

– who contribute to a strong **arts scene** and vibrant **nightlife**, during term time at least.

The university aside, the city hasn't had a lot of investment in recent decades – though being named a UNESCO **City of Literature** and winning ultra-fast broadband in a nationwide competition in 2014 means that the city's fortunes may be on the up. The once run down **Warehouse District**, sandwiched between Prince's Street and the railway, has become a canvas for **street artists** and is slowly filling with creative businesses and hip eateries.

Although Dunedin spreads out into the suburb-strung hills and surf beaches, the city has a compact and manageable heart, centred on **The Octagon**. This manicured, tree-lined green space is bordered by the **art gallery**, the ornate **Municipal Chambers** and the substantial **St Paul's Cathedral**. Further afield, the impressive new **Toitu Otago Settlers Museum** offers a fascinating glimpse into the city's past, while the **Chinese Gardens** offer contemplative calm. It is worth a look in the nearby **Dunedin Railway Station** even if you're not making a journey on the time-warped **Taieri Gorge Railway**.

Beer and chocolate are always winners, best experienced on the **Cadbury World** tour and **Speight's Brewery Tour**. North of the centre, **Olveston** gives a taste of Dunedin life from its heyday, a topic treated more formally in the **Otago Museum**. The **Botanic Garden** climbs up towards the lookout on **Signal Hill**, from where you can look down to **Otago Harbour**, a sheltered inlet 22km long and no wider than a river in places. The harbour is protected from the ocean by the wonderful **Otago Peninsula** (see p.607).

Local buses get you quickly to **Baldwin Street**, the world's steepest, and to the sandy beaches of **St Clair** and **St Kilda**, the former with good surfing and a cluster of cool cafés.

11

Brief history

From around 1300 AD, **Maori** fished the rich coastal waters of nearby bays, travelling inland in search of moa, ducks and freshwater fish, and trading with *iwi* further north. Eventually they formed a settlement near the harbour's mouth, calling it Otakou (pronounced "O-tar-go") and naming the headland at the harbour entrance after their great chieftain, Taiaroa – today a *marae* occupies the Otakou site. By the 1820s European whalers and sealers were seeking shelter in what was the only safe anchorage along this stretch of coast, unwittingly introducing foreign diseases. The local Maori population was decimated, dropping to a low of 110, but subsequent intermarriage bolstered numbers.

The Scots arrive

The New Zealand Company selected the Otago Harbour for a planned **Scottish settlement** as early as 1840 and purchased land from local Maori, but it wasn't until 1848 that the first migrant ships arrived, led by Captain William Cargill and the Reverend Thomas Burns, nephew of the Scottish poet Robert Burns. The arrival of English and Irish settlers soon made the Scots a minority, but their national fervour had already stamped its distinct character on the town.

The prospectors arrive

In 1861, a lone Australian prospector discovered **gold** at a creek near present-day Lawrence, about 100km west of Dunedin. Within three months, diggers were pouring in from Australia, and as the main port of entry Dunedin found itself in the midst of a gold rush. The port was expanded, and the population doubled in six months, trebling in three years and making the city briefly New Zealand's largest. The newfound wealth spurred a building boom that resulted in much of the city's most iconic architecture, including the university.

By the 1870s gold mania had largely subsided, but the area sustained its economic primacy through **shipping**, railway development and farming. Decline began during the early twentieth century, when the opening of the Panama Canal in 1914 made

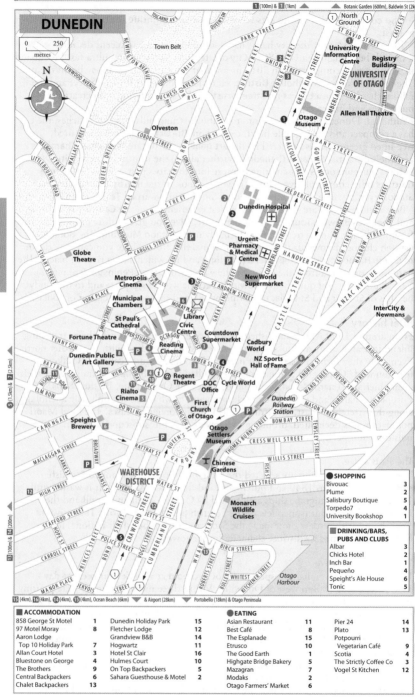

DUNEDIN

Botanic Garden (600m), Baldwin St (2k)

North Ground

Town Belt

University Information Centre

Registry Building

UNIVERSITY OF OTAGO

Olveston

Allen Hall Theatre

Otago Museum

Dunedin Hospital

Urgent Pharmacy & Medical Centre

Globe Theatre

New World Supermarket

Metropolis Cinema

InterCity & Newmans

Municipal Chambers

St Paul's Cathedral

Library

Fortune Theatre

Civic Centre

Countdown Supermarket

Cadbury World

Dunedin Public Art Gallery

Reading Cinema

NZ Sports Hall of Fame

Regent Theatre

DOC Office

Cycle World

Rialto Cinema

Dunedin Railway Station

First Church of Otago

Speights Brewery

Otago Settlers Museum

WAREHOUSE DISTRICT

Chinese Gardens

Monarch Wildlife Cruises

Otago Harbour

15 (4km), 16 (4km), 14 (4km), 15 (4km), Ocean Beach (6km)   & Airport (28km)   Portobello (18km) & Otago Peninsula

● SHOPPING

Bivouac	3
Plume	2
Salisbury Boutique	5
Torpedo7	4
University Bookshop	1

■ DRINKING/BARS, PUBS AND CLUBS

Albar	3
Chicks Hotel	2
Inch Bar	1
Pequeño	4
Speight's Ale House	6
Tonic	5

■ ACCOMMODATION

858 George St Motel	1	Dunedin Holiday Park	15
97 Motel Moray	8	Fletcher Lodge	12
Aaron Lodge		Grandview B&B	14
Top 10 Holiday Park	7	Hogwartz	11
Allan Court Hotel	3	Hotel St Clair	16
Bluestone on George	4	Hulmes Court	10
The Brothers	9	On Top Backpackers	5
Central Backpackers	6	Sahara Guesthouse & Motel	2
Chalet Backpackers	13		

● EATING

Asian Restaurant	11	Pier 24	14
Best Café	8	Plato	13
The Esplanade	15	Potpourri	
Etrusco	10	Vegetarian Café	9
The Good Earth	1	Scotia	4
Highgate Bridge Bakery	5	The Strictly Coffee Co	3
Mazagran	7	Vogel St Kitchen	12
Modaks	2		
Otago Farmers' Market	6		

Auckland a more economic port for British shipping. In the 1980s, the improvement in world gold prices and the development of equipment enabling large-scale recovery of gold from low-yielding soils re-established **mining** in the hinterland. New Zealand's largest gold-mining operation is located an hour's drive north of Dunedin at Macraes' vast open-pit mine.

The Octagon

Dunedin's diminutive central plaza is **The Octagon**, laid out in 1846 and ringed by a blend of well-preserved buildings and modern additions. The sloping site is presided over by a **statue of Robert Burns**, symbol of Dunedin's Scottish origins. On summer Fridays (10am–4pm), the area hosts **market** stalls selling local crafts, and at all times there are people huddled over phones and laptops making use of The Octagon's **free wi-fi**.

Dunedin Public Art Gallery

30 The Octagon • Daily 10am–5pm • Free • ☎ 03 477 3240, ⓦ dunedin.art.museum

Although **Dunedin Public Art Gallery** was founded in 1884 – making it the country's oldest gallery – its current incarnation is the work of City Council architects in 1996. This gleaming space was fashioned out of six Victorian buildings, all elegantly refurbished to create a light, modern split-level space with several exhibition areas. In the foyer a spiral staircase from the department store that once occupied the site winds up to Neil Dawson's *Cones*, five of them chasing each other across the ceiling. The gallery hosts a great rotating collection of early and contemporary pieces from New Zealand and further afield, along with temporary exhibits and an outpost of Wellington's **Nga Taonga Sound & Vision Archive** (see p.421), where you can watch Kiwi movies, documentaries and TV programmes on individual computer screens.

11

Municipal Chambers

The Octagon is dominated by the 1880 **Municipal Chambers**, a grand structure with an Italianate clock tower, all constructed from limestone on a base of Port Chalmers breccia. It's a fine example of the handiwork of Scottish architect **Robert A. Lawson**, whose influence can be seen in many of Dunedin's public buildings.

St Paul's Cathedral

Daily 10am–4pm • Free

Beside the Municipal Chambers rise the twin white-stone spires of **St Paul's Cathedral**, one of Dunedin's finest buildings and the seat of Anglican worship in the city. The stone-vaulted Gothic Revival nave, entirely constructed from Oamaru stone, was consecrated in 1919. The vaulted ceiling is the only one of its kind in New Zealand, and much of the stained glass in the impressive windows is original. The Modernist chancel and large organ were added in 1971.

Regent Theatre

17 The Octagon • ☎ 03 477 8597, ⓦ regenttheatre.co.nz

Across The Octagon, directly opposite St Paul's, a fine 1876 facade announces the **Regent Theatre**, originally a hotel, then a cinema and finally a theatre. The theatre hosts international shows and the Royal New Zealand Ballet, as well as live music. Inside, elaborate nineteenth-century plasterwork and marble staircases are juxtaposed with 1920s stained-glass windows and geometric balustrades.

First Church of Otago

415 Moray Place • Heritage Centre: Oct–May Mon–Fri 10am–4pm, Sat 10am–2pm; June–Sept Mon–Sat 10.30am–2.30pm • Free

The 60m-high stone spire of the **First Church of Otago** is visible throughout the city.

Robert A. Lawson's neo-Gothic building is generally recognized as the most impressive of New Zealand's nineteenth-century churches, with particular praise given to the wooden gabled ceiling and, above the pulpit, a brightly coloured rose window. Behind the altar, the **Heritage Centre** explores the history of the church and its prime movers.

Toitu Otago Settlers Museum

31 Queens Gardens • Daily: Oct–March 10am–5pm; April–Sept 10am–4pm; Thurs 10am–8pm year-round • Free • ☎ 03 477 5052, ⓦ toituosm.com

A $38 million revamp has transformed the **Toitu Otago Settlers Museum** into one of Dunedin's most worthwhile attractions. The collection narrates two centuries of colonial and social history with artefacts ranging from whaling boats to washing machines. The transport-related displays are particularly strong, and the entire experience is enhanced by the museum's innovative use of technology and plenty of hands-on exhibits.

The museum complex is composed of three buildings: the original neo-Georgian brick heritage building, a 1939 Art Deco former bus depot and the dramatic glass-walled entrance foyer containing *Josephine*, a restored 1872 double-ended Fairlie steam engine, New Zealand's oldest locomotive.

Chinese Gardens

Corner of Rattray and Cumberland sts • Daily 10am–5pm and Thurs 10–8pm • $9; audio guides $5 • ☎ 03 477 3248, ⓦ dunedinchinesegarden.com

Dunedin's **Chinese Gardens** opened in 2008, the culmination of a major project marking the contribution of the Chinese gold-miners and their descendants to the life of the city. It is one of a handful of classical Chinese gardens outside China and everything – from the 970 tonnes of limestone used in construction to the pavilions with their flying eaves – was shipped here from Shanghai. Ranged round a contemplative pond, it seems a world away from the surrounding city, a sensation only deepened by the opportunity to drink tea, eat steamed buns and play Go in the gardens' teahouse.

Dunedin Railway Station

22 Anzac Ave

Impossible to miss thanks to its towers, turrets and minarets, the resplendent **Dunedin Railway Station** took over twenty years to build on reclaimed swampland; it was finally completed in 1906. The walls of its exquisitely preserved **foyer** glisten with green, yellow and cream majolica tiles made especially for New Zealand Rail by Royal Doulton, and the mosaic floor celebrates the steam engine and consists of more than 700,000 tiny squares of porcelain. On the upstairs balcony, two stained-glass windows depict approaching trains, their headlights gleaming from all angles.

The station no longer sees regular passenger services, though it is the terminus for the Taieri Gorge Railway (see box, p.606).

New Zealand Sports Hall of Fame

Daily 10am–4pm • $6 • ☎ 03 477 7775, ⓦ nzhalloffame.co.nz

The station's upper floor houses a hagiographic collection of memorabilia relating to the 170 members of the **New Zealand Sports Hall of Fame**. The objects are taken from disciplines ranging from yachting to sheep shearing, with – as you'd expect – an excellent section on rugby that includes the likes of an arm guard used by revered player Colin Meads to play a test match with a broken arm.

Hocken Library

) Anzac Ave • Mon–Fri 9am–5pm, Tues until 9pm, Sat 9am–noon; tours Wed 2pm • Free • ☎ 03 479 8874, ⓦ library.otago.ac.nz/hocken

The **Hocken Library** is the university's extensive research facility, open to the public and built around an impressive New Zealand and Pacific collection assembled in the late nineteenth century by Dr Thomas Morland Hocken, a Dunedin physician and one of the country's first historians. The collection is housed in an Art Deco former butter factory where there are fascinating temporary exhibitions on the first floor, and free behind-the-scenes tours on Wednesday afternoons.

Cadbury World

80 Cumberland St • Mon–Fri for 75min tours; Sat & Sun, plus public holidays and Christmas to mid-Jan when production lines are closed r 45min tours; bookings recommended • 75min tours $22; 45min tours $16 • ☎ 03 467 7967, ⓦ cadburyworld.co.nz

Diverting displays on the history of chocolate and a chance to nibble on cacao beans (bitter and highly caffeinated but not unpleasant) set the scene for tours enthusiastically led by purple-clad guides. On the full tour you'll don hairnets and head into the factory (wear closed shoes), where you'll see lines producing chocolate buttons, boxed assortments, and Easter eggs. Both tours stop at the rather gratuitous "chocolate waterfall" set up for visitors, and everyone gets liberally showered with free samples.

11

Speight's Brewery

00 Rattray St • Oct–March noon, 2pm, 4pm, 5pm, 6pm & 7pm; April–Sept noon, 2pm, 4pm & 6pm • $28; bookings essential • ☎ 03 477 7697, ⓦ speights.co.nz

New Zealand's "liquid gold", Speight's Gold Medal Ale, has been brewed in Dunedin since the late 1880s, and remains one of the country's biggest-selling beers. Sample it and five other brews at the end of the **Speight's Brewery Tour**, an informative 90min meander around one of New Zealand's oldest breweries, established in 1876. Much of the recently refurbished brewery building dates from 1940, while the brick chimney (topped by a stone beer barrel) is visible from across the city.

Beside the tour entrance is a **spigot** fed by the same sweet-tasting artesian water that is used to brew the beer. Locals stop regularly to fill water bottles.

Olveston

2 Royal Terrace, 15min walk northwest of The Octagon • Daily 9.30am, 10.45am, noon, 1.30pm, 2.45pm & 4pm for 1hr guided tours only; bookings recommended • $19 • ☎ 03 477 3320, ⓦ olveston.co.nz

Dunedin's showpiece historic home is **Olveston**, a fine Edwardian four-storey manor built around 1906 for Jewish businessman and collector, David Theomin. The last-surviving family member, his daughter Dorothy, lived there until her death in 1966, after which the house was bequeathed to the City of Dunedin. It remains just as she left it: you could easily imagine her walking in through the door as you tour the house, which is a treasure-trove of art and antiques. The family were passionate about travel, art and music, and their tastes are reflected in everything from Arts and Crafts fireplaces, English oak panelling and Venetian glassware to Japanese and Delft porcelain. A kosher kitchen, elegant gardens and David Theomin's 1921 Fiat Tourer complete the scene.

Otago Museum

19 Great King St • Daily 10am–5pm; highlights tour daily 2pm • Free; highlights tour donation; Discovery World Tropical Forest $10 • ☎ 03 474 7474, ⓦ otagomuseum.govt.nz

If you're heading south from Dunedin, make sure to visit the absorbing **Otago Museum**, and its fascinating "Southern Land, Southern People" gallery for context on life and natural history in the southern half of the South Island. Boulders give an idea of the rock that underlies the region, while related displays draw in a fossilized plesiosaur skeleton and the influence of Oamaru stone on the region's architecture. Everything is knitted neatly together, with a discussion on climate illustrated by a Maori flax rain cape, and coverage of the region's fish, calling on the experience of whitebaiters.

Elsewhere look out for the **Animal Attic**, a deeply Victorian display of macabre skeletons and stuffed beasts – the chickens have even escaped to roost among the rafters. The **Pacific Cultures gallery** contains some excellent exhibits from Polynesia and Melanesia – keep an eye out for the coconut fibre and shark tooth armour from Kiribati – and there's a decent collection of Maori artefacts in the Tangata Whenua gallery. The humid, 28°C **Tropical Forest** section is a great place to escape a cold Dunedin day among a thousand butterflies.

11 University of Otago

Campus accessed from the corner of Cumberland and Union sts • Information centre: 9am–4.30pm daily

New Zealand's oldest university, the **University of Otago** was founded by Scottish settlers in 1869. Based on the design of Glasgow University, it quickly expanded into a complex of imposing Gothic bluestone buildings, foremost among them the **Clocktower** building. The best bits are concentrated along Leith Street; for a more thorough look, follow the self-guided walk detailed in the *University Tour* booklet (available from the i-SITE and university information centre). Note that if your visit falls in the summer holidays (Dec–Feb) you'll miss the usual studenty vibe.

Dunedin Botanic Garden

2km north of The Octagon along Great King St • Sunrise–sunset • Free

The serene **Dunedin Botanic Garden** was established in 1863 at the foot of Signal Hill. Split in half by Lindsay Creek, visitor facilities are centred in the flat **Lower Garden**. The steep **Upper Garden** contains an arboretum filled with now-mature trees planted in the nineteenth century to learn which species would flourish here for forestry purposes. Further up the hill there's also a sprawling rhododendron dell and an aviary, home to native birds as well as a garrulous flock of parrots.

Lower Garden

Information centre & Winter Garden daily 10am–4pm; Alpine House daily 9am–4pm • ☎ 03 471 9275

The lower half of the Botanic Garden holds the steamy Winter Garden, its glasshouses filled with a profusion of tropical plants. Outside you can stroll through formal rose and herb gardens, and the expansive parklands that insulate the garden from the surrounding city. A volunteer-run information centre sits between the tea kiosk and the Winter Garden.

Signal Hill

Signal Hill Rd, 7km northeast of The Octagon • #11 Opoho bus from George St Stand 7 stops 2km short of the summit and goes via the north end of the Botanic Garden

The 393m summit of **Signal Hill**, just north of the Botanic Garden, is crowned by a scenic reserve with magnificent views over Dunedin and the upper harbour from the Centennial Memorial. Constructed to commemorate the century of British sovereignty (1840–1940) that followed the signing of the Treaty of Waitangi, the memorial is flanked by two powerful bronze figures symbolizing the past and the future. Embedded in the podium is a tribute to Dunedin's namesake: a chunk of the rock upon which Edinburgh Castle was built.

Baldwin Street

4.5km north of the city centre; follow Great King St until it becomes North Rd then look for road signs • #9 Normanby and #28 St Clair–Normanby services run past the foot of Baldwin St from Princes St Stand 2

Dunedin rejoices in the world's steepest street, the dead-straight **Baldwin Street**, which, with a *Guinness Book of Records*-verified maximum gradient of 1 in 2.86, has a slope of almost 19 degrees. The views from the top aren't bad, but the highlight is walking up, something achieved in about five minutes, under the bemused gaze of residents. As part of Dunedin's Chocolate Carnival (held in mid-July; see box, p.604), the street has hosted the annual Cadbury Jaffa Race since 2002, which sees thousands of giant Jaffas (tangerine-coloured candy-coated chocolate balls) rolled downhill for charity.

Ocean Beach & Around

5km south of the city centre

The contiguous suburbs of **St Clair** and **St Kilda** back onto **Ocean Beach**, a long, wild sweep of sand enclosed by two volcanic headlands. The St Clair end is excellent for surfing (see box, p.600); further east, St Kilda is your best for swimming. Both ends are served by frequent buses from The Octagon.

St Clair Hot Salt Water Pool

The Esplanade • Oct–late March Mon–Fri 6am–7pm, Sat & Sun 7am–7pm • $6 • ☎ 03 455 6352

St Clair beach meets the cliffs at its western end beside the 25m **St Clair Hot Salt Water Pool**, the last open-air pool of its kind in the country. Filled with seawater heated to 28°C, it has a real community feel with all sorts of folk down for their constitutional. The pool's small café has the best views along the beach.

St Kilda and Tomahawk Beach

About 1km east of the saltwater baths, St Clair merges into **St Kilda**, where the beach is reasonably safe for swimming as long as you keep between the flags; it is patrolled in summer.

At the beach's eastern end, a headland separates Ocean Beach from the smaller **Tomahawk Beach** (not safe for swimming), at low tide often dotted with horses and buggies preparing for trotting races.

ARRIVAL AND DEPARTURE   DUNEDIN

By plane Dunedin Airport, 22km southwest of town on SH1 then 7km along SH86, is served by domestic flights as well as direct international flights from Australia. Shuttle buses, including Super Shuttle (☎ 0800 748885, ⓦ supershuttle.co.nz; $30 for 1, $40 for 2), drop off at city-centre accommodation. A taxi is about $80.

Destinations Auckland (3 daily; 1hr 50min); Brisbane (3 weekly; 3hr 35min); Christchurch (7 daily; 1hr); Wellington (5 daily; 1hr 40min).

By train Dunedin has no main-line passenger trains, just the scenic Taieri Gorge Railway (see box, p.606).

Destinations Middlemarch (1–2 weekly; 2hr 30min); Pukerangi (1–2 daily; 2hr).

By bus Dunedin is a regional hub for bus services. InterCity/Newmans (7 Halsey St) runs to Christchurch via Oamaru and

Timaru, Queenstown via Alexandra and Cromwell, Wanaka and Te Anau via Gore. Atomic and Alpine Connexions (☎ 03 443 9120, ⓦ alpineconnexions.co.nz) both run from Dunedin Railway Station to Queenstown and Wanaka, while NakedBus (630 Princes St) goes to Christchurch and Invercargill. Catch-A-Bus South (☎ 03 479 9960, ⓦ catchabussouth.co.nz) operate a door-to-door service between Dunedin, Gore and Invercargill; Knightrider (☎ 0800 287874, ⓦ knightrider.co.nz) runs to Christchurch.

Destinations Alexandra (4 daily; 3hr); Balclutha (4 daily; 1hr); Christchurch (6 daily; 6hr); Cromwell (4 daily; 3hr 30min); Gore (4 daily; 3hr); Invercargill (4–5 daily; 3hr 30min); Lawrence (4 daily; 1hr 30min); Oamaru (6 daily; 2hr); Queenstown (4 daily; 4–5hr); Te Anau (daily; 4h 30min); Wanaka (2–3 daily; 4hr).

INFORMATION

Tourist information i-SITE, 26 Princes St (Dec–March Mon–Fri 8.30am–6pm, Sat & Sun 8.45am–6pm;

April–Nov daily 8.30am–5pm; ☎ 03 474 3300). Handles transport, accommodation and trips, and stocks the

11

DUNEDIN TOURS AND ACTIVITIES

Dunedin's guided and self-guided **walks** are a great way to get to know another side of the city. On the city fringes, there's **surf** at St Clair and forested **mountain-bike** trails on the Signal Hill Reserve, just 3km northeast of The Octagon (free trail map from bike rental shops; see below). Half- and full-day biking routes are listed in the free *Fat Tyre Trails* leaflet, with some of the trails accessible from the city centre.

TOURS AND WALKS

City Walks ☎0800 925571, ⓦcitywalks.co.nz. Guided heritage walks around Dunedin's historic centre (Mon–Sat 10.30am; 2hr; $30) or the Warehouse District (Mon–Sat 1.30pm; 2hr; $30). An abridged version of the morning tour runs each afternoon, enlivened by a snack of whisky and haggis. (Mon–Sat 4.30pm; 1hr; $30).

Dunedin Literary Walk ☎03 470 1109, ⓦresearchwrite.co.nz/LiteraryWalk. The enthusiastic Jennie Coleman leads these 2hr explorations (daily 10.15am & 2.15pm; $30) of the city's literary heritage, with a "virtual" alternative in wet weather.

Hair Raiser Tours ☎0800 428683, ⓦhairraisertours.com. Entertainingly spooky walking tours such as the Underbelly Crime Walk (Mon–Sat 10.30am; $30), the Ghost Walk (daily: Oct–March 8pm; April–Sept 6pm; $30) and a graveyard tour of the city's Northern Cemetery (daily: Oct–March 9.30pm; April–Sept 8pm; $30).

Street Art Trail ⓦdunedinstreetart.com. Pick up a map from the i-SITE and head off on this self-guided walk around Dunedin's graffitied precincts. The trail, thoughtfully bracketed by excellent cafés and passing the Vogel St Kitchen (see p.603), winds from the Octagon down into the Warehouse District, where the street art is concentrated.

SURFING

Esplanade Surf School Eastern end of the Esplanade, by the St Clair Surf Rescue Station ☎0800 484141, ⓦespsurfschool.co.nz. Cool-water surfing lessons with wetsuit, board and sunscreen supplied (group lessons $60/90min; private lessons $120/90min); equipment hire is available too ($40/2hr for board and wetsuit).

MOUNTAIN BIKING

Offtrack ☎0800 633872, ⓦofftrack.co.nz. Brilliant half-day guided rides on some of Dunedin's finest singletrack and 4WD tracks ($70), plus scenic day-rides in the Catlins ($110) and a tough-but-fun day-trip ($130) on the Dunstan Road in the Maniototo.

informative *Dunedin: Selected Walks* leaflet ($4), which details 19 walks around the city.
DOC 77 Stuart St (Mon–Fri 8.30am–5pm; ☎03 477 0677).

Website Dunedin has an unusually good promotional website, ⓦdunedinnz.com, filled with information on events and things to do in the city.

GETTING AROUND

By bus The city has an efficient, if initially confusing, bus system (generally Mon–Fri 7.30am–11pm, Sat & Sun limited services; ⓦwww.orc.govt.nz). Buses are numbered and change numbers depending on which direction they're travelling in; fortunately routes are more usually identified by their destination. The most useful is the Normanby–St Clair run (#28 northbound, #8 southbound), which goes from the beach right through the city, past the Botanic Garden, to the foot of Baldwin St.

Bus fares Fares are zoned: the central city is Zone One ($2), Portobello is Zone Seven ($6.70). All buses pass through the centre of town, stopping at different stands around The Octagon, or along Princes and George sts.

By car Dunedin operates a one-way system running north–south through the city affecting Cumberland, Castle, Great King and Crawford sts.

Parking Parking is seldom a problem, with inexpensive meters and restricted zones in the centre and free long-term street parking outside the downtown core.

Car rental The international agencies are complemented by good home-grown companies including Hirepool, 66 Cumberland St (☎03 471 9747, ⓦhirepool.co.nz), and Ace at Dunedin Airport (☎0800 502277, ⓦacerentalcars.co.nz).

By taxi Call Dunedin Taxis (☎03 477 7777).

By bike Cycle World, 67 Stuart St (☎03 477 7473, ⓦcycleworld.co.nz), rents road and mountain bikes from $35/half-day or $50/day. Dunedin Bike Hire (☎0800 480680, ⓦibikehire.co.nz) hires out electric ($80/day) and standard bikes (from $40/day), with free delivery and pick-up. The city is developing a network of cycle trails and lanes; the only section currently rideable takes you halfway to Port Chalmers.

ACCOMMODATION

There's a broad choice of accommodation in Dunedin, most of it near the city centre. If you prefer something more rural, consider the **Otago Peninsula** (see p.608). **Freedom camping** is allowed in Dunedin City Council car parks all over the region provided you are self-contained and legally parked, and there are no more than three campervans in a 50m radius.

CENTRAL DUNEDIN

858 George St Motel 858 George St ☎03 474 0047, ⌂858georgestreetmotel.co.nz. A beautifully designed modern motel based on Victorian townhouses, with thirteen big, luxurious units and larger suites with their own kitchens. Free wi-fi. Studios **$140**, suites **$160**

97 Motel Moray 97 Moray Place ☎03 477 2050, ⌂97motel.co.nz. Very central motel that's better than it looks from the street, with 40 rooms in the main high-rise block (formerly student halls) or in a new two-storey building. There's plenty of parking and the spacious rooms have comfortable beds and kitchenettes, making it a good central option. **$130**

Allan Court Motel 590 George St ☎03 477 7526, ⌂allancourt.co.nz. Central and well-kept 1980s-built motel with spacious rooms, mostly one- and two-bedroom apartments, recently refitted bathrooms and nice touches such as free newspapers and wi-fi. **$145**

★Bluestone on George 571 George St ☎03 477 9201, ⌂bluestonedunedin.co.nz. Fifteen classy studio apartments with state-of-the-art kitchens, stylish bathrooms, in-room laundries and tasteful understated decor. If you manage to prise yourself from the sumptuous beds there's even a small gym, courtyard and lounge. **$210**

The Brothers 295 Rattray St ☎03 477 0043, ⌂brothershotel.co.nz. Fifteen-room boutique hotel tastefully converted from a 1920s Christian Brothers' residence. Pared-down contemporary decor, with many of the compact rooms opening onto verandas with splendid city views; one is in the former chapel. A spacious lounge has more views, Sky TV and free wi-fi. Continental breakfast included. **$160**

Central Backpackers 243 Moray Place ☎0800 123687 ⌂centralbackpackers.co.nz. Efficiently-run forty-bed BBH hostel with a mixed clientele. Along with free wi-fi and a DVD lounge with Playstation there are backpack-size security lockers and a friendly cat. Dorms **$28**, doubles **$70**

Chalet Backpackers 296 High St ☎03 479 2075, ⌂chaletbackpackers.co.nz. Light fills the mostly four-bed (no bunks) dorms at this comfortable hostel with pleasing harbour views, good kitchen and dining facilities, comfy singles ($43), doubles and small dorms, plus a pool table and piano. Occasional winter closures. Dorms **$29**, rooms **$66**

Fletcher Lodge 276 High St ☎03 477 5552, ⌂fletcherlodge.co.nz. Attention is devoted to guests' comfort at this elegant lodge set in an English baronial-style home built in 1924 for leading Kiwi industrialist Sir James Fletcher. The five rooms and suites are complemented by an adjacent pair of well-appointed and fully equipped apartments – you get independence but miss out on the splendour of the main house. Doubles **$335**, apartments **$650**

Grandview B&B 360 High St ☎03 472 9472, ⌂grandview.co.nz. Very welcoming B&B in an 1850s house with great views over the city and five rooms, three of which are en-suite. A good continental breakfast is included but there's also a full guest kitchen, an honesty bar and barbecue on the deck plus an infrared sauna ($5) and free internet. Doubles **$139**, en suites **$179**

★Hogwartz 277 Rattray St ☎03 474 1487, ⌂hogwartz.co.nz. Welcoming BBH hostel in the former Catholic bishop's residence close to the centre of town. The dorms are bunk-free, some rooms have city views and it has all the facilities you'll need from a laundry service to the sunny deck. The hostel also offers a handful of attractive self-contained studios in two adjacent cottages (from $96). Occasional winter closures. Dorms **$29**, en-suite doubles **$80**

Hulmes Court 52 Tennyson St ☎03 477 5319, ⌂hulmes.co.nz. The style of this pair of houses (one Edwardian, the other a grander 1860 Victorian affair) is a bit higgledy-piggledy but the price is right. Just a short climb from The Octagon with big, individually themed rooms (several en-suite), off-street parking, free internet, and continental breakfast served in the sunny drawing room. Rooms **$115**, en suites **$145**

On Top Backpackers Corner of Filleul St and Moray Place ☎0800 668672, ⌂ontopbackpackers.co.nz. Purpose-built 90-bed hostel with a lively atmosphere aided by the bar and pool hall downstairs. Along with slightly cramped six- to eight-bed dorms there are a number of en-suite doubles, plus TV, BBQ terrace and a bright, open-plan kitchen/common room. A basic continental breakfast is included. Discounts for YHA and BBH cardholders. Dorms **$27**, en suites **$89**

Sahara Guesthouse & Motel 619 George St ☎03 477 6662, ⌂dunedin-accommodation.co.nz. Pragmatic rather than romantic, the rooms at this 1863 guesthouse largely share facilities, though the standard motel units ($99) have their own bathrooms and kitchenettes and there are some comfortable newish deluxe studios ($109). Off-street parking. Shared-bath doubles **$70**, en-suite doubles **$90**

11

ST CLAIR

Hotel St Clair 24 Esplanade ☎03 456 0555, ⓦhotelstclair.com. This modern, stylish 26-room hotel and its *Pier 24* restaurant have become the focal point for St Clair, with smart clean lines, luxury fittings and spacious rooms, all with bathtubs and minibars. The cheapest sea-view rooms fill up quickly; book in advance. **$205**

CAMPSITES AND HOLIDAY PARKS

Aaron Lodge Top 10 Holiday Park 162 Kaikorai Valley Rd, 2.5km west of the city centre ☎0800 879227, ⓦaaronlodgetop10.co.nz. A sheltered, fairly spacious and well-tended site in the hills, with the Top 10 chain' usual wide range of accommodation options and on-site entertainment. Camping **$36**, powered sites **$36** (both pe site)

Dunedin Holiday Park 41 Victoria Rd ☎03 455 4690 ⓦdunedinholidaypark.co.nz. Lying alongside St Kilda Beach, this well-appointed park is a 5min drive from th city centre. There's a wide range of accommodation available if the weather precludes camping, plus free wi-f and a playground. Camping **$36**, powered sites **$40** (bot per site)

EATING

Dunedin enjoys a pretty decent range of eating options, from cafés to fine restaurants, most of which are concentrate around The Octagon and along George Street. Interesting outliers can be found in suburban Roslyn and beachy St Clair. Fo staples, visit the Countdown supermarket at 309 Cumberland St.

CENTRAL DUNEDIN

Asian Restaurant 43 Moray Place ☎03 477 6673. Nothing flash, but zingy, fun and always busy, dishing up MSG-free classics such as fried noodles ($7, large $10) and roast duck ($17 for a half-bird). Licensed and BYO. Mon–Sat noon–2pm & 5–10pm or later, Sun 5–10pm.

Best Café 30 Lower Stuart St ☎03 477 8059. Time-warped Dunedin stalwart where mains are served with bread, curled butter and no frills. The menu covers eight species of fresh fish, served with chips and coleslaw (1 piece for $11–18.50; 2 pieces for $16–26), and there's shrimp cocktail ($10) on the menu if you feel inspired by the retro surroundings, with Bluff oysters and whitebait patties in season. Licensed and BYO. Mon–Thurs 11.30am–2.30pm & 5–8pm, Fri & Sat 11.30am–2.30pm & 5–9pm.

Etrusco First floor, 8 Moray Place ☎03 477 3737, ⓦetrusco.co.nz. Cheap, cheerful and hugely popular Italian-run pizza and pasta restaurant (medium dishes $15–20; large $20–30) somewhat ostentatiously located in an airy and lovingly restored building. Feels like it has barely changed since the 1980s – in a good way. Daily 5.30–10pm or later.

The Good Earth 765 Cumberland St ☎03 471 8554. Art adorns the white walls of this predominantly organic and Fairtrade café with park views through big windows. Stop in for a coffee and a melt-in-your-mouth sun-dried tomato, feta and rocket scone ($4), or lunch on Moroccan chicken on couscous and preserved lemon salad ($16) or polenta-crusted frittata with salad ($14). Mon–Fri 7am–5pm, Sat & Sun 8am–5pm.

Mazagran 36 Moray Place ☎03 477 9959. If immaculate espresso is your goal head straight for this tiny café where everything is roasted on the premises. The barista decides which blend to use every morning and you can buy a dozen styles of freshly roasted beans. Mon–Fri 8am–5pm, Sa 10am–2pm.

★**Modaks** 337 George St ☎03 477 6563. Edgy an funky café with pop art lining the walls, plus great espress and chewy cinnamon pinwheel scones. The menu ha plenty of vegetarian and vegan dishes, and imaginative breakfasts – try their Mexican eggs breakfast ($15) serve with delicious gluten-free jalapeño bread. Mon–Fr 7.30am–6pm, Sat & Sun 8am–6pm.

Otago Farmers' Market Dunedin Railway Station ca park ⓦotagofarmersmarket.org.nz. Every Saturda morning the station car park comes alive with fruit, veg an food vendors from around the district at this always popular market. Saturday 8am–noon.

★**Plato** 2 Birch St ☎03 477 4235, ⓦplatocafe.co.nz Dunedin's cooler grown-ups find their way across th overpasses and railway tracks to fill this consistentl excellent bistro in a 1960s former seafarers' hostel – a lo rectangular room lined with shelves of quirky *tchotchkes* The menu changes constantly, but expect sophisticate flavours – even humble fish and chips ($34) is dressed u with a kelp crust and finished with lemon butter. Lunc Wed–Sat noon–2pm; brunch Sun 11am–3pm; dinne daily 6–10pm or later.

Potpourri Vegetarian Café 97 Stuart St ☎03 47 9983, ⓦpotpourrivegetariancafe.co.nz. You don't nee to be veggie to appreciate this established vegetarian café where the bare brick walls are decorated with botanica etchings. Delicious seed-and-fruit slices and muffin complement light meals (all under $10) and mor substantial dishes such as bean burrito and salad ($15) Mon–Fri 8.30am–3pm, Sat 9am–3pm.

★**Scotia** 199 Upper Stuart St ☎03 477 7704 ⓦscotiadunedin.co.nz. The cosy ambience of a converte Victorian terraced house is an appropriate setting for thi restaurant and bar with a distinct Scottish angle. There's a

11

fine collection of whiskies, friendly and efficient service, and Kiwi bistro food with nods to Scottish cuisine in the form of cullen skink (smoked fish chowder; $15), haggis, neeps and tatties (entrée $16; main $26) and Cranachan fool (raspberries, honeyed oats and whisky cream $14). Tues–Sat 5pm–late.

The Strictly Coffee Co 23 Bath St ☎ 03 479 0017, ✺ www.strictlycoffee.co.nz. If not the best coffee in town then in company with it, sold by the cup or the kilo in an industrial-chic, cherry-red daytime café filled with chrome coffee grinders. Enjoy the great crusty rolls and wraps and the little courtyard. Mon–Fri 7.30am–4pm.

Vogel St Kitchen 76 Vogel St ☎ 03 477 3623, ✺ vogelstkitchen.nz. Head to graffiti-covered Vogel Street and Dunedin's coolest eating establishment for coffee, cake and hot meals. Save for the "Otakou" pizza (topped with southern clams and muttonbird; $18.50); the menu is unadventurous but delicious and well-executed, with pasta and steak sandwiches for lunch (main $19–24; 11am–3pm); breakfast and wood-fired pizzas (all $18.50) are served all day. Fully licensed with Emerson's on tap. Tues–Thurs 7.30am–4pm, Fri 7.30am–late, Sat 8.30am–late, Sun 8.30–4pm.

ROSYLN

★**Highgate Bridge Bakery** 300 Highgate ☎ 03 474 9222. Known to locals as "The Friday Shop" for its limited opening hours, this plain-looking bakery sells superb pastries, tarts, quiches and gourmet prepared meals. Get here early: Albert Roux-trained chef, Jim Byars, shuts up shop when he's sold out, which can happen as early as 9am. Prices from $5 for a small quiche. Fri 7.30am–4pm.

ST CLAIR

★**The Esplanade** 2 Esplanade ☎ 03 456 2544, ✺ esplanade.co. This stylish Italian café and restaurant starts the day with a tasty selection of brunch dishes — the baked eggs are particularly good. Later in the day, sate your appetite with well-executed Italian classics from antipasti ($8–12) to pizzas and pasta ($21–26). Daily 9am–late.

Pier 24 24 Esplanade ☎ 03 456 0555, ✺ hotelstclair .com. Chic modern restaurant that ranks among Dunedin's finest with wonderful views out to the St Clair surf. Just about casual enough to nip in for a drink, it's really about the Asian-inflected food: seared tuna with a Szechuan pepper rub ($22) or miso-glazed roast king salmon ($34). Daily 7am–9pm or later.

DRINKING, NIGHTLIFE AND ENTERTAINMENT

Like all good university cities, drinking is taken seriously here. A number of the city's dozens of **pubs** and **bars** serve English- and German-style beers from Dunedin's premier micro-brewery, Emerson's. Local **bands** play at weekends (at the places below and *Chicks* in Port Chalmers), although once the students head home for the summer holidays (late Nov–early March) the dancefloors can look forlorn.

PUBS, BARS AND CLUBS

Albar 135 Stuart St ☎ 03 479 2468. Inviting, popular Scottish-themed bar with a good selection of whiskies, European and Kiwi bottled beers and local craft beers on tap. The otherwise authentic tapas menu ($5–9) includes a haggis-and-oatcakes dish, there's Celtic music on Tues nights and whisky tastings. Mon–Sat 11am–late, Sun noon–late.

Inch Bar 8 Bank St ☎ 03 473 6496. For a change from the downtown vibe, head for this intimate neighbourhood watering hole with speciality beers (including Emerson's and Tuatara on tap), a select range of tapas from pork skewers with chimichurri sauce ($8) to a big bowl of *patatas bravas* ($10) and regular live acts. Daily 3–11pm or later; closed Mon in winter.

★**Pequeño** Down the alley beside 12 Moray Place ☎ 03 477 7830, ✺ pequeno.co.nz. All low lighting, leather sofas and banquettes around the fire. Excellent wine and cocktails and Thurs-night live jazz (usually swing or funk). Mon–Fri 5pm–1am or later, Sat 7pm–2am or later.

Speight's Ale House 200 Rattray St ☎ 03 471 9050, ✺ thealehouse.co.nz. Popular and spacious Speight's-owned pub right by the brewery with good beer and food served in rural-kitsch decor. Daily 11.30am–late.

Tonic 138 Princes St ☎ 03 471 9194, ✺ tonicbar.co.nz.

RUGBY IN DUNEDIN

There's no surer way to get a real taste of Dunedin in party mode than to attend a **rugby match** at the new 30,000-seater Forsyth Barr Stadium (✺ forsythbarrstadium.co.nz) at 130 Anzac Avenue, 2km east of The Octagon. The city is proud of having the world's only fully roofed, natural-turf stadium, but its $200 million construction (in time for the 2011 Rugby World Cup) was controversial and put huge strains on the local ratepayers. Highlanders Super 15 games are held here regularly during the season (late Feb–July) and there are occasional All Black Games (generally May–Oct). For schedules and ticket sales visit the Champions of the World store, 8 George St (Mon–Fri 9am–6pm, Sat 10am–5pm, Sun 11am–4pm; ☎ 03 477 7852).

11

DUNEDIN FESTIVALS

Arts Festival Dunedin
ⓦartsfestivaldunedin.co.nz. Biennial mid- to high-brow arts festival with opera, plays and plenty of music. Late September to early October every even year.

Cadbury's Chocolate Carnival
ⓦchocolatecarnival.co.nz. Sweet-toothed travellers shouldn't miss Dunedin's chocolate carnival; a week of cocoa-themed events that climaxes in the Jaffa race down Baldwin St. Mid-July.

Fringe Festival
ⓦdunedinfringe.org.nz. Ten-day arts and culture festival with street performers, short films, comedy and exhibitions. Generally takes place in mid-March.

New Zealand International Film Festival
ⓦnzff.co.nz. The Dunedin leg of the nationwide cinema festival features the usual mix of oddball and pre-release mainstream movies, all shown at the Regent and Rialto cinemas. Early to mid-August.

A wonderful little bar with a beer from every decent Kiwi micro-brewery you can think of, Emerson's on tap, a decent wine list, antipasto platters ($19) and friendly regulars. Tues–Fri 4pm–late, Sat 6pm–late.

THEATRE, CINEMA AND CLASSICAL MUSIC
In addition to its festivals, Dunedin has a lively year-round theatre scene. Public recitals are held by the University of Otago's music department (check with the i-SITE).

CINEMAS
Metropolis Cinema Town Hall, Moray Place ☎03 471 9635, ⓦmetrocinema.co.nz. With only 56 seats this is a delightful place to watch art-house and more commercial movies for just $13. Popcorn is out, but you're welcome to take your coffee in with you.

Reading Cinemas 33 The Octagon ☎03 974 6700, ⓦreadingcinemas.co.nz. Multiplex screening all the latest mainstream films, with a fully licensed bar.

Rialto 11 Moray Place ☎03 474 2200, ⓦrialto.co.nz. Another run-of-the-mill cinema screening Hollywood blockbusters, plus occasional art-house releases.

THEATRES
Allen Hall 90 Union St East ☎03 479 8825. Campus theatre that showcases the talents of the university's drama students. Shows are often of an alternative bent and don't cost much.

Fortune Theatre 231 Stuart St ☎03 477 8323, ⓦfortunetheatre.co.nz. Converted from a neo-Gothic church, the Fortune divides its programme between new works by Kiwi playwrights, fringe theatre, popular Broadway-style plays and occasional musicals. Tickets around $40. Closed Jan to mid-Feb.

Globe 104 London St ☎03 477 3274, ⓦglobetheatre .org.nz. This small and intimate venue features contemporary plays, classical drama and experimental works. Tickets around $22.

Regent 18 The Octagon ☎03 477 8597, ⓦregenttheatre.co.nz. The city's largest and most ornate theatre, hosting musicals, ballets, touring plays, comedians, the New Zealand Symphony Orchestra, Dunedin's Southern Sinfonia and the city's film festival.

SHOPPING

Bivouac 171 George St ☎03 477 3679, ⓦbivouac .co.nz. Quality selection of tramping, mountaineering and skiing gear for rent and for sale. Mon–Fri 9am–5.30pm, Sat & Sun 10am–4pm.

Plume 310 George St ☎03 477 9358, ⓦplumestore.co.nz. Top women's fashion store run by Margi Robertson, founder of top Kiwi label Nom*D. Everything from Workshop to Comme des Garçons along with local labels Zambesi and, naturally Nom*D. Mon–Fri 9am–5.30pm, Sat 9am–4.30pm.

★**Salisbury Boutique** 104 Bond St ☎03 477 3933, ⓦsalisburyboutique.co.nz. Cool designer shop in an upcoming part of town, good for home-grown designer clothes, jewellery, art and homewares. Thurs & Fri 4–8pm, Sat 11am–8pm.

Torpedo7 70 Stuart St ☎03 474 1211, ⓦtorpedo7 .co.nz. Outdoor equipment shop with Dunedin's biggest range of camping, skiing, cycling and general sporting equipment. Mon–Thurs 9am–5.30pm, Fri 9am–6pm, Sat 9.30am–4pm, Sun 10.30am–4pm.

University Bookshop 378 Great King St, opposite the Otago Museum ☎03 477 6976, ⓦunibooks.co.nz. Comprehensive independent bookshop covering two floors, with the bargains located upstairs. Mon–Fri 8.30am–5.30pm, Sat 10am–4pm, Sun 11am–3pm.

DIRECTORY

Banks and foreign exchange The major banks are clustered on George and Princes sts, all with ATMs. On Saturday try the ANZ, corner of George and Hanover sts, which is open 10am–2pm. On

Sundays and public holidays you can change money at the i-SITE.

Internet access Wi-fi is free in the library (below) and around The Octagon, or try A1 Internet Café (daily, 9.30am–late; $1 for 12min), opposite the i-SITE.

Library Dunedin Public Library, corner of John and Stewart sts (Mon–Fri 9.30am–8pm, Sat & Sun 11am–4pm; ☎ 03 474 3690), has newspapers and free internet.

Medical treatment Dunedin Hospital, 201 Great King St (☎ 03 474 0999); emergencies only. After-hours doctors are available at 95 Hanover St (daily 8am–10pm; ☎ 03 479 2900).

Pharmacy After-hours service at Urgent Pharmacy, 95 Hanover St (daily 10am–10pm; ☎ 03 477 6344).

Post office 310 Moray Place (Mon–Fri 8.30am–5.30pm, Sat 9am–1pm).

Port Chalmers and around

Container cranes loom over the small, quirky town of **PORT CHALMERS**, 12km northeast of Dunedin and reached along the winding western shore of Otago Harbour. Arranged on hills around a container port and cruise-ship berth, the town has a vibrant artistic community, with the **Hotere Sculpture Garden**, legacy of the late painter and sculptor **Ralph Hotere** (a long-time resident of Port Chalmers) perched at the end of Constitution Street. The whole place has a delightful lost-in-time feel, with many fine nineteenth-century buildings along George Street, the main drag, and a modest amount of renovation has made way for a few cool shops and cafés. Two late Victorian churches vie for attention with the cranes: the elegant stone-spired Presbyterian **Iona Church** on Mount Street, and the nuggety bluestone Anglican **Holy Trinity**, on Scotia Street, designed by Robert A. Lawson.

For a little exercise tackle the **Port Chalmers Peninsula Circuit** (4km loop; 1hr; mostly flat) with views across to Goat Island and Quarantine Island in the harbour with the Otago Peninsula beyond: pick up a map from the library.

Brief history

Chosen in 1844 as the port to serve the proposed Scottish settlement that would become Dunedin, Port Chalmers became the embarkation point for several **Antarctic expeditions**, including those of Captain Scott, who set out from here in 1901 and again for his ill-fated attempt on the Pole in 1910. The first trial shipment of **frozen meat** to Britain was sent from Port Chalmers in 1882 and today the export of wool, meat and timber, and reception of cruise ships is its chief business.

Port Chalmers Maritime Museum

19 Beach St • Mon–Fri 10am–3pm, Sat & Sun 1–4pm • Donation • ☎ 03 472 8233, ⓦ portmuseum.org.nz

George Street meets the port at the small **museum** housed in an 1877 former post office. Brimming with maritime artefacts, models and local settler history, museum highlights include a display of navigational equipment. Outside stands a newly built boatshed, a replica of one that stood nearby until it was demolished to make way for the container port; of particular interest is the nineteenth-century passenger cabin inside, complete with portholes and a glossy wooden vanity stand.

Orokonui Ecosanctuary

600 Blueskin Rd, 6km north of Port Chalmers • Daily 9.30am–4.30pm; 1–2hr guided tours daily at 11am and 1.30pm; booking essential • $16; 1hr tour $30; 2hr tour $45 • ☎ 03 482 1755, ⓦ orokonui.org.nz

Modelled on the Zealandia: the Karori Sanctuary Experience attraction in Wellington (see p.425), the **Orokonui Ecosanctuary** is a welcome addition to the pantheon of wildlife activities within easy reach of Dunedin. Start at the visitor centre, all eco-designed using secondhand shipping containers and wood milled on-site. Solar panels heat roof rainwater for washing, and wastewater is treated and used for

11

RIDING DUNEDIN'S SCENIC RAILWAYS

Dunedin's splendid railway station marks the start of two wonderfully scenic train trips, both run by Dunedin Railways (☎03 477 4449, ⓦ taieri.co.nz). One threads inland through the craggy Taieri Gorge while the other winds along a spectacular coastal route north to Palmerston.

THE TAIERI GORGE RAILWAY

The Taieri Gorge Railway stretches 77km northwest from Dunedin through rugged hill country. Constructed between 1879 and 1921, the line once carried supplies a total of 235km from Dunedin to the old gold-town of Cromwell, returning with farm produce, fruit and livestock bound for the port. Commercial traffic stopped in 1990, and much of the route was turned into the Otago Central Rail Trail (see box, p.743), but the most dramatic section – through the schist strata of the Taieri Gorge – continues to offer a rewarding rail journey at any time of year.

Most trains run to **Pukerangi** (58km from Dunedin), a lonely wayside halt near the highest point of the track (250m) where you wait a few minutes then head back. Less frequent services continue a further 19km to the old gold-town of **Middlemarch** (see p.749).

RIDING THE TAIERI GORGE

The air-conditioned train is made up of a mix of modern steel carriages with large panoramic windows and nostalgic, **refurbished 1920s wooden cars**. Storage is available for backpacks and bicycles, and there's a licensed snack bar on board.

In summer there are usually two trains a day from Dunedin to Pukerangi and back (Oct–April daily except Fri & Sun 9.30am & 2.30pm; $89 return, $59 one way; 4hr return), with the train continuing beyond Pukerangi to Middlemarch twice each week (Oct–April Fri & Sun 9.30am; $110 return, $73 one way; 6hr return). A daily service continues through most of the winter with occasional closures; check online for the latest timetables.

TAIERI GORGE AND RAIL TRAIL COMBOS

As well as the day-trips, the Taieri Gorge trip makes an excellent way to start your journey inland towards Wanaka and Queenstown (both $195). Coaches meet the train at Pukerangi or Middlemarch and head through the Maniototo (see p.745) to Queenstown ($148); book through Dunedin Railways.

Cyclists can take the train ($10 surcharge per bike) then hop straight onto the Otago Central Rail Trail. If you don't have your own bike, get in touch with Offtrack (see box, p.600) or one of the rail trail specialists (see box, p.743).

THE SEASIDER

A completely different but equally picturesque rail journey, The *Seasider* leaves Dunedin Railway Station and runs along the main northbound line 66km up the coast to Palmerston. It initially follows the flank of Otago Harbour then winds through Port Chalmers to Blueskin Bay with tunnels, bridges and great coastal views all the way. The train ($89 return; $59 one way; 4hr return) runs sporadic days throughout the year (check the website for times) and stops for 45min for coffee in Palmerston.

irrigation. The place is packed with information and the café offers wonderful views of the valley, but the real treats are just the other side of the 8.7km predator-exclusion fence, protecting three square kilometres of regenerating bush, some of it over a century old, containing reintroduced native birds, **tuatara** and skinks. Among the birds you are likely to encounter are tomtit, South Island riflemen, saddleback, bellbird, tui, fantail and kaka.

You can take a self-guided walk through the sanctuary along a number of well-marked trails (including one long path down the valley that leads to the country's tallest tree, a huge blue gum tree), but will learn and probably see more on a **guided tour** with the freedom to roam afterwards. Either drive here (30min from Dunedin) or come on a wildlife tour (see box opposite), as no public buses visit.

Aramoana

The tiny settlement of **Aramoana**, on a sand-dune spit at the mouth of Otago Harbour 12km north of Port Chalmers, was catapulted into the Kiwi psyche in 1990 when one David Gray shot 13 of his neighbours before being shot by police. The story of the massacre is told in Robert Sarkies' 2006 film *Out of the Blue*. Pop out there if you fancy a walk on wild, often deserted **beaches** with views across the mouth of Otago Harbour towards Taiaroa Head and the possibility of seeing yellow-eyed penguins and sea lions.

ARRIVAL AND INFORMATION

PORT CHALMERS AND AROUND

By bus The #14 bus runs from Dunedin to Port Chalmers, leaving from Stand 4 opposite the Countdown supermarket in Cumberland St, dropping you off on George St, Port Chalmers main street, about 25min later; the #13 makes the return run, with sporadic Sunday services on both routes.

Tourist information Port Chalmers Library, 20 Beach St (Mon–Wed & Fri 9.30am–5.30pm, Thurs 9.30am–8pm, Sat 11am–2pm; ☎03 474 3690), has local leaflets and free internet.

ACCOMMODATION AND EATING

As well as the places to eat listed below you'll find several scenic picnic spots dotted along Peninsula Beach Road, just round from the harbour.

★ **Billy Browns** 423 Aramoana Rd, Hamilton Bay, 5km north of Port Chalmers ☎03 472 8323, ⓦbillybrowns.co.nz. Quirkily designed first-class hostel isolated on farmland, in an area where you probably wouldn't stay were the accommodation not so brilliant. It has stunning views, a log fire, stacks of vinyl, and made-up beds but no TV or internet. It sleeps just eight, so book ahead. Dorms $30, rooms $75

Carey's Bay Historic Hotel 17 Macandrew Rd, 1km north of town ☎03 472 8022, ⓦcareysbayhotel.co.nz. Maritime bar in an 1874 bluestone building with a restaurant specializing in seafood; try the great chowder ($18) or platters laden with scallops, mussels, squid and prawns ($28.50–48). Occasional live music. Daily 10.30am–10pm, with winter evening closures.

Chicks Hotel 2 Mount St ☎03 472 5074. Top live music venue and pub, in an atmospheric 1876 stone

DUNEDIN AND OTAGO PENINSULA NATURE TOURS

Even if you have your own wheels there's a lot to be said for exploring the area on an informative guided tour.

4 Nature Tours ☎03 472 7647, ⓦ4nature.co.nz. Nature and wildlife oriented tours focussed on the western side of Otago Harbour, such as their Ecosanctuary and Wading Birds Tour (4–5hr; $120) visiting Orokonui.

Elm Wildlife Tours ☎0800 356563, ⓦelmwildlifetours.co.nz. Excellent, ecologically minded, guided bus tours (usually 5–6hr; $107) leave Dunedin in the afternoon and visit a private conservation area where you'll see yellow-eyed penguins and fur seals, along with a host of other species. Trips can include an Albatross Centre tour ($142), an hour-long Monarch Cruise ($146), or everything combined (8hr; $217). Families, backpackers and students save $10 on all trips.

Monarch Wildlife Cruises & Tours 20 Fryatt St, Dunedin ☎0800 666272, ⓦwildlife.co.nz. A converted fishing boat with licensed galley is put to good use running short cruises around Taiaroa Head (Oct–March 5 daily; April–Sept 1–2 daily; 1hr; $49) from the Wellers Rock jetty, near the tip of the Otago Peninsula. This can be combined with a trip to the Albatross Centre ($85) or Penguin Place ($89). If you're not planning to drive out along the peninsula, opt for the Wildlife Tour (8.30am & 3.30pm; 4hr; $90), which leaves from the wharf in Dunedin, cruises around Taiaroa Head then drops you at Wellers Rock, returning to Dunedin by bus. Various albatross- and penguin-centre combos are available.

Wild Earth Adventures ☎03 489 1951, ⓦwildearth.co.nz. For an often magical perspective on the coast and its wildlife, take a sea-kayaking tour around Taiaroa Head or Portobello (both 4hr; $115), spending around two hours on the water. Among the other trips a particular favourite is the Twilight Tour (Oct–March; 3–5hr; $115), with wildlife, quiet and the lights of Dunedin in the background.

building with a hanging sign depicting a skull and crossbones. Generally open if a band is playing and for jam sessions. A bit of a schlep from Dunedin, but well worth it. Open most Fri & Sat nights.

★ **Port Royale** 10 George St ☎ 03 472 8283. Cool spot

looking out onto the main street, a great place to enjoy excellent coffee and a muffin or for simple lunches such pea, ham and potato pie with salad ($12) or a piled-high bagel ($12–14) in the sheltered courtyard. Mon–F 8am–4pm, Sat & Sun 8.30am–4pm.

The Otago Peninsula

The 35km-long crooked finger of the **OTAGO PENINSULA**, running northeast from Dunedin, divides Otago Harbour from the Pacific Ocean. With sweeping views of the harbour, the sea and Dunedin against its dramatic backdrop of hills, the peninsula offers outstanding year-round **marine wildlife viewing** that's probably the most condensed and varied in the country.

The prime wildlife viewing spots are concentrated at the peninsula's tip, **Taiaroa Head** (less than an hour's drive from Dunedin), where cold waters forced up by the continental shelf provide a rich and constant food source. The majestic **royal albatross** breeds here in the world's only mainland albatross colony. Also concentrated on the headland's shores are **penguins** (the little blue and the rare yellow-eyed) and **southern fur seals**, while the cliffs are home to other seabirds including three species of **shag**, **muttonbirds** (sooty shearwaters) and various species of gull. New Zealand **sea lions** sometimes loll on beaches, while offshore, orca and **whales** can occasionally be seen. A one time, it was possible to get close to the wildlife by simply walking down to one of the beaches; today, the disturbance caused by increasing visitor numbers means that some beaches are only open to those on the peninsula's excellent wildlife tours. That said, it's still possible to wander along **Sandfly Bay** (see box, p.610) and see sea lions an a handful of yellow-eyed penguins, while **Pilots Beach** is home to a colony of adolescent male fur seals and open until dusk, when it is closed to allow the beach's blue penguins to return to their nests in peace.

Around the head of Otago Harbour, **Portobello Road** shakes off Dunedin's southern suburbs and weaves its way along the peninsula's shoreline past little bays, many punctuated by stilt-mounted boathouses. On the top of the ridge, narrow **Highcliff Road** offers an even better vantage point over the hills and shore as it rolls towards the accommodation and eating nexus of **Portobello**. Beyond Portobello, Harington Point Road continues to Taiaroa Head.

Apart from wildlife spotting there's appeal in the beautiful woodland gardens of **Glenfalloch**, the exemplary grounds of **Larnach Castle** and several **scenic walks** to spectacular views and unusual land formations created by lava flows.

GETTING AROUND AND INFORMATION   THE OTAGO PENINSULA

By car The peninsula is best accessed with your own wheels, either via Portobello Road, which snakes along the western shoreline, or the inland Highcliff Road, which winds up and over the hills.

By bus The #18 Peninsula bus (3–9 daily; $6.70) runs along the coast road as far as Portobello (35min) from

Stand 5 outside the New World supermarket c Cumberland St. On weekdays a couple of services continu to Harington Point, within 2km of Taiaroa Head; the #1 bus returns to the city.

Tourist information Pick up the free *Visitor's Guide to th Otago Peninsula* from the Dunedin i-SITE (see p.599).

Glenfalloch Garden

430 Portobello Rd, 10km east of Dunedin • Daily dawn–dusk; café Sept–April 11am–3.30pm • $5 • ☎ 03 476 1006, ⊛ glenfalloch.co.nz

The peaceful **Glenfalloch Garden** contains 12 hectares of mature garden and bush, surrounding a homestead built in 1871 and a great licensed café. Between mid-September and mid-October the garden – recently recognized as a "Garden of National Significance" – is ablaze with rhododendrons, azaleas and camellias.

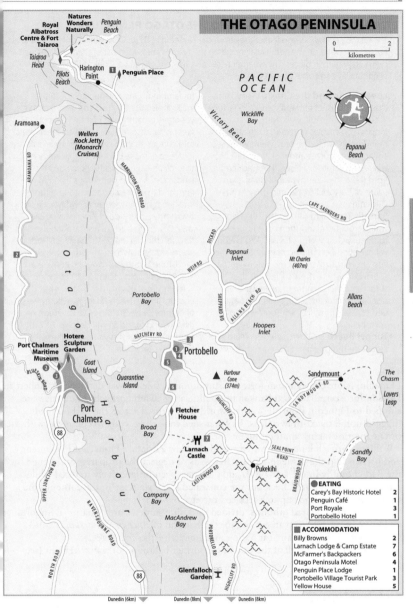

THE OTAGO PENINSULA

0   2
kilometres

Royal Albatross Centre & Fort Taiaroa
Natures Wonders Naturally
Penguin Beach
Taiaroa Head
Pilots Beach
Harington Point
Penguin Place
Aramoana
Wellers Rock Jetty (Monarch Cruises)

PACIFIC OCEAN
Wickliffe Bay
Victory Beach
Papanui Beach

ARAMOANA RD
HARINGTON POINT ROAD
DICKARD
WEIR RD
SHEPPARD RD
ALLANS BEACH RD
CAPE SAUNDERS RD

Otago
Portobello Bay
Papanui Inlet
Mt Charles (407m)
Allans Beach
Hoopers Inlet

Hotere Sculpture Garden
Port Chalmers Maritime Museum
Goat Island
Quarantine Island
HATCHERY RD
Portobello
Harbour Cone (374m)
Sandymount
The Chasm
Lovers Leap

BLUESKIN ROAD
Port Chalmers
88

Harbour
Fletcher House
Broad Bay
Larnach Castle
Pukekihi
SANDYMOUNT RD
SEAL POINT ROAD
BRAIDWOOD RD
HIGHCLIFF RD
CASTLEWOOD RD
Sandfly Bay

UPPER JUNCTION ROAD
RAVENSBOURNE ROAD
NORTH ROAD
Company Bay
MacAndrew Bay
PORTOBELLO RD
HIGHCLIFF RD
88
Glenfalloch Garden

EATING
Carey's Bay Historic Hotel   2
Penguin Café   1
Port Royale   3
Portobello Hotel   1

ACCOMMODATION
Billy Browns   2
Larnach Lodge & Camp Estate   7
McFarmer's Backpackers   6
Otago Peninsula Motel   4
Penguin Place Lodge   1
Portobello Village Tourist Park   3
Yellow House   5

Dunedin (6km)   Dunedin (8km)   Dunedin (8km)

Larnach Castle

145 Camp Rd, Company Bay • Daily 9am–5pm; gardens daily Oct–March 9am–7pm; April–Sept 9am–5pm • Castle and gardens $29; gardens only $13.50 • ☏ 03 476 1616, ⓦ larnachcastle.co.nz • Take the Peninsula bus either to Company Bay, from where it's a 5km signposted walk uphill, or to Broad Bay and a steeper 2km walk

At **Company Bay**, Castlewood Road runs 4km inland to the 1871 Gothic Revival **Larnach Castle**, which sits high on a hill commanding great views across the harbour to

WALKS AROUND DUNEDIN AND THE OTAGO PENINSULA

The *Otago Peninsula Tracks* leaflet (free from the Dunedin i-SITE or DOC office) briefly describes two dozen walks on the peninsula (including the first two below), most of them well defined but pretty steep in places. The weather here can turn cold or wet very quickly, even on the sunniest days, so come prepared.

Lovers Leap and the Chasm (3km; 1hr; closed Sept & Oct for lambing). Wonderfully accessible peninsula walk, forming an easy loop which crosses farmland to sheer cliffs that drop 200m to the sea, where you'll see collapsed sea caves and rock faces of layered volcanic lava flows. The track begins from the end of Sandymount Road, 8km south of Portobello (a 25min drive from Dunedin).

Sandfly Bay (3km return; 1hr). Pleasant walk across farmland then down the dunes to the beach, a wonderful place to watch yellow-eyed penguins come ashore in the late afternoon. Make for the colony at the south end where there's a hide and, in summer, a DOC ranger to make sure people don't disturb the birds. Start at the end of Seal Point Rd, 7km southwest of Portobello.

Tunnel Beach (1.5km return; 1hr; 140m ascent on the way back; closed Sept & Oct for lambing). One of Dunedin's best local walks is also the shortest and least strenuous, yet offers breathtaking coastal views of creamy sandstone cliffs and islets weathered into curious shapes. Untouched by lava flows, it gives a glimpse of Dunedin's geology before the volcanic eruptions that changed the landscape. A steep path drops through farmland to impressive sandstone clifftops and a magnificent sea arch. Additionally, for two hours either side of low tide, you can walk down the steps of a short tunnel carved through the cliff in the 1870s, which leads to a pretty sandy beach on the other side with sandstone buttresses towering above – an atmospheric spot for a picnic.

The route starts from the car park at the end of Tunnel Beach Road, 7km southwest of central Dunedin. Buses to Corstophine (New World Stand 5) will drop you 1.7km from the start of the walk; get off at Stenhope Crescent.

Dunedin. More château than fort, this sumptuous residence was designed by Robert A. Lawson for Australian-born banker and politician William Larnach. Materials were shipped to Dunedin from all over the world then punted across the harbour and dragged uphill by ox-drawn sleds. Its outer shell took three years to complete, with the ornate interior taking another nine.

William Larnach later committed suicide in New Zealand's Houses of Parliament, and his son sold the castle in 1906. After years of neglect the property was rescued by the Barker family in the late 1960s and has since been progressively restored while remaining their home. Check out the concealed spiral staircase in the corner of the third floor, which leads up to a terraced turret.

The castle's manicured **grounds**, divided into nine gardens, are of national importance and quite beautiful; keep an eye out for the handful of *Alice in Wonderland* statues, such as one of the Cheshire cat hiding in an ancient Atlas cedar tree.

You can refresh yourself at the café in the former ballroom, or stay overnight (see p.612).

Fletcher House

727 Portobello Rd, 15km northeast of Dunedin • Christmas–Easter daily 11am–4pm; Easter–Christmas Sat & Sun 11am–4pm • $4 • ☏ 0800 528767, ⓦ fletchertrust.co.nz

As you head along Portobello Road towards the tip of the peninsula, devote a few minutes to **Fletcher House**, a small Edwardian villa built by James Fletcher, founder of the Fletcher construction conglomerate. Built entirely of native wood, with rimu ceilings and floors, in 1909, it became the family home of the Broad Bay storekeeper and has now been lovingly restored to its original state.

> **OBSERVING WILDLIFE**
> When **observing wildlife**, respect the animals by staying well away from them (at least 10m), and keeping quiet and still. **Penguins** are especially frightened by people and they may be reluctant to come ashore (even if they have chicks to feed) if you are on or near the beach and visible. In summer, keep to the track as they're extremely vulnerable to stress while nesting and moulting. Never get between a **seal** or **sea lion** and the sea; these animals can be aggressive and move quickly.

Penguin Place

45 Pakihau Rd, off Harington Point Rd, 3km south of Taiaroa Head • Oct–March 10.15am–late afternoon & April–Sept 3.15–late afternoon for 90min tours; bookings essential • $52 • ☎ 03 478 0286, ⓦ penguinplace.co.nz

The wonderful **Penguin Place** penguin-conservation project gives you the rare privilege of entering a protected nesting area of around twenty yellow-eyed penguins. Carefully controlled and informative tours begin with a talk about penguins and their conservation, then a guide takes you to the beachside colony where well-camouflaged trenches lead to several hides among the dunes. These allow extraordinary proximity to the penguins and excellent photo opportunities. Proceeds from the tours are used to fund the penguin rehabilitation centre and habitat restoration projects. You can also **stay** overnight (see p.613).

Taiaroa Head

The world's only mainland albatross colony occupies **Taiaroa Head**, a wonderland of wildlife that also served as a fortified outpost against threats imagined and real.

Royal albatross can be spied in flight all year round from anywhere on the headland, and a short signposted walk from the Royal Albatross Centre car park leads to a **cliff-edge viewing area** with spectacular views of a spotted shag colony.

Royal Albatross Centre

1260 Harington Point Rd • Daily 11.30am–dusk • Free; albatross tour 60min, $45; unique tour 90min, $50; bookings recommended • ☎ 0800 528767, ⓦ albatross.org.nz

To see interesting displays on local wildlife and history (or just to grab a coffee) head into the **Royal Albatross Centre**. You can buy tickets here for the excellent **Albatross Tour** which includes an introductory film and time to view the birds from an enclosed area in the reserve (binoculars provided), where there is also closed-circuit TV of the far side of the colony. The **best months** for viewing are generally January and February, when the chicks hatch, and April to August, when parent birds feed their chicks. By September the chicks and adults are ready to depart and new breeding pairs start to arrive.

Fort Taiaroa

30min guided tour daily on demand • $20 • ☎ 0800 528767

The Royal Albatross Centre is the starting point for tours around **Fort Taiaroa**, a historic warren of tunnels and gun emplacements originally built in 1885 when an attack from Tsarist Russia was feared, and re-armed during World War II. The main attraction is the restored Armstrong Disappearing Gun, which was raised by a hand-pumped water ram and used its recoil to swing back into the gun pit. The fort is accessed through a web of tunnels beneath the albatross colony and can be visited on a stand-alone basis, or as part of the centre's Unique Taiaroa tour.

Pilots Beach

Blue Penguin Encounter: Oct–April nightly at dusk • $25 • ☎ 0800 528767, ⓦ bluepenguins.co.nz

For many summers, visitors after a free wildlife encounter have headed down to **Pilots Beach**, on the western side of Taiaroa Head (follow the footpath to the shore from the

THE YELLOW-EYED PENGUIN

Found only in southern New Zealand, the endangered **yellow-eyed penguin**, or *hoiho*, is considered the most ancient of all living penguins but today numbers only around four thousand. It evolved in forests free of predators, but human disturbance, loss of habitat and the introduction of ferrets, stoats and cats have had a devastating effect. The small mainland population of just a few hundred occupies nesting areas dotted along the wild southeast coast of the South Island (from Oamaru to the Catlins), while there are further colonies in the coastal forest margins of Stewart Island and offshore islets, and New Zealand's sub-Antarctic Auckland and Campbell islands.

Male and female adults are identical in colouring, with pink webbed feet and a bright yellow band that encircles the head, sweeping over their pale yellow eyes. Standing around 65cm high and weighing 5–6kg – making them the third-largest penguin species after the Emperor and the King – they have a **life expectancy** of up to twenty-five years. Their **diet** consists of squid and small fish, and hunting takes them up to 40km offshore and to depths of 100m.

Maori named the bird **hoiho**, meaning "the noise shouter", because of the distinctive high-pitched calls (an exuberant trilling) it makes at night when greeting its mate at the nest. Unlike other penguins, the yellow-eyed does not migrate after its first year, but stays near its home beach, making daily fishing trips and returning as daylight fails.

The penguins' **breeding season** lasts from mid-August to early March. Eggs are laid between mid-September and mid-October, and both parents share incubation duties for about 43 days. The eggs hatch in November and for the next six weeks the chicks are constantly guarded against predators. By the time the down-covered chicks are six or seven weeks old, their rapid growth gives them voracious appetites and both parents must fish daily to satisfy them. The fledglings enter the sea for the first time in late February or early March and journey up to 500km north to winter feeding grounds. Fewer than fifteen percent of fledged chicks reach breeding age, but those that do return to the colony of their birth.

Royal Albatross Centre car park), where southern fur seals loll on the shore in daytime and over a hundred little blue penguins come ashore around dusk.

While it's still possible to walk down to the beach in daylight, evening access is only possible on an authorized **Blue Penguin Encounter** tour, comprising a short guided walk from the Albatross Centre (where tickets are sold) down to a couple of low-impact viewing platforms among the sand dunes.

Natures Wonders Naturally

Taiaroa Head, 1.5km past the Albatross Centre • Daily 10.15am until 1hr before sunset for 1hr tours • $55 • ☎ 0800 246446, ⓦ natureswonders.co.nz

The peninsula road ends at **Natures Wonders Naturally**, a headland farm which endlessly enthusiastic owner, Perry Reid, has turned into one of the finest opportunities to see wildlife up close. There's no animal feeding or nesting boxes, just wild animals sometimes literally within arm's reach. The 8WD argos used to transport you around the 6km of often-steep farm tracks seem a little incongruous (and noisy) but get you to a fabulous viewing spot for cliff-dwelling spotted shags, in among a fur seal colony and to a hide above a beach where blue and yellow-eyed penguins waddle up to their sand-dune nests at just about any time of day.

ACCOMMODATION
THE OTAGO PENINSULA

Larnach Lodge & Camp Estate Larnach Castle ☎ 03 476 1616, ⓦ larnachcastle.co.nz. Cosy up in the converted stables, containing six shared-bath rooms, or in the *Larnach Lodge*'s twelve grander themed rooms, some of which have great harbour views. Just outside the grounds the modern *Camp Estate* has five sumptuous rooms ($460) in a modern house designed like a Scottish manor house,

with long harbour views and in-room fireplaces. All room rates include castle admission, breakfast and the chance to book a three-course dinner in the castle's grand dining room ($69/person plus wine). Stables **$160**, lodge **$290**

McFarmer's Backpackers 774 Portobello Rd ☎ 03 478 0389, ✉ mcfarmers@xtra.co.nz. Homey harbourside accommodation with a cosy backpacker lodge, plus a

THE ROYAL ALBATROSS

The majestic **albatross**, one of the world's largest seabirds, has long been the subject of reverence and superstition: the embodiment of a dead sea-captain's soul, condemned to drift the oceans forever. A solitary creature, the albatross spends most of its life on the wing or at sea.

Second only in size to the wandering albatross, the graceful **royal albatross** has a wingspan of up to 3m. They can travel 190,000km a year at speeds of up to 120kph, and have a life expectancy of 60 years. The albatross mates for life, but male and female separate to fly in opposite directions around the world, returning to the same breeding grounds once every two years, and arriving within days of one another. The female lays one egg (weighing up to 500g) per breeding season, and the parents both incubate it over a period of eleven weeks.

Once the chick has hatched, the parents take turns feeding it and guarding it against stoats, ferrets, wild cats and rats. Almost a year from the start of the breeding cycle, the fledgling takes flight and the parents leave the colony and return to sea only to start the cycle again a year later, while their offspring will remain at sea for up to five years before it next touches terra firma, making landfall in the same spot it hatched.

11

two-bedroom cottage. It's a peaceful spot with no wi-fi, phone or TV; admiring the scenery and watching the lambs is the order of the day. Occasional winter closures. Dorms $33, cottage $125

Otago Peninsula Motel 1724 Highcliff Rd, Portobello ☎03 478 0666, ⓦotagopeninsulamotel.co.nz. A comfortable modern motel in the heart of Portobello. All six rooms have harbour views and spa baths, and wi-fi is free. $160

Penguin Place Lodge 45 Pakihau Rd ☎03 478 0286, ⓦpenguinplace.co.nz. On the hill above Penguin Place, this simple, comfy backpackers has harbour views from many of its colourful doubles and twins. You can rent bedding ($5/stay/bed) or use your own; check-in before

6pm in summer, 4pm in winter. Per person $30

Portobello Village Tourist Park 27 Hereweka St, Portobello ☎03 478 0359, ⓦportobellopark.co.nz. Modest campsite with simple but spotless facilities, budget rooms ($60) and more upscale tourist flats (from $115) with bathroom, TV and kitchenette. Linen $5/person/night. Camping $16, powered sites $18

Yellow House 822 Portobello Rd, 1km southwest of Portobello ☎03 478 1001, ⓦyellowhouse.co.nz. Classy lemon-hued B&B with one beautiful airy room and the "starry suite" with a glass roof and spa bath in its own wing. There are fine harbour views, two cats and an excellent full breakfast made with eggs laid on the property. Double $220, suite $275

EATING

Penguin Café 1726 Highcliff Rd, Portobello ☎03 478 1055, ⓦpenguincafe.net.nz. While the interior is rather plain, this café serves excellent Mazagran coffee and a wide range of teas, delicious cakes, and hot dishes including penguin-shaped pikelets ($8–14) plus home-made ice cream and great pies. Free wi-fi. Daily: summer 8am–4pm; winter 9am–4pm.

Portobello Hotel 2 Harington Point Rd, Portobello ☎03 478 0759. Classic Kiwi pub where you sit in the bar or the slightly more salubrious dining conservatory, tucking into blue cod fishcakes ($17.50) or a focaccia steak sandwich ($18.50); a vegetarian option is usually available. Daily 11.30am–10pm or later.

The Catlins Coast

The rugged coastal route linking Dunedin and Invercargill is one of the less-travelled highways on the South Island, traversing some of the country's wildest scenery along the **Catlins Coast**. It is part of the **Southern Scenic Route** (ⓦsouthernscenicroute.co.nz), which continues on to Te Anau in Fiordland.

The region is home to swathes of native forest, most protected as the **Catlins Forest Park**, consisting of rimu, rata, kamahi and silver beech. Roaring southeasterlies and the remorseless sea have shaped the coastline into plunging cliffs, windswept headlands, white-sand beaches, rocky bays and gaping caves, many of which are accessible to visitors. **Wildlife** abounds, including several rare species of marine bird and mammal, and the region rings with birdsong for most of the year.

THE CATLINS COAST

● EATING
Blue Cod Blues	5
The Lumberjack	2
Niagara Falls Café	4
The Point Café	1
The Whistling Frog	3

■ ACCOMMODATION
Catlins Beach House	13
Curio Bay Holiday Houses & Penguin Paradise	11
Curio Bay Holiday Park	14
Kaka Point Camping Ground	2
McLean Falls Holiday Park	10
Mohua Park	5
Molyneux House	1
Newhaven Holiday Park	6
Nugget View & Kaka Point Motels	3
Purakaunui Bay	8
Slope Point Backpackers	12
Southern Secret Motel	9
The Split Level	4
Surat Bay Lodge	6
Wrights Mill Lodge	7

The best way to enjoy the **Catlins Coast** is to invest at least a couple of days and take it easy. From Nugget Point in South Otago (just southeast of Balclutha) to Waipapa Point in Southland (60km southeast of Invercargill), the wild landscape stretches unbroken, dense rainforest succumbing to open scrub as you cut through deep valleys and pass rocky bays and inlets. The coast is home to **penguins** (both blue and yellow-eyed), **dolphins**, many species of seabird and, at certain times of year, migrating **whales**. Elephant **seals**, fur seals, and increasingly, the rare New Zealand **sea lion** are found among the sand dunes, and **birds** – tui, resonant bellbirds and fantails – are abundant in the mossy depths of the forest. Even colourful rarities such as kakariki and mohua can be seen if you're patient.

Brief history

The Catlins, one of the last refuges of the flightless moa, was a thriving hunting ground for **Maori** but by 1700 they had moved on, to be supplanted by European **whalers and sealers** in the 1830s. Two decades later, having decimated marine mammal stocks, they too departed. Meanwhile, in 1840, Captain Edward Cattlin arrived to investigate the navigability of the river that bears his (misspelt) name, cannily purchasing a tract of land from the chief of the Ngai Tahu. Boatloads of **loggers** soon followed, lured by the great podocarp forests. Cleared valleys were settled and bush millers supplied Dunedin with much of the wood needed for housing – in 1872 more timber was exported from the Catlins than anywhere else in New Zealand. From 1879 the rail line from Balclutha began to extend into the region, bringing sawmills, schools and farms with it. Milling continued into the 1930s, but gradually dwindled and today's tiny settlements are shrunken remnants of the once-prosperous logging industry.

11

INFORMATION

THE CATLINS COAST

Tourist information i-SITE, 4 Clyde St, Balclutha (Nov–March Mon–Fri 8.30am–5pm, Sat & Sun 9.30am–3pm; April–Oct Mon–Fri 8.30am–5pm, Sat & Sun 10am–2pm; ☎03 418 0388, ⓦdestinationclutha.com). There is no i-SITE in the Catlins, so if you're approaching from the north, make full use of this i-SITE in the gateway town of Balclutha, 80km southwest of Dunedin. It has all the usual information and booking facilities plus internet access.

Services There are no banks or ATMs in the Catlins; many places accept credit and debit cards but bring plenty of cash. There are very few petrol stations, and most pumps close around 5pm; fill up before you set off, then at Owaka (24hr card operated), Papatowai or Tokanui. Mobile phone coverage is poor away from the main settlements.

Opening hours Lodging and restaurant opening days and hours vary seasonally and from year to year; check directly or with the visitor centres.

GETTING AROUND

By car and tour The region is linked by SH92, which is sealed all the way, though virtually all the Catlins' attractions are reached on narrow gravel roads. Without your own transport, visit on a guided tour.

anywhere, and there are Milford Sound and Stewart Island add-ons. Sector fares are also available with Dunedin–Catlins–Invercargill starting at $199.

TOURS

Bottom Bus ☎03 477 9083, ⓦtravelheadfirst.com. Hop-on, hop-off service offered (three times a week in summer) as a supplementary trip by Kiwi Experience (though it attracts less of the booze-bus crowd). It loops from Queenstown to Dunedin, Invercargill via the Catlins then on to Queenstown over 3–7 days ($315). You can start

Catlins Wildlife Trackers Mohua Park ☎0800 2285467, ⓦcatlins-ecotours.co.nz. Entertaining and inspirational private tours (half-day tours $125/person) led by committed conservationists sharing in-depth knowledge about the local ecology, history and geology. Their only multi-day tour is the Catlins Traverse (Nov–March on demand; 30km; $1200 per person, min. 2 people), a two-day/three-night guided trek with all accommodation, food and transport included. Advance bookings essential.

ACCOMMODATION AND EATING

Outside the main settlement of Owaka you'll only find a smattering of places to stay, the best of them listed in the text.

Freedom camping Travellers in campervans have traditionally appreciated the abundance of peaceful wayside spots for sneaky overnight stays, but a combination of sheer numbers and misuse of these sites means freedom camping is now banned in the area and instant fines have been imposed.

Self-catering Throughout the region you'll find very few worthwhile restaurants and cafés. It pays to bring your own supplies and self-cater where possible. You can get groceries in Owaka, there are small general stores at Kaka Point and Papatowai and a tiny store selling sweets and ice cream at *Curio Bay Holiday Park* (see p.621).

Kaka Point

22km south of Balclutha

The first stop inside the Catlins is **KAKA POINT**, a tiny holiday community with golden sands patrolled by lifeguards in summer, making it a good swimming and surfing spot. Just behind the township a scenic reserve of native forest is accessible on an easy loop track (2.5km; 30min) that can be accessed from the top of Tarata Street or Rata Street.

ACCOMMODATION AND EATING   **KAKA POINT**

Kaka Point Camping Ground 34 Tarata St ☎03 412 8801, ⓦkakapointcamping.co.nz. Grassy hilltop campsite with plenty of tree shelter. Facilities are basic, but it's got all the essentials, plus free wi-fi and cheap cabins (doubles $56). Camping **$29** for two, powered sites **$32** for two

Molyneux House 2 Rimu St ☎03 412 8002, ⓦmolyneuxhouse.co.nz. Very comfy B&B in a modern house offering just one deluxe suite with its own kitchen and great sea views from the deck. Continental breakfast ingredients provided and there's free wi-fi. **$190**

Nugget View & Kaka Point Motels 11 Rata St ☎03

412 8602, ⓦcatlins.co.nz. Comfortable place with a range of spacious self-contained units, almost all with decking and wonderful ocean views. The owner also offers small-group tours ($40; $35 for guests; 2hr 30min) around Nugget Point to see penguins and seals and get a taste of the local history. Economy units **$100**, studios **$135**

The Point Café 58 Esplanade ☎03 412 8800. This decent-enough café/pub is the only spot for a coffee, seafood chowder ($16) or blue cod and chips ($18), but works best for a beer while watching the breakers (and feeding the sandflies) on the deck. Daily 11am–10pm.

Nugget Point

9km south of Kaka Point

The Catlins proper kicks off with a bang at dramatic **Nugget Point**, a steep-sided, windswept promontory rising 133m above the sea. Just offshore lie **The Nuggets**, jagged stacks of wave-pounded rock whose layers have been tilted vertical over time. It is an impressive sight, visited on an easy, 900m track (30min return) which ends at a still-functioning 1870 lighthouse, from where you can gaze down on lively groups of honking southern fur seals. A short path leads from the car park to a clifftop viewpoint that overlooks a nesting colony of royal spoonbills.

Roaring Bay

At **Roaring Bay** you can watch **yellow-eyed penguins** as they leave their nests at sunrise and descend the steep grassy cliffs to the sea or as they return two hours before dark. Their progress is slow, so you need plenty of patience and insect repellent, and binoculars come in handy. A modern viewing hide is accessed along a 500m path from a parking area just before the road end.

Cannibal Bay

The long crescent of sand known as **Cannibal Bay** (named by an early explorer who thought human bones he found here were evidence of human feasting; in fact it was a Maori burial site) is a haul-out spot for New Zealand sea lions. To reach it from Nugget Point you'll need to backtrack 6km then turn onto the sealed road towards Owaka, before heading out to the coast again along a narrow, winding gravel road until you reach the cluster of huts at the northern end of the bay. Keep at least 10m away from any sea lions and back off quickly if they rear up and roar.

FROM TOP NUGGET POINT (P.616); YELLOW-EYED PENGUIN (P.612) >

Owaka and around

The only settlement of any size within the Catlins is the farming town of **OWAKA**, 18km southwest of Kaka Point and little more than a crossroads where you'll find a few places to stay, three restaurant/cafés and petrol.

Owaka Museum

10 Campbell St • Mon–Fri 9.30am–1pm & 1.30–4.30pm, Sat & Sun 10am–4pm • $5 • ☎ 03 415 8323, ⓦ owakamuseum.org.nz

A well-curated local museum with evocative exhibits on the area's significance to Maori and the coast's shipwrecks as well as sealer and whaler Captain Cattlin. The Owaka library is on-site and the staff can supply advertising and walks leaflets for the area.

Jack's Blowhole

10km southeast from Owaka

A gravel waterside drive runs to Jack's Bay, from where a farmland track (20–30min each way) leads up a valley and along the cliffs to **Jack's Blowhole**, an impressively wide 55m-deep hole in the ground, which connects with the sea through a 200m-long tunnel. Effectively the collapsed roof of a cave, the bottom of the blowhole is washed by surf at high tide when plumes of spray waft up.

Mohua Park

744 Catlins Valley Rd, 10km southwest of Owaka then 7.5km inland • Daily 9am–5pm • Donations welcome • ☎ 03 415 8613

Spend an hour or so checking out this delightful, remnant patch of forest in a transition zone where beech forest meets native podocarp, with patches of regenerating bush thick with native fuchsia. Nip into the 1920s homestead to pick up a leaflet detailing several trails that are typically alive with native birds. Engaging and knowledgeable owners Fergus and Mary Sutherland have displays on rat and stoat control and particularly on efforts to help the endangered **mohua** further establish itself in the area. In 2014 the historic Tawanui railway station – two tiny weatherboard huts – was relocated to the park and now contains displays on the settlement and railway's history.

Purakaunui Falls

Purakaunui Falls Rd, 15km southwest of Owaka • 20min return walk

If there has been a good bit of rain recently (not unknown in these parts) don't miss this gorgeous 20m-high, three-tiered waterfall in a scenic reserve of silver beech and podocarp. It is well signposted off the main road and accessed along a pleasant nature trail to a picnic area and viewing platform.

Matai Falls

Papatowai Hwy, 18km southwest of Owaka • 20–30min return walk

The easy walk to **Matai Falls** is as much a reason to visit as the fairly modest but pretty falls themselves. It winds through Table Hill Scenic Reserve among 10m-high native fuchsia trees, easily identified by their peeling pinkish bark and, in early summer, small red-and-blue trumpet flowers.

INFORMATION

OWAKA AND AROUND

Tourist information Catlins Information Centre, inside the Owaka Museum, 10 Campbell St (Mon–Fri 9.30am–1pm & 1.30–4.30pm, Sat & Sun 10am–4pm; ☎ 03 415 8371, ⓦ cluthanz.com). Dispenses useful updates on eating and sleeping options, as well as DOC information.

ACCOMMODATION

★ **Mohua Park** 744 Catlins Valley Rd, 10km southwest then 7.5km inland ☎ 03 415 8613, ⓦ catlinsmohuapark .co.nz. Four magically peaceful eco-cottages isolated on the edge of bush overlooking farmland. The cottages are self-catering, so bring supplies, or join owners Fergus and Mary Sutherland for home-cooked breakfast ($25) or dinner ($75, including wine); picnic lunches. **$190**

★ **Newhaven Holiday Park** 324 Newhaven Rd, Surat

THE CATLINS RIVER-WISP LOOP TRACK

The only long tramp in the Catlins, the **Catlins River-Wisp Loop Track** is essentially two twelve-kilometre routes linked in a circuit with multiple access points, enabling energetic types to do the whole 24km loop in a single day, while others can amble along shorter sections from either end.

The first half, Catlins River Walk (12km; 5–6hr), is a well-formed tramping track that links the *Tawanui Campsite*, 18km west of Owaka, with The Wisp, where there is a picnic area and toilet. The trail runs over several swingbridges and through silver beech forest; in December & January the forest around Tawanui is hung with the scarlet flowers of native mistletoe. From The Wisp, the Wisp Loop Walk (12km; 4–5hr) runs along forestry roads and over higher ground back to Tawanui, with the Rocky Knoll extension track giving access to the Rata Range, with great views over the Owaka Valley. See the DOC website ⓦ doc.govt.nz for more details.

Bay, 5km east of Owaka ☎03 415 8834, ⓦnewhavenholiday.com. Delightful, small campsite bordering the estuary and just a 2min walk from the beach. Simple cabins and self-contained tourist flats come ranged around a central grassy area, and there's a vaguely 70's-styled retro caravan ($55) available too. Camping $16, cabins $66

Purakaunui Bay Purakaunui Bay Rd, 17km south of Owaka. A DOC toilets-and-water site right on the coast with dramatic views of the cliffs, fire-pits and a ready supply of driftwood, plus good surfing. Cosgrove Island nature reserve is just offshore. $6

The Split Level 9 Waikawa Rd ☎03 415 8304, ⓦthesplitlevel.co.nz. There's little advantage to staying right in Owaka, but if you need to then try this warm and spacious 1970s house with a quad-share dorm, a twin and a double, all a decent distance from the well-appointed kitchen/lounge. There are also en-suite motel units ($76) in a separate building. Dorm $30, doubles $68

Surat Bay Lodge Surat Bay Rd, 5km east of Owaka ☎03 415 8099, ⓦsuratbay.co.nz. Backpacker beds in a peaceful spot with good views, where the Catlins Estuary meets the beach. The owners will pick you up from Owaka, bikes and kayaks are free to use for guests; there's free wi-fi too. Dorms $30, rooms $76

EATING

The Lumberjack 3 Saunders St ☎03 415 8747, ⓦlumberjackbarandcafe.co.nz. This establishment is probably the best of Owaka's middling trio of places to eat and drink. The menu is pretty old-fashioned but it's a good spot for a decent ribeye steak with a choice of three sauces plus veg ($30) beside the big open fire. Daily 10am–9pm or later, some winter closures.

Papatowai and around

Heading southwest through the Catlins on the Papatowai Highway (SH92) you cross the Tahakopa River into the small settlement of **PAPATOWAI**, 26km south of Owaka, with its general store, quirky gallery and a couple of good walks.

Lost Gypsy Gallery

Papatowai Hwy • Sept–April generally daily 10am–5pm, often closed Wed • Free; "theatre" $5

Wild nature aside, the real highlight of the Catlins is the **Lost Gypsy Gallery**, a cheerful old bus beside the main road containing a wonderland of Blair Somerville's animatronics – machines and toys ingeniously constructed from recycled materials and old electrical components. Almost everything in the bus is for sale (from teabag dunkers to dancing penguins) but Somerville showcases his best work in the **Winding Thoughts Theatre … of Sorts**, just behind the bus. This highly amusing treasure-trove of wacky and often interactive home-made inventions includes: a pedal-powered TV; a paua-shell waterwheel; a wonderful organ with each key activating sounds from an amazing array of objects; and just about anything imaginable in who-would-ever-think-of-that combinations. There's also a welcome **coffee** kiosk on-site, and **Catlins Kayaks** (ⓔcatlinskayaks@gmail.com) rent kayaks ($45; up to 3hrs) and stand-up paddleboards ($25; 1hr) from a caravan in the gallery car park.

Florence Hill Lookout

Papatowai Hwy, 2.5km southwest of Papatowai

Stop briefly at the roadside **Florence Hill Lookout**, which presents a fabulous panoramic view of Tautuku Bay, a magnificent crescent of pale sand backed by extensive forest. At the far end you can pick out the **Frances Pillars**, wave-lashed rock pinnacles made of conglomerate rock.

Tautuku Boardwalk and Lake Wilkie

Papatowai Hwy, 5km southwest of Papatowai

Birders will appreciate a stroll along the **Tautuku Boardwalk** (20–30min return), a raised walkway nature trail over some estuarine marshes into fernbird territory. Others might prefer the walk to **Lake Wilkie** (20min return) through mature forest with interpretive signs explaining forest succession. The lake is a glacial remnant that has gradually shrunk as the forest has encroached.

Cathedral Caves

Papatowai Hwy, 10km southwest of Papatowai then 3km off the main road · Accessible 2hr either side of low tide when open · $5

The ever-popular **Cathedral Caves** are the grandest of the fifteen or so caves that punctuate this part of the coast, their soaring walls created by furious seas. The path – which winds down through mixed woodland to a beautiful, broad beach – is only open for two hours either side of low tide. The caves lie at the western end of the beach; allow an hour for the walk down and back. Seasonal changes in the tides mean that the caves are closed each winter when the waves scour out much of the sand, generally reopening sometime between October and December: check the access situation at local visitor centres, or check the sign at the entrance.

McLean Falls

Rewcastle Rd, 11km southwest of Papatowai then 3km off the main road · 30–40min return walk

The picturesque 22m-high **McLean Falls** are the most impressive and beautiful of the falls hereabouts and reached along a rainforest walk through podocarp and fuchsia, the climb steepening as you approach the waterfall. The best time to visit is late afternoon when sun strikes the forest around the main cascade. The falls were named after an early landowner who once came here to bathe.

ACCOMMODATION AND EATING   PAPATOWAI

★**McLean Falls Holiday Park** 27 Rewcastle Rd ☎03 415 8338, ⓦ catlinsnz.com. Excellent and professionally-run complex with sheltered campsites and powered sites, sharing communal barbecue areas, a cramped kitchen and a TV lounge. There are dorm beds available ($39pp), but the cute backpacker cabins ($80), with their own table and chairs on the tiny porch are a better deal if you're travelling in a pair; you'll need sleeping bags. There's a range of plusher accommodation from compact "Kiwiana" cabins ($90) to roomy one-bedroom chalets ($195). Camping $22 powered sites $24.50

Southern Secret Motel 2510 Papatowai Hwy, Papatowai ☎03 415 8777, ⓦ southernsecretmotel .co.nz. Though it looks like an ordinary home on the outside, this motel has four fabulous rooms done out in Pacific colours with mosquito-net-draped wrought-iron beds and a free library of over 950 videos. The same people offer *Erehwon* and *Lancewood*, two eclectically decorated cottages, where a single-night surcharge of

$10/person applies. Motels $110, self-contained cottage $135

The Whistling Frog 27 Rewcastle Rd ☎03 415 8338, ⓦ whistlingfrogcafe.com. Some of the best dining in the Catlins is at this cosy and welcoming café and bar at the *McLean Falls Holiday Park*. As well as the standard range of Kiwi breakfasts, expect the likes of steak, mushroom and ale pie ($24) and delicious vegetarian arancini balls ($19). There's wine by the glass and a good selection of beers, plus home-brew on tap. Daily 8.30am–9pm or later.

Wrights Mill Lodge 865 Tahakopa Valley Rd, 9km northwest of Papatowai ☎03 204 8424, ⓦ catlins accommodation.co.nz. In an out-of-the-way location, deep in the tranquil Tahakopa Valley, with beautiful and reasonably priced rooms set amid beautiful gardens. The four double rooms (no dorms) share a bathroom in a century-old house with a sunny veranda and barbecue area. $90

Waikawa

There's not much to the fishing village of **WAIKAWA**, 38km west of Papatowai – just a few houses, the pretty, white, former Waikawa St Marys Anglican Church and a museum.

Waikawa Museum

604 Niagara Waikawa Highway • Daily summer 10am–5pm; winter 10am–4pm • Donation • ☎ 03 246 8464

To learn something of the seafaring and logging life hereabouts, visit the small **Waikawa Museum** which also has a small case containing a bible with a bullet hole and the bullet, which penetrated the unfortunate World War I rifleman carrying it. The museum doubles as the area's visitor centre, with material on the Hector's dolphins (see box, p.622) that come in close to the shore at nearby Curio Bay.

EATING   WAIKAWA

Blue Cod Blues Niagara Waikawa Rd, Waikawa. Top-quality burgers ($7–10) and blue cod and chips ($8.50) from a nicely kitted-out wayside caravan with the odd table or two outside. Generally Mon 11am–2pm, Fri–Sun 11am–2pm & 4.30–7pm; daily in high summer.

★ **Niagara Falls Café** 256 Niagara Waikawa Rd, 4km north of Waikawa ☎ 03 246 8577, ⓦ niagarafallscafe .co.nz. Great licensed café in Niagara's refurbished old schoolhouse surrounded by gardens and lawns. Everything is prepared on-site from natural ingredients and generally cooked as plainly as possible to bring out the flavours. Stop in for superb coffee and carrot cake, a whitebait entrée ($25; available seasonally), blue cod with salad and house-baked bread ($27) or rack of lamb ($34.50). Wheat- and dairy-free options are available and select Kiwi wines all come by the glass. Daily 9am–11pm, but check for winter closures.

11

Curio Bay and Porpoise Bay

5km southwest of Waikawa • For surfing here, contact Catlins Surf (☎ 03 246 8552, ⓦ catlins-surf.co.nz), who rent boards and wetsuits ($40/3hr), offer surfing lessons ($50/90min) and give you a chance to try stand-up paddleboarding ($75/2hr 30min)

Contrasting seascapes come together at a windswept headland that separates two of the most beautiful bays in a region packed with such things. To the northeast, the beautiful sandy crescent of **Porpoise Bay** forms superb rolling breakers where **Hector's dolphins** love to surf. To the south, the rocky wave-cut platform of **Curio Bay** is littered with the remains of a **petrified forest**, with fossilized Jurassic trees clearly visible at low tide. Over 170 million years ago, when most of New Zealand still lay beneath the sea, this would have been a broad, forested floodplain. Today, the seashore, composed of several layers of forest buried under blankets of volcanic mud and ash, is littered with fossilized tree stumps and fallen logs. Steps lead to a beach where, in places, you can even pick out ancient tree rings. Return at sunrise or just before dusk when up to a dozen **yellow-eyed penguins** stagger ashore to their burrows in the bushes at the back of Curio Bay.

ACCOMMODATION   CURIO BAY AND PORPOISE BAY

★ **Catlins Beach House** 499 Curio Bay Rd ☎ 03 246 8340, ⓦ catlinsbeachhouse.co.nz. Step off the lawn onto the beach at this wonderfully chilled-out hostel in a self-contained house with a pot-belly log burner and room for just nine in two doubles (one en suite) and a bunkroom. Dorms $30, double $70

Curio Bay Holiday Houses & Penguin Paradise ☎ 03 246 8552, ⓦ catlins-surf.co.nz. The energetic owner of Catlins Surf (see above) operates a selection of four fully self-contained beachside holiday homes around Porpoise Bay as well as the backpacker-friendly *Penguin Paradise* in nearby Waikawa. All of the holiday homes are available by the night with linen and towels provided, while backpackers can enjoy a "room and surf class" deal for just $75. *Penguin Paradise* $28, holiday homes from $120

Curio Bay Holiday Park 601 Curio Bay Rd ☎ 03 246 8897, ⓔ valwhyte@hotmail.com. Wonderfully sited campsite where tent and powered sites come nestled into dense flax enclaves to protect you from the sometimes ferocious winds. There are views across both Porpoise Bay and Curio Bay, and a tiny store sells supplies. Showers are $2 and for guests only. Camping/site $10, powered sites $15

11

THE NEW ZEALAND SEA LION AND HECTOR'S DOLPHIN

Two extremely rare species – the New Zealand sea lion and Hector's dolphin – are found only in New Zealand's waters.

New Zealand sea lions (*Phocarctos hookeri*, a.k.a. Hooker's sea lion) mostly live around the sub-Antarctic Auckland Islands, 460km south of the South Island, but some breeding also takes place on the Otago Peninsula, along the Catlins Coast and around Stewart Island. The large, adult male sea lions are black to dark brown, have a mane over their shoulders, weigh up to 400kg and reach lengths of over 3m. Adult females are buff to silvery grey and much smaller – less than half the weight and just under 2m. Barracuda, red cod, octopus, skate and, in spring, paddle crabs make up their diet, with New Zealand sea lions submerging for four or five minutes, usually to depths of 200m or less, although they have been known to dive as deep as 500m. Pups are born on the beach, then moved by the mother at about six weeks to grassy swards, shrubland or forest, and suckled for up to a year.

Sea lions prefer to haul out on sandy beaches and in summer spend much of the day flicking sand over themselves to keep cool. Unlike seals they don't fear people. If you encounter one on land, give it a wide berth of at least 10m (30m during the Dec–Feb breeding season), and if it rears up and roars, back off calmly but quickly – they can move fast and bite.

The **Hector's dolphin** (*Cephalarhynchus hectori*), with its distinctive black and white markings, is the smallest dolphin in the world and, with a population around 7000, is also one of the rarest. It's only found in New Zealand's inshore waters – mostly around the coast of the South Island – with eastern concentrations around Banks Peninsula, Te Waewae Bay and Porpoise Bay, plus western communities between Farewell Spit and Haast. They roam up to 8km from shore in winter but in summer prefer shallow waters within 1km of the coastline, catching mullet, arrowsquid, red cod, stargazers and crabs. Female dolphins are typically a little larger than the males, growing to 1.2–1.4m and weighing 40–50kg. They give birth from November to mid-February, and calves stay with their mothers for up to two years.

In summer and autumn, the tiny resident population at Porpoise Bay regularly enters the surf zone and even comes within 10m of the beach. Hector's dolphins are shy and being disturbed can impact on feeding, which in turn affects their already low breeding rate. If you're spending time around them, be sure to follow DOC rules (posted locally), which forbid touching, feeding, surrounding and chasing dolphins and encourage you to keep a respectful distance. Swimming around pods with juveniles is also forbidden, which in practice means avoiding all pods in summertime.

Slope Point

16km west of Curio Bay

Slope Point is the southernmost land on the South Island, some 7km further south than Bluff. A walk through sheep paddocks (40min return) brings you to a wind-lashed promontory that's totally exposed to the southern ocean. A sign advises that it is still 4803km to the South Pole.

ACCOMMODATION

SLOPE POINT

Slope Point Backpackers 164 Slope Point Rd ☏ 03 246 8420, ⊙ slopepoint.co.nz. Friendly and great-value hostel on a working sheep farm where kids (of all ages) are welcome to check out the animals. There's a selection of doubles, dorm rooms and a self-contained unit ($90), plus camping ($15/person) and a couple of powered sites. Dorms $25, doubles $50

Waipapa Point

26km west of Curio Bay

Waipapa Point is the site of New Zealand's worst civilian shipwreck, in 1881, when 131 lives were lost on SS *Tararua*. The lighthouse that now stands on the point was erected soon after and you might spot sea lions on the golden beach and around the rocky platform at its foot.

The **western continuation** of the **Southern Scenic Route**, from Invercargill to Te Anau via Tuatapere, is covered in the Fiordland chapter (see p.780).

Gore

The quiet Southland farming town of **GORE**, 70km west of Balclutha and 65km northeast of Invercargill, is a pleasant transit point at the intersection of routes from Dunedin to Te Anau and Invercargill. Dominated by the Hokonui Hills, Gore spans the Mataura River ("reddish swirling water"), and claims to be the **brown trout capital** of the world – celebrated by an enormous fish statue in the town centre. It also claims to be New Zealand's home of **country music** (not that anyone is fighting them for the honour), a scene that is most accessible during **Gold Guitar Week** (late May and early June; ☏03 208 1978, Ⓦgoldguitars.co.nz) when hundreds of would-be country stars and a few established performers roll into town for a weekend of low-key entertainment.

11

Hokonui Moonshine Museum

Hokonui Heritage Centre, 16 Hokonui Drive • Mon–Fri 8.30am–5pm, Sat 9.30am–4pm, Sun 1–4pm • $5

The entertaining **Hokonui Moonshine Museum** details decades of illicit whisky distillation deep in the local bush-covered hills. This "sly grogging" began in 1836 and reached a peak during a regional half-century of Prohibition that started in 1903. Alcohol freedom is still restricted in these parts, with all liquor sales and profits managed by a licensing trust. The visit ends with a dram of whisky loosely based on the old Hokonui recipe. In odd-numbered years, Gore hosts the biennial **Hokonui Moonshiners' Festival** (Ⓦmoonshinefest.co.nz), with live music by local bands.

The Heritage Centre also holds the **Gore Historical Museum**, a high-quality collection of Victorian costume, vintage homewares and angling paraphernalia.

Eastern Southland Art Gallery

14 Hokonui Drive • Mon–Fri 10am–4.30pm, Sat & Sun 1–4pm • Free

Art lovers shouldn't miss the **Eastern Southland Art Gallery** with its nationally significant collection. The permanent exhibition centres on a fascinating collection of art bequeathed by expat Kiwi sexologist, Dr John Money, with Congolese ceremonial helmets and ranks of life-size Bambara ancestral figures displayed alongside richly coloured oils by Rita Angus and works by Dutch émigré Theo Schoon, who incorporated Maori iconography into his painting long before it was fashionable. Also on permanent display are career-spanning pieces gifted to the museum by one of New Zealand's most famous painters, the late Ralph Hotere.

Old Mandeville Airfield

SH94, 17km west of Gore • Museum Mon–Fri 9.30am–4.30pm, Sat & Sun 11am–3pm • $10; flights from $95/10min–$220/30min • ☏03 208 9755, Ⓦcroydonaircraft.com

Fans of vintage aircraft shouldn't miss the **Old Mandeville Airfield**, where you can watch the restoration of vintage planes, take to the air in a Tiger Moth or a de Havilland biplane and have a leisurely wander around the brand-new **museum** containing a fleet of beautifully restored vintage aeroplanes. Refuel at the airfield café, *The Moth*.

ARRIVAL AND INFORMATION
GORE

By bus Gore lies on the major bus route between Dunedin, Invercargill and Te Anau, with buses stopping outside the Heritage Centre.

Destinations Dunedin (4 daily; 3hr); Invercargill (4 daily; 1hr); Te Anau (daily; 1hr 45min).
Tourist information 16 Hokonui Drive, inside the

Hokonui Heritage Centre (Mon–Fri 8.30am–5pm, Sat 9.30am–4pm, Sun 1–4pm; ☎03 203 9288, ☯gorenz .com), with free maps and leaflets available from a barrel outside.

Trout fishing During the fishing season (Nov–April) you can pit your wits against a brown trout with tackle rented from B&B Sports, 65 Main St (☎03 208 0801); they also sell fishing licences ($25/day).

ACCOMMODATION

Gore Motor Camp 35 Broughton St, 2km south of the Heritage Centre ☎03 208 4919, ☯gorecamp@xtra.co.nz. This open grassy campsite backs onto SH1, though you'll need to follow signs down Kitchener St to find the actual entrance. In addition to powered and non-powered campsites, there are a couple of very reasonably priced cabins. Free pick-ups from the town centre for two or more travellers, and occasional discounts available. Camping $̲1̲5̲, cabins $̲6̲5̲

Wentworth Heights 86a Wentworth St, off SH1 3km northeast of town ☎03 208 6476, ☯wentworthheights .co.nz. Very comfortable semirural B&B with fabulous breakfasts, hot tub, and a warm welcome that few can match. Host Barry Perkins is also a fishing guide with great local knowledge. $̲1̲6̲5̲

EATING

The Green Room 59 Irk St ☎03 208 1005. Casual wood-floored café next to Gore's St John Theatre that's good for soup, quiches, frittatas or just a coffee and a slice of cake. Mon–Sat 7.30am–4.30pm.

The Howl of the Moon 2 Main St ☎03 208 3851. This cavernous but friendly joint serves coffee and snacks all day, with hot meals cooked to order at lunch and dinner, with the steak-and-lamb-rack orientated menu making occasional forays into more exotic territory, with jerk chicken with roasted corn ($29) and coconut cheesecake ($11). Light meals available for $20. Mon–Sat 7.30am–4.30pm.

The Thomas Green 30 Medway St ☎03 208 9295, ☯thethomasgreen.co.nz. City style comes to eastern Southland at this flash restaurant of mirrors, smart lighting and green and black chesterfields tucked behind the facade of a heritage building. The food is upscale pub style with the likes of zucchini and feta tart ($18) and lemon and thyme-glazed chicken breast ($29). Daily 10am–10pm or later.

Invercargill

Many visitors pass straight through **INVERCARGILL**, regarding it as little more than a way station en route to Stewart Island or the Catlins Coast. But the city warrants a little more time. Settled in the mid-1850s, it sprawls over an exposed stretch of flat land at the head of the New River Estuary. In 2000, community contributions allowed its main centre of learning, the Southern Institute of Technology (SIT), to offer free tuition for New Zealand and Australian residents (with lower than usual fees for international students) on all of its courses. As a result, Invercargill's population swelled to 50,000, and its arts scene and nightlife gained new impetus. More recently, the exploration of a possible oil and gas deposit in the Great South Basin off the Southland coast has led to new investment in the town, with the prospect of more to come.

To the south, at the tip of a small peninsula, lies **Bluff**, the departure point for ferries to **Stewart Island** (see p.630).

Southland Museum and Art Gallery

108 Gala St, beside Queens Park • Mon–Fri 9am–5pm, Sat & Sun 10am–5pm • Donation • ☎03 219 9069, ☯southlandmuseum.com

Invercargill's chief attraction is the **Southland Museum and Art Gallery**, a giant white pyramid housing a well-laid-out collection over three levels. Upstairs, the fascinating "Beyond the Roaring Forties" exhibit focuses on New Zealand's **sub-Antarctic islands**, tiny windswept clusters lying hundreds of kilometres apart between New Zealand and Antarctica. They're the only obstacles in the way of the westerly gales that rage through these latitudes. Displays cover the shipwreck victims who have clung on to the islands, sometimes for years, sealers who subsisted while almost wiping out their quarry, meteorological teams who have weathered the storms with the albatross and penguins, and plants from the daisy, lily and carrot families which have adapted to form swathes of gigantic **megaherbs**.

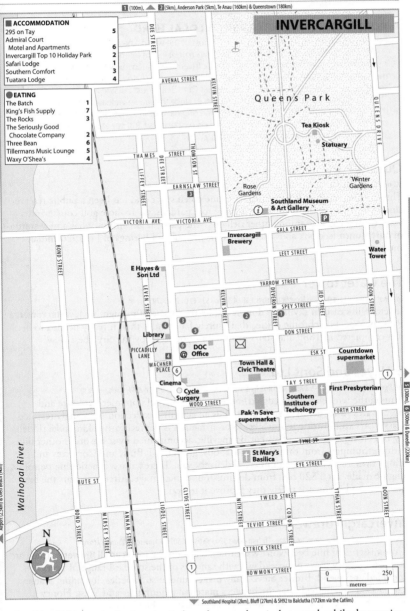

1 (100m), **2** (5km), Anderson Park (5km), Te Anau (160km) & Queenstown (180km)

INVERCARGILL

■ ACCOMMODATION
295 on Tay	5
Admiral Court Motel and Apartments	6
Invercargill Top 10 Holiday Park	2
Safari Lodge	1
Southern Comfort	3
Tuatara Lodge	4

● EATING
The Batch	1
King's Fish Supply	7
The Rocks	3
The Seriously Good Chocolate Company	2
Three Bean	6
Tillermans Music Lounge	5
Waxy O'Shea's	4

Queens Park

Tea Kiosk

Statuary

Winter Gardens

Rose Gardens

Southland Museum & Art Gallery

Invercargill Brewery

Water Tower

E Hayes & Son Ltd

Library

DOC @ Office

Town Hall & Civic Theatre

Countdown supermarket

Cinema

Cycle Surgery

Southern Institute of Techology

First Presbyterian

Pak 'n Save supermarket

St Mary's Basilica

Waihopai River

Airport (2.5km) & Oreti Beach (9km)

Southland Hospital (2km), Bluff (27km) & SH92 to Balclutha (172km via the Catlins)

5 (300m), **6** (500m) & Dunedin (220km)

11

metres 0 250

Southland's history is also imaginatively and comprehensively treated, while downstairs, Maori artefacts include a post-European-contact carved figure wearing a military cap and a couple of intricately carved *waka huia* treasure boxes. Burt Munro's exploits (see box, p.626) get glowing coverage alongside a replica bike made for *The World's Fastest Indian*.

Don't miss the **tuatara** – small, dinosaurian reptiles found nowhere else in the world – including Henry, who is thought to be well over a hundred years old. You can observe them in the glassed-in tuatarium at the back of the museum's ground floor.

BURT MUNRO – INVERCARGILL'S LOCAL HERO

Few New Zealanders, let alone anyone in the rest of the world, knew about Burt Munro (1899–1978) until Roger Donaldson's *The World's Fastest Indian* hit movie screens in 2005. All of a sudden everyone had heard of this eccentric Invercargill mechanic who, in 1967, aged 68, set the under-1000cc speed record of 295kph (183mph) on a 1920 Indian Scout bike. He had spent years modifying the bike and testing it at Oreti Beach, just outside Invercargill.

His stock has been rising around the town ever since the movie's release, with a display in the museum, a statue outside Queens Park, the original bike in E. Hayes and Sons Ltd shop, and the annual Burt Munro Challenge, four days of speedway and street racing, a hill climb and, of course, beach racing each November.

Queens Park

Main entrance on Gala St

The vast **Queens Park** is Invercargill's prime green space and has been a public reserve since 1869. Today there are lovely formal rose gardens, an 18-hole golf course and a walk-through aviary, among other delights. The park's main entrance has a new **statue of Burt Munro** (see box above) cocooned in streamlined fairings of his 1920 Indian motorcycle.

The water tower

Corner of Doon and Leet sts • Sun & public holidays 1.30–4.30pm • $2 • ☎ 03 211 1679

Invercargill's eastern skyline is dominated by the ornate 40m-high brick **water tower**, a Romanesque, polychrome edifice that's surely far grander than it really needed to be. It was completed in 1889 and stairs inside allow you to enjoy the city's best view.

E. Hayes and Sons Ltd

168 Dee St • Mon–Fri 7.30am–5.30pm, Sat 9am–4pm, Sun 10am–4pm • Free • ☎ 03 218 2059, ⓦ ehayes.co.nz

Among the wrenches and hedge trimmers in Invercargill's premier hardware and homewares store, **E. Hayes and Sons Ltd**, is an eccentric collection of lovingly restored classic cars and historic motorbikes. Star attraction is the record-breaking bike ridden by Burt Munro (see box above) at Bonneville, accompanied by some of his other bikes, British thumpers from the 1950s and 1960s, gleaming T-Birds and Corvettes and the shop's own 1956 Morris-Commercial delivery van. There's also a functioning petrol engine made, for a $20 bet, from detritus found in a garage. After two years the bet was won and if you ask nicely they'll prove it to you.

Invercargill Brewery

72 Leet St • Mon–Sat 10am–6pm; tours Mon–Fri 1pm • Tours $20 • ☎ 03 214 5070, ⓦ invercargillbrewery.co.nz

Connoisseurs of fine beer won't want to miss out on the **Invercargill Brewery**. There are walk-in brewery tours on weekdays, with samples of the standard range of beers included at the end. Brewer Steve Nally makes nine or so varieties, including Stanley Green Pale Ale, named after the brewer's maternal grandfather and Wasp Honey Pilsner, flavoured with a touch of kamahi honey from the Catlins.

Anderson Park Art Gallery

McIvor Rd, just off SH6, 7km north of the city centre • Gardens daily 8am–dusk • Free • Take a taxi ($25 one way) or rent a bike (see opposite)

On the outskirts of Invercargill, the beautiful grounds of **Anderson Park** provide the setting for the atmospheric **Anderson Park Art Gallery**, housed in a 1925 neo-Georgian mansion built for local businessman Robert Anderson. At the time of writing, the Cecil Wood-designed building was closed for major earthquake-proofing work. Until the house reopens in 2016, the collection – one of the country's most interesting independent collections of New Zealand art – has been moved elsewhere. The gardens themselves are still worth a visit in summer; look for the 1920s *wharepuni* tucked away behind the main house. This traditional timber meetinghouse was once used by the Andersons for dances, and has a doorway and porch decorated with carvings by Tene Waitere, a renowned Rotorua carver.

Oreti Beach

10km west of town, along Dunns Rd

The road from Invercargill to **Oreti Beach** literally finishes on the beach. Continuing isn't recommended, especially since this will invalidate any rental agreement, but locals drive out there all the time, either taking the dog for a high-speed walk or doing doughnuts in their souped-up Japanese cars.

This beautiful broad expanse of fine sand sweeps 30km right around to the seaside resort of Riverton in the west, giving great views of Stewart Island and Bluff. Burt Munro used the beach for many of his speed motorbike trials. In summer, it's popular for swimming (surf patrols operate when busy), yachting and waterskiing, but windy days can cause violent sandstorms.

ARRIVAL AND DEPARTURE INVERCARGILL

By plane Stewart Island planes and Air New Zealand flights from Wellington and Christchurch land at Invercargill's airport, 3.5km southwest of the city centre. For transport into town use Blue Star taxis (☎ 03 217 7777; $20). Airport parking costs $16 for the first day, $7 for the second, eventually dropping to a flat rate of $5/day from day five onwards.

Destinations Christchurch (5–7 daily; 1hr 15min); Stewart Island (3 daily; 20min); Wellington (1–2 daily; 1hr 50min).

By bus InterCity and NakedBus stop outside the i-SITE. Catch-A-Bus South (☎ 03 479 9960, ⊚ catchabussouth .co.nz) pick-up from accommodation and Invercargill airport on their daily runs to Dunedin.

Destinations Dunedin (4–5 daily; 3hr 30min); Gore (4 daily; 1hr); Queenstown (2 daily; 4hr).

INFORMATION

Tourist information i-SITE, 108 Gala St (Mon–Fri 8am–5pm, Sat & Sun 8.30am–4pm; ☎ 03 211 0895, ⊚ southlandnz.com). Excellent visitor centre in the foyer of the Southland Museum, where you can pick up the *What's On* guide (good for local events listings) and the *Invercargill*

Heritage Trail leaflet, which details some distinctive architecture around the city centre.

DOC Level 7, 33 Don St (Mon–Fri 8am–4.30pm; ☎ 03 211 2400). Information on walks and wildlife in the Catlins, Stewart Island and Fiordland.

GETTING AROUND

By bus At the i-SITE, pick up the *Invercargill City Bus Timetable* outlining the city's bus routes (Mon–Sat only; ⊚ bussmart.co.nz), which cost just $1 to ride Mon–Fri 9am–2.30pm and all day Sat.

By bike Rental is cheapest from the i-SITE ($20/half-day), but you'll get cycle trail maps and good-quality mountain bikes from Cycle Surgery, 21 Tay St (☎ 03 218 8055), for $35/day.

ACCOMMODATION

Invercargill has a plethora of places to stay, with motels lining the SH1 just outside the town centre; prices are generally reasonable. **Freedom camping** is not allowed in town or anywhere nearby – the nearest DOC site is at Colac Bay.

295 on Tay 295 Tay St ☎ 0800 295295, ⊚ 295ontay .co.nz. Very comfortable modern motel; the bland but pleasant rooms all have full kitchens, heated towel rails, electric blankets, minibars and hairdryers; downstairs units have spa baths too. $130

Admiral Court Motel & Apartments 327 Tay St

☎ 0800 111122, ⊚ admiralcourt.co.nz. Seventeen spotless, fully self-contained units with extras, including breakfast delivered to your door, plungers with freshly ground coffee, free wi-fi, and transport to and from the airport. A handful of units also have bathtubs. $120

Invercargill Top 10 Holiday Park 77 McIvor

Rd, 6km north of the city centre ☎ 03 215 9032, ⓦ invercargilltop10.co.nz. Upscale parkland campsite with the typically high-standard Top 10 facilities, including a gas BBQ and pizza oven. Camping and powered sites $40 per site

★ **Safari Lodge** 51 Herbert St ☎ 0800 885557, ⓦ safarilodge.co.nz. Decorated with mementos of the owners' years in Mozambique, this luxurious four-room B&B is reminiscent of a Victorian explorer's mansion. The rooms are tastefully decorated and all have four-poster beds, while amenities include a billiards table and hot tub. Be sure to check out the lovely vintage cars in the garage. Full breakfast and sundowners included. $280

★ **Southern Comfort** 30 Thomson St ☎ 03 218 3838,

ⓔ coupers@xtra.co.nz. Suburban BBH hostel in a neatly kept Victorian villa set among manicured lawns where a kids' playhouse has been put to use as a tiny double room ($60). There's a great modern kitchen and free luggage storage for those tramping on Stewart Island. Dorms $30, doubles $70

Tuatara Lodge 30 Dee St ☎ 0800 488282, ⓦ tuataralodge.co.nz. High-ceilinged hostel in a converted bank building, right in the heart of town. While it's a little shabby around the edges, the rooms are decent (although some are windowless) and guests get a discount in the excellent café on the ground floor. Limited off-street parking. Dorms $25, doubles $69

EATING AND DRINKING

11

Invercargill specializes in wholesome food in farmhand quantities, though a little delicacy is beginning to show through. If you're self-catering, look out for local **seafood**, including excellent Bluff oysters (fresh April–Oct) and blue cod, as well as **muttonbird**. A number of the city's **bars** transform into dance venues as the evening wears on, though the town is usually quiet until Thursday night, and liveliest during university termtime.

★ **The Batch** 173 Spey St ☎ 03 214 6357. Invercargill's nicest modern café is in a light airy space with sofas and comfy chairs. They serve great coffee and brunch dishes including coconut muesli with apple and berry compote ($13.50) and mince and poached eggs on toast ($17), along with the best-looking cakes in town. Mon–Thurs 7am–4.30pm, Fri 7am–8pm, Sat & Sun 8am–4pm.

King's Fish Supply 59 Ythan St ☎ 03 218 8450, ⓦ kingsfish.co.nz. You can buy the fresh seafood on display to take away (priced by weight) or have it cooked to order while you wait (extra $1); they also do incredibly cheap, delicious fish and chips ($8). Mon & Tues 8am–7pm, Wed–Sat 8am–8pm, Sun 4–8pm.

The Rocks Courtville Place, 101 Dee St ☎ 03 218 7597, ⓦ shop5rocks.com. Longtime locals' favourite with bare brick walls and varied menu stretching from Sicilian seafood stew to ribeye steak finished with Kikorangi blue cheese sauce (both $36.50). The more limited lunchtime menu has plenty of lower-priced options, with mains $18–23. Tues–Sat 11am–2pm & 5–10pm or later.

The Seriously Good Chocolate Company 147 Spey St ☎ 03 218 8060, ⓦ seriouslygoodchocolate.com. This petite café is a perfectly good spot for a sausage roll or

muffin and a coffee, but that would be missing the point. Sup on a super-rich hot chocolate while you choose from their fabulous selection of inventive creations all made on-site. Boxes of chocolates include a selection flavoured with Central Otago wines, or with a Kiwiana theme (chocolate in the shape of a muttonbird and flavoured with caramel and salt). Mon & Tues 8am–4pm, Wed–Fri 8am–5pm.

Three Bean 73 Dee St ☎ 03 214 1914. Popular breakfast and lunch café dishing up zingy coffee and a well-made bacon and egg bagel ($13) along with excellent cakes, scones and muffins. Good magazines and free wi-fi. Mon–Fri 7am–4pm, Sat 8.30am–2pm.

Tillermans Music Lounge 16 Don St ☎ 03 218 9240. Behind this anonymous doorway on Don Street lies a popular bar with pool tables; it's a focal point for (often fairly offbeat) live music. Fri & Sat 11pm–3am.

Waxy O'Shea's 90 Dee St ☎ 03 214 0313, ⓦ waxys .co.nz. Convivial and more convincing-than-average Irish bar with good – and occasionally live – music. They do a decent bangers and mash for $17.50 or steak and Guiness hotpot for $20. Daily 11am–10pm or later.

DIRECTORY

Internet Wi-fi is free at the museum/i-SITE and in the library.

Left luggage The i-SITE will hold bags during the day but not overnight (free).

Library 50 Dee St (Mon–Fri 9am–7pm, Sat & Sun 10am–4pm; ☎ 03 211 1444).

Medical treatment Southland Hospital, on Kew Rd (☎ 03 218 1949), has a 24hr accident and emergency department. For illness and minor accidents outside

surgery hours, contact the After Hours Doctors, 40 Clyde St (☎ 03 218 8821; Mon–Fri 6pm–6am, Sat & Sun 9am–4pm; appointment required).

Pharmacy Inside the Countdown supermarket on Tay St (Mon–Thurs 8.30am–8pm, Fri 8.30am–9pm, Sat 9am–6pm).

Police 117 Don St (☎ 03 211 0400).

Post office 51 Don St, near the junction with Kelvin St (Mon–Fri 8.30am–5pm, Sat 9am–1pm).

Bluff

The small but busy fishing town and port of **BLUFF**, 27km south of Invercargill, occupies a slender-waisted peninsula with its man-made harbour on one side and the wild Foveaux Strait on the other. Continuously settled since 1824, Bluff is the oldest European town in New Zealand and is starting to show its age. Parts look decidedly run down and, while most visitors are here to hop on the ferry to **Stewart Island**, the place has a great setting, a long history and some fine short walks. Unless you have your own vehicle, seeing the town will involve a good deal of walking, as it spreads along the shoreline for about 6km.

Bluff's famous oysters (see box, p.630) are celebrated at the annual **Bluff Oyster & Food Festival** (third weekend in May; ⊛bluffoysterfest.co.nz), an event the local organizers claim is "unsophisticated and proud of it".

Bluff Maritime Museum

241 Foreshore Rd, 1km north of the ferry dock • Mon–Fri 10am–4.30pm, Sat & Sun in summer 1–5pm • $2

Bluff's small **Bluff Maritime Museum** contains historical displays focusing on whaling, the harbour development, oyster harvesting and shipwrecks. Pride of place is given to a triple-expansion steam engine and the 1909 oyster boat, *Monica II*, which sits outside the building.

Stirling Point

SH1, 2km south of the ferry dock

State Highway 1 ends at **Stirling Point**, not the South Island's most southerly point (that's Slope Point in the Catlins), but a fine spot with a multi-armed signpost that balances Cape Reinga's at the other end of the country. It marks the distance to major cities around the world, as well as the equator (5133km) and the South Pole (4810km). This is the southern limit of the Te Araroa long-distance trail from Cape Reinga. For something much more manageable, Stirling Point is the start of a couple of short **walks** (see below).

Nearby, a massive **anchor chain sculpture** disappears into the sea, symbolically linking Stirling Point with Russell Beck's near-identical sculpture at Lee Bay on Stewart Island. In Maori lore, the South Island is demigod Maui's canoe, and Stewart Island is *Te Punga o Te Waka a Maui*, "The Anchor Stone of Maui's Canoe".

Some walks

There are a couple of good **walks** from the car park at Stirling Point. The Foveaux Walkway (6.6km; 2hr one way; mostly flat) loops back towards town and has great coastal views. The Topuni Track (2km one way; 45min; 265m ascent) is fairly steep and climbs to Bluff Hill Lookout for 360-degree views encompassing Stewart Island, 35km away. The lookout is also accessible by road from Bluff: follow Lee Street, opposite the ferry wharf, uphill for 3km.

ARRIVAL AND INFORMATION   BLUFF

By bus Stewart Island Experience (☎0800 000511, ⊛stewartislandexperience.co.nz) runs a regular bus service from Invercargill ($24 each way), to connect with the ferry. For details on sailings to Stewart Island, see p.635.

Tourist information Bluff's maritime museum acts as a de facto visitor centre. Check out ⊛bluff.co.nz and pick up a *Bluff Heritage Trail* leaflet at Invercargill's i-SITE.

ACCOMMODATION AND EATING

Bluff Lodge 120 Gore St ☎03 212 7106, ⊛blufflodge .co.nz. Super-handy for the Stewart Island ferries, this peeling 1899 former post office now has five- and seven-bed dorms and three doubles, all sharing kitchen and bathroom facilities. The rooms are nothing fancy, but you can't complain at these prices. Linen is $5/person extra. Dorms $20, doubles $45

FOVEAUX STRAIT, BLUFF OYSTERS AND MUTTONBIRDS

Foveaux Strait, between the South Island and Stewart Island, has a fearsome reputation as a rough stretch of water, right in the path of the Roaring Forties with no land east or west until you hit South America. Mostly flat-floored and just 20–30m deep, this causes waves to rear up and compounds the discomfort of ferry passengers and those out harvesting the strait's bounty.

The best-known foodstuff pulled from the waters hereabouts is the sweet **Bluff oyster**, a highly sought after delicacy dredged from April until September then processed in local oyster sheds before being sent all over the country.

Foveaux Strait is also home to a cluster of overgrown rocks known as the Titi or **Muttonbird Islands**, where local Maori have the traditional right to harvest sooty shearwater chicks in April and early May. Traditionally the birds were packed into kelp bags and preserved in their own fat mixed with salt. The muttonbirds' flesh (*titi* in Maori) is regarded as a delicacy, though a taste for the anchovy-duck flavour is something few Pakeha acquire.

11

Lands End Stirling Point ☎03 212 7575, ⓦlandsendhotel.co.nz. Overlooking Stirling Point's famous signpost, most of the stylish rooms here have brilliant views on clear days; happily there's heating for when the weather is less clement. All rooms are en suite with a continental breakfast in the café downstairs included. $160

Johnson's Oysters 8 Foreshore Rd ☎03 212 8665. Between June and August you can buy Bluff oysters direct at factory prices from several spots on Bluff's waterfront including this venerable establishment. Daily 9am–4pm.

Stewart Island

The Foveaux Strait separates the South Island from New Zealand's third main island, **STEWART ISLAND**, a genuinely special place of rare birds, bountiful seas and straight-talking people.

Most of Stewart Island is uninhabited and characterized by bush-fringed bays, sandy coves, windswept beaches and a rugged interior of rimu forest and granite outcrops. It is known in Maori as Rakiura ("The Land of Glowing Skies"), although the jury is still out on whether this refers to the aurora australis – a.k.a. **southern lights** – occasionally seen in the night sky throughout the year, or the fabulous sunsets. With the creation of **Rakiura National Park** in 2002 a full 85 percent of the island is now protected.

Almost the entire population of four hundred lives in the sole town, **Oban**, where boats dock, planes land and the parrot-shriek of kaka provides the soundtrack. There's not much to do in town, but the slow island ways can quickly get into your blood and you may well want to stay longer than you had planned, especially if you're drawn to serious wilderness **tramping**, abundant **wildlife** in unspoilt surroundings and **sea-kayaking** around the flooded valley of **Paterson Inlet**.

Since 2013 a $5 **visitor levy** has been charged for Stewart Island. This is typically included in your flight or ferry ticket; the funds thus raised are used to maintain and improve visitor facilities.

Brief history

Maori had been here for centuries before Captain Cook came by in 1770 and erroneously marked Rakiura as a peninsula on his charts. The island was later named after William Stewart, the first officer on a sealing vessel that visited in 1809. With the arrival of Europeans, felling rimu became the island's economic mainstay, supporting three thousand people in the 1930s. Now almost all of Stewart Island's residents live from **conservation** work, **fishing** (crayfish, blue cod and paua), **fish farming** (salmon and mussels) and tourism.

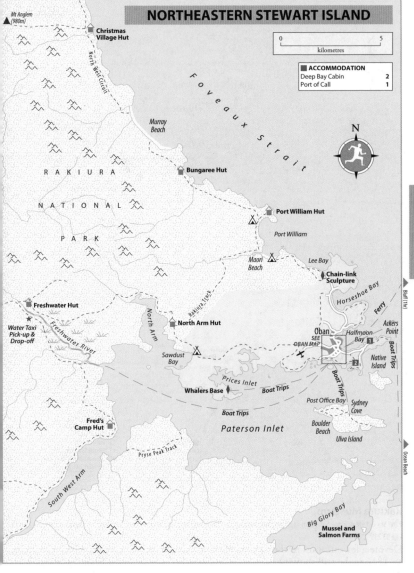

NORTHEASTERN STEWART ISLAND

■ ACCOMMODATION	
Deep Bay Cabin	2
Port of Call	1

11

Oban (Halfmoon Bay)

Scattered around Halfmoon Bay, **OBAN** (also commonly known as Halfmoon Bay) comprises little more than a few dozen houses, a visitor centre, a tiny museum, a couple of stores and cafés, and a hotel with a bar. More houses straggle away up the surrounding hills, surrounded by bush alive with native birds. Without trying, you'll see tui and kereru and small flocks of squawking **kaka**, large rusty-brown native parrots that are almost never seen elsewhere in the country.

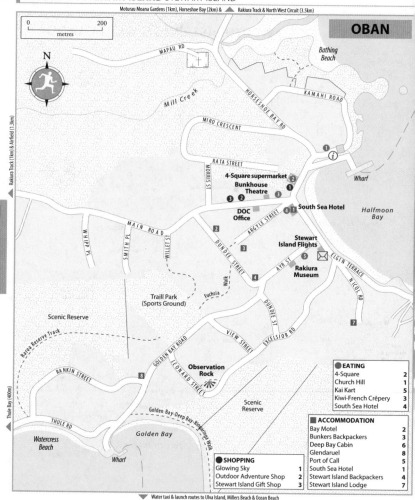

Moturau Moana Gardens (1km), Horseshoe Bay (2km) & ▲ Rakiura Track & North West Circuit (3.5km)

OBAN

0   200
metres

N

Bathing
Beach

MAPAU RD

Mill Creek

HORSESHOE BAY RD

KAMAHI ROAD

MIRO CRESCENT

RATA STREET

MORRIS ST

4-Square supermarket
Bunkhouse
Theatre

Wharf

DOC
Office

South Sea Hotel

Halfmoon
Bay

MAIN ROAD

WHIPP PL

SMITH PL

WILLET ST

DUNDEE STREET

ANGLYE STREET

Stewart
Island Flights

ELGIN TERRACE

AYR ST

Rakiura
Museum

N (OL RD)

Trail Park
(Sports Ground)

Fuchsia Walk

Scenic Reserve

Baron Reserve Track

RANKIN STREET

VIEW STREET

DUNDEE ST

EXCELSIOR RD

Observation
Rock

GOLDEN BAY ROAD

LEONARD STREET

Thule Bay (400m)

THULE RD

Golden Bay-Deep Bay-Ringaringa Walk

Watercress
Beach

Golden Bay

Scenic
Reserve

Wharf

● **SHOPPING**
Glowing Sky — 1
Outdoor Adventure Shop — 2
Stewart Island Gift Shop — 3

● **EATING**
4-Square — 2
Church Hill — 1
Kai Kart — 5
Kiwi-French Crêpery — 3
South Sea Hotel — 4

■ **ACCOMMODATION**
Bay Motel — 2
Bunkers Backpackers — 3
Deep Bay Cabin — 6
Glendaruel — 8
Port of Call — 5
South Sea Hotel — 1
Stewart Island Backpackers — 4
Stewart Island Lodge — 7

Rakiura Track (1km) & Airfield (1.3km)

11

Water taxi & launch routes to Ulva Island, Millers Beach & Ocean Beach

Rakiura Museum

9 Ayr St • Oct–May Mon–Sat 10am–1.30pm, Sun noon–2pm; June–Sept Mon–Fri 10am–noon, Sat 10am–1.30pm, Sun noon–2pm • $2 • ☎ 03 219 1221

Devote a few minutes to the **Rakiura Museum**, which focuses on local history including an 1816 globe still showing Stewart Island attached to the South Island, as Cook had depicted it. The small Maori collection contains a rare necklace made from several hundred dolphin teeth, while two giant sperm whale teeth add bite to a whaling display that includes delicate examples of scrimshaw.

Observation Rock

Excelsior Rd, 20min walk from central Oban

A short path through the bush leads to **Observation Rock**, a hilltop clearing with a wonderful panorama of Paterson Inlet and the island's highest peak, Mount Anglem. As the sun sets you may be treated to a dozen or so kaka screeching and flying about.

Ulva Island

Paterson Inlet, 2km offshore • Daylight hours • Free

The birdlife in Oban is pretty special, but it pales next to that on the 2km-long, low **Ulva Island**, an open wildlife sanctuary that's been cleared of introduced predators through sustained local effort. On a series of easy walks to secluded beaches you'll see more native birdlife than almost anywhere else in New Zealand. The place is full of birdsong, its dense temperate rainforest alive with endangered saddleback, bellbirds, kaka, yellow- and red-crowned parakeets, tui, fantails, pigeons and robins, which approach visitors with fearless curiosity.

Everyone lands at **Post Office Bay**, whose former post office, over 100 years old, is a remnant from the days when Ulva Island was the hub of the Paterson Inlet logging community. Armed with DOC's *Ulva Island: Te Wharawhara* booklet ($2), you can find your own way along trails, though naturalist guidance on one of the tours (see box, p.634) means you'll spot a lot more. There's a pleasant picnic shelter beside the sand beach at **Sydney Cove**. For information on how to get to the island, see p.636.

11

Whalers Base

On the shores of Paterson Inlet, 7km west of Oban • If you're not visiting as part of a guided trip, catch a water taxi ($50 return); operators will fix a time to pick you up from Millers Beach

Whalers Base is another wildlife-rich destination that can be included on boat and guided **kayaking trips**. A one-time overwintering spot for Norwegian whalers, it is accessed via **Millers Beach**, from where an easy twenty-minute coastal walk heads north from the beachside picnic shelter through native bush. Several eerie relics remain from 1924–32 when a fleet of Antarctic whaling ships was repaired here, and the beach is

---

SHORT WALKS AROUND OBAN

Over a dozen short walks around Oban are covered in the DOC's *Stewart Island/Rakiura short walks* leaflet ($2); a couple of the nicest are right in town.

Fuchsia and Raroa Reserve Track (2km one way; 30min). This little-used trail winds through fuchsia forest filled with tui, bellbirds, kaka and pigeons, then comes out at Traill Park. Cross the rugby pitch and head down through rimu forest to Watercress Beach.

Golden Bay–Deep Bay–Ringaringa (6km loop; 1hr 30min–2hr). Skirting east from Golden Bay, the track follows the coast to Deep Bay and then joins the gravel road to cross over to Ringaringa Beach. From here, follow the road and then signs across a stile to Ringaringa Point where a rough granite cross stands in memory of an early Lutheran missionary, Reverend Wohlers, and his wife.

Harrold Bay and Ackers Point Lighthouse (4km return; 2hr). An easy, well-graded coastal walk that offers the chance to see little blue penguins and muttonbirds returning to their nests at dusk (Nov–Feb). Trace the road around the south side of Halfmoon Bay, then follow the signs. Near the start of the track, you can follow a brief diversion to Harrold Bay, the site of a simple stone house built in 1835, and thus one of the oldest European buildings in New Zealand. The main track continues through coastal forest to a lighthouse and lookout point from where you can watch the penguins make the arduous climb to their nests hidden in the bush. Take a torch, and remember to keep the beam pointed to the ground to avoid disturbing the birds.

Horseshoe Point (5km loop; 2hr 30min). This pretty walk starts from Bragg Bay, 2km north of Oban, near the gently neglected Moturau Moana Native Garden. The clear trail winds and rolls along the coast, dipping steeply down to cross secluded Dead Man's Beach, then climbing again as you round Horseshoe Point. Once past the point the path broadens and levels out for the walk into Horseshoe Bay, passing through stands of fern trees and huge cypress trees, above cove after kelp-filled cove. Turn left onto the paved Horseshoe Bay Road to return to the starting point and Oban.

littered with objects left behind: old drums, cables, giant iron propellers, a boiler out in the water and, at the far end, a wrecked sailing ship deliberately sunk by the whaling company to create a wharf.

Mason Bay

Access from Oban by flight (see p.636) or by taking a water taxi (see p.636) to *Freshwater Hut* ($60 one way; 40min) then walking (15km; 3–4hr; flat but often flooded – check conditions before departure)

Stewart Island has become synonymous with **kiwi spotting** in the wild, something that is difficult to do on mainland New Zealand. There are kiwi spotting trips out of Oban, but the more adventurous option is to get yourself to **Mason Bay**, on the west coast, where you can stay overnight in the DOC hut (see p.637) and head out after dark in the hope of finding these elusive creatures. You'll almost certainly hear them, and have a fair chance of seeing them provided you don't go crashing about in the bush: just pick a spot and wait. Take a torch, but keep the beam pointed to the ground to avoid disturbing the birds.

STEWART ISLAND ADVENTURE TRIPS AND TOURS

The dispersed nature of the sights on Stewart Island makes it well suited to guided trips and tours. Both **Ulva Island** and **Whalers Base** form part of various boat tours that take in Paterson Inlet and beyond. Energetic visitors can explore more thoroughly by sea-kayaking around the inlet's scattered bays and islands; on extended trips it's even possible to paddle out to four water-accessible DOC huts. Bottlenose dolphins and fur seals are frequent visitors and the tidal flats attract wading birds. There's also a chance to see kiwi in the wild without having to cross the island to Mason Bay.

The waters around Stewart Island are highly changeable; only extremely experienced kayakers should venture into these waters unaccompanied.

Bravo Adventure Cruises T 03 219 1144, W kiwispotting.co.nz. Evening trips geared around spotting the Stewart Island brown kiwi (a subspecies of the mainland birds). Four-hour trips ($140) leave from the Oban wharf around dusk bound for Glory Bay (35min), from where you walk across an isthmus to the dark, windswept Ocean Beach where the birds come to forage for tiny crustaceans. Great care is taken to avoid disturbing these timid birds. Trips are weather dependent and extremely popular – even David Attenborough has been on one – so reserve well ahead. You'll need warm clothing, sturdy footwear and reasonable fitness as there's about 2hr of walking.

Phil's Sea Kayaks T 03 219 1444, E philskayak@observationrocklodge.co.nz. Excellent paddling trips around Paterson Inlet or along the coast north of Halfmoon Bay. Explore narrow inlets overhung by bush and see plenty of birdlife; exact itineraries are tailored to suit conditions and paddlers' experience, with prices from $90 for a 2hr sunset trip and $145 for a guided half-day tour, with hot drinks and buns included.

Stewart Island Experience T 0800 000511, W stewartislandexperience.co.nz. The main player on the island runs a number of trips and offers small discounts to those taking multiple trips. Their Paterson Inlet Cruise (Nov–April daily; 2hr 30min; $90) journeys around the outer reaches of the inlet and includes a 45min guided nature walk around Ulva Island. The Village and Bays Tour (2–3 daily; 1hr 30min; $45) gets you onto a minibus and gives you the lie of the land.

Stewart Island Fishing T 03 219 1334, W stewartislandfishing.com. The good ship *Tequila* takes to the waves twice a day to give passengers a taste of life aboard a commercial fishing vessel (4hr; $80); learn to set and haul in cod pots, and see how the catch is processed before casting out a hand line and (hopefully) catching your own blue cod to take home. Hot drinks and waterproofs provided.

Ulva's Guided Walks T 03 219 1216, W ulva.co.nz. Ulva Goodwillie was named after the island she now visits regularly on excellent 3–4hr guided walks ($125) which include plenty of botanizing and local Maori stories. Ulva also leads half-day trips to the former Maori settlement and early sealing site at Port William ($155) with lots of seabird spotting, and teams up with other companies to offer the Birding Bonanza, designed to pack in an evening kiwi-spotting expedition, a morning at Ulva island and an afternoon catamaran cruise (generally Mon eve–Tues afternoon; $395). Book through the Stewart Island Gift Shop on Main St.

Rakiura Track

39km loop; 2–3 days

Stewart Island's most popular overnight track is the relatively gentle **Rakiura Track**, one of New Zealand's Great Walks. This makes a circuit from Oban, though you can shave 7km off the route by getting someone to drop you off and pick you up at the road-ends. DOC's *Rakiura Track* leaflet is adequate for route finding; for information on accommodation along the track, see p.637.

You can walk in either direction at any time of the year and there is no limit on the number of nights you can stay, but the majority of people walk anticlockwise. This gets the best coastal walking in early around Maori Bay and Port William, site of the first hut. The track then contours around a forested ridge to reach Paterson Inlet and the *North Arm Hut* before the final push back to Oban.

North West Circuit

125km; 9–11 days

It is a very big step up from the Rakiura Track to the **North West Circuit** around the island's northern arm: only the hardiest (masochistic) trampers should consider attempting it. The boggy terrain is energy sapping even in good weather and thigh-deep mud is not uncommon. Added to that, unless you organize a boat or charter flight to drop food at one of the coastal huts, you'll have to carry all your supplies.

The track itself alternates between open coast and forested hill country, offering a side trip (11km return; 6hr) to the 980m summit of Mount Anglem. DOC's *North West and Southern Circuit Tracks* leaflet gives a good overview, pinpointing the **ten huts** (see p.637) which are mostly sited on the coast; there are no campsites. Make sure to stop in at the Oban DOC office if you're planning to hike the circuit, as the trail is frequently rerouted after storms.

11

ARRIVAL AND DEPARTURE   STEWART ISLAND

By plane Many people choose to fly to Stewart Island from Invercargill, which avoids the nasty sea crossing but can still be a bumpy ride. Stewart Island Fights (☎03 218 9129, ⓦstewartislandflights.com) charges $117.50 one way or $203 return, with discounts available for BBH, YHA and student-card holders. You can also go standby ($125 return); put your name down on the list first thing on the day you want to fly to stand the best chance. Flights land 3km west of town; transfer between Oban's airfield and the centre of town is included in the price of your ticket. The luggage allowance is 15kg/person; camping gas and fuels aren't allowed.
Destinations Bluff (on demand; 20min); Invercargill (3 daily; 20min).

By ferry Foveaux Strait has a reputation for trying the stomachs of even the hardiest sailors, but if you're bringing a lot of luggage, want to carry camping stove fuel or just need to save money it is the way to go. Stewart Island Experience (☎0800 000511, ⓦstewart islandexperience.co.nz) has fast catamarans ($75 one way, $130 return) running between Bluff and the wharf in central Oban, leaving Bluff at 8am and 5pm (4.30pm in winter), with extra services in summer. A connecting bus picks up from Invercargill city and airport, costing $24 each way. There's secure parking at the Bluff terminal for around $8/night.
Destinations Bluff (2–4 daily; 1hr).

INFORMATION

DOC office/Rakiura National Park Visitor Centre Main Rd, Oban (Boxing Day–April daily 8am–5pm; May–Oct Mon–Fri 8.30am–4.30pm, Sat & Sun 10am–2pm; Nov–Dec 24 Mon–Fri 8am–5pm, Sat & Sun 9am–4pm; ☎03 219 0009, ⓦdoc.govt.nz). As well as all the usual DOC information there are excellent displays on the island's tracks, natural history, pioneering life on the island, pest control on Ulva Island, plus some fascinating DVDs and rainy-day reading material.
Tourist information Oban Visitor Centre, The Wharf (daily; Nov–April 7.30am–6.30pm; May–Oct 8am–5pm;

☎03 219 0056). General island information with an emphasis on Stewart Island Experience trips and ferry crossings.
Weather and equipment Year-round, come prepared for all weather (often in the same day). This is particularly true for trampers who need to be ready for whatever the Stewart Island can throw at them: winds come straight across the southern ocean from Antarctica. Take several layers of clothing to cope with sun and rain, and don't forget sandfly repellent.

GETTING AROUND

Oban is a pleasant place to **walk** around, and unless you are staying in one of the more distant lodges you won't need any land transport. There are no roads outside the immediate vicinity of Oban, so straying further afield requires flying, taking a water taxi or walking.

By plane Stewart Island Flights (☎03 218 9129, ⓦ stewartislandflights.com) offer a "Coast to Coast" loop, flying from Oban to the beach at Mason Bay (weather and tide permitting), the quickest way to reach this remote spot. It costs $217.50 for the flight there and water taxi back, with a two-adult minimum: call them as they can often hook you up with others to make up numbers.

By car and bike Stewart Island Experience (☎0800 000511, ⓦ stewartislandexperience.co.nz) rent small cars ($65/4hr; $95/8–24hr), scooters ($60/4hr) and basic mountain bikes ($29/4hr; $39/8–24hr).

By boat Water taxis (typically speedboats with powerful outboard motors, carrying six to ten people) give great flexibility. A handful of companies offer broadly similar services, including Ulva Island Ferry (☎03 219 1013) who operate a regular service to Ulva Island (Mon–Sat only departing Golden Bay Wharf at 9am, noon and 4pm; departing Ulva at noon, 4pm and 6pm; $20 return). All other companies run to Ulva Island on demand ($25 return; 10min) and to pretty much anywhere else you want to go: try Stewart Island Water Taxi (☎03 219 1394, ⓦ stewartislandwatertaxi.co.nz) or Ruggedy Range (☎03 219 1066, ⓦ ruggedyrange.com).

ACCOMMODATION

The island is never crowded (with only around 35,000 overnight visitors a year), but it's wise to book in advance if you visit between mid-December and mid-February. Likewise, huts can be busy Nov–March, so it's a good idea to bring a tent.

OBAN

Oban's range of accommodation is broadish, although finding a place in high season can be difficult, particularly if you're on a tight budget – book in advance.

Bay Motel 9 Dundee St ☎03 219 1119, ⓦ baymotel .co.nz. Top-class 13-room motel where each fully self-contained unit has access to a deck with views over town and the bay. Quality furnishings, free transfers and great service. $175

★**Bunkers Backpackers** 13 Argyle St ☎027 738 1796, ⓦ bunkersbackpackers.co.nz. The shoes-off policy gives a relaxed and welcoming feel to this hostel in a large double-fronted villa where everyone hangs out discussing plans in the lounge or around the barbecue. As well as comfy shared-bath doubles and twins there are four- and seven-bed dorms. Amenities include free wi-fi and internet, free local calls and stacks of DVDs. Dorms $34, doubles $80

★**Deep Bay Cabin** 22 Deep Bay ☎03 219 1219, ⓔ ewanjengell@xtra.co.nz. Tiny and snug, this self-contained wooden cabin is hidden in the bush with four bunks, kitchen and a pot-bellied stove. There's a decent long-drop loo and a hand-pumped shower. Roughly a 20min walk from town and a great good-value spot for getting away from it all. $60

★**Glendaruel** 38 Golden Bay Rd ☎03 219 1092, ⓦ glendaruel.co.nz. Comfortable and welcoming B&B a 10min walk from town, surrounded by native bush. The three rooms – one of which is a well-priced single ($120) – are all en-suite. Guests have their own lounge with telescope, and the owner will do her best to ensure you have a great time on the island. $240

★**Port of Call** Jensen Bay 2.5km east of town ☎03 219 1394, ⓦ portofcall.co.nz. Choose from a boutique B&B ($385) with a single room in a large, sun-filled, contemporary house overlooking the bay; a self-catering *bach* just across the road sleeping three with a full kitchen and use of a car; or the rustic and romantic, self-contained Turner Cottage, enveloped in bush on the hill above Oban. Breakfast can be delivered wherever you stay ($35 for two) and transfers are included. *Bach* $250, cottage $175

South Sea Hotel 25 Elgin Terrace ☎03 219 1059, ⓦ stewart-island.co.nz. Century-old waterfront pub containing old-fashioned shared-bath rooms with TV; three rooms have sea views ($115) but these are also directly above the noisy bar. Light sleepers may prefer the four shared-bath doubles ($115) in a cottage and nine more modern en-suite units with their own kitchens ($165), both located behind the pub itself. Shared-bath doubles $90

Stewart Island Backpackers 18 Ayr St ☎03 219 1114, ⓦ stewartislandbackpackers.com. It's nothing swanky, but the island's largest hostel offers large communal areas, ranks of comfortable-enough shared-bath doubles and twins and four-share dorms ranged around a central courtyard. Campers can pitch their tents ($20) in the sheltered back garden and use the hostel facilities. Dorms $36, doubles $76

Stewart Island Lodge 14 Nichol Rd ☎0800 656501, ⓦ stewartislandlodge.co.nz. You're really looked after at this very well-appointed lodge with six rooms all opening out onto a deck with superb views over Halfmoon Bay. The vistas are matched by those from the guest lounge where breakfast is served. Free wi-fi. Closed June–Aug. Shoulder season rates ($195) Sept, Oct, April & May. $240

DOC HUTS

Freshwater On the North West Circuit and handy on the way to Mason Bay this 16-bunk hut is accessible by water taxi from

Oban. No bookings; buy hut tickets from DOC in Oban. $5

Mason Bay Kiwi-spotters base themselves at this twenty-bunk hut tucked in behind the dunes, with heating and camping outside. No bookings; buy hut tickets from DOC in Oban. Hut $5, camping free

North West Circuit There are ten huts along the North West Circuit including the two on the Rakiura Track (see p.635). The remaining eight huts (including *Freshwater*; see opposite) cost $5 a night (DOC backcountry hut pass valid) or you can buy a

North West Circuit Pass ($35), which entitles you to ten hut nights in all huts except those on the Rakiura Track. Huts $5

Rakiura Track Hikers must book and pre-pay for the two huts (*Port William* and *North Arm*) and three campsites (*Maori Beach*, *Port William* and *North Arm*). Book online (there is a free computer for this in the Oban DOC office) or get DOC staff to do it for you ($2 booking fee). The huts are equipped with mattresses, wood stoves for heating only, running water and toilets; you'll need your own cooker. Huts $22, camping $6

EATING AND DRINKING

4-Square 20 Elgin Terrace ☎ 03 219 1069. Small supermarket with a surprisingly good range on offer for those self-catering. There is also a selection of packaged sandwiches, and they do a packed lunch deal ($11–13) if you book a day ahead. Daily 7.30am–7pm.

★ **Church Hill** 36 Kamahi Rd ☎ 03 219 1123. The island's most sophisticated dining is hidden away in a hilltop villa just above the ferry pier. The menu emphasizes local seafood, with starters including steamed green-lipped mussels ($18.50) and oysters ($21), and mains such as baked blue cod with brown butter and *kumara rösti* ($36), accompanied by an excellent wine list. Vegetarian options available; reservations recommended. Nov–Easter daily 5.30–10pm.

★ **Kai Kart** Ayr St ☎ 03 219 1225. Billy Connolly once stopped by this fabulously quirky old Pie Kart, a glorified caravan decked out with leadlights and fresh flowers. You can order superb blue cod fish and chips ($10) or a fancy

burger ($12–16) to eat inside or at the outdoor picnic tables, or get takeaway and tantalize the seagulls at the adjacent beach. Nov–Easter daily 11.30am–2.30pm & 5–9pm.

Kiwi-French Crêpery 6 Main Rd ☎ 03 219 1422. The KFC is a cosy little café/restaurant dishing up French-style buckwheat crêpes in a range of classic and Kiwi-fied fillings including ham and cheese, cheese, pesto and sunflower seeds (both $18), or Nutella ($12.50). They also have espresso and cake. Oct–May daily 8am–6pm or to 8.30pm if there are bookings.

South Sea Hotel 25 Elgin Terrace ☎ 03 219 1059. The island's pub is very much its social centre. Muffins and coffee are served throughout the day, while lunch- and dinnertimes bring hearty portions of tasty pub food – and naturally their beer-battered cod and chips ($25) is particularly good. The lively bar has a Sunday pub quiz that shouldn't be missed. Breakfast 7–10.30am, lunch 11.30am–2pm, dinner 5.30–8pm.

SHOPPING

Glowing Sky Elgin Terrace ☎ 03 219 1518, ⓦ glowingsky.co.nz. The original outlet of this manufacturer of stylish New Zealand merino wool gear, perfect for outdoor pursuits and the street. They now have outlets in Wanaka, Waiheke Island, Dunedin and Invercargill (where the stuff is actually made), but this is where it all started. Their home store has a good range and clearance rails. Daily 10am–5pm, later in summer.

Outdoor Adventure Shop 14 Main St ☎ 03 219 1066,

ⓦ stewartislandoutdoorshop.co.nz. If you've forgotten any crucial items of tramping gear, pop along to this shop to see if they can help. They have a range of equipment for sale or rent, including pack liners and gaiters.

Stewart Island Gift Shop 20 Main St ☎ 03 219 1453. This large shop is a cornucopia of great non-tacky souvenirs and gifts inspired by the island and everything is made in New Zealand by local artists and craftspeople. Oct–May daily 10.30am–5pm.

DIRECTORY

Banks The island's only ATM, inside the 4-Square, doesn't accept international cards at present; fortunately most businesses take credit and debit cards, the water taxis being the only notable exception. Cash is available from the *Kiwi-French Crêpery* for a $3 fee and with a purchase.

Cinema The Bunkhouse Theatre (10 Main St; ☎ 027 867 9381, ⓦ bunkhousetheatre.co.nz) shows *A Local's Tail* (40min; $10) – a quirky look at the island's history and culture, "narrated" by a Staffordshire bull terrier – three times daily between Labour Day and Easter.

Internet There's good free internet available outside the community centre as well as in most of the

accommodation and restaurants. If you don't have your own device head to the *South Sea Hotel* ($8/hr) or DOC office ($2.50/15min).

Left luggage Available at the DOC (small $10, rucksack size $20; no time limit), with access only during the office's open hours.

Phone coverage Mobile coverage is good in Oban, fair around the bays to the northeast of Oban right to the island's northern tip, and sporadic everywhere else.

Post office Stewart Island Flights depot, Elgin St (Oct–March Mon–Fri 7.30am–5pm, Sat & Sun 8.30am–4pm; April–Sept daily 8.30am–4pm).

11

The West Coast

PANCAKE ROCKS, PUNAKAIKI

The West Coast

The Southern Alps run down the backbone of the South Island, both defining and isolating the West Coast. A narrow, rugged and largely untamed strip 400km long and barely 30km wide, the West Coast is home to just 32,000 people. Turbulent rivers cascade from the mountains through lush bush, past crystal lakes and dark-green paddocks before spilling into the Tasman Sea, its coastline fringed by atmospheric, surf-pounded beaches and backed by the odd tiny shack or, more often, nothing at all. But what really sets "the Coast" apart is the interaction of settlers with their environment. Coasters, many descended from early gold and coal miners, have long been proud of their ability to coexist with the landscape and their reputation for independent-mindedness and intemperate drinking. Stories abound of late-night boozing way past closing time, and your fondest memories of the West Coast might be chance encounters in the pub.

12

No discussion of the West Coast would be complete without mention of the torrential **rainfall**, which descends with tropical intensity for days at a time; waterfalls cascade from rocks and the bush becomes vibrant with colour. Such soakings have a detrimental effect on the soil, retarding decomposition and producing a peat-like top layer with all the minerals leached out. The result is **pakihi**, scrubby, impoverished and poor-looking paddocks that characterize much of the West Coast's cleared land. The downpours alternate with abundant sunshine, while today's "gold rushes" occur during the springtime rush to catch **whitebait**, when fishermen swarm around the river-mouths trying to net this culinary prize on the rising tide.

The boom-and-bust nature of the West Coast's mining has produced scores of ghost towns and spawned its three largest settlements – **Westport**, **Greymouth** and **Hokitika**. The real pleasure of the West Coast, though, lies in smaller places such as **Karamea**, on the southern limit of the Kahurangi National Park, or **Okarito**, by a tranquil lagoon. With the exception of a couple of decent museums and a handful of man-made sights, the West Coast's appeal is in its scenic beauty – the drive, either up or down the coast, is iconic, matching any great road trip in the world. The **Oparara Basin**, near Karamea, and the **Paparoa National Park**, south of Westport, hold some of the country's finest limestone formations, including huge arched spans and the famous Pancake Rocks, while in the Westland National Park the frosty white tongues of the **Franz Josef** and **Fox**

HIKING ON FOX GLACIER

Highlights

❶ Karamea and the Oparara Basin Set a day aside to explore this remote area's caves harbouring moa bones, vast limestone arches and placid streams that are great for cooling off. **See p.653**

❷ Pancake Rocks Layered like a stack of pancakes, this geological curiosity is gorgeous at any time but it's especially spectacular when high seas set the blowholes into action. See p.658

❸ Okarito The tiny settlement that inspired Keri Hulme's Booker Prize-winning novel *The Bone*

People offers a rare opportunity to spot kiwis in the wild, and take a boat trip on the limpid lagoon. See p.671

❹ Glacier adventures Hiking on and around icy glaciers is an awe-inspiring experience, and expeditions are run with great enthusiasm at both Fox and Franz Josef. **See p.676 & p.679**

❺ The Gillespie Pass Tramp Get into the West Coast's Great Outdoors on this great three-day tramp through the South Westland wilderness. **See p.684**

HIGHLIGHTS ARE MARKED ON THE MAP ON P.642

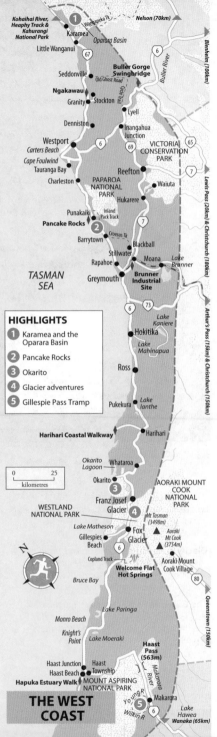

HIGHLIGHTS

1. Karamea and the Oparara Basin
2. Pancake Rocks
3. Okarito
4. Glacier adventures
5. Gillespie Pass Tramp

THE WEST COAST

---

glaciers poke down the flanks of the Southern Alps toward dense emerald bush and the sea.

Since this is New Zealand there's no shortage of **activities**, including thrilling fly-in **rafting** trips down the West Coast's steep rivers. The limestone bedrock makes for some adventurous **caving**, and there's plenty of **hiking**, with the Heaphy Track to the north, several excellent trails around Punakaiki and a stack of tramps around the glaciers.

Most people visit from November to April, but in **winter** temperatures are relatively mild, skies are more frequently cloud-free and pesky **sandflies** are less active. The West Coast never feels crowded but in the off season, accommodation is more plentiful, although some businesses close and excursions that require minimum numbers may be harder to arrange. Motels in particular are generally substantially more expensive than elsewhere on the South Island, and the area's remoteness means that food prices tend to be somewhat higher – consider stocking up on basics beforehand.

GETTING AROUND

By car and bike The simplest and most rewarding way to see the West Coast is with your own vehicle. The wind and wet can make cycling a chore but the distances between towns aren't off-putting and accommodation is plentiful between the main settlements.

By train and bus Public transport is fairly restrictive; trains only penetrate as far as Greymouth, while bus services are scarce and only stop at places on the main road, SH6. However, with patience and forward planning it's possible to see much of interest, especially if you're prepared to walk from bus drop-off points. The main West Coast bus routes run from Nelson to Fox Glacier, and between Franz Josef and Queenstown. InterCity run daily services along both sectors, with Atomic piggybacking on the same service (though they do use their own fleet for a daily Greymouth–Christchurch run). While NakedBus runs daily services from Queenstown to the glaciers, the company operates just three buses each week north of Franz Josef to Nelson.

Brief history

Westland has a long history of Maori habitation around its coastal fringes, river-mouths and sheltered bays. The main settlements are believed to have been the Hokitika area, with its abundant *pounamu* (greenstone), where communities lived on fish and forest birds. Beaches, river valleys and mountain passes provided the main access, as the Tasman Sea made offshore canoe journeys hazardous.

European arrival and the gold rush

Captain Cook sailed up the West Coast in 1770, describing it as "an inhospitable shore … As far as the eye could reach the prospect was wild, craggy and desolate". Little here then for early European explorers such as Thomas Brunner and Charles Heaphy, who made forays in 1846–47, led by Kehu, a Maori guide. They returned without finding the cultivable land they sought, and after a shorter trip in 1861 Henry Harper, the first bishop of Christchurch, wrote, "I doubt if such a wilderness will ever be colonized except through the discovery of **gold**." Prophetic words – within two years reports were circulating of flecks in West Coast rivers and a year later Greymouth and Hokitika were experiencing gold rushes. The boom was soon over but modern mining techniques (and sky-high gold prices) have rendered the old goldfields profitable once more, and today there are active mines outside Reefton and Ross.

Coal and environmental awareness

Coal eventually took gold's place and laid the foundation for more permanent towns; the West Coast still produces half the country's output. Recent decades, however, have seen a greater awareness of the Coast's fragile **ecosystems** – a situation that gave rise to tension between the Coasters and the government, particularly regarding native timber felling and its impact on the area's unique environment.

12

Along the Buller River

Stretching 169km from its source at Lake Rotoiti to its mouth at Westport, the **Buller River**'s blue-green waters reflect sunlight dappled through riverside beech forests as they swirl through one of the grandest of New Zealand's river canyons, the **Buller Gorge**. The river was used as a thoroughfare by Maori, who called it Kawatiri, meaning "deep and swift", and helped early European explorers to navigate its rapids; nowadays the same qualities lure rafters to several stretches. Gold was discovered along the Buller in 1858, sparking a gold rush centred on **Lyell**, whose remains can be visited on the **Lyell Walkway**, at the southern end of the **Old Ghost Road cycle trail**.

SH6 from Nelson passes through Murchison (see p.490) and follows the river 11km to **O'Sullivan's Bridge**, where you turn right to remain on SH6 as it enters the Upper Buller Scenic Reserve towards Lyell.

Buller Gorge Swingbridge

SH6, 6km west of O'Sullivan's Bridge • Daily: summer 8am–7pm; winter 9am–5.30pm; jetboats in summer hourly 10am–4pm; in winter by arrangement • Bridge $10; zip line $30–60; gold panning $12.50; jetboat $105/40min • ☎ 03 523 9809, ⓦ bullergorge.co.nz

The **Buller Gorge Swingbridge** is an adventure heritage park hybrid, accessed by New Zealand's longest (110m) swingbridge. Crossing high above the river, it parallels a fun 160m-long zip line, on which you can shoot across the river sitting or horizontal, Superman-style. The far bank is crisscrossed by a variety of **bushwalks** (15min–1hr) taking in a fault line that was the epicentre of the 1929 Murchison earthquake, gold-mine workings and the Ariki Falls (1hr return). You can also pan for gold or catch a jetboat ride.

Lyell and the Lyell Walkway

SH6, 20km southwest of Buller Gorge Swingbridge

The grassy site of the former gold-mining town of **Lyell** sits high above the Buller River on flats beside Lyell Creek. In its 1890s heyday it supported five hotels, two banks, two churches and a newspaper, all serving a population of three thousand. Fires and the

---

THE OLD GHOST ROAD

The 85km-long **Old Ghost Road** (ⓦ oldghostroad.org.nz) cycle and tramping track links the Buller and Mokihinui valleys, joining pack tracks that were optimistically started from trailheads in Lyell and Seddonville in the 1870s and later abandoned, half-finished, when the gold rush petered out.

The track, which crosses the corrugated junction between the Lyell and Glasgow ranges, was open to trampers at the time of writing, with two sections deep in the forested hills between Ghost Lake and Goat Creek expected to be opened to mountain-bikers midway through 2015. Upon completion, the challenging trail will be rideable in 2–4 days for experienced bikers, 5 days for trampers. With the exception of two existing DOC huts, accommodation – either in communal huts ($15/person) and "sleepouts" (unheated private bunkrooms sleeping four; $90) – must be booked online through the official website.

---

gradual decline in gold mining saw off the settlement but the remains can be visited along the **Lyell Walkway**, which passes terraces where huts stood, sobering slabs askew in the cemetery (15min return), and the ten-hammer Croesus quartz stamping battery (1hr 30min return). From the Croesus battery, it's possible to continue uphill along the first leg of the Old Ghost Road (see box above) to the Old Dray Road Loop (9km, 2–3hr), which takes in several further abandoned gold towns. A peaceful DOC **campsite** ($6) sits just off the SH6 at Lyell.

The Lower Buller Gorge

At **Inangahua Junction**, 17km west of Lyell, SH69 cuts south to Reefton, while SH6 continues west towards Westport through the **Lower Buller Gorge**, the narrowest and most dramatic section. The road hugs the cliff face in places, most notably at **Hawks Crag**, where the rock has been hewn to form an overhang – the fact that the water level rose several metres above this carved-out section during a 1926 flood will give you some idea of the volume of water that can surge down the gorge.

Reefton

Located beside the Inangahua River at the intersection of roads from Westport, Greymouth and Christchurch, **REEFTON** owes its existence to rich gold-bearing quartz veins known as **reefs**. These were exploited so heavily in the 1870s that some considered Reefton "the most brisk and businesslike place in the colony". It was also the first place in New Zealand, and one of the first in the world, to install electric street lighting powered by a hydroelectric generator. Such forward thinking abated and Reefton weathered poorly; an old gold mine that reopened on the outskirts of town in 2007 brought with it an influx of hope and money but was expected to close by October 2015. Unless you're a keen **angler** (there's excellent fly-fishing in these parts), once you've undertaken the town's historic walks and peeked at the museum you'll probably want to press on down the Grey Valley.

Town walks

Two walks link the specific points of interest around town. The elegiac, self-guided **Historic Reefton Walk** (40min) meanders around Reefton's grid of streets visiting once-grand buildings; the route is outlined in a leaflet available from the i-SITE visitor centre. In the centre of town, on the corner of Walsh Street and Broadway, the so-called "Bearded Miners" entertain visitors at an old **miner's cottage** and smithy (daily, pretty much when they feel like it; donation) by firing up the forge and helping you pan for gold.

The pleasant **Powerhouse Walk** (40min), leading past the ruined generator that once powered Reefton's famous streetlights, is slightly more uplifting, perhaps because of its course along the Inangahua River – the signposted route starts just southeast of town on the road towards Springs Junction.

12

Blacks Point Museum

Blacks Point, on SH7 towards Springs Junction • Oct–April Wed–Fri & Sun 9am–noon & 1–4pm, Sat 1–4pm • $5 • ☎ 03 732 8446

The water for Reefton's original hydroelectric scheme was diverted 2km from town at Blacks Point, where the **Blacks Point Museum** occupies a former Wesleyan chapel. The museum charts the district's cultural and mining history and shows a DVD, on request, promoting the modern mining operation nearby. Outside, an ancient water-driven gold battery that once crushed quartz can be cranked into action for a small fee ($2).

ARRIVAL AND DEPARTURE
REEFTON

By bus East West Coaches (☎03 789 6251, ⓦeastwestcoaches.co.nz) stop near the i-SITE on Broadway, Reefton's main street, on their Westport–Christchurch run.

Destinations Christchurch (6 weekly; 4hr); Westport (6 weekly; 1hr).

INFORMATION

Tourist information i-SITE/DOC, 67–69 Broadway (Mon–Fri 9am–4.30pm, Sat 9.30am–2pm; Sun 9.30am–1pm; ☎03 732 8391, ⓦreefton.co.nz). The combined i-SITE and DOC office has internet access ($6/hr), informative displays on local industries and a small replica gold mine; gold-bugs can rent pans and shovels ($5/day).

Pick up a leaflet detailing Reefton's historic walks and former mining trails nearby, which have been converted to walking or mountain-biking trails.
Banks There is a branch of BNZ inside the i-SITE (Mon–Fri 9am–12.30pm and 1.30–4.30pm), and an ATM outside the same building.

ACCOMMODATION

The Old Bread Shop 155 Buller Rd ☎03 732 8420, ⓦreeftonbackpackers.co.nz. Cosy, unpretentious backpackers in a former bakery with loads of DVDs plus free internet terminals and wi-fi. Trev, the owner, holds fly-fishing lessons and can point guests to prime fishing locations on the surrounding rivers. No credit cards. Dorms $18, doubles $50
The Old Nurses Home 104 Shiel St ☎03 732 8881, ✉info@reeftonaccommodation.co.nz. Popular with domestic visitors, Reefton's rambling and faintly institutional former nurses' home offers small but pleasant twins and doubles with communal bathrooms. Singles $55, doubles $80
Reef Cottage B&B Inn 51–55 Broadway ☎03 732 8440, ⓦreefcottage.co.nz. The fanciest place to stay in town, with four beautifully decorated Victorian- and 1920s-style doubles all with en-suite and an appealing café (see p.646), where breakfast is included. $130

12

WESTLAND'S ENDANGERED FOREST

If gold and coal built the West Coast's foundations, the **timber industry** supported its structure, with many Coasters relying on the seemingly limitless forests for their livelihood, producing pit props and sluicing flumes. Many miners became loggers, felling native hardwood trees that take centuries to mature.

Few expressed any concern for the plight of Westland's magnificent stands of **beech** and **podocarp** until the 1970s, when environmental groups rallied in opposition to government proposals to log the West Coast's state forests commercially, in an effort to support towns like Reefton, that had been abandoned by the mining industry. It wasn't until the 1986 **West Coast Accord** between the government, local authorities, conservationists and the timber industry that an uneasy truce prevailed. In the 1980s and 1990s most of the forests were selectively logged, using helicopters to pluck out the mature trees without destroying those nearby. While this preserved the appearance of the forest, it was little comfort for New Zealand's endangered **birds** – particularly kaka, kakariki (yellow-crowned parakeet), morepork (native owl) and rifleman – and long-tailed **bats**, all of which nest in holes in older trees.

In 1999, Labour leader Helen Clark honoured her election pledge and banned the logging of native forests on public land. Precious West Coast jobs were lost and the government stepped in with the $120 million fund, which helped support local economies. Still, thousands felt betrayed in this traditionally Labour-voting part of the world, but a resurgent farming sector, higher property prices and increased tourism gave Clark breathing space, until the economic downturn and 2008 general election, which she lost to the National Party's John Key. Logging publicly-owned native forest has been banned in New Zealand since 2002.

Reefton Domain Motor Camp 1 Ross St, at the top of Broadway ☎ 03 732 8477. This central campsite has hook-ups and a grassy campsite beside the Inangahua River, close to the local swimming pool. Camping $\overline{\$15}$, powered sites $\overline{\$20}$

Slab Hut Creek 1km off SH7, 8km south of Reefton. The primitive Slab Hut Creek DOC campsite is situated south down the Grey Valley and east off the SH7 in a former gold-mining area where you can try your luck fossicking. $\overline{\$5}$

EATING

Alfresco's 16 Broadway ☎ 03 732 8513. Welcoming place serving mining-themed dishes including "Snowy Battery" (ribeye steak topped with crumbed mussels) and "Prohibition Pork" (hot sliced ham with pineapple sauce), plus equally aptly named pizzas, including the seafood-topped "Quartz Reef" (mains $22.50–30). Daily lunch & dinner.

Miner's Crib 54 Broadway ☎ 03 732 8458. Dependable calorie-rich fare from this chip shop includes a decent

range of seafood (cod, John Dory and gurnard, plus crumbed shellfish), but they're best known for their burgers ($6–10). Tues & Wed 4.30–8pm, Thurs–Sun 11.30am–2pm and 4.30–9pm.

Reef Cottage Café 51–55 Broadway ☎ 03 732 8440. Warmed by an open fire, this timber cottage is an atmospheric spot for cooked breakfasts and light meals including home-made soups, quiches and crispy bacon butties (dishes $6–18.50). Daily breakfast & lunch.

The Grey Valley

Southwest of Reefton, SH7 follows the **Grey Valley**, cut off from the Tasman Sea by the rugged Paparoa Range and hemmed in by the Southern Alps. From both sides, the bush is gradually reclaiming the mine workings that once characterized the region. Nothing has stepped in to replace them, however, and yet the small communities continue to tick over, eking a living from dairy farming and inquisitive visitors keen to explore the former mining towns of **Waiuta** and **Blackball** and to walk the **Croesus Track**.

Waiuta

Along the Grey Valley from Reefton, the first diversion of any consequence is 24km south, where **Hukarere** marks the junction for **WAIUTA**, a ghost town seventeen partly sealed kilometres east. This was the last of the West Coast's great gold towns, reaching a population of 6000 in the 1930s.

Its end came when a mineshaft collapsed in 1951, burying large deposits of gold-bearing reef-quartz almost 900m down, where it was uneconomic to extract them. Miners left for jobs on the coast, Australian companies bought most of the mining equipment and many houses were carted off, whole or piecemeal. Today three cottages remain, along with a barber's shop and the original post office. The rolling country,

---

BLACKBALL: BIRTHPLACE OF NEW ZEALAND'S LABOUR MOVEMENT

During the first three decades of the twentieth century, the whole of the Grey Valley was a hotbed of nascent socialism, as organizers moved along the valley, pressing unbending mine managers to address atrocious working conditions. In 1908, Blackball miner, Pat Hickey, refused to finish eating a pie within the fifteen minutes allotted for the miners' "crib" (lunch) break – his protest aimed at extending the break to thirty minutes, as was standard in neighbouring mines.

Hickey and six of his colleagues were summarily sacked, sparking what came to be known as the "cribtime strike", a three-month **walkout**, during which the workers were fined £75 for their action. None could pay, and although the bailiffs tried to auction their possessions, the workers banded together refusing to bid – one then bought all the goods for a fraction of their worth and redistributed them to their original owners. The strike continued until the West Coast's weather stepped in, flooding two mines nearby and forcing managers at unflooded Blackball to agree to the miners' demands – though the £75 was later extracted from their wages. The struggle led to the formation of the **Miners' Federation**, which later evolved into the **Federation of Labour**, the country's principal **trade union**. Eric Beardsley's historical novel *Blackball 08* gives a passionate portrayal of the strike.

pocked by waste heaps, is slowly being colonized by gorse and brambles, but the cypresses and poplars that once delineated gardens and the fruit trees that filled them remain; sadly the whippet track, croquet lawns and swimming pool have fared less well. It's wonderfully atmospheric for just mooching around, guided by the invaluable **Waiuta leaflet** (from the Reefton i-SITE) and strategically placed interpretive panels – you can see the lot in a couple of hours.

Blackball

Sleepy **BLACKBALL** is a former gold- and coal-mining village spread across a plateau at the foot of the Paparoa Range, 11km northeast of Stillwater. Today commuters and neo-hippies coexist with gnarled part-time hunters and prospectors. Blackball owes its existence to alluvial gold discovered in Blackball Creek in 1864, but gold returns quickly diminished and the town was sustained by its coal mines, which helped to stake the town's place in the nation's history as birthplace of the **labour movement** (see box opposite) before the mines closed in 1964.

These days – apart from its famous salami (see p.648) – Blackball's rustic tranquillity is its main draw, along with excellent walking through the gold workings of Blackball Creek and up onto the wind-blasted tops of the Paparoa Range along the **Croesus Track** (see p.648). There's a small information centre next to *Formerly The Blackball Hilton* (see below), where you can pick up a free sketch map of the area.

Moana and Lake Brunner

From Stillwater, the sealed Arnold Valley–Lake Brunner road runs 55km southeast to link up with SH73 between Greymouth and Arthur's Pass. Roughly halfway the road passes **Lake Brunner**, a filled glacial hollow celebrated for its trout fishing. The village of **MOANA** on the north shore is popular with holidaying Kiwis but not brimming with diversions (or facilities). By late summer the lake is surprisingly warm and makes for good **swimming**, or you can stroll along a couple of easy paths. At the end of town, a slender swingbridge over the fledgling Arnold River leads to the riverside **Rakaitane Track** (45min loop) and the **Lake Side Track** (60min return), the latter with good mountain views.

Brunner Industrial Site

SH7, 2km west of Stillwater • Unrestricted access

A tall brick chimney marks the **Brunner Industrial Site**. Roadside information panels mark the path to a fine old suspension bridge (foot traffic only), which crosses the swirling Grey River to the remaining buildings and the ruins of the skilfully crafted beehive coking ovens.

On his explorations in the late 1840s, Thomas Brunner noted a seam of riverside coal, and by 1885 the valley was producing half of New Zealand's high-grade coal and exporting firebricks throughout Australasia. In 1896 New Zealand's worst mining disaster (with 65 dead, many buried in nearby Stillwater) heralded the area's decline; the site was abandoned in the 1940s and only exhumed from dense bush in the early 1980s.

ARRIVAL AND DEPARTURE   THE GREY VALLEY

By train and bus The TranzAlpine train (see p.524) stops at Moana's lakeshore station on Ana St at 11.47am on its way to Greymouth, and again at 2.42pm on its return to Christchurch. Atomic Shuttles' (☎03 349 0697, ⊕ atomictravel.co.nz) daily Christchurch–Greymouth buses also stop here. With no regular public transport, you'll have to find your own way to and from Waiuta and Blackball.

ACCOMMODATION

Formerly The Blackball Hilton 26 Hart St, Blackball ☎03 732 4705, ⊕ blackballhilton.co.nz. The last of the mining-era hotels opened as the Dominion in 1910, and subsequently operated as the Hilton – ostensibly named after the former mine manager remembered in Hilton St nearby – until challenged by the international hotel chain

THE CROESUS TRACK

Prospectors seeking new claims gradually pushed their way up Blackball Creek. The scant remains of their efforts are now the principal interest on the **Croesus Track**, the first half of which is easily explored in a day from Blackball. The whole track over the 1200m Paparoa Range to Barrytown, on the coast 30km north of Greymouth, takes two gentle days or one eight-hour slog. DOC's informative *Croesus Track* leaflet shows adequate detail for walkers.

ACCESS AND ACCOMMODATION

The track **starts** at Smoke-ho car park, at the end of a rough but passable road 8km north of Blackball, and **finishes** opposite on the SH6 in Barrytown, where there is a daily bus in each direction. The most convenient approach to arrange a Blackball drop-off and Barrytown pick-up through *Formerly The Blackball Hilton* (see p.647, contact the hotel for prices), as there is no accommodation in Barrytown. The only hut is the first-come, first-served **Ces Clarke Hut** (16 bunks; $15), with panoramic views, mattresses and a coal-burning stove.

THE TRACK

Much of the track was designed to accommodate tramways, so walkers enjoy a gentle, steady grade as the path winds through podocarp forest festooned with ferns, mosses and vines, gradually giving way to hardier silver beech then alpine tussock above the tree line. Sea mist commonly cloaks the tops during the middle of the day. Half an hour from the Smoke-ho car park, a side path (10min return) leads to the former site of the **Minerva Battery**. Immediately after the junction, the main path crosses Clarke Creek on a modern swingbridge above the remains of a wooden predecessor. Another half-hour on, a detour leads to two clearings that once contained **Perotti's Mill** (10min return) and the **Croesus Battery** (50min return). Another hour on, you'll come to Garden Gully junction, where a side path leads to the 1930s **Garden Gully Hut** (5min return) and the **Garden Gully Battery** (30min return). The main track turns sharply west before reaching the **Ces Clarke Hut**, on the tree line: fill your water bottles here, as there is no other supply. The top of the ridge near Mount Ryall (1220m) lies two undulating hours beyond, a little more if you run off to climb **Croesus Knob** (1204m). The broad ridge offers wonderful views of the coast, reached in under three hours by a steep and hard-to-follow path that dives through the bush to Barrytown.

of the same name. Apart from lively drinking with locals, the hotel offers a range of decent rooms with shared bathrooms; a continental breakfast is included. The pub serves coffee, lunches and dinner (mains $20–30), which might include Blackball salami. $110

Lake Brunner Hotel 34 Ahau St, Moana ☎ 03 738 0083, ⓦ lakebrunnerresort.net.nz. Block of swanky modern studio units overlooking the lake from Moana's main street, though not all rooms have lake views. The cheaper rooms have basic kitchenettes; there's a bar/restaurant on-site. $145

EATING

★ **Blackball Salami Co** 11 Hilton St, Blackball ☎ 03 732 4111, ⓦ blackballsalami.co.nz. For picnic supplies, call in at this excellent shop to feast on delicious venison sausages, chorizo, various salamis (of which 150 go to Antarctic bases every year) and other delectable morsels. Mon–Fri 8am–4pm, Sat 9am–2pm.

Station House Café 34 Koe St, Moana ☎ 03 738 0158, ⓦ lakebrunner.net. Opposite the railway station, this licensed restaurant/café opens onto a timber deck with umbrella-shaded tables and stunning lake and mountain views (weather permitting). It serves a tempting range of lunches and dinners (mains around $30). Daily 10.30am–9pm in summer.

Westport

Like a proud fly caught in amber, **WESTPORT** remains fixed in time, despite government money and the council's zealous desire to modernize. Diversions are scarce, except at the seal colony at **Cape Foulwind**, on the brain-clearing walk to the old lighthouse beyond or exploring the ghostly former coal towns of the **Rochfort Plateau**. Were Westport – once known as "Worstport" – not a transport interchange, few would stay in this workaday harbour as the temptations of the Heaphy Track (see box, pp.488–489) and Karamea, 100km north, are too strong. However, time spent here is made tolerable by good-value accommodation, an engaging museum, some adventure activities and an outstanding restaurant, *The Town House* (p.651), that could hold its own in Auckland, Wellington and well beyond.

Brief history

Westport was the first of the West Coast towns, established by one **Reuben Waite** in 1861 beside the mouth of the Buller River, where he made his living provisioning Buller Gorge prospectors. When the miners moved on to richer pickings in Otago, Waite upped sticks and headed south to help found Greymouth. Westport turned to coal and engineers channelled the river to scour out a **port**. Although the coal industry has now ceased to be a major employer, Westport battles on, with a respectable-sized fishing fleet and the odd ship laden with the produce of the huge Cape Foulwind cement works, itself fuelled by coal from the opencast mine at Stockton.

Coaltown

Inside the i-SITE, 123 Palmerston St • Nov–April daily 9am–5pm; May–Oct Mon–Fri 9am–4.30pm, Sat & Sun 10am–4pm • $10 • ☏ 03 789 6658

Westport's coal-mining past is brought to life at **Coaltown**, where imaginatively presented and engaging exhibits concentrate on the Buller coalfield. Great films and

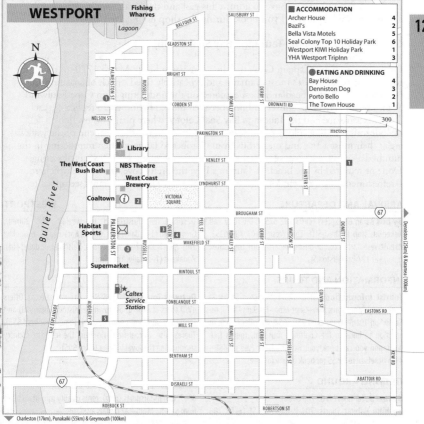

photographs of the workings in their heyday are dramatically complemented by huge pieces of mine equipment, including a coal wagon on tracks angled at an unsettling forty-five degrees, a braking drum from the Denniston incline (see p.652), a mock mine tunnel and a host of smaller relics – early carbon monoxide detectors containing stuffed canaries and the like.

West Coast Brewery

10 Lyndhurst St • Mon & Tues 9.30am–5pm, Wed–Fri 9.30am–6pm • Tours Mon–Fri 3.30pm, $10 • ☎ 03 789 6201, ⊛ westcoastbrewery.co.nz

Before leaving town, check out the preservative- and chemical-free beers made at the **West Coast Brewery**. Originally famed for its signature Green Fern Organic Lager, the brewery now focuses on craft beers – including an English-style bitter – that are distributed nationwide. Tours include tastings of five brews, but if you don't have time for the full shebang, just turn up with an empty bottle and they'll fill it with your choice of ale.

The West Coast Bush Bath

114 Palmerston St • Mon–Fri 9am–5pm, Sat 10am–2pm • $40 for 90min • ☎ 03 789 8828, ⊛ thesoapbox.co.nz

In true entrepreneurial West Coast spirit the owner of a soap shop has transformed his back block into **The West Coast Bush Bath**, where an open-air double bathtub is screened by bark and ferns imported from the bush outside town. Prices include soap or bubble bath plus glasses for wine, but you'll need to bring your own towel. It's not the best location but you have to admire his gall and the locals love it. After-hours access is possible, provided you book during the shop hours given above.

Cape Foulwind and the Tauranga Bay Seal Colony

12km west of town on Cape Foulwind Rd

Once again we have Captain Cook, battling heavy weather in March 1770, to thank for the naming of Westport's most dramatic and evocatively titled stretch of coastline, **Cape Foulwind**, its exposed headlands best explored on the undulating 4km Cape Foulwind Walkway. It's perfect for sunset ambling between the old lighthouse, a replica of Abel Tasman's astrolabe and the **Tauranga Bay Seal Colony**, where platforms overlook a malodorous breeding colony of fur seals. The animals, at the southern end of the walkway, are at their most active and numerous from October to January, often numbering in the hundreds – a welcome recovery after the decimation wrought by 150 years of sealing. Don't be tempted by the beach at Tauranga Bay; the pretty cove's waters are treacherous – refreshment of a different kind is available at the *Bay House* restaurant (see opposite).

ARRIVAL AND DEPARTURE
WESTPORT

By bus Karamea Express (☎ 03 782 6757), InterCity and NakedBus stop at the i-SITE; East-West (☎ 03 789 6251, ⊛ eastwestcoaches.co.nz) buses depart from the Caltex garage at 197 Palmerston St.

Destinations Christchurch (6 weekly; 4hr 30min); Greymouth (1–2 daily; 2hr 20min); Karamea (5–6 weekly; 2hr); Murchison (1–2; 1hr 30min); Nelson (1–2 daily; 4hr); Punakaiki (1–2 daily; 1hr 15min).

INFORMATION AND TOURS

Tourist information i-SITE, 123 Palmerston St (Oct–April daily 9am–5pm; May–Sept Mon–Fri 9am–4.30pm, Sat & Sun 10am–4pm; ☎ 03 789 6658, ⊛ buller.co.nz). In addition to housing the Coaltown museum, there's free wi-fi, and you can book your Heaphy Track (see pp.488–499) tickets here for $5 (or book online for free).

Outwest Tours ☎ 0800 688937, ⊛ outwest.co.nz. Offers 4WD tours of near-ghost town Denniston (6hrs; $95) and Stockton's modern open-pit coal mine (5–6hrs; $55). There's also a coal-free trip into the remote country surrounding the Awakiri River (6hrs; $95).

GETTING AROUND

By taxi Buller Taxis (☎ 03 789 6900).
By bike Habitat Sports, 204 Palmerston St (☎ 03 788

8002, ⊛ habitatsports.co.nz), rents quality mountain bikes from $15/hr. Multi-day rentals available.

ACCOMMODATION

Book ahead if you plan to visit in mid-February, when the town hosts the Buller Gorge Marathon.

Archer House 75 Queen St ☎03 789 8778, ⓦarcherhouse.co.nz. A lovely 1890 villa with multiple antique-filled lounges, set in beautiful gardens, and retaining many ornate Victorian details including a wraparound veranda. Two rooms are en suite, while one has a private bathroom across the hallway; rates include continental breakfast. Doubles $\overline{$225}$

Bazil's 54–56 Russell St ☎03 789 6410, ⓦbazils.com. Cheerful, busy backpackers with doubles, twins and a mass of dorms (some very cramped); there's a pleasant garden with a patch of lawn for tents, a TV room and a covered BBQ area. Surfing lessons available. Dorms $\overline{$29}$, doubles $\overline{$68}$

Bella Vista Motels 314 Palmerston St ☎0800 235528, ⓦstaybellavista.co.nz. A modern, business-like motel familiar from terracotta-and-cream *Bella Vista Motels* nationwide, with comfortable but bland rooms. Sky TV and limited cooking facilities available. Doubles $\overline{$130}$, spa doubles $\overline{$140}$

Seal Colony Top 10 Holiday Park 57 Marine Parade, Carters Beach, 5km west of town ☎0508 937 876, ⓦtop10westport.co.nz. Spacious, fully equipped site, with cabins and comfortable motel units, situated a stone's throw from the beach. Camping $\overline{$38}$, powered sites $\overline{$40}$

Westport KIWI Holiday Park 31 Domett St ☎03 789 7043, ⓦwestportholidaypark.co.nz. Smallish, low-key motor park partly hemmed in by native bush and surrounded by suburbia, a 10min walk from the town centre with its own 18-hole mini golf course. Camping $\overline{$16}$, powered sites $\overline{$36}$

YHA Westport TripInn 72 Queen St ☎03 789 7367, ⓦtripinn.co.nz. Friendly owners and an energetic refurbishment policy have breathed new life into this rambling 64-room YHA Associate backpackers. Quiet and relaxed with a great deck, BBQ, well-equipped kitchen, TV room and wi-fi; there are camping spots in the garden. Dorms $\overline{$29}$, rooms $\overline{$72}$

EATING, DRINKING AND NIGHTLIFE

Westport's pubs adhere to the West Coast tradition of aggressive weekend drinking; head to *The Town House* if you're looking for something more sophisticated.

★Bay House Tauranga Bay, 12km from Westport ☎03 789 4151 ⓦbayhouse.co.nz. If the seal colony isn't enough to lure you out here, this beautiful restaurant and café ought to do the trick. With a terrace and views of the bay, plus a brunch and dinner menu of appetizing dishes like seafood chowder with fennel oil ($14), and aubergine and tomato tart ($16), it's popular with visitors and locals alike. Wed–Sun 10am–3.30pm & 5.30–8.30pm.

Denniston Dog 18 Wakefield St ☎03 789 8885. The only café/bar that isn't just a pub with a percolator offers a good range of beers, coffee and some excellent light and main meals ($17–38) with thoughtful side dishes; venison comes with parsnip mash, and salmon with buttery new potatoes. Limited vegetarian options. Daily lunch & dinner.

Porto Bello 62 Palmerston St ☎03 789 5570. A classy bar and grill serving $20 pizzas and meals with a faintly American twist (mains $17–30) spanning Cajun chicken salad, gumbo and seafood. Daily 5pm–late.

★The Town House Corner of Cobden and Palmerston sts ☎03 789 7133, ⓦthetownhouse.co. World-class café/restaurant serving great coffee, breakfast, brunch, lunch and excellent evening meals (mains $24–32) featuring produce from small, local producers and its own kitchen garden. The menu changes regularly, but expect the likes of *chermoula* marinated chicken on cannellini bean mash or caramelized onion and Gaalburn goat's cheese tarte tatin. It's all served up in the stylish interior or on the sunny deck. Tues–Fri 11.30am–late, Sat 10am–late, Sun 10am–4pm.

CINEMA

NBS Theatre 105 Palmerston St ☎03 789 4219 ⓦnbstheatre.co.nz. If the nightlife is too raucous elsewhere, head along to this modern two-screen cinema, which shows local and international films.

12

Westport to Karamea

The Karamea Road (SH67) runs north from Westport to Karamea, parallel to the coast and pinched between the pounding Tasman breakers and bush-clad hills. The journey takes almost two hours if you don't stop, passing through meagre hamlets with barely a shop or pub. However, there are some interesting diversions – not least the coal towns around Westport such as **Denniston** – and great off-the-grid accommodation en route. North of the **Mokihinui River**, the road leaves the coastal strip, twisting and climbing over **Karamea Bluff** before descending again into a rich apron of dairying land, the surrounding hills cloaked in thick vegetation characterized by marauding cabbage trees and nikau palms. At the northern foot of the bluff, **Little Wanganui** marks the turn-off for the start of the **Wangapeka** (52km; 3–5days) and **Leslie–Karamea** (62km; 6–9 days) tracks, which traverse the southern half of Kahurangi National Park (see pp.488–489).

Charles Heaphy and Thomas Brunner surveyed the region in 1846, paving the way for the gold-miners, who arrived two decades later. Pioneers established themselves at **Karamea**, now the base for visiting the fine limestone country of the **Oparara Basin** and the final stretch of the **Heaphy Track** (see pp.488–489).

Note that there's little mobile phone coverage and **no fuel** between Westport and Karamea – and that the only fuel in Karamea itself is only available from the visitor centre during opening hours. Fill up before leaving Westport.

Denniston

Museum/visitor centre year-round by appointment 11am–3pm • Donation • ☎ 03 789 9755

Westport historically thrived on supplying inhospitably sited coal-mining towns where fresh vegetables were hard to grow and sheep reluctant to thrive. Foremost among these settlements was the now semi-ghost town of **DENNISTON**, 9km east of Waimangaroa off SH67, the setting for Jenny Pattrick's 2003 bestselling historical novel *The Denniston Rose*, located high on the Rochfort Plateau and once famous for its gravity-powered tramway (see box below).

The region peaked at around 2500 inhabitants in 1910, but the accessible coal eventually played out in the late 1960s. Since then, houses have been carted off and the bush has engulfed what remains – a post office, a fire station, half a dozen scattered houses (three or four of them occupied) and a treasure-trove of industrial archeology centred on a gaunt winding derrick. There are great views in fine weather, but a blanket of cloud and damp fog adds a suitably ethereal quality.

Apart from these, the only real sight of note is the old schoolhouse, which has been turned into a small "Friends of the Hill" **museum** and **visitor centre**, containing historical photos and old mining machinery. It all comes alive when you talk to curator Gary James, who is usually happy to open up. For guided tours of Denniston, see p.650.

Granity

The tiny community of **GRANITY**, 12km north of Waimangaroa, makes for a good place to break your journey as you head further north on SH67. Stop in at the *Granity Drifter's Café* at 97 Torea St (☎ 03 782 8808; Wed–Sun 9am–4pm), which has wi-fi and regular gigs in addition to a short menu of hot meals and a cabinet of sticky cakes; in fine weather there's an outsized **chess-set** in the back garden.

THE DENNISTON SELF-ACTING INCLINE

John Rochfort discovered the rich Coalbrook-Dale Seam in 1859 and the plateau was soon humming with activity, spurred on by the construction of the **Denniston Self-Acting Incline** in 1879. This impressive, gravity-powered tramway was the steepest in the world, lowering coal-filled wagons 518m over 1.7km and hauling up empty ones. Throughout its 88-year lifespan, over a thousand tonnes of coal a day would rattle at a prodigious 70km/hr down to Conn's Creek for the trip into Westport. Initially goods, machinery and even people came up the incline, but after four unfortunates were flung to their deaths, a path was constructed in 1884, easing some of the hardship of plateau life.

The incline closed in 1967, but fit and ambitious visitors can still get an idea of what was involved by tackling the **Denniston Bridle Track** (5km one way; 3hr up, 2hr down), which begins at Conn's Creek, 2km inland from Waimangaroa and traces the 1884 path roughly parallel to the incline.

Ngakawau and around

About 3km north of Granity a huge modern coal depot in **Ngakawau** signals the start of the **Charming Creek Walk** (5km one way; 2hr; 100m ascent), which follows an old railway, used for timber and coal extraction between 1914 and 1958. The first half-hour is dull, but things improve dramatically after the S-shaped Irishman's Tunnel, which has great views of the boulder-strewn river below and, after a swingbridge river crossing, the Mangatini Falls. From here to the picnic stop by the remains of Watson's Mills is the most interesting section of the walk and is as far as most people get (2–3hr return).

ACCOMMODATION WESTPORT TO KARAMEA

GRANITY

Granity Sands Backpackers 94 Torea St ☏ 03 782 8558. Arty, eco-conscious backpackers footsteps from the beach, with board games, books, comfy sofas ranged around a huge fireplace, and rambling, rather overgrown gardens. Dorms $20, doubles $50

Miners on Sea 117 Torea St ☏ 03 782 8664. A small collection of chic modern cabins facing the sea; the four-star options are a little overpriced ($195), but their backpacker "pods" are far more reasonable, as long as you can face sharing facilities. $65

NGAKAWAU AND AROUND

Ngakawau's best accommodation is across the river, well north of the village.

Gentle Annie 15km north of Ngakaway on SH67 and 3km down a side road ☏ 03 782 1826. Relaxed,

beautifully sited spot near the mouth of the Mokihinui River, beside Gentle Annie Beach. Spread-out accommodation ranges from flax-girt campsites to well-equipped family cottages with sea views; the *Cowshed Café* (call for opening times) serves coffee and wood-fired pizzas, and there are bushwalks, a maze and kayaks for hire. Camping $12, cottages $130

★ **The Old Slaughterhouse** 2km north of Hector, just off SH67 ☏ 03 782 8333, ⓦ oldslaughterhouse.co.nz. A relaxing wood-built hostel perched on the hillside with vast ocean views, welcoming hosts, good bushwalks and Hector's dolphins regularly playing in the surf below. It would be a crime to shatter the peace with TV, internet, washing machines or hairdryers, so they don't – plus it saves their precious hydro-generated power. Access is via a steep 10min walk off SH67, though the owners will carry your bags on a quad bike. Dorms $34, doubles $84

12

Karamea

Despite its isolation, virtually at the end of the road (to continue any distance north you'd have to go on foot along the Heaphy Track), there's no shortage of things to do in **KARAMEA**, 100km north of Westport. The southern section of the **Kahurangi National Park** easily justifies a day or two and the **Oparara Basin** (see p.654) rewards exploration.

Back in 1874, this was very much **frontier territory**, with the Karamea River port providing the only link with the outside world. Settlers eked a living from **gold** and **flax**, barely supported by the poorly drained *pakihi* soils. They persevered, opening up the first road to Westport just in time for the 1929 Murchison **earthquake**, which silted up the harbour and cut the settlement's only road link for years. The most recent natural upheavals came in April 2014, when Cyclone Ita uprooted swathes of venerable beech and kahikatea trees in the surrounding hills.

ARRIVAL AND DEPARTURE KARAMEA

By bus Karamea Express minibus services ply the Karamea–Westport route (Mon–Sat; $35 each way; ☏ 03 782 6757), picking up from accommodation in Karamea around 8am, departing from Westport at 11.30am for the

return journey. Karamea Connections (☏ 03 782 6767, ⓦ karameaconnections.co.nz) runs on demand to the Heaphy Track at Kohaihai ($15) and other nearby trailheads.

INFORMATION AND TOURS

Tourist information Market Cross, 2km east of the centre (Jan–April daily 9am–5pm; May–Dec Mon–Fri 9am–5pm, Sat & Sun 9am–1pm; ☏ 03 782 6652, ⓦ karameainfo .co.nz). Provides internet access ($2/30min) for booking Heaphy Track huts, among other things. The Heaphy Track is

generally walked from north to south; see pp.488–489 for more detail. Pick up the DOC-produced *Karamea* leaflet, which has details of a dozen or so good walks nearby.

Karamea Outdoor Adventures Market Cross, opposite the information centre (☏ 03 782 6181,

ⓦ karameaadventures.co.nz). Rents bikes, kayaks, inner tubes and "river bugs" (one-man dinghies with paddles worn like gloves) for exploring Flagstaff Lagoon and nearby rivers. Contact in advance for prices and bookings.

ACCOMMODATION

Karamea Domain On SH67 between The Last Resort and the Karamea Village Hotel ☎ 03 782 6069. Basic site utilizing the showers and toilets of the town's sports field, with a kitchen, day-shelter and bunkroom. Showers cost $4 paid via honesty box. Camping $14, powered sites $15

Karamea Farm Baches 17 Wharf Rd ☎ 03 782 6838, ⓦ karameamotels.com. Seven quirky, colourful motel-style units that come equipped with full kitchens and spacious bedrooms. Run by the same people as *Rongo* backpackers, your fourth night here is free, and they'll lay on post-Heaphy feasts if you're travelling with a crowd. $90

The Last Resort 71 Waverley St (SH67) ☎ 0800 505042, ⓦ lastresort.co.nz. Based around an imaginatively styled main lodge holding a restaurant and bar, with comfortable accommodation in five-bed dorms, simple but attractive lodge rooms (including a few cheaper rooms with shared bathrooms, $72), and attractive studios ($130) with basic kitchenettes. Dorms $37, doubles $107

Rongo 130 Waverley St (SH67) ☎ 03 782 6667, ⓦ rongobackpackers.com. Rainbow-painted, timber-floored hostel in grounds that house an organic veggie garden, a (very) rustic bush bath and an elderly collie dog. Art and music play a big part in the hostel's daily life – it even runs a community radio station (107.5FM). Stay three nights and the fourth is free. Dorms $30, doubles $75

Wangapeka Backpackers Retreat and Farmstay Wangapeka Valley Rd ☎ 03 782 6663, ⓦ wangapeka .co.nz. Cosy homestay on a working farm with native bush and welcoming, well-informed hosts, who will ensure you make the most of the beautiful surroundings. If you need to refuel post-tramp, consider going for a half-board deal (dorms with breakfast and dinner $45, doubles $125). Dorms $20, doubles $75

EATING AND DRINKING

Karamea's **eating** options are limited; there's a small **supermarket** at Market Cross.

Karamea Village Hotel Corner of Waverley St and Wharf Rd ☎ 03 782 6800. Karamea's revamped pub is the best place to eat in town thanks to its enormous pub meals (mains $16–29), and especially, its good-value fish and chips ($10) and great whitebait patties ($16). Daily 10am–late.

The Last Resort 71 Waverley St (SH67) ☎ 0800 505042, ⓦ lastresort.co.nz. Karamea's most formal dining (though that's not saying much) with good-value burgers and steaks (mains $20–34) and a couple of forays into more exciting territory with dishes like Thai chicken curry and duck confit. Tearoom staples available all day; evening bookings advised. Daily 7.30am–late.

The Oparara Basin

Kahurangi National Park's finest limestone formations lie 10km north of Karamea, and fifteen rolling kilometres inland from the Karamea–Kohaihai road in the **Oparara Basin**. This compact area of **karst** topography is characterized by sinkholes, underground streams, caves and bridges created over millennia by the action of faintly acidic streams on the jointed rock. The region is home to New Zealand's largest native **spider**, the harmless, 15cm-diameter *Spelungula cavernicola* (found only in caves around Kahurangi National Park), and to a rare species of ancient and primitive carnivorous **snail** that grows up to 70mm across and dines on earthworms. Tea-coloured rivers course gently over bleached boulders and, in faster-flowing sections, the rare **whio** (blue duck) swims for its supper. If your interest in geology is fleeting, the Oparara Basin still makes a superb place for day **walks** or a **picnic** – just make sure to bring some insect repellent.

Honeycomb Hill Caves

10km north of Karamea then 16km east along McCallums Mill Rd · Tours depart from the Upper Oparara Car Park at the far end of McCallums Mill Road daily 10am; 2hr 30min; minimum 2 people · $95 · Transfers available from Karamea, $25 · ☎ 03 782 6652, ⓦ oparara.co.nz

The Oparara Basin is home to the **Honeycomb Hill Caves**, which have become a valuable key to understanding New Zealand's fauna. The sediment on the cave floor has helped preserve the ancient skeletons of birds, most of them killed when they fell through holes in the roof. The bones of over fifty species have been found here, including those of Haast's eagle, the largest eagle ever known, with a wingspan of up to 4m.

The cave system can only be visited on the excellent and educational **Honeycomb Hill Caves Tour** which explores just some of the 15km of passages. It used to be possible to combine cave trips with the **Honeycomb Hill Arch Kayak Tour**, a gorgeous paddle through bush and under a broad limestone arch. These trips had been temporarily suspended at the time of research, after Cyclone Ita filled the river with tree trunks – it's worth checking to see if these have restarted.

Crazy Paving and Box Canyon caves

Accessed via a 5min track from the Upper Oparara Car Park

As is common in limestone areas, the watercourses alter frequently, leaving behind dry caves such as the **Crazy Paving** and more capacious **Box Canyon Caves** (about 10min return) near the Honeycomb Hill Caves. Both are good for spider- and fossil-spotting: take a torch and mind the slippery floors.

Oparara Arch and Moria Gate Arch

Signposted from the Oparara Car Park 3km before the caves

The two most spectacular examples of limestone architecture can be reached via beautiful, short bushwalks near the Oparara River. The largest is the **Oparara Arch** (2km, 40min return), a vast two-tiered rock bridge 43m high,

KARAMEA & THE OPARARA BASIN

ACCOMMODATION		EATING AND DRINKING	
Karamea Domain	3	Karamea Village Hotel	1
Karamea Farm Baches	2	The Last Resort	2
The Last Resort	4		
Rongo	1		
Wangapeka Backpackers Retreat and Farmstay	5		

79m wide and 219m long, which erupts from the bush defying any attempt at photography. On the opposite side of the road, a trail (2.2km, 30min return) leads to the lovely **Moria Gate Arch**, named decades before *Lord of the Rings* fever swept the land. The trail, initially through high-canopied native forest, ends in a short cave scramble (torch handy but not essential) to a sandy riverbank under the arch. This can be combined with a visit to limpid **Mirror Tarn** (4km, 90min for both); even if you don't complete the loop it's worth pressing on to a viewpoint just beyond the cave scramble, where there's a great view back to the rock formation.

Kohaihai River

At the end of the road, 17km north of Karamea

Visitors with no aspirations to tramp the full length of Heaphy Track can sample the final few coastal kilometres from the mouth of the Kohaihai River, where there's river (but not sea) swimming, a beautifully sited DOC **campsite** ($6) and an abundance of maddening sandflies (consider buying sandfly "armour" – close-weave mesh jackets, $39 from Westport's i-SITE). In the heat of the day, you're better off heading for the cool of the **Nikau Walk** (1km, 40min loop), which winds through a shady grove dense with nikau palms, tree ferns and magnificent gnarled old rata dripping in epiphytes. When it cools off, either continue along the Heaphy to **Scott's Beach** (6.5km, 2hr return), or return to the southern side of the Kohaihai River and the **Zig-Zag Track** (1.2km, 40min return), which switchbacks up to an expansive coastal lookout.

Paparoa National Park and around

South of Westport, SH67 crosses the Buller River and picks up the SH6, the main West Coast road. This stretch of coast is home to the Paparoa Range, a 1500m granite and gneiss ridge inlaid with limestone that separates the dramatic coastal strip from the valleys of the Grey and Inangahua rivers. In 1987, the coastal limestone country was designated the **Paparoa National Park**, one of the country's smallest and least known. The highlight is undoubtedly **Pancake Rocks**, where crashing waves have forced spectacular blowholes through a stratified stack of weathered limestone. But to skip the rest would be to miss out on a mysterious world of disappearing rivers, sinkholes, caves and limestone bluffs, which are best seen on the area's excellent **hiking trails**.

Maori often stopped while travelling the coast in search of *pounamu* (greenstone), and early **European explorers** followed suit seeking agricultural land. Charles Heaphy, Thomas Brunner and two Maori guides came through in 1846, finding little to detain them, but within twenty years this stretch was alive with **gold** prospectors at work on the black sands at **Charleston**.

Visitor services are centred on **Punakaiki** and Pancake Rocks, where bus passengers get a quick glimpse and others pause for the obligatory photos. A couple of days spent here will be well rewarded with a stack of wonderful walks, horseriding or canoeing up delightful limestone gorges.

Mitchells Gully Gold Mine

SH6, 22km south of Westport • Usually 9am–4pm • $15 • ☏ 03 789 6257

Mitchells Gully Gold Mine, a historic, family-run mine dating back to 1866, demonstrates the time-honoured methods used to extract fine gold held in a cement-like mass of oxidized iron sand. Along with mining paraphernalia, you can ride in an ore tram, and see a restored overshot wheel driving a stamping battery and working water races.

Charleston and Underwater Adventures

SH6, 26km south of Westport • Nile River Rainforest Train (2–3 daily) $20; Underworld Rafting caving trip (4hr) $175; Glowworm Cave Tour (3hr) $110; Adventure Caving (5hr) $330 • ☏ 03 788 8168, ⓦ caverafting.com

The most intensive mining in this region went on at **CHARLESTON**, once a rollicking boom town of around 18,000 people, but now a one-horse town without the horse. Instead, it's the base for Underworld Adventures. Tours in the surrounding area include the adult- and child-pleasing **Nile River Rainforest Train**, a gentle 25-minute journey on a modern narrow-gauge train through native bush. The train is also part of the hugely enjoyable Underworld Rafting **caving trip**, incorporating a bushwalk through a dramatic valley of limestone bluffs before delving underground decked out in wetsuit and caver's helmet with a rubber inner tube. An informative guided walk through the Metro cave system finishes with a float through a dreamlike, flooded glowworm cave and out to a gorgeous ravine into the Nile River, where depending on water levels you can shoot the rapids or just drift downstream. For more timid spelunkers there's the **Glowworm Cave Tour**, while adrenaline seekers should opt for the full-on **Adventure Caving**, which requires a 30m abseil and numerous tight squeezes, scrambles and climbs to explore the Te Tahi cave system.

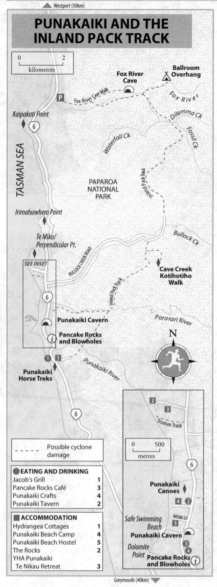

PUNAKAIKI AND THE INLAND PACK TRACK

12

★**Beaconstone** Birdsferry Rd, 1km off SH6 9km north of Charleston ☎027 431 0491, ⓦbeaconstoneecolodge.co.nz. One of the West Coast's best hostels, set in a hundred acres of native bush threaded by walking trails. Great-value accommodation includes a separate cottage with mountain views, and attractive dorms and doubles with ecofriendly features including composting toilets and solar power. Closed May–Sept, cash only; BBH registered. Dorms **$31**, doubles **$78**

Te Miko

SH6, 27km south of Charleston

The 50m-high cliffs of Te Miko were tagged Perpendicular Point by Charles Heaphy, who in 1846 recorded climbing the cliff on two stages of ladders constructed of shaky and rotten rata vines while his dog was hoisted on a rope. Te Miko remained an impenetrable barrier to pack animals until 1866, when a new Westport–Greymouth telegraph line prompted the forging of the **Inland Pack Track** (see box opposite). The coast road, finally completed in 1927, now climbs over Te Miko, passing the **Irimahuwhero Point Lookout**, with stupendous views along the coast past the layered rocks of the Te Miko cliff.

Punakaiki and the Pancake Rocks

SH6, 32km south of Charleston

The **Pancake Rocks** and blowholes at **PUNAKAIKI** are often all visitors see of the Paparoa National Park, as they tumble off the bus opposite the twenty-minute paved loop track that leads to the rocks. Layers of limestone have weathered to resemble an immense stack of giant pancakes, the result of **stylobedding**, a chemical process in which the pressure of overlying sediments creates bands of varying durability. Subsequent uplift and weathering has accentuated this effect to create photogenic formations. The edifice is undermined by huge sea caverns where the surf surges in, sending spumes of brine spouting up through vast **blowholes**: visit at high tide when a good swell from the south or southwest sees the blowholes at their best.

Some walks and swims

Further examples of Paparoa's karst landscape are on show on a number of walks. At the **Punakaiki Cavern**, 500m to the north, you'll find a few glowworms (go after dark: torch essential) and, 2km beyond that, the **Truman Track**

PAPAROA WALKS AND THE INLAND PACK TRACK

The best way to truly appreciate the dramatic limestone scenery of the Paparoa is on the region's walking trails. Unfortunately, the longest and best of Paparoa's tramps, the **Inland Pack Track** (27km; 2–3 days; see map opposite), was seriously damaged by 2014's **Cyclone Ita**, closing the Bullock Creek to Fossil Creek section for the forseeable future. Check at the Punakaiki DOC office for the latest trail status and consider tackling one of the area's shorter walks if the Inland Pack Track is still closed by the time you read this.

SHORTER WALKS

Punakaiki–Pororari Rivers Loop (12km; 3hr 30min; 100m ascent). A delightful route that follows the initial (open) stretch of the Inland Pack Track as far as the Pororari River, which is then followed downstream between some magnificent limestone cliffs to return to Punakaiki.

Fox River Cave Walk (10km; 2hr 30min; 100m ascent). This walk traces the last few kilometres of the Inland Pack Track from the Fox Rivermouth as far as the caves and returns the same way.

INLAND PACK TRACK PRACTICALITIES

The Inland Pack Track starts 1km south of the Punakaiki visitor centre beside the south bank of the Punakaiki River. DOC's *Inland Pack Track* leaflet provides enough information for the tramp; the 1:50,000 *Paparoa National Park* map is also very handy.

The track is best walked south to north, which eliminates the risk of missing the critical turn-off up Fossil Creek. There are no huts along the way, just a massive rock **bivvy** known as the Ballroom Overhang at the end of a long first day. You're advised to carry a **tent** for protection from voracious sandflies, and to avoid a wet night in the open if the rivers flood. **Campfires** are permitted at the Ballroom Overhang, but DOC recommends carrying a stove as most of the usable wood has already been burned. Be sure to check the **weather** forecast with DOC and fill out an **intentions form**.

Punakaiki River to Bullock Creek

(9.5km; 4hr; 220m ascent, 100m descent). The track rises to a low saddle then descends to ford the Pororari River, continuing with views inland to the Paparoa Range before reaching Bullock Creek. This should be forded with care – in flood conditions it is impassable.

Bullock Creek to Fox River (10km; 3–4hr; 100m ascent, 150m descent). While the trail through this section may have been altered after the cyclone, the original trail skirted swampland before climbing to a ridge and descending gradually to Fossil Creek, which was followed by wading from pool to pool, occasionally clambering over fallen tree trunks. After 30min, Fossil Creek meets the main tributary of the Fox River, Dilemma Creek, by a small sign – keep your eyes peeled. This is the most dramatic section of the trip but potentially the most dangerous, with eighteen fords to cross between gravel banks in the bed of Dilemma Creek: if you have any doubts about the first crossing, turn back, as they only get worse. The lower river has carved out a deep canyon between gleaming white vertical cliffs and, if you can find a

patch of sun, this makes a great place to rest. The track resumes by a sign on the true left bank just above the confluence with the Fox River; a steep bluff on the right makes a useful landmark.

Fox River to Ballroom Overhang (1km; 30min each way; negligible ascent). A signposted track crosses to the true right bank of the Fox River below the confluence, then crosses several more times to the vast limestone Ballroom Overhang with its 100m-long lip. It could easily provide shelter for a hundred or more campers, and has a long-drop toilet.

Fox River to Fox Rivermouth (5km; 2hr; 100m descent). From the Ballroom Overhang, return the same way you came, back to the river confluence. From there, the track runs to the Fox Rivermouth. A short distance along, a sign points across the river to the interesting Fox River Cave (30min). Meanwhile, the Inland Pack Track crosses to the car park by the Fox Rivermouth, some 12km by road from your starting point; southbound **buses** currently pass around 11.45am and 3.55pm.

12

(30min return) runs down from the highway to a small beach hemmed in by rock platforms.

Apart from the rocks, there's good **swimming** in the Pororari and Punakaiki rivers, and at the southern end of Pororari Beach – where there's also decent **surfing**.

ARRIVAL AND INFORMATION   PUNAKAIKI

By bus North- and south-bound buses run by InterCity and NakedBus stop for half an hour opposite the Pancake Rocks, by the DOC/i-SITE, allowing enough time for a quick look.

Tourist information Punakaiki's DOC/i-SITE is on SH6 (daily: Dec–April 9am–6pm; May–Nov 9am–4.30pm; ☎03 731 1895, ⍵doc.govt.nz). DOC's Paparoa National Park visitor centre is also an i-SITE, with displays on all aspects of the park, information on activities, walking maps, leaflets, and staff who can help with bookings.

Services Punakaiki has no fuel and no ATMs, so come prepared.

TOURS

Punakaiki Canoes SH6, 1km north of the Pancake Rocks ☎03 731 1870, ⍵riverkayaking.co.nz. Friendly outfit renting kayaks (from $40/2hr) from their base beside the Pororari River; guided trips by arrangement (from $70).

Punakaiki Horse Treks SH6, 600m south of the Pancake Rocks ☎03 731 1839, ⍵pancake-rocks.co.nz. No experience is necessary for these horse treks, which see you riding into the Punakaiki Valley and stopping for refreshments before heading back to the beach to trot through the surf. Oct–April only (3hr; $165).

ACCOMMODATION

Hydrangea Cottages SH6 ☎03 731 1839, ⍵pancake -rocks.co.nz. Six gorgeous cottages set above the road, most with sea views. The real appeal, though, is the self-catering cottages themselves, all beautifully constructed with native timbers and local stone, several with outside bathtubs and private verandas. $220

Punakaiki Beach Camp SH6 ☎03 731 1894, ⍵punakaikibeachcamp.co.nz. Attractive, grassy campsite roamed by wekas and pukekos, with a range of tent sites and campervan hook-ups plus a handful of cabins. It's handily positioned close to the beach and *Punakaiki Tavern*. Camping $17, powered sites $20

★**Punakaiki Beach Hostel** 4 Webb St ☎03 731 1852, ⍵punakaikibeachhostel.co.nz. Cheery, timber beachhouse-style backpackers right by the sand with great communal areas, board games and a TV-free policy; you can buy home-made bread, muffins and a few essentials from their tuck shop. There's an assortment of room types (including one double in a fantastic house truck); comfy

dorm beds come with reading lights and power points. Dorms $28, doubles $75

The Rocks Hartmount Place ☎03 731 1141, ⍵therockshomestay.com. Welcoming homestay, with three comfortable en-suite rooms; it's worth paying a bit more for the "Sea" room ($233) with its sea view, though the library and conservatory also have panoramic views. There's free wi-fi and rates include breakfast. No self-catering facilities. $205

YHA Punakaiki Te Nikau Retreat Hartmount Place, 200m north of the Truman Track and 3km north of the i-SITE ☎03 731 1111, ⍵tenikauretreat.co.nz. Associate YHA hostel in a rustic spot with buildings scattered around a hillside thick with nikau palms; most rooms have bathroom and kitchen facilities close by – check when booking if you wish to avoid inadvertent night-time bush excursions. There are dorms and attractive doubles plus some standalone cottages ($100); you can buy fresh bread, muffins and eggs on-site. Dorms $28, doubles $75

EATING

Punakaiki has a limited supply of **eating** options. There's no shop for supplies, so bring everything if you're self-catering.

Jacob's Grill Punakaiki Resort SH6, 700m south of the i-SITE ☎03 731 1168, ⍵punakaiki-resort.co.nz. Easily the swankiest place in Punakaiki, overlooking the sea, with elegantly presented fare such as scallops in white wine and cream sauce, followed by venison medallions with potato gratin (mains $28–38), though if they're busy you'll need to be staying at the resort to get a table. Daily lunch & dinner by reservation.

Pancake Rocks Café SH6, next to the i-SITE ☎03 731 1873. Popular with the tour buses, this place serves "West Coast" breakfasts (bacon, eggs, sausages, hash browns and toast; $18.50), as well as good home-made pies,

sandwiches and cakes; their fluffy pancake stacks ($17.50), served all day and topped with fruit compote or bacon and maple syrup, are particularly good. Daily summer 8am–5.30pm, winter 8am–4pm.

Punakaiki Crafts SH6, by the i-SITE. Craft shop with a small café serving coffee, tea, cakes and slices. Daily 9am– at least 4pm.

Punakaiki Tavern SH6, 1km north of the i-SITE ☎03 731 1188, ⍵punakaikitavern.co.nz. No-frills pub with good-value, simple, well-portioned meals ranging from vast cooked breakfasts to steaks, burgers, and bangers and mash (mains $18.50–26). Daily 8am–late.

12

Punakaiki to Greymouth

Punakaiki to Greymouth is a spectacular drive, pushed onto the sea cliffs by the intrusive ramparts of the Paparoa Range. Tragedy struck the area in 2010 when explosions rocked the Pike River coalmine, 46km north of Greymouth, trapping and killing 29 miners inside.

Photos aside, the only reasons to stop are to visit the **Barrytown knife maker**, 2662 Coast Rd/SH6, who will guide you through the intricacies of making your own blade, from hot steel to honed slicer, in a day ($150; around 9.30am–4pm; ☎0800 256433, ⓦbarrytownknifemaking.com). Tiny **RAPAHOE**, 34km south of Punakaiki, has about the safest bathing beach on the coast and a reputation for gemstones. Follow the track to the excellent vantage point of **Point Elizabeth** (5km, 2hr return).

Greymouth

The Grey River forces its way through a break in the coastal Rapahoe Range and over two treacherous sandbars to the sea at **GREYMOUTH**, the West Coast's largest settlement. The drab, workaday town has few highlights but attracts a decent flow of visitors thanks to its position at the end of the line for the *TranzAlpine* Railway and as a convenient stop for drivers (an increasing number of people take the train from Christchurch and pick up a rental car here).

Greymouth, like Hokitika, has a reputation for high-quality greenstone carving (see box, p.668). Once you've checked out the greenstone galleries and the brewery, and strolled along the waterfront, do what you came for and move on, particularly in winter when **The Barber**, a razor-sharp katabatic wind that whistles down the Grey Valley, envelops the town in thick icy fog.

12

Brief history

Greymouth began to take shape during the early years of the **gold rush** on land purchased in 1860 by James Mackay, who bought most of the West Coast from the Poutini Ngai Tahu people for £150. The town's defining feature is the river, which is deceptively calm and languid through most of the summer but awesome after heavy rains. Devastating **floods** swept through Greymouth in 1887, 1905, 1936, 1977 and 1988; since the town was last inundated a flood wall has successfully held back most of the waters.

Shades of Jade

16 Tainui St • Sept–April: Mon–Fri 8.30am–5pm, Sat 10am–2.30pm, Sun 11am–2.30pm; May–Aug by appointment only • ☎ 03 768 0794, ⓦ shadesofjade.co.nz

One of the town's jade gallery/shops well worth a visit is **Shades of Jade**, a charming spot where the local carver keeps the prices down, with traditional and modern designs in New Zealand *pounamu*, shell and bone. There's a workshop in the store, and the friendly owner is happy to show you stones and explain carving techniques.

History House Museum

27 Gresson St • Mon–Fri 10am–4pm, Sat 10am–2pm • $6 • ☎ 03 768 4028, ⓦ greydc.govt.nz

Despite presentation that owes much to the office photocopier, Greymouth's **History House Museum** does a good job of relating the Grey District's history, particularly prior to 1920, through maritime, gold- and coal-mining and timber-milling memorabilia and stacks of photos from the town's heyday. Take time to leaf through the books of newspaper articles and photographs that are piled in each room: stories of shipwrecks and claim-jumping that give a sense of just how recently Greymouth was a frontier town.

12

GREYMOUTH

Point Elizabeth Track (6km)

COBDEN

NELSON QUAY

COBDEN BRIDGE

Blaketown Beach

BLAKETOWN

COMKLEY ST
COLLINS ST
DOYLE ST
O'GRADY ST
PACKERS QUAY
RIGG ST
BLAKE STREET
REDD STREET
STEER AVE
PRESTON ROAD
RALEIGH ST

West Coast Wilderness Trail

Erua Moana

Grey River

GRESSON ST

Shades of Jade

MAWHERA QUAY

Bus Stop

JOHNSTON

MACKAY ST

Train Station

WHALL ST

MOUNT ST

History House Museum

GUINNESS ST

ARNEY ST

LEONARD ST

HERBERT ST

Wild West Adventures

CHAPEL ST

LORD ST

Victoria Park

PUKETANI ST

Monteith's Brewing Company

TURUMAHA ST

TAINUI ST

MURRAY ST

ALEXANDER ST

Memorial Park

FREYBERG TERR

Lake Karoro

Anzac Park

COWPER STREET

FRANKLIN ST

WINNIE ST

Terminal

Greymouth Airport

AERODROME RD

WATER WALK ROAD

HIGH STREET

New World Supermarket

SHAKESPEARE STREET

BUCCLEUGH ST

PALMERSTON ST

LYDIA ST

MARLBOROUGH ST

MARSDEN RD

Rugby Park

NELSON ST

BYRON ST

MILTON RD

JOYCE CR

CHESTERFIELD ST

TASMAN ST

MIRO

Shantytown (9km) & Hokitika (40km)

N

0 — 500
metres

■ ACCOMMODATION	
Duke Hostel	1
Global Village	4
Greymouth Seaside Top 10 Holiday Park	5
Noah's Ark	2
Rosewood	3

● EATING AND DRINKING	
Ali's	3
Bonzai Pizzeria	4
DP One Café	2
Monteith's Brewing Company	5
Speight's Ale House	1

Monteith's Brewing Company

Corner of Turumaha and Herbert sts • Daily 10am–8pm; guided tours at 10.30am, 3pm, 4.30pm & 6pm • Guided tours $20 • ☎ 03 768 4149, ⓦ monteiths.co.nz

Monteith's Brewing Company's shiny new brewery attracts a steady stream of beer aficionados. While locals come here for the excellent food and drink (see p.665), it's possible to work up a thirst on a tour of the brewhouse, where the company's "Brewer's Series" craft ales are produced. The small production runs mean that you're unlikely to see the bottling plant in action, but there's a good chance of

RAFTING THE WILD WEST COAST RIVERS

Kayakers and rafters visit New Zealand's West Coast to experience some of the country's most thrilling and scenic whitewater trips. Steep rivers spill dramatically out of the alpine wilderness, fed by the prodigious quantity of rain that guarantees solid flows most of the time. The steepness of the terrain means you're in constantly thrilling if not downright scary territory (generally Grade III–V).

ACCESS

Few of the region's rivers had been kayaked or rafted until the 1980s, when access became possible by helicopter. Many rafting trips still require **helicopter access**, so costs are relatively high, and prices often depend on numbers – getting a group together can save you a packet.

BOOKING AND SEASONS

Though their popularity is increasing, trips are still comparatively infrequent and you should **book** as far in advance as possible. The main **season** is November to April, though rafting is generally possible from early September to late May, and there is a minimum age of 13 years (15 for some of the more frightening runs).

RIVERS

The **most commonly rafted rivers** are (from north to south) the Karamea (Grade III+), the Mokihinui (Grade IV), the Arahura (Grade IV), the Whitcombe (Grade V), the Hokitika (Grade III–IV), the Wanganui (Grade III), the Perth (Grade V) and the Whataroa (Grade IV).

OUTFITTERS

Eco Rafting Franz Josef ☎03 755 4254, ⓦecorafting.co.nz. Enthusiastic guides take small groups on wilderness rafting trips, boating at rivers along the length of the West Coast, including the Whataroa River near Franz Josef. They organize drive-in rafting trips (from $90) but the heli-rafting (from $350) and overnight trips (from $450) are particularly popular.
Ultimate Descents 38 Waller St, Murchison ☎0800 748377, ⓦrivers.co.nz. Specialists in rafting the top half of South Island, with one-day heli-rafting trips on the Karamea ($500) and two-day trips on the Mokihinui ($900), among others.
Wild West Adventures 8 Whall St, Greymouth ☎0508 286 877, ⓦfun-nz.com. Offers a wide range of trips, from hardcore heli-rafting (from $485) to tamer trips (from $175), on most of the rivers listed above.

12

seeing the brewers at work on the morning tours. Take care though – the tour includes four 200ml glasses of beer, and even one glass of their *Doppelbock* could put you over the legal limit for driving.

Point Elizabeth Track

6km north of Greymouth • 5km return; 90min

Choose a fine evening for this pleasant walk; the **Point Elizabeth Track** follows the coast through stands of nikau to a lookout, from where you may spot Hector's dolphins or fur seals. Double back from here, or continue another 3km to Rapahoe (see p.661) and pick up a bus from there back to town (2 daily). While it's not strictly necessary, the *Point Elizabeth Walkway* leaflet, available from Greymouth's i-SITE ($2), is a good guide to the walk's history and geography.

ARRIVAL AND DEPARTURE

GREYMOUTH

By train The *TranzAlpine* train (see box, p.524), Greymouth's only passenger service, stops at the Mackay St station.
Destinations Arthur's Pass (daily; 2hr 15min); Christchurch (daily; 4hr 20min).
By bus InterCity buses running south to Hokitika and Franz Josef, or north to Westport and Nelson, depart shortly after the arrival of the *TranzAlpine* train. Atomic,

InterCity and NakedBus all stop outside the railway station on Mackay St.
Destinations Arthur's Pass (2 daily; 1hr 30min); Christchurch (2 daily; 4hr 30min); Fox Glacier (1–2 daily; 3hr 45min–4hr 30min); Franz Josef (1–2 daily; 3hr–3hr 30min); Hokitika (3–5 daily; 45min); Murchison (daily; 4hr); Punakaiki (1–2 daily; 1hr); Westport (1–2 daily; 2hr 30min).

GREYMOUTH TOURS AND ACTIVITIES

Activities around Greymouth cover a wide variety of bases, with the almost-completed **West Coast Wilderness Trail** (ⓦ westcoastwildernesstrail.co.nz), a cycle trail linking Ross, Hokitika and Greymouth, soon to join their ranks.

On Yer Bike 511 SH6, 5km north of Greymouth ⓣ 0800 669372, ⓦ onyerbike.co.nz. Offers adrenaline-charged activities on a private estate including "extreme off-roading" in 8WD amphibious tank-style Argos (from $50/30min), quad bikes ($115/hr) and go-karts, with free transport from Greymouth.

Shantytown Rutherglen Rd, Paroa, 10km south of town ⓣ 0800 742689, ⓦ shantytown.co.nz. If you're travelling with kids, you might want to consider a visit to this re-created gold-rush village heritage park

($31.50) where activities include a steam train and panning for gold. Daily 8.30am–5pm.

Wild West Adventures 8 Whall St, Greymouth ⓣ 0508 286 877, ⓦ fun-nz.com. Runs some of the best activities in town, notably Taniwha Cave Rafting (5hr; 1hr 30min–2hr underground; $185), an undemanding caving trip where wetsuits and cavers' lamps are provided for a gentle float on inner tubes through a cavern lit by glowworms, which finishes with a warm-up soak in a hot tub. They also offer a more energy-intensive range of guided hikes and bike-rides, plus rafting trips.

INFORMATION

Tourist information Inside the train station on Mackay St (Mon–Fri 9am–5pm, Sat & Sun 9.30am–4pm; ⓣ 03 768 5101, ⓦ greydistrict.co.nz). The combined i-SITE and West

Coast Travel Centre has free wi-fi and provides the *Central West Coast* visitor guide which contains a good street map.

GETTING AROUND

By bike Greymouth's hostels all lend bikes to guests free of charge. Rentals are available from Mann Cycles (ⓣ 03 768 0255) on Mackay St from $15/hr.

By car Several major car rental companies have offices inside the i-SITE.

ACCOMMODATION

Greymouth has several great **backpackers** but few other standout places to stay. **Book** ahead around local events: the Kumara Races (second weekend in Jan), the Coast to Coast Race (second weekend in Feb; see box opposite), Hokitika's Wildfoods Festival (second weekend in March) and the Around Brunner Cycle Race (third weekend in April).

Duke Hostel 27 Guinness St ⓣ 03 768 9470, ⓦ duke .co.nz. As long as you can stand the purple-and-green paint job, this is an excellent hostel: smoothly organized in a central location with well-equipped doubles, comfortable beds and knowledgeable and helpful hosts who offer free soup nightly, as well as toast and jam each morning and complimentary wi-fi. Dorms $29, doubles $72

★ **Global Village** 42 Cowper St ⓣ 03 768 7272, ⓦ globalvillagebackpackers.co.nz. Light and spacious, well-equipped hostel backing onto parkland and a river. The rooms are imaginatively decorated in tribal themes with artefacts from around the world, the bathrooms have been decorated with large colourful mosaics, and there's a range of tempting activities: free bikes and kayaks, low-cost sauna, spa and small gym, and a BBQ out back most fine evenings. All beds are made up and there are some single-sex dorms and camping spots ($18). Dorms $28, rooms $70

Greymouth Seaside Top 10 Holiday Park 2 Chesterfield St ⓣ 0800 867104, ⓦ top10greymouth .co.nz. The more central and better of the two motor parks, right by the beach with the excellent facilities (adventure playground, games room, etc.), expected of the Top 10 chain. Camping and powered sites $46

Noah's Ark 16 Chapel St ⓣ 03 768 4868, ⓦ noahsarkbackpackers.co.nz. Large but homey hostel in a two-storey villa with great verandas and a spacious lounge with Sky TV. Rooms and dorms are lavishly decorated with animal themes and there are free bikes and a spa. Dorms $27, doubles $70

★ **Rosewood** 20 High St ⓣ 0800 185748. Appealing B&B in a beautiful two-storey 1920s home – look for the flag outside – with wood panelling, leadlight windows and tasteful decor. Rooms are en suite or have private bathroom; rates include cooked breakfasts. Doubles $185

EATING AND DRINKING

Greymouth's quiet centre has plenty of good cafés, but little in the way of proper restaurants – you may find yourself self-catering come dinnertime, whether you plan to or not.

THE COAST TO COAST RACE

Kiwis are mad on multisport and punch above their weight on the international circuit; every weekend you'll see scores of people honing their biking, running and paddling skills. The ultimate goal of all local multisporters is the gruelling 243km **Coast to Coast Race** (second weekend in Feb; ⓦ coasttocoast.co.nz), which requires a pre-dawn start from the beach near Kumara Junction, 17km south of Greymouth. A 3km run leads to a 55km cycle uphill to Otira where jelly-kneed contenders tackle the most gruelling section, a 33km run up and down the boulder-strewn creek beds of the Southern Alps, before kayaking for several hours down Canterbury's braided Waimakariri River and cycling the final 70km to Sumner.

From humble beginnings in 1983 – when it was the world's first major multisport event – the Coast to Coast has blossomed into a professional affair with over a thousand competitors. Serious contenders engage a highly organized support crew and specialized gear; only the most high-tech bikes will do and designers build racing kayaks especially for Waimakariri conditions. Most competitors take two days, but around 150 elite triathletes compete in "The Longest Day", tackling the same course in under 24 hours. Mere mortals – though admittedly extremely fit ones – can also compete by forming two-person teams sharing the disciplines. The course record is an astonishing 10hr 34min and 37 seconds, unbroken since 1994.

Ali's 9 Tainui St ☎ 03 768 5858. Unpretentious, licensed café serving snacks, lunches and dinners including Thai curries and tasty pasta dishes ($18.50–29) plus snacks such as potato, spinach and feta fritters ($11.50). Tues–Sun 9am–9pm, Mon 9am–4.30pm.

Bonzai Pizzeria 31 Mackay St ☎ 03 768 4170. Cheerful licensed restaurant (mains $14–24) with tearoom staples through the day, including delightfully squidgy cakes and vast quiches in addition to the deep-pan pizzas for lunch and dinner. Mon & Tues 7.30am–4.30pm, Wed–Sat 7.30am–late.

DP One Café 126 Mawhera Quay. Cool café, with local artists' work on the walls and pre-loved furniture, serving cooked breakfasts, filled bagels and salads ($8–15), along with good coffee, tea and smoothies. Daily 8.30am–4pm.

★ **Monteith's Brewing Company** Corner of Turumaha and Herbert sts ☎ 03 768 4149, ⓦ monteiths.co.nz. Attached to the brewery itself, this popular café with indoor and outdoor seating serves an appealing range of tapas, peppered venison and blue cheese sliders, sticky baby back ribs and beer battered fries ($7–15), all of which can be paired with the brewery's ales. Daily 10am–8pm.

Speight's Ale House 130 Mawhera Quay ☎ 03 768 0667, ⓦ speights.co.nz. Cavernous restaurant/bar in a 1909 Edwardian Baroque former government building with a menu of hearty dishes (mains $17–32): whitebait patties, "great mates drunken steak" (rump steak) and Stewart Island battered blue cod – matched to beers from the Speight's range. Daily 11am–late, food served until 9pm.

Hokitika

South of Greymouth, SH6 hugs a desolate stretch of coast with little of abiding interest until **HOKITIKA**, 40km away. "Hoki" is markedly more interesting than Greymouth, due to its location on a long, driftwood-strewn beach, some engaging activities – including Sock World Hokitika's strangely seductive sock-making machine museum and an atmospheric glowworm dell – and proximity to good bushwalks in the surrounding area, not least of which is the spectacular Hokitika Gorge (see p.669).

Despite its long, windswept dark-sand beach, the town is primarily renowned for its crafts scene, and is something of an artists' enclave, with a slew of studios, galleries and shops where you can see weaving, carving (greenstone or bone) or glass-blowing in action or buy the high-quality results of the artists' labours.

Brief history

Like other West Coast towns, Hokitika owes its existence to the **gold rushes** of the 1860s. Within months of the initial discoveries near Greymouth in 1864, fields had been opened up on the tributaries of the Hokitika River, and Australian diggers and Irish hopefuls trekked to the West Coast to get their share. Within two years Hokitika had a population of 6000 (compared with today's 4000), streets packed with hotels,

and a steady export of over a tonne of gold a month – a booming period evoked in Eleanor Catton's 2013 Booker Prize-winning novel, *The Luminaries*.

Despite a treacherous sandbar at the Hokitika river-mouth, the **port** briefly became the country's busiest, with ships tied up four deep along Gibson Wharf. As gold grew harder to find and more sluicing water was needed, the enterprise eventually became uneconomic and was replaced by dairying and the timber industry. The port closed in 1954, only to be smartened up in the 1990s for the town's Heritage Trail.

Hokitika Museum

Carnegie Building, 17 Hamilton St · Daily: summer 10am–5pm; winter 10am–2pm · $6 · ☎ 03 755 6898

Hokitika's leading role in the West Coast gold rushes rightly occupies much of the **Hokitika Museum**, with a fascinating film about the period showing on loop. There are also worthwhile displays on *pounamu* and the West Coast's whitebait fanatics, as well as plenty of period photographs depicting the dangers of crossing the Hokitika River bar and the difficulties of building the region's roads.

Sock World Hokitika

27 Sewell St · Daily 9am–5pm · Free · ☎ 03 755 7251, 🌐 autoknitter.com

For an entirely different, charming and quirky experience pop into **Sock World Hokitika**, a working museum that houses a display of vintage knitting machines and a great range of woolly foot-warmers. The friendly, knowledgeable staff will give you a rundown on the largest collection of fully restored sock-knitting machines known to man, some capable of knocking up ten pairs an hour.

National Kiwi Centre

64 Tancred St • Daily: summer 9.30am–5pm; winter 9.30am–4.30pm; eel feeding 10am, noon and 3pm • $22 • ☎ 03 755 5251, ⓦ thenationalkiwicentre.co.nz

Firmly on the tour bus circuit, the modest, privately-run **National Kiwi Centre** holds a dimly-lit nocturnal house, where you can watch a small collection of kiwis scurrying about and sifting the leaf litter for insects. In the aquarium next door you can watch tuatara, a rare "living dinosaur", sunning themselves in summer, and feed giant long-finned eels at fixed times throughout the day.

ARRIVAL AND DEPARTURE   HOKITIKA

Fuel gets more expensive south along the coast, so fill up before leaving Hokitika.

By plane Hokitika's tiny airport is 2km east of the centre, with regular flights to Christchurch.
Destinations Christchurch (2–4 daily; 35min).
By bus InterCity and NakedBus stop outside the i-SITE on Weld St.
Destinations Arthur's Pass (1–2 daily; 3hr 30min); Christchurch (daily; 5hr 30min); Fox Glacier (1–2 daily; 2hr 30min); Franz Josef (1–2 daily; 2hr); Greymouth (1–2 daily; 45min); Nelson (1–2 daily; 7hr); Punakaiki (1–2 daily; 1hr 45min); Ross (1–2 daily; 30min); Whataroa (1–2 daily; 1hr 30min).

INFORMATION AND TOURS

Tourist information i-SITE 36 Weld St (Dec–March daily 9am–6pm; April–Nov daily 9am–5pm; ☎ 03 755 6166, ⓦ hokitika.org). Does DOC bookings and is your best source of information about the new Westland Wilderness Trail, a four-day, off-road cycle trail linking Greymouth and Ross.
Services The banks on Revell Street are the last before Wanaka, more than 400km to the southeast, although there are now a couple of ATMs en route.
Tours Wilderness Wings (at the airport; ☎ 0800 755 8118, ⓦ wildernesswings.co.nz) offer a number of scenic flights, including over the glaciers (35min; $285) and as far as Milford Sound (3hr; $975); two people minimum. Leaflets for the self-guided Hokitika Heritage Walk can be picked up at the i-SITE office; walks cover the town's historic landmarks, including the Gibson Quay area, a former riverside dock that makes for a pleasant evening stroll, the Signal Station Lookout, the 1897 Custom House and a reconstructed schooner, the *Tambo*, which stands as memorial to ships lost on the sandbar.

ACCOMMODATION

Accommodation in Hokitika is seldom hard to find, though you should book ahead during the Kumara Races (second weekend in Jan), for all of February including around the Coast to Coast race (see box, p.665) and during the Wildfoods Festival (see box, p.669).

252 Beachside 252 Revell St ☎ 03 755 8773, ⓦ 252beachside.co.nz. Old-fashioned motel and campervan park a block from the beach with a swimming pool and enclosed play area, with a row of dated but comfortable studios and a handful of basic cabins. The friendly owners have reams of information on activities in and around town. Powered sites $40, studios $135

★**Awatuna Homestead** SH6, 13km north of Hokitika ☎ 03 755 6834, ⓦ awatunahomestead.co.nz. Welcoming B&B with three tasteful, comfortable rooms and one self-catering apartment. A relaxing spot with assorted animals, home-grown veggies, plenty of books, outdoor bath, a track down to the beach and evening storytelling sessions; evening meals by arrangement. Rooms $290, apartment $360

Beachfront Hotel 111 Revell St ☎ 03 755 8344, ⓦ beachfronthotel.co.nz. With fifty rooms in two blocks, this is Hokitika's largest hotel. Rooms in the older block are rather average; the pick of the bunch are the modern first-floor rooms in the "Oceanview" building next door with full wall-windows and balconies just 50m from the water's edge. Doubles $165, ocean-view $180

★**Drifting Sands** 197 Revell Street ☎ 03 755 7654, ⓦ driftingsands.kiwi. A sleekly designed "boutique hostel", with great beds, a coal-fire-warmed lounge and a pebbly path straight to the beach. If your tent can stand up to Hokitika's sea breezes, it's possible to camp in the garden ($18). Dorms $32, doubles $86

Mountain Jade 41 Weld St ☎ 03 755 5185, ⓦ mountainjadebackpackers.co.nz. Central and slightly tatty BBH hostel above the jade studio of the same name

GREENSTONE

Maori revere **pounamu** (hard nephrite jade) and **tangiwai** (softer, translucent bowenite), usually collectively known as **greenstone**. In Aotearoa's pre-European culture, it took the place of durable metals for practical, warfaring and decorative uses; adzes and chisels were used for carving, *mere* (clubs) for combat and as symbols of chieftainship, and pendants were fashioned for jewellery.

In Maori, the entire South Island is known as **Te Wahi Pounamu**, "the place of greenstone", with deposits found solely between Greymouth and Hokitika in the Taramakau and Arahura rivers, in Fiordland's Anita Bay – where the beautifully dappled *tangiwai* occurs – and the Lake Wakatipu region near Queenstown. When the Poutini Ngai Tahu arranged to sell most of Westland to James Mackay in 1860, the Arahura River, their main source of *pounamu*, was specifically excluded.

Greenstone's value has barely diminished. Mineral claims are jealously guarded, the export of greenstone is prohibited and no extraction is allowed from national parks; penalties include fines of up to $200,000 and two years in jail. **Price** is heavily dependent on quality, but rates of $100,000 a tonne are not unknown – and the sky's the limit when the stone is fashioned into sculpture and jewellery, although pendants can be picked up for as little as $20.

Hokitika is the main destination for greenstone shoppers; keep in mind that the larger **shops** and **galleries** are firmly locked into the tour-bus circuit so prices are kept high. Big shops are fine for learning about the quality of the stone and competence of the artwork but smaller places have more competitive deals. Buyers should ask about the origins of the raw material – insiders suspect that lots of greenstone sold in New Zealand is cheaper jade sourced overseas.

HOKITIKA ARTS AND CRAFTS

Pick up a free city map from the i-SITE showing the locations of Hokitika's growing collection of art and craft shops, studios and galleries; **greenstone** in particular is big business. The places listed below allow you to go beyond mere shopping and to see artisans at work.

Arahura Greenstone Tours ☏ 021 0239 4922, Ⓦ greenstonetours.co.nz. If you're done with the greenstone shops in town, head out to the Arahura River with Tangi, an experienced Maori carver, to learn about the Ngai Tahu's deep connection to greenstone and to search for your own piece of *pounamu* (2hr; $135).

Bonz 'n' Stonz Carving Studio 16 Hamilton St ☏ 0800 214949, Ⓦ bonz-n-stonz.co.nz. If you want to shape a piece of greenstone yourself, pop along to this excellent studio where you can learn to carve; the friendly and estimable Steve Gwaliasi guides you through the design and execution in what is a personal and very memorable experience (2–6hr; jade $150; bone $85;

shell $75 or $30/hr if you bring your own material).

Hokitika Glass Studio 9 Weld St ☏ 03 755 7775, Ⓦ hokitikaglass.co.nz. Glass-blowing is another long-standing Hoki tradition, best seen on weekdays at this studio, which produces a fine line in glass penguins. Daily 8.30am–5pm.

Tectonic Jade 67 Revell St ☏ 03 755 6644, Ⓦ tectonicjade.com. One of the more interesting jade shops around town, with a collection of traditional and original designs in unusual types of *pounamu*. There's a great café in-store too, though it's aimed at refreshing potential buyers, rather than the general public – purchases are rewarded with an excellent free coffee. Sept–March daily 9am–5.30pm.

with cheap dorms and a couple of cramped but comfortable doubles out back, overlooking the car park. Dorms $25, doubles $60

Shining Star 16 Richards Drive ☏ 03 755 8921, Ⓦ accommodationwestcoast.co.nz. There's no road between you and the beach at this neat, well-run site. The stylized geometric log cabins all have en suites; some also offer stunning sea views and cooking facilities, and there are pet llamas and a playground. Powered sites $40, cabins $95

Teichelmann's B&B 20 Hamilton St ☏ 03 755 8232, Ⓦ teichelmanns.co.nz. Comfortable and well appointed,

this history-filled central B&B has friendly hosts, a range of en-suite rooms and a romantic garden cottage with double spa bath overlooking a tiny fern-filled courtyard. A hearty breakfast is served. Doubles $245, cottage $255

YHA Hokitika Birdsong Backpackers 124 Kumara Junction, SH6, 3km north of town ☏ 03 755 7179, Ⓦ birdsong.co.nz. The most long-lived of the local hostels, the brightly decorated rooms in this small, friendly laidback spot all feature a painting of the bird they're named after. There are discounts for YHA/BBH members, outdoor bathtubs and ocean views from upstairs. Dorms $32, doubles $83

WILDFOODS FESTIVAL

In the last decade or so, Hokitika has become synonymous with the annual **Wildfoods Festival** (second Sat in March; advance tickets $35; ⓦ www.wildfoods.co.nz), when the population quadruples to celebrate bush tucker. Around fifty stalls in Cass Square sell delicacies such as marinated goat kebabs, smoked eel wontons, huhu grubs, "mountain oysters" (a.k.a. sheep's testicles) and, of course, whitebait, washed down with home-brewed beer and South Island wine.

EATING, DRINKING AND ENTERTAINMENT

For free evening entertainment, stroll to the **Glowworm Dell** about 1km north of the centre beside SH6. The *Hokitika Guardian*, available from the i-SITE and around town, has entertainment listings.

★ **Fat Pipi** 89 Revell St ⓣ 03 755 6373. The locally famed pizzas here include "Greenpiece" (zucchini, spinach, mushrooms, feta, olives and roast red pepper pesto), and the whopping "Whitebait", topped with a quarter-pound of whitebait folded into a beaten egg, with mozzarella, capers and lemon (all pizzas $20–26). You can takeaway, or eat-in – head to the back of the garden for a side of sea-view with your dinner. Daily 5–9pm.

Ocean View 111 Revell St ⓣ 03 755 8344. *Beachfront Hotel* restaurant with tasty à la carte evening meals such as pork fillet with roast garlic mash, plus there's a range of good-value light meals on offer (tiger prawn risotto and the like) with great sea views from window tables and the deck. Mains $19–37. Daily 6pm–late.

Stations Inn Blue Spur Rd ⓣ 03 755 5499, ⓦ stationsinnhokitika.co.nz. Hokitika's only fine dining is to be had here, 5km east of town on the way to Lake Kaniere. The menu changes seasonally to show off choice Kiwi produce, with elegant dishes including things like braised rabbit in a pastry shell with *kumara* mash, house-cured Marlborough salmon with home-made rye bread, and great beef and lamb dishes (mains $28–45). Tues–Sat 6pm–late.

Stella Café 84 Revell St ⓣ 03 755 5432. One of the town's most popular meeting spots, with great hot meals and coffee, though their cabinet food is somewhat uninspired. There's a climate-controlled room stocked with fancy cheese and chutney, plus stacks of magazines and an in-house beehive to keep you entertained. Cheese platters from $20 and cooked mains from $22. Daily 8.30am–4.30pm, open for dinner Thurs–Sat.

★ **West Coast Wine Co.** 108 Revell St ⓣ 03 755 5417, ⓦ westcoastwine.co.nz. Tiny bar in a wine shop with a delightful courtyard, where good wine, beer and cocktails are complemented by excellent coffee and supplemented by a short menu of sophisticated bar snacks (mostly $10). By the time you read this their new "cellar door" setup ought to be up and running at the *Fire House* on Hamilton Street. Wed & Thurs 3–8pm, Fri & Sat 3–10pm, Sun 2–6pm.

CINEMA

The Regent 23 Weld St ⓣ 03 755 8101, ⓦ hokitikaregent.com. A 1935 Art Deco theatre – with "cutting-edge technology" – screening mainstream movies.

Lake Kaniere

19km east of Hokitika

Some of the best bush scenery and **walks** around Hokitika are inland where the dairying hinterland meets the foothills of the Southern Alps. Minor roads (initially following Stafford Street out of town) make a good 70km scenic drive, shown in detail on DOC's **Central West Coast: Hokitika** leaflet ($2). The road passes the fishing, waterskiing and tramping territory of **Lake Kaniere**, a glacial lake with fantastic reflections of the mountains in the crystal water, several picnic sites and basic camping ($6) along its eastern side. The most popular walk is the **Kaniere Water Race Walkway** (9km one way; 3hr 30min; 100m ascent), starting from the lake's northern end and following a channel that used to supply water to the goldfields, through stands of regenerating rimu.

Hokitika Gorge

35km east of Hokitika

Lake Kaniere's eastern-shore road passes the magical **Dorothy Falls**, with giant moss-covered boulders in unearthly shades of green, and eventually loops westwards where a side road leads to the dazzling **Hokitika Gorge**. A gentle path (1.2km; 30min return) leads through glades of rimu and podocarp to a swingbridge over the exquisite turquoise-coloured Hokitika River.

From Hokitika to the glaciers

The main highway snuggles in close to the Southern Alps for most of the 135km to the glacier at Franz Josef. The journey through dairy farms and stands of selectively logged native bush is broken by a series of small settlements – **Ross**, **Pukekura** and **Harihari**. The most popular places to stop are **Whataroa**, to visit the **white heron** colony, and **Okarito**, where the laidback charm of the hamlet's lagoon and **kiwi-spotting** trips may give you pause.

Immediately **south** of Hokitika, it's less than 10km along SH6 to the **Mananui Tramline** (12km return; 4hr; mainly flat; DOC leaflet from the Hokitika i-SITE $2), which offers easy walking and cycling with picnic opportunities at a lakeside beach – cyclists have the option of completing the loop around the lake. A further 2km south along SH6 the **Mananui Bush Walkway** (20min return) leads through coastal forest remnants to dunes and there's a particularly nice DOC **camping** spot at **Lake Mahinapua**, accessed off SH6 1km south ($6). Those travelling with children may wish to stop at the Westcoast Treetop Walk, a few kilometres further south, but the high ticket prices will put off most.

Ross

At the village of **ROSS**, 26km south of Hokitika, a lake-filled hole is all that remains of an opencast mine that sought alluvial **gold** until the deposit was exhausted in 2004. The mining company has moved to a new site just south of town, but would dearly love to get at the gold-bearing gravels underneath the settlement itself. Leave time for the well-signposted **Water Race Walkway** (4km loop, 1hr) linking a clutch of historic buildings and the site of the area's first gold strike.

De Bakker Cottage
Bold St • Daily Dec–March 9am–4pm; April–Nov 9am–2pm • Free

Though Ross had over 3000 residents at its gold-rush peak, things had slowed considerably by 1909, when a couple of diggers prospecting less than 500m from the current visitor centre turned up the largest gold nugget ever found in New Zealand, the 3.1kg "**Honourable Roddy**", named after the then Minister of Mines. The nugget was bought by the government and given as a coronation gift in 1911 to Britain's George V, who melted it down to make a tea service. A replica of the fist-sized lump resides in the 1885 **Miner's Cottage**, surrounded by period photos and Victorian bric-a-brac.

Pukekura
Bushman's Centre daily 9am–5pm • Free; museum $4 • ☎ 03 755 4144, ⓦ pukekura.co.nz

A giant model sandfly hangs from the eaves of the **Bushman's Centre**, in the two-house hamlet of **PUKEKURA**, 23km south of Ross. The centre's cobwebby **museum** takes a light-hearted approach to timber milling, live deer capture, possum trapping (with a few morose live examples) and harvesting sphagnum moss for East Asian orchid growers. The museum may not be to your taste, but the centre's **café** (see p.672) and the rest areas around pretty **Lake Ianthe**, 6km to the south, make good stops.

Harihari

Tiny **HARIHARI**, 23km south of Pukekura, was the marshy landing site of **Guy Menzies**, who flew solo from Sydney to New Zealand in 1931, becoming the first to do so. Menzies ended up strapped in upside down in the mud of La Fontaine swamp, 10km northwest of town. A replica of Menzies' plane resides near the southern entrance to town in **Guy Menzies Park**. You might also want to turn onto Whanganui Flat Road and drive 20km (partly gravel) coastwards past Menzies' landing site to the delightful **Hari Hari Coastal Walkway** (8km loop; 2–3hr; negligible ascent), which runs past elaborate whitebaiting stands to the Doughboy Lookout (60m) with great views of the coast and the Southern Alps. After a short stretch of dramatic coastline you return though kahikatea forest and along the line of a tram track once used by loggers. Note that certain sections are only accessible for two hours either side of low tide.

Whataroa and the Waitangiroto Nature Reserve

SH6, 30km south of Harihari • White Heron Sanctuary Tours Oct–Feb 4 daily; 2hr 30min • $120; booking advised • ☎ 0800 523456, ⊕ whiteherontours.co.nz

From September to late February, graceful white herons (*kotuku*) arrive to breed at the Waitangiroto Nature Reserve near **WHATAROA**, the bird's only nesting site in the country. Sitting across the river in a two-storey hide, gazing on forty or so nesting pairs of herons and spoonbills going about the daily business of preening, fishing and mating is a truly memorable if slightly surreal experience that ends all too quickly. The only way to visit is with the professional **White Heron Sanctuary Tours**, with tours departing from their office in Whataroa. The trip includes a scenic jetboat ride on the pretty Waitangiroto River and about half an hour ogling the birds; binoculars are provided. Pick-ups from Franz Josef are available (enquire for prices).

Okarito

In 1642, Abel Tasman became the first European to set eyes on Aotearoa at **Okarito**, 13km off SH6 15km south of Whataroa, now a secluded hamlet dotted round the southern side of its eponymous lagoon. The discovery of gold in the mid-1800s sparked an eighteen-month boom that saw fifty stores and hotels spring up along the

12

OKARITO TOURS AND ACTIVITIES

Nature-focused kayaking trips and cruises departing from Okarito offer the chance for close encounters with the area's seventy species of birdlife including the kotuku (white heron) and royal spoonbill, while bushwalking tours have an excellent success rate for spotting the rare **Okarito kiwi**.

WALKS

Okarito Trig Walk (4km return; 1hr 30min; 150m ascent). This route begins at the southern end of town, climbing through the bush to a headland with fabulous views over the lagoon and out to the Southern Alps – mounts Cook and Tasman are visible on a clear day.

Three Mile Pack Track (10km return; 3hr 30min; 150m ascent). Starting from the same spot, stroll through the coastal forest on a meandering, well-marked trail, that once linked the gold rush towns of Okarito and Three Mile Lagoon. Once at Three Mile Lagoon, you can return the way you came, or head back to Okarito along the beach, if tides allow – times are posted at the start of the walk.

TOUR OPERATORS

Okarito Boat Tours The Strand ☎ 03 753 4223, ⊕ okaritoboattours.co.nz. If you don't want to paddle, opt for one of these peaceful, leisurely cruises through the lagoon and its feeder streams. Early tours (1hr 30min; $70)are great for photography and spotting birds, while later trips (1hr; $45) focus on the seductive scenery.

Okarito Kiwi Tours 53 The Strand ☎ 03 753 4330, ⊕ okaritokiwitours.co.nz. Wildlife of a different feather can usually be seen on these excellent, low-impact trips into the bush for kiwi spotting (3–5hr; $75). If it goes well you'll start shortly before dusk and

catch a glimpse of some of the extremely rare Okarito brown kiwi. To maximize the already high (95 percent) success rate, wear quiet clothes and sturdy boots.

Okarito Nature Tours The Strand ☎ 0800 652748, ⊕ okarito.co.nz. Runs great-value guided kayaking trips (2hr; $90; minimum two people) and rents double kayaks (2hr $50; half-day $60; overnight rentals also available) for exploring the lagoon and its forested side-channels. Call first to check tide conditions, but plan to go out in the morning when the water is calmest and the birdlife abundant and active.

lagoon's shores. Timber and flax milling sustained the place once the gold had gone, but still the community foundered, leaving a handful of holiday homes, a few dozen permanent residents and a lovely beach and lagoon, used as the setting for much of Keri Hulme's prize-winning novel, *The Bone People*.

INFORMATION

Tourist information 4 Aylmer St, Ross (daily: Dec–March 9am–4pm; April–Nov 9am–2pm; museum $2; ☎ 03 755 4077). The visitor centre museum shows an interesting video (included in admission) on the 1865 gold

FROM HOKITIKA TO THE GLACIERS

rush and rents gold pans ($10); if you're after a sure thing there's also on-site gold panning which includes guaranteed strike ($12.50).

ACCOMMODATION AND EATING

PUKEKURA

Bushman's Centre Café ☎ 03 755 4144, ⓦ pukekura .co.nz. Serves a "roadkill menu" that includes rabbit and possum pies (the latter technically paid for "by donation" since possums have been banished from Kiwi menus). It's possible to stay across the road either in the campsite or double rooms with shared bathroom and kitchen facilities. Café daily 9am–5pm. Camping $10, doubles $45

HARIHARI

Flaxbush Motel SH6 ☎ 03 753 3116, ⓔ flaxbush123 @xtra.co.nz. What with the park and the coastal walkway you may decide to stay, in which case treat yourself to this very welcoming spot, which is a Noah's Ark for unwell and injured wildlife (including, at the time of research, an inquisitive peacock); all rooms have self-catering facilities. Doubles $90, cottages $120

OKARITO

While Okarito Nature Tours sell hot drinks (and particularly

good coffee) from their offices, there are no proper cafés or shops in Okarito, so bring provisions.

Okarito Beach House & Royal Hostel The Strand ☎ 03 753 4080, ⓦ okaritobeachhouse.com. This huddle of buildings is Okarito's cosiest spot to stay, with comfy en-suite doubles and the "hutel" – a self-contained cottage – all decorated in beach-inspired style. Doubles $85, "hutel" $120

Okarito Community Campground Russell Street. This grassy beachside campsite has a day-shelter, coin-operated hot showers, and fire pits – perfect for driftwood campfires $12.50

The School House The Strand ☎ 03 752 0796, ⓦ doc .govt.nz. A memorial commemorating Okarito's settlers stands opposite this DOC-managed 1901 former schoolhouse. It sleeps up to 12 in single bunks (bring your own linen), and you'll need to book the entire place out to stay. There's a toilet and full kitchen, but you'll need to head to the campsite for showers. Closed June–Aug. $100

The glaciers

Around 150km south of Hokitika, two white rivers of ice force their way down to the thick rainforest of the coastal plain – ample justification for the region's inclusion in **Te Wahipounamu**, the South West New Zealand World Heritage Area. The glaciers form a palpable connection between the coast and the highest peaks of the Southern Alps. Within a handful of kilometres the terrain drops from over 3000m to near sea level, bringing with it **Franz Josef Glacier** and **Fox Glacier**, two of the largest and most impressive of the sixty-odd glaciers that creak off the South Island's icy spine, together forming the centrepiece of the rugged **Westland National Park**. Legend tells of the beautiful Hinehukatere who so loved the mountains that she encouraged her lover, Tawe, to climb alongside her. He fell to his death and Hinehukatere cried so copiously that her tears formed the glaciers, with Franz Josef known to Maori as Ka Riomata o Hinehukatere – "The Tears of the Avalanche Girl".

The area is also characterized by the West Coast's prodigious **precipitation**, with upwards of 5m being the typical yearly dump. These conditions, combined with the rakish angle of the western slopes of the Southern Alps, produce some of the world's fastest-moving glaciers; stand at the foot for half an hour or so and you're bound to see a piece peel off. But these phenomenal speeds haven't been enough to counteract melting, and both glaciers have receded several kilometres since Cook saw them at their greatest recent extent, towards the end of the Little Ice Age. Glaciers are receding

GLACIERS EXPLAINED

The existence of a **glacier** is a balancing act between competing forces: snowfall at the **névé**, high in the mountains, battles with rapid melting at the **terminal** lower down the valley, the victor determining whether the glacier will advance or retreat. Snowfall, metres thick, gradually compacts to form clear **blue ice**, accumulating until it starts to flow downhill under its own weight. Friction against the valley walls slows the sides while ice in the centre slips down the valley, giving the characteristic scalloped effect on the surface, which is especially pronounced on such vigorous glaciers as Franz Josef and Fox. Where a riverbed steepens, the river forms a rapid: under similar conditions, glaciers break up into an **icefall**, full of towering blocks of ice known as **seracs**, separated by **crevasses**.

The glaciers' surface is mottled with **rock debris** that has fallen from the friable valley walls, though pristine blue ice still gleams from beneath its gravel mantle in places. Even more rock is swept up in the glaciers' flow below the surface, and when the glacier retreats, this is deposited as **moraine**. Occasionally retreating glaciers leave behind huge chunks of ice which, on melting, form **kettle lakes** – Lake Wombat at Franz Josef is a good example.

The most telling evidence of past glacial movements is the location of the **trim line** on the valley wall, caused by the glacier scouring vegetation from the rockface. At Fox and Franz Josef, the advance associated with the eighteenth-century **Little Ice Age** left a very visible trim-line high up the valley wall, separating mature rata from scrub.

worldwide, but the two here sometimes buck the trend by advancing from time to time, typically around five years after a particularly big snowfall in the mountains.

The glaciers were already in full retreat when travellers started to battle their way down the coast to observe these wonders of nature. They were initially named "Victoria" and "Albert" respectively but, in 1865, geologist Julius von Haast renamed Franz Josef after the Austro-Hungarian emperor, and following a visit by prime minister William Fox in 1872, the other was bestowed with his name.

Activity in the glaciers is focussed in two small **villages**, which survive almost entirely on tourist traffic. Both lie close to the base of their respective glaciers and offer excellent plane and helicopter **flights**, now often incorporated in guided **glacier walks**. With your own transport, it makes sense to base yourself in one of the two villages and explore both glaciers from there. If you have to choose one, Franz Josef has a wider range of accommodation and restaurants, while Fox is quieter.

Franz Josef Glacier

FRANZ JOSEF GLACIER (Waiau) is the slightly larger of the two glacier villages. Though the glacier is no longer visible from the edge of the village, the Southern Alps tower above and developers have done what they can to create an alpine character with steeply pitched roofs and pine panelling. It's an appealing place, and small enough to make you feel almost like a local if you stay for more than a night or two – something that's easily done, considering the beautiful surroundings.

In Franz Josef you can hike to, on or around the glacier, kayak on nearby Lake Mapourika or take a scenic flight over the mountains. While it was once possible to get up on the glacier on foot, these days the instability of the terminal ice means that most glacier walks start with a helicopter drop on firmer terrain higher up, and the glacier's airspace buzzes with activity on fine days. Options are more limited when poor weather sets in, though kayaking excursions and straightforward glacier valley walks often go ahead whatever the weather.

Glacier Hot Pools

Cron St • Daily 1–9pm; last entry 8pm • Main pools $25; private pool $85/45min for two people • ☎ 0800 044044, ⓦ glacierhotpools.co.nz

When the weather's wet, the best bet is a soak in the specially constructed **Glacier Hot Pools**. Artificially heated to 36°C, 38°C and 40°C respectively, the three public pools are covered in semi-porous canopies and surrounded by native bush, most of which has been transported to the site. Private pools come with cabana-type sheds containing showers. The pools' restorative qualities come into their own when you need to banish the aches of hiking or yomping about around the glacier; combo deals are available with Franz Josef Glacier Guides (see box, p.676).

West Coast Wildlife Centre

Corner of Cowan and Cron sts• Daily from 9am; call for seasonal closing times • $35, valid for 24hr; "backstage pass" $55 • ☏ 03 752 0600, ⊛ wildkiwi.co.nz

The enormous building that once housed the Hukawai Glacier Centre is now home to the state-of-the-art **West Coast Wildlife Centre**, where you can see New Zealand's rarest kiwis, the rowi and Haast tokoeka, as they scurry around in a dimly-lit "nocturnal house". Part of BNZ's Operation Nest Egg from approximately July to February, you'll also see chicks incubating and brooding if you stump up for the behind-the-scenes tour, which leaves at fixed times each day.

ARRIVAL AND DEPARTURE   FRANZ JOSEF

By bus InterCity and NakedBus stop on the main road in the village (SH6; known here as Main Rd). Book tickets at Scott Base or the i-SITE.

Destinations Fox Glacier (4 daily; 30min); Greymouth (1–2 daily; 3hr 30min–4hr); Haast (2 daily; 2hr 30min–3hr 30min); Hokitika (1–2 daily; 1hr 45min–2hr 30min); Makarora (2 daily; 3–5hr); Queenstown (2 daily; 6hr–8hr 30min); Wanaka (2 daily; 5hr–6hr 30min).

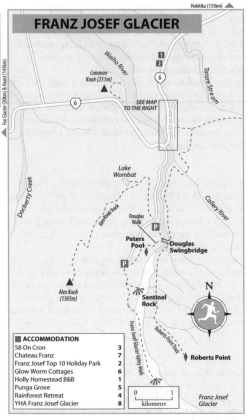

INFORMATION

Tourist information i-SITE/DOC SH6 (daily: Nov–March 8.30am–6pm; April–Oct 8.30am–5pm, closed noon–1pm Sat & Sun; ☎ 03 752 0796, ✉ westlandnpvc@doc.govt.nz). The combined office has stacks of leaflets on hikes in the area and gets daily weather reports and glacier updates; check with them before starting any serious walks.

Services There is an ATM but no banks. Get online at Scott Base on SH6 (daily 9am–6pm; $4/hr, wi-fi $4/day).

GETTING AROUND

By shuttle bus Glacier Valley Eco Tours (☎ 0800 999739, ⊕ glaciervalley.co.nz) offer a scheduled shuttle service from Scott Base to the glacier road-end (6 daily in summer; $12.50 return). Fox Bus (☎ 0800 369287) also run shuttle services on demand; the return trip to Fox Glacier costs $30.

ACCOMMODATION

With the region's popularity and a bus schedule that forces many people to overnight here, accommodation in Franz Josef is tight throughout the summer. Between November and March (and particularly February), you should aim to make **reservations** at least a week in advance, more for swankier places.

58 On Cron 58 Cron St ☎ 03 752 0627, ⊕ 58oncron .co.nz. Stylish units decorated with Italian fabrics and equipped with queen- or super-king-size beds; some rooms have spa baths. Guests have access to gas BBQs amid native bush gardens. Doubles $175, spa studios $200
Chateau Franz 8 Cron St ☎ 0800 728372, ⊕ sircedrics .co.nz. A popular backpacker-oriented complex with bags of character; common areas are festooned with old photographs and memorabilia. The dorms, among the cheapest beds in town, are slowly being upgraded; double rooms are good value too. Free soup and popcorn, fun common areas and a lively events schedule complete the package. Dorms $25, en-suite doubles $95
Franz Josef Top 10 Holiday Park SH6, 1km north of town ☎ 03 7520735, ⊕ franzjoseftop10.co.nz. High-spec rural campsite with a good range of tent and powered sites, cabins and units. Sites priced per person. Camping $44, powered sites $46
Glow Worm 27 Cron St ☎ 0800 151027, ⊕ sircedrics .co.nz. Small, homey hostel owned by the same crew as *Chateau Franz* with a well-equipped kitchen, six-bed dorms and nicer four-shares with their own bathrooms, plus comfy motel-style rooms. Free soup, popcorn and spa. Dorms $30, en-suite doubles $110
★ **Holly Homestead B&B** SH6, 1.5km north of town ☎ 03 752 0299, ⊕ hollyhomestead.co.nz. Comfort in an attractive two-storey 1920s home with five en-suite rooms, one being a super deluxe king suite (one with bathtub). The owners give a warm welcome, there's a deck with mountain views and rates include a delicious full breakfast. The caveats: it's only suitable for those 12 and over and is closed outside summer (call for seasonal openings). Doubles $265
Punga Grove 40 Cron St ☎ 03 752 0001, ⊕ pungagrove .co.nz. A choice of modern rooms ranging from nicely furnished doubles to vast two-bed apartments; the best, however, are the rainforest studios that back onto the bush and come with gas fires, underfloor heating and spa bath. $165, rainforest studios $220
Rainforest Retreat 46 Cron St ☎ 03 753 0220, ⊕ rainforestretreat.co.nz. Sprawling six-acre complex comprising a hotel, backpackers and campervan park (sites from $18 per person), plus the adjoining *Monsoon* bar and restaurant. The backpacker rooms are popular with rowdy bus tours, while the (mercifully quieter) hotel rooms are styled after luxurious log cabins. There's also a spa and sauna. Dorms $30, doubles $160
YHA Franz Josef 2 Cron St ☎ 03 752 0754, ✉ franzjosef@yha.co.nz. Modern, well-run hostel on the edge of town with the southernmost rooms overlooking bushland, where you'll hear a joyful dawn chorus. A spacious kitchen, clean comfortable rooms (some en suite), BBQ area and free sauna make it a decent choice. Dorms $27, doubles $88

EATING, DRINKING AND ENTERTAINMENT

Franz Josef's relatively remote location keeps prices high. Even if you're self-catering you can expect to pay over the odds for a limited stock of **groceries**.

Blue Ice Café Main Rd, between Cowan and Condon sts ☎ 03 752 0707. The modern and airy restaurant downstairs serves imaginative and tasty mains ($20–36) and pizzas to take away or eat in the unreconstructed upstairs bar, where the free pool table and music draw in a lively crowd most nights. Owns the village Hummerzine. Daily 8am–9pm, bar until late.
★ **King Tiger** 70 Cron St ☎ 03 752 0060, ⊕ kingtiger .co.nz. Decorated with photographs of Mahatma Gandhi and Mao Zedong, the menu (and decor) at this atmospheric "Eastern Eating House" sprawls from India to China by way

12

FRANZ JOSEF GLACIER TOURS AND ACTIVITIES

It's possible to walk to the glacier viewpoint independently, but to walk on the ice you'll need to take a guided trip. On any fine day the skies above Franz Josef are abuzz with choppers and light planes, which can make it rather noisy in the valley – kayaking trips further afield are a more tranquil experience.

WALKS

Glacier Valley Walk (6km return; 1hr 30min) This route is at the top of everyone's list of walks and starts at the car park 5km south of the village. The rough track crosses gravel beds left behind by past glacial retreats, giving you plenty of opportunity to observe small kettle lakes, the trim line high up the valley walls and a fault line cutting right across the valley (marked by deep gullies opposite each other). One of the best viewpoints is from the top of the glacier-scoured hump of Sentinel Rock, a ten-minute walk from the car park.

Douglas Walk (4km loop; 1hr) Reached from a car park halfway along the glacier access road, this circular walk passes through bush in various stages of regrowth to Peter's Pool, a serene kettle lake, and the Douglas Swingbridge.

Roberts Point Track (12km return; 5hr 30min; 950m ascent) Though closed at the time of writing, this excellent, adventurous track was expected to reopen by late 2015. One for more experienced trampers, the track leads from the Douglas Swingbridge past the Hendes Hut (a good lunch stop) to Roberts Point, high above the ice with stunning views. It's a bit of a slog and often slippery but well worth the effort.

Alex Knob Track (17km return; 8hr; 1000m ascent) Located on the other side of the glacial valley to the Roberts Point Track, this long but well-graded route climbs steadily above the glacier through several vegetation zones and offers more fine valley views; though long, it's less technical than the Roberts Point Track.

12

HIKING, HELI-HIKING AND ICE CLIMBING

Glacier Valley Eco Tours ☎0800 999739, ⓦglaciervalley.co.nz. Runs a series of very informative nature tours that will see you hiking through the glacier valleys at Franz Josef and Fox (both 3hrs; $75), climbing up onto the moraine, and exploring the glacier terminals. They also organise guided trips to Lake Matheson (3hr; $75) and a Lake Matheson-Fox glacier combo (5hr; $120).

Franz Josef Glacier Guides SH6 ☎0800 484337, ⓦfranzjosefglacier.com. This is the place to come if you want to get up onto the glacier itself – although the experience comes at a price. Their most popular trip, the

of Bangkok, but the Indian dishes are the stars, with delicious and reasonably priced curries – none over $20 – making it a great change from the norm. Daily 7.30am–late.

The Landing Corner of Main Rd and Cowan St ☎03 752 0229, ⓦthelandingbar.co.nz. Popular, swish-looking café/bar, with loads of outdoor seating (replete with blankets, ranks of patio heaters and a fire pit), serving substantial mains ($19.50–45) including a decent range of vegetarian options and lighter meals such as steamed mussels in white wine. Daily 7.30am–late.

Monsoon 46 Cron St ☎0800 873346, ⓦrainforestretreat.co.nz. Convivial drinking spot at the *Rainforest Retreat* (see p.675), serving Kiwi comfort food – think stuffed chicken with roast potatoes and coleslaw – until 9pm, when the serious business of drinking takes over (its motto: "it rains, we pour"). Daily 4.30pm–late.

Picnics European Bakery Main St ☎03 752 0667. A light dusting of sugar coats everything at this slightly chaotic bakery, though sinful piles of doughnuts ($4) and pies are ample compensation for any crunching underfoot. Daily 7.30am–5pm.

Fox Glacier

The village of **FOX GLACIER** (Weheka), 24km south of Franz Josef, is scattered over an outwash plain of the Fox and Cook rivers, and services the local farming community and passing sightseers. Everything of interest is beside SH6 or Cook Flat Road, which skirts the scenic Lake Matheson on the way to the former gold settlement and seal colony at Gillespies Beach. The foot of the glacier itself is around 6km to the southeast.

"Ice Explorer" (4hr; $325), starts with a quick helicopter ride to the upper part of the glacier, where you will spend up to three hours exploring the icefield – hopefully finding tunnels to explore, deep blue crevices into which to stare and a general sense of wonder and otherworldliness – rounded off by a return flight and a soak at the hot pools. They also offer heli-hiking (3 daily; 3hr; $429) trips, with a longer scenic flight and a gentler walk, as well as adventurous heli-ice climbing tours (5hr; $499).

SCENIC FLIGHTS AND SKYDIVING

Safety demands that specific flight paths must be followed, limiting what can be offered and forcing companies to compete on price; ask for youth, student, YHA, BBH, senior or just-for-the-sake-of-it discounts, most readily given if you can band together in a group of four to six and present yourselves as a ready-to-go plane or chopper load. Most people go by helicopter, with all operators regularly landing on a snowfield high above the glacier where the rotors are left running – hardly serene. Planes give you a longer flight with greater range for less money while a ski-plane landing on a snowfield is very rewarding, particularly the silence after they switch the engine off.

Air Safaris 6 Main Rd ☎0800 723274, ☻airsafaris .co.nz. For a slightly quieter experience than that offered by the helicopter operations around town, take a flight in one of Air Safari's turbo-prop flightseeing planes. Note that they don't do landings. Try their Grand Traverse (50min; $340).

Fox & Franz Josef Heliservices Alpine Adventure Centre Main Rd ☎0800 800793, ☻scenic-flights .co.nz. The cheapest operator hereabouts, offering one glacier and landing (20min; $195), two glaciers and landing (30min; $280), and two glaciers, landing and Mount Cook plus a quick nip across the main divide to see the Tasman Glacier (40min; $390).

Skydive Franz Scott Base Main Rd ☎0800 458677, ☻skydivefranz.co.nz. For the ultimate aerial adventure, book a tandem skydive – this is one of the few places in New Zealand where commercial tandem jumps from 19,000ft are permitted ($559); though lower drops are also available (13,000ft $319; 16,000ft $419).

KAYAKING

Glacier Country 46 Cron St ☎0800 423262, ☻glacierkayaks.com. Offers marvellous guided kayaking trips on the black waters of the kahikatea- and flax-fringed Lake Mapourika, 8km north of town (shuttle included). The most popular "Classic" trip (3 daily; 3hrs; $115) is best in the calm of the morning, with loads of photo opportunities in sun and/or rain. Deals are available if you wish to combine kayaking with a heli-hike or skydive.

ARRIVAL AND INFORMATION   FOX GLACIER

By bus InterCity and NakedBus buses stop by Fox Glacier Guides in the centre of the village.

Destinations Franz Josef (4 daily; 30min); Greymouth (1–2 daily; 4hr); Haast (2 daily; 2hr 30min); Hokitika (1–2 daily; 3hr); Makarora (daily; 4hr); Nelson (1–2 daily; 11hr); Queenstown (2 daily; 7hr 30min); Wanaka (2 daily; 5–6hr).

Tourist information DOC, SH6 (Mon–Fri 10am–2pm; ☎03 751 0807, ☻foxglacier@doc.govt.nz). The office has displays concentrating on lowland forests and glaciation; visit to get advice on conditions around the glacier valley.

GETTING AROUND

By shuttle bus Fox Glacier Shuttles & Tours (☎0800 369287) goes to the glacier ($15 return) and Lake Matheson ($18 return). They also go to Gillespies Beach (price on demand, depending on numbers) and Franz Josef for a very reasonable $30 return.

ACCOMMODATION

Fox's range of places to stay is limited; **book** as far ahead as you can and be prepared for resort prices. The basic, free DOC **campsite** at Gillespies Beach (see box, p.679) is popular in summer.

Fox Glacier Lodge Sullivan Rd ☎0800 369800, ☻foxglacierlodge.com. A pine-lined alpine chalet with attractively furnished en-suite rooms (where a buffet breakfast is included), a range of self-contained apartments and campervan hook-ups outside. Powered sites $20, doubles $185

Fox Glacier Top 10 Holiday Park Kerrs Rd ☎03 751 0821, ☻top10.co.nz. Comprehensive motor camp with

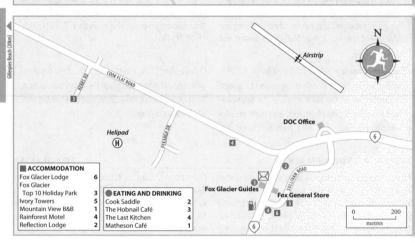

FOX GLACIER

12

ACCOMMODATION
Fox Glacier Lodge	6
Fox Glacier	
Top 10 Holiday Park	3
Ivory Towers	5
Mountain View B&B	1
Rainforest Motel	4
Reflection Lodge	2

● EATING AND DRINKING
Cook Saddle	2
The Hobnail Café	3
The Last Kitchen	4
Matheson Café	1

ranks of powered sites, spacious studio units, and great mountain views. Powered sites $45 (per vehicle), studio units $105

Ivory Towers Sullivan Rd ☎03 751 0838, ⓦivorytowerslodge.co.nz. Fox's most established backpackers is friendly, clean(ish) and colourfully decorated. Most dorms have both beds and bunks, while the pleasant doubles share the bathrooms. The kitchen has plenty of elbow room, there's a sauna, spa bath and a TV room for those rainy afternoons, plus bikes to rent. Dorms $27, doubles $74

Mountain View B&B 1 Williams Drive, 2km off SH6 ☎03 751 0770, ⓦfoxglaciermountainview.co.nz.

Welcoming, modern B&B with three en suites and a separate self-contained cottage in its own grounds on the edge of town with great mountain views. The decor is slightly dated, but rooms and beds are very comfortable, and a full breakfast is included. Doubles $180

Rainforest Motel 15 Cook Flat Rd, 200m off SH6 ☎03 751 0140, ⓦrainforestmotel.co.nz. Log cabins with attractive and well-priced studios and one-bedroom units, all with kitchens and plenty of space. Studios $130, units $145

Reflection Lodge 141 Cook Flat Rd, 1.5km off SH6 ☎03 751 0707, ⓦreflectionlodge.co.nz. So named

FOX GLACIER TOURS AND ACTIVITIES

Fox Glacier suffered from major ice collapses in 2014, which saw several ice-based tours suspended indefinitely – the best way to get onto the ice these days is to fly. The Fox Glacier airfield and helipads are quieter than those at Franz Josef, but a similar range of flights is on offer; Mount Cook is closer here, meaning that flights over the mountain here are shorter, and slightly cheaper.

WALKS

Don't miss the Fox Glacier just because you've already seen Franz Josef; the approaches are different and their characters distinct, the Fox Valley being less sheer but with more impressive rockfalls. Check the DOC's *Glacier Update* (posted at Fox Glacier Guides and the DOC office) before heading up the valley to check that the roads and trails around the glacier are open.

Te Weheka Walkway/Cycleway While drivers speed up the imaginatively named Glacier Access Road, it's possible for energetic types to walk or bike between the village and glacier; a broad gravel path connects the two, winding through dripping rainforest for 4km before joining the road for the last stretch, which is occasionally rerouted as "dead" ice under the roadway gradually melts.

Minnehaha Walk (1km; 20min loop) Branching off from Te Weheka Walkway is this short flat path through lush bush that's alive with glowworms after dark.

Fox Glacier Valley Walk The walk to the edge of the glacier begins from the car park at the end of Glacier Access Road. The rough 1.3km path leads over a series of landslips and creeks before climbing steeply up to a viewpoint with great views over the glacier's icy snout.

River Walk (2km; 30min) Halfway along the Glacier Access Road, this walk crosses a historic swingbridge to the Glacier Valley Viewpoint on Glacier View Road, which runs 3km along the opposite side of the Fox River.

Chalet Lookout Walk (4km; 1hr 30min return; 150m ascent) From the Glacier Valley Viewpoint, this route climbs relatively moderately for stupendous glacier and mountain views, passing the former site of The Chalet, a hut where Victorian tourists could lunch looking down at the terminal ice – sadly, both the hut and the ice below are no more. The path ends with an unbridged crossing of Mills Creek, which often floods the track after heavy rainfall, periodically closing it.

Lake Matheson Circuit (4.5km; 1hr 30min). It's difficult to imagine a New Zealand calendar or picture book without a photo of Mount Cook and Mount Tasman mirrored in Lake Matheson, 5km northwest of town along Cook Flat Road. A well-signposted boardwalk through lovely native bush encircles the lake, which was formed by an iceberg left when the Fox Glacier retreated 14,000 years ago, giving everyone a chance for that perfect image, especially those who venture out for sunrise. The *Matheson Café* (p.680), by the Lake Matheson car park, serves superb food.

Peak Viewpoint About 5km beyond Lake Matheson on the road to Gillespies Beach, Peak Viewpoint is ideal for fabulous fine-day views of the top of the Fox Glacier and the snowcapped mountains.

Walks from Gillespies Beach A 20km drive from Fox Glacier Village along Cook Flat Road brings you to Gillespies Beach, a former gold-mining settlement with a small cemetery and a simple DOC campsite. From the campsite an excellent walk threads north parallel to the beach, past the scant remains of a 1940s gold dredge (30min return), to Gillespies Lagoon (1hr 15min return), a short Miners' Tunnel (1hr 40min return) and an often muddy track continues to the Galway Beach Seal Colony (3.6km return, 3hr 30min), a winter haul-out for New Zealand fur seals.

GLACIER HIKING, HELI-HIKING AND ICE CLIMBING

Fox Glacier Guides 44 Main Rd (SH6) ☎0800 111600, ⓦfoxguides.co.nz. A smaller concern than the outfits operating on Franz Josef Glacier, Fox Glacier's recent instability meant that at the time of writing, the tours available were either gentle walks around the terminal face (2hr; $59) or full-on heli-adventures (heli-hiking, 4hr, $399; heli-ice climbing, 8–9hr, $499), flying up and over any unsafe sections.

SCENIC FLIGHTS AND SKYDIVING

Fox & Franz Josef Heliservices Inside Fox Glacier Guides ☎0800 800793, ⓦscenic-flights.co.nz. Besides similar deals to those on offer in Franz Josef (see box, p.676), here there's also the option to fly-by Mount Cook's west face (30min; $280).

Skydive NZ ☎0800 751 0080, ⓦskydivefox.co.nz. Flying out of Fox Glacier's tiny airstrip, with tandem skydives from 9000ft ($249) and 16,500ft ($399).

because of the glorious reflection of the mountains in the large garden pond, this romantic homestay offers just three pretty rooms in comfortable and spacious surroundings, plus it's run by a family of helicopter enthusiasts. **$210**

EATING AND DRINKING

Self-catering supplies are available at the Fox General Store (daily 8am–8pm) from a surprisingly wide range at unsurprisingly elevated prices.

Cook Saddle SH6 ☎ 03 751 0700, ⓦ cooksaddle.co.nz. A local favourite, this Western-inspired, all-wood saloon dishes out massive portions of good-quality food (mains $15–35) from lentil loaf to pork spare ribs, served at tealight-lit tables. There's regular live music in the summer and a pool table. Daily noon–late.

The Hobnail Café 44 Main Rd (SH6) ☎ 03 751 0825. In the alpine-chalet surroundings of Fox Glacier Guides, this café has a better-than-average selection of cabinet food, plus hearty, nicely presented breakfasts – their bubble and squeak topped with eggs and bacon ($14) is particularly good. Daily 8am–4pm.

★ **The Last Kitchen** Corner of Sullivans Rd and SH6 ☎ 03 751 0058. With an attractive interior and interesting variations of the usual suspects, often with Asian accents

– blue cod with coriander and cashew pesto with wok-fried veg ($27), for example – and a full liquor licence, this place hits the spot and has more atmosphere than most of the competition. Mains $21–33. Daily 11.30am–late.

★ **Matheson Café** Cook Flat Rd ☎ 03 751 0878, ⓦ lakematheson.com. Fantastic café/restaurant at the start of the walk around Lake Matheson, with mountain views through big picture windows. Fabulous breakfasts ($8.50–19.50) such as the salmon bagel Benedict reward an early walk, while lunches include a particularly fine lamb burger. Afternoon coffee and cake will coincide with the sun catching the mountains on fine days. Book ahead for summertime evening meals (mains $29–52) such as slow-cooked lamb shoulder with pea purée. Daily 8am–3pm, open until 9pm Nov–March.

12

South Westland and the Haast Pass

South of the glaciers, the West Coast feels even wilder. Many visitors do the run from the glaciers to Wanaka or Queenstown in a day, missing out on some fine remote country. Facilities aren't completely absent: many accommodation and eating places are clustered around **Haast**, and there's an increasing number of other pit stops along the way. There wasn't a road through here until 1965 and the final section of tarmac wasn't laid on the Haast Pass until 1995.

SH6 mostly runs inland, passing the start of the hike to the **Welcome Flat Hot Springs** (see box opposite) and through moss-clad rimu forests as far as **Knight's Point**, where it returns to the coast along the edge of the Haast Coastal Plain, whose stunning **coastal dune systems** shelter lakes and some fine stands of soaring kahikatea. The plain continues south past the scattered township of Haast to the site of the short-lived colonial settlement at **Jackson Bay**. From Haast, SH6 veers inland over the Haast Pass to the former timber town of **Makarora**, not strictly part of the West Coast but moist enough to share some of its characteristics and a base for the excellent **Gillespie Pass** Tramp.

Bruce Bay

SH6, 45km south of Fox Glacier

One place you might like to break your journey is **Bruce Bay**, where the road briefly parallels a long driftwood-strewn beach perfect for an atmospheric stroll. Recently tour bus drivers have been stopping long enough for their occupants to erect small cairns or etch their names on the rocks – though at least the former are quickly obliterated by high tide or good wind.

Paringa River and Lake Paringa

SH6, 17km south of Bruce Bay

Where SH6 crosses the **Paringa River** a plaque marks the southern limit of Thomas Brunner's 1846–48 explorations. Buses stop nearby at the *Salmon Farm* on SH6 for

> ## WELCOME FLAT HOT SPRINGS HIKE
>
> The most popular two-day hike in the region is the in-and-back jaunt to the **Welcome Flat Hot Springs**, a series of open-air pools where you're bound to find a spot that's just the right temperature for easing those bones. Almost everyone spends the night at DOC's adjacent **Welcome Flat Hut** (31 bunks; $15, camping $5; backcountry passes and hut tickets not valid); book online or at a DOC office.
>
> The track (detailed on DOC's *Copland Track to Welcome Flat Hut* leaflet) starts by a car park on SH6, 26km south of Fox Glacier; InterCity **buses** will drop off, and pick up pre-booked customers. From **SH6 to Welcome Flat** (18km; 7hr one way; 450m ascent) is a fairly tough tramp – following a clear path in places, orange triangles elsewhere – tracing the true right bank of the Copland River all the way to Welcome Flat, crossing numerous creeks by hopping from rock to rock or wading. If the creeks are high, as they commonly are, you may have to use the flood bridges, adding an hour or so – although it's recommended that you abandon the tramp if the first stream, Rough Creek, is too high to ford, as the river often floods the trail beyond after heavy rain.

an overpriced snack or lunch. A better bet is to pick up some delicious hot or cold smoked salmon to take away and continue 8km south to the northern shores of trout-filled **Lake Paringa** and DOC's simple but beautifully sited *Lake Paringa campsite* ($6).

The Monro Beach Walk
SH6, 19km south of Lake Paringa • 5km; 1hr 30min return

The **Monro Beach Walk** leads through lovely fern-filled forest to a rocky spot of shoreline where you might see rare **Fiordland crested penguins**, particularly in early morning and late afternoon. They're mainly around during the spring breeding season, but occasionally reappear between January and March, when they come ashore to moult – though even in the absence of penguins the scenery and serenity justify taking the walk.

Knight's Point and Ship Creek
Knight's Point is on SH6, 23km south of Lake Paringa

The highway finally returns to the coast at **Knight's Point**, where a roadside marker commemorates the linking of Westland and Otago by road in 1965. Ahead lies the **Haast Coastal Plain**, which kicks off at the tea-coloured **Ship Creek**, ten winding kilometres ahead, where a picnic area and information panels by a beautiful, long, surf-pounded beach mark the start of two lovely twenty-minute walks: the **Kahikatea Swamp Forest Walk**, a wheelchair-accessible loop upriver through swampy kahikatea (white pine) forest, and the **Dune Lake Walk** along the coast to a dune-trapped and reed-filled lake – the latter an opportunity to see how forests have gradually colonized the sandy coastal plain.

From Ship Creek it's only another 15km to the 700m-long Haast River Bridge, the longest single-lane bridge in the country, immediately before Haast Junction.

Haast

HAAST is initially a confusing place, with three tiny communities all taking the name: **Haast Junction**, at the intersection of SH6 and the minor road to Jackson Bay, **Haast Beach**, 4km along the Jackson Bay Road (see p.682), and **Haast Township**, the largest settlement, 3km along SH6 towards Haast Pass and Wanaka.

ARRIVAL AND INFORMATION   HAAST

By bus InterCity and NakedBus stop outside the *Fantail Café*, but you really need your own vehicle to get around.

Tourist information The DOC Visitor Centre is at the corner of SH6 and Jackson Bay Rd, Haast Junction (daily Nov–April 9am–6pm; May–Oct 9am–4.30pm; ☎03 750 0809, ✉haastvc@doc.govt.nz). Informative displays on all aspects of the local environment, plus the 20-minute *Edge* *of Wilderness* film (shown on demand; $3). Local information is also available at ⓦ haastnz.com.

Supplies Fuel is available in Haast Junction (24hr) and Haast Beach, and there's a small supermarket (with the only ATM) in Haast Township.

TOURS

Waiatoto River Nature Safaris Hannah's Homestead, Haast–Jackson Bay Rd ⓣ 0800 538723, ⓦ riversafaris .co.nz. Jetboat safaris (3 daily, Oct–late April; $199) comprising a 2hr wilderness ride up the Waiatoto River from its estuary into the heart of the mountains, with the emphasis on appreciating history and scenery.

Wanna Go Fishing Charters ⓣ 03 750 0134. Runs half- and full-day ($220–280/person) sea and freshwater fishing charters for a minimum of four.

ACCOMMODATION AND EATING

Haast gets busy between Christmas and late February so it pays to book ahead. Opening hours at Haast's eating establishments can vary.

Collyer House B&B Nolans Rd, Okuru, off SH6, 13km south of Haast Junction ⓣ 03 750 0022, ⓦ collyerhouse .co.nz. Welcoming luxury accommodation with four modern en suites, all with distant sea views and sizeable cooked breakfasts. Doubles $250

Fantail Café Marks Rd, Haast Township ⓣ 03 750 0055. Friendly but workaday tearoom spread across several rooms. Serves breakfasts (including bacon butties, $8), whitebait patties ($13), cakes, sandwiches and coffee. Daily 8am–4pm.

Haast Beach Holiday Park Jackson Bay Rd, Okuru, 15km south of Haast Junction ⓣ 03 750 0860, ⓦ haastpark.com. Simple holiday park close to the beach and the Hapuka Estuary Walk. Camping $15; powered sites $17 (both per person)

Hard Antler Bar Marks Rd, Haast Township ⓣ 03 750 0034. Locals' favourite, with antlers hanging from the rafters, ample bar meals (mains $20–30) including a hearty venison casserole, and $6 beers. Daily 11am–9pm.

Heritage Park Lodge Marks Rd, Haast Township ⓣ 03 750 0868, ⓦ heritageparklodge.co.nz. The pick of places to stay in the township, this well-tended motel offers spacious and comfortable studios with pure-wool blankets, some with self-catering facilities. $95

Wilderness Accommodation Haast Township ⓣ 03 750 0029, ⓦ wildernessaccommodation.co.nz. Good-value spot combining a backpacker hostel with a series of motel studio units, all with access to a plant- and board game-filled lounge and kitchen. Something of a character, the owner is knowledgeable about the area and rents scooters – ideal for getting out to Jackson Bay. Dorms $28, doubles $65

The road to Jackson Bay

A modest number of inquisitive tourists make it 50km south of Haast to the fishing village of Jackson Bay. Leaving Haast Junction, the canopies of windswept roadside trees bunch together like cauliflower heads down to and beyond **Haast Beach**, 4km south, where there's a small shop and fuel.

Hapuka Estuary Walk and around

10km from Haast Beach

Opposite the *Haast Beach Holiday Park* (see above), the **Hapuka Estuary Walk** (1km, 20min loop) follows a raised boardwalk over a brackish lagoon and through kowhai forest that gleams brilliant yellow in October and November. Sand dunes support rimu and kahikatea forest, and there are views out to the **Open Bay Islands**, once a major sealing area – it's now a **wildlife sanctuary** and breeding colony for fur seals and Fiordland crested penguins. Turn off after crossing Arawhata Bridge and follow the road for 3km to the easy one-hour return walk around **Lake Ellery**.

Jackson Bay

JACKSON BAY, 50km south of Haast on the Haast–Jackson Bay Road, is a former sealing station tucked into the curve of Jackson Head, which protects it from the worst of the westerlies. In 1875 it was chosen as the site of a town to rival Greymouth and Hokitika. Assisted migrants – Scandinavians, Germans, Poles and Italians – were expected to carve a living from tiny land allocations, with limited and irregular supplies. Sodden by rain, crops rotted, and people soon left in droves; a few stalwarts stayed, their descendants providing the core of today's residents, who eke out a meagre living from lobster and tuna fishing.

Try the **Wharekai Te Kou Walk** (1.6km, 40min return) across the low isthmus behind Jackson Head to Ocean Beach where you may see New Zealand fur seals. The **Smoothwater Track** (9.4km, 3–4hr return) traces an old settlers' track to the Smoothwater River, before following the river out to secluded Smoothwater Bay.

EATING AND DRINKING   JACKSON BAY

The Cray Pot ⊕ 03 750 0035. There are no facilities in Jackson Bay, except for this rustic diner in an old railway carriage. It doesn't sell crayfish, but it does dish up fantastic fresh-cooked fish and chips, seafood chowder and the like (mains $19–28) and mugs of tea or coffee. It's a great place to get away from the sandflies and gaze at the sea-tossed fishing boats through fake leadlight windows. Mid-Sept–April 12.30–3.30pm; seasonal openings can vary.

Haast Pass

SH6, east of Haast

From Haast it's nearly 150km over the **Haast Pass** (lower than both Arthur's Pass and Lewis Pass) to Wanaka – a journey from the rain-soaked forests of the West Coast to the parched, rolling grasslands of Central Otago. Ngai Tahu used the pass as a greenstone-trading route and probably introduced it to gold prospector Charles Cameron, the first Pakeha to cross in 1863; he was closely followed by the more influential **Julius Von Haast**, who modestly named it after himself.

The road starts beside the broad **Haast River**, which, as the road climbs, narrows to a series of churning cascades through the **Gates of Haast** – this stretch of the SH6 was closed for months in 2013 after a landslide destroyed the road, tragically sweeping two Canadian tourists and their car into the river below. Numerous short and well-signposted walks, mostly to waterfalls on tributaries, spur off at intervals. The most celebrated are the **Thunder Creek Falls**, the roadside **Fantail Falls**, and the **Blue Pools Walk**, where an aquamarine stream issues from a narrow, icy gorge; swim if you dare. Though there are few specific sights, it is a great area to linger awhile, **camping** in one of the DOC's toilets-and-water sites ($6/person): *Pleasant Flat*, 45km from Haast, or *Cameron Flat* 10km short of Makarora.

12

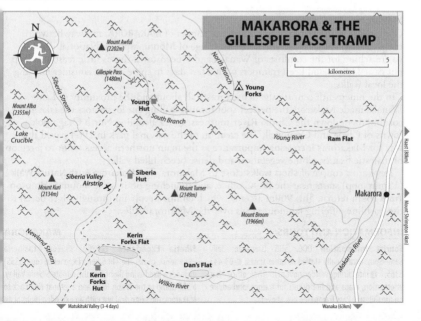

GILLESPIE PASS: THE WILKIN AND YOUNG VALLEYS CIRCUIT

This tramp over the 1501m Gillespie Pass links the upper valley of the **Young River** with that of the **Siberia Stream** and the **Wilkin River**. The scenery is a match for any of the more celebrated valleys further south, but is tramped by a fraction of the folk on the Routeburn or the Greenstone tracks.

Since a landslip dammed the north branch of the Young River in 2007, the valley has been open to trampers only on the condition that they avoid the entire river valley in the event of heavy rain, in case the potentially unstable dam gives way. Check at the DOC office if you're unsure whether to tackle it or not.

DOC's *Gillespie Pass, Wilkin Valley Tracks* leaflet ($2) has all the detail you need for the walk, though the Topo50 *Makarora* and *Mount Pollux* **maps** are useful. The route can be divided up into smaller chunks, using planes and jetboats (see below), but the full circuit (58km) takes three days – more likely four if you make the worthwhile side-trip to Lake Crucible.

ACCESS AND ACCOMMODATION

All the **huts** ($15; no advance booking) in the Wilkin and Young valleys are equipped with mattresses and heating (but not cooking) stoves; hut **tickets** and backcountry hut **passes** are available from the DOC office in Makarora (see below). The walk is typically done up the Young Valley and down the Wilkin and starts with a crossing of the braided Makarora River; if you don't fancy getting your feet wet or if you lack river-crossing experience, take a jetboat to the start (see p.685), or use the **Blue-Young Link Track**, an extension of the Blue Pools Track, which crosses the river via a swingbridge 9km north of Makarora, adding 2hr and 7km to the first day's walk.

At the other end, it's a good idea to prearrange a jetboat **pick-up** from Kerin Forks (see opposite), unless you want to take your chances with river crossings or a stand-by backflight out of Siberia Valley.

THE ROUTE

Day 1: Young and Makarora rivers confluence to Young Hut (20km; 6–7hr; 500m ascent) The Young Valley is signposted on the left of SH6, 2.5km north of Makarora. Cross the stile and follow orange poles to the confluence of the Young and Makarora rivers. Once you're across the Makarora, the track traces the true left bank of the Young River

12

Makarora

Comprising a smattering of buildings, the hamlet of **MAKARORA**, midway between Haast and Wanaka, lies on the northern fringe of Mount Aspiring National Park. If you're aching for the comforts of Wanaka and Queenstown there's little reason to stop, but casual hikers and keen trampers with a few days to spare should consider tackling the local walks.

In the nineteenth century the dense **forests** all about and the proximity of Lake Wanaka made Makarora the perfect spot for marshalling cut logs across the lake and coaxing them down the Clutha River southeast to the fledgling North Otago **gold towns** of Clyde and Cromwell. The creation of the national park in 1964 paved the way for Makarora's increasing importance as the main northern access point to a region of majestic beauty, alpine vegetation and dense beech-filled valleys.

There are a couple of **short walks** close to Makarora. The **Makarora Bush Nature Walk** (15min loop) starts near the DOC office, and branching off it is the **Mount Shrimpton Track** (6km return; 5hr; 900m ascent), which climbs steeply up through silver beech to the bushline, offering fabulous views over the Makarora Valley.

INFORMATION AND TOURS   MAKARORA

Tourist information DOC, SH6 (Dec–Feb daily 8am–5pm; occasionally staffed at other times; ☎03 443 8365, ✉mtaspiringgvc@doc.govt.nz). The office has information, maps and hut tickets for tramps, and advice on the Gillespie Pass Tramp (see box above).

Siberia Experience ☎0800 345666, ⌨siberia experience.co.nz. The 4hr Siberia Experience tour ($355) includes a fixed-wing flight into the remote Siberia Valley, a 3hr tramp to the Wilkin River and a jetboat ride back to Makarora; the same deal but with an extended flight of an

through beech forest to Young Forks, where there is a campsite (free). After the bridge, the track follows the South Branch, climbing steeply (100m), before traversing a series of unstable slips to reach Stag Creek. From here it's a steady climb up through forest to the Young Hut (20 bunks).

Day 2: Young Hut to Siberia Hut (12km; 6–8hr; 700m ascent, 1000m descent) You've another strenuous day ahead, first up to the tree line overlooked by the 2202m Mount Awful, apparently named in wonder rather than horror. Then it's over the Gillespie Pass, a steep and lengthy ascent eventually following snow poles to a saddle; it'll take four hours to reach this fabulous, barren spot with views across the snowcapped northern peaks of the Mount Aspiring National Park. Grassy slopes descend steeply to Gillespie Stream, which is followed to its confluence with the Siberia Stream, from where it's a gentle, undulating hour downstream to Siberia Hut, staffed by a warden in the summer. Keen trampers might tag on a side-trip to Lake Crucible (4–5hr return) before cantering down to the hut. You can spend two nights at Siberia Hut and do the Lake Crucible side-trip on the spare day.

Lake Crucible side-trip (14km; 6–7hr return; 500m ascent) From the Siberia Hut, follow the true left bank of the Siberia Stream a short distance until you see Crucible Stream cascading in a deep gash on the far side. Ford Siberia Stream and ascend through the bush along the path that enters the forest on the true left of Crucible Stream. It is hard going, and route-finding among the alpine meadows higher up can be difficult, but the deep alpine lake tucked under the skirts of Mount Alba and choked with small icebergs is ample reward. Planes fly in and out of the Siberia Valley airstrip, and you can take your chance on "backloading" flights out.

Day 3: Siberia Hut to Kerin Forks (7km; 2–3hr; 100m ascent) Enter the bush at the southern end of Siberia Flats on the true left bank of Siberia Stream and descend away from the stream then zigzag steeply down to the Wilkin River and the Kerin Forks Hut (10 bunks), where many trampers prearrange to be met by a jetboat. If it has rained heavily, fording the Makarora lower down will be impossible, so don't forgo the jetboat. The alternative is to walk from Kerin Forks to Makarora (15km; 4–5hr; 100m ascent, 200m descent), following the Wilkin River's true left bank, then crossing the Makarora upstream of the confluence.

12

extra 25min is $455, and there's a less energetic version (3hr 30min; $299) on offer too.

Wilkin River Jets ☎ 0800 538945, ⊚ wilkinriverjets .co.nz. Operates jetboat taxis to and from the Gillespie

Pass trailheads ($25 to the Young River Mouth, $110 from Kerin Forks, min 3 people), in addition to a range of standard jetboat trips and helicopter-hike-jetboat combos.

ACCOMMODATION AND EATING

Boundary Creek SH6. At the head of Lake Wanaka right by the lakeshore, this peaceful campsite has plenty of sheltered grass and gravel sites, along with toilets and tank water; it's basic but idyllically situated. **$6**

Makarora Tourist Centre SH6 ☎ 03 443 8372, ⊚ makarora.co.nz. Makarora's epicentre is this friendly jack-of-all-trades. The shop (daily 8am–5pm) sells fuel and

basic groceries, and there's a wood-beamed café/bar (daily 8am–late) serving breakfast, sandwiches and buffet lunches, plus basic steak, chicken and veggie evening meals (daily 5–8pm; mains $20–30). There's also camping ($12) and a range of good-value accommodation in A-frame huts. En-suite dorms **$30**, doubles **$70**

Queenstown, Wanaka and Central Otago

LAKE WAKATIPU AND PEAKS, QUEENSTOWN

13

Queenstown, Wanaka and Central Otago

Wedged between the sodden beech forests and plunging cliffs of Fiordland, the snowcapped peaks of the Southern Alps, the fertile plains of south Canterbury and the sheep country of Southland lies Queenstown, Wanaka and Central Otago, a region of matchless beauty with cold, glacier-carved lakes, barren hills and clear skies. The hub of the region is Queenstown, a flawed jewel with a legendary setting looking across Lake Wakatipu to the craggy heights of the Remarkables range. It has become New Zealand's adventure capital, offering the chance to indulge in just about every adrenaline-fuelled activity imaginable. Near neighbour Wanaka is Queenstown's more restrained cousin, draped around the placid waters of its eponymous lake. The whole region is riddled with the detritus of its nineteenth-century gold rushes, particularly in Central Otago, or "Central", as it is known to locals, the region centred around Cromwell and the big-sky landscapes of the Maniototo.

The whole region is shaped by its rivers and lakes. Meltwater and heavy rains course out of the mountains into the 70km lightning bolt of **Lake Wakatipu**, from which Queenstown and its environs get the moniker, the **Wakatipu Basin**. The lake drains east through the Kawarau River, which carves a rapids-strewn path through the Kawarau Gorge. Along the way it picks up the waters of the Shotover River from the goldfields of Skippers.

With a legendary setting looking across Lake Wakatipu to the craggy heights of **The Remarkables** range, **Queenstown** fills many roles. Bungy jumping, jetboating, rafting, skydiving, mountain biking, paragliding and many more activities have been honed into well-packaged, forcefully marketed products. But you don't need to do any of that. Many are happy to relax along the waterfront and dine at the best cafés and restaurants around. Film-makers have flocked here over the years to shoot major features: *The Lion, the Witch and the Wardrobe*, the *Lord of the Rings* trilogy and, more recently, *The Hobbit*.

OTAGO CENTRAL RAIL TRAIL

Highlights

❶ Nevis Bungy Test your nerve on the Nevis, at 134m New Zealand's highest bungy, done from a hut suspended high above a canyon. **See p.699**

❷ Shotover River Take a jetboat ride or rafting trip down through an iconic part of the New Zealand adventure landscape. **See p.700 & p.702**

❸ Ride Queenstown Pootle beside the lake as the sun drops, hurtle through the forest at Queenstown Bike Park or splash out on a wonderful heli-biking trip. **See p.701**

❹ The Routeburn Track Lush bush and alpine scenery combine to make this one of New

Zealand's best tramps. **See p.715**

❺ Wineries Over twenty Central Otago wineries offer tastings, particularly of sublime Pinot Noir, in the world's most southerly wine-growing area. **See p.727 & p.741**

❻ Canyoning Get intimate with one of the Matukituki Valley's verdant canyons, jumping, sliding and abseiling – about the most fun you can have in a wetsuit. **See p.734**

❼ Otago Central Rail Trail Absorb the rural pleasures of the Maniototo region on a gentle three-day cycle ride, taking in old tunnels and viaducts. **See p.743**

HIGHLIGHTS ARE MARKED ON THE MAP ON P.690

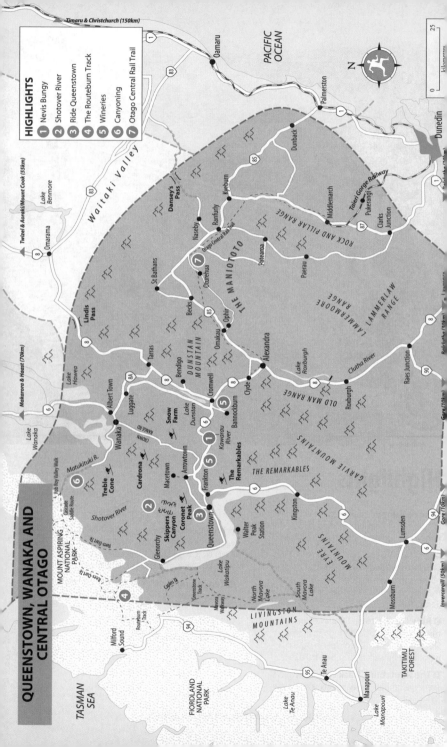

QUEENSTOWN, WANAKA AND CENTRAL OTAGO

HIGHLIGHTS

1. Nevis Bungy
2. Shotover River
3. Ride Queenstown
4. The Routeburn Track
5. Wineries
6. Canyoning
7. Otago Central Rail Trail

Timaru & Christchurch (150km)

Twizel & Aoraki/Mount Cook (55km)

Makarora & Haast (70km)

PACIFIC OCEAN

Oamaru

Dunback

Palmerston

Dunedin

To Fairlie (150km)

Waitaki Valley

Lake Benmore

Omarama

Lake Hawea

Lindis Pass

Tarras

St Bathans

Dansey's Pass

Naseby

Ranfurly

Kyeburn

Middlemarch

Taieri Gorge Railway

Pukerangi

Clarks Junction

ROCK AND PILLAR RANGE

Ourehua

Otago Central Rail Trail

Becks

Ophir

THE MANIOTOTO

Paerau

Patearoa

LAMMERLAW RANGE

LAMMERMOORE RANGE

Omakau

Alexandra

Clyde

Lake Roxburgh

OLD MAN RANGE

Clutha River

Roxburgh

Raes Junction

Balclutha (70km)

Lawrence

Gore (105km)

Gore (106km)

DUNSTAN MOUNTAIN

Bendigo

Cromwell

Lake Dunstan

Bannockburn

Kawarau River

Snow Farm

Albert Town

Luggate

Wanaka

CROWN RANGE RD

Cardrona

Treble Cone

Matukituki R.

Rob Roy Valley Walk

Cascade Saddle Route

MOUNT ASPIRING NATIONAL PARK

Rees-Dart Tk

Glenorchy

Routeburn Track

Greenstone Track

Caples Tk

Lake Wakatipu

Rees Dart Tk

Milford Sound

FIORDLAND NATIONAL PARK

Te Anau

Lake Te Anau

Lake Manapouri

Manapouri

Invercargill (150km)

TAKITIMU FOREST

Mossburn

Lumsden

EYRE MOUNTAINS

North Mavora Lake

South Mavora Lake

Mavora Walkway

LIVINGSTON MOUNTAINS

TASMAN SEA

Maetown

Arrowtown

Frankton

Skippers Canyon

Coronet Peak

Queenstown

The Remarkables

THE REMARKABLES

GARVIE MOUNTAINS

Kingston

Walter Peak Station

N

0 — 25 kilometres

Neighbouring **Arrowtown** wears its gold heritage well. There is something to delay most folk amid quaint streets, intimate restaurants, cool bars, indie cinema, historic Chinese gold settlements and day-long rides to the defunct gold mines around **Macetown**. All this provides a welcome break from Queenstown's high-pitched ambience but perhaps the perfect antidote is the great outdoors. Some of the country's most exalted multi-day tramps start from nearby **Glenorchy**, springboard for the magnificent **Routeburn Track**, the match of any in the country; the green and beautiful **Caples and Greenstone tracks** (combined to make a satisfying five-day circuit); and the rugged **Rees–Dart Track**, which opens up the challenging Cascade Saddle Route.

Glacially scoured, the three-sided pinnacle of Mount Aspiring, "the Matterhorn of the South", forms the centrepiece of the **Mount Aspiring National Park**. Permanently snowcapped, this alpine high country is linked by the alluring Matukituki Valley to the small resort town of **Wanaka** on the shores of **Lake Wanaka**. The town's laidback atmosphere stands in marked contrast to frenetic Queenstown, though there's no shortage of adventure operators vying to thrill you.

Lake Wanaka and Lake Wakatipu both ultimately feed the Clutha River which threads its way to the coast south of Dunedin passing through land transformed by New Zealand's first gold rushes. Numerous interesting relics remain around the modest centres of **Cromwell, Alexandra** and **Roxburgh**. Gold-miners fanned out to found tiny towns in the Maniototo: **St Bathans** and **Naseby** are particularly enjoyable places to idle among the boom-time remains.

From June to October the region's focus switches to **skiing**, with Queenstown acting as a base for the downhill resorts of **Coronet Peak** and the **Remarkables**, while Wanaka serves the **Cardrona** and **Treble Cone** fields, as well as the **Snow Farm** Nordic field.

Brief history

Early Maori certainly occupied Central Otago but numbers were small by the time Europeans first came to buy land for grazing in the 1830s. There was increased Pakeha interest in the area after the settlement of Dunedin in 1848, but everything turned around in 1861 when an Australian, Gabriel Read, kicked off New Zealand's greatest **gold rush** by unearthing a few flakes beside the Tuapeka River, south of Lawrence. Within weeks Dunedin had all but emptied and thousands were camping out on the **Tuapeka goldfield** around **Gabriels Gully**. In 1862 Californian prospectors Horatio Hartley and Christopher Reilly teased their first specks out of the Clutha River, bagging a 40kg haul in three months. This sparked off an even greater gold rush, this time centred on **Cromwell**, which mushroomed.

Gold in the Shotover

In 1862, Thomas Arthur and Harry Redfern struck lucky at what is now Arthur's Point, on the Shotover River 5km north of Queenstown. Word spread that prospectors were extracting over 10kg a day, and within months thousands were flocking from throughout New Zealand and Australia to work what was soon dubbed "The Richest River in the World".

The mother lode resides under **Mount Aurum**, tributaries of the Shotover carrying the ore down to the goldfields. The river-edge gravels had been all but worked out by 1864, necessitating ever more sophisticated extraction techniques (see box, p.692).

As mining continued in **Skippers Canyon** gold was found in what is now **Arrowtown**, the last of the major gold towns. Within a few years returns had dwindled, and as traders saw profits diminishing, **Chinese miners** were co-opted to pick over the tailings (discarded bits of rock and gravel) left behind by Europeans.

After the gold rush

Though the boom-and-bust cycle was rapid, some form of mining continued for the best part of forty years and the profits fuelled a South Island economy, which

13

GOLD FROM DIRT

The classic image of the felt-hatted old-timer panning merrily beside a stream is a true enough depiction of the first couple of years of the Otago gold rush. Initially all a miner needed was a pick and shovel, a pan, and preferably a special wooden box known as a "rocker" for washing the alluvial gravel. As the easily accessible gravel beds were worked out, ingenious schemes were devised to gain access to fresh pay dirt. On the Shotover River, steel sheets were driven into the riverbeds to divert the river, landslides were induced to temporarily dam the flow, and a tunnel was even bored through a bluff.

When pickings got thinner miners turned to **sluicing guns** that blasted the auriferous gravel free, ready for processing either by traditional hand-panning or its mechanical equivalent, where "riffle plates" caught the fine gravel and carpet-like matting trapped the fine flakes of gold. Eventually the scale of these operations put individual miners out of business and many pressed on to fresh fields.

Larger companies began building **gold dredges**, great clanking behemoths anchored to the riverbanks but floating free on the river. Buckets scooped out the river bottom, then the dredge processed the gravel and spat the "tailings" out of the back to pile up along the riversides.

Otago's alluvial gold starts its life underground embedded in quartz reefs, and when economic returns waned, miners sought the mother lode. **Reef quartz mining** required a considerable investment in machinery and whole towns sprang up to tunnel, hack out the ore and haul it on sledges to the stamper batteries. Here, a series of water-driven (and later steam-powered) hammers would pulverize the rock, which was then passed over copper plates smeared with mercury, and onto gold-catching blankets, before the remains were washed into the berdan – a special kind of cast-iron bowl. Gold was then separated from the mercury, a process subsequently made more efficient by using cyanide.

Although returns are far from spectacular, small-time panners still extract "colour" from the streams all over the province. There's very little appliance of science: instinct counts for much and fancy mining theories not at all. Bigger capital-intensive companies occasionally gauge the area's potential, and as one mining engineer pithily put it, "There's still a shitload of gold out there".

dominated New Zealand's exchequer. Dunedin's economy boomed, and the golden bounty funded the majority of the grand civic buildings there.

Eventually many **claims were abandoned** – not for lack of gold, but because of harsh winters, famine, war, a dip in the gold price, lack of sluicing water, or just lack of interest. The miners left behind a landscape littered with abandoned mines, perilous shafts and scattered bits of mysterious-looking machinery. For decades these just rusted elegantly as sheep farming and fruit growing became the mainstays of the economy. Now they have become one of the focal points for the all-important tourist industry.

Queenstown

Queenstown is New Zealand's premier commercialized resort town, superbly set by deep-blue Lake Wakatipu and hemmed in by craggy mountains. Kiwis and visitors complain that the town is too loud, crowded, expensive, big for its boots and the victim of devil-may-care development. There's some truth in this, with the faint screams of adrenaline-activity junkies piercing the tranquillity and the base thump of music providing the backdrop, but somehow Queenstown retains the air of a small-town idyll enhanced by a great selection of restaurants and some of the flashiest accommodation in the country.

Best taken in small doses, Queenstown is well worth using either as a base from which to plan lengthy forays into the surrounding countryside, or as a venue for sampling all manner of adventure activities. The most prominent of these is

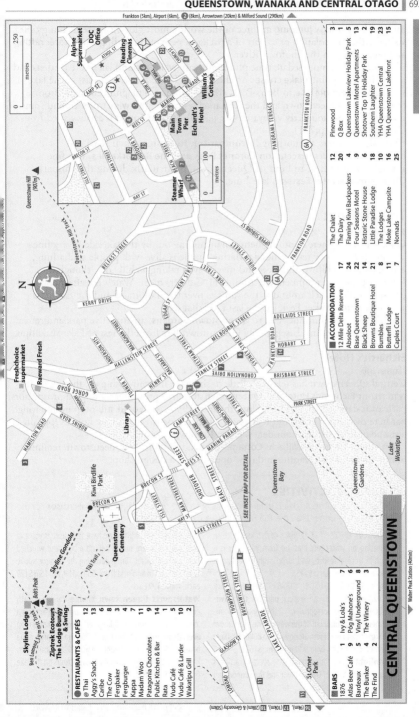

Frankton (5km), Airport (6km), 2 (8km), Arrowtown (20km) & Milford Sound (290km) ▲

● RESTAURANTS & CAFÉS

@ Thai	12
Aggy's Shack	13
Caribe	6
The Cow	8
Fergbaker	3
Fergburger	4
Kappa	7
Madam Woo	11
Patagonia Chocolates	9
Public Kitchen & Bar	14
Rata	1
Vudu Café	5
Vudu Café & Larder	10
Wakatipu Grill	2

■ ACCOMMODATION

The Chalet	17		Pinewood	3
The Dairy	24		Q Box	1
Four Seasons Motel	22		Queenstown Lakeview Holiday Park	5
Historic Stone House	14		Queenstown Motel Apartments	13
Little Paradise Lodge	21		Shotover Top 10 Holiday Park	2
The Lodges	8		Southern Laughter	19
Moke Lake Campsite	11		YHA Queenstown Central	23
Nomads	7		YHA Queenstown Lakefront	15

12 Mile Delta Reserve	17
Absoloot	24
Base Queenstown	22
Black Sheep	14
Browns Boutique Hotel	21
Bumbles	8
Butterfli Lodge	16
Caples Court	7

Flaming Kiwi Backpackers | 18
The Lodges | 10

7 BARS

1876	1	Ivy & Lola's	7
Atlas Beer Café	4	Pōg Mahone's	6
Bardeaux	5	Vinyl Underground	8
The Bunker	2	The Winery	3
The Find		

CENTRAL QUEENSTOWN

▼ Walter Peak Station (40min)

13

undoubtedly **bungy jumping** at three of the world's most gloriously scenic bungy sites, visited either in isolation or as part of a package, perhaps including **whitewater rafting** and **jetboating** on the Shotover River.

Visitors after a more sedate time plump for easy **walks** around lakeshore gardens and to hillside viewpoints; **lake cruises** on the elegant TSS *Earnslaw*, the last of the lake steamers; a **gondola ride** to Bob's Peak, which commands magnificent vistas from a cable car over Queenstown and the Remarkables range; and **wine tours** around some of the world's most southerly vineyards (see p.703). **Milford Sound** is easily visited from Queenstown (see p.771).

Frantic summers are nothing in comparison to winter, when Kiwi and international skiers descend on **Coronet Peak** and **the Remarkables**, two fine ski-fields within half an hour of Queenstown, particularly during the annual **Queenstown Winter Festival**, late June.

The lakefront

Beside Marine Parade

On a warm day there's nothing better than chilling out by the lakeside. Every fine afternoon the grassy reserve beside Marine Parade is alive with people sunbathing, eating fish and chips with a beer and maybe even taking a chilly dip, though the summer peak water temperature around 11°C deters most. Watch the afternoon parasailers, then stick around as the sun sets over the mountains and the *Earnslaw* steams towards Walter Peak for the last time that day.

Marine Parade continues east to **Queenstown Gardens**, an attractive parkland retreat that covers the peninsula separating Queenstown Bay from the rest of Lake Wakatipu.

Eichardt's Hotel

2 Marine Parade

Central Queenstown has relatively little to show for its gold-rush past, though the waterfront **Eichardt's Hotel** was Queenstown's original pub catering to gold prospectors, parts of it dating back to 1871. Until the mid-1990s you could still prop up the rough bar here over a few beers, but it is a now a super-expensive boutique hotel. Opposite is a statue of Queenstown founder, William Rees, with a ram.

Just along the street, **Williams Cottage** is the oldest house in Queenstown, retaining many original 1864 features and now operating as a design shop.

LAKESIDE ACTIVITIES

Lakeshore operators are keen to lure you onto their activities, and while several **cruises** ply the lake, none are better than the TSS *Earnslaw* (see p.697).

Flyboard ☏027 723 2964, ⊛flyboardqt.com. Levitating on water jets blasting from your feet is a laugh in tropical resorts, and surprisingly appealing in Wakatipu's 11°C waters. $115.

Hydro Attack ☏0508 493762, ⊛hydroattack .co.nz. Ride behind an expert pilot in this Kiwi-designed, 260-horsepower, shark-like semi-submersible, leaping out of the water, diving just under the surface and powering along at up to 80km/hr. Daily summer 8am–8pm, winter 9am–5pm ($169).

Paraflights Town Pier ☏0800 225520, ⊛paraflights .co.nz. Great views of Queenstown and the surrounding

mountains from 200m above Lake Wakatipu as you and your parachute are towed behind a boat and winched out on a rope. After 10min admiring the scenery, you're winched back in again, still dry. Solo $159, tandem $129 each, triple $99 each.

Watersports Queenstown Marine Parade, south end ☏027 787 9979, ⊛watersportsqueenstown .co.nz. Spend time paddling on Lake Wakatipu on everything from pedalboats ($20/20min) and aqua bikes ($15/20min) to paddleboards ($20/45min) and kayaks ($25/45min). Also guided kayak tours on the lake (half-day $139, full $249).

OPPOSITE JETBOATING ON THE SHOTOVER RIVER (P.702) >

13

Queenstown Cemetery

North of town, along Brecon St

As you make your way towards Bob's Peak, you'll pass Queenstown's **cemetery** – the final resting place of Queenstown pioneers Nicholas von Tunzelmann (who opened up the first pastoral lease in the area), hotelier Albert Eichardt and Henry Homer, discoverer of the Homer Saddle on the Milford Road.

Kiwi Birdlife Park

Brecon St, at the base of Bob's Peak • Daily: Nov–March 9am–5.30pm; March–Oct 9am–5pm; conservation show daily 11am & 3pm; kiwi feeding 10am, noon, 1.30pm & 4.30pm • $43 for two consecutive days, including audio tour; combo with Skyline gondola $69 • ☎ 03 442 8059, Ⓦ kiwibird.co.nz

Preserving New Zealand's native fauna is what drives this family-owned wildlife park, which is set among a compact knot of mixed native and exotic bush, laced with paths, ponds and lawns interspersed with walk-in aviaries and reptile houses. The focus is on breed-for-release programmes co-managed with the Department of Conservation which see some of New Zealand's rarest birds and reptiles – kiwi, whio (native blue ducks), pateke (brown teal), buff weka and Otago skinks – raised until they can look after themselves in the wild.

Be sure to time your visit around **kiwi feeding** in the nocturnal houses and the hugely entertaining thirty-minute **Conservation Shows** when kakariki (native parakeets), kereru (wood pigeons) and tuatara come out to play. If you miss one of these "Encounters" your ticket lets you return another day.

Bob's Peak

The Skyline Gondola and the Tiki Trail are both accessed from the end of Brecon St • Gondola daily 9am–9.30pm • $30 return • ☎ 03 441 0101, Ⓦ skyline.co.nz

For easy access to superb views of Queenstown, Lake Wakatipu, the Remarkables and Cecil and Walter peaks, head up to **Bob's Peak** whose conifer-clad slopes rise immediately behind the town. The sedate **Skyline Gondola** whisks you up 450m, depositing you at the Skyline Complex, base for a number of activities. In addition to those covered below, there's fantastic mountain biking in **Queenstown Bike Park** (see box, p.701).

Bob's Peak-based activities such as **bungy jumping**, **swinging** and **tandem paragliding** don't include the gondola ride in their prices. If you'd rather save money and get some exercise, follow the steep **Tiki Trail** (1hr; 450m ascent) up through the trees.

Skyline Luge

Daily 10am–dusk • Gondola plus one ride $39, two rides $42, five rides $53

Excellent fun can be had following this pair of 800m-long twisting concrete tracks (one Scenic, one Advanced) on a wheeled plastic buggy with a primitive braking system. Take it easy on your first attempt, then let rip on subsequent runs.

Ziptrek Ecotours

Tours run several times daily • 2hr Moa tour $135; 3hr Kea tour $185 • ☎ 0800 947 8735, Ⓦ ziptrek.co.nz

One way to get down from Bob's Peak is with **Ziptrek Ecotours**, a slightly odd synthesis of soft adventure – a series of zip lines (flying foxes) through the Douglas firs – combined with instruction on ecological awareness. If you're already an eco-convert then it can all seem a bit unnecessary, and if you're not then it is plain preachy. Still, zipping through the trees and learning to flip upside down is fun.

The **Moa** uses the first four lines (three of 100m and one of 300m) and finishes a short walk from the gondola top terminal. The **Kea** adds two much longer and steeper

WALKS AROUND QUEENSTOWN

When hard-sell adventure activities in Queenstown get a bit oppressive, a few hours away can be wonderfully therapeutic. The majority of the walks outlined below – listed in ascending order of difficulty – are well covered by DOC's *Wakatipu Walks* brochure (downloadable from ⓦ doc.govt.nz). Serious multi-day tramps in the region are centred on Wanaka (see p.728) and Glenorchy (see p.712).

One Mile Creek Walkway (50m ascent; 6km return; 1hr 30min). Fairly easy walk heading through a gully filled with beech forest before following a 1924 pipeline from Queenstown's first hydroelectric scheme. The route starts on the lakefront by the Fernhill roundabout and offers an opportunity to acquaint yourself with fuchsia, lancewood and native birds – principally fantails, bellbirds and tui.

Queenstown Hill Walk (500m ascent; 5km return; 2–3hr). Starting from the top of Belfast Street, this is a fairly steep climb through mostly exotic trees to panoramic views from the 907m Queenstown Hill.

Ben Lomond Summit Track (1400m ascent; 11km return; 6–8hr). A full-day tramp scaling Ben Lomond, one of the highest mountains in the region (1748m) and consequently subject to inclement weather, especially in winter when the track can be snow-covered. Start by the One Mile Creek Walk or use the Skyline Gondola and walk up past the paragliding launch site to join the track, which climbs through alpine tussock to reveal expansive views. Gentler slopes approach Ben Lomond Saddle, from where it's a steep final haul to the summit.

Ben Lomond–Moonlight Track (1400m ascent; 16km one way; 8–10hr). A demanding, difficult-to-follow route (especially in snow) combining the ascent to Ben Lomond Saddle with a poled subalpine route to the site of the former gold town of Sefferstown and the eastern section of the Moonlight Track to Arthur's Point. Organize someone to pick you up at Arthur's Point or endure a 5km slog back to Queenstown.

zip lines and finishes near the bottom terminal of the gondola. Wear closed shoes, and either walk up the Tiki Trail or pay extra for the gondola ride.

TSS Earnslaw

Steamer Wharf • Daily early July to mid-May; 1hr 30min • cruise only $55 • ☏ 0800 656 501, ⓦ realjourneys.co.nz

The coal-fired 1912 **TSS Earnslaw**, the last and largest of the lake steamers, is one of Queenstown's most enduring images. Wherever you are, the encircling mountains echo the shrill sound of the steam whistle as the beautifully restored relic slogs manfully out from Steamer Wharf.

Burnished brass and polished wood predominate even around the gleaming steam engine, which is open for inspection. Crowds usually cluster around the piano at the back of the boat for a music-hall singsong that can make the return journey a delight (or seem interminable, depending on your persuasion).

Walter Peak High Country Farm

Cruise and farm tour $75 • Cruise, farm tour and BBQ lunch $95 • Cruise, dinner and farm show $120 • Cruise and horse trekking mid-Sept–April $116 • Guided cycling Nov–April $219 • Independent cycling $70 • Mavora High Country Tour Nov–April $246

The *Earnslaw* cruises all head to **Walter Peak High Country Farm**, a tourist enclave nestling in the southwestern crook of Lake Wakatipu with various activities which can be added to your cruise.

Most people take the **farm tour** – an entertaining if sanitized vignette of farm life, with demonstrations of dog handling and sheepshearing. This comes with tea and scones on the lawn, or you can upgrade to a superb **BBQ lunch** with meats grilled to perfection in front of you (and lots of imaginative salads). The **Evening BBQ** is much the same deal with the meal followed by a sheepshearing demo.

13

IT'S RAINING. WHAT CAN WE DO?

If the weather turns foul and you don't fancy the virtual reality rides and haunted house along Shotover Street, then try these:

Alpine Aqualand 33 Joe O'Connell Drive, Frankton ☎ 03 450 9005, ⓦ sportrec.qldc.govt.nz. Indoor pool with hydroslides, lazy river etc. $8. Mon–Fri 6am–9pm, Sat & Sun 8am–8pm.

Caddyshack City 25 Brecon St ☎ 03 442 6642. Indoor minigolf. $19.50. Daily 10am–5pm or considerably later.

Onsen Hot Pools 160 Arthur's Point Rd ☎ 03 442 5707, ⓦ onsen.co.nz. Romantic, elegant artificially-heated tubs on a hillside overlooking the Shotover River. A 1hr session costs $44 each for 2 or $35 each for 4. Book ahead, and get the free shuttle from Shotover St. Daily 11am–10pm.

There's also a taste of **horse trekking** plus tea and scones; the **Mavora High Country Tour** involves a minibus trip along the gravel road to the pretty Mavora Lakes where key *LOTR* scenes were filmed; and gentle **guided cycling** around Mavora Lakes.

ARRIVAL AND DEPARTURE
QUEENSTOWN

By plane Queenstown's airport (ⓦ queenstownairport .co.nz) is at Frankton, 7km northeast of the city. As well as domestic flights you can get here from eastern Australia with Air New Zealand, Qantas, Jetstar and Virgin Australia. Most flights are met by the door-to-door Super Shuttle ($20 for one person; $26 for two). You can also get into town using the Connectabus (see below). Queenstown Taxis (☎ 03 450 3000) charge around $35 for the ride into town. Most major car rental companies have offices at the airport or nearby.

Destinations Auckland (6 daily; 1hr 50min); Christchurch (4 daily; 1hr); Wellington (2 daily; 1hr 45min).

By bus Buses arrive close to the junction of Camp and Shotover sts from where it's less than 100m to the i-SITE and barely a 15min walk to most hotels and hostels.

Bus services Atomic runs to Christchurch, Dunedin and up the coast to Greymouth; InterCity/Newmans operates the most extensive services to all major destinations;

and both Wanaka Connexions (☎ 03 443 9120, ⓦ alpineconnexions.co.nz) and Connect Wanaka (☎ 0800 405 066, ⓦ connectabus.com) go to Wanaka. The latter travels over the spectacular Crown Range. Trampers are well served by Tracknet (☎ 0800 483 262, ⓦ tracknet.net), who run fairly frequently to Te Anau, Milford Sound and the Milford Track, the Routeburn Track and Invercargill; and Info&Track (☎ 0800 462 248, ⓦ infotrack.co.nz) who serve Glenorchy, the Rees–Dart, Greenstone/Caples and Routeburn tracks.

Destinations Alexandra (4 daily; 1hr 30min); Aoraki/ Mount Cook (1 daily; 4–5hr); Arrowtown (14 daily; 30–40min); Christchurch (3–4 daily; 7–8hr); Cromwell (8 daily; 1hr); Dunedin (4 daily; 4–5hr); Franz Josef Glacier (2 daily; 7–8hr); Glenorchy (2–5 daily; 1hr); Greymouth (1 daily; 9hr); Invercargill (1 daily; 3hr); Te Anau (3 daily; 2hr 15min); Tekapo (3–4 daily; 3–4hr); Wanaka (9 daily; 1hr 30min).

GETTING AROUND

Everywhere you are likely to want to go in central Queenstown can be reached **on foot**. Most activities take place out of town but operators run courtesy buses to the sites, usually picking up centrally or from accommodation en route.

By bus Connectabus (☎ 03 441 4471, ⓦ connectabus .com) operates from O'Connells Mall on Camp St. The most useful service goes from Queenstown to Frankton (every 15–20min) and on to the airport. From Frankton there's a service to Arrowtown (roughly hourly), though there's also a direct service from Queenstown to Arrowtown via Arthur's Point (7 daily). One-way fares from Queenstown are: airport ($10), Arrowtown ($13), and an all-day-pass ($29) and seven-day pass ($43) can be bought on board.

By car Parking can be tight in the centre of town, though you'll usually find a free all-day spot a few streets away. Numerous car rental companies around

town and at the airport offer good deals: look for advertised rates.

By taxi There are taxi ranks on Camp St, at the top end of the Mall, and on Shotover St. Alternatively, book with Blue Bubble Taxis (☎ 03 450 3000).

By bike One of the best ways to explore the area is by bike. The massive range of opportunities is listed in the box on p.701.

By Segway A great way to get your bearings and have a little fun is to take one of the tours run by Segway on Q (☎ 0800 734 386, ⓦ segwayonq.co.nz) who cover a lot of ground on their 1hr tour ($85), and throw in a few more anecdotes and history for their 2hr jaunt ($119).

BUNGY JUMPING AND SWINGING

Even visitors who had no intention of parting with a large wad of cash to dangle on the end of a thick latex strand find themselves **bungy jumping** in Queenstown: magnificent scenery and zealous promotion get to most people. The sport's commercial originator, **AJ Hackett**, runs all three local jumps and adds in **swinging**. This presents an alternative to bungy jumping but still includes that stomach-in-your-mouth freefall sensation, with the bonus of a massive swoop through the air on the end of a rope. Bragging T-shirts and swing caps are included and your fifteen minutes of hair-raising fame will be recorded in all manner of formats ($45 for photos or $80 to add video).

The Ledge Bungy + Swing AJ Hackett ☎ 0800 286 495, ⊚ bungy.co.nz. Launching yourself off a 47m bungy platform in the pines near the top of the Skyline Gondola feels like you are diving out over Queenstown. A body harness allows you to do a running jump, and if they aren't too busy you may be able to jump with all manner of "toys" (surfboards, bikes and the like) to add that extra dimension. The same site hosts the Ledge Swing. Walk the Tiki Trail to the site (free) or pay for the Skyline Gondola. The opening hours allow for night jumps and swings in winter. Generally summer 1–7pm; winter 4–9pm. Bungy $195; swing $160.

Kawarau Bungy + Zipride AJ Hackett ☎ 0800 286 495, ⊚ bungy.co.nz. It may only be a modest 43m but this is the original commercial bungy site (see p.726) and the only place around Queenstown where you can do a water touch. They also operate a Zipride. Either call in on your way along SH6 or get one of the frequent buses out from Queenstown (a 2hr 30min round trip) at no extra cost. Bungy $195.

The Nevis Bungy + Swing AJ Hackett ☎ 0800 286 495 ⊚ bungy.co.nz. Some say that with bungy jumping it is only the first metre that counts, but size does matter and the Nevis is New Zealand's highest, a massive 134m with eight seconds of freefall. Jumpers launch from a partly glass-bottomed gondola strung way out over the Nevis River, a tributary of the Kawarau 32km east of Queenstown. Access is via private property so spectators have to fork out $50, though this does give you a ride out to the launch gondola and a wonderful view. The adjacent Nevis Swing carves a 300m arc. Several Queenstown departures (daily 8.40am–3.20pm) visit the Nevis site: allow a 4hr round trip. Bungy $275; swing $195; swing and bungy combo $375.

Shotover Canyon Swing 37 Shotover St ☎ 0800 279 464, ⊚ canyonswing.co.nz. A direct competitor to AJ Hackett's smaller or more distant swings, with a total of 60m fall in a huge (109m radius) sweeping arc over the Shotover River and the chance to impress the rafters below. Launch yourself forwards, backwards, seated in a chair or sixty other ways, even with a bin over your head. One spectator comes free and you'll only need to set aside 2hr. 3–10 departures daily; $215, second swing $35.

INFORMATION

i-SITE Corner of Camp and Shotover sts (daily 8.30am–7pm ☎ 03 442 4100, ⊚ queenstowninformation.co.nz). There are numerous visitor-centre-cum-booking offices along Shotover St, all with products to push, but only the i-SITE offers impartial advice and bookings for just about everything.

DOC 50 Stanley St (daily: Nov–April 8.30am–5.30pm; May–Oct 8.30am–4.30pm; ☎ 03 442 7935, ⊚ queenstownvc@doc.govt.nz). The place to go for all tramping, Great Walks and National Park information.

Left luggage Queenstown airport has luggage lockers ($6 for each 24hr period).

TOURS AND ACTIVITIES

There can be few places in the world with such an amazing choice of things to do. Top of many people's lists is bungy jumping (see box above) or getting wet in the Shotover and Kawarau rivers (see box, p.700). A massive range of biking options is covered in the box on p.701 and the rest of the tours and activities are covered below. Then again, you could simply go for a walk (see box, p.697) and in winter head for the slopes (see box, p.704.).

With so much on offer, it's tempting to be frugal elsewhere and blow the budget in Queenstown, but in reality most activities here are more expensive than in other parts of the country. To get the most action for the least money, check out one of the numerous **combo deals** such as the Awesome Foursome ($655), combining the 134m Nevis Bungy, the Shotover Jet, a helicopter flight and rafting the Shotover.

BALLOONING

Sunrise Balloons ☎ 0800 468 247, ⊚ ballooningnz.com.

Gorgeous daybreak flights climbing as high as 2000m to gawp at the stunning mountain before landing for

13

RAFTING, RIVER SURFING AND WHITEWATER SLEDGING

Some of the most thrilling activities around Queenstown take place on or in the water – sometimes a bit of both. Only the gentler Family Adventures gives you much chance of a dry run.

While rafters bob around high on their inflatable perches, **river surfers** and sledgers get right in the thick of it in a wetsuit, a helmet and fins, being encouraged to view their independence and freedom of movement as virtues rather than hazards. What look like ripples to rafters become huge waves: things work best if you are both confident in water and a decent swimmer. There isn't a lot to choose between river surfing (using a foam boogie board and surfing as many of the rapids' standing waves as possible), and **whitewater sledging** (where you snuggle your arms and upper body into a plastic "sledge", gaining manoeuvrability in return for more difficulty surfing waves. Indeed one company now runs both activities.

THE RIVERS

Rafting action mostly takes place on the **Shotover River** (Grade III–IV) with rapids revelling in names such as The Squeeze, The Anvil and The Toilet. They reach their apotheosis in the demanding Mother-in-Law rapid, usually bypassed at low water by diverting through the 170m Oxenbridge Tunnel (see p.709). The 14km rafted section flows straight out of the mountains and its level fluctuates considerably. In October and November, snowmelt ensures good flows and a bumpy ride; by late summer low flows can make it a bit tame for hardened rafters, though it is still scenic and fun for first-timers. The upper reaches of the Shotover are much tamer (Grade I–II), ideal for family rafting.

The Shotover flows into the larger **Kawarau River** (Grade II–III). Rafters run the 7km "Dog Leg" section negotiating four rapids (exciting but not truly frightening), ending with the potentially nasty Chinese Dog Leg, said to be the longest commercially rafted rapid in New Zealand. **River surfers** and **whitewater sledgers** run a swirling 5km lower section of the Kawarau downstream from the little Roaring Meg power station (Grade II–III). A few times a year there are also rafting trips on the remote, fly-in **Landsborough River** (Grade III).

Queenstown Rafting 35 Shotover St ☎ 0800 723 8464, ⓦ rafting.co.nz. Although there appear to be three whitewater-rafting companies in town, all rafts are in fact operated by Queenstown Rafting, who run the Shotover either driving in along the Skippers Road (half-day; $209), or more quickly by chopper ($309). In winter it is too cold for most people and all runs are shorter heli-access trips. They also run the Kawarau (half-day; $209, or $309 with heli-access), and one or twice a month in summer run the Landsborough (3 days; $1695), a fly-in, raft-out wilderness trip with camping beside the river – it's more about the whole experience than the whitewater.

Family Adventures ☎ 0800 472 384, ⓦ familyadventures.co.nz. A dramatic drive into Skippers Canyon is followed by an hour and a half floating in rafts down the mostly calm (Grade I–II) waters of the upper Shotover River past gold-mining relics. Great for kids but equally enjoyable for those without. You don't even need to paddle. Daily Oct–April; 5hr total; adults $179; kids (ages 3–17) $120.

Frogz Whitewater Sledging ☎ 0800 737 468, ⓦ frogz.co.nz. Whitewater sledging making two runs down the Roaring Meg section of the Kawarau. Run from Queenstown, though Wanaka sledgers can meet at the put-in. Daily Sept–May; 5hr with 2hr on the water; $215.

Serious Fun River Surfing ☎ 0800 737 468, ⓦ riversurfing.co.nz. River levels determine whether you run the Dog Leg or two runs down the Roaring Meg section of the Kawarau River. Either way, the 4hr trips give around 2hr on the water. Daily Sept–May. Kids 8–11 inclusive get a "private guide". $215.

champagne and pastries (3–4hr including around 1hr flight time; July to mid-May daily, weather permitting; $475). Queenstown and Arrowtown pick-ups.

CANYONING

Alta 8 Duke St ☎ 03 442 4994, ⓦ alta.co.nz. High-end bike hire offering hardtails (half-day $29, full-day $49), freeride ($69/$109) and downhill ($89/$139) models.

Around the Basin Bike Tours ☎ 0508 782 9253, ⓦ aroundthebasin.co.nz. Rents hardtail bikes for $55 a day if you also use their drop-off and pick-up bike shuttle service to points along the Queenstown Trails. Great for one-way rides, say from Queenstown to Arrowtown or Arrowtown to Gibbston (both $35 for 1, $60 for 2). Also family packages with a support vehicle and guided rides.

Canyoning Queenstown 39 Camp St ☎ 03 441 3003, ⓦ canyoning.co.nz. Swim across pools, slide down rocks and jump off cliffs in narrow canyons , protected only by a wetsuit, helmet and climbing harness. Queenstown Adventurer (Oct–April 1–2 daily; 3–4hr; $195) explores Twelve Mile Delta just out of town. For a bit more commitment, go for the Routeburn Explorer (Oct–April 1 daily; 7hr; $275) which involves walking the first twenty minutes of the Routeburn Track then launching yourself into a water-sculpted, narrow canyon full of jumps and slides. Also offers even more intense trips and heli-canyoning.

BIKING THE WAKATIPU BASIN

Queenstown is now a fully-fledged cycling hotspot with everything from gentle rides along smooth lakeside paths and supreme cross-country single-track to gondola-assisted downhill mayhem and glorious guided heli-biking. All the bike shops in Queenstown (and a couple more in Arrowtown) are staffed by keen riders who will point to the best the region has to offer. Everything comes together over Easter when the town hosts the ten-day **Queenstown Bike Festival** (Ⓦqueenstownbikefestival.com).

QUEENSTOWN TRAIL

The Queenstown Trail (Ⓦqueenstowntrail.co.nz) is a network of over 110km of easy-riding trails linking Queenstown and Lake Wakatipu with Frankton, Arrowtown and Gibbston; free maps are widely available and routes are marked on the *Around Queenstown* map (p.710). Principally designed to get riders around the area while avoiding roads, the trails are mostly broad gravel and fairly flat or gently undulating, though there is the odd steep hill. From Queenstown, the lakeshore is the obvious starting point, with a slightly more adventurous extension to Jack's Point. From Arrowtown, thread your way along the Arrow River, past the Kawarau Bungy site and into the vineyards around Gibbston. If the riding or the wine samples undermine your pedalling ability you can even phone for a lift home with *Around the Basin* or *QBT*.

QUEENSTOWN BIKE PARK

Ride up the 4WD road if you want but pretty much everyone chucks their bike on the Skyline Gondola (see p.696) for repeated downhill runs on tracks crafted by the fine folks at the Queenstown Mountain Bike Club (Ⓦqueenstownmtb.co.nz). A pricey downhill bike isn't really necessary for the relatively gentle Hammy's Track, but will be appreciated on the intermediate Vertigo and Original tracks and is essential for the remaining bulk of the park – extreme downhill black runs. Newcomers can expect 7–8 runs in half a day though the full-day record apparently stands at 41 descents.

The Skyline Gondola (closed to bikes 25 Dec–8 Jan) offers various passes from $60 for half a day.

CROSS-COUNTRY TRAILS

The Wakatipu Basin is so packed with great trails that it is hard to single out favourites. For a 4–6hr circuit, look no further than the **Moonlight Trail** which loops past Moke Lake and around the back of Ben Lomond to Arthur's Point; you'll feel like you've been on a remote adventure just a few kilometres from Queenstown.

Head up the Coronet Peak road to access a great sequence of intermediate trails, kicking off with Rude Rock and linking with Zoot, then following the narrow Pack Track right down into Skippers Canyon.

AROUND THE MOUNTAINS TRAIL

Though it won't be complete until 2016, people are already riding sections of the generally easy Around the Mountains trail (Ⓦnzcycletrail.com/around-mountains; 180km; 4–5 days), which loops south of Queenstown utilizing the TSS *Earnslaw* to cross the lake. Rent bikes in Queenstown and organize the ride yourself, or engage the services of Around the Mountains (Ⓦaroundthemountains.co.nz).

RENTALS AND TOURS

What you rent depends on where you'll be riding. Cruisers go fine on the smooth paths between Queenstown and Frankton but for most of the Queenstown Trail you'll appreciate a hardtail MTB. Cross-country trails are more comfortable on a full-suspension or freeride bike and for Queenstown Bike Park you'll be strongly encouraged to go for a high-spec downhill bike complete with full-face helmet and body armour.

13

Charge About Queenstown ☎ 0800 324 536, ⓦ chargeabout.co.nz. Tackle the Queenstown Trail on an electrically assisted bike (both half-day $79, full-day $119). A handful of recharge stations allow you to grab a coffee while the bike tops up. Rent from Alta (see p.700).

Cycle de Vine ☎ 0800 328 897, ⓦ cycledevine.co.nz. Gentle 4hr guided tours along the Queenstown Trail on retro cruisers with a little Gibbston wine tasting. $155

Fat Tyre ☎ 0800 328 897, ⓦ fat-tyre.co.nz. Guided ride specialist offering a variety of single-track mountain-biking packages with up to five hours in the saddle, including an excellent trip in the Dunstan Mountains above Cromwell (5hr; $229). Also all-day heli-rides ($549) that are scenic, challenging and great fun.

Outside Sports 9 Shotover St ☎ 03 441 0074, ⓦ outsidesports.co.nz. Major bike-rental operation with everything from hardtails (half-day $35; full day $55) through full suspension (half-day $55; full day $85) to serious downhillers (half-day $79; full day $119) and high-spec demo machines (half-day $99; full day $149).

QBT ☎ 0800245 3829, ⓦ queenstownbiketaxis.co.nz. Bike shuttle service mainly aimed at downhillers and cross-country MTBers. Kick off with their 9am and 1pm departures to Coronet Peak for the Rude Rock and Zoot combo ($60).

Rabbit Ridge 1820 SH6, Gibbston ☎ 0508 743 372, ⓦ rabbitridge.co.nz. Family-oriented bike park with 40km of trails, bike rentals and shuttles back to the top. Access is just $10 a day. Daily 9am–5pm or later.

Revolution Tours ☎ 0800 274 334, ⓦ revolutiontours .co.nz. Experience backcountry riding on a deluxe four-day three-night trip on the western side of Lake Wakatipu and up to Paradise, with short riding days, and nights in homesteads. $1685.

Torpedo 7 Corner of Camp and Shotover sts ☎ 03 409 0409, ⓦ torpedo7.co.nz/queenstown-bike-rental. Decent rental bikes at modest prices: hardtail (half-day $35; full day $55); full suspension (half-day $55; full day $79); downhill (half-day $79; full day $119). Gondola combo deals cut prices further.

Vertigo 4 Brecon St ☎ 0800 837 8446, ⓦ vertigobikes .co.nz. Downhill and cross-country experts offering bike shuttles, skills clinics, rental of quality hardtails (half-day $39, full day $59), freeride ($89/$59) and downhill bikes ($79/$119). They offer a Queenstown Bike Park intro

session ($159) with bike, half-day gondola ticket and two guided rides; plus all manner of fabulous heli-biking in the Remarkables (4hr; $399).

HORSERIDING

Ben Lomond Horse Treks ☎ 0800 236 566, ⓦ nzhorsetreks.co.nz. Backcountry horse trekking for those with a little experience. Great scenery and fun riding on trips ranging from an easy trek around Moke Lake (1hr 30min; $80) to the gold-mining heritage of the Historical Mining Sites (3–4hr; $190). Free Queenstown pick-up and drop-off. Daily Oct–April.

JETBOATING

There are strong arguments for spending your jetboating dollar on better-value wilderness trips elsewhere, but Queenstown does offer the following excellent options.

Dart River Jet Safaris ☎ 0800 327 853, ⓦ dartriver .co.nz. Excellent and very popular jetboating (3hr from Glenorchy; 6hr from Queenstown; $219 from either town), picking routes through braided riverbeds amid grand snowcapped mountains on the edge of Mount Aspiring National Park. Includes a 4WD coach past *Lord of the Rings* and *The Hobbit* locations. Their Funyak Safari (7hr from Glenorchy, 9hr from Queenstown; $319) adds in a rapid-free downstream paddle in inflatable canoes with a buffet lunch stop at the beautiful Rockburn Chasm, filled with calm, clear water. Open year-round.

Shotover Jet Corner of Camp and Shotover sts ☎ 0800 746 868, ⓦ shotoverjet.com. Slick, touristy and pricey but the thrills come thick and fast. Courtesy buses take you out to Arthur's Point, 5km north of Queenstown, where super-powerful jetboats thrust downstream along the Shotover Canyon. Perilously close shaves with rocks and canyon walls plus several 360-degree turns and periodic dousings guarantee that a twenty-minute trip is enough for most (daily 8.30am–5pm or later; $129).

Skippers Canyon Jet ☎ 0800 226 966, ⓦ skipperscanyonjet.com. A great way to combine exploring the Skippers Road (see p.711) with jetboating among the ancient gold workings of the upper Shotover River. Trips (2–3 daily; 3hr) cost $129 and there are various combos. For an extra $20 you get to add in the best of their off-road tour, and the Skippers Quest combo ($309) which tacks on a

---

LORD OF THE RINGS AND THE HOBBIT TOURS

Queenstown and the surrounding area boast the country's highest concentration of *Lord of the Rings* and *The Hobbit* film locations – some instantly recognizable, others so digitally manipulated you'll really need to stand there with a still from the film to work out just what was and wasn't used. Just about anyone who runs adventure trips around the Wakatipu Basin will tag "as seen in *The Lord of the Rings*" or "venturing into Middle-Earth" in their promotional material, but if you really want to stand where Frodo stood, check out the companies listed under Off-Road and 4WD Tours (see p.703), Jetboating (see p.702) and Scenic Flights (see p.703).

whitewater-rafting trip down the Shotover River. This saves $30 on the two trips done individually and means you can pack them both into 4hr 30min.

SCENIC, OFF-ROAD AND 4WD TOURS

Lord of the Rings Tours ☎ 0800 568759, ☏ lordoftheringstours.co.nz. Locations, costumes, filming gossip and a stack of locations are blended in tours around Queenstown (3hr 30min for $170 or 7hr for $299), up the lake to Glenorchy (6hr; $249), or covering the region by road and helicopter (7hr; $1650).

Nomad Safaris 37 Shotover St ☎ 0800 688222, ☏ nomadsafaris.co.nz. Easily the biggest 4WD tour operator, Nomad run Land Rovers on trips into Macetown (see p.724), Skippers Canyon (see p.711) and on several *LOTR* trips under their Safaris of the Scenes banner, with frequent stops to envisage *LOTR* scenes being shot. Tour either the Wakatipu Basin around Queenstown (4hr; $175) or Glenorchy (4hr; $175) with fewer but arguably more spectacular sites. Nomad will also let you get behind the wheel of a Land Rover for some real off-roading.

Off Road Adventures 61a Shotover St ☎ 0800 633 7623, ☏ offroad.co.nz. Not just pootling along in a line of quad-bikes, this is serious off-road fun on a variety of terrains. Packages range from straightforward, family-oriented quad-bike trips (3hr; $199) to the tougher Adventure Tour (3hr; $269), taking quad bikes on steep trails on a 11,000-acre high-country station, with stacks more adrenaline and scenic options. Often undercuts the opposition.

Paradise Safaris 37 Shotover St ☎ 0800 462 248, ☏ infotrack.co.nz. Budget 4WD tour to Glenorchy and Paradise includes Maori legends and gold-mining history as they uncover parts of Lothlórien, Isengard and so forth either in half a day ($145) or a full day ($299).

PARAGLIDING AND HANG-GLIDING

A fine day with a little breeze is all it needs to fill the skies above Queenstown with tandem paragliders descending from Bob's Peak. You get longer flights 10km northeast of town from Coronet Peak down to the Flight Park on Malaghans Road.

Extreme Air ☎ 021 156 3256, ☏ extremeair.co.nz. If pretending to be a bird becomes addictive, learn how to paraglide or hang-glide properly. Day-courses from $250.

G Force Paragliding ☎ 0800 759 688, ☏ nzgforce .com. Call in advance if you want to fly at a particular time, but otherwise just get yourself to the top station of the gondola and wait your turn – like a taxi rank. How many acrobatic manoeuvres are executed during the ten to fifteen minutes you're airborne is largely down to you, your jump guide and the conditions. If you don't see anyone in the air during the main operating times, don't bother with the gondola ride, as the weather's probably being uncooperative. Daily 9am–5pm or later. $199; at 9am $179, both excluding gondola.

NZone 35 Shotover St ☎ 0800 376 796, ☏ nzoneskydive .co.nz. Queenstown is an expensive place to go tandem skydiving, but the fabulous views over Lake Wakatipu and the jump site at the foot of the Remarkables do compensate considerably. Jumps from 12,000ft (45 seconds freefall; $339) and 15,000ft (65 seconds; $439).

Skytrek 45 Camp St ☎ 0800 759 873, ☏ skytrek.co.nz. Experienced tandem operators flying paragliders (15min flight; $190) and hang-gliders (10–20min flight; $210) from the Coronet Peak base buildings in summer. If you're keen you can even take an instruction flight ($235) where you get to fly the hang-glider except for the take-off and landing. In winter they paraglide from the top of Coronet Peak ski lifts ($210) and hang-glide above Glenorchy ($210).

SCENIC FLIGHTS

Numerous companies offer scenic flights, either fixed-wing or in a helicopter. Adventure combos often link the activities with a chopper flight, and both modes are used to reach Milford Sound. If neither of these satisfies consider a stand-alone flight.

Air Milford ☎ 0800 462252, ☏ airmilford.co.nz. Milford Sound flight specialists with all sorts of options such as the classic fly/cruise/fly (4hr; $569), often significantly discounted if you take the 8am early bird flight.

Glenorchy Air ☎ 0800 676264, ☏ trilogytrail.com. The main company who flew *LOTR* cast and crew around. As well as flightseeing trips to Milford Sound and around Aoraki/Mt Cook, options include the Two Ring Trilogy trail (2hr 30min; $385), flying past *LOTR* locations.

Heliworks ☎ 0800 464354, ☏ heliworks.co.nz. These folk did the chopper flying for the cast and now run a wide range of *LOTR* scenic flights, starting at $480 for 45 minutes, including one landing. Stacks of other scenic flights, too.

VIA FERRATA AND ROCK CLIMBING

Climbing Queenstown 36 Shotover St ☎ 0800 254 6246, ☏ climbingqueenstown.com. Get a sense of rock climbing on via ferrata (daily 9am & 1.30pm; 4hr; $159), a system originally used in Europe to move troops quickly across mountainous terrain during the two world wars. Suitably harnessed up, you make your own way up a trail of steel rungs drilled into a series of cliff faces just above Queenstown. Previous experience isn't necessary, and more demanding routes are available for the gung-ho. The company also offers more conventional rock-climbing trips and courses.

WINE TOURS

Appellation Central Wine Tours ☎ 03 442 0246, ☏ appellationcentral.co.nz. To really learn about the area's wines and winemakers, join these informative and

13

WINTER IN QUEENSTOWN

Two ski-fields – **Coronet Peak** and the smaller **Remarkables** – within easy reach of numerous quality hotels, great restaurants and plenty of après-ski combine to make Queenstown New Zealand's premier **ski destination**. The highlight of the season is the ten-day **Queenstown Winter Festival** (Ⓦ winterfestival.co.nz), around the end of June or early July, which, as well as all the conventional ski/snowboard events, has snow sculpture, ski-golf and great entertainment. Just before the September school holidays pack the place out, they also squeeze in the **Gay Ski Week** (Ⓦ gayskiweekqt.com).

INFORMATION AND PASSES

Both ski areas (and Mount Hutt) are run by the same company, whose website (Ⓦ nzski.com) has snow reports and plenty of other practical information. One-day lift passes are specific to each area, the Superpass ($98) works for both Coronet and The Remarks, and the NZSki **season ticket** (early-bird $999) covers all three fields.

ACCOMMODATION AND EQUIPMENT

Neither ski area has **accommodation** on site, but frequent shuttle buses ($18 return to either field) run to and from Queenstown. For **ski rental** visit the excellent (if pricey) Browns, 39 Shotover St (Ⓣ 03 442 4003, Ⓦ brownsnz.com), or the cheaper Outside Sports, 9 Shotover St (Ⓣ 03 441 0074, Ⓦ outsidesports.co.nz).

Coronet Peak Ⓣ 03 442 4620. First opened in 1947, Coronet Peak, 18km north of Queenstown, was New Zealand's first true ski destination. Snow-making equipment extends its season into spring, when cobalt blue skies and stunning scenery earn it an enviable reputation. Its range of runs for skiers and riders of all abilities, and almost 500 vertical metres of skiing, only add to its popularity. Throughout the season, which typically starts in early June and sometimes makes it into October, buses from Queenstown shuttle back and forth along the sealed access road (no toll). Passes for daytime skiing (9am–4pm) cost $98; floodlit skiing (July to mid-Sept Fri & Sat 4–9pm) goes for $51.

The Remarkables Ⓣ 03 442 4615. This hill, 28km east of Queenstown, occupies three mountain basins tucked in behind the wrinkled face of the Remarkables. It is best known for learner and intermediate terrain, but there are also good runs for advanced skiers, and rapid access to some excellent country for off-piste ski touring. Though the bottom of the lifts is 500m higher than at Coronet Peak, more snow is required to cover the tussock, giving a slightly shorter season (late June to early Oct). At 350m, the total vertical descent from the lifts is also less than at Coronet, but you gain an extra 120m by taking the Homeward Run – a long stretch of off-piste with sparkling scenery – to the 14km unsealed access road (no toll), where frequent free buses shuttle you back up to the chairlift. A day-pass costs $95.

fun small-group tours calling at wineries in Gibbston and around Bannockburn and Cromwell. Their afternoon Boutique Wine Tour (noon–5pm; $185) includes lunch at one of the four wineries, but enthusiasts will want to go for the more leisurely, full-day Gourmet Wine Tour (9.30am–4.30pm; $230) taking in five vineyards, a mid-morning cheese tasting, lunch at one of the wineries plus the Gibbston Valley cave tour (see p.727). They pick up from Queenstown and Arrowtown.

ACCOMMODATION

Queenstown has the widest selection of places to stay in this corner of New Zealand, but such is the demand in the middle of summer or at the height of the ski season, that rooms can be hard to come by and prices high. Reserve several days ahead from Christmas to the end of February, longer if you're particular about where you stay. Accommodation at both ends of the spectrum is excellent, with abundant **boutique lodges**, classy **hotels** and budget **hostels**. Things are tougher in the middle where there are few modestly priced, convenient **motels** and **B&Bs**. Some hotels offer good deals in what passes for Queenstown's off-season (essentially April, May & Nov). Almost everywhere is close to the centre, though you might fancy staying out towards Glenorchy or even in **Arrowtown**.

CENTRAL QUEENSTOWN

Absoloot 50 Beach Rd Ⓣ 03 442 9522, Ⓦ absoloot .co.nz; map p.693. Lively hostel right in the centre with a lounge and some rooms sporting excellent lake views.

Dorms are mostly six-bunk with bathroom, TV and fridge though there are also 4-shares ($35): some doubles and queens have en-suite ($125) and there's free wi-fi. Regular poker nights, pool competitions, backpacker bar discounts and bike and board storage. Dorms $\overline{\$29}$, double $\overline{\$98}$

Base Queenstown 49 Shotover St ☎03 441 1185, ⓦstayatbase.co.nz; map p.693. Massive, 300-plus-bed hostel with a busy booking desk and 24hr reception. The kitchen is a bit small but the hostel has its own restaurant/bar. Dorms have secure lockers, a toilet and shower, women can stay in the Sanctuary section ($29) and there's a decent range of en-suite doubles and twins with TV ($109). Wi-fi $4 a day. Dorms $\overline{\$27}$, doubles $\overline{\$79}$

Black Sheep 13 Frankton Rd ☎0800 743 3778, ⓦblacksheepbackpackers.co.nz; map p.693. Long-established hostel in a converted motel that's great value, particularly in the off-season (April–June & Sept–Dec) when all accommodation is $4/person cheaper. Most dorms are six-bed and along with deluxe king rooms ($85) there's a great deck with barbecue, spa pool and a relaxed atmosphere (no drinking after 9pm). Free wi-fi. Dorms $\overline{\$29}$, doubles $\overline{\$75}$

Browns Boutique Hotel 26 Isle St ☎03 441 2050, ⓦbrownshotel.co.nz; map p.693. Close to town and yet in a peaceful setting, all ten rooms at this classy lodge have great views from their small balconies across town to the Remarkables. Everything is beautifully appointed, including the luxurious guest lounge with an open fire and the terrace where breakfast is served in summer. $\overline{\$365}$

Bumbles 2 Brunswick St ☎0800 286 2537, ⓦbumbles backpackers.co.nz; map p.693. Among the best hostels in town, and nicely set just across the road from the lakefront, offering great views from most rooms and common areas. There's a spacious kitchen, BBQ area, off-street parking, free wi-fi and a couple of free cruiser bikes. Dorms $\overline{\$32}$, rooms $\overline{\$67}$

Butterfli Lodge 62 Thompson St ☎03 442 6367, ⓦbutterfli.co.nz; map p.693. Million-dollar views from a small house high on the hillside overlooking the lake. It's a bit of a slog up from town but the accommodation is intimate and friendly. Free wi-fi and there are a couple of tent sites ($18). Book early; two-night minimum. Dorms $\overline{\$30}$, doubles $\overline{\$69}$

Caples Court 20 Stanley St ☎0800 282275, ⓦcaplescourt.co.nz; map p.693. Delightful, comfortable motel with more spirit to its decor than most, and each room done in a different style. Most have a kitchen and a balcony and seven of the ten units have views over the town and/or lake. The others are tucked peacefully away beside a quiet garden. Two-night minimum at busy times. Garden units $\overline{\$140}$, lake view $\overline{\$170}$

★**The Chalet** 1 Dublin St ☎03 442 7117, ⓦchaletqueenstown.co.nz; map p.693. Swiss cottage from the outside, stylish boutique B&B within, this quiet seven-roomer is a great choice. Furnishings are high quality but understated, all rooms have little balconies and some overlook the lake and onto the mountains. Undoubtedly one of the best around. $\overline{\$225}$

The Dairy 10 Isle St ☎03 442 5164, ⓦthedairy.co.nz; map p.693. There's a refined air to this thirteen-room boutique hotel with delightful common areas hung with quality New Zealand artworks (several original) where you might sup something delightful from the extensive honesty bar. The rooms (some with bathtubs) are well appointed and tastefully decorated in modern styles. Breakfast and afternoon tea are served in the original dairy (corner shop). Pay the extra few dollars for a lake view. $\overline{\$465}$

★**Flaming Kiwi Backpackers** 39 Robins Rd ☎0800 555775, ⓦflamingkiwi.co.nz; map p.693. Keycard room entry, lockers with a phone and laptop charging socket inside, and international calls to many countries give a sense of the attention to detail at this central hostel which discourages partying (after 10pm is quiet time). Free cruiser bikes, Frisbees for disc golf and hot tub, and good off-street parking. Dorms $\overline{\$33}$, doubles $\overline{\$78}$

Four Seasons Motel 12 Stanley St ☎03 442 8953, ⓦqueenstownmotel.com; map p.693. Upgraded downtown motel with off-street parking, good kitchens, mountain views, a spa and one of the very few outdoor motel swimming pools in town (unfortunately beside the main road). $\overline{\$160}$

Historic Stone House 47 Hallenstein St ☎03 442 9812, ⓦhistoricstonehouse.co.nz; map p.693. Sister to *The Chalet*, this relaxing historic stone getaway has a pair of one-bedroom self-contained apartments and one three-bedroom apartment sleeping six with an open log fire. Stylish decor and a peaceful location. $\overline{\$225}$

The Lodges 8 Lake Esplanade ☎0508 473737, ⓦthelodges.co.nz; map p.693. Renovated lakeside apartments (from studios to three-bedroom) with kitchen, laundry and parking. Most have good lake views. $\overline{\$185}$

Nomads 5 Church St ☎03 441 3922, ⓦnomadsqueen stown.com; map p.693. Massive, modern hostel right in the heart of things, built to a high standard. The kitchen is piddly and the biggest dorms sleep 12, but there are 4-shares ($35) and the stylish en-suite double rooms with TV ($135) are excellent. There's also a female-only area, free sauna and spacious lounges. Dorms $\overline{\$29}$, doubles $\overline{\$110}$

★**Pinewood** 48 Hamilton Rd ☎0800 746396, ⓦpinewood.co.nz; map p.693. An extensive collection of new and older renovated self-contained buildings (all surrounded by lawns) a 10min walk from the centre, this friendly hostel has a spa bath with views ($10/30min) and en suites ($125) that collectively have their own kitchen and lounge areas. There's bike rental (from $29 half-day) and *The Hub*, which serves breakfast (for groups) and pizza in summer. Dorms $\overline{\$30}$, doubles $\overline{\$75}$

★**Queenstown Motel Apartments** 62 Frankton Rd ☎0800 661 6683, ⓦqma.co.nz; map p.693. Well-managed and good-value motel close to town with functional older units (some with good lake views) and

13

eighteen newer ones, all pale wood, bold colours and tasteful artworks (lakeview units $185). There's a strong environmental stance, with energy-saving light bulbs, double glazing and recycling bins in the kitchenettes. Free wi-fi. Old units $135, new units $165

Southern Laughter 4 Isle St ☎0800 5284 4837, ⓦsircedrics.co.nz; map p.693. Split over three buildings, this rabbit warren of a hostel has a wide variety of rooms (some sharing separate kitchen facilities), a free spa and free unlimited wi-fi all for pretty modest prices. Dorms $27, rooms $70

YHA Queenstown Central 48 Shotover St ☎03 442 7400, ⓦyha.co.nz; map p.693. Among the action, this YHA is more like a small hotel, with all rooms en-suite, even the 4-share dorms. Adequate kitchen facilities beside a lounge with nice lake views. Also has a 2-bedroom apartment. Dorms $38, doubles $110

YHA Queenstown Lakefront 88 Lake Esplanade ☎03 442 8413, ⓦyha.co.nz; map p.693. One of New Zealand's flagship YHA hostels, in a quiet location a 7min walk from town. The feel is surprisingly homey and accommodation is in spacious eight-bed dorms and four-shares ($35), plus twins and doubles. The excellent kitchen/dining area and separate TV and quiet lounges all have good lake views. Dorms $30, doubles $85

TOWARDS GLENORCHY

★**Little Paradise Lodge** Meilejohn Bay, 28km along Glenorchy Rd ☎03 442 6196, ⓦlittleparadise.co.nz; map p.710. Eccentric, alternative and charming guesthouse close to the lake amid Little Paradise Gardens (see p.712). The owner has lined the walls with stone and timber patterns including a frieze depicting New Zealand wildlife. Most of the furniture is handcrafted, goat-skins cover the floor and the toilet cistern is a fish tank. Accommodation is in a three-share room, standard doubles

and an en-suite chalet ($140). You can cook for yourself (breakfast available for $15), and there's kayak rental ($10) and free fishing gear. Share $45, doubles $120

CAMPING AND HOLIDAY PARKS

Freedom camping is restricted (see box below) but the Queenstown district has a few compact campsites with attendant cabins and several simple DOC sites that get pretty busy in Jan, Feb and March.

12 Mile Delta Campground 11km west of Queenstown towards Glenorchy ⓦ12miledelta.co.nz; map p.710. Hosted, lakeside DOC camping with room for 100 tents or vans, plus vault toilets and tap water amid regenerating scrub. Not the prettiest but good mountain views and lake access. No bookings. $10

Moke Lake 6km towards Glenorchy then 4km up Moke Lake Rd ⓦ12miledelta.co.nz; map p.710. The pick of the DOC sites in a quiet and beautiful mountain-girt setting with eighteen sites, lake water and vault toilets. No bookings. $10

Q Box 21 Bowen St ☎03 441 1567, ⓦqbox.co.nz; map p.693. Despite being tucked into a light industrial area this compact campsite is an appealing streamside place with lots of campervan spots (and a few marginal tent sites) ranged around showers, kitchen and lounge stylishly built into a corral of black shipping containers. Laundry, wi-fi and hook-ups available. Camping/site $30, powered sites $33

Queenstown Lakeview Holiday Park 45 Brecon St ☎0800 482 735, ⓦholidaypark.net.nz; map p.693. Vast, high-standard site that sprawls over the base of Bob's Peak with grassy (though not well-shaded) tent and van sites plus kitchen-less en-suite studios, fully self-contained units ($145) and relatively luxurious tourist flats and apartments ($195), many with great mountain views. Unlimited wi-fi $5 a day. Camping $25, studios $135

Shotover Top 10 Holiday Park 70 Arthur's Point Rd, 6km north of Queenstown ☎0800 786 222,

---

FREEDOM CAMPING AROUND QUEENSTOWN AND ARROWTOWN

Freedom camping is **banned** in Queenstown and Arrowtown and along much of the lakeshore around Queenstown, with "No Freedom Camping Zone" signs clearly posted on the approaches to built-up areas. Outside these areas, certified self-contained campervans can generally stay a maximum of two nights. For more information, pick up the local council's *Where Can I Camp?* leaflet or visit ⓦqldc.govt.nz. If you camp inside a banned area or freedom camp with a vehicle without wastewater facilities you may well get hit with a $200 instant fine.

There are still great spots to stop, though in summer you may want to arrive early to grab a prime position. Here are some good places to try:

Glenorchy Road Numerous small wayside parking areas line the road along Lake Wakatipu to Glenorchy, though you'll need to go at least 8km out of Queenstown to be legal.

Lake Hayes Reserve Space for a handful of vans on the northeastern shore of Lake Hayes off the

Arrowtown–Lake Hayes Road.

Shotover River East parking area Shotover Delta Rd. Gravel parking area for 4–5 vans beside the broad lower reaches of the Shotover River. Close to SH6, though this is fairly quiet at night.

shotoverholidaypark.co.nz; map p.710. Fairly spacious, family-oriented holiday park an easy drive or reasonably frequent bus ride from town with a wide range of deluxe cabins ($75), self-contained cabins ($110) and daily-serviced motel units ($150) plus a well-equipped kitchen and dining area and low-cost wi-fi. Camping, per site <u>$45</u>, cabins <u>$70</u>

EATING

Queenstown is blessed with the best range of eating places in this corner of New Zealand, many making the most of the town's climate and spilling out onto the pedestrianized streets and along the waterfront, where you can sit and watch the *Earnslaw* glide in. **Breakfast** and **snack** places generally close by 5pm, though some serve early **dinners**, while many restaurants double as bars as the evening wears on.

★**@Thai** Third Floor, 24 Church St ☎03 442 3683, atthai.co.nz; map p.693. Flavours zing around your mouth with every bite at this Thai restaurant that does all your curry and noodle favourites wonderfully. They also dish up the likes of prawn salad with chilli jam and cashew ($24) and *choo chee* – deep-fried blue cod topped with creamy red curry paste and kaffir lime leaves ($28). $15 lunch specials and smiling service too. Daily except Tues noon–10pm.

Aggy's Shack Corner of Marine Parade and Church St ☎03 442 4076; map p.693. You'll get the best fish and chips in town ($12) as well as marinated raw fish, sea urchin and even muttonbird and chips ($15) to enjoy at outdoor benches or on the grassy lakeshore. Daily 11am–10pm or later.

★**Caribe** 36 The Mall ☎03 442 6658; map p.693. Sunny beats surge out from this Latin kitchen and takeaway with some casual seating. Try Mexican favourites and Venezuelan *arepa*, maize flatbreads ($6–10) best stuffed with chicken and avocado or slow-cooked pork belly (both $10). Daily 11am–10pm.

The Cow Cow Lane ☎03 442 8588, thecowrestaurant .co.nz; map p.693. Be prepared to share a table at this longstanding stone-built pizzeria offering straightforward pasta dishes ($20–22) and traditional pizzas ($30 for a massive one). BYO & licensed. Daily noon–midnight.

Fergbaker 40 Shotover St ☎03 441 1206; map p.693. The perfect accompaniment to *Fergburger* next door, with everything from ready-made sandwiches and gourmet pies ($6), delectable breads, blueberry danishes, jalapeño bagels and chocolate éclairs. Everything to go including the espresso. Daily 6.30am–4.30am.

Fergburger 42 Shotover St ☎03 441 1232, fergburger.com; map p.693. There's always a cluster of hungry punters outside the swift and sweaty takeaway that has become something of a gold standard for Kiwi burgers. It dispenses massive, broad-ranging variations on meat in a bun (or non-meat in a bun) plus fries and/or a beer or plonk. The bacon, egg and hashbrowns Dawn Horn ($13) is a great kick-start to the day. Limited inside seating. Daily 8.30am–5am.

★**Kappa** Upstairs at 36a The Mall ☎03 441 1423; map p.693. Low-cost, no-nonsense Japanese place that's perfect for a sushi combo ($11), a bowl of soba or udon noodles ($11–16), a bento box lunch (from $15) or one of the specials – perhaps nori-flavoured blue cod and asparagus tempura ($17). Daily noon–2.30pm & 7.30–10pm.

★**Madam Woo** 5 The Mall ☎03 442 9200, madamwoo.co.nz; map p.693. Contemporary Malay and Chinese street food meets Queenstown sophistication in surroundings drawing on Southeast Asian night markets with a hint of *Raffles*. A table full of shared plates should definitely include tiger prawns and water chestnut dumplings ($9), the flavour-packed *percik* chicken ($14) and the steamed pork spare ribs with black bean-spiced sauce ($18). The lunch banquet ($35) is perfect. Daily noon–10pm or later.

Patagonia Chocolates 50 Beach St ☎442 9066, patagoniachocolates.co.nz; map p.693. Relaxed lakeview café notable for rich hot chocolate drinks (ginger, lavender, chilli), luscious cakes, delectable gelato (from $5) and hand-made chocolates. Free wi-fi during less busy hours. Daily 9am–10pm.

★**Public Kitchen & Bar** Steamer Wharf ☎03 442 5969, publickitchen.co.nz; map p.693. It is all about locavore dining from shared plates (small around $16, large $26) at this classy yet casual restaurant where tables spill out onto the lakeshore terrace. Expect the likes of venison *osso buco* with roast pumpkin purée, cider-roasted pork belly with caramelized pear or baked flounder with fennel and orange. Daily noon–11pm.

Rata 43 Ballarat St ☎03 442 9393, ratadining.co.nz; map p.693. Contemporary top-end restaurant by celebrity chef Josh Emmet set in a semi-industrial room. Dine on fairly complex modern New Zealand dishes such as Merino lamb with spiced aubergine, globe artichoke and parmesan beignets ($39). Almost 30 wines (many Central Otago) by the glass. The three-course set lunch (daily noon–3pm; $30) is light but good value. Daily noon–11pm.

★**Vudu Café** 23 Beach St ☎03 442 5357, vudu .co.nz; map p.693. It's seen many a worthy challenger come and go but this relaxed café remains the town's best. The booths are comfy, there are magazines to pore over and the food is great, whether an inexpensive breakfast, quiche, scrumptious muffins and good coffee, or more substantial offerings such as a field mushroom and lentil burger ($17) or a venison burger ($17). The breakfast *quesadilla* ($17.50) is a local favourite. Daily 8am–5pm.

13

Vudu Café & Larder 16 Rees St ☎ 03 441 8370, ⓦ vudu.co.nz; map p.693. Larger and more urban chic sister of its original up the street, adorned with a big photo of Queenstown in the 1950s and with limited lakeside seating. Great juices, smoothies and organic coffee, plus the likes of free-range eggs with smoked warehou fish cakes with Ickes beetroot ($19), butternut and tofu *laksa* ($18) and lots of wraps. Daily 7.30am–6pm.

★**Wakatipu Grill** Peninsula Rd ☎ 03 450 9400, ⓦ queenstown.hilton.com; map p.710. Make a special journey (perhaps by water taxi) to this fine restaurant inside the *Hilton Queenstown*. Settle into booths or grab a terrace table overlooking the lake and tuck into half a dozen Stewart Island oysters ($25) perhaps followed by Perendale lamb with caramelized fennel and semi-dried Pinot Noir grapes ($38). Daily 6–10.30am & 4–11pm.

GROCERIES

For groceries, try the Alpine Supermarket, 6 Shotover St (Mon–Sat 7am–10pm, Sun 9am–10pm); Fresh Choice, 64 George Rd (daily 7am–midnight); or the more gourmet Raeward Fresh, 53 Robins Rd (Mon–Sat 8am–6.30pm, Sun 10am–6pm). There's also Remarkables Market (Hawthorn Drive, Frankton; late Oct–early April Sat 9am–2pm; ⓦ remarkablesmarket.co.nz; map p.710), a farmers' market-style affair with loads of good food, arts and crafts.

DRINKING, NIGHTLIFE AND ENTERTAINMENT

Queenstown claims to have more bars per head of population than anywhere else in the country, and plenty of backpackers end up binge drinking in bar/clubs that border on being cattle markets. Decent touring bands are rare, movies are mostly mainstream and there's little highbrow culture. Still, if you are in the mood, it can be lots of fun. Find out what's on in the free entertainment weekly *The Source* (ⓦ thesourceonline.com).

1876 45 Ballarat St ☎ 03 409 2178, ⓦ 1876.co.nz; map p.693. Lively pub in the town's original stone courthouse building with lots of streetside tables in the sun. Their food and drink lunch combos (from $13.50) are great value or dine on their classic burger and fries ($20) or beer-battered blue cod and fries ($28). DJs play Wed–Sun. Daily noon–11pm or much later.

★**Atlas Beer Café** Steamer Wharf, Beach St ☎ 03 442 5995, ⓦ atlasbeercafe.com; map p.693. Cosy bar popular with the locals who sit in its windows to watch the *Earnslaw* as she comes in to dock. Emerson's is always on tap along with a changing roster of excellent guest beers. Their tapas are equally good but it is their signature rump steak, chips and salad ($19.50) that really flies out the door. Some of your beer money goes to support the local mountain-bike club. Daily 10am–2am.

★**Bardeaux** 5 Eureka Arcade ☎ 03 442 8284, ⓦ goodgroup.co.nz; map p.693. Seductive little cocktail bar, with big sofas, a roaring fire and a broad selection of excellent whisky and wine. Relaxed early on, but picks up big time after 11pm. Daily 4pm–4am.

The Bunker Cow Lane ☎ 03 441 8030, ⓦ thebunker .co.nz; map p.693. A stylish upstairs cocktail bar with cool music – anything from jazz to ambient. Daily 5pm–4am.

The Find 53 Shotover St ☎ 03 442 6757, ⓦ theworldbar .co.nz; map p.693. When the long-running *World Bar* burnt down the management soon "found" this space. Meet friends over one of their cocktails served in a teapot with shot glasses (half-price during happy hour 9–10pm) and head back here at the end of a bar crawl for an alcohol-soaking pulled pork burger ($15). On the veranda overlooking the street you can play music from your phone through their speaker tree. Daily noon–4am.

Ivy and Lola's 88 Beach St ☎ 03 441 2155, ⓦ ivyandlolas.com; map p.693. Busy lakeside restaurant and bar that catches plenty of daytime sun. Ideal for a bubble and squeak breakfast ($18) or a beef *rendang* curry with *roti* ($22) but primarily a place to while away the afternoon over a beer or wine. Daily 8am–11pm.

Póg Mahone's 14 Rees St ☎ 03 442 5382, ⓦ pogmahones.co.nz; map p.693. One of the better Irish bars you'll come across, typically crowded with folk clamouring for draught Guinness and hearty bar meals such as beef fillet in a whisky and pepper sauce ($36) and Irish stew with soda bread and veg ($20). Check the blackboards outside for all manner of midweek two-for-one discounts and the 6–7pm happy hour. Warm yourself by the open fire, soak up the sun on the lakeside or come for live music (nightly from 9pm). Daily 11am–1am or later.

Vinyl Underground 12 Church St ☎ 021 112 4061; map p.693. Intimate subterranean music venue with DJs or live music (rock, hip-hop, dubstep) every night, fun staff and a pool table. Where the best bands play. Daily 10pm–4am.

The Winery 14 Beach St, ☎ 03 409 2226, ⓦ thewinery .co.nz; map p.693. If you don't have time to head out to the wineries in Gibbston or Bannockburn, call in to try over eighty wines dispensed by sophisticated vending machines. Try what you fancy in sample (mostly $2–5), half-glass ($5–18) or full-glass quantities ($10–35), then hang out on the leather chairs, perhaps while snacking on a cheeseboard ($28–34). Whiskies are dispensed in the same manner. Daily 10.30am–10.30pm.

MAORI PERFORMANCES AND CINEMA

Kiwi Haka Bob's Peak Complex ☎ 03 441 0101, ⓦ skyline.co.nz; map p.693. This half-hour Maori concert performance takes place daily at 5.15pm, 6pm, 7.15pm &

8pm ($39, excluding gondola ride). Reservations essential. **Reading Cinemas** 11 The Mall ☎03 442 9990.

Mainstream movies. Head to Arrowtown (see p.720) if you're after something more arty.

DIRECTORY

Banks and exchange All major banks have a branch and ATM around the centre.

Internet Aside from hostel facilities, info centres along Shotover St often lure punters in with free wi-fi, or try the Global Gossip hotspot at Nomad, 5 Church St. MCinternet, upstairs in O'Connell's Shopping Centre, 30 Camp St (daily 8.30am–11pm), have rows of computers and wi-fi at cheap rates.

Library 10 Gorge Rd (Mon–Sat 10am–5pm; ☎03 441 0600).

Luggage storage Many lodgings will hold gear for you while you're away from Queenstown, especially if you're staying on your return. Info&Track, 37 Shotover St (☎0800 462 248, ⓦinfotrack.co.nz), charge $5/item/night (day storage $3).

Luggage transfer Track walkers wanting to transfer extra luggage can engage Info&Track, 37 Shotover St (☎0800 462 248, ⓦinfotrack.co.nz), who work with Tracknet (☎0800 483 262, ⓦtracknet.net) to get bags from Queenstown to Te Anau ($15 a bag) or Milford Sound ($25).

Medical treatment Queenstown Medical Centre, 9 Isle St (☎03 441 0500), and Lakes District Hospital, 20 Douglas St, Frankton (☎03 441 0015).

Outdoor Gear Info&Track (37 Shotover St ☎0800 462 248, ⓦinfotrack.co.nz; map p.693) rents gear such as packs ($7/day), sleeping bags ($7), two-person cooksets ($5) and tents ($10). Small Planet (17 Shotover St ☎03 442 6393, ⓦsmallplanetsports.com; map p.693) carries new and used gear, including snowboards, ski gear, climbing, camping and tramping stuff and books – all at good prices and with competitive buy-back deals. The staff are all qualified guides, and, if you've got something to get rid of, will hawk it for a twenty-five percent cut. The company also hires out tents ($12/day), climbing harnesses ($8/day), crampons ($10/day), avalanche transceivers ($10/day) and GoPro cameras ($39/day).

Pharmacy Wilkinsons Pharmacy, corner of The Mall and Rees St (daily 8.30am–10pm; ☎03 442 7313).

Police 11 Camp St (☎03 441 1600).

Post office 13 Camp St (Mon–Fri 8.30am–5.30pm, Sat 9am–4pm). Has poste restante facilities.

Around Queenstown

The commercial pressures of Queenstown drop away as soon as you leave, especially when heading towards Glenorchy via **Moke Lake**, or pause a while beside the lake at **Bob's Cove** and admire the quirky plantings at **Little Paradise Gardens**. There's more rugged exploration beside the churning **Shotover River**, once the scene of frenetic gold mining. The tourist mother lode is now mined through rafting trips, jetboating, mountain-bike rides and 4WD tours. The Shotover rises in the Richardson Mountains north of Queenstown and picks up speed to surge through its deepest and narrowest section, **Skippers Canyon**, and into the Kawarau River downstream from Lake Wakatipu. The Skippers Road, which follows the Shotover River only in its upper reaches, branches off Coronet Peak Road 12km north of Queenstown. It is approached along Malaghans Road through **Arthur's Point**.

Arthur's Point

Gorge Road leaves central Queenstown through a small industrial area bound for **Arthur's Point**, 5km north, where the parabolic concrete Edith Cavell Bridge spans the Shotover River. The Shotover Jet (see box, p.702) performs its antics in the gorge below, and Shotover rafting trips finish here.

Oxenbridge Tunnel

Oxenbridge Tunnel Rd, Arthur's Point

The finale of a Shotover rafting trip is a passage through the 170m-long **Oxenbridge Tunnel**, which was dug around 1911 to divert the river's flow and allow panning of the gold-bearing riverbed. After three years of drilling the miners reaped meagre rewards, returning only 2.5kg of gold. The tunnel exit is along Oxenbridge Tunnel Road.

AROUND QUEENSTOWN

ACCOMMODATION
12 Mile Delta Reserve	5
Hilton Queenstown	2
Kinloch Lodge	1
Little Paradise Lodge	4
Moke Lake campsite	3

Cromwell (50km), Wanaka (110km) & SH-8

Wanaka (20km)

Roaring Meg Power Station

Nevis Bungy

Nevis River

Kawarau River

Peregrine

Cardrona River

Crown Range (1076m)

Brennan Wines

Gibbston Valley

Cardrona

Crown Range Saddle (1076m)

Kawarau Bungy Centre

Ben Nevis (2240m)

CHALK ROAD

Arrow River Bridges Trail

The Remarkables

Arrowtown

Amisfield

Lake Hayes

THE REMARKABLES

Macetown

Millbrook Resort

Coronet Peak (1651m)

Twin Rivers Trail

Jack's Point Trail

Arrow River

Coronet Peak

Edith Cavell Bridge & Oxenbridge Tunnel

Arthurs Point

Frankton

Kelvin Heights

Skippers Township (Ghost town)

Skippers Canyon

SKIPPERS ROAD

Moonlight Track

Ben Lomond (1748m)

Queenstown

Lake McKenzie Road

Shotover River

Stony Creek

Sefferstown (Ghost town)

Ben Lomond Summit Tk

Moke Lake

Bob's Cove

Earnslaw Cruise

Walter Peak Station

Mt Aurum (2234m)

RICHARDSON MOUNTAINS

Mt Nicholas Station

Little Paradise Gardens

Lake Wakatipu

Rees-Dart Track

Rees River

Diamond Lake

Paradise

MOUNT ASPIRING NATIONAL PARK

Dart River

Glenorchy

Routeburn Track

Greenstone River

Caples River

Caples Track

Greenstone Track

Routeburn Shelter

The Divide

0 — 10 kilometres

The Skippers Road

Rental vehicles are not insured on the treacherous **Skippers Road**, a narrow, winding ribbon of dirt track that locals tend to hare around, leaving little space for oncoming traffic. That's a shame, because it accesses a wonderful area of gold-rush relics that are well worth exploring. You'll get a bit of flavour of the area on Shotover rafting and Skippers Canyon Jet trips (see p.702), since both start up this way, but a full exploration is better covered on a historically-oriented 4WD tour (see p.703).

From the start near Coronet Peak, the Skippers Road descends numerous hairpin bends to the river, then shadows it, negotiating **Pinchers Bluff**, where the road was cut from a near-vertical cliff face, to what remains of Skippers township. There are no shops, cafés or much else along the whole route.

Brief history

As the gold-panners gave way to gravity-fed water chutes, mechanical sieves and floating dredges, the construction of a decent road became crucial. From 1863, Chinese navvies spent over twenty years hacking away with pick and shovel at the Skippers Road; those who stuck out the harsh conditions began building quarters more substantial than the standard-issue canvas tents. Meanwhile, entrepreneurially minded pioneers began to exploit the boom, building twenty-seven hotels along the 40km of road, and selling fresh fruit and vegetables at extortionate prices to miners often suffering from scurvy.

By the turn of the twentieth century the river was worked out, though a few miners stayed on. Even today a couple of die-hards make a living from gold panning and sluicing, and in 1999, for a few days after flooding, happy prospectors were finding up to $600's worth in a couple of hours.

Skippers township

29km north of Queenstown

The Skipper Road wends its way upstream to the 1901 **Skippers Bridge**, the first high-level bridge to be built over the Shotover, and consequently the only one to survive the winter floods, which had swept away past efforts.

Just over the bridge you'll find the remnants of **Skippers township**, which once had a population of 1500, though they all legged it once the gold ran out. The **old schoolhouse** has been restored and there are ruins of a few more buildings scattered around, making it a bleak, haunted place.

ACCOMMODATION
THE SKIPPERS ROAD

Skippers campsite Simple DOC campsite occupying a remote and grassy site near the old schoolhouse and cemetery with great views of the surrounding hills. There are toilets (flush in summer) and tap water but you'll need to bring everything else with you. **$6**

West towards Glenorchy

New Zealand is blessed with hundreds of beautiful stretches of road, but few outdo the 45km run beside Lake Wakatipu from Queenstown to Glenorchy. Glorious mountain scenery abounds, often at its best with a sprinkling of snow or brooding storm clouds up ahead. There are lots of wayside halts to stop and admire the view, but few real reasons to stop with the exception of **Bob's Cove** and **Little Paradise Gardens**.

Moke Lake

6km towards Glenorchy from Queenstown then 4km up the partly dirt Moke Lake Road

This gorgeous little lake comes surrounded by mountains, and if the DOC campsite (see p.706) and adjacent Ben Lomond Horse Treks (see p.702) are not too busy it can be a supremely peaceful picnic spot that feels a million miles away from the bustle of

13

Queenstown. Come January the water is usually warm enough for swimming and if you bring you own gear there's good kayaking and fishing. Fans of Jane Campion's *Top of the Lake* series will recognize this as the location for the women's commune scenes.

Bob's Cove

Glenorchy Rd, 14km west of Queenstown

The lakeside road from Queenstown to Glenorchy is one of the best of many excellent drives in the district. After shaking off the suburbs, the first stop is **Bob's Cove**, the best place to observe the lake's **seiche**, a poorly understood phenomenon (rare but not unknown elsewhere in the world) which causes the lake level to fluctuate by around 150mm every five minutes. Place a stick at the water's edge and watch the change.

A short **nature walk** (30–40min return) leads through bush that's alive with bellbirds to the remains of an 1870s lime kiln.

Little Paradise Gardens

Glenorchy Rd, 30km west of Queenstown • Roughly 9am–5pm; if the sign is out they're open • Oct–April $14, May–Sept $10, including tea or coffee and a biscuit • ☎ 03 442 6196, ⊛ littleparadise.co.nz

A delightful, semi-wild haven where everything is made and tended by Swiss owner Thomas Schneider, who has a fine sense of the oddball. Full of roses, lilies, daffodils, plum trees and any plant that takes Schneider's fancy, the place is almost always a riot of colour, but there's nothing sterile or formal here, just grassy paths weaving past the frog and lily pond, a stream threading among concrete sculptures in yoga positions and the home-made fountain sundial. It stands right on the 45th parallel, equidistant from the equator and the South Pole.

Glenorchy

The town of **GLENORCHY** is picturesquely sited on the delta where the Rees and Dart rivers flow into Lake Wakatipu. It makes a perfect retreat from Queenstown, 46km to the southeast, though for many it is simply a staging post for some of the finest **tramping** in New Zealand – a circuit of the Rees and Dart rivers, the Routeburn Track and the Greenstone and Caples tracks. While a fair number of tourists pass through each day (many to ride the Dart River Jet Safari), Glenorchy itself remains tiny, with just a petrol station, a post office, a couple of pubs and cafés and limited accommodation; though if even this is too much, aim for **Kinloch**, a self-contained retreat just 3km from Glenorchy by water, but 25km distant by road.

When you arrive you'll recognize the place instantly if you've seen the 2013 mini-series *Top of the Lake* directed by local resident Jane Campion. Glenorchy is gloriously and gloomily portrayed as the fictional village of Laketop and virtually the entire series was shot on location in Glenorchy and Queenstown. The mountain and lake surroundings may be less recognizable but provide the backdrop for numerous top-end car adverts and Hollywood movies as well as the expected Jackson/Tolkien scenes. If you need to see specific shooting sites, join the Queenstown-based Safari of the Scenes trips run by Nomad Safaris (see p.703).

Brief history

The Glenorchy region's fantastic scenery owes a debt to beds of ancient sea-floor sediments laid down some 220–270 million years ago and metamorphosed into the grey-green schists and *pounamu* (greenstone) of the Forbes and Humboldt mountains. The western and northern flanks of the Forbes Mountains were shaped by the Dart Glacier, now a relatively short tongue of ice which, at its peak 18,000 years ago, formed the root of the huge glacial system that gouged out the floor of Lake Wakatipu. For a map of the area, see p.716.

13

GLENORCHY ACTIVITIES

Almost all the activities in and around Glenorchy are pitched at the Queenstown crowd. Busloads arrive to be decanted onto the Dart River Jet Safari (see p.702). Routeburn and Dart canyoning transport passes straight through and most operators don't even offer a discount if you join their trip in Glenorchy.

WALKING
Glenorchy Walkway (2km loop; 30–40min; flat). To get a feel for the area, follow the pleasant stroll from the wharf at the end of Islay Street along the edge of Lake Wakatipu and through the wetlands around the lagoon.

HORSERIDING
High Country Horses Priory Rd, 10km north of town ☎ 03 442 9915, ⓦ high-country-horses.co.nz. Glenorchy has always been a horsey town, and although it isn't the cheapest place to ride, the scenery is matchless. Join the Paradise on the Rees ride (2.5hr riding; $165, $185 ex-Queenstown) with a couple of river crossings and lots of *LOTR* locations, or the more committing Mountain High, River Deep (5–6hr riding; $305) which adds a climb into the mountains and a gold mine. Trips run all year.

KAYAKING
Kayak Kinloch ☎ 03 442 4900, ⓦ kinlochlodge .co.nz. Guided sit-on-top kayaking trips on moody Lake Wakatipu are run from *Kinloch Lodge*. Explore the quiet braids of the Dart River (1hr at sunrise or sunset; $40), or stay on the lake for two-hour paddles (10am & 2pm; $80) that include a visit to the site of the region's original sawmill and delicious home-baking, topped off with a dip in the outdoor hot tub. Summer only.

Rippled Earth ☎ 0800 474 775, ⓦ rippledearth .co.nz. Great guided kayaking trips to Pigeon of Pig islands with 45min paddling each way (3hr $125, $145 ex-Queenstown) or paddle to *Kinloch Lodge* for dinner with a return at twilight (Dec to mid-March; 3hr; 3hr $160, $180 ex-Queenstown).

In pre-European times the plain beside the combined delta of the Rees and Dart rivers was known as **Kotapahau**, "the place of revenge killing", a reference perhaps to fights between rival *hapu* over the esteemed *pounamu* which littered an area centred on the bed of the Dart River. There's still greenstone up there, but most is protected within the bounds of the Mount Aspiring National Park.

The first **Europeans** to penetrate the area were gold prospectors, government surveyors and nearby run-holders in search of fresh grazing. The fledgling community of Glenorchy served these disparate groups, along with teams of sawmillers and workers from a mine extracting scheelite, a tungsten ore used in armaments manufacture. Despite the lack of road access, **tourists** began to arrive early in the twentieth century, cruising across Lake Wakatipu on the TSS *Earnslaw* before being decanted into charabancs for the 20km jolt north to the Arcadia homestead at **Paradise**, north of Glenorchy – an admittedly beautiful spot, though the name apparently comes from the abundance of paradise ducks in the area.

ARRIVAL AND DEPARTURE · GLENORCHY

By car and bus It is a beautiful drive from Queenstown to Glenorchy and you can continue from there to the major trailheads (which all have parking areas). But many hikes end a long way from where they start so it makes sense to leave your vehicle in either Queenstown or Glenorchy and use shuttle buses to get to the trailheads.

Bus destinations Dart trailhead (1–2 daily; 40min); Greenstone/Caples trailhead (1–2 daily; 50min); Queenstown (2–4 daily; 1hr); Rees trailhead (1–2 daily; 40min); Routeburn Shelter (2–3 daily; 30min).

BUS/TRANSPORT COMPANIES
Buckley Transport ☎ 03 442 8215, ⓦ buckleytransport.co.nz. Track transport getting you to Routeburn Shelter by 9.15am for an early start ($45 from Queenstown; operates all year). They also run a service to and from the far end of the Routeburn Track to Queenstown (arrives at The Divide at noon, departs at 2pm; $80 one way) and offer a pick-up-and-drop-off Routeburn package for $115. Operates all year.

Info&Track ☎ 0800 462 248, ⓦ infotrack.co.nz. The main tramp trailhead operator running between

13

Queenstown and Glenorchy ($21 each way; $15 for bikes) and continuing to the trailheads for the Dart ($52), Greenstone/Caples ($52), Rees ($52) and Routeburn ($47). Their Routeburn Track loop package costs $119. Operates late Oct–late April only.

Kinloch Lodge ☎03 442 4900, ⓦkinlochlodge.co.nz. Runs a boat from Glenorchy (Dec–March Mon–Sat at 12.30pm; free) and on-demand ($15/person each way; minimum two), though lunch and accommodation guests ride free.

Glenorchy Journeys ☎0800 495 687, ⓦglenorchyjourneys.co.nz. Glenorchy-based operator linking all the trailheads to Glenorchy and Queenstown at very competitive prices.

INFORMATION

Tourist information Nothing very formal but ask for advice at the *Glenorchy Hotel* (42 Mull St; ☎03 442 9902) or at the *Trading Post* (café 13 Mull St; ☎03 442 7084, ⓦfacebook.com/glenorchytradingpost).

ACCOMMODATION

Aside from Glenorchy, consider staying around the lake at Kinloch, an excellent, peaceful retreat close to the trailheads for the Greenstone, Caples and Routeburn tracks – there's also a campsite at the start of the latter.

GLENORCHY

Camp Glenorchy 2 Oban St, Glenorchy ⓦglenorchy marketplace.co.nz. Glenorchy's accommodation mainstay was closed for redevelopment at the time of writing but hopes to reopen with bunkhouse cabins, campervan hook-ups and a few tent sites.

Glenorchy Freedom Camping Site southern end of Benmore Place, Glenorchy. Extensive site among mature willows for self-contained campers, with a 2-night max. Arrive early in summer to snag one of the prime lakeside, mountain-view spots. **Free**

Glenorchy Lake House 13 Mull St, Glenorchy ☎03 442 7048, ⓦglenorchylakehouse.co.nz. Central two-room lodge with sumptuous fittings and bedding, deep baths, a spacious lounge with mountain views and a big hot tub outside. With a supplied breakfast tray, guests have the place to themselves. Dinner is available at *Kinloch Lodge*, who run a boat across the lake. **$295**

The Lodge Glenorchy Cnr Mull and Argyle sts, Glenorchy ☎03 442 9968, ⓔgraham@the lodgeglenorchy.co.nz. Comfortable renovated rooms with fridge, tea- and coffee-making facilities and free wi-fi. Ask for the pitched-roof rooms upstairs which are lighter and have better views. **$140**

Precipice Creek 48 Nereus Way, Rees Valley, 6km north of Glenorchy ☎0800 442994, ⓦexperience glenorchy.co.nz. For spectacular views from gorgeous ensuite rooms separate from the main house visit this Czech-run B&B with all the comforts you might expect, plus a delicious home-made breakfast. **$280**

Sylvan campsite 23km northwest of Glenorchy near the start of the Routeburn. Simple but very pleasant DOC campsite beside the burbling Route Burn with BBQ pits, picnic tables and a vault toilet. Camp in the shade of beech trees, gather stream water (which should be treated) and don't miss the easy walk to Lake Sylvan. **$6**

KINLOCH

Kinloch campsite A small and very pleasant lakeside DOC campsite tucked away in the trees by *Kinloch Lodge*, with a toilet, BBQ area, picnic table and stream water (which should be treated). **$6**

★**Kinloch Lodge** 862 Kinloch Rd, 26km by road from Glenorchy ☎03 442 4900, ⓦkinlochlodge .co.nz. Enthusiastically run, the original 1868 Heritage Lodge houses small but comfortable Victorian-styled rooms ($160 with free wi-fi) with shared bathrooms and a lovely deck that catches the morning sun. Rooms around a pleasant lawn constitute the adjacent *Wilderness Lodge*, a self-catering associate YHA section with bunks and neat rooms, one of which is en-suite ($150). There's bike rental ($10/hr, $50/day), fishing rod rental ($15/day), guided kayak trips and transport to the track ends. They also run Routeburn and Greenstone/Caples track transfers which are free if you stay two nights. Dorms **$35**, rooms **$90**

EATING

Café at The Trading Post 13 Mull St ☎03 442 7084, ⓦfacebook.com/glenorchytradingpost. Organic Fairtrade coffee, restorative fruit smoothies ($7) and delightful cream teas ($7.50) are just the ticket at this friendly little shop. Eat in or out on the grass. Daily 9am–4pm.

Glenorchy Café (aka The GYC) 27 Mull St ☎03 442 9978. Convivial café in the former post office with lots of cosy nooks, a bar and plenty of outdoor seating. Ever popular for its GYC full breakfast ($19.50), soups, gourmet pizzas (Sat evenings only) and other home-made treats. Daily 8.30am–5pm, and until 10pm on Sat in summer.

Kinloch Lodge Restaurant ☎03 442 4900, ⓦkinlochlodge.co.nz. The heart of the lodge, this cosy spot with a lake-view deck serves a great range of breakfasts and the likes of wild venison burger and fries ($20). Dinner (by reservation) stretches from a plate of nachos ($18) that's enough for two small appetites or one hungry tramper, to grilled salmon with caper salsa and greens from the garden ($36). Summer daily 8–9.30am, noon–3pm & 6.30–7.30pm.

The Routeburn Track

ⓦ doc.govt.nz/routeburntrack

The fame of the 32km-long **Routeburn Track** – one of New Zealand's Great Walks – is eclipsed only by that of the Milford Track (see p.771), yet arguably it is superior, with better-spaced huts, more varied scenery and a route mostly above the bushline, away from sandflies. Straddling the spine of the Humboldt Mountains, the Routeburn provides access to many of the southwestern wilderness's most archetypal features: forested valleys rich with birdlife (including the rare yellow-headed mohua) and plunging waterfalls are combined with river flats, lakes and spectacular mountain scenery. It is regarded as a moderate three-day tramp and anyone who can carry a backpack for five or six hours a day should be fine. That said, the track passes through subalpine country, and snowfall and flooding can sometimes close it, even in summer. The **main hiking season** is between October and late April, though the track stays open all year. In **winter** the Routeburn becomes a much more serious undertaking, with the track often snowbound and extremely slippery, the huts unheated and the risk of avalanche high. Return day-trips from Routeburn Shelter to Routeburn Falls Hut and from The Divide to the Lake Mackenzie Hut are much better bets.

Most people walk the Routeburn Track westwards from Glenorchy to The Divide. To return to Queenstown from here is a journey approaching 300km, but anyone with a day or two extra to spare can avoid backtracking by making a three- to five-day **Routeburn combo** loop via the Greenstone or Caples tracks.

Routeburn Shelter to Routeburn Falls Hut

9km; 2hr 30min–4hr; 550m ascent

The first 7km follows Route Burn steadily uphill on a metre-wide track, though it's never strenuous. You will already have experienced a wide variety of scenery – river flats, waterfalls and open beech forest – by the time you reach the **Routeburn Flats Hut** and nearby campsite, the latter superbly sited on the edge of wide alluvial flats. Only a few tents are permitted and campers can make use of an open fireplace and a small shelter.

Hut users are better off making the first day a little longer and tackling the steeper and rougher 2km-long leg to the magnificently sited **Routeburn Falls Hut**, perched on the bushline above a precipice with eastward views looking back to Routeburn Flats and Sugar Loaf (1329m).

Routeburn Falls Hut to Lake Mackenzie Hut

11km; 4–6hr; 300m ascent, 350m descent

Most of this long, exposed section is spent above the bushline among the subalpine snow tussock of the Harris Saddle (1255m) and passing through bog country, where sundews, bladderworts and orchids thrive. You might even catch sight of chamois around the saddle. The track climbs gradually enough to the **Harris Saddle Shelter** (2–3hr), which has toilets; on a clear day, drop your pack here and climb up to the 1515m summit of **Conical Hill** (2km return; at least 1hr; 260m ascent) for superb views down into the Hollyford Valley and along it to Martin Bay and the Tasman Sea.

Continuing from the shelter, you cross from Mount Aspiring National Park into Fiordland National Park and skirt high along the edge of the Hollyford Valley, before

13

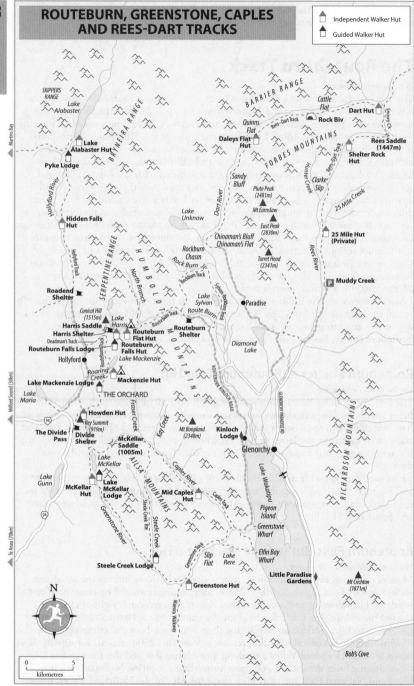

ROUTEBURN, GREENSTONE, CAPLES AND REES-DART TRACKS

Independent Walker Hut

Guided Walker Hut

switchbacking down through silver beech, fuchsia and ribbonwood to **Lake Mackenzie Hut** (50 bunks). The campsite is a short way from the hut, near the lake.

Lake Mackenzie Hut to The Divide

12km; 4–5hr 30min; 300m net descent

The track continues for 9km along the mountainside through a grassy patch of ribbonwood, known as The Orchard, and past the cascading Earland Falls to the **Howden Hut** at the junction of the Greenstone and Caples tracks (the latter handy for turning the tramp into a five-day Glenorchy-based circuit).

The final stretch initially climbs for twenty minutes to a point where you can make a half-hour excursion to Key Summit for views of three major river systems – the Hollyford, the Eglinton and the Greenstone. From the **Key Summit** (919m) turn-off, the track descends through silver beech to the car park and shelter at The Divide.

ARRIVAL AND DEPARTURE

THE ROUTEBURN TRACK

By bus You can drive to the Routeburn Shelter trailhead, but unless you're doing a day-walk it makes sense to use the trailhead buses (see p.713). These drop off at Routeburn Shelter at around 7.30am, 10am and 2pm, giving flexibility to hike to either Routeburn Flats hut or continue to Routeburn Falls huts, and even offering ample opportunity to explore the north branch of Route Burn. Routeburn Shelter drop-offs cost $26 from Glenorchy and $47 from Queenstown. At The Divide (the western end of the Routeburn Track) catch one of the several buses running between Te Anau and Milford

Sound. The best bet is Tracknet (☎0800 483 262, ⓦtracknet.net), with services to Te Anau (10.10am, 1.30pm, 3.15pm & 5.45pm; $39) and to Milford Sound (8.30am, 11am & 2.45pm; $35).

By car For two or more people wanting to walk the Routeburn and return to Queenstown it may be cheaper and more convenient to use EasyHike (☎0800 327 944, ⓦeasyhike.co.nz; $285/vehicle), who drive your vehicle from Routeburn Shelter to The Divide so it's there for you when you finish – they then run the Routeburn to get back to their own vehicle.

INFORMATION AND TOURS

Information The DOC in Queenstown will have the latest weather forecast and track conditions, or check ⓦdoc.govt .nz/routeburntrack. DOC's *Routeburn Track* brochure is adequate but the 1:40,000 *Routeburn, Greenstone and Caples* NewTopo map ($23) is better. Note that the DOC do not track trampers' whereabouts: let someone know your intentions through ⓦadventuresmart.org.nz.

GUIDED WALKS

Ultimate Hikes ☎0800 659 255, ⓦultimatehikes .co.nz. Walk the track in guided comfort with excellent

interpretation, return transport from Queenstown, all meals, hot showers and two nights in lodges equipped with duvets and a pay bar. Rates are for a four-share shared-bath room (Dec–March $1370; Nov & April $1225) or private en-suite room ($1620/$1475). The pace is fairly leisurely and walkers only carry their personal effects (no food or camping equipment). They also offer the shorter Routeburn Encounter day-walk (Nov–late April daily; 10hr; $175) and pricey, extended combinations with the Greenstone and Milford tracks.

ACCOMMODATION

Booking There's a compulsory booking system for the huts and campsites during the tramping season, which guarantees you a bed and allows people to stay up to two nights in a particular hut. Book three months ahead if you need a specific departure date or are part of a large group. It is easiest to book online (ⓦdoc.govt.nz/routeburntrack) from July 1 for the following season, though it is also possible to book at DOC visitor centres, in person or by phone. If the track is closed due to bad weather or track conditions, full refunds are given but new bookings can only be made if there is space. Changes can be made to existing bookings ($10 fee) before you start, again, if space allows.

Huts The four huts along the track are equipped with flush toilets, running water (which should be treated), and gas rings: you'll need to carry your own pans, plates and food. During the main Oct–late April season the huts are staffed by a warden, and the Backcountry Hut Pass is not valid. Outside the main season the huts are unheated, have no gas and cannot be booked, but the Backcountry Hut Pass is valid. Per person/night Oct–late April $54, per person/ night in winter $15

Camping A limited number of campsites with pit toilets and water exist close to the Routeburn Flats and Lake Mackenzie huts; campers are not allowed to use hut facilities. $18

13

Greenstone and Caples tracks

The **Greenstone Track** (36km; 2–3 days) and **Caples Track** (27km; 2 days) run roughly parallel to each other. Both are easy, following gently graded, parallel river valleys where the wilderness experience is moderated by grazing cattle from the high-country stations along the Lake Wakatipu shore. The Greenstone occupies the broader, U-shaped valley carved out by one arm of the huge Hollyford Glacier. The Caples runs over the subalpine McKellar Saddle and down the Caples Valley, where the river is bigger and the narrow base of the valley forces the path closer to it.

The Greenstone and Caples can be done as a loop from Greenstone car park, 6km south of *Kinloch Lodge*, but more commonly people combine the Routeburn Track with either the Greenstone or the Caples: both are described here as a follow-up to the Routeburn. The tracks are open year-round and hut booking details don't change with seasons. In **winter**, the lower-level Greenstone and Caples tracks make a less daunting prospect than the Routeburn: the McKellar Saddle is often snow-covered but at least the huts are heated (see opposite).

Along the Greenstone

Beginning from the **Howden Hut**, after twenty minutes the track passes the primitive but free Greenstone Saddle campsite. For the next 7km (2hr–2hr 30min) the Greenstone continues beside Lake McKellar to **McKellar Hut** (24 bunks), just outside the Fiordland National Park.

McKellar Hut to Greenstone Hut
17km; 4hr 30min–6hr 30min; 100m descent

This easy track starts by crossing the Greenstone River and follows the true left bank down a broad, grazed valley mostly along river flats and through the lower slopes of the beech forests. A swingbridge then crosses Steele Creek, and the track continues for two more hours to the **Greenstone Hut** (20 bunks), a good base for exploring the gentle **Mavora Walkway** to the south. It will take you two or three days, passing through open tussock country and beech forest, to reach Mavora Lakes from here; a couple of huts ($5) provide accommodation en route.

Greenstone Hut to Greenstone car park
10km; 3–5hr; 100m descent

The track follows the true left bank as the valley narrows and the river heads into a long gorge. The river soon meets the Caples River, an enticing series of deep pools that make great swimming holes. A swingbridge gives access to the left bank of the Caples River and the Caples Track; turn right to Greenstone car park (20–30min), or left to Mid Caples Hut (see below).

Along the Caples

Beginning again at Howden Hut, the first long day (21km; 6–7hr) on the Caples Track includes a very steep bush-clad zigzag up to **McKellar Saddle** (1005m); you can't shorten the day since camping is not allowed along the way. The descent mostly follows snow poles, crossing and recrossing the infant Caples River before regaining beech forest; beyond here is a stretch of grassland and **Mid Caples Hut** (24 bunks). Greenstone Wharf is within a day's walk beyond.

Mid Caples Hut to Greenstone Wharf
7km; 2–3hr; 100m descent

The path reaches a short but dramatic gorge, crosses it and follows the true left bank, continuing alongside the bush edge and crossing grassy clearings before arriving at the junction with the Greenstone Track, from where it is only twenty minutes to the car park at **Greenstone Wharf**.

ARRIVAL AND DEPARTURE	GREENSTONE AND CAPLES TRACKS

By car There's a car park near Greenstone Wharf which is useful if you're planning a Greenstone & Caples loop.
By bus If you're combining with the Routeburn you'll want to use the trailhead buses (see p.713). Info&Track ($36 to

Glenorchy, $52 to Queenstown) and *Kinloch Lodge* both call by at noon while Glenorchy Journeys ($35/55) visit at 8am, noon and 4pm. Book ahead if you're coming off the track and hope to be picked up.

INFORMATION

Information Use DOC's *Greenstone and Caples Tracks* leaflet, together with the 1:40,000 *Routeburn, Greenstone and Caples* NewTopo map ($23). Queenstown DOC will have

the latest weather forecast and track conditions, or check ⓦ doc.govt.nz. Let someone know your intentions through ⓦ adventuresmart.org.nz.

ACCOMMODATION

Booking These tracks are far less popular than the Routeburn so reservations are neither necessary nor possible.
Huts Huts (two on the Greenstone, one on the Caples) are heated by wood-burning stoves but there are no gas rings so you'll need a cooking stove as well as pots and food. The

Backcountry Pass is valid, or bring backcountry hut tickets. $\overline{\underline{\$15}}$
Camping Campers are encouraged to camp next to the huts and use the outside facilities. Free camping is allowed in both valleys along the fringes of the bush, at least 50m away from the track and not on the open flats. $\overline{\underline{\$5}}$

Rees–Dart Track

The **Rees–Dart Track** (58km; 3–4 days) forms a Glenorchy-centred loop and is the toughest of the major tramps in the area, covering rugged terrain and requiring six to eight hours of effort each day. It follows the standard Kiwi tramp formula of ascending one river valley, crossing the pass and descending into another, but adds an excellent side trip to the Cascade Saddle. The hike is straightforward enough between December and April, but in winter the Rees–Dart is really only for mountaineers.

Muddy Creek car park to Shelter Rock Hut

17km; 6–7hr; 400m ascent
The track follows a 4WD road across grass and gravel flats beside the braided lower Rees, and requires a couple of foot-soaking stream crossings. Press on across Twenty-five Mile Creek and over more river flats for another hour or so, with the Forbes Mountains straight ahead. Just past Hunter Creek, the Rees Valley steepens appreciably and becomes cloaked in beech forests, which continue sporadically until just below the tree line. Head on for 1km until you hit tussock country, where one final crossing of the Rees River, now a large stream, takes you to the **Shelter Rock Hut** (22 bunks).

Shelter Rock Hut to Dart Hut

9km; 4–6hr; 600m ascent, 450m descent
The second day is the shortest but one of the toughest, scaling the 1447m Rees Saddle. Stick to the true left bank of the Rees, traversing subalpine scrub and gravel banks for a couple of kilometres, before crossing the river and climbing to a tussock basin and the saddle. Descend across snow grass beside Snowy Creek, which churns down a narrow gorge to your right. A kilometre or so later the track crosses a swingbridge to the true right bank, commencing a loose and rocky descent past a long series of cascades to another crossing of Snowy Creek, just above its confluence with the Dart River. There

13

are **camping spots** in the grassy areas on the true right bank and accommodation at **Dart Hut** (32 bunks); many stay two nights here, giving time to explore the **Cascade Saddle route** (see box, p.733).

Dart Hut to Daleys Flat Hut

16km; 5–7hr; 450m descent

The track from Dart Hut climbs high above the river and stays there for 3km, passing through beech forest before dropping to Cattle Flat, 5km of grassed alluvial ridges traced by a winding and energy-sapping but easy-to-follow route. At the end of Cattle Flat, the track returns to the bush and runs parallel to the river until it reaches the beautiful grassy expanse of Quinns Flat (lovely in late-afternoon light), where the track turns inland. Within half an hour you reach the sandfly-ridden **Daleys Flat Hut** (20 bunks), redeemed by its pleasant location on the edge of a clearing.

Daleys Flat Hut to Chinaman's Bluff

16km; 5–7hr; 100m ascent, 150m descent

The walk skips through the bush for around 4km then skirts a lake created by a landslip in 2014. The track then climbs steeply over Sandy Bluff before dropping to river level for an easy walk across the flats and along the river to Chinaman's Bluff. Track Transport pick up from here, though you can continue on foot from Chinaman's Bluff to **Paradise car park** (6km; 2hr; negligible descent) along a 4WD track.

ARRIVAL AND DEPARTURE   REES–DART TRACK

By car You can drive to the Rees trailhead at Muddy Creek car park, 22km north of Glenorchy, and to the Dart trailhead at Paradise car park, 23km north of Glenorchy. A 4WD road continues to Chinaman's Bluff, 30km north of Glenorchy.

By bus Convenient shuttle buses run from either Queenstown or Glenorchy (see p.712), and bus timetables

make it easiest to tramp up the Rees and down the Dart. Info&Track will get you to the Rees trailhead around 10am and pick up from the Chinaman's Bluff at 2pm ($104 for both from Queenstown). Glenorchy Journeys drop at the Rees at 8am & 10am and pick up at Chinaman's Bluff on demand ($110 for same).

INFORMATION

Information The DOC in Queenstown will have the latest weather forecast and track conditions; check ⓦdoc.govt .nz. DOC's *The Rees–Dart Track* leaflet is fine but the

detailed 1:40,000 *Rees–Dart Track* NewTopo map ($23) adds contours. Let someone know your intended hiking route and dates through ⓦadventuresmart.org.nz.

ACCOMMODATION

There is no reservation system for the Rees–Dart, so bunks are first-come, first-served basis.

Huts The three huts come with heating stove but no gas rings. Bring all cooking gear. Hut wardens are present from Nov–April. The Backcountry Pass is valid, or bring backcountry hut tickets. $15

Camping Permitted anywhere along the track (free), except for the fragile, subalpine section between Shelter Rock Hut and Dart Hut. You are encouraged to camp outside the huts where you can use the toilets. $5

Arrowtown and around

ARROWTOWN, at the confluence of the Arrow River and Bush Creek 23km northeast of Queenstown, still has the feel of an old gold town, though on busy summer days any lingering authenticity is swamped by the tourists prowling the sheepskin, greenstone and gold of its souvenir shops. Nonetheless the town is very much a living community, with grocers' shops, pubs and a post office and a great range of accommodation and superb places to eat. Arrowtown has a permanent (and increasingly wealthy)

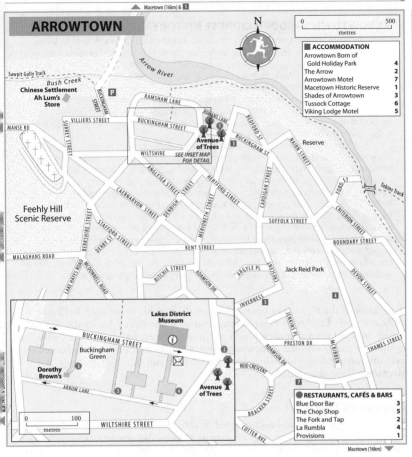

population of 2500, but in summer, when holiday homes are full and tourists arrive in force, it comes close to regaining the 7000-strong peak attained during the **gold rush**.

The best way to appreciate Arrowtown is to linger on after the crowds have gone. If you're visiting from Queenstown and not staying over, consider coming for lunch, spend the afternoon hiking, swimming in the river or biking up to the former mining settlement of **Macetown**, then catch a movie and dinner, making sure you get the last bus back.

If you can, visit in late April when the town is at its best, the trees golden and the streets alive during the ten-day **Autumn Festival** (ⓦarrowtownautumnfestival.org.nz), with all manner of historic walks, street theatre and hoedowns.

Brief history

In August 1862, a shearer employed by William Rees known as Jack Tewa or **Maori Jack**, discovered gold on the Arrow River. He wasn't particularly interested in gold mining but word soon spread to those who were, particularly the American **William Fox** who soon dominated proceedings, managing to keep his claim secret while recovering over 100kg of ore. Jealous prospectors tried to follow him to the lode, but he gave them the slip, on one occasion leaving his tent and provisions behind in

ARROWTOWN'S HIDDEN CHINESE HISTORY

The initial wave of miners who came to Arrowtown in the early 1860s were fortune-seekers intent on a fast buck. When gold was discovered on the West Coast, most of them hot-footed it to Greymouth or Hokitika, leaving a much-depleted community that lacked the economic wherewithal to support the businesses which had mushroomed around the miners.

The solution was to import **Chinese labour**; the first Chinese arrived in Otago in 1866, their number reaching 5000 by 1870. The Chinese were kept separate (settling along Bush Creek) and forced to pick over abandoned mining claims of European miners. Even Chinese employed on municipal projects such as the Presbyterian church got only half the wages paid to Europeans doing the same job.

A ray of light is cast amid the prevailing bigotry by newspaper reports, which suggest that many citizens found the Chinese business conduct "upright and straightforward" and their demeanour "orderly and sober" – perhaps surprisingly in what was an almost entirely male community. Most men carried dreams of earning their fortune and returning home, but wives came along later with members of the extended family. Few realized their dreams, but around ninety percent did return home, many in a box, sent to an early grave by overwork and poor living conditions. Many more were driven out in the early 1880s when recession brought racial jealousies to a head, resulting in the enactment of a punitive poll tax on foreign residents. There was little workable gold by this time and those Chinese who stayed mostly became market gardeners or merchants and drifted away, mainly to Auckland, though the Arrowtown community remained viable into the 1920s. Once the Chinese had left or died, the Bush Creek settlement was abandoned and largely destroyed by repeated flooding.

the middle of the night. The town subsequently bore his name until Fox's gave way to Arrowtown. The Arrow River became known as the richest for its size in the world – a reputation that drew scores of Chinese miners (see box above), who lived in the now partly restored **Arrowtown Chinese Settlement**. Prospectors fanned out over the surrounding hills, where brothers Charley and John Mace set up **Macetown**, now abandoned.

Avenue of Trees

Twin rows of sycamores and oaks, planted in 1867, have grown to overshadow the tiny miners' cottages along the photogenic **Avenue of Trees**, Arrowtown's defining image. The sixty or so period cottages are unusually small and close together, the chronic lack of timber undoubtedly being a factor. The sheltering hills give Arrowtown parched summers and snowy winters, thrown into sharp relief by autumn, when the deciduous trees planted by the mining community cast golden shadows on a central knot of picturesque miners' cottages. A few have been turned into boutique businesses and cafés.

Lakes District Museum

49 Buckingham St • Daily 8.30am–5pm • $8 • ☎ 03 442 1824, ⓦ museumqueenstown.com

Artefacts found during the 1983 Chinese Settlement dig are displayed inside the **Lakes District Museum**, which covers the lives of the gold-miners and their families, with a particular emphasis on the Chinese community. Opium smoking remained legal in New Zealand until 1901, some twenty years after games of chance – *fantan* and *pakapoo* – were proscribed. Technophiles also get a look-in, with displays on the quartz-reef mining used at Macetown and on one of the country's earliest hydro schemes, which once supplied mining communities in Skippers and Macetown with power. Down in the basement are displays on the old brewery, a bakery, a print room and a school room.

FROM TOP ARROWTOWN (P.720); THE TSS *EARNSLAW* (P.697) >

13

Arrowtown Chinese Settlement

Western end of Buckingham St • Open entry • Free

This string of heavily restored buildings hugging a narrow willow-draped section of Bush Creek is easily the best preserved of New Zealand's Chinese communities, and provides an insight into a fascinating, shameful episode in the country's history. Many of the buildings were intended as temporary retreats – with tin, sod and timber the principal materials – only becoming permanent homes as miners aged. Little was left standing when an archeological dig began in 1983, and many of the dwellings languish in a state of graceful decay, fleetingly brought back to life by interpretation panels.

Ah Lum's Store

The best-preserved Chinese building is **Ah Lum's Store**, built in 1883 for Wong Hop Lee and leased from 1909 to 1927 to Ah Lum, one of the pillars of the Chinese community in its later years. By this time integration was making inroads: Ah Lum sold European as well as Chinese goods, and operated an opium den and bank.

Macetown

16km north of Arrowtown, accessed on foot (see box below), bike (in around 2hr) or high-clearance 4WD vehicle

As gold fever swept through Otago in the early 1860s, prospectors fanned out, clawing their way up every creek and gully in search of a flash in the pan. In 1862, alluvial gold was found at Twelve Mile, sparking the rush to what later became known as **Macetown**, now a ghost town and a popular destination for mountain-bikers, horse-trekkers and trampers.

At its peak, Macetown boasted a couple of hotels, a post office and a school, but when the gold ran out it couldn't fall back on farming in the way that Arrowtown and Queenstown did and, like Skippers (see p.711), it died. All that remains of the town are a couple of stone buildings – the restored schoolmaster's house and the bakery. The surrounding creeks and gullies are littered with the twisted and rusting remains of gold batteries, making a fruitful hunting ground for industrial archeology fans.

ARROWTOWN AND MACETOWN WALKS AND RIDES

Arrowtown's museum stocks the *Cycle & Walking Trails around Arrowtown* leaflet ($1), which illustrates all the walks listed below. They fan out into gold country where abandoned cottage sites sprout **fruit bushes** – blackberry, blackcurrant, gooseberry, raspberry and elderberry. In autumn apples, pears and plums weigh down tree branches, and you can spend a lazy afternoon gorging on fruit. The surrounding hills are speckled with **rose bushes**: according to folklore, these were planted by miners seeking vitamin C (rosehips are one of the richest sources); others contend that they were planted primarily for their root systems, which could be fashioned into briar pipes.

Macetown Ride (32km return; 4–6hr; 300m ascent). Set a full day aside, pack a picnic and head for Macetown. The route mostly follows the 4WD drive track but diverts onto single-track to avoid all the river crossings. You can get to Macetown with dry-ish feet, enjoy the atmosphere then hurtle back to Arrowtown for a well-earned beer.

Sawpit Gully (5km loop; 2–3hr; 300m ascent). You'll need reasonable fitness for Arrowtown's classic walking loop hike, best done anticlockwise. Along the way beech forest turns to subalpine tussock and back to forest as you pass decayed evidence of gold mining, broken-down water races, mine tailings and the odd stone hut. Views of the Remarkables and Lake Hayes are stunning. You initially follow the Arrow River Trail parallel to the Macetown road then turn left into Sawpit Gully and loop back to Arrowtown.

Tobins Track (4.5km return; 1hr+; 260m ascent). Bike and walking route offering the quickest way to get great views over Arrowtown and Lake Hayes. Starts the end of Ford St and climbs steadily. Walk back the way you came or cycle down the single-track to meet the Queenstown trail back to town.

13

The 4WD road includes 22 fords of the Arrow River and, on first acquaintance, the place isn't massively exciting. But the grassy plateau makes a great camping spot. Indeed, arriving for a couple of days with a tent and provisions is the best way to experience Macetown's unique atmosphere.

ARRIVAL AND GETTING AROUND

By bus Connectabus (☏ 0800 405 066, ⊚ connectabus .com) operates services throughout the Wakatipu basin. Either get the #11 from Queenstown to the Frankton hub or the #10 to Arrowtown, or come direct via Arthur's Point on the #8. The one-way fare is $13, a day-pass costs $20, a seven-day card is $43, and the last bus back to Queenstown leaves at 10.05pm.

Destinations Queenstown (14 daily; 30–40min).

By bike Arrowtown Bike Hire, 59 Buckingham St (☏ 0800

ARROWTOWN AND AROUND

224 473, ⊚ arrowtownbikehire.co.nz) offer hardtails (half-day $35, full day $49) that are fine for use on the Queenstown Trail network. A ride to Gibbston is perfect and they'll do van pick-ups ($50) if you overdo it at the wineries and don't want to ride back. The workshop-based Arrow Bikes, 4/9 Bush Creek Rd (☏ 03 409 8140, ⊚ www .arrowbikes.co.nz) rent 29er hardtails (half-day $35, full day $50) they're happy to see used on the Macetown track. They'll also deliver to your Arrowtown accommodation.

INFORMATION, TOURS AND ACTIVITIES

Information centre 49 Buckingham St, inside the Lakes District Museum (daily 8.30am–5pm; ☏ 03 442 1824, ⊚ museumqueenstown.com and ⊚ arrowtown.com). Pick up the *Historic Buildings of Arrowtown* booklet ($1), the informative *Arrowtown Chinese Settlement* booklet ($4) and the detailed *Macetown and the Arrow Gorge* booklet ($4). It also has internet access and wi-fi (both $5/hr).

Gold panning Rent a pan ($3 for as long as you want from the Lakes District Museum) and try your luck along the Arrow River, or be assured of a fleck or three by dipping your pan in the salted troughs at *Dudley's Cottage*, 4 Buckingham St, beside the Chinese Settlement ($10 a go).

Guided walks The Lakes District Museum, 49 Buckingham St, is the starting point for Arrowtown Time Walks (Nov–April daily 1.30pm; 1hr 30min, $20; ☏ 03 442 1824,

⊚ arrowtowntimewalks.com), giving an entertaining look at the town's social history. There's a visit to the old gaol and a chance to follow the footsteps of Nelson Mandela, who visited in 1999.

Nomad Safaris ☏ 0800 688222, ⊚ nomadsafaris .co.nz. Major operator running trips from Queenstown (4hr; $175) heading up the Arrow River, crossing it over twenty times on the rough road into Macetown. Arrowtown pick-ups available.

Southern Explorer ☏ 0800 493975, ⊚ southern explorer.co.nz. Small Arrowtown-based company offering a 4WD Arrowtown tour (2.5hr; $99) which includes gold panning and visiting *LOTR* locations. Their Macetown trips (4hr; $185) include all the river crossings and really bring the history of the area to life.

ACCOMMODATION

Most of Arrowtown's accommodation is of a high standard and usually less busy than in Queenstown. There is currently no hostel, though the holiday park has budget rooms.

The Arrow 63 Manse Rd ☏ 03 409 8600, ⊚ thearrow .co.nz. Delightful private hotel that has a perfect blend of historic stone cottage (where wine is served each evening) and modern chic rooms with polished concrete floors. Big windows reveal views of the hills, appreciated each morning as your breakfast is delivered to your room. $375

Arrowtown Born of Gold Holiday Park 12 Centennial Ave ☏ 03 442 1876, ⊚ arrowtownholidaypark.co.nz. Spacious campsite with a modern kitchen and ablutions block and tennis court, and handy for the nearby community swimming pool. Backpacker-style lodge rooms sleep 4 ($65 for 2 plus $20 each extra; bring own bedding or rent from them) and there are self-contained flats ($140). Camping $18, studios $120

Arrowtown Motel 48 Adamson Drive ☏ 0800 246 538, ⊚ arrowtownmotel.co.nz. New owners have brought a sense of style (and their black labrador, Baxter) to this

fully-renovated 1970s motel. There's free wi-fi, a BBQ and playground area and the Queenstown bus stops outside. Studios $129, 1-bedroom unit $139

Macetown Historic Reserve 15km up a serious 4WD road from Arrowtown. A grassy DOC-run campsite among gold-town remains sheltered by low stone walls and willow, sycamore and apple trees. Facilities are limited to long-drop toilets, and you'll have to get your water from a stream. Free

★ **Shades of Arrowtown** 9 Merioneth St ☏ 03 442 1613, ⊚ shadesofarrowtown.co.nz. Tastefully decorated modern motel set in leafy surrounds in the heart of town. There's a good range of units (most with kitchenette or full kitchen), plus a self-contained cottage sleeping six. Units $115, cottage $200

Viking Lodge Motel 21 Inverness Crescent ☏ 0800 181 900, ⊚ vikinglodge.co.nz. One of Arrowtown's best-value

13

motels, featuring an outdoor pool and a cluster of one- and two-bedroom A-frame chalets with well-equipped kitchens and Sky TV. There's also a children's play area featuring a trampoline. **$145**

EATING, DRINKING AND ENTERTAINMENT

Blue Door Bar 18 Buckingham St ☎03 442 0130. Stylish, cool bar in a 140-year-old cellar with a log fire. The intimate cocktail tenor gives way to Wednesday-night jam sessions when a covers band blazes away in the corner and half the town seems to pack the alley outside. Daily 5pm–late.

The Chop Shop 44 Buckingham St ☎03 442 1116. Tucked away at the back of an alley this clever café brings five-star quality to breakfast and lunch. Sure you can get eggs, but try the likes of steamed pork belly dumplings with pickled ginger ($16) or crispy shrimp *huevos rancheros* with avocado salsa ($24). Daily 8am–4pm.

★**The Fork and Tap** 51 Buckingham St ☎03 442 1860, ⓦtheforkandtap.co.nz. Locals' favourite, in a stone-built 1865 former bank and spilling out into the shady garden bar. Hand-crafted beers and an excellent selection of Central Otago wines will complement lunchtime salads, sandwiches and platters. Quality pub dinners include blue cod and chips ($27), pizzas ($25) and wild rabbit and mushroom hotpot ($24). Irish music sessions Wednesday night. Daily 11am–11pm.

★**La Rumbla** Post Office Precinct, 54 Buckingham St ☎03 442 0509, ⓦfacebook.com/larumbla.arrowtown. They've hit on a winning combination at this casual tapas-style place: beautifully prepared food served as generous "shared plates" at very reasonable prices. Add in cocktails, well-priced wines and occasional DJs and live music and it is hard to beat. Tues–Sun 4–10pm or later.

★**Provisions** 65 Buckingham St ☎03 442 0714, ⓦprovisions.co.nz. Delightful little café in a historic miner's cottage with a sunny terrace and garden. Mouth-watering counter food (mostly using their own range of chutneys, vinegars and sauces) is supplemented by the likes of devilled kidneys on toast ($18.50) or seasonal salads. The sticky buns and gingerbread are legendary. Licensed. Daily 9am–5pm.

CINEMA

Dorothy Brown's 18 Buckingham St ☎03 442 1964, ⓦdorothybrowns.com. This wonderful little two-screen independent cinema is almost too good to be true. Watch mainstream and more arty films from stupendously comfortable seats (40-seat theatre $18.50; 15-seat theatre $15.50) and you can take your wine and snacks in with you.

Gibbston

After the **Kawarau River** flows out of Lake Wakatipu, it picks up the waters of the Shotover River before plunging into the **Kawarau Gorge**. The river stays confined for the next 30km before spilling into Lake Dunstan by Cromwell's Goldfields Mining Centre (see p.739).

The valley is a major destination for Queenstown's whitewater rafting, sledging and bungy operators, but the **Gibbston** region, essentially the first 12km of the gorge, has an enviable reputation for its wineries. Although far more grapes are now grown around 30km west near Cromwell and Bannockburn (see p.741), Gibbston pioneered the craft and remains a wine showcase. Half a dozen places have cellar doors open for tasting, a couple with good restaurants.

You can drive to them all, but you'll appreciate the experience a lot more if you join one of the **wine tours** that depart from Queenstown (see p.703).

Kawarau Bridge Bungy Centre

SH6, 23km east of Queenstown • Daily 9.30am–5pm • Site entry free; zipride $50; age restrictions apply • For details of all Queenstown area bungy sites, see box, p.699

Almost everyone stops to watch the antics at the **Kawarau Bridge Bungy Centre**, right beside SH6. The original road through the gorge crossed the river here on the 1880 **Kawarau Gorge Suspension Bridge**, which in 1988 became the world's first commercial bungy site. It remains the most frequently jumped site, and the only place hereabouts where you can get dunked in a river. The scene, at busy times, is a ghoulish production line of bungy initiates being trundled out and tour buses disgorging spectators to fill the viewing platforms.

13

ALL HAIL TO PINOT NOIR – THE CENTRAL OTAGO WINE STORY

It is only since the 1980s that **grapes** have been grown commercially in Central Otago, one of the world's most southerly wine-growing regions. The vineyards lie close to the 45th parallel, and a continental climate of hot dry summers, long cold winters and some of the largest daily temperature variations in New Zealand makes for tough growing conditions. This results in low yields, forcing wineries to go for quality boutique wines sold at prices which seem high (mostly $25–40) until you taste them.

The steep schist and gravel slopes on the southern banks of the Kawarau River were recognized as potential sites for vineyards as early as 1864, when French miner **Jean Désiré Feraud**, bored of his gold claim at Frenchman's Point near Alexandra, planted grapes from cuttings brought over from Australia. His wines won awards, but by the early 1880s he'd decamped to Dunedin. No more grapes were grown until 1976, when the *Rippon Vineyard* was planted outside Wanaka (see p.728). It was another five years before the Kawarau Gorge was recognized as ideally suited to the cultivation of Pinot Gris, Riesling and particularly **Pinot Noir grapes**, with Alan Brady releasing the first commercial wines from *Gibbston Valley Winery* in 1987. Since then, free-draining river terraces with good sun and a bit of a slope to drain off the winter chill air have been exploited throughout the region. Local winemakers have garnered shelves full of trophies, especially for the elegant, fruit-driven Pinot Noirs which make up the bulk of production. Still, volumes are low with the whole Otago region only producing a tiny 2.5 percent of the country's output.

Dozens of cellar doors showcase the goods, all explained on the free and widely available *Central Otago Wine Map*.

If you're going to bungy anywhere (and are not too bothered that at 43m this is nowhere near the highest jump) then this is the one to do. The location is superb and you've always got an audience. You get a bragging T-shirt and free transport from Queenstown if needed. Kids and anyone not up for the real thing can go on the 130m-long **Kawarau Zipride**, a 130m-long cableway beside the Kawarau River that can be tackled seated, Superman style or even upside down. At the far end a complicated pulley system flips you around and tows you back up to the top – no walking.

EATING AND DRINKING GIBBSTON

The following wineries all have **tastings**, and some have excellent on-site **restaurants**. They're listed in increasing distance from Queenstown.

Amisfield 10 Lake Hayes Rd ☎ 03 442 0556, ⓦ amisfield .co.nz; map p.710. There is a definite sense of occasion to dining at this chic modern winery, artfully combining local schist with big windows, recycled timbers and plenty of courtyard seating. Put a few hours aside for lunch or early dinner, perhaps going for the popular "trust the chef" option with seven dishes served over three courses ($65; with wine matches and dessert $120). Tasting (five wines for $8, fee waived with lunch or wine purchase) includes their renowned estate-grown Amisfield Pinot Noir. The Connectabus between Frankton and Arrowtown passes right outside. Tastings daily 10am–6pm; bistro daily 11.30am–8pm (last booking 6pm).

Gibbston Valley 1820 Gibbston Valley Hwy (SH6) ☎ 03 442 6910, ⓦ gibbstonvalley.com; map p.710. Gibbston's winery features tasting ($5 for three tastes), plus a couple of tours ($15, or $25 with better wines) which visit a "cave" blasted 80m into the hillside in the late 1980s. There's also a popular daytime garden and conservatory restaurant, and a cheesery (ⓦ gvcheese.co.nz) with the wine-washed Monk's Gold and signature Pecorino-style Balfour. The cheesery also has a small café with free wi-fi. Daily: Dec–Feb 10am–6pm; March–Nov 10am–5pm.

Peregrine 2127 Gibbston Valley Hwy (SH6) ☎ 03 442 4000, ⓦ peregrinewines.co.nz; map p.710. Nestled under a huge steel and plastic structure designed to mimic both the peregrine's wing and the angled layering of the local schist, this stylish winery has free tastings with views of the elegantly industrial barrel room and cutaway soil profiles from the Gibbston, Lowburn and Bendigo sub-regions. Superb wine too. Daily 10am–5pm.

Brennan Wines 86 Gibbston Back Rd ☎ 03 442 4315, ⓦ brennanwines.co.nz; map p.710. Engaging little family winery with free samples of almost a dozen wines supped in their comfy tasting room overlooking the schisty crags of Nevis Bluff. Nibbles and platters are best consumed out among the vines with a glass or two. Daily 11am–5pm.

13

Wanaka and around

The absence of hard-sell conveyor-belt tourism gives **WANAKA** (pronounced evenly as Wa-Na-Ka) a more relaxed feel than Queenstown. Only 55km northeast of its neighbour (but over an hour by road), Wanaka remains an eminently manageable place, with the tenor of an overgrown village and a feeling of light and spaciousness – an excellent place in which to chill out for a few days. There's no beating the setting, draped around the southern shores of **Lake Wanaka** at the point where the hummocky, poplar-studded hills of Central Otago rub up against the dramatic peaks of the Mount Aspiring National Park (though not Mount Aspiring itself).

Founded in the 1860s as a service centre for the local run-holders and itinerant gold-miners, the town didn't really take off until the prosperous middle years of the twentieth century, when camping and caravanning Kiwis discovered its warm, dry summer climate. Though still only home to around 7000 people, it is now one of New Zealand's fastest-growing towns, with extensive developments and new housing subdivisions popping up everywhere. But although central Wanaka is a pleasant place to café cruise or relax on the foreshore, there are no sights as such, and you'll need to head out of town for museums, a micro-brewery, vineyards and adventure activities – including canyoning.

With the jagged summits of the Southern Alps mirrored in Lake Wanaka's waters, the lure of **Mount Aspiring National Park** is strong and Wanaka makes a perfect base for easy walks and hard tramps.

During the winter months, Wanaka's relative calm is shattered by the arrival of skiers and snowboarders eager to explore the downhill **ski-fields** of **Treble Cone** and **Cardrona**, and the Nordic terrain at the **Snow Farm** (see box, p.730).

Lake Wanaka waterfront

One of the real pleasures of Wanaka is spending time simply chilling out on the waterfront, a kilometre or so of grassy reserve-backed soft-gravel beach with wonderful mountain views. In summer it is full of people sunbathing, swimming out to the pontoon, picnicking, feeding the ducks and renting various watercraft such as sit-on-top kayaks and pedalboats.

Rippon Vineyard

246 Mount Aspiring Rd, 3km west of town • Daily: Dec–April 11am–5pm; July–Nov noon–5pm • ☎ 03 443 8084, ⓦ rippon.co.nz • Drive from Wanaka or walk in 40min alongside the lakeside Glendhu Bay Track, then uphill through the vines

Central Otago's oldest winery, established in 1982, offers interesting wines in a stupendously scenic setting. Views from the hilltop tasting room sweep down across the vines towards the lake with the mountains behind. Managed on organic and biodynamic principles with no irrigation, the estate produces very good Pinot Noir sampled at free tastings. Also try their Riesling and the rare Osteiner Riesling hybrid.

Stuart Landsborough's Puzzling World

188 SH84, almost 2km east of town • Daily: Nov–April 8.30am–5.30pm; May–Oct 8.30am–5pm • $14 for the maze or the illusion rooms, $17.50 for both • ☎ 03 443 7489, ⓦ puzzlingworld.co.nz

A line of monkey puzzle trees heralds **Stuart Landsborough's Puzzling World**, with its complex wooden "Great Maze" comprising 1500m of dead-end passageways packed into a dense labyrinth. Your mission is to reach all four corner towers, either in any order (30min–1hr) or in a specific sequence (at least 1hr), then find your way out again. Much of the rest of the place delights in optical illusions, including the "Hall of Following Faces", with arrays of moulded images of famous people – Einstein, Mother

WANAKA

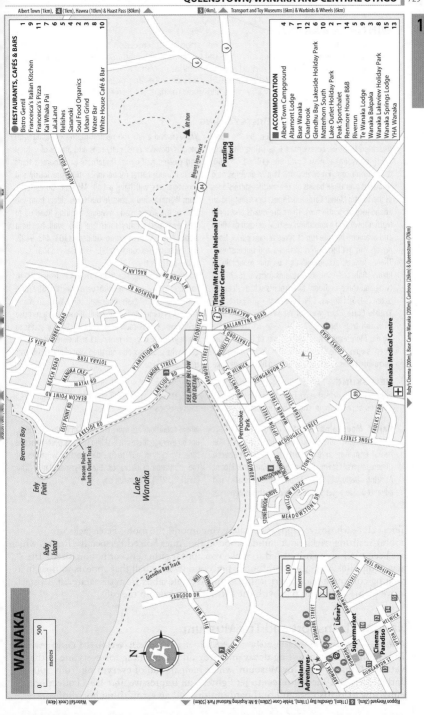

● RESTAURANTS, CAFÉS & BARS	
Bistro Gentil	1
Francesca's Italian Kitchen	9
Francesca's Pizza	11
Kai Whaka Pai	7
LaLaLand	6
Relishes	5
Sasanoki	4
Soul Food Organics	2
Urban Grind	3
Water Bar	8
White House Café & Bar	10

■ ACCOMMODATION	
Albert Town Campground	4
Altamont Lodge	7
Base Wanaka	11
Clearbrook	12
Glendhu Bay Lakeside Holiday Park	6
Matterhorn South	10
Lake Outlet Holiday Park	2
Peak Sportchalet	1
Renmore House B&B	14
Riverrun	5
Te Wanaka Lodge	9
Wanaka Bakpaka	3
Wanaka Lakeview Holiday Park	8
Wanaka Springs Lodge	15
YHA Wanaka	13

Albert Town (1km), 4 (1km), Hawea (10km) & Haast Pass (80km)

5 (4km), Transport and Toy Museums (6km) & Warbirds & Wheels (6km)

Rippon Vineyard (2km), 6 (1km), Glendhu Bay (11km), Treble Cone (20km) & Mt Aspiring National Park (50km)

Ruby's Cinema (200m), Base Camp Wanaka (200m), Cardrona (26km) & Queenstown (70km)

Waterfall Creek (4km)

13

WINTER IN WANAKA

In June Wanaka gets geared up for winter, watersports instructors don baggy snowboarder pants and frequent shuttle buses run up to the ski-fields. If you plan to drive up there you'll need tyre chains, which can be rented at petrol stations in Wanaka. The bike rental shops (see p.732) all switch to ski rental, starting at $38/day for skis, boots and poles or $45/day for board and boots. Combined multi-day lift passes allow you to share your time between Cardrona and Treble Cone.

DOWNHILL AND CROSS-COUNTRY SKIING

Cardrona Alpine Resort Reached by a 12km unsealed toll-free access road branching off 24km south of Wanaka, near Cardrona ☎ 0800 440800, ⓦ cardrona.com. Predominantly family-oriented field sprawled over three basins on the southeastern slopes of the 1934m Mount Cardrona. Expect dry snow and an abundance of gentle runs. There are quads and three learner tows, and a maximum vertical descent of 600m and everyone has the run of three terrain parks. Non-drivers can get buses from Wanaka and Queenstown. There's limited accommodation on the mountain in luxury, fully self-contained studios for two ($270), or two- and three-bedroom apartments which sleep up to ten ($455). Lift pass $99. Late June–early Oct.

Treble Cone 22km west of Wanaka, accessed by a 7km toll-free road ☎ 03 443 7443, ⓦ treblecone .co.nz. More experienced skiers tend to frequent the steep slopes here. Its appeal lies in its range of uncrowded runs spectacularly located high above Lake Wanaka, and a full 700 vertical metres of skiing with moguls, powder runs, gully runs and plenty of natural and created half-pipes. Three new-ish groomed trails make it much better for beginners than previously and snowboarders will have a ball. Morning buses leave from Wanaka, and a shuttle bus takes skiers from the start of the access road on Mount Aspiring Road up to the tows. Backcountry tours are also available from Treble Cone, with Aspiring Guides (☎ 03 443 9422, ⓦ aspiringguides.com; $199). Lift pass $105. Late June–early Oct.

Snow Farm Across the valley from Cardrona, 24km south of Wanaka, then 13km up a winding dirt road ☎ 03 443 7542, ⓦ snowfarmnz.com. With so many Kiwi skiers committed to downhill, it comes as a surprise to discover a cross-country ski area. At $40 for access to the field and $30 for ski rental, it's an inexpensive way to get on the snow, negotiating the 55km of marked Nordic trails. July–Sept.

HELI-SKIING

Heli-skiing is not cheap, but there's no other way of getting to runs of up to 1200 vertical metres across virgin snow on any of seven mountain ranges.

Harris Mountains Heli-Ski ☎ 03 442 6722, ⓦ heliski.co.nz. Offers over 400 different runs on 200 peaks – mainly in the Harris Mountains between Queenstown's Crown Range and Wanaka's Mount Aspiring National Park. Strong intermediate and advanced skiers get the most out of the experience, where conditions are more critical than at the ski-fields, but on average there's heli-skiing seventy percent of the time, typically in four- to five-day weather windows. Of the multitude of packages, the most popular is "The Classic" ($925), a four-run day.

Teresa etc – whose eyes appear to follow you around the room. Peter Jackson's hobbit-realizing tricks can be understood in the Ames Forced Perspective Room, which has been carefully manipulated to make you appear either ent- or hobbit-sized. The new Sculptillusion Gallery confounds perception with a ball that appears to float in a rotating coil and a parallax trick that seems to create a box from disparate bits of steel. Leave plenty of time to play with the frustrating puzzles in the café.

National Transport and Toy Museum

891 Wanaka–Luggate Hwy (SH6), 9km southeast of town • Daily 8.30am–5pm • $15; family $35 • ☎ 03 443 8765, ⓦ nttmuseum.co.nz

The emphasis is on arresting decay and providing something for everyone at the **National Transport and Toy Museum**, where hangars full of everything from 500 Barbie dolls and Meccano sets to jet fighters, an impressive *Star Wars* collection, a shiny row of British Seagull outboard motors and an astonishing hoard of cars,

13

trucks and bikes are preserved by Wanaka's dry climate. Some machines are well-kept examples of stuff still puttering around New Zealand roads, but there's also exotica such as a Centurion tank, Velocette and BSA bikes, a yellow-fur-covered Morris Minor and the Solar Kiwi Racer, an aluminium and glass-fibre bullet-shaped car powered by solar panels on its roof.

Warbirds & Wheels

11 Lloyd Dunn Ave, Wanaka Airport, 9km southeast of town • Daily: Nov–April 9am–5pm; May–Oct 9am–4pm • $20 • ☎ 03 443 7010, ⓦ warbirdsandwheels.com

The year-round face of the Warbirds Over Wanaka festival (see box, p.737), **Warbirds & Wheels** displays several warplanes in half a hangar, among them a Strikemaster training plane, a World War II Hurricane and a Skyhawk that did service in the New Zealand Air Force until 2002. The museum honours the festival's colourful founder, aircraft owner and originator of the 1980s live-deer-capture industry, **Sir Tim Wallis**.

The other half of the hangar houses 25 classic cars. Displays change every six months and you can usually see restoration going on in the workshop.

The Cardrona Valley

The discovery of gold at Arrowtown in 1862 quickly brought prospectors along the Crown Range and into the **Cardrona Valley**, where gold was discovered later that year.

WALKS AROUND WANAKA

There are some great walks and more serious hikes around Wanaka. No special gear is required, just robust shoes, wet-weather gear, sun protection and DOC's *Wanaka Outdoor Pursuits* leaflet ($3.50, downloadable free from DOC), which has a good map.

Beacon Point–Clutha Outlet Circuit (16km; 3–5hr; mostly flat). Long but undemanding riverbank and lakeside walk (or ride) which starts from Wanaka and follows the shore to Eely Point (15min), a sheltered bay popular for boating and picnics. Beyond Eely Point is Bremner Bay and the continuation of the waterfront path to Beacon Point (a further 30min). Either return the same way or continue along Beacon Point Road to the *Lake Outlet Holiday Park* and pick up the Outlet Track, which runs 4km to Alison Avenue, then down to SH6 not far from the Albert Town bridge. By following SH6 this can be turned into a loop back to Wanaka, passing the base of Mount Iron. **Diamond Lake Track** (7km; 2hr 30min–3hr; 400m ascent). A fine local walk with great lake and mountain views, starting at the car park 18km west of Wanaka on the Mount Aspiring Rd. There are a couple of short variations, but to get the views you'll need to tackle the summit of Rocky Mountain (775m). **Glendhu Bay Track** (12.5km one way; 3–4hr; negligible ascent). The westbound equivalent of the Beacon Point–Clutha Outlet Circuit leaves Roy's Bay, heading through Wanaka Station Park and past Rippon Vineyard to Waterfall Creek and on to Glendhu Bay following lakeside terraces. The trail is open to hikers and bikers: just go as far as you fancy and head back. **Mount Iron Track** (4.5km return; 1hr 30min; 240m ascent). The most accessible of Wanaka's hilltop walks climbs a 549m outcrop, its western and northern slopes ground smooth by the glacier that scoured its southern face. The path through farmland and the bird-filled manuka woodland of the Mount Iron Scenic Reserve starts 1500m east of Wanaka on SH84, climbing the steep southern face to the summit. Here you can enjoy magnificent panoramic views, before following the path down the east face of Mount Iron towards the entrance to Puzzling World (see p.728). **Roy's Peak Track** (16km return; 4–6hr; 1100m ascent). A more challenging prospect, winding up to the 1578m summit for wonderful views over Lake Wanaka and surrounding glaciers and mountains. The path starts 7km west of Wanaka on the Mount Aspiring Rd, but is closed during the lambing season (Oct 1–Nov 10).

13

Five years on, the Europeans legged it to new fields on the West Coast, leaving the dregs to Chinese immigrants, who themselves had drifted away by 1870.

Tiny **CARDRONA**, 25km south of Wanaka, comprises little more than a few cottages, a long-forgotten cemetery, the *Cardrona Hotel* (see p.738) and the similarly ancient former post office and store.

South from here, the road twists over the **Crown Range Road** (SH89), the quickest and most direct route from Wanaka to Queenstown, though it is sometimes snow-bound in winter and trailers are discouraged. Nonetheless, on a fine day the drive past the detritus of the valley's gold-mining heyday is a rewarding one, with views across bald, mica-studded hills to the tussock high country beyond. At the 1076m pass, a great **viewpoint** overlooks Queenstown and Lake Wakatipu, before it switchbacks down towards SH6, Arrowtown and Queenstown.

The Matukituki Valley and Mount Aspiring National Park

The **Matukituki Valley** is Wanaka's outdoor playground, a 60km tentacle reaching from the parched Otago landscapes around Lake Wanaka to the steep alpine skirts of Mount Aspiring, which at 3033m is New Zealand's highest peak outside the Aoraki/Mount Cook National Park. Extensive high-country stations run sheep on the riverside meadows, briefly glimpsed by skiers bound for Treble Cone, rock climbers making for the roadside crags, and trampers and mountaineers hot-footing it to the **Mount Aspiring National Park**.

The park is one of the country's largest, extending from the Haast Pass in the north, where there are tramps around Makarora (see p.684), to the head of Lake Wakatipu in the south, where the Rees–Dart Track and parts of the Routeburn Track fall within its bounds. The pyramidal Mount Aspiring forms the centrepiece of the park, rising with classical beauty over the ice-smoothed broad valleys and creaking glaciers. It was first climbed in 1909 using heavy hemp rope and without the climbing hardware used by today's mountaineers, who still treat it as one of the grails of Kiwi mountaineering ambition.

Travelling along the unsealed section of the Mount Aspiring Road beside the Matukituki River, you don't get to see much of Aspiring, as Mount Avalanche and Avalanche Glacier get in the way. Still, craggy mountains remain tantalizingly present all the way to the **Raspberry Creek**, where a car park and public toilets mark the start of a number of magnificent tramps (see box, p.733) into the heart of the park. For information on how to get to the park, see below.

ARRIVAL AND DEPARTURE

WANAKA AND AROUND

By bus Buses all stop outside the log cabin at 100 Ardmore St. Alpine Connexions (☎ 03 443 9120, ⊛ alpineconnexions .co.nz) link to Dunedin and Queenstown, some with connections at Cromwell, while Connect Wanaka (☎ 0800 405 066, ⊛ connectabus.com) links to Queenstown over the Crown Range: both Queenstown runs call at Queenstown Airport. Atomic (☎ 0508 108 359, ⊛ atomictravel.co.nz) runs to Dunedin and to Christchurch with a change at Cromwell. InterCity/Newmans pass

through on their Queenstown–Cromwell–Franz Josef run but not on their Queenstown–Christchurch run (though you can join it at Cromwell or Tarras), The taxi fare to Tarras is included in the fare but on this run it is usually much cheaper to go with NakedBus.

Destinations Christchurch (2–3 daily; 7–8hr); Cromwell (4 daily; 45min–1hr); Dunedin (1–2 daily; 4hr–4hr 30min); Franz Josef Glacier (1–2 daily; 7hr); Queenstown (9 daily; 1hr 30min).

GETTING AROUND

Wanaka is compact and you can walk everywhere in the centre. Most accommodation is less than fifteen minutes away on foot, but you may want transport for longer excursions.

By bike Many hostels and B&Bs have knockabout bikes for guests' use but for serious riding you'll want to visit the bike

rental places. Outside Sports, 17 Dunmore St (daily 9am–6pm longer in midwinter and summer in peak season; ☎ 03 443

13

WALKS IN THE MATUKITUKI VALLEY

DOC's *Matukituki Valley Tracks* and *Dart & Rees Valleys* leaflets ($2 each or downloadable free from ⓦdoc.govt.nz) are fine for these walks: get hold of the *Aspiring Flats* topo50 map (CA11; $9 from DOC) if you like contour lines. The routes are manageable for fit and experienced trampers, but the climatic differences in the park are extreme – the half-metre of rain that falls each year in the Matukituki Valley does not compare with the six metres that fall on the western side of the park, so go prepared. The hikes start at the Raspberry Creek car park, about an hour's drive from Wanaka.

Several **huts** in this area are owned by the New Zealand Alpine Club (NZAC) but are open to all: pay at the DOC visitor centre in Wanaka.

Raspberry Creek to Aspiring Hut (9km one way; 2hr 30min–3hr; 100m ascent). A popular and mostly pastoral day-walk starting along a 4WD track which climbs from the Raspberry Creek car park beside the western branch of the Matukituki River, only heading away from the river to avoid bluffs en route to Downs Creek, from where you get fabulous views up to the Rob Roy Glacier and Mount Avalanche. Brides Veil Falls is a brief distraction before the historic Cascade Hut, followed 20min later by the relatively luxurious stone-built Aspiring Hut (NZAC; 38 bunks; $30, with gas), a common base camp for mountaineers off to the peaks around Mount Aspiring. There's camping ($5) near the hut.

Rob Roy Valley Walk (10km return; 3–4hr; 300m ascent). This justly popular there-and-back hike is shorter and steeper than the walk to Aspiring Hut and more spectacular, striking through beech forest to some magnificent alpine scenery, snowfields and glaciers. From the Raspberry Creek car park, follow the true right bank of the Matukituki for 15min to a swingbridge; cross to the true left bank that leads on to the Rob Roy stream, which cuts through a small gorge into the beech forest. Gradually the woods give way to alpine vegetation – and the Rob Roy Glacier nosing down into the head of the valley. Eco Wanaka Adventures (☎0800 926 326, ⓦecowanaka.co.nz) run an all-day guided trip here including a picnic lunch ($250).

Aspiring Hut to Pearl Flat (5km; 1hr 30min; 100m ascent). For an excellent day out from Aspiring Hut, explore the headwaters of the Matukituki River to the north. Follow the river as it weaves in and out of the bush to Pearl Flat. Return from here or continue to the head of the valley (see below).

Cascade Saddle Route (4–5 days one way). One of the most challenging of the local tramps connects the Matukituki Valley's Aspiring Hut to Glenorchy's Rees–Dart Track (see p.719), via a magnificent alpine crossing with panoramic views of the Dart Glacier and the Barrier Range. You should have previous alpine experience, carry full waterproofs, and be prepared to turn back if conditions are unfavourable, though specialized mountaineering equipment is not usually needed from January to March. Check ⓦdoc.govt.nz for the latest info and a downloadable leaflet. From Aspiring Hut to Dart Hut (17km; 8–11hr; 1350m ascent), you rise above the tree line onto the steep tussock and snow-grass ridge, which is treacherous when wet or snowy. The route is marked by orange snow poles, which lead you to a steel pylon (1835m) that marks the top of the ridge, down to Cascade Creek and across it, before climbing gently to the meadows around Cascade Saddle. There is a toilet at Cascade Creek for campers. Non-campers will have to press on another four or five hours, past the rubble-topped Dart Glacier, to Dart Hut where you join the Rees–Dart Track for the last two days back to Glenorchy.

7966, ⓦoutsidesports.co.nz) have road ($30/4hr, $50/day), hardtails ($30/$50) and fully-sprung models ($50/$75). Racers Edge, 99 Ardmore St (daily: summer 9am–6pm; winter 7.30am–7pm; ☎03 443 7882, ⓦracersedge.co.nz), rents hardtails ($30 a half-day, $50 full) and fully sprung and road bikes ($45/$60). Both also operate ski rental and tuning services in winter. If style is more important than performance, rent a vintage cruiser from Hellcat Cycles (☎022 069 6387, ⓦhellcatcycles.com; $40/day).

By bus Alpine Connexions (☎03 443 9120,

ⓦalpineconnexions.co.nz) run the 55km along Mount Aspiring Rd to the national park's main trailhead at Raspberry Creek once or twice daily from Oct–April. Bookings essential. $40 each way. KT sightseeing (☎0800 272700, ⓦkts ightseeing.co.nz) charge $70 return for the same journey.

By car Wanaka Rentacar, 2 Brownston St (☎03 443 6641, ⓦwanakarentacar.co.nz), have the cheapest range of vehicles, starting at around $40/day, with unlimited kilometres for longer rentals.

By taxi Yello! (☎0800 443 5555).

13

INFORMATION

Information i-SITE, 103 Ardmore St (daily: Dec–March 8.30am–6pm; April–Nov 9am–5pm; ☎ 03 443 1233, �🖥 lake wanaka.co.nz). The DOC Tititea/Mount Aspiring National Park visitor centre is at the corner of SH84 and Ballantyne Rd, 500m east of central Wanaka (Nov–Easter daily 8am–5pm; Easter–Oct Mon–Fri 8.30am–5pm, Sat 9.30am–4pm; ☎ 03

443 7660, ✉ mtaspiringvc@doc.govt.nz).
Gear rental Outside Sports (17 Dunmore St; ☎ 03 4437966, �🖥 outsidesports.co.nz) stocks pretty much everything and does rentals including backpacks ($10/ day), sleeping bags ($10), mats ($5), hiking boots ($8), trekking poles ($5) and cooking stoves ($5).

TOURS AND ACTIVITIES

Magnificent scenery, clear skies and competitive prices make Wanaka an excellent place to get airborne, and with a beautiful lake and a number of decent rivers there's plenty of opportunity for getting wet in style. Most accommodation and numerous agents around town handle **bookings**, or you can contact the activity operator direct.

CANYONING

Deep Canyon 100 Ardmore St ☎ 03 443 7922, �🖥 deepcanyon.co.nz. Experienced guides take small groups into narrow canyons following a creek downstream with heaps of jumps, rockslides and abseils. Warm, protective clothing helps ease the sense of vulnerability, and the day is rounded off with a bush picnic. First-timers should opt for Niger Stream (7–8hr; $240), down a gorgeous stream with plenty of jumping into deep pools. Abseiling experience ensures you get the best from Big Nige (8hr; $305), which covers the same territory as the Niger Stream trip but starts further upstream with some big rappels. With one of these under your belt, even more adventurous trips are possible.

ROCK CLIMBING AND MOUNTAINEERING

Aspiring Guides ☎ 0800 754868, ⍵ aspiringguides .com. Professional mountaineering with five-day heli-in/ walk-out ascents of Mount Aspiring ($4200) as well as excellent seven-day Summit Weeks ($2990) where you get a guide to help tackle whatever peaks or learn whatever skills you need.
Basecamp Wanaka 50 Cardrona Valley Rd, 2km south of town ☎ 03 443 1110, ⍵ basecampwanaka.co.nz. Two climbing experiences in one. Inside is the child-oriented Clip 'N Climb ($20/hr; kids $10–16; bring trainers), where an auto-belay system allows you to climb against the clock, do a face-to-face race, or climb in the dark with UV-lit holds. The superbly sculpted outdoor wall ($20; $15 with your own harness) is pretty close to climbing on real rock. Lessons available. Mon–Fri noon–8pm, Sat, Sun & all public and school holidays 10am–6pm.
Wanaka Rock Climbing ☎ 03 443 6411, ⍵ wanakarock.co.nz. Wanaka's dry, sunny climate is ideal for rock climbing, and these guys run full-day introductory courses involving top-roping, seconding and abseiling for two to four people (half-day $140 each; full day $210), and offer private guiding ($345/day).

SKYDIVING AND PARAGLIDING

Skydive Lake Wanaka Wanaka Airport ☎ 0800

786877, ⍵ skydivewanaka.com. A 10min scenic flight can be combined with 45–60 seconds of freefall on a wonderful tandem skydive ($329 from 12,000ft; $429 from 15,000ft). Free pick-ups from Queenstown.
Wanaka Paragliding ☎ 0800 359754, ⍵ wanaka paragliding.co.nz. A gentle but spectacular approach to viewing the tremendous scenery is a tandem flight from high on Treble Cone ski-field down to the lakeside (800m descent) with 15–20min in the air. Trips ($215) take 2hr from Wanaka and transport is included.

SCENIC FLIGHTS

Scenic flights from Wanaka to Milford Sound tend to be a few dollars more expensive than those from Queenstown, but they do spend half an hour more flying over a wider range of stunning scenery, including Mount Aspiring, the Olivine Ice Plateau and the inaccessible lakes of Alabaster, McKerrow and Tutoko. Most local accommodation receives daily bulletins on Milford weather and flight conditions.
Alpine Helicopters ☎ 03 443 4000, ⍵ alpineheli .co.nz. Milford Sound flights with one landing (2hr; $795), or add in the West Coast and an additional landing (2.5– 3hr; $1195).
Southern Alps Air ☎ 0800 345666, ⍵ southernalpsair .co.nz. Excellent Milford Sound flight/cruise/flight combo (4hr total; $490) plus scenic flights around Mt Aspiring (40min; $240) and transport deals to link to their Siberia Experience and Blue Pools trips in Makarora (see p.684).

BIKING

Wanaka has several shops (see p.732) renting bikes and selling the *Lake Wanaka Cycling Map* ($2), which details local off-road rides. Pick of the local biking routes include the excellent Albert Town–Luggate circuit and the beautiful, gentle Beacon Point–Clutha Outlet track (see box, p.731).
Wanaka Bike Tours ☎ 0800 743 369, ⍵ wanakabiketours.co.nz. Dedicated guided riding company offering escorted rides along the Lakeside and Clutha tracks ($150–199), backcountry rides ($249) and even heli-biking (various options from $399).

CRUISES, KAYAKING, RAFTING AND JETBOATING

Eco Wanaka Adventures ☎0800 926326, ⓦecowanaka.co.nz. A wonderfully informative and scenic cruise (daily 9am & 1.30pm; 4hr; $195) across Lake Wanaka to Mou Waho island nature reserve and its population of buff weka. The nature walk highlight is "high tea" overlooking the island's picturesque lake-within-a-lake, and you can even plant a tree, helping Mou Waho's regeneration.

Lakeland Adventures 100 Ardmore St ☎03 443 7495, ⓦlakelandadventures.co.nz. Has all manner of waterborne activities including a gentle cruise to Stephensons Island (2hr; $95) where you can stroll briefly. Also rents kayaks ($15 per person/hr) and assorted aquatic toys.

Pioneer Rafting ☎03 443 1246, ⓦecoraft.co.nz. Rafting on the Grade II Upper Clutha (daily Sept–April; half-day $165, full day $225), where trips involve bobbing along choppy water with emphasis on appreciating the scenery and gold panning. Suitable for families.

Wanaka Kayaks ☎0800 926925, ⓦwanakakayaks .co.nz. Kayak and paddleboard specialists renting from the beach ($20–25 per person/hr), running no-experience-necessary kayak trips on the lake (half-day $95, day $189 including BBQ lunch) and down the Clutha River (3hr; $149). They also run a paddleboard school with various short courses (including SUP yoga) possibly leading to a paddleboard trip down the river (2hr; $95).

Wanaka River Journeys ☎0800 544555, ⓦwanakariverjourneys.co.nz. Great-value jetboating tours (1–2 daily; 3–4hr; $229) which thunder up the Matukituki River, providing great views of Mount Aspiring, the Avalanche Glacier, Mount Avalanche and the rest, with a knowledgeable guide and bushwalk.

FISHING

Lake Wanaka and nearby lakes and rivers are popular territory for quinnat salmon and brown and rainbow trout fishing. There's a maximum bag of six fish per day and you'll require the sport fishing licence ($25/day, $123 for the season for Kiwis, $160 for foreigners; ⓦfishandgame.org.nz), obtainable online or from tackle shops such as Hamills, 10 Helwick St (☎03 443 8094, ⓦhamillswanakafishinghunting.co.nz) who rent fishing tackle packages ($20/day). Unless you really know your bait, you'll have a better chance of catching your supper with a fishing guide – rates start around $650 a half-day or $800 day.

HORSERIDING

Timber Creek Equestrian Centre 386 Cardrona Valley Rd, near Rippon Vineyard ☎03 443 2933. Gentle rides through Rippon Vineyard with a stop for tasting (1hr 45min; $89). Very civilized.

4WD TRIPS

Ridgeline Adventures ☎0800 234000, ⓦridgelinenz .com. Get a sense of how a high-country station operates on Wild Hills Safari (4h; $225) which takes you high up onto remote farmland with long views over Lake Wanaka. Photography tours and chopper and jetboat combos also available.

ACCOMMODATION

For a diminutive place, Wanaka has a great range of accommodation, particularly luxury lodges. You should have no problem finding a bed, except during the peak months of January, February, July and August, and during events (see box, p.737) when **booking** is essential and prices rise. **Freedom camping** is not allowed in town or along the lakefront.

Altamont Lodge 121 Mount Aspiring Rd, 2km west of Wanaka ☎03 443 8864, ⓦaltamontlodge.co.nz. For hostel prices without the dorms or backpacker vibe, head for this tramping-cum-ski-lodge with a pine-panelled alpine atmosphere, communal cooking and lounge areas, a spa pool, drying rooms, spacious lawns, tennis court and ski-tuning facilities. Twins, doubles and triples are fairly functional, with shared bathrooms. $79

Base Wanaka 73 Brownston St ☎03 443 4291, ⓦstayatbase.co.nz. Purpose-built hostel in the heart of town; the kitchen is cramped but there's also a bar serving budget meals. The smart rooms feature upscale women-only dorms ($33). Has internet and a busy booking desk. Dorms $27, en-suite doubles $90

Clearbrook 72 Helwick ☎0800 443 441, ⓦclearbrook .co.nz. Afternoon sun streams in to the studios, one- and two-bedroom apartments at this classy motel with tastefully decorated luxury units ranged along the burbling Bullock Creek. All units have TV/DVD, full kitchen with dishwasher, laundry and balconies with mountain views. All are great value including the separate three-bedroom houses sleeping six ($385). $155

Matterhorn South 56 Brownston St ☎03 443 1119, ⓦmatterhornsouth.co.nz. Combined hostel and budget lodge, with an appealing backpacker section featuring dorms of various sizes and "Hobbit Room" garden shed. The more upmarket lodge section has modern, en-suite four-shares with TV and fridge, and access to an excellent kitchen and comfortable lounge. Dorms $29, doubles $75

Peak Sportchalet 36 Hunter Crescent, 2km north of town ☎03 443 6990, ⓦpeak-sportchalet.co.nz. Purpose-built self-contained studio and two-bedroom chalet in a peaceful part of town, run by a charming German couple who provide a buffet breakfast ($10 extra).

13

There's an individual touch to the decor, bathrooms get under-floor heating and everywhere is super-insulated. The studio is great for couples; the chalet for a family or two couples. Studio $140, one-bedroom chalet $160

Renmore House B&B 44 Upton St **☎**03 443 6566, **ⓦ**renmore-house.co.nz. Large purpose-built house, centrally located beside the waters of Bullock Creek, with three plush en-suite rooms all fitted out to a high standard. There are bikes for guests' use and the hosts (and cat) are genial and welcoming. $270

★Riverrun 86 Halliday Rd, 5km east of Wanaka **☎**03 443 9049 , **ⓦ**riverrun.co.nz. Stylish lodge, wonderfully sited on ancient river flats with trails through sheep paddocks down to the Clutha River. The thoughtfully conceived modern house uses lots of recycled timber and contains five beautifully appointed en-suite rooms, sunny verandas and a common dining area where most guests stay for a four-course dinner ($100), the match of any restaurant in Wanaka. Rates (which reduce for 3-night stays) include breakfast and pre-dinner drinks. $400

★Te Wanaka Lodge 23 Brownston St **☎**03 443 9224, **ⓦ**tewanaka.co.nz. Welcoming thirteen-room lodge built around a large walnut tree. Comfortable rooms all have private entrances and Sky TV. A cedar hot tub shares the peaceful garden with a delightful small cottage. There's a hearty breakfast served around a communal table and even an honesty bar with a good wine selection. The owners are friendly and highly knowledgeable about all things outdoors. Free wi-fi. $220

★Wanaka Bakpaka 117 Lakeside Rd **☎**03 443 7837, **ⓦ**wanakabakpaka.co.nz. Beautifully maintained low-key hostel a 5min walk from town, with great lake and mountain views (doubles with views are $90), a peaceful atmosphere, summer BBQs and bike rental ($19/day). Plenty of room for sitting out in the afternoon sun. Dorms $29, doubles $70

Wanaka Springs Lodge 21 Warren St **☎**03 443 8421, **ⓦ**wanakasprings.com. Classy, purpose-built, boutique lodge with comfortable, beautifully decorated rooms, stylish communal areas, free liqueurs and a spa pool in the native garden. The hosts have good local knowledge. Small discounts for two-night stays or longer. $310

★YHA Wanaka Purple Cow 94 Brownston St **☎**03 443 1880, **ⓦ**yha.co.nz. Large and inviting hostel where dorms (up to six beds) and rooms all come with their own bathroom. Also several en-suite doubles ($98), some with lake view and TV/DVD ($108), and a couple of deluxe motel units complete with iPod dock ($125). Sit and gaze at the fabulous lake view through the big picture windows, play pool (free), watch the nightly movie or rent a bike. Dorms $29, doubles $88

CAMPSITES AND HOLIDAY PARKS

Albert Town Campground SH6, 6km northeast of Wanaka. Open, informal camping area on the banks of the swift-flowing Clutha River with tap water and flush toilets. There's plenty of shade but it gets very busy for four weeks from Boxing Day. $7

Glendhu Bay Lakeside Holiday Park Camp 1127 Mount Aspiring Rd, 12km west of Wanaka **☎**03 443 7243, **ⓦ**glendhubaymotorcamp.co.nz. Beautifully situated family campsite with numerous pitches strung along the lakeshore, a bunkhouse sleeping 16 ($20) and fabulous views across to Mount Aspiring. Facilities include a popular boat ramp. Camping $16, cabins $50

★Lake Outlet Holiday Park 197 Lake Outlet Rd, 6km from Wanaka **☎**03 443 7478, **ⓦ**lakeoutlet.co.nz. Spacious and stunningly sited campsite at the point where Lake Wanaka becomes the Clutha River, in a great position for strolls along the lake or river frontage. Along with tent and powered sites there are simple cabins (some with a lounge) and a cottage sleeping 6 ($250). Rent a bike ($20 for 3hr) and ride the Outlet Track. Camping $14, cabins $55

Wanaka Lakeview Holiday Park 212 Brownston St **☎**03 443 7883, **ⓦ**wanakalakeview.co.nz. The closest campsite to town is a 10min walk from the centre and has tent sites, cabins and a self-contained flat ($100). Camping $18, standard cabins $50

EATING AND ENTERTAINMENT

Skiers and the healthy influx of summer tourists have determined the style and number of places to eat and drink in Wanaka. Unless you strike it lucky and catch a band passing through, entertainment extends to movies and one nightclub.

Bistro Gentil 76a Golf Course Rd **☎**03 443 2299, **ⓦ**bistrogentil.co.nz. Classy modern French restaurant with an elegant interior (hung with contemporary New Zealand art) and a terrace with long views towards the lake and mountains. Expect the likes of duck liver parfait with whipped orange butter ($20) followed by slow-cooked Cardrona lamb rump with a potato purée and sherry jus ($42). Trust-the-chef weekend lunches (3 courses for $55) are a little lighter, and self-serve wine dispensers let you sample a good range before committing to a full glass. Daily 11.30am–10pm or later.

★Francesca's Italian Kitchen 93 Ardmore St **☎**03 443 5599, **ⓦ**fransitalian.co.nz. Always buzzing with folk tucking into their famed polenta fries with truffle oil ($7) or wonderful pizzas ($20–25), this modern take on a traditional Italian joint artfully also turns super-fresh ingredients into starters like beef carpaccio with reggiano and anchovies ($20). Don't miss out on their wonderfully crisp cannoli ($4 each). Daily noon–3pm & 5–9pm or later.

13

Francesca's Pizza Brownston St ☎0800 464 74992, ⓦfrancescaspizzas.com. Mobile wood-fired pizza trailer that was the originator of *Francesca's Italian Kitchen*. Try the Tartufi with mushrooms, parmesan and truffle oil ($20). Daily 4–9pm.

Kai Whaka Pai Corner of Ardmore & Helwick sts ☎03 443 7795. Wanaka's liveliest daytime eating spot is a favourite with locals who come for chocolate cookies, breakfasts and fine coffee. On summer evenings the emphasis is on beer and wine, seated at tables on the street perhaps eating pulled beef burger ($19) or thin-crust pizza ($22). Taps dispense several of the local Wanaka Beerworks brews. Daily 7am–11pm.

LaLaLand 99 Ardmore St ☎03 443 4911, ⓦfacebook .com/lalalandwanaka. Mixology reaches its Wanaka apotheosis at this cute little cocktail bar. Come for a sundowner on the deck overlooking the lake or stick around until it really kicks off. Daily 4–2.30pm.

★**Relishes** 99 Ardmore St ☎03 443 9018, ⓦrelishescafe.co.nz. Long-standing, pretension-free Wanaka favourite that's always good for coffee and cake but serves a delicious smoked salmon breakfast *quesedilla* ($19) and the likes of horopito-crusted lamb with beetroot gnocchi and sage butter ($35) for dinner. Daily 7am–10pm or later.

Sasanoki 26 Ardmore St ☎03 443 6474. Eat in or take away from this modest Japanese kitchen, serving excellent udon noodles, sashimi and *donburi*, mostly $12–14. Grab a bento box and a sake for under $25. Mon–Fri 11.30am–2.30pm & 5.30–9pm, Sat 5.30–9pm.

Soul Food Organics 74 Ardmore St ☎03 443 7885. Unpretentious indoor and courtyard eating in this café and wholefood shop specializing in vegetarian, dairy- and gluten-free dishes. Drop by for excellent plunger coffee and muffins, vegetable omelette breakfasts ($14), winter soups, summer salad bar and tasty juices and smoothies such as raw cacao, date and banana thick shake ($10). Mon–Fri 8am–6pm, Sat & Sun 8am–4pm.

Urban Grind 73 Ardmore St ☎03 443 6748, ⓦurbangrind.co.nz. Start the day with smashed avocado with slow-roasted tomato on ciabatta ($13) in this smart modern bare-brick café with outsized lampshades. Pork belly sliders ($15) and blue cod croquettes ($14) work as an appetizer for thin-crust pizza ($20–23) washed down with a four-beer sample paddle ($13). Daily 8am–11pm.

Water Bar 145 Ardmore St ☎03 443 4345, ⓦwaterbarwanaka.co.nz. Happy hour (5.30–6.30pm) is the time to hit this fairly generic waterfront bar, especially on Friday when the $4 beers (and free pork buns while they last) extend to 7.30pm. Daily 11am–2am.

★**White House Café & Bar** 33 Dunmore St ☎03 443 9595. The owner sometimes rubs people up the wrong way, and building maintenance is a little lax, but these are easily outweighed by the wonderful meals when it's on form. A lot of love goes into loosely Mediterranean-influenced dishes such as mackerel, olive, new potato and avocado salad ($35), or ribeye with beetroot relish, silverbeet and fried potato ($40). Leave room for dessert, which might be ginger loaf with figs and blue cheese. Tues–Sun 6–10pm or later.

WANAKA FESTIVALS

New Year's Eve The youthful revelry of yesteryear has mostly been curtailed in recent times, and the new year is welcomed in with a family-oriented celebration.

Rippon Festival (ⓦripponfestival.co.nz). One-day rock, roots and reggae festival with a top Kiwi line-up and a magical setting with superb lake and mountain backdrop. There's always a lively after-party. Tickets around $135. First Saturday in February every even-numbered year.

A&P Show (ⓦwanakashow.co.nz). Town meets country at Wanaka's showgrounds on the lakefront with everything from calf-wrangling demos and biggest pumpkin competitions to the perfect Victoria sponge and a Jack Russell race in which up to 100 dogs chase a rabbit dragged around behind a man on a horse. Heaps of food, drink and fun, but accommodation is hard to come by. Third weekend in March.

Warbirds Over Wanaka (☎0800 496 620, ⓦwarbirdsoverwanaka.com). Wanaka Airport plays host to New Zealand's premier air show – three days of airborne craft doing their thing watched by over 50,000 people. Tickets: Fri $60, Sat $85, Sun $85, three days $180. Easter every even-numbered year.

Festival of Colour (ⓦfestivalofcolour.co.nz). A biennial celebration of visual art, dance, music, theatre and the like, with top Kiwi acts, including the symphony orchestra, performing all over town. Lots of free stuff, or buy tickets for individual performances. Mid-April in odd-numbered years.

Rhythm & Alps (ⓦrhythmandalps.co.nz). Around 10,000 typically attend this bass-heavy two-day music festival in the Cardrona Valley, 16km south of Wanaka. Loads of great music (Bastille and London Elektricity and lots of Kiwi acts in 2014); on-site camping logistics that get better by the year. $159 ($229 with camping).

13

THE CARDRONA VALLEY

Cardrona Hotel Cardrona ☎ 03 443 8153, ⓦ cardronahotel.co.nz. Stop for a bite or a beer at this 1863 survivor which, after years of neglect, was spruced up and reopened in 1984, although the frontage is held in a state of arrested decay. In winter, skiers sink into the chesterfields around the fire, while in summer the beer garden bursts into life. There's a great range of drinks, meals such as beef burger and fries ($20) or Asian-style pork belly ($29), plus B&B accommodation. Restaurant and bar daily 10am–10pm or later.

CINEMAS

Cinema Paradiso 72 Brownston St ☎ 03 443 1505, ⓦ paradiso.net.nz. The screens might have gone digital but you still sit in sagging old sofas, armchairs, airline seats or even a bisected Austin A30 at this quirky two-screener in a former Catholic church. The films range from Hollywood to art house, and there's always an interval during which everyone tucks into cookies, ice cream, coffee or booze from the on-site café. Adults $15.

Ruby's 50 Cardrona Valley Rd, 2km south of town ☎ 03 443 6901, ⓦ rubyscinema.co.nz. A chic pair of mini, digital cinemas (37-seat & 12-seat) entered through an intimate cocktail bar with Loren, Newman and Hepburn on the wall. Grab yourself a cocktail, wine or craft beer and a few nibbles and repair to the cinemas' huge leather recliners. Adults $18.50.

DIRECTORY

Internet Wanaka Internet, 3 Helwick St (generally daily 9am–7pm; ☎ 03 443 7429), charge $7/hr for a super-fast connection and the ability to log out and back in without losing time or data allowance.

Medical treatment Wanaka Medical Centre, 23 Cardrona Valley Road (☎ 03 443 0710, ⓦ wanakamedicalcentre .co.nz). Clinic Mon–Fri 8.30am–6pm plus 24hr emergency care.

Pharmacy Wanaka Pharmacy, 41 Helwick St (daily 8.30am–7pm; ☎ 03 443 8000).

Post office 39 Ardmore St (Mon–Fri 8.30am–5pm, Sat 9am–noon).

Along the Clutha River

Lake Wanaka is drained by the **Clutha River** (Mata-au in Maori), New Zealand's highest volume river and, at 338km, its second longest. The flow is interrupted along the way by major dams at Clyde and Roxburgh as the river and SH8 squeeze between the Old Man Range to the east, and the Knobby Range to the west.

The Clutha's middle reaches flow through the **Central Otago goldfields**, a fascinatingly historic region, southeast of Queenstown and Wanaka, where the barren and beautiful high country is peppered with gold-town ruins from the 1860s.

The boom towns were mostly moribund by the early twentieth century, but a few struggled on, mostly growing **stone fruit** and, later, grapes for what has become a burgeoning **wine region** (see p.741). With wine comes food and the region is increasingly establishing itself as a **foodie** haven. The range of activities seems pale compared to Queenstown or Wanaka, but **mountain biking** is hitting its straps with great rides all over the place and a few operators keen to rent you a bike or lead superb tours.

The reconstructed nineteenth-century settlement of **Cromwell**, 50km east of Queenstown, probably won't delay you long, but is a good jumping-off point for the former mining town of **Bendigo** and the wineries of **Bannockburn**. The twin towns of **Clyde** and **Alexandra** have fashioned themselves as bases for the popular Otago Central Rail Trail and some newer variants, while **Lawrence** relishes its position as the gold rush's hometown.

SH8 follows the Clutha River pretty closely and is typically plied by four buses a day running between Dunedin and Queenstown.

Cromwell

The uninspiring service town of **CROMWELL**, 60km east of Queenstown, does its best to celebrate its gold-mining roots while hopping on the back of the region's food and wine renaissance. Sadly, almost all of Cromwell's historic core is submerged below the shimmering surface of **Lake Dunstan**, formed behind the Clyde Dam, 20km downstream (see p.741). Cromwell may only be 120km from the coast, but this is as far from the sea as you can get in New Zealand, something that gives the area something of a continental climate that's perfect for fruit growing. A 13m-high, fibreglass **fruit sculpture** beside the highway highlights the long-time importance of nectarines, peaches, apples and pears, though these days cherries and grapes are probably more important.

Brief history

Soon after Hartley and Reilly's (see p.691) 1862 discovery of **gold**, a settlement sprouted at "The Junction" at the fork of the Kawarau and Clutha rivers. Local stories tell that it was later renamed when a government survey party dubbed it Cromwell to spite local Irish immigrant workers. Miners low on provisions planted the first fruit trees in the region, little expecting Cromwell to become the centre of the Otago **stone fruit** orchard belt.

Cromwell Historic Precinct

Melmore Terrace • ⓦ cromwellheritageprecinct.co.nz

Lake Dunstan laps at the toes of **Cromwell Historic Precinct**, a short street of restored old shopfronts, most of which would now be submerged had they not been dismantled and rebuilt on the water's edge. It all feels a bit fake, but on a fine day you can spend a happy hour browsing the art, craft and gourmet food shops before retiring for a libation to *Armando's*.

Highlands Motorsport Park

SH6 & Sandflat Rd, 3km southeast of Cromwell • Daily 9am–5pm • Go Karts $35, Dirt Buggies $40, Fastlaps $295, Lamborghini $149, Yourlaps $295 • ☎ 03 445 4052, ⓦ highlands.co.nz

With no real motorsport tradition it was a bit of a surprise when, in 2013, the town opened a **motor racing circuit** with aspirations to host the New Zealand Grand Prix sometime in the future. But mostly the two tracks are a playground for those with a need for speed. There's everything from self-drive Go Karts and Dirt Buggies to Fastlaps in a race-spec Porsche, a quick (very quick) spin in a Lamborghini Superleggera, and Yourlaps, in which you drive a grunty Suzuki Swift Sport seven times around the track to see if you can get yourself on the leaderboard.

National Motorsport Museum

Daily 9am–5pm • $20

Small but fascinating insight into New Zealand's illustrious (at least in parts) motor-racing past with plenty of coverage of Kiwi legends Bruce McLaren (founder of F1 team McLaren) and 1967 F1 champion Denny Hulme. There are usually a couple of newer McLarens on display along with racers through the years in all sorts of shapes and forms. One highlight is the 1906 Darracq, the last survivor from the original Grand Prix at La Mans.

The Nose

Daily 11am–4pm; $15

Hone your wine-tasting skills by watching a short movie intro to the region's wine history then visiting the aroma room. Here you compare the wine you're drinking with a massive array of aromas in little vials – citrus, clove, leather, truffle, liquorice etc.

Goldfields Mining Centre

SH6, 7km west of Cromwell • Daily 9am–5.30pm; guided tour departs on the hour • $20; guided tour $25 • ☎ 0800 111038, ⓦ goldfieldsmining.co.nz

A footbridge across the Kawarau River accesses the **Goldfields Mining Centre**, a former mine site scattered along a river terrace. Among the old huts, flumes and rusty

13

machinery, the most engaging part of the centre is the Chinese Village, ironically constructed as a film set in the early 1990s. You can take a **self-guided tour** in an hour or so, but it is far more informative to join the one-hour **guided tour** on which you get to handle some large gold nuggets, see a stamper battery cranked up using a water-powered Pelton wheel and try your hand at extracting a flake or two.

The site is also home to the *Wild Earth* restaurant and wine tasting (see below).

ARRIVAL AND DEPARTURE CROMWELL

By bus Cromwell acts as a hub for InterCity/Newmans, Alpine Connexions, Atomic, NakedBus and Catch-A-Bus, all stopping centrally on Lode Lane right by The Mall. You may well have to change buses here.

Destinations Alexandra (4 daily; 30min); Dunedin (4 daily; 3hr 30min); Lawrence (4 daily; 2hr); Queenstown (7 daily; 1hr); Wanaka (5 daily; 45min).

INFORMATION AND ACTIVITIES

Information i-SITE, 2d The Mall (daily: Nov–March 9am–7pm; April–Oct 9am–5pm; ☎03 445 0212, ⊕cromwell.org.nz). The region's main visitor centre provides the free and comprehensive *Discover Cromwell* and

Walk Cromwell leaflets (both downloadable from their site) and contains a small museum packed with gold-mining memorabilia.

ACCOMMODATION

Burn Cottage Retreat 168 Burn Cottage Rd, 3km north of town ☎03 445 3050, ⊕burncottageretreat.co.nz. Three high-standard self-contained cottages plus one B&B room, peacefully set surrounded by vineyards and a hosta garden. Cottages have sunny decks with barbecue and there's always a bowl of walnuts from their trees. B&B $195, cottages $200

The Chalets 102 Barry Ave ☎03 445 1260, ⊕thechaletscromwell.co.nz. New and enthusiastic management look set to turn this spacious and somewhat run-down 1970s former workers' camp into a quality campsite and backpackers. There are no dorms, just doubles and twins. Already popular with fruit pickers, it should get better and better. Camping $15, doubles $70

Colonial Manor Motel 14 Barry Ave ☎0800 428648,

⊕colonialmanor.co.nz. You'll be well looked after at this clean and welcoming motel roughly midway between the town centre and the historic precinct. Good range of rooms including spa suites. $130

Cromwell Top 10 Holiday Park 1 Alpha St ☎0800 107275, ⊕cromwellholidaypark.co.nz. Large, quality campsite on the edge of town with a range of en-suite cabins ($75) and motel units ($140). Facilities include hot tub, TV room and kids' playground with jumping pillow. Camping, per site $40, cabins $75

Lowburn Freedom Camping SH6, 4km north of Cromwell. Large lakeside gravel parking area with toilets where freedom camping is allowed for up to three nights. Free

EATING AND DRINKING

Armando's Italian Kitchen 71 Melrose Place, Old Cromwell Town ☎03 445 0303, ⊕armandoskitchen .com. Thin-crust pizza ($22), risottos and delicious gelato combine with Kiwi café staples in this casual joint overlooking the lake. Daily 9am–4pm.

Mrs Jones' Orchard SH6, 5km west of town ☎03 445 0275, ⊕mrsjonesorchard.co.nz. Tour buses disgorge at the fruit stalls that encircle Cromwell, but especially at this place, which is stacked with fresh and dried fruit, the former blended to make wonderful fruit ice creams, best consumed in the adjacent rose garden. Daily 8am–5pm or later.

delicious white port. Bring a picnic and eat in the grounds. Daily 10am–5pm.

Wild Earth Restaurant Goldfields Mining Centre ☎03 445 4841. Stroll over the bridge across the Kawarau River to access this tasting room for top-quality Wild Earth wines, particularly Pinot Noir ($5 for 5 tastes, refunded with purchase). Wine-matched meals cooked in old French oak Pinot Noir barrels are served on the grass overlooking the river. Try the mussels on the half-shell ($15), tequila-cured salmon ($18) or grilled haloumi stack with aubergine ($17). Daily 10am–5pm.

Wooing Tree 64 Shortcut Rd ☎03 445 4142, ⊕wooingtree.co.nz. Casual little family-run winery right in Cromwell where the easy-drinking wines (available for free tasting) are a perfect accompaniment to lunches in the neat grounds. Grab a salmon or cheese platter (both $20), a BLT ($15) and help a citrus tart down with a glass of their delicate *Tickled Pink* dessert wine. Daily 10am–5pm.

WINERIES

Aurum Wines SH6, 2km north of Cromwell ☎03 445 3620, ⊕aurumwines.co.nz. Welcoming Kiwi-French-run winery producing quality Pinot Noirs along with an unusual repertoire including a Blanc de Blanc bubbly and a

Bannockburn

13

There are remote clusters of cottage foundations and sluicings all over Central Otago, and dedicated ruin hounds can poke around the detritus in places such as the **Nevis Valley** and **Bendigo** (ask locally), but the most extensive workings are found at **BANNOCKBURN**, a scattered hamlet 9km southwest of Cromwell that's now more famous for its wineries.

Bannockburn Sluicings

Felton Rd • Open access • Free

Download the *Walk Cromwell* leaflet from the Cromwell i-SITE website and make for the **Bannockburn Sluicings**, a tortured landscape that was once home to two thousand people, washing away the land to reveal the gold-rich seams below. Interpretive signs punctuate a ninety-minute **self-guided trail** that starts 1500m along Felton Road and weaves up to Stewart Town, home to dilapidated mud-brick huts and ageing pear and apricot trees.

The Wineries

Exploring mine workings is thirsty work, and you'll welcome the chance to sample the Bannockburn **wineries**; founded in the early 1990s, they have quickly established themselves as some of New Zealand's best. Almost a dozen are open for tasting; call in advance if you're visiting in winter. For informed guidance, join Queenstown-based Appellation Central Wine Tours (see p.703).

EATING AND DRINKING BANNOCKBURN

Carrick 247 Cairnmuir Rd ⊕03 445 3480, ⓦcarrick .co.nz. Fully organic winery overlooking Bannockburn Inlet that's good for tastings of their excellent wines ($5 refunded with purchase) or lunch of confit duck leg, quinoa and kale or slow-roasted crispy pork belly, bok choy, garlic, miso and potato (both $29). Expect sophisticated Pinot Noir, and estate-grown Chardonnay, Riesling, Pinot Gris and even (unusually this far south) Sauvignon Blanc. Daily 11am–5pm.

Felton Road Felton Rd ⊕03 445 0885, ⓦfeltonroad .com. There's no food or anything fancy at this cellar door overlooking the vines, just free tasting of all but the pricier wines from one of the region's classiest producers. Mon–Fri 2–5pm.

★**The Kitchen** 430a Bannockburn Rd ⊕03 445 1553, ⓦfacebook.com/thekitchenbannockburn. Casual but classy café in a modern corrugated-iron shed, with fresh flowers and attentive staff. Expect great coffee, sumptuous cakes and the likes of *croque monsieur* ($11) and top-quality bacon butties ($15). Seasonal produce grown out the back makes its way onto the very short weekend dinner menu (mains $30). Wed–Sun 9am–3pm plus Fri & Sat 6–9.30pm, when bookings are recommended.

Mt Difficulty 73 Felton Rd ⊕03 445 3445, ⓦmtdifficulty.co.nz. Great wines and a perfect place to taste them, either at the cellar door or in the restaurant overlooking the vines and the sluicings. Sample their platters ($30 & $55) or mains such as Pinot Noir-roasted duck with Portobello mushrooms ($35). Tasting daily 10.30am–4.30pm or later. Restaurant daily noon–4pm.

Clyde

SH8 cuts southeast from Cromwell through 20km of the bleak and windswept **Cromwell Gorge**, hugging the banks of Lake Dunstan to peaceful **CLYDE**. With several good places to stay and eat, this small former gold town makes a great base for forays around the region and on to the Otago Central Rail Trail (see box, p.743).

Since the mid-1980s, Clyde has been dominated by the giant grey hydroelectric **Clyde Dam**, 1km north of town, which generates five percent of New Zealand's power and provides water for irrigation. Initially controversial, the dam is nevertheless considered something of an engineering marvel, with special "slip joints" providing the dam wall with flexibility in case of earthquakes.

Clyde Museum and the Herb Factory Museum

5 Blyth St and 10 Fache St • both Oct–April Tues–Sun 2–4pm • Individually $3, combined $5

Clyde's original 1864 stone courthouse is flanked by the **Clyde Museum**, worth a peek for its intriguing coverage of Clyde's botched Great Gold Robbery of 1870 when one George Rennie tried to make off with £13,000 in bullion and banknotes.

A couple of streets away, the **Herb Factory Museum** was established in the 1930s as New Zealand's first, and thrived by making use of the common thyme that still grows wild in abundance hereabouts.

ARRIVAL AND DEPARTURE CLYDE

By bus Buses stop in Clyde on demand, pulling up on Sunderland St, which is where you'll find many of the town's accommodation, restaurants and amenities.

ACCOMMODATION

Dunstan House 29 Sunderland St ☎03 449 2295, ⓦdunstanhouse.co.nz. Comfy B&B in a former stagecoach stop with bags of character. Rooms are imaginatively decorated (half en suite and some with claw-foot bath), some opening out onto a wraparound veranda on the first floor, where miners once rode their horses, after a glass or two. There's plenty of bike storage, and a piano in the lounge. Shared bath **$130**, en suite **$170**

Hartley Arms 25 Sutherland St ☎03 449 270, ⓦhartleyarms.co.nz. Clyde's cheapest rooms with just one double and two four-bed bunk rooms all sharing bathroom, laundry and cooking facilities. Friendly and informative hosts. Closed July & Aug. Per person including continental breakfast **$45**

★**Olivers** 34 Sutherland St ☎03 449 2600 & ☎0800 131070, ⓦoliverscentralotago.co.nz. Don't pass up the opportunity to stay in this gorgeous eleven-room reworking of a former homestead right in the heart of town. Five of the rooms are in the former stables, which open out into a central courtyard, and all are completely different – schist wall, half-tester bed, claw-foot bath – while maintaining the same balance of modern comfort with period style. The five wonderfully spacious premium rooms are especially gorgeous. Superb breakfast included. **$215**, premium **$365**

EATING AND ENTERTAINMENT

The Bank Café 31 Sunderland St ☎03 449 2955. Streetside tables catch the morning sun at this central café, offering great coffee, eggs Benedict ($16) and lamb wrap ($13) and a friendly smile. Daily 9am–4pm.

Clyde Bistro 6 Naylor St ☎03 449 3089, ⓦclydebistro .co.nz. After a day in the saddle who can pass up a classic wood-fired pizza ($22) and a glass of local Pinot? Summer daily 4pm–late; winter Wed–Sun 4.30 to not quite so late.

Clyde Cinema 6a Naylor St ☎03 449 2379, ⓦclydecinema.co.nz. Sink into leather seats with a glass of wine for the latest mainstream and independent releases. Tickets $16.50.

Post Office Café & Bar 2 Blyth St ☎03 449 2488. This 1865 former post office serves the Post Office dark ale in its bar, but the place is best for its peaceful garden where you can tuck into hearty dishes such as nachos ($15) or lamb with vegetables ($31). Daily 10am–10pm.

Alexandra

ALEXANDRA (affectionately known as Alex), 10km southeast of Clyde, sprang up during the 1862 gold rush, and flourished for four years before turning into a quiet, prosperous, service town for the fruit growers of Central Otago. Throughout the summer you'll find fruit stalls selling some delectable apricots, peaches and nectarines, and in December and January some of the world's finest cherries.

Central Stories

21 Centennial Ave • Daily 10am–4pm • Donation • ☎03 448 6230, ⓦcentralstories.com

A huge water wheel marks the fascinating **Central Stories**, a social and natural history museum covering everything from the creation of the region's distinctive schist tors to viticulture in the world's southernmost wine region. Learn about the heart-rending mystery of James Horn, whose father's deathbed letter will bring a lump to your throat, and the sorry tale of the rabbits, introduced into the area in 1909, which did what rabbits do – so well that they became a menace throughout the South Island. To combat the problem, the town holds an **Easter Bunny Shoot** every year, and hunters from all over New Zealand congregate on Good Friday for the slaughter.

BIKE CENTRAL

Following on from the pioneering Otago Central Rail Trail, Central Otago now has an enviable selection of easy-riding routes to explore and an elaborate array of operators keen to offer everything from straight bike hire to all-in luxury accommodation and transport packages. The main players are listed below.

OTAGO CENTRAL RAIL TRAIL

One of the finest ways to explore the Maniototo is to **cycle** the Otago Central Rail Trail (OCRT), a largely flat 150km route from Clyde to Middlemarch that passes through all the main towns except for St Bathans and Naseby. It follows the hard-packed gravel trackbed of the former **Otago Central Branch railway line** and includes modified rail bridges and viaducts (several spanning over 100m), beautiful valleys and long agricultural plains.

Passenger trains ran through the Maniototo until 1990, a continuation of what is now the Taieri Gorge Railway (see box, p.606), but it wasn't until early 2000 that the trail opened, galvanizing a dying region. All sorts of accommodation has sprung up to cater to bikers' needs. Pubs and cafés located where the trail crosses roads aren't shy to advertise the opportunity to take a break.

The trail takes most people 3–4 days and combining the ride with the **Taieri Gorge Railway** makes a great way to travel between Clyde and Dunedin.

If you're just out to pick the **highlights**, aim for a couple of 10km stretches, both with tunnels, viaducts and interesting rock formations: Lauder–Auripo in the northern section, and Daisybank–Hyde in the east. A torch is handy for the tunnels.

The widely available *Otago Central Rail Trail* leaflet (free) outlines the route and elevation profile. The most comprehensive information on the web is at ⓦotagocentralrailtrail.co.nz, though a couple of commercial sites offer good practical information; try ⓦotagorailtrail.co.nz and ⓦrailtrail.co.nz.

ROXBURGH GORGE TRAIL

The **Roxburgh Gorge Trail** (10km+13km+10km; 1 day; ⓦroxburghgorge.co.nz) has piggy-backed on the popularity of the Otago Central Rail Trail, but suffers from being discontinuous at present. The route follows the Clutha River south from Alexandra to Lake Roxburgh Village but the middle section hasn't been built yet. Clutha River Cruises (☎0800 258842, ⓦclutharivercruises .co.nz) can jetboat you across the gap for $95, but it is probably easier to just ride the first 10km from Alex to Doctor's Point then back again. It is a lovely ride through a schist chasm where in spring the hillsides are a riot of yellow lupin and lilac thyme blooms. Keep your eyes peeled for evidence of old mine workings and the stone shack of the people who once worked the river.

CLUTHA GOLD TRAIL

The southern end of the Roxburgh Gorge Trail continues as the **Clutha Gold Trail** (73km; 2–3 days; ⓦcluthagold.co.nz) which largely follows the Clutha River before veering away to Lawrence.

BIKE RENTAL AND PACKAGES

Altitude Bikes ☎03 448 8917, ⓦaltitudebikes .co.nz. Alexandra-based operator offering a one-day, 47km OCRT highlights package with transport and bike rental ($89), a fully supported 4-day package including B&B accommodation ($649) and all manner of freedom ride, bike rental and customized packages.

Bike It Now! 23 Holloway St, Clyde ☎0800 245366, ⓦbikeitnow.co.nz. Relative newcomer to the scene offering 27.5 and 29er bikes (from $50 a day) for use on guided and self-guide trips on all the local trails. Their 3-day OCRT package with bike, transport and simple accommodation ($500) can be upgraded to more comfy digs ($585) and includes bag transfers. A boutique 5-night variation costs $1075.

Cycle Surgery ☎0800 292534, ⓦcyclesurgery.co.nz. Middlemarch-based company offering just about everything you might want to do from upright, step-through unisex bike rental ($35/day; tandems $70; panniers $5) and minibus shuttles to custom packages possibly including Taieri Gorge tickets, accommodation, bag transfers and meals. They cater for a wide range of budgets.

Cycle Trail Tours ☎0800 429253, ⓦnotarailtrail .co.nz. Guided trip specialist on the Roxburgh (1 day; $329) and Clutha Gold (2 days; $599) trails.

Trail Journeys ☎0800 030381, ⓦtrailjourneys.co.nz. With over 500 bikes, this Clyde-based operator dominates the OCRT scene. They offer bike rental and shuttle transport but specialize in itinerary planning, piecing together accommodation, bag transport and the like.

By bus InterCity, Atomic and Wanaka Connexions all stop outside the i-SITE. Catch-A-Bus picks up wherever you want.

Destinations Dunedin (4 daily; 3hr); Lawrence (4 daily; 1hr 15min); Queenstown (4 daily; 1hr 30min); Ranfurly (1–2 daily; 1hr).

INFORMATION AND ACTIVITIES

Information i-SITE, 21 Centennial Ave in Central Stories (daily: Nov–Easter 9am–6pm; Easter–Oct 9am–5pm; ☎ 03 448 9515, ⓦ centralotagonz.com).

Altitude Bikes 88 Centennial Ave ☎ 03 448 8917, ⓦ altitudebikes.co.nz. An abundance of treeless hills makes Alex a good base for mountain biking. Altitude Adventures rent mountain bikes from $40/day to get you out on the singletrack, and staff have the expertise for

getting you on the Otago Central Rail Trail (see box, p.743). They also run guided singletrack tours requiring intermediate skills or better: probably the best is the half-day Knobby Range ($155) across high-country tussock and down steep rocky trails with a ride to the start minimizing the amount of climbing. Mon–Fri 9am–5pm.

ACCOMMODATION

Alexandra Garden Court 51 Manuherikia Rd ☎ 0800 736116, ⓦ alexgardencourtmotel.co.nz. Quiet budget motel on the edge of town with landscaped grounds, swimming pool, kids' play area and very clean, if not particularly stylish, units. **$120**

Asure Avenue Motel 117 Centennial Ave ☎ 0800 758899, ⓦ avenue-motel.co.nz. Very comfortable and central motel with tastefully decorated units and suites (some with spa bath). Units **$130**, suites **$150**

Marj's Place 5 Theyers St, 1km northwest ☎ 03 448 7098, ⓦ marjsplace.co.nz. Marj is the mother hen at this very welcoming hostel-cum-homestay in three houses on a quiet street. Homestay guests share a bathroom but get robes, a sauna and a spa bath plus access to a well-equipped kitchen with dishwasher. Most backpackers stay across the road, and there are great long-stay rates for fruit pickers. Dorms **$30**, doubles **$70**

EATING

★**Courthouse Café** 8 Centennial Ave ☎ 03 448 7818, ⓦ packingshedcompany.com. Licensed café in (and on the sunny lawns around) Alex's 1878 former courthouse, serving delicious home-baked food such as honey chicken salad ($21) plus a bunch of fresh salads, smoothies, cakes and coffee. Dec–March Mon–Fri 7.30am–8pm, Sat & Sun 8am–8pm; April–Nov Mon–Fri 7.30am–4.30pm,

Sat & Sun 8am–4pm.

Nosh Nosh Swigs Limerick St, in the car park behind Furniture Court ⓦ noshnoshswigs.co.nz. Gourmet burgers plus soups, salads, sodas and sundaes to eat in, out in the courtyard or take away. The lamb shoulder, falafel and gurnard burgers ($14) are all excellent. Wine and beer too. No bookings. Tues–Sat noon–9pm, Sun 5–9pm.

Roxburgh

The bland former gold town of **Roxburgh**, 40km south of Alexandra, sits hemmed in by vast orchards that yield bountiful crops of peaches, apricots, apples, raspberries and strawberries, all harvested by an annual influx of seasonal pickers. The season's surplus is sold from a phalanx of roadside stalls from early December through to May. If you've a hankering for a stomach filler, stop in at **Jimmy's Pies** (143 Scotland St, SH8), whose product, made here since 1960, is sold all over the South Island.

Lawrence

From Roxburgh, SH8 runs 60km southeast to **LAWRENCE**, Otago's original 1861 gold town where, in May 1861, Australian Gabriel Read struck pay dirt. Twelve thousand gold-seekers scrambled to try their luck in the gold-rich Gabriel's Gully but the boom was over in barely a year. Its legacy is a sleepy farming town of barely 550 souls and a smattering of Victorian buildings, hastily constructed in a variety of materials and styles. A few have now been converted into chichi **galleries** that provide some reason to linger.

Gabriel's Gully Historic Reserve

3.5km north along Gabriel's Gully Rd • Open access • Free

Gabriel's Gully Road leads 3.5km north of Lawrence to **Gabriel's Gully Historic Reserve**, where a series of plaques explaining the old workings should take you an hour or so to explore. A climb up the steep rise of **Jacob's Ladder** gives a good view of the gully, long since filled with tailings that reach nearly 20m in depth. It is possible to visit Gabriel's Gully as part of a farmland loop walk from town (8.5km loop; 2hr 30min), returning along a ridge.

ARRIVAL AND INFORMATION
LAWRENCE

By bus InterCity, Atomic and Alpine Connexions all stop in the centre of town.

Destinations Alexandra (4 daily; 1hr 15min); Cromwell (4 daily; 2hr); Dunedin (4 daily; 1hr 20min).

Tourist information Goldfields Museum, 17 Ross Place

(daily 9.30am–4.30pm; ☎03 485 9222, ⓦ lawrence .co.nz). A combined information centre and museum that brings something of the heady early gold-rush days to life through imaginative displays. They also have free wi-fi.

The Maniototo

The most interesting route to the east coast from Alexandra is through the **Maniototo**, flat high country shared by three shallow valleys – the Manuherikia River, the Ida Burn and the Taieri River – and the low, craggy ranges that separate them. Despite easy road access, the Maniototo feels like a windswept and ambient world apart.

Many come to cycle the **Otago Central Rail Trail** (see box, p.743), but former gold-mining communities such as **St Bathans** and **Naseby** are worth sampling for their calm seclusion and subtle reminders of how greed transforms the land. Much of the area's pleasure is in even smaller places – the post office at **Ophir** or the old engineering works in the **Ida Valley** – and in the dozens of small cottages, many abandoned – a testimony to the harsh life in these parts.

Brief history

Predictably, Europeans first came in search of gold. They found it near **Naseby**, but returns swiftly declined and farming on the plains became more rewarding. This was especially true when **railway** developers looking for the easiest route from Dunedin to Alexandra chose a way up the Taieri Gorge and across the Maniototo. In 1898, the line arrived in **Ranfurly**, which soon took over from Naseby as the area's main administrative centre. With the closure of the rail line in 1990 an already moribund area withered further until the **Otago Central Rail Trail** caught on. In recent years, environmentalists have battled to save the landscape from **Project Hayes**, which would have been New Zealand's largest wind farm, a battle only won when the power company Meridian Energy backed down in 2012.

GETTING AROUND
THE MANIOTOTO

By car and bike Driving or riding is the best way to see the Maniototo as public transport is very limited.

By train The Taieri Gorge Railway (see box, p.606) runs daily from Dunedin to the Otago Rail Trail. On Fri and Sun it stops in Middlemarch, but on other days it turns around at Pukerangi and you'll have to cycle the 18km along the road to reach Middlemarch.

By bus Trail Journeys (Oct–April daily; May–Sept on demand; ☎0800 030 381, ⓦ trailjourneys.co.nz) runs a service between Clyde and Middlemarch primarily for Rail Trail riders. Alpine Connexions (Oct–April daily; May–Sept daily except Tues & Sat; ☎03 443 9120, ⓦ alpineconnexions.co.nz) will also pick up from the train at Pukerangi or Middlemarch and run through the Maniototo to Wanaka and Queenstown.

Omakau and Ophir

Heading northeast from Alexandra, you climb steadily onto the high-country plain. After 25km, turn down Ophir Bridge Road which crosses a historic little **suspension**

13

GRAHAME SYDNEY

Many New Zealanders only know the Maniototo through the works of Dunedin-born Realist painter **Grahame Sydney** (Ⓦ grahamesydney.com), who spends much of his time in the region. His broad, big-sky landscapes of goods sheds amid parched fields and letterboxes at lonely crossroads are universally accessible, and instantly recognizable to anyone visiting the region.

Prints and postcards of his work are found throughout the Maniototo and beyond, and originals hang in most of the country's major galleries. At first glance many of the works are unemotional renditions, but reflection reveals great poignancy. As he says, "I'm the long stare, not the quick glimpse".

bridge across the Manuherikia River and continues 1km to **Ophir**, the region's original gold town. It still has its imposing and operational 1886 **Post & Telegraph Office** (Mon–Fri 9am–noon). **Omakau**, 2km to the north, has basic services.

ACCOMMODATION AND EATING
OMAKAU AND OPHIR

Chatto Creek Tavern 1544 SH85, 10km southwest of Omakau ☎ 03 447 3710, Ⓦ chattocreektavern.co.nz. Classic Rail Trail stop with old-fashioned but comfortably rustic rooms in a 130-year-old schist pub. Lots of memorabilia and quality pub meals such as blue cod and chips or pulled pork in Lebanese bread with horseradish sour cream (both $22). Bunkroom, including breakfast $50, double B&B $120

Muddy Creek Café 2 Harvey St, Omakau ☎ 03 447 3344. Good casual café with fish and chips ($16), pumpkin lasagne ($15), espresso and cakes, plus takeaway burgers and toasted sandwiches. Mon–Sat 8.30am–7pm, Sun 10am–7pm.

Pitches Store 45 Swindon St, Ophir ☎ 03 447 3240, Ⓦ pitches-store.co.nz. This former general merchants' building now houses some of the classiest accommodation in the Maniototo, the rough-hewn stone walls contrasting nicely with the sophisticated modern decor. Out front, the café/restaurant isn't quite as good as it would like to think it is, but still offers an imaginative seasonal menu a few steps above most of what's available locally – think pan-seared squid and ramen noodles ($19) followed by Merino lamb rump with *pommes duchesse* ($37) and a cheese platter ($15–21). Restaurant Nov–April daily 10am–9pm; May–Oct Thurs, Sun & Mon 10am–4pm, Fri & Sat 10am–9pm. $280

Oturehura

The main SH85 avoids the Ida Valley, but it is worth turning off at Omakau and detouring past a couple of the Maniototo's most interesting historical sights at **Oturehura**.

Hayes Engineering Works

Hayes Rd, Oturehura • Sept–May daily 10am–5pm • $10; check website for "operating days" when there are guided tours $15 • ☎ 03 444 5801, Ⓦ hayesengineering.co.nz

All over the world, wire fences are still tensioned by parallel wire strainers designed by Ernest Hayes in 1902 at the **Hayes Engineering Works**, a site based around a frozen-in-time corrugated-iron workshop. Everything is as it was in 1952 when the company decamped to Christchurch – in the gloom, cutters and drill presses are linked by belts and pulleys to overhead shafts originally driven by wind, then hydro power and now the power-takeoff from an ancient tractor (still fired up on operating days).

Alongside the workshop stands the original 1890 mud-brick **cottage** (now a small museum and café) Ernest shared with his wife, Hannah. An integral part of the company, she set off on lengthy sales trips on her bicycle wearing an ankle-length skirt.

Next door is the somewhat idiosyncratic house they designed and built, decked out precisely as it was in the 1920s. They were engineers, not carpenters, so broken doors are fixed with metal bracing and one doorjamb was fitted with steel springs to prevent the door slamming shut.

Gilchrist's General Store

3353 Ida Valley Rd, Oturehua • Mon–Fri 7.30am–5.30pm, Sat 8am–4pm & Sun 10am–2pm • Free • ☎ 03 444 5808

Poke your head in to this working museum, a still operational 1929 grocery shop and post office lined with the original wooden shelving laden with ancient (and new) groceries. The place was once the hub of the valley, with twelve staff, but saw hard times and almost closed before being revived. Buy a pie, browse the books or just wander in for a chat.

EATING	OTUREHURA

★ **Ida Valley Kitchen** 3407 Ida Valley Rd ☎ 03 444 5030. Stop for an excellent coffee or a huge chunk of wonderful carrot cake at the region's best café. Sausage rolls and the likes of beef bourguignon pies ($8) and pesto chicken wraps ($14) are served in the smart interior or sunny garden. Sept–May daily 9am–4pm.

St Bathans

Gallery ☎ 03 447 3518, ⓦ stbathansgallery.co.nz

The picturesque former gold town of **ST BATHANS** is out on a limb 80km north of Alexandra and accessed 17km along St Bathans Loop Road from Becks. St Bathans boomed in 1863, but when the gold ran out in the 1930s everything went with it. These days it's virtually a ghost town, with just six residents and an attractive straggle of ancient buildings along the single road. The former post office exhibits photography, prints and engraving as **St Bathan's Gallery**.

Blue Lake

The few remaining dwellings overlook the striking **Blue Lake** where mineral-rich water has flooded a crater left by the merciless sluicing of Kildare Hill, once 120m high but now entirely washed away. A short track leads from the *Vulcan* to a vantage point over the azure waters, now used for swimming and boating.

ACCOMMODATION AND EATING	ST BATHANS

St Bathans Domain campsite Loop Rd, 1.3km northwest of St Bathans. Simple DOC site with water and toilets. **Free**
St Bathan's Jail and Constables Cottage Loop Rd ☎ 0800 555016, ⓦ stbathansnz.co.nz. Choose from a 3-bedroom 1864 house with modern bathroom and kitchen and lovely gardens overlooking the Blue Lake, or self-contained unit just behind with simple continental

breakfast included. Cottage **$220**, jail **$145**
Vulcan Hotel Loop Rd ☎ 03 447 3629. Atmospheric 1882 hotel where local farmers and visitors prop up the wooden bar. Grab a BLT ($15) or dine on venison in port with cranberry sauce ($38), either in the dark bar or shady garden. You can also stay, though the nicest room (#1) is reputed to be haunted. Bar & restaurant daily 9am–9pm. **$120**

Naseby

The small settlement of **NASEBY**, 25km east of St Bathans and 9km off SH85, clings to the Maniototo some 600m above sea level. At its 4000-strong peak in 1865, Naseby was the largest gold-mining town hereabouts, but today numbers have dropped to around 100 huddled in a collection of small houses (many of them originally built of sun-dried mud brick by miners), with a shop, a garage, a couple of pubs, a café and a campsite.

The museums

Early Settlers Museum Dec–April Wed–Sun 1–4pm; donation • **Jubilee Museum** daily 10am–5pm; included with Early Settlers Museum or $2 token from the general store

The story of the town and wider region is told through the tiny **Maniototo Early Settlers Museum**, corner of Earne and Leven streets, which is packed with black-and-white photos of past residents and also contains a small collection of items left by Chinese miners. Across the street, the **Jubilee Museum** houses the remains of an old watchmaker's shop together with displays on the local gold rush of the 1860s and 1870s.

Information Naseby Information Centre, 16 Derwent St (Christmas to mid-Jan daily 10am–4.30pm; rest of year Fri–Mon 11am–2pm; ☎ 03 444 9961, ⊚ nasebyinfo.org .nz). Located in the former post office this volunteer-run place has the *A Walk Through History* map of town and walking maps of the forest.

One Tree Hill Track The visitor centre has maps showing three local walks, the best being this one (1600m; 1hr return), which starts on Brooms Street in town and snakes uphill along the eastern side of Hogburn Gully, past dramatic honey-coloured cliffs entirely carved by water.

Mountain biking If you've got your own wheels pick up a map from the information centre and head into the forest, threaded with lots of great single-track, mostly undulating without seriously steep climbs.

Naseby Curling International 1057 Channel Rd ☎ 03 444 9878, ⊚ curling.co.nz. Naseby is New Zealand's home of curling. This occasionally takes place outside on cold winter days but most activity is at this indoor year-round venue where instruction is usually available ($30 for 1hr 30min). Daily 10am–5pm.

Ancient Briton Hotel 16 Leven St ☎ 03 444 9992, ⊚ ancientbriton.co.nz. Classic Kiwi pub with a convivial bar, a sunny garden and solid bar meals such as burger and chips ($17) and roast pork belly with Asian greens ($28). An annexe outside has pleasant rooms. Free wi-fi. **$105**

Black Forest Café 7 Derwent St ☎ 03 444 9820. Cosy café with good coffee and muffins, great cheese scones and light meals such as eggs Benedict ($18) and frittata ($12). Evening meals by arrangement. Daily 9am–4pm.

Larchview Holiday Park 8 Swimming Dam Rd ☎ 03 444 9904, ⊚ larchviewholidaypark.co.nz. Pretty and tranquil forest campsite a 5min walk from town and across the road from the popular swimming dam complete with springboard. Also has a self-contained house ($90). Camping **$13**, cabins **$52**

Naseby Lodge Cnr of Derwent and Oughter sts ☎ 03 444 8222, ⊚ nasebylodge.co.nz. A delightful modern cluster of mud-brick and corrugated-iron one- and two-bedroom self-contained units clustered around the straw bale-built 2000ft restaurant which serves quality steak, chicken and fish mains for around $30. Lodge and restaurant nightly Dec–April, weekends only for rest of year. **$170**

Old Doctors Residence 58 Derwent St ☎ 03 444 9775, ⊚ olddoctorsresidence.co.nz. A fabulous B&B where the customers get treated like prodigal children. Luxurious accommodation is in the mud-brick former dairy or a suite comprising the former doctor's surgery and the waiting room. There's a cosy guest lounge and wine tasting with food matches each evening. **$295**

Dansey's Pass

The gravel Kyeburn Diggings Road runs east out of Naseby 16km to the *Dansey's Pass Coach Inn*. From here, the 50km north to Duntroon on SH83 is narrow, winding and unsuitable for medium and large campervans. But the route is barren and beautiful, one of the last untouched high-country passes with open hillsides covered in tussock. It is sometimes closed by snow between June and September: check in Naseby before setting out.

Old gold workings are visible from the roadside, where water-jets from sluices have distorted the schist and tussock landscape, leaving rock dramatically exposed.

★ **Dansey's Pass Coach Inn** 781 Kyeburn Diggings, 16km east of Naseby ☎ 03 444 9048, ⊚ danseyspass .co.nz. Charming wayside inn with a bit of Wild West feel that's the only relic of the once 2000-strong gold-rush community. It was built from local schist stone in 1862 (the stonemason was reputedly paid a pint of beer for each stone laid). Stop in for a beer on leather sofas around the fire, grab lunch (perhaps grilled salmon on potato cake; $20) on the grass across the road or stay for dinner of lamb backstrap with Moroccan chutney ($30) in the conservatory restaurant. They close early if things are quiet, so call ahead before making a special journey. The nineteen rooms are Victorian styled and there's free wi-fi. Daily 8am–10pm or later. Double **$140**, en suite **$160**

Ranfurly

Centennial Milk Bar Tues–Sun: Oct–Dec 1–4pm, Jan–May 11am–4pm • $2 donation

RANFURLY is the largest settlement on the Maniototo, though that's not saying much. It has enjoyed a resurgence, thanks to being roughly midway along the rail trail and a rather desperate attempt to brand itself as New Zealand's **Rural Art Deco** centre. In truth, the only vaguely noteworthy building is the sleek cream-and-green-painted 1948 Centennial Milk Bar on Charlemont Street East, which now operates as an Art Deco furnishings store. The town goes all out to make the best of what it has, particularly during the **Rural Art Deco Weekend** at the end of February.

INFORMATION RANFURLY

i-SITE 3 Charlemont St East (daily: Oct–May 9am–5.30pm; June–Sept 9am–5pm; ☎ 03 444 1005, ⓦ maniototo .co.nz). Visitor centre housed in the former train station

which has a free audiovisual show on the region and pictorial displays tracing the history of the town and the Otago Central Railway.

ACCOMMODATION AND EATING

Komako 634 Waipiata–Naseby Rd, 3km south of town ☎ 03 444 9324, ⓦ komako.net.nz. Peony garden (blooming Oct–Dec) with three gorgeous cabins right by the Rail Trail and surrounded by great views. Accommodation and dinner deals ($100/person), which could be a gourmet barbecue or a roast. **$120**

Maniototo Lodge 3 Ranfurly–Patearoa Rd, 1km south of Ranfurly ☎ 03 444 9600, ⓦ maniototolodge.co.nz. Very welcoming B&B in a solid-brick former presbytery with three shared-bath guest rooms equipped with robes. There's home-baking, a full cooked breakfast, courtesy local transport and as much local advice as you fancy. Per person, **$80**

Old Post Office Backpackers 11 Pery St ☎ 03 444

9588, ⓦ oldpobackpackers.co.nz. Clean, comfortable and well-run hostel sleeping twenty in a variety of doubles, twins and five-bed dorms. Continental breakfast ($11) available. Be sure to call ahead in winter. Dorms **$33**, rooms **$75**

Ranfurly Holiday Park Corner of Reade and Pery sts ☎ 0800 726 387, ⓦ ranfurlyholidaypark.co.nz. Relaxed, spacious and central campsite ($15), with pitches, power and units. Cabins **$48**, motel units **$105**

Ranfurly Lion Hotel 10 Charlemont St East ☎ 03 444 9140, ⓦ ranfurlyhotel.co.nz. A good hotel restaurant in Art Deco surroundings serving the likes of roasts ($20) and fish and chips ($25). Daily 7.30am–10pm.

Middlemarch

ⓦ middlemarch.co.nz

At Kyeburn, 15km east of Ranfurly, SH85 (locally known as "The Pigroot") heads for the coast over to Palmerston while SH87 branches south, slowly winding through the eastern Maniototo between the Rock and Pillar Range and the Taieri River. Fifty barren yet scenic kilometres south, you'll reach the tiny community of **MIDDLEMARCH**, at the end of the Rail Trail and the Friday- and Sunday-only terminus of the **Taieri Gorge Railway** (see box, p.606). There's not much to it, but a number of local farms provide B&B accommodation, mostly for rail trailers.

ACCOMMODATION AND EATING MIDDLEMARCH

Annandale 1 Snow St ☎ 03 464 3131, ⓦ annandalebnb .co.nz. Lovely, central B&B in a characterful villa with comfortable rooms, modern bathrooms (one with a bath) all surrounded by well-kept garden. Fruit is preserved for their continental breakfast. **$130**

Kissing Gate Café 2 Swansea St (SH87) ☎ 03 464 3224. Grab a coffee or a light lunch at this pretty café in an old wooden cottage and its surrounding garden. Mon–Thurs 8.30am–4pm, Fri, Sat & Sun 8.30am–5pm.

The Lodge 24 Conway St ☎ 027 228 4789, ⓔ thelodge @middlemarch.co.nz. Modest but comfortable B&B accommodation in a central old villa with continental breakfast included. Add $30 for en-suite. **$100**

Middlemarch Holiday Park 26 Mold St ☎ 03 464 3776, ⓦ middlemarchholidaypark.co.nz. Bikers are always welcome at this modest site on the outskirts of Middlemarch which also has motel units ($95). Camping **$20**, cabins **$65**

Fiordland

HALL ARM, DOUBTFUL SOUND

Fiordland

For all New Zealand's grandeur, no other region matches the concentration of stupendous landscapes found in its southwestern corner, Fiordland. Almost the entire region (and most of the area covered in this chapter) falls within the 12,500-square-kilometre Fiordland National Park, which stretches from Martins Bay, once the site of New Zealand's remotest settlement, to the southern forests of Waitutu and Preservation Inlet, where early gold prospectors set up a couple of short-lived towns. This raw, heroic landscape embraces New Zealand's two deepest lakes, its highest rainfall, fifteen hairline fiords and some of the world's rarest birds. Such wonder is acknowledged by the United Nations, who gathered the park – along with Mount Aspiring National Park, parts of Westland and the Aoraki/Mount Cook area – into the Te Wahipounamu World Heritage Area.

One persistent feature of Fiordland is the **rain**. Milford Sound is particularly favoured, being deluged with up to 7m of rainfall a year – one of the highest in the world. Fortunately the area's settlements are in a rain shadow and receive less than half the precipitation of the coast. Happily, **Milford Sound** is particularly beautiful when it's raining, with ribbons of water plunging from hanging valleys into the fiords where colonies of red and black coral grow and dolphins, fur seals and Fiordland crested penguins cavort. Many visitors who fly in from Queenstown see little else, but a greater sense of remoteness is gained by driving there along the achingly scenic **Milford Road** from the lakeside town of **Te Anau**. Better still, hike the **Milford Track**, widely promoted as the "finest walk in the world", though others in the region – particularly the **Hollyford Track** and the **Kepler Track** – are equally strong contenders.

A second lakeside town, **Manapouri**, is the springboard for trips to the West Arm hydroelectric power station, **Doubtful Sound** and the isolated fiords to the south. From Manapouri, the **Southern Scenic Route** winds through the western quarter of Southland via minor towns along the southwestern coast. The main stops here are Tuatapere, base for the excellent **Hump Ridge Track**, and pretty coastal **Riverton**.

Brief history

Fiordland's complex geology evolved over the last 500 million years. The beds of granite that underlay the region were compressed and heated deep within the earth's

LAKE TE ANAU

Highlights

❶ Te Anau Watch the inspirational film *Ata Whenua: Shadowland*, shot from a helicopter above Fiordland, then book a flight to see for yourself. **See p.755**

❷ Milford Sound Experience Milford's world-famous waters on a cruise or kayak, dwarfed by the fiord's soaring cliffs. **See p.765**

❸ The Milford Track Brave the rain and the sandflies to find out why this beautiful four-day tramp was billed "The Finest Walk in the World". **See p.773**

❹ Doubtful Sound Soak up scenic grandeur and superb wildlife from a kayak or small cruise boat, without the tourist bustle of Milford Sound. **See p.779**

❺ Hump Ridge Track Escape the Great Walks' crowds on this varied and beautiful, yet little-visited trail. **See p.782**

HIGHLIGHTS ARE MARKED ON THE MAP ON P.754

crust, forming layers of gneiss hard enough to form fiord-side cliffs a thousand metres high where softer rocks would crumble. Glaciers scoured the entire region during the last ice age, giving valleys the classic U-shaped profile that was later invaded by the sea, creating the steep-sided fiords.

After experiencing the dual challenges of Fiordland's copious rainfall and vicious **sandflies** (*namu*), you'll appreciate why there is little evidence of permanent Maori

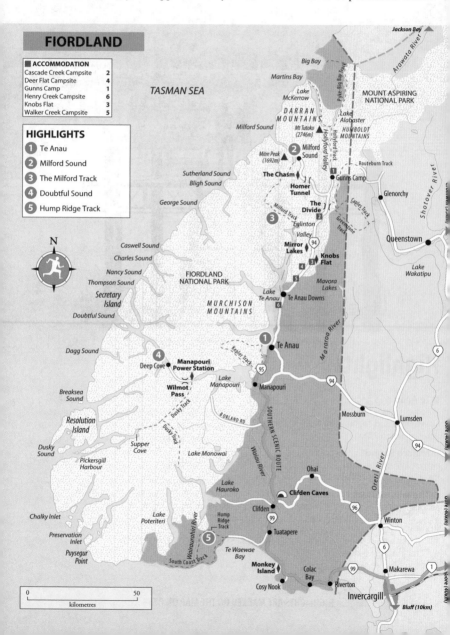

FIORDLAND

◼ ACCOMMODATION
Cascade Creek Campsite	2
Deer Flat Campsite	4
Gunns Camp	1
Henry Creek Campsite	6
Knobs Flat	3
Walker Creek Campsite	5

HIGHLIGHTS

1. Te Anau
2. Milford Sound
3. The Milford Track
4. Doubtful Sound
5. Hump Ridge Track

TU-TO-RAKI-WHANOA AND TE NAMU

In Maori legend Fiordland was created when the demi-god **Tu-to-Raki-whanoa** hewed the rough gashes of the southern fiords around Preservation Inlet and Dusky Sound with his *ko* (digging stick), leaving Resolution and Secretary islands where his feet stood. He honed his skill as he worked north, reaching perfection with the more sharply defined Milford Sound (Piopiotahi).

After creating this spectacular landscape, he was visited by Hine-nui-te-po, goddess of death, who feared the vista created by Tu was so wonderful that people would want to live here forever. As a deterrent, she freed *namu* (**sandflies**) at Te Namu-a-Te-Hine-nui-te-po (Sandfly Point), at the end of the Milford Track. The pesky bugs have certainly had the desired effect – in 1773, when Cook entered Dusky Sound, he was already familiar with the sandfly:

The most mischievous animal here is the small black sandfly which are exceedingly numerous and are so troublesome that they exceed everything of the kind I ever met with...

14

---

settlement, though they spent summers hunting here and passed through in search of greenstone (*pounamu*). **Cook** was equally suspicious of Fiordland when, in 1770, he sailed up the coast on his first voyage to New Zealand: anchorages were hard to find; the glowering sky put him off entering Dusky Sound; slight, shifting winds discouraged entry into what he dubbed Doubtful Harbour; and he missed Milford Sound altogether.

Paradoxically for a region that's now the preserve of hardy trampers and anglers, the southern fiords region was once the best charted in the country. Cook returned in 1773, after four months battling the southern oceans, and spent six weeks in Dusky Sound. His midshipman, George Vancouver, returned in 1791, with bloodthirsty sealers and whalers hot on his heels. Over the mountains, **Europeans** seized, or paid a pittance for, land on the eastern shores of Lake Te Anau and Manapouri though it offered meagre grazing, while **explorers** headed for the interior, conferring their names on the passes, waterfalls and valleys they came across – Donald Sutherland lent his name to New Zealand's highest waterfall and Quintin McKinnon scaled the Mackinnon Pass (but failed to persuade cartographers to spell his name correctly).

GETTING AROUND

By bus Almost all of Fiordland's buses ply the corridor from Queenstown through Te Anau to Milford Sound: most are tour buses, stopping at scenic spots and regaling passengers with a jocular commentary; others are scheduled services that disgorge trampers at the trailheads. Unless you are very pushed for time don't be persuaded to visit Milford from Queenstown, as it is an arduous journey that will lessen the Milford Sound experience – it's much better to stay overnight in Milford or visit from Te Anau.

By plane The only flights you are likely to take are scenic jaunts (see p.771) to Milford Sound from Queenstown or Wanaka.

Te Anau

Ringed by snowcapped peaks, the gateway town to Fiordland, **TE ANAU** (pronounced Teh AHN-ow), stretches along the shores of its eponymous lake, one of New Zealand's grandest and deepest. To the west, the lake's watery fingers claw deep into bush-cloaked mountains so remote that their most celebrated inhabitant, the **takahe**, was thought extinct for half a century.

The main way-station on the route to Milford Sound, Te Anau is an ideal base and recuperation spot for the numerous tramps, including several of the most famous and worthwhile in the country. Top of most people's list is the **Milford Track**, which starts at the head of the lake, while the **Kepler Track** (see p.761) starts closer to town.

14

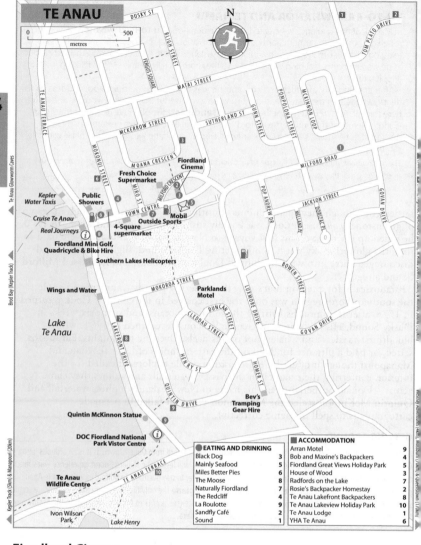

Fiordland Cinema

7 The Lane • Daily 9am–8pm; 4–10 screenings daily • $10; $1 off with voucher from the i-SITE • ☎ 03 249 8844, ⊗ fiordlandcinema.co.nz

Don't leave town without visiting the **Fiordland Cinema**, which presents the 32-minute *Ata Whenua: Shadowland*. Filmed mostly from a helicopter, it shows Fiordland at its majestic best throughout the seasons with wonderful cinematography, an original soundtrack and no ponderous voiceover. Pick of the scenes are the snow-tipped mountain summits rising up out of a sea of clouds, and dropping from a forested gully out over a perpendicular waterfall. You'll want to go straight out for a heli-flight (bookable in the foyer). Screenings are interspersed with a selection of mainstream movies, the chairs are big and comfy, and you can take your espresso, beer or wine in with you.

Te Anau Wildlife Centre

SH95 • Open access; takahe feeding daily: summer 9.30am; winter 10.30am • $1–2 donation

At DOC's **Te Anau Wildlife Centre** you can amble through the park-like setting, and glimpse some of New Zealand's rarest birds, most of which are injured or captive-bred. Look out for kakariki (parakeets), whio (blue duck), kea and kaka (indigenous parrots). The largest enclosure belongs to a couple of takahe (see box below); they can be hard to spot among the tussocks – your best chance of seeing them is at the daily feeding session.

14

Te Anau Glowworm Caves

Daily tours: Nov–March 2pm, 5.45pm, 7pm & 8.15pm; April–Sept 2pm, 7pm; 2hr 15min • $75 • ☎ 0800 656501, ⍵ realjourneys.co.nz

If you're not planning to visit the more impressive underground attractions at Waitomo, head to **Te Anau Glowworm Caves**. The town's full Maori name, Te Ana-au, means "cave with a current of swirling water" and it was a search for the town's namesake which led to their rediscovery in 1948. The tour feels a little processed but includes a pretty cruise to the western side of Lake Te Anau from the jetty adjacent to the visitor centre. Guides then lead you underground in small groups, spending thirty minutes walking through the Aurora cave system, followed by a short underground boat ride through a glittering glowworm-festooned cavern and past a couple of noisy waterfalls.

ARRIVAL AND DEPARTURE

TE ANAU

By bus InterCity/Newmans/Great Sights run Queenstown–Te Anau–Milford and Te Anau–Gore–Balclutha–Dunedin daily. NakedBus operates early morning buses from Te Anau to Milford Sound, Queenstown and Invercargill. Tracknet (☎ 0800 483262, ⍵ tracknet.net) run Queenstown–Te Anau–Milford and back twice daily plus Kepler Track and Manapouri shuttles and summer-only buses to Tuatapere and Invercargill. Buses pick up and drop off at central accommodation. Topline Tours (☎ 03 249 8059, ⍵ toplinetours.co.nz) serve the Kepler Track and Manapouri on demand.

Destinations The Divide (3–4 daily; 1hr); Dunedin (daily; 4hr 30min); Invercargill (2 daily; 4hr); Manapouri (4 daily; 20min); Milford Sound (at least 7 daily; 2hr 30min); Queenstown (at least 7 daily; 2hr 15min); Tuatapere (3 weekly in summer; 1hr 30min).

THE TAKAHE

For half a century the flightless blue-green **takahe** was thought extinct. These plump, turkey-sized birds – close relatives of the smaller pukeko – were once common throughout New Zealand but after the arrival of Maori their territory became restricted to the southern extremities of the South Island, and by the time Europeans came only a few were spotted, by early settlers in Fiordland. No sightings were recorded after 1898; the few trampers and ornithologists who claimed to have seen its tracks or heard its call in remote Fiordland valleys were dismissed as cranks.

One keen birder, **Geoffrey Orbell**, pieced together the sketchy evidence and concentrated his search on the **Murchison Mountains**, a virtual island surrounded on three sides by the western arms of Lake Te Anau and on the fourth by the Main Divide. In 1948, he was rewarded with the first takahe sighting in fifty years. However, the few remaining birds seemed doomed: deer were chomping their way through the grasses on which the takahe feed. Culling the deer averted the immediate crisis but did not halt the decline caused by stoats.

Takahe often lay three eggs but seldom manage to raise more than one chick. By removing any "surplus" eggs and hand-rearing them (often using hand-puppets to stop the chicks imprinting on their carers), DOC were able to gradually increase the population; recently efforts have turned to fostering chicks with birds whose own broods have failed. In addition, DOC has established several populations on predator-free sanctuary islands – Maud Island in the Marlborough Sounds, Mana Island and Kapiti Island northwest of Wellington, Maungatautiri near Hamilton and Tiritiri Matangi and Motutapu in Auckland's Hauraki Gulf – where the birds are breeding well. The total population is around 260 birds today, and it is hoped that takahe can be removed from the critically endangered list in the next decade.

14

TE ANAU TOURS AND ACTIVITIES

Kicking around Te Anau before a big tramp provides a good opportunity to explore some of the local **short walks** or get out **on the lake**. Short cruises access the Kepler or Milford tracks (see p.761 & p.773), and if you're not up to a multi-day hike then consider a one-day guided walk along them, though walks along the Milford Road are equally rewarding (see box, p.776).

DAY-WALKS FROM TE ANAU

DOC visitor centre to Control Gates (4km one way; 50min; flat). Easy lakeside walk past the Te Anau Wildlife Centre to the point where the Waiau River flows out of Lake Te Anau towards Lake Manapouri. The Control Gates mark the start of the Kepler Track (see p.761).

Control Gates to Brod Bay (5km one way; 1hr 30min; gently undulating). The first section of the Kepler Track goes to Dock Bay (30min) where there's good swimming (and toilets), and on through mountain and silver beech forest to the campsite at Brod Bay.

Control Gates to Rainbow Reach (9.5km one way; 2hr 30min–3hr 30min; mostly flat). Follow the course of the upper Waiau River through stands of beech, crossing a swingbridge just before Rainbow Reach. By using the Tracknet buses to the Control Gates and back from Rainbow Reach (see p.762) you can

extend this walk, continuing on to *Moturau Hut* (6km one way from Rainbow Reach; 1.5–2hr) beside Lake Manapouri and walking back to Rainbow Reach; a wetland viewing platform halfway makes a less ambitious target.

Brod Bay to Kepler summit (20km return; 7–9hr; 1000m ascent). Catch the Kepler Water Taxi across the lake to Brod Bay ($25) then hike the steep first third of the Kepler Track past *Luxmore Hut* to the summit of Mt Luxmore (1471m), then return, probably walking all the way back to Te Anau. A full but rewarding day.

Milford Track Day-Walk Ultimate Hikes (see p.776) run easy day-walks beside the Clinton River at the start of the Milford Track. Trips involve a bus to Te Anau Downs, boat to Glade Wharf, 5–6hr hiking and lunch at Ultimate Hikes' *Glade House*. Daily Nov–April from Te Anau ($195) and Queenstown ($295).

LAKE CRUISES, JETBOATING AND KAYAKING

Cruise Te Anau ☎03 249 8005, ⊛cruiseteanau. co.nz. Scenic cruises aboard a restored kauri motor launch (summer daily 10am, 1pm & 5pm; 3hr; $90) plus overnight cruises including meals (4pm–9.30am; $275).

Luxmore Jet ☎0800 253826, ⊛luxmorejet.co .nz. One-hour jetboat ride ($99) past three *Lord of the Rings* locations on the placid Waiau River. Several departures daily.

FLIGHTS

Air Fiordland ☎0800 107505, ⊛airfiordland.com. One of the best deals offered here involves taking a bus to Milford Sound, a cruise and a flight back over the Milford Track (from Te Anau: 6hr; $485; from Queenstown: 9hr; $535).

Southern Lakes Helicopters 79 Lakefront Drive ☎0508 249 7167, ⊛southernlakeshelicopters .co.nz. Helicopter flights from a waterside heli-pad start at $195 for 25min and range up to a couple of hours, including scenic flights over Milford, Doubtful and Dusky sounds. They'll even fly you up to the

Luxmore Hut on the Kepler Track (see p.761), leaving you to walk downhill to Brod Bay, where a water taxi will ferry you back to Te Anau ($185).

Wings & Water Lakefront Drive ☎03 249 7405, ⊛wingsandwater.co.nz. Floatplane flights are ideal for an aerial view of southern Fiordland. "Round the Lake" (15min; $145), Kepler Track overflights (20min; $225) and Doubtful Sound overflights (40min; $310) are among the options. One worthwhile combo involves jetboating down the Waiau River to Lake Manapouri and flying back to Te Anau (1hr; $240).

QUAD BIKING AND HORSERIDING

Westray Adventures 55 Ramparts Rd, off SH94 5km west of Te Anau ☎03 249 9079, ⊛fiordlandhorse treks.com. Ninety-minute quad-biking trips ($99) across a sheep station with great mountain views outside

Te Anau, with transfers included. If you fancy something lower-octane, opt for one of their horse treks (2–3hr; $95) up to a viewpoint overlooking Lake Te Anau. No experience necessary for either form of transport.

SKY-WATCHING

Astronomy Fiordland ☎05 0826 7667, ⊛astronomyfiordland.co.nz. Excellent trips to the dark skies just out of town using a mobile telescope to view

planets, distant galaxies and all manner of astronomical curiosities. Trips ($45) start just after dark (around 10.30pm in midsummer) and last an hour and a half.

INFORMATION

Tourist information i-SITE, Corner of Town Centre and Lakefront Drive ☏ 03 249 8900, ⓦ fiordland.org.nz. The best source of general information adjoins the Real Journeys booking office. Daily 8.30am–6pm.

DOC Fiordland National Park Visitor Centre, Lakefront Drive, 500m south of town centre ☏ 03 249 7924, ⓔ fiordlandvc @doc.govt.nz. Stacks of track and hut information, some useful tramping supplies and a Great Walks booking office (☏ 03 249 8514, ⓔ greatwalksbooking@doc.govt.nz). Outside stands a statue of Milford Track explorer Quintin McKinnon. Daily: Nov to April 8am–5pm; May–Oct 8.30am–4.30pm.

Outdoor gear rental Available from several places including Bev's Tramping Gear Hire, 16 Homer St (☏ 03 249 7389, ⓦ bevs-hire.co.nz; Mon–Sat 9am–noon & 5.30–7pm, Sun 5.30–7pm). Individual items are charged by the day, but the per track rates are better value if you need gear for anything longer than an overnighter (sleeping bags $15/night or $30/track); their Great Walks Package ($150 for 3–4 days), which has everything you need, except boots and food, is another good option. Outside Sports, 38 Town Centre (☏ 03 249 8195, ⓦ outsidesports.co.nz), have a full range of gear including tents, backpacks and sleeping bags ($30 each for 4 days).

14

GETTING AROUND

By bus There's a plethora of transport to the local trailheads, mostly with Tracknet and Topline Tours (see p.778).

By bike Rentals are available from backpackers, Fiordland Mini Golf, Quadricycle & Bike Hire, 7 Mokonui St ($24/half-day; $30/day; ☏ 03 249 7211), and Outside Sports, 38

Town Centre ($30/half-day, $50/day; ☏ 03 249 8195, ⓦ outsidesports.co.nz).

By car For Milford trips, rent a car from Rent-a-dent ($89/day), at *Parklands Motel*, 16 Mokoroa St (☏ 0800 736823, ⓦ rentadent.co.nz).

ACCOMMODATION

Motels dominate the length of Lakefront Drive and Quintin Drive, a block back. **Rates** drop dramatically between June and August, and may be negotiable in the shoulder seasons (mid-April to May & Sept). **Freedom camping** is banned within 10km of Te Anau and there are No Camping signs in likely-looking parking spots well beyond that. There are, however, a couple of cheap DOC sites.

Arran Motel 64 Quintin Drive ☏ 03 249 8826, ⓦ arranmotel.co.nz. Attractive studios, one- and two-bedroom units, some with cooking facilities, plus unlimited free wi-fi. Continental breakfast available ($10.50). **$155**

Bob and Maxine's Backpackers 20 Paton Place, off Oraka St ☏ 03 931 3161, ⓔ bob.anderson@woosh .co.nz. Barn-like purpose-built backpackers in a new suburb on the edge of town with simple but spacious and thoughtfully designed six-bunk dorms and one en-suite twin. The hospitable Bob and Maxine provide stacks of DVDs, free local calls, fresh fruit, bikes and dirt-cheap track drop-offs. Cash only. Dorms **$33**, twin **$86**

House of Wood 44 Moana Crescent ☏ 03 249 8404. Homey alpine chalet-style B&B a 2min walk from the town centre. In the best possible way, staying here is just like staying at your gran's, with slightly dated timber-lined rooms (most are en-suite), floral carpets, a cosy lounge, free use of bikes, and filling breakfasts with home-made jam. **$155**

Radfords on the Lake 56 Lakefront Drive ☏ 03 249 9186, ⓦ radfordsonthelake.co.nz. Modern, scrupulously clean and well-managed motel with everything done to the highest standard. Some of the pretty rooms have great views, plus there's free wi-fi, oodles of TV channels and plenty of parking spots. **$249**

★**Rosie's Backpacker Homestay** 23 Tom Plato Drive ☏ 03 249 8431, ⓦ rosiesbackpackers.co.nz. This small, relaxed backpackers sleeps just twelve in a family home with lake and mountain views – and even after twenty

years of sharing their home with travellers, Rosie and her family are still warm, enthusiastic hosts. Book early as it fills up fast. Closed June & July. Dorms **$33**, doubles **$78**

Te Anau Lakefront Backpackers 48 Lakefront Drive ☏ 03 249 7713, ⓦ teanaubackpackers.co.nz. Ageing but friendly and well-organized 110-bed hostel spread across three buildings centred on a former motel. Dorms mostly come with their own bathroom and kitchen and some have great lake views. Pairs of doubles and twins generally share a kitchen and bathroom and there's a good barbecue area, which helps reduce pressure on the main kitchen. They're well set up for trampers, with $5/item gear storage, and you can camp ($18) on the back lawn. Dorms **$30**, doubles **$78**

★**Te Anau Lodge** 52 Howden St ☏ 03 249 7477, ⓦ teanaulodge.com. Extremely comfortable accommodation in a substantially upgraded former convent. Rooms, many with superb mountain views, are styled in keeping with its 1920s origins and all are quite different; the deluxe rooms ($350) are particularly lovely. An excellent breakfast is served in the wood-panelled former chapel, complete with organ keyboard; afternoon tea and cake are laid on in the commodious upstairs lounge. **$240**

YHA Te Anau 29 Mokonui St ☏ 03 249 7847, ⓔ teanau @yha.co.nz. Modern and comfortable two-storey hostel close to the town centre with large three- to eight-bed dorms, doubles (en suites $100), free gear storage, helpful staff, lounge with a separate TV room and an outdoors deck. There's a self-catering family cottage with double and

14

twin rooms that can be booked separately or together. Dorms $\overline{\$34}$, doubles $\overline{\$94}$

CAMPSITES

Fiordland Great Views Holiday Park SH94, 2km east of town ☎ 03 249 7059, ⓦ fiordlandgreatviewsholiday park.co.nz. The cheapest of Te Anau's big holiday parks is set well back from the lake but has good long mountain views from some of the sites. Facilities are pretty good, the kindly owner does cheap Kepler Track transfers (in a London black cab no less), and organizes day-trips to Milford ($145) for

guests that includes a good cruise, underwater observatory and lunch. Cabins ($54) and self-catering units ($120) available. Camping $\overline{\$16}$, powered sites $\overline{\$18}$

Te Anau Lakeview Holiday Park 77 Manapouri Rd, 1km south of town centre ☎ 03 249 7457, ⓦ teanauholidaypark.co.nz. Vast, very well equipped complex with spacious tent and campervan areas, the *Steamers Beach* backpackers, lots of single rooms, modern facilities including a sauna, and a huge range of cabins and units including some gorgeous new Marakura rooms ($229) with lake views. Camping $\overline{\$18}$, dorms $\overline{\$29}$

EATING AND DRINKING

Eating options are improving in Te Anau, while self-caterers have two well-stocked supermarkets to explore. Given that many visitors are embarking on or coming off tramps, drinking is low-key.

Black Dog 7 The Lane ☎ 03 249 8844. City-slicker cocktail bar in little old Te Anau. Dress up a little – although the locals don't seem to bother, at least you'll match the decor – and go for one of the cocktails ($10). Happy hour 5.30–6.30pm; 5.30–10pm or later.

★**Mainly Seafood** Te Anau Terrace ☎ 027 516 5555, ⓦ mainlyseafood.co.nz. The blue cod burger ($12) from this friendly takeaway slips down a treat especially on a fine evening when you can tuck in watching the sunset. The venison burger ($11) is equally good and the mixed seafood Fisherman's Basket ($22.50) could be shared unless you've just finished a big hike. Mon 4–9pm, Tues–Sun 11.30am–9pm.

Miles Better Pies 2 Milford Rd ☎ 03 249 9044. Unpretentious place with pretty decent pies in a range of fillings such as venison, steak and pepper, and Thai chicken (all $6.50) plus a few vegetarian and sweet varieties, all to eat in or take away to the lakefront. Daily 6.30am–6pm.

The Moose 84 Lakefront Drive ☎ 03 249 7100. Rambunctious locals' haunt with low-cost drink deals, plus live music on summer Saturdays, named in honour of the ten Canadian moose calves that were released at Dusky Sound in the 1900s. Standard Kiwi pub grub in more-than-healthy portions, with lunches under $20, evening meals for less than $30 and a $15 Sunday roast deal. Daily 11am–11pm or later.

Naturally Fiordland 62 Town Centre ☎ 03 249 7111. While it's not the most authentic of Te Anau's four pizzerias, the pizzas here have good crispy bases with gently Kiwified toppings, and all pizzas come in 9" and 12" versions; try The Godfather (spinach, sun-dried tomatoes, olives, salami and feta; $17.80/$23.80) or a Little Sicily (a margherita with fresh

tomatoes and herbs; $9.80/$16.80). Pasta, coffee and cakes available too. Licensed. Daily 9am–11.30pm.

★**The Redcliff** 12 Mokonui St ☎ 03 249 7431, ⓦ theredcliff.co.nz. This cosy timber cottage houses a semiformal restaurant that produces the best meals in Fiordland and a welcoming bar with seating in the garden out front and a nice little window nook. Dinner might be wild hare backstrap with glazed baby carrots ($32) or prime ribeye steak with truffle salt potato skins and mushroom mousse ($40); a single, unspecified vegetarian option is available. Oct–May daily 5–9.30pm.

La Roulotte Lakeside Drive, opposite the DOC visitor centre ☎ 024 027 4353. This cheery caravan may have moved by the time you read this, but it's worth seeking them out for a delicious crêpe or savoury galette (from $6), washed down with home-made soda or a cup of "sock coffee" (no flat whites here). Daily 9am–4pm.

Sandfly Café 9 The Lane ☎ 03 249 9529. The best of Te Anau's underwhelming range of cafés is laidback and has heaps of sunny, roadside seating. They serve good coffee, a range of cooked breakfasts with the likes of steak sandwiches ($16) for lunch, along with piles of appealing snacks in their cabinets. Daily 7am–4.30pm.

Sound 225 Milford Road ☎ 03 249 8437. Although this cool takeaway had just opened at the time of research it was already a big hit with the locals, thanks to its fancy burgers served in brioche buns (expect combinations like Fiordland venison with mushroom duxelle or beef with blue cheese and crispy onions, both around $15), though the menu also runs to salad, chicken wings and fish. Daily 11.30am–9pm or later.

DIRECTORY

Banks Banks with ATMs are along Town Centre.

Left luggage If your accommodation can't help, *Lakeview Holiday Park* offer luggage storage at $10/locker for as long as you need.

Pharmacy Fiordland Community Pharmacy (70 Town

Centre; ☎ 03 249 9268) is open Mon–Fri 8.30–6pm, Sat & Sun 9am–5pm.

Post office Paper Plus on Town Centre, Mon–Fri 8.30am–6pm, Sat 9.30am–5.30pm.

Showers The Te Anau Terrace public toilet

(8.30am–6.30pm) also has showers ($5), as well as shampoo and conditioner ($5) and towels ($6) to get you looking lovely post-tramp.

Vehicle storage Safer Parking, 48 Caswell Rd (☎ 03 249 7198, ⓦ saferparking.co.nz), offer secure parking ($9/ night) while you're on a tramp. Tracknet and Real Journeys can pick up here for Milford Track, Milford Sound and Doubtful Sound transfers.

The Kepler Track

45–70km; 3–4 days

The **Kepler Track** was created in 1988 and designated as one of New Zealand's Great Walks. It was intended to take the load off the Milford and Routeburn tracks and has been so successful it has become equally popular. Tracing a wide loop through the Kepler Mountains on the western side of Lake Te Anau, the track has one full day of exposed subalpine ridge walking, some lovely virgin beech forest and has the advantage of being accessible on foot from Te Anau. Typically walked **anticlockwise**, getting most of the climbing out of the way early, the track ranges from as little as 45km – if you use boats and buses – to 70km for the full Te Anau–Te Anau walk.

Well graded and maintained throughout – to the extent that you barely need to look where you are treading – it is still lengthy and strenuous, particularly the long haul up to *Luxmore Hut*. The section between the *Luxmore* and *Iris Burn* huts is occasionally closed after snowfall.

Top athletes complete the 60km **Kepler Challenge** (first Sat in Dec), a run around the track, in under five hours. The current record, set by Martin Dent in 2013, is 4:33:37.

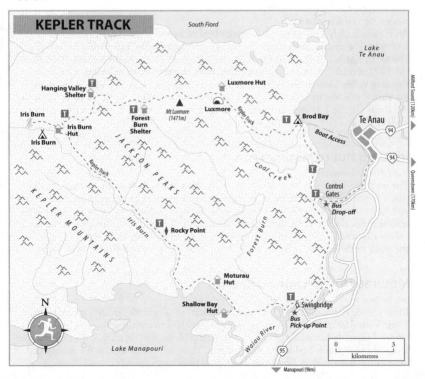

Te Anau to Control Gates

5km; 1hr; flat

Most people get the bus to the Control Gates, but it is possible to walk, first heading south along Lakefront Drive, then right and following the lakeshore until the final right-turn to the **Control Gates**, which regulate the water flow between lakes Te Anau and Manapouri. It's not a particularly interesting walk, but pretty enough.

Control Gates to Brod Bay

5.6km; 1hr–1hr 30min; flat

The track follows the lakeshore around Dock Bay and over Coal Creek, passing through predominantly beech and kamahi forests but with a fine stand of tree ferns. **Brod Bay** has good swimming off a sandy beach and makes a lovely place to camp.

Brod Bay to Luxmore Hut

8.2km; 3–4hr; 880m ascent

Non-campers must press on from Brod Bay, following a signpost midway along the beach. The path climbs fairly steeply; after a couple of hours you sidle below limestone bluffs, from where it is almost another hour to the bushline and fine views over Te Anau and Manapouri lakes and the surrounding mountains. **Luxmore Hut** is almost one hour above the bushline. A 10min side trip from the hut visits the short and fairly unexciting Luxmore Cave, its ceiling hung with skinny stalactites.

Luxmore Hut to Iris Burn Hut

14.6km; 5–6hr; 300m ascent, 900m descent

An exposed, high-level section where any hint of bad weather should be treated seriously. The track climbs to the highest point of the tramp, Luxmore Saddle (1400m), just below the summit of Mount Luxmore (from where you can hike up to the 1471m peak), then descends to **Forest Burn Shelter** before following a ridge to **Hanging Valley Shelter** and turning sharply south to trace another open ridge towards **Iris Burn** – reached by zigzagging west into the forested Hanging Valley then following the stream to the hut and campsite in a large tussock clearing. It's worth doing the easy walk to the Iris Burn waterfall (40min return).

Iris Burn Hut to Moturau Hut

16.2km; 4–6hr; 300m descent

The track from the *Iris Burn Hut* passes over a low saddle before descending steadily past a large landslip and through beech forest and riverside clearings. About halfway you pass toilets at **Rocky Point**, then enter a short gorge before hugging the river for several magical kilometres. Just before Iris Burn spills into Lake Manapouri, the track swings east and skirts Shallow Bay to the pleasant lakeside **Moturau Hut**. If you're doing the track in three days, press on to the bus pick-up at Rainbow Reach, 6km further on.

Moturau Hut to Rainbow Reach

6km; 1hr 30min; flat

Most people finish their walk at **Rainbow Reach**, an easy walk through gentle beech forest from *Moturau Hut*. Keen trampers might want to continue on foot back to the Control Gates (additional 9.5km; 2–3hr; negligible ascent) on a track through mature lowland beech forest beside the Waiau River. There are opportunities for fishing and swimming, but the river flows swiftly, so pick your spot carefully.

ARRIVAL AND DEPARTURE

THE KEPLER TRACK

By bus The Kepler Track starts at the Control Gates, 5km southwest of Te Anau. Most people catch the Tracknet bus (Oct–April only; $6; ☎0800 483262, ⓦtracknet.net), which picks up at accommodation around town at 8.30am and 9.30am, dropping off at the Control Gates. On the last day, most trampers stop 9.5km short of the Control Gates at the swingbridge over the Waiau's Rainbow Reach. Tracknet pick up at Rainbow Reach at 10am, 3pm and 5pm; it costs $16 for both trips.

By boat You can skip 5km of lakeside walking (and make a relaxed first day start) by boating across to Brod Bay from Te Anau wharf with Kepler Water Taxi (8.30am & 9.30am or by arrangement; $25; ☎03 249 8364 ⓔstevsaunders @xtra.co.nz).

INFORMATION

Maps The trail information given in DOC's *Kepler Track* brochure (free) is adequate, but for more detailed information consult either the 1:55,000 *Kepler Track* map by NewTopo ($9.90) or the 1:40,000 *Kepler Track* map by Craig Potton Publishing ($25), both available from the National Park Visitor Centre.

Weather and track conditions The Te Anau National Park Visitor Centre has the latest weather forecast and track conditions. If you're hiking the Kepler Track in winter, see the winter-specific page at ⓦdoc.govt.nz /keplertrack.

Safety DOC do not track trampers' whereabouts. Let someone know your intentions through ⓦadventuresmart.org.nz. Locator beacons are available for $30/3 days from Bev's Tramping Gear (see p.759) or the Mobil garage in Te Anau.

ACCOMMODATION

Booking Hut bookings are mandatory during Great Walk season (late Oct–late April). You can walk in either direction, retrace your steps and stay up to two nights in a particular hut. Book as far ahead as possible – three months if you need a specific departure date or are part of a large group. It is easiest to book online (ⓦdoc.govt.nz) from July 1 for the following season, though it is also possible to book by mail and in person at DOC visitor centres ($2). If the track is closed due to bad weather or track conditions, full refunds are given; however, new bookings can only be made if there is space. Changes can be made to existing bookings before you start ($10/ booking).

Huts The three main huts – *Luxmore* (54 bunks), *Iris Burn* (50 bunks) and *Moturau* (40 bunks) – have a warden, gas rings and flush toilets: you'll need to carry your own pans and plates. Trampers are discouraged from using the simple and very small *Shallow Bay Hut*, just off the track beside Lake Manapouri. During the main season the Backcountry Hut Pass is not valid. Outside the main season, the huts lose their warden, gas rings and running water, reverting to pit toilets until spring; during this period the Backcountry Hut Pass is valid. Great Walk season $54, off season $15

Camping Campers are forced to tackle the Kepler in one very short and two very long days using the campsites at Brod Bay and Iris Burn. Both have 15 pitches, pit toilets and water. Great Walk season $18, off season **Free**

Milford Road

The 120km **Milford Road** (SH94), from Te Anau to Milford Sound, is one of the world's finest scenic highways. The two-hour drive can easily take a day if you grab every photo opportunity, and longer if you explore some of the excellent hiking trails outlined in the *Fiordland Day Walks* booklet, available free from the National Park Visitor Centre in Te Anau. Anywhere else the initial drive beside Lake Te Anau would be considered gorgeous, but it is nothing compared to the Eglinton Valley, where the road penetrates steeper into bush-clad mountains, winding through a subalpine wonderland to the seemingly impassable bare rock walls at the head of the Hollyford Valley. The rough-hewn Homer Tunnel cuts through to the sheer-walled Cleddau Valley before the road descends steeply to Milford Sound.

There's very little habitation along the way, and no shops or petrol, but lots of great camping.

Brief history

Maori parties long used the Milford Road route on their way to seek *pounamu* at Anita Bay at the mouth of Milford Sound, but no road existed until two hundred

14

MILFORD ROAD SAFETY

With all the fabulous scenery along the Milford Road it is easy for drivers to lose concentration. Bear in mind that there is heavy bus traffic Milford-bound from 11am to noon and Te Anau-bound between 3 and 5pm. Apart from the store in the Hollyford Valley, 8km off your route, there is nowhere to buy **food** until you reach Milford, so go prepared. There are single **petrol** and diesel pumps in Milford, but they often run out, so fill up in Te Anau before you leave.

In winter (May–Oct or Nov) the subalpine section of the Milford Road is one of the world's most **avalanche-prone**. Since the last avalanche death on the road in 1983, a sophisticated monitoring system has been put in place and explosives are dropped from helicopters to loosen dangerous accumulations of snow while the road is closed. At this time, motorists are required to carry chains (available from service stations in Te Anau for $30/day). If there is a risk of snowfall you'll be stopped at the small kiosk five minutes' drive out of Te Anau to make sure that you have them and know how to fit them – and sent back to Te Anau if you don't. It's not uncommon for people to be stuck in Milford if the road does close. Always check weather forecasts with the DOC office in Te Anau before setting out; check the road status at Ⓦ milfordroad.co.nz.

---

unemployment-relief workers with shovels and wheelbarrows were put to the task in 1929. The greatest challenge was the Homer Tunnel, which wasn't finally completed until 1953 when the road officially opened.

Eglinton Valley

Heading north from Te Anau, there's little reason to stop in the first 30km to the harbour at **Te Anau Downs**, where boats leave for the start of the Milford Track. The road then cuts east away from the lake, before veering north into the **Eglinton Valley** through occasional stands of beech, interspersed with open flats of red tussock grass. Once grazed, these plains are now returning to their natural state with bush regenerating at the margins, though in November and December the flats are ablaze with pink, purple and white lupins – a pest, but a beautiful one.

Mirror Lakes

Particularly picturesque mountains hem the valley and, when the weather is calm, are reflected in the roadside **Mirror Lakes**, 58km north of Te Anau. Even without the reflective stillness it is a beautiful spot with boardwalks leading down to flax-fringed waters, originally the bed of the Eglinton River.

The Divide

84km north of Te Anau

As you get nearer to the head of the valley the road steepens to **The Divide**, which at 532m is the lowest east–west crossing of the Southern Alps. This is the start/finish of the Greenstone, Caples and Routeburn tracks, the last of which can be followed to Key Summit (see box, p.766). The car park has toilets and a walkers' shelter with a notice board advertising the times of passing buses to Milford Sound (3 daily; 1hr 15min) and Te Anau (3–4 daily; 1hr), although it is better to prearrange a pick-up as there is no mobile reception up here.

Pressing on a couple of kilometres towards Milford, you descend briefly into the top end of the Hollyford River, best seen from a popular **viewpoint** just before the Hollyford Road shoots off north.

SHORTENING THE WAY TO MILFORD

Everyone wants to go to Milford Sound, but it is a long way from the rest of the country, so boosters are forever promoting ways to shorten the journey.

In the 1990s the Ngai Tahu *iwi* hoped to install a monorail along the Greenstone Valley, the shortest route from Queenstown to The Divide, just 40km east of Milford Sound. An alliance of greenies and outdoor enthusiasts raised enough public concern to scupper that, although the idea was briefly resuscitated by a Queenstown-based tour operator in 2014.

The next strategy proposed the construction of an 11km-long **tunnel** linking the start of the Routeburn Track with the Hollyford Valley, which would have shipped passengers from Queenstown to Milford Sound by bus in a little over two hours. Despite having more legs than some of the other schemes mooted, the government rejected this plan in 2013, due to the heavy environmental toll it would take inside the national park.

The idea of linking Milford to the West Coast by road has been kicking around since the 1870s, when connecting Jacksons Bay to Milford via the Hollyford Valley was considered key to opening up this rugged region. The **Hollyford Valley Road** was approved in 1936, but only 16km of it was ever built, today's Lower Hollyford Road. At the time of writing a new proposal to construct an 80km **toll road** along the northern Fiordland coast was gaining momentum, with foreign investors in line to stump up much of the $230m cost – though it remains to be seen if the plans will ever be approved.

14

The Hollyford Valley

The Milford Road drops down from The Divide into the **Hollyford Valley**, which runs 80km from its headwaters in the Darran Mountains north to the Tasman Sea at Martins Bay. The 16km gravel Lower Hollyford Road provides access to the Hollyford Track, the Lake Marian walk and the tiny settlement of **Gunns Camp** (aka Hollyford Camp), 8km along the valley road. This former roading camp now has simple accommodation (see p.768), a museum devoted to the characters who have called the valley home, and a **shop** selling trampers' supplies along with postcards, books, maps and some rare bowenite pendants. The road runs 8km beyond Gunns Camp to the beginning of the Hollyford Track. It is also the start of a short, steep walk to **Humboldt Falls** (30min return), a ribbon-thin cascade tumbling 200m.

Gunns Camp Museum

Daily: Oct–March 8am–8pm; April–Sept 9am–7pm • $2, free to guests

If you're at all interested in the region's history, set half an hour aside for this small but fascinating collection of pioneer artefacts, intriguing paraphernalia relating to the one-time community at Martins Bay, stuff on the devastating floods that periodically afflict the region, and the building of the Milford Road and the Homer Tunnel. A nice shot shows former owner, the late Murray Gunn, sitting in his kitchen back in 1989.

Homer Tunnel

After the Hollyford turn-off, the Milford Road continues west towards the Hollyford's source, climbing all the while through ever more stunted beech trees to the huge glacial cirque of the Gertrude Valley. It is a magnificent spot, frequently strung with waterfalls and resounding to the sound of curious **kea**: do not feed them, as human food can kill them.

The road then cuts to the sea via the 1200m-long **Homer Tunnel**, which punctures the headwall of the Gertrude Valley. Construction was started in 1935, but was badly planned from the start. Working at a one-in-ten downhill gradient, the builders soon hit water and were forced to pump it out continuously; a pilot tunnel allowing the water to drain westwards was finished in 1948. After a concerted push, the tunnel was completed in 1953, opening Milford Sound to road traffic for the first time. Each April, uninhibited locals compete in a race through the tunnel naked (apart from running shoes).

14

HIKES FROM THE MILFORD ROAD

Old-timers grumble about tourists wasting their time, effort and money on prize tramps like the Milford and the Routeburn when there are so many excellent, easily accessible walks along the Milford Road.

Lake Gunn Nature Walk (3km loop; 45min; negligible ascent). Wheelchair-accessible nature walk with interpretive panels. Starts 78km north of Te Anau.

The Divide to Key Summit (5km return; 2–3hr; 400m ascent). Panoramic views (when it's not raining) over the Hollyford Valley and across to the Darran and Humboldt mountains are the reward for this tramp along the western portion of the Routeburn Track, branching off the Great Walk for the final climb up to the 918m summit. Starts 83km north of Te Anau.

Lake Marian (5km return; 2–3hr; 400m ascent). Picturesque ascent to a scenic alpine lake, passing pretty cataracts (30–40min return), where cantilevered boardwalks jut out of the rockface. Once past the falls the path climbs steeply to Lake Marian's hanging valley and superb views of the surrounding mountains. Starts 1km along Lower Hollyford Rd, 88km north of Te Anau.

Gertrude Saddle Route (10km return; 3–5hr; 600m ascent). This tramp starts relatively gently up the dramatic Gertrude Valley, ringed by sheer rock walls. The track then becomes a steep route and is unmarked above the snowline; you'll need decent navigation skills and the Topo50 *Hollyford* map to find your way through the cairns misleadingly erected by other trampers. Past Black Lake the route is exposed and dangerous after rain or snow, but those who make it to the saddle are rewarded with a wonderful view of Milford Sound and the 2756m Mount Tutoko, Fiordland's highest peak. Starts 98km north of Te Anau, from a car park just before the eastern end of the Homer Tunnel.

Despite recent improvements, the tunnel remains rough-hewn, narrow and dark. During peak periods in the summer **traffic lights** dictate one-way traffic (expect a wait of up to 15min), but for the rest of the time you'll need to look out for oncoming vehicles.

The Chasm

The Homer Tunnel emerges at the top of a series of switchbacks down to the Cleddau River. Almost 10km on from the tunnel all buses stop at **The Chasm**, while their passengers stroll (15min return) to the near-vertical rapids where the Cleddau has scoured out a deep, narrow channel. Tantalizing glimpses through the foliage reveal sculpted rocks hollowed out by churning water or eroded into freestanding ribs that resemble flying buttresses. From here it is another 10km to Milford Sound.

ACCOMMODATION   **MILFORD ROAD**

Campers will want to spend a night or two in one of the dozen simple DOC **campsites** along the Milford Road either on the grassy flats of the Eglinton Valley or the bush nearby. All have vault toilets and giardia-free stream water, and most have fireplaces. All are outlined in DOC's free *Conservation Campsites* booklet: some of the best are listed below, in order of distance from Te Anau.

Henry Creek SH94, 23km north of Te Anau on the Milford Rd. The first of the Milford Road DOC sites is attractive with (almost) lakeside gravel sites well spaced along the lakeshore and sheltered camping among the beech trees. Vault toilets and lake water. $6

Walker Creek SH94, 47km north of Te Anau. Small DOC site with valley views just 2km inside the national park. There's stream water, toilets and picnic tables plus plenty of room for campervans in secluded spots. $6

Deer Flat SH94, 59km north of Te Anau. The pitches at

this DOC campsite are scattered around, with a couple of sites sheltered by patches of beech, the remainder on grassy flats nearby. Toilets and picnic tables available. $6

★ **Knobs Flat** SH94, 62km north of Te Anau ☏ 03 249 9122, ⊕ knobsflat.co.nz. Six very comfortable motel-style units in a remote location with great valley views from the verandas, and no TV or mobile phone reception. Guided nature walks through the Eglinton Valley are available ($20/hr; $75/half-day) and there's camping (no powered sites) with showers ($5 for non-guests) and a

THE HOLLYFORD TRACK

Long, but mostly flat, the **Hollyford Track** (56km; 3–4 days one way) runs from the end of the Hollyford Valley road to Martins Bay following Fiordland's longest valley.

The joy of the Hollyford is not in the sense of achievement that comes from scaling alpine passes, but in the appreciation of the dramatic mountain scenery and the kahikatea, rimu and matai **bush** with an understorey of wineberry, fuchsia and fern. At the northern end of Martins Bay, Long Reef has a resident **fur seal** colony, and from September to December you might spot rare Fiordland crested **penguins** (tawaki) nesting among the scrub and rocks.
The track is a one-way tramp, requiring three to four days' backtracking – unless you're flash enough to fly out from the airstrip at Martins Bay or tough enough to continue around a long, difficult and remote loop known as the **Pyke–Big Bay Route** (144km; 9–10 days total; consult DOC's *Pyke–Big Bay Route* leaflet for details).

SEASONS AND SAFETY

The track is open year-round, but muddy in winter. Jetboats (see below) only run on Lake McKerrow during the guided walk season. Pick up DOC's *Hollyford Track* leaflet and visit DOC in Te Anau for the latest conditions. Locator beacons are available from Bev's Tramping Gear (see p.759) or the Mobil garage in Te Anau.

ACCESS, ACCOMMODATION AND GUIDED WALKS

Access the Hollyford Road end from Te Anau with Tracknet **buses** (Nov–April Mon, Wed & Fri; $55; ⓣ 0800 483262, ⓦ tracknet.net). Guided walkers **fly** out from Martins Bay over spectacular mountains to Milford Sound. You can join them, or get back-flights into Martins Bay, with several companies (see p.772). On the way back you can avoid most of the long day's walk beside the attractive but samey Lake McKerrow with Hollyford Track's **jetboat service** between Martins Bay and the head of Lake McKerrow (late Oct to mid-April; around $110).

There is no **booking** system for the track. Most DOC **huts** cost $15/night and the Backcountry Hut Pass is valid. All have twelve bunks except *Alabaster Hut* (26) and *Martins Bay Hut* (24). Carry all cooking gear. **Camping** ($5) is permitted next to all huts.

Trips & Tramps ⓣ 0800 305807, ⓦ tripsandtramps.com. The handiest access package is with this outfit, who will book your flight and organize transport between Milford Sound airport and your vehicle at the Hollyford Road end ($225; $280 from Te Anau).

Hollyford Track Guided Walk ⓣ 0800 832226, ⓦ hollyfordtrack.com. Perfect if you hate carrying a pack and prefer comfortable lodgings and having hearty meals cooked for you. Knowledgeable guides lead small groups on these three-day hikes with nights spent at the relatively luxurious *Martins Bay Lodge* and *Pyke Lodge*. The price ($1995) includes a jetboat journey along Lake McKerrow, , and a helicopter flight out of Martins Bay. Late Oct to mid-April.

THE ROUTE

Road End to Hidden Falls Hut (9km; 2–3hr; negligible ascent). After the first swingbridge, the track follows a disused road along Swamp Creek and then the Hollyford River, passing Hollyford Track Guided Walks' *Sunshine Hut* before before arriving at *Hidden Falls Hut*.

Hidden Falls Hut to Alabaster Hut (10km; 3–4hr; 100m ascent). Keen walkers can push on from *Hidden Falls Hut* through ribbonwood and beech forest, over Little Homer Saddle and past 60m-high Little Homer Falls, passing another private hut before arriving at the DOC hut at Lake Alabaster.

Alabaster Hut to Demon Trail Hut (15km; 3–4hr; negligible ascent). Backtrack from *Alabaster Hut* to the swingbridge over the Pyke River, following a poorly maintained and often muddy path towards Lake McKerrow. After several hours, you will pass a side path to the nicely sited *McKerrow Island Hut*, before continuing beside the lake to *Demon Trail Hut*.

Demon Trail Hut to Hokuri Hut (10km; 5–6hr; 100m ascent). The most technical day following the shore of Lake McKerrow on rough, undulating ground with some tricky stream crossings to the twelve-bunk *Hokuri Hut*.

Hokuri Hut to Martins Bay Hut (13km; 4–5hr; negligible ascent). Passing the scant remains of Jamestown, a cattle-ranching settlement that prospered in the 1870s, and the small airstrip and lodge used by Hollyford Track Guided Walk's tours, you'll stumble across some of the dozen dwellings that comprise Martins Bay; whitebaiters and hunters stay here occasionally, although there are no permanent residents. Continuing parallel to Martins Bay, which you'll glimpse across the Hollyford River and groves of wind-shorn trees, you reach the *Martins Bay Hut*.

14

well-equipped camp kitchen. A flax-girt bush bath makes a great spot for star-gazing. Camping $15, doubles $130

Cascade Creek SH94, 77km north of Te Anau. The closest DOC site to Milford Sound that's suitable for campers – still over 40km away. Fly-fishing possible. $6

Gunns Camp 8km along Lower Hollyford Rd ⓦgunnscamp.org.nz. The only accommodation in these parts is this huddle of simple 1930s cabins that served as families' quarters for the long-suffering road-builders. An

ongoing revamp includes a modern lounge and kitchen block, but the place retains its spirit – basic and with bags of character. Cabins generally have single beds or six-berth bunks ($25/bed); linen is available to rent, but you'll need a sleeping bag. There's generator power (7–9am & 6–10pm) and wood-fired showers, but no refrigeration, landline, mobile coverage or internet; very basic supplies are available from the small shop. Camping $15, double cabins $65

Milford Sound

The most northerly and celebrated of Fiordland's fifteen fiords is **Milford Sound** (Piopiotahi) with its vertical sides towering 1200m above the sea and waterfalls plunging from hanging valleys. Some 16km long and mostly less than 1km wide, it is also one of the slenderest fiords – and yes, it is misnamed. Sounds are drowned river valleys whereas this is very much a glacially formed fiord. It is a wondrous place, though it is difficult to grasp its heroic scale unless your visit coincides with that of one of the great cruise liners – even these formidable vessels are totally dwarfed.

Perhaps counterintuitively, Milford is at its best in the rain, something that happens on over 180 days a year giving a massive 7m of **annual rainfall**. Within minutes of a torrential downpour every cliff-face sprouts a waterfall and the place looks even more magical as ethereal mist descends. Indeed, Milford warrants repeated visits: in bright sunshine (yes, it does happen), on a rainy day and even under a blanket of snow.

None of the other fiords quite matches Milford for its spectacular **beauty**, but what makes Milford special is its **accessibility**. The tiny airport hardly rests as planes buzz in and out, while busloads of visitors are disgorged from buses onto cruises – all day in the summer and around the middle of the day in spring and autumn.

The crowds can certainly detract from the grandeur, but don't let that put you off. Driving to Milford Sound and admiring it from the land just doesn't cut it; you need to get out on the water, either on a cruise or in a kayak.

Brief history

Maori know Milford Sound as **Piopiotahi** ("a single thrush"), and attribute its creation to the god Tu-te-Raki-whanoa, who was called away before he could carve a route into the interior, leaving high rock walls. These precipitous routes are now known as the

---

MILFORD'S FRAGILE ECOSYSTEM

The predations of today's influx of visitors and the operation of a small fishing fleet have necessitated strategies to preserve the **fragile ecosystem**. Like all fiords, Milford Sound has an entrance sill at its mouth, in this case only 70m below the surface – by comparison, the deepest point is almost 450m. This minimizes the water's natural recirculation and hinders the mixing of seawater and the vast quantities of fresh water that pour into the fiord, creating the strange phenomenon of **deep water emergence**. The less-dense tannin-stained fresh surface layer (generally 2–6m deep) builds up, further diminishing the penetration of light, which is already reduced by the all-day shadow cast by the fiord walls. The result is a narrow band of fragile, light-shy red and black **corals** just 10m below the surface – these normally grow only at much greater depths, but thrive here in the dark conditions. Unfortunately, Milford's fishing fleet use crayfish pots, which tend to shear off anything that grows on the fiord's walls. A marine reserve has been set up along the northern shore, where all such activity is prohibited, but really this is far too small and conservation groups are campaigning for its extension.

TUATAPERE HUMP RIDGE TRACK (P.782) >

14

Homer and Mackinnon passes, probably first used by Maori who came to collect *pounamu* from Anita Bay at the mouth of the fiord. The first European known to have sailed into Piopiotahi was sealer John Grono who, in 1823, named the fiord Milford Haven after his home port in south Wales. The main river flowing into the Welsh Milford is the Cleddau, so naturally the river at the head of the fiord is likewise named.

The earliest settler was Scot **Donald Sutherland**, who arrived with his dog, John O'Groat, in 1877; he promptly planned a series of thatched huts beside the freshwater basin of what he called the "City of Milford", funding his explorations by guiding small numbers of visitors who had heard tell of the scenic wonder.

All visitors arrived by boat or walked the Milford Track until 1953 when the road through the Homer Tunnel was finally completed, paving the way for the phalanxes of buses that today disgorge tourists onto cruises.

Milford Sound village

The settlement of Milford Sound is tiny, comprising little more than a small airstrip, fishing harbour, outsized cruise terminal, post office, pub/café and a couple of lodges.

You're pretty much surrounded by water here, and should waste little time getting out on it, but if tales of his pioneering days have inspired you, pay homage at **Donald Sutherland's grave**, hidden among the staff accommodation behind the pub. Alternatively take a five-minute **walk** up to a lookout behind *Mitre Peak Lodge*, or the **Piopiotahi Foreshore Walk**, which runs from the main car park along the fiord's sandy shore returning through beech woods to the settlement (30min loop; flat).

Mitre Peak

The view of Milford Sound is dominated by the iconic, triangular, glaciated pinnacle of **Mitre Peak** (1692m), named for its resemblance to a bishop's mitre. It actually doesn't look much like one, but pioneering Victorians were undoubtedly desperate to find an alternative to its Maori name, *Rahotu*, which some coyly translate as "member of upstanding masculinity" (though it really doesn't look much like one of those either).

Sinbad Gully

The left side of Mitre Peak plunges into **Sinbad Gully**, a vast hanging valley that was the last Fiordland refuge of the world's largest parrot, the **kakapo**. A handful were found here in 1981 and added to the genetically limited Steward Island kakapo, now all protected on predator-free islands. A stoat-trapping programme hopes to make Sinbad Gully safe enough to release kakapo back into the wild here.

Lady Bowen Falls and Stirling Falls

After heavy rain, Milford Sound can feel like a chasm of waterfalls but there are really only two major falls that keep going long after the rain stops – both best seen from the water. Right by Milford Sound village, the 164m **Lady Bowen Falls** is an impressive sight at any time, but truly thunders after heavy rain sending a vast spume of spray over any who approach.

Halfway along the fiord, the 155m **Stirling Falls** is almost as impressive and features on most cruise-boat itineraries and some kayak trips.

Milford Discovery Centre and Underwater Observatory

Harrison Cove, optional stop on most cruises; 30–45min stop • $36 • ☎ 0800 264536, ⓦ southerndiscoveries.co.nz

About a third of the way along the fiord is the recently revamped **Milford Discovery**

Centre and Underwater Observatory, a floating platform moored to a sheer rock wall in the marine reserve. A spiral staircase takes you 10m down through the relatively lifeless freshwater surface layer to a circular gallery where windows look out into the briny heart of the fiord. Sharks and seals occasionally swim by, but most of the action happens immediately outside in window-box "gardens", specially grown from rare, locally gathered **coral** and plant species. Lights pick out colourful fish, tubeworms, sea fans, huge starfish, and rare red and black coral (the latter actually white when alive). Unless you're an experienced diver this is the only chance you'll get to see these corals, which elsewhere in the world grow only at depths greater than 40m.

Topside, there's diverting interpretation on the Milford Road, the construction of the Homer Tunnel and the building of the centre in the mid-1990s.

14

ARRIVAL AND DEPARTURE   MILFORD SOUND

Milford Sound is on most visitors' itineraries, and during the season (Oct–April) there are plenty of operators to get you there from almost anywhere in the country. You can drive yourself along the Milford Road (see p.763), catch a bus the same way or fly direct from Queenstown or Wanaka. Several companies combine forces offering coach/cruise/flight combos (see box below).

BY BUS

Numerous luxury tour buses make the 5hr journey from Queenstown to Milford Sound via Te Anau (complete with frequent photo stops and a relentless commentary), stopping briefly for a cruise before heading back to Queenstown – a hurried twelve- to thirteen-hour day usually starting around 7am. A more palatable option is to base yourself in Te Anau and catch a bus from there – it's a leisurely eight hours to the Milford and back, allowing you to concentrate on the most interesting section of the Milford Road and the cruise. The cheapest buses don't include cruises, leaving you to arrange your own upon arrival. Buses between Milford and The Divide are run by Tracknet (☎ 0800 483262, ☻ tracknet.net).
Destinations The Divide (3 daily; 45min); Queenstown (at least 7 daily; 4hr 45min–5hr 30min); Te Anau (at least 7 daily; 2hr 15min–2hr 45min).

BUS COMPANIES

BBQ Bus ☎ 03 442 1045, ☻ milford.net.nz. A great option from Queenstown, with stops for short bushwalks, a BBQ in the Hollyford Valley and a Milford cruise (or flight option). Oct–April daily; May, Aug & Sept five weekly ($195). Also available from Te Anau ($165).
Fiordland Tours ☎ 0800 247249, ☻ fiordlandtours .co.nz. Te Anau-based owner-operator running small-bus

tours to Milford Sound with accommodation pick-ups, good commentary, cruise and home baking ($169; lunch $20 extra).
Jucy ☎ 0800 500121, ☻ jucycruize.co.nz. Budget trip from Queenstown for late-ish risers. Departs 8.15am, joins the 3.15pm Jucy Cruise and stops for a quick meal in Te Anau on the way back, returning 9pm ($159).
Milford Sound Select ☎ 0800 477479, ☻ milfordsoundselect.co.nz. Mid-sized glass-roofed coaches are a nice touch on these very competitively priced coach/cruise/coach tours from Queenstown ($179).
Real Journeys ☎ 0800 656501, ☻ realjourneys.co.nz. Upmarket coach/cruise/coach tours from Queenstown using wedge-shaped, glass-roofed coaches with slightly angled seats that give the best all-round views, and on-board wi-fi. There's good interpretation and a multilingual commentary. Operates all year ($226) with pick-ups in Te Anau ($170).
Tracknet ☎ 03 249 7777, ☻ tracknet.net. Budget transport between Te Anau and Milford Sound, though you'll have to put up with detours to the trailheads. Oct–April three times daily ($49 each way).
Trips & Tramps ☎ 0800 305807, ☻ tripsandtramps .co.nz. Te Anau-based, small-bus interactive, nature-oriented trips start from a coach, cruise and walk option where you can either do a 2hr self-guided walk up Key Summit (see box,

---

COACH, CRUISE AND FLIGHT COMBOS TO MILFORD SOUND

If you can't face a full-day coach/cruise/coach trip from Queenstown to Milford Sound, and want a superb flight over the South Island's icy spine as well as seeing the gorgeous Milford Road from the ground, opt for a fly/cruise/coach or coach/cruise/flight combo. Flights are far more likely to get cancelled due to bad weather so if the morning is looking fine it makes sense to fly in and coach out. Many operators offer such combos that, perhaps counter-intuitively, cost more than flying both ways. Typical prices are: Air Fiordland ($535), Milford Sound Select ($599) and Real Journeys ($584).

14

MILFORD SOUND CRUISES AND ACTIVITIES

There's little point visiting Milford Sound and not spending time on the water, and fortunately there are numerous worthwhile ways to do just that.

DAY-CRUISES

The dramatic view from the shore of Milford Sound pales beside the spectacle from the water. The majority of cruises explore the full length of Milford Sound, all calling at waterfalls, a seal colony and overhanging rock faces; at **Stirling Falls**, boats nose up to the base of the falls, while suitably attired passengers are encouraged to edge out onto the bowsprit and collect an earful of water.

The simplest option is one of the 1.5–3hr **day-cruises** (summer 20-plus daily; winter 10 daily; best booked a few days in advance in Jan, Feb & March) either on a large and comfortable catamaran or one of the more intimate small boats. Most cruise companies vary their **fares** during the day, with those leaving between 11am and 2pm around 20–30 percent more expensive than those at, say, 9am or 3pm. Otherwise, costs vary according to the size of boat, duration of trip and degree of interpretation, but all offer the same beautiful backdrop.

Cruise Milford ☎ 0800 645367, ⓦ cruisemilfordnz .com. With the smallest boats on the sound (max. 40 passengers), this new family-run cruise operator is a promising alternative should you wish to escape the tour groups that dominate elsewhere. 1hr 45min cruises cost $70–$85.

Go Orange ☎ 0800 246672, ⓦ goorange.co.nz. Real Journeys' budget-friendly sister company offers good-value 2hr cruises ($55–70), with free snacks and full packed lunches ($20–$25) available; they also offer a handful of kayaking trips.

Jucy Cruize ☎ 0800 500121, ⓦ jucycruize.co.nz. Fun, budget-oriented cruises (90min–1hr 45min;

$45–79) on a catamaran that takes up to 200 passengers, although it's rare for them to be that full. Sustenance is provided by an on-board branch of *Pita Pit*.

Mitre Peak Cruises ☎ 0800 744633, ⓦ mitrepeak .com. With smallish boats (max. 75) and more personal service, there's undoubted appeal to these 2hr cruises ($70–82) and they're deservedly popular.

Real Journeys ☎ 0800 656501, ⓦ realjourneys .co.nz. The biggest cruise operator with a wide range of boats and professional service. Choose a basic scenic cruise (1hr 40min; $72–96) or a more leisurely nature cruise (2hr; $88–98); lunches ($17–$33) available, but Indian and o-bento meals must be preordered.

p.766) or join a nature guide on a few show walks (10hr; $159, picnic lunch included). Another great two-day option throws kayaking into the mix ($335, accommodation not included).

BY PLANE

Visitors really pushed for time can do a simple overflight of Milford Sound from either Queenstown or Wanaka (typically around $370), but you really should land and take a cruise. Flights are, of course, weather dependent and operators won't fly you in to Milford unless they are fairly confident of getting you out again.

Air Fiordland ☎ 0800 103404, ⓦ airfiordland.com. Te

Anau-based airline doing 4hr fly/cruise/fly trips from both Te Anau and Queenstown ($470 from either).

Real Journeys ☎ 0800 656501, ⓦ realjourneys.co.nz. Major Fiordland operator flying from Queenstown and using their own cruise boats (overflight $360; fly/cruise/fly from $430).

Wanaka Flightseeing ☎ 03 443 8787, ⓦ flightseeing .co.nz. Fly/cruise/fly trips from Wanaka give especially good views of Mt Aspiring and the Olivine Ice Plateau en route (4hr; $490).

Destinations Queenstown (at least 10 daily; 35min); Wanaka (2–3 daily; 40min).

ACCOMMODATION AND EATING

Blue Duck Bar SH94 ☎ 03 249 7982. Fairly uninspiring pub with pool tables, sports TV and a short menu of pizzas, chicken burger and chips, and spaghetti Bolognese (all around $19). Meals served 5–9pm. Daily: Nov–March noon–11pm or later; April–Oct 4–9pm.

Blue Duck Café SH94 ☎ 03 249 7931. Café that's good for espresso, muffins, sandwiches, pies and ice cream, though the buffet lunches ($18–22) are less tempting. Get

a corner seat for views of Mitre Peak (or to watch the weather sweeping along the fiord). Daily: Nov–March 8.30am–4.30pm; April–Oct 9am–4pm.

Milford Sound Lodge 1.5km back from the wharf ☎ 03 249 8071, ⓦ milfordlodge.com. Book in advance to stay at this well-run lodge with campsites (tents $22; campervans $25), spacious dorms, twins and doubles (with shared bathrooms). If you're splashing out, opt for one of

Southern Discoveries ☎0800 264536, ⓦsoutherndiscoveries.co.nz. Mainstream options ranging from a basic cruise (1hr 45min; $59–92) to their Discover More cruise (3hr; $99) with lunch and a visit to the Milford Discovery Centre included.

OVERNIGHT CRUISES

Overnight cruises are all run by Real Journeys (☎0800 656501, ⓦrealjourneys.co.nz), who operate two motor cruisers each offering a slightly different experience. Both operate daily in summer from around 4.30pm–9.15am and involve a leisurely cruise around Milford Sound, usually anchoring for a while in **Anita Bay** (Te-Wahi-Takiwai, "the place of Takiwai"), a former greenstone-gathering place at the fiord's mouth, but still sheltered from the wrath of the Tasman Sea. There's a chance to go kayaking, good meals and a night spent at anchor in sheltered Harrison Cove. Coach transfers or coach-flight combos are available from Queenstown and Te Anau.

Milford Wanderer The 36 berths in this backpacker-oriented boat are mostly in cramped twin rooms that share bathrooms (though there are also a couple of quad-shares). All are equipped with sheets, duvets and towels, and a hearty three-course set meal (drinks extra) helps iron out the kinks. Nov–March only, twin-share $335, quad-share $285.

Milford Mariner Fairly luxurious 60-berth boat with reasonably comfortable twin or double en-suite cabins; dinner is a three-course buffet meal. Nov–March $415; Sept, Oct & April to mid-May $291.

KAYAKING

The elemental nature of Milford Sound can best be appreciated by **kayaking**, possibly seeing wildlife up close and even paddling in the spray from waterfalls.

★**Rosco's Milford Sound Sea Kayaks** 72 Town Centre, Te Anau ☎0800 476726, ⓦroscosmilfordkayaks.com. Extensive range of Milford Sound-based kayaking trips with expert and friendly guides, including the wonderful Morning Glory (18km; 6hr; $195), with a dawn start, long paddle then a water taxi back. The afternoon Twilighter Classic (12km; 5hr; $179) follows a similar format, will probably involve more wind and waves and usually has smaller groups. Trips mostly run mid-Oct to mid-April, with the Sunriser (12km; 5hr; $149) available year-round.

---

their gorgeous chalets (from $290) with large windows, underfloor heating and soft, super king-sized beds. The excellent in-house *Piopio Café* and comfortable lounge are ample compensation for the cramped kitchen and pricey shop. Dorms $33, doubles $99

Mitre Peak Lodge ☎03 249 7907. Ultimate Hikes' guided walkers get priority at this prominent 35-room 1950s hotel. Others can phone to fill any remaining rooms, which are a bit dated, though those with great Mitre Peak views also have modernized bathrooms. Checkout time is 8.30am; open Nov to mid-April. $200, fiord-view $250

The Milford Track

54km; 4 days

More than any other Great Walk, the **Milford Track** is a Kiwi icon. Its exalted reputation is part accident and part history but there's no doubt that the Milford Track is wonderful and includes some of Fiordland's finest scenery. The track starts at the head of Lake Te Anau and follows the Clinton River into the heart of the mountains, climbing over the spectacular Mackinnon Pass before tracing the Arthur River to Milford Sound.

Some disparage the track as over-regimented, expensive and not especially varied, while others complain that the huts are badly spaced and lurk below the tree line among the sandflies. While these criticisms aren't unfounded – the tramp costs around $370 in hut and transport fees alone – the track is well managed and maintained, the huts clean and unobtrusive, and because everyone's going in the same direction you can charge ahead (or lag behind) and hike all day without seeing a soul. The Milford is also tougher than many people expect, packing the only hard climb and a dash for the boat at Milford Sound into the last two days.

Brief history

It is likely that **Maori** paced the Arthur and Clinton valleys in search of *pounamu*, but there is little direct evidence. The first **Europeans** to explore were Scotsmen Donald Sutherland and John Mackay who in 1880 blazed a trail up the Arthur

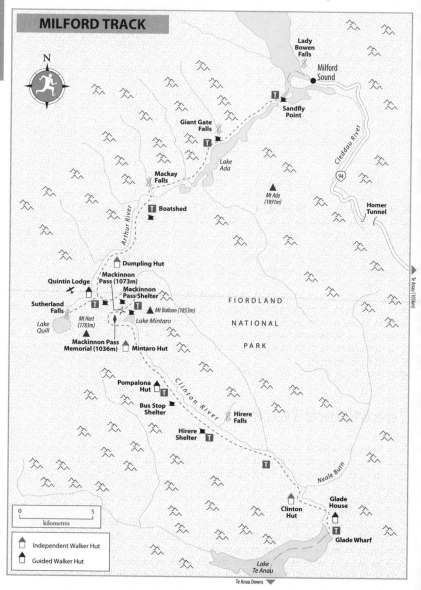

MILFORD TRACK

Lady Bowen Falls

Milford Sound

Sandfly Point

Giant Gate Falls

Lake Ada

Mackay Falls

Mt Ada (1891m)

Arthur River

Boatshed

Homer Tunnel

Cleddau River

94

Te Anau (105km)

Dumpling Hut

Quintin Lodge

Mackinnon Pass (1073m)

Mackinnon Pass Shelter

Sutherland Falls

Mt Hart (1783m)

Mt Balloon (1853m)

Lake Mintaro

Lake Quill

Mackinnon Pass Memorial (1036m)

Mintaro Hut

FIORDLAND

NATIONAL

PARK

Clinton River

Pompalona Hut

Bus Stop Shelter

Hirere Falls

Hirere Shelter

Neale Burn

Glade House

Clinton Hut

Glade Wharf

0   5
kilometres

Independent Walker Hut

Guided Walker Hut

Lake Te Anau

Te Anau Downs

Valley from Milford Sound. The story goes that while working their way up the valley they came upon the magnificent Mackay Falls and tossed a coin to decide who would name it, on the understanding that the loser would name the next waterfall. Mackay won the toss but rued his good fortune when, days later, they stumbled across the much more famous and lofty Sutherland Falls. They may well have climbed the adjacent Mackinnon Pass, but the honour of naming it went to **Quintin McKinnon** who, with his companion Ernest Mitchell, reached it in 1888 after having been commissioned by the Otago Chief Surveyor, C.W. Adams, to cut a path up the Clinton Valley.

14

Tourists arrive

The route was finally pushed through in mid-October 1888 and the first **tourists** followed a year later, guided by McKinnon. The greatest fillip came in 1908 when a writer submitted her account of the Milford Track to the editor of London's *Spectator*. She had declared it "A Notable Walk" but, in a fit of editorial hyperbole, the editor retitled the piece "The Finest Walk in the World". From 1903 until 1966 the government held a monopoly on the track, allowing only guided walkers; the huts were supplied by packhorses, a system that wasn't retired until 1969.

Wider **public access** was only achieved after the Otago Tramping Club challenged the government's policy by tramping the Milford in 1964. Huts were built in 1966 and the first independent parties came through later that year.

Glade Wharf to Clinton Hut

5km; 1–1hr 30min; 50m ascent

The first day is a doddle, starting along a 2km 4WD track that serves **Glade House** (guided walkers only). The path then crosses a swingbridge to the true right bank of the gentle, meandering Clinton River; keen anglers can spend an hour or two fishing for trout in the deep pools. The track runs through dense beech forest, only occasionally giving glimpses of the mountains ahead beyond **Clinton Hut**, where there are a handful of good swimming holes nearby.

Clinton Hut to Mintaro Hut

16.5km; 4–7hr; 350m ascent

The track follows the right bank of the Clinton River to its source, Lake Mintaro, and the *Mintaro Hut*. Again, it's easy going and by the time you reach a short side track to Hidden Lake, Mackinnon Pass should be visible. The track steepens a little to Bus Stop Shelter, flattens out to **Pompolona Hut** (guided walkers only), and is a further hour to **Mintaro Hut** where, if it looks like it will be a good sunset, you should drop your pack and head up Mackinnon Pass.

Mintaro Hut to Dumpling Hut

14km; 5–7hr; 550m ascent; 1030m descent

The walk to this point does little to prepare you for the third day. Though the surface of the broad path is firm and well-graded, less-experienced bushwalkers will find the haul up to **Mackinnon Pass** (1hr 30min–2hr) very strenuous. Long breath-catching pauses provide an opportunity to admire the wonderful alpine scenery, notably the headwall of the Clinton Valley, a sheer glacial cirque of grey granite. As the bush drops away behind you, the slope eases to the saddle at Mackinnon Pass, a great place to eat lunch, though you'll have the company of kea and the incessant buzzing of pleasure flights from Milford. A memorial to McKinnon and Mitchell marks the low point of the saddle, from where the path

14

turns east and climbs to a day-shelter (with toilets and, in summer, a gas ring) just below the dramatic form of Mount Balloon.

From here it's all downhill, and steeply too, initially skirting the flank of Mount Balloon then following the path beside the picturesque Roaring Burn down to the Arthur River. The confluence is marked by **Quintin Hut** (guided walkers only), which was originally built by the Union Steamship Company as an overnight shelter for sightseers from Milford visiting the Sutherland Falls. Though it remains a private hut, toilets and shelter are provided for independent walkers – who mostly dump their packs for the walk to the base of the 580m Sutherland Falls (4km return; 1hr–1hr 30min; 50m ascent), the highest in New Zealand. **Dumpling Hut** is another hour's walk from *Quintin Hut*.

Dumpling Hut to Sandfly Point

18km; 5–6hr; 125m descent

You're in for an early start and a steady walk to meet your launch (the last boat departs at 4pm). After rain this can be a magnificent walk, the valley walls streaming with waterfalls and the Arthur River in spate. The track follows the tumbling river for a couple of hours to the **Boatshed** (toilets), before crossing the Arthur River by swingbridge and cutting inland to the magnificent **Mackay Falls**. Though much smaller than the Sutherland Falls, they are equally impressive, particularly after rain. Don't miss Bell Rock, a water-hollowed boulder that you can crawl inside. The track subsequently follows Lake Ada, created by a centuries-old landslip, and named by Sutherland after his Scottish girlfriend. A small lunch shelter midway along its shore heralds Giant Gate Falls, which are best viewed from the swingbridge that crosses the river at the foot of the falls. From here it is roughly an hour and a half to the shelter at **Sandfly Point** along a good, broad track, the work of convicts put to work building it in the 1890s.

ARRIVAL AND DEPARTURE   MILFORD TRACK

By bus and boat Both ends of the Milford Track can only be approached by boat, and arrangements must be made at the same time as accommodation passes are issued. Independent walkers need to catch the Tracknet bus (30min; $36) from Te Anau to the harbour at Te Anau Downs, 30km north of Te Anau, then the Real Journeys launch across Lake Te Anau to Glade Wharf (10.30am and 1pm; 1hr; $81). There are early departures, but since the first day's walk is very easy, it is possible to make a late start

using the 12.15pm bus and the 1pm launch. At the Milford end of the track, catch the launch from the aptly named Sandfly Point to Milford Sound (Nov–April daily 2pm, 3pm & 4pm; 20min; $45). Tracknet buses back to Te Anau can be picked up at 9.30am, 2.30pm and 5pm (2hr; $49). An off-season option is with Cruise Te Anau (☏03 249 8005, ⓦcruiseteanau.co.nz) who offer a full transportation package for $180 (April–Nov only).

INFORMATION AND TOURS

Seasons Hiking the track outside the main Oct–April season is not recommended since transport to the trailheads is very limited, some footbridges are removed and huts have no heating. Still, bookings are not required and the Backcountry Hut Pass is valid.

Leaflets and maps DOC's *Milford Track* brochure (free) is adequate, though for detailed information consult the 1:40,000 *Milford Track Map and Track Guide* ($24.90) or 1:38,000 NewTopo map ($22.90), both available from the Fiordland National Park Visitor Centre.

Weather and track conditions DOC in Te Anau have the latest weather forecast and track conditions.

Safety DOC do not keep track of trampers' whereabouts. Let someone know your intentions through ⓦadventuresmart.org.nz. Due to the presence of

avalanche zones along the track, anyone walking out of season should check conditions with DOC before setting out. Locator beacons are available for $30/3 days from Bev's Tramping Gear (see p.759) or the Mobil garage in Te Anau.

GUIDED WALKS

Milford Track Guided Walk ☏0800 659255, ⓦultimatehikes.co.nz. For many years, the only way to walk the Milford Track was on a guided walk. Some argue that this is still the best approach, with just your personal effects to carry and comfortable beds in clean, plain huts with hot showers, duvets, three-course dinners with wine and cooked breakfasts. Accommodation is in shared bunkrooms or double en-suites. Staff prepare the huts, cook the meals, make up the lunches and tidy up after you.

The five-day, four-night package includes a pre-track briefing in Queenstown, trailhead transport, accommodation and food on the track, a night at the *Mitre Peak Lodge* and a Milford Sound cruise (Nov–April daily departures). The same company also runs guided walks on the Routeburn Track. A single-room supplement of $600 applies, with small discounts available very early and late in the season. Bunk/person $2195, double/person $2605

ACCOMMODATION

Booking There's a rigid system of advance hut booking during the main hiking season (late Oct–late April). You can only walk the track from south to north, spending the first night at *Clinton Hut*, the second at *Mintaro* and the third at *Dumpling*. No backtracking or second nights are allowed. It is easiest to book free online (☉ doc.govt.nz) from July 1 for the following season, though it is also possible to book by mail and in person ($2) through the Great Walks Booking Desk (PO Box 29, Te Anau ☏ 03 249 8514, ✉ greatwalksbooking@doc.govt.nz). Pick up your accommodation passes from DOC in Te Anau up to two days in advance; you must get them before 9am if you're on the 10.30am boat or 11am if you're on the afternoon boat. Numbers are limited to forty per day, so you'll need to book well in advance; a couple of months if you are adaptable, six if you need a specific departure date or are part of a large group. If the track is closed due to bad weather or track conditions full refunds are made.

Huts and camping During the season, the three 40-bunk huts all have wardens and are equipped with flush toilets, running water (which must be treated), heaters and gas rings, but not pans and plates; the cost is $162 for the three nights. Outside the main season these huts lose their warden and gas rings, go back to pit toilets and cost $15. There is no camping on the Milford Track.

Manapouri and Lake Manapouri

Even among New Zealand's bountiful supply of beautiful lakes, **Lake Manapouri** shines, its long, indented shoreline contorted into three distinct arms and clad with thick bush tangled with ferns. The lake sits at 178m and has a vast catchment area, guzzling all the water that flows down the Upper Waiau River from Lake Te Anau and unwittingly creating a massive hydroelectric generating capacity – something that almost led to its downfall (see box below).

ELECTRICITY, ALUMINIUM AND BRICKBATS

Lake Manapouri's **hydroelectric** potential had long been recognized, but nothing was done until the 1950s. An Australian firm, Comalco, wanted to smelt their Queensland bauxite into **aluminium** – a power-hungry process – as cheaply and reliably as possible, and alighted upon **Lake Manapouri**. They approached the New Zealand government, who agreed to build a power station on the lake, at taxpayers' expense, while Comalco built a smelter at Tiwai Point, near Bluff, 170km to the southeast.

The scheme entailed blocking the lake's natural outlet into the Lower Waiau River and chiselling out a vast powerhouse 200m underground beside Lake Manapouri's West Arm, where the flow would be diverted down a 10km tailrace tunnel to Deep Cove on Doubtful Sound. By the time the fledgling **environmental movement** had rallied its supporters, the scheme was well under way, but the government underestimated the anger that would be unleashed by its secondary plan to boost water storage and power production by raising the water level in the lake by more than 8m. The threat to the natural beauty of the lake sparked **nationwide protests**, though the 265,000-signature petition prepared by the "Save Manapouri Campaign" failed to change the government's mind. It was only after the 1972 elections, when Labour unseated the National Party, that the policy was changed and the lake saved. The full saga is recounted in Neville Peat's *Manapouri Saved* (see p.823).

The **Manapouri Underground Power Station** took eight years to build. Completed in 1971, it remains one of the most ambitious projects ever carried out in New Zealand. Eighty percent of its output goes straight to the **smelter** – which consumes around fifteen percent of all the electricity used in the country, and it is widely perceived to be an unnecessary drain on the country's resources. Because of the unexpectedly high friction in the original tailrace tunnel the power station had always run below 85-percent capacity, and to boost power production a second parallel tailrace tunnel was built in the late 1990s.

The small village of **MANAPOURI**, 20km south of Te Anau, wraps prettily around the shores of the lake at the head of the Waiau River, which the hydroelectric shenanigans have turned into a narrow arm of the lake now known as Pearl Harbour.

Apart from cruises and kayak trips, the only thing to do in Manapouri is to saunter along a few minor walks: accommodation and eating options are very limited.

14

Manapouri Underground Power Station

Oct–April daily at 12.30–1.30pm • Tours 3–4hr • $77

Real Journeys (see box, p.780) are the only ones with access to the impressive, if controversial, Manapouri Underground Power Station. After a lake cruise, you can get a sense of the scale of the place from a scale model in the visitor centre, then a bus takes you down a narrow, 2km-long tunnel to a viewing platform in the Machine Hall. All you see are the exposed sections of seven whirring turbines and panels assaulting you with statistics before you're whisked back to the bus.

ARRIVAL, INFORMATION AND TOURS

MANAPOURI

By bus Topline Tours (☎0508 249 8059, ⓦtoplinetours .co.nz) run between Te Anau and Manapouri (Oct–April daily on demand; $20). Real Journeys buses from Te Anau connecting with boats to West Arm and Doubtful Sound may also take extras ($42), but only if their cruise passengers don't fill the bus.
Destinations Te Anau (1–2 daily; 20min).
Tourist information Pearl Harbour (daily: Nov–Feb 7.30am–6pm; March–Oct 8.30am–5.30pm; ☎0800

656501, ⓦrealjourneys.co.nz). The Real Journeys booking office for Doubtful Sound trips also has some local information.
Manapouri Lake Cruises ☎03 249 6893, ⓦmanapourilakecruises.co.nz. A local boat-owner and a pianist have joined forces for these short cruises each afternoon (2hr; $75) and evening (3hr; $95–125), which see the motor yacht moor in a quiet cove for refreshments (coffee and cake or wine and cheese) and a classical piano recital.

GETTING AROUND

By boat You can get around Manapouri on foot, but to access the best walking tracks you need to get across the Waiau River, which is less than 100m across.
Adventure Kayak & Cruise 33 Waiau St, next to the Mobil station ☎0800 324966, ⓦfiordlandadventure .co.nz. This Doubtful Sound kayak tour operator also rents out single and double kayaks ($50/day; wetsuits, thermals

and VHF radio included) from their Manapouri office. Oct–April daily 9am–4.30pm.
Adventure Manapouri ☎03 249 8070, ⓦadventuremanapouri.co.nz. Runs a regular water taxi across the Waiau (Oct–April daily at 11am & 3pm; $15 return), a shuttle on demand ($20 return), and rents rowing boats ($30/day).

ACCOMMODATION

★**Freestone Backpackers** 270 Hillside Rd (SH99), 3km east of Manapouri ☎03 249 6893, ⓦfreestone

.co.nz. With its hillside setting, fabulous lake and mountain views, horses and chickens and accommodation in comfy

---

> ## MANAPOURI WALKS
>
> The following are covered in more depth in DOC's *Fiordland Day Walks* booklet. See "Getting around" for boat access to the Hope Arm and Circle tracks.
>
> **Circle Track** (7km; 3–4hr loop; 330m ascent). Manapouri's most popular walk contours west around the lakeshore before turning southeast to climb the ridge to a point with stupendous views over the lake, then heads north back to the start.
> **Hope Arm and Back Valley loop** (15km loop; 6–7hr; 200m ascent). Lovely exploration of the podocarp and beech forest west of Manapouri, with great lake views and an
>
> optional (and often muddy) side trip to Lake Rakatu (extra 2hr). Best done as an overnighter, sleeping at beachside *Hope Arm Hut* (12 bunks; $5) or *Back Valley Hut* (4 bunks; free)
> **Pearl Harbour to Fraser's Beach** (30min one way). Easy lakeshore track through beech forest, partly following the Old Coach Road Walk with fantails and silvereye flitting about the undergrowth; the views are magnificent on a clear evening.

wooden chalets (one en suite, $86), this doesn't really feel like a hostel. Chalets have pot-bellied stoves, verandas and basic cooking facilities. Guests qualify for locals' rates on the friendly owner's concert cruises (see box, p.780). Dorms $30, doubles $66

Manapouri Lakeview Motor Inn 68 Cathedral Drive ☎03 249 6652, ⓦmanapouri.com. This classic Kiwi motor lodge has great lake and mountain views from every room – even the budget ones. The standard studios ($130)

are crammed full of beds; unless you need them, you're better off stumping up for one of the more attractive superior studios ($135). Budget rooms $96

Possum Lodge 13 Murrell Ave ☎03 249 6623, ⓦpossumlodge.co.nz. An appealingly old-fashioned, peaceful and well-maintained campsite and hostel among beech trees where the Waiau River meets the lake. Some powered sites ($37 per site) plus retro 1940s motel units ($110). Camping $32 (per site), dorms $23

14

EATING

Lakeview Café 68 Cathedral Drive, at the Manapouri Lakeview Motor Inn ☎03 249 6652. True to its name, there are great vistas across Lake Manapouri from the picture windows and benches on the lawn outside this traditional Kiwi pub. The usual suspects are all here, but

they're done nicely – try the dukkah-sprinkled lamb chops and mash ($28.50); vegetarians could go for their tasty falafel burger ($23.50). Take away available. Meals served daily 11am–9.30pm.

Doubtful Sound

It was the building of the Manapouri hydro scheme that opened up **Doubtful Sound** to visitors. What was previously the preserve of the odd yacht and a few deerstalkers and trampers is now accessible to anyone prepared to take a boat across Lake Manapouri and a bus over the Wilmot Pass. Amid pristine beauty, wildlife is a major attraction, not least the resident pod of sixty-odd **bottlenose dolphins**, who frequently come to play around ships' bows and cavort near kayakers. **Fur seals** loll on the outer islands, **Fiordland crested penguins** arrive to breed in October and November, and the bush, which comes right down to the water's edge, is alive with kaka, kiwi and other rare bird species.

Like Milford, Doubtful Sound gets a huge amount of **rain**, but don't let that put you off – the place is at its best when the cliffs spring waterfalls everywhere you look after a downpour.

Though the rock architecture is a little less dramatic than Milford Sound, it easily makes up for this with its isolation. Travel between Manapouri to Doubtful Sound takes two hours, so to fully appreciate the beauty and isolation of the area it really pays to maximize your time there by staying overnight. Costs are unavoidably high and you need to be self-sufficient, but any inconvenience is easily outweighed by the glorious solitude – although it's becoming more popular for that very reason.

Brief history

Cook spotted Doubtful Sound in 1770 but didn't enter, as he was "doubtful" of his ability to sail out again in the face of winds buffeted by the steep-walled fiord. The breeze was more favourable for the joint leaders of a Spanish expedition, Malaspina and Bauza, who in 1793 sailed in and named Febrero Point, Malaspina Reach and Bauza Island. Sealers soon decimated the colonies of fur seals and few people visited the area until the 1960s when the hydro scheme required the construction of the 21km gravel **Wilmot Pass** supply road, which links Manapouri's West Arm with Doubtful Sound's Deep Cove.

Dusky Sound

Captain Cook spent six weeks in **Dusky Sound**, 40km south of Doubtful Sound, on his second voyage in 1773, while his crew recovered from an arduous crossing of the Southern Ocean. Time was mostly spent at Pickersgill Harbour where, at Astronomer's Point, it is still possible to see where Cook's astronomer had trees felled so he could get

14

DOUBTFUL SOUND CRUISES AND KAYAK TRIPS

Spending the day (or preferably a couple of days) on Doubtful Sound is an unmissable experience, and the overall quality of the kayak and cruise operators makes it even more pleasurable.

Adventure Kayak and Cruise ☎0800 324966, ⓦ fiordlandadventure.co.nz. Good-value kayak trips including a full-day guided trip ($245) with 4–5hr paddling on Doubtful Sound and a two-day trip ($385) where you camp beside the fiord. A great combo ($285) includes the guided day on Doubtful Sound then on the way back you set up camp beside Lake Manapouri, the guide leaves and next day you paddle yourselves back to Manapouri. Operates Nov–late March.

Deep Cove Charters ☎0800 249682, ⓦ deepcovecharters.co.nz. For a small-boat overnight experience opt for excellent trips aboard the twelve-berth *Seafinn*, a modern cruiser with lots of space and a dedicated crew. As well as exploring the fiord and watching wildlife you can kayak and fish. Chris, the skipper, will probably check his crayfish pots and the catch may end up on the lunch table. All meals are included and accommodation is in slightly cramped doubles/twins with shared bathroom. Operates Nov–March. Per adult prices: Bunk $500, twin-share $600, double $650.

Go Orange ☎0800 246672, ⓦ goorange.co.nz. A subsidiary of Real Journeys, these budget-oriented day-trips ($225) are the cheapest way to experience Doubtful Sound, with a 3hr cruise on the fiord, complete with breezy commentary and a variety of lunch options (from $20). The boat is smaller than some, taking a maximum of 45 passengers.

Real Journeys Overnight Cruise ☎0800 656501, ⓦ realjourneys.co.nz. Spend the night anchored in Doubtful Sound aboard the *Fiordland Navigator*, a modern cruiser that's designed to look like an old-fashioned three-masted scow. The trip doesn't visit the power station but you're away from Manapouri for a full 24hr, time enough to immerse yourself in this extraordinary landscape by kayaking or even swimming. Food and accommodation are excellent. Operates mid-Sept to mid-May and there's a ten-percent YHA discount. Per adult prices: quad-share $375, double or twin-share $595, single $1041.

Real Journeys Wilderness Cruise ☎0800 656501, ⓦ realjourneys.co.nz. Doubtful Sound's original day-trip involves a boat trip across Lake Manapouri, a visit to the underground power station and a bus ride to Deep Cove. You then board a catamaran for the three-hour cruise out to the mouth of the fiord (where fur seals loll on the rocks) and back, making forays into the fiord's serene "arms" (where your wildlife-spotting chances are best) before the bus and boat trip back. Year-round; 1–2 daily; cruise $265; preordered lunch $17.

Sea Kayak Fiordland ☎0800 200434, ⓦ seakayakfiordland.co.nz. Now part of the Real Journeys empire, these energetic and awe-inspiring overnight kayaking trips ($399) give you maximum time on the water with 4–6hr days paddling quality fibreglass sea kayaks either side of a night spent at a simple bush camp beside the fiord, with three-, four- and five-day trips also available. No experience is needed but the minimum age is 16 and you'll need to bring your own food. Daily Nov–late April. They also do occasional yacht-supported six-day/five-night kayaking trips to Dusky Sound ($2750) – a real wilderness experience.

an accurate fix on the stars. Not far from here is the site where 1790s castaways built the first European-style house and boat in New Zealand. Marooned by the fiord's waters, nearby Pigeon Island shelters the ruins of a house built by **Richard Henry**, a pioneer of New Zealand's conservation movement, who battled here from 1894 to 1908 to save endangered native birds from introduced stoats and rats.

ARRIVAL AND DEPARTURE — **DUSKY SOUND**

By tour Very few trips come down this way, making it all the more rewarding if you make the effort. Real Journeys (☎0800 656501, ⓦ realjourneys.co.nz) operate several tours in the area, the shortest and cheapest of which is their Dusky Sound Discovery Expedition (book well in advance; 4–5 days; $1950–$2150), which sees you cruising around Breaksea and Dusky sounds before hopping on a helicopter back to Manapouri.

The Southern Scenic Route

ⓦ southernscenicroute.co.nz

While in Fiordland, don't miss out on the beautiful fringe country, where the fertile sheep paddocks of Southland butt up against the remote country of Fiordland National

Park. The region's towns are linked by the underrated, pastoral charms of the **Southern Scenic Route**, a series of small roads where sheep are the primary traffic hazard. From Te Anau it runs via Manapouri to SH99, following the valley of the Waiau River to the cave-pocked limestone country around **Clifden**. A minor road cuts west to Lake Hauroko, access point for the Dusky Track, while the Southern Scenic Route continues south through the small service town of **Tuatapere** (the base for hiking the **Hump Ridge and South Coast tracks**), to estuary-side **Riverton** and on to Invercargill.

Clifden

CLIFDEN, 90km south of Te Anau, is barely a town at all but is of passing interest for the historic **Clifden Suspension Bridge**, one of the longest in the South Island, built over the Waiau River in 1899 and still open to foot traffic. Amateur spelunkers should allow time to tackle the **Clifden Caves** nearby.

Clifden Caves

1km along Clifden Gorge Road • Open access • Free

Maori once camped on summer foraging trips at the **Clifden Caves**, which are signposted around 1km north of the bridge along SH96. With no one to guide you there's a palpable sense of adventure when tackling this labyrinth lined with flowstone and stalactite formations and dotted with glowworms. The passages are not too tight but you'll need to crouch, scramble and climb several short ladders, following a series of reflective strips; modest scrambling skills are handy. Let someone know your intentions, and go with at least one other person. Wear clothes you don't mind getting dirty and take at least two torches – you can expect to be underground for 1.5 to 2hr.

Lake Hauroko

Lake Hauroko, at the end of a long dirt road, 32km west of Clifden, is New Zealand's deepest lake (462m), and far enough off the beaten track (20km of gravel road) that you can skinny dip. Low bush-clad hills surrounding the lake create the "sounding winds" immortalized in its name. The lake sits at the southern end of the epic **Dusky Track** – one of the longest and most remote in New Zealand, and much tougher than any of the Great Walks. Experienced trampers considering tackling it should obtain information and condition reports from DOC offices in the region. At First Bay, the road-end, there's just a parking area and toilets, though you can **camp** some 7km back from the lake at DOC's *Thicket Burn* campsite (free), just a grassy field with toilets and tap water.

JETBOATING TRIPS AROUND LAKE HAUROKO

To explore the beautiful wilderness area around Lake Hauroko, engage one of the companies running wilderness **jetboating trips** on the lake and along the 27km of the Grade III **Wairaurahiri River** down to the coast. Both companies listed below only run when numbers demand, so call several days ahead and hope to hook up with others.

Humpridge Jet ☎ 0800 270556, ⊕ river-jet.co.nz. Runs a full-day sightseeing trip down to the coast ($225; BBQ lunch $25 extra) with around 3hr of jetboating, some short walks and plenty of tales of hunting, fishing and live-deer capture back in the 1980s. You can use them as pick-up or drop-off for the South Coast Track ($180 one way).

Wairaurahiri Jet ☎ 0800 376174, ⊕ wjet.co.nz. There's a more polished feel to trips run by this operator, who do a full-day trip to the coast with a barbecue lunch at *Waitutu Lodge* (6hr; $249), tramper transport ($189 one way) and summer twilight trips (3hr; $179) across Lake Hauroko and partway down the Wairaurahiri River.

14

THE HUMP RIDGE AND SOUTH COAST TRACKS

Tuatapere is the base for two excellent and markedly different hiking experiences: the traditional **South Coast Track** and the **Hump Ridge Track**, with its engaging combination of coastal walking, historic remains, subalpine country and relatively sophisticated huts. The two hikes are cursorily covered in DOC's *Southern Fiordland Tracks* **leaflet**.

Both tracks share historically interesting kilometres of coastal walking, following a portion of the 1896 track cut 100km along the south coast to gold-mining settlements around the southernmost fiord of Preservation Inlet. This paved the way for woodcutters, who arrived en masse in the 1920s. Logs were transported to the mills on tramways, which crossed the burns and gullies on viaducts – four of the finest have been faithfully restored, including the 125m bridge over Percy Burn that stands 35m high in the middle. The remains of the former mill village of **Port Craig** – wharf, rusting machinery, crumbling fireplaces – are equally fascinating.

The **trailhead** for both tracks is the Rarakau car park, 20km west of Tuatapere, accessible by bus ($45 return) organized through the Hump Ridge Track office; there's also secure parking available ($5/day).

Jetboat operators (see box, p.781) will pick up and drop off at the Wairaurahiri rivermouth ($189/person one way), enabling you to return to Tuatapere by jetboat and minibus.

THE SOUTH COAST TRACK

The **South Coast Track** slices through the largest area of lowland rainforest in New Zealand. Although it is easy going it takes the best part of four days to reach Big River and you'll just have to turn around and walk back unless you prearrange a jetboat up the Wairaurahiri River. A popular alternative is to make a three-day excursion, staying at DOC's *Port Craig School Hut* ($15), and exploring the environs. Three more huts ($5 each) spaced four to seven hours' walk apart provide accommodation, and camping is free.

Rarakau to Port Craig School Hut (20km; 5–7hr; negligible ascent). The first leg follows either the old logging road or, tide permitting, the beach – which should shave half an hour off your walking time – before winding through the forest to Port Craig.
Port Craig School Hut to Wairaurahiri Hut (16km; 4–6hr; 200m ascent). Here the track follows the old tramway, crossing three of the restored viaducts (the largest, Percy Burn Viaduct, is currently closed for long-term maintenance work), before dropping down to the Wairaurahiri River. Alternatively, stay on the banks of the Wairaurahiri River at the private *Waitutu Lodge* (book through the Tuatapere information centre; $30; ⓦwaitutu.co.nz): take sleeping bag and food.
Wairaurahiri Hut to Waitutu Hut (13km; 4–6hr; negligible ascent). This section of the path largely follows the coastal flats across Maori land to *Waitutu Hut* (12 bunks; $5) on the true right bank of the *Waitutu River*. Fit and experienced trampers with camping equipment might want to continue from Waitutu Hut to the end of the track at Big River (12km; 5–7hr; negligible ascent), where DOC's *Westies Hut* (free) nestles in the mouth of a cave.

THE HUMP RIDGE TRACK

The privately managed 62km Hump Ridge Track (book in advance ☎0800 486774, ⓦhumpridgetrack.co.nz or at the office in Tuatapere, see opposite) is done in three days with nights spent at two comfortable 32-bunk lodges equipped with lights, gas cookers, cooking pots and eating utensils, eight-bunk rooms, a beer and wine license (you can't bring your own), flush toilets, porridge cooked by the lodge manager and hot showers ($10). There's even helicopter **bag transfer** (max 15kg; $100/leg), that's especially good for the first leg, saving you the biggest ascent when the bag is heaviest.

Tuatapere

TUATAPERE, thinly spread on the banks of the Waiau River 14km south of Clifden, is the largest town in southwestern Southland (though that's not saying much) and makes a good base for exploring the southern limits of Fiordland. It was once a major sawmilling town, but a single sawmill and one stand of beech/podocarp forest is the only evidence that the town could once have justified its epithet of "The Hole in the Bush". As logging declined, the community banded together to create the excellent

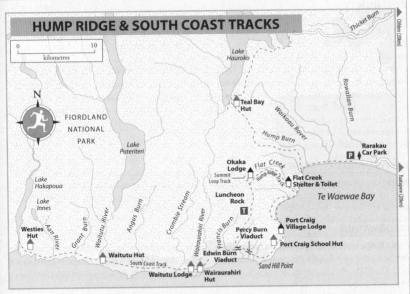

HUMP RIDGE & SOUTH COAST TRACKS

The tramp is occasionally muddy in places and when off the boardwalks it feels like a real "trampers" track. It requires a good level of fitness and it isn't for beginners or under-10s. Everyone walks the track anticlockwise, starting and finishing at Rarakau.

Summer **season** (late Oct to mid-April) accommodation packages range from the tramping-style **Freedom Walk** ($170; bring sleeping bag and food) which includes one night in each lodge, upgradable to a double or twin with sheets and duvets (add $100/room/night). To add a night in Tuatapere, first-day heli-packing and hot showers go for the Prime Package (departs Thurs; $450), or opt for a four-day **guided walk** (departs Fri; $1645) with meals, a short chopper flight, full heli-packing, a private room at the lodges and a night's B&B accommodation in Tuatapere. **Outside the season** lodge facilities are cut back and heli-packing is not available.

Rarakau to Okaka Lodge (21km; 7–9hr; 900m ascent). After great coastal walking you turn inland along boardwalks through open forest with a thick undergrowth of crown ferns. Glimpse views through the beech forest as you climb steeply up a ridge to the open tops with fabulous views back across Te Waewae Bay. Allow time to explore the adjacent Summit Loop Track (30min) along boardwalks past picturesque sandstone tors and delicate alpine plants.

Okaka Lodge to Port Craig Lodge (21km; 7–9hr; 100m ascent; 900m descent). The track follows the Hump Ridge, staying high for several hours with magical views before descending to the South Coast Track by Edwin Burn Viaduct. You then follow an old tramway to the majestic Percy Burn Viaduct and on to Port Craig.

Port Craig Lodge to Rarakau (20km; 5–7hr; undulating). Wander through towering coastal rimu and down on to sandy beaches, and back along the coast to Rarakau.

Hump Ridge Track, to encourage travellers to the area. The South Coast Track visits some of the same area, and both can be combined with jetboating along the Wairaurahiri River and Lake Hauroko.

The bush makes a last stand at a riverside clump of beech, kahikatea and totara on **The Domain** – staff at the information centre will point the way – where an easy walkway winds through the trees.

14

Brief history

Maori legend records the great explorer Tamatea's canoe *Takitimu* being wrecked on the Waiau River bar at Te Waewae Bay, where it turned to stone, the line of its petrified hull forming the Takitimu Mountains to the north of Tuatapere. While Maori set up summer foraging camps in the area, permanent settlement in Tuatapere dates from the arrival of European **pioneers** around 1885. By 1909 the **railway** had arrived from Invercargill, bringing with it steam-powered haulers that made short work of clearing the surrounding forests. More recently, foresters' attention shifted west to the fringes of the Fiordland National Park where, in the 1970s, the Maori owners proposed clear-cutting stands of ancient rimu. Environmentalists prevailed upon the Conservation Minister who eventually, in 1996, agreed to pay compensation in return for a sustainable management policy.

ARRIVAL AND DEPARTURE   TUATAPERE

By bus Trips & Tramps (☎ 0800 305807, ⊛ tripsandtramps .com) run the region's only bus service, operating between Te Anau and Tuatapere (Nov–late April Mon & Thurs only).

There is no bus between Tuatapere and Invercargill. Destinations Manapouri (2 weekly; 1hr 25min); Te Anau (2 weekly; 1hr 45min).

INFORMATION

Hump Ridge Track booking office and information centre 31 Orawia Rd (daily Oct–April 7.30am–6pm; ☎ 03 226 6739). Primarily set up for Hump Ridge Track hikers with a small selection of tramping essentials and

plenty of trail information. They can store valuables while you're in the wilds, and help with local accommodation and transport. Its small Bushman's Museum (donation) gives a rose-tinted version of pioneer history.

ACCOMMODATION AND EATING

Last Light Lodge & Café 2 Clifden Hwy ☎ 03 226 6667, ⊛ lastlightlodge.com. Once a forestry camp, this complex has been nicely converted into a holiday camp, with small, basic rooms, three-bed dorms, and a few tent ($14) and campervan ($16) sites. The café is excellent, with plenty of seating outside, internet and a range of tasty dishes served all day – think salmon and scallop penne ($25) or smoked chicken panini ($10). Café daily 8am–9pm or later. Dorms $30, doubles $70
Tuatapere Motel & Shooters Backpackers Holiday Park 73 Main St ☎ 0800 009993, ⊛ tuatapereaccommodation.co.nz. Slightly soulless but well-equipped combination of four spacious modern motel

units, a backpackers with spa pool ($25/hr) and some tent sites ($18) and hook-ups ($19). Dorms $30, doubles $65
★ **Yesteryear Café** 3a Orawia Rd ☎ 03 226 6682. The owner, Helen, whips up delightful home-made food in this former bakery decked out with a cornucopia of early twentieth-century kitchenware – a tribute to her and her husband's grandmothers, whose four jam pots hang on the wall. If you're in luck, she'll fire up the old coal range for pikelets with raspberry jam and cream, but otherwise there are pies, mince on toast ($9) and delectable date scones to keep you occupied – all to a soundtrack of golden oldies on the 1970s turntable. Oct–April daily 7am–5pm.

Monkey Island

23km south of Tuatapere

South of Tuatapere, SH99 follows the wind-ravaged cliffs behind the wide and moody Te Waewae Bay, where fierce southerlies have sculpted the much-photographed macrocarpa trees into extravagantly windswept forms. About 3km beyond the small town of Orepuki, signs point to **Monkey Island** where there's a good beach and basic camping (free) with vault toilets nearby.

Cosy Nook

29km south of Tuatapere

A further 4km south along SH99, signs point 5km west to **Cosy Nook**, a wonderfully picturesque cove hemmed in by granite boulders, which looks quite unlike anywhere else in the country – you could easily imagine it along Scotland's west coast. Indeed, one apocryphal story has a former resident, George Thomson, naming it after his Highland home village. The spot was site of one of the largest Maori settlements along this stretch of coast, with a *pa* (fort) on Matariki Island at the cove's mouth, though today all you'll see is a huddle of rustic holiday homes.

Colac Bay

37km southeast of Tuatapere

The highway regains the coast at the quiet community of **Colac Bay**, a name eighteenth-century whalers derived from the name of the local Maori chief, Korako. Apart from swimming and a nationally renowned surf break the only reason to stop is to get some rest – self-contained **campervans** are allowed to park overnight on Colac Foreshore Road between the boat ramp and shelter shed (2 nights max; free).

Riverton

RIVERTON (Aparima), 12km east of Colac Bay, is one of the country's oldest settlements. Frequented by whalers as early as the 1790s, the town was formally established in 1836 by another whaler, John Howell – who is also credited with kick-starting New Zealand's now formidable sheep-farming industry. The small town is strung along a spit between the sea and the Jacob's River Estuary (actually the mouth of the Aparima and Pourakino rivers), where fishing boats still harbour.

Beyond Riverton, SH99 heads into the hinterland of **Invercargill**, 40km away.

Te Hikoi: Southern Journey

172 Palmerston St • Daily: Oct–March 10am–5pm; April–Sept 10am–4pm • $6 • ☎ 03 234 8260, ⓦ tehikoi.co.nz

If you've any interest in the cultural history of the south coast, devote an hour to this well-presented, modern museum, which kicks off with an excellent fifteen-minute movie focusing on the unsettling times of early European contact. The tableau of a Maori muttonbirders' camp isn't entirely convincing but the tales of harvesting on the Titi Islands and the Maori seasonal food-gathering calendar show just how tough it was in these southern climes. Europeans didn't have it much easier, sealing, whaling and hacking out a living from the bush – to ease the hardship, some brewed rum from cabbage trees. There's also coverage of the Chinese gold-mining community at Round Hill, and diverting videos of old-timers reminiscing about growing up in the area.

EATING

RIVERTON

★**Mrs Clark's Café** 108 Palmerston St ☎ 03 234 8600. The best coffee and cakes in town, served in lively surroundings with interesting music and a glorious display of toast racks around the walls. Try the home-style baked beans on wholegrain toast ($14) or the blue cod fishcakes with salad ($19). Sun–Thurs 8am–3pm, Fri & Sat 8am–late.

The **eastern continuation** of the **Southern Scenic Route**, along the Catlins Coast to Dunedin, is covered in the "Dunedin to Stewart Island" chapter, p.613.

MAORI CARVING

Contexts

History

Many New Zealanders of European descent have long thought of their country as a model of humanitarian colonization. Maori often take a different view, however, informed by the repeated theft of land and erosion of rights that were supposedly guaranteed by a treaty. Schoolroom histories have generally been faithful to the European view, even to the point of influencing Maori mythology. In the last couple of decades, however, revisionist historians have largely discredited what many older New Zealanders know as fact. Much that is presented as tradition turns out to be the late nineteenth-century scholarship of historians who bent research to fit their theories and, in some cases, even destroyed evidence. What follows is inextricably interwoven with Maori legend and can be understood more fully with reference to the section on *Maoritanga* (see p.801).

Pre-European history

It's thought that the ancestors of modern **Maori** arrived from Polynesia in double-hulled canoes between 1200 and 1300 AD. Their journey was planned to the extent that they took with them the *kuri* (dog) and food plants such as taro (a starchy tuber), yam and *kumara* (sweet potato). The notion of a legendary "**Great Fleet**" of seven canoes arriving in 1350 AD seems most likely to be a Victorian adaptation of Maori oral history, which has been readopted into contemporary Maori legend.

The Polynesians found a land so much colder than their tropical home that many of their crops and plants wouldn't grow. Fortunately there was an abundance of marine life and large flightless birds, particularly in the South Island, where most settled. The people of this **Archaic Period** are often misleadingly known as "Moa Hunters" and while some undoubtedly lived off these birds, the moa wasn't present in other areas. By around 1350 settlements had been established all around the coast, but it was only later that there's evidence of horticulture, suggesting a later migration bringing plants for cultivation, or the beginning of successful year-round food storage, allowing a settled living pattern rather than the earlier hunters' short-lived campsites.

Either way, this marks the beginning of the **Classic Period** when *kainga* (villages) grew up close to the *kumara* grounds, often supported by *pa* (fortified villages) where the people could retreat when under attack. As tasks became more specialized and hunting and horticulture took up less time, the arts – particularly carving and weaving (see pp.804–806) – flourished and warfare became endemic. The decline of easily caught birdlife and the relative ease of growing *kumara* in the warmer North Island marked the beginning of a northward population shift. When the Europeans arrived,

1200–1300 AD	c.1350	1642
Arrival of first Polynesians.	The traditional date of arrival of the "Great Fleet" from Hawaiki.	Dutchman Abel Tasman sails past the West Coast and anchors in Golden Bay.

> ## POLYNESIAN MIGRATION
>
> Modern scholarship suggests that humans from Southeast Asia first explored the South Pacific around five thousand years ago, gradually evolving a distinct culture as they filtered down through the Indonesian archipelago. A thousand years of progressive island-hopping got them as far as Tonga and Samoa, where a distinctly **Polynesian** society continued to evolve, honing seafaring skills to the point where lengthy sea journeys were possible. Around a thousand years ago, Polynesian culture reached its classical apotheosis in the **Society Islands** west of Tahiti, widely thought to be the hub for a series of migrations heading southwest across thousands of kilometres of open ocean, past the Cook Islands, eventually striking land in what is now known as New Zealand (Aotearoa).

95 percent of the population was located in the North Island, mostly in the northern reaches, with coastal settlements reaching down to Hawke's Bay and Wanganui.

European contact and the Maori response

Many **Europeans** were convinced of the existence of a *terra australis incognita*, an unknown southern land, and wanted to trade there. In 1642, Dutchman **Abel Tasman**, working for the Dutch East India Company, became the first European to catch sight of Aotearoa. He anchored in Golden Bay, where a small boat being rowed between Tasman's two ships was intercepted by a Maori war canoe and four sailors were killed. Without setting foot on land Tasman fled up the west coast of the North Island, going on to add Tonga and Fiji to European maps. Aotearoa was subsequently named Nieuw Zeeland after the Dutch maritime province.

Nieuw Zeeland was ignored for over a century until 1769, when **James Cook** (see box opposite) paid the first of three extensive visits. Cook found Maori a **sophisticated people** with a highly formalized social structure and skills to turn stone and wood into fabulously carved canoes, weapons and meeting houses – yet they had no wheels, roads, metalwork, pottery or animal husbandry. After initial unfortunate encounters near Gisborne (see p.372) and Napier (see p.385), Cook managed to strike up friendly, constructive relations. The original settlers now found that their tribal allegiance wasn't enough to differentiate them from the Europeans and subsequently began calling themselves **Maori** (meaning "normal" or "not distinctive") while referring to the newcomers as **Pakeha** ("foreign").

On the Coromandel Peninsula, Cook deviated from instructions and unfurled the British flag, claiming formal possession without the consent of Maori, but was still able to return twice in 1773 and 1777. The French were also interested – on his 1769 voyage Cook had passed **Jean François Marie de Surville** in a storm without either knowing of the other's presence.

The establishment of the Botany Bay penal colony in neighbouring Australia aroused the first commercial interest in New Zealand and from the 1790s to the 1830s New Zealand was part of the Australian frontier. By 1830 the coast was dotted with semi-permanent **sealing** communities which, within thirty years, had almost clubbed the seals into extinction. The British navy rapidly felled giant kauri trees for its ships' masts, while others supplied Sydney shipbuilders. By the 1820s **whalers** had moved in, basing

1769	1830s	1835
Englishman James Cook circumnavigates both main islands.	Sealing and whaling stations dotted around the coast.	Independence of the United Tribes of NZ proclaimed.

themselves at Kororareka (now Russell), where they could recruit Maori crew and provision their ships. This combination of rough whalers, escaped convicts from Australia and assorted miscreants and adventurers combined to turn Russell into a lawless place populated by what Darwin, on his visit in 1835, found to be "the very refuse of Society".

Before long, the Maori way of life had been entirely disrupted. **Intertribal fighting** soon broke out on a scale never seen before. Hongi Hika (see box, p.790) was the first off the mark, but the quest for new territory also fuelled the actions of Ngati Toa's **Te Rauparaha** (see p.256), who soon controlled the southern half of the North Island.

The huge demand for **firearms** drove Maori to sell the best of their food, relocating to unhealthy areas close to flax swamps, where flax production could be increased. Even highly valued tribal treasures – *pounamu* (greenstone) clubs and the preserved heads of chiefs taken in battle – were traded. European **diseases** swept through the Maori population, alcohol and tobacco became widespread, Maori women were prostituted to Pakeha sailors, and the tribal structure began to crumble.

Into this scene stepped the **missionaries** in 1814, the brutal New South Wales magistrate **Samuel Marsden** arriving in the Bay of Islands a transformed man with a mission to bring Christianity and "civilization" to Maori, and to save the souls of the sealers and whalers. Subsequently Anglicans, Wesleyans and Catholics all set up missions throughout the North Island, ostensibly to protect Maori from the worst of the exploitation and campaigning in both London and Sydney for more policing of Pakeha actions. In exchange, they destroyed fine artworks considered too sexually explicit and demanded that Maori abandon cannibalism and slavery; in short, Maori were expected to trade in their *Maoritanga* and become "**Europeans**". By the 1830s, self-confidence and the belief in Maori ways was in rapid decline: the *tohunga* (priest) was powerless over new European diseases which could often be cured by the missionaries, and some Maori had started to believe Pakeha that the Maori race was dying out.

The push for colonization

Despite Cook's discovery claim in 1769, imperial cartographers had never marked New Zealand as a British possession and it was with some reluctance – informed by the perception of an overextended empire only marginally under control – that New South Wales law was nominally extended to New Zealand in 1817. The effect was minimal; the New South Wales governor had no official representation on this side of

---

JAMES COOK

Yorkshireman Lieutenant (later Captain) **James Cook** was a meticulous **navigator** who sailed the *Endeavour* into the Pacific to observe the transit of Venus across the sun. Following Admiralty instructions he then continued west, arriving at "the Eastern side of the Land discover'd by Tasman" where he observed the "Genius, Temper, Disposition and Number of the Natives" and encouraged his botanists, Banks and Solander, to collect numerous samples.

On three voyages between 1769 and 1777 Cook spent a total of ten months around the coast of Aotearoa, leaving his mark with numerous place names. Some of his **charts** were in use well into the twentieth century, and his only significant errors were showing Banks Peninsula as an island and Stewart Island as a peninsula.

1840	**1840s**	**1852**
Treaty of Waitangi. Capital moved from Kororareka to Auckland.	Cities of Auckland, Christchurch, Dunedin, Nelson, New Plymouth, Wanganui and Wellington established.	NZ becomes a self-governing colony divided into six provinces.

HONGI HIKA

Hongi Hika from Ngapuhi *iwi* of the Bay of Islands was the first Maori chief to appreciate the value of firearms, and had already acquired several when missionary Thomas Kendall met him in 1814. By this time he was encouraging his people to grow crops that could be traded with Pakeha for guns.

In 1820 Hongi Hika travelled to England with Thomas Kendall to work on *A grammar and vocabulary of the language of New Zealand*. While he was there he briefly became the toast of London society and was presented to George IV as an "equal". Having little use for most of the gifts showered upon him, he traded them for 300 muskets. Eager to emulate the supreme power of the imperial king, Hongi Hika set about subduing much of the North Island, using the often badly maintained and inexpertly aimed guns to rattle the enemy, who were then slaughtered with the traditional *mere*. Warriors abandoned the old fighting season – the lulls between hunting and tending the crops – and set off to settle old scores, resulting in a massive loss of life.

the Tasman and was powerless to act. Unimpressed, by 1831 a small group of northern Maori chiefs decided to petition the British monarch to become a "friend and the guardian of these islands", a letter that was later used to justify Britain's intervention.

Britain's response was to send the less-than-competent **James Busby** as British Resident in 1833, with a brief to encourage trade, stay on good terms with the missionaries and Maori, and apprehend escaped convicts for return to Sydney. Convinced that New Zealand was becoming a drain on the colony's economy, the New South Wales governor withheld guns and troops, and Busby was unable to enforce his will. Busby was also duped by Baron de Thierry, a Briton of French parents, who claimed he had bought most of the Hokianga district from Hongi Hika and styled himself the "sovereign chief of New Zealand", to "save" Maori from the degradation he foresaw under British dominion. In a panic, Busby misguidedly persuaded 35 northern chiefs to proclaim themselves as the "**United Tribes of New Zealand**" in 1835. As far as the Foreign Office was concerned, this allowed Britain to disclaim responsibility for the actions of its subjects.

By the late 1830s there were around two thousand Pakeha in New Zealand, the largest concentration around Kororareka in the Bay of Islands. Most were British, but French Catholics also consolidated their tentative toehold, and in 1839 British-born James Clendon was appointed American consul. Meanwhile, **land speculators** and colonists began taking an interest. The Australian emancipationist, William Charles Wentworth, had "bought" the South Island and Stewart Island for a few hundred pounds (the largest private land deal in history, subsequently quashed by government order) and British settlers were already setting sail. The British admiralty finally took notice when the Australian convict settlements, originally intended simply as an out-of-sight, out-of-mind solution to their bulging prisons, looked set to become a valuable possession.

A combination of these pressures and Busby's exaggeration of the Maori inability to manage their own affairs goaded the British government into action. The result was the 1840 **Treaty of Waitangi** (see box opposite & p.165), a document that purported to guarantee continued Maori control of their lands, rights and possessions in return for their loss of sovereignty, a concept open for misinterpretation. The annexed lands became a dependency of New South Wales until New Zealand was declared a separate colony a year later.

1858	1860–65	1860s	1865
Settlers outnumber Maori.	New Zealand Wars between Pakeha and Maori.	Major gold rushes in the South Island.	Capital moved from Auckland to Wellington.

Settlement and the early pioneers

Even before the Treaty was signed, there were moves to found a settlement in Port Nicholson, the site of Wellington, on behalf of the New Zealand Company. This was the brainchild of **Edward Gibbon Wakefield**, who hoped to stem American-style egalitarianism and use New Zealand as the proving ground for his theory of "scientific colonization". This aimed to preserve the English squire-and-yokel class structure but ended up encouraging absentee landlordism.

Between 1839 and 1843 the New Zealand Company dispatched nearly 19,000 settlers to "**planned settlements**" in Wellington, Wanganui, Nelson and New Plymouth. This was the core of Pakeha immigration, the only substantial non-Wakefield settlement being **Auckland**, a scruffy collection of waterside shacks which, to the horror of New Zealand Company officials, became the capital after the signing of the Treaty of Waitangi.

The company couldn't buy land direct from Maori, but the government bought up huge tracts and sold it on, often for ten or twenty times what they paid for it. In 1850 the New Zealand Company foundered, leaving settlements which, subject to the hard

---

THE TREATY OF WAITANGI

IN ENGLISH

The main points set out in the **English treaty** are as follows:
- The chiefs cede sovereignty of New Zealand to the Queen of England.
- The Queen guarantees the chiefs "full exclusive and undisturbed possession of their Lands and Estates Forests Fisheries and other properties which they may collectively or individually possess".
- The Crown retains the right of pre-emption over Maori lands.
- The Queen extends the rights and privileges of British subjects to Maori.

IN MAORI

However, the **Maori translation** presents numerous possibilities for misunderstanding, since Maori is a more idiomatic and metaphorical language, where words can take on several meanings. The main points of contention include the following:
- The preamble of the English version cites the main **objectives** of the treaty being to protect Maori interests, to provide for British settlement and to set up a government to maintain peace and order. On the other hand, the main thrust of the Maori version is that the all-important rank and status of the chiefs and tribes will be maintained.
- The concept of **sovereignty** in the Maori version is translated as *kawanatanga* (governorship), a word Maori linked to their experience of the toothless reign of James Busby (see opposite). It seems unlikely that the chiefs realized just what they were giving away.
- In the Maori text, the Crown guaranteed the *tangata whenua* (people of the land) the possession of their properties for as long as they wished to keep them. In English this was expressed in terms of **individual rights** over property. This is perhaps the most wilful mistranslation and, in practice, there were long periods when Maori were coerced into selling their **land**, and when they refused, lands were simply taken.
- **Pre-emption** was translated as *hokonga* – a term simply meaning "buying and selling", with no explanation of the Crown's exclusive right to buy Maori land, which was clearly spelled out in the English version. This has resulted in considerable friction over Maori being unable to sell any land that the government didn't want, even if they had a buyer.
- The implications of **British citizenship** may not have been well understood: it is not clear whether Maori realized they would be bound by British law.

1867	1870s	1876
Maori men given the vote.	Wool established as the mainstay of the NZ economy.	Abolition of provincial governments. Power centralized in Wellington.

realities of colonial life, had failed to conform to Wakefield's lofty theories and were filled with sturdy workers from labouring and lower-middle-class backgrounds.

In 1852 New Zealand achieved self-government and divided the country into six **provinces** – Auckland, New Plymouth, Wellington, Nelson, Canterbury and Otago. In addition to taking over land sales, it encouraged migrants with free passage, land grants and guaranteed employment on road construction schemes – a call heeded by those hoping for a better life away from the drudgery of working-class Britain. Maori still held the best land, growing potatoes and wheat for both local consumption and export to Australia, where the Victorian gold rush had created a huge demand. Pakeha were barely able to compete, and the slump in export prices in the mid-1850s saw many look to **pastoralism**. The Crown helped by halving the price of land, allowing poorer settlers to become landowners but simultaneously paving the way for the creation of huge pastoral runs and putting further pressure on Maori land.

Maori resistance and the New Zealand Wars

The first five years after the signing of the Treaty were a disaster, first under Governor Hobson then the ineffectual FitzRoy. Relations between Maori and Pakeha began to deteriorate immediately, as the capital was moved from Kororareka to Auckland and duties were imposed in the Bay of Islands. The consequent loss of trade from passing ships precipitated the first tangible expression of dissent, a famous series of incidents involving the Ngapuhi leader **Hone Heke**, who repeatedly felled the most fundamental symbol of British authority, the flagstaff at Russell. The situation improved to some degree with the appointment of **George Grey**, the most able of New Zealand's governors, who did more than anyone else to shape the country's early years. Soon Maori began to adapt their culture to accommodate Pakeha – selling crops, operating flour mills and running coastal shipping. Grey encouraged the process by establishing mission schools, erecting hospitals where Maori could get free treatment, and providing employment on public works. In short, he upheld the spirit of the Treaty, thereby gaining enormous respect among Maori. Sadly, he failed to set up any mechanism to perpetuate his policies after he left for the governorship of Cape Town in 1853.

Under **New Zealand's constitution**, enacted in 1852, Maori were excluded from political decision-making and prevented from setting up their own form of government; although British subjects in name, they had few of the practical benefits and yet were increasingly expected to comply with British law. By now it was clear that Maori had been duped by the Treaty of Waitangi: one chief explained that they thought they were transferring the "shadow of the land" while "the substance of the land remains with us", and yet he now conceded "the substance of the land goes to the Europeans, the shadow only will be our portion". Growing **resistance** to land sales came at a time when settler communities were expanding and demanding to buy huge tracts of pastoral land. With improved communications Pakeha became more self-reliant and dismissive of Maori, who began to lose faith in the government and fell back on traditional methods of handling their affairs. Self-government had given landowners the vote, but since Maori didn't hold individual titles to their land they were denied suffrage. Maori and Pakeha aspirations seemed completely at odds and there was a growing **sense of betrayal**, which helped replace tribal animosities with a tenuous unity. In 1854, a month before

1882	1893	1910s
First refrigerated meat shipment to Europe. Lamb becomes increasingly important.	Full women's suffrage: a world first.	Rise of organized labour under the socialist Red Federation. Strikes at Blackball, Waihi and Auckland.

New Zealand's first parliament, Maori held intertribal meetings to discuss a response to the degradation of their culture and the rapid loss of their land. The eventual upshot was the 1858 election of the ageing **Te Wherowhero**, head chief of the Waikatos, as the Maori "King", the leader of the **King Movement** (see box, p.217) behind which Maori could rally to hold back the flood of Pakeha settlement. Most were moderates making peaceful overtures that Pakeha chose to regard as rebellious.

Matters came to a head in 1860, when the government used troops to enforce a bogus purchase of land at Waitara, near New Plymouth. The fighting at Taranaki soon consumed the whole of the North Island in the **New Zealand Wars**, once known by Pakeha as the Maori Wars and by Maori as *te riri Pakeha* (foreigners' anger). Maori were divided, with some settling old grievances by siding with the government against their traditional enemies. Through the early 1860s the number of Pakeha troops was tripled to around 3000, providing an effective force against less coordinated Maori forces. Though there were notable Maori successes, the final result was inevitable. Fighting had abated by the end of the 1860s but peace wasn't finally declared until 1881.

British soldiers had been lured into service with offers of land and free passage and, in a further affront to defeated Maori, many were settled in the solidly Maori Waikato. Much of the most fertile land was **confiscated** – in the Waikato, the Bay of Plenty and Taranaki – with little regard to the owners' allegiances during the conflict. By 1862 individuals could buy land directly from Maori, who were forced to limit the stated ownership first to ten individuals and later to just one owner. With their collective power smashed, voracious land agents lured Maori into debt then offered to buy their land to "save" them.

Between 1860 and 1881, the **non-Maori population** rose from 60,000 to 470,000, swamping and marginalizing Maori society. An Anglo-Saxon worldview came to dominate all aspects of New Zealand life, and by 1871 the Maori language was no longer used for teaching in schools.

Meanwhile, as the New Zealand Wars raged in the North Island, **gold fever** had struck the South, with discoveries near Queenstown in 1861 and later along the West Coast. For the best part of a decade, gold was New Zealand's major export, but its most noticeable effect was on population distribution: by 1858 the shrinking Maori population had been outstripped by rapidly swelling Pakeha numbers, most settling in the South Island where relations with Maori played a much smaller part.

Consolidation and social reform

The 1870s were dominated by the policies of Treasurer Julius Vogel, who started a **programme of public works** funded by borrowing on a massive scale. Within a decade previously scattered towns in separately governed provinces were transformed into a single country unified by improved roads, an expanding rail system, 7000km of telegraph wires and numerous public institutions. Almost all the remaining farmable land was bought up or leased from Maori and acclimatization societies sprang up with the express aim of anglicizing the New Zealand countryside and improving **farming**. With no extensive market close enough to make perishable produce profitable, **wool** became the main export, stimulated by the development of the Corriedale sheep, a Romney-Lincoln cross with a long fleece. Wool continued as the mainstay until 1882,

1914–18	1917	1920s
NZ takes part in World War I with terrible loss of life.	Temperance Movement closes pubs at 6pm. Only repealed in 1967.	Initial prosperity evaporates as the Great Depression takes hold.

when the first **refrigerated meat shipment** left for Britain, signalling a turning point in the economy and the establishment of New Zealand as Britain's offshore larder, a role it maintained until the 1970s.

From 1879 until 1896 New Zealand slid into a "long depression", mostly overseen by the conservative "Continuous Ministry" – the last government composed of colonial gentry. During this time **trade unionism** began influencing the political scene and bolstered the Liberal Pact (a Liberal and Labour alliance). In 1890 the alliance wrested power and ushered in an era of unprecedented social change. Its first leader, **John Ballance**, firmly believed in state intervention and installed socialist **William Pember Reeves** as his Minister of Labour. Reeves was instrumental in pushing through sweeping reforms to working hours and factory conditions that were so progressive that no further changes were made to labour laws until 1936. When Ballance died in 1892 he was replaced by **Richard "King Dick" Seddon**, who introduced a graduated income tax and repealed property tax, hoping to break up some of the large estates. New Zealand was already being tagged the "social laboratory of the world", but more was to come.

In 1893, New Zealand was the first nation in the world to enact full **female suffrage**, (see box below), followed five years later by the introduction of an **old age pension**. Fabian Beatrice Webb, in New Zealand that same year, declared that "it is delightful to see a country with no millionaires and hardly any slums".

By the early twentieth century, the Pakeha standard of living was one of the highest in the world. But things were not so rosy for Maori, whose numbers had plummeted from an estimated 200,000 at Cook's first visit to around 50,000 in 1896. However, as resistance to European diseases grew, numbers started rising, accompanied by a new confidence buoyed by the rise of Maori parliamentary leadership. **Apirana Ngata**, **Maui Pomare** and **Te Rangi Hiroa** (**Peter Buck**), who were committed to working within the administrative and legislative framework of government, became convinced that the

---

ACCIDENTAL SUFFRAGE

In 1893, New Zealand became the first nation on earth to grant women the vote. Other territories (South Australia, Wyoming etc) had led the way with limited **women's suffrage**, but New Zealand threw the net wider. It is something New Zealanders are inordinately proud of even though it came about more by accident than any free-thinking principle.

When a radical electoral reform bill was up for consideration, Prime Minister Seddon let an amendment pass on the assumption that it would be rejected by the Legislative Council (an upper house which survived until 1950). Seddon then ordered a Liberal Party councillor to change his vote, his interference causing the ire of two other councillors who then voted for the bill, allowing it to pass by twenty votes to eighteen. It's also contended that female suffrage was approved in response to the powerful quasi-religious temperance movement, which hoped to "purify and improve the tone of our politics", effectively giving married couples double the vote of the unmarried man, who was often seen as a drunken layabout. Regardless of the rationale, New Zealand set a precedent and other major Western nations eventually followed suit – Finland in 1906, all Australian states by 1908, Britain in 1918, and the US in 1920. It wasn't until 1919, however, that New Zealand women were given the right to stand for parliament, and they were not eligible to be appointed to the New Zealand Legislative Council until 1941.

1935	1941	1947
M.J. Savage's Labour government ushers in the world's first Welfare State.	Bombing of Pearl Harbor and World War II begins New Zealand's military realignment with the Pacific region.	Full independence from Britain.

survival of *Maoritanga* depended on shedding those aspects of the traditional lifestyle that impeded their acceptance of the modern world.

Seddon died in 1906 and the flame went out of the Liberal torch, though the party was to stay in power another six years. This era saw the rise of the "**Red Feds**", international socialists of the Red Federation who began to organize Kiwi labour. They rejected the arbitration system that had kept wage rises below the level of inflation for a decade, and encouraged **strikes**. The longest was at Blackball on the West Coast, where prime movers in the formation of the Federation of Miners, and subsequently the Federation of Labour, led a three-month stoppage.

The 1912 election was won by William Massey's Reform Party, with the support of the farmers or "cow cockies". Allegiances were now substantially polarized and 1912 and 1913 saw bitter fighting at a series of strikes at the gold mines of Waihi, the docks at Timaru and the wharves of Auckland. As workers opposed to the arbitration system withdrew their labour, owners organized scab labour, while the hostile Farmers' Union recruited mounted "special constables" to help the government. Protected by naval and military forces, they decisively smashed the Red Feds. The Prime Minister even handed out medals to strike-breaking dairy farmers.

Coming of age

Though New Zealand had started off as the unwanted offspring of Mother England, it had soon transformed itself into a devoted daughter who could be relied upon in times of crisis. New Zealand had supported Britain in South Africa at the end of the nineteenth century and was now called upon to do the same in **World War I**. Locally born Pakeha now outnumbered immigrants and, in 1907, New Zealand had traded its self-governing colony status for that of a Dominion. This gave the country control over its foreign policy, but did not stop New Zealanders flocking to the war effort. Altogether ten percent of the population was involved, 100,000 fighting in the trenches of Gallipoli, Passchendaele and elsewhere. Seventeen thousand were killed.

At home, the **Temperance Movement** was back in action, attempting to curb vice in the army brought on by drink. Plebiscites in 1911, 1914 and 1919 narrowly averted national prohibition but the "wowsers" succeeded to the point that from 1917 pubs would close at 6pm for the duration of the war, though it wasn't repealed until 1967. This "**Six o'clock swill**" – frenetic after-work consumption in which the ability to tank down as much beer as possible was raised to an art form – probably did more to hinder New Zealand's social development than anything else (and the emphasis on quantity over quality encouraged breweries to churn out dreadful watery brews).

The wartime boom economy continued until around 1920 as Britain's demand for food remained high. Pakeha **returned servicemen** were rehabilitated on newly acquired farmland; Maori returned servicemen got nothing.

New Zealand continued to grow, with ongoing improvements in infrastructure – hydroelectric dams and roads – and enormous improvements in farming techniques, such as the application of superphosphate fertilizers, sophisticated milking machines and tractors. Yet it was ill-prepared for the **Great Depression**. The already high national debt skyrocketed as export income dropped and the Reform government cut pensions, health care and public works' expenditure. The budget was balanced at the cost of producing

1950	1951	1960s
Parliament's upper house abolished.	NZ joins ANZUS military pact with the US and Australia.	Start of immigration from Pacific Islands. Major urbanization of Maori population.

huge numbers of unemployed. Prime Minister Forbes dictated "no pay without work" and sent thousands of men to primitive rural relief camps for unnecessary tasks such as planting trees and draining swamps, resulting in lines of ragged men awaiting their relief money, malnourished children in schools and former soldiers panhandling in the streets.

Throughout the 1920s the Labour Party had watered down some of its socialist policies in an attempt to woo the middle-ground voter. In 1935 it was swept to power and ushered in New Zealand's second era of massive social change, picking up where Seddon left off. Labour's leader **Michael Joseph Savage** felt that "Social Justice must be the guiding principle and economic organization must adapt itself to social needs", a sentiment translated by a contemporary commentator as aiming "to turn capitalism quite painlessly into a nicer sort of capitalism which will eventually become indistinguishable from socialism". Salaries reduced during the depression were restored; public works programmes were rekindled, with workers on full pay rather than "relief"; income was redistributed through graduated taxation; and in two rapid bursts of legislation Labour built the model **Welfare State**, the first in the world and the most comprehensive and integrated. State houses were built and let at low rental, pensions were increased, a national health service provided free medicines and health care, and family benefits supplemented the income of those with children.

Maori welfare was also on the agenda, with living standards raised to the Pakeha level, partly by increasing pensions and unemployment payments. Legal changes paved the way for Maori land to be farmed using Pakeha agricultural methods, while maintaining communal ownership. In return, the newly formed **Ratana Party**, who held all four of the Maori parliamentary seats, supported Labour, keeping them in office until 1949.

New Zealand's perception of its world position changed dramatically in 1941 when the Japanese bombed Hawaii's Pearl Harbor. The country was forced to recognize its position half a globe away from Britain and in the military sphere of America. As in World War I, large numbers of troops were called up, amounting to a third of the male labour force, but casualties were fewer and on the home front the economy continued to boom. By the 1940s New Zealand was the world's most prosperous country, with an enviable quality of life and welfare safety-net.

More years of prosperity

The Reform Party and the remnants of the Liberals eventually combined to form the National Party which, in 1949, wrested power from Labour. With McCarthyite rhetoric, National branded the more militant unionists as Communists and succeeded in breaking much of the power of the unions during the violent 1951 **Waterfront Lock-out**. From the late 1940s until the mid-1980s, **National** became New Zealand's main party of government, interrupted only by two three-year stints with Labour in power. The country's underlying conservatism had now found its expression. Most were happy with the government's strong-arm tactics, which emasculated the militant unions.

Notions of the prosperous "Kiwi ideal" had huge appeal for Brits still suffering rationing after World War II, and between 1947 and 1975, 77,000 Brits became "**ten pound poms**", making use of the New Zealand government's assisted passage to fill Kiwi job vacancies.

By most measures New Zealand's wealth was evenly spread, with few truly rich and relatively few poor. The exception were Maori. Responding to the urban

1972–75	1975	1970s–80s
NZ economy struggles to cope with huge oil price hikes and Britain's entry into the Common Market.	Waitangi Tribunal established to consider Maori land claims.	Contentious sporting relations culminate in massive protests as a racially selected South African Springbok rugby team tours NZ.

labour shortages and good wages after World War II, many now took part in a **Maori migration** to the cities, especially Auckland. Yet by the 1970s, unemployment, unrest and a disproportionate prison population were exposing weaknesses in the Pakeha belief that the country's race relations were the best in the world. Pakeha took great pride in Maori bravery, skill, generosity, sporting prowess and good humour, but were unable to set aside the discrimination which kept Maori out of professional jobs.

On the economic front, major changes took place under **Walter Nash**'s 1957–60 Labour government, when New Zealand embarked on a programme designed to relieve the country's dependence on exports. A steel rolling mill, oil refinery, gin distillery, aluminium smelter and glass factory were all set up. When **Keith Holyoake** helmed the next National government, in 1960, Britain was still by far New Zealand's biggest export market but was making overtures to the economically isolationist European Common Market. Britain was no longer the guardian she once was and in the **military** sphere New Zealand began to court Pacific allies, mainly through the ANZUS pact, which provided for mutual defence of Australia, New Zealand and the US.

Dithering in the face of adversity

In 1972 Britain finally joined the Common Market and New Zealand felt betrayed. Later the same year **oil prices** quadrupled in a few months and the treasury found itself with mounting fuel bills and decreasing export receipts. The Labour government were defeated in 1975 by National's obstreperous and pugnacious **Robert "Piggy" Muldoon**, who denounced Labour's borrowing and then outdid them. In short order New Zealand had dreadful domestic and foreign debt, unemployment was the highest for decades, and the unthinkable was happening – the standard of living was falling. People began to leave in their thousands and the "brain drain" almost reached crisis point. Muldoon's solution was to "**Think Big**", a catch-all term for a number of capital-intensive petrochemical projects designed to utilize New Zealand's abundant natural gas to produce ammonia, urea fertilizer, methanol and synthetic petrol. It made little economic sense. Rather than use local technology and labour to convert vehicles to run on compressed natural gas (a system already up and running), Muldoon paid international corporations to design huge prefabricated processing plants which were then shipped to New Zealand for assembly, mostly around New Plymouth.

Factory outfalls often jeopardized traditional Maori shellfish beds, and a new **spirit of protest** saw *iwi* win significant concessions. Maori began to question the philosophy of Pakeha life and looked to the Treaty of Waitangi to correct their grievances. These were aired at occupations of traditional land at Bastion Point in Auckland and at Raglan, and through a petition delivered to parliament after a march across the North Island.

Maori also found expression in the formation of **gangs** – particularly Black Power and the Mongrel Mob – along the lines graphically depicted in Lee Tamahori's film *Once Were Warriors* (see p.818), which was originally written about South Auckland life in the 1970s. Fortified suburban homes still exist and such gangs continue to be influential among Maori youth.

1984	1985	1987
The "Hikoi" land march brings Maori grievances into political focus.	French secret service agents bomb Greenpeace flagship the *Rainbow Warrior* in Auckland Harbour.	New Zealand becomes a Nuclear-Free Zone.

Race relations were never Muldoon's strong suit and when large numbers of illegal **Polynesian immigrants** from South Pacific islands – particularly Tonga, Samoa and the Cook Islands – started arriving in Auckland he responded by instructing the police to conduct random "dawn raids" checking for "over-stayers", many of whom were deported.

Muldoon took a hands-off approach when it came to sporting contacts with apartheid South Africa and in 1976 let rugby administrators send an All Blacks team over to play racially selected South African teams. African nations responded by boycotting the Montréal Olympics, making New Zealand an international pariah. New Zealand signed the 1977 Gleneagles Agreement requiring it to "vigorously combat the evil of apartheid" and yet in 1981 the New Zealand Rugby Union courted a **Springbok Tour**, which sparked New Zealand's greatest civil disturbance since the labour riots of the 1920s.

Economic and electoral reform

Muldoon's big-spending economic policies proved unsuccessful, and in 1984 Labour was returned to power under **David Lange**. Just as National had eschewed traditional right-wing economics in favour of a "managed economy", Labour now addressed the dire economic problems by turning one of the world's most regulated economies into one governed by market forces. The long-standing belief that the state should provide for those least able to help themselves was cast aside as exchange controls were abolished, state benefits were cut, the maximum income-tax rate was halved and a Goods and Services Tax was introduced. Unemployment doubled to twelve percent, a quarter of manufacturing jobs were lost, and the moderately well-off benefited at the expense of the poor.

In other spheres Labour's views weren't so right-wing. One of Lange's first acts was to refuse US ships entry to New Zealand ports unless they declared that they were nuclear-free. The Americans refused and withdrew support for New Zealand's defence safety net, the **ANZUS** pact. Lange also gave **legal recognition to the Treaty of Waitangi**, for the first time since the middle of the nineteenth century. Now, Maori grievances dating back to 1840 could be addressed.

The rise in apparent income created consumer confidence and the economy boomed until the stock market crash of 1987, which hit New Zealand especially hard. In 1990 National's **Jim Bolger** took the helm, and throughout the deep recession National continued Labour's free-market reforms, cutting welfare programmes and weakening the unions by passing the **Employment Contracts Act**, under which individual workplaces came to their own agreements on wages and conditions. By the middle of the 1990s the economy had improved dramatically and what for a time had been considered a foolhardy experiment was seen by monetarists as a model for open economies the world over. Meanwhile, the gap between rich and poor continued to widen.

Political change

In 1996, New Zealand experienced its first MMP election (see box opposite), which brought a new Maori spirit into parliament, with far more Maori MPs than ever before.

1990–96	1997	1999
Continuation of free-market reforms and further dismantling of the welfare state.	National's Jenny Shipley becomes NZ's first female prime minister.	Labour's Helen Clark becomes NZ's second female prime minister, and the first elected in her own right.

Bolger's poor handling of the first MMP coalition government saw him supplanted in a palace coup, with **Jenny Shipley** becoming New Zealand's first female prime minister. In the 1999 election, the **Green Party** came out of left field, long-sidelined but newly resurgent under MMP. They racked up six seats and helped form a government under Labour's **Helen Clark** – the country's first elected female prime minister. The 1999 election brought New Zealand's first Rastafarian MP, **Nandor Tanczos**, resplendent in waist-length dreads and a hemp suit, and **Georgina Beyer**, the world's first transgender MP.

The Labour-led coalition stopped logging of West Coast beech forests and replaced the Employment Contracts Act with more worker-friendly legislation but failed to deliver on education and health care. Still, Labour was returned with an increased majority at the 2002 election.

Labour's popularity remained high until the 2003 **foreshore and seabed debate** in which Labour forced through legislation ostensibly guaranteeing beach-access to all, by declaring that the land in question was owned by the Crown. Maori perceived this as an affront to their sovereignty, and traditionally Labour-supporting Maori voters turned to the newly established **Maori Party**, co-led by former Labour MP **Tariana Turia**. At the 2005 election the Maori Party won four of the seven Maori seats but Labour was still able to cobble together a coalition without Maori Party support.

This, combined with the perception of the Labour government having outstayed its welcome after nearly a decade in power, saw a resurgent National Party, under former currency trader **John Key**, form a coalition government following the 2008 election.

FIRST-PAST-THE-POST, MMP AND MAORI SEATS

In the troubled economic times of 1993, when dissatisfaction with both major parties was running high, New Zealand voted to abandon its long-standing, Westminster-style, first-past-the-post voting system in favour of Mixed Member Proportional representation (MMP). This gave smaller parties an opportunity to have a greater influence, and New Zealand's Parliament has become all the more colourful for it.

Of the 120 MPs elected, around half represent their own area of the country ("electorate" or "seat") and half are elected from party lists. Voters get **two votes**. The first is for a person, who you hope will become your electorate MP. The second is for a party and is generally considered the more important as it determines the overall make-up of Parliament. A party's representation in Parliament is made up from the number of electorate seats they win plus a number of their list MPs determined by their percentage of the party vote.

To get any seats at all, small parties must exceed the threshold of five percent of the party vote, or win a constituency seat. If they win a seat, their representation is proportional to their party vote even if it's under five percent.

To further complicate matters, Maori voters can choose to vote either within the general system described above, or for one of the seven **Maori seats** which cover the country. All parties are entitled to field candidates in both general and Maori constituencies, though parties championing Maori concerns tend to win.

A **referendum** on New Zealand's electoral system was held at the same time as the 2011 general election, during which Kiwis resoundingly voted to retain the MMP system.

2003	2003	2008
Privy Council in London replaced by a Supreme Court as NZ's highest legal body.	Continued immigration from East Asia brings the Asian population up to ten percent of the nation.	New Zealand becomes first developed country to sign a free trade agreement with China.

Recent history

When much of the rest of the developed world struggled with the Global Financial Crisis from 2008, New Zealand fared reasonably well. Lefties will cite sound financial management under Labour but much of the credit goes to **booming international dairy prices**, particularly powdered milk, which almost doubled from 2007 to 2008 and remained high until 2014. Sheep farmers everywhere were converting to dairying and even arable regions like the Canterbury Plains now sprout cows on grassy circles created by kilometre-long irrigation booms. With high nutrient loads leaching into depleted watercourses this is unsustainable in the long term, and perhaps the 2015 drop in milk prices may turn farmers away from such practices.

In the early 1990s, 15 percent of Kiwi dairy exports went to the UK and only 0.5 percent to China. Now those stats are reversed with the UK taking only 0.3 percent and China snaffling 23 percent. Much of that change has come about since 2008 when New Zealand became the first developed nation to sign a **free trade agreement** with China. In 2013, China became New Zealand's biggest trade partner (with $12 billion annually) just pipping Australia ($11 billion) with the USA ($6 billion), Japan ($4 billion) and Korea ($2 billion) as distant followers.

Firmly ensconced in Parliament, National sought to take control of Auckland by amalgamating a barely functional patchwork of seven councils under one unitary authority. To National's chagrin, this "Supercity" voted left-leaning **Len Brown** as its first mayor in 2010. Auckland Council carries considerable heft and relations with the National Government have been fraught, especially over the council's approach to tackling the house prices that make Auckland one of the world's least affordable places to live. The two parties have also clashed over funding for the **City Rail Link**, Brown's dream of significantly improving Auckland's train system with a 3.4km-long $1 billion tunnel under the CBD. National's refusal to commit government funds threatens the 2021 completion date.

Late 2010 wasn't a happy time. A 7.1 magnitude **earthquake** hitting Christchurch in September was followed by the loss of 29 men after an explosion at a botched coal-mine development at **Pike River** on the West Coast in November. These were trumped in February 2011 when 185 people were killed by a massive aftershock in Christchurch (see box, p.511).

On the political front, Key's government repealed the Foreshore and Seabed Act in 2011 prompting Maori Party firebrand MP Hone Harawira to break away and form the **Mana Party**. Harawira took the Northland Maori seat of Te Tai Tokerau at the 2011 election and remained a thorn in the side of both the National government and the Maori Party. He lost his seat in 2014 after forming a disastrous alliance with the Internet party, founded by German Mega mogul, **Kim Dotcom**.

In opposition, a succession of Labour leaders have failed to dent John Key's popularity. Clark lieutenant **Phil Goff** fell after the 2011 election, **David Shearer** got rolled and, in 2014, Labour suffered its worst loss at the ballot box since 1922 under David Cunliffe. After polling under 25 percent and returning just 32 members in a 121-seat parliament, former union leader **Andrew Little** took over at Labour's helm.

2010–11	2011	2014
Christchurch struck by severe earthquakes. The most devastating, in February 2011, kills 185 people.	New Zealand hosts – and wins – the Rugby World Cup. The country rejoices.	National re-elected for a third term under John Key, the first time any party has won an outright majority under MMP.

Maoritanga

When the Pakeha first came to this Island, the first thing he taught the Maori was Christianity. They made parsons and priests of several members of the Maori race, and they taught these persons to look up and pray; and while they were looking up the Pakehas took away our land.

Mahuta, the son of the Maori King Tawhiao, addressing the New Zealand Legislative Council in 1903

Contemporary Maori culture has seen a dramatic resurgence in recent decades, though it struggles in a broadly Anglo-European-dominated New Zealand. Around fifteen percent of the country's population identify as Maori, and many Pakeha also have Maori forebears. Indeed, Maori–Pakeha marriage since the early nineteenth century has created a complex interracial pool – a fact that led one academic to speculate "race relations will be worked out in the bedrooms of New Zealand". Ancestry remains the foundation of Maoridom but a sense of belonging is increasingly important and centres on Maoritanga. This embodies Maori lifestyle – embracing Maori social structure, ethics, customs, legends, art and language.

Maori in the modern world

New Zealand's Maori make up a vital part of all walks of life – as lawyers, MPs, university lecturers, sporting, musical and media identities and even as the Governor-General. That said, average incomes are lower than those of Pakeha, almost half of all prison inmates are Maori and only around a quarter of Maori achieve post-school qualifications. These, along with dreadful health statistics, are among the imbalances that activists and politicians are working to redress.

Many Pakeha have long cited scenes of Maori and Pakeha elbow-to-elbow at the bar and Maori rugby players in the scrum alongside their Pakeha brothers as evidence of a harmonious existence. Yet this has ignored an undercurrent of Maori dissatisfaction over their treatment since the arrival of Europeans; the policy of **assimilation** relied on Maori conforming to the Pakeha way of doing things, making no concession to *Maoritanga*. Maori adapted quickly to European ways but were rewarded with the near-loss of their language and the loss of their **land**. It is impossible to overestimate the importance of this: Maori spirituality invests every tree, hill and bay with a kind of supernatural life of its own, drawn from past events and the actions of the ancestors. It is by no means fanciful to equate the loss of land with the diminution of Maori life force.

It's only really since the 1980s that the paternal Pakeha view has been challenged, with the country adopting **biculturalism**. As Maori rediscover their heritage and Pakeha comprehend what has been around for generations, knowledge of *Maoritanga* and some understanding of the language is considered desirable and advantageous. Recent governments have increasingly fostered a take-up in the learning of Maori language, resurgence in Maori arts and crafts and a growing pride in the culture by both Maori and Pakeha.

The sluggish pace of change led to an increase in Maori activism. The debate effectively led to the 2004 birth of the centrist Maori Party, and more recently the radical Mana Party. Activist Tame Iti and others obviously felt this was way too little and established a camp in the Urewera hills. During a strong-arm 2007 raid there was a "lock-down" of the local community at nearby Ruatoki and those arrested were charged as terrorists (later commuted to firearms offences). If anything, the then-Labour government's botched response heightened calls for greater self-determination.

Maori legend

Maori culture remains primarily oral with chants, storytelling and oratory central to ceremonial and daily life. Different tribal groups had different sets of stories, or at least variations on common themes, but European historians with pet theories often distorted the tales they heard and destroyed conflicting evidence, creating their own Maori folklore. Over time many of these stories have been taken back into Maori tradition, resulting in a patchwork of authentic and bowdlerized legends and helping create a common Maori identity.

Creation

From the primal nothingness of **Te Kore** sprang **Ranginui**, the sky father, and **Papatuanuku**, the earth mother. They had numerous offspring, including: **Haumia Tiketike**, the god of the fern root and food from the forest; **Rongo**, the god of the *kumara* and cultivation; **Tu Matauenga**, the god of war; **Tangaroa**, the god of the oceans and sea life; **Tawhirimatea**, the god of the winds; and **Tane Mahuta**, the god of the forests. Through long centuries of darkness the brothers argued over whether to separate their parents and create light. Tawhirimatea opposed the idea and fled to the skies where his anger is manifested in thunder and lightning, while Tane Mahuta succeeded in parting the two, allowing life to flourish. Ranginui's tears filled the oceans, and even now it is his grief that brings the dew, mist and rain.

Having created the creatures of the sea, the air and the land, the gods turned their attentions to humans and, realizing that they were all male, decided to create a female. They fashioned clay into a form resembling their mother and **Tane** breathed life into the nostrils of the Dawn Maiden, **Hinetitama**.

Maui the trickster and Kupe the navigator

Maori mythology is littered with demigods, none more celebrated than **Maui-Tikitiki-a-Taranga**, whose exploits are legend throughout Polynesia. With an armoury of spells, guile and boundless mischief, Maui gained a reputation as a trickster, using his abilities to turn situations to his advantage. Equipped with the powerful magic jawbone of his grandmother, he set about taming his world, believing himself invincible. He even took on the sun, which passed so swiftly through the heavens that people had no time to tend their fields. Maui, with the aid of his older brothers, plaited strong ropes and

---

MAUI FISHES UP THE NORTH ISLAND

Maui's greatest work was the creation of **Aotearoa**. Because of his reputation for mischief, Maui's brothers often left him behind when they went fishing, but one morning he stowed away, revealing himself far out to sea and promising to improve their catch. Maui egged them on until they were beyond the normal fishing grounds before dropping anchor. In no time at all Maui's brothers filled the canoe with fish, but Maui still had some fishing to do. They scorned his hook (secretly armed with a chip of his grandmother's jawbone) and wouldn't lend him any bait, so Maui struck his own nose and smeared the hook with his blood. Soon he hooked a fabulous fish that, as it broke the surface, stretched into the distance all around them. Chanting an incantation, Maui got the fish to lie quietly and it became the North Island, Te ika a Maui, the fish of Maui. As Maui went to make an offering to the gods, his brothers began to cut up the fish and eat it, hacking mountains and valleys into the surface. To fit in with the legend, the South Island is often called Te waka a Maui, the canoe of Maui, and Stewart Island the anchor, Te punga o te waka a Maui.

tied them across the sun's pit before dawn. The sun rose into the net and Maui beat the sun with his magic jawbone, imploring it not to go so fast. The sun weakened and agreed to Maui's request. Maui's legendary antics extend to the creation of Aotearoa (see box opposite).

Maori trace their ancestry back to **Hawaiki**, the source of the Polynesian diaspora, for which the Society Islands and the Cook Islands are likely candidates. According to legend, the first visitor to Aotearoa was **Kupe**, the great Polynesian navigator. He was determined to kill a great octopus that kept stealing his bait; drawn ever further out to sea in pursuit, he finally reached landfall on the uninhabited shores of Aotearoa, the "land of the long white cloud". He named numerous features of the land before returning to Hawaiki with instructions for retracing his voyage.

Social structure and customs

Maori society is **tribal**, though mass migration from homelands to the cities has eroded tribal affiliations. In urban situations the finer points of *Maoritanga* have been rediscovered and the basic tenets remain strong, with formal protocol ruling ceremonies from funeral wakes to meetings.

The most fundamental grouping in Maori society is the extended family or **whanau** (literally "birthing"), spanning immediate relatives to cousins, uncles and nieces. A dozen or so *whanau* form localized subtribes or **hapu** (literally "gestation or pregnancy"), comprising extended families of common descent. *Hapu* were originally economically autonomous and today continue to conduct communal activities, typically through *marae* (see p.804). Neighbouring *hapu* are likely to belong to the same tribe or **iwi** (literally "bones"), a looser association of Maori spread over large geographical areas. The thirty-odd major *iwi* are tenuously linked by common ancestry, traced back to semi-legendary canoes, or *waka*. In troubled times, *iwi* from the same *waka* would band together for protection. Together these are the **tangata whenua**, "the people of the land", a term that may refer to Maori people as a whole, or just to one *hapu* if local concerns are being aired.

The literal meanings of *whanau*, *hapu* and *iwi* can be viewed as a metaphor for the Maori view of their relationship with their ancestors or **tupuna**, existing through their genetic inheritors, the past forming part of the present. Hence the respect accorded the **whakapapa**, an individual's genealogy tracing descent from the gods via one of the migratory *waka* and through the *tupuna*. The *whakapapa* is often recited on formal occasions such as **hui** (meetings).

Maori traditional life is informed by the parallel notions of **tapu** (taboo) and **noa** (mundane, not *tapu*). This belief system is designed to impose a code of conduct: transgressing *tapu* brings ostracism, ill fortune and sickness. Objects, places, actions and people can be *tapu*, demanding extra respect; the body parts of a chief, especially the head, menstruating women, sacred items, earrings, pendants, hair combs, burial sites, and the knowledge contained in the *whakapapa* are all *tapu*. The productivity of fishing grounds and forests was traditionally maintained by imposing *tapu* at critical times. The direct opposite of *tapu* is *noa*, a term applied to ordinary items that, by implication, are considered safe; a new building is *tapu* until a special ceremony renders it *noa*.

People, animals and artefacts, whether *tapu* or *noa*, possess **mauri** (life force), **wairua** (spirit) and **mana**, a term loosely translated as prestige but embodying wider concepts of power, influence, charisma and goodwill. Birthright brings with it a degree of *mana* that can then be augmented through brave deeds or lost through inaction. Wartime cannibalism was partly ritual and by eating an enemy's heart a warrior absorbed his *mauri*. Likewise personal effects gain *mana* from association with the *mana* of their owner, accruing more when passed to descendants. Any slight on the *mana* of an individual was felt by the *hapu*, who must then exact **utu** (a need to balance any action with an equal reaction), a compunction that often led to bloody feuds, sometimes escalating to war and further enhancing the *mana* of the victors. Pakeha found this a hard concept to grasp and deeds that they considered deceitful or treacherous could be considered correct in Maori terms.

The responsibility for determining *tapu* falls to the **tohunga** (priest or expert), the most exalted of many specialists in *Maoritanga*, conversant with tribal history, sacred lore and the *whakapapa*, and considered to be the earthly presence of the power of the gods.

Marae

The rituals of *hapu* life – **hui**, **tangi** (funeral wakes) and **powhiri** (formal welcomes) – are conducted on the **marae**, a combined community, cultural and social centre where the cultural values, protocols, customs and vitality of *Maoritanga* find their fullest expression. Strictly, a *marae* is a courtyard, but the term is often applied to a whole complex, comprising the **whare runanga** (meeting house, or *whare nui*), *whare manuhiri* (house for visitors), *whare kai* (eating house) and an old-fashioned **pataka** (raised storehouse). *Marae* belonging to one or more *hapu* are found all over the country, while pan-tribal urban *marae* exist to help Maori who have lost their roots.

Visitors, whether Maori or Pakeha, may not enter *marae* without invitation, so unless you're personally invited, you're most likely to visit on a commercially run **tour** (see box, p.806). Invited guests are expected to provide some form of **koha** (donation) towards the upkeep of the *marae*, usually included in tour fees. Remember, the *marae* is sacred and due reverence must be accorded the **kawa** (protocols).

Arts and crafts

The origins of **Maori art** lie in eastern Polynesia but half a millennium of isolated development has resulted in unique forms of expression. Eastern Polynesia has no suitable clay, so Maori forebears had no skills for pottery and focused on wood, stone and weaving, occasionally using naturalistic designs but more often the **stylized forms** that make Maori art unmistakeable.

As with other *taonga* (treasures), many examples were taken by Victorian and later collectors, but there is determined effort by *iwi* and Te Puni Kokiri (the Ministry of Maori Development) to restore *taonga* to New Zealand, including severed heads scattered through museums around the world.

Woodcarving

Maori handiworks' greatest expression is **woodcarving**. The essence of great Maori woodcarving is that as much care is given to the production of a humble water bailer as to the pinnacle of Maori creativity, *waka* (canoes) and *whare whakairo* (carved houses). Early examples of woodcarving feature the sparse, rectilinear styles of ancient eastern Polynesia, but by the fifteenth century these were replaced by the cursive style, employed by more traditional carvers today. In Northland, kauri wood was used, while elsewhere durable, easily worked totara was the material of choice. Carvers worked with shells and sharp stones in the earliest times, but the artist's scope increased with the invention of tools fashioned from **pounamu** (greenstone, a form of jade; see box, p.668). Some would say that the quality of the work declined after European arrival: not just through the demand for quickly executed "tourist art", but as a consequence of pressure to remove the phallic imagery found obscene by missionaries. As early as 1844, carving had been abandoned in areas with a strong missionary presence, and it continued to decline until the 1920s when Maori parliamentarian Apirana Ngata established Rotorua's pan-tribal **Maori Arts and Crafts Institute** – a foundation on which *Maoritanga* could be rebuilt.

> ### WHARE
> Originally the chief's residence, the *whare* gradually adopted the symbolism of the *waka* – some incorporated wood from *waka*. Each meeting house is a tangible manifestation of the *whakapapa*, usually representing a synthesis of the ancestors: the ridge-pole, the backbone; the rafters, the ribs; the interior, the belly; the gable, the head; and the barge-boards, the arms, often with finger-like decoration. Inside, all wooden surfaces are carved and the spaces filled with intricate woven-flax panels, *tukutuku*.

The role of carver has always been highly respected, with seasoned and skilled exponents having the status of *tohunga* and travelling the country to carve and teach. The work is *tapu* and *noa* objects must be kept away – cooked food is not allowed nearby, and carvers have to brush away shavings rather than blow them – though women, previously banned, can now become carvers.

Maori carving exhibits a distinctive **style**. Relief forms are hewn from a single piece of wood with no concession to natural form, shapes or blemishes. Landscapes are symbolized not actually depicted, perspective is not represented, and figures stand separately. Unadorned wood is rare, carvers creating a stylistic bed of swirling spirals, curving organic forms based on fern fronds or seashells and interlocking latticework. Superimposed on this are key elements, often inlaid with paua shell.

The most common is the ancestor figure, the **hei tiki**, a distorted human form, either male, female or of indeterminate gender. Almost as common is the mythical *manaia*, a beaked birdlike form with an almost human profile. Secondary motifs include the *pakake* (whale) and *moko* (lizard).

While the same level of craftsmanship was applied to all manner of tools, weapons and ornaments, it reached its most exalted expression in *waka taua* (**war canoes**), the focus of community pride and endeavour. Gunwales, bailers and paddles are fabulously decorated but the most detailed work is reserved for the prow and sternpost, usually a matrix of spirals interwoven with *manaia* figures. As guns and the European presence altered the balance of tribal warfare in the 1860s, the *waka taua* was superseded in importance by the *whare whakairo* (carved meeting house).

Greenstone carving

Maori carvers also work in **pounamu** (greenstone), supplied by pre-European trade routes originating in the West Coast and Fiordland; indeed, the South Island became known as Te Wai Pounamu, the Greenstone Water. The stone was fashioned into adzes, chisels and clubs for hand-to-hand combat, tools that took on a ritual significance and demanded decoration. *Pounamu*'s hardness dictates a more restrained carving style and *mere* and *patu* tend to be only partly worked, leaving large sweeping surfaces ending in a flourish of delicate swirls. Ornamental pieces range from simple drop pendants worn as earrings or neck decoration to *hei tiki*, worn as a breast pendant. Like other personal items, especially those worn close to the body, an heirloom *tiki* possesses the *mana* of the ancestors and absorbs the wearer's *mana*, becoming *tapu*.

Tattooing

A stylistic extension of the carver's craft is exhibited in *moko*, ornamental and ceremonial **tattooing** that almost died out with European contact. Women had *moko* on the lips and chin, high-ranking men had their faces completely covered, along with their buttocks and thighs; the greater the extent and intricacy of the *moko*, the greater the status. A symmetrical pattern of traditional elements, crescents, spirals, fern fronds and other organic forms, was gouged into the flesh with an *uhi* (chisel) and mallet, then soot rubbed into the wound. In the last couple of decades the tradition of full-face *moko* has been revived, as a symbol of *Maoritanga* and an art form in its own right; since 1999, *moko* artists have been eligible for government funding.

EXPERIENCING MAORI CULTURE

The most direct and popular introduction to Maori culture is a **concert and hangi** (feast), best experienced in Rotorua.

Both the concert and *hangi* once took place on a traditional *marae* though these days it is usually at some dedicated site or even inside a hotel. *Kawa* (*protocols*) governing behaviour dictate that *manuhiri* (visitors) must be challenged to determine friendly intent before being allowed onto the *marae*. As visitors, you elect a "chief" who represents you during this *wero*, where a fearsome warrior bears down on you with twirling *taiaha* (long club), flicking tongue and bulging eyes. Once a ritual gift has been accepted, the women make the *karanga* (welcoming call), breaking the *tapu*, followed by their *powhiri* (sung welcome). This acts as a prelude to ceremonial touching of noses, *hongi*, binding the *manuhiri* and the *tangata whenua* physically and spiritually.

And so begins the concert, performed in traditional costume. Highlights are the men's *haka* and the women's *poi* dance, in which tennis-ball-sized bulrush clumps are twirled rhythmically. The concert is followed by the *hangi*, a feast traditionally steamed in an earth oven or, in Rotorua, over a geothermal vent. Typically visits include learning at least a few words of the Maori language.

Beyond commercial concert and *hangi* ensembles, the following tours and lodgings offer opportunities to dig deeper into Maori culture. The website ⓦinz.maori.nz is also a handy resource to find Maori tourism operators around the country.

Footprints Waipoua Northland. See p.192.
Kapiti Island near Wellington. See p.258.
Maori Tours Kaikoura. See p.503.
TIME Unlimited tours Auckland. See p.80.
Maraehako Bay Retreat East Cape. See p.363.
Tipuna Tours East Cape. See p.374.

Weaving and clothing

While men carved, women concentrated on weaving and producing clothing. When Polynesians arrived in these cool, damp islands their paper mulberry plants didn't thrive and they were forced to look for alternatives. They found *harakeke* (New Zealand **flax**), the foundation of Maori fibre-work. The long, strong and pliable fibres, growing on marshy land all over the country, were used as fishing lines, as cordage for axe-heads and as floor matting. With the arrival of the Pakeha, Maori adopted European clothes, but they continued to wear cloaks on formal occasions and today these constitute the basis for contemporary designs.

Used in something close to their raw form for *raranga* (plaiting), flax fibres made *kete*, handle-less baskets for collecting shellfish and *kumara*, triangular canoe sails, sandals and *whariki*, patterned floor mats still used in meeting houses. For finer work, trimming, soaking and beating flax, a laborious process, produced stronger and more pliable fibre.

Most flax was neutral but Maori design requires some **colouring**: black is achieved by soaking in a dilute extract of hinau tree bark then rubbing with a black swamp sediment, *paru*; red-brown ranges of colours require boiling in dyes derived from the tanekaha tree bark and fixing by rolling in hot ashes; while the less-popular yellow tint is produced from the bark of the Coprosma species. Today synthetic dyes are used to create green.

Natural and coloured fibres are both used in *whatu kakahu* (**cloak-weaving**), the crowning achievement of Maori women's art, the finest cloaks ranking alongside prized *taonga*; the immense war canoe now in the Auckland Museum was once exchanged for a fine cloak. The technique is sometimes referred to as finger-weaving as no loom is used. The women work downwards from a base warp strung between two sticks. Complex weaving techniques produce a huge array of different textures, often decorated with *taniko* (coloured borders), cord tags tacked onto the cloth at intervals and, most impressively, **feathers**. Feather cloaks (*kahu huruhu*) don't appear to have been common before European contact, though heroic tales often feature key players in iridescent garments. The appeal of the bright yellow feathers of the huia probably saw to its demise, and most other brightly coloured birds are now too rare to use for cloaks, so new feather cloaks are rarely made.

You'll come across some fine examples in museums, the base cloth often completely covered by a dense layer of kiwi feathers bordered by zigzag patterns of tui, native pigeon and parakeet. More robust, *para* (rain capes) were made using the water-repellent leaves of the cabbage tree and a form of coarse canvas that could reportedly resist spear thrusts was used for *pukupuku* (war cloaks). Some *pukupuku* were turned into *kahu kuri* (dog-skin cloaks) with the addition of strips of dog skin, arranged vertically so that the natural fur colours produced distinctive patterns.

Weaving and plaiting are again popular; cloaks are an important element of formal occasions, whether on the *marae* for *hui* and *tangi*, or elsewhere for receiving academic or state honours. Old forms are reproduced directly or raided as inspiration for contemporary designs that interpret traditional elements in the light of modern fashion.

The haka, Maori dance and Maori music

The use of the *haka* (see box below) by what are often predominantly Pakeha sides might seem inappropriate but it is entrenched in Kiwi culture; there was a considerable backlash in 1996 when the All Blacks coach suggested the *haka* should be changed to mollify those Maori *iwi* who had been decimated by Te Rauparaha. The new, specially written *Kapa O Pango haka* was unveiled in 2005 but it hasn't completely replaced the Te Rauparaha version.

The drums of eastern Polynesia didn't make it to New Zealand, so both chants and the *haka* go unaccompanied. Along with the traditional bone flute, Pakeha added the guitar to accompany **waiata** (songs), relatively modern creations whose impact comes from tone, rhythm and lyrics. The impassioned delivery can seem at odds with music that's often based on Victorian hymns: perhaps the best known are *Pokarekare ana* and *Haere Ra*, both post-European-contact creations. Outside the tourist concert party, Maori music has developed enormously in recent years to the point where there are tribal and Maori-language music stations almost exclusively playing music written and performed by Maori, often with a hip-hop or R & B influence and a Pacific twist. For more on music, see box, p.819.

THE HAKA

Before every international rugby match, New Zealand's All Blacks put the wind up the opposition by performing an intimidating thigh-slapping, eye-bulging, tongue-poking chant. Traditionally this has been the Te Rauparaha *haka*, just one of many such Maori posture dances, designed to display fitness, agility and ferocity. The Te Rauparaha *haka* was reputedly composed early in the nineteenth century by the warrior Te Rauparaha (p.256), who was hiding from his enemies in the *kumara* pit of a friendly chief. Hearing noise above and then being blinded by light he thought his days were numbered, but as his eyes became accustomed to the sun he saw the hairy legs of his host and was so relieved he performed the *haka* on the spot.

Touring teams have performed the *haka* at least since the 1905 All Blacks tour of Britain, and since the 1987 World Cup for home matches as well. The performance is typically led by a player of Maori descent chanting:

Ringa pakia Slap the hands against the thighs	**Hope whai ake** Let the hip follow
Uma tiraha Puff out the chest	**Waewae takahia kia kino** Stamp the feet as hard as you can
Turi whatia Bend the knees	

After a pause for effect the rest of the team join in with:

Ka Mate! Ka Mate! It is death! It is death!	**Whakawhiti te ra** Keep abreast!
Ka Ora! Ka Ora! It is life! It is life!	**A upane ka upane!** The rank! Hold fast!
Tenei te ta ngata puhuru huru This is the hairy man	**A upane kaupane whiti te ra!** Into the sun that shines!
Nana nei i tiki mai Who caused the sun to shine	

Landscapes and wildlife

Despite its relatively small size, New Zealand is bursting with enormous diversity: subtropical forests, volcanic basins, boiling mud pools, geysers, rugged white-silica- and gold-sand-fringed coastlines and spectacular alpine regions. These landscapes support an extraordinary variety of animals and plant life, with almost ninety percent of the flora not found anywhere else in the world. Many habitats, plants and wildlife are easily accessible, protected within national parks and scenic reserves.

The Shaky Isles

The earliest rocks are thought to have originated in the continental forelands of Australia and Antarctica, part of Gondwanaland, a massive supercontinent to which New Zealand belonged. Oceanic islands were created by continental drift, the movement of the large plates that form the earth's crust, which created an island arc and oceanic trench about 100 million years ago.

Roughly 26 million years ago, New Zealand rose further from the sea and today's landscape evolved, through **volcanic** activity and continuous movement along fault lines, particularly the Alpine Fault of the South Island. On the boundary between the Australian and Pacific tectonic plates, New Zealand's North Island has the two plates crashing into one another, the Pacific plate pushed beneath the Australian to produce prolific volcanic activity. Conversely under the South Island the Pacific plate rides over the Australian, causing **mountain building** and creating the Southern Alps. This unique island combination generates about four hundred **earthquakes** a year, although only a quarter are big enough to be noticed, and has earned New Zealand the nickname "the Shaky Isles". In 2010 and 2011, severe quakes struck the Canterbury region around Christchurch, causing extensive damage and loss of life (see box, p.511). The volcanoes on the North Island periodically become impressively active: White Island (just off the coast of the Bay of Plenty) blows steam, while Mount Ruapehu recently erupted in 2006 and 2007.

The end of isolation

New Zealand's flora and fauna evolved untouched until the first human reached Aotearoa, probably around 800 years ago. Before the arrival of Maori, the land was covered in thick **forest** composed of hundreds of tree species, and the only mammals were seals, whales and dolphins round the coast, and a couple of types of **bat**. Land mammals were nonexistent, a unique situation, which allowed **birds** to take their place in the food chain; with no predators, many gradually lost the ability to fly.

CONSERVATION AND WILDLIFE ORGANIZATIONS AND WEBSITES

Department of Conservation ⓦdoc.govt .nz. Government department charged with conserving New Zealand's natural and historic heritage.
Forest and Bird Protection Society ⓦforestandbird.org.nz. New Zealand's leading independent conservation organization.

NZ Birds ⓦnzbirds.com. Comprehensive site on everything feathery.
Kiwis for Kiwis ⓦkiwisforkiwi.org. Independent charity campaigning to save the national bird from extinction.

THE SCOURGE OF THE BUSH: MAMMALIAN PESTS

Since human habitation began, 43 indigenous bird species have become extinct and New Zealand is now home to about eleven percent of the world's most endangered species. Settlement and the introduction of non-native plants and animals are responsible for devastating this country's unique ecosystem.

POSSUMS

Visitors to New Zealand soon become familiar with the nocturnal **possum** (officially brushtail opossum or *Trichosurus vulpecula*), if only as roadkill. Live specimens usually show up when you are tramping, their eyes reflecting your torchlight around huts at night. Although they look cute they are pests, causing enormous damage to flora and fauna, stunting trees by munching new shoots, eating native birds' eggs and killing chicks. Consequently, New Zealanders have an almost pathological hatred of this introduced Australian marsupial, and greenies who would never dream of wearing any other fur happily don possum garments.

Before the start of controlled European migration in 1840, enterprising individuals were liberating these cat-sized Australian natives in New Zealand, with the aim of establishing a fur industry. Releases stopped around 1930 but control measures were not introduced until 1951, when a bounty was paid on all possums with their skins intact. Until the late 1980s possums were killed for their fur, but successful anti-fur lobbying saw prices plummet. Hunting tailed off and possum numbers skyrocketed. There are now in excess of **thirty million** possums, which currently eat their way through some 10,000 tonnes of vegetation every night, and are known carriers of bovine TB – endangering the dairy, beef and deer industries.

Possums are so widespread that hunting barely has any effect and the government is forced to spend around $60 million a year on possum control. The most cost-effective is aerial drops of **1080 poison**, a controversial substance banned in almost every other country in the world. Farmers claim it kills their stock and the native birds it is designed to protect. Certainly native birds do die, but the decimation of the possum population allows such an increase in avian breeding success that bird numbers soon exceed their pre-poisoning levels.

WILD PIGS, DEER, TAHR AND CHAMOIS

When James Cook sailed around New Zealand in the 1770s he released **pigs** so that on return voyages there would be something tasty to eat. These feral pigs (known as "Captain Cookers") are still rooting up the ground, although pig hunting keeps numbers down.

The forest understorey is hammered by the seven **deer** species introduced for sport from 1851 to the 1930s, and even today there are illegal releases of deer by hunters. Authorities are reluctant to advocate complete removal because of the political strength of the hunting lobby. In the first half of the twentieth century, the government also introduced the Himalayan **tahr**, a goat-like animal, and European **chamois**, both of which inhabit the high country of the South Island.

RABBITS AND MUSTELIDS

Rabbits were introduced to New Zealand from the 1840s, and though they don't pose a particular threat to native wildlife, the means used to try and stem the population certainly does. From the 1880s **ferrets**, weasels and stoats were introduced, but instead of targeting rabbits, these members of the mustelid family found the flightless birdlife easier prey.

DOGS, CATS, RATS AND MICE

Uncontrolled **dogs** can't resist playing with any flightless birds they might come across, and studies suggest they are responsible for 76 percent of adult brown kiwi deaths alone. There are an estimated 1.2 million **cats** in New Zealand, a quarter of them feral, and they kill numerous birds and lizards.

The *kiore* or Polynesian **rat** has been largely displaced by more aggressive Norway and ship rats, living everywhere from the treetops to the leaf litter, who ravage small bird and insect populations as well as devouring plant seeds and suppressing growth in the bush. **Mice** play a similarly devastating role.

When Maori came, with their dogs and rats, and then Pakeha, with all their introduced species, the birds could not compete. Those that survived (see box, pp.812–813) now cling precariously to existence.

Maori impact pales in comparison with the devastation wreaked by **Europeans**. Cook's first exploratory visits left a legacy of wild pigs, sheep and potatoes, while in the early 1800s whalers and sealers bloodied the coastal waters, while logging campaigns cleared vast tracts of native trees for grazing cattle. Pioneers continued to tamper with the delicately balanced ecosystem in an attempt to create a "New England". **Acclimatization societies** sprung up in the late 1800s to introduce familiar animals and plants from settlers' European homelands – New Zealand would never have become the successful pastoral nation it is without the grasses, pollinating birds, bees and butterflies, sheep and cattle. But many releases were disastrous, either out-competing native plants and birds or killing them.

The lowlands

Archetypal paddocks full of **sheep**, often backed by shelter belts of macrocarpa trees, are within sight of the airports. Sheep number about 30 million, less than half the population of thirty years ago, with much of their grazing land turned over to other uses, particularly dairying. Elsewhere, land has been redeveloped for horticulture or **vineyards**, with vintners sometimes co-producing **olives**. Optimistic souls plant oak and hazel trees in the hope of creating a truffle industry.

Throughout both farmed and forested New Zealand you'll see native **cabbage trees** (*ti kouka*) with thin grey trunks (up to 10m high) topped by spear-shaped leaves and clusters of white flowers. Captain Cook and his men ate the leaf shoots, finding them vaguely cabbage-like.

Lowland forests

Much of the thick forest that greeted Maori and early settlers was burned, logged, or cleared for farming, but pockets of **native bush** survive. The forests of Northland, the Coromandel Peninsula, the west coasts of both islands and on Stewart Island contain a wonderful variety of native trees. There are also sixty endemic native flowering plant species in lowland areas, whose blooms are almost all white or yellow. With no pollinating bees to attract there was little need for vibrant petals.

The **kauri** is the king of the forest, rising to 30m, two-thirds of it comprising straight, branchless trunk. It lives for over two thousand years and has long been revered by Maori canoe-builders, who enacted solemn ceremonies before cutting them down. European shipbuilders used them for masts and many more were turned into house floorboards. The tree was also the source of kauri gum, dug and exported in the early twentieth century. In recent decades the kauri has been struck by **kauri dieback**, with whole forests succumbing to the fungus-like pathogen *Phytophthora taxon Agathis* (PTA). As scientists try to work out how to control it, authorities attempt to control its spread to unaffected pockets, particularly the Coromandel Peninsula.

Open spaces along forest edges and riverbanks are often alive with tui (see box, pp.812–813) sucking nectar from golden clusters of **kowhai**, the national flower, which hang from trees whose wood was once fashioned into Maori canoe paddles and adze handles.

The North Island and the top third of the South are home to New Zealand's only native palm, the **nikau**. Its slender branchless stem bears shiny leaves, up to 30cm, long, pink spiky flowers and red berries, used by European settlers as pellets in the absence of ammunition.

Irregularly branched, growing to 20m, the **pohutukawa** is found as far south as Otago, in forests around the coast and at lake edges. Typically it bears festive, bright crimson blossoms around Christmas. Another red-blooming tree is the gnarled **rata**,

THE KIWI

Flightless, dull brown in colour and distinctly odd looking, the kiwi is New Zealand's much-loved national symbol. Stout, muscular, shy and nocturnal, it is a member of the ratite family – which includes the ostrich, emu, rhea, cassowary and the long-extinct moa – and is one of the few birds in the world with a well-developed sense of **smell**. At night you might hear them snuffling around, using the nostrils at the end of their bill to detect earthworms, beetles, cicada larvae, spiders and koura (freshwater crayfish), berries and the occasional frog. Armed with sensitive bristles at the base of its bill and a highly developed sense of hearing, the kiwi can detect other birds and animals on its territory and will readily attack them with its claws. The females are bigger than the males and lay huge eggs, weighing a fifth of their body weight. After eighty days, the eggs hatch and the chicks live off the rich yolk; neither parent feeds them and they emerge from the nest totally independent. They sleep for up to twenty hours a day, which explains why they normally live to the age of 20 or 25.

Sadly there are probably fewer than 70,000 birds left and numbers in the wild are dropping. Kiwi are most easily seen in **kiwi houses** around the country in places such as Auckland Zoo, Otorohanga, Napier, Wellington and Hokitika. The best opportunities for seeing **kiwi in the wild** are:

Trounson Forest Northland. See p.195.
Tiritiri Matangi Auckland. See p.136.
Kapiti Island near Wellington. See p.256.

Okarito near Franz Josef. See p.671.
Mason Bay Stewart Island. See p.634.

KIWI SPECIES

Kiwi have traditionally been divided into three species – brown, little spotted and great spotted – but genetic research in recent decades subdivided new species off from the brown kiwi.

Great spotted kiwi Going by the Maori name *roa*, this is the largest kiwi species, with adult males averaging 2.4kg and females 3.3kg. They are the most rugged kiwi, and are happiest in subalpine regions with wet, mossy vegetation. Smaller birds range down into lowland and coastal beech forests. European explorers told stories of kiwi the size of turkeys with powerful spurs on their legs, whose call was the loudest. Their harsh home has also helped keep them relatively safe from mammalian pests. Living mostly in the northern half of the South Island, the population of around 15,000 is in slow decline.

Little spotted kiwi Also known as Kiwi Pukupuku, this is the smallest of the kiwi, with adults weighing 1100–1300g. The main population (around 1200 birds) is on Kapiti Island. Mellow and docile by nature, pairs often share daytime shelter, going their separate ways to feed, grunting to one another as they pass. They rarely probe for food, instead finding prey on the ground or in the forest litter. The best time to hear them is just after dark from high points around an island. Listen carefully for the male's shrill whistle and the female's gentle purr.

Brown kiwi These medium-sized kiwi are the most widespread, particularly in the central and northern North Island, where there are around 25,000 birds. They are famous for their bad temper and for being tough fighters of intruders on their territory. They live in a wide range of vegetation, including exotic forests and rough farmland.

Rowi (aka Okarito brown). Originally considered a subspecies of the brown kiwi, this is the rarest kiwi, with only around 375 surviving in the wild, all in the 11,000-hectare south Okarito Kiwi Sanctuary in South Westland. They're greyish in colour, often with patches of white feathers on their face. Males and females share incubation – unlike most kiwi, where the male does the lion's share.

Tokoeka The most numerous kiwi species with an estimated 30,000 birds. The rarest form is the small Haast tokoeka (around 400 left), which are most common around Haast's bushline and in subalpine grasslands, even digging their burrows in snow. The Northern Fiordland, Southern Fiordland and Stewart Island tokoeka are all larger and in steady decline. They are one of the most primitive and the most communal kiwi, sometimes seen poking about along the tideline within a few metres of one another.

found mostly in South Island forests but occasionally popping up around the North Island.

New Zealand is also known for its unusual family of pine species, or **podocarps**. One such is the majestic **rimu** (red pine), which grows to 60m, with small green flowers, red cones and tiny green or black fruit. It was heavily milled for its timber (the charcoal was mixed with oil and rubbed into Maori tattoo incisions) but is still widespread throughout mixed forests. Other podocarps include **matai** (black pine), **miro** (brown pine), **kahikatea** (white pine), and **totara**, which grow for up to a thousand years. The trunks were used by Maori to make war canoes while strips of the thick brown bark were woven into baskets.

Below the canopy of these trees you'll find an enormous variety of **tree ferns**, many hard to tell apart. The most famous, adopted as the national emblem, is the **ponga** (silver fern). Reaching about 10m in height, its long fronds are dull green on top and silvery white underneath.

The lowland forest is prime habitat for the bulk of New Zealand's endangered birds (see box below).

NEW ZEALAND'S RARE AND ENDANGERED WILDLIFE

New Zealand has 69 birds and many more plants on the IUCN Red List of Globally Threatened Species (🌐 redlist.org). Among developed countries, only the United States has more. Of the birds, some 37 percent of New Zealand species (the world's highest percentage) are regarded as globally threatened, including most of the following.

BIRDS

Bellbird (*korimako*) Relatively common in forest and shrub, the shy, pale green bellbird is noted for its distinctive musical call.

Black stilt (*kaki*) This thin black bird with round eyes and long red legs is incredibly shy – if you do see one in the wild, keep well away. It is one of the world's rarest wading birds. Usually found in swamps and beside riverbeds, the best place to see them is in the specially created reserve near Twizel (see p.584).

Blue duck (*whio*) Uniquely among ducks, the *whio* (sometimes known as the torrent duck) spends most of its time in mountain streams, where it dives for food. One of four endemic species with no close relatives anywhere in the world, you can spot it by its blue-grey plumage, with chestnut on both breast and flanks. It also has an unusual bill with a black flexible membrane along each side, and yellow eyes (as seen on the $10 note). Its Maori name represents the male bird's call.

Fantail (*piwakawaka*) Relatively common forest dweller, seen constantly opening and closing the tail that gives it its name. It often flies alongside walkers on trails, not out of a desire for company but to feed on the insects disturbed.

Kaka Large parrot closely related to the kea, though it does not venture from its favoured lowland forest environments. You can recognize the bird by its colour: bronze with a crimson belly and underside of the tail and wings.

Kakapo The world's only flightless parrot, kakapo were once so widespread they were kept as pets. Now there are around 125 birds left, all on a couple of predator-free islands off the coast of Fiordland (off-limits to tourists).

Kakariki Bright green parakeets that come in yellow-crowned, red-crowned and orange-crowned varieties. Found at most wildlife sanctuaries and on offshore islands.

Kea The world's only alpine parrot. See box, p.565.

Kereru (a.k.a. *kukupa*) With adults weighing in at around 650g, this is the world's second-largest pigeon. Its metallic green, purple and bronze colouring and pure white breast is often seen flashing through low-lying forests with its distinctive noisy wing-slaps. It is a very ancient New Zealand species, which seems to have no relatives elsewhere.

Kiwi See box, p.811.

Kokako Rare slate-grey bird with distinctive blue wattles (patches of skin) on each cheek. An abysmal flyer, it lives mainly in protected forests and mainland islands where trapping keeps predator numbers low. Closely related to the saddleback (see opposite) and featured on the $50 note.

Rivers, lakes and wetlands

High mountains and plentiful rain mean that New Zealand is not short of rivers. Canterbury and the Waitaki sport distinctive **braided rivers**, their wide shingle beds and multiple channels providing a breeding ground for many birds, insects, fish and plants. Numerous lakes provide rich habitats; many of New Zealand's **wetlands**, on the other hand, have been drained for agriculture and property development, although some are preserved as national parks and scenic reserves. It's in low wetland areas that you're likely to come across the tallest of the native trees, the kahikatea (white pine), which reaches over 60m.

One bird you're bound to see in the vicinity of a lake is the **pukeko** (swamp hen), a bird still in the process of losing the power of flight. Also found in parts of Australia, the pukeko is mostly dark and mid-blue with large feet and an orange beak, and lets out a high-pitched screech if disturbed.

New Zealand is renowned for its freshwater fishing, with massive brown and rainbow **trout** and **salmon** swarming through the fast-flowing streams. All introduced species, these fish have adapted so well to their conditions that they grow much

Morepork (*ruru*) New Zealand's only native owl, this small brown bird is usually heard in the bush at night, and occasionally in town and city gardens. Both Maori and Pakeha names are supposed to represent its call.

New Zealand falcon (*karearea*) Seen occasionally in the north of the North Island but more often in the high country of the Southern Alps, Fiordland and the forests of Westland. New Zealand's only native raptor has a heavily flecked breast, chestnut thighs and a pointed head (as seen on the $20 note). Conservationists and winegrowers hope to reintroduce it to the Marlborough Plains where it may deter smaller, nuisance birds.

Robin There are three species of native robin, all glimpsed as they flit around the forest, often fearlessly pecking the dirt around your feet. They range from black with a cream or yellow breast to all black. Their prolonged and distinctive song lasts for up to thirty minutes, with only brief pauses for breath.

Saddleback (*tieke*) This rare but pretty thrush-sized bird is mostly black except for a tan-coloured saddle.

Stitchbird (*hihi*) Small with a slightly curved beak and distinctive yellow and white patches on its sides. There are thought to be a few left, some on Kapiti Island and Tiritiri Matangi, where you can see them using the feeding stations.

Takahe Rare turkey-sized bird once thought extinct (see p.757).

Tui With its white throat and mostly green and purple velvet-like body, the tui is renowned for mimicking the calls of other birds and for its copious consumption of nectar and fruit. Its song has greater range than the bellbird and contains rather unmusical squeaks, croaks and strangled utterances.

Weka About the most common flightless native, the weka is a little like a kiwi but slimmer, far less shy, and generally dark brown with marked golden flecks, especially on its heavily streaked breast. Like the kiwi, the weka grubs around at dusk but can be seen regularly during the day: many are bold enough to approach trampers and take titbits from their hands. The bird's whistle is a loud and distinctive "kooo-li". There are four subspecies found in a variety of habitats throughout the country.

OTHER SPECIES

Tuatara This nocturnal lizard-like creature is a throwback to the age of dinosaurs and remains little changed over 260 million years. The tuatara lives on insects, small mammals and birds' eggs, a diet that sees them grow to 60cm in length and keeps them alive for well over a hundred years. Best viewed in a zoo or kiwi house.

Weta A relatively common grasshopper-like insect that has lived in lowland forests for 190 million years. Several species live in the bush but they're hard to spot so you're most likely to see them in caves or zoos. The most impressive species is the giant weta (*wetapunga*), which ranks as the heaviest insect in the world, weighing up to 71g, and is said to have been the inspiration for Ridley Scott's *Alien*.

larger here than other places in the world; as a result, many native species have been driven out. Another delicacy found in New Zealand's waters is native **eels**, which, despite spending most of their lives in New Zealand rivers, migrate over 2000km to breed in the waters off Tonga.

Keeping anglers company along the riverbanks of the Mackenzie Country and Canterbury are the perilously rare **black stilts** (see box, pp.812-813). The **common pied stilt**, a black-and-white bird, has been more successful in resisting introduced predators.

Another inhabitant of the Canterbury braided riverbank is the **wrybill**. This small white-and-grey bird uses its unique bent bill to turn over stones or pull out crustaceans from mud. The wrybill's close cousin, the **banded dotterel**, favours riverbanks, lakes, open land with sparse vegetation and coastal lagoons and beaches. A small, brown-and-white bird with a dark or black band around its neck, it breeds only in New Zealand, though it does migrate to Australia. Around fast-flowing streams you might see the increasingly rare **blue duck** (see box, pp.812-813).

The highlands

With most of the lowland forests cleared for farming, you need to get into the hills to appreciate the picture that greeted Maori and early European immigrants. The best bets are the Tongariro, Whanganui, Taranaki, Nelson Lakes, Arthur's Pass and Aoraki/ Mount Cook national parks – all cloaked in highland forests, particularly native beech trees, which, unlike northern hemisphere varieties, are evergreen. The 20m-high **mountain beech** (*tawhairauriki*) grows close to the top of the tree line and has sharp dark leaves and little red flowers. Also at high altitudes, often in mixed stands, are **silver beech** (*tawhai*), whose grey trunks grow up to 30m. Slightly lower altitudes are favoured by black and red beech. Often mixed in with them, the thin, straggly **manuka** (tea tree) grows in both alpine regions and on seashores.

New Zealand has five hundred species of flowering alpine plant that grow nowhere else in the world. Most famous is the large white-flowered yellow-centred **Mount Cook lily**, the world's largest buttercup. It flowers from November to January. On the high ground of the South Island is the **vegetable sheep**, a white, hairy plant that grows low along the ground and, at a great distance, could just about be mistaken for a grazing animal.

Among alpine caves and rock crevices you might come across the black **alpine weta** (also known as the "Mount Cook flea"). Fewer species of bird inhabit the high country, but those that do are fascinating. In the Southern Alps you'll hear and see the raucous **kea** and perhaps the **New Zealand falcon** (for both see box, pp.812-813). Subalpine areas host smaller birds like the yellow-and-green **rock wren** and the **rifleman**, a tiny green and blue bird with spiralling flight. Such areas are also the natural home of two of the country's rarest birds, the **takahe** and the **kakapo** (see box, pp.812-813), neither seen outside tightly controlled areas.

The coast, islands and sea

New Zealand's indented coastline, battered by the Tasman Sea and the Pacific Ocean, is a meeting place for warm and cold currents, which makes for an environment suited to an enormous variety of fish. The warm currents, populated by hoki, kahawai, snapper, orange roughy and trevally, attract tropical fish like barracuda, marlin, sharks and tuna. The cold Antarctic currents bring blue and red cod, blue and red moki, and fish that can tolerate a considerable range of temperatures, such as the tarakihi, grouper and bass.

Marine mammals also grace these waters: the rare **humpback whale** is an occasional visitor to Kaikoura and Cook Strait, while **sperm whales** are common year-round in the deep sea trench near Kaikoura. **Orca** are seen regularly wherever there are dolphins, seals and other whales. Another frequent visitor is the **pilot whale**: up to two hundred pass by Farewell Spit each year; they're also seen in Cook Strait and the Bay of Plenty.

Common dolphins congregate all year round in the Bay of Plenty, Bay of Islands and around the Coromandel Peninsula. Of the three other species seen in New Zealand, **bottlenose dolphins** hang around Kaikoura and Whakatane most of the year, while **dusky dolphins**, the most playful, can be spotted near the shore of the Marlborough Sounds, Fiordland and Kaikoura from October to May. At any time of year you might get small schools of tiny **Hector's dolphins** accompanying your boat around Banks Peninsula, the Catlins and Invercargill.

Until recently there were few opportunities to see the Hooker's (or "New Zealand") **sea lion** except on remote Antarctic islands, but these rare animals, with their round noses and deep, wet eyes, now appear around the Catlins and Otago Peninsula. The larger New Zealand **fur seal** is in much greater abundance around the coast. You're most likely to come across them in the Sugar Loaf Marine Reserve off New Plymouth, around the Northland coast, in the Bay of Plenty, near Kaikoura, around the Otago Peninsula and in the Abel Tasman National Park. Both seals and sea lions can become aggressive during the breeding season (Dec–Feb), so remember to keep your distance (at least 30m). **Elephant seals** still breed in the Catlins; more extensive colonies exist on the offshore islands.

New Zealand has the world's greatest diversity of seabirds, with over 140 species drawn by the coast's fish-rich waters. Sadly, it also has the highest number of threatened breeding species, perhaps the most famous being the graceful royal albatross. A far more common sight is **little blue penguins**, which you'll see on any boat journey. The large **yellow-eyed penguin** is confined to parts of the east coast of the South Island, from Christchurch to the Catlins, while the **Fiordland crested penguin**, with its thick yellow eyebrows, is rarely seen outside Fiordland and Stewart Island. Other common seabirds include **gannets**, their yellow heads and white bodies unmistakeable as they dive into shoals of fish; and **cormorants** and **shags** (mostly grey or black), usually congregating on cliffs and rocky shores. On and around islands you're also likely to see the **sooty shearwater, titi** (also known as "muttonbirds"), while the **black oystercatchers** and the black-and-white **variable oystercatchers**, both with orange cigar beaks and stooping gait, can be spotted searching in pairs for food on the foreshore.

SANCTUARIES, PARKS AND RESERVES

NORTH ISLAND

Bushy Park Wanganui. See p.238.
Goat Island Marine Reserve Northland. See p.145.
Kapiti Island near Wellington. See p.256.
Parry Kauri Park Northland. See p.144.
Poor Knights Islands Marine Reserve Northland. See p.157.
Pukaha Mount Bruce National Wildlife Centre Wairarapa. See p.402.

Rangitoto and Motutapu islands Auckland. See p.119.
Tiritiri Matangi Auckland. See p.136.
Waipoua and Trounson kauri forests Northland. See p.195.
Zealandia: The Karori Sanctuary Experience Wellington. See p.425.

SOUTH ISLAND

Abel Tasman National Park See p.472.
Aoraki/Mount Cook National Park See p.578.
Fiordland National Park See p.752.
Kura Tawhiti Castle Hill Reserve. See p.562.
Mason Bay Stewart Island. See p.634.

Motuara Island Marlborough Sounds. See p.453.
Oamaru Blue Penguin Colony See p.547.
Orokonui Ecosanctuary near Dunedin. See p.605.
Ulva Island off Stewart Island. See p.633.

Green issues

New Zealand comes with an enviable reputation for being **clean and green**, but this is more by accident than design. With a population of 4.5 million and a relatively short recorded history, you might expect human impact to be limited, but in less than a thousand years (mostly the last 150) humans have converted three-quarters of the land to farming and commercial forestry. Just ten percent of native forest remains, while generous winds and flushing rainfall conveniently dispose of much of the country's **pollution**.

Land usage

European settlers and, later, returning World War I veterans spent years taming steep bush-covered hills only suitable for raising sheep. These **farms** were profitable when wool and lamb prices were high, but in recent years have become uneconomic; thus some areas are being allowed to revert to their natural state, through the **tenure review** process, opening them up to the public as parks and reserves. Far more often, marginal lands are planted with introduced **pines** and logged every 25 years, reducing them to barren fields of stumps. Meanwhile, the ever-growing need for housing, roads and associated infrastructure gobbles up productive farmland and threatens fragile wetland.

Pollution

In large parts of New Zealand you can inhale lungfuls of fresh air and gaze at crystal-clear lakes and rivers, but all is not idyllic. Due to poor public transport New Zealand's **car ownership** rates are some of the highest in the world. New Zealand also imports huge numbers of secondhand cars from Japan that would not be allowed off the boat in other countries, and there is no requirement for regular vehicle emission testing.

Mountain streams and alpine tarns look so clean and fresh you'll be tempted to drink straight from them. In most cases this is fine, but the water might also harbour **giardia**, an intestinal parasite that can easily ruin your holiday. It is best to treat all drinking water. Freshwater rivers have recently become prey to the **didymo** algae (*Didymoshenia geminata*); boaties, anglers and kayakers should thoroughly clean all their gear before moving to another river to prevent it spreading. Additionally, modern intensive **farming** techniques, particularly the use of fertilizers, have polluted many lowland rivers and streams. On the bright side, **industrial pollution** is a relatively minor issue, but only because there is little manufacturing.

The search for power

With a population growing ever more power-hungry and a lack of major investment over the last thirty years, New Zealand's power supplies are inadequate. Green **hydro** and **geothermal power** account for only two-thirds of electricity supply, compared to eighty percent in the late twentieth century, and even these clean generation methods are contentious: hydro reservoirs have destroyed natural habitats, especially riverbanks where threatened birds live. More geothermal stations are planned but over-extraction detrimentally affects geysers and boiling mud pools.

Building coal power stations (and converting to oil and gas stations) could make New Zealand electricity self-sufficient for over a hundred years, but at a considerable cost to the environment. Clean emission technologies are strenuously debated. **Wind energy** meets resistance from those complaining of noise and visual pollution, and installed capacity is very low. For decades no one dared suggest New Zealand should invest in **nuclear power**, but the power pinch and the need to follow Kyoto commitments is eroding long-held resistance.

The good news is that, despite government vacillation and the paramount interests of big business, an ever-increasing number of New Zealanders are working to preserve the country's unique environment.

Film and music

New Zealand has two film industries. The landscape provided the backdrop for internationally financed blockbusters, primarily Peter Jackson's *The Lord of the Rings* trilogy in the early 2000s and his three Hobbit films a decade later. Miniatures powerhouse Weta Workshop and postproduction unit, Park Road Post, have become familiar names and lent their skills to the likes of *The Chronicles of Narnia*, and the Avatar movies by James Cameron, who partly lives locally. Tax breaks and tweaked labour-rules have so far kept the work coming New Zealand's way.

Like most small countries, New Zealand lacks the resources and infrastructure to sustain a large-scale film industry but still manages to produce some fine movies. Between 1988 and 1994 alone, *The Navigator*, *An Angel at My Table*, *The Piano*, *Once Were Warriors* and *Heavenly Creatures* all rightly gained international recognition. Success has been patchy since but there's always hope for another "golden age of Kiwi cinema". Some tout 2014 as a new beginning with *The Dark Horse*, *What We Do in the Shadows*, *The Dead Lands*, *Housebound* and *The Pa Boys* all earning critical acclaim and seeing success at the box office.

★**An Angel at My Table** *Jane Campion, 1990*. Winner of the Special Jury prize at the Venice Film Festival. One of the most inspiring films New Zealand has produced, based on the brilliant autobiographies of Janet Frame (see p.547).

Bad Blood *Mike Newell, 1981*. A New Zealand/British collaboration set in New Zealand in World War II that relates the true story of Stan Graham, a Hokitika man who breaks the law by refusing to hand in his rifle. The ensuing events give rise to a discussion of the Kiwi spirit.

★**Bad Taste** *Peter Jackson, 1988*. Winner of the Special Jury prize at the Paris Film Festival. Aliens visit earth to pick up flesh for an intergalactic fast-food chain and have a wild old time.

Black Sheep *Jonathan King, 2006*. Festival favourite telling the story of sheep-phobic Harry, who returns to the family farm where he discovers his brother has been playing with the sheep, genetically, and has inadvertently created man-eating weresheep.

★**Boy** *Taika Waititi, 2010*. New Zealand's highest grossing movie is a coming-of-age drama set on the East Cape. Set in 1984, it finishes with the cast doing a brilliant Thriller-style *haka* to "Poi E", a huge hit that year.

★**Came a Hot Friday** *Ian Mune, 1984*. The best comedy to come out of New Zealand, based on the novel by Ronald Hugh Morrieson (see p.237), concentrating on two incompetent confidence tricksters whose luck runs out in a sleepy country town.

Crush *Alison Maclean, 1992*. Offbeat, angst-ridden psychological drama set around Rotorua, where the boiling mud and gushing geysers underline the tensions and sexual chaos that arise when an American femme fatale enters the lives of a New Zealand family.

★**The Dark Horse** *James Robertson, 2014*. Cliff Curtis is masterful as Genesis Potini in the true story of this Maori chess genius who struggles with bipolar disorder and a dysfunctional family. Deeply affecting and beautifully developed.

The Dead Lands *Toa Fraser, 2014*. Ultra-violence Maori-style. Set in pre-Pakeha Aotearoa, this bloody tale of honour and *utu* could be a standard coming-of-age movie if the director didn't seize every chance to showcase the traditional martial art of *mau rakau*.

Desperate Remedies *Peter Wells and Stewart Main, 1993*. This visually stimulating movie comments wryly on the melodramatic intrigues and desires of a group of Victorians on the edge of Britain's empire.

Eagle Versus Shark *Taika Waititi, 2007*. A low-key, well-realized love story starring Jemaine "Flight of the Conchords" Clement, with similar quirky humour.

Fifty Ways of Saying Fabulous *Stewart Main, 2005*. Clever adaptation of the book of the same name (see p.821) that grabs the spirit of the original and wrings out lots of laughs as well as poignancy.

★**Forgotten Silver** *Peter Jackson, 2000*. Jackson, at his tongue-in-cheek best, constructs a fake documentary about a Kiwi movie pioneer, who invents film, sound, colour and the biblical epic, from flax, in the bush on the West Coast.

Goodbye Pork Pie *Geoff Murphy, 1980*. New Zealand's favourite comedy/road movie following the adventures of two young men in a yellow mini, the cops they infuriate, and the mixed bag of characters they encounter.

★**Heavenly Creatures** *Peter Jackson, 1994.* Oscar-nominated account of the horrific Parker/Hulme matricide in the 1950s following the increasingly self-obsessed life of two adolescent girls. An evocative and explosive film that brings all Jackson's subversive humour to bear on the strait-laced real world and the girls' fantastic imaginary one. Kate Winslet's film debut.

The Hobbit *Peter Jackson, 2012–14.* Big budget, battle-heavy fantasy trilogy turning a four-hour epic of Bilbo's journey There and Back Again into eight hours of movie. Shot on location around the country, with miniatures and postproduction in Wellington.

Housebound *Gerard Johnstone, 2014.* Kiwis do horror. With characteristic pragmatism and dry humour this film undermines every scary movie convention and ends up celebrating diversity. Nothing is what it seems. Great fun.

In My Father's Den *Brad McGann, 2004.* Depicts an emotional rough ride for an exhausted war journalist (Matthew Macfadyen) who returns home and becomes involved in an unexpected and engrossing journey of discovery that descends into murder mystery. From a novel by Maurice Gee (see p.821).

Insatiable Moon *Rosemary Riddell, 2010.* This low-budget Moondance winner was shot mainly round Ponsonby. It addresses issues of social evolution and progress, from the point of view of Arthur, street person and self-proclaimed Son of God. The community tries to close the care-in-the-community home in which Arthur lives and he becomes the catalyst of miraculous and magical events.

Kaikohe Demolition *Florian Habicht, 2004.* Even if demolition derbies are the furthest thing from your bucket list, check out this warm, low-budget doco of life in a small Northland town. A grower.

Lord of the Rings *Peter Jackson, 2001–03.* New Zealand hit the Hollywood big-time with Jackson's epic ten-hour Tolkien trilogy. The Kiwi scenery shone through the ground-breaking special effects and was as much a star as the actors.

★**The Navigator** *Vincent Ward, 1988.* An atmospheric and stylistically inventive movie employing all Ward's favourite themes and characters, including the innocent visionary, in this case a boy who leads five men through time from a fourteenth-century Cumbrian village to New Zealand in the twentieth century in a quest to save their homes.

Once Were Warriors *Lee Tamahori, 1994.* A surging fly-on-the-wall-style comment on the economically challenged Maori situation in modern south Auckland, bringing to mind the British kitchen-sink dramas of the 1950s and 1960s. More a study of class than a full-blown racial statement, it revels in human weakness and strength

of spirit against a background of urban decay. Based on a novel by Alan Duff (see p.821).

Operation 8 *Errol Wright and Abi King-Jones, 2011.* Doco based on the real events of October 2007, when government agencies used the 2002 Terrorism Suppression Act as justification for arresting a number of Maori activists and its repercussions on wider society.

The Orator *Tusi Tamaese, 2011.* New Zealand-financed Samoan-language film, selected for the Sundance Film Festival and winner of the Venice Horizons Award, dealing with the unconventional life of a farmer and his efforts to protect his plantation and family.

Out of the Blue *Robert Sarkies, 2006.* Based on the true events of the Aramouna Massacre, in which thirteen people lost their lives to a local unemployed gun collector. A dark tale, concentrating on the heroism of the out-gunned seaside-town police and inhabitants.

The Pa Boys *Hinemoa Grace, 2014.* Almost the entire population of Tolaga Bay turns out for this tale of how a Maori reggae band's road trip turns, almost successfully, into a demonstration of how ancestral actions still affect the land and families today.

Patu *Merata Mita, 1983.* A powerful documentary recording the year of opposition to the 1981 Springbok rugby tour of New Zealand, which goes some way to showing the extraordinary passions ignited.

★**The Piano** *Jane Campion, 1993.* With Holly Hunter, Harvey Keitel, Sam Neill and Anna Paquin. This moody winner of the Cannes Palme d'Or (and three Oscars) made Campion bankable in Hollywood. Its mixture of grand scenes and personal trauma knowingly synthesizes paperback romance, erotica and Victorian melodrama – and includes Keitel's stab at the worst Scottish accent of all time.

River Queen *Vincent Ward, 2005.* Production problems on the Whanganui River saw Ward depart before the project was finished, but what's left is a beautifully shot, over-simplified and uneven film worth a look just for the locations.

★**Scarfies** *Robert Sarkies, 2000.* A darkly funny story about students taking over a deserted house in Dunedin only to discover a massive dope crop in the basement. Things get progressively more unpleasant when the dope grower returns.

Sione's Wedding *Chris Graham, 2006.* Lovely feel-good comedy about four immature Samoan-Kiwi thirty-somethings required to find girlfriends to attend their mate's wedding.

Sleeping Dogs *Roger Donaldson, 1977.* Perhaps the birth of the real New Zealand film industry, based on C.K. Stead's book *Smith's Dream*. Sam Neill plays a paranoid antihero hunted by repressive state forces. A slick thriller, which rushes to a violent conclusion.

Two Little Boys *Robert Sarkies, 2012.* A black comedy that becomes ever blacker as two former friends, a hot

CONTEMPORARY KIWI MUSIC

Many people would have been hard pressed to name a single Kiwi contemporary band or artist until the meteoric rise of **Lorde**. Apparently from nowhere (well, Devonport actually) this wise-beyond-her-years 16-year-old arrived almost fully formed in mid-2013 with the release of "Royals", a #1 hit worldwide. With the release of her *Pure Heroine* album and the use of "Yellow Flicker Beat" as the lead song of movie *The Hunger Games: Mockingjay – Part 1*, Lorde's reputation grew. Bruce Springsteen even opened one of his 2014 Auckland concerts with a cover of "Royals".

Lorde may never be royal but the country doesn't lack rock royalty. Foremost among them is singer-songwriter **Dave Dobbyn** whose tunes provide the "soundtrack of the nation" both from his bands Th' Dudes and DD Smash and from his enduring solo career. Some consider the catchy Slice of Heaven (recorded with Herbs) an unofficial national anthem, while Loyal rings out whenever some national sporting team appear. Several of his songs appear on *The Great New Zealand Songbook* (Sony; 2009), a double CD – "Last Century" and "This Century" – that showcases a diverse cross section of Kiwi artists. Other high fliers on the all-time Kiwi playlist are **Tim Finn**, who founded seminal 1970s ban Split Enz, later joined by his brother **Neil Finn** who went on to helm Crowded House. Both have successful solo careers and are sometimes joined on stage by Neil's son, **Liam Finn**, one of New Zealand's most talented singer-songwriters and multi-instrumentalists.

There's always been plenty of indie rock with the jangly pop of **The Chills** threatening to break internationally in the mid-1980s. Subsequently bands like The Datsuns and the Mint Chicks have kept the flame burning.

The new millennium saw an explosion of Kiwi roots, reggae, dub and electronica with Pacifica influences, which continues to be fundamental to minorities as a mode of expression, with artists such as Katchafire, Trinity Roots, **Salmonella Dub**, the Black Seeds and **Fat Freddy's Drop** among the most successful. Salmonella Dub's **Tiki Taane** subsequently went solo, creating Always on My Mind, one of New Zealand's most successful songs ever. He also incorporates elements of Maori chants and instruments perhaps best heard on Tangaroa off his second album, *Past*, *Present*, *Future*.

Country and folk music have generally been quite fringe, though for the last thirty-odd years **The Topp Twins**, New Zealand's favourite yodelling lesbian sisters, have managed to cut through the prejudice with leftie politics and plenty of humour. The genre has gained wider acceptance with the rise of the Christchurch and Lyttelton scene which revolves around folkie songsmiths **The Eastern**, Delaney Davidson and Lindon Puffin.

Catching a gig is one of the best ways to tap into the country's music scene – Ⓦ amplifier .co.nz lists upcoming shows, has downloads and sells CDs.

---

meat pie and ginger cat lead to the premature death of a Scandinavian footballer.

The Ugly *Scott Reynold, 1996*. Rave US reviews greeted this edgy comment on incarceration, reform and mistrust revolving around a serial killer who has been locked away and wants to convince the world he is cured.

Utu *Geoff Murphy, 1983*. This Kiwi classic portrays a Maori warrior in the late 1800s who sets out to revenge himself on the conquerors of New Zealand, in the form of a Pakeha farmer. A tense, well-acted representation of modern and historic issues.

Vigil *Vincent Ward, 1984*. Dark, rain-soaked story portraying a young girl's sexual awakening and her negative reaction to a stranger who is trying to seduce her mother.

Whakataratara Paneke *Don C. Selwyn, 2001*. The Maori *Merchant of Venice*, with English subtitles, an ambitious home-grown film that brings much local acting talent to the screen in an involved, if overly long, epic.

★**Whale Rider** *Niki Caro, 2002*. Uplifting tale of 12-year-old Pai (Keisha Castle-Hughes) trying to win over her conservative Maori grandfather and claim the birthright denied her as a girl. Shot in the East Cape village of Whangara.

★**What We Do in the Shadows** *Jermaine Clement and Taika Waititi, 2014*. Fly-on-the-wall comedy about house-sharing vampires in Wellington, the mundanity of their daily routine, and the fights they have with the local werewolf gang. Funny and sharp as their teeth.

★**The World's Fastest Indian** *Roger Donaldson, 2005*. Feel-good movie about old codger Burt Munro, who in real life proved you don't have to be young to achieve your dreams – though being barmy helps. Anthony Hopkins in the lead role is marvellous and even does a passable Invercargill accent.

Books

Kiwis publish extensively, including a disproportionate number of glossy picture books, wildlife guides and things with "Middle Earth" in the title. Modern authors, inheritors of an increasingly confident tradition, regularly produce excellent novels, poems and factual material.

HISTORY, SOCIETY AND POLITICS

Carol Archie and Hineani Melbourne (eds) *Maori Sovereignty: The Maori Perspective*; and its companion volume *Maori Sovereignty: The Pakeha Perspective*. Everyone from grass-roots activists to statesmen gets a voice in these two volumes, one airing the widely divergent Maori visions of sovereignty, the other covering equally disparate Pakeha views. They assume a good understanding of Maori structures and recent New Zealand history but are highly instructive nonetheless.

Mark Beehre *Men Alone – Men Together*. Photographer and oral historian Mark Beehre documents the diverse lives of 45 gay men, recounting key events in their lives and those in New Zealand's social history before, during and after homosexual law reform.

James Belich *The New Zealand Wars*. Well-researched, in-depth study re-examining the Victorian and Maori interpretations of the colonial wars. A book for committed historians. *Paradise Reforged* is a history of New Zealanders from 1880 to 2000, concentrating on their relationship with the outside world.

Alistair Campbell *Maori Legends*. A brief, accessible retelling of selected stories with some evocative illustrations.

Garth Cartwright *Sweet As: Journeys in a New Zealand Summer*. Brickbats and bouquets are liberally handed out (often about different aspects of the same place) as the London-based music journalist visits his boyhood haunts and the wider Kiwi landscape. Art, music, politics and fish and chips are the main themes.

Ron Crosby *The Musket Wars*. Account of the massive nineteenth-century upsurge in inter-*iwi* conflict, exacerbated by the introduction of the musket, which led to the death of 23 percent of the Maori population, a proportion greater even than that suffered by Russia in World War II.

★**Joan Druett** *Tupaia*. Fascinating tale of the Polynesian chief who joined James Cook's first visit to New Zealand and helped the great navigator communicate with Maori.

Alan Duff *Out of the Mist and Steam*. A vivid memoir of the *Once Were Warriors* author's life that falls short of autobiography, but gives the reader a good idea of the basis of inspiration for his novels.

A.K. Grant *Corridors of Paua*. A light-hearted look at the turbulent and fraught political history of the country from 1984 to the introduction of MMP in 1996.

Mark Inglis *Legs on Everest*. In 2006, 24 years after losing both lower legs to frostbite on Mt Cook, Inglis became the first double amputee to climb to the summit of Mt Everest. An inspirational read.

Hamish Keith *The Big Picture: A History of New Zealand Art from 1642*. A fascinating and rewarding tome for anybody interested in the progression from early Maori art through European influence to today's fusion of styles.

★**Michael King** *The Penguin History of New Zealand*. Published in 2003, this is a highly readable general history of New Zealand, from Maori oral history to uneasy Maori–Pakeha relations and the Maori renaissance. *Death of the Rainbow Warrior* is a brilliant account of the farcical, and ultimately tragic, efforts of the French secret service to sabotage Greenpeace's campaign against French nuclear testing.

Gareth Morgan & Susan Guthrie *Are We There Yet?* Wealthy activist Morgan gives his view on the way forward as a nation, proposing compulsory Maori language learning in primary schools; an Upper House of Parliament with half the members elected by Maori; and changing the country's name to Aotearoa New Zealand. Some sound ideas which have rarked up the talkback stations.

★**Claudia Orange** *The Story of the Treaty*. A concise illustrated exploration of the history and myths behind what many believe to be the most important document in New Zealand history, the Treaty of Waitangi.

Margaret Orbell *A Concise Encyclopaedia of Maori Myth and Legend*. A comprehensive rundown on many tales and their backgrounds that rewards perseverance, though a little dry.

Jock Phillips *A Man's Country? The Image of the Pakeha Male*. Classic treatise on mateship and the Kiwi bloke, an exploration of formative pioneering years, rugby, wartime camaraderie and the family-man ideal.

Anne Salmond *Amiria: The Life Story of Maori Women*. Reprinted classic describing the traditional values passed on to the author, set against a background of tribal history and contemporary race relations.

D.C. Starzecka (ed) *Maori Art and Culture*. A kind of Maori culture primer, with concise and interesting coverage of Maori history, culture, social structure, carving and weaving.

K. Taylor and P. Moloney (eds) *On the Left: Essays on Socialism in New Zealand*. Comprehensive collection of political essays spanning over a century that shows why New Zealand society has such a strong egalitarian spine.

Chris Trotter *No Left Turn*. Wonderful episodic history of New Zealand that convincingly argues that the country has been continuously shaped by "greed, bigotry and right-wing politics".

Dorothy Urlich Cloher *Hongi Hika*. Compelling biography dealing with the foremost Maori leader at the time of the first contact between Maori and the Europeans, and his subsequent participation in the Musket Wars.

FICTION

Graeme Aitken *Fifty Ways of Saying Fabulous*. Extremely funny book about burgeoning homosexuality in a young farm boy, who lives in a world where he is expected to clean up muck and play rugby.

Eric Beardsley *Blackball 08*. Entertaining and fairly accurate historical novel set in the West Coast coal-mining town of Blackball during New Zealand's longest labour dispute.

★**Graham Billing** *Forbrush and the Penguins*. Described as the first serious novel to come out of Antarctica, this is a compelling description of one man's lonely vigil over a colony of penguins.

Samuel Butler *Erewhon*. Initially set in the Canterbury high country (where Butler ran a sheep station), but increasingly devoted to a satirical critique of mid-Victorian Britain.

Eleanor Catton *The Luminaries*. This complex whodunit set in gold-rush Hokitika in 1866 won the 2013 Man Booker Prize. At over 800 pages it is the longest winner and at 28 Catton was the youngest author. Part of its genius is the author's success at constraining the narrative within a straitjacket defined by chapter length, zodiac signs and lunar cycles.

Paul Cleave *The Cleaner*. Debut novel from Christchurch-based crime writer (and New Zealand's best-selling author) who turns his city into a grim and dysfunctional backdrop for complex tales taken from many perspectives. Continue with the sequel *Victim Joe* or his series centred on retired cop Carl Schroder.

Nigel Cox *Tarzan Presley*. Amusing reworking of the Tarzan myth where the hero grows up in New Zealand and then becomes the king of rock'n'roll – nothing if not ambitious.

★**Ian Cross** *The God Boy*. Widely considered to be New Zealand's equivalent to *The Catcher in the Rye*, about a young boy trapped between two parents who hate each other and the violent consequences.

★**Barry Crump** *A Good Keen Man; Hang on a Minute Mate; Bastards I Have Met; Forty Yarns and a Song; The Adventures of Sam Cash*. Just a few of the many New Zealand bushman books by the Kiwi equivalent of Banjo Paterson, who writes with humour, tenderness and style about the male-dominated world of hunting, shooting, fishing, drinking, and telling stories. Worth reading for a picture of a now-past New Zealand lifestyle.

Alan Duff *Once Were Warriors*. Shocking and violent social-realist book set in 1970s south Auckland and adapted in the 1990s for Lee Tamahori's film of the same name. Well intentioned and passionate.

Laurence Fearnley *The Hut Builder*. Mannered fiction concerning the life of a Kiwi poet, whose work never makes an appearance, and who happens to climb Mt Cook with Edmund Hillary.

★**Janet Frame** *An Angel at My Table*. Though one of New Zealand's most accomplished novelists, Frame is perhaps best known for this three-volume autobiography, dramatized in Jane Campion's film, which with wit and a self-effacing honesty gives a poignant insight into both the author and her environment. Her superb novels and short stories use humour alongside highly disturbing combinations of events and characters to overthrow readers' preconceptions. For starters, try *Faces in the Water, Scented Gardens for the Blind, Towards Another Summer* and *Owls Do Cry*.

Maurice Gee *Crime Story; Going West; Prowlers; The Plumb Trilogy*. Novels from an underrated but highly talented writer. Despite the misleadingly light titles, Gee's focus is social realism, taking an unflinching, powerful look at motivation and unravelling relationships.

★**Patricia Grace** *Potiki*. Poignant, poetic and exquisitely written tale of a Maori community redefining itself while its land is threatened by coastal development. *Baby No Eyes* is a magical weaving of real events with stories of family history told from four points of view. *Dogside Story*, shortlisted for the 2001 Booker Prize, is a wonderful story about the power of the land and the strength of *whanau* at the turn of the millennium. *Tu* is an astonishing novel about the Maori Battalion fighting in Italy in World War II, drawn from the experiences of the author's father and other relatives.

Peter Hawes *Leapfrog with Unicorns* and *Tasman's Lay*. Two from an unsung hero, cult figure and probably only member of the absurdist movement in New Zealand, who writes with great energy, wit and surprising discipline about almost anything that takes his fancy. Hawes has also written the not-to-be-missed *Inca Girls Aren't Easy*, a series of joyous, sad and slippery tales, under the name W.P. Hearst. A brilliant late addition to Hawes' eccentric canon, *Royce, Royce the People's Choice*, is a sort of *Old Man and the Sea* mixed with *Moby Dick*.

★**Keri Hulme** *The Bone People*. The winner of the 1985 Booker Prize, and an extraordinary first novel, set along the wild beaches of the South Island's West Coast. Mysticism, myth and earthy reality are transformed into a haunting tale peopled with richly drawn characters.

★**Witi Ihimaera** *Bulibasha – King of the Gypsies*. The best introduction to one of the country's finest Maori authors. A rollicking good read, energetically exploring the life of a rebellious teenager in 1950s rural New Zealand – it's an intense look at adolescence, cultural choices, family ties and the abuse of power, culminating in a masterful twist. Look out also for *The Matriarch* and *The Uncle Story*, *Whale Rider* (adapted into a highly successful film) and *Star Dancer* by the same author.

Lloyd Jones *Mister Pip*. Intriguing 2007 Booker-shortlisted novel dealing with an unreported war on a remote South Pacific island where the schoolchildren's futures are entwined with a boy called Pip and a man named Dickens. Jones' 2009 collection of short stories, *The Man in the Shed*, showcases his sharp observations about contemporary NZ life.

Shonagh Koea *The Grandiflora Tree*. A savagely witty yet deeply moving study of the conventions of widowhood, with a peculiar love story thrown in. First novel from a journalist and short-story writer renowned for her astringent humour.

★**Katherine Mansfield** *The Collected Stories of Katherine Mansfield*. All 73 short stories sit alongside fifteen unfinished fragments in this 780-page tome of concise, penetrating examinations of human behaviour in apparently trivial situations, often transmitting a painfully pessimistic view of the world – startlingly modern considering when they were written in the early twentieth century.

Craig Marriner *Stonedogs*. Frenetic, feral, culturally fraught tale of gang-controlled drug running between Rotorua, Auckland and Northland, portraying "a New Zealand the tourists and executives had better pray they never stumble upon".

★**Ngaio Marsh** *Opening Night*; *Artists in Crime*; *Vintage Murder*. Just a selection from the doyenne of New Zealand crime fiction, who since 1934 has been airing her Anglophile sensibilities and killing off innumerable individuals in the name of entertainment, before solving the crimes with Inspector Allen. Perfect mindless reading matter for planes, trains and buses.

Owen Marshall *Drybread*. Sparingly written novel set between Christchurch and Central Otago that examines love and loss through its two protagonists: a mother returning to New Zealand to flee a court order from the US and an emotionally scarred local journalist pursuing her story.

★**Ronald Hugh Morrieson** *Came a Hot Friday*. Superb account of the idiosyncrasies of country folk and the two smart spielers who enter their lives, in a visceral gothic comedy thriller focusing on crime and sex in a small town. Also worth checking out are *The Scarecrow*, *Predicament* and *Pallet on the Floor*, all of which reveal Morrieson to have been the outstanding genius of this very New Zealand take on the genre.

Frank Sargeson *The Stories of Frank Sargeson*. Though not well known outside New Zealand, Sargeson is a giant of Kiwi literature. His writing, from the 1930s to the 1980s, is incisive and sharply observed, with dialogue true to the metre of New Zealand speech. This work brings together some of his finest short stories. *Once is Enough*, *More than Enough* and *Never Enough!* make up the complete auto-biography of a man sometimes even more colourful than his characters; Michael King wrote a fine biography, *Frank Sargeson: A Life*.

★**Maurice Shadbolt** *Strangers and Journeys*. On publication in 1972 this became a defining novel in New Zealand's literary ascendancy and its sense of nationhood. A tale of two families, with finely wrought characters, whose lives interweave through three generations – very New Zealand, very human and not overly epic. Later works, which consolidated Shadbolt's reputation, include *Monday's Warriors*, *Season of the Jew* and *The House of Strife*.

C.K. Stead *The Singing Whakapapa*. Highly regarded author of many books and critical essays who is little known outside New Zealand and Australia. This powerful novel focuses on an early missionary and a dissatisfied modern descendant searching for meaning in his own life. *All Visitors Ashore* is a masterpiece based around the harbourfront strike of 1951 and slyly alluding to Stead's literary contemporaries, while *Mansfield* is an evocative fictional musing about New Zealand's most famous short-story writer.

★**Damien Wilkins** *The Miserables*. One of the best novels to come out of New Zealand, shorn of much of the colonial baggage of many writers and surprisingly mature for a first novel, it sharply evokes middle-class New Zealand life from the 1960s to the 1980s through finely wrought characters.

ANTHOLOGIES

Warwick Brown *100 New Zealand Artists*. Companion to the *Picador Book of Contemporary New Zealand Fiction*, but also allows room for sculptors, printmakers, photographers and graphic artists.

James Burns (ed) *Novels and Novelists 1861–1979, a Bibliography*. A sweeping and comprehensive introduction to the history of the New Zealand novel and the authors who made it a powerful art form.

Bill Manhire (ed) *100 New Zealand Poems*. Manageable selection that provides an excellent introduction to the poetry of the nation and the characters who penned the rhymes and verses.

★**Owen Marshall** (selected by) *Essential New Zealand Short Stories*. A representative collection of fascinating tales by some of New Zealand's best-known and finest authors, including Frame, Ihimera, Mansfield, Shadbolt, Stead and Gee.

★ **Ian Wedde and Harvey McQueen** (eds) *The Penguin Book of New Zealand Verse*. A comprehensive collection of verse from the earliest European settlers to contemporary poets, and an excellent introduction to Kiwi poetry; highlights are works by James K. Baxter, Janet Frame, C.K. Stead, Sam Hunt, Keri Hulme, Hirini Melbourne and Apirana Taylor.

REFERENCE AND SPECIALIST GUIDES

John Kent *North Island Trout Fishing Guide* and *South Island Trout Fishing Guide*. Laden with information on access, seasons and fishing style, and illustrated with maps of the more important rivers.

FLORA, FAUNA AND THE ENVIRONMENT

★ **Andrew Crowe** *Which Native Tree?* Great little book, ideal for identifying New Zealand's common native trees – though not tree ferns – with diagrams of tree shape, photos of leaves and fruit and an idea of geographic extent.

John Dawson & Rob Lucas *New Zealand's Native Trees*. This magisterial tome is beautifully photographed and covers everything from distribution to detailed identification. *Their Field Guide to New Zealand's Native Trees* is more backpack-friendly.

Gerald Durrell *Two in the Bush*. Almost half of this slim volume is devoted to Durrell's 1962 visit while filming for a BBC wildlife documentary. Dated but a fascinating insight into both the times, the environment and the wildlife – mostly kaka, tuatara, takahe and penguins.

Julian Fitter *Guide to Wild New Zealand*. Fabulous collection of all the flora and fauna you are ever likely to encounter in an easy-to-manage package – the perfect field guide for experts and amateurs alike.

Susanne & John Hill *Richard Henry of Resolution Island*. Comprehensive and very readable account of a man widely regarded as New Zealand's first conservationist. The book also serves as a potted history of this underpopulated area of Fiordland, peopled by many of the key explorers.

Leonie Johnson & Tony Ward *Organic Explorer*. Small guide to the best in organic, eco- and vegetarian spots around the country with everything from wholefood shops and organic wineries to ecolodges.

Rod Morris & Hal Smith *Wild South: Saving New Zealand's Endangered Birds*. A fascinating companion volume to a 1980s TV series following a band of dedicated individuals trying to preserve a dozen of New Zealand's wonderfully exotic bird species, including the kiwi, kakapo, takahe and kea.

Neville Peat *Manapouri Saved*. Full and heartening coverage of one of New Zealand's earliest environmental battles when, in the 1960s, a petition signed by ten percent of the country succeeded in persuading the government to cancel its hydroelectric plans for Lake Manapouri.

Tim Rainger *The Good New Zealand Beach Guide: North Island*. If golden strands, point breaks and surfcasting are your thing, don't miss this guide full of great photos, helpful maps and a few tall tales. No sign of a South Island companion volume yet.

Paul Schofield & Brent Stephenson *Birds of New Zealand: A Photographic Guide*. One for the campervan bookshelf, this is a complete guide to 365 species with over a thousand superb photos.

Kerry-Jayne Wilson *Flight of the Huia*. Focusing on Jurassic frogs and bizarre creatures such as the Alpine parrot, this book studies faunal change in New Zealand and current conservation issues.

TRAMPING, CYCLING AND ADVENTURE SPORTS

★ **Shaun Barnett** *Tramping in New Zealand*. Clear, concise and nicely photographed guide to forty of the best multi-day hikes in the country including most of the Great Walks. The maps show the terrain beautifully and there's a companion volume covering *100 Day Walks in New Zealand* with similar production values.

Graham Charles *New Zealand Whitewater: 180 Great Kayaking Runs*. A comprehensive and entertaining guide to New Zealand's kayaking rivers with maps and details on access, supplemented by quick reference panels with grades, timings, and handy tips.

Paul, Simon and Jonathan Kennett *Classic New Zealand Mountain Bike Rides*. All you need to know about off-road biking in New Zealand, with details of over three hundred rides. The brothers also publish *Classic New Zealand Road Rides*, *The New Zealand Cycle Trails* and others. Paul Kennett runs the ⓦ mountainbike.co.nz site.

Moir's Guide Away from the Great Walks, this is the most comprehensive guide to tramping in the South Island. It comes divided into two volumes: *North*, covering hikes between Lake Ohau and Lake Wakatipu; and *South*, which concentrates on walks around the southern lakes and fiords including the Kepler Track, plus the less popular Dusky and George Sound tracks.

Nigel Rushton *Pedallers' Paradise*. Separate lightweight *North Island* and *South Island* volumes covering recommended routes with distances, gradient profiles and places to grab a scone along the way.

Wavetrack New Zealand Surfing Guide *New Zealand Surfing Guide*. Pragmatic handbook to the prime surf spots around the New Zealand coast, with details on access, transport, the best wind and tide conditions and expected swells.

Language

English and *te reo Māori*, the Māori language, share joint status as New
Zealand's official languages, but on a day-to-day basis all you'll need is
English, or its colourful Kiwi variant. All Māori speak English fluently, often
slipping in numerous Māori terms that in time become part of everyday
Kiwi parlance. Mainstream TV and radio coverage of any event that has
significance to Māori is likely to be littered with words totally alien to
foreigners, but well understood by Anglophone Kiwis. It is initially confusing,
but with the aid of our Glossary (see p.827) you'll soon find yourself using
Māori terms all the time.

A basic knowledge of Māori pronunciation will make you more comprehensible and
some understanding of the roots of place names can be helpful. You'll need to become
something of an expert to appreciate much of the wonderful oral history, and stories
told through *waiata* (songs), but learning a few key terms will enhance any Māori
cultural events you may attend.

To many Brits and North Americans, **Kiwi English** is barely distinguishable from
its trans-Tasman cousin, "Strine", sharing much of the same lexicon of slang terms,
but with a softer accent. Australians have no trouble distinguishing the two accents,
repeatedly highlighting the vowel shift which turns "bat" into "bet", makes "yes" sound
like "yis" and causes "fish" to come out as "fush". There is very little regional variation;
only residents of Otago and Southland – the southern quarter of the South Island
– distinguish themselves with a rolled "r", courtesy of their predominantly Scottish
forebears. Throughout the land, Kiwis add an upward inflection to statements, making
them sound like questions; most are not, and to highlight those that are, some add the
interrogative "eh?" to the end of the sentence, a trait most evident in the North Island,
especially among Māori.

Māori

For the 30,000–50,000 native speakers and additional 100,000 who speak it as a
second tongue, **Māori** is very much a living language. It is gaining strength all the time
as both Māori and Pākehā increasingly appreciate the cultural value of *te reo*, a language
central to *Māoritanga* and forming the basis of a huge body of magnificent songs,
chants and legends, lent a poetic quality by its hypnotic and lilting rhythms.

Māori is a member of the East Polynesian group of languages and shares both
grammar and vocabulary with those spoken throughout most of the South Pacific.
Similarities are so pronounced that Tupaia, a Tahitian crew member on Captain Cook's
first Pacific voyage in 1769, was able to communicate freely with the Aotearoa Māori
they encountered. The Treaty of Waitangi was written in both English and Māori, but
te reo soon began to lose ground to the point where, by the late nineteenth century, its
use was proscribed in schools. Māori parents keen for their offspring to do well in the
Pākehā world frequently promoted the use of English, and Māori declined further,
exacerbated by the mid-twentieth-century migration to the cities. The language reached
its nadir in the 1970s when perhaps only ten percent of Māori spoke their language
fluently. The tide began to turn towards the end of the decade with the inception of
kōhanga reo **pre-schools** (literally "language nests") where **Māoritanga** is taught and
activities are conducted in Māori. The national roll is around 9000 pupils. Originally a
Māori initiative, it now has some crossover and a few progressive Pākehā parents

introduce their kids to biculturalism at an early age. Fortunate *kōhanga reo* graduates can progress to the small number of state-funded Māori-language primary schools known as *kura kaupapa*. For decades, Māori has been taught as an option in secondary schools, and there are now state-funded tertiary institutions operated by Māori, offering graduate programmes in Māori studies.

The success of these programmes has bred a young generation of Māori-speakers frequently far more fluent than their parents who, determined to recover their heritage, are attending Māori evening classes. Legal parity means that Māori is now finding its way into officialdom too, with government departments all adopting Māori names and many government and council documents being printed in both languages. Local Māori-language **radio stations** are now commonplace in the northern half of the North Island where the majority of Māori live (check out ⓦirirangi.net for locations and frequencies). But the real boost came in 2004 with the launching of **Māori Television**. Substantially government funded and less ratings-driven than its competitors, it still has relatively low ratings but is well worth tuning into for a very different take on what's going on. Partly in English, partly in Māori and occasionally a synthesis of the two, there's a wonderful cross-fertilization of styles. You can expect everything from movies and sitcoms to discussion panels on Māori issues and lifestyle programmes such as *Kai Time on the Road* (a cooking and Māori food show). There's even *Dora Matatoa*, the kids' show *Dora the Explorer* dubbed into an engaging mix of Māori and Spanish, and an animated show for pre-schoolers.

In your day-to-day dealings you won't need **to speak Māori**, though both native speakers and Pākehā may well greet you with *kia ora* ("hi, hello"), or less commonly *haere mai* ("welcome"). On ceremonial occasions, such as *marae* visits, you'll hear the more formal greeting *tēnā koe* (said to one person) or *tena koutou katoa* (to a group).

Māori words used in place names are listed below, while those in common use are listed in the general Glossary (see p.827). If you are interested in learning a little more, the best handy reference is Patricia Turoa's *The Collins Māori Phrase Book*, which has helpful notes on pronunciation, handy phrases and a useful Māori–English and English–Māori vocabulary. Online resources include ⓦkorero.maori.nz and ⓦmaoridictionary.co.nz.

MĀORI PLACE NAMES

The following is a list of some of the most common words and elements you will see in **town and place names** throughout New Zealand.

Ao	Cloud	**Nui**	Big
Ara	Road or path	**O**	The place of
Awa	River or valley	**One**	Sand, beach
Hau	Wind	**Pā**	Fortified settlement
Ika	Fish	**Pae**	Ridge
Iti	Small	**Papa**	Flat, earth, floor
Kai	Food or eat	**Pātere**	Chants
Kāinga	Home, village	**Puke**	Hill
Kare	Rippling	**Puna**	Spring
Kino	Bad	**Raki**	North
Mā	White, clear	**Rangi**	Sky
Manga	Stream	**Roa**	Long, high
Manu	Bird	**Roto**	Lake
Mata	Headland	**Rua**	Hole, cave, pit, two
Maunga	Mountain	**Runga**	Top
Mihi	Speeches or greetings	**Tahu**	Light
Moana	Sea, lake	**Tai**	Sea
Motu	Island or anything isolated	**Tāne**	Man
Muri	End	**Tapu**	Sacred

Tara	Peak	**Waka**	Canoe
Te	The	**Whanga**	Bay, body of water
Tomo	Cave	**Whenua**	Land or country
Wai	Water		

Pronunciation

Pākehā – and consequently most visitors – may still have a distorted impression of Māori pronunciation, which is usually mutated into an anglicized form. Until the 1970s there was little attempt to get it right, but with the rise in Māori consciousness since the 1980s, coupled with a sense of political correctness, many Pākehā now make some attempt at Māori pronunciation. As a visitor you will probably get away with just about anything, but by sticking to a few simple rules and keeping your ears open, apparently unfathomable place names will soon trip off your tongue.

Māori was solely a spoken language before the arrival of British and French missionaries in the early nineteenth century, who transcribed it using only fifteen letters of the Roman alphabet. The eight **consonants**, h, k, m, n, p, r, t and w, and the digraph **ng** are pronounced much as they are in English. The five **vowels** come in long and short forms; the long form is sometimes signified in print by a macron – the flat bar above the letter that we've used in this section of the book – but usually it is simply a case of learning by experience which sound to use. When two vowels appear together they are both pronounced, though substantially run together. For example, "Māori" should be written with a macron on the "a" and be pronounced with the first two vowels separate, turning the commonly used but incorrect "Mow-ree" into something more like "Maao-ri".

Here are a few **pronunciation** pointers to help you get it right:

- Long compound words can be split into syllables which all end in a vowel. Waikaremoana comes out as Wai-kare-**moana**. Scanning our list of place-name elements should help a great deal.
- All syllables are stressed evenly, so it is not **Wai**-ka re-**moana** or Wai-kare-**moana** but a flat Wai-kare-**moana**.
- Māori words don't take an "s" to form a plural, so you'll find many plural nouns in this book – kiwi, tui, kauri, Māori – in what appears to be a singular form; about the only exception is Kiwis (as people), a Māori word wholly adopted into English.
- **Ng** is pronounced much as in "sing".
- **Wh** sounds either like an aspirated "f" as in "off", or like the "wh" in "why", depending on who is saying what and in which part of the country.

Glossary

ANZAC Australian and New Zealand Army Corps; every town in New Zealand has a memorial to ANZAC casualties from both world wars.

Aotearoa Māori for New Zealand, the land of the long white cloud.

Ariki Supreme chief of an *iwi*.

Aroha Love.

Bach (pronounced "batch") Holiday home, originally a bachelor pad at work camps and now something of a Kiwi institution that can be anything from shack to palatial waterside residence.

Back-blocks Remote areas.

Bludger Someone who doesn't pull their weight or pay their way, a sponger.

Bro Brother, term of endearment widely used by Māori.

BYO Bring Your Own (bottle to drink).

Captain Cooker Wild pig, probably descended from pigs released in the Marlborough Sounds on Cook's first voyage.

Chilly bin Insulated cool box for carrying picnic supplies.

Choice Fantastic.

Chook Chicken.

Chunder Vomit.

Coaster (Ex-) resident of the West Coast of the South Island.

Cocky Farmer, comes in "Cow" and "Sheep" variants.

Crib South Island name for a *bach*.

Crook Unwell.

Cuz or **Cuzzy** Short for cousin, see "bro".

Dag Wag or entertaining character.

Dairy Corner shop selling just about everything, open seven days and sometimes 24 hours.

Dob in Reporting one's friends and neighbours to the police; there is currently a dobber's charter encouraging drivers to report one another for dangerous driving.

DOC Department of Conservation. Operators of the national parks, conservation policy, track administration and much more.

Docket Receipt.

Domain Grassy reserve, open to the public.

EFTPOS Card-based debit system found in shops, bars and restaurants.

Feijoa Fleshy, tomato-sized fruit with melon-like flesh and a tangy, perfumed flavour.

Footie Rugby, usually union rather than league, never soccer.

Freezing works Slaughterhouse.

Godzone New Zealand, short for "God's own country".

Good as (gold) First rate, excellent.

Greasies Takeaway food, especially fish and chips.

Greenstone A type of nephrite jade known in Māori as *pounamu*.

Haere mai Welcome.

Haka Māori dance performed in threatening fashion before All Blacks rugby games.

Handle Large glass of beer.

Hangi Māori feast cooked in an earth oven (see box, p.41).

Hapū Māori subtribal unit. Several make up an *iwi*.

Harakeke Flax.

Hard case See "dag".

Hikoi Walk (often as a protest).

Hogget The meat from a year-old sheep. Older and more tasty (though less succulent) than lamb, but not as tough as mutton.

Hollywood A faked or exaggerated sporting injury used to gain advantage.

Hongi Māori greeting, performed by pressing noses together.

Hoon Lout, yob or delinquent.

Hori Offensive word for a Māori.

Hot dog A battered sausage on a stick, dipped in tomato ketchup. What the rest of the world knows as a hot dog is known here as an American hot dog.

Hui Māori gathering or conference.

Iwi Largest of Māori tribal groupings.

Jafa Just Another Fucking Aucklander. Semi-derogatory term now (over)used as a noun. "He's a bloody Jafa".

Jandals Ubiquitous Kiwi footwear, thongs or flip-flops.

Jug Litre of beer.

Ka kite See you later.

Ka pai It is good, well done.

Kai Māori word for food, used in general parlance.

Kaimoana Seafood.

Kāinga Village.

Karanga Call for visitors to come forward on a *marae*.

Kaumatuā Māori elders, old people.

Kawa-Marae Etiquette or protocol on a *marae*.

Kete Traditional basket made of plaited harakeke.

Kia ora Hello, thank you.

Kiore Polynesian rat.

kiwi The national bird and mascot of NZ, always set lower case.

Kiwi An alternative label for a New Zealander.

Kiwifruit In New Zealand they are always called kiwifruit, never "kiwis". Golden-fleshed kiwifruit are also available, and less acidic than their green counterparts.

Koha Donation, gift or present.

Kōhanga Reo Pre-school Māori language immersion (literally "language nest").

Kuia Female Māori elder.

Kūmara Sweet potato.

Kurī Polynesian dog, now extinct.

Lay-by Practice of putting a deposit on goods until they can be fully paid for.

Lucked in In luck. What "Lucked out" means elsewhere in the world.

Lucked out Out of luck. The meaning completely reversed on its way across the Pacific.

Mana Māori term indicating status, esteem, prestige or authority, and in wide use among all Kiwis.

Manaia Stylized bird or lizard forms used extensively in Māori carving.

Manuhiri Guest or visitor, particularly to a *marae*.

Māoritanga Māori culture and custom, the Māori way of doing things.

Marae Place for conducting ceremonies in front of a meeting house – literally "courtyard". Also a general term for a settlement centred on the meeting house.

Mauri Life force or life principle.

Mere War club, usually of greenstone.

Metalled Graded road surface of loose stones found all over rural New Zealand.

MMP Mixed Member Proportional representation – New Zealand's electoral system.

Moko Old form of tattooing on body and face that has seen a resurgence among Māori.

Muttonbird Gull-sized sooty shearwater that was a major component of the pre-European Māori diet and tastes like oily and slightly fishy mutton – hence the name.

Ngāti Tribal prefix meaning "the descendants (or people) of". Also Ngāi and Āti.

OE Overseas experience, usually a year spent abroad by Kiwis in their early twenties.

Pā Fortified village of yore, now usually an abandoned terraced hillside.

Paddock Field.

Pākehā A non-Māori, usually white and not usually expressed with derogatory intent. Literally "foreign" though it can also be translated as "flea" or "pest". It may also be a corruption of *pakePākehā*, which are mythical human-like beings with fair skins.

Pashing Kissing or snogging.

Patu Short fighting club.

Pāua The muscular foot of the abalone, often minced and served as a fritter, while the wonderful iridescent shell is used for jewellery and decoration.

Pavlova Meringue dessert with a fruit and cream topping.

Pike out To chicken out or give up.

Piss Beer.

Pissed Drunk.

Podocarp Family of pine, native to New Zealand including rimu, kahikatea, matai, miro, totara etc.

Pōhutukawa Gnarled native tree found around the coast of the upper North Island. Blooms bright red in mid-December and is sometimes known as New Zealand's Christmas Tree.

Poms Folk from Britain; not necessarily offensive.

Pounamu New Zealand greenstone, a unique type of jade.

Pōwhiri Traditional welcome onto a *marae*.

Pūhā Māori term for "sow thistle", a leafy plant traditionally gathered by Māori and eaten like spinach.

Puku Māori for stomach, often used as a term of endearment for someone amply endowed.

Rangatira General term for a Māori chief.

Rapt Well-pleased.

Rattle your dags Hurry up.

Root Vulgar term for sex.

Rooted To be very tired or beyond repair, as in "she's rooted, mate" – your car is irreparable.

Rough as guts Uncouth, roughly made or operating badly, as in "she's running rough as guts, mate".

Sealed road Bitumen-surfaced road.

Section Block of land usually surrounding a house.

She'll be right Everything will work out fine.

Shout To buy a round of drinks or generally to treat folk.

Skull To knock back beer quickly.

Smoko Tea break.

Snarler, snag Sausage.

Squiz A look, as in "Give us a squiz".

Stoked Very pleased.

Sweet Cool.

Taiaha Long-handled club.

Tall poppy Someone who excels. "Cutting down tall poppies" is to bring overachievers back to earth – every Kiwi's perceived duty.

Tamarillo Slightly bitter, deep-red fruit, often known as a tree tomato.

Tāne Man.

Tangata whenua The people of the land, local or original inhabitants.

Tangi Mourning or funeral.

Taniwha Fearsome water spirit of Māori legend.

Taonga Treasures, prized possessions.

Tapu Forbidden or taboo. Frequently refers to sacred land.

Te reo Māori Māori language.

Tikanga Māori customs, ethics and etiquette – the Māori way of doing things.

Tiki Māori pendant depicting a distorted human figure.

Tiki tour Guided tour.

Togs Swimming costume.

Tohunga Māori priests, experts in *Māoritanga*.

True Left On the left facing downstream.

True Right On the right when facing downstream.

Tukutuku Knotted latticework panels decorating the inside of a meeting house.

Tupuna Ancestors; of great spiritual importance to Māori.

Ute Car-sized pick-up truck, short for "utility".

Varsity University.

Vegemite or **Marmite** Dark, savoury yeast-extract spreads. There's always debate between those who love Vegemite (Australian) and those who prefer Kiwi Marmite – sweeter and more appealing than its British equivalent – and of course those who loathe all of the above.

Wahine Woman.

Waiata Māori action songs.

Wairua Spirit.

Waka Māori canoe.

Waratah Stake, a term used to describe snow poles on tramps.

Wero Challenge before entering a *marae*.

Whakapapa Family tree or genealogical relationship.

Whānau Extended family group.

Whare Māori for a house.

Whare rūnanga Meeting house.

Whare whakairo Carved house.

Wop-wops Remote areas.

Small print and index

A ROUGH GUIDE TO ROUGH GUIDES

Published in 1982, the first Rough Guide – to Greece – was a student scheme that became a publishing phenomenon. Mark Ellingham, a recent graduate in English from Bristol University, had been travelling in Greece the previous summer and couldn't find the right guidebook. With a small group of friends he wrote his own guide, combining a highly contemporary, journalistic style with a thoroughly practical approach to travellers' needs.

The immediate success of the book spawned a series that rapidly covered dozens of destinations. And, in addition to impecunious backpackers, Rough Guides soon acquired a much broader readership that relished the guides' wit and inquisitiveness as much as their enthusiastic, critical approach and value-for-money ethos.

These days, Rough Guides include recommendations from budget to luxury and cover more than 120 destinations around the globe, as well as producing an ever-growing range of ebooks.

Visit **roughguides.com** to find all our latest books, read articles, get inspired and share travel tips with the Rough Guides community.

Rough Guide credits

Editor: David Leffman
Layout: Anita Singh
Cartography: Rajesh Chhibber
Picture editor: Rhiannon Furbear-Williams
Proofreader: Diane Margolis
Managing editor: Keith Drew
Assistant editor: Payal Sharotri
Production: Nicole Landau

Cover design: Nicole Newman, Anita Singh
Photographer: Paul Whitfield
Editorial assistant: Freya Godfrey
Senior pre-press designer: Dan May
Programme manager: Gareth Lowe
Publisher: Joanna Kirby
Publishing director: Georgina Dee

Publishing information

This ninth edition published September 2015 by
Rough Guides Ltd,
80 Strand, London WC2R 0RL
11, Community Centre, Panchsheel Park,
New Delhi 110017, India
Distributed by Penguin Random House
Penguin Books Ltd,
80 Strand, London WC2R 0RL
Penguin Group (USA)
345 Hudson Street, NY 10014, USA
Penguin Group (Australia)
250 Camberwell Road, Camberwell,
Victoria 3124, Australia
Penguin Group (NZ)
67 Apollo Drive, Mairangi Bay, Auckland 1310,
New Zealand
Penguin Group (South Africa)
Block D, Rosebank Office Park, 181 Jan Smuts Avenue,
Parktown North, Gauteng, South Africa 2193
Rough Guides is represented in Canada by Tourmaline
Editions Inc. 662 King Street West, Suite 304, Toronto,
Ontario M5V 1M7
Printed in Singapore

© Rough Guides 2015
Maps © Rough Guides
No part of this book may be reproduced in any form
without permission from the publisher except for the
quotation of brief passages in reviews.
848pp includes index
A catalogue record for this book is available from the
British Library
ISBN: 978-0-24118-670-1
The publishers and authors have done their best to ensure
the accuracy and currency of all the information in **The
Rough Guide to New Zealand**, however, they can accept
no responsibility for any loss, injury, or inconvenience
sustained by any traveller as a result of information or
advice contained in the guide.
1 3 5 7 9 8 6 4 2

MIX
Paper from
responsible sources
FSC www.fsc.org   FSC™ C018179

Help us update

We've gone to a lot of effort to ensure that the ninth
edition of **The Rough Guide to New Zealand** is accurate
and up-to-date. However, things change – places get
"discovered", opening hours are notoriously fickle,
restaurants and rooms raise prices or lower standards. If
you feel we've got it wrong or left something out, we'd like
to know, and if you can remember the address, the price,
the hours, the phone number, so much the better.

Please send your comments with the subject line
"Rough Guide New Zealand Update" to ✉ mail
@uk.roughguides.com. We'll credit all contributions and
send a copy of the next edition (or any other Rough Guide
if you prefer) for the very best emails.

Find more travel information, connect with fellow
travellers and plan your trip on ⓦ roughguides.com.

ABOUT THE AUTHORS

Joanna James started her career as a commodity broker in London before a dislike of commuting and a chronic case of wanderlust intervened. She escaped to Asia and worked in a series of very odd jobs – one of which included inspecting Chinese pig farms for a UN agency – before settling into life as an itinerant writer and photographer. When she's not somewhere else, Jo lives on a small island in Hong Kong with her husband, and has contributed to the Rough Guides to China, Myanmar, Malaysia, Singapore & Brunei, and New Zealand. Follow her travels at ⚲ little-yak.com.

Alison Mudd studied Classics at Cambridge before deciding to spend less time in libraries and more time exploring. She fell in love with New Zealand on her first visit (with the Rough Guide) and served an informal seven-year apprenticeship, covering photography, app production and article-writing, before updating this edition. When she's not writing, she's travelling (usually in America, Africa and Europe), ideally by kayak or on foot.

Helen Ochyra is a freelance travel writer who has been visiting New Zealand for over a decade. As well as working on guidebooks for Rough Guides, she writes regular features for numerous newspapers, magazines and websites, both in the UK, where she is based, and worldwide.

Paul Whitfield spent his formative years studying and working in New Zealand and after some time living in Britain co-authored the original edition of the NZ Rough Guide. Since then he has moved back to his adopted home and spends his time updating several Rough Guides, doing photography commissions around the world. Until recently he also went kayaking, rock climbing and mountain biking though the arrival of daughter, Freya, has put a temporary (?) hold on that.

Acknowledgements

Jo James: To everyone who helped during my research, whether knowingly or unknowingly, voluntarily or involuntarily, thank you. Extra special thanks go to Jo, Adam, Otis and all the McAulays in Wellington; Jeannie, Steve and John in Auckland; Paul, Marion and Freya in Arrowtown; Suzanne in Dunedin; Adin at Arrowtown Bikes and Jarrad in Milford (beers next time!).

Alison Mudd: Thanks to all the operators I visited, people I stayed with, other travellers and i-SITE staff (particularly the guys at Te Aroha and Opotiki); you all shared tips, enthusiasm, gossip (and cake) along the way. The YHA team were, as always, great, as were Ace Rentals. Heartfelt gratitude and love to Gerry and Sally at The Great Ponsonby Art Hotel, and Graeme and Jan at Bay Cottages, Kaikoura. Thanks (for more than you'll know) to Pihi and whanau, Sean, Reg for the tow and bees, Rose and Bruce, Iliana, Matt, Helene, Paul, and especially Kweenie at Kaikoura YHA. Dedicated to my friends and family – especially Kate and Clare for prodding, Mum, Dan and Celia for tlc, Dad and Mel's advice, Grassy's enthusiasm and Steven for having such unshakeable confidence. Oh – and

David for being such a calm and skilled editor. First and last, to Tony: il miglior fabbro.

Helen Ochyra: Judith Watson and Zoe Macfarlane for organising my Jucy van rental and my husband Douglas Whelpdale for driving it!

Paul Whitfield: I'd like to thank everyone I met on research trips throughout New Zealand, especially those who suggested great restaurants to check out, waxed lyrical about hotels and hostels and shared experiences. Special thanks go out to the helpful and knowledgeable staff of i-SITEs and visitor centres across the land. Cheers too to friends who have sussed out top places and passed on their impressions, especially Phil & Wendy in Arrowtown for their invaluable guidance over good Central Otago wine, Meg at RiverRun in Wanaka and Colin, Allan and Deryl for sterling advice on Great Barrier Island. Lastly, huge gratitude is due to Marion for helping with the restaurant reviewing and wine sampling, and Kim and Helen for looking after Freya during my long absences around the country and in the study.

Readers' updates

Thanks to all the readers who have taken the time to write in with comments and suggestions (and apologies if we've inadvertently omitted or misspelt anyone's name):

David Armour, Phil Avery, Laura Bennitt, Frances Boyson, Tertia Cumming, Peter Davies & Sylvia Welberry, Louise Elliott, Bolette & Joergen Fokdal, Teresa & Joe Howarth, Julie and Tom, Dirk Kruwinnus, Frances Landeryou, Michael Lloyd, Etelka Pieper, Petrina Quinn, Ian J. Roche, Philipp Roessler, Sam Smith & Aurélie Detrez, Mary & Geoff Stoddart, Gianfranco Vallese, Keith Walker & Nicola Grahamslaw

Photo credits

All photos © Rough Guides except the following:
(Key: t-top; c-centre; b-bottom; l-left; r-right)

p.1 AWL Images: Danita Delimont Stock
p.2 AWL Images: Doug Pearson
p.4 Getty Images: David Clapp
p.5 Getty Images: Picturegarden
p.9 AWL Images: Doug Pearson (c); Alamy: Graham Warman (b)
p.10 Corbis: Bill Ross
p.11 Alamy: nobleIMAGES
p.12 4Corners: Massimo Ripani/SIME
p.14 Robert Harding Picture Library: Matthew Williams-Ellis
p.15 Getty Images: ML Harris (t); Getty Images: Bill Hatcher (b)
p.16 Getty Images: Gerard Soury (t); AWL Images: David Wall (c); Getty Images: Darryl Torckler (b)
p.17 Alamy: David Wall (t); Alamy: David Wall (b)
p.18 Alamy: Ignacio Palacios (cl); Getty Images: age Fotostock (cr) Alamy: Peter Szekely (b)
p.19 Alamy: Greg Balfour Evans (t); Alamy: LOOK Die Bildagentur der Fotografen (b)
p.20 Alamy: Greg Balfour Evans (t); Alamy: Rolf Hicker Photography (c); Alamy: Chris McLennan (b)
p.21 Getty Images: Colin Monteath (bl)
p.22 Alamy: Andrew Court (t)
p.23 Alamy Images: Jon Arnold Images Ltd (tl); Alamy: Henk Meijer (bl); Alamy: Ben Lewis (br)
p.24 4Corners: Riccardo Spila
p.25 Alamy Images: Jon Arnold Images Ltd (tl)
p.26 Getty Images: John Lamb
p.68 Getty Images: Scott E Barbour
p.71 Alamy: David Wall
p.91 Getty Images: Andrew Watson (t); Getty Images: Lasting Images (b)
p.133 Alamy: David Hancock
p.141 Alamy: Vincent Lowe
p.159 Alamy: Louise Heusinkveld (t)
p.200 AWL Images: Doug Pearson
p.203 Alamy Images: Andrew Bain
p.223 Alamy: Ian Woolcock

p.243 Alamy: Chris McLennan (t); Alamy: Mark Boulton (b)
p.260 Robert Harding Picture Library: Stuart Black
p.263 Alamy: David Wall
p.283 Corbis: Alex Wallace/www.photonewzealand.com (t); Alamy: Ernie Janes (b)
p.313 Alamy: David Wall
p.329 Alamy: Darren Newbery (t)
p.368 Getty Images: Danita Delimont
p.371 AWL Images: Danita Delimont Stock
p.393 Getty Images: Kevin Schafer (t); Getty Images: Lasting Images (b)
p.413 Alamy: Greg Balfour Evans
p.419 Getty Images: Travel Ink (b)
p.435 Alamy Images: Jon Sparks (b)
p.487 Alamy: David Wall
p.506 Alamy: Terry Whittaker
p.509 Alamy: David Wall
p.545 Alamy Images: age fotostock
p.555 Alamy: David Wall
p.588 Alamy: Ian Dagnall
p.591 Robert Harding Picture Library: Frans Lanting/Mint Images
p.638 Alamy: ScotStock
p.641 Getty Images: Bo Tornvig Olsen
p.657 Alamy: Chris McLennan (b)
p.723 Alamy Images: 42pix Premier (t); Alamy: William Robinson (b)
p.750 Alamy: David Wall
p.753 Getty Images: Jason Hosking
p.769 Alamy Images: Jason Friend
p.786 Alamy: Tips Images

Front cover & spine Lake Pukaki and Mount Cook National Park © Corbis/Frans Lemmens
Back cover Auckland skyline (t) © AWL Images: Doug Pearson; Yellow-eyed penguin (l) © AWL Images: Marco Simoni; Sea kayak near Doctors Point ® © AWL Images: David Wall

Index

Maps are marked in **grey**

Map symbols

The symbols below are used on maps throughout the book

- − − − Chapter division boundary
- Motorway
- Major road
- Minor road
- Pedestrian road
- 4 Wheel drive
- Railway
- Ferry route
- Footpath
- River
- ✈ Airport
- ✈ Airport (regional)
- Fuel station
- T Toilets
- P Parking
- ★ Bus stop
- ♦ Point of interest
- @ Internet access

- ⓘ Tourist office
- ✉ Post office
- ✚ Hospital
- ☏ Telephone
- ♈ Garden
- Golf course
- Winery
- ♨ Castle
- ♕ Museum
- Ski area
- Swimming pool
- Surf/beach
- Waterfall
- ▲ Peak
- Bridge
- Cave
- ∴ Ruins
- Waterfall

- Mountain range
- Gorge
- Viewpoint
- Lighthouse
- Campsite
- Hut/hide
- Boat
- ⚓ Boat stop
- ● − ● Cable car
- Church
- Stadium
- Building
- Park/forest
- Beach
- Cemetery
- Glacier

Listings key

- ■ Accommodation
- ● Restaurant/café
- ■ Bar/pub/club
- ● Shop